AF662809

# The Complete Reference

# Java™

## Thirteenth Edition

## About the Authors

Best-selling author **Herbert Schildt** has written extensively about programming for over three decades and is a leading authority on the Java language. Called "one of the world's foremost authors of books about programming" by *International Developer* magazine, his books have sold millions of copies worldwide and have been translated into all major foreign languages. He is the author of numerous books on Java, including *Java: A Beginner's Guide, Herb Schildt's Java Programming Cookbook, Introducing JavaFX 8 Programming,* and *Swing: A Beginner's Guide.* He has also written extensively about C, C++, and C#. Featured as one of the rock star programmers in Ed Burns' book *Secrets of the Rock Star Programmers: Riding the IT Crest,* Schildt is interested in all facets of computing, but his primary focus is computer languages. Schildt holds both BA and MCS degrees from the University of Illinois.

**Dr. Danny Coward** has worked on all editions of the Java platform. He led the definition of Java Servlets into the first version of the Java EE platform and beyond, web services into the Java ME platform, and the strategy and planning for Java SE 7. He helped found JavaFX technology and designed the Java WebSocket API in Java EE. From coding in Java, to designing APIs with industry experts, to serving for several years as an executive to the Java Community Process, he has a uniquely broad perspective into multiple aspects of Java technology. In addition, he is the author of two books on Java programming: *Java WebSocket Programming* and *Java EE 7: The Big Picture.* More recently, he has been applying his knowledge of Java to scale Java-based services for one of the world's most successful software companies. Dr. Coward holds bachelor's, master's, and doctorate degrees in mathematics from the University of Oxford.

## About the Technical Editor

**Simon Ritter** is the deputy CTO of Azul. Simon joined Sun Microsystems in 1996 and spent time working in both Java development and consultancy. He has been presenting Java technologies to developers since 1999, focusing on the core Java platform as well as client and embedded applications. At Azul, he continues to help people understand Java and the JVM.

Simon is a Java Champion and two-time recipient of the JavaOne Rockstar award. In addition, he represents Azul on the JCP Executive Committee, the OpenJDK Vulnerability Group, and the JSR Expert Group since Java SE 9.

# The Complete Reference

# Java™ Thirteenth Edition

Herbert Schildt
Dr. Danny Coward

McGraw Hill Education (India) Private Limited

**Java™: The Complete Reference, Thirteenth Edition**



**McGraw Hill Education (India) Reprint 2024**

Seventh reprint 2025

Reprinted in India by arrangement with McGraw Hill LLC.

Sales territories: India, Pakistan, Nepal, Bangladesh, Sri Lanka and Bhutan

**Library of Congress Control Number: 2023948899**

**ISBN-13: 978-93-5532-647-8**
**ISBN-10: 93-5532-647-5**

**07 08 09 10 11 RAJ 29 28 27 26 25**

Published by McGraw Hill Education (India) Private Limited,
Anjana Complex No: 5/90 A, Butt Road, St. Thomas Mount, Chennai – 600016, Tamil Nadu, India,
Printed and bound in India at Rajkamal Electric Press, Kundli, Sonepat, Haryana.

Visit us at: www.mheducation.co.in

Write to us at: professional.india@mheducation.com

CIN: U80302TN2010PTC111532
Toll free Number: 1800 103 5875

# Contents at a Glance

# Contents

## Part II The Java Library

## Part IV Applying Java

# Foreword

Having written extensively about programming for nearly four decades, the time has come for me to retire. As a result, this edition of *Java: The Complete Reference* was prepared by Dr. Danny Coward. Danny is a Java expert, a published author, and the technical editor on several previous editions of this book. When it came time for me to retire, he generously agreed to take on the task of fully revising this book for JDK 21. As a result, all revisions, updates, and new material, such as coverage of **record** patterns, pattern matching for **switch**, and sequenced collections, were prepared and written by Danny. Revising a book of this size is no small task, and I want thank Danny for all his efforts in preparing this, the thirteenth edition of *Java: The Complete Reference.*

I also want to thank everyone at McGraw Hill. To become a successful writer requires a successful publisher. Each needs the other to create a quality book. (In other words, writing and publishing form two sides of the same coin.) Of course, a publisher is only as good as its people. Over these many years, I have been fortunate to have worked with some of the very best. Although there are far too many to name them all, I want to give special thanks to Wendy Rinaldi, Lisa McClain, Patty Mon, Jeff Pepper, and Scott Rogers. Friends, it's been one grand adventure and a wonderful time. All the best, and many thanks!

—HERBERT SCHILDT

# Preface

Java is one of the world's most important and widely used computer languages. Furthermore, it has held that distinction for many years. Unlike some other computer languages whose influence has waned with the passage of time, Java's has grown stronger. Java leapt to the forefront of Internet programming with its first release. Each subsequent version has solidified that position. Today, it is still the first and best choice for developing web-based applications. It is also a powerful, general-purpose programming language suitable for a wide variety of purposes. Simply put: much of the modern world runs on Java code. Java really is that important.

A key reason for Java's success is its agility. Since its original 1.0 release, Java has continually adapted to changes in the programming environment and to changes in the way that programmers program. Most importantly, it has not just followed the trends, it has helped create them. Java's ability to accommodate the fast rate of change in the computing world is a crucial part of why it has been and continues to be so successful.

Since this book was first published in 1996, it has gone through several editions, each reflecting the ongoing evolution of Java. This is the thirteenth edition, and it has been updated for Java SE 21 (JDK 21). As a result, this edition of the book contains a substantial amount of new material, updates, and changes. Of special interest are the discussions of the following key features that have been added to the Java platform since the previous edition of this book:

- Pattern matching in **switch**
- Record patterns
- Sequenced collections
- Virtual threads

Collectively, these constitute a substantial set of new features that significantly expand the range, scope, and expressiveness of the platform. The first two features are additions to the Java language itself. Pattern matching in **switch** expands the expressiveness of the **switch** statement to look for values matching a number of patterns, while record patterns allows pattern matching with Java records in **instanceof** expressions for concise and powerful forms of data processing. The additional APIs in Sequenced Collections defines the idea of the *encounter order* on several of the familiar Java Collection classes, while also providing uniform APIs to manage their first and last elements and for processing their elements backwards. Virtual Threads allow developers to create Java threads in their traditional form but that are managed by Java, not by the underlying OS, thereby opening up the possibilities to scale applications that require large numbers of threads more gracefully. Collectively, these new features fundamentally expand the ways in which you can design and implement solutions.

## A Book for All Programmers

This book is for all programmers, whether you are a novice or an experienced pro. The beginner will find its carefully paced discussions and many examples especially helpful. Its in-depth coverage of Java's more advanced features and libraries will appeal to the pro. For both, it offers a lasting resource and handy reference.

## What's Inside

This book is a comprehensive guide to the Java language, describing its syntax, keywords, and fundamental programming principles. Significant portions of the Java API library are also examined. The book is divided into four parts, each focusing on a different aspect of the Java programming environment.

Part I presents an in-depth tutorial of the Java language. It begins with the basics, including such things as data types, operators, control statements, and classes. It then moves on to inheritance, packages, interfaces, exception handling, and multithreading including the new virtual threading. Next, it describes annotations, enumerations, autoboxing, generics, modules, and lambda expressions. I/O is also introduced. The final chapter in Part I covers several recently added features: records, sealed classes and interfaces, the enhanced **switch**, including pattern matching, record patterns, pattern matching with **instanceof**, and text blocks.

Part II examines key aspects of Java's standard API library. Topics include strings, I/O, networking, the standard utilities, the Collections Framework (including the newly added Sequenced Collections), the AWT, event handling, imaging, concurrency (including the Fork/Join Framework), regular expressions, and the stream library.

Part III offers three chapters that introduce Swing.

Part IV contains two chapters that show examples of Java in action. The first discusses Java Beans. The second presents an introduction to servlets.

## Special Thanks

I thank my many mentors as a programmer and designer in Java. Bill Shannon, for teaching me to always strive for the best way to solve a problem; Graham Hamilton, for showing me what it means to be a thought leader' and James Gosling, for bringing out the magic in everyday work.

Thank you to Simon Ritter for his thoughtful and expert technical reviews for the updates to this book, both the detail and the bigger picture.

I give special thanks to Herb Schildt. In creating and maintaining this valuable and comprehensive book with such care and expertise over some 12 editions, he has helped so very many of his readers become skilled and knowledgeable Java programmers. I have enjoyed working with him as a technical reviewer for a number of past editions of this work and am grateful for his thoughtful guidance in my updates to this thirteenth edition.

DANNY COWARD

# PART I

# The Java Language

CHAPTER

# 1 The History and Evolution of Java

To fully understand Java, one must understand the reasons behind its creation, the forces that shaped it, and the legacy that it inherits. Like the successful computer languages that came before, Java is a blend of the best elements of its rich heritage combined with the innovative concepts required by its unique mission. While the remaining chapters of this book describe the practical aspects of Java—including its syntax, key libraries, and applications—this chapter explains how and why Java came about, what makes it so important, and how it has evolved over the years.

Although Java has become inseparably linked with the online environment of the Internet, it is important to remember that Java is first and foremost a programming language. Computer language innovation and development occur for two fundamental reasons:

- To adapt to changing environments and uses
- To implement refinements and improvements in the art of programming

As you will see, the development of Java was driven by both elements in nearly equal measure.

## Java's Lineage

Java is related to C++, which is a direct descendant of C. Much of the character of Java is inherited from these two languages. From C, Java derives its syntax. Many of Java's object-oriented features were influenced by C++. In fact, several of Java's defining characteristics come from—or are responses to—its predecessors. Moreover, the creation of Java was deeply rooted in the process of refinement and adaptation that has been occurring in computer programming languages for the past several decades. For these reasons, this section reviews the sequence of events and forces that led to Java. As you will see, each innovation in language design was driven by the need to solve a fundamental problem that the preceding languages could not solve. Java is no exception.

## The Birth of Modern Programming: C

The C language shook the computer world. Its impact should not be underestimated, because it fundamentally changed the way programming was approached and thought about. The creation of C was a direct result of the need for a structured, efficient, high-level language that could replace assembly code when creating systems programs. As you may know, when a computer language is designed, trade-offs are often made, such as the following:

- Ease-of-use versus power
- Safety versus efficiency
- Rigidity versus extensibility

Prior to C, programmers usually had to choose between languages that optimized one set of traits or the other. For example, although FORTRAN could be used to write fairly efficient programs for scientific applications, it was not very good for system code. And while BASIC was easy to learn, it wasn't very powerful, and its lack of structure made its usefulness questionable for large programs. Assembly language can be used to produce highly efficient programs, but it is not easy to learn or use effectively. Further, debugging assembly code can be quite difficult.

Another compounding problem was that early computer languages such as BASIC, COBOL, and FORTRAN were not designed around structured principles. Instead, they relied upon the GOTO as a primary means of program control. As a result, programs written using these languages tended to produce "spaghetti code"—a mass of tangled jumps and conditional branches that make a program virtually impossible to understand. While languages like Pascal are structured, they were not designed for efficiency, and failed to include certain features necessary to make them applicable to a wide range of programs. (Specifically, given the standard dialects of Pascal available at the time, it was not practical to consider using Pascal for systems-level code.)

So, just prior to the invention of C, no one language had reconciled the conflicting attributes that had dogged earlier efforts. Yet the need for such a language was pressing. By the early 1970s, the computer revolution was beginning to take hold, and the demand for software was rapidly outpacing programmers' ability to produce it. A great deal of effort was being expended in academic circles in an attempt to create a better computer language. But, and perhaps most importantly, a secondary force was beginning to be felt. Computer hardware was finally becoming common enough that a critical mass was being reached. No longer were computers kept behind locked doors. For the first time, programmers were gaining virtually unlimited access to their machines. This allowed the freedom to experiment. It also allowed programmers to begin to create their own tools. On the eve of C's creation, the stage was set for a quantum leap forward in computer languages.

Invented and first implemented by Dennis Ritchie on a DEC PDP-11 running the UNIX operating system, C was the result of a development process that started with an older language called BCPL, developed by Martin Richards. BCPL influenced a language called B, invented by Ken Thompson, which led to the development of C in the 1970s.

For many years, the de facto standard for C was the one supplied with the UNIX operating system and described in *The C Programming Language* by Brian Kernighan and Dennis Ritchie (Prentice-Hall, 1978). C was formally standardized in December 1989, when the American National Standards Institute (ANSI) standard for C was adopted.

The creation of C is considered by many to have marked the beginning of the modern age of computer languages. It successfully synthesized the conflicting attributes that had so troubled earlier languages. The result was a powerful, efficient, structured language that was relatively easy to learn. It also included one other, nearly intangible aspect: it was a *programmer's* language. Prior to the invention of C, computer languages were generally designed either as academic exercises or by bureaucratic committees. C is different. It was designed, implemented, and developed by real, working programmers, reflecting the way that they approached the job of programming. Its features were honed, tested, thought about, and rethought by the people who actually used the language. The result was a language that programmers liked to use. Indeed, C quickly attracted many followers who had a near-religious zeal for it. As such, it found wide and rapid acceptance in the programmer community. In short, C is a language designed by and for programmers. As you will see, Java inherited this legacy.

## C++: The Next Step

During the late 1970s and early 1980s, C became the dominant computer programming language, and it is still widely used today. Since C is a successful and useful language, you might ask why a need for something else existed. The answer is *complexity*. Throughout the history of programming, the increasing complexity of programs has driven the need for better ways to manage that complexity. C++ is a response to that need. To better understand why managing program complexity is fundamental to the creation of C++, consider the following.

Approaches to programming have changed dramatically since the invention of the computer. For example, when computers were first invented, programming was done by manually toggling in the binary machine instructions by use of the front panel. As long as programs were just a few hundred instructions long, this approach worked. As programs grew, assembly language was invented so that a programmer could deal with larger, increasingly complex programs by using symbolic representations of the machine instructions. As programs continued to grow, high-level languages were introduced that gave the programmer more tools with which to handle complexity.

The first widespread language was, of course, FORTRAN. While FORTRAN was an impressive first step, at the time it was hardly a language that encouraged clear and easy-to-understand programs. The 1960s gave birth to *structured programming*. This is the method of programming championed by languages such as C. The use of structured languages enabled programmers to write, for the first time, moderately complex programs fairly easily. However, even with structured programming methods, once a project reaches a certain size, its complexity exceeds what a programmer can manage. By the early 1980s, many projects were pushing the structured approach past its limits. To solve this problem, a new way to program was invented, called *object-oriented programming (OOP)*. Object-oriented programming is discussed in detail later in this book, but here is a brief definition: OOP is a programming methodology that helps organize complex programs through the use of inheritance, encapsulation, and polymorphism.

In the final analysis, although C is one of the world's great programming languages, there is a limit to its ability to handle complexity. Once the size of a program exceeds a certain point, it becomes so complex that it is difficult to grasp as a totality. While the precise size at which this occurs differs, depending upon both the nature of the program and the programmer, there is always a threshold at which a program becomes unmanageable. C++ added features that enabled this threshold to be broken, allowing programmers to comprehend and manage larger programs.

C++ was invented by Bjarne Stroustrup in 1979, while he was working at Bell Laboratories in Murray Hill, New Jersey. Stroustrup initially called the new language "C with Classes." However, in 1983, the name was changed to C++. C++ extends C by adding object-oriented features. Because C++ is built on the foundation of C, it includes all of C's features, attributes, and benefits. This is a crucial reason for the success of C++ as a language. The invention of C++ was not an attempt to create a completely new programming language. Instead, it was an enhancement to an already highly successful one.

### The Stage Is Set for Java

By the end of the 1980s and the early 1990s, object-oriented programming using C++ took hold. Indeed, for a brief moment it seemed as if programmers had finally found the perfect language. Because C++ blended the high efficiency and stylistic elements of C with the object-oriented paradigm, it was a language that could be used to create a wide range of programs. However, just as in the past, forces were brewing that would, once again, drive computer language evolution forward. Within a few years, the World Wide Web and the Internet would reach critical mass. This event would precipitate another revolution in programming.

## The Creation of Java

Java was conceived by James Gosling, Patrick Naughton, Chris Warth, Ed Frank, and Mike Sheridan at Sun Microsystems, Inc., in 1991. It took 18 months to develop the first working version. This language was initially called "Oak," but was renamed "Java" in 1995. Between the initial implementation of Oak in the fall of 1992 and the public announcement of Java in the spring of 1995, many more people contributed to the design and evolution of the language. Bill Joy, Arthur van Hoff, Jonathan Payne, Frank Yellin, and Tim Lindholm were key contributors to the maturing of the original prototype.

Somewhat surprisingly, the original impetus for Java was not the Internet! Instead, the primary motivation was the need for a platform-independent (that is, architecture-neutral) language that could be used to create software to be embedded in various consumer electronic devices, such as microwave ovens and remote controls. As you can probably guess, many different types of CPUs are used as controllers. The trouble with C and C++ (and most other languages at the time) is that they are designed to be compiled for a specific target. Although it is possible to compile a C++ program for just about any type of CPU, to do so requires a full C++ compiler targeted for that CPU. The problem is that compilers are expensive and time-consuming to create. An easier—and more cost-efficient—solution was needed. In an attempt to find such a solution, Gosling and others began work on a portable, platform-independent language that could be used to produce code that would run on a variety of CPUs under differing environments. This effort ultimately led to the creation of Java.

About the time that the details of Java were being worked out, a second, and ultimately more important, factor was emerging that would play a crucial role in the future of Java. This second force was, of course, the World Wide Web. Had the Web not taken shape at about the same time that Java was being implemented, Java might have remained a useful but obscure language for programming consumer electronics. However, with the emergence of the World Wide Web, Java was propelled to the forefront of computer language design, because the Web, too, demanded portable programs.

Most programmers learn early in their careers that portable programs are as elusive as they are desirable. While the quest for a way to create efficient, portable (platform-independent) programs is nearly as old as the discipline of programming itself, it had taken a back seat to other, more pressing problems. Further, because (at that time) much of the computer world had divided itself into the three competing camps of Intel, Macintosh, and UNIX, most programmers stayed within their fortified boundaries, and the urgent need for portable code was reduced. However, with the advent of the Internet and the Web, the old problem of portability returned with a vengeance. After all, the Internet consists of a diverse, distributed universe populated with various types of computers, operating systems, and CPUs. Even though many kinds of platforms are attached to the Internet, users would like them all to be able to run the same program. What was once an irritating but low-priority problem had become a high-profile necessity.

By 1993, it became obvious to members of the Java design team that the problems of portability frequently encountered when creating code for embedded controllers are also found when attempting to create code for the Internet. In fact, the same problem that Java was initially designed to solve on a small scale could also be applied to the Internet on a large scale. This realization caused the focus of Java to switch from consumer electronics to Internet programming. So, while the desire for an architecture-neutral programming language provided the initial spark, the Internet ultimately led to Java's large-scale success.

As mentioned earlier, Java derives much of its character from C and C++. This is by intent. The Java designers knew that using the familiar syntax of C and echoing the object-oriented features of C++ would make their language appealing to the legions of experienced C/C++ programmers. In addition to the surface similarities, Java shares some of the other attributes that helped make C and C++ successful. First, Java was designed, tested, and refined by real, working programmers. It is a language grounded in the needs and experiences of the people who devised it. Thus, Java is a programmer's language. Second, Java is cohesive and logically consistent. Third, except for those constraints imposed by the Internet environment, Java gives you, the programmer, full control. If you program well, your programs reflect it. If you program poorly, your programs reflect that, too. Put differently, Java is not a language with training wheels. It is a language for professional programmers.

Because of the similarities between Java and C++, it is tempting to think of Java as simply the "Internet version of C++." However, to do so would be a large mistake. Java has significant practical and philosophical differences. While it is true that Java was influenced by C++, it is not an enhanced version of C++. For example, Java is neither upwardly nor downwardly compatible with C++. Of course, the similarities with C++ are significant, and if you are a

C++ programmer, then you will feel right at home with Java. One other point: Java was not designed to replace C++. Java was designed to solve a certain set of problems. C++ was designed to solve a different set of problems. Both will coexist for many years to come.

As mentioned at the start of this chapter, computer languages evolve for two reasons: to adapt to changes in environment and to implement advances in the art of programming. The environmental change that prompted Java was the need for platform-independent programs destined for distribution on the Internet. However, Java also embodies changes in the way that people approach the writing of programs. For example, Java enhanced and refined the object-oriented paradigm used by C++, added integrated support for multithreading, and provided a library that simplified Internet access. In the final analysis, though, it was not the individual features of Java that made it so remarkable. Rather, it was the language as a whole. Java was the perfect response to the demands of the then newly emerging, highly distributed computing universe. Java was to Internet programming what C was to system programming: a revolutionary force that changed the world.

### The C# Connection

The reach and power of Java continues to be felt throughout the world of computer language development. Many of its innovative features, constructs, and concepts have become part of the baseline for any new language. The success of Java is simply too important to ignore.

Perhaps the most important example of Java's influence is C#. Created by Microsoft to support the .NET Framework, C# is closely related to Java. For example, both share the same general syntax, support distributed programming, and utilize the same object model. There are, of course, differences between Java and C#, but the overall "look and feel" of these languages is very similar. This "cross-pollination" from Java to C# is the strongest testimonial to date that Java redefined the way we think about and use a computer language.

### Longevity

Even as Java has broadened its range and power, other general-purpose computer languages have been created. Some are inspired by the success of Java, often emulating some of its features, even some running on its virtual machine. Some address perceived weaknesses of Java in novel ways. These newer languages include Kotlin, which uses the same bytecode representation but aims to be simpler and easier to learn, and Ruby, a dynamically interpreted language with a straightforward syntax to allow applications to be developed quickly. Other languages include Go, Scala, and Rust. With each year that passes the list grows. But one constant in the near three decades since Java was released has been its popularity with developers. This has kept it at or near the top of the most widely used languages for computing. Perhaps this is testimony to how well Java has continued to evolve to meet the changing needs of developers and the work they do.

## How Java Impacted the Internet

The Internet helped catapult Java to the forefront of programming, and Java, in turn, had a profound effect on the Internet. In addition to simplifying web programming in general, Java innovated a new type of networked program called the applet that changed the way the online world thought about content. Java also addressed some of the thorniest issues associated with the Internet: portability and security. Let's look more closely at each of these.

## Java Applets

At the time of Java's creation, one of its most exciting features was the applet. An *applet* is a special kind of Java program that is designed to be transmitted over the Internet and automatically executed inside a Java-compatible web browser. If the user clicks a link that contains an applet, the applet will download and run in the browser. Applets were intended to be small programs. They were typically used to display data provided by the server, handle user input, or provide simple functions, such as a loan calculator, that execute locally, rather than on the server. In essence, the applet allowed some functionality to be moved from the server to the client.

The creation of the applet was important because, at the time, it expanded the universe of objects that could move about freely in cyberspace. In general, there are two very broad categories of objects that are transmitted between the server and the client: passive information and dynamic, active programs. For example, when you read your e-mail, you are viewing passive data. Even when you download a program, the program's code is still only passive data until you execute it. By contrast, the applet is a dynamic, self-executing program. Such a program is an active agent on the client computer, yet it is initiated by the server.

In the early days of Java, applets were a crucial part of Java programming. They illustrated the power and benefits of Java, added an exciting dimension to web pages, and enabled programmers to explore the full extent of what was possible with Java. Although it is likely that there are still applets in use today, over time they became less important. For reasons that will be explained, beginning with JDK 9, the phase-out of applets began, with applet support being removed by JDK 11.

## Security

As desirable as dynamic, networked programs are, they can also present serious problems in the areas of security and portability. Obviously, a program that downloads and executes on the client computer must be prevented from doing harm. It must also be able to run in a variety of different environments and under different operating systems. As you will see, Java solved these problems in an effective and elegant way. Let's look a bit more closely at each, beginning with security.

As you are likely aware, every time you download a "normal" program, you are taking a risk, because the code you are downloading might contain a virus, Trojan horse, or other harmful code. At the core of the problem is the fact that malicious code can cause its damage because it has gained unauthorized access to system resources. For example, a virus program might gather private information, such as credit card numbers, bank account balances, and passwords, by searching the contents of your computer's local file system. In order for Java to enable programs to be safely downloaded and executed on the client computer, it was necessary to prevent them from launching such an attack.

Java achieved this protection by enabling you to confine an application to the Java execution environment and prevent it from accessing other parts of the computer. (You will see how this is accomplished shortly.) The ability to download programs with a degree of confidence that no harm will be done may have been the single most innovative aspect of Java.

### Portability

Portability is a major aspect of the Internet because there are many different types of computers and operating systems connected to it. If a Java program were to be run on virtually any computer connected to the Internet, there needed to be some way to enable that program to execute on different systems. In other words, a mechanism that allows the same application to be downloaded and executed by a wide variety of CPUs, operating systems, and browsers is required. It is not practical to have different versions of the application for different computers. The *same* application code must work on *all* computers. Therefore, some means of generating portable executable code was needed. As you will soon see, the same mechanism that helps ensure security also helps create portability.

## Java's Magic: The Bytecode

The key that allowed Java to solve both the security and the portability problems just described is that the output of a Java compiler is not executable code. Rather, it is bytecode. *Bytecode* is a highly optimized set of instructions designed to be executed by what is called the *Java Virtual Machine (JVM)*, which is part of the Java Runtime Environment (JRE). In essence, the original JVM was designed as an *interpreter for bytecode*. This may come as a bit of a surprise since many modern languages are designed to be compiled into executable code because of performance concerns. However, the fact that a Java program is executed by the JVM helps solve the major problems associated with web-based programs. Here is why.

Translating a Java program into bytecode makes it much easier to run a program in a wide variety of environments because only the JVM needs to be implemented for each platform. Once a JRE exists for a given system, any Java program can run on it. Remember, although the details of the JVM will differ from platform to platform, all understand the same Java bytecode. If a Java program were compiled to native code, then different versions of the same program would have to exist for each type of CPU connected to the Internet. This is, of course, not a feasible solution. Thus, the execution of bytecode by the JVM is the easiest way to create truly portable programs.

The fact that a Java program is executed by the JVM also helps to make it secure. Because the JVM is in control, it manages program execution. Thus, it is possible for the JVM to create a restricted execution environment, called the *sandbox*, that contains the program, preventing unrestricted access to the machine. Safety is also enhanced by certain restrictions that exist in the Java language.

In general, when a program is compiled to an intermediate form and then interpreted by a virtual machine, it runs slower than it would run if compiled to executable code. However, with Java, the differential between the two is not so great. Because bytecode has been highly optimized, the use of bytecode enables the JVM to execute programs much faster than you might expect.

Although Java was designed as an interpreted language, there is nothing about Java that prevents on-the-fly compilation of bytecode into native code in order to boost performance. For this reason, the HotSpot technology was introduced not long after Java's initial release. HotSpot provides a just-in-time (JIT) compiler for bytecode. When a JIT compiler is part of the JVM, selected portions of bytecode are compiled into executable code in real time, on a piece-by-piece, demand basis. It is important to understand that an entire Java program is not compiled into executable code all at once. Instead, a JIT compiler compiles code as it is needed, during execution. Furthermore, not all sequences of bytecode are compiled—only those that will benefit from compilation. The remaining code is simply interpreted. However, the just-in-time approach still yields a significant performance boost. Even when dynamic compilation is applied to bytecode, the portability and safety features still apply, because the JVM is still in charge of the execution environment.

One other point: There has been experimentation with an *ahead-of-time* compiler for Java. Such a compiler can be used to compile bytecode into native code *prior* to execution by the JVM, rather than on-the-fly. Some previous versions of the JDK supplied an experimental ahead-of-time compiler; however, JDK 17 has removed it. Ahead-of-time compilation is a specialized feature, and it does not replace Java's traditional approach just described. Because of the highly specialized nature of ahead-of-time compilation, it is not discussed further in this book.

## Moving Beyond Applets

At the time of this writing, it has been nearly three decades since Java's original release. Over those years, many changes have taken place. At the time of Java's creation, the Internet was a new and exciting innovation; web browsers were undergoing rapid development and refinement; the modern form of the smart phone had not yet been invented; and the near ubiquitous use of computers was still a few years off. As you would expect, Java has also changed and so, too, has the way that Java is used. Perhaps nothing illustrates the ongoing evolution of Java better than the applet.

As explained previously, in the early years of Java, applets were a crucial part of Java programming. They not only added excitement to a web page, they were also a highly visible part of Java, which added to its charisma. However, applets rely on a Java browser plug-in. Thus, for an applet to work, the browser must support it. Over the past few years, support for the Java browser plug-in has been waning. Simply put, without browser support, applets are not viable. Because of this, beginning with JDK 9, the phase-out of applets was begun, with support for applets being deprecated. In the language of Java, *deprecated* means that a feature is still available but flagged as obsolete. Thus, a deprecated feature should not be used for new code. The phase-out became complete with the release of JDK 11 because run-time support for applets was removed. Beginning with JDK 17, the entire Applet API was deprecated for removal.

As a point of interest, a few years after Java's creation an alternative to applets was added to Java. Called Java Web Start, it enabled an application to be dynamically downloaded from a web page. It was a deployment mechanism that was especially useful for larger Java applications that were not appropriate for applets. The difference between an applet and a Web Start application is that a Web Start application runs on its own, not inside the browser.

Thus, it looks much like a "normal" application. It does, however, require that a stand-alone JRE that supports Web Start is available on the host system. Beginning with JDK 11, Java Web Start support has been removed.

Given that neither applets nor Java Web Start are supported by modern versions of Java, you might wonder what mechanism should be used to deploy a Java application. At the time of this writing, part of the answer is to use the **jlink** tool added by JDK 9. It can create a complete run-time image that includes all necessary support for your program, including the JRE. Another part of the answer is the **jpackage** tool. Added by JDK 16, it can be used to create a ready-to-install application. Although a detailed discussion of deployment strategies is outside the scope of this book, it is something that you will want to pay close attention to going forward.

## A Faster Release Schedule

Another major change has recently occurred in Java, but it does not involve changes to the language or the run-time environment. Rather, it relates to the way that Java releases are scheduled. In the past, major Java releases were typically separated by two or more years. However, subsequent to the release of JDK 9, the time between major Java releases has been decreased. Today, major releases occur every six months.

Each major release, called a *feature release,* includes those features ready at the time of the release. This increased *release cadence* enables new features and enhancements to be available to Java programmers in a timely fashion. Furthermore, it allows Java to respond quickly to the demands of an ever-changing programming environment. Simply put, the faster release schedule promises to be a very positive development for Java programmers.

In addition, feature releases include new features that are available to developers if they explicitly enable them to try them out but that have not yet been finalized. There are two types of these features. First, Preview Features are APIs and/or new language syntax that are fully designed and implemented but may yet be refined before being formally included in a future release based on feedback from developers trying them out. The second type of such experimental features is Incubator Modules, which is a feature that is still evolving significantly and may or may not make it into a future release. Both types of "nonfinal" features give strong indications of what is to come next in feature releases.

With a cadence that is now every two years, a feature release will also be one that is supported (and thus remains viable) for a period of time longer than the six months until the next feature release. Such a release is called a long-term support release (LTS). An LTS release will be supported (and thus remain viable) for a period of time longer than six months. The first LTS release was JDK 11. The second LTS release was JDK 17 and the third JDK 21, for which this book has been updated. Because of the stability that an LTS release offers, it is likely that its feature set will define a baseline of functionality for a number of years. Consult Oracle for the latest information concerning long-term support and the LTS release schedule.

Currently, feature releases are scheduled for March and September of each year. As a result, JDK 10 was released in March 2018, which was six months after the release of JDK 9. The next release (JDK 11) was in September 2018. JDK 11 was an LTS release. This was followed by JDK 12 in March 2019, JDK 13 in September 2019, and so on. At the time of this writing, the latest release is JDK 21, which is an LTS release. Again, it is anticipated that every six months a new feature release will take place. Of course, you will want to consult the latest release schedule information.

At the time of this writing, there are a number of new Java features on the horizon. Because of the faster release schedule, it is very likely that several of them will be added to Java over the next few years. You will want to review the information and release notes provided by each six-month release in detail. It is truly an exciting time to be a Java programmer!

# Servlets: Java on the Server Side

Client-side code is just one half of the client/server equation. Not long after the initial release of Java, it became obvious that Java would also be useful on the server side. One result was the *servlet*. A servlet is a small program that executes on the server.

Servlets are used to create dynamically generated content that is then served to the client. For example, an online store might use a servlet to look up the price for an item in a database. The price information is then used to dynamically generate a web page that is sent to the browser. Although dynamically generated content was available through mechanisms such as CGI (Common Gateway Interface), the servlet offered several advantages, including increased performance.

Because servlets (like all Java programs) are compiled into bytecode and executed by the JVM, they are highly portable. Thus, the same servlet can be used in a variety of different server environments. The only requirements are that the server support the JVM and a servlet container. Today, server-side code in general constitutes a major use of Java.

# The Java Buzzwords

No discussion of Java's history is complete without a look at the Java buzzwords. Although the fundamental forces that necessitated the invention of Java are portability and security, other factors also played an important role in molding the final form of the language. The key considerations were summed up by the Java team in the following list of buzzwords:

- Simple
- Secure
- Portable
- Object-oriented
- Robust
- Multithreaded
- Architecture-neutral
- Interpreted
- High performance
- Distributed
- Dynamic

Two of these buzzwords have already been discussed: secure and portable. Let's examine what each of the others implies.

## Simple

Java was designed to be easy for the professional programmer to learn and use effectively. Assuming that you have some programming experience, you will not find Java hard to master. If you already understand the basic concepts of object-oriented programming, learning Java will be even easier. Best of all, if you are an experienced C++ programmer, moving to Java will require very little effort. Because Java inherits the C/C++ syntax and many of the object-oriented features of C++, most programmers have little trouble learning Java.

## Object-Oriented

Although influenced by its predecessors, Java was not designed to be source-code compatible with any other language. This allowed the Java team the freedom to design with a blank slate. One outcome of this was a clean, usable, pragmatic approach to objects. Borrowing liberally from many seminal object-software environments of the last few decades, Java managed to strike a balance between the purist's "everything is an object" paradigm and the pragmatist's "stay out of my way" model. The object model in Java is simple and easy to extend, while primitive types, such as integers, were kept as high-performance nonobjects.

## Robust

The multiplatformed environment of the Web places extraordinary demands on a program, because the program must execute reliably in a variety of systems. Thus, the ability to create robust programs was given a high priority in the design of Java. To gain reliability, Java restricts you in a few key areas to force you to find your mistakes early in program development. At the same time, Java frees you from having to worry about many of the most common causes of programming errors. Because Java is a strictly typed language, it checks your code at compile time. However, it also checks your code at run time. Many hard-to-track-down bugs that often turn up in hard-to-reproduce run-time situations are simply impossible to create in Java. Knowing that what you have written will behave in a predictable way under diverse conditions is a key feature of Java.

To better understand how Java is robust, consider two of the main reasons for program failure: memory management mistakes and mishandled exceptional conditions (that is, run-time errors). Memory management can be a difficult, tedious task in traditional programming environments. For example, in C/C++, the programmer will often manually allocate and free dynamic memory. This sometimes leads to problems, because programmers will either forget to free memory that has been previously allocated or, worse, try to free some memory that another part of their code is still using. Java virtually eliminates these problems by managing memory allocation and deallocation for you. (In fact, deallocation is completely automatic, because Java provides garbage collection for unused objects.) Exceptional conditions in traditional environments often arise in situations such as division by zero or "file not found," and they must be managed with clumsy and hard-to-read constructs. Java helps in this area by providing object-oriented exception handling. In a well-written Java program, all run-time errors can—and should—be managed by your program.

### Multithreaded

Java was designed to meet the real-world requirement of creating interactive, networked programs. To accomplish this, Java supports multithreaded programming, which allows you to write programs that do many things simultaneously. The Java run-time system comes with an elegant yet sophisticated solution for multiprocess synchronization that enables you to construct smoothly running interactive systems. Java's easy-to-use approach to multithreading allows you to think about the specific behavior of your program, not the multitasking subsystem.

### Architecture-Neutral

A central issue for the Java designers was that of code longevity and portability. At the time of Java's creation, one of the main problems facing programmers was that no guarantee existed that if you wrote a program today, it would run tomorrow—even on the same machine. Operating system upgrades, processor upgrades, and changes in core system resources can all combine to make a program malfunction. The Java designers made several hard decisions in the Java language and the Java Virtual Machine in an attempt to alter this situation. Their goal was "write once; run anywhere, any time, forever." To a great extent, this goal was accomplished.

### Interpreted and High Performance

As described earlier, Java enables the creation of cross-platform programs by compiling into an intermediate representation called Java bytecode. This code can be executed on any system that implements the Java Virtual Machine. Most previous attempts at cross-platform solutions have done so at the expense of performance. As explained earlier, the Java bytecode was carefully designed so that it would be easy to translate directly into native machine code for very high performance by using a just-in-time compiler. Java run-time systems that provide this feature lose none of the benefits of the platform-independent code.

### Distributed

Java is designed for the distributed environment of the Internet because it handles TCP/IP protocols. In fact, accessing a resource using a URL is not much different from accessing a file. Java also supports *Remote Method Invocation (RMI)*. This feature enables a program to invoke methods across a network.

### Dynamic

Java programs carry with them substantial amounts of run-time type information that is used to verify and resolve accesses to objects at run time. This makes it possible to dynamically link code in a safe and expedient manner. This is crucial to the robustness of the Java environment, in which small fragments of bytecode may be dynamically updated on a running system.

## The Evolution of Java

The initial release of Java was nothing short of revolutionary, but it did not mark the end of Java's era of rapid innovation. Unlike most other software systems that usually settle into a pattern of small, incremental improvements, Java continued to evolve at an explosive pace.

Soon after the release of Java 1.0, the designers of Java had already created Java 1.1. The features added by Java 1.1 were more significant and substantial than the increase in the minor revision number would have you think. Java 1.1 added many new library and language features, introduced anonymous and inner classes, redefined the way events are handled, and reconfigured many features of the 1.0 library. It also deprecated (rendered obsolete) several features originally defined by Java 1.0. Thus, Java 1.1 both added to and subtracted from attributes of its original specification.

The next major release of Java was Java 2, where the "2" indicates "second generation." The creation of Java 2 was a watershed event, marking the beginning of Java's "modern age." The first release of Java 2 carried the version number 1.2. It may seem odd that the first release of Java 2 used the 1.2 version number. The reason is that it originally referred to the internal version number of the Java libraries, but then was generalized to refer to the entire release. With Java 2, Sun repackaged the Java product as J2SE (Java 2 Platform Standard Edition), and the version numbers began to be applied to that product.

Java 2 added support for a number of new features, such as Swing and the Collections Framework, and it enhanced the Java Virtual Machine and various programming tools. Java 2 also contained a few deprecations. The most important affected the **Thread** class in which the methods **suspend( )**, **resume( )**, and **stop( )** were deprecated.

J2SE 1.3 was the first major upgrade to the original Java 2 release. For the most part, it added to existing functionality and "tightened up" the development environment. In general, programs written for version 1.2 and those written for version 1.3 are source-code compatible. Although version 1.3 contained a smaller set of changes than the preceding three major releases, it was nevertheless important.

The release of J2SE 1.4 further enhanced Java. This release contained several important upgrades, enhancements, and additions. For example, it added the new keyword **assert**, chained exceptions, and a channel-based I/O subsystem. It also made changes to the Collections Framework and the networking classes. In addition, numerous small changes were made throughout. Despite the significant number of new features, version 1.4 maintained nearly 100 percent source-code compatibility with prior versions.

The next release of Java was J2SE 5, and it was revolutionary. Unlike most of the previous Java upgrades, which offered important, but measured improvements, J2SE 5 fundamentally expanded the scope, power, and range of the language. To grasp the magnitude of the changes that J2SE 5 made to Java, consider the following list of its major new features:

- Generics
- Annotations
- Autoboxing and auto-unboxing
- Enumerations
- Enhanced, for-each style **for** loop
- Variable-length arguments (varargs)
- Static import
- Formatted I/O
- Concurrency utilities

This is not a list of minor tweaks or incremental upgrades. Each item in the list represented a significant addition to the Java language. Some, such as generics, the enhanced **for**, and varargs, introduced new syntax elements. Others, such as autoboxing and auto-unboxing, altered the semantics of the language. Annotations added an entirely new dimension to programming. In all cases, the impact of these additions went beyond their direct effects. They changed the very character of Java itself.

The importance of these new features is reflected in the use of the version number "5." The next version number for Java would normally have been 1.5. However, the new features were so significant that a shift from 1.4 to 1.5 just didn't seem to express the magnitude of the change. Instead, Sun elected to increase the version number to 5 as a way of emphasizing that a major event was taking place. Thus, it was named J2SE 5, and the developer's kit was called JDK 5. However, in order to maintain consistency, Sun decided to use 1.5 as its internal version number, which is also referred to as the *developer version* number. The "5" in J2SE 5 is called the *product version* number.

The next release of Java was called Java SE 6. Sun once again decided to change the name of the Java platform. First, notice that the "2" was dropped. Thus, the platform was now named *Java SE*, and the official product name was *Java Platform, Standard Edition 6*. The Java Development Kit was called JDK 6. As with J2SE 5, the 6 in Java SE 6 is the product version number. The internal, developer version number is 1.6.

Java SE 6 built on the base of J2SE 5, adding incremental improvements. Java SE 6 added no major features to the Java language proper, but it did enhance the API libraries, added several new packages, and offered improvements to the run time. It also went through several updates during its (in Java terms) long life cycle, with several upgrades added along the way. In general, Java SE 6 served to further solidify the advances made by J2SE 5.

Java SE 7 was the next release of Java, with the Java Development Kit being called JDK 7, and an internal version number of 1.7. Java SE 7 was the first major release of Java after Sun Microsystems was acquired by Oracle. Java SE 7 contained many new features, including significant additions to the language and the API libraries. Upgrades to the Java run-time system that support non-Java languages were also included, but it is the language and library additions that were of most interest to Java programmers.

The new language features were developed as part of *Project Coin*. The purpose of Project Coin was to identify a number of small changes to the Java language that would be incorporated into JDK 7. Although these features were collectively referred to as "small," the effects of these changes have been quite large in terms of the code they impact. In fact, for many programmers, these changes may well have been the most important new features in Java SE 7. Here is a list of the language features added by JDK 7:

- A **String** can now control a **switch** statement.
- Binary integer literals.
- Underscores in numeric literals.
- An expanded **try** statement, called ***try-with-resources***, that supports automatic resource management. (For example, streams can be closed automatically when they are no longer needed.)
- Type inference (via the *diamond* operator) when constructing a generic instance.

- Enhanced exception handling in which two or more exceptions can be caught by a single **catch** (multi-catch) and better type checking for exceptions that are rethrown.
- Although not a syntax change, the compiler warnings associated with some types of varargs methods were improved, and you have more control over the warnings.

As you can see, even though the Project Coin features were considered small changes to the language, their benefits were much larger than the qualifier "small" would suggest. In particular, the **try**-*with-resources* statement has profoundly affected the way that stream-based code is written. Also, the ability to use a **String** to control a **switch** statement was a long-desired improvement that simplified coding in many situations.

Java SE 7 made several additions to the Java API library. Two of the most important were the enhancements to the NIO Framework and the addition of the Fork/Join Framework. NIO (which originally stood for *New I/O*) was added to Java in version 1.4. However, the changes added by Java SE 7 fundamentally expanded its capabilities. So significant were the changes that the term *NIO.2* is often used.

The Fork/Join Framework provides important support for *parallel programming*. Parallel programming is the name commonly given to the techniques that make effective use of computers that contain more than one processor, including multicore systems. The advantage that multicore environments offer is the prospect of significantly increased program performance. The Fork/Join Framework addressed parallel programming by:

- Breaking down large computing tasks into a number of smaller tasks that can be executed in parallel
- Automatically making use of multiple processors

Therefore, by using the Fork/Join Framework, you can design applications that automatically take advantage of the processors available in the execution environment. Of course, not all algorithms lend themselves to parallelization, but for those that do, a significant improvement in execution speed can be obtained.

The next release of Java was Java SE 8, with the developer's kit being called JDK 8. It has an internal version number of 1.8. JDK 8 was a significant upgrade to the Java language because of the inclusion of a far-reaching new language feature: the *lambda expression*. The impact of lambda expressions was, and will continue to be, profound, changing both the way that programming solutions are conceptualized and how Java code is written. As explained in detail in Chapter 15, lambda expressions add functional programming features to Java. In the process, lambda expressions can simplify and reduce the amount of source code needed to create certain constructs, such as some types of anonymous classes. The addition of lambda expressions also caused a new operator (the –>) and a new syntax element to be added to the language.

The inclusion of lambda expressions has also had a wide-ranging effect on the Java libraries, with new features being added to take advantage of them. One of the most important was the new stream API, which is packaged in **java.util.stream**. The stream API supports pipeline operations on data and is optimized for lambda expressions. Another new package was **java.util.function**. It defines a number of *functional interfaces*, which provide additional support for lambda expressions. Other new lambda-related features are found throughout the API library.

Another lambda-inspired feature affects **interface**. Beginning with JDK 8, it is now possible to define a default implementation for a method specified by an interface. If no implementation for a default method is created, then the default defined by the interface is used. This feature enables interfaces to be gracefully evolved over time because a new method can be added to an interface without breaking existing code. It can also streamline the implementation of an interface when the defaults are appropriate. Other new features in JDK 8 include a new time and date API, type annotations, and the ability to use parallel processing when sorting an array, among others.

The next release of Java was Java SE 9. The developer's kit was called JDK 9. With the release of JDK 9, the internal version number is also 9. JDK 9 represented a major Java release, incorporating significant enhancements to both the Java language and its libraries. Like the JDK 5 and JDK 8 releases, JDK 9 affected the Java language and its API libraries in fundamental ways.

The primary new JDK 9 feature was *modules*, which enable you to specify the relationship and dependencies of the code that comprises an application. Modules also add another dimension to Java's access control features. The inclusion of modules caused a new syntax element and several keywords to be added to Java. Furthermore, a tool called **jlink** was added to the JDK, which enables a programmer to create a run-time image of an application that contains only the necessary modules. A new file type, called JMOD, was created. Modules also have a profound affect on the API library because, beginning with JDK 9, the library packages are now organized into modules.

Although modules constitute a major Java enhancement, they are conceptually simple and straightforward. Furthermore, because pre-module legacy code is fully supported, modules can be integrated into the development process on your timeline. There is no need to immediately change any preexisting code to handle modules. In short, modules added substantial functionality without altering the essence of Java.

In addition to modules, JDK 9 included many other new features. One of particular interest is JShell, which is a tool that supports interactive program experimentation and learning. (An introduction to JShell is found in Appendix B.) Another interesting upgrade is support for private interface methods. Their inclusion further enhanced JDK 8's support for default methods in interfaces. JDK 9 added a search feature to the **javadoc** tool and a new tag called **@index** to support it. As with previous releases, JDK 9 contained a number of enhancements to Java's API libraries.

As a general rule, in any Java release, it is the new features that receive the most attention. However, there was one high-profile aspect of Java that was deprecated by JDK 9: applets. Beginning with JDK 9, applets were no longer recommended for new projects. As explained earlier in this chapter, because of waning browser support for applets (and other factors), JDK 9 deprecated the entire applet API.

The next release of Java was Java SE 10 (JDK 10), which was released in March 2018. The primary new language feature added by JDK 10 was support for *local variable type inference*. With local variable type inference, it is now possible to let the type of a local variable be inferred from the type of its initializer, rather than being explicitly specified. To support this new capability, the context-sensitive keyword **var** was added to Java. Type inference can streamline code by eliminating the need to redundantly specify a variable's type when it can be inferred from its initializer. It can also simplify declarations in cases in which the type is difficult to discern or cannot be explicitly specified. Local variable type inference has become a common part of the contemporary programming environment. Its inclusion in Java helps keep Java up to date with evolving trends in language design. Along with a number of other changes, JDK 10 also redefined the Java version string, changing the meaning of the version numbers so that they better align with the new time-based release schedule.

The next version of Java was Java SE 11 (JDK 11). It was released in September 2018, which was six months after JDK 10. JDK 11 was an LTS release. The primary new language feature in JDK 11 was support for the use of **var** in a lambda expression. Along with a number of tweaks and updates to the API in general, JDK 11 added a new networking API, which will be of interest to a wide range of developers. Called the *HTTP Client API,* it is packaged in **java.net.http**, and it provides enhanced, updated, and improved networking support for HTTP clients. Also, another execution mode was added to the Java launcher that enables it to directly execute simple single-file programs. JDK 11 also removed some features. Perhaps of the greatest interest because of its historical significance is the removal of support for applets. Recall that applets were first deprecated by JDK 9. With the release of JDK 11, applet support has been removed. Support for another deployment-related technology called Java Web Start was also removed from JDK 11. As the execution environment has continued to evolve, both applets and Java Web Start were rapidly losing relevance. Another key change in JDK 11 is that JavaFX was no longer included in the JDK. Instead, this GUI framework has become a separate open-source project. Because these features are no longer part of the JDK, they are not discussed in this book.

Between the JDK 11 LTS and the next LTS release (JDK 17) were five feature releases: JDK 12 through JDK 16. JDK 14 added support for the **switch** expression, which is a **switch** that produces a value and which was included in JDK 12 in preview form. Other enhancements to **switch** were also included. Text blocks, which are essentially string literals that can span more than one line, were added by JDK 15, after being previewed in JDK 13. JDK 16 enhanced **instanceof** with pattern matching and added a new type of class called a *record* along with the new context-sensitive keyword **record**. A record provides a convenient means of aggregating data. JDK 16 also supplied a new application packaging tool called **jpackage**.

JDK 17 was the second LTS release. Its major new feature was the ability to seal classes and interfaces. Sealing gives you control over the inheritance of a class and the inheritance and implementation of an interface. To this end, it adds the context-sensitive keywords **sealed**, **permits**, and **non-sealed**, which is the first hyphenated Java keyword. JDK 17 marks the applet API as deprecated for removal in a future release.

At the time of this writing, Java SE 21 (JDK 21) is the latest version of Java and the third LTS Java release. Thus, it is of particular importance. Its major new features are both to the language and to the APIs. The language additions of patterns in **switch** statements and record patterns enhance the power of Java to express complex data processing procedures concisely. The API additions of Sequenced Collections bring a uniform way to deal with collections with a well-defined order in which the elements are processed, while virtual threads offer a new way for the Java platform to manage Java threads efficiently, with an API model that is entirely consistent with the existing operating system managed thread model.

JDK 21 also includes several preview features, such as string templates and structured concurrency. These features are still undergoing development and may evolve further in future releases, but are available for experimentation by developers in this release.

One other point about the evolution of Java: Beginning in 2006, the process of open-sourcing Java began, which resulted in the OpenJDK project: a home for the reference implementation of Java and now also home for the ongoing evolution of Java through its formal process for proposing, refining, and integrating new features in Java, called Java Enhancement Proposals (JEP). Today, other open-source implementations of the JDK are also available. Open-sourcing further contributes to the dynamic nature of Java development. In the final analysis, Java's legacy of innovation is secure. Java remains the vibrant, nimble language that the programming world has come to expect.

The material in this book has been updated through JDK 21. Many new Java features, updates, and additions are described throughout. As the preceding discussion has highlighted, however, the history of Java programming is marked by dynamic change. You will want to review the new features in each subsequent Java release. Simply put: The evolution of Java continues!

## A Culture of Innovation

Since the beginning, Java has been at the center of a culture of innovation. Its original release redefined programming for the Internet. The Java Virtual Machine (JVM) and bytecode changed the way we think about security and portability. Portable code made the Web come alive. The Java Community Process (JCP) redefined the way that new ideas are assimilated into the language. The world of Java has never stood still for very long. JDK 21 is the latest release in Java's ongoing, dynamic history.

CHAPTER

# 2 An Overview of Java

As in all other computer languages, the elements of Java do not exist in isolation. Rather, they work together to form the language as a whole. However, this interrelatedness can make it difficult to describe one aspect of Java without involving several others. Often a discussion of one feature implies prior knowledge of another. For this reason, this chapter presents a quick overview of several key features of Java. The material described here will give you a foothold that will allow you to write and understand simple programs. Most of the topics discussed will be examined in greater detail in the remaining chapters of Part I.

## Object-Oriented Programming

Object-oriented programming (OOP) is at the core of Java. In fact, all Java programs are to at least some extent object-oriented. OOP is so integral to Java that it is best to understand its basic principles before you begin writing even simple Java programs. Therefore, this chapter begins with a discussion of the theoretical aspects of OOP.

### Two Paradigms

All computer programs consist of two elements: code and data. Furthermore, a program can be conceptually organized around its code or around its data. That is, some programs are written around "what is happening" and others are written around "who is being affected." These are the two paradigms that govern how a program is constructed. The first way is called the *process-oriented model.* This approach characterizes a program as a series of linear steps (that is, code). The process-oriented model can be thought of as *code acting on data*. Procedural languages such as C employ this model to considerable success. However, as mentioned in Chapter 1, problems with this approach appear as programs grow larger and more complex.

To manage increasing complexity, the second approach, called *object-oriented programming*, was conceived. Object-oriented programming organizes a program around its data (that is, objects) and a set of well-defined interfaces to that data. An object-oriented program can be characterized as *data controlling access to code*. As you will see, by switching the controlling entity to data, you can achieve several organizational benefits.

## Abstraction

An essential element of object-oriented programming is *abstraction*. Humans manage complexity through abstraction. For example, people do not think of a car as a set of tens of thousands of individual parts. They think of it as a well-defined object with its own unique behavior. This abstraction allows people to use a car to drive to the grocery store without being overwhelmed by the complexity of the individual parts. They can ignore the details of how the engine, transmission, and braking systems work. Instead, they are free to utilize the object as a whole.

A powerful way to manage abstraction is through the use of hierarchical classifications. This allows you to layer the semantics of complex systems, breaking them into more manageable pieces. From the outside, the car is a single object. Once inside, you see that the car consists of several subsystems: steering, brakes, sound system, seat belts, heating, cellular phone, and so on. In turn, each of these subsystems is made up of more specialized units. For instance, the system you interact with through a car's dashboard controls may consist of a media system, navigation interface, and vehicle monitoring display. The point is that you manage the complexity of the car (or any other complex system) through the use of hierarchical abstractions.

Hierarchical abstractions of complex systems can also be applied to computer programs. The data from a traditional process-oriented program can be transformed by abstraction into its component objects. A sequence of process steps can become a collection of messages between these objects. Thus, each of these objects describes its own unique behavior. You can treat these objects as concrete entities that respond to messages telling them to *do something*. This is the essence of object-oriented programming.

Object-oriented concepts form the heart of Java just as they form the basis for human understanding. It is important that you understand how these concepts translate into programs. As you will see, object-oriented programming is a powerful and natural paradigm for creating programs that survive the inevitable changes accompanying the life cycle of any major software project, including conception, growth, and aging. For example, once you have well-defined objects and clean, reliable interfaces to those objects, you can gracefully decommission or replace parts of an older system without fear.

## The Three OOP Principles

All object-oriented programming languages provide mechanisms that help you implement the object-oriented model. They are encapsulation, inheritance, and polymorphism. Let's take a look at these concepts now.

### Encapsulation

*Encapsulation* is the mechanism that binds together code and the data it manipulates, and it keeps both safe from outside interference and misuse. One way to think about encapsulation is as a protective wrapper that prevents the code and data from being arbitrarily accessed by other code defined outside the wrapper. Access to the code and data inside the wrapper is tightly controlled through a well-defined interface. To relate this to the real world, consider the automatic transmission on an automobile. It encapsulates hundreds of bits of information about your engine, such as how much you are accelerating, the pitch of the surface you are on, and the position of the shift lever. You, as the user, have only one method of affecting this complex encapsulation: by moving the gear-shift lever. You can't affect the transmission by using the turn signal or windshield wipers, for example. Thus, the gear-shift lever is a well-defined (indeed, unique) interface to the transmission. Further, what occurs inside the transmission does not affect objects outside the transmission. For example, shifting gears does not turn on the headlights! Because an automatic transmission is encapsulated, dozens of car manufacturers can implement one in any way they please. However, from the driver's point of view, they all work the same. This same idea can be applied to programming. The power of encapsulated code is that everyone knows how to access it and thus can use it regardless of the implementation details—and without fear of unexpected side effects.

In Java, the basis of encapsulation is the class. Although the class will be examined in great detail later in this book, the following brief discussion will be helpful now. A *class* defines the structure and behavior (data and code) that will be shared by a set of objects. Each object of a given class contains the structure and behavior defined by the class, as if it were stamped out by a mold in the shape of the class. For this reason, objects are sometimes referred to as *instances of a class*. Thus, a class is a logical construct; an object has physical reality.

When you create a class, you will specify the code and data that constitute that class. Collectively, these elements are called *members* of the class. Specifically, the data defined by the class are referred to as *member variables* or *instance variables*. The code that operates on that data is referred to as *member methods* or just *methods*. (If you are familiar with C/C++, it may help to know that what a Java programmer calls a *method*, a C/C++ programmer calls a *function*.) In properly written Java programs, the methods define how the member variables can be used. This means that the behavior and interface of a class are defined by the methods that operate on its instance data.

Since the purpose of a class is to encapsulate complexity, there are mechanisms for hiding the complexity of the implementation inside the class. Each method or variable in a class may be marked private or public. The *public* interface of a class represents everything that external users of the class need to know, or may know. The *private* methods and data can only be accessed by code that is a member of the class. Therefore, any other code that is not a member of the class cannot access a private method or variable. Since the private members of a class may only be accessed by other parts of your program through the class's public methods, you can ensure that no improper actions take place. Of course, this means that the public interface should be carefully designed not to expose too much of the inner workings of a class (see Figure 2-1).

## Inheritance

*Inheritance* is the process by which one object acquires the properties of another object. This is important because it supports the concept of hierarchical classification. As mentioned earlier, most knowledge is made manageable by hierarchical (that is, top-down) classifications. For example, a Golden Retriever is part of the classification *dog*, which in turn is part of the *mammal* class, which is under the larger class *animal*. Without the use of hierarchies, each object would need to define all of its characteristics explicitly. However, by use of inheritance, an object need only define those qualities that make it unique within its class. It can inherit its general attributes from its parent. Thus, it is the inheritance mechanism that makes it possible for one object to be a specific instance of a more general case. Let's take a closer look at this process.

Most people naturally view the world as made up of objects that are related to each other in a hierarchical way, such as animals, mammals, and dogs. If you wanted to describe animals in an abstract way, you would say they have some attributes, such as size, intelligence, and type of skeletal system. Animals also have certain behavioral aspects; they eat, breathe, and sleep. This description of attributes and behavior is the class definition for animals.

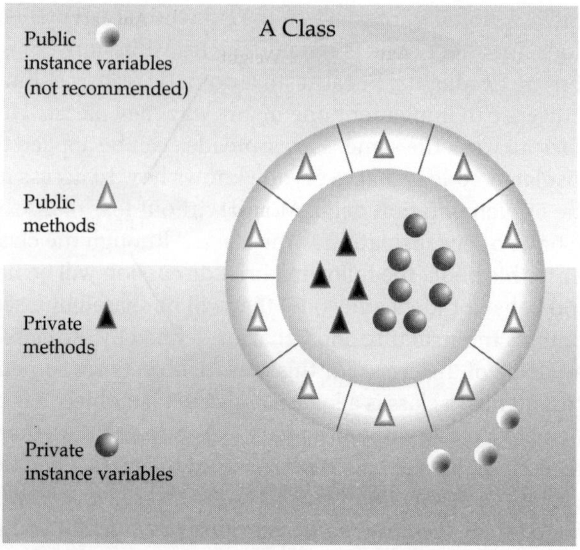


**Figure 2-1** Encapsulation: public methods can be used to protect private data.

If you wanted to describe a more specific class of animals, such as mammals, they would have more specific attributes, such as type of teeth and mammary glands. This is known as a *subclass* of animals, where animals are referred to as mammals' *superclass*.

Since mammals are simply more precisely specified animals, they *inherit* all of the attributes from animals. A deeply inherited subclass inherits all of the attributes from each of its ancestors in the *class hierarchy*.

Inheritance interacts with encapsulation as well. If a given class encapsulates some attributes, then any subclass will have the same attributes *plus* any that it adds as part of its specialization (see Figure 2-2). This is a key concept that lets object-oriented programs grow in complexity linearly rather than geometrically. A new subclass inherits all of the attributes of all of its ancestors. It does not have unpredictable interactions with the majority of the rest of the code in the system.

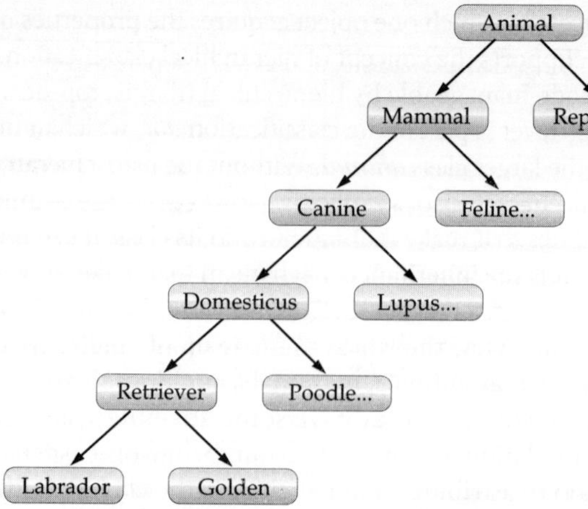

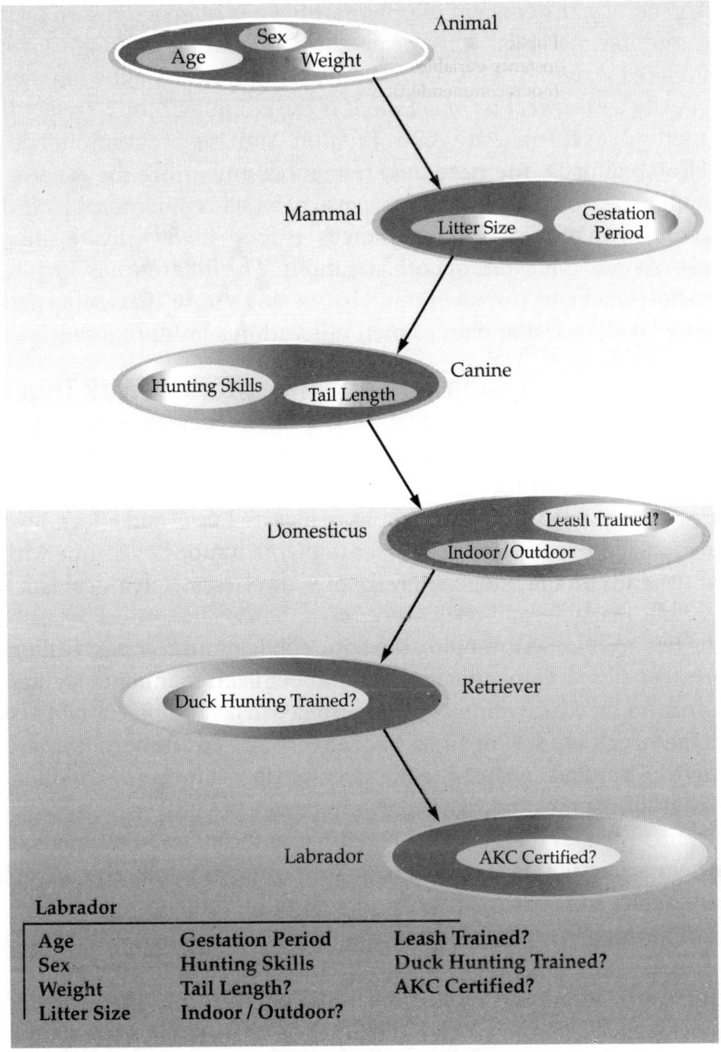


**Figure 2-2** Labrador inherits the encapsulation of all its superclasses.

## Polymorphism

*Polymorphism* (from Greek, meaning "many forms") is a feature that allows one interface to be used for a general class of actions. The specific action is determined by the exact nature of the situation. Consider a stack (which is a last-in, first-out list). You might have a program that requires three types of stacks. One stack is used for integer values, one for floating-point values, and one for characters. The algorithm that implements each stack is the same, even though the data being stored differs. In a non-object-oriented language, you would be required to create three different sets of stack routines, with each set using different names. However, because of polymorphism, in Java you can specify a general set of stack routines that all share the same names.

More generally, the concept of polymorphism is often expressed by the phrase "one interface, multiple methods." This means that it is possible to design a generic interface to a group of related activities. This helps reduce complexity by allowing the same interface to be used to specify a *general class of action*. It is the compiler's job to select the *specific action* (that is, method) as it applies to each situation. You, the programmer, do not need to make this selection manually. You need only remember and utilize the general interface.

Extending the dog analogy, a dog's sense of smell is polymorphic. If the dog smells a cat, it will bark and run after it. If the dog smells its food, it will salivate and run to its bowl. The same sense of smell is at work in both situations. The difference is what is being smelled—that is, the type of data being operated upon by the dog's nose! This same general concept can be implemented in Java as it applies to methods within a Java program.

## Polymorphism, Encapsulation, and Inheritance Work Together

When properly applied, polymorphism, encapsulation, and inheritance combine to produce a programming environment that supports the development of far more robust and scalable programs than does the process-oriented model. A well-designed hierarchy of classes is the basis for reusing the code in which you have invested time and effort developing and testing. Encapsulation allows you to migrate your implementations over time without breaking the code that depends on the public interface of your classes. Polymorphism allows you to create clean, sensible, readable, and resilient code.

Of the two real-world examples, the automobile more completely illustrates the power of object-oriented design. Dogs are fun to think about from an inheritance standpoint, but cars are more like programs. All drivers rely on inheritance to drive different types (subclasses) of vehicles. Whether the vehicle is a school bus, a Mercedes sedan, a Porsche, or the family minivan, drivers can all more or less find and operate the steering wheel, the brakes, and the accelerator. After a bit of gear grinding, most people can even manage the difference between a stick shift and an automatic, because they fundamentally understand their common superclass, the transmission.

People interface with encapsulated features on cars all the time. The brake and gas pedals hide an incredible array of complexity with an interface so simple you can operate them with your feet! The implementation of the engine, the style of brakes, and the size of the tires have no effect on how you interface with the class definition of the pedals.

The final attribute, polymorphism, is clearly reflected in the ability of car manufacturers to offer a wide array of options on basically the same vehicle. For example, you can get an antilock braking system or traditional brakes, power or rack-and-pinion steering, and a 4-, 6-, or 8-cylinder engine, or an EV. Either way, you will still press the brake pedal to stop, turn the steering wheel to change direction, and press the accelerator when you want to move. The same interface can be used to control a number of different implementations.

As you can see, it is through the application of encapsulation, inheritance, and polymorphism that the individual parts are transformed into the object known as a car. The same is also true of computer programs. By the application of object-oriented principles, the various parts of a complex program can be brought together to form a cohesive, robust, maintainable whole.

As mentioned at the start of this section, every Java program is object-oriented. Or, put more precisely, every Java program involves encapsulation, inheritance, and polymorphism. Although the short sample programs shown in the rest of this chapter and in the next few chapters may not seem to exhibit all of these features, they are nevertheless present.

As you will see, many of the features supplied by Java are part of its built-in class libraries, which do make extensive use of encapsulation, inheritance, and polymorphism.

# A First Simple Program

Now that the basic object-oriented underpinning of Java has been discussed, let's look at some actual Java programs. Let's start by compiling and running the short sample program shown here. As you will see, this involves a little more work than you might imagine.

```
/*
   This is a simple Java program.
   Call this file "Example.java".
*/
class Example {
  // Your program begins with a call to main().
  public static void main(String[] args) {
    System.out.println("This is a simple Java program.");
  }
}
```

**NOTE** The descriptions that follow use the standard Java SE Development Kit (JDK), which is available from Oracle. (Open source versions are also available.) If you are using an integrated development environment (IDE), then you will need to follow a different procedure for compiling and executing Java programs. In this case, consult your IDE's documentation for details.

## Entering the Program

For some computer languages, the name of the file that holds the source code to a program is immaterial. However, this is not the case with Java. The first thing that you must learn about Java is that the name you give to a source file is very important. For this example, the name of the source file should be **Example.java**. Let's see why.

In Java, a source file is officially called a *compilation unit*. It is a text file that contains (among other things) one or more class definitions. (For now, we will be using source files that contain only one class.) The Java compiler requires that a source file use the **.java** filename extension.

As you can see by looking at the program, the name of the class defined by the program is also **Example**. This is not a coincidence. In Java, all code must reside inside a class. By convention, the name of the main class should match the name of the file that holds the program. You should also make sure that the capitalization of the filename matches the class name. The reason for this is that Java is case-sensitive. At this point, the convention that filenames correspond to class names may seem arbitrary. However, this convention makes it easier to maintain and organize your programs. Furthermore, as you will see later in this book, in some cases, it is required.

## Compiling the Program

To compile the **Example** program, execute the compiler, **javac**, specifying the name of the source file on the command line, as shown here:

```
C:\>javac Example.java
```

The **javac** compiler creates a file called **Example.class** that contains the bytecode version of the program. As discussed earlier, the Java bytecode is the intermediate representation of your program that contains instructions the Java Virtual Machine will execute. Thus, the output of **javac** is not code that can be directly executed.

To actually run the program, you must use the Java application launcher called **java**. To do so, pass the class name **Example** as a command-line argument, as shown here:

```
C:\>java Example
```

When the program is run, the following output is displayed:

```
This is a simple Java program.
```

When Java source code is compiled, each individual class is put into its own output file named after the class and using the **.class** extension. This is why it is a good idea to give your Java source files the same name as the class they contain—the name of the source file will match the name of the **.class** file. When you execute **java** as just shown, you are actually specifying the name of the class that you want to execute. It will automatically search for a file by that name that has the **.class** extension. If it finds the file, it will execute the code contained in the specified class.

---

**NOTE** Beginning with JDK 11, Java provides a way to run some types of simple programs directly from a source file, without explicitly invoking **javac**. This technique, which can be useful in some situations, is described in Appendix C. For the purposes of this book, it is assumed that you are using the normal compilation process just described.

## A Closer Look at the First Sample Program

Although **Example.java** is quite short, it includes several key features that are common to all Java programs. Let's closely examine each part of the program.

The program begins with the following lines:

```
/*
   This is a simple Java program.
   Call this file "Example.java".
*/
```

This is a *comment*. Like most other programming languages, Java lets you enter a remark into a program's source file. The contents of a comment are ignored by the compiler. Instead, a comment describes or explains the operation of the program to anyone who is reading its source code. In this case, the comment describes the program and reminds you that the source file should be called **Example.java**. Of course, in real applications, comments generally explain how some part of the program works or what a specific feature does.

Java supports three styles of comments. The one shown at the top of the program is called a *multiline comment*. This type of comment must begin with /* and end with */. Anything between these two comment symbols is ignored by the compiler. As the name suggests, a multiline comment may be several lines long.

The next line of code in the program is shown here:

```
class Example {
```

This line uses the keyword **class** to declare that a new class is being defined. **Example** is an *identifier* that is the name of the class. The entire class definition, including all of its members, will be between the opening curly brace ({) and the closing curly brace (}). For the moment, don't worry too much about the details of a class except to note that in Java, all program activity occurs within one. This is one reason why all Java programs are (at least a little bit) object-oriented.

The next line in the program is the *single-line comment*, shown here:

```
// Your program begins with a call to main().
```

This is the second type of comment supported by Java. A *single-line comment* begins with a // and ends at the end of the line. As a general rule, programmers use multiline comments for longer remarks and single-line comments for brief, line-by-line descriptions. The third type of comment, a *documentation comment*, will be discussed in the "Comments" section later in this chapter.

The next line of code is shown here:

```
public static void main(String[] args) {
```

This line begins the **main( )** method. As the comment preceding it suggests, this is the line at which the program will begin executing. As a general rule, a Java program begins execution by calling **main( )**. The full meaning of each part of this line cannot be given now, since it involves a detailed understanding of Java's approach to encapsulation. However, since most of the examples in the first part of this book will use this line of code, let's take a brief look at each part now.

The **public** keyword is an *access modifier*, which allows the programmer to control the visibility of class members. When a class member is preceded by **public**, then that member may be accessed by code outside the class in which it is declared. (The opposite of **public** is **private**, which prevents a member from being used by code defined outside of its class.) In this case, **main( )** must be declared as **public**, since it must be called by code outside of its class when the program is started. The keyword **static** allows **main( )** to be called without having to instantiate a particular instance of the class. This is necessary since **main( )** is called by the Java Virtual Machine before any objects are made. The keyword **void** simply tells the compiler that **main( )** does not return a value. As you will see, methods may also return values. If all this seems a bit confusing, don't worry. All of these concepts will be discussed in detail in subsequent chapters.

As stated, **main( )** is the method called when a Java application begins. Keep in mind that Java is case-sensitive. Thus, **Main** is different from **main**. It is important to understand that the Java compiler will compile classes that do not contain a **main( )** method. But **java** has no way to run these classes. So, if you had typed **Main** instead of **main**, the compiler would still compile your program. However, **java** would report an error because it would be unable to find the **main( )** method.

Any information that you need to pass to a method is received by variables specified within the set of parentheses that follow the name of the method. These variables are called *parameters*. If there are no parameters required for a given method, you still need to include the empty parentheses. In **main( )**, there is only one parameter, albeit a complicated one. **String[ ] args** declares a parameter named **args**, which is an array of instances of the class **String**. (*Arrays* are collections of objects of the same type.) Objects of type **String** store character strings. In this case, **args** receives any command-line arguments present when the program is executed. This program does not make use of this information, but other programs shown later in this book will.

The last character on the line is the {. This signals the start of **main( )**'s body. All of the code that comprises a method will occur between the method's opening curly brace and its closing curly brace.

One other point: **main( )** is simply a starting place for your program. A complex program will have dozens of classes, only one of which will need to have a **main( )** method to get things started. Furthermore, for some types of programs, you won't need **main( )** at all. However, for most of the programs shown in this book, **main( )** is required.

The next line of code is shown here. Notice that it occurs inside **main( )**.

```
System.out.println("This is a simple Java program.");
```

This line outputs the string "This is a simple Java program." followed by a new line on the screen. Output is actually accomplished by the built-in **println( )** method. In this case, **println( )** displays the string that is passed to it. As you will see, **println( )** can be used to display other types of information, too. The line begins with **System.out**. While too complicated to explain in detail at this time, briefly, **System** is a predefined class that provides access to the system, and **out** is the output stream that is connected to the console.

As you have probably guessed, console output (and input) is not used frequently in most real-world Java applications. Since most modern computing environments are graphical in nature, console I/O is used mostly for simple utility programs, demonstration programs, and server-side code. Later in this book, you will learn other ways to generate output using Java. But for now, we will continue to use the console I/O methods.

Notice that the **println( )** statement ends with a semicolon. Many statements in Java end with a semicolon. As you will see, the semicolon is an important part of the Java syntax.

The first } in the program ends **main( )**, and the last } ends the **Example** class definition.

## A Second Short Program

Perhaps no other concept is more fundamental to a programming language than that of a variable. As you may know, a variable is a named memory location that may be assigned a value by your program. The value of a variable may be changed during the execution of the program. The next program shows how a variable is declared and how it is assigned a value. The program also illustrates some new aspects of console output. As the comments at the top of the program state, you should call this file **Example2.java**.

```
/*
   Here is another short example.
   Call this file "Example2.java".
*/

class Example2 {
  public static void main(String[] args) {
    int num; // this declares a variable called num

    num = 100; // this assigns num the value 100

    System.out.println("This is num: " + num);

    num = num * 2;
```

```
    System.out.print("The value of num * 2 is ");
    System.out.println(num);
  }
}
```

When you run this program, you will see the following output:

```
This is num: 100
The value of num * 2 is 200
```

Let's take a close look at why this output is generated. The first new line in the program is shown here:

```
int num; // this declares a variable called num
```

This line declares an integer variable called **num**. Java (like many other languages) requires that variables be declared before they are used.

Following is the general form of a variable declaration:

*type var-name;*

Here, *type* specifies the type of variable being declared, and *var-name* is the name of the variable. If you want to declare more than one variable of the specified type, you may use a comma-separated list of variable names. Java defines several data types, including integer, character, and floating-point. The keyword **int** specifies an integer type.

In the program, the line

```
num = 100; // this assigns num the value 100
```

assigns to **num** the value 100. In Java, the assignment operator is a single equal sign.

The next line of code outputs the value of **num** preceded by the string "This is num:".

```
System.out.println("This is num: " + num);
```

In this statement, the plus sign causes the value of **num** to be appended to the string that precedes it, and then the resulting string is output. (Actually, **num** is first converted from an integer into its string equivalent and then concatenated with the string that precedes it. This process is described in detail later in this book.) This approach can be generalized. Using the + operator, you can join together as many items as you want within a single **println( )** statement.

The next line of code assigns **num** the value of **num** times 2. Like most other languages, Java uses the * operator to indicate multiplication. After this line executes, **num** will contain the value 200.

Here are the next two lines in the program:

```
System.out.print ("The value of num * 2 is ");
System.out.println (num);
```

Several new things are occurring here. First, the built-in method **print( )** is used to display the string "The value of num * 2 is ". This string is not followed by a newline. This means that when the next output is generated, it will start on the same line. The **print( )** method is just like **println( )**, except that it does not output a newline character after each call. Now look at the call to **println( )**. Notice that **num** is used by itself. Both **print( )** and **println( )** can be used to output values of any of Java's built-in types.

# Two Control Statements

Although Chapter 5 will look closely at control statements, two are briefly introduced here so that they can be used in sample programs in Chapters 3 and 4. They will also help illustrate an important aspect of Java: blocks of code.

## The if Statement

The Java **if** statement works much like the IF statement in any other language. It determines the flow of execution based on whether some condition is true or false. Its simplest form is shown here:

if(*condition*) *statement*;

Here, *condition* is a Boolean expression. (A Boolean expression is one that evaluates to either true or false.) If *condition* is true, then the statement is executed. If *condition* is false, then the statement is bypassed. Here is an example:

```
if(num < 100) System.out.println("num is less than 100");
```

In this case, if **num** contains a value that is less than 100, the conditional expression is true, and **println( )** will execute. If **num** contains a value greater than or equal to 100, then the **println( )** method is bypassed.

As you will see in Chapter 4, Java defines a full complement of relational operators that may be used in a conditional expression. Here are a few:

| Operator | Meaning |
|---|---|
| < | Less than |
| > | Greater than |
| == | Equal to |

Notice that the test for equality is the double equal sign.

Here is a program that illustrates the **if** statement:

```
/*
  Demonstrate the if.

  Call this file "IfSample.java".
*/
class IfSample {
  public static void main(String[] args) {
    int x, y;

    x = 10;
    y = 20;

    if(x < y) System.out.println("x is less than y");

    x = x * 2;
    if(x == y) System.out.println("x now equal to y");
```

```
    x = x * 2;
    if(x > y) System.out.println("x now greater than y");

    // this won't display anything
    if(x == y) System.out.println("you won't see this");
  }
}
```

The output generated by this program is shown here:

```
x is less than y
x now equal to y
x now greater than y
```

Notice one other thing in this program. The line

```
int x, y;
```

declares two variables, **x** and **y**, by use of a comma-separated list.

## The for Loop

Loop statements are an important part of nearly any programming language because they provide a way to repeatedly execute some task. As you will see in Chapter 5, Java supplies a powerful assortment of loop constructs. Perhaps the most versatile is the **for** loop. The simplest form of the **for** loop is shown here:

for*(initialization; condition; iteration) statement;*

In its most common form, the *initialization* portion of the loop sets a loop control variable to an initial value. The *condition* is a Boolean expression that tests the loop control variable. If the outcome of that test is true, *statement* executes and the **for** loop continues to iterate. If it is false, the loop terminates. The *iteration* expression determines how the loop control variable is changed each time the loop iterates. Here is a short program that illustrates the **for** loop:

```
/*
  Demonstrate the for loop.

  Call this file "ForTest.java".
*/
class ForTest {
  public static void main(String[] args) {
    int x;

    for(x = 0; x<10; x = x+1)
      System.out.println("This is x: " + x);
  }
}
```

This program generates the following output:

```
This is x: 0
This is x: 1
This is x: 2
This is x: 3
```

```
This is x: 4
This is x: 5
This is x: 6
This is x: 7
This is x: 8
This is x: 9
```

In this example, **x** is the loop control variable. It is initialized to zero in the initialization portion of the **for**. At the start of each iteration (including the first one), the conditional test **x < 10** is performed. If the outcome of this test is true, the **println( )** statement is executed, and then the iteration portion of the loop is executed, which increases **x** by 1. This process continues until the conditional test is false.

As a point of interest, in professionally written Java programs you will almost never see the iteration portion of the loop written as shown in the preceding program. That is, you will seldom see statements like this:

```
x = x + 1;
```

The reason is that Java includes a special increment operator that performs this operation more efficiently. The increment operator is ++. (That is, two plus signs back to back.) The increment operator increases its operand by one. By use of the increment operator, the preceding statement can be written like this:

```
x++;
```

Thus, the **for** in the preceding program will usually be written like this:

```
for(x = 0; x<10; x++)
```

You might want to try this. As you will see, the loop still runs exactly the same as it did before.

Java also provides a decrement operator, which is specified as – –. This operator decreases its operand by one.

## Using Blocks of Code

Java allows two or more statements to be grouped into *blocks of code*, also called *code blocks*. This is done by enclosing the statements between opening and closing curly braces. Once a block of code has been created, it becomes a logical unit that can be used any place that a single statement can. For example, a block can be a target for Java's **if** and **for** statements. Consider this **if** statement:

```
if(x < y) { // begin a block
  x = y;
  y = 0;
} // end of block
```

Here, if **x** is less than **y**, then both statements inside the block will be executed. Thus, the two statements inside the block form a logical unit, and one statement cannot execute without the other also executing. The key point here is that whenever you need to logically link two or more statements, you do so by creating a block.

Let's look at another example. The following program uses a block of code as the target of a **for** loop:

```
/*
  Demonstrate a block of code.

  Call this file "BlockTest.java"
*/
class BlockTest {
  public static void main(String[] args) {
    int x, y;

    y = 20;

    // the target of this loop is a block
    for(x = 0; x<10; x++) {
      System.out.println("This is x: " + x);
      System.out.println("This is y: " + y);
      y = y - 2;
    }
  }
}
```

The output generated by this program is shown here:

```
This is x: 0
This is y: 20
This is x: 1
This is y: 18
This is x: 2
This is y: 16
This is x: 3
This is y: 14
This is x: 4
This is y: 12
This is x: 5
This is y: 10
This is x: 6
This is y: 8
This is x: 7
This is y: 6
This is x: 8
This is y: 4
This is x: 9
This is y: 2
```

In this case, the target of the **for** loop is a block of code and not just a single statement. Thus, each time the loop iterates, the three statements inside the block will be executed. This fact is, of course, evidenced by the output generated by the program.

As you will see later in this book, blocks of code have additional properties and uses. However, the main reason for their existence is to create logically inseparable units of code.

# Lexical Issues

Now that you have seen several short Java programs, it is time to more formally describe the atomic elements of Java. Java programs are a collection of whitespace, identifiers, literals, comments, operators, separators, and keywords. The operators are described in the next chapter. The others are described next.

## Whitespace

Java is a free-form language. This means that you do not need to follow any special indentation rules. For instance, the **Example** program could have been written all on one line or in any other strange way you felt like typing it, as long as there was at least one whitespace character between each token that was not already delineated by an operator or separator. In Java, whitespace includes a space, tab, newline, or form feed.

## Identifiers

Identifiers are used to name things, such as classes, variables, and methods. An identifier may be any descriptive sequence of uppercase and lowercase letters, numbers, or the underscore and dollar-sign characters. (The dollar-sign character is not intended for general use.) They must not begin with a number, lest they be confused with a numeric literal. Again, Java is case-sensitive, so **VALUE** is a different identifier than **Value**. Some examples of valid identifiers are

| AvgTemp | count | a4 | $test | this_is_ok |
|---|---|---|---|---|

Invalid identifier names include these:

| 2count | high-temp | Not/ok |
|---|---|---|

**NOTE** Beginning with JDK 9, the underscore cannot be used by itself as an identifier.

## Literals

A constant value in Java is created by using a *literal* representation of it. For example, here are some literals:

| 100 | 98.6 | 'X' | "This is a test" |
|---|---|---|---|

Left to right, the first literal specifies an integer, the next is a floating-point value, the third is a character constant, and the last is a string. A literal can be used anywhere a value of its type is allowed.

## Comments

As mentioned, there are three types of comments defined by Java. You have already seen two: single-line and multiline. The third type is called a *documentation comment.* This type of comment is used to produce an HTML file that documents your program. The documentation comment begins with a /** and ends with a */. Documentation comments are explained in Appendix A.

## Separators

In Java, there are a few characters that are used as separators. The most commonly used separator in Java is the semicolon. As you have seen, it is often used to terminate statements. The separators are shown in the following table:

| Symbol | Name | Purpose |
|---|---|---|
| ( ) | Parentheses | Used to contain lists of parameters in method definition and invocation. Also used for defining precedence in expressions, containing expressions in control statements, and surrounding cast types. |
| { } | Braces | Used to contain the values of automatically initialized arrays. Also used to define a block of code, for classes, methods, and local scopes. |
| [ ] | Brackets | Used to declare array types. Also used when dereferencing array values. |
| ; | Semicolon | Terminates statements. |
| , | Comma | Separates consecutive identifiers in a variable declaration. Also used to chain statements together inside a **for** statement. |
| . | Period | Used to separate package names from subpackages and classes. Also used to separate a variable or method from a reference variable. |
| :: | Colons | Used to create a method or constructor reference. |
| ... | Ellipsis | Indicates a variable-arity parameter. |
| @ | At-sign | Begins an annotation. |

## The Java Keywords

There are 68 keywords currently defined in the Java language (see Table 2-1). These keywords, combined with the syntax of the operators and separators, form the foundation of the Java language. The Java language limits the uses of its keywords and divides them into two categories: 51 *reserved words* and 17 *contextual keywords*. Reserved words cannot be used as identifiers, for example, variable, class, or method names. Contextual keywords have special meanings for the specific language feature that defines them but can be used elsewhere. Keywords support features added to Java over the past few years. Ten relate to modules: **exports**, **module**, **open**, **opens**, **provides**, **requires**, **to**, **transitive**, **uses**, and **with** Records are declared by **record**; sealed classes and interfaces use **sealed**, **non-sealed**, and **permits**; **yield** and **when** are used by the enhanced **switch**; and **var** supports local variable type inference. Because keywords are context-sensitive, existing programs were unaffected by their addition. Also, beginning with JDK 9, an underscore by itself is considered a keyword in order to prevent its use as the name of something in your program. Since JDK 17, **strictfp** has been rendered obsolete because it has no effect.

The keywords **const** and **goto** are reserved but not used. In the early days of Java, several other keywords were reserved for possible future use. However, the current specification for Java defines only the keywords shown in Table 2-1.

| abstract | assert | boolean | break | byte | case |
|---|---|---|---|---|---|
| catch | char | class | const | continue | default |
| do | double | else | enum | exports | extends |
| final | finally | float | for | goto | if |
| implements | import | instanceof | int | interface | long |
| module | native | new | non-sealed | open | opens |
| package | permits | private | protected | provides | public |
| record | requires | return | sealed | short | static |
| strictfp | super | switch | synchronized | this | throw |
| throws | to | transient | transitive | try | uses |
| var | void | volatile | when | while | with |
| yield | _ | | | | |

**Table 2-1** Java Keywords

In addition to the keywords, Java reserves three other names that have been part of Java from the start: **true**, **false**, and **null**. These are values defined by Java. You may not use these words for the names of variables, classes, and so on.

## The Java Class Libraries

The sample programs shown in this chapter make use of two of Java's built-in methods: **println( )** and **print( )**. As mentioned, these methods are available through **System.out**. **System** is a class predefined by Java that is automatically included in your programs. In the larger view, the Java environment relies on several built-in class libraries that contain many built-in methods that provide support for such things as I/O, string handling, networking, and graphics. The standard classes also provide support for a graphical user interface (GUI). Thus, Java as a totality is a combination of the Java language itself plus its standard classes. As you will see, the class libraries provide much of the functionality that comes with Java. Indeed, part of becoming a Java programmer is learning to use the standard Java classes. Throughout Part I of this book, various elements of the standard library classes and methods are described as needed. In Part II, several class libraries are described in detail.

CHAPTER

# 3 Data Types, Variables, and Arrays

This chapter examines three of Java's most fundamental elements: data types, variables, and arrays. As with all modern programming languages, Java supports several types of data. You may use these types to declare variables and to create arrays. As you will see, Java's approach to these items is clean, efficient, and cohesive.

## Java Is a Strongly Typed Language

It is important to state at the outset that Java is a strongly typed language. Indeed, part of Java's safety and robustness comes from this fact. Let's see what this means. First, every variable has a type, every expression has a type, and every type is strictly defined. Second, all assignments, whether explicit or via parameter passing in method calls, are checked for type compatibility. There are no automatic coercions or conversions of conflicting types as in some languages. The Java compiler checks all expressions and parameters to ensure that the types are compatible. Any type mismatches are errors that must be corrected before the compiler will finish compiling the class.

## The Primitive Types

Java defines eight *primitive* types of data: **byte**, **short**, **int**, **long**, **char**, **float**, **double**, and **boolean**. The primitive types are also commonly referred to as *simple* types, and both terms will be used in this book. These can be put in four groups:

- **Integers** This group includes **byte**, **short**, **int**, and **long**, which are for whole-valued signed numbers.
- **Floating-point numbers** This group includes **float** and **double**, which represent numbers with fractional precision.
- **Characters** This group includes **char**, which represents symbols in a character set, like letters and numbers.
- **Boolean** This group includes **boolean**, which is a special type for representing true/false values.

You can use these types as-is or to construct arrays or your own class types. Thus, they form the basis for all other types of data that you can create.

The primitive types represent single values—not complex objects. Although Java is otherwise completely object-oriented, the primitive types are not. They are analogous to the simple types found in most other non-object-oriented languages. The reason for this is efficiency. Making the primitive types into objects would have degraded performance too much.

The primitive types are defined to have an explicit range and mathematical behavior. Languages such as C and C++ allow the size of an integer to vary based upon the dictates of the execution environment. However, Java is different. Because of Java's portability requirement, all data types have a strictly defined range. For example, an **int** is always 32 bits, regardless of the particular platform. This allows programs to be written that are guaranteed to run *without porting* on any machine architecture. While strictly specifying the size of an integer may cause a small loss of performance in some environments, it is necessary in order to achieve portability.

Let's look at each type of data in turn.

# Integers

Java defines four integer types: **byte**, **short**, **int**, and **long**. All of these are signed, positive and negative values. Java does not support unsigned, positive-only integers. Many other computer languages support both signed and unsigned integers. However, Java's designers felt that unsigned integers were unnecessary. Specifically, they felt that the concept of *unsigned* was used mostly to specify the behavior of the *high-order bit*, which defines the *sign* of an integer value. As you will see in Chapter 4, Java manages the meaning of the high-order bit differently, by adding a special "unsigned right shift" operator. Thus, the need for an unsigned integer type was eliminated.

The *width* of an integer type should not be thought of as the amount of storage it consumes, but rather as the *behavior* it defines for variables and expressions of that type. The Java run-time environment is free to use whatever size it wants, as long as the types behave as you declared them. The width and ranges of these integer types vary widely, as shown in this table:

| Name | Width | Range |
|---|---|---|
| **long** | 64 | –9,223,372,036,854,775,808 to 9,223,372,036,854,775,807 |
| **int** | 32 | –2,147,483,648 to 2,147,483,647 |
| **short** | 16 | –32,768 to 32,767 |
| **byte** | 8 | –128 to 127 |

Let's look at each type of integer.

## byte

The smallest integer type is **byte**. This is a signed 8-bit type that has a range from –128 to 127. Variables of type **byte** are especially useful when you're working with a stream of data from a network or file. They are also useful when you're working with raw binary data that may not be directly compatible with Java's other built-in types.

Byte variables are declared by use of the **byte** keyword. For example, the following declares two **byte** variables called **b** and **c**:

```
byte b, c;
```

## short

**short** is a signed 16-bit type. It has a range from –32,768 to 32,767. It is probably the least-used Java type. Here are some examples of **short** variable declarations:

```
short s;
short t;
```

## int

The most commonly used integer type is **int**. It is a signed 32-bit type that has a range from –2,147,483,648 to 2,147,483,647. In addition to other uses, variables of type **int** are commonly employed to control loops and to index arrays. Although you might think that using a **byte** or **short** would be more efficient than using an **int** in situations in which the larger range of an **int** is not needed, this may not be the case. The reason is that when **byte** and **short** values are used in an expression, they are *promoted* to **int** when the expression is evaluated. (Type promotion is described later in this chapter.) Therefore, **int** is often the best choice when an integer is needed.

## long

**long** is a signed 64-bit type and is useful for those occasions where an **int** type is not large enough to hold the desired value. The range of a **long** is quite large. This makes it useful when big, whole numbers are needed. For example, here is a program that computes the number of miles that light will travel in a specified number of days:

```
// Compute distance light travels using long variables.
class Light {
  public static void main(String[] args) {
    int lightspeed;
    long days;
    long seconds;
    long distance;

    // approximate speed of light in miles per second
    lightspeed = 186000;

    days = 1000; // specify number of days here

    seconds = days * 24 * 60 * 60; // convert to seconds

    distance = lightspeed * seconds; // compute distance

    System.out.print("In " + days);
    System.out.print(" days light will travel about ");
    System.out.println(distance + " miles.");
  }
}
```

This program generates the following output:

```
In 1000 days light will travel about 16070400000000 miles.
```

Clearly, the result could not have been held in an **int** variable.

# Floating-Point Types

Floating-point numbers, also known as *real* numbers, are used when evaluating expressions that require fractional precision. For example, calculations such as square root, or transcendentals such as sine and cosine, result in a value whose precision requires a floating-point type. Java implements the standard (IEEE 754) set of floating-point types and operators. There are two kinds of floating-point types, **float** and **double**, which represent single- and double-precision numbers, respectively. Their width and ranges are shown here:

| Name | Width in Bits | Approximate Range |
|---|---|---|
| **double** | 64 | 4.9e–324 to 1.8e+308 |
| **float** | 32 | 1.4e–045 to 3.4e+038 |

Each of these floating-point types is examined next.

## float

The type **float** specifies a *single-precision* value that uses 32 bits of storage. Single precision is faster on some processors and takes half as much space as double precision, but will become imprecise when the values are either very large or very small. Variables of type **float** are useful when you need a fractional component but don't require a large degree of precision. For example, **float** can be useful when representing dollars and cents.

Here are some sample **float** variable declarations:

```
float hightemp, lowtemp;
```

## double

Double precision, as denoted by the **double** keyword, uses 64 bits to store a value. Double precision is actually faster than single precision on some modern processors that have been optimized for high-speed mathematical calculations. All transcendental math functions, such as **sin( )**, **cos( )**, and **sqrt( )**, return **double** values. When you need to maintain accuracy over many iterative calculations, or are manipulating large-valued numbers, **double** is the best choice.

Here is a short program that uses **double** variables to compute the area of a circle:

```
// Compute the area of a circle.
class Area {
  public static void main(String[] args) {
    double pi, r, a;
```

```
    r = 10.8; // radius of circle
    pi = 3.1416; // pi, approximately
    a = pi * r * r; // compute area

    System.out.println("Area of circle is " + a);
  }
}
```

## Characters

In Java, the data type used to store characters is **char**. A key point to understand is that Java uses *Unicode* to represent characters. Unicode defines a fully international character set that can represent all of the characters found in all human languages. It is a unification of dozens of character sets, such as Latin, Greek, Arabic, Cyrillic, Hebrew, Katakana, Hangul, and many more. At the time of Java's creation, Unicode required 16 bits. Thus, in Java **char** is a 16-bit type. The range of a **char** is 0 to 65,535. There are no negative **char**s. The standard set of characters known as ASCII still ranges from 0 to 127 as always, and the extended 8-bit character set, ISO-Latin-1, ranges from 0 to 255. Since Java is designed to allow programs to be written for worldwide use, it makes sense that it would use Unicode to represent characters. Of course, the use of Unicode is somewhat inefficient for languages such as English, German, Spanish, and French, whose characters can easily be contained within 8 bits. But such is the price that must be paid for global portability.

---

**NOTE** More information about Unicode can be found at https://home.unicode.org.

Here is a program that demonstrates **char** variables:

```
// Demonstrate char data type.
class CharDemo {
  public static void main(String[] args) {
    char ch1, ch2;

    ch1 = 88; // code for X
    ch2 = 'Y';

    System.out.print("ch1 and ch2: ");
    System.out.println(ch1 + " " + ch2);
  }
}
```

This program displays the following output:

```
ch1 and ch2: X Y
```

Notice that **ch1** is assigned the value 88, which is the ASCII (and Unicode) value that corresponds to the letter *X*. As mentioned, the ASCII character set occupies the first 127 values in the Unicode character set. For this reason, all the "old tricks" that you may have used with characters in other languages will work in Java, too.

Although **char** is designed to hold Unicode characters, it can also be used as an integer type on which you can perform arithmetic operations. For example, you can add two characters together or increment the value of a character variable. Consider the following program:

```
// char variables behave like integers.
class CharDemo2 {
  public static void main(String[] args) {
    char ch1;

    ch1 = 'X';
    System.out.println("ch1 contains " + ch1);

    ch1++; // increment ch1
    System.out.println("ch1 is now " + ch1);
  }
}
```

The output generated by this program is shown here:

```
ch1 contains X
ch1 is now Y
```

In the program, **ch1** is first given the value *X*. Next, **ch1** is incremented. This results in **ch1** containing *Y*, the next character in the ASCII (and Unicode) sequence.

**NOTE** In the formal specification for Java, **char** is referred to as an *integral type*, which means that it is in the same general category as **int**, **short**, **long**, and **byte**. However, because its principal use is for representing Unicode characters, **char** is commonly considered to be in a category of its own.

# Booleans

Java has a primitive type, called **boolean**, for logical values. It can have only one of two possible values, **true** or **false**. This is the type returned by all relational operators, as in the case of **a < b**. **boolean** is also the type *required* by the conditional expressions that govern the control statements such as **if** and **for**.

Here is a program that demonstrates the **boolean** type:

```
// Demonstrate boolean values.
class BoolTest {
  public static void main(String[] args) {
    boolean b;

    b = false;
    System.out.println("b is " + b);
    b = true;
    System.out.println("b is " + b);

    // a boolean value can control the if statement
    if(b) System.out.println("This is executed.");

    b = false;
    if(b) System.out.println("This is not executed.");
```

```
    // outcome of a relational operator is a boolean value
    System.out.println("10 > 9 is " + (10 > 9));
  }
}
```

The output generated by this program is shown here:

```
b is false
b is true
This is executed.
10 > 9 is true
```

There are three interesting things to notice about this program. First, as you can see, when a **boolean** value is output by **println( )**, "true" or "false" is displayed. Second, the value of a **boolean** variable is sufficient, by itself, to control the **if** statement. There is no need to write an **if** statement like this:

```
if(b == true) ...
```

Third, the outcome of a relational operator, such as <, is a **boolean** value. This is why the expression **10>9** displays the value "true." Further, the extra set of parentheses around **10>9** is necessary because the + operator has a higher precedence than the >.

# A Closer Look at Literals

Literals were mentioned briefly in Chapter 2. Now that the built-in types have been formally described, let's take a closer look at them.

## Integer Literals

Integers are probably the most commonly used type in the typical program. Any whole number value is an integer literal. Examples are 1, 2, 3, and 42. These are all decimal values, meaning they are describing a base 10 number. Two other bases that can be used in integer literals are *octal* (base eight) and *hexadecimal* (base 16). Octal values are denoted in Java by a leading zero. Normal decimal numbers cannot have a leading zero. Thus, the seemingly valid value 09 will produce an error from the compiler, since 9 is outside of octal's 0 to 7 range. A more common base for numbers used by programmers is hexadecimal, which matches cleanly with modulo 8 word sizes, such as 8, 16, 32, and 64 bits. You signify a hexadecimal constant with a leading zero-x (**0x** or **0X**). The range of a hexadecimal digit is 0 to 15, so *A* through *F* (or *a* through *f*) are substituted for 10 through 15.

Integer literals create an **int** value, which in Java is a 32-bit integer value. Since Java is strongly typed, you might be wondering how it is possible to assign an integer literal to one of Java's other integer types, such as **byte** or **long**, without causing a type mismatch error. Fortunately, such situations are easily handled. When a literal value is assigned to a **byte** or **short** variable, no error is generated if the literal value is within the range of the target type. An integer literal can always be assigned to a **long** variable. However, to specify a **long** literal, you will need to explicitly tell the compiler that the literal value is of type **long**. You do this by appending an upper- or lowercase *L* to the literal. For example, 0x7fffffffffffffffL or

9223372036854775807L, is the largest **long**. An integer can also be assigned to a **char** as long as it is within range.

You can also specify integer literals using binary. To do so, prefix the value with **0b** or **0B**. For example, this specifies the decimal value 10 using a binary literal:

```
int x = 0b1010;
```

Among other uses, the addition of binary literals makes it easier to enter values used as bitmasks. In such a case, the decimal (or hexadecimal) representation of the value does not visually convey its meaning relative to its use. The binary literal does.

You can embed one or more underscores in an integer literal. Doing so makes it easier to read large integer literals. When the literal is compiled, the underscores are discarded. For example, given

```
int x = 123_456_789;
```

the value given to **x** will be 123,456,789. The underscores will be ignored. Underscores can only be used to separate digits. They cannot come at the beginning or the end of a literal. It is, however, permissible for more than one underscore to be used between two digits. For example, this is valid:

```
int x = 123___456___789;
```

The use of underscores in an integer literal is especially useful when encoding such things as telephone numbers, customer ID numbers, part numbers, and so on. They are also useful for providing visual groupings when specifying binary literals. For example, binary values are often visually grouped in four-digits units, as shown here:

```
int x = 0b1101_0101_0001_1010;
```

## Floating-Point Literals

Floating-point numbers represent decimal values with a fractional component. They can be expressed in either standard or scientific notation. *Standard notation* consists of a whole number component followed by a decimal point followed by a fractional component. For example, 2.0, 3.14159, and 0.6667 represent valid standard-notation floating-point numbers. *Scientific notation* uses a standard-notation floating-point number plus a suffix that specifies a power of 10 by which the number is to be multiplied. The exponent is indicated by an *E* or *e* followed by a decimal number, which can be positive or negative. Examples include 6.022E23, 314159E–05, and 2e+100.

Floating-point literals in Java default to **double** precision. To specify a **float** literal, you must append an *F* or *f* to the constant. You can also explicitly specify a **double** literal by appending a *D* or *d*. Doing so is, of course, redundant. The default **double** type consumes 64 bits of storage, while the smaller **float** type requires only 32 bits.

Hexadecimal floating-point literals are also supported, but they are rarely used. They must be in a form similar to scientific notation, but a **P** or **p**, rather than an **E** or **e**, is used. For example, 0x12.2P2 is a valid floating-point literal. The value following the **P**, called the *binary exponent*, indicates the power-of-two by which the number is multiplied. Therefore, **0x12.2P2** represents 72.5.

You can embed one or more underscores in a floating-point literal. This feature works the same as it does for integer literals, which were just described. Its purpose is to make it easier to read large floating-point literals. When the literal is compiled, the underscores are discarded. For example, given

```
double num = 9_423_497_862.0;
```

the value given to **num** will be 9,423,497,862.0. The underscores will be ignored. As is the case with integer literals, underscores can only be used to separate digits. They cannot come at the beginning or the end of a literal. It is, however, permissible for more than one underscore to be used between two digits. It is also permissible to use underscores in the fractional portion of the number. For example,

```
double num = 9_423_497.1_0_9;
```

is legal. In this case, the fractional part is **.109**.

## Boolean Literals

Boolean literals are simple. There are only two logical values that a **boolean** value can have, **true** and **false**. The values of **true** and **false** do not convert into any numerical representation. The **true** literal in Java does not equal 1, nor does the **false** literal equal 0. In Java, the Boolean literals can only be assigned to variables declared as **boolean** or used in expressions with Boolean operators.

## Character Literals

Characters in Java are indices into the Unicode character set. They are 16-bit values that can be converted into integers and manipulated with the integer operators, such as the addition and subtraction operators. A literal character is represented inside a pair of single quotes. All of the visible ASCII characters can be directly entered inside the quotes, such as '*a*', '*z*', and '@'. For characters that are impossible to enter directly, there are several escape sequences that allow you to enter the character you need, such as '\'' for the single-quote character itself and '**\n**' for the newline character. There is also a mechanism for directly entering the value of a character in octal or hexadecimal. For octal notation, use the backslash followed by the three-digit number. For example, '*141*' is the letter '*a*'. For hexadecimal, you enter a backslash-u ( **\u**), then exactly four hexadecimal digits. For example, '*u0061*' is the ISO-Latin-1 '*a*' because the top byte is zero. '*ua432*' is a Japanese Katakana character. Table 3-1 shows the character escape sequences.

## String Literals

String literals in Java are specified like they are in most other languages—by enclosing a sequence of characters between a pair of double quotes. Examples of string literals are

"Hello World"
"two\nlines"
" \"This is in quotes\""

| Escape Sequence | Description |
| --- | --- |
| \ddd | Octal character (ddd) |
| \uxxxx | Hexadecimal Unicode character (xxxx) |
| \' | Single quote |
| \" | Double quote |
| \\ | Backslash |
| \r | Carriage return |
| \n | New line (also known as line feed) |
| \f | Form feed |
| \t | Tab |
| \b | Backspace |
| \s | Space (added by JDK 15) |
| *endofline* | Continue line (applies only to text blocks; added by JDK 15) |

**Table 3-1** Character Escape Sequences

The escape sequences and octal/hexadecimal notations that were defined for character literals work the same way inside of string literals. One important thing to note about Java string literals is that they must begin and end on the same line, even if the line wraps. For string literals there is no line-continuation escape sequence as there is in some other languages. (It is useful to point out that beginning with JDK 15, Java added a feature called a *text block*, which gives you more control and flexibility when multiple lines of text are needed. See Chapter 17.)

**NOTE** As you may know, in some other languages strings are implemented as arrays of characters. However, this is not the case in Java. Strings are actually object types. As you will see later in this book, because Java implements strings as objects, Java includes extensive string-handling capabilities that are both powerful and easy to use.

# Variables

The variable is the basic unit of storage in a Java program. A variable is defined by the combination of an identifier, a type, and an optional initializer. In addition, all variables have a scope, which defines their visibility, and a lifetime. These elements are examined next.

## Declaring a Variable

In Java, all variables must be declared before they can be used. The basic form of a variable declaration is shown here:

*type identifier* [ = *value* ][, *identifier* [= *value* ] ...];

Here, *type* is one of Java's atomic types, or the name of a class or interface. (Class and interface types are discussed later in Part I of this book.) The *identifier* is the name of the variable. You can initialize the variable by specifying an equal sign and a value. Keep in mind that the initialization expression must result in a value of the same (or compatible) type as that specified for the variable. To declare more than one variable of the specified type, use a comma-separated list.

Here are several examples of variable declarations of various types. Note that some include an initialization.

```
int a, b, c;            // declares three ints, a, b, and c.
int d = 3, e, f = 5;    // declares three more ints, initializing
                        // d and f.
byte z = 22;            // initializes z.
double pi = 3.14159;    // declares an approximation of pi.
char x = 'x';           // the variable x has the value 'x'.
```

The identifiers that you choose have nothing intrinsic in their names that indicates their type. Java allows any properly formed identifier to have any declared type.

## Dynamic Initialization

Although the preceding examples have used only constants as initializers, Java allows variables to be initialized dynamically, using any expression valid at the time the variable is declared.

For example, here is a short program that computes the length of the hypotenuse of a right triangle given the lengths of its two opposing sides:

```
// Demonstrate dynamic initialization.
class DynInit {
  public static void main(String[] args) {
    double a = 3.0, b = 4.0;

    // c is dynamically initialized
    double c = Math.sqrt(a * a + b * b);

    System.out.println("Hypotenuse is " + c);
  }
}
```

Here, three local variables—**a**, **b**, and **c**—are declared. The first two, **a** and **b**, are initialized by constants. However, **c** is initialized dynamically to the length of the hypotenuse (using the Pythagorean theorem). The program uses another of Java's built-in methods, **sqrt( )**, which is a member of the **Math** class, to compute the square root of its argument. The key point here is that the initialization expression may use any element valid at the time of the initialization, including calls to methods, other variables, or literals.

## The Scope and Lifetime of Variables

So far, all of the variables used have been declared at the start of the **main( )** method. However, Java allows variables to be declared within any block. As explained in Chapter 2, a block is begun with an opening curly brace and ended by a closing curly brace. A block defines a *scope*. Thus, each time you start a new block, you are creating a new scope. A scope determines what objects are visible to other parts of your program. It also determines the lifetime of those objects.

It is not uncommon to think in terms of two general categories of scopes: global and local. However, these traditional scopes do not fit well with Java's strict, object-oriented model. While it is possible to create what amounts to being a global scope, it is by far the exception, not the rule. In Java, the two major scopes are those defined by a class and those defined by a method. Even this distinction is somewhat artificial. However, since the class scope has several unique properties and attributes that do not apply to the scope defined by a method, this distinction makes some sense. Because of the differences, a discussion of class scope (and variables declared within it) is deferred until Chapter 6, when classes are described. For now, we will only examine the scopes defined by or within a method.

The scope defined by a method begins with its opening curly brace. However, if that method has parameters, they too are included within the method's scope. A method's scope ends with its closing curly brace. This block of code is called the *method body*.

As a general rule, variables declared inside a scope are not visible (that is, accessible) to code that is defined outside that scope. Thus, when you declare a variable within a scope, you are localizing that variable and protecting it from unauthorized access and/or modification. Indeed, the scope rules provide the foundation for encapsulation. A variable declared within a block is called a *local variable*.

Scopes can be nested. For example, each time you create a block of code, you are creating a new, nested scope. When this occurs, the outer scope encloses the inner scope. This means that objects declared in the outer scope will be visible to code within the inner scope. However, the reverse is not true. Objects declared within the inner scope will not be visible outside it.

To understand the effect of nested scopes, consider the following program:

```
// Demonstrate block scope.
class Scope {
  public static void main(String[] args) {
    int x; // known to all code within main

    x = 10;
    if(x == 10) { // start new scope
      int y = 20; // known only to this block

      // x and y both known here.
      System.out.println("x and y: " + x + " " + y);
      x = y * 2;
    }
    // y = 100; // Error! y not known here

    // x is still known here.
    System.out.println("x is " + x);
  }
}
```

As the comments indicate, the variable **x** is declared at the start of **main( )**'s scope and is accessible to all subsequent code within **main( )**. Within the **if** block, **y** is declared. Since a block defines a scope, **y** is only visible to other code within its block. This is why outside of its block, the line **y = 100;** is commented out. If you remove the leading comment symbol, a compile-time error will occur, because **y** is not visible outside of its block. Within the **if** block, **x** can be used because code within a block (that is, a nested scope) has access to variables declared by an enclosing scope.

Within a block, variables can be declared at any point but are valid only after they are declared. Thus, if you define a variable at the start of a method, it is available to all of the code within that method. Conversely, if you declare a variable at the end of a block, it is effectively useless, because no code will have access to it. For example, this fragment is invalid because **count** cannot be used prior to its declaration:

```
// This fragment is wrong!
count = 100; // oops! cannot use count before it is declared!
int count;
```

Here is another important point to remember: variables are created when their scope is entered, and destroyed when their scope is left. This means that a variable will not hold its value once it has gone out of scope. Therefore, variables declared within a method will not hold their values between calls to that method. Also, a variable declared within a block will lose its value when the block is left. Thus, the lifetime of a variable is confined to its scope.

If a variable declaration includes an initializer, then that variable will be reinitialized each time the block in which it is declared is entered. For example, consider the next program:

```
// Demonstrate lifetime of a variable.
class LifeTime {
  public static void main(String[] args) {
    int x;

    for(x = 0; x < 3; x++) {
      int y = -1; // y is initialized each time block is entered
      System.out.println("y is: " + y); // this always prints -1
      y = 100;
      System.out.println("y is now: " + y);
    }
  }
}
```

The output generated by this program is shown here.

```
y is: -1
y is now: 100
y is: -1
y is now: 100
y is: -1
y is now: 100
```

As you can see, **y** is reinitialized to –1 each time the inner **for** loop is entered. Even though it is subsequently assigned the value 100, this value is lost.

One last point: Although blocks can be nested, you cannot declare a variable to have the same name as one in an outer scope. For example, the following program is illegal:

```
// This program will not compile
class ScopeErr {
  public static void main(String[] args) {
    int bar = 1;
    {              // creates a new scope
      int bar = 2; // Compile-time error - bar already defined!
    }
  }
}
```

# Type Conversion and Casting

If you have previous programming experience, then you already know that it is fairly common to assign a value of one type to a variable of another type. If the two types are compatible, then Java will perform the conversion automatically. For example, it is always possible to assign an **int** value to a **long** variable. However, not all types are compatible, and thus, not all type conversions are implicitly allowed. For instance, there is no automatic conversion defined from **double** to **byte**. Fortunately, it is still possible to obtain a conversion between incompatible types. To do so, you must use a *cast*, which performs an explicit conversion between incompatible types. Let's look at both automatic type conversions and casting.

## Java's Automatic Conversions

When one type of data is assigned to another type of variable, an *automatic type conversion* will take place if the following two conditions are met:

- The two types are compatible.
- The destination type is larger than the source type.

When these two conditions are met, a *widening conversion* takes place. For example, the **int** type is always large enough to hold all valid **byte** values, so no explicit cast statement is required.

For widening conversions, the numeric types, including integer and floating-point types, are compatible with each other. However, there are no automatic conversions from the numeric types to **char** or **boolean**. Also, **char** and **boolean** are not compatible with each other.

As mentioned earlier, Java also performs an automatic type conversion when storing a literal integer constant into variables of type **byte**, **short**, **long**, or **char**.

## Casting Incompatible Types

Although the automatic type conversions are helpful, they will not fulfill all needs. For example, what if you want to assign an **int** value to a **byte** variable? This conversion will not be performed automatically, because a **byte** is smaller than an **int**. This kind of conversion is sometimes called a *narrowing conversion*, since you are explicitly making the value narrower so that it will fit into the target type.

To create a conversion between two incompatible types, you must use a cast. A *cast* is simply an explicit type conversion. It has this general form:

(*target-type*) *value*

Here, *target-type* specifies the desired type to convert the specified value to. For example, the following fragment casts an **int** to a **byte**. If the integer's value is larger than the range of a **byte**, it will be reduced modulo (the remainder of an integer division by) the **byte**'s range.

```
int a;
byte b;
// …
b = (byte) a;
```

A different type of conversion will occur when a floating-point value is assigned to an integer type: *truncation*. As you know, integers do not have fractional components. Thus, when a floating-point value is assigned to an integer type, the fractional component is lost. For example, if the value 1.23 is assigned to an integer, the resulting value will simply be 1. The 0.23 will have been truncated. Of course, if the size of the whole number component is too large to fit into the target integer type, then that value will be reduced modulo the target type's range.

The following program demonstrates some type conversions that require casts:

```
// Demonstrate casts.
class Conversion {
  public static void main(String[] args) {
    byte b;
    int i = 257;
    double d = 323.142;

    System.out.println("\nConversion of int to byte.");
    b = (byte) i;
    System.out.println("i and b " + i + " " + b);

    System.out.println("\nConversion of double to int.");
    i = (int) d;
    System.out.println("d and i " + d + " " + i);

    System.out.println("\nConversion of double to byte.");
    b = (byte) d;
    System.out.println("d and b " + d + " " + b);
  }
}
```

This program generates the following output:

```
Conversion of int to byte.
i and b 257 1

Conversion of double to int.
d and i 323.142 323

Conversion of double to byte.
d and b 323.142 67
```

Let's look at each conversion. When the value 257 is cast into a **byte** variable, the result is the remainder of the division of 257 by 256 (the range of a **byte**), which is 1 in this case. When the **d** is converted to an **int**, its fractional component is lost. When **d** is converted to a **byte**, its fractional component is lost, *and* the value is reduced modulo 256, which in this case is 67.

# Automatic Type Promotion in Expressions

In addition to assignments, there is another place where certain type conversions may occur: in expressions. To see why, consider the following. In an expression, the precision required of an intermediate value will sometimes exceed the range of either operand. For example, examine the following expression:

```
byte a = 40;
byte b = 50;
byte c = 100;
int d = a * b / c;
```

The result of the intermediate term **a * b** easily exceeds the range of either of its **byte** operands. To handle this kind of problem, Java automatically promotes each **byte**, **short**, or **char** operand to **int** when evaluating an expression. This means that the subexpression **a * b** is performed using integers—not bytes. Thus, 2,000, the result of the intermediate expression, **50 * 40**, is legal even though **a** and **b** are both specified as type **byte**.

As useful as the automatic promotions are, they can cause confusing compile-time errors. For example, this seemingly correct code causes a problem:

```
byte b = 50;
b = b * 2; // Error! Cannot assign an int to a byte!
```

The code is attempting to store 50 * 2, a perfectly valid **byte** value, back into a **byte** variable. However, because the operands were automatically promoted to **int** when the expression was evaluated, the result has also been promoted to **int**. Thus, the result of the expression is now of type **int**, which cannot be assigned to a **byte** without the use of a cast. This is true even if, as in this particular case, the value being assigned would still fit in the target type.

In cases where you understand the consequences of overflow, you should use an explicit cast, such as

```
byte b = 50;
b = (byte)(b * 2);
```

which yields the correct value of 100.

## The Type Promotion Rules

Java defines several *type promotion* rules that apply to expressions. They are as follows: First, all **byte**, **short**, and **char** values are promoted to **int**, as just described. Then, if one operand is a **long**, the whole expression is promoted to **long**. If one operand is a **float**, the entire expression is promoted to **float**. If any of the operands are **double**, the result is **double**.

The following program demonstrates how each value in the expression gets promoted to match the second argument to each binary operator:

```
class Promote {
  public static void main(String[] args) {
    byte b = 42;
    char c = 'a';
    short s = 1024;
    int i = 50000;
    float f = 5.67f;
    double d = .1234;
    double result = (f * b) + (i / c) - (d * s);
    System.out.println((f * b) + " + " + (i / c) + " - " + (d * s));
    System.out.println("result = " + result);
  }
}
```

Let's look closely at the type promotions that occur in this line from the program:

```
double result = (f * b) + (i / c) - (d * s);
```

In the first subexpression, **f * b**, **b** is promoted to a **float** and the result of the subexpression is **float**. Next, in the subexpression **i/c**, **c** is promoted to **int**, and the result is of type **int**. Then, in **d * s**, the value of **s** is promoted to **double**, and the type of the subexpression is **double**. Finally, these three intermediate values, **float**, **int**, and **double**, are considered. The outcome of **float** plus an **int** is a **float**. Then the resultant **float** minus the last **double** is promoted to **double**, which is the type for the final result of the expression.

# Arrays

An *array* is a group of like-typed variables that are referred to by a common name. Arrays of any type can be created and may have one or more dimensions. A specific element in an array is accessed by its index. Arrays offer a convenient means of grouping related information.

## One-Dimensional Arrays

A *one-dimensional array* is, essentially, a list of like-typed variables. To create an array, you first must create an array variable of the desired type. The general form of a one-dimensional array declaration is

*type*[ ] *var-name*;

Here, *type* declares the element type (also called the base type) of the array. The element type determines the data type of each element that comprises the array. Thus, the element type for the array determines what type of data the array will hold. For example, the following declares an array named **month_days** with the type "array of int":

```
int[] month_days;
```

Although this declaration establishes the fact that **month_days** is an array variable, no array actually exists. To link **month_days** with an actual, physical array of integers, you must allocate one using **new** and assign it to **month_days**. **new** is a special operator that allocates memory.

You will look more closely at **new** in a later chapter, but you need to use it now to allocate memory for arrays. The general form of **new** as it applies to one-dimensional arrays appears as follows:

*array-var* = new *type* [*size*];

Here, *type* specifies the type of data being allocated, *size* specifies the number of elements in the array, and *array-var* is the array variable that is linked to the array. That is, to use **new** to allocate an array, you must specify the type and number of elements to allocate. The elements in the array allocated by **new** will automatically be initialized to zero (for numeric types), **false** (for **boolean**), or **null** (for reference types, which are described in a later chapter). This example allocates a 12-element array of integers and links them to **month_days**:

```
month_days = new int[12];
```

After this statement executes, **month_days** will refer to an array of 12 integers. Further, all elements in the array will be initialized to zero.

Let's review: Obtaining an array is a two-step process. First, you must declare a variable of the desired array type. Second, you must allocate the memory that will hold the array, using **new**, and assign it to the array variable. Thus, in Java all arrays are dynamically allocated. If the concept of dynamic allocation is unfamiliar to you, don't worry. It will be described at length later in this book.

Once you have allocated an array, you can access a specific element in the array by specifying its index within square brackets. All array indexes start at zero. For example, this statement assigns the value 28 to the second element of **month_days**:

```
month_days[1] = 28;
```

The next line displays the value stored at index 3:

```
System.out.println(month_days[3]);
```

Putting together all the pieces, here is a program that creates an array of the number of days in each month:

```
// Demonstrate a one-dimensional array.
class Array {
  public static void main(String[] args) {
    int[] month_days;
    month_days = new int[12];
    month_days[0] = 31;
    month_days[1] = 28;
    month_days[2] = 31;
    month_days[3] = 30;
    month_days[4] = 31;
    month_days[5] = 30;
    month_days[6] = 31;
```

```
    month_days[7] = 31;
    month_days[8] = 30;
    month_days[9] = 31;
    month_days[10] = 30;
    month_days[11] = 31;
    System.out.println("April has " + month_days[3] + " days.");
  }
}
```

When you run this program, it prints the number of days in April. As mentioned, Java array indexes start with zero, so the number of days in April is **month_days[3]**, or 30.

It is possible to combine the declaration of the array variable with the allocation of the array itself, as shown here:

```
int[] month_days = new int[12];
```

This is the way that you will normally see it done in professionally written Java programs.

Arrays can be initialized when they are declared. The process is much the same as that used to initialize the simple types. An *array initializer* is a list of comma-separated expressions surrounded by curly braces. The commas separate the values of the array elements. The array will automatically be created large enough to hold the number of elements you specify in the array initializer. There is no need to use **new**. For example, to store the number of days in each month, the following code creates an initialized array of integers:

```
// An improved version of the previous program.
class AutoArray {
  public static void main(String[] args) {

    int[] month_days = { 31, 28, 31, 30, 31, 30, 31, 31, 30, 31,
                         30, 31 };
    System.out.println("April has " + month_days[3] + " days.");
  }
}
```

When you run this program, you see the same output as that generated by the previous version.

Java strictly checks to make sure you do not accidentally try to store or reference values outside of the range of the array. The Java run-time system will check that all array indexes are in the correct range. For example, the run-time system will check the value of each index into **month_days** to make sure that it is between 0 and 11, inclusive. If you try to access elements outside the range of the array (negative numbers or numbers greater than the length of the array), you will cause a run-time error.

Here is one more example that uses a one-dimensional array. It finds the average of a set of numbers.

```
// Average an array of values.
class Average {
  public static void main(String[] args) {
    double[] nums = {10.1, 11.2, 12.3, 13.4, 14.5};
    double result = 0;
    int i;
```

```
    for(i=0; i<5; i++)
      result = result + nums[i];
    System.out.println("Average is " + result / 5);
  }
}
```

## Multidimensional Arrays

In Java, *multidimensional arrays* are implemented as arrays of arrays. To declare a multidimensional array variable, specify each additional index using another set of square brackets. For example, the following declares a two-dimensional array variable called **twoD**:

```
int[][] twoD = new int[4][5];
```

This allocates a 4-by-5 array and assigns it to **twoD**. Internally, this matrix is implemented as an *array* of *arrays* of **int**. Conceptually, this array will look like the one shown in Figure 3-1.

The following program numbers each element in the array from left to right, top to bottom, and then displays these values:

```
// Demonstrate a two-dimensional array.
class TwoDArray {
  public static void main(String[] args) {
    int[][] twoD= new int[4][5];
    int i, j, k = 0;

    for(i=0; i<4; i++)
      for(j=0; j<5; j++) {
        twoD[i][j] = k;
        k++;
      }

    for(i=0; i<4; i++) {
      for(j=0; j<5; j++)
        System.out.print(twoD[i][j] + " ");
      System.out.println();
    }
  }
}
```

This program generates the following output:

```
0 1 2 3 4
5 6 7 8 9
10 11 12 13 14
15 16 17 18 19
```

When you allocate memory for a multidimensional array, you need only specify the memory for the first (leftmost) dimension. You can allocate the remaining dimensions separately.

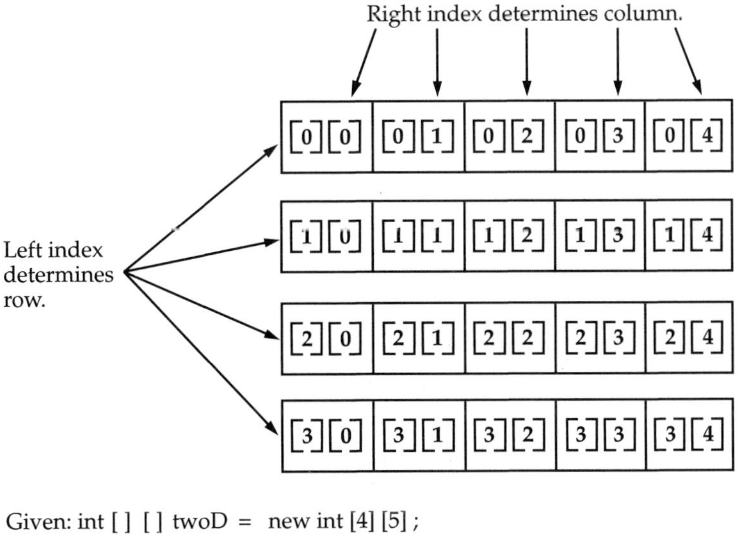


**Figure 3-1** A conceptual view of a 4-by-5, two-dimensional array

For example, this following code allocates memory for the first dimension of **twoD** when it is declared. It allocates the second dimension separately.

```
int[][] twoD = new int[4][];
twoD[0] = new int[5];
twoD[1] = new int[5];
twoD[2] = new int[5];
twoD[3] = new int[5];
```

While there is no advantage to individually allocating the second dimension arrays in this situation, there may be in others. For example, when you allocate dimensions individually, you do not need to allocate the same number of elements for each dimension. As stated earlier, since multidimensional arrays are actually arrays of arrays, the length of each array is under your control. For example, the following program creates a two-dimensional array in which the sizes of the second dimension are unequal:

```
// Manually allocate differing size second dimensions.
class TwoDAgain {
  public static void main(String[] args) {
    int[][] twoD = new int[4][];
    twoD[0] = new int[1];
    twoD[1] = new int[2];
    twoD[2] = new int[3];
    twoD[3] = new int[4];

    int i, j, k = 0;
```

```
    for(i=0; i<4; i++)
      for(j=0; j<i+1; j++) {
      twoD[i][j] = k;
      k++;
    }

    for(i=0; i<4; i++) {
      for(j=0; j<i+1; j++)
        System.out.print(twoD[i][j] + " ");
      System.out.println();
    }
  }
}
```

This program generates the following output:

```
0
1 2
3 4 5
6 7 8 9
```

The array created by this program looks like this:

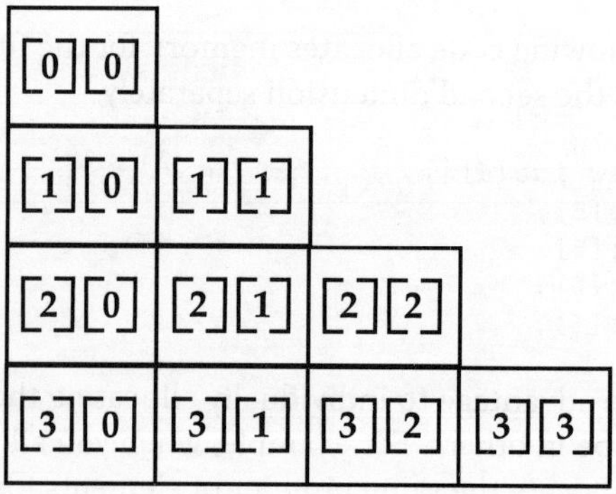


The use of uneven (or irregular) multidimensional arrays may not be appropriate for many applications, because it runs contrary to what people expect to find when a multidimensional array is encountered. However, irregular arrays can be used effectively in some situations. For example, if you need a very large two-dimensional array that is sparsely populated (that is, one in which not all of the elements will be used), then an irregular array might be a perfect solution.

It is possible to initialize multidimensional arrays. To do so, simply enclose each dimension's initializer within its own set of curly braces. The following program creates a matrix where each element contains the product of the row and column indexes. Also notice that you can use expressions as well as literal values inside of array initializers.

```
// Initialize a two-dimensional array.
class Matrix {
  public static void main(String[] args) {
```

```
    double[][] m = {
      { 0*0, 1*0, 2*0, 3*0 },
      { 0*1, 1*1, 2*1, 3*1 },
      { 0*2, 1*2, 2*2, 3*2 },
      { 0*3, 1*3, 2*3, 3*3 }
    };
    int i, j;

    for(i=0; i<4; i++) {
      for(j=0; j<4; j++)
        System.out.print(m[i][j] + " ");
      System.out.println();
    }
  }
}
```

When you run this program, you will get the following output:

```
0.0  0.0  0.0  0.0
0.0  1.0  2.0  3.0
0.0  2.0  4.0  6.0
0.0  3.0  6.0  9.0
```

As you can see, each row in the array is initialized as specified in the initialization lists.

Let's look at one more example that uses a multidimensional array. The following program creates a 3-by-4-by-5, three-dimensional array. It then loads each element with the product of its indexes. Finally, it displays these products.

```
// Demonstrate a three-dimensional array.
class ThreeDMatrix {
  public static void main(String[] args) {
    int[][][] threeD = new int[3][4][5];
    int i, j, k;

    for(i=0; i<3; i++)
      for(j=0; j<4; j++)
        for(k=0; k<5; k++)
          threeD[i][j][k] = i * j * k;

    for(i=0; i<3; i++) {
      for(j=0; j<4; j++) {
        for(k=0; k<5; k++)
          System.out.print(threeD[i][j][k] + " ");
        System.out.println();
      }
      System.out.println();
    }
  }
}
```

This program generates the following output:

```
0 0 0 0 0
0 0 0 0 0
0 0 0 0 0
0 0 0 0 0

0 0 0 0 0
0 1 2 3 4
0 2 4 6 8
0 3 6 9 12

0 0 0 0 0
0 2 4 6 8
0 4 8 12 16
0 6 12 18 24
```

## Alternative Array Declaration Syntax

There is a second form that may be used to declare an array:

*type var-name*[ ];

Here, the square brackets follow the array variable name, and not the type specifier. For example, the following two declarations are equivalent:

```
int al[] = new int[3];
int[] a2 = new int[3];
```

The following declarations are also equivalent:

```
char twod1[][] = new char[3][4];
char[][] twod2 = new char[3][4];
```

This alternative declaration form offers convenience when converting code from C/C++ to Java. It also lets you declare both array and non-array variables in a single declaration statement. Today, the alternative form of array declaration is less commonly used, but it is still important that you are familiar with it because both forms of array declaration are legal in Java.

# Introducing Type Inference with Local Variables

Not long ago, a new feature called *local variable type inference* was added to the Java language. To begin, let's review two important aspects of variables. First, all variables in Java must be declared prior to their use. Second, a variable can be initialized with a value when it is declared. Furthermore, when a variable is initialized, the type of the initializer must be the same as (or convertible to) the declared type of the variable. Thus, in principle, it would not be necessary to specify an explicit type for an initialized variable because it could be inferred by the type of its initializer. Of course, in the past, such inference was not supported, and all variables required an explicitly declared type, whether they were initialized or not. Today, that situation has changed.

Beginning with JDK 10, it is now possible to let the compiler infer the type of a local variable based on the type of its initializer, thus avoiding the need to explicitly specify the type. Local variable type inference offers a number of advantages. For example, it can streamline code by eliminating the need to redundantly specify a variable's type when it can be inferred from its initializer. It can simplify declarations in cases in which the type name is quite lengthy, such as can be the case with some class names. It can also be helpful when a type is difficult to discern or cannot be denoted. (An example of a type that cannot be denoted is the type of an anonymous class, discussed in Chapter 25.) Furthermore, local variable type inference has become a common part of the contemporary programming environment. Its inclusion in Java helps keep Java up to date with evolving trends in language design. To support local variable type inference, the context-sensitive keyword **var** was added.

To use local variable type inference, the variable must be declared with **var** as the type name and it must include an initializer. For example, in the past you would declare a local **double** variable called **avg** that is initialized with the value 10.0 as shown here:

```
double avg = 10.0;
```

Using type inference, this declaration can now also be written like this:

```
var avg = 10.0;
```

In both cases, **avg** will be of type **double**. In the first case, its type is explicitly specified. In the second, its type is inferred as **double** because the initializer 10.0 is of type **double**.

As mentioned, **var** is context-sensitive. When it is used as the type name in the context of a local variable declaration, it tells the compiler to use type inference to determine the type of the variable being declared based on the type of the initializer. Thus, in a local variable declaration, **var** is a placeholder for the actual, inferred type. However, when used in most other places, **var** is simply a user-defined identifier with no special meaning. For example, the following declaration is still valid:

```
int var = 1;  // In this case, var is simply a user-defined identifier.
```

In this case, the type is explicitly specified as **int** and **var** is the name of the variable being declared. Even though it is context-sensitive, there are a few places in which the use of **var** is illegal. It cannot be used as the name of a class, for example.

The following program puts the preceding discussion into action:

```
// A simple demonstration of local variable type inference.
class VarDemo {
  public static void main(String[] args) {

    // Use type inference to determine the type of the
    // variable named avg. In this case, double is inferred.
    var avg = 10.0;
    System.out.println("Value of avg: " + avg);

    // In the following context, var is not a predefined identifier.
    // It is simply a user-defined variable name.
    int var = 1;
    System.out.println("Value of var: " + var);
```

```
        // Interestingly, in the following sequence, var is used
        // as both the type of the declaration and as a variable name
        // in the initializer.
        var k = -var;
        System.out.println("Value of k: " + k);
    }
}
```

Here is the output:

```
Value of avg: 10.0
Value of var: 1
Value of k: -1
```

The preceding example uses **var** to declare only simple variables, but you can also use **var** to declare an array. For example:

```
var myArray = new int[10]; // This is valid.
```

Notice that neither **var** nor **myArray** has brackets. Instead, the type of **myArray** is inferred to be **int[ ]**. Furthermore, you *cannot* use brackets on the left side of a **var** declaration. Thus, both of these declarations are invalid:

```
var[] myArray = new int[10]; // Wrong
var myArray[] = new int[10]; // Wrong
```

In the first line, an attempt is made to bracket **var**. In the second, an attempt is made to bracket **myArray**. In both cases, the use of the brackets is wrong because the type is inferred from the type of the initializer.

It is important to emphasize that **var** can be used to declare a variable only when that variable is initialized. For example, the following statement is incorrect:

```
var counter; // Wrong! Initializer required.
```

Also, remember that **var** can be used only to declare local variables. It cannot be used when declaring instance variables, parameters, or return types, for example.

Although the preceding discussion and examples have introduced the basics of local variable type inference, they haven't shown its full power. As you will see in Chapter 7, local variable type inference is especially effective in shortening declarations that involve long class names. It can also be used with generic types (see Chapter 14), in a **try**-with-resources statement (see Chapter 13), and with a **for** loop (see Chapter 5).

## Some var Restrictions

In addition to those mentioned in the preceding discussion, several other restrictions apply to the use of **var**. Only one variable can be declared at a time; a variable cannot use **null** as an initializer; and the variable being declared cannot be used by the initializer expression.

Although you can declare an array type using **var**, you cannot use **var** with an array initializer. For example, this is valid:

```
var myArray = new int[10]; // This is valid.
```

However, this is not:

```
var myArray = { 1, 2, 3 }; // Wrong
```

As mentioned earlier, **var** cannot be used as the name of a class. It also cannot be used as the name of other reference types, including an interface, enumeration, or annotation, or as the name of a generic type parameter, all of which are described later in this book. Here are two other restrictions that relate to Java features described in subsequent chapters but mentioned here in the interest of completeness. Local variable type inference cannot be used to declare the exception type caught by a **catch** statement. Also, neither lambda expressions nor method references can be used as initializers.

**NOTE** At the time of this writing, a number of readers of this book will be using Java environments that don't support local variable type inference. So that as many of the code examples as possible will compile and run for all readers, local variable type inference will not be used by most of the programs in the remainder of this edition of the book. Using the full declaration syntax also makes it very clear at a glance what type of variable is being created, which is important for the sample code. Of course, going forward, you should consider the use of local variable type inference where appropriate in your own code.

# A Few Words About Strings

As you may have noticed, in the preceding discussion of data types and arrays there has been no mention of strings or a string data type. This is not because Java does not support such a type—it does. It is just that Java's string type, called **String**, is not a primitive type. Nor is it simply an array of characters. Rather, **String** defines an object, and a full description of it requires an understanding of several object-related features. As such, it will be covered later in this book, after objects are described. However, so that you can use simple strings in sample programs, the following brief introduction is in order.

The **String** type is used to declare string variables. You can also declare arrays of strings. A quoted string constant can be assigned to a **String** variable. A variable of type **String** can be assigned to another variable of type **String**. You can use an object of type **String** as an argument to **println( )**. For example, consider the following fragment:

```
String str = "this is a test";
System.out.println(str);
```

Here, **str** is an object of type **String**. It is assigned the string "this is a test". This string is displayed by the **println( )** statement.

As you will see later, **String** objects have many special features and attributes that make them quite powerful and easy to use. However, for the next few chapters, you will be using them only in their simplest form.

CHAPTER

# 4 Operators

Java provides a rich operator environment. Most of its operators can be divided into the following four groups: arithmetic, bitwise, relational, and logical. Java also defines some additional operators that handle certain special situations. This chapter describes all of Java's operators except for the type comparison operator **instanceof**, which is examined in Chapter 13, and the arrow operator (–>), which is described in Chapter 15.

## Arithmetic Operators

Arithmetic operators are used in mathematical expressions in the same way that they are used in algebra. The following table lists the arithmetic operators:

| Operator | Result |
|---|---|
| + | Addition (also unary plus) |
| – | Subtraction (also unary minus) |
| * | Multiplication |
| / | Division |
| % | Modulus |
| ++ | Increment |
| += | Addition assignment |
| – = | Subtraction assignment |
| *= | Multiplication assignment |
| /= | Division assignment |
| %= | Modulus assignment |
| – – | Decrement |

The operands of the arithmetic operators must be of a numeric type. You cannot use them on **boolean** types, but you can use them on **char** types, since the **char** type in Java is, essentially, a subset of **int**.

## The Basic Arithmetic Operators

The basic arithmetic operations—addition, subtraction, multiplication, and division—all behave as you would expect for all numeric types. The unary minus operator negates its single operand. The unary plus operator simply returns the value of its operand. Remember that when the division operator is applied to an integer type, there will be no fractional component attached to the result.

The following simple sample program demonstrates the arithmetic operators. It also illustrates the difference between floating-point division and integer division.

```
// Demonstrate the basic arithmetic operators.
class BasicMath {
  public static void main(String[] args) {
    // arithmetic using integers
    System.out.println("Integer Arithmetic");
    int a = 1 + 1;
    int b = a * 3;
    int c = b / 4;
    int d = c - a;
    int e = -d;
    System.out.println("a = " + a);
    System.out.println("b = " + b);
    System.out.println("c = " + c);
    System.out.println("d = " + d);
    System.out.println("e = " + e);

    // arithmetic using doubles
    System.out.println("\nFloating Point Arithmetic");
    double da = 1 + 1;
    double db = da * 3;
    double dc = db / 4;
    double dd = dc - a;
    double de = -dd;
    System.out.println("da = " + da);
    System.out.println("db = " + db);
    System.out.println("dc = " + dc);
    System.out.println("dd = " + dd);
    System.out.println("de = " + de);
  }
}
```

When you run this program, you will see the following output:

```
Integer Arithmetic
a = 2
b = 6
c = 1
d = -1
e = 1

Floating Point Arithmetic
da = 2.0
db = 6.0
```

```
dc = 1.5
dd = -0.5
de = 0.5
```

## The Modulus Operator

The modulus operator, **%**, returns the remainder of a division operation. It can be applied to floating-point types as well as integer types. The following sample program demonstrates the **%**:

```
// Demonstrate the % operator.
class Modulus {
  public static void main(String[] args) {
    int x = 42;
    double y = 42.25;

    System.out.println("x mod 10 = " + x % 10);
    System.out.println("y mod 10 = " + y % 10);
  }
}
```

When you run this program, you will get the following output:

```
x mod 10 = 2
y mod 10 = 2.25
```

## Arithmetic Compound Assignment Operators

Java provides special operators that can be used to combine an arithmetic operation with an assignment. As you probably know, statements like the following are quite common in programming:

```
a = a + 4;
```

In Java, you can rewrite this statement as shown here:

```
a += 4;
```

This version uses the += *compound assignment operator*. Both statements perform the same action: they increase the value of **a** by 4.

Here is another example,

```
a = a % 2;
```

which can be expressed as

```
a %= 2;
```

In this case, the %= obtains the remainder of **a** /2 and puts that result back into **a**.

There are compound assignment operators for all of the arithmetic, binary operators. Thus, any statement of the form

*var = var op expression*;

can be rewritten as

*var op= expression*;

The compound assignment operators provide two benefits. First, they save you a bit of typing, because they are "shorthand" for their equivalent long forms. Second, in some cases they are more efficient than are their equivalent long forms. For these reasons, you will often see the compound assignment operators used in professionally written Java programs.

Here is a sample program that shows several *op*= assignments in action:

```
// Demonstrate several assignment operators.
class OpEquals {
  public static void main(String[] args) {
    int a = 1;
    int b = 2;
    int c = 3;

    a += 5;
    b *= 4;
    c += a * b;
    c %= 6;
    System.out.println("a = " + a);
    System.out.println("b = " + b);
    System.out.println("c = " + c);
  }
}
```

The output of this program is shown here:

```
a = 6
b = 8
c = 3
```

## Increment and Decrement

The ++ and the – – are Java's increment and decrement operators, respectively. They were introduced in Chapter 2. Here they will be discussed in detail. As you will see, they have some special properties that make them quite interesting. Let's begin by reviewing precisely what the increment and decrement operators do.

The increment operator increases its operand by one. The decrement operator decreases its operand by one. For example, this statement:

```
x = x + 1;
```

can be rewritten like this by use of the increment operator:

```
x++;
```

Similarly, this statement:

```
x = x - 1;
```

is equivalent to

```
x--;
```

These operators are unique in that they can appear both in *postfix* form, where they follow the operand as just shown, and *prefix* form, where they precede the operand. In the foregoing examples, there is no difference between the prefix and postfix forms. However, when the increment and/or decrement operators are part of a larger expression, then a subtle, yet powerful, difference between these two forms appears. In the prefix form, the operand is incremented or decremented before the value is obtained for use in the expression. In postfix form, the previous value is obtained for use in the expression, and then the operand is modified. For example:

```
x = 42;
y = ++x;
```

In this case, **y** is set to 43 as you would expect, because the increment occurs *before* **x** is assigned to **y**. Thus, the line **y = ++x;** is the equivalent of these two statements:

```
x = x + 1;
y = x;
```

However, when written like this,

```
x = 42;
y = x++;
```

the value of **x** is obtained before the increment operator is executed, so the value of **y** is 42. Of course, in both cases **x** is set to 43. Here, the line **y = x++;** is the equivalent of these two statements:

```
y = x;
x = x + 1;
```

The following program demonstrates the increment operator:

```
// Demonstrate ++.
class IncDec {
  public static void main(String[] args) {
    int a = 1;
    int b = 2;
    int c;
    int d;
    c = ++b;
    d = a++;
    c++;
    System.out.println("a = " + a);
    System.out.println("b = " + b);
    System.out.println("c = " + c);
    System.out.println("d = " + d);
  }
}
```

The output of this program follows:

```
a = 2
b = 3
c = 4
d = 1
```

## The Bitwise Operators

Java defines several *bitwise operators* that can be applied to the integer types: **long**, **int**, **short**, **char**, and **byte**. These operators act upon the individual bits of their operands. They are summarized in the following table:

| Operator | Result |
|---|---|
| ~ | Bitwise unary NOT |
| & | Bitwise AND |
| \| | Bitwise OR |
| ^ | Bitwise exclusive OR |
| >> | Shift right |
| >>> | Shift right zero fill |
| << | Shift left |
| &= | Bitwise AND assignment |
| \|= | Bitwise OR assignment |
| ^= | Bitwise exclusive OR assignment |
| >>= | Shift right assignment |
| >>>= | Shift right zero fill assignment |
| <<= | Shift left assignment |

Since the bitwise operators manipulate the bits within an integer, it is important to understand what effects such manipulations may have on a value. Specifically, it is useful to know how Java stores integer values and how it represents negative numbers. So, before continuing, let's briefly review these two topics.

All of the integer types are represented by binary numbers of varying bit widths. For example, the **byte** value for 42 in binary is 00101010, where each position represents a power of two, starting with $2^0$ at the rightmost bit. The next bit position to the left would be $2^1$, or 2, continuing toward the left with $2^2$, or 4, then 8, 16, 32, and so on. So 42 has 1 bits set at positions 1, 3, and 5 (counting from 0 at the right); thus, 42 is the sum of $2^1 + 2^3 + 2^5$, which is 2 + 8 + 32.

All of the integer types (except **char**) are signed integers. This means that they can represent negative values as well as positive ones. Java uses an encoding known as *two's complement*, which means that negative numbers are represented by inverting (changing 1's to 0's and vice versa) all of the bits in a value, then adding 1 to the result. For example, –42 is represented by inverting all of the bits in 42, or 00101010, which yields 11010101, then adding 1, which results in 11010110, or –42. To decode a negative number, first invert all of the bits, then add 1. For example, –42, or 11010110 inverted, yields 00101001, or 41, so when you add 1 you get 42.

The reason Java (and most other computer languages) uses two's complement is easy to see when you consider the issue of *zero crossing*. Assuming a **byte** value, zero is represented by 00000000. In one's complement, simply inverting all of the bits creates 11111111, which creates negative zero. The trouble is that negative zero is invalid in integer math. This problem is solved by using two's complement to represent negative values. When using two's complement, 1 is added to the complement, producing 100000000. This produces a 1 bit too far to the left to fit back into the **byte** value, resulting in the desired behavior, where –0 is the same as 0, and 11111111 is the encoding for –1. Although we used a **byte** value in the preceding example, the same basic principle applies to all of Java's integer types.

Because Java uses two's complement to store negative numbers—and because all integers are signed values in Java—applying the bitwise operators can easily produce unexpected results. For example, turning on the high-order bit will cause the resulting value to be interpreted as a negative number, whether this is what you intended or not. To avoid unpleasant surprises, just remember that the high-order bit determines the sign of an integer no matter how that high-order bit gets set.

## The Bitwise Logical Operators

The bitwise logical operators are &, |, ^, and ~. The following table shows the outcome of each operation. In the discussion that follows, keep in mind that the bitwise operators are applied to each individual bit within each operand.

| A | B | A \| B | A & B | A ^ B | ~A |
|---|---|---|---|---|---|
| 0 | 0 | 0 | 0 | 0 | 1 |
| 1 | 0 | 1 | 0 | 1 | 0 |
| 0 | 1 | 1 | 0 | 1 | 1 |
| 1 | 1 | 1 | 1 | 0 | 0 |

### The Bitwise NOT

Also called the *bitwise complement*, the unary NOT operator, ~, inverts all of the bits of its operand. For example, the number 42, which has the following bit pattern:

00101010

becomes

11010101

after the NOT operator is applied.

## The Bitwise AND

The AND operator, &, produces a 1 bit if both operands are also 1. A zero is produced in all other cases. Here is an example:

```
  00101010  42
&00001111  15
_________
  00001010  10
```

## The Bitwise OR

The OR operator, |, combines bits such that if either of the bits in the operands is a 1, then the resultant bit is a 1, as shown here:

```
  00101010  42
| 00001111  15
_________
  00101111  47
```

## The Bitwise XOR

The XOR operator, ^, combines bits such that if exactly one operand is 1, then the result is 1. Otherwise, the result is zero. The following example shows the effect of the ^. This example also demonstrates a useful attribute of the XOR operation. Notice how the bit pattern of 42 is inverted wherever the second operand has a 1 bit. Wherever the second operand has a 0 bit, the first operand is unchanged. You will find this property useful when performing some types of bit manipulations.

```
  00101010  42
^ 00001111  15
_________
  00100101  37
```

## Using the Bitwise Logical Operators

The following program demonstrates the bitwise logical operators:

```
// Demonstrate the bitwise logical operators.
class BitLogic {
  public static void main(String[] args) {
    String[] binary = {
      "0000", "0001", "0010", "0011", "0100", "0101", "0110", "0111",
      "1000", "1001", "1010", "1011", "1100", "1101", "1110", "1111"
    };
    int a = 3; // 0 + 2 + 1 or 0011 in binary
    int b = 6; // 4 + 2 + 0 or 0110 in binary
    int c = a | b;
    int d = a & b;
    int e = a ^ b;
    int f = (~a & b)|(a & ~b);
    int g = ~a & 0x0f;
```

```
    System.out.println("         a = " + binary[a]);
    System.out.println("         b = " + binary[b]);
    System.out.println("       a|b = " + binary[c]);
    System.out.println("       a&b = " + binary[d]);
    System.out.println("       a^b = " + binary[e]);
    System.out.println("~a&b|a&~b = " + binary[f]);
    System.out.println("        ~a = " + binary[g]);
  }
}
```

In this example, **a** and **b** have bit patterns that present all four possibilities for two binary digits: 0-0, 0-1, 1-0, and 1-1. You can see how the | and **&** operate on each bit by the results in **c** and **d**. The values assigned to **e** and **f** are the same and illustrate how the ^ works. The string array named **binary** holds the human-readable, binary representation of the numbers 0 through 15. In this example, the array is indexed to show the binary representation of each result. The array is constructed such that the correct string representation of a binary value **n** is stored in **binary[n]**. The value of **~a** is ANDed with **0x0f** (0000 1111 in binary) in order to reduce its value to less than 16, so it can be printed by use of the **binary** array. Here is the output from this program:

```
        a = 0011
        b = 0110
      a|b = 0111
      a&b = 0010
      a^b = 0101
~a&b|a&~b = 0101
       ~a = 1100
```

## The Left Shift

The left shift operator, **<<**, shifts all of the bits in a value to the left a specified number of times. It has this general form:

*value* << *num*

Here, *num* specifies the number of positions to left-shift the value in *value*. That is, the << moves all of the bits in the specified value to the left by the number of bit positions specified by *num*. For each shift left, the high-order bit is shifted out (and lost), and a zero is brought in on the right. This means that when a left shift is applied to an **int** operand, bits are lost once they are shifted past bit position 31. If the operand is a **long**, then bits are lost after bit position 63.

Java's automatic type promotions produce unexpected results when you are shifting **byte** and **short** values. As you know, **byte** and **short** values are promoted to **int** when an expression is evaluated. Furthermore, the result of such an expression is also an **int**. This means that the outcome of a left shift on a **byte** or **short** value will be an **int**, and the bits shifted left will not be lost until they shift past bit position 31. Furthermore, a negative **byte** or **short** value will be sign-extended when it is promoted to **int**. Thus, the high-order bits will be filled with 1's. For these reasons, to perform a left shift on a **byte** or **short** implies that you must discard the high-order bytes of the **int** result. For example, if you left-shift a **byte** value, that value will first be promoted to **int** and then shifted. This means that you must discard the top three bytes of the result if what you want is the result of a shifted **byte** value. The easiest way to do this is to simply cast the result back into a **byte**. The following program demonstrates this concept:

```
// Left shifting a byte value.
class ByteShift {
  public static void main(String[] args) {
    byte a = 64, b;
    int i;

    i = a << 2;
    b = (byte) (a << 2);

    System.out.println("Original value of a: " + a);
    System.out.println("i and b: " + i + " " + b);
  }
}
```

The output generated by this program is shown here:

```
Original value of a: 64
i and b: 256 0
```

Since **a** is promoted to **int** for the purposes of evaluation, left-shifting the value 64 (0100 0000) twice results in **i** containing the value 256 (1 0000 0000). However, the value in **b** contains 0 because after the shift, the low-order byte is now zero. Its only 1 bit has been shifted out.

Since each left shift has the effect of doubling the original value, programmers frequently use this fact as an efficient alternative to multiplying by 2. But you need to watch out. If you shift a 1 bit into the high-order position (bit 31 or 63), the value will become negative. The following program illustrates this point:

```
// Left shifting as a quick way to multiply by 2.
class MultByTwo {
  public static void main(String[] args) {
    int i;
    int num = 0xFFFFFFE;

    for(i=0; i<4; i++) {
      num = num << 1;
      System.out.println(num);
    }
  }
}
```

The program generates the following output:

```
536870908
1073741816
2147483632
-32
```

The starting value was carefully chosen so that after being shifted left 4 bit positions, it would produce –32. As you can see, when a 1 bit is shifted into bit 31, the number is interpreted as negative.

## The Right Shift

The right shift operator, >>, shifts all of the bits in a value to the right a specified number of times. Its general form is shown here:

*value* >> *num*

Here, *num* specifies the number of positions to right-shift the value in *value*. That is, the >> moves all of the bits in the specified value to the right the number of bit positions specified by *num*.

The following code fragment shifts the value 32 to the right by two positions, resulting in **a** being set to **8**:

```
int a = 32;
a = a >> 2; // a now contains 8
```

When a value has bits that are "shifted off," those bits are lost. For example, the next code fragment shifts the value 35 to the right two positions, which causes the two low-order bits to be lost, resulting again in **a** being set to 8:

```
int a = 35;
a = a >> 2; // a contains 8
```

Looking at the same operation in binary shows more clearly how this happens:

00100011 35
>> 2
00001000 8

Each time you shift a value to the right, it divides that value by two—and discards any remainder. In some cases, you can take advantage of this for high-performance integer division by 2.

When you are shifting right, the top (leftmost) bits exposed by the right shift are filled in with the previous contents of the top bit. This is called *sign extension* and serves to preserve the sign of negative numbers when you shift them right. For example, –8 >> 1 is –4, which, in binary, is

11111000 –8
>> 1
11111100 –4

It is interesting to note that if you shift –1 right, the result always remains –1, since sign extension keeps bringing in more ones in the high-order bits.

Sometimes it is not desirable to sign-extend values when you are shifting them to the right. For example, the following program converts a **byte** value to its hexadecimal string representation. Notice that the shifted value is masked by ANDing it with **0x0f** to discard any sign-extended bits so that the value can be used as an index into the array of hexadecimal characters.

```
// Masking sign extension.
class HexByte {
  static public void main(String[] args) {
    char[] hex = {
      '0', '1', '2', '3', '4', '5', '6', '7',
      '8', '9', 'a', 'b', 'c', 'd', 'e', 'f'
    };

    byte b = (byte) 0xf1;

   System.out.println("b = 0x" + hex[(b >> 4) & 0x0f] + hex[b & 0x0f]);
  }
}
```

Here is the output of this program:

```
b = 0xf1
```

## The Unsigned Right Shift

As you have just seen, the >> operator automatically fills the high-order bit with its previous contents each time a shift occurs. This preserves the sign of the value. However, sometimes this is undesirable. For example, if you are shifting something that does not represent a numeric value, you may not want sign extension to take place. This situation is common when you are working with pixel-based values and graphics. In these cases, you will generally want to shift a zero into the high-order bit no matter what its initial value was. This is known as an *unsigned shift.* To accomplish this, you will use Java's unsigned, shift-right operator, **>>>**, which always shifts zeros into the high-order bit.

The following code fragment demonstrates the **>>>**. Here, **a** is set to –1, which sets all 32 bits to 1 in binary. This value is then shifted right 24 bits, filling the top 24 bits with zeros, ignoring normal sign extension. This sets **a** to 255.

```
int a = -1;
a = a >>> 24;
```

Here is the same operation in binary form to further illustrate what is happening:

11111111 11111111 11111111 11111111   –1 in binary as an **int**
>>>24
00000000 00000000 00000000 11111111   255 in binary as an **int**

The >>> operator is often not as useful as you might like, since it is only meaningful for 32- and 64-bit values. Remember, smaller values are automatically promoted to **int** in expressions. This means that sign extension occurs and that the shift will take place on a 32-bit rather than on an 8- or 16-bit value. That is, one might expect an unsigned right shift on a **byte** value to zero-fill beginning at bit 7. But this is not the case, since it is a 32-bit value that is actually being shifted. The following program demonstrates this effect:

```
// Unsigned shifting a byte value.
class ByteUShift {
  static public void main(String[] args) {
    char[] hex = {
      '0', '1', '2', '3', '4', '5', '6', '7',
      '8', '9', 'a', 'b', 'c', 'd', 'e', 'f'
    };
    byte b = (byte) 0xf1;
    byte c = (byte) (b >> 4);
    byte d = (byte) (b >>> 4);
    byte e = (byte) ((b & 0xff) >> 4);

    System.out.println("              b = 0x"
      + hex[(b >> 4) & 0x0f] + hex[b & 0x0f]);
    System.out.println("         b >> 4 = 0x"
      + hex[(c >> 4) & 0x0f] + hex[c & 0x0f]);
    System.out.println("        b >>> 4 = 0x"
      + hex[(d >> 4) & 0x0f] + hex[d & 0x0f]);
    System.out.println("(b & 0xff) >> 4 = 0x"
      + hex[(e >> 4) & 0x0f] + hex[e & 0x0f]);
  }
}
```

The following output of this program shows how the >>> operator appears to do nothing when dealing with bytes. The variable **b** is set to an arbitrary negative **byte** value for this demonstration. Then **c** is assigned the **byte** value of **b** shifted right by four, which is 0xff because of the expected sign extension. Then **d** is assigned the **byte** value of **b** unsigned shifted right by four, which you might have expected to be 0x0f but is actually 0xff because of the sign extension that happened when **b** was promoted to **int** before the shift. The last expression sets **e** to the **byte** value of **b** masked to 8 bits using the AND operator, then shifted right by four, which produces the expected value of 0x0f. Notice that the unsigned shift right operator was not used for **d**, since the state of the sign bit after the AND was known.

```
              b = 0xf1
         b >> 4 = 0xff
        b >>> 4 = 0xff
(b & 0xff) >> 4 = 0x0f
```

## Bitwise Operator Compound Assignments

All of the binary bitwise operators have a compound form similar to that of the algebraic operators, which combines the assignment with the bitwise operation. For example, the following two statements, which shift the value in **a** right by four bits, are equivalent:

```
a = a >> 4;
a >>= 4;
```

Likewise, the following two statements, which result in **a** being assigned the bitwise expression **a** OR **b**, are equivalent:

```
a = a | b;
a |= b;
```

The following program creates a few integer variables and then uses compound bitwise operator assignments to manipulate the variables:

```
class OpBitEquals {
  public static void main(String[] args) {
    int a = 1;
    int b = 2;
    int c = 3;

    a |= 4;
    b >>= 1;
    c <<= 1;
    a ^= c;
    System.out.println("a = " + a);
    System.out.println("b = " + b);
    System.out.println("c = " + c);
  }
}
```

The output of this program is shown here:

```
a = 3
b = 1
c = 6
```

## Relational Operators

The *relational operators* determine the relationship that one operand has to the other. Specifically, they determine equality and ordering. The relational operators are shown here:

| Operator | Result |
|---|---|
| == | Equal to |
| != | Not equal to |
| > | Greater than |
| < | Less than |
| >= | Greater than or equal to |
| <= | Less than or equal to |

The outcome of these operations is a **boolean** value. The relational operators are most frequently used in the expressions that control the **if** statement and the various loop statements.

Any type in Java, including integers, floating-point numbers, characters, and Booleans can be compared using the equality test, ==, and the inequality test, **!=**. Notice that in Java equality is denoted with two equal signs, not one. (Remember: a single equal sign is the assignment operator.) Only numeric types can be compared using the ordering operators. That is, only integer, floating-point, and character operands may be compared to see which is greater or less than the other.

As stated, the result produced by a relational operator is a **boolean** value. For example, the following code fragment is perfectly valid:

```
int a = 4;
int b = 1;
boolean c = a < b;
```

In this case, the result of **a<b** (which is **false**) is stored in **c**.

If you are coming from a C/C++ background, please note the following. In C/C++, these types of statements are very common:

```
int done;
//...
if(!done)... // Valid in C/C++
if(done)...  // but not in Java.
```

In Java, these statements must be written like this:

```
if(done == 0)... // This is Java-style.
if(done != 0)...
```

The reason is that Java does not define true and false in the same way as C/C++. In C/C++, true is any nonzero value and false is zero. In Java, **true** and **false** are nonnumeric values that do not relate to zero or nonzero. Therefore, to test for zero or nonzero, you must explicitly employ one or more of the relational operators.

# Boolean Logical Operators

The Boolean logical operators shown here operate only on **boolean** operands. All of the binary logical operators combine two **boolean** values to form a resultant **boolean** value.

| Operator | Result |
|---|---|
| & | Logical AND |
| \| | Logical OR |
| ^ | Logical XOR (exclusive OR) |
| \|\| | Short-circuit OR |
| && | Short-circuit AND |
| ! | Logical unary NOT |
| &= | AND assignment |
| \|= | OR assignment |
| ^= | XOR assignment |

| Operator | Result |
|---|---|
| == | Equal to |
| != | Not equal to |
| ?: | Ternary if-then-else |

The logical Boolean operators, **&**, **|**, and **^**, operate on **boolean** values in the same way that they operate on the bits of an integer. The logical **!** operator inverts the Boolean state: **!true == false** and **!false == true**. The following table shows the effect of each logical operation:

| A | B | A \| B | A & B | A ^ B | !A |
|---|---|---|---|---|---|
| False | False | False | False | False | True |
| True | False | True | False | True | False |
| False | True | True | False | True | True |
| True | True | True | True | False | False |

Here is a program that is almost the same as the **BitLogic** example shown earlier, but it operates on **boolean** logical values instead of binary bits:

```
// Demonstrate the boolean logical operators.
class BoolLogic {
  public static void main(String[] args) {
    boolean a = true;
    boolean b = false;
    boolean c = a | b;
    boolean d = a & b;
    boolean e = a ^ b;
    boolean f = (!a & b) | (a & !b);
    boolean g = !a;
    System.out.println("        a = " + a);
    System.out.println("        b = " + b);
    System.out.println("      a|b = " + c);
    System.out.println("      a&b = " + d);
    System.out.println("      a^b = " + e);
    System.out.println("!a&b|a&!b = " + f);
    System.out.println("       !a = " + g);
  }
}
```

After running this program, you will see that the same logical rules apply to **boolean** values as they did to bits. As you can see from the following output, the string representation of a Java **boolean** value is one of the literal values **true** or **false**:

```
        a = true
        b = false
      a|b = true
      a&b = false
      a^b = true
!a&b|a&!b = true
       !a = false
```

## Short-Circuit Logical Operators

Java provides two interesting Boolean operators not found in some other computer languages. These are secondary versions of the Boolean AND and OR operators, and are commonly known as *short-circuit* logical operators. As you can see from the preceding table, the OR operator results in **true** when **A** is **true**, no matter what **B** is. Similarly, the AND operator results in **false** when **A** is **false**, no matter what **B** is. If you use the **||** and **&&** forms rather than the **|** and **&** forms of these operators, Java will not bother to evaluate the right-hand operand when the outcome of the expression can be determined by the left operand alone. This is very useful when the right-hand operand depends on the value of the left one in order to function properly. For example, the following code fragment shows how you can take advantage of short-circuit logical evaluation to be sure that a division operation will be valid before evaluating it:

```
if (denom != 0 && num / denom > 10)
```

Since the short-circuit form of AND (**&&**) is used, there is no risk of causing a run-time exception when **denom** is zero. If this line of code were written using the single **&** version of AND, both sides would be evaluated, causing a run-time exception when **denom** is zero.

It is standard practice to use the short-circuit forms of AND and OR in cases involving Boolean logic, leaving the single-character versions exclusively for bitwise operations. However, there are exceptions to this rule. For example, consider the following statement:

```
if(c==1 & e++ < 100) d = 100;
```

Here, using a single **&** ensures that the increment operation will be applied to **e** whether **c** is equal to 1 or not.

---

**NOTE** The formal specification for Java refers to the short-circuit operators as the *conditional-and* and the *conditional-or*.

# The Assignment Operator

You have been using the assignment operator since Chapter 2. Now it is time to take a formal look at it. The *assignment operator* is the single equal sign, =. The assignment operator works in Java much as it does in any other computer language. It has this general form:

*var* = *expression*;

Here, the type of *var* must be compatible with the type of *expression*.

The assignment operator does have one interesting attribute that you may not be familiar with: it allows you to create a chain of assignments. For example, consider this fragment:

```
int x, y, z;

x = y = z = 100; // set x, y, and z to 100
```

This fragment sets the variables **x**, **y**, and **z** to 100 using a single statement. This works because the = is an operator that yields the value of the right-hand expression. Thus, the value of **z = 100** is 100, which is then assigned to **y**, which in turn is assigned to **x**. Using a "chain of assignment" is an easy way to set a group of variables to a common value.

## The ? Operator

Java includes a special *ternary* (three-way) *operator* that can replace certain types of if-then-else statements. This operator is the **?**. It can seem somewhat confusing at first, but the **?** can be used very effectively once mastered. The **?** has this general form:

*expression1* ? *expression2* : *expression3*

Here, *expression1* can be any expression that evaluates to a **boolean** value. If *expression1* is **true**, then *expression2* is evaluated; otherwise, *expression3* is evaluated. The result of the **?** operation is that of the expression evaluated. Both *expression2* and *expression3* are required to return the same (or compatible) type, which can't be **void**.

Here is an example of the way that the **?** is employed:

```
ratio = denom == 0 ? 0 : num / denom;
```

When Java evaluates this assignment expression, it first looks at the expression to the *left* of the question mark. If **denom** equals zero, then the expression *between* the question mark and the colon is evaluated and used as the value of the entire **?** expression. If **denom** does not equal zero, then the expression *after* the colon is evaluated and used for the value of the entire **?** expression. The result produced by the **?** operator is then assigned to **ratio**.

Here is a program that demonstrates the **?** operator. It uses it to obtain the absolute value of a variable.

```
// Demonstrate ?.
class Ternary {
  public static void main(String[] args) {
    int i, k;

    i = 10;
    k = i < 0 ? -i : i; // get absolute value of i
    System.out.print("Absolute value of ");
    System.out.println(i + " is " + k);

    i = -10;
    k = i < 0 ? -i : i; // get absolute value of i
    System.out.print("Absolute value of ");
    System.out.println(i + " is " + k);
  }
}
```

The output generated by the program is shown here:

```
Absolute value of 10 is 10
Absolute value of -10 is 10
```

## Operator Precedence

Table 4-1 shows the order of precedence for Java operators, from highest to lowest. Operators in the same row are equal in precedence. In binary operations, the order of evaluation is left to right (except for assignment, which evaluates right to left). Although they are technically separators, the [ ], ( ), and **.** can also act like operators. In that capacity, they would have the highest precedence. Also, notice the arrow operator (->). It is used in lambda expressions.

## Using Parentheses

*Parentheses* raise the precedence of the operations that are inside them. This is often necessary to obtain the result you desire. For example, consider the following expression:

```
a >> b + 3
```

This expression first adds 3 to **b** and then shifts **a** right by that result. That is, this expression can be rewritten using redundant parentheses like this:

```
a >> (b + 3)
```

However, if you want to first shift **a** right by **b** positions and then add 3 to that result, you will need to parenthesize the expression like this:

```
(a >> b) + 3
```

| **Highest** | | | | | | |
|---|---|---|---|---|---|---|
| ++ (postfix) | – – (postfix) | | | | | |
| ++ (prefix) | – – (prefix) | ~ | ! | + (unary) | – (unary) | (*type-cast*) |
| * | / | % | | | | |
| + | – | | | | | |
| >> | >>> | << | | | | |
| > | >= | < | <= | instanceof | | |
| == | != | | | | | |
| & | | | | | | |
| ^ | | | | | | |
| \| | | | | | | |
| && | | | | | | |
| \|\| | | | | | | |
| ?: | | | | | | |
| -> | | | | | | |
| = | op= | | | | | |
| **Lowest** | | | | | | |

**Table 4-1** The Precedence of the Java Operators

In addition to altering the normal precedence of an operator, parentheses can sometimes be used to help clarify the meaning of an expression. For anyone reading your code, a complicated expression can be difficult to understand. Adding redundant but clarifying parentheses to complex expressions can help prevent confusion later. For example, which of the following expressions is easier to read?

```
a | 4 + c >> b & 7
(a | (((4 + c) >> b) & 7))
```

One other point: parentheses (redundant or not) do not degrade the performance of your program. Therefore, adding parentheses to reduce ambiguity does not negatively affect your program.

# CHAPTER 5 Control Statements

A programming language uses *control* statements to cause the flow of execution to advance and branch based on changes to the state of a program. Java's program control statements can be put into the following categories: selection, iteration, and jump. *Selection* statements allow your program to choose different paths of execution based upon the outcome of an expression or the state of a variable. *Iteration* statements enable program execution to repeat one or more statements (that is, iteration statements form loops). *Jump* statements allow your program to execute in a nonlinear fashion. All of Java's control statements are examined here.

## Java's Selection Statements

Java supports two selection statements: **if** and **switch**. These statements allow you to control the flow of your program's execution based upon conditions known only during run time. You will be pleasantly surprised by the power and flexibility contained in these two statements.

### if

The **if** statement was introduced in Chapter 2. It is examined in detail here. The **if** statement is Java's conditional branch statement. It can be used to route program execution through two different paths. Here is the general form of the **if** statement:

if (*condition*) *statement1*;
else *statement2*;

Here, each *statement* may be a single statement or a compound statement enclosed in curly braces (that is, a *block*). The *condition* is any expression that returns a **boolean** value. The **else** clause is optional.

The **if** works like this: If the *condition* is true, then *statement1* is executed. Otherwise, *statement2* (if it exists) is executed. In no case will both statements be executed. For example, consider the following:

```
int a, b;
//...
if(a < b) a = 0;
else b = 0;
```

Here, if **a** is less than **b**, then **a** is set to zero. Otherwise, **b** is set to zero. In no case are they both set to zero.

Most often, the expression used to control the **if** will involve the relational operators. However, this is not technically necessary. It is possible to control the **if** using a single **boolean** variable, as shown in this code fragment:

```
boolean dataAvailable;
//...
if (dataAvailable)
  ProcessData();
else
  waitForMoreData();
```

Remember, only one statement can appear directly after the **if** or the **else**. If you want to include more statements, you'll need to create a block, as in this fragment:

```
int bytesAvailable;
// ...
if (bytesAvailable > 0) {
  ProcessData();
  bytesAvailable -= n;
} else
  waitForMoreData();
```

Here, both statements within the **if** block will execute if **bytesAvailable** is greater than zero.

Some programmers find it convenient to include the curly braces when using the **if**, even when there is only one statement in each clause. This makes it easy to add another statement at a later date, and you don't have to worry about forgetting the braces. In fact, forgetting to define a block when one is needed is a common cause of errors. For example, consider the following code fragment:

```
int bytesAvailable;
// ...
if (bytesAvailable > 0) {
  ProcessData();
  bytesAvailable -= n;
} else
  waitForMoreData();
  bytesAvailable = n;
```

It seems clear that the statement **bytesAvailable = n;** was intended to be executed inside the **else** clause, because of the indentation level. However, as you recall, whitespace is insignificant to Java, and there is no way for the compiler to know what was intended. This code will compile without complaint, but it will behave incorrectly when run. The preceding example is fixed in the code that follows:

```
int bytesAvailable;
// ...
if (bytesAvailable > 0) {
  ProcessData();
  bytesAvailable -= n;
} else {
```

```
    waitForMoreData();
    bytesAvailable = n;
  }
```

## Nested ifs

A *nested* **if** is an **if** statement that is the target of another **if** or **else**. Nested **if**s are very common in programming. When you nest **if**s, the main thing to remember is that an **else** statement always refers to the nearest **if** statement that is within the same block as the **else** and that is not already associated with an **else**. Here is an example:

```
if(i == 10) {
  if(j < 20) a = b;
  if(k > 100) c = d; // this if is
  else a = c;        // associated with this else
}
else a = d;          // this else refers to if(i == 10)
```

As the comments indicate, the final **else** is not associated with **if(j<20)** because it is not in the same block (even though it is the nearest **if** without an **else**). Rather, the final **else** is associated with **if(i==10)**. The inner **else** refers to **if(k>100)** because it is the closest **if** within the same block.

## The if-else-if Ladder

A common programming construct that is based upon a sequence of nested **if**s is the *if-else-if* ladder. It looks like this:

if(*condition*)<br>
  *statement*;<br>
else if(*condition*)<br>
  *statement*;<br>
else if(*condition*)<br>
  *statement*;<br>
.<br>
.<br>
.<br>
else<br>
  *statement*;

The **if** statements are executed from the top down. As soon as one of the conditions controlling the **if** is **true**, the statement associated with that **if** is executed, and the rest of the ladder is bypassed. If none of the conditions is true, then the final **else** statement will be executed. The final **else** acts as a default condition; that is, if all other conditional tests fail, then the last **else** statement is performed. If there is no final **else** and all other conditions are **false**, then no action will take place.

Here is a program that uses an **if-else-if** ladder to determine which season a particular month is in:

```
// Demonstrate if-else-if statements.
class IfElse {
  public static void main(String[] args) {
```

```
    int month = 4; // April
    String season;

    if(month == 12 || month == 1 || month == 2)
      season = "Winter";
    else if(month == 3 || month == 4 || month == 5)
      season = "Spring";
    else if(month == 6 || month == 7 || month == 8)
      season = "Summer";
    else if(month == 9 || month == 10 || month == 11)
      season = "Autumn";
    else
      season = "Bogus Month";

    System.out.println("April is in the " + season + ".");
  }
}
```

Here is the output produced by the program:

```
April is in the Spring.
```

You might want to experiment with this program before moving on. As you will find, no matter what value you give **month**, one and only one assignment statement within the ladder will be executed.

## The Traditional switch

The **switch** statement is Java's multiway branch statement. It provides an easy way to dispatch execution to different parts of your code based on the value of an expression. As such, it often provides a better alternative than a large series of **if-else-if** statements.

At the outset, it is necessary to state that beginning with JDK 14, the **switch** has been significantly enhanced and expanded with several new features that go far beyond its traditional form. The traditional form of **switch** has been part of Java from the beginning and is, therefore, in widespread use. Furthermore, it is the form that will work in all Java development environments and for all readers. Because of the substantial nature of the recent **switch** enhancements, they are described in Chapter 17, in the context of other recent additions to Java. Here, the traditional form of the **switch** is examined. Here is the general form of a traditional **switch** statement:

switch (*expression*) {
  case *value1*:
    // statement sequence
    break;
  case *value2*:
    // statement sequence
    break;
  .
  .
  .

```
    case valueN :
      // statement sequence
      break;
    default:
      // default statement sequence
  }
```

For versions of Java prior to JDK 7, *expression* must resolve to type **byte**, **short**, **int**, **char**, or an enumeration. (Enumerations are described in Chapter 12.) Today, *expression* can also be of type **String**, and beginning with JDK 21, in some situations, it can be an object reference (see Chapter 17). Each value specified in the **case** statements must be a unique constant expression (such as a literal value). Duplicate **case** values are not allowed. The type of each value must be compatible with the type of *expression*.

The traditional **switch** statement works like this: The value of the expression is compared with each of the values in the **case** statements. If a match is found, the code sequence following that **case** statement is executed. If none of the constants matches the value of the expression, then the **default** statement is executed. However, the **default** statement is optional. If no **case** matches and no **default** is present, then no further action is taken.

The **break** statement is used inside the **switch** to terminate a statement sequence. When a **break** statement is encountered, execution branches to the first line of code that follows the entire **switch** statement. This has the effect of "jumping out" of the **switch**.

Here is a simple example that uses a **switch** statement:

```
// A simple example of the switch.
class SampleSwitch {
  public static void main(String[] args) {
    for(int i=0; i<6; i++)
      switch(i) {
        case 0:
          System.out.println("i is zero.");
          break;
        case 1:
          System.out.println("i is one.");
          break;
        case 2:
          System.out.println("i is two.");
          break;
        case 3:
          System.out.println("i is three.");
          break;
        default:
          System.out.println("i is greater than 3.");
      }
  }
}
```

The output produced by this program is shown here:

```
i is zero.
i is one.
i is two.
```

```
i is three.
i is greater than 3.
i is greater than 3.
```

As you can see, each time through the loop, the statements associated with the **case** constant that matches **i** are executed. All others are bypassed. After **i** is greater than 3, no **case** statements match, so the **default** statement is executed.

The **break** statement is optional. If you omit the **break**, execution will continue on into the next **case**. It is sometimes desirable to have multiple **cases** without **break** statements between them. For example, consider the following program:

```
// In a switch, break statements are optional.
class MissingBreak {
  public static void main(String[] args) {
    for(int i=0; i<12; i++)
      switch(i) {
        case 0:
        case 1:
        case 2:
        case 3:
        case 4:
          System.out.println("i is less than 5");
          break;
        case 5:
        case 6:
        case 7:
        case 8:
        case 9:
          System.out.println("i is less than 10");
          break;
        default:
          System.out.println("i is 10 or more");
      }
  }
}
```

This program generates the following output:

```
i is less than 5
i is less than 5
i is less than 5
i is less than 5
i is less than 5
i is less than 10
i is less than 10
i is less than 10
i is less than 10
i is less than 10
i is 10 or more
i is 10 or more
```

As you can see, execution falls through each **case** until a **break** statement (or the end of the **switch**) is reached.

While the preceding example is, of course, contrived for the sake of illustration, omitting the **break** statement has many practical applications in real programs. To sample its more realistic usage, consider the following rewrite of the season example shown earlier. This version uses a **switch** to provide a more efficient implementation.

```
// An improved version of the season program.
class Switch {
  public static void main(String[] args) {
    int month = 4;
    String season;

    switch (month) {
      case 12:
      case 1:
      case 2:
        season = "Winter";
        break;
      case 3:
      case 4:
      case 5:
        season = "Spring";
        break;
      case 6:
      case 7:
      case 8:
        season = "Summer";
        break;
      case 9:
      case 10:
      case 11:
        season = "Autumn";
        break;
      default:
        season = "Bogus Month";
    }
    System.out.println("April is in the " + season + ".");
  }
}
```

As mentioned, you can also use a string to control a **switch** statement. For example:

```
// Use a string to control a switch statement.

class StringSwitch {
  public static void main(String[] args) {

    String str = "two";

    switch(str) {
      case "one":
        System.out.println("one");
        break;
      case "two":
        System.out.println("two");
        break;
      case "three":
```

```
        System.out.println("three");
        break;
      default:
        System.out.println("no match");
        break;
    }
  }
}
```

As you would expect, the output from the program is

```
two
```

The string contained in **str** (which is "two" in this program) is tested against the **case** constants. When a match is found (as it is in the second **case**), the code sequence associated with that sequence is executed.

Being able to use strings in a **switch** statement streamlines many situations. For example, using a string-based **switch** is an improvement over using the equivalent sequence of **if/else** statements. However, switching on strings can be more expensive than switching on integers. Therefore, it is best to switch on strings only in cases in which the controlling data is already in string form. In other words, don't use strings in a **switch** unnecessarily.

## Nested switch Statements

You can use a **switch** as part of the statement sequence of an outer **switch**. This is called a *nested* **switch**. Since a **switch** statement defines its own block, no conflicts arise between the **case** constants in the inner **switch** and those in the outer **switch**. For example, the following fragment is perfectly valid:

```
switch(count) {
  case 1:
    switch(target) { // nested switch
      case 0:
        System.out.println("target is zero");
        break;
      case 1: // no conflicts with outer switch
        System.out.println("target is one");
        break;
    }
    break;
  case 2: // ...
```

Here, the **case 1:** statement in the inner switch does not conflict with the **case 1:** statement in the outer switch. The **count** variable is compared only with the list of cases at the outer level. If **count** is 1, then **target** is compared with the inner list cases.

In summary, there are three important features of the **switch** statement to note:

- The **switch** differs from the **if** in that **switch** can only test for equality, whereas **if** can evaluate any type of Boolean expression. That is, the **switch** looks only for a match between the value of the expression and one of its **case** constants.

- No two **case** constants in the same **switch** can have identical values. Of course, a **switch** statement and an enclosing outer **switch** can have **case** constants in common.
- A **switch** statement is usually more efficient than a set of nested **if**s.

The last point is particularly interesting because it gives insight into how the Java compiler works. When it compiles a **switch** statement, the Java compiler will inspect each of the **case** constants and create a "jump table" that it will use for selecting the path of execution depending on the value of the expression. Therefore, if you need to select among a large group of values, a **switch** statement will run much faster than the equivalent logic coded using a sequence of **if-else**s. The compiler can do this because it knows that the **case** constants are all the same type and simply must be compared for equality with the **switch** expression. The compiler has no such knowledge of a long list of **if** expressions.

**REMEMBER** Recently, the capabilities and features of **switch** have been substantially expanded beyond those offered by the traditional **switch** just described. Refer to Chapter 17 for details on the enhanced **switch**.

# Iteration Statements

Java's iteration statements are **for**, **while**, and **do-while**. These statements create what we commonly call *loops*. As you probably know, a loop repeatedly executes the same set of instructions until a termination condition is met. As you will see, Java has a loop to fit any programming need.

## while

The **while** loop is Java's most fundamental loop statement. It repeats a statement or block while its controlling expression is true. Here is its general form:

```
while(condition) {
  // body of loop
}
```

The *condition* can be any Boolean expression. The body of the loop will be executed as long as the conditional expression is true. When *condition* becomes false, control passes to the next line of code immediately following the loop. The curly braces are unnecessary if only a single statement is being repeated.

Here is a **while** loop that counts down from 10, printing exactly ten lines of "tick":

```
// Demonstrate the while loop.
class While {
  public static void main(String[] args) {
    int n = 10;

    while(n > 0) {
      System.out.println("tick " + n);
      n--;
    }
  }
}
```

When you run this program, it will "tick" ten times:

```
tick 10
tick 9
tick 8
tick 7
tick 6
tick 5
tick 4
tick 3
tick 2
tick 1
```

Since the **while** loop evaluates its conditional expression at the top of the loop, the body of the loop will not execute even once if the condition is false to begin with. For example, in the following fragment, the call to **println()** is never executed:

```
int a = 10, b = 20;

while(a > b)
  System.out.println("This will not be displayed");
```

The body of the **while** (or any other of Java's loops) can be empty. This is because a *null statement* (one that consists only of a semicolon) is syntactically valid in Java. For example, consider the following program:

```
// The target of a loop can be empty.
class NoBody {
  public static void main(String[] args) {
    int i, j;

    i = 100;
    j = 200;

    // find midpoint between i and j
    while(++i < --j); // no body in this loop

    System.out.println("Midpoint is " + i);
  }
}
```

This program finds the midpoint between **i** and **j**. It generates the following output:

```
Midpoint is 150
```

Here is how this **while** loop works. The value of **i** is incremented, and the value of **j** is decremented. These values are then compared with one another. If the new value of **i** is still less than the new value of **j**, then the loop repeats. If **i** is equal to or greater than **j**, the loop stops. Upon exit from the loop, **i** will hold a value that is midway between the original values of **i** and **j**.

(Of course, this procedure only works when **i** is less than **j** to begin with.) As you can see, there is no need for a loop body; all of the action occurs within the conditional expression itself. In professionally written Java code, short loops are frequently coded without bodies when the controlling expression can handle all of the details itself.

## do-while

As you just saw, if the conditional expression controlling a **while** loop is initially false, then the body of the loop will not be executed at all. However, sometimes it is desirable to execute the body of a loop at least once, even if the conditional expression is false to begin with. In other words, there are times when you would like to test the termination expression at the end of the loop rather than at the beginning. Fortunately, Java supplies a loop that does just that: the **do-while**. The **do-while** loop always executes its body at least once, because its conditional expression is at the bottom of the loop. Its general form is

```
do {
  // body of loop
} while (condition);
```

Each iteration of the **do-while** loop first executes the body of the loop and then evaluates the conditional expression. If this expression is true, the loop will repeat. Otherwise, the loop terminates. As with all of Java's loops, *condition* must be a Boolean expression.

Here is a reworked version of the "tick" program that demonstrates the **do-while** loop. It generates the same output as before.

```
// Demonstrate the do-while loop.
class DoWhile {
  public static void main(String[] args) {
    int n = 10;

    do {
      System.out.println("tick " + n);
      n--;
    } while(n > 0);
  }
}
```

The loop in the preceding program, while technically correct, can be written more efficiently as follows:

```
do {
  System.out.println("tick " + n);
} while(--n > 0);
```

In this example, the expression (**– –n > 0**) combines the decrement of **n** and the test for zero into one expression. Here is how it works. First, the **– –n** statement executes, decrementing **n** and returning the new value of **n**. This value is then compared with zero. If it is greater than zero, the loop continues; otherwise, it terminates.

The **do-while** loop is especially useful when you process a menu selection, because you will usually want the body of a menu loop to execute at least once. Consider the following program, which implements a very simple help system for Java's selection and iteration statements:

```
// Using a do-while to process a menu selection
class Menu {
  public static void main(String[] args)
    throws java.io.IOException {
    char choice;

    do {
      System.out.println("Help on: ");
      System.out.println("  1. if");
      System.out.println("  2. switch");
      System.out.println("  3. while");
      System.out.println("  4. do-while");
      System.out.println("  5. for\n");
      System.out.println("Choose one:");
      choice = (char) System.in.read();
    } while( choice < '1' || choice > '5');

    System.out.println("\n");

    switch(choice) {
      case '1':
        System.out.println("The if:\n");
        System.out.println("if(condition) statement;");
        System.out.println("else statement;");
        break;
      case '2':
        System.out.println("The switch:\n");
        System.out.println("switch(expression) {");
        System.out.println("  case constant:");
        System.out.println("    statement sequence");
        System.out.println("    break;");
        System.out.println("  //...");
        System.out.println("}");
        break;
      case '3':
        System.out.println("The while:\n");
        System.out.println("while(condition) statement;");
        break;
      case '4':
        System.out.println("The do-while:\n");
        System.out.println("do {");
        System.out.println("  statement;");
        System.out.println("} while (condition);");
        break;
      case '5':
        System.out.println("The for:\n");
        System.out.print("for(init; condition; iteration)");
        System.out.println(" statement;");
        break;
    }
  }
}
```

Here is a sample run produced by this program:

```
Help on:
  1. if
  2. switch
  3. while
  4. do-while
  5. for
Choose one:
4
The do-while:
do {
  statement;
} while (condition);
```

In the program, the **do-while** loop is used to verify that the user has entered a valid choice. If not, then the user is reprompted. Since the menu must be displayed at least once, the **do-while** is the perfect loop to accomplish this.

A few other points about this example: Notice that characters are read from the keyboard by calling **System.in.read( )**. This is one of Java's console input functions. Although Java's console I/O methods won't be discussed in detail until Chapter 13, **System.in.read( )** is used here to obtain the user's choice. It reads characters from standard input (returned as integers, which is why the return value was cast to **char**). By default, standard input is line buffered, so you must press ENTER before any characters that you type will be sent to your program.

Java's console input can be a bit awkward to work with. Further, most real-world Java programs will use a graphical user interface (GUI). For these reasons, console input is not used much in this book. However, it is useful in this context. One other point to consider: Because **System.in.read( )** is being used, the program must specify the **throws java.io.IOException** clause. This line is necessary to handle input errors. It is part of Java's exception handling features, which are discussed in Chapter 10.

## for

You were introduced to a simple form of the **for** loop in Chapter 2. As you will see, it is a powerful and versatile construct.

There are two forms of the **for** loop. The first is the traditional form that has been in use since the original version of Java. The second is the newer "for-each" form, added by JDK 5. Both types of **for** loops are discussed here, beginning with the traditional form.

Here is the general form of the traditional **for** statement:

for(*initialization*; *condition*; *iteration*) {
  // body
}

If only one statement is being repeated, there is no need for the curly braces.

The **for** loop operates as follows. When the loop first starts, the *initialization* portion of the loop is executed. Generally, this is an expression that sets the value of the *loop control variable*, which acts as a counter that controls the loop. It is important to understand that the initialization expression is executed only once. Next, *condition* is evaluated. This must be a Boolean expression.

It usually tests the loop control variable against a target value. If this expression is true, then the body of the loop is executed. If it is false, the loop terminates. Next, the *iteration* portion of the loop is executed. This is usually an expression that increments or decrements the loop control variable. The loop then iterates, first evaluating the conditional expression, then executing the body of the loop, and then executing the iteration expression with each pass. This process repeats until the controlling expression is false.

Here is a version of the "tick" program that uses a **for** loop:

```
// Demonstrate the for loop.
class ForTick {
  public static void main(String[] args) {
    int n;

    for(n=10; n>0; n--)
      System.out.println("tick " + n);
  }
}
```

## Declaring Loop Control Variables Inside the for Loop

Often the variable that controls a **for** loop is needed only for the purposes of the loop and is not used elsewhere. When this is the case, it is possible to declare the variable inside the initialization portion of the **for**. For example, here is the preceding program recoded so that the loop control variable **n** is declared as an **int** inside the **for**:

```
// Declare a loop control variable inside the for.
class ForTick {
  public static void main(String[] args) {

    // here, n is declared inside of the for loop
    for(int n=10; n>0; n--)
      System.out.println("tick " + n);
  }
}
```

When you declare a variable inside a **for** loop, there is one important point to remember: the scope of that variable ends when the **for** statement does. (That is, the scope of the variable is limited to the **for** loop.) Outside the **for** loop, the variable will cease to exist. If you need to use the loop control variable elsewhere in your program, you will not be able to declare it inside the **for** loop.

When the loop control variable will not be needed elsewhere, most Java programmers declare it inside the **for**. For example, here is a simple program that tests for prime numbers. Notice that the loop control variable, **i**, is declared inside the **for** since it is not needed elsewhere.

```
// Test for primes.
class FindPrime {
  public static void main(String[] args) {
    int num;
    boolean isPrime;

    num = 14;
```

```
    if(num < 2) isPrime = false;
    else isPrime = true;

    for(int i=2; i <= num/i; i++) {
      if((num % i) == 0) {
        isPrime = false;
        break;
      }
    }

    if(isPrime) System.out.println("Prime");
    else System.out.println("Not Prime");
  }
}
```

## Using the Comma

There will be times when you will want to include more than one statement in the initialization and iteration portions of the **for** loop. For example, consider the loop in the following program:

```
class Sample {
  public static void main(String[] args) {
    int a, b;

    b = 4;
    for(a=1; a<b; a++) {
      System.out.println("a = " + a);
      System.out.println("b = " + b);
      b--;
    }
  }
}
```

As you can see, the loop is controlled by the interaction of two variables. Since the loop is governed by two variables, it would be useful if both could be included in the **for** statement itself, instead of **b** being handled manually. Fortunately, Java provides a way to accomplish this. To allow two or more variables to control a **for** loop, Java permits you to include multiple statements in both the initialization and iteration portions of the **for**. Each statement is separated from the next by a comma.

Using the comma, the preceding **for** loop can be more efficiently coded, as shown here:

```
// Using the comma.
class Comma {
  public static void main(String[] args) {
    int a, b;

    for(a=1, b=4; a<b; a++, b--) {
      System.out.println("a = " + a);
      System.out.println("b = " + b);
    }
  }
}
```

In this example, the initialization portion sets the values of both **a** and **b**. The two comma-separated statements in the iteration portion are executed each time the loop repeats. The program generates the following output:

```
a = 1
b = 4
a = 2
b = 3
```

## Some for Loop Variations

The **for** loop supports a number of variations that increase its power and applicability. The reason it is so flexible is that its three parts—the initialization, the conditional test, and the iteration—do not need to be used for only those purposes. In fact, the three sections of the **for** can be used for any purpose you desire. Let's look at some examples.

One of the most common variations involves the conditional expression. Specifically, this expression does not need to test the loop control variable against some target value. In fact, the condition controlling the **for** can be any Boolean expression. For example, consider the following fragment:

```
boolean done = false;

for(int i=1; !done; i++) {
  // ...
  if(interrupted()) done = true;
}
```

In this example, the **for** loop continues to run until the **boolean** variable **done** is set to **true**. It does not test the value of **i**.

Here is another interesting **for** loop variation. Either the initialization or the iteration expression or both may be absent, as in this next program:

```
// Parts of the for loop can be empty.
class ForVar {
  public static void main(String[] args) {
    int i;
    boolean done = false;

    i = 0;
    for( ; !done; ) {
      System.out.println("i is " + i);
      if(i == 10) done = true;
      i++;
    }
  }
}
```

Here, the initialization and iteration expressions have been moved out of the **for**. Thus, parts of the **for** are empty. While this is of no value in this simple example—indeed, it would be considered quite poor style—there can be times when this type of approach makes sense.

For example, if the initial condition is set through a complex expression elsewhere in the program or if the loop control variable changes in a nonsequential manner determined by actions that occur within the body of the loop, it may be appropriate to leave these parts of the **for** empty.

Here is one more **for** loop variation. You can intentionally create an infinite loop (a loop that never terminates) if you leave all three parts of the **for** empty. For example:

```
for( ; ; ) {
  // ...
}
```

This loop will run forever because there is no condition under which it will terminate. Although there are some programs, such as operating system command processors, that require an infinite loop, most "infinite loops" are really just loops with special termination requirements. As you will soon see, there is a way to terminate a loop—even an infinite loop like the one shown—that does not make use of the normal loop conditional expression.

## The For-Each Version of the for Loop

A second form of **for** implements a "for-each" style loop. As you may know, contemporary language theory has embraced the for-each concept, and it has become a standard feature that programmers have come to expect. A for-each style loop is designed to cycle through a collection of objects, such as an array, in strictly sequential fashion, from start to finish. In Java, the for-each style of **for** is also referred to as the *enhanced* **for** loop.

The general form of the for-each version of the **for** is shown here:

for(*type itr-var* : *collection*) *statement-block*

Here, *type* specifies the type and *itr-var* specifies the name of an *iteration variable* that will receive the elements from a collection, one at a time, from beginning to end. The collection being cycled through is specified by *collection*. There are various types of collections that can be used with the **for**, but the only type used in this chapter is the array. (Other types of collections that can be used with the **for**, such as those defined by the Collections Framework, are discussed later in this book.) With each iteration of the loop, the next element in the collection is retrieved and stored in *itr-var*. The loop repeats until all elements in the collection have been obtained.

Because the iteration variable receives values from the collection, *type* must be the same as (or compatible with) the elements stored in the collection. Thus, when iterating over arrays, *type* must be compatible with the element type of the array.

To understand the motivation behind a for-each style loop, consider the type of **for** loop that it is designed to replace. The following fragment uses a traditional **for** loop to compute the sum of the values in an array:

```
int[] nums = { 1, 2, 3, 4, 5, 6, 7, 8, 9, 10 };
int sum = 0;

for(int i=0; i < 10; i++) sum += nums[i];
```

To compute the sum, each element in **nums** is read, in order, from start to finish. Thus, the entire array is read in strictly sequential order. This is accomplished by manually indexing the **nums** array by **i**, the loop control variable.

The for-each style **for** automates the preceding loop. Specifically, it eliminates the need to establish a loop counter, specify a starting and ending value, and manually index the array. Instead, it automatically cycles through the entire array, obtaining one element at a time, in sequence, from beginning to end. For example, here is the preceding fragment rewritten using a for-each version of the **for**:

```
int[] nums = { 1, 2, 3, 4, 5, 6, 7, 8, 9, 10 };
int sum = 0;

for(int x: nums) sum += x;
```

With each pass through the loop, **x** is automatically given a value equal to the next element in **nums**. Thus, on the first iteration, **x** contains 1; on the second iteration, **x** contains 2; and so on. Not only is the syntax streamlined, but it also prevents boundary errors.

Here is an entire program that demonstrates the for-each version of the **for** just described:

```
// Use a for-each style for loop.
class ForEach {
  public static void main(String[] args) {
    int[] nums = { 1, 2, 3, 4, 5, 6, 7, 8, 9, 10 };
    int sum = 0;

    // use for-each style for to display and sum the values
    for(int x : nums) {
      System.out.println("Value is: " + x);
      sum += x;
    }

    System.out.println("Summation: " + sum);
  }
}
```

The output from the program is shown here:

```
Value is: 1
Value is: 2
Value is: 3
Value is: 4
Value is: 5
Value is: 6
Value is: 7
Value is: 8
Value is: 9
Value is: 10
Summation: 55
```

As this output shows, the for-each style **for** automatically cycles through an array in sequence from the lowest index to the highest.

Although the for-each **for** loop iterates until all elements in an array have been examined, it is possible to terminate the loop early by using a **break** statement. For example, this program sums only the first five elements of **nums**:

```
// Use break with a for-each style for.
class ForEach2 {
  public static void main(String[] args) {
    int sum = 0;
    int[] nums = { 1, 2, 3, 4, 5, 6, 7, 8, 9, 10 };

    // use for to display and sum the values
    for(int x : nums) {
      System.out.println("Value is: " + x);
      sum += x;
      if(x == 5) break; // stop the loop when 5 is obtained
    }
    System.out.println("Summation of first 5 elements: " + sum);
  }
}
```

This is the output produced:

```
Value is: 1
Value is: 2
Value is: 3
Value is: 4
Value is: 5
Summation of first 5 elements: 15
```

As is evident, the **for** loop stops after the fifth element has been obtained. The **break** statement can also be used with Java's other loops, and it is discussed in detail later in this chapter.

There is one important point to understand about the for-each style loop. Its iteration variable is "read-only" as it relates to the underlying array. An assignment to the iteration variable has no effect on the underlying array. In other words, you can't change the contents of the array by assigning the iteration variable a new value. For example, consider this program:

```
// The for-each loop is essentially read-only.
class NoChange {
  public static void main(String[] args) {
    int[] nums = { 1, 2, 3, 4, 5, 6, 7, 8, 9, 10 };

    for(int x: nums) {
      System.out.print(x + " ");
      x = x * 10; // no effect on nums
    }

    System.out.println();

    for(int x : nums)
      System.out.print(x + " ");

    System.out.println();
  }
}
```

The first **for** loop increases the value of the iteration variable by a factor of 10. However, this assignment has no effect on the underlying array **nums**, as the second **for** loop illustrates. The output, shown here, proves this point:

```
1 2 3 4 5 6 7 8 9 10
1 2 3 4 5 6 7 8 9 10
```

## Iterating Over Multidimensional Arrays

The enhanced version of the **for** also works on multidimensional arrays. Remember, however, that in Java, multidimensional arrays consist of *arrays of arrays*. (For example, a two-dimensional array is an array of one-dimensional arrays.) This is important when iterating over a multidimensional array, because each iteration obtains the *next array*, not an individual element. Furthermore, the iteration variable in the **for** loop must be compatible with the type of array being obtained. For example, in the case of a two-dimensional array, the iteration variable must be a reference to a one-dimensional array. In general, when using the for-each **for** to iterate over an array of *N* dimensions, the objects obtained will be arrays of *N*–1 dimensions. To understand the implications of this, consider the following program. It uses nested **for** loops to obtain the elements of a two-dimensional array in row-order, from first to last.

```
// Use for-each style for on a two-dimensional array.
class ForEach3 {
  public static void main(String[] args) {
    int sum = 0;
    int[][] nums = new int[3][5];

    // give nums some values
    for(int i = 0; i < 3; i++)
      for(int j = 0; j < 5; j++)
        nums[i][j] = (i+1)*(j+1);

    // use for-each for to display and sum the values
    for(int[] x : nums) {
      for(int y : x) {
        System.out.println("Value is: " + y);
        sum += y;
      }
    }
    System.out.println("Summation: " + sum);
  }
}
```

The output from this program is shown here:

```
Value is: 1
Value is: 2
Value is: 3
Value is: 4
Value is: 5
Value is: 2
Value is: 4
Value is: 6
Value is: 8
Value is: 10
```

```
Value is: 3
Value is: 6
Value is: 9
Value is: 12
Value is: 15
Summation: 90
```

In the program, pay special attention to this line:

```
for(int[] x: nums) {
```

Notice how **x** is declared. It is a reference to a one-dimensional array of integers. This is necessary because each iteration of the **for** obtains the next *array* in **nums**, beginning with the array specified by **nums[0]**. The inner **for** loop then cycles through each of these arrays, displaying the values of each element.

## Applying the Enhanced for

Since the for-each style **for** can only cycle through an array sequentially, from start to finish, you might think that its use is limited, but this is not true. A large number of algorithms require exactly this mechanism. One of the most common is searching. For example, the following program uses a **for** loop to search an unsorted array for a value. It stops if the value is found.

```
// Search an array using for-each style for.
class Search {
  public static void main(String[] args) {
    int[] nums = { 6, 8, 3, 7, 5, 6, 1, 4 };
    int val = 5;
    boolean found = false;

    // use for-each style for to search nums for val
    for(int x : nums) {
      if(x == val) {
        found = true;
        break;
      }
    }

    if(found)
      System.out.println("Value found!");
  }
}
```

The for-each style **for** is an excellent choice in this application because searching an unsorted array involves examining each element in sequence. (Of course, if the array were sorted, a binary search could be used, which would require a different style loop.) Other types of applications that benefit from for-each style loops include computing an average, finding the minimum or maximum of a set, looking for duplicates, and so on.

Although we have been using arrays in the examples in this chapter, the for-each style **for** is especially useful when operating on collections defined by the Collections Framework, which is described in Part II. More generally, the **for** can cycle through the elements of any collection of objects, as long as that collection satisfies a certain set of constraints, which are described in Chapter 20.

## Local Variable Type Inference in a for Loop

As explained in Chapter 3, JDK 10 introduced a feature called *local variable type inference,* which allows the type of a local variable to be inferred from the type of its initializer. To use local variable type inference, the type of the variable is specified as **var** and the variable must be initialized. Local variable type inference can be used in a **for** loop when declaring and initializing the loop control variable inside a traditional **for** loop, or when specifying the iteration variable in a for-each **for**. The following program shows an example of each case:

```
// Use type inference in a for loop.
class TypeInferenceInFor {
  public static void main(String[] args) {

    // Use type inference with the loop control variable.
    System.out.print("Values of x: ");
    for(var x = 2.5; x < 100.0; x = x * 2)
      System.out.print(x + " ");

    System.out.println();

    // Use type inference with the iteration variable.
    int[] nums = { 1, 2, 3, 4, 5, 6};
    System.out.print("Values in nums array: ");
    for(var v : nums)
      System.out.print(v + " ");

    System.out.println();
  }
}
```

The output is shown here:

```
Values of x: 2.5 5.0 10.0 20.0 40.0 80.0
Values in nums array: 1 2 3 4 5 6
```

In this example, loop control variable **x** in this line:

```
for(var x = 2.5; x < 100.0; x = x * 2)
```

is inferred to be type **double** because that is the type of its initializer. Iteration variable **v** is this line:

```
for(var v : nums)
```

inferred to be of type **int** because that is the element type of the array **nums**.

One last point: Because a number of readers will be working in environments that predate JDK 10, local variable type inference will not be used by most of the **for** loops in the remainder of this edition of this book. You should, of course, consider it for new code that you write.

## Nested Loops

Like all other programming languages, Java allows loops to be nested. That is, one loop may be inside another. For example, here is a program that nests **for** loops:

```
// Loops may be nested.
class Nested {
  public static void main(String[] args) {
    int i, j;

    for(i=0; i<10; i++) {
      for(j=i; j<10; j++)
        System.out.print(".");
      System.out.println();
    }
  }
}
```

The output produced by this program is shown here:

```
..........
.........
........
.......
......
.....
....
...
..
.
```

# Jump Statements

Java supports three jump statements: **break**, **continue**, and **return**. These statements transfer control to another part of your program. Each is examined here.

---

**NOTE** In addition to the jump statements discussed here, Java supports one other way that you can change your program's flow of execution: through exception handling. Exception handling provides a structured method by which run-time errors can be trapped and handled by your program. It is supported by the keywords **try**, **catch**, **throw**, **throws**, and **finally**. In essence, the exception handling mechanism allows your program to perform a nonlocal branch. Since exception handling is a large topic, it is discussed in its own chapter, Chapter 10.

## Using break

In Java, the **break** statement has three uses. First, as you have seen, it terminates a statement sequence in a **switch** statement. Second, it can be used to exit a loop. Third, it can be used as a "civilized" form of goto. The last two uses are explained here.

## Using break to Exit a Loop

By using **break**, you can force immediate termination of a loop, bypassing the conditional expression and any remaining code in the body of the loop. When a **break** statement is encountered inside a loop, the loop is terminated and program control resumes at the next statement following the loop. Here is a simple example:

```
// Using break to exit a loop.
class BreakLoop {
  public static void main(String[] args) {
    for(int i=0; i<100; i++) {
      if(i == 10) break; // terminate loop if i is 10
      System.out.println("i: " + i);
    }
    System.out.println("Loop complete.");
  }
}
```

This program generates the following output:

```
i: 0
i: 1
i: 2
i: 3
i: 4
i: 5
i: 6
i: 7
i: 8
i: 9
Loop complete.
```

As you can see, although the **for** loop is designed to run from 0 to 99, the **break** statement causes it to terminate early, when **i** equals 10.

The **break** statement can be used with any of Java's loops, including intentionally infinite loops. For example, here is the preceding program coded by use of a **while** loop. The output from this program is the same as just shown.

```
// Using break to exit a while loop.
class BreakLoop2 {
  public static void main(String[] args) {
    int i = 0;

    while(i < 100) {
      if(i == 10) break; // terminate loop if i is 10
      System.out.println("i: " + i);
      i++;
    }
    System.out.println("Loop complete.");
  }
}
```

When used inside a set of nested loops, the **break** statement will only break out of the innermost loop. For example:

```
// Using break with nested loops.
class BreakLoop3 {
  public static void main(String[] args) {
    for(int i=0; i<3; i++) {
      System.out.print("Pass " + i + ": ");
      for(int j=0; j<100; j++) {
        if(j == 10) break; // terminate loop if j is 10
        System.out.print(j + " ");
      }
      System.out.println();
    }
    System.out.println("Loops complete.");
  }
}
```

This program generates the following output:

```
Pass 0: 0 1 2 3 4 5 6 7 8 9
Pass 1: 0 1 2 3 4 5 6 7 8 9
Pass 2: 0 1 2 3 4 5 6 7 8 9
Loops complete.
```

As you can see, the **break** statement in the inner loop only causes termination of that loop. The outer loop is unaffected.

Here are two other points to remember about **break**. First, more than one **break** statement may appear in a loop. However, be careful. Too many **break** statements have the tendency to destructure your code. Second, the **break** that terminates a **switch** statement affects only that **switch** statement and not any enclosing loops.

---

**REMEMBER** **break** was not designed to provide the normal means by which a loop is terminated. The loop's conditional expression serves this purpose. The **break** statement should be used to cancel a loop only when some sort of special situation occurs.

## Using break as a Form of Goto

In addition to its uses with the **switch** statement and loops, the **break** statement can also be employed by itself to provide a "civilized" form of the goto statement. Java does not have a goto statement because it provides a way to branch in an arbitrary and unstructured manner. This usually makes goto-ridden code hard to understand and hard to maintain. It also prohibits certain compiler optimizations. There are, however, a few places where the goto is a valuable and legitimate construct for flow control. For example, the goto can be useful when you are exiting from a deeply nested set of loops. To handle such situations, Java defines an expanded form of the **break** statement. By using this form of **break**, you can, for example, break out of one or more blocks of code. These blocks need not be part of a loop or a **switch**. They can be any block. Further, you can specify precisely where execution will resume, because this form of **break** works with a label. As you will see, **break** gives you the benefits of a goto without its problems.

The general form of the labeled **break** statement is shown here:

break *label*;

Most often, *label* is the name of a label that identifies a block of code. This can be a stand-alone block of code but it can also be a block that is the target of another statement. When this form of **break** executes, control is transferred out of the named block. The labeled block must enclose the **break** statement, but it does not need to be the immediately enclosing block. This means, for example, that you can use a labeled **break** statement to exit from a set of nested blocks. But you cannot use **break** to transfer control out of a block that does not enclose the **break** statement.

To name a block, put a label at the start of it. A *label* is any valid Java identifier followed by a colon. Once you have labeled a block, you can then use this label as the target of a **break** statement. Doing so causes execution to resume at the *end* of the labeled block. For example, the following program shows three nested blocks, each with its own label. The **break** statement causes execution to jump forward, past the end of the block labeled **second**, skipping the two **println( )** statements.

```
// Using break as a civilized form of goto.
class Break {
  public static void main(String[] args) {
    boolean t = true;

    first: {
      second: {
        third: {
          System.out.println("Before the break.");
          if(t) break second; // break out of second block
          System.out.println("This won't execute");
        }
        System.out.println("This won't execute");
      }
      System.out.println("This is after second block.");
    }
  }
}
```

Running this program generates the following output:

```
Before the break.
This is after second block.
```

One of the most common uses for a labeled **break** statement is to exit from nested loops. For example, in the following program, the outer loop executes only once:

```
// Using break to exit from nested loops
class BreakLoop4 {
  public static void main(String[] args) {
    outer: for(int i=0; i<3; i++) {
      System.out.print("Pass " + i + ": ");
      for(int j=0; j<100; j++) {
        if(j == 10) break outer; // exit both loops
        System.out.print(j + " ");
```

```
      }
      System.out.println("This will not print");
    }
    System.out.println("Loops complete.");
  }
}
```

This program generates the following output:

```
Pass 0: 0 1 2 3 4 5 6 7 8 9 Loops complete.
```

As you can see, when the inner loop breaks to the outer loop, both loops have been terminated. Notice that this example labels the **for** statement, which has a block of code as its target.

Keep in mind that you cannot break to any label that is not defined for an enclosing block. For example, the following program is invalid and will not compile:

```
// This program contains an error.
class BreakErr {
  public static void main(String[] args) {

    one: for(int i=0; i<3; i++) {
      System.out.print("Pass " + i + ": ");
    }

    for(int j=0; j<100; j++) {
      if(j == 10) break one; // WRONG
      System.out.print(j + " ");
    }
  }
}
```

Since the loop labeled **one** does not enclose the **break** statement, it is not possible to transfer control out of that block.

## Using continue

Sometimes it is useful to force an early iteration of a loop. That is, you might want to continue running the loop but stop processing the remainder of the code in its body for this particular iteration. This is, in effect, a goto just past the body of the loop, to the loop's end. The **continue** statement performs such an action. In **while** and **do-while** loops, a **continue** statement causes control to be transferred directly to the conditional expression that controls the loop. In a **for** loop, control goes first to the iteration portion of the **for** statement and then to the conditional expression. For all three loops, any intermediate code is bypassed.

Here is a sample program that uses **continue** to cause two numbers to be printed on each line:

```
// Demonstrate continue.
class Continue {
  public static void main(String[] args) {
    for(int i=0; i<10; i++) {
      System.out.print(i + " ");
```

```
            if (i%2 == 0) continue;
            System.out.println("");
        }
    }
}
```

This code uses the **%** operator to check if **i** is even. If it is, the loop continues without printing a newline. Here is the output from this program:

```
0 1
2 3
4 5
6 7
8 9
```

As with the **break** statement, **continue** may specify a label to describe which enclosing loop to continue. Here is a sample program that uses **continue** to print a triangular multiplication table for 0 through 9:

```
// Using continue with a label.
class ContinueLabel {
  public static void main(String[] args) {
outer: for (int i=0; i<10; i++) {
         for(int j=0; j<10; j++) {
           if(j > i) {
             System.out.println();
             continue outer;
           }
           System.out.print(" " + (i * j));
         }
       }
       System.out.println();
  }
}
```

The **continue** statement in this example terminates the loop counting **j** and continues with the next iteration of the loop counting **i**. Here is the output of this program:

```
 0
 0 1
 0 2 4
 0 3 6 9
 0 4 8 12 16
 0 5 10 15 20 25
 0 6 12 18 24 30 36
 0 7 14 21 28 35 42 49
 0 8 16 24 32 40 48 56 64
 0 9 18 27 36 45 54 63 72 81
```

Good uses of **continue** are rare. One reason is that Java provides a rich set of loop statements that fit most applications. However, for those special circumstances in which early iteration is needed, the **continue** statement provides a structured way to accomplish it.

## return

The last control statement is **return**. The **return** statement is used to explicitly return from a method. That is, it causes program control to transfer back to the caller of the method. As such, it is categorized as a jump statement. Although a full discussion of **return** must wait until methods are discussed in Chapter 6, a brief look at **return** is presented here.

At any time in a method, the **return** statement can be used to cause execution to branch back to the caller of the method. Thus, the **return** statement immediately terminates the method in which it is executed. The following example illustrates this point. Here, **return** causes execution to return to the Java run-time system, since it is the run-time system that calls **main( )**:

```
// Demonstrate return.
class Return {
  public static void main(String[] args) {
    boolean t = true;

    System.out.println("Before the return.");

    if(t) return; // return to caller

    System.out.println("This won't execute.");
  }
}
```

The output from this program is shown here:

```
Before the return.
```

As you can see, the final **println( )** statement is not executed. As soon as **return** is executed, control passes back to the caller.

One last point: In the preceding program, the **if(t)** statement is necessary. Without it, the Java compiler would flag an "unreachable code" error because the compiler would know that the last **println( )** statement would never be executed. To prevent this error, the **if** statement is used here to trick the compiler for the sake of this demonstration.

# CHAPTER 6

# Introducing Classes

The class is at the core of Java. It is the logical construct upon which the entire Java language is built because it defines the shape and nature of an object. As such, the class forms the basis for object-oriented programming in Java. Any concept you wish to implement in a Java program must be encapsulated within a class.

Because the class is so fundamental to Java, this and the next few chapters will be devoted to it. Here, you will be introduced to the basic elements of a class and learn how a class can be used to create objects. You will also learn about methods, constructors, and the **this** keyword.

## Class Fundamentals

Classes have been used since the beginning of this book. However, until now, only the most rudimentary form of a class has been shown. The classes created in the preceding chapters primarily exist simply to encapsulate the **main( )** method, which has been used to demonstrate the basics of the Java syntax. As you will see, classes are substantially more powerful than the limited ones presented so far.

Perhaps the most important thing to understand about a class is that it defines a new data type. Once defined, this new type can be used to create objects of that type. Thus, a class is a *template* for an object, and an object is an *instance* of a class. Because an object is an instance of a class, you will often see the two words *object* and *instance* used interchangeably.

### The General Form of a Class

When you define a class, you declare its exact form and nature. You do this by specifying the data that it contains and the code that operates on that data. While very simple classes may contain only code or only data, most real-world classes contain both. As you will see, a class's code defines the interface to its data.

A class is declared by use of the **class** keyword. The classes that have been used up to this point are actually very limited examples of its complete form. Classes can (and usually do) get much more complex. A simplified general form of a **class** definition is shown here:

```
class classname {
  type instance-variable1;
  type instance-variable2;
  // ...
  type instance-variableN;

  type methodname1(parameter-list) {
    // body of method
  }
  type methodname2(parameter-list) {
    // body of method
  }
  // ...
  type methodnameN(parameter-list) {
    // body of method
  }
}
```

The data, or variables, defined within a **class** are called *instance variables.* The code is contained within *methods.* Collectively, the methods and variables defined within a class are called *members* of the class. In most classes, the instance variables are acted upon and accessed by the methods defined for that class. Thus, as a general rule, it is the methods that determine how a class's data can be used.

Variables defined within a class are called instance variables because each instance of the class (that is, each object of the class) contains its own copy of these variables. Thus, the data for one object is separate and unique from the data for another. We will come back to this point shortly, but it is an important concept to learn early.

All methods have the same general form as **main( )**, which we have been using thus far. However, most methods will not be specified as **static** or **public**. Notice that the general form of a class does not specify a **main( )** method. Java classes do not need to have a **main( )** method. You only specify one if that class is the starting point for your program. Further, some kinds of Java applications don't require a **main( )** method at all.

## A Simple Class

Let's begin our study of the class with a simple example. Here is a class called **Box** that defines three instance variables: **width**, **height**, and **depth**. Currently, **Box** does not contain any methods (but some will be added soon).

```
class Box {
  double width;
  double height;
  double depth;
}
```

As stated, a class defines a new type of data. In this case, the new data type is called **Box**. You will use this name to declare objects of type **Box**. It is important to remember that a class declaration only creates a template; it does not create an actual object. Thus, the preceding code does not cause any objects of type **Box** to come into existence.

To actually create a **Box** object, you will use a statement like the following:

```
Box mybox = new Box(); // create a Box object called mybox
```

After this statement executes, **mybox** will refer to an instance of **Box**. Thus, it will have "physical" reality. For the moment, don't worry about the details of this statement.

As mentioned earlier, each time you create an instance of a class, you are creating an object that contains its own copy of each instance variable defined by the class. Thus, every **Box** object will contain its own copies of the instance variables **width**, **height**, and **depth**. To access these variables, you will use the *dot* (.) operator. The dot operator links the name of the object with the name of an instance variable. For example, to assign the **width** variable of **mybox** the value 100, you would use the following statement:

```
mybox.width = 100;
```

This statement tells the compiler to assign the copy of **width** that is contained within the **mybox** object the value of 100. In general, you use the dot operator to access both the instance variables and the methods within an object. One other point: Although commonly referred to as the dot *operator*, the formal specification for Java categorizes the . as a separator. However, since the use of the term "dot operator" is widespread, it is used in this book.

Here is a complete program that uses the **Box** class:

```
/* A program that uses the Box class.

   Call this file BoxDemo.java
*/
class Box {
  double width;
  double height;
  double depth;
}

// This class declares an object of type Box.
class BoxDemo {
  public static void main(String[] args) {
    Box mybox = new Box();
    double vol;

    // assign values to mybox's instance variables
    mybox.width = 10;
    mybox.height = 20;
    mybox.depth = 15;

    // compute volume of box
    vol = mybox.width * mybox.height * mybox.depth;

    System.out.println("Volume is " + vol);
  }
}
```

You should call the file that contains this program **BoxDemo.java**, because the **main( )** method is in the class called **BoxDemo**, not the class called **Box**. When you compile this program, you will find that two **.class** files have been created, one for **Box** and one for **BoxDemo**. The Java compiler automatically puts each class into its own **.class** file. It is not necessary for both the **Box** and the **BoxDemo** class to actually be in the same source file. You could put each class in its own file, called **Box.java** and **BoxDemo.java**, respectively.

To run this program, you must execute **BoxDemo.class**. When you do, you will see the following output:

```
Volume is 3000.0
```

As stated earlier, each object has its own copies of the instance variables. This means that if you have two **Box** objects, each has its own copy of **depth, width**, and **height**. It is important to understand that changes to the instance variables of one object have no effect on the instance variables of another. For example, the following program declares two **Box** objects:

```
// This program declares two Box objects.

class Box {
  double width;
  double height;
  double depth;
}

class BoxDemo2 {
  public static void main(String[] args) {
    Box mybox1 = new Box();
    Box mybox2 = new Box();
    double vol;

    // assign values to mybox1's instance variables
    mybox1.width = 10;
    mybox1.height = 20;
    mybox1.depth = 15;

    /* assign different values to mybox2's
       instance variables */
    mybox2.width = 3;
    mybox2.height = 6;
    mybox2.depth = 9;

    // compute volume of first box
    vol = mybox1.width * mybox1.height * mybox1.depth;
    System.out.println("Volume is " + vol);

    // compute volume of second box
    vol = mybox2.width * mybox2.height * mybox2.depth;
    System.out.println("Volume is " + vol);
  }
}
```

The output produced by this program is shown here:

```
Volume is 3000.0
Volume is 162.0
```

As you can see, **mybox1**'s data is completely separate from the data contained in **mybox2**.

# Declaring Objects

As just explained, when you create a class, you are creating a new data type. You can use this type to declare objects of that type. However, obtaining objects of a class is a two-step process. First, you must declare a variable of the class type. This variable does not define an object. Instead, it is simply a variable that can *refer* to an object. Second, you must acquire an actual, physical copy of the object and assign it to that variable. You can do this using the **new** operator. The **new** operator dynamically allocates (that is, allocates at run time) memory for an object and returns a reference to it. This reference is, essentially, the address in memory of the object allocated by **new**. This reference is then stored in the variable. Thus, in Java, all class objects must be dynamically allocated. Let's look at the details of this procedure.

In the preceding sample programs, a line similar to the following is used to declare an object of type **Box**:

```
Box mybox = new Box();
```

This statement combines the two steps just described. It can be rewritten like this to show each step more clearly:

```
Box mybox; // declare reference to object
mybox = new Box(); // allocate a Box object
```

The first line declares **mybox** as a reference to an object of type **Box**. At this point, **mybox** does not yet refer to an actual object. The next line allocates an object and assigns a reference to it to **mybox**. After the second line executes, you can use **mybox** as if it were a **Box** object. But in reality, **mybox** simply holds, in essence, the memory address of the actual **Box** object. The effect of these two lines of code is depicted in Figure 6-1.

## A Closer Look at new

As just explained, the **new** operator dynamically allocates memory for an object. In the context of an assignment, it has this general form:

*class-var* = new *classname* ( );

Here, *class-var* is a variable of the class type being created. The *classname* is the name of the class that is being instantiated. The class name followed by parentheses specifies the *constructor* for the class. A constructor defines what occurs when an object of a class is created. Constructors are an important part of all classes and have many significant attributes. Most real-world classes explicitly define their own constructors within their class definition. However, if no explicit constructor is specified, then Java will automatically supply a default constructor. This is the case with **Box**. For now, we will use the default constructor. Soon, you will see how to define your own constructors.

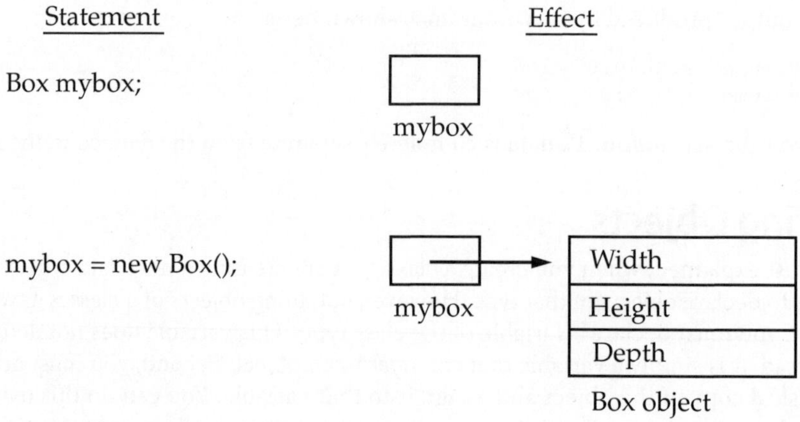


**Figure 6-1** Declaring an object of type **Box**

At this point, you might be wondering why you do not need to use **new** for such things as integers or characters. The answer is that Java's primitive types are not implemented as objects. Rather, they are implemented as "normal" variables. This is done in the interest of efficiency. As you will see, objects have many features and attributes that require Java to treat them differently than it treats the primitive types. By not applying the same overhead to the primitive types that applies to objects, Java can implement the primitive types more efficiently. Later, you will see object versions of the primitive types that are available for your use in those situations in which complete objects of these types are needed.

It is important to understand that **new** allocates memory for an object during run time. The advantage of this approach is that your program can create as many or as few objects as it needs during the execution of your program. However, since memory is finite, it is possible that **new** will not be able to allocate memory for an object because insufficient memory exists. If this happens, a run-time exception will occur. (You will learn how to handle exceptions in Chapter 10.) For the sample programs in this book, you won't need to worry about running out of memory, but you will need to consider this possibility in real-world programs that you write.

Let's once again review the distinction between a class and an object. A class creates a new data type that can be used to create objects. That is, a class creates a logical framework that defines the relationship between its members. When you declare an object of a class, you are creating an instance of that class. Thus, a class is a logical construct. An object has physical reality. (That is, an object occupies space in memory.) It is important to keep this distinction clearly in mind.

## Assigning Object Reference Variables

Object reference variables act differently than you might expect when an assignment takes place. For example, what do you think the following fragment does?

```
Box b1 = new Box();
Box b2 = b1;
```

You might think that **b2** is being assigned a reference to a copy of the object referred to by **b1**. That is, you might think that **b1** and **b2** refer to separate and distinct objects. However, this would be wrong. Instead, after this fragment executes, **b1** and **b2** will both refer to the *same* object. The assignment of **b1** to **b2** did not allocate any memory or copy any part of the original object. It simply makes **b2** refer to the same object as does **b1**. Thus, any changes made to the object through **b2** will affect the object to which **b1** is referring, since they are the same object.

This situation is depicted here:

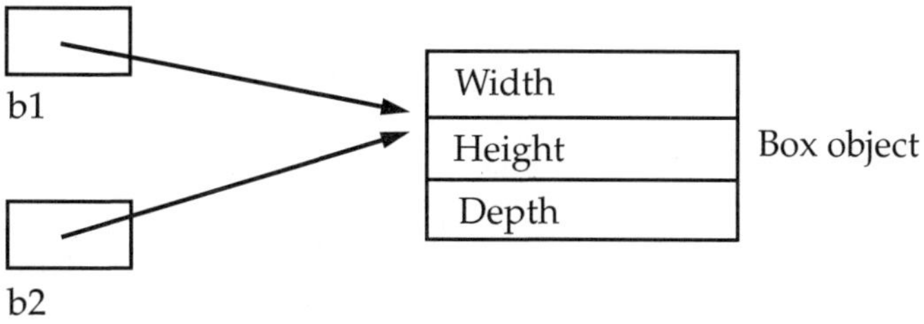


Although **b1** and **b2** both refer to the same object, they are not linked in any other way. For example, a subsequent assignment to **b1** will simply *unhook* **b1** from the original object without affecting the object or affecting **b2**. For example:

```
Box b1 = new Box();
Box b2 = b1;
// ...
b1 = null;
```

Here, **b1** has been set to **null**, but **b2** still points to the original object.

---

**REMEMBER** When you assign one object reference variable to another object reference variable, you are not creating a copy of the object, you are only making a copy of the reference.

## Introducing Methods

As mentioned at the beginning of this chapter, classes usually consist of two things: instance variables and methods. The topic of methods is a large one because Java gives them so much power and flexibility. In fact, much of the next chapter is devoted to methods. However, there are some fundamentals that you need to learn now so that you can begin to add methods to your classes.

This is the general form of a method:

*type name*(*parameter list*) {
  // body of method
}

Here, *type* specifies the type of data returned by the method. This can be any valid type, including class types that you create. If the method does not return a value, its return type must be **void**. The name of the method is specified by *name*. This can be any legal identifier other than those already used by other items within the current scope. The *parameter-list* is a sequence of type and identifier pairs separated by commas. Parameters are essentially variables that receive the value of the arguments passed to the method when it is called. If the method has no parameters, then the parameter list will be empty.

Methods that have a return type other than **void** return a value to the calling routine using the following form of the **return** statement:

return *value*;

Here, *value* is the value returned.

In the next few sections, you will see how to create various types of methods, including those that take parameters and those that return values.

## Adding a Method to the Box Class

Although it is perfectly fine to create a class that contains only data, it rarely happens. Most of the time, you will use methods to access the instance variables defined by the class. In fact, methods define the interface to most classes. This allows the class implementor to hide the specific layout of internal data structures behind cleaner method abstractions. In addition to defining methods that provide access to data, you can also define methods that are used internally by the class itself.

Let's begin by adding a method to the **Box** class. It may have occurred to you while looking at the preceding programs that the computation of a box's volume was something that was best handled by the **Box** class rather than the **BoxDemo** class. After all, since the volume of a box is dependent upon the size of the box, it makes sense to have the **Box** class compute it. To do this, you must add a method to **Box**, as shown here:

```
// This program includes a method inside the box class.

class Box {
  double width;
  double height;
  double depth;

  // display volume of a box
  void volume() {
    System.out.print("Volume is ");
    System.out.println(width * height * depth);
  }
}

class BoxDemo3 {
  public static void main(String[] args) {
    Box mybox1 = new Box();
    Box mybox2 = new Box();

    // assign values to mybox1's instance variables
    mybox1.width = 10;
    mybox1.height = 20;
    mybox1.depth = 15;
```

```
    /* assign different values to mybox2's
       instance variables */
    mybox2.width = 3;
    mybox2.height = 6;
    mybox2.depth = 9;

    // display volume of first box
    mybox1.volume();

    // display volume of second box
    mybox2.volume();
  }
}
```

This program generates the following output, which is the same as the previous version.

```
Volume is 3000.0
Volume is 162.0
```

Look closely at the following two lines of code:

```
mybox1.volume();
mybox2.volume();
```

The first line here invokes the **volume( )** method on **mybox1**. That is, it calls **volume( )** relative to the **mybox1** object, using the object's name followed by the dot operator. Thus, the call to **mybox1.volume( )** displays the volume of the box defined by **mybox1**, and the call to **mybox2.volume( )** displays the volume of the box defined by **mybox2**. Each time **volume( )** is invoked, it displays the volume for the specified box.

If you are unfamiliar with the concept of calling a method, the following discussion will help clear things up. When **mybox1.volume( )** is executed, the Java run-time system transfers control to the code defined inside **volume( )**. After the statements inside **volume( )** have executed, control is returned to the calling routine, and execution resumes with the line of code following the call. In the most general sense, a method is Java's way of implementing subroutines.

There is something very important to notice inside the **volume( )** method: the instance variables **width**, **height**, and **depth** are referred to directly, without preceding them with an object name or the dot operator. When a method uses an instance variable that is defined by its class, it does so directly, without explicit reference to an object and without use of the dot operator. This is easy to understand if you think about it. A method is always invoked relative to some object of its class. Once this invocation has occurred, the object is known. Thus, within a method, there is no need to specify the object a second time. This means that **width**, **height**, and **depth** inside **volume( )** implicitly refer to the copies of those variables found in the object that invokes **volume( )**.

Let's review: When an instance variable is accessed by code that is not part of the class in which that instance variable is defined, it must be done through an object, by use of the dot operator. However, when an instance variable is accessed by code that is part of the same class as the instance variable, that variable can be referred to directly. The same thing applies to methods.

## Returning a Value

While the implementation of **volume( )** does move the computation of a box's volume inside the **Box** class where it belongs, this is not the best way to do it. For example, what if another part of your program wanted to know the volume of a box but not display its value? A better way to implement **volume( )** is to have it compute the volume of the box and return the result to the caller. The following example, an improved version of the preceding program, does just that:

```
// Now, volume() returns the volume of a box.

class Box {
  double width;
  double height;
  double depth;

  // compute and return volume
  double volume() {
    return width * height * depth;
  }
}

class BoxDemo4 {
  public static void main(String[] args) {
    Box mybox1 = new Box();
    Box mybox2 = new Box();
    double vol;

    // assign values to mybox1's instance variables
    mybox1.width = 10;
    mybox1.height = 20;
    mybox1.depth = 15;

    /* assign different values to mybox2's
       instance variables */
    mybox2.width = 3;
    mybox2.height = 6;
    mybox2.depth = 9;

    // get volume of first box
    vol = mybox1.volume();
    System.out.println("Volume is " + vol);

    // get volume of second box
    vol = mybox2.volume();
    System.out.println("Volume is " + vol);
  }
}
```

As you can see, when **volume( )** is called, it is put on the right side of an assignment statement. On the left is a variable, in this case **vol**, that will receive the value returned by **volume( )**. Thus, after

```
vol = mybox1.volume();
```

executes, the value of **mybox1.volume( )** is 3000 and this value then is stored in **vol**.

There are two important things to understand about returning values:

- The type of data returned by a method must be compatible with the return type specified by the method. For example, if the return type of some method is **boolean**, you could not return an integer.
- The variable receiving the value returned by a method (such as **vol**, in this case) must also be compatible with the return type specified for the method.

One more point: The preceding program can be written a bit more efficiently because there is actually no need for the **vol** variable. The call to **volume( )** could have been used in the **println( )** statement directly, as shown here:

```
System.out.println("Volume is" + mybox1.volume());
```

In this case, when **println( )** is executed, **mybox1.volume( )** will be called automatically and its value will be passed to **println( )**.

## Adding a Method That Takes Parameters

While some methods don't need parameters, most do. Parameters allow a method to be generalized. That is, a parameterized method can operate on a variety of data and/or be used in a number of slightly different situations. To illustrate this point, let's use a very simple example. Here is a method that returns the square of the number 10:

```
int square()
{
  return 10 * 10;
}
```

While this method does, indeed, return the value of 10 squared, its use is very limited. However, if you modify the method so that it takes a parameter, as shown next, then you can make **square( )** much more useful.

```
int square(int i)
{
  return i * i;
}
```

Now, **square( )** will return the square of whatever value it is called with. That is, **square( )** is now a general-purpose method that can compute the square of any integer value, rather than just 10.

Here is an example:

```
int x, y;
x = square(5); // x equals 25
x = square(9); // x equals 81
y = 2;
x = square(y); // x equals 4
```

In the first call to **square( )**, the value 5 will be passed into parameter **i**. In the second call, **i** will receive the value 9. The third invocation passes the value of **y**, which is 2 in this example. As these examples show, **square( )** is able to return the square of whatever data it is passed.

It is important to keep the two terms *parameter* and *argument* straight. A *parameter* is a variable defined by a method that receives a value when the method is called. For example, in **square( )**, **i** is a parameter. An *argument* is a value that is passed to a method when it is invoked. For example, **square(100)** passes 100 as an argument. Inside **square( )**, the parameter **i** receives that value.

You can use a parameterized method to improve the **Box** class. In the preceding examples, the dimensions of each box had to be set separately by use of a sequence of statements, such as:

```
mybox1.width = 10;
mybox1.height = 20;
mybox1.depth = 15;
```

While this code works, it is troubling for two reasons. First, it is clumsy and error prone. For example, it would be easy to forget to set a dimension. Second, in well-designed Java programs, instance variables should be accessed only through methods defined by their class. In the future, you can change the behavior of a method, but you can't change the behavior of an exposed instance variable.

Thus, a better approach to setting the dimensions of a box is to create a method that takes the dimensions of a box in its parameters and sets each instance variable appropriately. This concept is implemented by the following program:

```
// This program uses a parameterized method.

class Box {
  double width;
  double height;
  double depth;

  // compute and return volume
  double volume() {
    return width * height * depth;
  }

  // sets dimensions of box
  void setDim(double w, double h, double d) {
    width = w;
    height = h;
```

```
    depth = d;
  }
}

class BoxDemo5 {
  public static void main(String[] args) {
    Box mybox1 = new Box();
    Box mybox2 = new Box();
    double vol;

    // initialize each box
    mybox1.setDim(10, 20, 15);
    mybox2.setDim(3, 6, 9);

    // get volume of first box
    vol = mybox1.volume();
    System.out.println("Volume is " + vol);

    // get volume of second box
    vol = mybox2.volume();
    System.out.println("Volume is " + vol);
  }
}
```

As you can see, the **setDim( )** method is used to set the dimensions of each box. For example, when

```
mybox1.setDim(10, 20, 15);
```

is executed, 10 is copied into parameter **w**, 20 is copied into **h**, and 15 is copied into **d**. Inside **setDim( )** the values of **w**, **h**, and **d** are then assigned to **width**, **height**, and **depth**, respectively.

For many readers, the concepts presented in the preceding sections will be familiar. However, if such things as method calls, arguments, and parameters are new to you, then you might want to take some time to experiment before moving on. The concepts of the method invocation, parameters, and return values are fundamental to Java programming.

# Constructors

It can be tedious to initialize all of the variables in a class each time an instance is created. Even when you add convenience methods like **setDim( )**, it would be simpler and more concise to have all of the setup done at the time the object is first created. Because the requirement for initialization is so common, Java allows objects to initialize themselves when they are created. This automatic initialization is performed through the use of a constructor.

A *constructor* initializes an object immediately upon creation. It has the same name as the class in which it resides and is syntactically similar to a method. Once defined, the constructor is automatically called when the object is created, before the **new** operator completes. Constructors look a little strange because they have no return type, not even **void**. This is because the implicit return type of a class's constructor is the class type itself.

It is the constructor's job to initialize the internal state of an object so that the code creating an instance will have a fully initialized, usable object immediately.

You can rework the **Box** example so that the dimensions of a box are automatically initialized when an object is constructed. To do so, replace **setDim( )** with a constructor. Let's begin by defining a simple constructor that sets the dimensions of each box to the same values. This version is shown here:

```
/* Here, Box uses a constructor to initialize the
   dimensions of a box.
*/
class Box {
  double width;
  double height;
  double depth;

  // This is the constructor for Box.
  Box() {
    System.out.println("Constructing Box");
    width = 10;
    height = 10;
    depth = 10;
  }

  // compute and return volume
  double volume() {
    return width * height * depth;
  }
}

class BoxDemo6 {
  public static void main(String[] args) {
    // declare, allocate, and initialize Box objects
    Box mybox1 = new Box();
    Box mybox2 = new Box();

    double vol;

    // get volume of first box
    vol = mybox1.volume();
    System.out.println("Volume is " + vol);

    // get volume of second box
    vol = mybox2.volume();
    System.out.println("Volume is " + vol);
  }
}
```

When this program is run, it generates the following results:

```
Constructing Box
Constructing Box
Volume is 1000.0
Volume is 1000.0
```

As you can see, both **mybox1** and **mybox2** were initialized by the **Box( )** constructor when they were created. Since the constructor gives all boxes the same dimensions, 10 by 10 by 10, both **mybox1** and **mybox2** will have the same volume. The **println( )** statement inside **Box( )** is for the sake of illustration only. Most constructors will not display anything. They will simply initialize an object.

Before moving on, let's reexamine the **new** operator. As you know, when you allocate an object, you use the following general form:

*class-var* = new *classname* ( );

Now you can understand why the parentheses are needed after the class name. What is actually happening is that the constructor for the class is being called. Thus, in the line

```
Box mybox1 = new Box();
```

**new Box( )** is calling the **Box( )** constructor. When you do not explicitly define a constructor for a class, then Java creates a default constructor for the class. This is why the preceding line of code worked in earlier versions of **Box** that did not define a constructor. When using the default constructor, all non-initialized instance variables will have their default values, which are zero, **null**, and **false**, for numeric types, reference types, and **boolean**, respectively. The default constructor is often sufficient for simple classes, but it usually won't do for more sophisticated ones. Once you define your own constructor, the default constructor is no longer used.

## Parameterized Constructors

While the **Box( )** constructor in the preceding example does initialize a **Box** object, it is not very useful—all boxes have the same dimensions. What is needed is a way to construct **Box** objects of various dimensions. The easy solution is to add parameters to the constructor. As you can probably guess, this makes it much more useful. For example, the following version of **Box** defines a parameterized constructor that sets the dimensions of a box as specified by those parameters. Pay special attention to how **Box** objects are created.

```
/* Here, Box uses a parameterized constructor to
   initialize the dimensions of a box.
*/
class Box {
  double width;
  double height;
  double depth;

  // This is the constructor for Box.
  Box(double w, double h, double d) {
    width = w;
    height = h;
    depth = d;
  }

  // compute and return volume
  double volume() {
```

```
    return width * height * depth;
  }
}

class BoxDemo7 {
  public static void main(String[] args) {
    // declare, allocate, and initialize Box objects
    Box mybox1 = new Box(10, 20, 15);
    Box mybox2 = new Box(3, 6, 9);

    double vol;

    // get volume of first box
    vol = mybox1.volume();
    System.out.println("Volume is " + vol);

    // get volume of second box
    vol = mybox2.volume();
    System.out.println("Volume is " + vol);
  }
}
```

The output from this program is shown here:

```
Volume is 3000.0
Volume is 162.0
```

As you can see, each object is initialized as specified in the parameters to its constructor. For example, in the following line,

```
Box mybox1 = new Box(10, 20, 15);
```

the values 10, 20, and 15 are passed to the **Box( )** constructor when **new** creates the object. Thus, **mybox1**'s copy of **width, height**, and **depth** will contain the values 10, 20, and 15, respectively.

## The this Keyword

Sometimes a method will need to refer to the object that invoked it. To allow this, Java defines the **this** keyword. **this** can be used inside any method to refer to the *current* object. That is, **this** is always a reference to the object on which the method was invoked. You can use **this** anywhere a reference to an object of the current class's type is permitted.

To better understand what **this** refers to, consider the following version of **Box( )**:

```
// A redundant use of this.
Box(double w, double h, double d) {
  this.width = w;
  this.height = h;
  this.depth = d;
}
```

This version of **Box( )** operates exactly like the earlier version. The use of **this** is redundant but perfectly correct. Inside **Box( )**, **this** will always refer to the invoking object. While it is redundant in this case, **this** is useful in other contexts, one of which is explained in the next section.

## Instance Variable Hiding

As you know, it is illegal in Java to declare two local variables with the same name inside the same or enclosing scopes. Interestingly, you can have local variables, including formal parameters to methods, that overlap with the names of the class's instance variables. However, when a local variable has the same name as an instance variable, the local variable *hides* the instance variable. This is why **width**, **height**, and **depth** were not used as the names of the parameters to the **Box( )** constructor inside the **Box** class. If they had been, then **width,** for example, would have referred to the formal parameter, hiding the instance variable **width**. While it is usually easier to simply use different names, there is another way around this situation. Because **this** lets you refer directly to the object, you can use it to resolve any namespace collisions that might occur between instance variables and local variables. For example, here is another version of **Box( )**, which uses **width**, **height**, and **depth** for parameter names and then uses **this** to access the instance variables by the same name:

```
// Use this to resolve name-space collisions.
Box(double width, double height, double depth) {
  this.width = width;
  this.height = height;
  this.depth = depth;
}
```

A word of caution: The use of **this** in such a context can sometimes be confusing, and some programmers are careful not to use local variables and formal parameter names that hide instance variables. Of course, other programmers believe the contrary—that it is a good convention to use the same names for clarity—and use **this** to overcome the instance variable hiding. It is a matter of taste which approach you adopt.

# Garbage Collection

Since objects are dynamically allocated by using the **new** operator, you might be wondering how such objects are destroyed and their memory released for later reallocation. In some languages, such as traditional C++, dynamically allocated objects must be manually released by use of a **delete** operator. Java takes a different approach; it handles deallocation for you automatically. The technique that accomplishes this is called *garbage collection.* It works like this: when no references to an object exist, that object is assumed to be no longer needed, and the memory occupied by the object can be reclaimed. There is no need to explicitly destroy objects. Garbage collection only occurs sporadically (if at all) during the execution of your program. It will not occur simply because one or more objects exist that are no longer used. Furthermore, different Java run-time implementations will take varying approaches to garbage collection, but for the most part, you should not have to think about it while writing your programs.

## A Stack Class

While the **Box** class is useful to illustrate the essential elements of a class, it is of little practical value. To show the real power of classes, this chapter will conclude with a more sophisticated example. As you recall from the discussion of object-oriented programming (OOP) presented in Chapter 2, one of OOP's most important benefits is the encapsulation of data and the code that manipulates that data. As you have seen, the class is the mechanism by which encapsulation is achieved in Java. By creating a class, you are creating a new data type that defines both the nature of the data being manipulated and the routines used to manipulate it. Further, the methods define a consistent and controlled interface to the class's data. Thus, you can use the class through its methods without having to worry about the details of its implementation or how the data is actually managed within the class. In a sense, a class is like a "data engine." No knowledge of what goes on inside the engine is required to use the engine through its controls. In fact, since the details are hidden, its inner workings can be changed as needed. As long as your code uses the class through its methods, internal details can change without causing side effects outside the class.

To see a practical application of the preceding discussion, let's develop one of the archetypal examples of encapsulation: the stack. A *stack* stores data using first-in, last-out ordering. That is, a stack is like a stack of plates on a table—the first plate put down on the table is the last plate to be used. Stacks are controlled through two operations traditionally called *push* and *pop*. To put an item on top of the stack, you will use push. To take an item off the stack, you will use pop. As you will see, it is easy to encapsulate the entire stack mechanism.

Here is a class called **Stack** that implements a stack for up to ten integers:

```
// This class defines an integer stack that can hold 10 values
class Stack {
  int[] stck = new int[10];
  int tos;

  // Initialize top-of-stack
  Stack() {
    tos = -1;
  }

  // Push an item onto the stack
  void push(int item) {
    if(tos==9)
      System.out.println("Stack is full.");
    else
      stck[++tos] = item;
  }

  // Pop an item from the stack
  int pop() {
    if(tos < 0) {
       System.out.println("Stack underflow.");
```

```
            return 0;
        }
        else
            return stck[tos--];
    }
}
```

As you can see, the **Stack** class defines two data items, two methods, and a constructor. The stack of integers is held by the array **stck**. This array is indexed by the variable **tos**, which always contains the index of the top of the stack. The **Stack( )** constructor initializes **tos** to –1, which indicates an empty stack. The method **push( )** puts an item on the stack. To retrieve an item, call **pop( )**. Since access to the stack is through **push( )** and **pop( )**, the fact that the stack is held in an array is actually not relevant to using the stack. For example, the stack could be held in a more complicated data structure, such as a linked list, yet the interface defined by **push( )** and **pop( )** would remain the same.

The class **TestStack**, shown here, demonstrates the **Stack** class. It creates two integer stacks, pushes some values onto each, and then pops them off.

```
class TestStack {
  public static void main(String[] args) {
    Stack mystack1 = new Stack();
    Stack mystack2 = new Stack();

    // push some numbers onto the stack
    for(int i=0; i<10; i++) mystack1.push(i);
    for(int i=10; i<20; i++) mystack2.push(i);

    // pop those numbers off the stack
    System.out.println("Stack in mystack1:");
    for(int i=0; i<10; i++)
       System.out.println(mystack1.pop());

    System.out.println("Stack in mystack2:");
    for(int i=0; i<10; i++)
       System.out.println(mystack2.pop());
  }
}
```

This program generates the following output:

```
Stack in mystack1:
9
8
7
6
5
4
3
2
1
0
```

```
Stack in mystack2:
19
18
17
16
15
14
13
12
11
10
```

As you can see, the contents of each stack are separate.

One last point about the **Stack** class. As it is currently implemented, it is possible for the array that holds the stack, **stck**, to be altered by code outside of the **Stack** class. This leaves **Stack** open to misuse or mischief. In the next chapter, you will see how to remedy this situation.

CHAPTER

# 7 A Closer Look at Methods and Classes

This chapter continues the discussion of methods and classes begun in the preceding chapter. It examines several topics relating to methods, including overloading, parameter passing, and recursion. The chapter then returns to the class, discussing access control, the use of the keyword **static**, and one of Java's most important built-in classes: **String**.

## Overloading Methods

In Java, it is possible to define two or more methods within the same class that share the same name, as long as their parameter declarations are different. When this is the case, the methods are said to be overloaded, and the process is referred to as *method overloading.* Method overloading is one of the ways that Java supports polymorphism. If you have never used a language that allows the overloading of methods, then the concept may seem strange at first. But as you will see, method overloading is one of Java's most exciting and useful features.

When an overloaded method is invoked, Java uses the type and/or number of arguments as its guide to determine which version of the overloaded method to actually call. Thus, overloaded methods must differ in the type and/or number of their parameters. While overloaded methods may have different return types, the return type alone is insufficient to distinguish two versions of a method. When Java encounters a call to an overloaded method, it simply executes the version of the method whose parameters match the arguments used in the call.

Here is a simple example that illustrates method overloading:

```
// Demonstrate method overloading
class OverloadDemo {
  void test() {
    System.out.println("No parameters");
  }

  // Overload test for one integer parameter.
  void test(int a) {
    System.out.println("a: " + a);
  }
```

```
  // Overload test for two integer parameters.
  void test(int a, int b) {
    System.out.println("a and b: " + a + " " + b);
  }

  // Overload test for a double parameter
  double test(double a) {
    System.out.println("double a: " + a);
    return a*a;
  }
}

class Overload {
  public static void main(String[] args) {
    OverloadDemo ob = new OverloadDemo();
    double result;

    // call all versions of test()
    ob.test();
    ob.test(10);
    ob.test(10, 20);
    result = ob.test(123.25);
    System.out.println("Result of ob.test(123.25): " + result);
  }
}
```

This program generates the following output:

```
No parameters
a: 10
a and b: 10 20
double a: 123.25
Result of ob.test(123.25): 15190.5625
```

As you can see, **test( )** is overloaded four times. The first version takes no parameters, the second takes one integer parameter, the third takes two integer parameters, and the fourth takes one **double** parameter. The fact that the fourth version of **test( )** also returns a value is of no consequence relative to overloading, since return types do not play a role in overload resolution.

When an overloaded method is called, Java looks for a match between the arguments used to call the method and the method's parameters. However, this match need not always be exact. In some cases, Java's automatic type conversions can play a role in overload resolution. For example, consider the following program:

```
// Automatic type conversions apply to overloading.
class OverloadDemo {
  void test() {
    System.out.println("No parameters");
  }

  // Overload test for two integer parameters.
  void test(int a, int b) {
    System.out.println("a and b: " + a + " " + b);
  }
```

```
  // Overload test for a double parameter
  void test(double a) {
    System.out.println("Inside test(double) a: " + a);
  }
}

class Overload {
  public static void main(String[] args) {
    OverloadDemo ob = new OverloadDemo();
    int i = 88;

    ob.test();
    ob.test(10, 20);

    ob.test(i); // this will invoke test(double)
    ob.test(123.2); // this will invoke test(double)
  }
}
```

This program generates the following output:

```
No parameters
a and b: 10 20
Inside test(double) a: 88.0
Inside test(double) a: 123.2
```

As you can see, this version of **OverloadDemo** does not define **test(int)**. Therefore, when **test( )** is called with an integer argument inside **Overload**, no matching method is found. However, Java can automatically convert an integer into a **double**, and this conversion can be used to resolve the call. Therefore, after **test(int)** is not found, Java elevates **i** to **double** and then calls **test(double)**. Of course, if **test(int)** had been defined, it would have been called instead. Java will employ its automatic type conversions only if no exact match is found.

Method overloading supports polymorphism because it is one way that Java implements the "one interface, multiple methods" paradigm. To understand how, consider the following. In languages that do not support method overloading, each method must be given a unique name. However, frequently you will want to implement essentially the same method for different types of data. Consider the absolute value function. In languages that do not support overloading, there are usually three or more versions of this function, each with a slightly different name. For instance, in C, the function **abs( )** returns the absolute value of an integer, **labs( )** returns the absolute value of a long integer, and **fabs( )** returns the absolute value of a floating-point value. Since C does not support overloading, each function has its own name, even though all three functions do essentially the same thing. This makes the situation more complex, conceptually, than it actually is. Although the underlying concept of each function is the same, you still have three names to remember. This situation does not occur in Java, because each absolute value method can use the same name. Indeed, Java's standard class library includes an absolute value method, called **abs( )**. This method is overloaded by Java's **Math** class to handle all numeric types. Java determines which version of **abs( )** to call based upon the type of argument.

The value of overloading is that it allows related methods to be accessed by use of a common name. Thus, the name **abs** represents the *general action* that is being performed.

It is left to the compiler to choose the right *specific* version for a particular circumstance. You, the programmer, need only remember the general operation being performed. Through the application of polymorphism, several names have been reduced to one. Although this example is fairly simple, if you expand the concept, you can see how overloading can help you manage greater complexity.

When you overload a method, each version of that method can perform any activity you desire. There is no rule stating that overloaded methods must relate to one another. However, from a stylistic point of view, method overloading implies a relationship. Thus, while you can use the same name to overload unrelated methods, you should not. For example, you could use the name **sqr** to create methods that return the *square* of an integer and the *square root* of a floating-point value. But these two operations are fundamentally different. Applying method overloading in this manner defeats its original purpose. In practice, you should only overload closely related operations.

## Overloading Constructors

In addition to overloading normal methods, you can also overload constructor methods. In fact, for most real-world classes that you create, overloaded constructors will be the norm, not the exception. To understand why, let's return to the **Box** class developed in the preceding chapter. Following is the latest version of **Box**:

```
class Box {
  double width;
  double height;
  double depth;

  // This is the constructor for Box.
  Box(double w, double h, double d) {
    width = w;
    height = h;
    depth = d;
  }

  // compute and return volume
  double volume() {
    return width * height * depth;
  }
}
```

As you can see, the **Box( )** constructor requires three parameters. This means that all declarations of **Box** objects must pass three arguments to the **Box( )** constructor. For example, the following statement is currently invalid:

```
Box ob = new Box();
```

Since **Box( )** requires three arguments, it's an error to call it without them. This raises some important questions. What if you simply wanted a box and did not care (or know) what its initial dimensions were? Or, what if you want to be able to initialize a cube by specifying only one value that would be used for all three dimensions? As the **Box** class is currently written, these other options are not available to you.

Fortunately, the solution to these problems is quite easy: simply overload the **Box** constructor so that it handles the situations just described. Here is a program that contains an improved version of **Box** that does just that:

```
/* Here, Box defines three constructors to initialize
   the dimensions of a box various ways.
*/
class Box {
  double width;
  double height;
  double depth;

  // constructor used when all dimensions specified
  Box(double w, double h, double d) {
    width = w;
    height = h;
    depth = d;
  }

  // constructor used when no dimensions specified
  Box() {
    width = -1;  // use -1 to indicate
    height = -1; // an uninitialized
    depth = -1;  // box
  }

  // constructor used when cube is created
  Box(double len) {
    width = height = depth = len;
  }

  // compute and return volume
  double volume() {
    return width * height * depth;
  }
}

class OverloadCons {
  public static void main(String[] args) {
    // create boxes using the various constructors
    Box mybox1 = new Box(10, 20, 15);
    Box mybox2 = new Box();
    Box mycube = new Box(7);

    double vol;

    // get volume of first box
    vol = mybox1.volume();
    System.out.println("Volume of mybox1 is " + vol);

    // get volume of second box
    vol = mybox2.volume();
    System.out.println("Volume of mybox2 is " + vol);
```

```
    // get volume of cube
    vol = mycube.volume();
    System.out.println("Volume of mycube is " + vol);
  }
}
```

The output produced by this program is shown here:

```
Volume of mybox1 is 3000.0
Volume of mybox2 is -1.0
Volume of mycube is 343.0
```

As you can see, the proper overloaded constructor is called based upon the arguments specified when **new** is executed.

## Using Objects as Parameters

So far, we have only been using simple types as parameters to methods. However, it is both correct and common to pass objects to methods. For example, consider the following short program:

```
// Objects may be passed to methods.
class Test {
  int a, b;

  Test(int i, int j) {
    a = i;
    b = j;
  }

  // return true if o is equal to the invoking object
  boolean equalTo(Test o) {
    if(o.a == a && o.b == b) return true;
    else return false;
  }
}

class PassOb {
  public static void main(String[] args) {
    Test ob1 = new Test(100, 22);
    Test ob2 = new Test(100, 22);
    Test ob3 = new Test(-1, -1);

    System.out.println("ob1 == ob2: " + ob1.equalTo(ob2));
    System.out.println("ob1 == ob3: " + ob1.equalTo(ob3));
  }
}
```

This program generates the following output:

```
ob1 == ob2: true
ob1 == ob3: false
```

As you can see, the **equalTo( )** method inside **Test** compares two objects for equality and returns the result. That is, it compares the invoking object with the one that it is passed. If they contain the same values, then the method returns **true**. Otherwise, it returns **false**. Notice that the parameter **o** in **equalTo( )** specifies **Test** as its type. Although **Test** is a class type created by the program, it is used in just the same way as Java's built-in types.

One of the most common uses of object parameters involves constructors. Frequently, you will want to construct a new object so that it is initially the same as some existing object. To do this, you must define a constructor that takes an object of its class as a parameter. For example, the following version of **Box** allows one object to initialize another:

```
// Here, Box allows one object to initialize another.

class Box {
  double width;
  double height;
  double depth;

  // Notice this constructor. It takes an object of type Box.
  Box(Box ob) { // pass object to constructor
    width = ob.width;
    height = ob.height;
    depth = ob.depth;
  }

  // constructor used when all dimensions specified
  Box(double w, double h, double d) {
    width = w;
    height = h;
    depth = d;
  }

  // constructor used when no dimensions specified
  Box() {
    width = -1;  // use -1 to indicate
    height = -1; // an uninitialized
    depth = -1;  // box
  }

  // constructor used when cube is created
  Box(double len) {
    width = height = depth = len;
  }

  // compute and return volume
  double volume() {
    return width * height * depth;
  }
}

class OverloadCons2 {
  public static void main(String[] args) {
    // create boxes using the various constructors
    Box mybox1 = new Box(10, 20, 15);
```

```
        Box mybox2 = new Box();
        Box mycube = new Box(7);

        Box myclone = new Box(mybox1); // create copy of mybox1

        double vol;

        // get volume of first box
        vol = mybox1.volume();
        System.out.println("Volume of mybox1 is " + vol);

        // get volume of second box
        vol = mybox2.volume();
        System.out.println("Volume of mybox2 is " + vol);

        // get volume of cube
        vol = mycube.volume();
        System.out.println("Volume of cube is " + vol);

       // get volume of clone
        vol = myclone.volume();
        System.out.println("Volume of clone is " + vol);
    }
}
```

As you will see when you begin to create your own classes, providing many forms of constructors is usually required to allow objects to be constructed in a convenient and efficient manner.

## A Closer Look at Argument Passing

In general, there are two ways that a computer language can pass an argument to a subroutine. The first way is *call-by-value*. This approach copies the *value* of an argument into the formal parameter of the subroutine. Therefore, changes made to the parameter of the subroutine have no effect on the argument. The second way an argument can be passed is *call-by-reference*. In this approach, a reference to an argument (not the value of the argument) is passed to the parameter. Inside the subroutine, this reference is used to access the actual argument specified in the call. This means that changes made to the parameter will affect the argument used to call the subroutine. As you will see, although Java uses call-by-value to pass all arguments, the precise effect differs between whether a primitive type or a reference type is passed.

When you pass a primitive type to a method, it is passed by value. Thus, a copy of the argument is made, and what occurs to the parameter that receives the argument has no effect outside the method. For example, consider the following program:

```
// Primitive types are passed by value.
class Test {
  void meth(int i, int j) {
    i *= 2;
    j /= 2;
  }
}
```

```
class CallByValue {
  public static void main(String[] args) {
    Test ob = new Test();

    int a = 15, b = 20;

    System.out.println("a and b before call: " +
                       a + " " + b);

    ob.meth(a, b);

    System.out.println("a and b after call: " +
                       a + " " + b);
  }
}
```

The output from this program is shown here:

```
a and b before call: 15 20
a and b after call: 15 20
```

As you can see, the operations that occur inside **meth( )** have no effect on the values of **a** and **b** used in the call; their values here did not change to 30 and 10.

When you pass an object to a method, the situation changes dramatically, because objects are passed by what is effectively call-by-reference. Keep in mind that when you create a variable of a class type, you are only creating a reference to an object. Thus, when you pass this reference to a method, the parameter that receives it will refer to the same object as that referred to by the argument. This effectively means that objects act as if they are passed to methods by use of call-by-reference. Changes to the object inside the method *do* affect the object used as an argument. For example, consider the following program:

```
// Objects are passed through their references.

class Test {
  int a, b;

  Test(int i, int j) {
    a = i;
    b = j;
  }

  // pass an object
  void meth(Test o) {
    o.a *= 2;
    o.b /= 2;
  }
}

class PassObjRef {
  public static void main(String[] args) {
    Test ob = new Test(15, 20);
```

```
        System.out.println("ob.a and ob.b before call: " +
                           ob.a + " " + ob.b);

        ob.meth(ob);

        System.out.println("ob.a and ob.b after call: " +
                           ob.a + " " + ob.b);
    }
}
```

This program generates the following output:

```
ob.a and ob.b before call: 15 20
ob.a and ob.b after call: 30 10
```

As you can see, in this case, the actions inside **meth( )** have affected the object used as an argument.

**REMEMBER** When an object reference is passed to a method, the reference itself is passed by use of call-by-value. However, since the value being passed refers to an object, the copy of that value will still refer to the same object that its corresponding argument does.

## Returning Objects

A method can return any type of data, including class types that you create. For example, in the following program, the **incrByTen( )** method returns an object in which the value of **a** is ten greater than it is in the invoking object.

```
// Returning an object.
class Test {
  int a;

  Test(int i) {
    a = i;
  }

  Test incrByTen() {
    Test temp = new Test(a+10);
    return temp;
  }
}

class RetOb {
  public static void main(String[] args) {
    Test ob1 = new Test(2);
    Test ob2;

    ob2 = ob1.incrByTen();
    System.out.println("ob1.a: " + ob1.a);
    System.out.println("ob2.a: " + ob2.a);
```

```
    ob2 = ob2.incrByTen();
    System.out.println("ob2.a after second increase: "
                        + ob2.a);
  }
}
```

The output generated by this program is shown here:

```
ob1.a: 2
ob2.a: 12
ob2.a after second increase: 22
```

As you can see, each time **incrByTen( )** is invoked, a new object is created, and a reference to it is returned to the calling routine.

The preceding program makes another important point: Since all objects are dynamically allocated using **new**, you don't need to worry about an object going out of scope because the method in which it was created terminates. The object will continue to exist as long as there is a reference to it somewhere in your program. When there are no references to it, the object will be reclaimed the next time garbage collection takes place.

# Recursion

Java supports *recursion*. Recursion is the process of defining something in terms of itself. As it relates to Java programming, recursion is the attribute that allows a method to call itself. A method that calls itself is said to be *recursive*.

The classic example of recursion is the computation of the factorial of a number. The factorial of a number *N* is the product of all the whole numbers between 1 and *N*. For example, 3 factorial is 1 × 2 × 3, or 6. Here is how a factorial can be computed by use of a recursive method:

```
// A simple example of recursion.
class Factorial {
  // this is a recursive method
  int fact(int n) {
    int result;

    if(n==1) return 1;
    result = fact(n-1) * n;
    return result;
  }
}

class Recursion {
  public static void main(String[] args) {
    Factorial f = new Factorial();

    System.out.println("Factorial of 3 is " + f.fact(3));
    System.out.println("Factorial of 4 is " + f.fact(4));
    System.out.println("Factorial of 5 is " + f.fact(5));
  }
}
```

The output from this program is shown here:

```
Factorial of 3 is 6
Factorial of 4 is 24
Factorial of 5 is 120
```

If you are unfamiliar with recursive methods, then the operation of **fact( )** may seem a bit confusing. Here is how it works. When **fact( )** is called with an argument of 1, the function returns 1; otherwise, it returns the product of **fact(n–1)*n**. To evaluate this expression, **fact( )** is called with **n–1**. This process repeats until **n** equals 1 and the calls to the method begin returning.

To better understand how the **fact( )** method works, let's go through a short example. When you compute the factorial of 3, the first call to **fact( )** will cause a second call to be made with an argument of 2. This invocation will cause **fact( )** to be called a third time with an argument of 1. This call will return 1, which is then multiplied by 2 (the value of **n** in the second invocation). This result (which is 2) is then returned to the original invocation of **fact( )** and multiplied by 3 (the original value of **n**). This yields the answer, 6. You might find it interesting to insert **println( )** statements into **fact( )**, which will show at what level each call is and what the intermediate answers are.

When a method calls itself, new local variables and parameters are allocated storage on the stack, and the method code is executed with these new variables from the start. As each recursive call returns, the old local variables and parameters are removed from the stack, and execution resumes at the point of the call inside the method. Recursive methods could be said to "telescope" out and back.

Recursive versions of many routines may execute a bit more slowly than the iterative equivalent because of the added overhead of the additional method calls. A large number of recursive calls to a method could cause a stack overrun. Because storage for parameters and local variables is on the stack and each new call creates a new copy of these variables, it is possible that the stack could be exhausted. If this occurs, the Java run-time system will cause an exception. However, this is typically not an issue unless a recursive routine runs wild.

The main advantage to recursive methods is that they can be used to create clearer and simpler versions of several algorithms than can their iterative relatives. For example, the QuickSort sorting algorithm is quite difficult to implement in an iterative way. Also, some types of AI-related algorithms are most easily implemented using recursive solutions.

When writing recursive methods, you must have an **if** statement somewhere to force the method to return without the recursive call being executed. If you don't do this, once you call the method, it will never return. This is a very common error in working with recursion. Use **println( )** statements liberally during development so that you can watch what is going on and abort execution if you see that you have made a mistake.

Here is one more example of recursion. The recursive method **printArray( )** prints the first **i** elements in the array **values**.

```
// Another example that uses recursion.

class RecTest {
  int[] values;
```

```
  RecTest(int i) {
    values = new int[i];
  }

  // display array -- recursively
  void printArray(int i) {
    if(i==0) return;
    else printArray(i-1);
    System.out.println("[" + (i-1) + "] " + values[i-1]);
  }
}

class Recursion2 {
  public static void main(String[] args) {
    RecTest ob = new RecTest(10);
    int i;

    for(i=0; i<10; i++) ob.values[i] = i;

    ob.printArray(10);
  }
}
```

This program generates the following output:

```
[0] 0
[1] 1
[2] 2
[3] 3
[4] 4
[5] 5
[6] 6
[7] 7
[8] 8
[9] 9
```

## Introducing Access Control

As you know, encapsulation links data with the code that manipulates it. However, encapsulation provides another important attribute: *access control*. Through encapsulation, you can control what parts of a program can access the members of a class. By controlling access, you can prevent misuse. For example, allowing access to data only through a well-defined set of methods, you can prevent the misuse of that data. Thus, when correctly implemented, a class creates a "black box" that may be used, but the inner workings of which are not open to tampering. However, the classes that were presented earlier do not completely meet this goal. For example, consider the **Stack** class shown at the end of Chapter 6. While it is true that the methods **push( )** and **pop( )** do provide a controlled interface to the stack, this interface is not enforced. That is, it is possible for another part of the program to bypass these methods and access the stack directly. Of course, in the wrong hands, this could lead to trouble. In this section, you will be introduced to the mechanism by which you can precisely control access to the various members of a class.

How a member can be accessed is determined by the *access modifier* attached to its declaration. Java supplies a rich set of access modifiers. Some aspects of access control are related mostly to inheritance or packages. (A *package* is, essentially, a grouping of classes.) These parts of Java's access control mechanism will be discussed in subsequent chapters. Here, let's begin by examining access control as it applies to a single class. Once you understand the fundamentals of access control, the rest will be easy.

---

**NOTE** The modules feature added by JDK 9 can also impact accessibility. Modules are described in Chapter 16.

Java's access modifiers are **public**, **private**, and **protected**. Java also defines a default access level. **protected** applies only when inheritance is involved. The other access modifiers are described next.

Let's begin by defining **public** and **private**. When a member of a class is modified by **public**, then that member can be accessed by any other code. When a member of a class is specified as **private**, then that member can only be accessed by other members of its class. Now you can understand why **main( )** has always been preceded by the **public** modifier. It is called by code that is outside the program—that is, by the Java run-time system. When no access modifier is used, then by default the member of a class is public within its own package, but cannot be accessed outside of its package. (Packages are discussed in Chapter 9.)

In the classes developed so far, all members of a class have used the default access mode. However, this is not what you will typically want to be the case. Usually, you will want to restrict access to the data members of a class—allowing access only through methods. Also, there will be times when you will want to define methods that are private to a class.

An access modifier precedes the rest of a member's type specification. That is, it must begin a member's declaration statement. Here is an example:

```
public int i;
private double j;

private int myMethod(int a, char b) { //...
```

To understand the effects of public and private access, consider the following program:

```
/* This program demonstrates the difference between
   public and private.
*/
class Test {
  int a; // default access
  public int b; // public access
  private int c; // private access

  // methods to access c
  void setc(int i) { // set c's value
    c = i;
  }
  int getc() { // get c's value
    return c;
  }
}
```

```
class AccessTest {
  public static void main(String[] args) {
    Test ob = new Test();

    // These are OK, a and b may be accessed directly
    ob.a = 10;
    ob.b = 20;

    // This is not OK and will cause an error
//  ob.c = 100; // Error!

    // You must access c through its methods
    ob.setc(100); // OK
    System.out.println("a, b, and c: " + ob.a + " " +
                       ob.b + " " + ob.getc());
  }
}
```

As you can see, inside the **Test** class, **a** uses default access, which for this example is the same as specifying **public**. **b** is explicitly specified as **public**. Member **c** is given private access. This means that it cannot be accessed by code outside of its class. So, inside the **AccessTest** class, **c** cannot be used directly. It must be accessed through its public methods: **setc( )** and **getc( )**. If you were to remove the comment symbol from the beginning of the following line,

```
// ob.c = 100; // Error!
```

then you would not be able to compile this program because of the access violation.

To see how access control can be applied to a more practical example, consider the following improved version of the **Stack** class shown at the end of Chapter 6:

```
// This class defines an integer stack that can hold 10 values.
class Stack {
  /* Now, both stck and tos are private. This means
     that they cannot be accidentally or maliciously
     altered in a way that would be harmful to the stack.
  */
  private int[] stck = new int[10];
  private int tos;

  // Initialize top-of-stack
  Stack() {
    tos = -1;
  }

  // Push an item onto the stack
  void push(int item) {
    if(tos==9)
      System.out.println("Stack is full.");
    else
      stck[++tos] = item;
  }
```

```
    // Pop an item from the stack
    int pop() {
      if(tos < 0) {
        System.out.println("Stack underflow.");
        return 0;
      }
      else
        return stck[tos--];
    }
  }
```

As you can see, now both **stck**, which holds the stack, and **tos**, which is the index of the top of the stack, are specified as **private**. This means that they cannot be accessed or altered except through **push( )** and **pop( )**. Making **tos** private, for example, prevents other parts of your program from inadvertently setting it to a value that is beyond the end of the **stck** array.

The following program demonstrates the improved **Stack** class. Try removing the commented-out lines to prove to yourself that the **stck** and **tos** members are, indeed, inaccessible.

```
class TestStack {
  public static void main(String[] args) {
    Stack mystack1 = new Stack();
    Stack mystack2 = new Stack();

    // push some numbers onto the stack
    for(int i=0; i<10; i++) mystack1.push(i);
    for(int i=10; i<20; i++) mystack2.push(i);

    // pop those numbers off the stack
    System.out.println("Stack in mystack1:");
    for(int i=0; i<10; i++)
       System.out.println(mystack1.pop());

    System.out.println("Stack in mystack2:");

    for(int i=0; i<10; i++)
       System.out.println(mystack2.pop());

    // these statements are not legal
    // mystack1.tos = -2;
    // mystack2.stck[3] = 100;
  }
}
```

Although methods will usually provide access to the data defined by a class, this does not always have to be the case. It is perfectly proper to allow an instance variable to be public when there is good reason to do so. For example, most of the simple classes in this book were created with little concern about controlling access to instance variables for the sake of simplicity. However, in most real-world classes, you will need to allow operations on data only through methods. The next chapter will return to the topic of access control. As you will see, it is particularly important when inheritance is involved.

## Understanding static

There will be times when you will want to define a class member that will be used independently of any object of that class. Normally, a class member must be accessed only in conjunction with an object of its class. However, it is possible to create a member that can be used by itself, without reference to a specific instance. To create such a member, precede its declaration with the keyword **static**. When a member is declared **static**, it can be accessed before any objects of its class are created, and without reference to any object. You can declare both methods and variables to be **static**. The most common example of a **static** member is **main( )**. **main( )** is declared as **static** because it must be called before any objects exist.

Instance variables declared as **static** are, essentially, global variables. When objects of its class are declared, no copy of a **static** variable is made. Instead, all instances of the class share the same **static** variable.

Methods declared as **static** have several restrictions:

- They can only directly call other **static** methods of their class.
- They can only directly access **static** variables of their class.
- They cannot refer to **this** or **super** in any way. (The keyword **super** relates to inheritance and is described in the next chapter.)

If you need to do computation in order to initialize your **static** variables, you can declare a **static** block that gets executed exactly once, when the class is first loaded. The following example shows a class that has a **static** method, some **static** variables, and a **static** initialization block:

```
// Demonstrate static variables, methods, and blocks.
class UseStatic {
  static int a = 3;
  static int b;

  static void meth(int x) {
    System.out.println("x = " + x);
    System.out.println("a = " + a);
    System.out.println("b = " + b);
  }

  static {
    System.out.println("Static block initialized.");
    b = a * 4;
  }

  public static void main(String[] args) {
    meth(42);
  }
}
```

As soon as the **UseStatic** class is loaded, all of the **static** statements are run. First, **a** is set to **3**, then the **static** block executes, which prints a message and then initializes **b** to **a*4** or **12**. Then **main( )** is called, which calls **meth( )**, passing **42** to **x**. The three **println( )** statements refer to the two **static** variables **a** and **b**, as well as to the parameter **x**.

Here is the output of the program:

```
Static block initialized.
x = 42
a = 3
b = 12
```

Outside of the class in which they are defined, **static** methods and variables can be used independently of any object. To do so, you need only specify the name of their class followed by the dot operator. For example, if you wish to call a **static** method from outside its class, you can do so using the following general form:

*classname.method*( )

Here, *classname* is the name of the class in which the **static** method is declared. As you can see, this format is similar to that used to call non-**static** methods through object-reference variables. A **static** variable can be accessed in the same way—by use of the dot operator on the name of the class. This is how Java implements a controlled version of global methods and global variables.

Here is an example. Inside **main( )**, the **static** method **callme( )** and the **static** variable **b** are accessed through their class name **StaticDemo**.

```
class StaticDemo {
  static int a = 42;
  static int b = 99;

  static void callme() {
    System.out.println("a = " + a);
  }
}

class StaticByName {
  public static void main(String[] args) {
    StaticDemo.callme();
    System.out.println("b = " + StaticDemo.b);
  }
}
```

Here is the output of this program:

```
a = 42
b = 99
```

## Introducing final

A field can be declared as **final**. Doing so prevents its contents from being modified, making it, essentially, a constant. This means that you must initialize a **final** field when it is declared. You can do this in one of two ways: First, you can give it a value when it is declared. Second, you can assign it a value within a constructor. The first approach is probably the most common. Here is an example:

```
final int FILE_NEW = 1;
final int FILE_OPEN = 2;
final int FILE_SAVE = 3;
final int FILE_SAVEAS = 4;
final int FILE_QUIT = 5;
```

Subsequent parts of your program can now use **FILE_OPEN**, etc., as if they were constants, without fear that a value has been changed. It is a common coding convention to choose all uppercase identifiers for **final** fields, as this example shows.

In addition to fields, both method parameters and local variables can be declared **final**. Declaring a parameter **final** prevents it from being changed within the method. Declaring a local variable **final** prevents it from being assigned a value more than once.

The keyword **final** can also be applied to methods, but its meaning is substantially different than when it is applied to variables. This additional usage of **final** is explained in the next chapter, when inheritance is described.

## Arrays Revisited

Arrays were introduced earlier in this book, before classes had been discussed. Now that you know about classes, an important point can be made about arrays: they are implemented as objects. Because of this, there is a special array attribute that you will want to take advantage of. Specifically, the size of an array—that is, the number of elements that an array can hold—is found in its **length** instance variable. All arrays have this variable, and it will always hold the size of the array. Here is a program that demonstrates this property:

```
// This program demonstrates the length array member.
class Length {
  public static void main(String[] args) {
    int[] a1 = new int[10];
    int[] a2 = {3, 5, 7, 1, 8, 99, 44, -10};
    int[] a3 = {4, 3, 2, 1};

    System.out.println("length of a1 is " + a1.length);
    System.out.println("length of a2 is " + a2.length);
    System.out.println("length of a3 is " + a3.length);
  }
}
```

This program displays the following output:

```
length of a1 is 10
length of a2 is 8
length of a3 is 4
```

As you can see, the size of each array is displayed. Keep in mind that the value of **length** has nothing to do with the number of elements that are actually in use. It only reflects the number of elements that the array is designed to hold.

You can put the **length** member to good use in many situations. For example, here is an improved version of the **Stack** class. As you might recall, the earlier versions of this class always created a ten-element stack. The following version lets you create stacks of any size. The value of **stck.length** is used to prevent the stack from overflowing.

```
// Improved Stack class that uses the length array member.
class Stack {
  private int[] stck;
  private int tos;

  // allocate and initialize stack
  Stack(int size) {
    stck = new int[size];
    tos = -1;
  }

  // Push an item onto the stack
  void push(int item) {
    if(tos==stck.length-1) // use length member
      System.out.println("Stack is full.");
    else
      stck[++tos] = item;
  }

  // Pop an item from the stack
  int pop() {
    if(tos < 0) {
      System.out.println("Stack underflow.");
      return 0;
    }
    else
      return stck[tos--];
  }
}

class TestStack2 {
  public static void main(String[] args) {
    Stack mystack1 = new Stack(5);
    Stack mystack2 = new Stack(8);

    // push some numbers onto the stack
    for(int i=0; i<5; i++) mystack1.push(i);
    for(int i=0; i<8; i++) mystack2.push(i);

    // pop those numbers off the stack
    System.out.println("Stack in mystack1:");
    for(int i=0; i<5; i++)
      System.out.println(mystack1.pop());

    System.out.println("Stack in mystack2:");
    for(int i=0; i<8; i++)
      System.out.println(mystack2.pop());
  }
}
```

Notice that the program creates two stacks: one five elements deep and the other eight elements deep. As you can see, the fact that arrays maintain their own length information makes it easy to create stacks of any size.

# Introducing Nested and Inner Classes

It is possible to define a class within another class; such classes are known as *nested classes.* The scope of a nested class is bounded by the scope of its enclosing class. Thus, if class B is defined within class A, then B does not exist independently of A. A nested class has access to the members, including private members, of the class in which it is nested. However, the enclosing class does not have access to the members of the nested class. A nested class that is declared directly within its enclosing class scope is a member of its enclosing class. It is also possible to declare a nested class that is local to a block.

There are two types of nested classes: *static* and *inner.* A static nested class is one that has the **static** modifier applied. Because it is static, it must access the non-static members of its enclosing class through an object. That is, it cannot refer to non-static members of its enclosing class directly.

The second type of nested class is the *inner* class. An inner class is a non-static nested class. It has access to all of the variables and methods of its outer class and may refer to them directly in the same way that other non-static members of the outer class do.

The following program illustrates how to define and use an inner class. The class named **Outer** has one instance variable named **outer_x**, one instance method named **test( )**, and defines one inner class called **Inner**.

```
// Demonstrate an inner class.
class Outer {
  int outer_x = 100;

  void test() {
    Inner inner = new Inner();
    inner.display();
  }

  // this is an inner class
  class Inner {
    void display() {
      System.out.println("display: outer_x = " + outer_x);
    }
  }
}

class InnerClassDemo {
  public static void main(String[] args) {
    Outer outer = new Outer();
    outer.test();
  }
}
```

Output from this application is shown here:

```
display: outer_x = 100
```

In the program, an inner class named **Inner** is defined within the scope of class **Outer**. Therefore, any code in class **Inner** can directly access the variable **outer_x**. An instance method named **display( )** is defined inside **Inner**. This method displays **outer_x** on the standard output stream. The **main( )** method of **InnerClassDemo** creates an instance of class **Outer** and invokes its **test( )** method. That method creates an instance of class **Inner**, and the **display( )** method is called.

It is important to realize that an instance of **Inner** can be created only in the context of class **Outer**. The Java compiler generates an error message otherwise. In general, an inner class instance is often created by code within its enclosing scope, as the example does.

As explained, an inner class has access to all of the members of its enclosing class, but the reverse is not true. Members of the inner class are known only within the scope of the inner class and may not be used by the outer class. For example:

```
// This program will not compile.
class Outer {
  int outer_x = 100;

  void test() {
    Inner inner = new Inner();
    inner.display();
  }

  // this is an inner class
  class Inner {
    int y = 10; // y is local to Inner

    void display() {
      System.out.println("display: outer_x = " + outer_x);
    }
  }

  void showy() {
    System.out.println(y); // error, y not known here!
  }
}

class InnerClassDemo {
  public static void main(String[] args) {
    Outer outer = new Outer();
    outer.test();
  }
}
```

Here, **y** is declared as an instance variable of **Inner**. Thus, it is not known outside of that class and it cannot be used by **showy( )**.

Although we have been focusing on inner classes declared as members within an outer class scope, it is possible to define inner classes within any block scope. For example, you can define a nested class within the block defined by a method or even within the body of a **for** loop, as this next program shows:

```
// Define an inner class within a for loop.
class Outer {
  int outer_x = 100;

  void test() {
    for(int i=0; i<10; i++) {
      class Inner {
        void display() {
          System.out.println("display: outer_x = " + outer_x);
        }
      }
      Inner inner = new Inner();
      inner.display();
    }
  }
}

class InnerClassDemo {
  public static void main(String[] args) {
    Outer outer = new Outer();
    outer.test();
  }
}
```

The output from this version of the program is shown here:

```
display: outer_x = 100
display: outer_x = 100
display: outer_x = 100
display: outer_x = 100
display: outer_x = 100
display: outer_x = 100
display: outer_x = 100
display: outer_x = 100
display: outer_x = 100
display: outer_x = 100
```

While nested classes are not applicable to all situations, they are particularly helpful when handling events. We will return to the topic of nested classes in Chapter 25. There you will see how inner classes can be used to simplify the code needed to handle certain types of events. You will also learn about *anonymous inner classes*, which are inner classes that don't have a name.

One point of interest: Nested classes were not allowed by the original 1.0 specification for Java. They were added by Java 1.1.

## Exploring the String Class

Although the **String** class will be examined in depth in Part II of this book, a short exploration of it is warranted now, because we will be using strings in some of the sample programs shown toward the end of Part I. **String** is probably the most commonly used class in Java's class library. The obvious reason for this is that strings are a very important part of programming.

The first thing to understand about strings is that every string you create is actually an object of type **String**. Even string constants are actually **String** objects. For example, in the statement

```
System.out.println("This is a String, too");
```

the string "This is a String, too" is a **String** object.

The second thing to understand about strings is that objects of type **String** are immutable; once a **String** object is created, its contents cannot be altered. While this may seem like a serious restriction, it is not, for two reasons:

- If you need to change a string, you can always create a new one that contains the modifications.
- Java defines peer classes of **String**, called **StringBuffer** and **StringBuilder**, that allow strings to be altered, so all of the normal string manipulations are still available in Java. (**StringBuffer** and **StringBuilder** are described in Part II of this book.)

Strings can be constructed in a variety of ways. The easiest is to use a statement like this:

```
String myString = "this is a test";
```

Once you have created a **String** object, you can use it anywhere that a string is allowed. For example, this statement displays **myString**:

```
System.out.println(myString);
```

Java defines one operator for **String** objects: +. It is used to concatenate two strings. For example, the statement

```
String myString = "I" + " like " + "Java.";
```

results in **myString** containing "I like Java."

The following program demonstrates the preceding concepts:

```
// Demonstrating Strings.
class StringDemo {
  public static void main(String[] args) {
    String strOb1 = "First String";
    String strOb2 = "Second String";
    String strOb3 = strOb1 + " and " + strOb2;

    System.out.println(strOb1);
```

```
    System.out.println(strOb2);
    System.out.println(strOb3);
  }
}
```

The output produced by this program is shown here:

```
First String
Second String
First String and Second String
```

The **String** class contains several methods that you can use. Here are a few. You can test two strings for equality by using **equals( )**. You can obtain the length of a string by calling the **length( )** method. You can obtain the character at a specified index within a string by calling **charAt( )**. The general forms of these three methods are shown here:

boolean equals(*secondStr*)
int length( )
char charAt(*index*)

Here is a program that demonstrates these methods:

```
// Demonstrating some String methods.
class StringDemo2 {
  public static void main(String[] args) {
    String strOb1 = "First String";
    String strOb2 = "Second String";
    String strOb3 = strOb1;

    System.out.println("Length of strOb1: " +
                       strOb1.length());

    System.out.println("Char at index 3 in strOb1: " +
                       strOb1.charAt(3));

    if(strOb1.equals(strOb2))
      System.out.println("strOb1 == strOb2");
    else
      System.out.println("strOb1 != strOb2");

    if(strOb1.equals(strOb3))
      System.out.println("strOb1 == strOb3");
    else
      System.out.println("strOb1 != strOb3");
  }
}
```

This program generates the following output:

```
Length of strOb1: 12
Char at index 3 in strOb1: s
strOb1 != strOb2
strOb1 == strOb3
```

Of course, you can have arrays of strings, just like you can have arrays of any other type of object. For example:

```
// Demonstrate String arrays.
class StringDemo3 {
  public static void main(String[] args) {
    String[] str = { "one", "two", "three" };

    for(int i=0; i<str.length; i++)
      System.out.println("str[" + i + "]: " +
                          str[i]);
  }
}
```

Here is the output from this program:

```
str[0]: one
str[1]: two
str[2]: three
```

As you will see in the following section, string arrays play an important part in many Java programs.

## Using Command-Line Arguments

Sometimes you will want to pass information into a program when you run it. This is accomplished by passing *command-line arguments* to **main( )**. A command-line argument is the information that directly follows the program's name on the command line when it is executed. To access the command-line arguments inside a Java program is quite easy—they are stored as strings in a **String** array passed to the **args** parameter of **main( )**. The first command-line argument is stored at **args[0]**, the second at **args[1]**, and so on. For example, the following program displays all of the command-line arguments that it is called with:

```
// Display all command-line arguments.
class CommandLine {
  public static void main(String[] args) {
    for(int i=0; i<args.length; i++)
      System.out.println("args[" + i + "]: " +
                          args[i]);
  }
}
```

Try executing this program, as shown here:

```
java CommandLine this is a test 100 -1
```

When you do, you will see the following output:

```
args[0]: this
args[1]: is
args[2]: a
args[3]: test
args[4]: 100
args[5]: -1
```

**REMEMBER** All command-line arguments are passed as strings. You must convert numeric values to their internal forms manually, as explained in Chapter 19.



## Varargs: Variable-Length Arguments

Modern versions of Java include a feature that simplifies the creation of methods that need to take a variable number of arguments. This feature is called *varargs*, and it is short for *variable-length arguments*. A method that takes a variable number of arguments is called a *variable-arity method*, or simply a *varargs method*.

Situations that require that a variable number of arguments be passed to a method are not unusual. For example, a method that opens an Internet connection might take a user name, password, filename, protocol, and so on, but supply defaults if some of this information is not provided. In this situation, it would be convenient to pass only the arguments to which the defaults did not apply. Another example is the **printf( )** method that is part of Java's I/O library. As you will see in Chapter 22, it takes a variable number of arguments, which it formats and then outputs.

In the early days of Java, variable-length arguments could be handled two ways, neither of which was particularly pleasing. First, if the maximum number of arguments was small and known, then you could create overloaded versions of the method, one for each way the method could be called. Although this works and is suitable for some cases, it applies to only a narrow class of situations.

In cases where the maximum number of potential arguments was larger, or unknowable, a second approach was used in which the arguments were put into an array, and then the array was passed to the method. This approach, which you may still find in older legacy code, is illustrated by the following program:

```
// Use an array to pass a variable number of
// arguments to a method. This is the old-style
// approach to variable-length arguments.
class PassArray {
  static void vaTest(int[] v) {
    System.out.print("Number of args: " + v.length +
                     " Contents: ");

    for(int x : v)
      System.out.print(x + " ");
    System.out.println();
  }

  public static void main(String[] args)
  {
    // Notice how an array must be created to
    // hold the arguments.
    int[] n1 = { 10 };
    int[] n2 = { 1, 2, 3 };
    int[] n3 = { };

    vaTest(n1); // 1 arg
    vaTest(n2); // 3 args
    vaTest(n3); // no args
  }
}
```

The output from the program is shown here:

```
Number of args: 1 Contents: 10
Number of args: 3 Contents: 1 2 3
Number of args: 0 Contents:
```

In the program, the method **vaTest( )** is passed its arguments through the array **v**. This old-style approach to variable-length arguments does enable **vaTest( )** to take an arbitrary number of arguments. However, it requires that these arguments be manually packaged into an array prior to calling **vaTest( )**. Not only is it tedious to construct an array each time **vaTest( )** is called, it is potentially error-prone. The varargs feature offers a simpler, better option.

A variable-length argument is specified by three periods (...). For example, here is how **vaTest( )** is written using a vararg:

```
static void vaTest(int ... v) {
```

This syntax tells the compiler that **vaTest( )** can be called with zero or more arguments. As a result, **v** is implicitly declared as an array of type **int[ ]**. Thus, inside **vaTest( )**, **v** is accessed using the normal array syntax. Here is the preceding program rewritten using a vararg:

```
// Demonstrate variable-length arguments.
class VarArgs {

  // vaTest() now uses a vararg.
  static void vaTest(int ... v) {
    System.out.print("Number of args: " + v.length +
                     " Contents: ");

    for(int x : v)
      System.out.print(x + " ");

    System.out.println();
  }

  public static void main(String[] args)
  {
    // Notice how vaTest() can be called with a
    // variable number of arguments.
    vaTest(10);       // 1 arg
    vaTest(1, 2, 3); // 3 args
    vaTest();         // no args
  }
}
```

The output from the program is the same as the original version.

There are two important things to notice about this program. First, as explained, inside **vaTest( )**, **v** is operated on as an array. This is because **v** *is* an array. The ... syntax simply tells the compiler that a variable number of arguments will be used and that these arguments will be stored in the array referred to by **v**. Second, in **main( )**, **vaTest( )** is called with different numbers of arguments, including no arguments at all. The arguments are automatically put in an array and passed to **v**. In the case of no arguments, the length of the array is zero.

A method can have "normal" parameters along with a variable-length parameter. However, the variable-length parameter must be the last parameter declared by the method. For example, this method declaration is perfectly acceptable:

```
int doIt(int a, int b, double c, int ... vals) {
```

In this case, the first three arguments used in a call to **doIt( )** are matched to the first three parameters. Then, any remaining arguments are assumed to belong to **vals**.

Remember, the varargs parameter must be last. For example, the following declaration is incorrect:

```
int doIt(int a, int b, double c, int ... vals, boolean stopFlag) { // Error!
```

Here, there is an attempt to declare a regular parameter after the varargs parameter, which is illegal.

There is one more restriction to be aware of: there must be only one varargs parameter. For example, this declaration is also invalid:

```
int doIt(int a, int b, double c, int ... vals, double ... morevals) { // Error!
```

The attempt to declare the second varargs parameter is illegal.

Here is a reworked version of the **vaTest( )** method that takes a regular argument and a variable-length argument:

```
// Use varargs with standard arguments.
class VarArgs2 {

  // Here, msg is a normal parameter and v is a
  // varargs parameter.
  static void vaTest(String msg, int ... v) {
    System.out.print(msg + v.length +
                     " Contents: ");

    for(int x : v)
      System.out.print(x + " ");

    System.out.println();
  }

  public static void main(String[] args)
  {
    vaTest("One vararg: ", 10);
    vaTest("Three varargs: ", 1, 2, 3);
    vaTest("No varargs: ");
  }
}
```

The output from this program is shown here:

```
One vararg: 1 Contents: 10
Three varargs: 3 Contents: 1 2 3
No varargs: 0 Contents:
```

## Overloading Vararg Methods

You can overload a method that takes a variable-length argument. For example, the following program overloads **vaTest( )** three times:

```
// Varargs and overloading.
class VarArgs3 {

  static void vaTest(int ... v) {
    System.out.print("vaTest(int ...): " +
                     "Number of args: " + v.length +
                     " Contents: ");

    for(int x : v)
      System.out.print(x + " ");

    System.out.println();
  }

  static void vaTest(boolean ... v) {
    System.out.print("vaTest(boolean ...) " +
                     "Number of args: " + v.length +
                     " Contents: ");

    for(boolean x : v)
      System.out.print(x + " ");

    System.out.println();
  }

  static void vaTest(String msg, int ... v) {
    System.out.print("vaTest(String, int ...): " +
                     msg + v.length +
                     " Contents: ");

    for(int x : v)
      System.out.print(x + " ");

    System.out.println();
  }

  public static void main(String[] args)
  {
    vaTest(1, 2, 3);
    vaTest("Testing: ", 10, 20);
    vaTest(true, false, false);
  }
}
```

The output produced by this program is shown here:

```
vaTest(int ...): Number of args: 3 Contents: 1 2 3
vaTest(String, int ...): Testing: 2 Contents: 10 20
vaTest(boolean ...) Number of args: 3 Contents: true false false
```

This program illustrates both ways that a varargs method can be overloaded. First, the types of its vararg parameter can differ. This is the case for **vaTest(int ...)** and **vaTest(boolean ...)**. Remember, the **...** causes the parameter to be treated as an array of the specified type. Therefore, just as you can overload methods by using different types of array parameters, you can overload vararg methods by using different types of varargs. In this case, Java uses the type difference to determine which overloaded method to call.

The second way to overload a varargs method is to add one or more normal parameters. This is what was done with **vaTest(String, int ...)**. In this case, Java uses both the number of arguments and the type of the arguments to determine which method to call.

---

**NOTE** A varargs method can also be overloaded by a non-varargs method. For example, **vaTest(int x)** is a valid overload of **vaTest( )** in the foregoing program. This version is invoked only when one **int** argument is present. When two or more **int** arguments are passed, the varargs version **vaTest (int...v)** is used.

## Varargs and Ambiguity

Somewhat unexpected errors can result when overloading a method that takes a variable-length argument. These errors involve ambiguity because it is possible to create an ambiguous call to an overloaded varargs method. For example, consider the following program:

```
// Varargs, overloading, and ambiguity.
//
// This program contains an error and will
// not compile!
class VarArgs4 {

  static void vaTest(int ... v) {
    System.out.print("vaTest(int ...): " +
                     "Number of args: " + v.length +
                     " Contents: ");

    for(int x : v)
      System.out.print(x + " ");

    System.out.println();
  }

  static void vaTest(boolean ... v) {
    System.out.print("vaTest(boolean ...) " +
                     "Number of args: " + v.length +
                     " Contents: ");

    for(boolean x : v)
      System.out.print(x + " ");

    System.out.println();
  }

  public static void main(String[] args)
  {
    vaTest(1, 2, 3); // OK
    vaTest(true, false, false); // OK
```

```
    vaTest(); // Error: Ambiguous!
  }
}
```

In this program, the overloading of **vaTest( )** is perfectly correct. However, this program will not compile because of the following call:

```
vaTest(); // Error: Ambiguous!
```

Because the vararg parameter can be empty, this call could be translated into a call to **vaTest(int ...)** or **vaTest(boolean ...)**. Both are equally valid. Thus, the call is inherently ambiguous.

Here is another example of ambiguity. The following overloaded versions of **vaTest( )** are inherently ambiguous even though one takes a normal parameter:

```
static void vaTest(int ... v) { // ...

static void vaTest(int n, int ... v) { // ...
```

Although the parameter lists of **vaTest( )** differ, there is no way for the compiler to resolve the following call:

```
vaTest(1)
```

Does this translate into a call to **vaTest(int ...)**, with one varargs argument, or into a call to **vaTest(int, int ...)** with no varargs arguments? There is no way for the compiler to answer this question. Thus, the situation is ambiguous.

Because of ambiguity errors like those just shown, sometimes you will need to forego overloading and simply use two different method names. Also, in some cases, ambiguity errors expose a conceptual flaw in your code, which you can remedy by more carefully crafting a solution.

# Local Variable Type Inference with Reference Types

As you saw in Chapter 3, beginning with JDK 10, Java supports local variable type inference. Recall that when using local variable type inference, the type of the variable is specified as **var** and the variable must be initialized. Earlier examples have shown type inference with primitive types, but it can also be used with reference types. In fact, type inference with reference types constitutes a primary use. Here is a simple example that declares a **String** variable called **myStr**:

```
var myStr = "This is a string";
```

Because a quoted string is used as an initializer, the type **String** is inferred.

As explained in Chapter 3, one of the benefits of local variable type inference is its ability to streamline code, and it is with reference types where such streamlining is most apparent.

The reason for this is that many class types in Java have rather long names. For example, in Chapter 13, you will learn about the **FileInputStream** class, which is used to open a file for input operations. In the past, you would declare and initialize a **FileInputStream** using a traditional declaration like the one shown here:

```
FileInputStream fin = new FileInputStream("test.txt");
```

With the use of **var**, it can now be written like this:

```
var fin = new FileInputStream("test.txt");
```

Here, **fin** is inferred to be of type **FileInputStream** because that is the type of its initializer. There is no need to explicitly repeat the type name. As a result, this declaration of **fin** is substantially shorter than writing it the traditional way. Thus, the use of **var** streamlines the declaration. This benefit becomes even more apparent in more complex declarations, such as those involving generics. In general, the streamlining attribute of local variable type inference helps lessen the tedium of entering long type names into your program.

Of course, the streamlining aspect of local variable type inference must be used carefully to avoid reducing the readability of your program and, thus, obscuring its meaning. For example, consider a declaration such as the one shown here:

```
var x = o.getNext();
```

In this case, it may not be immediately clear to someone reading your code what the type of **x** is. In essence, local variable type inference is a feature that you should use wisely.

As you would expect, you can also use local variable type inference with user-defined classes, as the following program illustrates. It creates a class called **MyClass** and then uses local variable type inference to declare and initialize an object of that class.

```
// Local variable type inference with a user-defined class type.
class MyClass {
  private int i;

  MyClass(int k) { i = k;}

  int geti() { return i; }
  void seti(int k) { if(k >= 0) i = k; }
}

class RefVarDemo {
  public static void main(String[] args) {
    var mc = new MyClass(10); // Notice the use of var here.

    System.out.println("Value of i in mc is " + mc.geti());
    mc.seti(19);
    System.out.println("Value of i in mc is now " + mc.geti());
  }
}
```

The output of the program is shown here:

```
Value of i in mc is 10
Value of i in mc is now 19
```

In the program, pay special attention to this line:

```
var mc = new MyClass(10); // Notice the use of var here.
```

Here, the type of **mc** will be inferred as **MyClass** because that is the type of the initializer, which is a new **MyClass** object.

As explained earlier in this book, for the benefit of readers working in Java environments that do not support local variable type inference, it will not be used by most examples in the remainder of this edition of this book. This way, the majority of examples will compile and run for the largest number of readers.

CHAPTER

# 8 Inheritance

Inheritance is one of the cornerstones of object-oriented programming because it allows the creation of hierarchical classifications. Using inheritance, you can create a general class that defines traits common to a set of related items. This class can then be inherited by other, more specific classes, each adding those things that are unique to it. In the terminology of Java, a class that is inherited is called a *superclass*. The class that does the inheriting is called a *subclass*. Therefore, a subclass is a specialized version of a superclass. It inherits all of the members defined by the superclass and adds its own, unique elements.

## Inheritance Basics

In order to have your class inherit from a superclass, you simply incorporate the definition of the superclass into your class using the **extends** keyword. To see how, let's begin with a short example. The following program creates a superclass called **A** and a subclass called **B**. Notice how the keyword **extends** is used to create a subclass of **A**.

```
// A simple example of inheritance.

// Create a superclass.
class A {
  int i, j;

  void showij() {
    System.out.println("i and j: " + i + " " + j);
  }
}

// Create a subclass by extending class A.
class B extends A {
  int k;

  void showk() {
    System.out.println("k: " + k);
  }
```

```
  void sum() {
    System.out.println("i+j+k: " + (i+j+k));
  }
}

class SimpleInheritance {
  public static void main(String[] args) {
    A superOb = new A();
    B subOb = new B();

    // The superclass may be used by itself.
    superOb.i = 10;
    superOb.j = 20;
    System.out.println("Contents of superOb: ");
    superOb.showij();
    System.out.println();

    /* The subclass has access to all public members of
       its superclass. */
    subOb.i = 7;
    subOb.j = 8;
    subOb.k = 9;
    System.out.println("Contents of subOb: ");
    subOb.showij();
    subOb.showk();
    System.out.println();

    System.out.println("Sum of i, j and k in subOb:");
    subOb.sum();
  }
}
```

The output from this program is shown here:

```
Contents of superOb:
i and j: 10 20

Contents of subOb:
i and j: 7 8
k: 9

Sum of i, j and k in subOb:
i+j+k: 24
```

As you can see, the subclass **B** includes all of the members of its superclass, **A**. This is why **subOb** can access **i** and **j** and call **showij( )**. Also, inside **sum( )**, **i** and **j** can be referred to directly, as if they were part of **B**.

Even though **A** is a superclass for **B**, it is also a completely independent, stand-alone class. Being a superclass for a subclass does not mean that the superclass cannot be used by itself. Further, a subclass can be a superclass for another subclass.

The general form of a **class** declaration that inherits a superclass is shown here:

class *subclass-name* extends *superclass-name* {
  // body of class
}

You can only specify one superclass for any subclass that you create. Java does not support the inheritance of multiple superclasses into a single subclass. You can, as stated, create a hierarchy of inheritance in which a subclass becomes a superclass of another subclass. However, no class can be a superclass of itself.

## Member Access and Inheritance

Although a subclass includes all of the members of its superclass, it cannot access those members of the superclass that have been declared as **private**. For example, consider the following simple class hierarchy:

```
/* In a class hierarchy, private members remain
   private to their class.

   This program contains an error and will not
   compile.
*/

// Create a superclass.
class A {
  int i; // default access
  private int j; // private to A

  void setij(int x, int y) {
    i = x;
    j = y;
  }
}

// A's j is not accessible here.
class B extends A {
  int total;

  void sum() {
    total = i + j; // ERROR, j is not accessible here
  }
}

class Access {
  public static void main(String[] args) {
    B subOb = new B();

    subOb.setij(10, 12);

    subOb.sum();
    System.out.println("Total is " + subOb.total);
  }
}
```

This program will not compile because the use of **j** inside the **sum( )** method of **B** causes an access violation. Since **j** is declared as **private**, it is only accessible by other members of its own class. Subclasses have no access to it.

---

**REMEMBER** A class member that has been declared as private will remain private to its class. It is not accessible by any code outside its class, including subclasses.

## A More Practical Example

Let's look at a more practical example that will help illustrate the power of inheritance. Here, the final version of the **Box** class developed in the preceding chapter will be extended to include a fourth component called **weight**. Thus, the new class will contain a box's width, height, depth, and weight.

```
// This program uses inheritance to extend Box.
class Box {
  double width;
  double height;
  double depth;

  // construct clone of an object
  Box(Box ob) { // pass object to constructor
    width = ob.width;
    height = ob.height;
    depth = ob.depth;
  }

  // constructor used when all dimensions specified
  Box(double w, double h, double d) {
    width = w;
    height = h;
    depth = d;
  }

  // constructor used when no dimensions specified
  Box() {
    width = -1;  // use  -1 to indicate
    height = -1; // an uninitialized
    depth = -1;  // box
  }

  // constructor used when cube is created
  Box(double len) {
    width = height = depth = len;
  }

  // compute and return volume
  double volume() {
    return width * height * depth;
  }
}

// Here, Box is extended to include weight.
class BoxWeight extends Box {
```

```
  double weight; // weight of box

  // constructor for BoxWeight
  BoxWeight(double w, double h, double d, double m) {
    width = w;
    height = h;
    depth = d;
    weight = m;
  }
}

class DemoBoxWeight {
  public static void main(String[] args) {
    BoxWeight mybox1 = new BoxWeight(10, 20, 15, 34.3);
    BoxWeight mybox2 = new BoxWeight(2, 3, 4, 0.076);
    double vol;

    vol = mybox1.volume();
    System.out.println("Volume of mybox1 is " + vol);
    System.out.println("Weight of mybox1 is " + mybox1.weight);
    System.out.println();

    vol = mybox2.volume();
    System.out.println("Volume of mybox2 is " + vol);
    System.out.println("Weight of mybox2 is " + mybox2.weight);
  }
}
```

The output from this program is shown here:

```
Volume of mybox1 is 3000.0
Weight of mybox1 is 34.3

Volume of mybox2 is 24.0
Weight of mybox2 is 0.076
```

**BoxWeight** inherits all of the characteristics of **Box** and adds to them the **weight** component. It is not necessary for **BoxWeight** to re-create all of the features found in **Box**. It can simply extend **Box** to meet its own purposes.

A major advantage of inheritance is that once you have created a superclass that defines the attributes common to a set of objects, it can be used to create any number of more specific subclasses. Each subclass can precisely tailor its own classification. For example, the following class inherits **Box** and adds a color attribute:

```
// Here, Box is extended to include color.
class ColorBox extends Box {
  int color; // color of box

  ColorBox(double w, double h, double d, int c) {
    width = w;
    height = h;
    depth = d;
    color = c;
  }
}
```

Remember, once you have created a superclass that defines the general aspects of an object, that superclass can be inherited to form specialized classes. Each subclass simply adds its own unique attributes. This is the essence of inheritance.

## A Superclass Variable Can Reference a Subclass Object

A reference variable of a superclass can be assigned a reference to any subclass derived from that superclass. You will find this aspect of inheritance quite useful in a variety of situations. For example, consider the following:

```
class RefDemo {
  public static void main(String[] args) {
    BoxWeight weightbox = new BoxWeight(3, 5, 7, 8.37);
    Box plainbox = new Box();
    double vol;

    vol = weightbox.volume();
    System.out.println("Volume of weightbox is " + vol);
    System.out.println("Weight of weightbox is " +
                       weightbox.weight);
    System.out.println();

    // assign BoxWeight reference to Box reference
    plainbox = weightbox;

    vol = plainbox.volume(); // OK, volume() defined in Box
    System.out.println("Volume of plainbox is " + vol);

    /* The following statement is invalid because plainbox
       does not define a weight member. */
//  System.out.println("Weight of plainbox is " + plainbox.weight);
  }
}
```

Here, **weightbox** is a reference to **BoxWeight** objects, and **plainbox** is a reference to **Box** objects. Since **BoxWeight** is a subclass of **Box**, it is permissible to assign **plainbox** a reference to the **weightbox** object.

It is important to understand that it is the type of the reference variable—not the type of the object that it refers to—that determines what members can be accessed. That is, when a reference to a subclass object is assigned to a superclass reference variable, you will have access only to those parts of the object defined by the superclass. This is why **plainbox** can't access **weight** even when it refers to a **BoxWeight** object. If you think about it, this makes sense, because the superclass has no knowledge of what a subclass adds to it. This is why the last line of code in the preceding fragment is commented out. It is not possible for a **Box** reference to access the **weight** field, because **Box** does not define one.

Although the preceding may seem a bit esoteric, it has some important practical applications—two of which are discussed later in this chapter.

## Using super

In the preceding examples, classes derived from **Box** were not implemented as efficiently or as robustly as they could have been. For example, the constructor for **BoxWeight** explicitly initializes the **width**, **height**, and **depth** fields of **Box**. Not only does this duplicate code found in its superclass, which is inefficient, but it implies that a subclass must be granted access to these members. However, there will be times when you will want to create a superclass that keeps the details of its implementation to itself (that is, that keeps its data members private). In this case, there would be no way for a subclass to directly access or initialize these variables on its own. Since encapsulation is a primary attribute of OOP, it is not surprising that Java provides a solution to this problem. Whenever a subclass needs to refer to its immediate superclass, it can do so by use of the keyword **super**.

**super** has two general forms. The first calls the superclass's constructor. The second is used to access a member of the superclass that has been hidden by a member of a subclass. Each use is examined here.

### Using super to Call Superclass Constructors

A subclass can call a constructor defined by its superclass by use of the following form of **super**:

super(*arg-list*);

Here, *arg-list* specifies any arguments needed by the constructor in the superclass. **super( )** must always be the first statement executed inside a subclass's constructor.

To see how **super( )** is used, consider this improved version of the **BoxWeight** class:

```
// BoxWeight now uses super to initialize its Box attributes.
class BoxWeight extends Box {
  double weight; // weight of box

  // initialize width, height, and depth using super()
  BoxWeight(double w, double h, double d, double m) {
    super(w, h, d); // call superclass constructor
    weight = m;
  }
}
```

Here, **BoxWeight( )** calls **super( )** with the arguments **w**, **h**, and **d**. This causes the **Box** constructor to be called, which initializes **width**, **height**, and **depth** using these values. **BoxWeight** no longer initializes these values itself. It only needs to initialize the value unique to it: **weight**. This leaves **Box** free to make these values **private** if desired.

In the preceding example, **super( )** was called with three arguments. Since constructors can be overloaded, **super( )** can be called using any form defined by the superclass. The constructor executed will be the one that matches the arguments. For example, here is a complete implementation of **BoxWeight** that provides constructors for the various ways that a box can be constructed. In each case, **super( )** is called using the appropriate arguments. Notice that **width, height**, and **depth** have been made private within **Box**.

```
// A complete implementation of BoxWeight.
class Box {
  private double width;
  private double height;
  private double depth;

  // construct clone of an object
  Box(Box ob) { // pass object to constructor
    width = ob.width;
    height = ob.height;
    depth = ob.depth;
  }

  // constructor used when all dimensions specified
  Box(double w, double h, double d) {
    width = w;
    height = h;
    depth = d;
  }

  // constructor used when no dimensions specified
  Box() {
    width = -1;  // use -1 to indicate
    height = -1; // an uninitialized
    depth = -1;  // box
  }

  // constructor used when cube is created
  Box(double len) {
    width = height = depth = len;
  }

  // compute and return volume
  double volume() {
    return width * height * depth;
  }
}

// BoxWeight now fully implements all constructors.
class BoxWeight extends Box {
  double weight; // weight of box

  // construct clone of an object
  BoxWeight(BoxWeight ob) { // pass object to constructor
    super(ob);
    weight = ob.weight;
  }

  // constructor when all parameters are specified
  BoxWeight(double w, double h, double d, double m) {
```

```
    super(w, h, d); // call superclass constructor
    weight = m;
  }

  // default constructor
  BoxWeight() {
    super();
    weight = -1;
  }

  // constructor used when cube is created
  BoxWeight(double len, double m) {
    super(len);
    weight = m;
  }
}

class DemoSuper {
  public static void main(String[] args) {
    BoxWeight mybox1 = new BoxWeight(10, 20, 15, 34.3);
    BoxWeight mybox2 = new BoxWeight(2, 3, 4, 0.076);
    BoxWeight mybox3 = new BoxWeight(); // default
    BoxWeight mycube = new BoxWeight(3, 2);
    BoxWeight myclone = new BoxWeight(mybox1);
    double vol;

    vol = mybox1.volume();
    System.out.println("Volume of mybox1 is " + vol);
    System.out.println("Weight of mybox1 is " + mybox1.weight);
    System.out.println();

    vol = mybox2.volume();
    System.out.println("Volume of mybox2 is " + vol);
    System.out.println("Weight of mybox2 is " + mybox2.weight);
    System.out.println();

    vol = mybox3.volume();
    System.out.println("Volume of mybox3 is " + vol);
    System.out.println("Weight of mybox3 is " + mybox3.weight);
    System.out.println();

    vol = myclone.volume();
    System.out.println("Volume of myclone is " + vol);
    System.out.println("Weight of myclone is " + myclone.weight);
    System.out.println();

    vol = mycube.volume();
    System.out.println("Volume of mycube is " + vol);
    System.out.println("Weight of mycube is " + mycube.weight);
    System.out.println();
  }
}
```

Part I

This program generates the following output:

```
Volume of mybox1 is 3000.0
Weight of mybox1 is 34.3

Volume of mybox2 is 24.0
Weight of mybox2 is 0.076

Volume of mybox3 is -1.0
Weight of mybox3 is -1.0

Volume of myclone is 3000.0
Weight of myclone is 34.3

Volume of mycube is 27.0
Weight of mycube is 2.0
```

Pay special attention to this constructor in **BoxWeight**:

```
// construct clone of an object
BoxWeight(BoxWeight ob) { // pass object to constructor
  super(ob);
  weight = ob.weight;
}
```

Notice that **super( )** is passed an object of type **BoxWeight**—not of type **Box**. This still invokes the constructor **Box(Box ob)**. As mentioned earlier, a superclass variable can be used to reference any object derived from that class. Thus, we are able to pass a **BoxWeight** object to the **Box** constructor. Of course, **Box** only has knowledge of its own members.

Let's review the key concepts behind **super( )**. When a subclass calls **super( )**, it is calling the constructor of its immediate superclass. Thus, **super( )** always refers to the superclass immediately above the calling class. This is true even in a multileveled hierarchy. Also, **super( )** must always be the first statement executed inside a subclass constructor.

## A Second Use for super

The second form of **super** acts somewhat like **this**, except that it always refers to the superclass of the subclass in which it is used. This usage has the following general form:

super.*member*

Here, *member* can be either a method or an instance variable.

This second form of **super** is most applicable to situations in which member names of a subclass hide members by the same name in the superclass. Consider this simple class hierarchy:

```
// Using super to overcome name hiding.
class A {
  int i;
}

// Create a subclass by extending class A.
```

```
class B extends A {
  int i; // this i hides the i in A

  B(int a, int b) {
    super.i = a; // i in A
    i = b; // i in B
  }

  void show() {
    System.out.println("i in superclass: " + super.i);
    System.out.println("i in subclass: " + i);
  }
}

class UseSuper {
  public static void main(String[] args) {
    B subOb = new B(1, 2);

    subOb.show();
  }
}
```

This program displays the following:

```
i in superclass: 1
i in subclass: 2
```

Although the instance variable **i** in **B** hides the **i** in **A**, **super** allows access to the **i** defined in the superclass. As you will see, **super** can also be used to call methods that are hidden by a subclass.

# Creating a Multilevel Hierarchy

Up to this point, we have been using simple class hierarchies that consist of only a superclass and a subclass. However, you can build hierarchies that contain as many layers of inheritance as you like. As mentioned, it is perfectly acceptable to use a subclass as a superclass of another. For example, given three classes called **A**, **B**, and **C**, **C** can be a subclass of **B**, which is a subclass of **A**. When this type of situation occurs, each subclass inherits all of the traits found in all of its superclasses. In this case, **C** inherits all aspects of **B** and **A**. To see how a multilevel hierarchy can be useful, consider the following program. In it, the subclass **BoxWeight** is used as a superclass to create the subclass called **Shipment**. **Shipment** inherits all of the traits of **BoxWeight** and **Box**, and it adds a field called **cost**, which holds the cost of shipping such a parcel.

```
// Extend BoxWeight to include shipping costs.

// Start with Box.
class Box {
  private double width;
  private double height;
  private double depth;
```

```
    // construct clone of an object
    Box(Box ob) { // pass object to constructor
      width = ob.width;
      height = ob.height;
      depth = ob.depth;
    }

    // constructor used when all dimensions specified
    Box(double w, double h, double d) {
      width = w;
      height = h;
      depth = d;
    }

    // constructor used when no dimensions specified
    Box() {
      width = -1;  // use -1 to indicate
      height = -1; // an uninitialized
      depth = -1;  // box
    }

    // constructor used when cube is created
    Box(double len) {
      width = height = depth = len;
    }

    // compute and return volume
    double volume() {
      return width * height * depth;
    }
  }

  // Add weight.
  class BoxWeight extends Box {
    double weight; // weight of box

    // construct clone of an object
    BoxWeight(BoxWeight ob) { // pass object to constructor
      super(ob);
      weight = ob.weight;
    }

    // constructor when all parameters are specified
    BoxWeight(double w, double h, double d, double m) {
      super(w, h, d); // call superclass constructor
      weight = m;
    }

    // default constructor
    BoxWeight() {
      super();
      weight = -1;
    }
```

```
  // constructor used when cube is created
  BoxWeight(double len, double m) {
    super(len);
    weight = m;
  }
}

// Add shipping costs.
class Shipment extends BoxWeight {
  double cost;

  // construct clone of an object
  Shipment(Shipment ob) { // pass object to constructor
    super(ob);
    cost = ob.cost;
  }

  // constructor when all parameters are specified
  Shipment(double w, double h, double d,
           double m, double c) {
    super(w, h, d, m); // call superclass constructor
    cost = c;
  }

  // default constructor
  Shipment() {
    super();
    cost = -1;
  }

  // constructor used when cube is created
  Shipment(double len, double m, double c) {
    super(len, m);
    cost = c;
  }
}

class DemoShipment {
  public static void main(String[] args) {
    Shipment shipment1 =
               new Shipment(10, 20, 15, 10, 3.41);
    Shipment shipment2 =
               new Shipment(2, 3, 4, 0.76, 1.28);

    double vol;

    vol = shipment1.volume();
    System.out.println("Volume of shipment1 is " + vol);
    System.out.println("Weight of shipment1 is "
                        + shipment1.weight);
    System.out.println("Shipping cost: $" + shipment1.cost);
    System.out.println();
```

```
    vol = shipment2.volume();
    System.out.println("Volume of shipment2 is " + vol);
    System.out.println("Weight of shipment2 is "
                        + shipment2.weight);
    System.out.println("Shipping cost: $" + shipment2.cost);
  }
}
```

The output of this program is shown here:

```
Volume of shipment1 is 3000.0
Weight of shipment1 is 10.0
Shipping cost: $3.41

Volume of shipment2 is 24.0
Weight of shipment2 is 0.76
Shipping cost: $1.28
```

Because of inheritance, **Shipment** can make use of the previously defined classes of **Box** and **BoxWeight**, adding only the extra information it needs for its own, specific application. This is part of the value of inheritance; it allows the reuse of code.

This example illustrates one other important point: **super( )** always refers to the constructor in the closest superclass. The **super( )** in **Shipment** calls the constructor in **BoxWeight**. The **super( )** in **BoxWeight** calls the constructor in **Box**. In a class hierarchy, if a superclass constructor requires arguments, then all subclasses must pass those arguments "up the line." This is true whether or not a subclass needs arguments of its own.

**NOTE** In the preceding program, the entire class hierarchy, including **Box**, **BoxWeight**, and **Shipment**, is shown all in one file. This is for your convenience only. In Java, all three classes could have been placed into their own files and compiled separately. In fact, using separate files is the norm, not the exception, in creating class hierarchies.

## When Constructors Are Executed

When a class hierarchy is created, in what order are the constructors for the classes that make up the hierarchy executed? For example, given a subclass called **B** and a superclass called **A**, is **A**'s constructor executed before **B**'s, or vice versa? The answer is that in a class hierarchy, constructors complete their execution in order of derivation, from superclass to subclass. Further, since **super( )** must be the first statement executed in a subclass's constructor, this order is the same whether or not **super( )** is used. If **super( )** is not used, then the default or parameterless constructor of each superclass will be executed. The following program illustrates when constructors are executed:

```
// Demonstrate when constructors are executed.

// Create a super class.
class A {
  A() {
    System.out.println("Inside A's constructor.");
  }
}
```

```
// Create a subclass by extending class A.
class B extends A {
  B() {
    System.out.println("Inside B's constructor.");
  }
}

// Create another subclass by extending B.
class C extends B {
  C() {
    System.out.println("Inside C's constructor.");
  }
}

class CallingCons {
  public static void main(String[] args) {
    C c = new C();
  }
}
```

The output from this program is shown here:

```
Inside A's constructor
Inside B's constructor
Inside C's constructor
```

As you can see, the constructors are executed in order of derivation.

If you think about it, it makes sense that constructors complete their execution in order of derivation. Because a superclass has no knowledge of any subclass, any initialization it needs to perform is separate from and possibly prerequisite to any initialization performed by the subclass. Therefore, it must complete its execution first.

# Method Overriding

In a class hierarchy, when a method in a subclass has the same name and type signature as a method in its superclass, then the method in the subclass is said to *override* the method in the superclass. When an overridden method is called through its subclass, it will always refer to the version of that method defined by the subclass. The version of the method defined by the superclass will be hidden. Consider the following:

```
// Method overriding.
class A {
  int i, j;
  A(int a, int b) {
    i = a;
    j = b;
  }

  // display i and j
  void show() {
    System.out.println("i and j: " + i + " " + j);
  }
}
```

```
class B extends A {
  int k;

  B(int a, int b, int c) {
    super(a, b);
    k = c;
  }

  // display k - this overrides show() in A
  void show() {
    System.out.println("k: " + k);
  }
}

class Override {
  public static void main(String[] args) {
    B subOb = new B(1, 2, 3);

    subOb.show(); // this calls show() in B
  }
}
```

The output produced by this program is shown here:

```
k: 3
```

When **show( )** is invoked on an object of type **B**, the version of **show( )** defined within **B** is used. That is, the version of **show( )** inside **B** overrides the version declared in **A**.

If you wish to access the superclass version of an overridden method, you can do so by using **super**. For example, in this version of **B**, the superclass version of **show( )** is invoked within the subclass's version. This allows all instance variables to be displayed.

```
class B extends A {
  int k;

  B(int a, int b, int c) {
    super(a, b);
    k = c;
  }

  void show() {
    super.show(); // this calls A's show()
    System.out.println("k: " + k);
  }
}
```

If you substitute this version of **A** into the previous program, you will see the following output:

```
i and j: 1 2
k: 3
```

Here, **super.show( )** calls the superclass version of **show( )**.

Method overriding occurs *only* when the names and the type signatures of the two methods are identical. If they are not, then the two methods are simply overloaded. For example, consider this modified version of the preceding example:

```
// Methods with differing type signatures are overloaded - not
// overridden.
class A {
  int i, j;

  A(int a, int b) {
    i = a;
    j = b;
  }

  // display i and j
  void show() {
    System.out.println("i and j: " + i + " " + j);
  }
}

// Create a subclass by extending class A.
class B extends A {
  int k;

  B(int a, int b, int c) {
    super(a, b);
    k = c;
  }

  // overload show()
  void show(String msg) {
    System.out.println(msg + k);
  }
}

class Override {
  public static void main(String[] args) {
    B subOb = new B(1, 2, 3);

    subOb.show("This is k: "); // this calls show() in B
    subOb.show(); // this calls show() in A
  }
}
```

The output produced by this program is shown here:

```
This is k: 3
i and j: 1 2
```

The version of **show( )** in **B** takes a string parameter. This makes its type signature different from the one in **A**, which takes no parameters. Therefore, no overriding (or name hiding) takes place. Instead, the version of **show( )** in **B** simply overloads the version of **show( )** in **A**.

## Dynamic Method Dispatch

While the examples in the preceding section demonstrate the mechanics of method overriding, they do not show its power. Indeed, if there were nothing more to method overriding than a name space convention, then it would be, at best, an interesting curiosity, but of little real value. However, this is not the case. Method overriding forms the basis for one of Java's most powerful concepts: *dynamic method dispatch*. Dynamic method dispatch is the mechanism by which a call to an overridden method is resolved at run time, rather than compile time. Dynamic method dispatch is important because this is how Java implements run-time polymorphism.

Let's begin by restating an important principle: a superclass reference variable can refer to a subclass object. Java uses this fact to resolve calls to overridden methods at run time. Here is how. When an overridden method is called through a superclass reference, Java determines which version of that method to execute based upon the type of the object being referred to at the time the call occurs. Thus, this determination is made at run time. When different types of objects are referred to, different versions of an overridden method will be called. In other words, *it is the type of the object being referred to* (not the type of the reference variable) that determines which version of an overridden method will be executed. Therefore, if a superclass contains a method that is overridden by a subclass, then when different types of objects are referred to through a superclass reference variable, different versions of the method are executed.

Here is an example that illustrates dynamic method dispatch:

```
// Dynamic Method Dispatch
class A {
  void callme() {
    System.out.println("Inside A's callme method");
  }
}

class B extends A {
  // override callme()
  void callme() {
    System.out.println("Inside B's callme method");
  }
}

class C extends A {
  // override callme()
  void callme() {
    System.out.println("Inside C's callme method");
  }
}

class Dispatch {
  public static void main(String[] args) {
    A a = new A(); // object of type A
    B b = new B(); // object of type B
    C c = new C(); // object of type C
```

```
    A r; // obtain a reference of type A

    r = a; // r refers to an A object
    r.callme(); // calls A's version of callme

    r = b; // r refers to a B object
    r.callme(); // calls B's version of callme

    r = c; // r refers to a C object
    r.callme(); // calls C's version of callme
  }
}
```

The output from the program is shown here:

```
Inside A's callme method
Inside B's callme method
Inside C's callme method
```

This program creates one superclass called **A** and two subclasses of it, called **B** and **C**. Subclasses **B** and **C** override **callme( )** declared in **A**. Inside the **main( )** method, objects of type **A**, **B**, and **C** are declared. Also, a reference of type **A**, called **r**, is declared. The program then in turn assigns a reference to each type of object to **r** and uses that reference to invoke **callme( )**. As the output shows, the version of **callme( )** executed is determined by the type of object being referred to at the time of the call. Had it been determined by the type of the reference variable, **r**, you would see three calls to **A**'s **callme( )** method.

---

**NOTE** Readers familiar with C++ or C# will recognize that overridden methods in Java are similar to virtual functions in those languages.

## Why Overridden Methods?

As stated earlier, overridden methods allow Java to support run-time polymorphism. Polymorphism is essential to object-oriented programming for one reason: it allows a general class to specify methods that will be common to all of its derivatives, while allowing subclasses to define the specific implementation of some or all of those methods. Overridden methods are another way that Java implements the "one interface, multiple methods" aspect of polymorphism.

Part of the key to successfully applying polymorphism is understanding that the superclasses and subclasses form a hierarchy that moves from lesser to greater specialization. Used correctly, the superclass provides all elements that a subclass can use directly. It also defines those methods that the derived class must implement on its own. This allows the subclass the flexibility to define its own methods, yet still enforces a consistent interface. Thus, by combining inheritance with overridden methods, a superclass can define the general form of the methods that will be used by all of its subclasses.

Dynamic, run-time polymorphism is one of the most powerful mechanisms that object-oriented design brings to bear on code reuse and robustness. The ability of existing code libraries to call methods on instances of new classes without recompiling while maintaining a clean abstract interface is a profoundly powerful tool.

## Applying Method Overriding

Let's look at a more practical example that uses method overriding. The following program creates a superclass called **Figure** that stores the dimensions of a two-dimensional object. It also defines a method called **area( )** that computes the area of an object. The program derives two subclasses from **Figure**. The first is **Rectangle** and the second is **Triangle**. Each of these subclasses overrides **area( )** so that it returns the area of a rectangle and a triangle, respectively.

```
// Using run-time polymorphism.
class Figure {
  double dim1;
  double dim2;

  Figure(double a, double b) {
    dim1 = a;
    dim2 = b;
  }

  double area() {
    System.out.println("Area for Figure is undefined.");
    return 0;
  }
}

class Rectangle extends Figure {
  Rectangle(double a, double b) {
    super(a, b);
  }

  // override area for rectangle
  double area() {
    System.out.println("Inside Area for Rectangle.");
    return dim1 * dim2;
  }
}

class Triangle extends Figure {
  Triangle(double a, double b) {
    super(a, b);
  }

  // override area for right triangle
  double area() {
    System.out.println("Inside Area for Triangle.");
    return dim1 * dim2 / 2;
  }
}

class FindAreas {
  public static void main(String[] args) {
    Figure f = new Figure(10, 10);
    Rectangle r = new Rectangle(9, 5);
```

```
    Triangle t = new Triangle(10, 8);
    Figure figref;

    figref = r;
    System.out.println("Area is " + figref.area());

    figref = t;
    System.out.println("Area is " + figref.area());

    figref = f;
    System.out.println("Area is " + figref.area());
  }
}
```

The output from the program is shown here:

```
Inside Area for Rectangle.
Area is 45
Inside Area for Triangle.
Area is 40
Area for Figure is undefined.
Area is 0
```

Through the dual mechanisms of inheritance and run-time polymorphism, it is possible to define one consistent interface that is used by several different, yet related, types of objects. In this case, if an object is derived from **Figure**, then its area can be obtained by calling **area( )**. The interface to this operation is the same no matter what type of figure is being used.

## Using Abstract Classes

There are situations in which you will want to define a superclass that declares the structure of a given abstraction without providing a complete implementation of every method. That is, sometimes you will want to create a superclass that only defines a generalized form that will be shared by all of its subclasses, leaving it to each subclass to fill in the details. Such a class determines the nature of the methods that the subclasses must implement. One way this situation can occur is when a superclass is unable to create a meaningful implementation for a method. This is the case with the class **Figure** used in the preceding example. The definition of **area( )** is simply a placeholder. It will not compute and display the area of any type of object.

As you will see as you create your own class libraries, it is not uncommon for a method to have no meaningful definition in the context of its superclass. You can handle this situation two ways. One way, as shown in the previous example, is to simply have it report a warning message. While this approach can be useful in certain situations—such as debugging—it is not usually appropriate. You may have methods that must be overridden by the subclass in order for the subclass to have any meaning. Consider the class **Triangle**. It has no meaning if **area( )** is not defined. In this case, you want some way to ensure that a subclass does, indeed, override all necessary methods. Java's solution to this problem is the *abstract method*.

You can require that certain methods be overridden by subclasses by specifying the **abstract** type modifier. These methods are sometimes referred to as *subclasser responsibility* because they have no implementation specified in the superclass. Thus, a subclass must override them—it cannot simply use the version defined in the superclass. To declare an abstract method, use this general form:

abstract *type name*(*parameter-list*);

As you can see, no method body is present.

Any class that contains one or more abstract methods must also be declared abstract. To declare a class abstract, you simply use the **abstract** keyword in front of the **class** keyword at the beginning of the class declaration. There can be no objects of an abstract class. That is, an abstract class cannot be directly instantiated with the **new** operator. Such objects would be useless, because an abstract class is not fully defined. Also, you cannot declare abstract constructors or abstract static methods. Any subclass of an abstract class must either implement all of the abstract methods in the superclass or be declared **abstract** itself.

Here is a simple example of a class with an abstract method, followed by a class which implements that method:

```
// A Simple demonstration of abstract.
abstract class A {
  abstract void callme();

  // concrete methods are still allowed in abstract classes
  void callmetoo() {
    System.out.println("This is a concrete method.");
  }
}

class B extends A {
  void callme() {
    System.out.println("B's implementation of callme.");
  }
}

class AbstractDemo {
  public static void main(String[] args) {
    B b = new B();

    b.callme();
    b.callmetoo();
  }
}
```

Notice that no objects of class **A** are declared in the program. As mentioned, it is not possible to instantiate an abstract class. One other point: class **A** implements a concrete method called **callmetoo( )**. This is perfectly acceptable. Abstract classes can include as much implementation as they see fit.

Although abstract classes cannot be used to instantiate objects, they can be used to create object references, because Java's approach to run-time polymorphism is implemented through the use of superclass references. Thus, it must be possible to create a reference to an abstract class so that it can be used to point to a subclass object. You will see this feature put to use in the next example.

Using an abstract class, you can improve the **Figure** class shown earlier. Since there is no meaningful concept of area for an undefined two-dimensional figure, the following version of the program declares **area( )** as abstract inside **Figure**. This, of course, means that all classes derived from **Figure** must override **area( )**.

```
// Using abstract methods and classes.
abstract class Figure {
  double dim1;
  double dim2;

  Figure(double a, double b) {
    dim1 = a;
    dim2 = b;
  }

  // area is now an abstract method
  abstract double area();
}

class Rectangle extends Figure {
  Rectangle(double a, double b) {
    super(a, b);
  }

  // override area for rectangle
  double area() {
    System.out.println("Inside Area for Rectangle.");
    return dim1 * dim2;
  }
}

class Triangle extends Figure {
  Triangle(double a, double b) {
    super(a, b);
  }

  // override area for right triangle
  double area() {
    System.out.println("Inside Area for Triangle.");
    return dim1 * dim2 / 2;
  }
}

class AbstractAreas {
  public static void main(String[] args) {
  // Figure f = new Figure(10, 10); // illegal now
    Rectangle r = new Rectangle(9, 5);
    Triangle t = new Triangle(10, 8);
    Figure figref; // this is OK, no object is created

    figref = r;
    System.out.println("Area is " + figref.area());
```

```
    figref = t;
    System.out.println("Area is " + figref.area());
  }
}
```

As the comment inside **main( )** indicates, it is no longer possible to declare objects of type **Figure**, since it is now abstract. And, all subclasses of **Figure** must override **area( )**. To prove this to yourself, try creating a subclass that does not override **area( )**. You will receive a compile-time error.

Although it is not possible to create an object of type **Figure**, you can create a reference variable of type **Figure**. The variable **figref** is declared as a reference to **Figure**, which means that it can be used to refer to an object of any class derived from **Figure**. As explained, it is through superclass reference variables that overridden methods are resolved at run time.

# Using final with Inheritance

The keyword **final** has three uses. First, it can be used to create the equivalent of a named constant. This use was described in the preceding chapter. The other two uses of **final** apply to inheritance. Both are examined here.

## Using final to Prevent Overriding

While method overriding is one of Java's most powerful features, there will be times when you will want to prevent it from occurring. To disallow a method from being overridden, specify **final** as a modifier at the start of its declaration. Methods declared as **final** cannot be overridden. The following fragment illustrates **final**:

```
class A {
  final void meth() {
    System.out.println("This is a final method.");
  }
}

class B extends A {
  void meth() { // ERROR! Can't override.
    System.out.println("Illegal!");
  }
}
```

Because **meth( )** is declared as **final**, it cannot be overridden in **B**. If you attempt to do so, a compile-time error will result.

Methods declared as **final** can sometimes provide a performance enhancement: The compiler is free to *inline* calls to them because it "knows" they will not be overridden by a subclass. When a small **final** method is called, often the Java compiler can copy the bytecode for the subroutine directly inline with the compiled code of the calling method, thus eliminating the costly overhead associated with a method call. Inlining is an option only with **final** methods. Normally, Java resolves calls to methods dynamically, at run time. This is called *late binding*. However, since **final** methods cannot be overridden, a call to one can be resolved at compile time. This is called *early binding*.

## Using final to Prevent Inheritance

Sometimes you will want to prevent a class from being inherited. To do this, precede the class declaration with **final**. Declaring a class as **final** implicitly declares all of its methods as **final**, too. As you might expect, it is illegal to declare a class as both **abstract** and **final** since an abstract class is incomplete by itself and relies upon its subclasses to provide complete implementations.

Here is an example of a **final** class:

```
final class A {
  //...
}

// The following class is illegal.
class B extends A { // ERROR! Can't subclass A
  //...
}
```

As the comments imply, it is illegal for **B** to inherit **A** since **A** is declared as **final**.

**NOTE** Beginning with JDK 17, the ability to *seal* a class was added to Java. Sealing offers fine-grained control over inheritance. Sealing is described in Chapter 17.

# Local Variable Type Inference and Inheritance

As explained in Chapter 3, JDK 10 added local variable type inference to the Java language, which is supported by the context-sensitive keyword **var**. It is important to have a clear understanding of how type inference works within an inheritance hierarchy. Recall that a superclass reference can refer to a derived class object, and this feature is part of Java's support for polymorphism. However, it is critical to remember that when using local variable type inference, the inferred type of a variable is based on the declared type of its initializer. Therefore, if the initializer is of the superclass type, that will be the inferred type of the variable. It does not matter if the actual object being referred to by the initializer is an instance of a derived class. For example, consider this program:

```
// When working with inheritance, the inferred type is the declared
// type of the initializer, which may not be the most derived type of
// the object being referred to by the initializer.

class MyClass {
  // ...
}

class FirstDerivedClass extends MyClass {
  int x;
  // ...
}
```

```
class SecondDerivedClass extends FirstDerivedClass {
  int y;
  // ...
}

class TypeInferenceAndInheritance {

  // Return some type of MyClass object.
  static MyClass getObj(int which) {
    switch(which) {
      case 0: return new MyClass();
      case 1: return new FirstDerivedClass();
      default: return new SecondDerivedClass();
    }
  }

  public static void main(String[] args) {

    // Even though getObj() returns different types of
    // objects within the MyClass inheritance hierarchy,
    // its declared return type is MyClass. As a result,
    // in all three cases shown here, the type of the
    // variables is inferred to be MyClass, even though
    // different derived types of objects are obtained.

    // Here, getObj() returns a MyClass object.
    var mc = getObj(0);

    // In this case, a FirstDerivedClass object is returned.
    var mc2 = getObj(1);

    // Here, a SecondDerivedClass object is returned.
    var mc3 = getObj(2);

    // Because the types of both mc2 and mc3 are inferred
    // as MyClass (because the return type of getObj() is
    // MyClass), neither mc2 nor mc3 can access the fields
    // declared by FirstDerivedClass or SecondDerivedClass.
//    mc2.x = 10; // Wrong! MyClass does not have an x field.
//    mc3.y = 10; // Wrong! MyClass does not have a y field.
  }
}
```

In the program, a hierarchy is created that consists of three classes, at the top of which is **MyClass**. **FirstDerivedClass** is a subclass of **MyClass**, and **SecondDerivedClass** is a subclass of **FirstDerivedClass**. The program then uses type inference to create three variables, called **mc**, **mc2**, and **mc3**, by calling **getObj( )**. The **getObj( )** method has a return type of **MyClass** (the superclass) but returns objects of type **MyClass**, **FirstDerivedClass**, or **SecondDerivedClass**, depending on the argument that it is passed. As the output shows, the inferred type is determined by the return type of **getObj( )**, not by the actual type of the object obtained. Thus, all three variables will be of type **MyClass**.

# The Object Class

There is one special class, **Object**, defined by Java. All other classes are subclasses of **Object**. That is, **Object** is a superclass of all other classes. This means that a reference variable of type **Object** can refer to an object of any other class. Also, since arrays are implemented as classes, a variable of type **Object** can also refer to any array.

**Object** defines the following methods, which means that they are available in every object.

| Method | Purpose |
|---|---|
| Object clone( ) | Creates a new object that is the same as the object being cloned. |
| boolean equals(Object *object*) | Determines whether one object is equal to another. |
| void finalize( ) | Called before an unused object is recycled. (Deprecated for removal by JDK 18.) |
| Class<?> getClass( ) | Obtains the class of an object at run time. |
| int hashCode( ) | Returns the hash code associated with the invoking object. |
| void notify( ) | Resumes execution of a thread waiting on the invoking object. |
| void notifyAll( ) | Resumes execution of all threads waiting on the invoking object. |
| String toString( ) | Returns a string that describes the object. |
| void wait( )<br>void wait(long *milliseconds*)<br>void wait(long *milliseconds*, int *nanoseconds*) | Waits on another thread of execution. |

The methods **getClass( )**, **notify( )**, **notifyAll( )**, and **wait( )** are declared as **final**. You may override the others. These methods are described elsewhere in this book. However, notice two methods now: **equals( )** and **toString( )**. The **equals( )** method compares two objects. It returns **true** if the objects are equal, and **false** otherwise. The precise definition of equality can vary, depending on the type of objects being compared. The **toString( )** method returns a string that contains a description of the object on which it is called. Also, this method is automatically called when an object is output using **println( )**. Many classes override this method. Doing so allows them to tailor a description specifically for the types of objects that they create.

One last point: Notice the unusual syntax in the return type for **getClass( )**. This relates to Java's *generics* feature, which is described in Chapter 14.

CHAPTER

# 9 Packages and Interfaces

This chapter examines two of Java's most innovative features: packages and interfaces. *Packages* are containers for classes. They are used to keep the class name space compartmentalized. For example, a package allows you to create a class named **List**, which you can store in your own package without concern that it will collide with some other class named **List** stored elsewhere. Packages are stored in a hierarchical manner and are explicitly imported into new class definitions. As you will see in Chapter 16, packages also play an important role with modules.

In previous chapters, you have seen how methods define the interface to the data in a class. Through the use of the **interface** keyword, Java allows you to fully abstract an interface from its implementation. Using **interface**, you can specify a set of methods that can be implemented by one or more classes. In its traditional form, the **interface** itself does not actually define any implementation. Although they are similar to abstract classes, **interfaces** have an additional capability: A class can implement more than one interface. By contrast, a class can only inherit a single superclass (abstract or otherwise).

## Packages

In the preceding chapters, the name of each sample class was taken from the same name space. This means that a unique name had to be used for each class to avoid name collisions. After a while, without some way to manage the name space, you could run out of convenient, descriptive names for individual classes. You also need some way to be assured that the name you choose for a class will be reasonably unique and not collide with class names chosen by other programmers. (Imagine a small group of programmers fighting over who gets to use the name "Foobar" as a class name. Or, imagine the entire Internet community arguing over who first named a class "Espresso.") Thankfully, Java provides a mechanism for partitioning the class name space into more manageable chunks. This mechanism is the package. The package is both a naming and a visibility control mechanism. You can define classes inside a package that are not accessible by code outside that package. You can also define class members that are exposed only to other members of the same package. This allows your classes to have intimate knowledge of each other but not expose that knowledge to the rest of the world.

## Defining a Package

To create a package is quite easy: simply include a **package** command as the first statement in a Java source file. Any classes declared within that file will belong to the specified package. The **package** statement defines a name space in which classes are stored. If you omit the **package** statement, the class names are put into the default package, which has no name. (This is why you haven't had to worry about packages before now.) While the default package is fine for short, sample programs, it is inadequate for real applications. Most of the time, you will define a package for your code.

This is the general form of the **package** statement:

package *pkg*;

Here, *pkg* is the name of the package. For example, the following statement creates a package called **mypackage**:

```
package mypackage;
```

Typically, Java uses file system directories to store packages, and that is the approach assumed by the examples in this book. For example, the **.class** files for any classes you declare to be part of **mypackage** must be stored in a directory called **mypackage**. Remember that case is significant, and the directory name must match the package name exactly.

More than one file can include the same **package** statement. The **package** statement simply specifies to which package the classes defined in a file belong. It does not exclude other classes in other files from being part of that same package. Most real-world packages are spread across many files.

You can create a hierarchy of packages. To do so, simply separate each package name from the one above it by use of a period. The general form of a multileveled package statement is shown here:

package *pkg1*[.*pkg2*[.*pkg3*]];

A package hierarchy must be reflected in the file system of your Java development system. For example, a package declared as

```
package a.b.c;
```

needs to be stored in **a\b\c** in a Windows environment. Be sure to choose your package names carefully. You cannot rename a package without renaming the directory in which the classes are stored.

## Finding Packages and CLASSPATH

As just explained, packages are typically mirrored by directories. This raises an important question: How does the Java run-time system know where to look for packages that you create? As it relates to the examples in this chapter, the answer has three parts. First, by default, the Java run-time system uses the current working directory as its starting point. Thus, if your package is in a subdirectory of the current directory, it will be found. Second, you can specify a directory path or paths by setting the **CLASSPATH** environmental variable.

Third, you can use the **-classpath** option with **java** and **javac** to specify the path to your classes. It is useful to point out that, beginning with JDK 9, a package can be part of a module, and thus found on the module path. However, a discussion of modules and module paths is deferred until Chapter 16. For now, we will use only class paths.

For example, consider the following package specification:

```
package mypack;
```

In order for a program to find **mypack**, the program can be executed from a directory immediately above **mypack**, or the **CLASSPATH** must be set to include the path to **mypack**, or the **-classpath** option must specify the path to **mypack** when the program is run via **java**.

When the last two options are used, the class path *must not* include **mypack** itself. It must simply specify the *path to* **mypack**. For example, in a Windows environment, if the path to **mypack** is

```
C:\MyPrograms\Java\mypack
```

then the class path to **mypack** is

```
C:\MyPrograms\Java
```

The easiest way to try the examples shown in this book is to simply create the package directories below your current development directory, put the **.class** files into the appropriate directories, and then execute the programs from the development directory. This is the approach used in the following example.

## A Short Package Example

Keeping the preceding discussion in mind, you can try this simple package:

```
// A simple package
package mypack;

class Balance {
  String name;
  double bal;

  Balance(String n, double b) {
    name = n;
    bal = b;
  }

  void show() {
    if(bal<0)
      System.out.print("--> ");
    System.out.println(name + ": $" + bal);
  }
}

class AccountBalance {
  public static void main(String[] args) {
    Balance[] current = new Balance[3];
```

```
        current[0] = new Balance("K. J. Fielding", 123.23);
        current[1] = new Balance("Will Tell", 157.02);
        current[2] = new Balance("Tom Jackson", -12.33);

        for(int i=0; i<3; i++) current[i].show();
    }
}
```

Call this file **AccountBalance.java** and put it in a directory called **mypack**.

Next, compile the file. Make sure that the resulting **.class** file is also in the **mypack** directory. Then, try executing the **AccountBalance** class, using the following command line:

```
java mypack.AccountBalance
```

Remember, you will need to be in the directory above **mypack** when you execute this command. (Alternatively, you can use one of the other two options described in the preceding section to specify the path **mypack**.)

As explained, **AccountBalance** is now part of the package **mypack**. This means that it cannot be executed by itself. That is, you cannot use this command line:

```
java AccountBalance
```

**AccountBalance** must be qualified with its package name.

# Packages and Member Access

In the preceding chapters, you learned about various aspects of Java's access control mechanism and its access modifiers. For example, you already know that access to a **private** member of a class is granted only to other members of that class. Packages add another dimension to access control. As you will see, Java provides many levels of protection to allow fine-grained control over the visibility of variables and methods within classes, subclasses, and packages.

Classes and packages are both means of encapsulating and containing the name space and scope of variables and methods. Packages act as containers for classes and other subordinate packages. Classes act as containers for data and code. The class is Java's smallest unit of abstraction. As it relates to the interplay between classes and packages, Java addresses four categories of visibility for class members:

- Subclasses in the same package
- Non-subclasses in the same package
- Subclasses in different packages
- Classes that are neither in the same package nor subclasses

The three access modifiers, **private**, **public**, and **protected**, provide a variety of ways to produce the many levels of access required by these categories. Table 9-1 sums up the interactions.

| | Private | No Modifier | Protected | Public |
|---|---|---|---|---|
| Same class | Yes | Yes | Yes | Yes |
| Same package subclass | No | Yes | Yes | Yes |
| Same package non-subclass | No | Yes | Yes | Yes |
| Different package subclass | No | No | Yes | Yes |
| Different package non-subclass | No | No | No | Yes |

**Table 9-1** Class Member Access

While Java's access control mechanism may seem complicated, we can simplify it as follows. Anything declared **public** can be accessed from different classes and different packages. Anything declared **private** cannot be seen outside of its class. When a member does not have an explicit access specification, it is visible to subclasses as well as to other classes in the same package. This is the default access. If you want to allow an element to be seen outside your current package, but only to classes that subclass your class directly, then declare that element **protected**.

Table 9-1 applies only to members of classes. A non-nested class has only two possible access levels: default and public. When a class is declared as **public**, it is accessible outside its package. If a class has default access, then it can only be accessed by other code within its same package. When a class is public, it must be the only public class declared in the file, and the file must have the same name as the class.

---

**NOTE** The modules feature can also affect accessibility. Modules are described in Chapter 16.

## An Access Example

The following example shows all combinations of the access control modifiers. This example has two packages and five classes. Remember that the classes for the two different packages need to be stored in directories named after their respective packages—in this case, **p1** and **p2.**

The source for the first package defines three classes: **Protection, Derived,** and **SamePackage.** The first class defines four **int** variables in each of the legal protection modes. The variable **n** is declared with the default protection, **n_pri** is **private, n_pro** is **protected,** and **n_pub** is **public.**

Each subsequent class in this example will try to access the variables in an instance of this class. The lines that will not compile due to access restrictions are commented out. Before each of these lines is a comment listing the places from which this level of protection would allow access.

The second class, **Derived,** is a subclass of **Protection** in the same package, **p1.** This grants **Derived** access to every variable in **Protection** except for **n_pri,** the **private** one. The third class, **SamePackage,** is not a subclass of **Protection,** but it is in the same package and also has access to all but **n_pri.**

This is file **Protection.java:**

```
package p1;

public class Protection {
  int n = 1;
  private int n_pri = 2;
  protected int n_pro = 3;
  public int n_pub = 4;

  public Protection() {
    System.out.println("base constructor");
    System.out.println("n = " + n);
    System.out.println("n_pri = " + n_pri);
    System.out.println("n_pro = " + n_pro);
    System.out.println("n_pub = " + n_pub);
  }
}
```

This is file **Derived.java:**

```
package p1;

class Derived extends Protection {
  Derived() {
    System.out.println("derived constructor");
    System.out.println("n = " + n);

// class only
// System.out.println("n_pri = "4 + n_pri);

   System.out.println("n_pro = " + n_pro);
   System.out.println("n_pub = " + n_pub);
  }
}
```

This is file **SamePackage.java:**

```
package p1;

class SamePackage {
  SamePackage() {

    Protection p = new Protection();
    System.out.println("same package constructor");
    System.out.println("n = " + p.n);

// class only
// System.out.println("n_pri = " + p.n_pri);

   System.out.println("n_pro = " + p.n_pro);
   System.out.println("n_pub = " + p.n_pub);
  }
}
```

Following is the source code for the other package, **p2**. The two classes defined in **p2** cover the other two conditions that are affected by access control. The first class, **Protection2**, is a subclass of **p1.Protection**. This grants access to all of **p1.Protection**'s variables except for **n_pri** (because it is **private**) and **n**, the variable declared with the default protection. Remember, the default only allows access from within the class or the package, not extra-package subclasses. Finally, the class **OtherPackage** has access to only one variable, **n_pub**, which was declared **public**.

This is file **Protection2.java**:

```
package p2;

class Protection2 extends p1.Protection {
  Protection2() {
    System.out.println("derived other package constructor");

//  class or package only
//  System.out.println("n = " + n);

//  class only
//  System.out.println("n_pri = " + n_pri);

    System.out.println("n_pro = " + n_pro);
    System.out.println("n_pub = " + n_pub);
  }
}
```

This is file **OtherPackage.java**:

```
package p2;

class OtherPackage {
  OtherPackage() {
    p1.Protection p = new p1.Protection();
    System.out.println("other package constructor");

//  class or package only
//  System.out.println("n = " + p.n);

//  class only
//  System.out.println("n_pri = " + p.n_pri);

//  class, subclass or package only
//  System.out.println("n_pro = " + p.n_pro);

    System.out.println("n_pub = " + p.n_pub);
  }
}
```

If you want to try these two packages, here are two test files you can use. The one for package **p1** is shown here:

```
// Demo package p1.
package p1;
```

```
// Instantiate the various classes in p1.
public class Demo {
  public static void main(String[] args) {
    Protection ob1 = new Protection();
    Derived ob2 = new Derived();
    SamePackage ob3 = new SamePackage();
  }
}
```

The test file for **p2** is shown next:

```
// Demo package p2.
package p2;

// Instantiate the various classes in p2.
public class Demo {
  public static void main(String[] args) {
    Protection2 ob1 = new Protection2();
    OtherPackage ob2 = new OtherPackage();
  }
}
```

## Importing Packages

Given that packages exist and are a good mechanism for compartmentalizing diverse classes from each other, it is easy to see why all of the built-in Java classes are stored in packages. There are no core Java classes in the unnamed default package; all of the standard classes are stored in some named package. Since classes within packages must be fully qualified with their package name or names, it could become tedious to type in the long dot-separated package path name for every class you want to use. For this reason, Java includes the **import** statement to bring certain classes, or entire packages, into visibility. Once imported, a class can be referred to directly, using only its name. The **import** statement is a convenience to the programmer and is not technically needed to write a complete Java program. If you are going to refer to a few dozen classes in your application, however, the **import** statement will save a lot of typing.

In a Java source file, **import** statements occur immediately following the **package** statement (if it exists) and before any class definitions. This is the general form of the **import** statement:

import *pkg1* [.*pkg2*].(*classname* | *);

Here, *pkg1* is the name of a top-level package, and *pkg2* is the name of a subordinate package inside the outer package separated by a dot (.). There is no practical limit on the depth of a package hierarchy, except that imposed by the file system. Finally, you specify either an explicit *classname* or a star (*), which indicates that the Java compiler should import the entire package. This code fragment shows both forms in use:

```
import java.util.Date;
import java.io.*;
```

All of the standard Java SE classes included with Java begin with the name **java**. The basic language functions are stored in a package called **java.lang**. Normally, you have to import every package or class that you want to use, but since Java is useless without much of the functionality in **java.lang**, it is implicitly imported by the compiler for all programs. This is equivalent to the following line being at the top of all of your programs:

```
import java.lang.*;
```

If a class with the same name exists in two different packages that you import using the star form, the compiler will remain silent, unless you try to use one of the classes. In that case, you will get a compile-time error and have to explicitly name the class specifying its package.

It must be emphasized that the **import** statement is optional. Any place you use a class name, you can use its *fully qualified name*, which includes its full package hierarchy. For example, this fragment uses an **import** statement:

```
import java.util.*;
class MyDate extends Date {
}
```

The same example without the **import** statement looks like this:

```
class MyDate extends java.util.Date {
}
```

In this version, **Date** is fully qualified.

As shown in Table 9-1, when a package is imported, only those items within the package declared as **public** will be available to non-subclasses in the importing code. For example, if you want the **Balance** class of the package **mypack** shown earlier to be available as a stand-alone class for general use outside of **mypack**, then you will need to declare it as **public** and put it into its own file, as shown here:

```
package mypack;

/* Now, the Balance class, its constructor, and its
   show() method are public. This means that they can
   be used by non-subclass code outside their package.
*/
public class Balance {
  String name;
  double bal;

  public Balance(String n, double b) {
    name = n;
    bal = b;
  }

  public void show() {
    if(bal<0)
```

```
      System.out.print("--> ");
    System.out.println(name + ": $" + bal);
  }
}
```

As you can see, the **Balance** class is now **public**. Also, its constructor and its **show( )** method are **public**, too. This means that they can be accessed by any type of code outside the **mypack** package. For example, here **TestBalance** imports **mypack** and is then able to make use of the **Balance** class:

```
import mypack.*;

class TestBalance {
  public static void main(String[] args) {

    /* Because Balance is public, you may use Balance
       class and call its constructor. */
    Balance test = new Balance("J. J. Jaspers", 99.88);

    test.show(); // you may also call show()
  }
}
```

As an experiment, remove the **public** specifier from the **Balance** class and then try compiling **TestBalance**. As explained, errors will result.

# Interfaces

Using the keyword **interface**, you can fully abstract a class's interface from its implementation. That is, using **interface**, you can specify what a class must do, but not how it does it. Interfaces are syntactically similar to classes, but they lack instance variables, and, as a general rule, their methods are declared without any body. In practice, this means that you can define interfaces that don't make assumptions about how they are implemented. Once it is defined, any number of classes can implement an interface. Also, one class can implement any number of interfaces.

To implement an interface, a class must provide the complete set of methods required by the interface. However, each class is free to determine the details of its own implementation. By providing the **interface** keyword, Java allows you to fully utilize the "one interface, multiple methods" aspect of polymorphism.

Interfaces are designed to support dynamic method resolution at run time. Normally, in order for a method to be called from one class to another, both classes need to be present at compile time so the Java compiler can check to ensure that the method signatures are compatible. This requirement by itself makes for a static and nonextensible classing environment. Inevitably in a system like this, functionality gets pushed up higher and higher in the class hierarchy so that the mechanisms will be available to more and more subclasses. Interfaces are designed to avoid this problem. They disconnect the definition of a method or set of methods from the inheritance hierarchy. Since interfaces are in a different hierarchy from classes, it is possible for classes that are unrelated in terms of the class hierarchy to implement the same interface. This is where the real power of interfaces is realized.

## Defining an Interface

An interface is defined much like a class. This is a simplified general form of an interface:

```
access interface name {
    return-type method-name1(parameter-list);
    return-type method-name2(parameter-list);

    type final-varname1 = value;
    type final-varname2 = value;
    //...
    return-type method-nameN(parameter-list);
    type final-varnameN = value;
}
```

When no access modifier is included, then default access results, and the interface is only available to other members of the package in which it is declared. When it is declared as **public**, the interface can be used by code outside its package. In this case, the interface must be the only public interface declared in the file, and the file must have the same name as the interface. *name* is the name of the interface, and can be any valid identifier. Notice that the methods that are declared have no bodies. They end with a semicolon after the parameter list. They are, essentially, abstract methods. Each class that includes such an interface must implement all of the methods.

Before continuing, an important point needs to be made. JDK 8 added a feature to **interface** that made a significant change to its capabilities. Prior to JDK 8, an interface could not define any implementation whatsoever. This is the type of interface that the preceding simplified form shows, in which no method declaration supplies a body. Thus, prior to JDK 8, an interface could define only "what," but not "how." JDK 8 changed this. Beginning with JDK 8, it is possible to add a *default implementation* to an interface method. Furthermore, JDK 8 also added static interface methods, and beginning with JDK 9, an interface can include private methods. Thus, it is now possible for **interface** to specify some behavior. However, such methods constitute what are, in essence, special-use features, and the original intent behind **interface** still remains. Therefore, as a general rule, you will still often create and use interfaces in which no use is made of these new features. For this reason, we will begin by discussing the interface in its traditional form. The newer interface features are described at the end of this chapter.

As the general form shows, variables can be declared inside interface declarations. They are implicitly **final** and **static**, meaning they cannot be changed by the implementing class. They must also be initialized. All methods and variables are implicitly **public**.

Here is an example of an interface definition. It declares a simple interface that contains one method called **callback( )** that takes a single integer parameter.

```
interface Callback {
  void callback(int param);
}
```

## Implementing Interfaces

Once an interface has been defined, one or more classes can implement that interface. To implement an interface, include the **implements** clause in a class definition, and then create the methods required by the interface. The general form of a class that includes the **implements** clause looks like this:

class *classname* [extends *superclass*] [implements *interface* [,*interface...*]] {
  // class-body
}

If a class implements more than one interface, the interfaces are separated with a comma. If a class implements two interfaces that declare the same method, then the same method will be used by clients of either interface. The methods that implement an interface must be declared **public**. Also, the type signature of the implementing method must match exactly the type signature specified in the **interface** definition.

Here is a small sample class that implements the **Callback** interface shown earlier:

```
class Client implements Callback {
  // Implement Callback's interface
  public void callback(int p) {

    System.out.println("callback called with " + p);
  }
}
```

Notice that **callback( )** is declared using the **public** access modifier.

---

**REMEMBER** When you implement an interface method, it must be declared as **public**.

It is both permissible and common for classes that implement interfaces to define additional members of their own. For example, the following version of **Client** implements **callback( )** and adds the method **nonIfaceMeth( )**:

```
class Client implements Callback {
  // Implement Callback's interface
  public void callback(int p) {
    System.out.println("callback called with " + p);
  }

  void nonIfaceMeth() {
    System.out.println("Classes that implement interfaces " +
                       "may also define other members, too.");
  }
}
```

### Accessing Implementations Through Interface References

You can declare variables as object references that use an interface rather than a class type. Any instance of any class that implements the declared interface can be referred to by such a variable. When you call a method through one of these references, the correct version will be called based on the actual instance of the interface being referred to. This is one of the key features of interfaces. The method to be executed is looked up dynamically at run time, allowing classes to be created later than the code that calls methods on them. The calling code can dispatch through an interface without having to know anything about the "callee." This process is similar to using a superclass reference to access a subclass object, as described in Chapter 8.

The following example calls the **callback( )** method via an interface reference variable:

```
class TestIface {
  public static void main(String[] args) {
    Callback c = new Client();
    c.callback(42);
  }
}
```

The output of this program is shown here:

```
callback called with 42
```

Notice that variable **c** is declared to be of the interface type **Callback**, yet it was assigned an instance of **Client**. Although **c** can be used to access the **callback( )** method, it cannot access any other members of the **Client** class. An interface reference variable has knowledge only of the methods declared by its **interface** declaration. Thus, **c** could not be used to access **nonIfaceMeth( )** since it is defined by **Client** but not **Callback**.

While the preceding example shows, mechanically, how an interface reference variable can access an implementation object, it does not demonstrate the polymorphic power of such a reference. To sample this usage, first create the second implementation of **Callback**, shown here:

```
// Another implementation of Callback.
class AnotherClient implements Callback {
  // Implement Callback's interface
  public void callback(int p) {
    System.out.println("Another version of callback");
    System.out.println("p squared is " + (p*p));
  }
}
```

Now, try the following class:

```
class TestIface2 {
  public static void main(String[] args) {
    Callback c = new Client();
    AnotherClient ob = new AnotherClient();

    c.callback(42);

    c = ob; // c now refers to AnotherClient object
    c.callback(42);
  }
}
```

The output from this program is shown here:

```
callback called with 42
Another version of callback
p squared is 1764
```

As you can see, the version of **callback( )** that is called is determined by the type of object that **c** refers to at run time. While this is a very simple example, you will see another, more practical one shortly.

## Partial Implementations

If a class includes an interface but does not fully implement the methods required by that interface, then that class must be declared as **abstract**. For example:

```
abstract class Incomplete implements Callback {
  int a, b;

  void show() {
    System.out.println(a + " " + b);
  }
  //...
}
```

Here, the class **Incomplete** does not implement **callback( )** and must be declared as **abstract**. Any class that inherits **Incomplete** must implement **callback( )** or be declared **abstract** itself.

# Nested Interfaces

An interface can be declared a member of a class or another interface. Such an interface is called a *member interface* or a *nested interface.* A nested interface can be declared as **public**, **private**, or **protected**. This differs from a top-level interface, which must either be declared as **public** or use the default access level, as previously described. When a nested interface is used outside of its enclosing scope, it must be qualified by the name of the class or interface of which it is a member. Thus, outside of the class or interface in which a nested interface is declared, its name must be fully qualified.

Here is an example that demonstrates a nested interface:

```
// A nested interface example.

// This class contains a member interface.
class A {
  // this is a nested interface
  public interface NestedIF {
    boolean isNotNegative(int x);
  }
}
```

```
// B implements the nested interface.
class B implements A.NestedIF {
  public boolean isNotNegative(int x) {
    return x < 0 ? false: true;
  }
}

class NestedIFDemo {
  public static void main(String[] args) {

    // use a nested interface reference
    A.NestedIF nif = new B();

    if(nif.isNotNegative(10))
      System.out.println("10 is not negative");
    if(nif.isNotNegative(-12))
      System.out.println("this won't be displayed");
  }
}
```



Notice that **A** defines a member interface called **NestedIF** and that it is declared **public**. Next, **B** implements the nested interface by specifying

```
implements A.NestedIF
```

Notice that the name is fully qualified by the enclosing class's name. Inside the **main( )** method, an **A.NestedIF** reference called **nif** is created, and it is assigned a reference to a **B** object. Because **B** implements **A.NestedIF**, this is legal.

## Applying Interfaces

To understand the power of interfaces, let's look at a more practical example. In earlier chapters, you developed a class called **Stack** that implemented a simple fixed-size stack. However, there are many ways to implement a stack. For example, the stack can be of a fixed size or it can be "growable." The stack can also be held in an array, a linked list, a binary tree, and so on. No matter how the stack is implemented, the interface to the stack remains the same. That is, the methods **push( )** and **pop( )** define the interface to the stack independently of the details of the implementation. Because the interface to a stack is separate from its implementation, it is easy to define a stack interface, leaving it to each implementation to define the specifics. Let's look at two examples.

First, here is the interface that defines an integer stack. Put this in a file called **IntStack.java**. This interface will be used by both stack implementations.

```
// Define an integer stack interface.
interface IntStack {
  void push(int item); // store an item
  int pop(); // retrieve an item
}
```

The following program creates a class called **FixedStack** that implements a fixed-length version of an integer stack:

```
// An implementation of IntStack that uses fixed storage.
class FixedStack implements IntStack {
  private int[] stck;
  private int tos;

  // allocate and initialize stack
  FixedStack(int size) {
    stck = new int[size];
    tos = -1;
  }

  // Push an item onto the stack
  public void push(int item) {
    if(tos==stck.length-1) // use length member
      System.out.println("Stack is full.");
    else
      stck[++tos] = item;
  }

  // Pop an item from the stack
  public int pop() {
    if(tos < 0) {
      System.out.println("Stack underflow.");
      return 0;
    }
    else
      return stck[tos--];
  }
}

class IFTest {
  public static void main(String[] args) {
    FixedStack mystack1 = new FixedStack(5);
    FixedStack mystack2 = new FixedStack(8);

    // push some numbers onto the stack
    for(int i=0; i<5; i++) mystack1.push(i);
    for(int i=0; i<8; i++) mystack2.push(i);

    // pop those numbers off the stack
    System.out.println("Stack in mystack1:");
    for(int i=0; i<5; i++)
       System.out.println(mystack1.pop());

    System.out.println("Stack in mystack2:");
    for(int i=0; i<8; i++)
       System.out.println(mystack2.pop());
  }
}
```

Following is another implementation of **IntStack** that creates a dynamic stack by use of the same **interface** definition. In this implementation, each stack is constructed with an initial length. If this initial length is exceeded, then the stack is increased in size. Each time more room is needed, the size of the stack is doubled.

```
// Implement a "growable" stack.
class DynStack implements IntStack {
  private int[] stck;
  private int tos;

  // allocate and initialize stack
  DynStack(int size) {
    stck = new int[size];
    tos = -1;
  }

  // Push an item onto the stack
  public void push(int item) {
    // if stack is full, allocate a larger stack
    if(tos==stck.length-1) {
      int[] temp = new int[stck.length * 2]; // double size
      for(int i=0; i<stck.length; i++) temp[i] = stck[i];
      stck = temp;
      stck[++tos] = item;
    }
    else
      stck[++tos] = item;
  }

  // Pop an item from the stack
  public int pop() {
    if(tos < 0) {
      System.out.println("Stack underflow.");
      return 0;
    }
    else
      return stck[tos--];
  }
}

class IFTest2 {
  public static void main(String[] args) {
    DynStack mystack1 = new DynStack(5);
    DynStack mystack2 = new DynStack(8);

    // these loops cause each stack to grow
    for(int i=0; i<12; i++) mystack1.push(i);
    for(int i=0; i<20; i++) mystack2.push(i);

    System.out.println("Stack in mystack1:");
    for(int i=0; i<12; i++)
       System.out.println(mystack1.pop());
```

```
    System.out.println("Stack in mystack2:");
    for(int i=0; i<20; i++)
      System.out.println(mystack2.pop());
  }
}
```

The following class uses both the **FixedStack** and **DynStack** implementations. It does so through an interface reference. This means that calls to **push( )** and **pop( )** are resolved at run time rather than at compile time.

```
/* Create an interface variable and
   access stacks through it.
*/
class IFTest3 {
  public static void main(String[] args) {
    IntStack mystack; // create an interface reference variable
    DynStack ds = new DynStack(5);
    FixedStack fs = new FixedStack(8);

    mystack = ds; // load dynamic stack
    // push some numbers onto the stack
    for(int i=0; i<12; i++) mystack.push(i);

    mystack = fs; // load fixed stack
    for(int i=0; i<8; i++) mystack.push(i);

    mystack = ds;
    System.out.println("Values in dynamic stack:");
    for(int i=0; i<12; i++)
      System.out.println(mystack.pop());

    mystack = fs;
    System.out.println("Values in fixed stack:");
    for(int i=0; i<8; i++)
      System.out.println(mystack.pop());
  }
}
```

In this program, **mystack** is a reference to the **IntStack** interface. Thus, when it refers to **ds**, it uses the versions of **push( )** and **pop( )** defined by the **DynStack** implementation. When it refers to **fs**, it uses the versions of **push( )** and **pop( )** defined by **FixedStack**. As explained, these determinations are made at run time. Accessing multiple implementations of an interface through an interface reference variable is the most powerful way that Java achieves run-time polymorphism.

## Variables in Interfaces

You can use interfaces to import shared constants into multiple classes by simply declaring an interface that contains variables that are initialized to the desired values. When you include that interface in a class (that is, when you "implement" the interface), all of those variable names will be in scope as constants. If an interface contains no methods, then any class that includes such an interface doesn't actually implement anything. It is as if that class were importing the constant fields into the class name space as **final** variables. The next example uses this technique to implement an automated "decision maker":

```
import java.util.Random;

interface SharedConstants {
  int NO = 0;
  int YES = 1;
  int MAYBE = 2;
  int LATER = 3;
  int SOON = 4;
  int NEVER = 5;
}

class Question implements SharedConstants {
  Random rand = new Random();
  int ask() {
    int prob = (int) (100 * rand.nextDouble());
    if (prob < 30)
      return NO;            // 30%
    else if (prob < 60)
      return YES;           // 30%
    else if (prob < 75)
      return LATER;         // 15%
    else if (prob < 98)
      return SOON;          // 13%

    else
      return NEVER;         // 2%
  }
}

class AskMe implements SharedConstants {
  static void answer(int result) {
    switch(result) {
      case NO:
        System.out.println("No");
        break;
      case YES:
        System.out.println("Yes");
        break;
      case MAYBE:
        System.out.println("Maybe");
        break;
      case LATER:
        System.out.println("Later");
        break;
      case SOON:
        System.out.println("Soon");
        break;
      case NEVER:
        System.out.println("Never");
        break;
```

```
    }
  }

  public static void main(String[] args) {
    Question q = new Question();

    answer(q.ask());
    answer(q.ask());
    answer(q.ask());
    answer(q.ask());
  }
}
```

Notice that this program makes use of one of Java's standard classes: **Random**. This class provides pseudorandom numbers. It contains several methods that allow you to obtain random numbers in the form required by your program. In this example, the method **nextDouble( )** is used. It returns random numbers in the range 0.0 to 1.0.

In this sample program, the two classes, **Question** and **AskMe**, both implement the **SharedConstants** interface where **NO**, **YES**, **MAYBE**, **SOON**, **LATER**, and **NEVER** are defined. Inside each class, the code refers to these constants as if each class had defined or inherited them directly. Here is the output of a sample run of this program. Note that the results are different each time it is run.

```
Later
Soon
No
Yes
```

**NOTE** The technique of using an interface to define shared constants, as just described, is controversial. It is described here for completeness.

## Interfaces Can Be Extended

One interface can inherit another by use of the keyword **extends**. The syntax is the same as for inheriting classes. When a class implements an interface that inherits another interface, it must provide implementations for all methods required by the interface inheritance chain. Following is an example:

```
// One interface can extend another.
interface A {
  void meth1();
  void meth2();
}

// B now includes meth1() and meth2() -- it adds meth3().
interface B extends A {
  void meth3();
}
```

```
// This class must implement all of A and B
class MyClass implements B {
  public void meth1() {
    System.out.println("Implement meth1().");
  }

  public void meth2() {
    System.out.println("Implement meth2().");
  }

  public void meth3() {
    System.out.println("Implement meth3().");
  }
}

class IFExtend {
  public static void main(String[] args) {
    MyClass ob = new MyClass();

    ob.meth1();
    ob.meth2();
    ob.meth3();
  }
}
```

As an experiment, you might want to try removing the implementation for **meth1( )** in **MyClass**. This will cause a compile-time error. As stated earlier, any class that implements an interface must implement all methods required by that interface, including any that are inherited from other interfaces.

## Default Interface Methods

As explained earlier, prior to JDK 8, an interface could not define any implementation whatsoever. This meant that for all previous versions of Java, the methods specified by an interface were abstract, containing no body. This is the traditional form of an interface and is the type of interface that the preceding discussions have used. The release of JDK 8 changed this by adding a new capability to **interface** called the *default method*. A default method lets you define a default implementation for an interface method. In other words, by use of a default method, it is possible for an interface method to provide a body, rather than being abstract. During its development, the default method was also referred to as an *extension method*, and you will likely see both terms used.

A primary motivation for the default method was to provide a means by which interfaces could be expanded without breaking existing code. Recall that there must be implementations for all methods defined by an interface. In the past, if a new method were added to a popular, widely used interface, then the addition of that method would break existing code because no implementation would be found for that new method. The default method solves this problem by supplying an implementation that will be used if no other implementation is explicitly provided. Thus, the addition of a default method will not cause preexisting code to break.

Another motivation for the default method was the desire to specify methods in an interface that are, essentially, optional, depending on how the interface is used. For example, an interface might define a group of methods that act on a sequence of elements. One of these methods might be called **remove( )**, and its purpose is to remove an element from the sequence. However, if the interface is intended to support both modifiable and nonmodifiable sequences, then **remove( )** is essentially optional because it won't be used by nonmodifiable sequences. In the past, a class that implemented a nonmodifiable sequence would have had to define an empty implementation of **remove( )**, even though it was not needed. Today, a default implementation for **remove( )** can be specified in the interface that does nothing (or throws an exception). Providing this default prevents a class used for nonmodifiable sequences from having to define its own, placeholder version of **remove( )**. Thus, by providing a default, the interface makes the implementation of **remove( )** by a class optional.

It is important to point out that the addition of default methods does not change a key aspect of **interface**: its inability to maintain state information. An interface still cannot have instance variables, for example. Thus, the defining difference between an interface and a class is that a class can maintain state information, but an interface cannot. Furthermore, it is still not possible to create an instance of an interface by itself. It must be implemented by a class. Therefore, even though, beginning with JDK 8, an interface can define default methods, the interface must still be implemented by a class if an instance is to be created.

One last point: As a general rule, default methods constitute a special-purpose feature. Interfaces that you create will still be used primarily to specify *what* and not *how*. However, the inclusion of the default method gives you added flexibility.

## Default Method Fundamentals

An interface default method is defined similar to the way a method is defined by a **class**. The primary difference is that the declaration is preceded by the keyword **default**. For example, consider this simple interface:

```
public interface MyIF {
  // This is a "normal" interface method declaration.
  // It does NOT define a default implementation.
  int getNumber();

  // This is a default method. Notice that it provides
  // a default implementation.
  default String getString() {
    return "Default String";
  }
}
```

**MyIF** declares two methods. The first, **getNumber( )**, is a standard interface method declaration. It defines no implementation whatsoever. The second method is **getString( )**, and it does include a default implementation. In this case, it simply returns the string "Default String". Pay special attention to the way **getString( )** is declared. Its declaration is preceded by the **default** modifier. This syntax can be generalized. To define a default method, precede its declaration with **default**.

Because **getString( )** includes a default implementation, it is not necessary for an implementing class to override it. In other words, if an implementing class does not provide its own implementation, the default is used. For example, the **MyIFImp** class shown next is perfectly valid:

```
// Implement MyIF.
class MyIFImp implements MyIF {
  // Only getNumber() defined by MyIF needs to be implemented.
  // getString() can be allowed to default.
  public int getNumber() {
    return 100;
  }
}
```

The following code creates an instance of **MyIFImp** and uses it to call both **getNumber( )** and **getString( )**:

```
// Use the default method.
class DefaultMethodDemo {
  public static void main(String[] args) {

    MyIFImp obj = new MyIFImp();

    // Can call getNumber(), because it is explicitly
    // implemented by MyIFImp:
    System.out.println(obj.getNumber());

    // Can also call getString(), because of default
    // implementation:
    System.out.println(obj.getString());
  }
}
```

The output is shown here:

```
100
Default String
```

As you can see, the default implementation of **getString( )** was automatically used. It was not necessary for **MyIFImp** to define it. Thus, for **getString( )**, implementation by a class is optional. (Of course, its implementation by a class will be *required* if the class uses **getString( )** for some purpose beyond that supported by its default.)

It is both possible and common for an implementing class to define its own implementation of a default method. For example, **MyIFImp2** overrides **getString( )**:

```
class MyIFImp2 implements MyIF {
  // Here, implementations for both getNumber( ) and getString( ) are provided.
  public int getNumber() {
    return 100;
  }
```

```
  public String getString() {
    return "This is a different string.";
  }
}
```

Now, when **getString( )** is called, a different string is returned.

## A More Practical Example

Although the preceding shows the mechanics of using default methods, it doesn't illustrate their usefulness in a more practical setting. To do this, let's once again return to the **IntStack** interface shown earlier in this chapter. For the sake of discussion, assume that **IntStack** is widely used and many programs rely on it. Further assume that we now want to add a method to **IntStack** that clears the stack, enabling the stack to be re-used. Thus, we want to evolve the **IntStack** interface so that it defines new functionality, but we don't want to break any preexisting code. In the past, this would be impossible, but with the inclusion of default methods, it is now easy to do. For example, the **IntStack** interface can be enhanced like this:

```
interface IntStack {
  void push(int item); // store an item
  int pop(); // retrieve an item

  // Because clear( ) has a default, it need not be
  // implemented by a preexisting class that uses IntStack.
  default void clear() {
    System.out.println("clear() not implemented.");
  }
}
```

Here, the default behavior of **clear( )** simply displays a message indicating that it is not implemented. This is acceptable because no preexisting class that implements **IntStack** would ever call **clear( )** because it was not defined by the earlier version of **IntStack**. However, **clear( )** can be implemented by a new class that implements **IntStack**. Furthermore, **clear( )** needs to be defined by a new implementation only if it is used. Thus, the default method gives you

- a way to gracefully evolve interfaces over time, and
- a way to provide optional functionality without requiring that a class provide a placeholder implementation when that functionality is not needed.

One other point: In real-world code, **clear( )** would have thrown an exception, rather than displaying an error message. Exceptions are described in the next chapter. After working through that material, you might want to try modifying **clear( )** so that its default implementation throws an **UnsupportedOperationException**.

## Multiple Inheritance Issues

As explained earlier in this book, Java does not support the multiple inheritance of classes. Now that an interface can include default methods, you might be wondering if an interface can provide a way around this restriction. The answer is, essentially, no. Recall that there is still a key difference between a class and an interface: a class can maintain state information (especially through the use of instance variables), but an interface cannot.

The preceding notwithstanding, default methods do offer a bit of what one would normally associate with the concept of multiple inheritance. For example, you might have a class that implements two interfaces. If each of these interfaces provides default methods, then some behavior is inherited from both. Thus, to a limited extent, default methods do support multiple inheritance of behavior. As you might guess, in such a situation, it is possible that a name conflict will occur.

For example, assume that two interfaces called **Alpha** and **Beta** are implemented by a class called **MyClass**. What happens if both **Alpha** and **Beta** provide a method called **reset( )** for which both declare a default implementation? Is the version by **Alpha** or the version by **Beta** used by **MyClass**? Or, consider a situation in which **Beta** extends **Alpha**. Which version of the default method is used? Or, what if **MyClass** provides its own implementation of the method? To handle these and other similar types of situations, Java defines a set of rules that resolves such conflicts.

First, in all cases, a class implementation takes priority over an interface default implementation. Thus, if **MyClass** provides an override of the **reset( )** default method, **MyClass**'s version is used. This is the case even if **MyClass** implements both **Alpha** and **Beta**. In this case, both defaults are overridden by **MyClass**'s implementation.

Second, in cases in which a class implements two interfaces that both have the same default method, but the class does not override that method, then an error will result. Continuing with the example, if **MyClass** implements both **Alpha** and **Beta**, but does not override **reset( )**, then an error will occur.

In cases in which one interface inherits another, with both defining a common default method, the inheriting interface's version of the method takes precedence. Therefore, continuing the example, if **Beta** extends **Alpha**, then **Beta**'s version of **reset( )** will be used.

It is possible to explicitly refer to a default implementation in an inherited interface by using this form of **super**. Its general form is shown here:

*InterfaceName*.super.*methodName( )*

For example, if **Beta** wants to refer to **Alpha**'s default for **reset( )**, it can use this statement:

```
Alpha.super.reset();
```

## Use static Methods in an Interface

Another capability added to **interface** by JDK 8 is the ability to define one or more **static** methods. Like **static** methods in a class, a **static** method defined by an interface can be called independently of any object. Thus, no implementation of the interface is necessary, and no instance of the interface is required, in order to call a **static** method. Instead, a **static** method is called by specifying the interface name, followed by a period, followed by the method name. Here is the general form:

*InterfaceName.staticMethodName*

Notice that this is similar to the way that a **static** method in a class is called.

The following shows an example of a **static** method in an interface by adding one to **MyIF**, shown in the previous section. The **static** method is **getDefaultNumber( )**. It returns zero.

```
public interface MyIF {
  // This is a "normal" interface method declaration.
  // It does NOT define a default implementation.
  int getNumber();

  // This is a default method. Notice that it provides
  // a default implementation.
  default String getString() {
    return "Default String";
  }

  // This is a static interface method.
  static int getDefaultNumber() {
    return 0;
  }
}
```

The **getDefaultNumber( )** method can be called as shown here:

```
int defNum = MyIF.getDefaultNumber();
```

As mentioned, no implementation or instance of **MyIF** is required to call **getDefaultNumber( )** because it is **static**.

One last point: **static** interface methods are not inherited by either an implementing class or a subinterface.

# Private Interface Methods

Beginning with JDK 9, an interface can include a private method. A private interface method can be called only by a default method or another private method defined by the same interface. Because a private interface method is specified **private**, it cannot be used by code outside the interface in which it is defined. This restriction includes subinterfaces because a private interface method is not inherited by a subinterface.

The key benefit of a private interface method is that it lets two or more default methods use a common piece of code, thus avoiding code duplication. For example, here is another version of the **IntStack** interface that has two default methods called **popNElements( )** and **skipAndPopNElements( )**. The first returns an array that contains the top *N* elements on the stack. The second skips a specified number of elements and then returns an array that contains the next *N* elements. Both use a private method called **getElements( )** to obtain an array of the specified number of elements from the stack.

```
// Another version of IntStack that has a private interface
// method that is used by two default methods.
interface IntStack {
  void push(int item); // store an item
  int pop(); // retrieve an item
```

```
  // A default method that returns an array that contains
  // the top n elements on the stack.
  default int[] popNElements(int n) {
    // Return the requested elements.
    return getElements(n);
  }

  // A default method that returns an array that contains
  // the next n elements on the stack after skipping elements.
  default int[] skipAndPopNElements(int skip, int n) {

    // Skip the specified number of elements.
    getElements(skip);

    // Return the requested elements.
    return getElements(n);
  }

  // A private method that returns an array containing
  // the top n elements on the stack
  private int[] getElements(int n) {
    int[] elements = new int[n];

    for(int i=0; i < n; i++) elements[i] = pop();
    return elements;
  }
}
```

Notice that both **popNElements( )** and **skipAndPopNElements( )** use the private **getElements( )** method to obtain the array to return. This prevents both methods from having to duplicate the same code sequence. Keep in mind that because **getElements( )** is private, it cannot be called by code outside **IntStack**. Thus, its use is limited to the default methods inside **IntStack**. Also, because **getElements( )** uses the **pop( )** method to obtain stack elements, it will automatically call the implementation of **pop( )** provided by the **IntStack** implementation. Thus, **getElements( )** will work for any stack class that implements **IntStack**.

Although the private interface method is a feature that you will seldom need, in those cases in which you *do* need it, you will find it quite useful.

# Final Thoughts on Packages and Interfaces

Although the examples we've included in this book do not make frequent use of packages or interfaces, both of these tools are an important part of the Java programming environment. Virtually all real programs that you write in Java will be contained within packages. A number will probably implement interfaces as well. It is important, therefore, that you be comfortable with their usage.

CHAPTER

# 10 Exception Handling

This chapter examines Java's exception-handling mechanism. An *exception* is an abnormal condition that arises in a code sequence at run time. In other words, an exception is a run-time error. In computer languages that do not support exception handling, errors must be checked and handled manually—typically through the use of error codes, and so on. This approach is as cumbersome as it is troublesome. Java's exception handling avoids these problems and, in the process, brings run-time error management into the object-oriented world.

## Exception-Handling Fundamentals

A Java exception is an object that describes an exceptional (that is, error) condition that has occurred in a piece of code. When an exceptional condition arises, an object representing that exception is created and *thrown* in the method that caused the error. That method may choose to handle the exception itself, or pass it on. Either way, at some point, the exception is *caught* and processed. Exceptions can be generated by the Java run-time system, or they can be manually generated by your code. Exceptions thrown by Java relate to fundamental errors that violate the rules of the Java language or the constraints of the Java execution environment. Manually generated exceptions are typically used to report some error condition to the caller of a method.

Java exception handling is managed via five keywords: **try**, **catch**, **throw**, **throws**, and **finally**. Briefly, here is how they work. Program statements that you want to monitor for exceptions are contained within a **try** block. If an exception occurs within the **try** block, it is thrown. Your code can catch this exception (using **catch**) and handle it in some rational manner. System-generated exceptions are automatically thrown by the Java run-time system. To manually throw an exception, use the keyword **throw**. Any exception that is thrown out of a method must be specified as such by a **throws** clause. Any code that absolutely must be executed after a **try** block completes is put in a **finally** block.

This is the general form of an exception-handling block:

```
try {
    // block of code to monitor for errors
}

catch (ExceptionType1 exOb) {
    // exception handler for ExceptionType1
}

catch (ExceptionType2 exOb) {
    // exception handler for ExceptionType2
}
// ...
finally {
    // block of code to be executed after try block ends
}
```

Here, *ExceptionType* is the type of exception that has occurred. The remainder of this chapter describes how to apply this framework.

**NOTE** There is another form of the **try** statement that supports *automatic resource management*. This form of **try**, called ***try**-with-resources*, is described in Chapter 13 in the context of managing files because files are some of the most commonly used resources.

## Exception Types

All exception types are subclasses of the built-in class **Throwable**. Thus, **Throwable** is at the top of the exception class hierarchy. Immediately below **Throwable** are two subclasses that partition exceptions into two distinct branches. One branch is headed by **Exception**. This class is used for exceptional conditions that user programs should catch. This is also the class that you will subclass to create your own custom exception types. There is an important subclass of **Exception**, called **RuntimeException**. Exceptions of this type are automatically defined for the programs that you write and include things such as division by zero and invalid array indexing.

The other branch is topped by **Error**, which defines exceptions that are not expected to be caught under normal circumstances by your program. Exceptions of type **Error** are used by the Java run-time system to indicate errors having to do with the run-time environment itself. Stack overflow is an example of such an error. This chapter will not be dealing with exceptions of type **Error**, because these are typically created in response to catastrophic failures that cannot usually be handled by your program.

The top-level exception hierarchy is shown here:

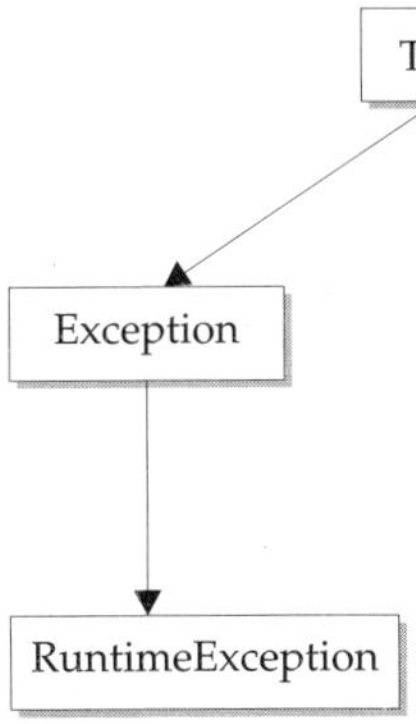


## Uncaught Exceptions

Before you learn how to handle exceptions in your program, it is useful to see what happens when you don't handle them. This small program includes an expression that intentionally causes a divide-by-zero error:

```
class Exc0 {
  public static void main(String[] args) {
    int d = 0;
    int a = 42 / d;
  }
}
```

When the Java run-time system detects the attempt to divide by zero, it constructs a new exception object and then *throws* this exception. This causes the execution of **Exc0** to stop, because once an exception has been thrown, it must be *caught* by an exception handler and dealt with immediately. In this example, we haven't supplied any exception handlers of our own, so the exception is caught by the default handler provided by the Java run-time system. Any exception that is not caught by your program will ultimately be processed by the default handler. The default handler displays a string describing the exception, prints a stack trace from the point at which the exception occurred, and terminates the program.

Here is the exception generated when this example is executed:

```
java.lang.ArithmeticException: / by zero
        at Exc0.main(Exc0.java:4)
```

Notice how the class name, **Exc0**; the method name, **main**; the filename, **Exc0.java**; and the line number, **4**, are all included in the simple stack trace. Also, notice that the type of exception thrown is a subclass of **Exception** called **ArithmeticException**, which more specifically describes what type of error happened. As discussed later in this chapter, Java supplies several built-in exception types that match the various sorts of run-time errors that can be generated. One other point: The exact output you see when running this and other sample programs in this chapter that use Java's built-in exceptions may vary slightly from what is shown because of differences between JDKs.

The stack trace will always show the sequence of method invocations that led up to the error. For example, here is another version of the preceding program that introduces the same error but in a method separate from **main( )**:

```
class Exc1 {
  static void subroutine() {
    int d = 0;
    int a = 10 / d;
  }
  public static void main(String[] args) {
    Exc1.subroutine();
  }
}
```

The resulting stack trace from the default exception handler shows how the entire call stack is displayed:

```
java.lang.ArithmeticException: / by zero
    at Exc1.subroutine(Exc1.java:4)
    at Exc1.main(Exc1.java:7)
```

As you can see, the bottom of the stack is **main**'s line 7, which is the call to **subroutine( )**, which caused the exception at line 4. The call stack is quite useful for debugging, because it pinpoints the precise sequence of steps that led to the error.

## Using try and catch

Although the default exception handler provided by the Java run-time system is useful for debugging, you will usually want to handle an exception yourself. Doing so provides two benefits. First, it allows you to fix the error. Second, it prevents the program from automatically terminating. Most users would be confused (to say the least) if your program stopped running and printed a stack trace whenever an error occurred! Fortunately, it is quite easy to prevent this.

To guard against and handle a run-time error, simply enclose the code that you want to monitor inside a **try** block. Immediately following the **try** block, include a **catch** clause that specifies the exception type that you wish to catch. To illustrate how easily this can be done, the following program includes a **try** block and a **catch** clause that processes the **ArithmeticException** generated by the division-by-zero error:

```
class Exc2 {
  public static void main(String[] args) {
    int d, a;

    try { // monitor a block of code.
     d = 0;
     a = 42 / d;
     System.out.println("This will not be printed.");
   } catch (ArithmeticException e) { // catch divide-by-zero error
     System.out.println("Division by zero.");
   }
```

```
    System.out.println("After catch statement.");
  }
}
```

This program generates the following output:

```
Division by zero.
After catch statement.
```

Notice that the call to **println( )** inside the **try** block is never executed. Once an exception is thrown, program control transfers out of the **try** block into the **catch** block. Put differently, **catch** is not "called," so execution never "returns" to the **try** block from a **catch**. Thus, the line "This will not be printed." is not displayed. Once the **catch** statement has executed, program control continues with the next line in the program following the entire **try/catch** mechanism.

A **try** and its **catch** statement form a unit. The scope of the **catch** clause is restricted to those statements specified by the immediately preceding **try** statement. A **catch** statement cannot catch an exception thrown by another **try** statement (except in the case of nested **try** statements, described shortly). The statements that are protected by **try** must be surrounded by curly braces. (That is, they must be within a block.) You cannot use **try** on a single statement.

The goal of most well-constructed **catch** clauses should be to resolve the exceptional condition and then continue on as if the error had never happened. For example, in the next program, each iteration of the **for** loop obtains two random integers. Those two integers are divided by each other, and the result is used to divide the value 12345. The final result is put into **a**. If either division operation causes a divide-by-zero error, it is caught, the value of **a** is set to zero, and the program continues.

```
// Handle an exception and move on.
import java.util.Random;

class HandleError {
  public static void main(String[] args) {
    int a=0, b=0, c=0;
    Random r = new Random();

    for(int i=0; i<32000; i++) {
      try {
        b = r.nextInt();
        c = r.nextInt();
        a = 12345 / (b/c);
      } catch (ArithmeticException e) {
        System.out.println("Division by zero.");
        a = 0; // set a to zero and continue
      }
      System.out.println("a: " + a);
    }
  }
}
```

## Displaying a Description of an Exception

**Throwable** overrides the **toString( )** method (defined by **Object**) so that it returns a string containing a description of the exception. You can display this description in a **println( )** statement by simply passing the exception as an argument. For example, the **catch** block in the preceding program can be rewritten like this:

```
catch (ArithmeticException e) {
  System.out.println("Exception: " + e);
  a = 0; // set a to zero and continue
}
```

When this version is substituted in the program, and the program is run, each divide-by-zero error displays the following message:

```
Exception: java.lang.ArithmeticException: / by zero
```

While it is of no particular value in this context, the ability to display a description of an exception is valuable in other circumstances—particularly when you are experimenting with exceptions or when you are debugging.

# Multiple catch Clauses

In some cases, more than one exception could be raised by a single piece of code. To handle this type of situation, you can specify two or more **catch** clauses, each catching a different type of exception. When an exception is thrown, each **catch** statement is inspected in order, and the first one whose type matches that of the exception is executed. After one **catch** statement executes, the others are bypassed, and execution continues after the **try/catch** block. The following example traps two different exception types:

```
// Demonstrate multiple catch statements.
class MultipleCatches {
  public static void main(String[] args) {
    try {
      int a = args.length;
      System.out.println("a = " + a);
      int b = 42 / a;
      int[] c = { 1 };
      c[42] = 99;
    } catch(ArithmeticException e) {
      System.out.println("Divide by 0: " + e);
    } catch(ArrayIndexOutOfBoundsException e) {
      System.out.println("Array index oob: " + e);
    }
    System.out.println("After try/catch blocks.");
  }
}
```

This program will cause a division-by-zero exception if it is started with no command-line arguments, since **a** will equal zero. It will survive the division if you provide a command-line argument, setting **a** to something larger than zero. But it will cause an **ArrayIndexOutOfBoundsException**, since the **int** array **c** has a length of 1, yet the program attempts to assign a value to **c[42]**.

Here is the output generated by running it both ways:

```
C:\>java MultipleCatches
a = 0
Divide by 0: java.lang.ArithmeticException: / by zero
After try/catch blocks.

C:\>java MultipleCatches TestArg
a = 1
Array index oob:  java.lang.ArrayIndexOutOfBoundsException:
Index 42 out of bounds for length 1
After try/catch blocks.
```

When you use multiple **catch** statements, it is important to remember that exception subclasses must come before any of their superclasses. This is because a **catch** statement that uses a superclass will catch exceptions of that type plus any of its subclasses. Thus, a subclass would never be reached if it came after its superclass. Further, in Java, unreachable code is an error. For example, consider the following program:

```
/* This program contains an error.

   A subclass must come before its superclass in
   a series of catch statements. If not,
   unreachable code will be created and a
   compile-time error will result.
*/
class SuperSubCatch {
  public static void main(String[] args) {
    try {
      int a = 0;
      int b = 42 / a;
     } catch(Exception e) {
       System.out.println("Generic Exception catch.");
     }
    /* This catch is never reached because
       ArithmeticException is a subclass of Exception. */
    catch(ArithmeticException e) { // ERROR - unreachable
      System.out.println("This is never reached.");
     }
  }
}
```

If you try to compile this program, you will receive an error message stating that the second **catch** statement is unreachable because the exception has already been caught. Since **ArithmeticException** is a subclass of **Exception**, the first **catch** statement will handle all **Exception**-based errors, including **ArithmeticException**. This means that the second **catch** statement will never execute. To fix the problem, reverse the order of the **catch** statements.

## Nested try Statements

The **try** statement can be nested. That is, a **try** statement can be inside the block of another **try**. Each time a **try** statement is entered, the context of that exception is pushed on the stack. If an inner **try** statement does not have a **catch** handler for a particular exception, the stack is unwound and the next **try** statement's **catch** handlers are inspected for a match. This continues until one of the **catch** statements succeeds, or until all of the nested **try** statements are exhausted. If no **catch** statement matches, then the Java run-time system will handle the exception. Here is an example that uses nested **try** statements:

```
// An example of nested try statements.
class NestTry {
  public static void main(String[] args) {
    try {
      int a = args.length;

      /* If no command-line args are present,
         the following statement will generate
         a divide-by-zero exception. */
      int b = 42 / a;

      System.out.println("a = " + a);

      try { // nested try block
        /* If one command-line arg is used,
           then a divide-by-zero exception
           will be generated by the following code. */
        if(a==1) a = a/(a-a); // division by zero

        /* If two command-line args are used,
           then generate an out-of-bounds exception. */
        if(a==2) {
          int[] c = { 1 };
          c[42] = 99; // generate an out-of-bounds exception
        }
      } catch(ArrayIndexOutOfBoundsException e) {
        System.out.println("Array index out-of-bounds: " + e);
      }

    } catch(ArithmeticException e) {
      System.out.println("Divide by 0: " + e);
    }
  }
}
```

As you can see, this program nests one **try** block within another. The program works as follows. When you execute the program with no command-line arguments, a divide-by-zero exception is generated by the outer **try** block. Execution of the program with one command-line argument generates a divide-by-zero exception from within the nested **try** block. Since the inner block does not catch this exception, it is passed on to the outer **try** block, where it is handled. If you execute the program with two command-line arguments, an array boundary exception is generated from within the inner **try** block. Here are sample runs that illustrate each case:

```
C:\>java NestTry
Divide by 0: java.lang.ArithmeticException: / by zero

C:\>java NestTry One
a = 1
Divide by 0: java.lang.ArithmeticException: / by zero

C:\>java NestTry One Two
a = 2
Array index out-of-bounds:
  java.lang.ArrayIndexOutOfBoundsException:
  Index 42 out of bounds for length 1
```

Nesting of **try** statements can occur in less obvious ways when method calls are involved. For example, you can enclose a call to a method within a **try** block. Inside that method is another **try** statement. In this case, the **try** within the method is still nested inside the outer **try** block, which calls the method. Here is the previous program recoded so that the nested **try** block is moved inside the method **nesttry( )**:

```
/* Try statements can be implicitly nested via
   calls to methods. */
class MethNestTry {
  static void nesttry(int a) {
    try { // nested try block
      /* If one command-line arg is used,
         then a divide-by-zero exception
         will be generated by the following code. */
       if(a==1) a = a/(a-a); // division by zero

       /* If two command-line args are used,
          then generate an out-of-bounds exception. */
      if(a==2) {
        int[] c = { 1 };
        c[42] = 99; // generate an out-of-bounds exception
      }
    } catch(ArrayIndexOutOfBoundsException e) {
      System.out.println("Array index out-of-bounds: " + e);
    }
  }

  public static void main(String[] args) {
    try {
      int a = args.length;

      /* If no command-line args are present,
         the following statement will generate
         a divide-by-zero exception. */
      int b = 42 / a;
      System.out.println("a = " + a);
```

```
      nesttry(a);
    } catch(ArithmeticException e) {
      System.out.println("Divide by 0: " + e);
    }
  }
}
```

The output of this program is identical to that of the preceding example.

## throw

So far, you have only been catching exceptions that are thrown by the Java run-time system. However, it is possible for your program to throw an exception explicitly, using the **throw** statement. The general form of **throw** is shown here:

throw *ThrowableInstance*;

Here, *ThrowableInstance* must be an object of type **Throwable** or a subclass of **Throwable**. Primitive types, such as **int** or **char**, as well as non-**Throwable** classes, such as **String** and **Object**, cannot be used as exceptions. There are two ways you can obtain a **Throwable** object: using a parameter in a **catch** clause or creating one with the **new** operator.

The flow of execution stops immediately after the **throw** statement; any subsequent statements are not executed. The nearest enclosing **try** block is inspected to see if it has a **catch** statement that matches the type of exception. If it does find a match, control is transferred to that statement. If not, then the next enclosing **try** statement is inspected, and so on. If no matching **catch** is found, then the default exception handler halts the program and prints the stack trace.

Here is a sample program that creates and throws an exception. The handler that catches the exception rethrows it to the outer handler.

```
// Demonstrate throw.
class ThrowDemo {
  static void demoproc() {
    try {
      throw new NullPointerException("demo");
    } catch(NullPointerException e) {
      System.out.println("Caught inside demoproc.");
      throw e; // rethrow the exception
    }
  }

  public static void main(String[] args) {
    try {
      demoproc();
    } catch(NullPointerException e) {
      System.out.println("Recaught: " + e);
    }
  }
}
```

This program gets two chances to deal with the same error. First, **main( )** sets up an exception context and then calls **demoproc( )**. The **demoproc( )** method then sets up another exception-handling context and immediately throws a new instance of **NullPointerException**, which is caught on the next line. The exception is then rethrown. Here is the resulting output:

```
Caught inside demoproc.
Recaught: java.lang.NullPointerException: demo
```

The program also illustrates how to create one of Java's standard exception objects. Pay close attention to this line:

```
throw new NullPointerException("demo");
```

Here, **new** is used to construct an instance of **NullPointerException**. Many of Java's built-in run-time exceptions have at least two constructors: one with no parameter and one that takes a string parameter. When the second form is used, the argument specifies a string that describes the exception. This string is displayed when the object is used as an argument to **print( )** or **println( )**. It can also be obtained by a call to **getMessage( )**, which is defined by **Throwable**.

## throws

If a method is capable of causing an exception that it does not handle, it must specify this behavior so that callers of the method can guard themselves against that exception. You do this by including a **throws** clause in the method's declaration. A **throws** clause lists the types of exceptions that a method might throw. This is necessary for all exceptions, except those of type **Error** or **RuntimeException**, or any of their subclasses. All other exceptions that a method can throw must be declared in the **throws** clause. If they are not, a compile-time error will result.

This is the general form of a method declaration that includes a **throws** clause:

*type method-name*(*parameter-list*) throws *exception-list*
{
  // body of method
}

Here, *exception-list* is a comma-separated list of the exceptions that a method can throw.

Following is an example of an incorrect program that tries to throw an exception that it does not catch. Because the program does not specify a **throws** clause to declare this fact, the program will not compile.

```
// This program contains an error and will not compile.
class ThrowsDemo {
  static void throwOne() {
    System.out.println("Inside throwOne.");
    throw new IllegalAccessException("demo");
  }
  public static void main(String[] args) {
    throwOne();
  }
}
```

To make this example compile, you need to make two changes. First, you need to declare that **throwOne( )** throws **IllegalAccessException**. Second, **main( )** must define a **try/catch** statement that catches this exception.

The corrected example is shown here:

```
// This is now correct.
class ThrowsDemo {
  static void throwOne() throws IllegalAccessException {
    System.out.println("Inside throwOne.");
    throw new IllegalAccessException("demo");
  }
  public static void main(String[] args) {
    try {
      throwOne();
    } catch (IllegalAccessException e) {
      System.out.println("Caught " + e);
    }
  }
}
```

Here is the output generated by running this sample program:

```
inside throwOne
caught java.lang.IllegalAccessException: demo
```

# finally

When exceptions are thrown, execution in a method takes a rather abrupt, nonlinear path that alters the normal flow through the method. Depending upon how the method is coded, it is even possible for an exception to cause the method to return prematurely. This could be a problem in some methods. For example, if a method opens a file upon entry and closes it upon exit, then you will not want the code that closes the file to be bypassed by the exception-handling mechanism. The **finally** keyword is designed to address this contingency.

**finally** creates a block of code that will be executed after a **try/catch** block has completed and before the code following the **try/catch** block. The **finally** block will execute whether or not an exception is thrown. If an exception is thrown, the **finally** block will execute even if no **catch** statement matches the exception. Any time a method is about to return to the caller from inside a **try/catch** block, via an uncaught exception or an explicit return statement, the **finally** clause is also executed just before the method returns. This can be useful for closing file handles and freeing up any other resources that might have been allocated at the beginning of a method with the intent of disposing of them before returning. The **finally** clause is optional. However, each **try** statement requires at least one **catch** or a **finally** clause.

Here is a sample program that shows three methods that exit in various ways, none without executing their **finally** clauses:

```
// Demonstrate finally.
class FinallyDemo {
  // Throw an exception out of the method.
  static void procA() {
    try {
      System.out.println("inside procA");
      throw new RuntimeException("demo");
```

```
    } finally {
      System.out.println("procA's finally");
    }
  }

  // Return from within a try block.
  static void procB() {
    try {
      System.out.println("inside procB");
      return;
    } finally {
      System.out.println("procB's finally");
    }
  }

  // Execute a try block normally.
  static void procC() {
    try {
      System.out.println("inside procC");
    } finally {
      System.out.println("procC's finally");
    }
  }

  public static void main(String[] args) {
    try {
      procA();
    } catch (Exception e) {
      System.out.println("Exception caught");
    }

    procB();
    procC();
  }
}
```

In this example, **procA( )** prematurely breaks out of the **try** by throwing an exception. The **finally** clause is executed on the way out. **procB( )**'s **try** statement is exited via a **return** statement. The **finally** clause is executed before **procB( )** returns. In **procC( )**, the **try** statement executes normally, without error. However, the **finally** block is still executed.

**REMEMBER** If a **finally** block is associated with a **try**, the **finally** block will be executed upon conclusion of the **try**.

Here is the output generated by the preceding program:

```
inside procA
procA's finally
Exception caught
inside procB
procB's finally
inside procC
procC's finally
```

## Java's Built-in Exceptions

Inside the standard package **java.lang**, Java defines several exception classes. A few have been used by the preceding examples. The most general of these exceptions are subclasses of the standard type **RuntimeException**. As previously explained, these exceptions need not be included in any method's **throws** list. In the language of Java, these are called *unchecked exceptions* because the compiler does not check to see if a method handles or throws these exceptions. The unchecked exceptions defined in **java.lang** are listed in Table 10-1. Table 10-2 lists those exceptions defined by **java.lang** that must be included in a method's **throws** list if that method can generate one of these exceptions and does not handle it itself. These are called *checked exceptions*. In addition to the exceptions in **java.lang**, Java defines several more that relate to its other standard packages.

| Exception | Meaning |
|---|---|
| ArithmeticException | Arithmetic error, such as divide-by-zero. |
| ArrayIndexOutOfBoundsException | Array index is out of bounds. |
| ArrayStoreException | Assignment to an array element of an incompatible type. |
| ClassCastException | Invalid cast. |
| EnumConstantNotPresentException | An attempt is made to use an undefined enumeration value. |
| IllegalArgumentException | Illegal argument used to invoke a method. |
| IllegalCallerException | A method cannot be legally executed by the calling code. |
| IllegalMonitorStateException | Illegal monitor operation, such as waiting on an unlocked thread. |
| IllegalStateException | Environment or application is in incorrect state. |
| IllegalThreadStateException | Requested operation not compatible with current thread state. |
| IndexOutOfBoundsException | Some type of index is out of bounds. |
| LayerInstantiationException | A module layer cannot be created. |
| NegativeArraySizeException | Array created with a negative size. |
| NullPointerException | Invalid use of a null reference. |
| NumberFormatException | Invalid conversion of a string to a numeric format. |
| SecurityException | Attempt to violate security. |
| StringIndexOutOfBoundsException | Attempt to index outside the bounds of a string. |
| TypeNotPresentException | Type not found. |
| UnsupportedOperationException | An unsupported operation was encountered. |

**Table 10-1** Java's Unchecked **RuntimeException** Subclasses Defined in **java.lang**

| Exception | Meaning |
|---|---|
| ClassNotFoundException | Class not found. |
| CloneNotSupportedException | Attempt to clone an object that does not implement the **Cloneable** interface. |
| IllegalAccessException | Access to a class is denied. |
| InstantiationException | Attempt to create an object of an abstract class or interface. |
| InterruptedException | One thread has been interrupted by another thread. |
| NoSuchFieldException | A requested field does not exist. |
| NoSuchMethodException | A requested method does not exist. |
| ReflectiveOperationException | Superclass of reflection-related exceptions. |

**Table 10-2** Java's Checked Exceptions Defined in **java.lang**



# Creating Your Own Exception Subclasses

Although Java's built-in exceptions handle most common errors, you will probably want to create your own exception types to handle situations specific to your applications. This is quite easy to do: just define a subclass of **Exception** (which is, of course, a subclass of **Throwable**). Your subclasses don't need to actually implement anything—it is their existence in the type system that allows you to use them as exceptions.

The **Exception** class does not define any methods of its own. It does, of course, inherit those methods provided by **Throwable**. Thus, all exceptions, including those that you create, have the methods defined by **Throwable** available to them. They are shown in Table 10-3. You may also wish to override one or more of these methods in exception classes that you create.

**Exception** defines four public constructors. Two support chained exceptions, described in the next section. The other two are shown here:

Exception( )
Exception(String *msg*)

The first form creates an exception that has no description. The second form lets you specify a description of the exception.

Although specifying a description when an exception is created is often useful, sometimes it is better to override **toString( )**. Here's why: The version of **toString( )** defined by **Throwable** (and inherited by **Exception**) first displays the name of the exception followed by a colon, which is then followed by your description. By overriding **toString( )**, you can prevent the exception name and colon from being displayed. This makes for a cleaner output, which is desirable in some cases.

| Method | Description |
|---|---|
| final void addSuppressed(Throwable *exc*) | Adds *exc* to the list of suppressed exceptions associated with the invoking exception. Primarily for use by the **try**-with-resources statement. |
| Throwable fillInStackTrace( ) | Returns a **Throwable** object that contains a completed stack trace. This object can be rethrown. |
| Throwable getCause( ) | Returns the exception that underlies the current exception. If there is no underlying exception, **null** is returned. |
| String getLocalizedMessage( ) | Returns a localized description of the exception. |
| String getMessage( ) | Returns a description of the exception. |
| StackTraceElement[ ] getStackTrace( ) | Returns an array that contains the stack trace, one element at a time, as an array of **StackTraceElement**. The method at the top of the stack is the last method called before the exception was thrown. This method is found in the first element of the array. The **StackTraceElement** class gives your program access to information about each element in the trace, such as its method name. |
| final Throwable[ ] getSuppressed( ) | Obtains the suppressed exceptions associated with the invoking exception and returns an array that contains the result. Suppressed exceptions are primarily generated by the **try**-with-resources statement. |
| Throwable initCause(Throwable *causeExc*) | Associates *causeExc* with the invoking exception as a cause of the invoking exception. Returns a reference to the exception. |
| void printStackTrace( ) | Displays the stack trace. |
| void printStackTrace(PrintStream *stream*) | Sends the stack trace to the specified stream. |
| void printStackTrace(PrintWriter *stream*) | Sends the stack trace to the specified stream. |
| void setStackTrace(StackTraceElement[ ] *elements*) | Sets the stack trace to the elements passed in *elements*. This method is for specialized applications, not normal use. |
| String toString( ) | Returns a **String** object containing a description of the exception. This method is called by **println( )** when outputting a **Throwable** object. |

**Table 10-3** The Methods Defined by **Throwable**

The following example declares a new subclass of **Exception** and then uses that subclass to signal an error condition in a method. It overrides the **toString( )** method, allowing a carefully tailored description of the exception to be displayed.

```
// This program creates a custom exception type.
class MyException extends Exception {
  private int detail;

  MyException(int a) {
    detail = a;
  }

  public String toString() {
    return "MyException[" + detail + "]";
  }
}

class ExceptionDemo {
  static void compute(int a) throws MyException {
    System.out.println("Called compute(" + a + ")");
    if(a > 10)
      throw new MyException(a);
    System.out.println("Normal exit");
  }

  public static void main(String[] args) {
    try {
      compute(1);
      compute(20);
    } catch (MyException e) {
      System.out.println("Caught " + e);
    }
  }
}
```

This example defines a subclass of **Exception** called **MyException**. This subclass is quite simple: It has only a constructor plus an overridden **toString( )** method that displays the value of the exception. The **ExceptionDemo** class defines a method named **compute( )** that throws a **MyException** object. The exception is thrown when **compute( )**'s integer parameter is greater than 10. The **main( )** method sets up an exception handler for **MyException**, then calls **compute( )** with a legal value (less than 10) and an illegal one to show both paths through the code. Here is the result:

```
Called compute(1)
Normal exit
Called compute(20)
Caught MyException[20]
```

## Chained Exceptions

A number of years ago, a feature was incorporated into the exception subsystem: *chained exceptions.* The chained exception feature allows you to associate another exception with an exception. This second exception describes the cause of the first exception. For example, imagine a situation in which a method throws an **ArithmeticException** because of an attempt to divide by zero. However, the actual cause of the problem was that an I/O error occurred, which caused the divisor to be set improperly. Although the method must certainly throw an **ArithmeticException**, since that is the error that occurred, you might also want to let the calling code know that the underlying cause was an I/O error. Chained exceptions let you handle this, and any other situation in which layers of exceptions exist.

To allow chained exceptions, two constructors and two methods were added to **Throwable**. The constructors are shown here:

Throwable(Throwable *causeExc*)
Throwable(String *msg*, Throwable *causeExc*)

In the first form, *causeExc* is the exception that causes the current exception. That is, *causeExc* is the underlying reason that an exception occurred. The second form allows you to specify a description at the same time that you specify a cause exception. These two constructors have also been added to the **Error**, **Exception**, and **RuntimeException** classes.

The chained exception methods supported by **Throwable** are **getCause( )** and **initCause( )**. These methods are shown in Table 10-3 and are repeated here for the sake of discussion.

Throwable getCause( )
Throwable initCause(Throwable *causeExc*)

The **getCause( )** method returns the exception that underlies the current exception. If there is no underlying exception, **null** is returned. The **initCause( )** method associates *causeExc* with the invoking exception and returns a reference to the exception. Thus, you can associate a cause with an exception after the exception has been created. However, the cause exception can be set only once. This means that you can call **initCause( )** only once for each exception object. Furthermore, if the cause exception was set by a constructor, then you can't set it again using **initCause( )**. In general, **initCause( )** is used to set a cause for legacy exception classes that don't support the two additional constructors described earlier.

Here is an example that illustrates the mechanics of handling chained exceptions:

```
// Demonstrate exception chaining.
class ChainExcDemo {
  static void demoproc() {

    // create an exception
    NullPointerException e =
      new NullPointerException("top layer");

    // add a cause
    e.initCause(new ArithmeticException("cause"));

    throw e;
  }
```

```
  public static void main(String[] args) {
    try {
      demoproc();
    } catch(NullPointerException e) {
      // display top level exception
      System.out.println("Caught: " + e);

      // display cause exception
      System.out.println("Original cause: " +
                          e.getCause());
    }
  }
}
```

The output from the program is shown here:

```
Caught: java.lang.NullPointerException: top layer
Original cause: java.lang.ArithmeticException: cause
```

In this example, the top-level exception is **NullPointerException**. To it is added a cause exception, **ArithmeticException**. When the exception is thrown out of **demoproc( )**, it is caught by **main( )**. There, the top-level exception is displayed, followed by the underlying exception, which is obtained by calling **getCause( )**.

Chained exceptions can be carried on to whatever depth is necessary. Thus, the cause exception can, itself, have a cause. Be aware that overly long chains of exceptions may indicate poor design.

Chained exceptions are not something that every program will need. However, in cases in which knowledge of an underlying cause is useful, they offer an elegant solution.

# Three Additional Exception Features

Beginning with JDK 7, three interesting and useful features have been part of the exception system. The first automates the process of releasing a resource, such as a file, when it is no longer needed. It is based on an expanded form of the **try** statement called ***try-with-resources***, and is described in Chapter 13 when files are introduced. The second feature is called *multi-catch*, and the third is sometimes referred to as *final rethrow* or *more precise rethrow*. These two features are described here.

The multi-catch feature allows two or more exceptions to be caught by the same **catch** clause. It is not uncommon for two or more exception handlers to use the same code sequence even though they respond to different exceptions. Instead of having to catch each exception type individually, you can use a single **catch** clause to handle all of the exceptions without code duplication.

To use a multi-catch, separate each exception type in the **catch** clause with the OR operator. Each multi-catch parameter is implicitly **final**. (You can explicitly specify **final**, if desired, but it is not necessary.) Because each multi-catch parameter is implicitly **final**, it can't be assigned a new value.

Here is a **catch** statement that uses the multi-catch feature to catch both **ArithmeticException** and **ArrayIndexOutOfBoundsException**:

```
catch(ArithmeticException | ArrayIndexOutOfBoundsException e) {
```

The following program shows the multi-catch feature in action:

```
// Demonstrate the multi-catch feature.
class MultiCatch {
  public static void main(String[] args) {
    int a=10, b=0;
    int[] vals = { 1, 2, 3 };

    try {
      int result = a / b; // generate an ArithmeticException

//      vals[10] = 19; // generate an ArrayIndexOutOfBoundsException

      // This catch clause catches both exceptions.
    } catch(ArithmeticException | ArrayIndexOutOfBoundsException e) {
      System.out.println("Exception caught: " + e);
    }

    System.out.println("After multi-catch.");
  }
}
```

The program will generate an **ArithmeticException** when the division by zero is attempted. If you comment out the division statement and remove the comment symbol from the next line, an **ArrayIndexOutOfBoundsException** is generated. Both exceptions are caught by the single **catch** statement.

The more precise rethrow feature restricts the type of exceptions that can be rethrown to only those checked exceptions that the associated **try** block throws, that are not handled by a preceding **catch** clause, and that are a subtype or supertype of the parameter. Although this capability might not be needed often, it is now available for use. For the more precise rethrow feature to be in force, the **catch** parameter must be either effectively **final**, which means that it must not be assigned a new value inside the **catch** block, or explicitly declared **final**.

## Using Exceptions

Exception handling provides a powerful mechanism for controlling complex programs that have many dynamic run-time characteristics. It is important to think of **try**, **throw**, and **catch** as clean ways to handle errors and unusual boundary conditions in your program's logic. Instead of using error return codes to indicate failure, use Java's exception handling capabilities. Thus, when a method can fail, have it throw an exception. This is a cleaner way to handle failure modes.

One last point: Java's exception-handling statements should not be considered a general mechanism for nonlocal branching. If you do so, it will only confuse your code and make it hard to maintain.

CHAPTER

# 11 Multithreaded Programming

Java provides built-in support for *multithreaded programming.* A multithreaded program contains two or more parts that can run concurrently. Each part of such a program is called a *thread*, and each thread defines a separate path of execution. Thus, multithreading is a specialized form of multitasking.

You are almost certainly acquainted with multitasking because it is supported by virtually all modern operating systems. However, there are two distinct types of multitasking: process-based and thread-based. It is important to understand the difference between the two. For many readers, process-based multitasking is the more familiar form. A *process* is, in essence, a program that is executing. Thus, *process-based* multitasking is the feature that allows your computer to run two or more programs concurrently. For example, process-based multitasking enables you to run the Java compiler at the same time that you are using a text editor or visiting a website. In process-based multitasking, a program is the smallest unit of code that can be dispatched by the scheduler.

In a *thread-based* multitasking environment, the thread is the smallest unit of dispatchable code. This means that a single program can perform two or more tasks simultaneously. For instance, a text editor can format text at the same time that it is printing, as long as these two actions are being performed by two separate threads. Thus, process-based multitasking deals with the "big picture," and thread-based multitasking handles the details.

Multitasking threads require less overhead than multitasking processes. Processes are heavyweight tasks that require their own separate address spaces. Interprocess communication is expensive and limited. Context switching from one process to another is also costly. Threads, on the other hand, are lighter weight. They share the same address space and cooperatively share the same heavyweight process. Interthread communication is inexpensive, and context switching from one thread to the next is lower in cost. While Java programs make use of process-based multitasking environments, process-based multitasking is not under Java's direct control. However, multithreaded multitasking is.

Multithreading enables you to write efficient programs that make maximum use of the processing power available in the system. One important way multithreading achieves this is by keeping idle time to a minimum. This is especially important for the interactive, networked environment in which Java operates because idle time is common. For example, the transmission rate of data over a network is much slower than the rate at which the computer can process it. Even local file system resources are read and written at a much slower pace than they can be processed by the CPU. And, of course, user input is much slower than the computer. In a single-threaded environment, your program has to wait for each of these tasks to finish before it can proceed to the next one—even though most of the time the program is idle, waiting for input. Multithreading helps you reduce this idle time because another thread can run when one is waiting.

If you have programmed for operating systems such as Windows, then you are already familiar with multithreaded programming. However, the fact that Java manages threads makes multithreading especially convenient because many of the details are handled for you.

## The Java Thread Model

The Java run-time system depends on threads for many things, and all the class libraries are designed with multithreading in mind. In fact, Java uses threads to enable the entire environment to be asynchronous. This helps reduce inefficiency by preventing the waste of CPU cycles.

The value of a multithreaded environment is best understood in contrast to its counterpart. Single-threaded systems often use an approach called an *event loop* with *polling*. In this model, a single thread of control runs in an infinite loop, polling a single event queue to decide what to do next. Once this polling mechanism returns with, say, a signal that a network file is ready to be read, then the event loop dispatches control to the appropriate event handler. Until this event handler returns, nothing else can happen in the program. This wastes CPU time. It can also result in one part of a program dominating the system and preventing any other events from being processed. In general, in a single-threaded environment, when a thread *blocks* (that is, suspends execution) because it is waiting for some resource, the entire program stops running. This is an example of how only being able to do one thing at a time, something common to all single-threaded systems, whatever approach they use, is an inefficient way to use the CPU.

The benefit of Java's multithreading is that the main loop/polling mechanism is eliminated. One thread can pause without stopping other parts of your program. For example, the idle time created when a thread reads data from a network or waits for user input can be utilized elsewhere. Multithreading allows animation loops to sleep for a second between each frame without causing the whole system to pause. When a thread blocks in a Java program, only the single thread that is blocked pauses. All other threads continue to run.

As most readers know, over the past few years, multicore systems have become commonplace. Of course, single-core systems are still in use. It is important to understand that Java's multithreading features work in both types of systems. In a single-core system, concurrently executing threads share the CPU, with each thread receiving a slice of CPU time. Therefore, in a single-core system, two or more threads do not actually run at the same time, but idle CPU time is utilized. However, in multicore systems, it is possible for two or more threads to actually execute simultaneously. In many cases, this can further improve program efficiency and increase the speed of certain operations.

Java has straddled these two CPU architectures with the thread model by implementing Java threads, each as a wrapper around an OS thread. Such Java threads are known as platform threads. For most developers, platform threads, when used correctly, give great scalability and performance characteristics. However, for some high-throughput server applications, particularly ones managing many connections simultaneously like a heavily trafficked web application, this model can lead to performance bottlenecks. For these special kinds of applications, JDK 21 has added a new way to map Java threads onto OS threads. Java threads using this new feature are called *virtual threads*. When an application uses virtual threads, the JVM is freed from tying each virtual thread one-to-one with an OS thread, offering greater efficiencies for highly multithreaded applications. While most developers will continue to use the default platform thread model, for those who do wish to explore virtual threads, fortunately, the programming model for the new virtual threads is the same as for platform threads. We'll cover virtual threads at the end of the chapter.

**NOTE** In addition to the multithreading features described in this chapter, you will also want to explore the Fork/Join Framework. It provides a powerful means of creating multithreaded applications that automatically scale to make best use of multicore environments. The Fork/Join Framework is part of Java's support for *parallel programming*, which is the name commonly given to the techniques that optimize some types of algorithms for parallel execution in systems that have more than one CPU. For a discussion of the Fork/Join Framework and other concurrency utilities, see Chapter 29. Java's traditional multithreading capabilities are described here.

Threads exist in several states. Here is a general description: A thread can be *running*. It can be *ready to run* as soon as it gets CPU time. A running thread can be *suspended*, which temporarily halts its activity. A suspended thread can then be *resumed*, allowing it to pick up where it left off. A thread can be *blocked* when waiting for a resource. At any time, a thread can be terminated, which halts its execution immediately. Once terminated, a thread cannot be resumed.

## Thread Priorities

Java assigns to each thread a priority that determines how that thread should be treated with respect to the others. Thread priorities are integers that specify the relative priority of one thread to another. As an absolute value, a priority is meaningless; a higher-priority thread doesn't run any faster than a lower-priority thread if it is the only thread running. Instead, a thread's priority is used to decide when to switch from one running thread to the next. This is called a *context switch*. The rules that determine when a context switch takes place are simple:

- *A thread can voluntarily relinquish control.* This occurs when explicitly yielding, sleeping, or when blocked. In this scenario, all other threads are examined, and the highest priority thread that is ready to run is given the CPU.
- *A thread can be preempted by a higher-priority thread.* In this case, a lower-priority thread that does not yield the processor is simply preempted—no matter what it is doing—by a higher-priority thread. Basically, as soon as a higher-priority thread wants to run, it does. This is called *preemptive multitasking*.

In cases where two threads with the same priority are competing for CPU cycles, the situation is a bit complicated. For some operating systems, threads of equal priority are time-sliced automatically in round-robin fashion. For other types of operating systems, threads of equal priority must voluntarily yield control to their peers. If they don't, the other threads will not run.

---

**CAUTION** Portability problems can arise from the differences in the way that operating systems context-switch threads of equal priority.

## Synchronization

Because multithreading introduces an asynchronous behavior to your programs, there must be a way for you to enforce synchronicity when you need it. For example, if you want two threads to communicate and share a complicated data structure, such as a linked list, you need some way to ensure that they don't conflict with each other. That is, you must prevent one thread from writing data while another thread is in the middle of reading it. For this purpose, Java implements an elegant twist on an age-old model of interprocess synchronization: the *monitor*. The monitor is a control mechanism first defined by C.A.R. Hoare. You can think of a monitor as a very small box that can hold only one thread. Once a thread enters a monitor, all other threads must wait until that thread exits the monitor. In this way, a monitor can be used to protect a shared asset from being manipulated by more than one thread at a time.

In Java, there is no class "Monitor"; instead, each object has its own implicit monitor that is automatically entered when one of the object's synchronized methods is called. Once a thread is inside a synchronized method, no other thread can call any other synchronized method on the same object. This enables you to write very clear and concise multithreaded code, because synchronization support is built into the language.

## Messaging

After you divide your program into separate threads, you need to define how they will communicate with each other. When programming with some other languages, you must depend on the operating system to establish communication between threads. This, of course, adds overhead. By contrast, Java provides a clean, low-cost way for two or more threads to talk to each other, via calls to predefined methods that all objects have. Java's messaging system allows a thread to enter a synchronized method on an object, and then wait there until some other thread explicitly notifies it to come out.

## The Thread Class and the Runnable Interface

Java's multithreading system is built upon the **Thread** class, its methods, and its companion interface, **Runnable**. **Thread** encapsulates a thread of execution. Since you can't directly refer to the ethereal state of a running thread, you will deal with it through its proxy, the **Thread** instance that spawned it. To create a new thread, your program will either extend **Thread** or implement the **Runnable** interface.

The **Thread** class defines several methods that help manage threads. Several of those used in this chapter are shown here:

| Method | Meaning |
|---|---|
| getName | Obtain a thread's name. |
| getPriority | Obtain a thread's priority. |
| isAlive | Determine if a thread is still running. |
| join | Wait for a thread to terminate. |
| run | Entry point for the thread. |
| sleep | Suspend a thread for a period of time. |
| start | Start a thread by calling its run method. |

Thus far, all the examples in this book have used a single thread of execution. The remainder of this chapter explains how to use **Thread** and **Runnable** to create and manage threads, beginning with the one thread that all Java programs have: the main thread.

# The Main Thread

When a Java program starts up, one thread begins running immediately. This is usually called the *main thread* of your program, because it is the one that is executed when your program begins. The main thread is important for two reasons:

- It is the thread from which other "child" threads will be spawned.
- Often, it must be the last thread to finish execution because it performs various shutdown actions.

Although the main thread is created automatically when your program is started, it can be controlled through a **Thread** object. To do so, you must obtain a reference to it by calling the method **currentThread( )**, which is a **public static** member of **Thread**. Its general form is shown here:

static Thread currentThread( )

This method returns a reference to the thread in which it is called. Once you have a reference to the main thread, you can control it just like any other thread.

Let's begin by reviewing the following example:

```
// Controlling the main Thread.
class CurrentThreadDemo {
  public static void main(String[] args) {
    Thread t = Thread.currentThread();

    System.out.println("Current thread: " + t);

    // change the name of the thread
    t.setName("My Thread");
    System.out.println("After name change: " + t);
```

```
      try {
        for(int n = 5; n > 0; n--) {
          System.out.println(n);
          Thread.sleep(1000);
        }
      } catch (InterruptedException e) {
        System.out.println("Main thread interrupted");
      }
    }
  }
```

In this program, a reference to the current thread (the main thread, in this case) is obtained by calling **currentThread( )**, and this reference is stored in the local variable **t**. Next, the program displays information about the thread. The program then calls **setName( )** to change the internal name of the thread. Information about the thread is then redisplayed. Next, a loop counts down from five, pausing one second between each line. The pause is accomplished by the **sleep( )** method. The argument to **sleep( )** specifies the delay period in milliseconds. Notice the **try/catch** block around this loop. The **sleep( )** method in **Thread** might throw an **InterruptedException**. This would happen if some other thread wanted to interrupt this sleeping one. This example just prints a message if it gets interrupted. In a real program, you would need to handle this differently. Here is the output generated by this program:

```
Current thread: Thread[main,5,main]
After name change: Thread[My Thread,5,main]
5
4
3
2
1
```

Notice the output produced when **t** is used as an argument to **println( )**. This displays, in order: the name of the thread, its priority, and the name of its group. By default, the name of the main thread is **main**. Its priority is 5, which is the default value, and **main** is also the name of the group of threads to which this thread belongs. A *thread group* is a data structure that controls the state of a collection of threads as a whole. After the name of the thread is changed, **t** is again output. This time, the new name of the thread is displayed.

Let's look more closely at the methods defined by **Thread** that are used in the program. The **sleep( )** method causes the thread from which it is called to suspend execution for the specified period of milliseconds. Its general form is shown here:

static void sleep(long *milliseconds*) throws InterruptedException

The number of milliseconds to suspend is specified in *milliseconds*. This method may throw an **InterruptedException**.

The **sleep( )** method has a second form, shown next, that allows you to specify the period in terms of milliseconds and nanoseconds:

static void sleep(long *milliseconds*, int *nanoseconds*) throws InterruptedException

This second form is useful only in environments that allow timing periods as short as nanoseconds.

As the preceding program shows, you can set the name of a thread by using **setName( )**. You can obtain the name of a thread by calling **getName( )** (but note that this is not shown in the program). These methods are members of the **Thread** class and are declared like this:

final void setName(String *threadName*)
final String getName( )

Here, *threadName* specifies the name of the thread.

# Creating a Thread

In the most general sense, you create a thread by instantiating an object of type **Thread**. Java defines two ways in which this can be accomplished:

- You can implement the **Runnable** interface.
- You can extend the **Thread** class itself.

The following two sections look at each method, in turn.

## Implementing Runnable

The easiest way to create a thread is to create a class that implements the **Runnable** interface. **Runnable** abstracts a unit of executable code. You can construct a thread on any object that implements **Runnable**. To implement **Runnable**, a class need only implement a single method called **run( )**, which is declared like this:

public void run( )

Inside **run( )**, you will define the code that constitutes the new thread. It is important to understand that **run( )** can call other methods, use other classes, and declare variables, just like the main thread can. The only difference is that **run( )** establishes the entry point for another, concurrent thread of execution within your program. This thread will end when **run( )** returns.

After you create a class that implements **Runnable**, you will instantiate an object of type **Thread** from within that class. **Thread** defines several constructors. The one that we will use is shown here:

Thread(Runnable *threadOb*, String *threadName*)

In this constructor, *threadOb* is an instance of a class that implements the **Runnable** interface. This defines where execution of the thread will begin. The name of the new thread is specified by *threadName*.

After the new thread is created, it will not start running until you call its **start( )** method, which is declared within **Thread**. In essence, **start( )** initiates a call to **run( )**. The **start( )** method is shown here:

void start( )

Here is an example that creates a new thread and starts it running:

```
// Create a second thread.
class NewThread implements Runnable {
  Thread t;
```

```
  NewThread() {
    // Create a new, second thread
    t = new Thread(this, "Demo Thread");
    System.out.println("Child thread: " + t);
  }

  // This is the entry point for the second thread.
  public void run() {
    try {
      for(int i = 5; i > 0; i--) {
        System.out.println("Child Thread: " + i);
        Thread.sleep(500);
      }
    } catch (InterruptedException e) {
      System.out.println("Child interrupted.");
    }
    System.out.println("Exiting child thread.");
  }
}

class ThreadDemo {
  public static void main(String[] args) {
    NewThread nt = new NewThread(); // create a new thread

    nt.t.start(); // Start the thread

    try {
      for(int i = 5; i > 0; i--) {
        System.out.println("Main Thread: " + i);
        Thread.sleep(1000);
      }
    } catch (InterruptedException e) {
      System.out.println("Main thread interrupted.");
    }
    System.out.println("Main thread exiting.");
  }
}
```

Inside **NewThread**'s constructor, a new **Thread** object is created by the following statement:

```
t = new Thread(this, "Demo Thread");
```

Passing **this** as the first argument indicates that you want the new thread to call the **run( )** method on the **this** object. Inside **main( )**, **start( )** is called, which starts the thread of execution beginning at the **run( )** method. This causes the child thread's **for** loop to begin. Next, the main thread enters its **for** loop. Both threads continue running, sharing the CPU in single-core systems, until their loops finish. The output produced by this program is as follows.(Your output may vary based upon the specific execution environment.)

```
Child thread: Thread[Demo Thread,5,main]
Main Thread: 5
Child Thread: 5
Child Thread: 4
```

```
Main Thread: 4
Child Thread: 3
Child Thread: 2
Main Thread: 3
Child Thread: 1
Exiting child thread.
Main Thread: 2
Main Thread: 1
Main thread exiting.
```

As mentioned earlier, in a multithreaded program, it is often useful for the main thread to be the last thread to finish running. The preceding program ensures that the main thread finishes last, because the main thread sleeps for 1000 milliseconds between iterations, but the child thread sleeps for only 500 milliseconds. This causes the child thread to terminate earlier than the main thread. Shortly, you will see a better way to wait for a thread to finish.

## Extending Thread

The second way to create a thread is to create a new class that extends **Thread**, and then to create an instance of that class. The extending class must override the **run( )** method, which is the entry point for the new thread. As before, a call to **start( )** begins execution of the new thread. Here is the preceding program rewritten to extend **Thread**:

```
// Create a second thread by extending Thread
class NewThread extends Thread {

  NewThread() {
    // Create a new, second thread
    super("Demo Thread");
    System.out.println("Child thread: " + this);
  }

  // This is the entry point for the second thread.
  public void run() {
    try {
      for(int i = 5; i > 0; i--) {
        System.out.println("Child Thread: " + i);
        Thread.sleep(500);
      }
    } catch (InterruptedException e) {
      System.out.println("Child interrupted.");
    }
    System.out.println("Exiting child thread.");
  }
}

class ExtendThread {
  public static void main(String[] args) {
    NewThread nt = new NewThread(); // create a new thread

    nt.start(); // start the thread
```

```
    try {
      for(int i = 5; i > 0; i--) {
        System.out.println("Main Thread: " + i);
        Thread.sleep(1000);
      }
    } catch (InterruptedException e) {
      System.out.println("Main thread interrupted.");
    }
    System.out.println("Main thread exiting.");
  }
}
```

This program generates the same output as the preceding version. As you can see, the child thread is created by instantiating an object of **NewThread**, which is derived from **Thread**.

Notice the call to **super( )** inside **NewThread**. This invokes the following form of the **Thread** constructor:

public Thread(String *threadName*)

Here, *threadName* specifies the name of the thread.

## Choosing an Approach

At this point, you might be wondering why Java has two ways to create child threads, and which approach is better. The answers to these questions turn on the same point. The **Thread** class defines several methods that can be overridden by a derived class. Of these methods, the only one that *must* be overridden is **run( )**. This is, of course, the same method required when you implement **Runnable**. Many Java programmers feel that classes should be extended only when they are being enhanced or adapted in some way. So, if you will not be overriding any of **Thread**'s other methods, it is probably best simply to implement **Runnable**. Also, by implementing **Runnable**, your thread class does not need to inherit **Thread**, making it free to inherit a different class. Ultimately, which approach to use is up to you. However, throughout the rest of this chapter, we will create threads by using classes that implement **Runnable**.

# Creating Multiple Threads

So far, you have been using only two threads: the main thread and one child thread. However, your program can spawn as many threads as it needs. For example, the following program creates three child threads:

```
// Create multiple threads.
class NewThread implements Runnable {
  String name; // name of thread
  Thread t;

  NewThread(String threadname) {
    name = threadname;
    t = new Thread(this, name);
    System.out.println("New thread: " + t);
  }
```

```
  // This is the entry point for thread.
  public void run() {
    try {
      for(int i = 5; i > 0; i--) {
        System.out.println(name + ": " + i);
        Thread.sleep(1000);
      }
    } catch (InterruptedException e) {
      System.out.println(name + "Interrupted");
    }
    System.out.println(name + " exiting.");
  }
}

class MultiThreadDemo {
  public static void main(String[] args) {
    NewThread nt1 = new NewThread("One");
    NewThread nt2 = new NewThread("Two");
    NewThread nt3 = new NewThread("Three");

    // Start the threads.
    nt1.t.start();
    nt2.t.start();
    nt3.t.start();

    try {
      // wait for other threads to end
      Thread.sleep(10000);
    } catch (InterruptedException e) {
      System.out.println("Main thread Interrupted");
    }

    System.out.println("Main thread exiting.");
  }
}
```

Sample output from this program is shown here. (Your output may vary based upon the specific execution environment.)

```
New thread: Thread[One,5,main]
New thread: Thread[Two,5,main]
New thread: Thread[Three,5,main]
One: 5
Two: 5
Three: 5
One: 4
Two: 4
Three: 4
One: 3
Three: 3
Two: 3
One: 2
Three: 2
```

```
Two: 2
One: 1
Three: 1
Two: 1
One exiting.
Two exiting.
Three exiting.
Main thread exiting.
```

As you can see, once started, all three child threads share the CPU. Notice the call to **sleep(10000)** in **main( )**. This causes the main thread to sleep for ten seconds and ensures that it will finish last.

## Using isAlive( ) and join( )

As mentioned, often you will want the main thread to finish last. In the preceding examples, this is accomplished by calling **sleep( )** within **main( )**, with a long enough delay to ensure that all child threads terminate prior to the main thread. However, this is hardly a satisfactory solution, and it also raises a larger question: How can one thread know when another thread has ended? Fortunately, **Thread** provides a means by which you can answer this question.

Two ways exist to determine whether a thread has finished. First, you can call **isAlive( )** on the thread. This method is defined by **Thread**, and its general form is shown here:

final boolean isAlive( )

The **isAlive( )** method returns **true** if the thread upon which it is called is still running. It returns **false** otherwise.

While **isAlive( )** is occasionally useful, the method that you will more commonly use to wait for a thread to finish is called **join( )**, shown here:

final void join( ) throws InterruptedException

This method waits until the thread on which it is called terminates. Its name comes from the concept of the calling thread waiting until the specified thread *joins* it. Additional forms of **join( )** allow you to specify a maximum amount of time that you want to wait for the specified thread to terminate.

Here is an improved version of the preceding example that uses **join( )** to ensure that the main thread is the last to finish. It also demonstrates the **isAlive( )** method.

```
// Using join() to wait for threads to finish.
class NewThread implements Runnable {
  String name; // name of thread
  Thread t;

  NewThread(String threadname) {
    name = threadname;
    t = new Thread(this, name);
    System.out.println("New thread: " + t);
  }
```

```
  // This is the entry point for thread.
  public void run() {
    try {
      for(int i = 5; i > 0; i--) {
        System.out.println(name + ": " + i);
        Thread.sleep(1000);
      }
    } catch (InterruptedException e) {
      System.out.println(name + " interrupted.");
    }
    System.out.println(name + " exiting.");
  }
}

class DemoJoin {
  public static void main(String[] args) {
    NewThread nt1 = new NewThread("One");
    NewThread nt2 = new NewThread("Two");
    NewThread nt3 = new NewThread("Three");

    // Start the threads.
    nt1.t.start();
    nt2.t.start();
    nt3.t.start();

    System.out.println("Thread One is alive: "
                        + nt1.t.isAlive());
    System.out.println("Thread Two is alive: "
                        + nt2.t.isAlive());
    System.out.println("Thread Three is alive: "
                        + nt3.t.isAlive());
    // wait for threads to finish
    try {
      System.out.println("Waiting for threads to finish.");
      nt1.t.join();
      nt2.t.join();
      nt3.t.join();
    } catch (InterruptedException e) {
      System.out.println("Main thread Interrupted");
    }

    System.out.println("Thread One is alive: "
                        + nt1.t.isAlive());
    System.out.println("Thread Two is alive: "
                        + nt2.t.isAlive());
    System.out.println("Thread Three is alive: "
                        + nt3.t.isAlive());

    System.out.println("Main thread exiting.");
  }
}
```

Sample output from this program is shown here. (Your output may vary based upon the specific execution environment.)

```
New thread: Thread[One,5,main]
New thread: Thread[Two,5,main]
New thread: Thread[Three,5,main]
Thread One is alive: true
Thread Two is alive: true
Thread Three is alive: true
Waiting for threads to finish.
One: 5
Two: 5
Three: 5
One: 4
Two: 4
Three: 4
One: 3
Two: 3
Three: 3
One: 2
Two: 2
Three: 2
One: 1
Two: 1
Three: 1
Two exiting.
Three exiting.
One exiting.
Thread One is alive: false
Thread Two is alive: false
Thread Three is alive: false
Main thread exiting.
```

As you can see, after the calls to **join( )** return, the threads have stopped executing.

## Thread Priorities

Thread priorities are used by the thread scheduler to decide when each thread should be allowed to run. In theory, over a given period of time, higher-priority threads get more CPU time than lower-priority threads. In practice, the amount of CPU time that a thread gets often depends on several factors besides its priority. (For example, how an operating system implements multitasking can affect the relative availability of CPU time.) A higher-priority thread can also preempt a lower-priority one. For instance, when a lower-priority thread is running and a higher-priority thread resumes (from sleeping or waiting on I/O, for example), it will preempt the lower-priority thread.

In theory, threads of equal priority should get equal access to the CPU. But you need to be careful. Remember, Java is designed to work in a wide range of environments. Some of those environments implement multitasking fundamentally differently than others. You should think of the thread priority as a polite suggestion to the thread scheduler as to how to prioritize your threads at times when the system resources are getting stretched. But the thread scheduler will likely have other factors to consider as well. So you should experiment with your application in a range of conditions if you are using thread priorities and not depend on it as if it were a strict rule.

To set a thread's priority, use the **setPriority( )** method, which is a member of **Thread**. This is its general form:

final void setPriority(int *level*)

Here, *level* specifies the new priority setting for the calling thread. The value of *level* must be within the range **MIN_PRIORITY** and **MAX_PRIORITY**. Currently, these values are 1 and 10, respectively. To return a thread to default priority, specify **NORM_PRIORITY**, which is currently 5. These priorities are defined as **static final** variables within **Thread**.

You can obtain the current priority setting by calling the **getPriority( )** method of **Thread**, shown here:

final int getPriority( )

Implementations of Java may have radically different behavior when it comes to scheduling. Most of the inconsistencies arise when you have threads that are relying on preemptive behavior, instead of cooperatively giving up CPU time. The safest way to obtain predictable, cross-platform behavior with Java is to use threads that voluntarily give up control of the CPU.

# Synchronization

When two or more threads need access to a shared resource, they need some way to ensure that the resource will be used by only one thread at a time. The process by which this is achieved is called *synchronization*. As you will see, Java provides unique, language-level support for it.

Key to synchronization is the concept of the monitor. A *monitor* is an object that is used as a mutually exclusive lock. Only one thread can *own* a monitor at a given time. When a thread acquires a lock, it is said to have *entered* the monitor. All other threads attempting to enter the locked monitor will be suspended until the first thread *exits* the monitor. These other threads are said to be *waiting* for the monitor. A thread that owns a monitor can reenter the same monitor if it so desires.

You can synchronize your code in either of two ways. Both involve the use of the **synchronized** keyword, and both are examined here.

## Using Synchronized Methods

Synchronization is easy in Java, because all objects have their own implicit monitor associated with them. To enter an object's monitor, just call a method that has been modified with the **synchronized** keyword. While a thread is inside a synchronized method, all other threads that try to call it (or any other synchronized method) on the same instance have to wait. To exit the monitor and relinquish control of the object to the next waiting thread, the owner of the monitor simply returns from the synchronized method.

To understand the need for synchronization, let's begin with a simple example that does not use it—but should. The following program has three simple classes. The first one, **Callme**, has a single method named **call( )**. The **call( )** method takes a **String** parameter called **msg**. This method tries to print the **msg** string inside of square brackets. The interesting thing to notice is that after **call( )** prints the opening bracket and the **msg** string, it calls **Thread.sleep(1000)**, which pauses the current thread for one second.

The constructor of the next class, **Caller**, takes a reference to an instance of the **Callme** class and a **String**, which are stored in **target** and **msg**, respectively. The constructor also creates a new thread that will call this object's **run( )** method. The **run( )** method of **Caller** calls the **call( )** method on the **target** instance of **Callme**, passing in the **msg** string. Finally, the **Synch** class starts by creating a single instance of **Callme**, and three instances of **Caller**, each with a unique message string. The same instance of **Callme** is passed to each **Caller**.

```
// This program is not synchronized.
class Callme {
  void call(String msg) {
    System.out.print("[" + msg);
    try {
      Thread.sleep(1000);
    } catch(InterruptedException e) {
      System.out.println("Interrupted");
    }
    System.out.println("]");
  }
}

class Caller implements Runnable {
  String msg;
  Callme target;
  Thread t;

  public Caller(Callme targ, String s) {
    target = targ;
    msg = s;
    t = new Thread(this);
  }

  public void run() {
    target.call(msg);
  }
}

class Synch {
  public static void main(String[] args) {
    Callme target = new Callme();
    Caller ob1 = new Caller(target, "Hello");
    Caller ob2 = new Caller(target, "Synchronized");
    Caller ob3 = new Caller(target, "World");
```

```
    // Start the threads.
    ob1.t.start();
    ob2.t.start();
    ob3.t.start();

    // wait for threads to end
    try {
      ob1.t.join();
      ob2.t.join();
      ob3.t.join();
    } catch(InterruptedException e) {
      System.out.println("Interrupted");
    }
  }
}
```

Here is the output produced by this program:

```
[Hello[Synchronized[World]
]
]
```

As you can see, by calling **sleep( )**, the **call( )** method allows execution to switch to another thread. This results in the mixed-up output of the three message strings. In this program, nothing exists to prevent all three threads from calling the same method, on the same object, at the same time. This is known as a *race condition*, because the three threads are racing each other to complete the method. This example used **sleep( )** to make the effects repeatable and obvious. In most situations, a race condition is more subtle and less predictable, because you can't be sure when the context switch will occur. This can cause a program to run right one time and wrong the next.

To fix the preceding program, you must *serialize* access to **call( )**. That is, you must restrict its access to only one thread at a time. To do this, you simply need to precede **call( )**'s definition with the keyword **synchronized**, as shown here:

```
class Callme {
  synchronized void call(String msg) {
  ...
```

This prevents other threads from entering **call( )** while another thread is using it. After **synchronized** has been added to **call( )**, the output of the program is as follows:

```
[Hello]
[Synchronized]
[World]
```

Any time that you have a method, or group of methods, that changes the internal state of an object in a multithreaded situation, you should consider using the **synchronized** keyword to guard the state from race conditions. Remember, once a thread enters any synchronized method on an instance, no other thread can enter any other synchronized method on the same instance. However, nonsynchronized methods on that instance will continue to be callable.

## The synchronized Statement

While creating **synchronized** methods within classes that you create is an easy and effective means of achieving synchronization, it will not work in all cases. To understand why, consider the following: Imagine that you want to synchronize access to objects of a class that was not designed for multithreaded access. That is, the class does not use **synchronized** methods. Further, this class was not created by you, but by a third party, and you do not have access to the source code. Thus, you can't add **synchronized** to the appropriate methods within the class. How can access to an object of this class be synchronized? Fortunately, the solution to this problem is quite easy: You simply put calls to the methods defined by this class inside a **synchronized** block.

This is the general form of the **synchronized** statement:

```
synchronized(objRef) {
  // statements to be synchronized
}
```

Here, *objRef* is a reference to the object being synchronized. A synchronized block ensures that a call to a synchronized method that is a member of *objRef*'s class occurs only after the current thread has successfully entered *objRef*'s monitor.

Here is an alternative version of the preceding example, using a synchronized block within the **run( )** method:

```
// This program uses a synchronized block.
class Callme {
  void call(String msg) {
    System.out.print("[" + msg);
    try {
      Thread.sleep(1000);
    } catch (InterruptedException e) {
      System.out.println("Interrupted");
    }
    System.out.println("]");
  }
}

class Caller implements Runnable {
  String msg;
  Callme target;
  Thread t;

  public Caller(Callme targ, String s) {
    target = targ;
    msg = s;
    t = new Thread(this);
  }

  // synchronize calls to call()
  public void run() {
    synchronized(target) { // synchronized block
      target.call(msg);
```

```
    }
  }
}

class Synch1 {
  public static void main(String[] args) {
    Callme target = new Callme();
    Caller ob1 = new Caller(target, "Hello");
    Caller ob2 = new Caller(target, "Synchronized");
    Caller ob3 = new Caller(target, "World");

    // Start the threads.
    ob1.t.start();
    ob2.t.start();
    ob3.t.start();

    // wait for threads to end
    try {
      ob1.t.join();
      ob2.t.join();
      ob3.t.join();
    } catch(InterruptedException e) {
      System.out.println("Interrupted");
    }
  }
}
```

Here, the **call( )** method is not modified by **synchronized**. Instead, the **synchronized** statement is used inside **Caller**'s **run( )** method. This causes the same correct output as the preceding example, because each thread waits for the prior one to finish before proceeding.

# Interthread Communication

The preceding examples unconditionally blocked other threads from asynchronous access to certain methods. This use of the implicit monitors in Java objects is powerful, but you can achieve a more subtle level of control through interthread communication. As you will see, this is especially easy in Java.

As discussed earlier, multithreading replaces event loop programming by dividing your tasks into discrete, logical units. Threads also provide a secondary benefit: they do away with polling. Polling is usually implemented by a loop that is used to check some condition repeatedly. Once the condition is true, appropriate action is taken. This wastes CPU time. For example, consider the classic queuing problem, where one thread is producing some data and another is consuming it. To make the problem more interesting, suppose that the producer has to wait until the consumer is finished before it generates more data. In a polling system, the consumer would waste many CPU cycles while it waited for the producer to produce. Once the producer was finished, it would start polling, wasting more CPU cycles waiting for the consumer to finish, and so on. Clearly, this situation is undesirable.

To avoid polling, Java includes an elegant interthread communication mechanism via the **wait( )**, **notify( )**, and **notifyAll( )** methods. These methods are implemented as **final** methods in **Object**, so all classes have them. All three methods can be called only from within a **synchronized** context. Although conceptually advanced from a computer science perspective, the rules for using these methods are actually quite simple:

- **wait( )** tells the calling thread to give up the monitor and go to sleep until some other thread enters the same monitor and calls **notify( )** or **notifyAll( )**.
- **notify( )** wakes up a thread that called **wait( )** on the same object.
- **notifyAll( )** wakes up all the threads that called **wait( )** on the same object. One of the threads will be granted access.

These methods are declared within **Object**, as shown here:

final void wait( ) throws InterruptedException
final void notify( )
final void notify All( )

Additional forms of **wait( )** exist that allow you to specify a period of time to wait.

Before working through an example that illustrates interthread communication, an important point needs to be made. Although **wait( )** normally waits until **notify( )** or **notifyAll( )** is called, there is a possibility that in very rare cases the waiting thread could be awakened due to a *spurious wakeup*. In this case, a waiting thread resumes without **notify( )** or **notifyAll( )** having been called. (In essence, the thread resumes for no apparent reason.) Because of this remote possibility, the Java API documentation recommends that calls to **wait( )** should take place within a loop that checks the condition on which the thread is waiting. The following example shows this technique.

Let's now work through an example that uses **wait( )** and **notify( )**. To begin, consider the following sample program that incorrectly implements a simple form of the producer/consumer problem. It consists of four classes: **Q**, the queue that you're trying to synchronize; **Producer**, the threaded object that is producing queue entries; **Consumer**, the threaded object that is consuming queue entries; and **PC**, the tiny class that creates the single **Q**, **Producer**, and **Consumer**.

```
// An incorrect implementation of a producer and consumer.
class Q {
  int n;

  synchronized int get() {
    System.out.println("Got: " + n);
    return n;
  }

  synchronized void put(int n) {
    this.n = n;
    System.out.println("Put: " + n);
  }
}

class Producer implements Runnable {
  Q q;
  Thread t;
```

```
  Producer(Q q) {
    this.q = q;
    t = new Thread(this, "Producer");
  }

  public void run() {
    int i = 0;

    while(true) {
      q.put(i++);
    }
  }
}

class Consumer implements Runnable {
  Q q;
  Thread t;

  Consumer(Q q) {
    this.q = q;
    t = new Thread(this, "Consumer");
  }

  public void run() {
    while(true) {
      q.get();
    }
  }
}

class PC {
  public static void main(String[] args) {
    Q q = new Q();
    Producer p = new Producer(q);
    Consumer c = new Consumer(q);

    // Start the threads.
    p.t.start();
    c.t.start();

    System.out.println("Press Control C to stop.");
  }
}
```

Although the **put( )** and **get( )** methods on **Q** are synchronized, nothing stops the producer from overrunning the consumer, nor will anything prevent the consumer from consuming the same queue value twice. Thus, you get the erroneous output shown here (the exact output will vary with processor speed and task load):

```
Put: 1
Got: 1
Got: 1
Got: 1
Got: 1
```

```
Got: 1
Put: 2
Put: 3
Put: 4
Put: 5
Put: 6
Put: 7
Got: 7
```

As you can see, after the producer put 1, the consumer started and got the same 1 five times in a row. Then, the producer resumed and produced 2 through 7 without letting the consumer have a chance to consume them.

The proper way to write this program in Java is to use **wait( )** and **notify( )** to signal in both directions, as shown here:

```
// A correct implementation of a producer and consumer.
class Q {
  int n;
  boolean valueSet = false;

  synchronized int get() {
    while(!valueSet)
      try {
        wait();

      } catch(InterruptedException e) {
        System.out.println("InterruptedException caught");
      }

      System.out.println("Got: " + n);
      valueSet = false;
      notify();
      return n;
  }

  synchronized void put(int n) {
    while(valueSet)
      try {
        wait();
      } catch(InterruptedException e) {
        System.out.println("InterruptedException caught");
      }

      this.n = n;
      valueSet = true;
      System.out.println("Put: " + n);
      notify();
  }
}

class Producer implements Runnable {
  Q q;
  Thread t;
```

```
  Producer(Q q) {
    this.q = q;
    t = new Thread(this, "Producer");
  }

  public void run() {
    int i = 0;

    while(true) {
      q.put(i++);
    }
  }
}

class Consumer implements Runnable {
  Q q;
  Thread t;

  Consumer(Q q) {
    this.q = q;
    t = new Thread(this, "Consumer");
  }

  public void run() {
    while(true) {
      q.get();
    }
  }
}

class PCFixed {
  public static void main(String[] args) {
    Q q = new Q();
    Producer p = new Producer(q);
    Consumer c = new Consumer(q);

    // Start the threads.
    p.t.start();
    c.t.start();

    System.out.println("Press Control-C to stop.");
  }
}
```

Inside **get( )**, **wait( )** is called. This causes its execution to suspend until **Producer** notifies you that some data is ready. When this happens, execution inside **get( )** resumes. After the data has been obtained, **get( )** calls **notify( )**. This tells **Producer** that it is okay to put more data in the queue. Inside **put( )**, **wait( )** suspends execution until **Consumer** has removed the item from the queue. When execution resumes, the next item of data is put in the queue, and **notify( )** is called. This tells **Consumer** that it should now remove it.

Here is some output from this program, which shows the clean synchronous behavior:

```
Put: 1
Got: 1
Put: 2
Got: 2
Put: 3
Got: 3
Put: 4
Got: 4
Put: 5
Got: 5
```

## Deadlock

A special type of error that you need to avoid that relates specifically to multitasking is *deadlock*, which occurs when two threads have a circular dependency on a pair of synchronized objects. For example, suppose one thread enters the monitor on object X and another thread enters the monitor on object Y. If the thread in X tries to call any synchronized method on Y, it will block as expected. However, if the thread in Y, in turn, tries to call any synchronized method on X, the thread waits forever, because to access X, it would have to release its own lock on Y so that the first thread could complete. Deadlock is a difficult error to debug for two reasons:

- In general, it occurs unpredictably, when the two threads time-slice in just the right way.
- It may involve more than two threads and two synchronized objects. (That is, deadlock can occur through a more convoluted sequence of events than just described.)

To understand deadlock fully, it is useful to see it in action. The next example creates two classes, **A** and **B**, with methods **foo( )** and **bar( )**, respectively, which pause briefly before trying to call a method in the other class. The main class, named **Deadlock**, creates an **A** and a **B** instance, and then calls **deadlockStart( )** to start a second thread that sets up the deadlock condition. The **foo( )** and **bar( )** methods use **sleep( )** as a way to force the deadlock condition to occur.

```
// An example of deadlock.
class A {
  synchronized void foo(B b) {
    String name = Thread.currentThread().getName();

    System.out.println(name + " entered A.foo");

    try {
      Thread.sleep(1000);
    } catch(Exception e) {
      System.out.println("A Interrupted");
    }

    System.out.println(name + " trying to call B.last()");
    b.last();
  }
```

```
  synchronized void last() {
    System.out.println("Inside A.last");
  }
}

class B {
  synchronized void bar(A a) {
    String name = Thread.currentThread().getName();
    System.out.println(name + " entered B.bar");

    try {
      Thread.sleep(1000);
    } catch(Exception e) {
      System.out.println("B Interrupted");
    }

    System.out.println(name + " trying to call A.last()");
    a.last();
  }

  synchronized void last() {
    System.out.println("Inside B.last");
  }
}

class Deadlock implements Runnable {
  A a = new A();
  B b = new B();
  Thread t;

  Deadlock() {
    Thread.currentThread().setName("MainThread");
    t = new Thread(this, "RacingThread");
  }

  void deadlockStart() {
    t.start();
    a.foo(b); // get lock on a in this thread.
    System.out.println("Back in main thread");
  }

  public void run() {
    b.bar(a); // get lock on b in other thread.
    System.out.println("Back in other thread");
  }

  public static void main(String[] args) {
    Deadlock dl = new Deadlock();

    dl.deadlockStart();
  }
}
```

When you run this program, you will see the output shown here, although whether **A.foo( )** or **B.bar( )** executes first will vary based on the specific execution environment.

```
MainThread entered A.foo
RacingThread entered B.bar
MainThread trying to call B.last()
RacingThread trying to call A.last()
```

Because the program has deadlocked, you need to press CTRL-C to end the program. You can see a full thread and monitor cache dump by pressing CTRL-BREAK on a PC. You will see that **RacingThread** owns the monitor on **b**, while it is waiting for the monitor on **a**. At the same time, **MainThread** owns **a** and is waiting to get **b**. This program will never complete. As this example illustrates, if your multithreaded program locks up occasionally, deadlock is one of the first conditions that you should check for.

## Suspending, Resuming, and Stopping Threads

Sometimes, suspending execution of a thread is useful. For example, a separate thread can be used to display the time of day. If the user doesn't want a clock, then its thread can be suspended. Whatever the case, suspending a thread is a simple matter. Once it's suspended, restarting the thread is also a simple matter.

The mechanisms to suspend, stop, and resume threads differ between early versions of Java, such as Java 1.0, and more modern versions, beginning with Java 2. Prior to Java 2, a program used **suspend( )**, **resume( )**, and **stop( )**, which are methods defined by **Thread**, to pause, restart, and stop the execution of a thread, respectively. Although these methods seem to be a perfectly reasonable and convenient approach to managing the execution of threads, they must not be used for new Java programs. Here's why. The **suspend( )** method of the **Thread** class was deprecated by Java 2 several years ago, and will be removed in a future release. This was done because **suspend( )** can sometimes cause serious system failures. Assume that a thread has obtained locks on critical data structures. If that thread is suspended at that point, those locks are not relinquished. Other threads that may be waiting for those resources can be deadlocked.

The **resume( )** method is also deprecated. It does not cause problems, but it cannot be used without the **suspend( )** method as its counterpart.

The **stop( )** method of the **Thread** class, too, was deprecated by Java 2, and will be removed in a future release. This was done because this method can sometimes cause serious system failures. Assume that a thread is writing to a critically important data structure and has completed only part of its changes. If that thread is stopped at that point, that data structure might be left in a corrupted state. The trouble is that **stop( )** causes any lock the calling thread holds to be released. Thus, the corrupted data might be used by another thread that is waiting on the same lock.

Because you can't now use the **suspend( )**, **resume( )**, or **stop( )** methods to control a thread, you might be thinking that no way exists to pause, restart, or terminate a thread. But, fortunately, this is not true. Instead, a thread must be designed so that the **run( )** method periodically checks to determine whether that thread should suspend, resume, or stop its own execution. Typically, this is accomplished by establishing a flag variable that indicates the execution state of the thread. As long as this flag is set to "running," the **run( )** method must continue to let the thread execute. If this variable is set to "suspend," the thread must pause.

If it is set to "stop," the thread must terminate. Of course, a variety of ways exist in which to write such code, but the central theme will be the same for all programs.

The following example illustrates how the **wait( )** and **notify( )** methods that are inherited from **Object** can be used to control the execution of a thread. Let us consider its operation. The **NewThread** class contains a **boolean** instance variable named **suspendFlag**, which is used to control the execution of the thread. It is initialized to **false** by the constructor. The **run( )** method contains a **synchronized** statement block that checks **suspendFlag**. If that variable is **true**, the **wait( )** method is invoked to suspend the execution of the thread. The **mysuspend( )** method sets **suspendFlag** to **true**. The **myresume( )** method sets **suspendFlag** to **false** and invokes **notify( )** to wake up the thread. Finally, the **main( )** method has been modified to invoke the **mysuspend( )** and **myresume( )** methods.

```
// Suspending and resuming a thread the modern way.
class NewThread implements Runnable {
  String name; // name of thread
  Thread t;
  boolean suspendFlag;

  NewThread(String threadname) {
    name = threadname;
    t = new Thread(this, name);
    System.out.println("New thread: " + t);
    suspendFlag = false;
  }

  // This is the entry point for thread.
  public void run() {
    try {
      for(int i = 15; i > 0; i--) {
        System.out.println(name + ": " + i);
        Thread.sleep(200);
        synchronized(this) {
          while(suspendFlag) {
            wait();
          }
        }
      }
    } catch (InterruptedException e) {
      System.out.println(name + " interrupted.");
    }
    System.out.println(name + " exiting.");
  }

  synchronized void mysuspend() {
    suspendFlag = true;
  }

  synchronized void myresume() {
    suspendFlag = false;
    notify();
  }
}
```

```
class SuspendResume {
  public static void main(String[] args) {
    NewThread ob1 = new NewThread("One");
    NewThread ob2 = new NewThread("Two");

    ob1.t.start(); // Start the thread
    ob2.t.start(); // Start the thread

    try {
      Thread.sleep(1000);
      ob1.mysuspend();
      System.out.println("Suspending thread One");
      Thread.sleep(1000);
      ob1.myresume();
      System.out.println("Resuming thread One");
      ob2.mysuspend();
      System.out.println("Suspending thread Two");
      Thread.sleep(1000);
      ob2.myresume();
      System.out.println("Resuming thread Two");
    } catch (InterruptedException e) {
      System.out.println("Main thread Interrupted");
    }

    // wait for threads to finish
    try {
      System.out.println("Waiting for threads to finish.");
      ob1.t.join();
      ob2.t.join();
    } catch (InterruptedException e) {
      System.out.println("Main thread Interrupted");
    }

    System.out.println("Main thread exiting.");
  }
}
```

When you run the program, you will see the threads suspend and resume. Later in this book, you will see more examples that use the modern mechanism of thread control. Although this mechanism may not appear as simple to use as the old way, nevertheless, it is the way required to ensure that run-time errors don't occur. It is the approach that *must* be used for all new code.

# Obtaining a Thread's State

As mentioned earlier in this chapter, a thread can exist in a number of different states. You can obtain the current state of a thread by calling the **getState( )** method defined by **Thread**. It is shown here:

Thread.State getState( )

It returns a value of type **Thread.State** that indicates the state of the thread at the time at which the call was made. **State** is an enumeration defined by **Thread**. (An enumeration is a list of named constants. It is discussed in detail in Chapter 12.) Here are the values that can be returned by **getState( )**:

| Value | State |
|---|---|
| BLOCKED | A thread that has suspended execution because it is waiting to acquire a lock. |
| NEW | A thread that has not begun execution. |
| RUNNABLE | A thread that either is currently executing or will execute when it gains access to the CPU. |
| TERMINATED | A thread that has completed execution. |
| TIMED_WAITING | A thread that has suspended execution for a specified period of time, such as when it has called **sleep( )**. This state is also entered when a timeout version of **wait( )** or **join( )** is called. |
| WAITING | A thread that has suspended execution because it is waiting for some action to occur. For example, it is waiting because of a call to a non-timeout version of **wait( )** or **join( )**. |

Figure 11-1 diagrams how the various thread states relate.

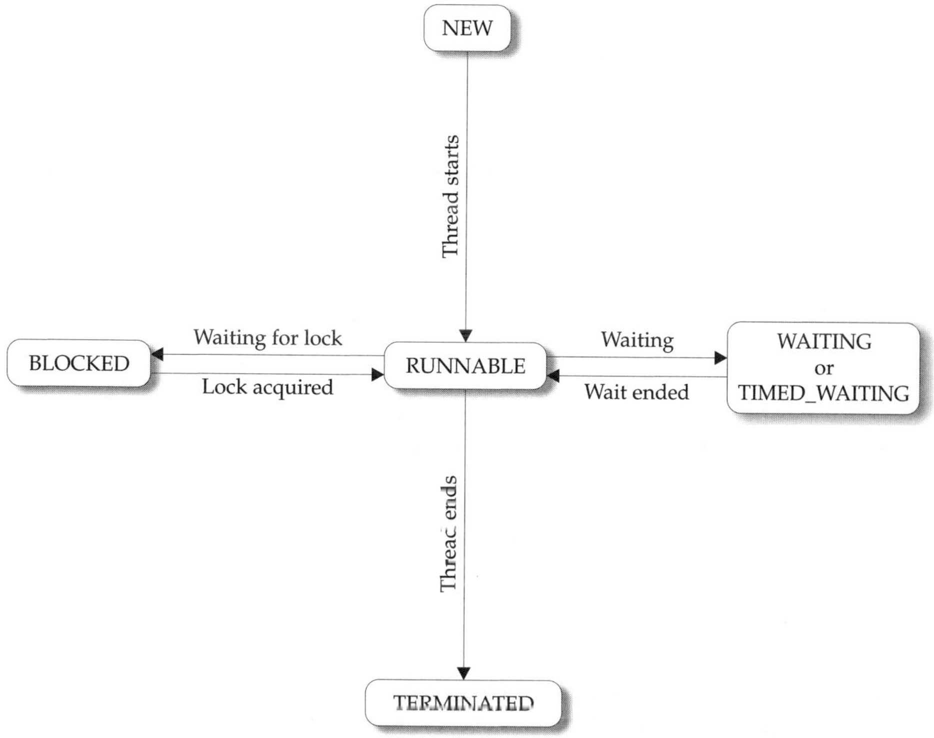


**Figure 11-1** Thread states

Given a **Thread** instance, you can use **getState( )** to obtain the state of a thread. For example, the following sequence determines if a thread called **thrd** is in the **RUNNABLE** state at the time **getState( )** is called:

```
Thread.State ts = thrd.getState();

if(ts == Thread.State.RUNNABLE) // ...
```

It is important to understand that a thread's state may change after the call to **getState( )**. Thus, depending on the circumstances, the state obtained by calling **getState( )** may not reflect the actual state of the thread only a moment later. For this (and other) reasons, **getState( )** is not intended to provide a means of synchronizing threads. It's primarily used for debugging or for profiling a thread's run-time characteristics.

## Using a Factory Method to Create and Start a Thread

In some cases, it is not necessary to separate the creation of a thread from the start of its execution. In other words, sometimes it is convenient to create and start a thread at the same time. One way to do this is to use a static factory method. A *factory method* is a method that returns an object of a class. Typically, factory methods are *static* methods of a class. They are used for a variety of reasons, such as to set an object to some initial state prior to use, to configure a specific type of object, or in some cases to enable an object to be reused. As it relates to creating and starting a thread, a factory method will create the thread, call **start( )** on the thread, and then return a reference to the thread. With this approach, you can create and start a thread through a single method call, thus streamlining your code.

For example, assuming the **ThreadDemo** program shown near the start of this chapter, adding the following factory method to **NewThread** enables you to create and start a thread in a single step:

```
// A factory method that creates and starts a thread.
public static NewThread createAndStart() {
  NewThread myThrd = new NewThread();
  myThrd.t.start();
  return myThrd;
}
```

Using **createAndStart( )**, you can now replace the sequence

```
NewThread nt = new NewThread(); // create a new thread
nt.t.start(); // Start the thread
```

with

```
NewThread nt = NewThread.createAndStart();
```

Now the thread is created and started in one step.

In cases in which you don't need to keep a reference to the executing thread, you can sometimes create and start a thread with one line of code, without the use of a factory method. For example, again assuming the **ThreadDemo** program, the following creates and starts a **NewThread** thread:

```
new NewThread().t.start();
```

However, in real-world applications, you will usually need to keep a reference to the thread, so the factory method is often a good choice.

# Virtual Threads

As mentioned at the beginning of this chapter, the Java platform implements Java threads as wrappers around the underlying OS's native threads. In this model, when the OS runs out of threads, so does Java! For high-throughput, high-scale applications such as application servers, which generally like to use a new thread for each new incoming request, this can be a performance bottleneck as to the number of requests the server can handle at the same time. JDK 21 has introduced a new way to map Java threads onto OS threads in which many Java threads can share the same OS thread. This is called *virtual threading*. By scheduling work on the OS in a more flexible way, high-scale server applications can perform better because they can handle more concurrent requests gracefully. The number of virtual Java threads an application can create is no longer limited to the number of OS threads available to Java.

Fortunately, the programming model for using platform threads and virtual threads is the same except for how the Java threads are first created and managed when the JVM terminates. All the examples so far have created threads that are platform threads, since these are the kind of threads that work well for most applications. You can determine what kind of thread is in use by the **Thread** class method

**boolean isVirtual( )**

which is **false** for platform threads and **true** for virtual threads.

In order to create a virtual thread in Java, you can use the static **Thread** method **ofVirtual( )**, from which you can obtain a **Thread.Builder** object from which to create virtual threads. For example, the code

```
Runnable myTask = // a task within the run() method
Thread myVirtualThread = Thread.ofVirtual().start(myTask);
```

shows a **Runnable** task being run on a virtual thread. The virtual thread is an instance of the Java **Thread** class you already learned about in this chapter, and so it has the same life cycle and API methods for managing execution. It is important to note that if you want to use virtual threads, you have to explicitly choose this API to do so.

The companion to **ofVirtual( )** is the static **Thread** method **ofPlatform( )**, which creates a **Thread.Builder** object from which you can create traditional platform threads. However, since platform threads are the default type of threads, the APIs that you have already seen create platform threads, such as

```
Runnable myTask = // a task within the run() method
Thread myThread = new Thread(task, "myTask");
```

or the default no argument constructor of the **Thread** class.

While virtual threads "look like" platform threads for the most part, they differ in that they are not named by default (their name variable is the empty string) and the JVM does not wait for them to finish their work when it exits.

If a virtual thread is waiting, the Java platform can schedule its OS thread to be useful for another virtual thread that needs attention. In this way, the Java platform can use OS threads more efficiently for applications that have tasks spending significant time waiting on network connections or blocking I/O. For applications mostly doing continuous processing, like large algorithmic calculations, virtual threads will likely not bring much benefit. So virtual threads, while easy to use because they "look like" traditional threads, bring performance benefits only for certain types of applications and will likely require judicious use together with performance testing to realize their full potential.

## Using Multithreading

The key to utilizing Java's multithreading features effectively is to think concurrently rather than serially. For example, when you have two subsystems within a program that can execute concurrently, make them individual threads. With the careful use of multithreading, you can create very efficient programs. A word of caution is in order, however: If you create too many threads, you can actually degrade the performance of your program rather than enhance it. Remember, some overhead is associated with context switching. If you create too many threads, more CPU time will be spent changing contexts than executing your program! One last point: To create compute-intensive applications that can automatically scale to make use of the available processors in a multicore system, consider using the Fork/Join Framework, which is described in Chapter 29.

CHAPTER

# 12 Enumerations, Autoboxing, and Annotations

This chapter examines three features that were not originally part of Java, but over time each has become a near indispensable aspect of Java programming: enumerations, autoboxing, and annotations. Originally added by JDK 5, each is a feature upon which Java programmers have come to rely because each offers a streamlined approach to handling common programming tasks. This chapter also discusses Java's type wrappers and introduces reflection.

## Enumerations

In its simplest form, an *enumeration* is a list of named constants that define a new data type and its legal values. Thus, an enumeration object can hold only a value that was declared in the list. Other values are not allowed. In other words, an enumeration gives you a way to explicitly specify the only values that a data type can legally have. Enumerations are commonly used to define a set of values that represent a collection of items. For example, you might use an enumeration to represent the error codes that can result from some operation, such as success, failed, or pending; or a list of the states that a device might be in, such as running, stopped, or paused. In early versions of Java, such values were defined using **final** variables, but enumerations offer a far superior approach.

Although Java enumerations might, at first glance, appear similar to enumerations in other languages, this similarity may be only skin deep because, in Java, an enumeration defines a class type. By making enumerations into classes, the capabilities of the enumeration are greatly expanded. For example, in Java, an enumeration can have constructors, methods, and instance variables. Because of their power and flexibility, enumerations are widely used throughout the Java API library.

## Enumeration Fundamentals

An enumeration is created using the **enum** keyword. For example, here is a simple enumeration that lists various apple varieties:

```
// An enumeration of apple varieties.
enum Apple {
  Jonathan, GoldenDel, RedDel, Winesap, Cortland
}
```

The identifiers **Jonathan**, **GoldenDel**, and so on are called *enumeration constants*. Each is implicitly declared as a public, static final member of **Apple**. Furthermore, their type is the type of the enumeration in which they are declared, which is **Apple** in this case. Thus, in the language of Java, these constants are called *self-typed*, in which "self" refers to the enclosing enumeration.

Once you have defined an enumeration, you can create a variable of that type. However, even though enumerations define a class type, you do not instantiate an **enum** using **new**. Instead, you declare and use an enumeration variable in much the same way as you do one of the primitive types. For example, this declares **ap** as a variable of enumeration type **Apple**:

```
Apple ap;
```

Because **ap** is of type **Apple**, the only values that it can be assigned (or can contain) are those defined by the enumeration. For example, this assigns **ap** the value **RedDel**:

```
ap = Apple.RedDel;
```

Notice that the symbol **RedDel** is preceded by **Apple**.

Two enumeration constants can be compared for equality by using the = = relational operator. For example, this statement compares the value in **ap** with the **GoldenDel** constant:

```
if(ap == Apple.GoldenDel) // ...
```

An enumeration value can also be used to control a **switch** statement. Of course, all of the **case** statements must use constants from the same **enum** as that used by the **switch** expression. For example, this **switch** is perfectly valid:

```
// Use an enum to control a switch statement.
switch(ap) {
  case Jonathan:
    // ...
  case Winesap:
    // ...
```

Notice that in the **case** statements, the names of the enumeration constants are used without being qualified by their enumeration type name. That is, **Winesap**, not **Apple.Winesap**, is used. This is because the type of the enumeration in the **switch** expression has already implicitly specified the **enum** type of the **case** constants. There is no need to qualify the constants in the **case** statements with their **enum** type name. In fact, attempting to do so will cause a compilation error.

When an enumeration constant is displayed, such as in a **println( )** statement, its name is output. For example, given the statement

```
System.out.println(Apple.Winesap);
```

the name **Winesap** is displayed.

The following program puts together all of the pieces and demonstrates the **Apple** enumeration:

```
// An enumeration of apple varieties.
enum Apple {
  Jonathan, GoldenDel, RedDel, Winesap, Cortland
}

class EnumDemo {
  public static void main(String[] args)
  {
    Apple ap;

    ap = Apple.RedDel;

    // Output an enum value.
    System.out.println("Value of ap: " + ap);
    System.out.println();

    ap = Apple.GoldenDel;

    // Compare two enum values.
    if(ap == Apple.GoldenDel)
      System.out.println("ap contains GoldenDel.\n");

    // Use an enum to control a switch statement.
    switch(ap) {
      case Jonathan:
        System.out.println("Jonathan is red.");
        break;
      case GoldenDel:
        System.out.println("Golden Delicious is yellow.");
        break;
      case RedDel:
        System.out.println("Red Delicious is red.");
        break;
      case Winesap:
        System.out.println("Winesap is red.");
        break;
      case Cortland:
        System.out.println("Cortland is red.");
        break;
    }
  }
}
```

The output from the program is shown here:

```
Value of ap: RedDel

ap contains GoldenDel.

Golden Delicious is yellow.
```

## The values( ) and valueOf( ) Methods

All enumerations automatically contain two predefined methods: **values( )** and **valueOf( )**. Their general forms are shown here:

public static *enum-type* [ ] values( )
public static *enum-type* valueOf(String *str* )

The **values( )** method returns an array that contains a list of the enumeration constants. The **valueOf( )** method returns the enumeration constant whose value corresponds to the string passed in *str*. In both cases, *enum-type* is the type of the enumeration. For example, in the case of the **Apple** enumeration shown earlier, the return type of **Apple.valueOf("Winesap")** is **Winesap**.

The following program demonstrates the **values( )** and **valueOf( )** methods:

```
// Use the built-in enumeration methods.

// An enumeration of apple varieties.
enum Apple {
  Jonathan, GoldenDel, RedDel, Winesap, Cortland
}

class EnumDemo2 {
  public static void main(String[] args)
  {
    Apple ap;

    System.out.println("Here are all Apple constants:");

    // use values()
    Apple[] allapples = Apple.values();
    for(Apple a : allapples)
      System.out.println(a);

    System.out.println();

    // use valueOf()
    ap = Apple.valueOf("Winesap");
    System.out.println("ap contains " + ap);

  }
}
```

The output from the program is shown here:

```
Here are all Apple constants:
Jonathan
GoldenDel
RedDel
Winesap
Cortland

ap contains Winesap
```

Notice that this program uses a for-each style **for** loop to cycle through the array of constants obtained by calling **values( )**. For the sake of illustration, the variable **allapples** was created and assigned a reference to the enumeration array. However, this step is not necessary because the **for** could have been written as shown here, eliminating the need for the **allapples** variable:

```
for(Apple a : Apple.values())
  System.out.println(a);
```

Now, notice how the value corresponding to the name **Winesap** was obtained by calling **valueOf( )**:

```
ap = Apple.valueOf("Winesap");
```

As explained, **valueOf( )** returns the enumeration value associated with the name of the constant represented as a string.

## Java Enumerations Are Class Types

As mentioned, a Java enumeration is a class type. Although you don't instantiate an **enum** using **new**, it otherwise has much the same capabilities as other classes. The fact that **enum** defines a class gives the Java enumeration extraordinary power. For example, you can give it constructors, add instance variables and methods, and even implement interfaces.

It is important to understand that each enumeration constant is an object of its enumeration type. Thus, when you define a constructor for an **enum**, the constructor is called when each enumeration constant is created. Also, each enumeration constant has its own copy of any instance variables defined by the enumeration. For example, consider the following version of **Apple**:

```
// Use an enum constructor, instance variable, and method.
enum Apple {
  Jonathan(10), GoldenDel(9), RedDel(12), Winesap(15), Cortland(8);

  private int price; // price of each apple

  // Constructor
  Apple(int p) { price = p; }

  int getPrice() { return price; }
}
```

```
class EnumDemo3 {
  public static void main(String[] args)
  {
    Apple ap;

    // Display price of Winesap.
    System.out.println("Winesap costs " +
                       Apple.Winesap.getPrice() +
                       " cents.\n");

    // Display all apples and prices.
    System.out.println("All apple prices:");
    for(Apple a : Apple.values())
      System.out.println(a + " costs " + a.getPrice() +
                         " cents.");
  }
}
```

The output is shown here:

```
Winesap costs 15 cents.

All apple prices:
Jonathan costs 10 cents.
GoldenDel costs 9 cents.
RedDel costs 12 cents.
Winesap costs 15 cents.
Cortland costs 8 cents.
```

This version of **Apple** adds three things. The first is the instance variable **price**, which is used to hold the price of each variety of apple. The second is the **Apple** constructor, which is passed the price of an apple. The third is the method **getPrice( )**, which returns the value of **price**.

When the variable **ap** is declared in **main( )**, the constructor for **Apple** is called once for each constant that is specified. Notice how the arguments to the constructor are specified, by putting them inside parentheses after each constant, as shown here:

```
Jonathan(10), GoldenDel(9), RedDel(12), Winesap(15), Cortland(8);
```

These values are passed to the **p** parameter of **Apple( )**, which then assigns this value to **price**. Again, the constructor is called once for each constant.

Because each enumeration constant has its own copy of **price**, you can obtain the price of a specified type of apple by calling **getPrice( )**. For example, in **main( )**, the price of a Winesap is obtained by the following call:

```
Apple.Winesap.getPrice( )
```

The prices of all varieties are obtained by cycling through the enumeration using a **for** loop. Because there is a copy of **price** for each enumeration constant, the value associated with one constant is separate and distinct from the value associated with another constant. This is a powerful concept, which is only available when enumerations are implemented as classes, as Java does.

Although the preceding example contains only one constructor, an **enum** can offer two or more overloaded forms, just as can any other class. For example, this version of **Apple** provides a default constructor that initializes the price to –1, to indicate that no price data is available:

```
// Use an enum constructor.
enum Apple {
  Jonathan(10), GoldenDel(9), RedDel, Winesap(15), Cortland(8);

  private int price; // price of each apple

  // Constructor
  Apple(int p) { price = p; }

  // Overloaded constructor
  Apple() { price = -1; }

  int getPrice() { return price; }
}
```

Notice that in this version, **RedDel** is not given an argument. This means that the default constructor is called, and **RedDel's** price variable is given the value –1.

Here are two restrictions that apply to enumerations. First, an enumeration can't inherit another class. Second, an **enum** cannot be a superclass. This means that an **enum** can't be extended. Otherwise, **enum** acts much like any other class type. The key is to remember that each of the enumeration constants is an object of the class in which it is defined.

## Enumerations Inherit Enum

Although you can't inherit a superclass when declaring an **enum**, all enumerations automatically inherit one: **java.lang.Enum**. This class defines several methods that are available for use by all enumerations. The **Enum** class is described in detail in Part II, but three of its methods warrant a discussion at this time.

You can obtain a value that indicates an enumeration constant's position in the list of constants. This is called its *ordinal value*, and it is retrieved by calling the **ordinal( )** method, shown here:

final int ordinal( )

It returns the ordinal value of the invoking constant. Ordinal values begin at zero. Thus, in the **Apple** enumeration, **Jonathan** has an ordinal value of 0, **GoldenDel** has an ordinal value of 1, **RedDel** has an ordinal value of 2, and so on.

You can compare the ordinal value of two constants of the same enumeration by using the **compareTo( )** method. It has this general form:

final int compareTo(*enum-type e*)

Here, *enum-type* is the type of the enumeration, and *e* is the constant being compared to the invoking constant. Remember, both the invoking constant and *e* must be of the same enumeration. If the invoking constant has an ordinal value less than *e*'s, then **compareTo( )**

returns a negative value. If the two ordinal values are the same, then zero is returned. If the invoking constant has an ordinal value greater than *e*'s, then a positive value is returned.

You can compare for equality an enumeration constant with any other object by using **equals( )**, which overrides the **equals( )** method defined by **Object**. Although **equals( )** can compare an enumeration constant to any other object, those two objects will be equal only if they both refer to the same constant, within the same enumeration. Simply having ordinal values in common will not cause **equals( )** to return true if the two constants are from different enumerations.

Remember, you can compare two enumeration references for equality by using = =.

The following program demonstrates the **ordinal( )**, **compareTo( )**, and **equals( )** methods:

```
// Demonstrate ordinal(), compareTo(), and equals().

// An enumeration of apple varieties.
enum Apple {
  Jonathan, GoldenDel, RedDel, Winesap, Cortland
}

class EnumDemo4 {
  public static void main(String[] args)
  {
    Apple ap, ap2, ap3;

    // Obtain all ordinal values using ordinal().
    System.out.println("Here are all apple constants" +
                       " and their ordinal values: ");
    for(Apple a : Apple.values())
      System.out.println(a + " " + a.ordinal());

    ap =  Apple.RedDel;
    ap2 = Apple.GoldenDel;
    ap3 = Apple.RedDel;

    System.out.println();

    // Demonstrate compareTo() and equals()
    if(ap.compareTo(ap2) < 0)
      System.out.println(ap + " comes before " + ap2);

    if(ap.compareTo(ap2) > 0)
      System.out.println(ap2 + " comes before " + ap);

    if(ap.compareTo(ap3) == 0)
      System.out.println(ap + " equals " + ap3);

    System.out.println();

    if(ap.equals(ap2))
      System.out.println("Error!");

    if(ap.equals(ap3))
      System.out.println(ap + " equals " + ap3);
```

```
    if(ap == ap3)
      System.out.println(ap + " == " + ap3);

  }
}
```

The output from the program is shown here:

```
Here are all apple constants and their ordinal values.
Jonathan 0
GoldenDel 1
RedDel 2
Winesap 3
Cortland 4

GoldenDel comes before RedDel
RedDel equals RedDel

RedDel equals RedDel
RedDel == RedDel
```

## Another Enumeration Example

Before moving on, we will look at a different example that uses an **enum**. In Chapter 9, we created an automated "decision maker" program. In that version, variables called **NO**, **YES**, **MAYBE**, **LATER**, **SOON**, and **NEVER** were declared within an interface and used to represent the possible answers. While there is nothing technically wrong with that approach, using an enumeration is a better choice. Here is an improved version of that program that uses an **enum** called **Answers** to define the answers. You should compare this version to the original in Chapter 9.

```
// An improved version of the "Decision Maker"
// program from Chapter 9. This version uses an
// enum, rather than interface variables, to
// represent the answers.

import java.util.Random;

// An enumeration of the possible answers.
enum Answers {
  NO, YES, MAYBE, LATER, SOON, NEVER
}

class Question {
  Random rand = new Random();
  Answers ask() {
  int prob = (int) (100 * rand.nextDouble());

    if (prob < 15)
      return Answers.MAYBE; // 15%
    else if (prob < 30)
      return Answers.NO;    // 15%
    else if (prob < 60)
      return Answers.YES;   // 30%
```

```
    else if (prob < 75)
      return Answers.LATER; // 15%
    else if (prob < 98)
      return Answers.SOON;  // 13%
    else
      return Answers.NEVER; // 2%
  }
}

class AskMe {
  static void answer(Answers result) {
    switch(result) {
      case NO:
        System.out.println("No");
        break;
      case YES:
        System.out.println("Yes");
        break;
      case MAYBE:
        System.out.println("Maybe");
        break;
      case LATER:
        System.out.println("Later");
        break;
      case SOON:
        System.out.println("Soon");
        break;
      case NEVER:
        System.out.println("Never");
        break;
    }
  }

  public static void main(String[] args) {
    Question q = new Question();
    answer(q.ask());
    answer(q.ask());
    answer(q.ask());
    answer(q.ask());
  }
}
```

## Type Wrappers

As you know, Java uses primitive types (also called simple types), such as **int** or **double**, to hold the basic data types supported by the language. Primitive types, rather than objects, are used for these quantities for the sake of performance. Using objects for these values would add an unacceptable overhead to even the simplest of calculations. Thus, the primitive types are not part of the object hierarchy, and they do not inherit **Object**.

Despite the performance benefit offered by the primitive types, there are times when you will need an object representation. For example, you can't pass a primitive type by reference to a method. Also, many of the standard data structures implemented by Java operate on objects, which means that you can't use these data structures to store primitive types. To handle these (and other) situations, Java provides *type wrappers*, which are classes that encapsulate a primitive type within an object. The type wrapper classes are described in detail in Part II, but they are introduced here because they relate directly to Java's autoboxing feature.

The type wrappers are **Double**, **Float**, **Long**, **Integer**, **Short**, **Byte**, **Character**, and **Boolean**. These classes offer a wide array of methods that allow you to fully integrate the primitive types into Java's object hierarchy. Each is briefly examined next.

## Character

**Character** is a wrapper around a **char**. The constructor for **Character** is

Character(char *ch*)

Here, *ch* specifies the character that will be wrapped by the **Character** object being created.

However, beginning with JDK 9, the **Character** constructor was deprecated, and beginning with JDK 16, it has been deprecated for removal. Today, it is strongly recommended that you use the static method **valueOf( )** to obtain a **Character** object. It is shown here:

static Character valueOf(char *ch*)

It returns a **Character** object that wraps *ch*.

To obtain the **char** value contained in a **Character** object, call **charValue( )**, shown here:

char charValue( )

It returns the encapsulated character.

## Boolean

**Boolean** is a wrapper around **boolean** values. It defines these constructors:

Boolean(boolean *boolValue*)
Boolean(String *boolString*)

In the first version, *boolValue* must be either **true** or **false**. In the second version, if *boolString* contains the string "true" (in uppercase or lowercase), then the new **Boolean** object will be true. Otherwise, it will be false.

However, beginning with JDK 9, the **Boolean** constructors were deprecated, and beginning with JDK 16, they have been deprecated for removal. Today, it is strongly recommended that you use the static method **valueOf( )** to obtain a **Boolean** object. It has the two versions shown here:

static Boolean valueOf(boolean *boolValue*)
static Boolean valueOf(String *boolString*)

Each returns a **Boolean** object that wraps the indicated value.

To obtain a **boolean** value from a **Boolean** object, use **booleanValue( )**, shown here:

boolean booleanValue( )

It returns the **boolean** equivalent of the invoking object.

## The Numeric Type Wrappers

By far, the most commonly used type wrappers are those that represent numeric values. These are **Byte**, **Short**, **Integer**, **Long**, **Float**, and **Double**. All of the numeric type wrappers inherit the abstract class **Number**. **Number** declares methods that return the value of an object in each of the different number formats. These methods are shown here:

byte byteValue( )
double doubleValue( )
float floatValue( )
int intValue( )
long longValue( )
short shortValue( )

For example, **doubleValue( )** returns the value of an object as a **double**, **floatValue( )** returns the value as a **float**, and so on. These methods are implemented by each of the numeric type wrappers.

All of the numeric type wrappers define constructors that allow an object to be constructed from a given value, or a string representation of that value. For example, here are the constructors defined for **Integer**:

Integer(int *num*)
Integer(String *str*)

If *str* does not contain a valid numeric value, then a **NumberFormatException** is thrown.

However, beginning with JDK 9, the numeric type-wrapper constructors were deprecated, and beginning with JDK 16, they have been deprecated for removal. Today, it is strongly recommended that you use one of the **valueOf( )** methods to obtain a wrapper object. The **valueOf( )** method is a static member of all of the numeric wrapper classes, and all numeric classes support forms that convert a numeric value or a string into an object. For example, here are two of the forms supported by **Integer**:

static Integer valueOf(int *val*)
static Integer valueOf(String *valStr*) throws NumberFormatException

Here, *val* specifies an integer value and *valStr* specifies a string that represents a properly formatted numeric value in string form. Each returns an **Integer** object that wraps the specified value. Here is an example:

```
Integer iOb = Integer.valueOf(100);
```

After this statement executes, the value 100 is represented by an **Integer** instance. Thus, **iOb** wraps the value 100 within an object. In addition to the forms of **valueOf( )** just shown, the integer wrappers, **Byte**, **Short**, **Integer**, and **Long**, also supply a form that lets you specify a radix.

All of the type wrappers override **toString( )**. It returns the human-readable form of the value contained within the wrapper. This allows you to output the value by passing a type wrapper object to **println( )**, for example, without having to convert it into its primitive type.

The following program demonstrates how to use a numeric type wrapper to encapsulate a value and then extract that value:

```
// Demonstrate a type wrapper.
class Wrap {
  public static void main(String[] args) {

    Integer iOb = Integer.valueOf(100);

    int i = iOb.intValue();

    System.out.println(i + " " + iOb); // displays 100 100
  }
}
```

This program wraps the integer value 100 inside an **Integer** object called **iOb**. The program then obtains this value by calling **intValue( )** and stores the result in **i**.

The process of encapsulating a value within an object is called *boxing*. Thus, in the program, this line boxes the value 100 into an **Integer**:

```
Integer iOb = Integer.valueOf(100);
```

The process of extracting a value from a type wrapper is called *unboxing*. For example, the program unboxes the value in **iOb** with this statement:

```
int i = iOb.intValue();
```

The same general procedure used by the preceding program to box and unbox values has been available for use since the original version of Java. However, today, Java provides a more streamlined approach, which is described next.

# Autoboxing

Modern versions of Java have included two important features: *autoboxing* and *auto-unboxing*. Autoboxing is the process by which a primitive type is automatically encapsulated (boxed) into its equivalent type wrapper whenever an object of that type is needed. There is no need to explicitly construct an object. Auto-unboxing is the process by which the value of a boxed object is automatically extracted (unboxed) from a type wrapper when its value is needed. There is no need to call a method such as **intValue( )** or **doubleValue( )**.

Autoboxing and auto-unboxing greatly streamline the coding of several algorithms, removing the tedium of manually boxing and unboxing values. They also help prevent errors. Moreover, they are very important to generics, which operate only on objects. Finally, autoboxing makes working with the Collections Framework (described in Part II) much easier.

With autoboxing, it is not necessary to manually construct an object in order to wrap a primitive type. You need only assign that value to a type-wrapper reference. Java automatically constructs the object for you. For example, here is the modern way to construct an **Integer** object that has the value 100:

```
Integer iOb = 100; // autobox an int
```

Notice that the object is not explicitly boxed. Java handles this for you, automatically.

To unbox an object, simply assign that object reference to a primitive-type variable. For example, to unbox **iOb**, you can use this line:

```
int i = iOb; // auto-unbox
```

Java handles the details for you.

Here is the preceding program rewritten to use autoboxing/unboxing:

```
// Demonstrate autoboxing/unboxing.
class AutoBox {
  public static void main(String[] args) {

    Integer iOb = 100; // autobox an int

    int i = iOb; // auto-unbox

    System.out.println(i + " " + iOb);  // displays 100 100
  }
}
```

## Autoboxing and Methods

In addition to the simple case of assignments, autoboxing automatically occurs whenever a primitive type must be converted into an object; auto-unboxing takes place whenever an object must be converted into a primitive type. Thus, autoboxing/unboxing might occur when an argument is passed to a method, or when a value is returned by a method. For example, consider this:

```
// Autoboxing/unboxing takes place with
// method parameters and return values.

class AutoBox2 {
  // Take an Integer parameter and return
  // an int value;
  static int m(Integer v) {
    return v ; // auto-unbox to int
  }

  public static void main(String[] args) {
    // Pass an int to m() and assign the return value
    // to an Integer.  Here, the argument 100 is autoboxed
    // into an Integer.  The return value is also autoboxed
    // into an Integer.
    Integer iOb = m(100);

    System.out.println(iOb);
  }
}
```

This program displays the following result:

```
100
```

In the program, notice that **m( )** specifies an **Integer** parameter and returns an **int** result. Inside **main( )**, **m( )** is passed the value 100. Because **m( )** is expecting an **Integer**, this value is automatically boxed. Then, **m( )** returns the **int** equivalent of its argument. This causes **v** to be auto-unboxed. Next, this **int** value is assigned to **iOb** in **main( )**, which causes the **int** return value to be autoboxed.

## Autoboxing/Unboxing Occurs in Expressions

In general, autoboxing and unboxing take place whenever a conversion into an object or from an object is required. This applies to expressions. Within an expression, a numeric object is automatically unboxed. The outcome of the expression is reboxed, if necessary. For example, consider the following program:

```
// Autoboxing/unboxing occurs inside expressions.

class AutoBox3 {
  public static void main(String[] args) {

    Integer iOb, iOb2;
    int i;

    iOb = 100;
    System.out.println("Original value of iOb: " + iOb);

    // The following automatically unboxes iOb,
    // performs the increment, and then reboxes
    // the result back into iOb.
    ++iOb;
    System.out.println("After ++iOb: " + iOb);

    // Here, iOb is unboxed, the expression is
    // evaluated, and the result is reboxed and
    // assigned to iOb2.
    iOb2 = iOb + (iOb / 3);
    System.out.println("iOb2 after expression: " + iOb2);

    // The same expression is evaluated, but the
    // result is not reboxed.
    i = iOb + (iOb / 3);
    System.out.println("i after expression: " + i);

  }
}
```

The output is shown here:

```
Original value of iOb: 100
After ++iOb: 101
iOb2 after expression: 134
i after expression: 134
```

In the program, pay special attention to this line:

```
++iOb;
```

This causes the value in **iOb** to be incremented. It works like this: **iOb** is unboxed, the value is incremented, and the result is reboxed.

Auto-unboxing also allows you to mix different types of numeric objects in an expression. Once the values are unboxed, the standard type promotions and conversions are applied. For example, the following program is perfectly valid:

```
class AutoBox4 {
  public static void main(String[] args) {

    Integer iOb = 100;
    Double dOb = 98.6;

    dOb = dOb + iOb;
    System.out.println("dOb after expression: " + dOb);
  }
}
```

The output is shown here:

```
dOb after expression: 198.6
```

As you can see, both the **Double** object **dOb** and the **Integer** object **iOb** participated in the addition, and the result was reboxed and stored in **dOb**.

Because of auto-unboxing, you can use **Integer** numeric objects to control a **switch** statement. For example, consider this fragment:

```
Integer iOb = 2;

switch(iOb) {
  case 1: System.out.println("one");
    break;
  case 2: System.out.println("two");
    break;
  default: System.out.println("error");
}
```

When the **switch** expression is evaluated, **iOb** is unboxed and its **int** value is obtained.

As the examples in the programs show, because of autoboxing/unboxing, using numeric objects in an expression is both intuitive and easy. In the early days of Java, such code would have involved casts and calls to methods such as **intValue( )**.

## Autoboxing/Unboxing Boolean and Character Values

As described earlier, Java also supplies wrappers for **boolean** and **char**. These are **Boolean** and **Character**. Autoboxing/unboxing applies to these wrappers, too. For example, consider the following program:

```
// Autoboxing/unboxing a Boolean and Character.

class AutoBox5 {
  public static void main(String[] args) {
```

```
    // Autobox/unbox a boolean.
    Boolean b = true;

    // Below, b is auto-unboxed when used in
    // a conditional expression, such as an if.
    if(b) System.out.println("b is true");

    // Autobox/unbox a char.
    Character ch = 'x'; // box a char
    char ch2 = ch; // unbox a char

    System.out.println("ch2 is " + ch2);
  }
}
```

The output is shown here:

```
b is true
ch2 is x
```

The most important thing to notice about this program is the auto-unboxing of **b** inside the **if** conditional expression. As you should recall, the conditional expression that controls an **if** must evaluate to type **boolean**. Because of auto-unboxing, the **boolean** value contained within **b** is automatically unboxed when the conditional expression is evaluated. Thus, with autoboxing/unboxing, a **Boolean** object can be used to control an **if** statement.

Because of auto-unboxing, a **Boolean** object can now also be used to control any of Java's loop statements. When a **Boolean** is used as the conditional expression of a **while**, **for**, or **do/while**, it is automatically unboxed into its **boolean** equivalent. For example, this is perfectly valid code:

```
Boolean b;
// ...
while(b) { // ...
```

## Autoboxing/Unboxing Helps Prevent Errors

In addition to the convenience that it offers, autoboxing/unboxing can also help prevent errors. For example, consider the following program:

```
// An error produced by manual unboxing.
class UnboxingError {
  public static void main(String[] args) {

    Integer iOb = 1000; // autobox the value 1000

    int i = iOb.byteValue(); // manually unbox as byte !!!

    System.out.println(i);   // does not display 1000 !
  }
}
```

This program displays not the expected value of 1000, but –24! The reason is that the value inside **iOb** is manually unboxed by calling **byteValue( )**, which causes the truncation of the value stored in **iOb**, which is 1000. This results in the garbage value of –24 being assigned to **i**. Auto-unboxing prevents this type of error because the value in **iOb** will always auto-unbox into a value compatible with **int**.

In general, because autoboxing always creates the proper object, and auto-unboxing always produces the proper value, there is no way for the process to produce the wrong type of object or value. In the rare instances where you want a type different than that produced by the automated process, you can still manually box and unbox values. Of course, the benefits of autoboxing/unboxing are lost. In general, you should employ autoboxing/unboxing. It is the way that modern Java code is written.

## A Word of Warning

Because of autoboxing and auto-unboxing, some might be tempted to use objects such as **Integer** or **Double** exclusively, abandoning primitives altogether. For example, with autoboxing/unboxing, it is possible to write code like this:

```
// A bad use of autoboxing/unboxing!
Double a, b, c;

a = 10.0;
b = 4.0;

c = Math.sqrt(a*a + b*b);

System.out.println("Hypotenuse is " + c);
```

In this example, objects of type **Double** hold values that are used to calculate the hypotenuse of a right triangle. Although this code is technically correct and does, in fact, work properly, it is a very bad use of autoboxing/unboxing. It is far less efficient than the equivalent code written using the primitive type **double**. The reason is that each autobox and auto-unbox adds overhead that is not present if the primitive type is used.

In general, you should restrict your use of the type wrappers to only those cases in which an object representation of a primitive type is required. Autoboxing/unboxing was not added to Java as a "back door" way of eliminating the primitive types.

# Annotations

Java provides a feature that enables you to embed supplemental information into a source file. This information, called an *annotation*, does not change the actions of a program. Thus, an annotation leaves the semantics of a program unchanged. However, this information can be used by various tools during both development and deployment. For example, an annotation might be processed by a source-code generator. The term *metadata* is also used to refer to this feature, but the term *annotation* is the most descriptive and more commonly used.

## Annotation Basics

An annotation is created through a mechanism based on the **interface**. Let's begin with an example. Here is the declaration for an annotation called **MyAnno**:

```
// A simple annotation type.
@interface MyAnno {
  String str();
  int val();
}
```

First, notice the @ that precedes the keyword **interface**. This tells the compiler that an annotation type is being declared. Next, notice the two members **str( )** and **val( )**. All annotations consist solely of method declarations. However, you don't provide bodies for these methods. Instead, Java implements these methods. Moreover, the methods act much like fields, as you will see.

An annotation cannot include an **extends** clause. However, all annotation types automatically extend the **Annotation** interface. Thus, **Annotation** is a super-interface of all annotations. It is declared within the **java.lang.annotation** package. It overrides **hashCode( )**, **equals( )**, and **toString( )**, which are defined by **Object**. It also specifies **annotationType( )**, which returns a **Class** object that represents the invoking annotation.

Once you have declared an annotation, you can use it to annotate something. Initially, annotations could be used only on declarations, and that is where we will begin. (JDK 8 added the ability to annotate type use, and this is described later in this chapter. However, the same basic techniques apply to both kinds of annotations.) Any type of declaration can have an annotation associated with it. For example, classes, methods, fields, parameters, and **enum** constants can be annotated. Even an annotation can be annotated. In all cases, the annotation precedes the rest of the declaration.

When you apply an annotation, you give values to its members. For example, here is an example of **MyAnno** being applied to a method declaration:

```
// Annotate a method.
@MyAnno(str = "Annotation Example", val = 100)
public static void myMeth() { // ...
```

This annotation is linked with the method **myMeth( )**. Look closely at the annotation syntax. The name of the annotation, preceded by an @, is followed by a parenthesized list of member initializations. To give a member a value, that member's name is assigned a value. Therefore, in the example, the string "Annotation Example" is assigned to the **str** member of **MyAnno**. Notice that no parentheses follow **str** in this assignment. When an annotation member is given a value, only its name is used. Thus, annotation members look like fields in this context.

## Specifying a Retention Policy

Before exploring annotations further, it is necessary to discuss *annotation retention policies*. A retention policy determines at what point an annotation is discarded. Java defines three such policies, which are encapsulated within the **java.lang.annotation.RetentionPolicy** enumeration. They are **SOURCE**, **CLASS**, and **RUNTIME**.

An annotation with a retention policy of **SOURCE** is retained only in the source file and is discarded during compilation.

An annotation with a retention policy of **CLASS** is stored in the **.class** file during compilation. However, it is not available through the JVM during run time.

An annotation with a retention policy of **RUNTIME** is stored in the **.class** file during compilation and is available through the JVM during run time. Thus, **RUNTIME** retention offers the greatest annotation persistence.

---

**NOTE** An annotation on a local variable declaration is not retained in the **.class** file.

A retention policy is specified for an annotation by using one of Java's built-in annotations: **@Retention**. Its general form is shown here:

@Retention(*retention-policy*)

Here, *retention-policy* must be one of the previously discussed enumeration constants. If no retention policy is specified for an annotation, then the default policy of **CLASS** is used.

The following version of **MyAnno** uses **@Retention** to specify the **RUNTIME** retention policy. Thus, **MyAnno** will be available to the JVM during program execution.

```
@Retention(RetentionPolicy.RUNTIME)
@interface MyAnno {
  String str();
  int val();
}
```

## Obtaining Annotations at Run Time by Use of Reflection

Although annotations are designed mostly for use by other development or deployment tools, if they specify a retention policy of **RUNTIME**, then they can be queried at run time by any Java program through the use of *reflection.* Reflection is the feature that enables information about a class to be obtained at run time. The reflection API is contained in the **java.lang .reflect** package. There are a number of ways to use reflection, and we won't examine them all here. We will, however, walk through a few examples that apply to annotations.

The first step to using reflection is to obtain a **Class** object that represents the class whose annotations you want to obtain. **Class** is one of Java's built-in classes and is defined in **java.lang**. It is described in detail in Part II. There are various ways to obtain a **Class** object. One of the easiest is to call **getClass( )**, which is a method defined by **Object**. Its general form is shown here:

final Class<?> getClass( )

It returns the **Class** object that represents the invoking object.

---

**NOTE** Notice the **<?>** that follows **Class** in the declaration of **getClass( )** just shown. This is related to Java's generics feature. **getClass( )** and several other reflection-related methods discussed in this chapter make use of generics. Generics are described in Chapter 14. However, an understanding of generics is not needed to grasp the fundamental principles of reflection.

After you have obtained a **Class** object, you can use its methods to obtain information about the various items declared by the class, including its annotations. If you want to obtain the annotations associated with a specific item declared within a class, you must first obtain an object that represents that item. For example, **Class** supplies (among others) the **getMethod( )**, **getField( )**, and **getConstructor( )** methods, which obtain information about a method, field, and constructor, respectively. These methods return objects of type **Method**, **Field**, and **Constructor**.

To understand the process, let's work through an example that obtains the annotations associated with a method. To do this, you first obtain a **Class** object that represents the class, and then you call **getMethod( )** on that **Class** object, specifying the name of the method. **getMethod( )** has this general form:

Method getMethod(String *methName*, Class<?> ... *paramTypes*)

The name of the method is passed in *methName*. If the method has arguments, then **Class** objects representing those types must also be specified by *paramTypes*. Notice that *paramTypes* is a varargs parameter. This means that you can specify as many parameter types as needed, including zero. **getMethod( )** returns a **Method** object that represents the method. If the method can't be found, **NoSuchMethodException** is thrown.

From a **Class**, **Method**, **Field**, or **Constructor** object, you can obtain a specific annotation associated with that object by calling **getAnnotation( )**. Its general form is shown here:

<A extends Annotation> getAnnotation(Class<A> *annoType*)

Here, *annoType* is a **Class** object that represents the annotation in which you are interested. The method returns a reference to the annotation. Using this reference, you can obtain the values associated with the annotation's members. The method returns **null** if the annotation is not found, which will be the case if the annotation does not have **RUNTIME** retention.

Here is a program that assembles all of the pieces shown earlier and uses reflection to display the annotation associated with a method:

```
import java.lang.annotation.*;
import java.lang.reflect.*;

// An annotation type declaration.
@Retention(RetentionPolicy.RUNTIME)
@interface MyAnno {
  String str();
  int val();
}

class Meta {

  // Annotate a method.
  @MyAnno(str = "Annotation Example", val = 100)
  public static void myMeth() {
    Meta ob = new Meta();

    // Obtain the annotation for this method
    // and display the values of the members.
```

```
    try {
      // First, get a Class object that represents
      // this class.
      Class<?> c = ob.getClass();

      // Now, get a Method object that represents
      // this method.
      Method m = c.getMethod("myMeth");

      // Next, get the annotation for this class.
      MyAnno anno = m.getAnnotation(MyAnno.class);

      // Finally, display the values.
      System.out.println(anno.str() + " " + anno.val());
    } catch (NoSuchMethodException exc) {
      System.out.println("Method Not Found.");
    }
  }

  public static void main(String[] args) {
    myMeth();
  }
}
```

The output from the program is shown here:

```
Annotation Example 100
```

This program uses reflection as described to obtain and display the values of **str** and **val** in the **MyAnno** annotation associated with **myMeth( )** in the **Meta** class. There are two things to pay special attention to. First, in the line

```
MyAnno anno = m.getAnnotation(MyAnno.class);
```

notice the expression **MyAnno.class**. This expression evaluates to a **Class** object of type **MyAnno**, the annotation. This construct is called a *class literal*. You can use this type of expression whenever a **Class** object of a known class is needed. For example, this statement could have been used to obtain the **Class** object for **Meta**:

```
Class<?> c = Meta.class;
```

Of course, this approach only works when you know the class name of an object in advance, which might not always be the case. In general, you can obtain a class literal for classes, interfaces, primitive types, and arrays. (Remember, the **<?>** syntax relates to Java's generics feature. It is described in Chapter 14.)

The second point of interest is the way the values associated with **str** and **val** are obtained when they are output by the following line:

```
System.out.println(anno.str() + " " + anno.val());
```

Notice that they are invoked using the method-call syntax. This same approach is used whenever the value of an annotation member is required.

## A Second Reflection Example

In the preceding example, **myMeth( )** has no parameters. Thus, when **getMethod( )** was called, only the name **myMeth** was passed. However, to obtain a method that has parameters, you must specify class objects representing the types of those parameters as arguments to **getMethod( )**. For example, here is a slightly different version of the preceding program:

```
import java.lang.annotation.*;
import java.lang.reflect.*;

@Retention(RetentionPolicy.RUNTIME)
@interface MyAnno {
  String str();
  int val();
}

class Meta {

  // myMeth now has two arguments.
  @MyAnno(str = "Two Parameters", val = 19)
  public static void myMeth(String str, int i)
  {
    Meta ob = new Meta();

    try {
      Class<?> c = ob.getClass();

      // Here, the parameter types are specified.
      Method m = c.getMethod("myMeth", String.class, int.class);

      MyAnno anno = m.getAnnotation(MyAnno.class);

      System.out.println(anno.str() + " " + anno.val());
    } catch (NoSuchMethodException exc) {
       System.out.println("Method Not Found.");
    }
  }

  public static void main(String[] args) {
    myMeth("test", 10);
  }
}
```

The output from this version is shown here:

```
Two Parameters 19
```

In this version, **myMeth( )** takes a **String** and an **int** parameter. To obtain information about this method, **getMethod( )** must be called as shown here:

```
Method m = c.getMethod("myMeth", String.class, int.class);
```

Here, the **Class** objects representing **String** and **int** are passed as additional arguments.

## Obtaining All Annotations

You can obtain all annotations that have **RUNTIME** retention that are associated with an item by calling **getAnnotations( )** on that item. It has this general form:

Annotation[ ] getAnnotations( )

It returns an array of the annotations. **getAnnotations( )** can be called on objects of type **Class**, **Method**, **Constructor**, and **Field**, among others.

Here is another reflection example that shows how to obtain all annotations associated with a class and with a method. It declares two annotations. It then uses those annotations to annotate a class and a method.

```
// Show all annotations for a class and a method.
import java.lang.annotation.*;
import java.lang.reflect.*;

@Retention(RetentionPolicy.RUNTIME)
@interface MyAnno {
  String str();
  int val();
}

@Retention(RetentionPolicy.RUNTIME)
@interface What {
  String description();
}

@What(description = "An annotation test class")
@MyAnno(str = "Meta2", val = 99)
class Meta2 {

  @What(description = "An annotation test method")
  @MyAnno(str = "Testing", val = 100)
  public static void myMeth() {
    Meta2 ob = new Meta2();

      try {
        Annotation[] annos = ob.getClass().getAnnotations();

        // Display all annotations for Meta2.
        System.out.println("All annotations for Meta2:");
        for(Annotation a : annos)
          System.out.println(a);

        System.out.println();

        // Display all annotations for myMeth.
        Method m = ob.getClass( ).getMethod("myMeth");
        annos = m.getAnnotations();
```

```
      System.out.println("All annotations for myMeth:");
      for(Annotation a : annos)
        System.out.println(a);

    } catch (NoSuchMethodException exc) {
       System.out.println("Method Not Found.");
    }
  }

  public static void main(String[] args) {
    myMeth();
  }
}
```

The output is shown here:

```
All annotations for Meta2:
@What(description=An annotation test class)
@MyAnno(str=Meta2, val=99)

All annotations for myMeth:
@What(description=An annotation test method)
@MyAnno(str=Testing, val=100)
```

The program uses **getAnnotations( )** to obtain an array of all annotations associated with the **Meta2** class and with the **myMeth( )** method. As explained, **getAnnotations( )** returns an array of **Annotation** objects. Recall that **Annotation** is a super-interface of all annotation interfaces and that it overrides **toString( )** in **Object**. Thus, when a reference to an **Annotation** is output, its **toString( )** method is called to generate a string that describes the annotation, as the preceding output shows.

## The AnnotatedElement Interface

The methods **getAnnotation( )** and **getAnnotations( )** used by the preceding examples are defined by the **AnnotatedElement** interface, which is defined in **java.lang.reflect**. This interface supports reflection for annotations and is implemented by the classes **Method**, **Field**, **Constructor**, **Class**, and **Package**, among others.

In addition to **getAnnotation( )** and **getAnnotations( )**, **AnnotatedElement** defines several other methods. Two have been available since annotations were initially added to Java. The first is **getDeclaredAnnotations( )**, which has this general form:

Annotation[ ] getDeclaredAnnotations( )

It returns all non-inherited annotations present in the invoking object. The second is **isAnnotationPresent( )**, which has this general form:

default boolean isAnnotationPresent(Class<? extends Annotation> *annoType*)

It returns **true** if the annotation specified by *annoType* is associated with the invoking object. It returns **false** otherwise. To these, JDK 8 added **getDeclaredAnnotation( )**, **getAnnotationsByType( )**, and **getDeclaredAnnotationsByType( )**. Of these, the last two automatically work with a repeated annotation.(Repeated annotations are discussed at the end of this chapter.)

## Using Default Values

You can give annotation members default values that will be used if no value is specified when the annotation is applied. A default value is specified by adding a **default** clause to a member's declaration. It has this general form:

*type member*( ) default *value*;

Here, *value* must be of a type compatible with *type*.

Here is **@MyAnno** rewritten to include default values:

```
// An annotation type declaration that includes defaults.
@Retention(RetentionPolicy.RUNTIME)
@interface MyAnno {
  String str() default "Testing";
  int val() default 9000;
}
```

This declaration gives a default value of "Testing" to **str** and 9000 to **val**. This means that neither value needs to be specified when **@MyAnno** is used. However, either or both can be given values if desired. Therefore, following are the four ways that **@MyAnno** can be used:

```
@MyAnno() // both str and val default
@MyAnno(str = "some string") // val defaults
@MyAnno(val = 100) // str defaults
@MyAnno(str = "Testing", val = 100) // no defaults
```

The following program demonstrates the use of default values in an annotation:

```
import java.lang.annotation.*;
import java.lang.reflect.*;

// An annotation type declaration that includes defaults.
@Retention(RetentionPolicy.RUNTIME)
@interface MyAnno {
  String str() default "Testing";
  int val() default 9000;
}

class Meta3 {

  // Annotate a method using the default values.
  @MyAnno()
  public static void myMeth() {
    Meta3 ob = new Meta3();

    // Obtain the annotation for this method
    // and display the values of the members.
    try {
      Class<?> c = ob.getClass();

     Method m = c.getMethod("myMeth");
```

```
      MyAnno anno = m.getAnnotation(MyAnno.class);

      System.out.println(anno.str() + " " + anno.val());
    } catch (NoSuchMethodException exc) {
      System.out.println("Method Not Found.");
    }
  }

  public static void main(String[] args) {
    myMeth();
  }
}
```

The output is shown here:

```
Testing 9000
```

## Marker Annotations

A *marker* annotation is a special kind of annotation that contains no members. Its sole purpose is to mark an item. Thus, its presence as an annotation is sufficient. The best way to determine if a marker annotation is present is to use the method **isAnnotationPresent( )**, which is defined by the **AnnotatedElement** interface.

Here is an example that uses a marker annotation. Because a marker interface contains no members, simply determining whether it is present or absent is sufficient.

```
import java.lang.annotation.*;
import java.lang.reflect.*;

// A marker annotation.
@Retention(RetentionPolicy.RUNTIME)
@interface MyMarker { }

class Marker {

  // Annotate a method using a marker.
  // Notice that no ( ) is needed.
  @MyMarker
  public static void myMeth() {
    Marker ob = new Marker();

    try {
      Method m = ob.getClass().getMethod("myMeth");

      // Determine if the annotation is present.
      if(m.isAnnotationPresent(MyMarker.class))
        System.out.println("MyMarker is present.");

    } catch (NoSuchMethodException exc) {
      System.out.println("Method Not Found.");
    }
  }
```

```
  public static void main(String[] args) {
    myMeth();
  }
}
```

The output, shown here, confirms that **@MyMarker** is present:

```
MyMarker is present.
```

In the program, notice that you do not need to follow **@MyMarker** with parentheses when it is applied. Thus, **@MyMarker** is applied simply by using its name, like this:

@MyMarker

It is not wrong to supply an empty set of parentheses, but they are not needed.

## Single-Member Annotations

A *single-member* annotation contains only one member. It works like a normal annotation, except that it allows a shorthand form of specifying the value of the member. When only one member is present, you can simply specify the value for that member when the annotation is applied—you don't need to specify the name of the member. However, in order to use this shorthand, the name of the member must be **value**.

Here is an example that creates and uses a single-member annotation:

```
import java.lang.annotation.*;
import java.lang.reflect.*;

// A single-member annotation.
@Retention(RetentionPolicy.RUNTIME)
@interface MySingle {
  int value(); // this variable name must be value
}

class Single {

  // Annotate a method using a single-member annotation.
  @MySingle(100)
  public static void myMeth() {
    Single ob = new Single();

    try {
      Method m = ob.getClass().getMethod("myMeth");

      MySingle anno = m.getAnnotation(MySingle.class);

      System.out.println(anno.value()); // displays 100

    } catch (NoSuchMethodException exc) {
       System.out.println("Method Not Found.");
    }
  }
```

```
  public static void main(String[] args) {
    myMeth();
  }
}
```

As expected, this program displays the value 100. In the program, **@MySingle** is used to annotate **myMeth( )**, as shown here:

```
@MySingle(100)
```

Notice that **value** = need not be specified.

You can use the single-value syntax when applying an annotation that has other members, but those other members must all have default values. For example, here the value **xyz** is added, with a default value of zero:

```
@interface SomeAnno {
  int value();
  int xyz() default 0;
}
```

In cases in which you want to use the default for **xyz**, you can apply **@SomeAnno**, as shown next, by simply specifying the value of **value** by using the single-member syntax:

```
@SomeAnno(88)
```

In this case, **xyz** defaults to zero, and **value** gets the value 88. Of course, to specify a different value for **xyz** requires that both members be explicitly named, as shown here:

```
@SomeAnno(value = 88, xyz = 99)
```

Remember, whenever you are using a single-member annotation, the name of that member must be **value**.

## The Built-In Annotations

Java defines many built-in annotations. Most are specialized, but nine are general purpose. Of these, four are imported from **java.lang.annotation**: **@Retention**, **@Documented**, **@Target**, and **@Inherited**. Five—**@Override**, **@Deprecated**, **@FunctionalInterface**, **@SafeVarargs**, and **@SuppressWarnings**—are included in **java.lang**. Each is described here.

**NOTE** **java.lang.annotation** also includes the annotations **Repeatable** and **Native**. **Repeatable** supports repeatable annotations, as described later in this chapter. **Native** annotates a field that can be accessed by native code.

### @Retention

**@Retention** is designed to be used only as an annotation to another annotation. It specifies the retention policy as described earlier in this chapter.

## @Documented

The **@Documented** annotation is a marker interface that tells a tool that an annotation is to be documented. It is designed to be used only as an annotation to an annotation declaration.

## @Target

The **@Target** annotation specifies the types of items to which an annotation can be applied. It is designed to be used only as an annotation to another annotation. **@Target** takes one argument, which is an array of constants of the **ElementType** enumeration. This argument specifies the types of declarations to which the annotation can be applied. The constants are shown here along with the type of declaration to which they correspond:

| Target Constant | Annotation Can Be Applied To |
|---|---|
| ANNOTATION_TYPE | Another annotation |
| CONSTRUCTOR | Constructor |
| FIELD | Field |
| LOCAL_VARIABLE | Local variable |
| METHOD | Method |
| MODULE | Module |
| PACKAGE | Package |
| PARAMETER | Parameter |
| RECORD_COMPONENT | A component of a record (added by JDK 16) |
| TYPE | Class, interface, or enumeration |
| TYPE_PARAMETER | Type parameter |
| TYPE_USE | Type use |

You can specify one or more of these values in a **@Target** annotation. To specify multiple values, you must specify them within a braces-delimited list. For example, to specify that an annotation applies only to fields and local variables, you can use this **@Target** annotation:

```
@Target( { ElementType.FIELD, ElementType.LOCAL_VARIABLE } )
```

If you don't use **@Target**, then the annotation can be used on any declaration. For this reason, it is often a good idea to explicitly specify the target or targets so as to clearly indicate the intended uses of an annotation.

## @Inherited

**@Inherited** is a marker annotation that can be used only on another annotation declaration. Furthermore, it affects only annotations that will be used on class declarations. **@Inherited** causes the annotation for a superclass to be inherited by a subclass. Therefore, when a request for a specific annotation is made to the subclass, if that annotation is not present in the subclass, then its superclass is checked. If that annotation is present in the superclass, and if it is annotated with **@Inherited**, then that annotation will be returned.

### @Override

**@Override** is a marker annotation that can be used only on methods. A method annotated with **@Override** must override a method from a superclass. If it doesn't, a compile-time error will result. It is used to ensure that a superclass method is actually overridden, and not simply overloaded.

### @Deprecated

**@Deprecated** indicates that a declaration is obsolete and not recommended for use. Beginning with JDK 9, **@Deprecated** also allows you to specify the Java version in which the deprecation occurred and whether the deprecated element is slated for removal.

### @FunctionalInterface

**@FunctionalInterface** is a marker annotation designed for use on interfaces. It indicates that the annotated interface is a functional interface. A *functional interface* is an interface that contains one and only one abstract method. Functional interfaces are used by lambda expressions. (See Chapter 15 for details on functional interfaces and lambda expressions.) If the annotated interface is not a functional interface, a compilation error will be reported. It is important to understand that **@FunctionalInterface** is not needed to create a functional interface. Any interface with exactly one abstract method is, by definition, a functional interface. Thus, **@FunctionalInterface** is purely informational.

### @SafeVarargs

**@SafeVarargs** is a marker annotation that can be applied to methods and constructors. It indicates that no unsafe actions related to a varargs parameter occur. It is used to suppress unchecked warnings on otherwise safe code as it relates to non-reifiable vararg types and parameterized array instantiation. (A non-reifiable type is, essentially, a generic type. Generics are described in Chapter 14.) It must be applied only to vararg methods or constructors. Methods must also be **static**, **final**, or **private**.

### @SuppressWarnings

**@SuppressWarnings** specifies that one or more warnings that might be issued by the compiler are to be suppressed. The warnings to suppress are specified by name, in string form.

## Type Annotations

As mentioned earlier, annotations were originally allowed only on declarations. However, for modern versions of Java, annotations can also be specified in most cases in which a type is used. This expanded aspect of annotations is called *type annotation*. For example, you can annotate the return type of a method, the type of **this** within a method, a cast, array levels, an inherited class, and a **throws** clause. You can also annotate generic types, including generic type parameter bounds and generic type arguments. (See Chapter 14 for a discussion of generics.)

Type annotations are important because they enable tools to perform additional checks on code to help prevent errors. Understand that, as a general rule, **javac** will not perform these checks, itself. A separate tool is used for this purpose, although such a tool might operate as a compiler plug-in.

A type annotation must include **ElementType.TYPE_USE** as a target. (Recall that valid annotation targets are specified using the **@Target** annotation, as previously described.) A type annotation applies to the type that the annotation precedes. For example, assuming some type annotation called **@TypeAnno**, the following is legal:

```
void myMeth() throws @TypeAnno NullPointerException { // ...
```

Here, **@TypeAnno** annotates **NullPointerException** in the **throws** clause.

You can also annotate the type of **this** (called the *receiver*). As you know, **this** is an implicit argument to all instance methods, and it refers to the invoking object. To annotate its type requires the use of another feature that was not originally part of Java. Beginning with JDK 8, you can explicitly declare **this** as the first parameter to a method. In this declaration, the type of **this** must be the type of its class; for example:

```
class SomeClass {
  int myMeth(SomeClass this, int i, int j) { // ...
```

Here, because **myMeth( )** is a method defined by **SomeClass**, the type of **this** is **SomeClass**. Using this declaration, you can now annotate the type of **this**. For example, again assuming that **@TypeAnno** is a type annotation, the following is legal:

```
int myMeth(@TypeAnno SomeClass this, int i, int j) { // ...
```

It is important to understand that it is not necessary to declare **this** unless you are annotating it. (If **this** is not declared, it is still implicitly passed, as it always has been.) Also, explicitly declaring **this** does not change any aspect of the method's signature because **this** is implicitly declared, by default. Again, you will declare **this** only if you want to apply a type annotation to it. If you do declare **this**, it *must* be the first parameter.

The following program shows a number of the places that a type annotation can be used. It defines several annotations, of which several are for type annotation. The names and targets of the annotations are shown here:

| Annotation | Target |
|---|---|
| @TypeAnno | ElementType.TYPE_USE |
| @MaxLen | ElementType.TYPE_USE |
| @NotZeroLen | ElementType.TYPE_USE |
| @Unique | ElementType.TYPE_USE |
| @What | ElementType.TYPE_PARAMETER |
| @EmptyOK | ElementType.FIELD |
| @Recommended | ElementType.METHOD |

Notice that **@EmptyOK**, **@Recommended**, and **@What** are not type annotations. They are included for comparison purposes. Of special interest is **@What**, which is used to annotate a generic type parameter declaration. The comments in the program describe each use.

```
// Demonstrate several type annotations.
import java.lang.annotation.*;
import java.lang.reflect.*;

// A marker annotation that can be applied to a type.
@Target(ElementType.TYPE_USE)
@interface TypeAnno { }

// Another marker annotation that can be applied to a type.
@Target(ElementType.TYPE_USE)
@interface NotZeroLen {
}

// Still another marker annotation that can be applied to a type.
@Target(ElementType.TYPE_USE)
@interface Unique { }

// A parameterized annotation that can be applied to a type.
@Target(ElementType.TYPE_USE)
@interface MaxLen {
  int value();
}

// An annotation that can be applied to a type parameter.
@Target(ElementType.TYPE_PARAMETER)
@interface What {
  String description();
}

// An annotation that can be applied to a field declaration.
@Target(ElementType.FIELD)
@interface EmptyOK { }

// An annotation that can be applied to a method declaration.
@Target(ElementType.METHOD)
@interface Recommended { }


// Use an annotation on a type parameter.
class TypeAnnoDemo<@What(description = "Generic data type") T> {

  // Use a type annotation on a constructor.
  public @Unique TypeAnnoDemo() {}

  // Annotate the type (in this case String), not the field.
  @TypeAnno String str;
```

```
  // This annotates the field test.
  @EmptyOK String test;

  // Use a type annotation to annotate this (the receiver).
  public int f(@TypeAnno TypeAnnoDemo<T> this, int x) {
    return 10;
  }

  // Annotate the return type.
  public @TypeAnno Integer f2(int j, int k) {
    return j+k;
  }

  // Annotate the method declaration.
  public @Recommended Integer f3(String str) {
    return str.length() / 2;
  }

  // Use a type annotation with a throws clause.
  public void f4() throws @TypeAnno NullPointerException {
    // ...
  }

  // Annotate array levels.
  String @MaxLen(10) [] @NotZeroLen [] w;

  // Annotate the array element type.
  @TypeAnno Integer[] vec;

  public static void myMeth(int i) {

    // Use a type annotation on a type argument.
    TypeAnnoDemo<@TypeAnno Integer> ob =
                       new TypeAnnoDemo<@TypeAnno Integer>();

    // Use a type annotation with new.
    @Unique TypeAnnoDemo<Integer> ob2 = new @Unique TypeAnnoDemo<Integer>();

    Object x = Integer.valueOf(10);
    Integer y;

    // Use a type annotation on a cast.
    y = (@TypeAnno Integer) x;
  }

  public static void main(String[] args) {
    myMeth(10);
  }

  // Use type annotation with inheritance clause.
  class SomeClass extends @TypeAnno TypeAnnoDemo<Boolean> {}
}
```

Although what most of the annotations in the preceding program refer to is clear, four uses require a bit of discussion. The first is the annotation of a method return type versus the annotation of a method declaration. In the program, pay special attention to these two method declarations:

```
// Annotate the return type.
public @TypeAnno Integer f2(int j, int k) {
  return j+k;
}

// Annotate the method declaration.
public @Recommended Integer f3(String str) {
  return str.length() / 2;
}
```

Notice that in both cases, an annotation precedes the method's return type (which is **Integer**). However, the two annotations annotate two different things. In the first case, the **@TypeAnno** annotation annotates **f2( )**'s return type. This is because **@TypeAnno** has its target specified as **ElementType.TYPE_USE**, which means that it can be used to annotate type uses. In the second case, **@Recommended** annotates the method declaration itself. This is because **@Recommended** has its target specified as **ElementType.METHOD**. As a result, **@Recommended** applies to the declaration, not the return type. Therefore, the target specification is used to eliminate what, at first glance, appears to be ambiguity between the annotation of a method declaration and the annotation of the method's return type.

One other thing about annotating a method return type: You cannot annotate a return type of **void**.

The second point of interest are the field annotations, shown here:

```
// Annotate the type (in this case String), not the field.
@TypeAnno String str;

// This annotates the field test.
@EmptyOK String test;
```

Here, **@TypeAnno** annotates the type **String**, but **@EmptyOK** annotates the field **test**. Even though both annotations precede the entire declaration, their targets are different, based on the target element type. If the annotation has the **ElementType.TYPE_USE** target, then the type is annotated. If it has **ElementType.FIELD** as a target, then the field is annotated. Thus, the situation is similar to that just described for methods, and no ambiguity exists. The same mechanism also disambiguates annotations on local variables.

Next, notice how **this** (the receiver) is annotated here:

```
public int f(@TypeAnno TypeAnnoDemo<T> this, int x) {
```

Here, **this** is specified as the first parameter and is of type **TypeAnnoDemo** (which is the class of which **f( )** is a member). As explained, an instance method declaration can explicitly specify the **this** parameter for the sake of applying a type annotation.

Finally, look at how array levels are annotated by the following statement:

```
String @MaxLen(10) [] @NotZeroLen [] w;
```

In this declaration, **@MaxLen** annotates the type of the first level, and **@NotZeroLen** annotates the type of the second level. In the declaration

```
@TypeAnno Integer[] vec;
```

the element type **Integer** is annotated.

## Repeating Annotations

Beginning with JDK 8, an annotation can be repeated on the same element. This is called *repeating annotations*. For an annotation to be repeatable, it must be annotated with the **@Repeatable** annotation, defined in **java.lang.annotation**. Its **value** field specifies the *container* type for the repeatable annotation. The container is specified as an annotation for which the **value** field is an array of the repeatable annotation type. Thus, to create a repeatable annotation, you must create a container annotation and then specify that annotation type as an argument to the **@Repeatable** annotation.

To access the repeated annotations using a method such as **getAnnotation( )**, you will use the container annotation, not the repeatable annotation. The following program shows this approach. It converts the version of **MyAnno** shown previously into a repeatable annotation and demonstrates its use.

```
// Demonstrate a repeated annotation.

import java.lang.annotation.*;
import java.lang.reflect.*;

// Make MyAnno repeatable.
@Retention(RetentionPolicy.RUNTIME)
@Repeatable(MyRepeatedAnnos.class)
@interface MyAnno {
  String str() default "Testing";
  int val() default 9000;
}

// This is the container annotation.
@Retention(RetentionPolicy.RUNTIME)
@interface MyRepeatedAnnos {
  MyAnno[] value();
}

class RepeatAnno {

  // Repeat MyAnno on myMeth().
  @MyAnno(str = "First annotation", val = -1)
  @MyAnno(str = "Second annotation", val = 100)
  public static void myMeth(String str, int i)
```

```
  {
    RepeatAnno ob = new RepeatAnno();

    try {
      Class<?> c = ob.getClass();

      // Obtain the annotations for myMeth().
      Method m = c.getMethod("myMeth", String.class, int.class);

      // Display the repeated MyAnno annotations.
      Annotation anno = m.getAnnotation(MyRepeatedAnnos.class);
      System.out.println(anno);

    } catch (NoSuchMethodException exc) {
       System.out.println("Method Not Found.");
    }
  }

  public static void main(String[] args) {
    myMeth("test", 10);
  }
}
```

The output is shown here:

```
@MyRepeatedAnnos(value={@MyAnno(val=-1, str="First annotation"),
@MyAnno(val=100, str="Second annotation")})
```

As explained, in order for **MyAnno** to be repeatable, it must be annotated with the **@Repeatable** annotation, which specifies its container annotation. The container annotation is called **MyRepeatedAnnos**. The program accesses the repeated annotations by calling **getAnnotation( )**, passing in the class of the container annotation, not the repeatable annotation, itself. As the output shows, the repeated annotations are separated by a comma. They are not returned individually.

Another way to obtain the repeated annotations is to use one of the methods in **AnnotatedElement** that can operate directly on a repeated annotation. These are **getAnnotationsByType( )** and **getDeclaredAnnotationsByType( )**. Here, we will use the former. It is shown here:

```
default <T extends Annotation> T[ ] getAnnotationsByType(Class<T> annoType)
```

It returns an array of the annotations of *annoType* associated with the invoking object. If no annotations are present, the array will be of zero length. Here is an example. Assuming the preceding program, the following sequence uses **getAnnotationsByType( )** to obtain the repeated **MyAnno** annotations:

```
Annotation[] annos = m.getAnnotationsByType(MyAnno.class);
for(Annotation a : annos)
  System.out.println(a);
```

Here, the repeated annotation type, which is **MyAnno**, is passed to **getAnnotationsByType( )**. The returned array contains all of the instances of **MyAnno** associated with **myMeth( )**, which, in this example, is two. Each repeated annotation can be accessed via its index in the array. In this case, each **MyAnno** annotation is displayed via a for-each loop.

## Some Restrictions

There are a number of restrictions that apply to annotation declarations. First, no annotation can inherit another. Second, all methods declared by an annotation must be without parameters. Furthermore, they must return one of the following:

- A primitive type, such as **int** or **double**
- An object of type **String** or **Class**
- An object of an **enum** type
- An object of another annotation type
- An array of a legal type.

Annotations cannot be generic. In other words, they cannot take type parameters. (Generics are described in Chapter 14.) Finally, annotation methods cannot specify a **throws** clause.

CHAPTER

# 13 I/O, Try-with-Resources, and Other Topics

This chapter introduces one of Java's most important packages, **java.io**, which supports Java's basic I/O (input/output) system, including file I/O. Support for I/O comes from Java's core API libraries, not from language keywords. For this reason, an in-depth discussion of this topic is found in Part II of this book, which examines several of Java's API packages. Here, the foundation of this important subsystem is introduced so that you can see how it fits into the larger context of the Java programming and execution environment. This chapter also examines the **try**-with-resources statement and several more Java keywords: **transient**, **volatile**, **instanceof**, **native**, **strictfp**, and **assert**. It concludes by discussing static import and describing another use for the **this** keyword.

## I/O Basics

As you may have noticed while reading the preceding 12 chapters, not much use has been made of I/O in the sample programs. In fact, aside from **print( )** and **println( )**, none of the I/O methods have been used significantly. The reason is simple: Most real applications of Java are not text-based, console programs. Rather, they are either graphically oriented programs that rely on one of Java's graphical user interface (GUI) frameworks, such as Swing, for user interaction, or they are web applications. Although text-based, console programs are excellent as teaching examples, they do not, as a general rule, constitute an important use for Java in the real world. Also, Java's support for console I/O is limited and somewhat awkward to use—even in simple sample programs. Text-based console I/O is just not that useful in real-world Java programming.

The preceding paragraph notwithstanding, Java does provide strong, flexible support for I/O as it relates to files and networks. Java's I/O system is cohesive and consistent. In fact, once you understand its fundamentals, the rest of the I/O system is easy to master. A general overview of I/O is presented here. A detailed description is found in Chapters 22 and 23.

## Streams

Java programs perform I/O through streams. A *stream* is an abstraction that either produces or consumes information. A stream is linked to a physical device by the Java I/O system. All streams behave in the same manner, even if the actual physical devices to which they are linked differ. Thus, the same I/O classes and methods can be applied to different types of devices. This means that an input stream can abstract many different kinds of input: from a disk file, a keyboard, or a network socket. Likewise, an output stream may refer to the console, a disk file, or a network connection. Streams are a clean way to deal with input/output without having every part of your code understand the difference between a keyboard and a network, for example. Java implements streams within class hierarchies defined in the **java.io** package.

**NOTE** In addition to the stream-based I/O defined in **java.io**, Java also provides buffer- and channel-based I/O, which are defined in **java.nio** and its subpackages. They are described in Chapter 23.

## Byte Streams and Character Streams

Java defines two types of I/O streams: byte and character. *Byte streams* provide a convenient means for handling input and output of bytes. Byte streams are used, for example, when reading or writing binary data. *Character streams* provide a convenient means for handling input and output of characters. They use Unicode and, therefore, can be internationalized. Also, in some cases, character streams are more efficient than byte streams.

The original version of Java (Java 1.0) did not include character streams and, thus, all I/O was byte-oriented. Character streams were added by Java 1.1, and certain byte-oriented classes and methods were deprecated. Although old code that doesn't use character streams is becoming increasingly rare, it may still be encountered from time to time. As a general rule, old code should be updated to take advantage of character streams where appropriate.

One other point: At the lowest level, all I/O is still byte-oriented. The character-based streams simply provide a convenient and efficient means for handling characters.

An overview of both byte-oriented streams and character-oriented streams is presented in the following sections.

### The Byte Stream Classes

Byte streams are defined by using two class hierarchies. At the top are two abstract classes: **InputStream** and **OutputStream**. Each of these abstract classes has several concrete subclasses that handle the differences among various devices, such as disk files, network connections, and even memory buffers. The non-deprecated byte stream classes in **java.io** are shown in Table 13-1. A few of these classes are discussed later in this section. Others are described in Part II of this book. Remember, to use the stream classes, you must import **java.io**.

| Stream Class | Meaning |
|---|---|
| BufferedInputStream | Buffered input stream |
| BufferedOutputStream | Buffered output stream |
| ByteArrayInputStream | Input stream that reads from a byte array |
| ByteArrayOutputStream | Output stream that writes to a byte array |
| DataInputStream | An input stream that contains methods for reading the Java standard data types |
| DataOutputStream | An output stream that contains methods for writing the Java standard data types |
| FileInputStream | Input stream that reads from a file |
| FileOutputStream | Output stream that writes to a file |
| FilterInputStream | Implements **InputStream** |
| FilterOutputStream | Implements **OutputStream** |
| InputStream | Abstract class that describes stream input |
| ObjectInputStream | Input stream for objects |
| ObjectOutputStream | Output stream for objects |
| OutputStream | Abstract class that describes stream output |
| PipedInputStream | Input pipe |
| PipedOutputStream | Output pipe |
| PrintStream | Output stream that contains **print( )** and **println( )** |
| PushbackInputStream | Input stream that allows bytes to be returned to the input stream |
| SequenceInputStream | Input stream that is a combination of two or more input streams that will be read sequentially, one after the other |

**Table 13-1** The Non-Deprecated Byte Stream Classes in **java.io**

The abstract classes **InputStream** and **OutputStream** define several key methods that the other stream classes implement. Two of the most important are **read( )** and **write( )**, which, respectively, read and write bytes of data. Each has a form that is abstract and must be overridden by derived stream classes.

## The Character Stream Classes

Character streams are defined by using two class hierarchies. At the top are two abstract classes: **Reader** and **Writer**. These abstract classes handle Unicode character streams. Java has several concrete subclasses of each of these. The character stream classes in **java.io** are shown in Table 13-2.

| Stream Class | Meaning |
|---|---|
| BufferedReader | Buffered input character stream |
| BufferedWriter | Buffered output character stream |
| CharArrayReader | Input stream that reads from a character array |
| CharArrayWriter | Output stream that writes to a character array |
| FileReader | Input stream that reads from a file |
| FileWriter | Output stream that writes to a file |
| FilterReader | Filtered reader |
| FilterWriter | Filtered writer |
| InputStreamReader | Input stream that translates bytes to characters |
| LineNumberReader | Input stream that counts lines |
| OutputStreamWriter | Output stream that translates characters to bytes |
| PipedReader | Input pipe |
| PipedWriter | Output pipe |
| PrintWriter | Output stream that contains **print( )** and **println( )** |
| PushbackReader | Input stream that allows characters to be returned to the input stream |
| Reader | Abstract class that describes character stream input |
| StringReader | Input stream that reads from a string |
| StringWriter | Output stream that writes to a string |
| Writer | Abstract class that describes character stream output |

**Table 13-2** The Character Stream I/O Classes in **java.io**

The abstract classes **Reader** and **Writer** define several key methods that the other stream classes implement. Two of the most important methods are **read( )** and **write( )**, which read and write characters of data, respectively. Each has a form that is abstract and must be overridden by derived stream classes.

## The Predefined Streams

As you know, all Java programs automatically import the **java.lang** package. This package defines a class called **System**, which encapsulates several aspects of the run-time environment. For example, using some of its methods, you can obtain the current time and the settings of various properties associated with the system. **System** also contains three predefined stream variables: **in**, **out**, and **err**. These fields are declared as **public**, **static**, and **final** within **System**. This means that they can be used by any other part of your program and without reference to a specific **System** object.

**System.out** refers to the standard output stream. By default, this is the console. **System.in** refers to standard input, which is the keyboard by default. **System.err** refers to the standard error stream, which also is the console by default. However, these streams may be redirected to any compatible I/O device.

**System.in** is an object of type **InputStream**; **System.out** and **System.err** are objects of type **PrintStream**. These are byte streams, even though they are typically used to read and write characters from and to the console. As you will see, you can wrap these within character-based streams, if desired.

The preceding chapters have been using **System.out** in their examples. You can use **System.err** in much the same way. As explained in the next section, use of **System.in** is a little more complicated.

## Reading Console Input

In the early days of Java, the only way to perform console input was to use a byte stream. Today, using a byte stream to read console input is still often acceptable, such as when used in sample programs. However, for commercial applications, the preferred method of reading console input is to use a character-oriented stream. This makes your program easier to internationalize and maintain.

In Java, console input is accomplished (either directly or indirectly) by reading from **System.in**. One way to obtain a character-based stream that is attached to the console is to wrap **System.in** in a **BufferedReader**. The **BufferedReader** class supports a buffered input stream. A commonly used constructor is shown here:

BufferedReader(Reader *inputReader*)

Here, *inputReader* is the stream that is linked to the instance of **BufferedReader** that is being created. **Reader** is an abstract class. One of its concrete subclasses is **InputStreamReader**, which converts bytes to characters.

Beginning with JDK 17, the precise way you obtain an **InputStreamReader** linked to **System.in** has changed. In the past, it was common to use the following **InputStreamReader** constructor for this purpose:

InputStreamReader(InputStream *inputStream*)

Because **System.in** refers to an object of type **InputStream**, it can be used for *inputStream*. Thus, the following line of code shows a common approach used in the past for creating a **BufferedReader** connected to the keyboard:

```
BufferedReader br = new BufferedReader(new InputStreamReader(System.in));
```

After this statement executes, **br** is a character-based stream that is linked to the console through **System.in**.

However, beginning with JDK 17, it is now recommended to explicitly specify the charset associated with the console when creating the **InputStreamReader**. A *charset* defines the way that bytes are mapped to characters. Normally, when a charset is not specified, the default charset of the JVM is used. However, in the case of the console, the charset used for console input may differ from this default charset. Thus, it is now recommended that this form of **InputStreamReader** constructor be used:

InputStreamReader(InputStream *inputStream*, Charset *charset*)

For *charset*, use the charset associated with the console. This charset is returned by **charset( )**, which is a new method added by JDK 17 to the **Console** class. (See Chapter 22.)

You obtain a **Console** object by calling **System.console( )**. It returns a reference to the console, or **null** if no console is present. Therefore, today the following sequence shows one way to wrap **System.in** in a **BufferedReader**:

```
Console con = System.console(); // get the console
if(con==null) return; // if no console present, return

BufferedReader br = new
    BufferedReader(new InputStreamReader(System.in, con.charset()));
```

Of course, in cases in which you know that a console will be present, the sequence can be shortened to:

```
BufferedReader br = new
    BufferedReader(new InputStreamReader(System.in,
                                         System.console().charset()));
```

Because a console is (obviously) required to run the examples in this book, this is the form we will use.

One other point: It is also possible to obtain a **Reader** that is already associated with the console by use of the **reader( )** method defined by **Console**. However, we will use the **InputStreamReader** approach as just described because it explicitly demonstrates the way that byte streams and character streams can interact.

## Reading Characters

To read a character from a **BufferedReader**, use **read( )**. The version of **read( )** that we will be using is

int read( ) throws IOException

Each time that **read( )** is called, it reads a character from the input stream and returns it as an integer value. It returns –1 when an attempt is made to read at the end of the stream. As you can see, it can throw an **IOException**.

The following program demonstrates **read( )** by reading characters from the console until the user types a "q." Notice that any I/O exceptions that might be generated are simply thrown out of **main( )**. Such an approach is common when reading from the console in simple sample programs such as those shown in this book, but in more sophisticated applications, you can handle the exceptions explicitly.

```
// Use a BufferedReader to read characters from the console.
import java.io.*;

class BRRead {
  public static void main(String[] args) throws IOException
  {
    char c;
    BufferedReader br = new BufferedReader(new
      InputStreamReader(System.in, System.console().charset()));

    System.out.println("Enter characters, 'q' to quit.");
    // read characters
```

```
    do {
      c = (char) br.read();
      System.out.println(c);
    } while(c != 'q');
  }
}
```

Here is a sample run:

```
Enter characters, 'q' to quit.
123abcq
1
2
3
a
b
c
q
```

This output may look a little different from what you expected because **System.in** is line buffered, by default. This means that no input is actually passed to the program until you press ENTER. As you can guess, this does not make **read( )** particularly valuable for interactive console input.

## Reading Strings

To read a string from the keyboard, use the version of **readLine( )** that is a member of the **BufferedReader** class. Its general form is shown here:

String readLine( ) throws IOException

As you can see, it returns a **String** object.

The following program demonstrates **BufferedReader** and the **readLine( )** method; the program reads and displays lines of text until you enter the word "stop":

```
// Read a string from console using a BufferedReader.
import java.io.*;

class BRReadLines {
  public static void main(String[] args) throws IOException
  {
    // create a BufferedReader using System.in
    BufferedReader br = new BufferedReader(new
      InputStreamReader(System.in, System.console().charset()));

    String str;
    System.out.println("Enter lines of text.");
    System.out.println("Enter 'stop' to quit.");
    do {
      str = br.readLine();
      System.out.println(str);
    } while(!str.equals("stop"));
  }
}
```

The next example creates a tiny text editor. It creates an array of **String** objects and then reads in lines of text, storing each line in the array. It will read up to 100 lines or until you enter "stop." It uses a **BufferedReader** to read from the console.

```
// A tiny editor.
import java.io.*;

class TinyEdit {
  public static void main(String[] args) throws IOException
  {
    // create a BufferedReader using System.in
    BufferedReader br = new BufferedReader(new
      InputStreamReader(System.in, System.console().charset()));

    String[] str = new String[100];
    System.out.println("Enter lines of text.");
    System.out.println("Enter 'stop' to quit.");
    for(int i=0; i<100; i++) {
      str[i] = br.readLine();
      if(str[i].equals("stop")) break;
    }
    System.out.println("\nHere is your file:");
    // display the lines
    for(int i=0; i<100; i++) {
      if(str[i].equals("stop")) break;
      System.out.println(str[i]);
    }
  }
}
```

Here is a sample run:

```
Enter lines of text.
Enter 'stop' to quit.
This is line one.
This is line two.
Java makes working with strings easy.
Just create String objects.
stop
Here is your file:
This is line one.
This is line two.
Java makes working with strings easy.
Just create String objects.
```

## Writing Console Output

Console output is most easily accomplished with **print( )** and **println( )**, described earlier, which are used in most of the examples in this book. These methods are defined by the class **PrintStream** (which is the type of object referenced by **System.out**). Even though **System.out** is a byte stream, using it for simple program output is still acceptable. However, a character-based alternative is described in the next section.

Because **PrintStream** is an output stream derived from **OutputStream**, it also implements the low-level method **write( )**. Thus, **write( )** can be used to write to the console. The simplest form of **write( )** defined by **PrintStream** is shown here:

void write(int *byteval*)

This method writes the byte specified by *byteval*. Although *byteval* is declared as an integer, only the low-order eight bits are written. Here is a short example that uses **write( )** to output the character "A" followed by a newline to the screen:

```
// Demonstrate System.out.write().
class WriteDemo {
  public static void main(String[] args) {
    int b;

    b = 'A';
    System.out.write(b);
    System.out.write('\n');
  }
}
```

You will not often use **write( )** to perform console output (although doing so might be useful in some situations) because **print( )** and **println( )** are substantially easier to use.

## The PrintWriter Class

Although using **System.out** to write to the console is acceptable, its use is probably best for debugging purposes or for sample programs, such as those found in this book. For real-world programs, the recommended method of writing to the console when using Java is through a **PrintWriter** stream. **PrintWriter** is one of the character-based classes. Using a character-based class for console output makes internationalizing your program easier.

**PrintWriter** defines several constructors. The one we will use is shown here:

PrintWriter(OutputStream *outputStream*, boolean *flushingOn*)

Here, *outputStream* is an object of type **OutputStream**, and *flushingOn* controls whether Java flushes the output stream every time a **println( )** method (among others) is called. If *flushingOn* is **true**, flushing automatically takes place. If **false**, flushing is not automatic.

**PrintWriter** supports the **print( )** and **println( )** methods. Thus, you can use these methods in the same way as you used them with **System.out**. If an argument is not a simple type, the **PrintWriter** methods call the object's **toString( )** method and then display the result.

To write to the console by using a **PrintWriter**, specify **System.out** for the output stream and automatic flushing. For example, this line of code creates a **PrintWriter** that is connected to console output:

```
PrintWriter pw = new PrintWriter(System.out, true);
```

The following application illustrates using a **PrintWriter** to handle console output:

```
// Demonstrate PrintWriter
import java.io.*;
```

```
public class PrintWriterDemo {
  public static void main(String[] args) {
    PrintWriter pw = new PrintWriter(System.out, true);

    pw.println("This is a string");
    int i = -7;
    pw.println(i);
    double d = 4.5e-7;
    pw.println(d);
  }
}
```

The output from this program is shown here:

```
This is a string
-7
4.5E-7
```

Remember, there is nothing wrong with using **System.out** to write simple text output to the console when you are learning Java or debugging your programs. However, using a **PrintWriter** makes your real-world applications easier to internationalize. Because no advantage is gained by using a **PrintWriter** in the sample programs shown in this book, we will continue to use **System.out** to write to the console.

## Reading and Writing Files

Java provides a number of classes and methods that allow you to read and write files. Before we begin, it is important to state that the topic of file I/O is quite large, and file I/O is examined in detail in Part II. The purpose of this section is to introduce the basic techniques that read from and write to a file. Although byte streams are used, these techniques can be adapted to the character-based streams.

Two of the most often-used stream classes are **FileInputStream** and **FileOutputStream**, which create byte streams linked to files. To open a file, you simply create an object of one of these classes, specifying the name of the file as an argument to the constructor. Although both classes support additional constructors, the following are the forms that we will be using:

FileInputStream(String *fileName*) throws FileNotFoundException
FileOutputStream(String *fileName*) throws FileNotFoundException

Here, *fileName* specifies the name of the file that you want to open. When you create an input stream, if the file does not exist, then **FileNotFoundException** is thrown. For output streams, if the file cannot be opened or created, then **FileNotFoundException** is thrown. **FileNotFoundException** is a subclass of **IOException**. When an output file is opened, any preexisting file by the same name is destroyed.

**NOTE** In situations in which a security manager is present, several of the file classes, including **FileInputStream** and **FileOutputStream**, will throw a **SecurityException** if a security violation occurs when attempting to open a file. By default, applications run via **java** do not use a security manager. For that reason, the I/O examples in this book do not need to watch for a possible **SecurityException**. However, other types of applications may use the security manager, and file I/O performed by such an application could generate a **SecurityException**. In that case, you will need to appropriately handle this exception. Be aware that JDK 17 deprecates the security manager for removal.

When you are done with a file, you must close it. This is done by calling the **close( )** method, which is implemented by both **FileInputStream** and **FileOutputStream**. It is shown here:

void close( ) throws IOException

Closing a file releases the system resources allocated to the file, allowing them to be used by another file. Failure to close a file can result in "memory leaks" because of unused resources remaining allocated.

---

**NOTE** The **close( )** method is specified by the **AutoCloseable** interface in **java.lang**. **AutoCloseable** is inherited by the **Closeable** interface in **java.io**. Both interfaces are implemented by the stream classes, including **FileInputStream** and **FileOutputStream**.

Before moving on, it is important to point out that there are two basic approaches that you can use to close a file when you are done with it. The first is the traditional approach, in which **close( )** is called explicitly when the file is no longer needed. This is the approach used by all versions of Java prior to JDK 7 and is, therefore, found in all pre-JDK 7 legacy code. The second is to use the **try**-with-resources statement added by JDK 7, which automatically closes a file when it is no longer needed. In this approach, no explicit call to **close( )** is executed. Since you may still encounter pre-JDK 7 legacy code, it is important that you know and understand the traditional approach. Furthermore, the traditional approach could still be the best approach in some situations. Therefore, we will begin with it. The automated approach is described in the following section.

To read from a file, you can use a version of **read( )** that is defined within **FileInputStream**. The one that we will use is shown here:

int read( ) throws IOException

Each time that it is called, it reads a single byte from the file and returns the byte as an integer value. **read( )** returns –1 when an attempt is made to read at the end of the stream. It can throw an **IOException**.

The following program uses **read( )** to input and display the contents of a file that contains ASCII text. The name of the file is specified as a command-line argument.

```
/* Display a text file.
   To use this program, specify the name
   of the file that you want to see.
   For example, to see a file called TEST.TXT,
   use the following command line.

   java ShowFile TEST.TXT
*/

import java.io.*;

class ShowFile {
  public static void main(String[] args)
  {
    int i;
    FileInputStream fin;
```

```
    // First, confirm that a filename has been specified.
    if(args.length != 1) {
      System.out.println("Usage: ShowFile filename");
      return;
    }

    // Attempt to open the file.
    try {
      fin = new FileInputStream(args[0]);
    } catch(FileNotFoundException e) {
      System.out.println("Cannot Open File");
      return;
    }

    // At this point, the file is open and can be read.
    // The following reads characters until EOF is encountered.
    try {
      do {
        i = fin.read();
        if(i != -1) System.out.print((char) i);
      } while(i != -1);
    } catch(IOException e) {
      System.out.println("Error Reading File");
   }

    // Close the file.
    try {
      fin.close();
    } catch(IOException e) {
        System.out.println("Error Closing File");
    }
  }
}
```

In the program, notice the **try/catch** blocks that handle the I/O errors that might occur. Each I/O operation is monitored for exceptions, and if an exception occurs, it is handled. Be aware that in simple programs or sample code, it is common to see I/O exceptions simply thrown out of **main( )**, as was done in the earlier console I/O examples. Also, in some real-world code, it can be helpful to let an exception propagate to a calling routine to let the caller know that an I/O operation failed. However, most of the file I/O examples in this book handle all I/O exceptions explicitly, as shown, for the sake of illustration.

Although the preceding example closes the file stream after the file is read, there is a variation that is often useful. The variation is to call **close( )** within a **finally** block. In this approach, all of the methods that access the file are contained within a **try** block, and the **finally** block is used to close the file. This way, no matter how the **try** block terminates, the file is closed. Assuming the preceding example, here is how the **try** block that reads the file can be recoded:

```
try {
  do {
    i = fin.read();
    if(i != -1) System.out.print((char) i);
  } while(i != -1);
```

```
} catch(IOException e) {
  System.out.println("Error Reading File");
} finally {
  // Close file on the way out of the try block.
  try {
    fin.close();
  } catch(IOException e) {
    System.out.println("Error Closing File");
  }
}
```

Although not an issue in this case, one advantage to this approach in general is that if the code that accesses a file terminates because of some non-I/O related exception, the file is still closed by the **finally** block.

Sometimes it's easier to wrap the portions of a program that open the file and access the file within a single **try** block (rather than separating the two) and then use a **finally** block to close the file. For example, here is another way to write the **ShowFile** program:

```
/* Display a text file.
   To use this program, specify the name
   of the file that you want to see.
   For example, to see a file called TEST.TXT,
   use the following command line.

   java ShowFile TEST.TXT

   This variation wraps the code that opens and
   accesses the file within a single try block.
   The file is closed by the finally block.
*/

import java.io.*;

class ShowFile {
  public static void main(String[] args)
  {
    int i;
    FileInputStream fin = null;

    // First, confirm that a filename has been specified.
    if(args.length != 1) {
      System.out.println("Usage: ShowFile filename");
      return;
    }

    // The following code opens a file, reads characters until EOF
    // is encountered, and then closes the file via a finally block.
    try {
      fin = new FileInputStream(args[0]);

      do {
        i = fin.read();
        if(i != -1) System.out.print((char) i);
      } while(i != -1);
```

```
      } catch(FileNotFoundException e) {
        System.out.println("File Not Found.");
      } catch(IOException e) {
        System.out.println("An I/O Error Occurred");
      } finally {
        // Close file in all cases.
        try {
          if(fin != null) fin.close();
        } catch(IOException e) {
          System.out.println("Error Closing File");
        }
      }
    }
  }
```

In this approach, notice that **fin** is initialized to **null**. Then, in the **finally** block, the file is closed only if **fin** is not **null**. This works because **fin** will be non-**null** only if the file is successfully opened. Thus, **close( )** is not called if an exception occurs while opening the file.

It is possible to make the **try/catch** sequence in the preceding example a bit more compact. Because **FileNotFoundException** is a subclass of **IOException**, it need not be caught separately. For example, here is the sequence recoded to eliminate catching **FileNotFoundException**. In this case, the standard exception message, which describes the error, is displayed.

```
try {
  fin = new FileInputStream(args[0]);

  do {
    i = fin.read();
    if(i != -1) System.out.print((char) i);
  } while(i != -1);

} catch(IOException e) {
  System.out.println("I/O Error: " + e);
} finally {
  // Close file in all cases.
  try {
    if(fin != null) fin.close();
  } catch(IOException e) {
    System.out.println("Error Closing File");
  }
}
```

In this approach, any error, including an error opening the file, is simply handled by the single **catch** statement. Because of its compactness, this approach is used by many of the I/O examples in this book. Be aware, however, that this approach is not appropriate in cases in which you want to deal separately with a failure to open a file, such as might be caused if a user mistypes a filename. In such a situation, you might want to prompt for the correct name, for example, before entering a **try** block that accesses the file.

To write to a file, you can use the **write( )** method defined by **FileOutputStream**. Its simplest form is shown here:

void write(int *byteval*) throws IOException

This method writes the byte specified by *byteval* to the file. Although *byteval* is declared as an integer, only the low-order eight bits are written to the file. If an error occurs during writing, an **IOException** is thrown. The next example uses **write( )** to copy a file:

```
/* Copy a file.
   To use this program, specify the name
   of the source file and the destination file.
   For example, to copy a file called FIRST.TXT
   to a file called SECOND.TXT, use the following
   command line.

   java CopyFile FIRST.TXT SECOND.TXT
*/

import java.io.*;

class CopyFile {
  public static void main(String[] args) throws IOException
  {
    int i;
    FileInputStream fin = null;
    FileOutputStream fout = null;

    // First, confirm that both files have been specified.
    if(args.length != 2) {
      System.out.println("Usage: CopyFile from to");
      return;
    }

    // Copy a File.
    try {
      // Attempt to open the files.
      fin = new FileInputStream(args[0]);
      fout = new FileOutputStream(args[1]);

      do {
        i = fin.read();
        if(i != -1) fout.write(i);
      } while(i != -1);

    } catch(IOException e) {
      System.out.println("I/O Error: " + e);
    } finally {
      try {
        if(fin != null) fin.close();
      } catch(IOException e2) {
        System.out.println("Error Closing Input File");
      }
```

```
        try {
          if(fout != null) fout.close();
        } catch(IOException e2) {
          System.out.println("Error Closing Output File");
        }
      }
    }
  }
```

In the program, notice that two separate **try** blocks are used when closing the files. This ensures that both files are closed, even if the call to **fin.close( )** throws an exception.

In general, notice that all potential I/O errors are handled in the preceding two programs by the use of exceptions. This differs from some computer languages that use error codes to report file errors. Not only do exceptions make file handling cleaner, but they also enable Java to easily differentiate the end-of-file condition from file errors when input is being performed.

# Automatically Closing a File

In the preceding section, the sample programs have made explicit calls to **close( )** to close a file once it is no longer needed. As mentioned, this is the way files were closed when using versions of Java prior to JDK 7. Although this approach is still valid and useful, JDK 7 added a feature that offers another way to manage resources, such as file streams, by automating the closing process. This feature, sometimes referred to as *automatic resource management*, or *ARM* for short, is based on an expanded version of the **try** statement. The principal advantage of automatic resource management is that it prevents situations in which a file (or other resource) is inadvertently not released after it is no longer needed. As explained, forgetting to close a file can result in memory leaks and could lead to other problems.

Automatic resource management is based on an expanded form of the **try** statement. Here is its general form:

try (*resource-specification*) {
  // use the resource
}

Typically, *resource-specification* is a statement that declares and initializes a resource, such as a file stream. It consists of a variable declaration in which the variable is initialized with a reference to the object being managed. When the **try** block ends, the resource is automatically released. In the case of a file, this means that the file is automatically closed. (Thus, there is no need to call **close( )** explicitly.) Of course, this form of **try** can also include **catch** and **finally** clauses. This form of **try** is called the ***try-with-resources*** statement.

**NOTE** Beginning with JDK 9, it is also possible for the resource specification of the **try** to consist of a variable that has been declared and initialized earlier in the program. However, that variable must be *effectively final*, which means that it has not been assigned a new value after being given its initial value.

The **try**-with-resources statement can be used only with those resources that implement the **AutoCloseable** interface defined by **java.lang**. This interface defines the **close( )** method. **AutoCloseable** is inherited by the **Closeable** interface in **java.io**. Both interfaces are implemented by the stream classes. Thus, **try**-with-resources can be used when working with streams, including file streams.

As a first example of automatically closing a file, here is a reworked version of the **ShowFile** program that uses it:

```
/* This version of the ShowFile program uses a try-with-resources
   statement to automatically close a file after it is no longer needed.
*/

import java.io.*;

class ShowFile {
  public static void main(String[] args)
  {
    int i;

    // First, confirm that a filename has been specified.
    if(args.length != 1) {
      System.out.println("Usage: ShowFile filename");
      return;
    }

    // The following code uses a try-with-resources statement to open
    // a file and then automatically close it when the try block is left.
    try(FileInputStream fin = new FileInputStream(args[0])) {

      do {
        i = fin.read();
        if(i != -1) System.out.print((char) i);
      } while(i != -1);

    } catch(FileNotFoundException e) {
      System.out.println("File Not Found.");
    } catch(IOException e) {
      System.out.println("An I/O Error Occurred");
    }

  }
}
```

In the program, pay special attention to how the file is opened within the **try** statement:

```
try(FileInputStream fin = new FileInputStream(args[0])) {
```

Notice how the resource specification portion of the **try** declares a **FileInputStream** called **fin**, which is then assigned a reference to the file opened by its constructor. Thus, in this version of the program, the variable **fin** is local to the **try** block, being created when the **try** is entered. When the **try** is left, the stream associated with **fin** is automatically closed by an implicit call to **close( )**. You don't need to call **close( )** explicitly, which means that you can't forget to close the file. This is a key advantage of using **try**-with-resources.

It is important to understand that a resource declared in the **try** statement is implicitly **final**. This means that you can't assign to the resource after it has been created. Also, the scope of the resource is limited to the **try**-with-resources statement.

Before moving on, it is useful to mention that beginning with JDK 10, you can use local variable type inference to specify the type of the resource declared in a **try**-with-resources statement. To do so, specify the type as **var**. When this is done, the type of the resource is inferred from its initializer. For example, the **try** statement in the preceding program can now be written like this:

```
try(var fin = new FileInputStream(args[0])) {
```

Here, **fin** is inferred to be of type **FileInputStream** because that is the type of its initializer. Because a number of readers will be working in Java environments that predate JDK 10, the **try**-with-resource statements in the remainder of this book will not make use of type inference so that the code works for as many readers as possible. Of course, going forward, you should consider using type inference in your own code.

You can manage more than one resource within a single **try** statement. To do so, simply separate each resource specification with a semicolon. The following program shows an example. It reworks the **CopyFile** program shown earlier so that it uses a single **try**-with-resources statement to manage both **fin** and **fout**.

```
/* A version of CopyFile that uses try-with-resources.
   It demonstrates two resources (in this case files) being
   managed by a single try statement.
*/

import java.io.*;

class CopyFile {
  public static void main(String[] args) throws IOException
  {
    int i;

    // First, confirm that both files have been specified.
    if(args.length != 2) {
      System.out.println("Usage: CopyFile from to");
      return;
    }

    // Open and manage two files via the try statement.
    try (FileInputStream fin = new FileInputStream(args[0]);
         FileOutputStream fout = new FileOutputStream(args[1]))
    {

      do {
        i = fin.read();
        if(i != -1) fout.write(i);
      } while(i != -1);

    } catch(IOException e) {
      System.out.println("I/O Error: " + e);
    }
  }
}
```

In this program, notice how the input and output files are opened within the **try** block:

```
try (FileInputStream fin = new FileInputStream(args[0]);
     FileOutputStream fout = new FileOutputStream(args[1]))
{
  // ...
```

After this **try** block ends, both **fin** and **fout** will have been closed. If you compare this version of the program to the previous version, you will see that it is much shorter. The ability to streamline source code is a side-benefit of automatic resource management.

There is one other aspect to **try**-with-resources that needs to be mentioned. In general, when a **try** block executes, it is possible that an exception inside the **try** block will lead to another exception that occurs when the resource is closed in a **finally** clause. In the case of a "normal" **try** statement, the original exception is lost, being preempted by the second exception. However, when using **try**-with-resources, the second exception is *suppressed*. It is not, however, lost. Instead, it is added to the list of suppressed exceptions associated with the first exception. The list of suppressed exceptions can be obtained by using the **getSuppressed( )** method defined by **Throwable**.

Because of the benefits that the **try**-with-resources statement offers, it will be used by many, but not all, of the sample programs in this edition of this book. Some of the examples will still use the traditional approach to closing a resource. There are several reasons for this. First, you may encounter legacy code that still relies on the traditional approach. It is important that all Java programmers be fully versed in, and comfortable with, the traditional approach when maintaining this older code. Second, it is possible that some programmers will continue to work in a pre-JDK 7 environment for a period of time. In such situations, the expanded form of **try** is not available. Finally, there may be cases in which explicitly closing a resource is more appropriate than the automated approach. For these reasons, some of the examples in this book will continue to use the traditional approach, explicitly calling **close( )**. In addition to illustrating the traditional technique, these examples can also be compiled and run by all readers in all environments.

**REMEMBER** A few examples in this book use the traditional approach to closing files as a means of illustrating this technique, which is widely used in legacy code. However, for new code, you will usually want to use the automated approach supported by the **try**-with-resources statement just described.

# The transient and volatile Modifiers

Java defines two interesting type modifiers: **transient** and **volatile**. These modifiers are used to handle somewhat specialized situations.

When an instance variable is declared as **transient**, its value need not persist when an object is stored. For example:

```
class T {
  transient int a; // will not persist
  int b; // will persist
}
```

Here, if an object of type **T** is written to a persistent storage area, the contents of **a** would not be saved, but the contents of **b** would.

The **volatile** modifier tells the compiler that the variable modified by **volatile** can be changed unexpectedly by other parts of your program. One of these situations involves multithreaded programs. In a multithreaded program, sometimes two or more threads share the same variable. For efficiency considerations, each thread can keep its own, private copy of such a shared variable. The real (or *master*) copy of the variable is updated at various times, such as when a **synchronized** method is entered. While this approach works fine, it may be inefficient at times. In some cases, all that really matters is that the master copy of a variable always reflects its current state. To ensure this, simply specify the variable as **volatile**, which tells the compiler that it must always use the master copy of a **volatile** variable (or, at least, always keep any private copies up to date with the master copy, and vice versa). Also, accesses to the shared variable must be executed in the precise order indicated by the program.

## Introducing instanceof

Sometimes, knowing the type of an object during run time is useful. For example, you might have one thread of execution that generates various types of objects, and another thread that processes these objects. In this situation, it might be useful for the processing thread to know the type of each object when it receives it. Another situation in which knowledge of an object's type at run time is important involves casting. In Java, an invalid cast causes a run-time error. Many invalid casts can be caught at compile time. However, casts involving class hierarchies can produce invalid casts that can be detected only at run time. For example, a superclass called A can produce two subclasses, called B and C. Thus, casting a B object into type A or casting a C object into type A is legal, but casting a B object into type C (or vice versa) isn't legal. Because an object of type A can refer to objects of either B or C, how can you know, at run time, what type of object is actually being referred to before attempting the cast to type C? It could be an object of type A, B, or C. If it is an object of type B, a run-time exception will be thrown. Java provides the run-time operator **instanceof** to answer this question.

Before we begin, it is necessary to state that **instanceof** was significantly enhanced by JDK 17 with a powerful new feature based on pattern matching. Here, the traditional form of **instanceof** is introduced. The enhanced form is covered in Chapter 17.

The traditional **instanceof** operator has this general form:

*objref* instanceof *type*

Here, *objref* is a reference to an instance of a class, and *type* is a class type. If *objref* is of the specified type or can be cast into the specified type, then the **instanceof** operator evaluates to **true**. Otherwise, its result is **false**. Thus, **instanceof** is the means by which your program can obtain run-time type information about an object.

The following program demonstrates **instanceof**:

```
// Demonstrate instanceof operator.
class A {
  int i, j;
}

class B {
  int i, j;
}

class C extends A {
```

```
  int k;
}

class D extends A {
  int k;
}

class InstanceOf {
  public static void main(String[] args) {
    A a = new A();
    B b = new B();
    C c = new C();
    D d = new D();
    if(a instanceof A)
      System.out.println("a is instance of A");
    if(b instanceof B)
      System.out.println("b is instance of B");
    if(c instanceof C)
      System.out.println("c is instance of C");
    if(c instanceof A)
      System.out.println("c can be cast to A");

    if(a instanceof C)
      System.out.println("a can be cast to C");

    System.out.println();

    // compare types of derived types
    A ob;

    ob = d; // A reference to d
    System.out.println("ob now refers to d");
    if(ob instanceof D)
      System.out.println("ob is instance of D");

    System.out.println();

    ob = c; // A reference to c
    System.out.println("ob now refers to c");

    if(ob instanceof D)
      System.out.println("ob can be cast to D");
    else
      System.out.println("ob cannot be cast to D");

    if(ob instanceof A)
      System.out.println("ob can be cast to A");

    System.out.println();

    // all objects can be cast to Object
    if(a instanceof Object)
      System.out.println("a may be cast to Object");
    if(b instanceof Object)
      System.out.println("b may be cast to Object");
    if(c instanceof Object)
      System.out.println("c may be cast to Object");
    if(d instanceof Object)
      System.out.println("d may be cast to Object");
  }
}
```

The output from this program is shown here:

```
a is instance of A
b is instance of B
c is instance of C
c can be cast to A

ob now refers to d
ob is instance of D

ob now refers to c
ob cannot be cast to D
ob can be cast to A

a may be cast to Object
b may be cast to Object
c may be cast to Object
d may be cast to Object
```

The **instanceof** operator isn't needed by most simple programs because, often, you know the type of object with which you are working. However, it can be very useful when you're writing generalized routines that operate on objects of a complex class hierarchy or that are created from code outside your direct control. As you will see, the pattern matching enhancements described in Chapter 17 streamline its use.

## strictfp

With the creation of Java 2 several years ago, the floating-point computation model was relaxed slightly. Specifically, the new model did not require the truncation of certain intermediate values that occur during a computation. This prevented overflow or underflow in some cases. By modifying a class, a method, or interface with **strictfp**, you could ensure that floating-point calculations (and thus all truncations) took place precisely as they did in earlier versions of Java. When a class was modified by **strictfp**, all the methods in the class were also modified by **strictfp** automatically. However, beginning with JDK 17, all floating-point computations are now strict, and **strictfp** is obsolete and no longer required. Its use will now generate a warning message.

For versions of Java prior to JDK 17, the following example illustrates **strictfp**. It tells Java to use the original floating-point model for calculations in all methods defined within **MyClass**:

```
strictfp class MyClass { //...
```

Frankly, most programmers never needed to use **strictfp** because it affected only a very small class of problems.

---

**REMEMBER** Beginning with JDK 17, **stricfp** has been rendered obsolete and its use will now generate a warning message.

## Native Methods

Although it is rare, occasionally you may want to call a subroutine that is written in a language other than Java. Typically, such a subroutine exists as executable code for the CPU and environment in which you are working—that is, native code. For example, you may want to call a native code subroutine to achieve faster execution time. Or, you may want to use a specialized, third-party library, such as a statistical package. However, because Java programs are compiled to bytecode, which is then interpreted (or compiled on the fly) by the Java run-time system, it would seem impossible to call a native code subroutine from within your Java program. Fortunately, this conclusion is false. Java provides the **native** keyword, which is used to declare native code methods. Once declared, these methods can be called from inside your Java program just as you call any other Java method.

To declare a native method, precede the method with the **native** modifier, but do not define any body for the method. For example:

```
public native int meth() ;
```

After you declare a native method, you must write the native method and follow a rather complex series of steps to link it with your Java code. Consult the Java documentation for current details.

---

**NOTE** JDK 21 introduces a more sophisticated API for using code libraries written in languages other than Java code. The new java.lang.foreign.* package contains an API that gives greater control over managing memory and calling functions in such libraries.

## Using assert

Another interesting keyword is **assert**. It is used during program development to create an *assertion*, which is a condition that should be true during the execution of the program. For example, you might have a method that should always return a positive integer value. You might test this by asserting that the return value is greater than zero using an **assert** statement. At run time, if the condition is true, no other action takes place. However, if the condition is false, then an **AssertionError** is thrown. Assertions are often used during testing to verify that some expected condition is actually met. They are not usually used for released code.

The **assert** keyword has two forms. The first is shown here:

assert *condition*;

Here, *condition* is an expression that must evaluate to a Boolean result. If the result is true, then the assertion is true and no other action takes place. If the condition is false, then the assertion fails and a default **AssertionError** object is thrown.

The second form of **assert** is shown here:

assert *condition: expr*;

In this version, *expr* is a value that is passed to the **AssertionError** constructor. This value is converted to its string format and displayed if an assertion fails. Typically, you will specify a string for *expr*, but any non-**void** expression is allowed as long as it defines a reasonable string conversion.

Here is an example that uses **assert**. It verifies that the return value of **getnum( )** is positive.

```
// Demonstrate assert.
class AssertDemo {
  static int val = 3;

  // Return an integer.
  static int getnum() {
    return val--;
  }

  public static void main(String[] args)
  {
    int n;

    for(int i=0; i < 10; i++) {
      n = getnum();

      assert n > 0; // will fail when n is 0

      System.out.println("n is " + n);
    }
  }
}
```

To enable assertion checking at run time, you must specify the **-ea** option. For example, to enable assertions for **AssertDemo**, execute it using this line:

```
java -ea AssertDemo
```

After compiling and running as just described, the program creates the following output:

```
n is 3
n is 2
n is 1
Exception in thread "main" java.lang.AssertionError
        at AssertDemo.main(AssertDemo.java:17)
```

In **main( )**, repeated calls are made to the method **getnum( )**, which returns an integer value. The return value of **getnum( )** is assigned to **n** and then tested using this **assert** statement:

```
assert n > 0; // will fail when n is 0
```

This statement will fail when **n** equals 0, which it will after the fourth call. When this happens, an exception is thrown.

As explained, you can specify the message displayed when an assertion fails. For example, if you substitute

```
assert n > 0 : "n is not positive!";
```

for the assertion in the preceding program, then the following output will be generated:

```
n is 3
n is 2
```

```
n is 1
Exception in thread "main" java.lang.AssertionError: n is not
positive!
        at AssertDemo.main(AssertDemo.java:17)
```

One important point to understand about assertions is that you must not rely on them to perform any action actually required by the program. The reason is that normally, released code will be run with assertions disabled. For example, consider this variation of the preceding program:

```
// A poor way to use assert!!!
class AssertDemo {
  // get a random number generator
  static int val = 3;

  // Return an integer.
  static int getnum() {
    return val--;
  }

  public static void main(String[] args)
  {
    int n = 0;

    for(int i=0; i < 10; i++) {

      assert (n = getnum()) > 0; // This is not a good idea!

      System.out.println("n is " + n);
    }
  }
}
```

In this version of the program, the call to **getnum( )** is moved inside the **assert** statement. Although this works fine if assertions are enabled, it will cause a malfunction when assertions are disabled because the call to **getnum( )** will never be executed! In fact, **n** must now be initialized because the compiler will recognize that it might not be assigned a value by the **assert** statement.

Assertions can be quite useful because they streamline the type of error checking that is common during development. For example, prior to **assert**, if you wanted to verify that **n** was positive in the preceding program, you had to use a sequence of code similar to this:

```
if(n < 0) {
   System.out.println("n is negative!");
   return; // or throw an exception
}
```

With **assert**, you need only one line of code. Furthermore, you don't have to remove the **assert** statements from your released code.

## Assertion Enabling and Disabling Options

When executing code, you can disable all assertions by using the **-da** option. You can enable or disable a specific package (and all of its subpackages) by specifying its name followed by three periods after the **-ea** or **-da** option. For example, to enable assertions in a package called **MyPack**, use

```
-ea:MyPack...
```

To disable assertions in **MyPack**, use

```
-da:MyPack...
```

You can also specify a class with the **-ea** or **-da** option. For example, this enables **AssertDemo** individually:

```
-ea:AssertDemo
```

# Static Import

Java includes a feature called *static import* that expands the capabilities of the **import** keyword. By following **import** with the keyword **static**, an **import** statement can be used to import the static members of a class or interface. When using static import, it is possible to refer to static members directly by their names, without having to qualify them with the name of their class. This simplifies and shortens the syntax required to use a static member.

To understand the usefulness of static import, let's begin with an example that does *not* use it. The following program computes the hypotenuse of a right triangle. It uses two static methods from Java's built-in math class **Math**, which is part of **java.lang**. The first is **Math.pow( )**, which returns a value raised to a specified power. The second is **Math.sqrt( )**, which returns the square root of its argument.

```
// Compute the hypotenuse of a right triangle.
class Hypot {
  public static void main(String[] args) {
    double side1, side2;
    double hypot;
    side1 = 3.0;
    side2 = 4.0;

    // Notice how sqrt() and pow() must be qualified by
    // their class name, which is Math.
    hypot = Math.sqrt(Math.pow(side1, 2) +
                      Math.pow(side2, 2));

    System.out.println("Given sides of lengths " +
                       side1 + " and " + side2 +
                       " the hypotenuse is " +
                       hypot);
  }
}
```

Because **pow( )** and **sqrt( )** are static methods, they must be called through the use of their class's name, **Math**. This results in a somewhat unwieldy hypotenuse calculation:

```
hypot = Math.sqrt(Math.pow(side1, 2) +
                  Math.pow(side2, 2));
```

As this simple example illustrates, having to specify the class name each time **pow( )** or **sqrt( )** (or any of Java's other math methods, such as **sin( )**, **cos( )**, and **tan( )**) is used can grow tedious.

You can eliminate the tedium of specifying the class name through the use of static import, as shown in the following version of the preceding program:

```
// Use static import to bring sqrt() and pow() into view.
import static java.lang.Math.sqrt;
import static java.lang.Math.pow;

// Compute the hypotenuse of a right triangle.
class Hypot {
  public static void main(String[] args) {
    double side1, side2;
    double hypot;

    side1 = 3.0;
    side2 = 4.0;

    // Here, sqrt() and pow() can be called by themselves,
    // without their class name.
    hypot = sqrt(pow(side1, 2) + pow(side2, 2));

    System.out.println("Given sides of lengths " +
                       side1 + " and " + side2 +
                       " the hypotenuse is " +
                       hypot);
  }
}
```

In this version, the names **sqrt** and **pow** are brought into view by these static import statements:

```
import static java.lang.Math.sqrt;
import static java.lang.Math.pow;
```

After these statements, it is no longer necessary to qualify **sqrt( )** or **pow( )** with their class name. Therefore, the hypotenuse calculation can more conveniently be specified, as shown here:

```
hypot = sqrt(pow(side1, 2) + pow(side2, 2));
```

As you can see, this form is considerably more readable.

There are two general forms of the **import static** statement. The first, which is used by the preceding example, brings into view a single name. Its general form is shown here:

import static *pkg.type-name.static-member-name*;

Here, *type-name* is the name of a class or interface that contains the desired static member. Its full package name is specified by *pkg*. The name of the member is specified by *static-member-name*.

The second form of static import imports all static members of a given class or interface. Its general form is shown here:

import static *pkg.type-name.**;

If you will be using many static methods or fields defined by a class, then this form lets you bring them into view without having to specify each individually. Therefore, the preceding program could have used this single **import** statement to bring both **pow( )** and **sqrt( )** (and *all other* static members of **Math** ) into view:

```
import static java.lang.Math.*;
```

Of course, static import is not limited just to the **Math** class or just to methods. For example, this brings the static field **System.out** into view:

```
import static java.lang.System.out;
```

After this statement, you can output to the console without having to qualify **out** with **System**, as shown here:

```
out.println("After importing System.out, you can use out directly.");
```

Whether importing **System.out** as just shown is a good idea is subject to debate. Although it does shorten the statement, it is no longer instantly clear to anyone reading the program that the **out** being referred to is **System.out**.

One other point: in addition to importing the static members of classes and interfaces defined by the Java API, you can also use static import to import the static members of classes and interfaces that you create.

As convenient as static import can be, it is important not to abuse it. Remember, the reason that Java organizes its libraries into packages is to avoid namespace collisions. When you import static members, you are bringing those members into the current namespace. Thus, you are increasing the potential for namespace conflicts and inadvertent name hiding. If you are using a static member once or twice in the program, it's best not to import it. Also, some static names, such as **System.out**, are so recognizable that you might not want to import them. Static import is designed for those situations in which you are using a static member repeatedly, such as when performing a series of mathematical computations. In essence, you should use, but not abuse, this feature.

## Invoking Overloaded Constructors Through this( )

When working with overloaded constructors, it is sometimes useful for one constructor to invoke another. In Java, this is accomplished by using another form of the **this** keyword. The general form is shown here:

this(*arg-list*)

When **this( )** is executed, the overloaded constructor that matches the parameter list specified by *arg-list* is executed first. Then, if there are any statements inside the original constructor, they are executed. The call to **this( )** must be the first statement within the constructor.

To understand how **this( )** can be used, let's work through a short example. First, consider the following class that *does not* use **this( )**:

```
class MyClass {
  int a;
  int b;

  // initialize a and b individually
  MyClass(int i, int j) {
    a = i;
    b = j;
  }

  // initialize a and b to the same value
  MyClass(int i) {
    a = i;
    b = i;
  }

  // give a and b default values of 0
  MyClass( ) {
    a = 0;
    b = 0;
  }
}
```

This class contains three constructors, each of which initializes the values of **a** and **b**. The first is passed individual values for **a** and **b**. The second is passed just one value, which is assigned to both **a** and **b**. The third gives **a** and **b** default values of zero.

By using **this( )**, it is possible to rewrite **MyClass** as shown here:

```
class MyClass {
  int a;
  int b;

  // initialize a and b individually
  MyClass(int i, int j) {
    a = i;
    b = j;
  }
```

```
  // initialize a and b to the same value
  MyClass(int i) {
    this(i, i); // invokes MyClass(i, i)
  }

  // give a and b default values of 0
  MyClass( ) {
    this(0); // invokes MyClass(0)
  }
}
```

In this version of **MyClass**, the only constructor that actually assigns values to the **a** and **b** fields is **MyClass(int, int)**. The other two constructors simply invoke that constructor (either directly or indirectly) through **this( )**. For example, consider what happens when this statement executes:

```
MyClass mc = new MyClass(8);
```

The call to **MyClass(8)** causes **this(8, 8)** to be executed, which translates into a call to **MyClass(8, 8)**, because this is the version of the **MyClass** constructor whose parameter list matches the arguments passed via **this( )**. Now, consider the following statement, which uses the default constructor:

```
MyClass mc2 = new MyClass();
```

In this case, **this(0)** is called. This causes **MyClass(0)** to be invoked because it is the constructor with the matching parameter list. Of course, **MyClass(0)** then calls **MyClass(0,0)** as just described.

One reason why invoking overloaded constructors through **this( )** can be useful is that it can prevent the unnecessary duplication of code. In many cases, reducing duplicate code decreases the time it takes to load your class because often the object code is smaller. This is especially important for programs delivered via the Internet in which load times are an issue. Using **this( )** can also help structure your code when constructors contain a large amount of duplicate code.

However, you need to be careful. Constructors that call **this( )** will execute a bit slower than those that contain all of their initialization code inline. This is because the call and return mechanism used when the second constructor is invoked adds overhead. If your class will be used to create only a handful of objects, or if the constructors in the class that call **this( )** will be seldom used, then this decrease in run-time performance is probably insignificant. However, if your class will be used to create a large number of objects (on the order of thousands) during program execution, then the negative impact of the increased overhead could be meaningful. Because object creation affects all users of your class, there will be cases in which you must carefully weigh the benefits of faster load time against the increased time it takes to create an object.

Here is another consideration: for very short constructors, such as those used by **MyClass**, there is often little difference in the size of the object code whether **this( )** is used or not. (Actually, there are cases in which no reduction in the size of the object code is achieved.)

This is because the bytecode that sets up and returns from the call to **this( )** adds instructions to the object file. Therefore, in these types of situations, even though duplicate code is eliminated, using **this( )** will not obtain significant savings in terms of load time. However, the added cost in terms of overhead to each object's construction will still be incurred. Therefore, **this( )** is most applicable to constructors that contain large amounts of initialization code, not those that simply set the value of a handful of fields.

There are two restrictions you need to keep in mind when using **this( )**. First, you cannot use any instance variable of the constructor's class in a call to **this( )**. Second, you cannot use **super( )** and **this( )** in the same constructor because each must be the first statement in the constructor.

## A Word About Value-Based Classes

Beginning with JDK 8, Java has included the concept of a *value-based* class, and a number of classes in the Java API have been classified as value-based. Value-based classes are defined by various rules and restrictions. Here are some examples. They must be final, and their instance variables must also be final. If **equals( )** determines that two instances of a value-based class are equal, one instance can be used in place of the other. Also, two equal but separately obtained instances of a value-based class may, in fact, be the same object. Very importantly, you should avoid using instances of a value-based class for synchronization. Additional rules and restrictions apply. Furthermore, the definition of value-based classes has evolved somewhat over time. Consult the Java documentation for the latest details on value-based classes, including which classes in the API library are documented as value-based.

# CHAPTER 14 Generics

Since the original 1.0 release in 1995, many new features have been added to Java. One that has had a profound and long-lasting impact is *generics*. Introduced by JDK 5, generics changed Java in two important ways. First, they added a new syntactical element to the language. Second, they caused changes to many of the classes and methods in the core API. Today, generics are an integral part of Java programming, and a solid understanding of this important feature is required. It is examined here in detail.

Through the use of generics, it is possible to create classes, interfaces, and methods that will work in a type-safe manner with various kinds of data. Many algorithms are logically the same no matter what type of data they are being applied to. For example, the mechanism that supports a stack is the same whether that stack is storing items of type **Integer**, **String**, **Object**, or **Thread**. With generics, you can define an algorithm once, independently of any specific type of data, and then apply that algorithm to a wide variety of data types without any additional effort. The expressive power generics added to the language fundamentally changed the way that Java code is written.

Perhaps the one feature of Java that was most significantly affected by generics is the *Collections Framework*. The Collections Framework is part of the Java API and is described in detail in Chapter 20, but a brief mention is useful now. A *collection* is a group of objects. The Collections Framework defines several classes, such as lists and maps, that manage collections. The collection classes had always been able to work with any type of object. The benefit that generics added is the ability to use the collection classes with complete type safety. Thus, in addition to being a powerful language element on its own, generics also enabled an existing feature to be substantially improved. This is another reason why generics were such an important addition to Java.

This chapter describes the syntax, theory, and use of generics. It also shows how generics provide type safety for some previously difficult cases. Once you have completed this chapter, you will want to examine Chapter 20, which covers the Collections Framework. There you will find many examples of generics at work.

# What Are Generics?

At its core, the term *generics* means *parameterized types*. Parameterized types are important because they enable you to create classes, interfaces, and methods in which the type of data upon which they operate is specified as a parameter. Using generics, it is possible to create a single class, for example, that automatically works with different types of data. A class, interface, or method that operates on a parameterized type is called *generic*, as in *generic class* or *generic method*.

It is important to understand that Java has always given you the ability to create generalized classes, interfaces, and methods by operating through references of type **Object**. Because **Object** is the superclass of all other classes, an **Object** reference can refer to any type object. Thus, in pre-generics code, generalized classes, interfaces, and methods used **Object** references to operate on various types of objects. The problem was that they could not do so with type safety.

Generics added the type safety that was lacking. They also streamlined the process, because it is no longer necessary to explicitly employ casts to translate between **Object** and the type of data that is actually being operated upon. With generics, all casts are automatic and implicit. Thus, generics expanded your ability to reuse code and let you do so safely and easily.

---

**CAUTION** *A Warning to C++ Programmers:* Although generics are similar to templates in C++, they are not the same. There are some fundamental differences between the two approaches to generic types. If you have a background in C++, it is important not to jump to conclusions about how generics work in Java.

# A Simple Generics Example

Let's begin with a simple example of a generic class. The following program defines two classes. The first is the generic class **Gen**, and the second is **GenDemo**, which uses **Gen**.

```
// A simple generic class.
// Here, T is a type parameter that
// will be replaced by a real type
// when an object of type Gen is created.
class Gen<T> {
  T ob; // declare an object of type T

  // Pass the constructor a reference to
  // an object of type T.
  Gen(T o) {
    ob = o;
  }

  // Return ob.
  T getOb() {
    return ob;
  }

  // Show type of T.
```

```
  void showType() {
    System.out.println("Type of T is " +
                       ob.getClass().getName());
  }
}

// Demonstrate the generic class.
class GenDemo {
  public static void main(String[] args) {
    // Create a Gen reference for Integers.
    Gen<Integer> iOb;

    // Create a Gen<Integer> object and assign its
    // reference to iOb. Notice the use of autoboxing
    // to encapsulate the value 88 within an Integer object.
    iOb = new Gen<Integer>(88);

    // Show the type of data used by iOb.
    iOb.showType();

    // Get the value in iOb. Notice that
    // no cast is needed.
    int v = iOb.getOb();
    System.out.println("value: " + v);

    System.out.println();

    // Create a Gen object for Strings.
    Gen<String> strOb = new Gen<String> ("Generics Test");

    // Show the type of data used by strOb.
    strOb.showType();

    // Get the value of strOb. Again, notice
    // that no cast is needed.
    String str = strOb.getOb();
    System.out.println("value: " + str);
  }
}
```

The output produced by the program is shown here:

```
Type of T is java.lang.Integer
value: 88

Type of T is java.lang.String
value: Generics Test
```

Let's examine this program carefully.

First, notice how **Gen** is declared by the following line:

```
class Gen<T> {
```

Here, **T** is the name of a *type parameter*. This name is used as a placeholder for the actual type that will be passed to **Gen** when an object is created. Thus, **T** is used within **Gen** whenever the type parameter is needed. Notice that **T** is contained within < >. This syntax can be generalized. Whenever a type parameter is being declared, it is specified within angle brackets. Because **Gen** uses a type parameter, **Gen** is a generic class, which is also called a *parameterized type*.

In the declaration of **Gen**, there is no special significance to the name **T**. Any valid identifier could have been used, but **T** is traditional. Furthermore, it is recommended that type parameter names be single-character capital letters. Other commonly used type parameter names are **V** and **E**. One other point about type parameter names: Beginning with JDK 10, you cannot use **var** as the name of a type parameter.

Next, **T** is used to declare an object called **ob**, as shown here:

```
T ob; // declare an object of type T
```

As explained, **T** is a placeholder for the actual type that will be specified when a **Gen** object is created. Thus, **ob** will be an object of the type passed to **T**. For example, if type **String** is passed to **T**, then in that instance, **ob** will be of type **String**.

Now consider **Gen**'s constructor:

```
Gen(T o) {
  ob = o;
}
```

Notice that its parameter, **o**, is of type **T**. This means that the actual type of **o** is determined by the type passed to **T** when a **Gen** object is created. Also, because both the parameter **o** and the member variable **ob** are of type **T**, they will both be of the same actual type when a **Gen** object is created.

The type parameter **T** can also be used to specify the return type of a method, as is the case with the **getOb( )** method, shown here:

```
T getOb() {
  return ob;
}
```

Because **ob** is also of type **T**, its type is compatible with the return type specified by **getOb( )**.

The **showType( )** method displays the type of **T** by calling **getName( )** on the **Class** object returned by the call to **getClass( )** on **ob**. The **getClass( )** method is defined by **Object** and is thus a member of all class types. It returns a **Class** object that corresponds to the type of the class of the object on which it is called. **Class** defines the **getName( )** method, which returns a string representation of the class name.

The **GenDemo** class demonstrates the generic **Gen** class. It first creates a version of **Gen** for integers, as shown here:

```
Gen<Integer> iOb;
```

Look closely at this declaration. First, notice that the type **Integer** is specified within the angle brackets after **Gen**. In this case, **Integer** is a *type argument* that is passed to **Gen**'s type parameter, **T**. This effectively creates a version of **Gen** in which all references to **T** are translated into references to **Integer**. Thus, for this declaration, **ob** is of type **Integer**, and the return type of **getOb( )** is of type **Integer**.

Before moving on, it's necessary to state that the Java compiler does not actually create different versions of **Gen**, or of any other generic class. Although it's helpful to think in these terms, it is not what actually happens. Instead, the compiler removes all generic type information, substituting the necessary casts, to make your code *behave as if* a specific version of **Gen** were created. Thus, there is really only one version of **Gen** that actually exists in your program. The process of removing generic type information is called *erasure*, and we will return to this topic later in this chapter.

The next line assigns to **iOb** a reference to an instance of an **Integer** version of the **Gen** class:

```
iOb = new Gen<Integer>(88);
```

Notice that when the **Gen** constructor is called, the type argument **Integer** is also specified. This is because the type of the object (in this case **iOb**) to which the reference is being assigned is of type **Gen<Integer>**. Thus, the reference returned by **new** must also be of type **Gen<Integer>**. If it isn't, a compile-time error will result. For example, the following assignment will cause a compile-time error:

```
iOb = new Gen<Double>(88.0); // Error!
```

Because **iOb** is of type **Gen<Integer>**, it can't be used to refer to an object of **Gen<Double>**. This type checking is one of the main benefits of generics because it ensures type safety.

---

**NOTE** As you will see later in this chapter, it is possible to shorten the syntax used to create an instance of a generic class. In the interest of clarity, we will use the full syntax at this time.

As the comments in the program state, the assignment

```
iOb = new Gen<Integer>(88);
```

makes use of autoboxing to encapsulate the value 88, which is an **int**, into an **Integer**. This works because **Gen<Integer>** creates a constructor that takes an **Integer** argument. Because an **Integer** is expected, Java will automatically box 88 inside one. Of course, the assignment could also have been written explicitly, like this:

```
iOb = new Gen<Integer>(Integer.valueOf(88));
```

However, there would be no benefit to using this version.

The program then displays the type of **ob** within **iOb**, which is **Integer**. Next, the program obtains the value of **ob** by use of the following line:

```
int v = iOb.getOb();
```

Because the return type of **getOb( )** is **T**, which was replaced by **Integer** when **iOb** was declared, the return type of **getOb( )** is also **Integer**, which unboxes into **int** when assigned to **v** (which is an **int**). Thus, there is no need to cast the return type of **getOb( )** to **Integer**.

Of course, it's not necessary to use the auto-unboxing feature. The preceding line could have been written like this, too:

```
int v = iOb.getOb().intValue();
```

However, the auto-unboxing feature makes the code more compact.

Next, **GenDemo** declares an object of type **Gen<String>**:

```
Gen<String> strOb = new Gen<String>("Generics Test");
```

Because the type argument is **String**, **String** is substituted for **T** inside **Gen**. This creates (conceptually) a **String** version of **Gen**, as the remaining lines in the program demonstrate.

## Generics Work Only with Reference Types

When declaring an instance of a generic type, the type argument passed to the type parameter must be a reference type. You cannot use a primitive type, such as **int** or **char**. For example, with **Gen**, it is possible to pass any class type to **T**, but you cannot pass a primitive type to a type parameter. Therefore, the following declaration is illegal:

```
Gen<int> intOb = new Gen<int>(53); // Error, can't use primitive type
```

Of course, not being able to specify a primitive type is not a serious restriction because you can use the type wrappers (as the preceding example did) to encapsulate a primitive type. Further, Java's autoboxing and auto-unboxing mechanism makes the use of the type wrapper transparent.

## Generic Types Differ Based on Their Type Arguments

A key point to understand about generic types is that a reference of one specific version of a generic type is not type compatible with another version of the same generic type. For example, assuming the program just shown, the following line of code is in error and will not compile:

```
iOb = strOb; // Wrong!
```

Even though both **iOb** and **strOb** are of type **Gen<T>**, they are references to different types because their type arguments differ. This is part of the way that generics add type safety and prevent errors.

## How Generics Improve Type Safety

At this point, you might be asking yourself the following question: Given that the same functionality found in the generic **Gen** class can be achieved without generics, by simply specifying **Object** as the data type and employing the proper casts, what is the benefit of making **Gen** generic? The answer is that generics automatically ensure the type safety of all operations involving **Gen**. In the process, they eliminate the need for you to enter casts and to type-check code by hand.

To understand the benefits of generics, first consider the following program that creates a non-generic equivalent of **Gen**:

```
// NonGen is functionally equivalent to Gen
// but does not use generics.
class NonGen {
  Object ob; // ob is now of type Object

  // Pass the constructor a reference to
  // an object of type Object
  NonGen(Object o) {
    ob = o;
  }

  // Return type Object.
  Object getOb() {
    return ob;
  }

  // Show type of ob.
  void showType() {
    System.out.println("Type of ob is " +
                       ob.getClass().getName());
  }
}

// Demonstrate the non-generic class.
class NonGenDemo {
  public static void main(String[] args) {
    NonGen iOb;

    // Create NonGen Object and store
    // an Integer in it. Autoboxing still occurs.
    iOb = new NonGen(88);

    // Show the type of data used by iOb.
    iOb.showType();

    // Get the value of iOb.
    // This time, a cast is necessary.
    int v = (Integer) iOb.getOb();
    System.out.println("value: " + v);

    System.out.println();

    // Create another NonGen object and
    // store a String in it.
    NonGen strOb = new NonGen("Non-Generics Test");

    // Show the type of data used by strOb
    strOb.showType();

    // Get the value of strOb.
    // Again, notice that a cast is necessary.
```

```
        String str = (String) strOb.getOb();
        System.out.println("value: " + str);

        // This compiles, but is conceptually wrong!
        iOb = strOb;
        v = (Integer) iOb.getOb(); // run-time error!
    }
}
```

There are several things of interest in this version. First, notice that **NonGen** replaces all uses of **T** with **Object**. This makes **NonGen** able to store any type of object, as can the generic version. However, it also prevents the Java compiler from having any real knowledge about the type of data actually stored in **NonGen**, which is bad for two reasons. First, explicit casts must be employed to retrieve the stored data. Second, many kinds of type mismatch errors cannot be found until run time. Let's look closely at each problem.

Notice this line:

```
int v = (Integer) iOb.getOb();
```

Because the return type of **getOb( )** is **Object**, the cast to **Integer** is necessary to enable that value to be auto-unboxed and stored in **v**. If you remove the cast, the program will not compile. With the generic version, this cast was implicit. In the non-generic version, the cast must be explicit. This is not only an inconvenience, but also a potential source of error.

Now, consider the following sequence from near the end of the program:

```
// This compiles, but is conceptually wrong!
iOb = strOb;
v = (Integer) iOb.getOb(); // run-time error!
```

Here, **strOb** is assigned to **iOb**. However, **strOb** refers to an object that contains a string, not an integer. This assignment is syntactically valid because all **NonGen** references are the same, and any **NonGen** reference can refer to any other **NonGen** object. However, the statement is semantically wrong, as the next line shows. Here, the return type of **getOb( )** is cast to **Integer**, and then an attempt is made to assign this value to **v**. The trouble is that **iOb** now refers to an object that stores a **String**, not an **Integer**. Unfortunately, without the use of generics, the Java compiler has no way to know this. Instead, a run-time exception occurs when the cast to **Integer** is attempted. As you know, it is extremely bad to have run-time exceptions occur in your code!

The preceding sequence can't occur when generics are used. If this sequence were attempted in the generic version of the program, the compiler would catch it and report an error, thus preventing a serious bug that results in a run-time exception. The ability to create type-safe code in which type-mismatch errors are caught at compile time is a key advantage of generics. Although using **Object** references to create "generic" code has always been possible, that code was not type safe, and its misuse could result in run-time exceptions. Generics prevent this from occurring. In essence, through generics, run-time errors are converted into compile-time errors. This is a major advantage.

# A Generic Class with Two Type Parameters

You can declare more than one type parameter in a generic type. To specify two or more type parameters, simply use a comma-separated list. For example, the following **TwoGen** class is a variation of the **Gen** class that has two type parameters:

```
// A simple generic class with two type
// parameters: T and V.
class TwoGen<T, V> {
  T ob1;
  V ob2;

  // Pass the constructor a reference to
  // an object of type T and an object of type V.
  TwoGen(T o1, V o2) {
    ob1 = o1;
    ob2 = o2;
  }

  // Show types of T and V.
  void showTypes() {
    System.out.println("Type of T is " +
                       ob1.getClass().getName());

    System.out.println("Type of V is " +
                       ob2.getClass().getName());
  }

  T getOb1() {
    return ob1;
  }

  V getOb2() {
    return ob2;
  }
}

// Demonstrate TwoGen.
class SimpGen {
  public static void main(String[] args) {

    TwoGen<Integer, String> tgObj =
      new TwoGen<Integer, String>(88, "Generics");

    // Show the types.
    tgObj.showTypes();

    // Obtain and show values.
    int v = tgObj.getOb1();
    System.out.println("value: " + v);

    String str = tgObj.getOb2();
    System.out.println("value: " + str);
  }
}
```

The output from this program is shown here:

```
Type of T is java.lang.Integer
Type of V is java.lang.String
value: 88
value: Generics
```

Notice how **TwoGen** is declared:

```
class TwoGen<T, V> {
```

It specifies two type parameters: **T** and **V**, separated by a comma. Because it has two type parameters, two type arguments must be passed to **TwoGen** when an object is created, as shown next:

```
TwoGen<Integer, String> tgObj =
  new TwoGen<Integer, String>(88, "Generics");
```

In this case, **Integer** is substituted for **T**, and **String** is substituted for **V**.

Although the two type arguments differ in this example, it is possible for both types to be the same. For example, the following line of code is valid:

```
TwoGen<String, String> x = new TwoGen<String, String> ("A", "B");
```

In this case, both **T** and **V** would be of type **String**. Of course, if the type arguments were always the same, then two type parameters would be unnecessary.

## The General Form of a Generic Class

The generics syntax shown in the preceding examples can be generalized. Here is the syntax for declaring a generic class:

class *class-name<type-param-list>* { // ...

Here is the full syntax for declaring a reference to a generic class and instance creation:

*class-name<type-arg-list> var-name* =
new *class-name<type-arg-list>(cons-arg-list)*;

## Bounded Types

In the preceding examples, the type parameters could be replaced by any class type. This is fine for many purposes, but sometimes it is useful to limit the types that can be passed to a type parameter. For example, assume that you want to create a generic class that contains a method that returns the average of an array of numbers. Furthermore, you want to use the class to obtain the average of an array of any type of number, including integers, **float**s, and **double**s. Thus, you want to specify the type of the numbers generically, using a type parameter. To create such a class, you might try something like this:

```
// Stats attempts (unsuccessfully) to
// create a generic class that can compute
```

```
// the average of an array of numbers of
// any given type.
//
// The class contains an error!
class Stats<T> {
  T[] nums; // nums is an array of type T

  // Pass the constructor a reference to
  // an array of type T.
  Stats(T[] o) {
    nums = o;
  }

  // Return type double in all cases.
  double average() {
    double sum = 0.0;
    for(int i=0; i < nums.length; i++)
      sum += nums[i].doubleValue(); // Error!!!

    return sum / nums.length;
  }
}
```

In **Stats**, the **average( )** method attempts to obtain the **double** version of each number in the **nums** array by calling **doubleValue( )**. Because all numeric classes, such as **Integer** and **Double**, are subclasses of **Number**, and **Number** defines the **doubleValue( )** method, this method is available to all numeric wrapper classes. The trouble is that the compiler has no way to know that you are intending to create **Stats** objects using only numeric types. Thus, when you try to compile **Stats**, an error is reported that indicates that the **doubleValue( )** method is unknown. To solve this problem, you need some way to tell the compiler that you intend to pass only numeric types to **T**. Furthermore, you need some way to *ensure* that *only* numeric types are actually passed.

To handle such situations, Java provides *bounded types*. When specifying a type parameter, you can create an upper bound that declares the superclass from which all type arguments must be derived. This is accomplished through the use of an **extends** clause when specifying the type parameter, as shown here:

<*T* extends *superclass*>

This specifies that *T* can only be replaced by *superclass*, or subclasses of *superclass*. Thus, *superclass* defines an inclusive, upper limit.

You can use an upper bound to fix the **Stats** class shown earlier by specifying **Number** as an upper bound, as shown here:

```
// In this version of Stats, the type argument for
// T must be either Number, or a class derived
// from Number.
class Stats<T extends Number> {
  T[] nums; // array of Number or subclass
```

```
  // Pass the constructor a reference to
  // an array of type Number or subclass.
  Stats(T[] o) {
    nums = o;
  }

  // Return type double in all cases.
  double average() {
    double sum = 0.0;

    for(int i=0; i < nums.length; i++)
      sum += nums[i].doubleValue();

    return sum / nums.length;
  }
}

// Demonstrate Stats.
class BoundsDemo {
  public static void main(String[] args) {

    Integer[] inums = { 1, 2, 3, 4, 5 };
    Stats<Integer> iob = new Stats<Integer>(inums);
    double v = iob.average();
    System.out.println("iob average is " + v);

    Double[] dnums = { 1.1, 2.2, 3.3, 4.4, 5.5 };
    Stats<Double> dob = new Stats<Double>(dnums);
    double w = dob.average();
    System.out.println("dob average is " + w);

    // This won't compile because String is not a
    // subclass of Number.
//    String[] strs = { "1", "2", "3", "4", "5" };
//    Stats<String> strob = new Stats<String>(strs);

//    double x = strob.average();
//    System.out.println("strob average is " + v);

  }
}
```

The output is shown here:

```
Average is 3.0
Average is 3.3
```

Notice how **Stats** is now declared by this line:

```
class Stats<T extends Number> {
```

Because the type **T** is now bounded by **Number**, the Java compiler knows that all objects of type **T** can call **doubleValue( )** because it is a method declared by **Number**. This is, by itself, a major advantage. However, as an added bonus, the bounding of **T** also prevents nonnumeric **Stats** objects from being created. For example, if you try removing the comments from the lines at the end of the program, and then try recompiling, you will receive compile-time errors because **String** is not a subclass of **Number**.

In addition to using a class type as a bound, you can also use an interface type. In fact, you can specify multiple interfaces as bounds. Furthermore, a bound can include both a class type and one or more interfaces. In this case, the class type must be specified first. When a bound includes an interface type, only type arguments that implement that interface are legal. When specifying a bound that has a class and an interface, or multiple interfaces, use the **&** operator to connect them. This creates an *intersection type*. For example:

```
class Gen<T extends MyClass & MyInterface> { // ...
```

Here, **T** is bounded by a class called **MyClass** and an interface called **MyInterface**. Thus, any type argument passed to **T** must be a subclass of **MyClass** and implement **MyInterface**. As a point of interest, you can also use a type intersection in a cast.

## Using Wildcard Arguments

As useful as type safety is, sometimes it can get in the way of perfectly acceptable constructs. For example, given the **Stats** class shown at the end of the preceding section, assume that you want to add a method called **isSameAvg( )** that determines if two **Stats** objects contain arrays that yield the same average, no matter what type of numeric data each object holds. For example, if one object contains the **double** values 1.0, 2.0, and 3.0, and the other object contains the integer values 2, 1, and 3, then the averages will be the same. One way to implement **isSameAvg( )** is to pass it a **Stats** argument, and then compare the average of that argument against the invoking object, returning true only if the averages are the same. For example, you want to be able to call **isSameAvg( )**, as shown here:

```
Integer[] inums = { 1, 2, 3, 4, 5 };
Double[] dnums = { 1.1, 2.2, 3.3, 4.4, 5.5 };

Stats<Integer> iob = new Stats<Integer>(inums);
Stats<Double> dob = new Stats<Double>(dnums);

if(iob.isSameAvg(dob))
  System.out.println("Averages are the same.");
else
  System.out.println("Averages differ.");
```

At first, creating **isSameAvg( )** seems like an easy problem. Because **Stats** is generic and its **average( )** method can work on any type of **Stats** object, it seems that creating **isSameAvg( )** would be straightforward. Unfortunately, trouble starts as soon as you try to declare a parameter of type **Stats**. Because **Stats** is a parameterized type, what do you specify for **Stats'** type parameter when you declare a parameter of that type?

At first, you might think of a solution like this, in which **T** is used as the type parameter:

```
// This won't work!
// Determine if two averages are the same.
boolean isSameAvg(Stats<T> ob) {
  if(average() == ob.average())
    return true;

  return false;
}
```

The trouble with this attempt is that it will work only with other **Stats** objects whose type is the same as the invoking object. For example, if the invoking object is of type **Stats<Integer>**, then the parameter **ob** must also be of type **Stats<Integer>**. It can't be used to compare the average of an object of type **Stats<Double>** with the average of an object of type **Stats<Short>**, for example. Therefore, this approach won't work except in a very narrow context and does not yield a general (that is, generic) solution.

To create a generic **isSameAvg( )** method, you must use another feature of Java generics: the *wildcard* argument. The wildcard argument is specified by the **?**, and it represents an unknown type. Using a wildcard, here is one way to write the **isSameAvg( )** method:

```
// Determine if two averages are the same.
// Notice the use of the wildcard.
boolean isSameAvg(Stats<?> ob) {
  if(average() == ob.average())
    return true;

  return false;
}
```

Here, **Stats<?>** matches any **Stats** object, allowing any two **Stats** objects to have their averages compared. The following program demonstrates this:

```
// Use a wildcard.
class Stats<T extends Number> {
  T[] nums; // array of Number or subclass

  // Pass the constructor a reference to
  // an array of type Number or subclass.
  Stats(T[] o) {
    nums = o;
  }

  // Return type double in all cases.
  double average() {
    double sum = 0.0;

    for(int i=0; i < nums.length; i++)
      sum += nums[i].doubleValue();
```

```
    return sum / nums.length;
  }

  // Determine if two averages are the same.
  // Notice the use of the wildcard.
  boolean isSameAvg(Stats<?> ob) {
    if(average() == ob.average())
      return true;

    return false;
  }
}

// Demonstrate wildcard.
class WildcardDemo {
  public static void main(String[] args) {
    Integer[] inums = { 1, 2, 3, 4, 5 };
    Stats<Integer> iob = new Stats<Integer>(inums);
    double v = iob.average();
    System.out.println("iob average is " + v);

    Double[] dums = { 1.1, 2.2, 3.3, 4.4, 5.5 };
    Stats<Double> dob = new Stats<Double>(dnums);
    double w = dob.average();
    System.out.println("dob average is " + w);

    Float[] fnums = { 1.0F, 2.0F, 3.0F, 4.0F, 5.0F };
    Stats<Float> fob = new Stats<Float>(fnums);
    double x = fob.average();
    System.out.println("fob average is " + x);

    // See which arrays have same average.
    System.out.print("Averages of iob and dob ");
    if(iob.isSameAvg(dob))
      System.out.println("are the same.");
    else
      System.out.println("differ.");

    System.out.print("Averages of iob and fob ");
    if(iob.isSameAvg(fob))
      System.out.println("are the same.");
    else
      System.out.println("differ.");
  }
}
```

The output is shown here:

```
iob average is 3.0
dob average is 3.3
fob average is 3.0
Averages of iob and dob differ.
Averages of iob and fob are the same.
```

One last point: It is important to understand that the wildcard does not affect what type of **Stats** objects can be created. This is governed by the **extends** clause in the **Stats** declaration. The wildcard simply matches any *valid* **Stats** object.

## Bounded Wildcards

Wildcard arguments can be bounded in much the same way that a type parameter can be bounded. A bounded wildcard is especially important when you are creating a generic type that will operate on a class hierarchy. To understand why, let's work through an example. Consider the following hierarchy of classes that encapsulate coordinates:

```
// Two-dimensional coordinates.
class TwoD {
  int x, y;

  TwoD(int a, int b) {
    x = a;
    y = b;
  }
}

// Three-dimensional coordinates.
class ThreeD extends TwoD {
  int z;

  ThreeD(int a, int b, int c) {
    super(a, b);
    z = c;
  }
}

// Four-dimensional coordinates.
class FourD extends ThreeD {
  int t;

  FourD(int a, int b, int c, int d) {
    super(a, b, c);
    t = d;
  }
}
```

At the top of the hierarchy is **TwoD**, which encapsulates a two-dimensional, XY coordinate. **TwoD** is inherited by **ThreeD**, which adds a third dimension, creating an XYZ coordinate. **ThreeD** is inherited by **FourD**, which adds a fourth dimension (time), yielding a four-dimensional coordinate.

Shown next is a generic class called **Coords**, which stores an array of coordinates:

```
// This class holds an array of coordinate objects.
class Coords<T extends TwoD> {
  T[] coords;

  Coords(T[] o) { coords = o; }
}
```

Notice that **Coords** specifies a type parameter bounded by **TwoD**. This means that any array stored in a **Coords** object will contain objects of type **TwoD** or one of its subclasses.

Now, assume that you want to write a method that displays the X and Y coordinates for each element in the **coords** array of a **Coords** object. Because all types of **Coords** objects have at least two coordinates (X and Y), this is easy to do using a wildcard, as shown here:

```
static void showXY(Coords<?> c) {
  System.out.println("X Y Coordinates:");
  for(int i=0; i < c.coords.length; i++)
    System.out.println(c.coords[i].x + " " +
                       c.coords[i].y);
  System.out.println();
}
```

Because **Coords** is a bounded generic type that specifies **TwoD** as an upper bound, all objects that can be used to create a **Coords** object will be arrays of type **TwoD**, or of classes derived from **TwoD**. Thus, **showXY( )** can display the contents of any **Coords** object.

However, what if you want to create a method that displays the X, Y, and Z coordinates of a **ThreeD** or **FourD** object? The trouble is that not all **Coords** objects will have three coordinates, because a **Coords<TwoD>** object will only have X and Y. Therefore, how do you write a method that displays the X, Y, and Z coordinates for **Coords<ThreeD>** and **Coords<FourD>** objects, while preventing that method from being used with **Coords<TwoD>** objects? The answer is the *bounded wildcard argument.*

A bounded wildcard specifies either an upper bound or a lower bound for the type argument. This enables you to restrict the types of objects upon which a method will operate. The most common bounded wildcard is the upper bound, which is created using an **extends** clause in much the same way it is used to create a bounded type.

Using a bounded wildcard, it is easy to create a method that displays the X, Y, and Z coordinates of a **Coords** object, if that object actually has those three coordinates. For example, the following **showXYZ( )** method shows the X, Y, and Z coordinates of the elements stored in a **Coords** object, if those elements are actually of type **ThreeD** (or are derived from **ThreeD**):

```
static void showXYZ(Coords<? extends ThreeD> c) {
  System.out.println("X Y Z Coordinates:");
  for(int i=0; i < c.coords.length; i++)
    System.out.println(c.coords[i].x + " " +
                       c.coords[i].y + " " +
                       c.coords[i].z);
  System.out.println();
}
```

Notice that an **extends** clause has been added to the wildcard in the declaration of parameter **c**. It states that the **?** can match any type as long as it is **ThreeD**, or a class derived from **ThreeD**. Thus, the **extends** clause establishes an upper bound that the **?** can match. Because of this bound, **showXYZ( )** can be called with references to objects of type **Coords<ThreeD>** or **Coords<FourD>**, but not with a reference of type **Coords<TwoD>**. Attempting to call **showXZY( )** with a **Coords<TwoD>** reference results in a compile-time error, thus ensuring type safety.

Here is an entire program that demonstrates the actions of a bounded wildcard argument:

```
// Bounded Wildcard arguments.

// Two-dimensional coordinates.
class TwoD {
  int x, y;

  TwoD(int a, int b) {
    x = a;
    y = b;
  }
}

// Three-dimensional coordinates.
class ThreeD extends TwoD {
  int z;

  ThreeD(int a, int b, int c) {
    super(a, b);
    z = c;
  }
}

// Four-dimensional coordinates.
class FourD extends ThreeD {
  int t;

  FourD(int a, int b, int c, int d) {
    super(a, b, c);
    t = d;
  }
}

// This class holds an array of coordinate objects.
class Coords<T extends TwoD> {
  T[] coords;

  Coords(T[] o) { coords = o; }
}

// Demonstrate a bounded wildcard.
class BoundedWildcard {
  static void showXY(Coords<?> c) {
    System.out.println("X Y Coordinates:");
    for(int i=0; i < c.coords.length; i++)
      System.out.println(c.coords[i].x + " " +
                         c.coords[i].y);
    System.out.println();
  }

  static void showXYZ(Coords<? extends ThreeD> c) {
    System.out.println("X Y Z Coordinates:");
    for(int i=0; i < c.coords.length; i++)
```

```
      System.out.println(c.coords[i].x + " " +
                         c.coords[i].y + " " +
                         c.coords[i].z);
    System.out.println();
  }

  static void showAll(Coords<? extends FourD> c) {
    System.out.println("X Y Z T Coordinates:");
    for(int i=0; i < c.coords.length; i++)
      System.out.println(c.coords[i].x + " " +
                         c.coords[i].y + " " +
                         c.coords[i].z + " " +
                         c.coords[i].t);
    System.out.println();
  }

  public static void main(String[] args) {
    TwoD[] td = {
      new TwoD(0, 0),
      new TwoD(7, 9),
      new TwoD(18, 4),
      new TwoD(-1, -23)
    };

    Coords<TwoD> tdlocs = new Coords<TwoD>(td);

    System.out.println("Contents of tdlocs.");
    showXY(tdlocs); // OK, is a TwoD
//  showXYZ(tdlocs); // Error, not a ThreeD
//  showAll(tdlocs); // Error, not a FourD

    // Now, create some FourD objects.
    FourD[] fd = {
      new FourD(1, 2, 3, 4),
      new FourD(6, 8, 14, 8),
      new FourD(22, 9, 4, 9),
      new FourD(3, -2, -23, 17)
    };

    Coords<FourD> fdlocs = new Coords<FourD>(fd);

    System.out.println("Contents of fdlocs.");
    // These are all OK
    showXY(fdlocs);
    showXYZ(fdlocs);
    showAll(fdlocs);
  }
}
```

The output from the program is shown here:

```
Contents of tdlocs.
X Y Coordinates:
0 0
```

```
7 9
18 4
-1 -23

Contents of fdlocs.
X Y Coordinates:
1 2
6 8
22 9
3 -2

X Y Z Coordinates:
1 2 3
6 8 14
22 9 4
3 -2 -23

X Y Z T Coordinates:
1 2 3 4
6 8 14 8
22 9 4 9
3 -2 -23 17
```

Notice these commented-out lines:

```
// showXYZ(tdlocs); // Error, not a ThreeD
// showAll(tdlocs); // Error, not a FourD
```

Because **tdlocs** is a **Coords(TwoD)** object, it cannot be used to call **showXYZ( )** or **showAll( )** because bounded wildcard arguments in their declarations prevent it. To prove this to yourself, try removing the comment symbols, and then attempt to compile the program. You will receive compilation errors because of the type mismatches.

In general, to establish an upper bound for a wildcard, use the following type of wildcard expression:

<? extends *superclass*>

where *superclass* is the name of the class that serves as the upper bound. Remember, this is an inclusive clause because the class forming the upper bound (that is, specified by *superclass*) is also within bounds.

You can also specify a lower bound for a wildcard by adding a **super** clause to a wildcard declaration. Here is its general form:

<? super *subclass*>

In this case, only classes that are superclasses of *subclass* are acceptable arguments. This is an inclusive clause.

## Creating a Generic Method

As the preceding examples have shown, methods inside a generic class can make use of a class's type parameter and are, therefore, automatically generic relative to the type parameter. However, it is possible to declare a generic method that uses one or more type parameters of its own. Furthermore, it is possible to create a generic method that is enclosed within a non-generic class.

Let's begin with an example. The following program declares a non-generic class called **GenMethDemo** and a static generic method within that class called **isIn( )**. The **isIn( )** method determines if an object is a member of an array. It can be used with any type of object and array as long as the array contains objects that are compatible with the type of the object being sought.

```
// Demonstrate a simple generic method.
class GenMethDemo {

  // Determine if an object is in an array.
  static <T extends Comparable<T>, V extends T> boolean isIn(T x, V[] y) {
    for(int i=0; i < y.length; i++)
      if(x.equals(y[i])) return true;

    return false;
  }

  public static void main(String[] args) {

    // Use isIn() on Integers.
    Integer[] nums = { 1, 2, 3, 4, 5 };

    if(isIn(2, nums))
      System.out.println("2 is in nums");

    if(!isIn(7, nums))
      System.out.println("7 is not in nums");

    System.out.println();

    // Use isIn() on Strings.
    String[] strs = { "one", "two", "three",
                      "four", "five" };

    if(isIn("two", strs))
      System.out.println("two is in strs");

    if(!isIn("seven", strs))
      System.out.println("seven is not in strs");

    // Oops! Won't compile! Types must be compatible.
//    if(isIn("two", nums))
//      System.out.println("two is in strs");
  }
}
```

The output from the program is shown here:

```
2 is in nums
7 is not in nums
```

```
two is in strs
seven is not in strs
```

Let's examine **isIn( )** closely. First, notice how it is declared by this line:

```
static <T extends Comparable<T>, V extends T> boolean isIn(T x, V[] y) {
```

The type parameters are declared *before* the return type of the method. Also note that **T** extends **Comparable<T>**. **Comparable** is an interface declared in **java.lang.** A class that implements **Comparable** defines objects that can be ordered. Thus, requiring an upper bound of **Comparable** ensures that **isIn( )** can be used only with objects that are capable of being compared. **Comparable** is generic, and its type parameter specifies the type of objects that it compares. (Shortly, you will see how to create a generic interface.) Next, notice that the type **V** is upper-bounded by **T**. Thus, **V** must either be the same as type **T**, or a subclass of **T**. This relationship enforces that **isIn( )** can be called only with arguments that are compatible with each other. Also notice that **isIn( )** is static, enabling it to be called independently of any object. Understand, though, that generic methods can be either static or non-static. There is no restriction in this regard.

Now, notice how **isIn( )** is called within **main( )** by use of the normal call syntax, without the need to specify type arguments. This is because the types of the arguments are automatically discerned, and the types of **T** and **V** are adjusted accordingly. For example, in the first call:

```
if(isIn(2, nums))
```

the type of the first argument is **Integer** (due to autoboxing), which causes **Integer** to be substituted for **T**. The base type of the second argument is also **Integer**, which makes **Integer** a substitute for **V**, too. In the second call, **String** types are used, and the types of **T** and **V** are replaced by **String**.

Although type inference will be sufficient for most generic method calls, you can explicitly specify the type argument if needed. For example, here is how the first call to **isIn( )** looks when the type arguments are specified:

```
GenMethDemo.<Integer, Integer>isIn(2, nums)
```

Of course, in this case, there is nothing gained by specifying the type arguments. Furthermore, JDK 8 improved type inference as it relates to methods. As a result, today there are fewer cases in which explicit type arguments are needed.

Now, notice the commented-out code, shown here:

```
//    if(isIn("two", nums))
//      System.out.println("two is in strs");
```

If you remove the comments and then try to compile the program, you will receive an error. The reason is that the type parameter **V** is bounded by **T** in the **extends** clause in **V**'s declaration. This means that **V** must be either type **T**, or a subclass of **T**. In this case, the first argument is of type **String**, making **T** into **String**, but the second argument is of type

**Integer**, which is not a subclass of **String**. This causes a compile-time type-mismatch error. This ability to enforce type safety is one of the most important advantages of generic methods.

The syntax used to create **isIn( )** can be generalized. Here is the syntax for a generic method:

*<type-param-list> ret-type meth-name* (*param-list*) { // ...

In all cases, *type-param-list* is a comma-separated list of type parameters. Notice that for a generic method, the type parameter list precedes the return type.

## Generic Constructors

It is possible for constructors to be generic, even if their class is not. For example, consider the following short program:

```
// Use a generic constructor.
class GenCons {
  private double val;

  <T extends Number> GenCons(T arg) {
    val = arg.doubleValue();
  }

  void showVal() {
    System.out.println("val: " + val);
  }
}

class GenConsDemo {
  public static void main(String[] args) {

    GenCons test = new GenCons(100);
    GenCons test2 = new GenCons(123.5F);

    test.showVal();
    test2.showVal();
  }
}
```

The output is shown here:

```
val: 100.0
val: 123.5
```

Because **GenCons( )** specifies a parameter of a generic type, which must be a subclass of **Number**, **GenCons( )** can be called with any numeric type, including **Integer**, **Float**, or **Double**. Therefore, even though **GenCons** is not a generic class, its constructor is generic.

## Generic Interfaces

In addition to generic classes and methods, you can also have generic interfaces. Generic interfaces are specified just like generic classes. Here is an example. It creates an interface called **MinMax** that declares the methods **min( )** and **max( )**, which are expected to return the minimum and maximum value of some set of objects.

```
// A generic interface example.

// A Min/Max interface.
interface MinMax<T extends Comparable<T>> {
  T min();
  T max();
}

// Now, implement MinMax
class MyClass<T extends Comparable<T>> implements MinMax<T> {
  T[] vals;

  MyClass(T[] o) { vals = o; }

  // Return the minimum value in vals.
  public T min() {
    T v = vals[0];

    for(int i=1; i < vals.length; i++)
      if(vals[i].compareTo(v) < 0) v = vals[i];

    return v;
  }

  // Return the maximum value in vals.
  public T max() {
    T v = vals[0];

    for(int i=1; i < vals.length; i++)
      if(vals[i].compareTo(v) > 0) v = vals[i];

    return v;
  }
}

class GenIFDemo {
  public static void main(String[] args) {
    Integer[] inums = {3, 6, 2, 8, 6 };
    Character[] chs = {'b', 'r', 'p', 'w' };

    MyClass<Integer> iob = new MyClass<Integer>(inums);
    MyClass<Character> cob = new MyClass<Character>(chs);

    System.out.println("Max value in inums: " + iob.max());
    System.out.println("Min value in inums: " + iob.min());
```

```
    System.out.println("Max value in chs: " + cob.max());
    System.out.println("Min value in chs: " + cob.min());
  }
}
```

The output is shown here:

```
Max value in inums: 8
Min value in inums: 2
Max value in chs: w
Min value in chs: b
```

Although most aspects of this program should be easy to understand, a couple of key points need to be made. First, notice that **MinMax** is declared like this:

```
interface MinMax<T extends Comparable<T>> {
```

In general, a generic interface is declared in the same way as is a generic class. In this case, the type parameter is **T**, and its upper bound is **Comparable**. As explained earlier, **Comparable** is an interface defined by **java.lang** that specifies how objects are compared. Its type parameter specifies the type of the objects being compared.

Next, **MinMax** is implemented by **MyClass**. Notice the declaration of **MyClass**, shown here:

```
class MyClass<T extends Comparable<T>> implements MinMax<T> {
```

Pay special attention to the way that the type parameter **T** is declared by **MyClass** and then passed to **MinMax**. Because **MinMax** requires a type that implements **Comparable**, the implementing class (**MyClass** in this case) must specify the same bound. Furthermore, once this bound has been established, there is no need to specify it again in the **implements** clause. In fact, it would be wrong to do so. For example, this line is incorrect and won't compile:

```
// This is wrong!
class MyClass<T extends Comparable<T>>
        implements MinMax<T extends Comparable<T>> {
```

Once the type parameter has been established, it is simply passed to the interface without further modification.

In general, if a class implements a generic interface, then that class must also be generic, at least to the extent that it takes a type parameter that is passed to the interface. For example, the following attempt to declare **MyClass** is in error:

```
class MyClass implements MinMax<T> { // Wrong!
```

Because **MyClass** does not declare a type parameter, there is no way to pass one to **MinMax**. In this case, the identifier **T** is simply unknown, and the compiler reports an error. Of course, if a class implements a *specific type* of generic interface, such as shown here:

```
class MyClass implements MinMax<Integer> { // OK
```

then the implementing class does not need to be generic.

The generic interface offers two benefits. First, it can be implemented for different types of data. Second, it allows you to put constraints (that is, bounds) on the types of data for which the interface can be implemented. In the **MinMax** example, only types that implement the **Comparable** interface can be passed to **T**.

Here is the generalized syntax for a generic interface:

interface *interface-name<type-param-list>* { // ...

Here, *type-param-list* is a comma-separated list of type parameters. When a generic interface is implemented, you must specify the type arguments, as shown here:

class *class-name<type-param-list>*
  implements *interface-name<type-arg-list>* {

# Raw Types and Legacy Code

Because support for generics did not exist prior to JDK 5, it was necessary to provide some transition path from old, pre-generics code. Furthermore, this transition path had to enable pre-generics code to remain functional while at the same time being compatible with generics. In other words, pre-generics code had to be able to work with generics, and generic code had to be able to work with pre-generics code.

To handle the transition to generics, Java allows a generic class to be used without any type arguments. This creates a *raw type* for the class. This raw type is compatible with legacy code, which has no knowledge of generics. The main drawback to using the raw type is that the type safety of generics is lost.

Here is an example that shows a raw type in action:

```
// Demonstrate a raw type.
class Gen<T> {

  T ob; // declare an object of type T

  // Pass the constructor a reference to
  // an object of type T.
  Gen(T o) {
    ob = o;
  }

  // Return ob.
  T getOb() {
    return ob;
  }
}

// Demonstrate raw type.
class RawDemo {
  public static void main(String[] args) {

    // Create a Gen object for Integers.
    Gen<Integer> iOb = new Gen<Integer>(88);
```

```
    // Create a Gen object for Strings.
    Gen<String> strOb = new Gen<String>("Generics Test");

    // Create a raw-type Gen object and give it
    // a Double value.
    Gen raw = new Gen(Double.valueOf(98.6));

    // Cast here is necessary because type is unknown.
    double d = (Double) raw.getOb();
    System.out.println("value: " + d);

    // The use of a raw type can lead to run-time
    // exceptions. Here are some examples.

    // The following cast causes a run-time error!
//    int i = (Integer) raw.getOb(); // run-time error

    // This assignment overrides type safety.
    strOb = raw; // OK, but potentially wrong
//    String str = strOb.getOb(); // run-time error

    // This assignment also overrides type safety.
    raw = iOb; // OK, but potentially wrong
//    d = (Double) raw.getOb(); // run-time error
  }
}
```

This program contains several interesting things. First, a raw type of the generic **Gen** class is created by the following declaration:

```
Gen raw = new Gen(Double.valueOf(98.6));
```

Notice that no type arguments are specified. In essence, this creates a **Gen** object whose type **T** is replaced by **Object**.

A raw type is not type safe. Thus, a variable of a raw type can be assigned a reference to any type of **Gen** object. The reverse is also allowed; a variable of a specific **Gen** type can be assigned a reference to a raw **Gen** object. However, both operations are potentially unsafe because the type checking mechanism of generics is circumvented.

This lack of type safety is illustrated by the commented-out lines at the end of the program. Let's examine each case. First, consider the following situation:

```
//    int i = (Integer) raw.getOb(); // run-time error
```

In this statement, the value of **ob** inside **raw** is obtained, and this value is cast to **Integer**. The trouble is that **raw** contains a **Double** value, not an integer value. However, this cannot be detected at compile time because the type of **raw** is unknown. Thus, this statement fails at run time.

The next sequence assigns to a **strOb** (a reference of type **Gen<String>**) a reference to a raw **Gen** object:

```
    strOb = raw; // OK, but potentially wrong
//    String str = strOb.getOb(); // run-time error
```

The assignment itself is syntactically correct, but questionable. Because **strOb** is of type **Gen<String>**, it is assumed to contain a **String**. However, after the assignment, the object referred to by **strOb** contains a **Double**. Thus, at run time, when an attempt is made to assign the contents of **strOb** to **str**, a run-time error results because **strOb** now contains a **Double**. Thus, the assignment of a raw reference to a generic reference bypasses the type-safety mechanism.

The following sequence inverts the preceding case:

```
    raw = iOb; // OK, but potentially wrong
//    d = (Double) raw.getOb(); // run-time error
```

Here, a generic reference is assigned to a raw reference variable. Although this is syntactically correct, it can lead to problems, as illustrated by the second line. In this case, **raw** now refers to an object that contains an **Integer** object, but the cast assumes that it contains a **Double**. This error cannot be prevented at compile time. Rather, it causes a run-time error.

Because of the potential for danger inherent in raw types, **javac** displays *unchecked warnings* when a raw type is used in a way that might jeopardize type safety. In the preceding program, these lines generate unchecked warnings:

```
Gen raw = new Gen(Double.valueOf(98.6));

strOb = raw; // OK, but potentially wrong
```

In the first line, it is the call to the **Gen** constructor without a type argument that causes the warning. In the second line, it is the assignment of a raw reference to a generic variable that generates the warning.

At first, you might think that this line should also generate an unchecked warning, but it does not:

```
raw = iOb; // OK, but potentially wrong
```

No compiler warning is issued because the assignment does not cause any *further* loss of type safety than had already occurred when **raw** was created.

One final point: You should limit the use of raw types to those cases in which you must mix legacy code with newer, generic code. Raw types are simply a transitional feature and not something that should be used for new code.

## Generic Class Hierarchies

Generic classes can be part of a class hierarchy in just the same way as a non-generic class. Thus, a generic class can act as a superclass or be a subclass. The key difference between generic and non-generic hierarchies is that in a generic hierarchy, any type arguments needed by a generic superclass must be passed up the hierarchy by all subclasses. This is similar to the way that constructor arguments must be passed up a hierarchy.

## Using a Generic Superclass

Here is a simple example of a hierarchy that uses a generic superclass:

```
// A simple generic class hierarchy.
class Gen<T> {
  T ob;

  Gen(T o) {
    ob = o;
  }

  // Return ob.
  T getOb() {
    return ob;
  }
}

// A subclass of Gen.
class Gen2<T> extends Gen<T> {
  Gen2(T o) {
    super(o);
  }
}
```

In this hierarchy, **Gen2** extends the generic class **Gen**. Notice how **Gen2** is declared by the following line:

```
class Gen2<T> extends Gen<T> {
```

The type parameter **T** is specified by **Gen2** and is also passed to **Gen** in the **extends** clause. This means that whatever type is passed to **Gen2** will also be passed to **Gen**. For example, this declaration,

```
Gen2<Integer> num = new Gen2<Integer>(100);
```

passes **Integer** as the type parameter to **Gen**. Thus, the **ob** inside the **Gen** portion of **Gen2** will be of type **Integer**.

Notice also that **Gen2** does not use the type parameter **T** except to support the **Gen** superclass. Thus, even if a subclass of a generic superclass would otherwise not need to be generic, it still must specify the type parameter(s) required by its generic superclass.

Of course, a subclass is free to add its own type parameters, if needed. For example, here is a variation on the preceding hierarchy in which **Gen2** adds a type parameter of its own:

```
// A subclass can add its own type parameters.
class Gen<T> {
  T ob; // declare an object of type T

  // Pass the constructor a reference to
  // an object of type T.
```

```
  Gen(T o) {
    ob = o;
  }

  // Return ob.
  T getOb() {
    return ob;
  }
}

// A subclass of Gen that defines a second
// type parameter, called V.
class Gen2<T, V> extends Gen<T> {
  V ob2;

  Gen2(T o, V o2) {
    super(o);
    ob2 = o2;
  }

  V getOb2() {
    return ob2;
  }
}

// Create an object of type Gen2.
class HierDemo {
  public static void main(String[] args) {

    // Create a Gen2 object for String and Integer.
    Gen2<String, Integer> x =
      new Gen2<String, Integer>("Value is: ", 99);

    System.out.print(x.getOb());
    System.out.println(x.getOb2());
  }
}
```

Notice the declaration of this version of **Gen2**, which is shown here:

```
class Gen2<T, V> extends Gen<T> {
```

Here, **T** is the type passed to **Gen**, and **V** is the type that is specific to **Gen2**. **V** is used to declare an object called **ob2**, and as a return type for the method **getOb2( )**. In **main( )**, a **Gen2** object is created in which type parameter **T** is **String**, and type parameter **V** is **Integer**. The program displays the following, expected, result:

```
Value is: 99
```

## A Generic Subclass

It is perfectly acceptable for a non-generic class to be the superclass of a generic subclass. For example, consider this program:

```
// A non-generic class can be the superclass
// of a generic subclass.

// A non-generic class.
class NonGen {
  int num;

  NonGen(int i) {
    num = i;
  }

  int getnum() {
    return num;
  }
}

// A generic subclass.
class Gen<T> extends NonGen {
  T ob; // declare an object of type T

  // Pass the constructor a reference to
  // an object of type T.
  Gen(T o, int i) {
    super(i);
    ob = o;
  }

  // Return ob.
  T getOb() {
    return ob;
  }
}

// Create a Gen object.
class HierDemo2 {
  public static void main(String[] args) {

    // Create a Gen object for String.
    Gen<String> w = new Gen<String>("Hello", 47);

    System.out.print(w.getOb() + " ");
    System.out.println(w.getnum());
  }
}
```

The output from the program is shown here:

```
Hello 47
```

In the program, notice how **Gen** inherits **NonGen** in the following declaration:

```
class Gen<T> extends NonGen {
```

Because **NonGen** is not generic, no type argument is specified. Thus, even though **Gen** declares the type parameter **T**, it is not needed by (nor can it be used by) **NonGen**. Thus, **NonGen** is inherited by **Gen** in the normal way. No special conditions apply.

## Run-Time Type Comparisons Within a Generic Hierarchy

Recall the run-time type information operator **instanceof** that was introduced in Chapter 13. As explained, **instanceof** determines if an object is an instance of a class. It returns true if an object is of the specified type or can be cast to the specified type. The **instanceof** operator can be applied to objects of generic classes. The following class demonstrates some of the type compatibility implications of a generic hierarchy:

```
// Use the instanceof operator with a generic class hierarchy.
class Gen<T> {
  T ob;

  Gen(T o) {
    ob = o;
  }

  // Return ob.
  T getOb() {
    return ob;
  }
}

// A subclass of Gen.
class Gen2<T> extends Gen<T> {
  Gen2(T o) {
    super(o);
  }
}

// Demonstrate run-time type ID implications of generic
// class hierarchy.
class HierDemo3 {
  public static void main(String[] args) {

    // Create a Gen object for Integers.
    Gen<Integer> iOb = new Gen<Integer>(88);
```

```
    // Create a Gen2 object for Integers.
    Gen2<Integer> iOb2 = new Gen2<Integer>(99);

    // Create a Gen2 object for Strings.
    Gen2<String> strOb2 = new Gen2<String>("Generics Test");

    // See if iOb2 is some form of Gen2.
    if(iOb2 instanceof Gen2<?>)
      System.out.println("iOb2 is instance of Gen2");

    // See if iOb2 is some form of Gen.
    if(iOb2 instanceof Gen<?>)
      System.out.println("iOb2 is instance of Gen");

    System.out.println();

    // See if strOb2 is a Gen2.
    if(strOb2 instanceof Gen2<?>)
      System.out.println("strOb2 is instance of Gen2");

    // See if strOb2 is a Gen.
    if(strOb2 instanceof Gen<?>)
      System.out.println("strOb2 is instance of Gen");

    System.out.println();

    // See if iOb is an instance of Gen2, which it is not.
    if(iOb instanceof Gen2<?>)
      System.out.println("iOb is instance of Gen2");

    // See if iOb is an instance of Gen, which it is.
    if(iOb instanceof Gen<?>)
      System.out.println("iOb is instance of Gen");
  }
}
```

The output from the program is shown here:

```
iOb2 is instance of Gen2
iOb2 is instance of Gen

strOb2 is instance of Gen2
strOb2 is instance of Gen

iOb is instance of Gen
```

In this program, **Gen2** is a subclass of **Gen**, which is generic on type parameter **T**. In **main( )**, three objects are created. The first is **iOb**, which is an object of type **Gen<Integer>**. The second is **iOb2**, which is an instance of **Gen2<Integer>**. Finally, **strOb2** is an object of type **Gen2<String>**.

Then, the program performs these **instanceof** tests on the type of **iOb2**:

```
// See if iOb2 is some form of Gen2.
if(iOb2 instanceof Gen2<?>)
  System.out.println("iOb2 is instance of Gen2");

// See if iOb2 is some form of Gen.
if(iOb2 instanceof Gen<?>)
  System.out.println("iOb2 is instance of Gen");
```

As the output shows, both succeed. In the first test, **iOb2** is checked against **Gen2<?>**. This test succeeds because it simply confirms that **iOb2** is an object of some type of **Gen2** object. The use of the wildcard enables **instanceof** to determine if **iOb2** is an object of any type of **Gen2**. Next, **iOb2** is tested against **Gen<?>**, the superclass type. This is also true because **iOb2** is some form of **Gen**, the superclass. The next few lines in **main( )** show the same sequence (and same results) for **strOb2**.

Next, **iOb**, which is an instance of **Gen<Integer>** (the superclass), is tested by these lines:

```
// See if iOb is an instance of Gen2, which it is not.
if(iOb instanceof Gen2<?>)
  System.out.println("iOb is instance of Gen2");

// See if iOb is an instance of Gen, which it is.
if(iOb instanceof Gen<?>)
  System.out.println("iOb is instance of Gen");
```

The first **if** fails because **iOb** is not some type of **Gen2** object. The second test succeeds because **iOb** is some type of **Gen** object.

## Casting

You can cast one instance of a generic class into another only if the two are otherwise compatible and their type arguments are the same. For example, assuming the foregoing program, this cast is legal:

```
(Gen<Integer>) iOb2 // legal
```

because **iOb2** includes an instance of **Gen<Integer>**. But, this cast:

```
(Gen<Long>) iOb2 // illegal
```

is not legal because **iOb2** is not an instance of **Gen<Long>**.

## Overriding Methods in a Generic Class

A method in a generic class can be overridden just like any other method. For example, consider this program in which the method **getOb( )** is overridden:

```
// Overriding a generic method in a generic class.
class Gen<T> {
  T ob; // declare an object of type T
```

```
  // Pass the constructor a reference to
  // an object of type T.
  Gen(T o) {
    ob = o;
  }

  // Return ob.
  T getOb() {
    System.out.print("Gen's getOb(): " );
    return ob;
  }
}

// A subclass of Gen that overrides getOb().
class Gen2<T> extends Gen<T> {

  Gen2(T o) {
    super(o);
  }

  // Override getOb().
  T getOb() {
    System.out.print("Gen2's getOb(): ");
    return ob;
  }
}

// Demonstrate generic method override.
class OverrideDemo {
  public static void main(String[] args) {

    // Create a Gen object for Integers.
    Gen<Integer> iOb = new Gen<Integer>(88);

    // Create a Gen2 object for Integers.
    Gen2<Integer> iOb2 = new Gen2<Integer>(99);

    // Create a Gen2 object for Strings.
    Gen2<String> strOb2 = new Gen2<String> ("Generics Test");

    System.out.println(iOb.getOb());
    System.out.println(iOb2.getOb());
    System.out.println(strOb2.getOb());
  }
}
```

The output is shown here:

```
Gen's getOb(): 88
Gen2's getOb(): 99
Gen2's getOb(): Generics Test
```

As the output confirms, the overridden version of **getOb( )** is called for objects of type **Gen2**, but the superclass version is called for objects of type **Gen**.

## Type Inference with Generics

Beginning with JDK 7, it became possible to shorten the syntax used to create an instance of a generic type. To begin, consider the following generic class:

```
class MyClass<T, V> {
  T ob1;
  V ob2;

  MyClass(T o1, V o2) {
    ob1 = o1;
    ob2 = o2;
  }
  // ...
}
```

Prior to JDK 7, to create an instance of **MyClass**, you would have needed to use a statement similar to the following:

```
MyClass<Integer, String> mcOb =
  new MyClass<Integer, String>(98, "A String");
```

Here, the type arguments (which are **Integer** and **String**) are specified twice: first, when **mcOb** is declared, and second, when a **MyClass** instance is created via **new**. Since generics were introduced by JDK 5, this is the form required by all versions of Java prior to JDK 7. Although there is nothing wrong, per se, with this form, it is a bit more verbose than it needs to be. In the **new** clause, the type of the type arguments can be readily inferred from the type of **mcOb**; therefore, there is really no reason that they need to be specified a second time. To address this situation, JDK 7 added a syntactic element that lets you avoid the second specification.

Today the preceding declaration can be rewritten as shown here:

```
MyClass<Integer, String> mcOb = new MyClass<>(98, "A String");
```

Notice that the instance creation portion simply uses <>, which is an empty type argument list. This is referred to as the *diamond* operator. It tells the compiler to infer the type arguments needed by the constructor in the **new** expression. The principal advantage of this type-inference syntax is that it shortens what are sometimes quite long declaration statements.

The preceding can be generalized. When type inference is used, the declaration syntax for a generic reference and instance creation has this general form:

*class-name<type-arg-list> var-name* = new *class-name*<>(*cons-arg-list*);

Here, the type argument list of the constructor in the **new** clause is empty.

Type inference can also be applied to parameter passing. For example, if the following method is added to **MyClass**,

```
boolean isSame(MyClass<T, V> o) {
  if(ob1 == o.ob1 && ob2 == o.ob2) return true;
  else return false;
}
```

then the following call is legal:

```
if(mcOb.isSame(new MyClass<>(1, "test"))) System.out.println("Same");
```

In this case, the type arguments for the argument passed to **isSame( )** can be inferred from the parameter's type.

Most of the examples in this book will continue to use the full syntax when declaring instances of generic classes. This way, the examples will work with any Java compiler that supports generics. Using the full-length syntax also makes it very clear precisely what is being created, which is important in sample code shown in a book. However, in your own code, the use of the type-inference syntax will streamline your declarations.

# Local Variable Type Inference and Generics

As just explained, type inference is already supported for generics through the use of the diamond operator. However, you can also use the local variable type inference feature added by JDK 10 with a generic class. For example, assuming **MyClass** used in the preceding section, this declaration:

```
MyClass<Integer, String> mcOb =
  new MyClass<Integer, String>(98, "A String");
```

can be rewritten like this using local variable type inference:

```
var mcOb = new MyClass<Integer, String>(98, "A String");
```

In this case, the type of **mcOb** is inferred to be **MyClass<Integer, String>** because that is the type of its initializer. Also notice that the use of **var** results in a shorter declaration than would be the case otherwise. In general, generic type names can often be quite long and (in some cases) complicated. The use of **var** is another way to substantially shorten such declarations. For the same reasons as just explained for the diamond operator, the remaining examples in this book will continue to use the full generic syntax, but in your own code the use of local variable type inference can be quite helpful.

# Erasure

Usually, it is not necessary to know the details about how the Java compiler transforms your source code into object code. However, in the case of generics, some general understanding of the process is important because it explains why the generic features work as they do— and why their behavior is sometimes a bit surprising. For this reason, a brief discussion of how generics are implemented in Java is in order.

An important constraint that governed the way that generics were added to Java was the need for compatibility with previous versions of Java. Simply put, generic code had to be compatible with preexisting, non-generic code. Thus, any changes to the syntax of the Java language, or to the JVM, had to avoid breaking older code. The way Java implements generics while satisfying this constraint is through the use of *erasure*.

In general, here is how erasure works: When your Java code is compiled, all generic type information is removed (erased). This means replacing type parameters with their bound type, which is **Object** if no explicit bound is specified, and then applying the appropriate casts (as determined by the type arguments) to maintain type compatibility with the types specified by the type arguments. The compiler also enforces this type compatibility. This approach to generics means that no type parameters exist at run time. They are simply a source-code mechanism.

## Bridge Methods

Occasionally, the compiler will need to add a *bridge method* to a class to handle situations in which the type erasure of an overriding method in a subclass does not produce the same erasure as the method in the superclass. In this case, a method is generated that uses the type erasure of the superclass, and this method calls the method that has the type erasure specified by the subclass. Of course, bridge methods only occur at the bytecode level, are not seen by you, and are not available for your use.

Although bridge methods are not something that you will normally need to be concerned with, it is still instructive to see a situation in which one is generated. Consider the following program:

```
// A situation that creates a bridge method.
class Gen<T> {
  T ob; // declare an object of type T

  // Pass the constructor a reference to
  // an object of type T.
  Gen(T o) {
    ob = o;
  }

  // Return ob.
  T getOb() {
    return ob;
  }
}

// A subclass of Gen.
class Gen2 extends Gen<String> {

  Gen2(String o) {
    super(o);
  }

  // A String-specific override of getOb().
  String getOb() {
    System.out.print("You called String getOb(): ");
    return ob;
  }
}
```

```
// Demonstrate a situation that requires a bridge method.
class BridgeDemo {
  public static void main(String[] args) {

    // Create a Gen2 object for Strings.
    Gen2 strOb2 = new Gen2("Generics Test");

    System.out.println(strOb2.getOb());
  }
}
```



In the program, the subclass **Gen2** extends **Gen**, but does so using a **String**-specific version of **Gen**, as its declaration shows:

```
class Gen2 extends Gen<String> {
```

Furthermore, inside **Gen2, getOb( )** is overridden with **String** specified as the return type:

```
// A String-specific override of getOb().
String getOb() {
  System.out.print("You called String getOb(): ");
  return ob;
}
```

All of this is perfectly acceptable. The only trouble is that because of type erasure, the expected form of **getOb( )** will be

```
Object getOb() { // ...
```

To handle this problem, the compiler generates a bridge method with the preceding signature that calls the **String** version. Thus, if you examine the class file for **Gen2** by using **javap**, you will see the following methods:

```
class Gen2 extends Gen<java.lang.String> {
  Gen2(java.lang.String);
  java.lang.String getOb();
  java.lang.Object getOb(); // bridge method
}
```

As you can see, the bridge method has been included. (The comment was added by the author and not by **javap**, and the precise output you see may vary based on the version of Java that you are using.)

There is one last point to make about this example. Notice that the only difference between the two **getOb( )** methods is their return type. Normally, this would cause an error, but because this does not occur in your source code, it does not cause a problem and is handled correctly by the JVM.

## Ambiguity Errors

The inclusion of generics gives rise to another type of error that you must guard against: *ambiguity*. Ambiguity errors occur when erasure causes two seemingly distinct generic declarations to resolve to the same erased type, causing a conflict. Here is an example that involves method overloading:

```
// Ambiguity caused by erasure on
// overloaded methods.
class MyGenClass<T, V> {
  T ob1;
  V ob2;

  // ...

  // These two overloaded methods are ambiguous
  // and will not compile.
  void set(T o) {
    ob1 = o;
  }

  void set(V o) {
    ob2 = o;
  }
}
```

Notice that **MyGenClass** declares two generic types: **T** and **V**. Inside **MyGenClass**, an attempt is made to overload **set( )** based on parameters of type **T** and **V**. This looks reasonable because **T** and **V** appear to be different types. However, there are two ambiguity problems here.

First, as **MyGenClass** is written, there is no requirement that **T** and **V** actually be different types. For example, it is perfectly correct (in principle) to construct a **MyGenClass** object as shown here:

```
MyGenClass<String, String> obj = new MyGenClass<String, String>()
```

In this case, both **T** and **V** will be replaced by **String**. This makes both versions of **set( )** identical, which is, of course, an error.

The second and more fundamental problem is that the type erasure of **set( )** reduces both versions to the following:

```
void set(Object o) { // ...
```

Thus, the overloading of **set( )** as attempted in **MyGenClass** is inherently ambiguous.

Ambiguity errors can be tricky to fix. For example, if you know that **V** will always be some type of **Number**, you might try to fix **MyGenClass** by rewriting its declaration as shown here:

```
class MyGenClass<T, V extends Number> { // almost OK!
```

This change causes **MyGenClass** to compile, and you can even instantiate objects like the one shown here:

```
MyGenClass<String, Number> x = new MyGenClass<String, Number>();
```

This works because Java can accurately determine which method to call. However, ambiguity returns when you try this line:

```
MyGenClass<Number, Number> x = new MyGenClass<Number, Number>();
```

In this case, since both **T** and **V** are **Number**, which version of **set( )** is to be called? The call to **set( )** is now ambiguous.

Frankly, in the preceding example, it would be much better to use two separate method names, rather than trying to overload **set( )**. Often, the solution to ambiguity involves the restructuring of the code, because ambiguity frequently means that you have a conceptual error in your design.

# Some Generic Restrictions

There are a few restrictions that you need to keep in mind when using generics. They involve creating objects of a type parameter, static members, exceptions, and arrays. Each is examined here.

## Type Parameters Can't Be Instantiated

It is not possible to create an instance of a type parameter. For example, consider this class:

```
// Can't create an instance of T.
class Gen<T> {
  T ob;

  Gen() {
    ob = new T(); // Illegal!!!
  }
}
```

Here, it is illegal to attempt to create an instance of **T**. The reason should be easy to understand: the compiler does not know what type of object to create. **T** is simply a placeholder.

## Restrictions on Static Members

No **static** member can use a type parameter declared by the enclosing class. For example, both of the **static** members of this class are illegal:

```
class Wrong<T> {
  // Wrong, no static variables of type T.
  static T ob;
```

```
  // Wrong, no static method can use T.
  static T getOb() {
    return ob;
  }
}
```

Although you can't declare **static** members that use a type parameter declared by the enclosing class, you can declare **static** generic methods, which define their own type parameters, as was done earlier in this chapter.

## Generic Array Restrictions

There are two important generics restrictions that apply to arrays. First, you cannot instantiate an array whose element type is a type parameter. Second, you cannot create an array of type-specific generic references. The following short program shows both situations:

```
// Generics and arrays.
class Gen<T extends Number> {
  T ob;

  T[] vals; // OK

  Gen(T o, T[] nums) {
    ob = o;

    // This statement is illegal.
    // vals = new T[10]; // can't create an array of T

    // But, this statement is OK.
    vals = nums; // OK to assign reference to existent array
  }
}

class GenArrays {
  public static void main(String[] args) {
    Integer[] n = { 1, 2, 3, 4, 5 };

    Gen<Integer> iOb = new Gen<Integer>(50, n);

    // Can't create an array of type-specific generic references.
    // Gen<Integer>[] gens = new Gen<Integer>[10]; // Wrong!

    // This is OK.
    Gen<?>[] gens = new Gen<?>[10]; // OK
  }
}
```

As the program shows, it's valid to declare a reference to an array of type **T**, as this line does:

```
T[] vals; // OK
```

But, you cannot instantiate an array of **T**, as this commented-out line attempts:

```
// vals = new T[10]; // can't create an array of T
```

The reason you can't create an array of **T** is that there is no way for the compiler to know what type of array to actually create.

However, you can pass a reference to a type-compatible array to **Gen( )** when an object is created and assign that reference to **vals**, as the program does in this line:

```
vals = nums; // OK to assign reference to existent array
```

This works because the array passed to **Gen** has a known type, which will be the same type as **T** at the time of object creation.

Inside **main( )**, notice that you can't declare an array of references to a specific generic type. That is, this line

```
// Gen<Integer>[] gens = new Gen<Integer>[10]; // Wrong!
```

won't compile.

You *can* create an array of references to a generic type if you use a wildcard, however, as shown here:

```
Gen<?>[] gens = new Gen<?>[10]; // OK
```

This approach is better than using an array of raw types, because at least some type checking will still be enforced.

## Generic Exception Restriction

A generic class cannot extend **Throwable**. This means that you cannot create generic exception classes.

CHAPTER

# 15 Lambda Expressions

During Java's ongoing development and evolution, many features have been added since its original 1.0 release. However, two stand out because they have profoundly reshaped the language, fundamentally changing the way that code is written. The first was the addition of generics, added by JDK 5. (See Chapter 14.) The second is the *lambda expression,* which is the subject of this chapter.

Added by JDK 8, lambda expressions (and their related features) significantly enhanced Java because of two primary reasons. First, they added new syntax elements that increased the expressive power of the language. In the process, they streamlined the way that certain common constructs are implemented. Second, the addition of lambda expressions resulted in new capabilities being incorporated into the API library. Among these new capabilities are the ability to more easily take advantage of the parallel processing capabilities of multicore environments, especially as it relates to the handling of for-each style operations, and the new stream API, which supports pipeline operations on data. The addition of lambda expressions also provided the catalyst for other new Java features, including the default method (described in Chapter 9), which lets you define default behavior for an interface method, and the method reference (described here), which lets you refer to a method without executing it.

In the final analysis, in much the same way that generics reshaped Java several years ago, lambda expressions continue to reshape Java today. Simply put, lambda expressions will impact virtually all Java programmers. They truly are that important.

## Introducing Lambda Expressions

Key to understanding Java's implementation of lambda expressions are two constructs. The first is the lambda expression itself. The second is the functional interface. Let's begin with a simple definition of each.

A *lambda expression* is, essentially, an anonymous (that is, unnamed) method. However, this method is not executed on its own. Instead, it is used to implement a method defined by a functional interface. Thus, a lambda expression results in a form of anonymous class. Lambda expressions are also commonly referred to as *closures.*

A *functional interface* is an interface that contains one and only one abstract method. Normally, this method specifies the intended purpose of the interface. Thus, a functional interface typically represents a single action. For example, the standard interface **Runnable** is a functional interface because it defines only one method: **run( )**. Therefore, **run( )** defines the action of **Runnable**. Furthermore, a functional interface defines the *target type* of a lambda expression. Here is a key point: a lambda expression can be used only in a context in which its target type is specified. One other thing: a functional interface is sometimes referred to as a *SAM type,* where SAM stands for Single Abstract Method.

---

**NOTE** A functional interface may specify any public method defined by **Object**, such as **equals( )**, without affecting its "functional interface" status. The public **Object** methods are considered implicit members of a functional interface because they are automatically implemented by an instance of a functional interface.

Let's now look more closely at both lambda expressions and functional interfaces.

## Lambda Expression Fundamentals

The lambda expression introduced a new syntax element and operator into the Java language. The new operator, sometimes referred to as the *lambda operator* or the *arrow operator,* is –>. It divides a lambda expression into two parts. The left side specifies any parameters required by the lambda expression. (If no parameters are needed, an empty parameter list is used.) On the right side is the *lambda body,* which specifies the actions of the lambda expression. The –> can be verbalized as "becomes" or "goes to."

Java defines two types of lambda bodies. One consists of a single expression, and the other type consists of a block of code. We will begin with lambdas that define a single expression. Lambdas with block bodies are discussed later in this chapter.

At this point, it will be helpful to look at a few examples of lambda expressions before continuing. Let's begin with what is probably the simplest type of lambda expression you can write. It evaluates to a constant value and is shown here:

```
() -> 123.45
```

This lambda expression takes no parameters; thus, the parameter list is empty. It returns the constant value 123.45. Therefore, it is similar to the following method:

```
double myMeth() { return 123.45; }
```

Of course, the method defined by a lambda expression does not have a name.

A slightly more interesting lambda expression is shown here:

```
() -> Math.random() * 100
```

This lambda expression obtains a pseudo-random value from **Math.random( )**, multiplies it by 100, and returns the result. It, too, does not require a parameter.

When a lambda expression requires a parameter, it is specified in the parameter list on the left side of the lambda operator. Here is a simple example:

```
(n) -> (n % 2)==0
```

This lambda expression returns **true** if the value of parameter **n** is even. Although it is possible to explicitly specify the type of a parameter, such as **n** in this case, often you won't need to do so because in many cases its type can be inferred. Like a named method, a lambda expression can specify as many parameters as needed.



## Functional Interfaces

As stated, a functional interface is an interface that specifies only one abstract method. If you have been programming in Java for some time, you might at first think that all interface methods are implicitly abstract. Although this was true prior to JDK 8, the situation has changed. As explained in Chapter 9, beginning with JDK 8, it is possible to specify a default implementation for a method declared in an interface. Private and static interface methods also supply an implementation. As a result, today, an interface method is abstract only if it does not specify an implementation. Because non-default, non-static, non-private interface methods are implicitly abstract, there is no need to use the **abstract** modifier (although you can specify it, if you like).

Here is an example of a functional interface:

```
interface MyNumber {
  double getValue();
}
```

In this case, the method **getValue( )** is implicitly abstract, and it is the only method defined by **MyNumber**. Thus, **MyNumber** is a functional interface, and its function is defined by **getValue( )**.

As mentioned earlier, a lambda expression is not executed on its own. Rather, it forms the implementation of the abstract method defined by the functional interface that specifies its target type. As a result, a lambda expression can be specified only in a context in which a target type is defined. One of these contexts is created when a lambda expression is assigned to a functional interface reference. Other target type contexts include variable initialization, **return** statements, and method arguments, to name a few.

Let's work through an example that shows how a lambda expression can be used in an assignment context. First, a reference to the functional interface **MyNumber** is declared:

```
// Create a reference to a MyNumber instance.
MyNumber myNum;
```

Next, a lambda expression is assigned to that interface reference:

```
// Use a lambda in an assignment context.
myNum = () -> 123.45;
```

When a lambda expression occurs in a target type context, an instance of a class is automatically created that implements the functional interface, with the lambda expression defining the behavior of the abstract method declared by the functional interface. When that method is called through the target, the lambda expression is executed. Thus, a lambda expression gives us a way to transform a code segment into an object.

In the preceding example, the lambda expression becomes the implementation for the **getValue( )** method. As a result, the following displays the value 123.45:

```
// Call getValue(), which is implemented by the previously assigned
// lambda expression.
System.out.println(myNum.getValue());
```

Because the lambda expression assigned to **myNum** returns the value 123.45, that is the value obtained when **getValue( )** is called.

In order for a lambda expression to be used in a target type context, the type of the abstract method and the type of the lambda expression must be compatible. For example, if the abstract method specifies two **int** parameters, then the lambda must specify two parameters whose type either is explicitly **int** or can be implicitly inferred as **int** by the context. In general, the type and number of the lambda expression's parameters must be compatible with the method's parameters; the return types must be compatible; and any exceptions thrown by the lambda expression must be acceptable to the method.

## Some Lambda Expression Examples

With the preceding discussion in mind, let's look at some simple examples that illustrate the basic lambda expression concepts. The first example puts together the pieces shown in the foregoing section.

```
// Demonstrate a simple lambda expression.

// A functional interface.
interface MyNumber {
  double getValue();
}

class LambdaDemo {
  public static void main(String[] args)
  {
    MyNumber myNum;  // declare an interface reference

    // Here, the lambda expression is simply a constant expression.
    // When it is assigned to myNum, a class instance is
    // constructed in which the lambda expression implements
    // the getValue() method in MyNumber.
    myNum = () -> 123.45;

    // Call getValue(), which is provided by the previously assigned
    // lambda expression.
    System.out.println("A fixed value: " + myNum.getValue());

    // Here, a more complex expression is used.
    myNum = () -> Math.random() * 100;
```

```
    // These call the lambda expression in the previous line.
    System.out.println("A random value: " + myNum.getValue());
    System.out.println("Another random value: " + myNum.getValue());

    // A lambda expression must be compatible with the method
    // defined by the functional interface. Therefore, this won't work:
//  myNum = () -> "123.03"; // Error!
  }
}
```

Sample output from the program is shown here:

```
A fixed value: 123.45
A random value: 88.90663650412304
Another random value: 53.00582701784129
```

As mentioned, the lambda expression must be compatible with the abstract method that it is intended to implement. For this reason, the commented-out line at the end of the preceding program is illegal because a value of type **String** is not compatible with **double**, which is the return type required by **getValue( )**.

The next example shows the use of a parameter with a lambda expression:

```
// Demonstrate a lambda expression that takes a parameter.

// Another functional interface.
interface NumericTest {
 boolean test(int n);
}

class LambdaDemo2 {
  public static void main(String[] args)
  {
    // A lambda expression that tests if a number is even.
    NumericTest isEven = (n) -> (n % 2)==0;

    if(isEven.test(10)) System.out.println("10 is even");
    if(!isEven.test(9)) System.out.println("9 is not even");

    // Now, use a lambda expression that tests if a number
    // is non-negative.
    NumericTest isNonNeg = (n) -> n >= 0;

    if(isNonNeg.test(1)) System.out.println("1 is non-negative");
    if(!isNonNeg.test(-1)) System.out.println("-1 is negative");
  }
}
```

The output from this program is shown here:

```
10 is even
9 is not even
1 is non-negative
-1 is negative
```

This program demonstrates a key fact about lambda expressions that warrants close examination. Pay special attention to the lambda expression that performs the test for evenness. It is shown again here:

```
(n) -> (n % 2)==0
```

Notice that the type of **n** is not specified. Rather, its type is inferred from the context. In this case, its type is inferred from the parameter type of **test( )** as defined by the **NumericTest** interface, which is **int**. It is also possible to explicitly specify the type of a parameter in a lambda expression. For example, this is also a valid way to write the preceding:

```
(int n) -> (n % 2)==0
```

Here, **n** is explicitly specified as **int**. Usually it is not necessary to explicitly specify the type, but you can in those situations that require it. Beginning with JDK 11, you can also use **var** to explicitly indicate local variable type inference for a lambda expression parameter.

This program demonstrates another important point about lambda expressions: A functional interface reference can be used to execute any lambda expression that is compatible with it. Notice that the program defines two different lambda expressions that are compatible with the **test( )** method of the functional interface **NumericTest**. The first, called **isEven**, determines if a value is even. The second, called **isNonNeg**, checks if a value is non-negative. In each case, the value of the parameter **n** is tested. Because each lambda expression is compatible with **test( )**, each can be executed through a **NumericTest** reference.

One other point before moving on: When a lambda expression has only one parameter, it is not necessary to surround the parameter name with parentheses when it is specified on the left side of the lambda operator. For example, this is also a valid way to write the lambda expression used in the program:

```
n -> (n % 2)==0
```

For consistency, this book will surround all lambda expression parameter lists with parentheses, even those containing only one parameter. Of course, you are free to adopt a different style.

The next program demonstrates a lambda expression that takes two parameters. In this case, the lambda expression tests if one number is a factor of another.

```
// Demonstrate a lambda expression that takes two parameters.

interface NumericTest2 {
  boolean test(int n, int d);
}

class LambdaDemo3 {
  public static void main(String[] args)
  {
    // This lambda expression determines if one number is
    // a factor of another.
    NumericTest2 isFactor = (n, d) -> (n % d) == 0;
```

```
    if(isFactor.test(10, 2))
      System.out.println("2 is a factor of 10");

    if(!isFactor.test(10, 3))
      System.out.println("3 is not a factor of 10");
  }
}
```

The output is shown here:

```
2 is a factor of 10
3 is not a factor of 10
```

In this program, the functional interface **NumericTest2** defines the **test( )** method:

```
boolean test(int n, int d);
```

In this version, **test( )** specifies two parameters. Thus, for a lambda expression to be compatible with **test( )**, the lambda expression must also specify two parameters. Notice how they are specified:

```
(n, d) -> (n % d) == 0
```

The two parameters, **n** and **d**, are specified in the parameter list, separated by commas. This example can be generalized. Whenever more than one parameter is required, the parameters are specified, separated by commas, in a parenthesized list on the left side of the lambda operator.

Here is an important point about multiple parameters in a lambda expression: If you need to explicitly declare the type of a parameter, then all of the parameters must have declared types. For example, this is legal:

```
(int n, int d) -> (n % d) == 0
```

But this is not:

```
(int n, d) -> (n % d) == 0
```

## Block Lambda Expressions

The body of the lambdas shown in the preceding examples consist of a single expression. These types of lambda bodies are referred to as *expression bodies*, and lambdas that have expression bodies are sometimes called *expression lambdas*. In an expression body, the code on the right side of the lambda operator must consist of a single expression. While expression lambdas are quite useful, sometimes the situation will require more than a single expression. To handle such cases, Java supports a second type of lambda expression in which the code on the right side of the lambda operator consists of a block of code that can contain more than one statement. This type of lambda body is called a *block body*. Lambdas that have block bodies are sometimes referred to as *block lambdas*.

A block lambda expands the types of operations that can be handled within a lambda expression because it allows the body of the lambda to contain multiple statements. For example, in a block lambda you can declare variables, use loops, specify **if** and **switch** statements, create nested blocks, and so on. A block lambda is easy to create. Simply enclose the body within braces as you would any other block of statements.

Aside from allowing multiple statements, block lambdas are used much like the expression lambdas just discussed. One key difference, however, is that you must explicitly use a **return** statement to return a value. This is necessary because a block lambda body does not represent a single expression.

Here is an example that uses a block lambda to compute and return the factorial of an **int** value:

```
// A block lambda that computes the factorial of an int value.

interface NumericFunc {
  int func(int n);
}

class BlockLambdaDemo {
  public static void main(String[] args)
  {

    // This block lambda computes the factorial of an int value.
    NumericFunc factorial = (n) ->  {
      int result = 1;

      for(int i=1; i <= n; i++)
        result = i * result;

      return result;
    };

    System.out.println("The factorial of 3 is " + factorial.func(3));
    System.out.println("The factorial of 5 is " + factorial.func(5));
  }
}
```

The output is shown here:

```
The factorial of 3 is 6
The factorial of 5 is 120
```

In the program, notice that the block lambda declares a variable called **result**, uses a **for** loop, and has a **return** statement. These are legal inside a block lambda body. In essence, the block body of a lambda is similar to a method body. One other point: When a **return** statement occurs within a lambda expression, it simply causes a return from the lambda. It does not cause an enclosing method to return.

Another example of a block lambda is shown in the following program. It reverses the characters in a string.

```
// A block lambda that reverses the characters in a string.

interface StringFunc {
  String func(String n);
}

class BlockLambdaDemo2 {
  public static void main(String[] args)
  {

    // This block lambda reverses the characters in a string.
    StringFunc reverse = (str) ->  {
      String result = "";
      int i;

      for(i = str.length()-1; i >= 0; i--)
        result += str.charAt(i);

      return result;
    };

    System.out.println("Lambda reversed is " +
                       reverse.func("Lambda"));
    System.out.println("Expression reversed is " +
                       reverse.func("Expression"));
  }
}
```

The output is shown here:

```
Lambda reversed is adbmaL
Expression reversed is noisserpxE
```

In this example, the functional interface **StringFunc** declares the **func( )** method. This method takes a parameter of type **String** and has a return type of **String**. Thus, in the **reverse** lambda expression, the type of **str** is inferred to be **String**. Notice that the **charAt( )** method is called on **str**. This is legal because of the inference that **str** is of type **String**.

## Generic Functional Interfaces

A lambda expression itself cannot specify type parameters. Thus, a lambda expression cannot be generic. (Of course, because of type inference, all lambda expressions exhibit some "generic-like" qualities.) However, the functional interface associated with a lambda expression can be generic. In this case, the target type of the lambda expression is determined, in part, by the type argument or arguments specified when a functional interface reference is declared.

To understand the value of generic functional interfaces, consider this: The two examples in the previous section used two different functional interfaces, one called **NumericFunc** and the other called **StringFunc**. However, both defined a method called **func( )** that took one parameter and returned a result. In the first case, the type of the parameter and return type was **int**. In the second case, the parameter and return type was **String**. Thus, the only difference between the two methods was the type of data they required. Instead of having two functional interfaces whose methods differ only in their data types, it is possible to declare one generic interface that can be used to handle both circumstances. The following program shows this approach:

```
// Use a generic functional interface with lambda expressions.

// A generic functional interface.
interface SomeFunc<T> {
  T func(T t);
}

class GenericFunctionalInterfaceDemo {
  public static void main(String[] args)
  {

    // Use a String-based version of SomeFunc.
    SomeFunc<String> reverse = (str) ->  {
      String result = "";
      int i;

      for(i = str.length()-1; i >= 0; i--)
        result += str.charAt(i);

      return result;
    };

    System.out.println("Lambda reversed is " +
                       reverse.func("Lambda"));
    System.out.println("Expression reversed is " +
                       reverse.func("Expression"));

    // Now, use an Integer-based version of SomeFunc.
    SomeFunc<Integer> factorial = (n) ->  {
      int result = 1;

      for(int i=1; i <= n; i++)
        result = i * result;

      return result;
    };

    System.out.println("The factorial of 3 is " + factorial.func(3));
    System.out.println("The factorial of 5 is " + factorial.func(5));
  }
}
```

The output is shown here:

```
Lambda reversed is adbmaL
Expression reversed is noisserpxE
The factorial of 3 is 6
The factorial of 5 is 120
```

In the program, the generic functional interface **SomeFunc** is declared as shown here:

```
interface SomeFunc<T> {
  T func(T t);
}
```

Here, **T** specifies both the return type and the parameter type of **func( )**. This means that it is compatible with any lambda expression that takes one parameter and returns a value of the same type.

The **SomeFunc** interface is used to provide a reference to two different types of lambdas. The first uses type **String**. The second uses type **Integer**. Thus, the same functional interface can be used to refer to the **reverse** lambda and the **factorial** lambda. Only the type argument passed to **SomeFunc** differs.

## Passing Lambda Expressions as Arguments

As explained earlier, a lambda expression can be used in any context that provides a target type. One of these is when a lambda expression is passed as an argument. In fact, passing a lambda expression as an argument is a common use of lambdas. Moreover, it is a very powerful use because it gives you a way to pass executable code as an argument to a method. This greatly enhances the expressive power of Java.

To pass a lambda expression as an argument, the type of the parameter receiving the lambda expression argument must be of a functional interface type compatible with the lambda. Although using a lambda expression as an argument is straightforward, it is still helpful to see it in action. The following program demonstrates the process:

```
// Use lambda expressions as an argument to a method.

interface StringFunc {
  String func(String n);
}

class LambdasAsArgumentsDemo {

  // This method has a functional interface as the type of
  // its first parameter. Thus, it can be passed a reference to
  // any instance of that interface, including the instance created
  // by a lambda expression.
  // The second parameter specifies the string to operate on.
  static String stringOp(StringFunc sf, String s) {
    return sf.func(s);
  }
```

```
public static void main(String[] args)
{
  String inStr = "Lambdas add power to Java";
  String outStr;

  System.out.println("Here is input string: " + inStr);

  // Here, a simple expression lambda that uppercases a string
  // is passed to stringOp( ).
  outStr = stringOp((str) -> str.toUpperCase(), inStr);
  System.out.println("The string in uppercase: " + outStr);

  // This passes a block lambda that removes spaces.
  outStr = stringOp((str) -> {
                   String result = "";
                   int i;

                   for(i = 0; i < str.length(); i++)
                   if(str.charAt(i) != ' ')
                     result += str.charAt(i);

                   return result;
                 }, inStr);

  System.out.println("The string with spaces removed: " + outStr);


  // Of course, it is also possible to pass a StringFunc instance
  // created by an earlier lambda expression. For example,
  // after this declaration executes, reverse refers to an
  // instance of StringFunc.
  StringFunc reverse = (str) -> {
    String result = "";
    int i;

    for(i = str.length()-1; i >= 0; i--)
      result += str.charAt(i);

    return result;
  };

  // Now, reverse can be passed as the first parameter to stringOp()
  // since it refers to a StringFunc object.
  System.out.println("The string reversed: " +
                   stringOp(reverse, inStr));
 }
}
```

The output is shown here:

```
Here is input string: Lambdas add power to Java
The string in uppercase: LAMBDAS ADD POWER TO JAVA
The string with spaces removed: LambdasaddpowertoJava
The string reversed: avaJ ot rewop dda sadbmaL
```

In the program, first notice the **stringOp( )** method. It has two parameters. The first is of type **StringFunc**, which is a functional interface. Thus, this parameter can receive a reference to any instance of **StringFunc**, including one created by a lambda expression. The second argument of **stringOp( )** is of type **String**, and this is the string operated on.

Next, notice the first call to **stringOp( )**, shown again here:

```
outStr = stringOp((str) -> str.toUpperCase(), inStr);
```

Here, a simple expression lambda is passed as an argument. When this occurs, an instance of the functional interface **StringFunc** is created and a reference to that object is passed to the first parameter of **stringOp( )**. Thus, the lambda code, embedded in a class instance, is passed to the method. The target type context is determined by the type of parameter. Because the lambda expression is compatible with that type, the call is valid. Embedding simple lambdas, such as the one just shown, inside a method call is often a convenient technique—especially when the lambda expression is intended for a single use.

Next, the program passes a block lambda to **stringOp( )**. This lambda removes spaces from a string. It is shown again here:

```
outStr = stringOp((str) -> {
                   String result = "";
                   int i;

                   for(i = 0; i < str.length(); i++)
                   if(str.charAt(i) != ' ')
                     result += str.charAt(i);

                   return result;
                 }, inStr);
```

Although this uses a block lambda, the process of passing the lambda expression is the same as just described for the simple expression lambda. In this case, however, some programmers will find the syntax a bit awkward.

When a block lambda seems overly long to embed in a method call, it is an easy matter to assign that lambda to a functional interface variable, as the previous examples have done. Then, you can simply pass that reference to the method. This technique is shown at the end of the program. There, a block lambda is defined that reverses a string. This lambda is assigned to **reverse**, which is a reference to a **StringFunc** instance. Thus, **reverse** can be used as an argument to the first parameter of **stringOp( )**. The program then calls **stringOp( )**, passing in **reverse** and the string on which to operate. Because the instance obtained by the evaluation of each lambda expression is an implementation of **StringFunc**, each can be used as the first parameter to **stringOp( )**.

One last point: In addition to variable initialization, assignment, and argument passing, the following also constitute target type contexts: casts, the **?** operator, array initializers, **return** statements, and lambda expressions themselves.

## Lambda Expressions and Exceptions

A lambda expression can throw an exception. However, it if throws a checked exception, then that exception must be compatible with the exception(s) listed in the **throws** clause of the abstract method in the functional interface. Here is an example that illustrates this fact. It computes the average of an array of **double** values. If a zero-length array is passed, however, it throws the custom exception **EmptyArrayException**. As the example shows, this exception is listed in the **throws** clause of **func( )** declared inside the **DoubleNumericArrayFunc** functional interface.

```
// Throw an exception from a lambda expression.

interface DoubleNumericArrayFunc {
  double func(double[] n) throws EmptyArrayException;
}

class EmptyArrayException extends Exception {
  EmptyArrayException() {
    super("Array Empty");
  }
}

class LambdaExceptionDemo {

  public static void main(String[] args) throws EmptyArrayException
  {
    double[] values = { 1.0, 2.0, 3.0, 4.0 };

    // This block lambda computes the average of an array of doubles.
    DoubleNumericArrayFunc average = (n) ->  {
      double sum = 0;

      if(n.length == 0)
        throw new EmptyArrayException();

      for(int i=0; i < n.length; i++)
        sum += n[i];

      return sum / n.length;
    };

    System.out.println("The average is " + average.func(values));

    // This causes an exception to be thrown.
    System.out.println("The average is " + average.func(new double[0]));
  }
}
```

The first call to **average.func( )** returns the value 2.5. The second call, which passes a zero-length array, causes an **EmptyArrayException** to be thrown. Remember, the inclusion of the **throws** clause in **func( )** is necessary. Without it, the program will not compile because the lambda expression will no longer be compatible with **func( )**.

This example demonstrates another important point about lambda expressions. Notice that the parameter specified by **func( )** in the functional interface **DoubleNumericArrayFunc** is an array. However, the parameter to the lambda expression is simply **n**, rather than **n**[ ]. Remember, the type of a lambda expression parameter will be inferred from the target context. In this case, the target context is **double**[ ], so the type of **n** will be **double**[ ]. It is not necessary (or legal) to specify it as **n**[ ]. It would be legal to explicitly declare it as **double**[ ] **n**, but doing so gains nothing in this case.

## Lambda Expressions and Variable Capture

Variables defined by the enclosing scope of a lambda expression are accessible within the lambda expression. For example, a lambda expression can use an instance or **static** variable defined by its enclosing class. A lambda expression also has access to **this** (both explicitly and implicitly), which refers to the invoking instance of the lambda expression's enclosing class. Thus, a lambda expression can obtain or set the value of an instance or **static** variable and call a method defined by its enclosing class.

However, when a lambda expression uses a local variable from its enclosing scope, a special situation is created that is referred to as a *variable capture*. In this case, a lambda expression may only use local variables that are *effectively final*. An effectively final variable is one whose value does not change after it is first assigned. There is no need to explicitly declare such a variable as **final**, although doing so would not be an error. (The **this** parameter of an enclosing scope is automatically effectively final, and lambda expressions do not have a **this** of their own.)

It is important to understand that a local variable of the enclosing scope cannot be modified by the lambda expression. Doing so would remove its effectively final status, thus rendering it illegal for capture.

The following program illustrates the difference between effectively final and mutable local variables:

```
// An example of capturing a local variable from the enclosing scope.

interface MyFunc {
  int func(int n);
}

class VarCapture {
  public static void main(String[] args)
  {
    // A local variable that can be captured.
    int num = 10;

    MyFunc myLambda = (n) -> {
      // This use of num is OK. It does not modify num.
      int v = num + n;

      // However, the following is illegal because it attempts
      // to modify the value of num.
//    num++;
```

```
      return v;
    };

    // The following line would also cause an error, because
    // it would remove the effectively final status from num.
//  num = 9;
  }
}
```

As the comments indicate, **num** is effectively final and can, therefore, be used inside **myLambda**. However, if **num** were to be modified, either inside the lambda or outside of it, **num** would lose its effectively final status. This would cause an error, and the program would not compile.

It is important to emphasize that a lambda expression can use and modify an instance variable from its invoking class. It just can't use a local variable of its enclosing scope unless that variable is effectively final.

# Method References

There is an important feature related to lambda expressions called the *method reference.* A method reference provides a way to refer to a method without executing it. It relates to lambda expressions because it, too, requires a target type context that consists of a compatible functional interface. When evaluated, a method reference also creates an instance of the functional interface.

There are different types of method references. We will begin with method references to **static** methods.

## Method References to static Methods

To create a **static** method reference, use this general syntax:

*ClassName::methodName*

Notice that the class name is separated from the method name by a double colon. The :: is a separator that was added to Java by JDK 8 expressly for this purpose. This method reference can be used anywhere in which it is compatible with its target type.

The following program demonstrates a **static** method reference:

```
// Demonstrate a method reference for a static method.

// A functional interface for string operations.
interface StringFunc {
  String func(String n);
}

// This class defines a static method called strReverse().
class MyStringOps {
  // A static method that reverses a string.
  static String strReverse(String str) {
```

```
    String result = "";
    int i;

    for(i = str.length()-1; i >= 0; i--)
      result += str.charAt(i);

    return result;
  }
}

class MethodRefDemo {

  // This method has a functional interface as the type of
  // its first parameter. Thus, it can be passed any instance
  // of that interface, including a method reference.
  static String stringOp(StringFunc sf, String s) {
    return sf.func(s);
  }

  public static void main(String[] args)
  {
    String inStr = "Lambdas add power to Java";
    String outStr;

    // Here, a method reference to strReverse is passed to stringOp().
    outStr = stringOp(MyStringOps::strReverse, inStr);

    System.out.println("Original string: " + inStr);
    System.out.println("String reversed: " + outStr);
  }
}
```

The output is shown here:

```
Original string: Lambdas add power to Java
String reversed: avaJ ot rewop dda sadbmaL
```

In the program, pay special attention to this line:

```
outStr = stringOp(MyStringOps::strReverse, inStr);
```

Here, a reference to the **static** method **strReverse( )**, declared inside **MyStringOps**, is passed as the first argument to **stringOp( )**. This works because **strReverse** is compatible with the **StringFunc** functional interface. Thus, the expression **MyStringOps::strReverse** evaluates to a reference to an object in which **strReverse** provides the implementation of **func( )** in **StringFunc**.

## Method References to Instance Methods

To pass a reference to an instance method on a specific object, use this basic syntax:

*objRef::methodName*

As you can see, the syntax is similar to that used for a **static** method, except that an object reference is used instead of a class name. Here is the previous program rewritten to use an instance method reference:

```
// Demonstrate a method reference to an instance method

// A functional interface for string operations.
interface StringFunc {
  String func(String n);
}

// Now, this class defines an instance method called strReverse().
class MyStringOps {
  String strReverse(String str) {
    String result = "";
    int i;

    for(i = str.length()-1; i >= 0; i--)
      result += str.charAt(i);

    return result;
  }
}

class MethodRefDemo2 {

  // This method has a functional interface as the type of
  // its first parameter. Thus, it can be passed any instance
  // of that interface, including method references.
  static String stringOp(StringFunc sf, String s) {
    return sf.func(s);
  }

  public static void main(String[] args)
  {
    String inStr = "Lambdas add power to Java";
    String outStr;

    // Create a MyStringOps object.
    MyStringOps strOps = new MyStringOps( );

    // Now, a method reference to the instance method strReverse
    // is passed to stringOp().
    outStr = stringOp(strOps::strReverse, inStr);

    System.out.println("Original string: " + inStr);
    System.out.println("String reversed: " + outStr);
  }
}
```

This program produces the same output as the previous version.

In the program, notice that **strReverse( )** is now an instance method of **MyStringOps**. Inside **main( )**, an instance of **MyStringOps** called **strOps** is created. This instance is used to create the method reference to **strReverse** in the call to **stringOp**, as shown again here:

```
outStr = stringOp(strOps::strReverse, inStr);
```

In this example, **strReverse( )** is called on the **strOps** object.

It is also possible to handle a situation in which you want to specify an instance method that can be used with any object of a given class—not just a specified object. In this case, you will create a method reference as shown here:

*ClassName::instanceMethodName*

Here, the name of the class is used instead of a specific object, even though an instance method is specified. With this form, the first parameter of the functional interface matches the invoking object and the second parameter matches the parameter specified by the method. Here is an example. It defines a method called **counter( )** that counts the number of objects in an array that satisfy the condition defined by the **func( )** method of the **MyFunc** functional interface. In this case, it counts instances of the **HighTemp** class.

```
// Use an instance method reference with different objects.

// A functional interface that takes two reference arguments
// and returns a boolean result.
interface MyFunc<T> {
  boolean func(T v1, T v2);
}

// A class that stores the temperature high for a day.
class HighTemp {
  private int hTemp;

  HighTemp(int ht) { hTemp = ht; }

  // Return true if the invoking HighTemp object has the same
  // temperature as ht2.
  boolean sameTemp(HighTemp ht2) {
    return hTemp == ht2.hTemp;
  }

  // Return true if the invoking HighTemp object has a temperature
  // that is less than ht2.
  boolean lessThanTemp(HighTemp ht2) {
    return hTemp < ht2.hTemp;
  }
}

class InstanceMethWithObjectRefDemo {

  // A method that returns the number of occurrences
  // of an object for which some criteria, as specified by
  // the MyFunc parameter, is true.
  static <T> int counter(T[] vals, MyFunc<T> f, T v) {
```

```
    int count = 0;

    for(int i=0; i < vals.length; i++)
      if(f.func(vals[i], v)) count++;

    return count;
  }

  public static void main(String[] args)
  {
    int count;

    // Create an array of HighTemp objects.
    HighTemp[] weekDayHighs = { new HighTemp(89), new HighTemp(82),
                                new HighTemp(90), new HighTemp(89),
                                new HighTemp(89), new HighTemp(91),
                                new HighTemp(84), new HighTemp(83) };

    // Use counter() with arrays of the class HighTemp.
    // Notice that a reference to the instance method
    // sameTemp() is passed as the second argument.
    count = counter(weekDayHighs, HighTemp::sameTemp,
                    new HighTemp(89));
    System.out.println(count + " days had a high of 89");

    // Now, create and use another array of HighTemp objects.
    HighTemp[] weekDayHighs2 = { new HighTemp(32), new HighTemp(12),
                                new HighTemp(24), new HighTemp(19),
                                new HighTemp(18), new HighTemp(12),
                                new HighTemp(-1), new HighTemp(13) };

    count = counter(weekDayHighs2, HighTemp::sameTemp,
                      new HighTemp(12));
    System.out.println(count + " days had a high of 12");


    // Now, use lessThanTemp() to find days when temperature was less
    // than a specified value.
    count = counter(weekDayHighs, HighTemp::lessThanTemp,
                      new HighTemp(89));
    System.out.println(count + " days had a high less than 89");

    count = counter(weekDayHighs2, HighTemp::lessThanTemp,
                      new HighTemp(19));
    System.out.println(count + " days had a high of less than 19");
  }
}
```

The output is shown here:

```
3 days had a high of 89
2 days had a high of 12
3 days had a high less than 89
5 days had a high of less than 19
```

In the program, notice that **HighTemp** has two instance methods: **sameTemp( )** and **lessThanTemp( )**. The first returns **true** if two **HighTemp** objects contain the same temperature. The second returns **true** if the temperature of the invoking object is less than that of the passed object. Each method has a parameter of type **HighTemp**, and each method returns a **boolean** result. Thus, each is compatible with the **MyFunc** functional interface because the invoking object type can be mapped to the first parameter of **func( )** and the argument mapped to **func( )**'s second parameter. Thus, when the expression

```
HighTemp::sameTemp
```

is passed to the **counter( )** method, an instance of the functional interface **MyFunc** is created in which the parameter type of the first parameter is that of the invoking object of the instance method, which is **HighTemp**. The type of the second parameter is also **HighTemp** because that is the type of the parameter to **sameTemp( )**. The same is true for the **lessThanTemp( )** method.

One other point: you can refer to the superclass version of a method by use of **super**, as shown here:

super::*name*

The name of the method is specified by *name*. Another form is

*typeName*.**super**::*name*

where *typeName* refers to an enclosing class or super interface.

## Method References with Generics

You can use method references with generic classes and/or generic methods. For example, consider the following program:

```
// Demonstrate a method reference to a generic method
// declared inside a non-generic class.

// A functional interface that operates on an array
// and a value, and returns an int result.
interface MyFunc<T> {
  int func(T[] vals, T v);
}

// This class defines a method called countMatching() that
// returns the number of items in an array that are equal
// to a specified value. Notice that countMatching()
// is generic, but MyArrayOps is not.
class MyArrayOps {
  static <T> int countMatching(T[] vals, T v) {
    int count = 0;

    for(int i=0; i < vals.length; i++)
      if(vals[i] == v) count++;

      return count;
  }
}
```

```
class GenericMethodRefDemo {

  // This method has the MyFunc functional interface as the
  // type of its first parameter. The other two parameters
  // receive an array and a value, both of type T.
  static <T> int myOp(MyFunc<T> f, T[] vals, T v) {
    return f.func(vals, v);
  }

  public static void main(String[] args)
  {
    Integer[] vals = { 1, 2, 3, 4, 2, 3, 4, 4, 5 };
    String[] strs = { "One", "Two", "Three", "Two" };
    int count;

    count = myOp(MyArrayOps::<Integer>countMatching, vals, 4);
    System.out.println("vals contains " + count + " 4s");

    count = myOp(MyArrayOps::<String>countMatching, strs, "Two");
    System.out.println("strs contains " + count + " Twos");
  }
}
```

The output is shown here:

```
vals contains 3 4s
strs contains 2 Twos
```

In the program, **MyArrayOps** is a non-generic class that contains a generic method called **countMatching( )**. The method returns a count of the elements in an array that match a specified value. Notice how the generic type argument is specified. For example, its first call in **main( )**, shown here:

```
count = myOp(MyArrayOps::<Integer>countMatching, vals, 4);
```

passes the type argument **Integer**. Notice that it occurs after the ::. This syntax can be generalized: When a generic method is specified as a method reference, its type argument comes after the :: and before the method name. It is important to point out, however, that explicitly specifying the type argument is not required in this situation (and many others) because the type argument would have been automatically inferred. In cases in which a generic class is specified, the type argument follows the class name and precedes the ::.

Although the preceding examples show the mechanics of using method references, they don't show their real benefits. One place method references can be quite useful is in conjunction with the Collections Framework, which is described later in Chapter 20. However, for completeness, a short, but effective, example that uses a method reference to help determine the largest element in a collection is included here. (If you are unfamiliar with the Collections Framework, return to this example after you have worked through Chapter 20.)

One way to find the largest element in a collection is to use the **max( )** method defined by the **Collections** class. For the version of **max( )** used here, you must pass a reference to the collection and an instance of an object that implements the **Comparator<T>** interface. This interface specifies how two objects are compared. It defines only one abstract method, called **compare( )**, that takes two arguments, each the type of the objects being compared. It must return greater than zero if the first argument is greater than the second, zero if the two arguments are equal, and less than zero if the first object is less than the second.

In the past, to use **max( )** with user-defined objects, an instance of **Comparator<T>** had to be obtained by first explicitly implementing it by a class, and then creating an instance of that class. This instance was then passed as the comparator to **max( )**. Beginning with JDK 8, it is now possible to simply pass a reference to a comparison method to **max( )** because doing so automatically implements the comparator. The following simple example shows the process by creating an **ArrayList** of **MyClass** objects and then finding the one in the list that has the highest value (as defined by the comparison method):

```
// Use a method reference to help find the maximum value in a collection.
import java.util.*;

class MyClass {
  private int val;

  MyClass(int v) { val = v; }

  int getVal() { return val; }
}

class UseMethodRef {
  // A compare() method compatible with the one defined by Comparator<T>.
  static int compareMC(MyClass a, MyClass b) {
    return a.getVal() - b.getVal();
  }

  public static void main(String[] args)
  {
    ArrayList<MyClass> al = new ArrayList<MyClass>();

    al.add(new MyClass(1));
    al.add(new MyClass(4));
    al.add(new MyClass(2));
    al.add(new MyClass(9));
    al.add(new MyClass(3));
    al.add(new MyClass(7));

    // Find the maximum value in al using the compareMC() method.
    MyClass maxValObj = Collections.max(al, UseMethodRef::compareMC);

    System.out.println("Maximum value is: " + maxValObj.getVal());
  }
}
```

The output is shown here:

```
Maximum value is: 9
```

In the program, notice that **MyClass** neither defines any comparison method of its own, nor does it implement **Comparator**. However, the maximum value of a list of **MyClass** items can still be obtained by calling **max( )** because **UseMethodRef** defines the static method **compareMC( )**, which is compatible with the **compare( )** method defined by **Comparator**. Therefore, there is no need to explicitly implement and create an instance of **Comparator**.

## Constructor References

Similar to the way that you can create references to methods, you can create references to constructors. Here is the general form of the syntax that you will use:

*classname*::new

This reference can be assigned to any functional interface reference that defines a method compatible with the constructor. Here is a simple example:

```
// Demonstrate a Constructor reference.

// MyFunc is a functional interface whose method returns
// a MyClass reference.
interface MyFunc {
   MyClass func(int n);
}

class MyClass {
  private int val;

  // This constructor takes an argument.
  MyClass(int v) { val = v; }

  // This is the default constructor.
  MyClass() { val = 0; }

  // ...

  int getVal() { return val; };
}

class ConstructorRefDemo {
  public static void main(String[] args)
  {
    // Create a reference to the MyClass constructor.
    // Because func() in MyFunc takes an argument, new
    // refers to the parameterized constructor in MyClass,
    // not the default constructor.
    MyFunc myClassCons = MyClass::new;

    // Create an instance of MyClass via that constructor reference.
    MyClass mc = myClassCons.func(100);
```

```
    // Use the instance of MyClass just created.
    System.out.println("val in mc is " + mc.getVal( ));
  }
}
```

The output is shown here:

```
val in mc is 100
```

In the program, notice that the **func( )** method of **MyFunc** returns a reference of type **MyClass** and has an **int** parameter. Next, notice that **MyClass** defines two constructors. The first specifies a parameter of type **int**. The second is the default, parameterless constructor. Now, examine the following line:

```
MyFunc myClassCons = MyClass::new;
```

Here, the expression **MyClass::new** creates a constructor reference to a **MyClass** constructor. In this case, because **MyFunc**'s **func( )** method takes an **int** parameter, the constructor being referred to is **MyClass(int v)** because it is the one that matches. Also notice that the reference to this constructor is assigned to a **MyFunc** reference called **myClassCons**. After this statement executes, **myClassCons** can be used to create an instance of **MyClass**, as this line shows:

```
MyClass mc = myClassCons.func(100);
```

In essence, **myClassCons** has become another way to call **MyClass(int v)**.

Constructor references to generic classes are created in the same fashion. The only difference is that the type argument can be specified. This works the same as it does for using a generic class to create a method reference: simply specify the type argument after the class name. The following illustrates this by modifying the previous example so that **MyFunc** and **MyClass** are generic:

```
// Demonstrate a constructor reference with a generic class.

// MyFunc is now a generic functional interface.
interface MyFunc<T> {
   MyClass<T> func(T n);
}

class MyClass<T> {
  private T val;

  // A constructor that takes an argument.
  MyClass(T v) { val = v; }

  // This is the default constructor.
  MyClass( ) { val = null;  }

  // ...
```

```
  T getVal() { return val; };
}

class ConstructorRefDemo2 {

  public static void main(String[] args)
  {
    // Create a reference to the MyClass<T> constructor.
    MyFunc<Integer> myClassCons = MyClass<Integer>::new;

    // Create an instance of MyClass<T> via that constructor reference.
    MyClass<Integer> mc = myClassCons.func(100);

    // Use the instance of MyClass<T> just created.
    System.out.println("val in mc is " + mc.getVal( ));
  }
}
```

This program produces the same output as the previous version. The difference is that now both **MyFunc** and **MyClass** are generic. Thus, the sequence that creates a constructor reference can include a type argument (although one is not always needed), as shown here:

```
MyFunc<Integer> myClassCons = MyClass<Integer>::new;
```

Because the type argument **Integer** has already been specified when **myClassCons** is created, it can be used to create a **MyClass<Integer>** object, as the next line shows:

```
MyClass<Integer> mc = myClassCons.func(100);
```

Although the preceding examples demonstrate the mechanics of using a constructor reference, no one would use a constructor reference as just shown because nothing is gained. Furthermore, having what amounts to two names for the same constructor creates a confusing situation (to say the least). However, to give you the flavor of a more practical usage, the following program uses a **static** method, called **myClassFactory( )**, that is a factory for objects of any type of **MyFunc** objects. It can be used to create any type of object that has a constructor compatible with its first parameter.

```
// Implement a simple class factory using a constructor reference.

interface MyFunc<R, T> {
  R func(T n);
}

// A simple generic class.
class MyClass<T> {
  private T val;

  // A constructor that takes an argument.
  MyClass(T v) { val = v; }
```

```
  // The default constructor. This constructor
  // is NOT used by this program.
  MyClass() { val = null; }
  // ...

  T getVal() { return val; };
}

// A simple, non-generic class.
class MyClass2 {
  String  str;

  // A constructor that takes an argument.
  MyClass2(String s) { str = s; }

  // The default constructor. This
  // constructor is NOT used by this program.
  MyClass2() { str = ""; }

  // ...

  String getVal() { return str; };
}

class ConstructorRefDemo3 {

  // A factory method for class objects. The class must
  // have a constructor that takes one parameter of type T.
  // R specifies the type of object being created.
  static <R,T> R myClassFactory(MyFunc<R, T> cons, T v) {
    return cons.func(v);
  }

  public static void main(String[] args)
  {
    // Create a reference to a MyClass constructor.
    // In this case, new refers to the constructor that
    // takes an argument.
    MyFunc<MyClass<Double>, Double> myClassCons = MyClass<Double>::new;

    // Create an instance of MyClass by use of the factory method.
    MyClass<Double> mc = myClassFactory(myClassCons, 100.1);

    // Use the instance of MyClass just created.
    System.out.println("val in mc is " + mc.getVal( ));

    // Now, create a different class by use of myClassFactory().
    MyFunc<MyClass2, String> myClassCons2 = MyClass2::new;

    // Create an instance of MyClass2 by use of the factory method.
    MyClass2 mc2 = myClassFactory(myClassCons2, "Lambda");
```

```
        // Use the instance of MyClass just created.
        System.out.println("str in mc2 is " + mc2.getVal( ));
    }
}
```

The output is shown here:

```
val in mc is 100.1
str in mc2 is Lambda
```

As you can see, **myClassFactory( )** is used to create objects of type **MyClass<Double>** and **MyClass2**. Although both classes differ—for example, **MyClass** is generic and **MyClass2** is not—both can be created by **myClassFactory( )** because they both have constructors that are compatible with **func( )** in **MyFunc**. This works because **myClassFactory( )** is passed the constructor for the object that it builds. You might want to experiment with this program a bit, trying different classes that you create. Also try creating instances of different types of **MyClass** objects. As you will see, **myClassFactory( )** can create any type of object whose class has a constructor that is compatible with **func( )** in **MyFunc**. Although this example is quite simple, it hints at the power that constructor references bring to Java.

Before moving on, it is important to mention a second form of the constructor reference syntax that is used for arrays. To create a constructor reference for an array, use this construct:

*type*[]::new

Here, *type* specifies the type of object being created. For example, assuming the form of **MyClass** as shown in the first constructor reference example (**ConstructorRefDemo**) and given the **MyArrayCreator** interface shown here:

```
interface MyArrayCreator<T> {
   T func(int n);
}
```

the following creates a two-element array of **MyClass** objects and gives each element an initial value:

```
MyArrayCreator<MyClass[]> mcArrayCons = MyClass[]::new;
MyClass[] a = mcArrayCons.func(2);
a[0] = new MyClass(1);
a[1] = new MyClass(2);
```

Here, the call to **func(2)** causes a two-element array to be created. In general, a functional interface must contain a method that takes a single **int** parameter if it is to be used to refer to an array constructor.

## Predefined Functional Interfaces

Up to this point, the examples in this chapter have defined their own functional interfaces so that the fundamental concepts behind lambda expressions and functional interfaces could be clearly illustrated. However, in many cases, you won't need to define your own functional interface because the package called **java.util.function** provides several predefined ones. Although we will look at them more closely in Part II, here is a sampling:

| Interface | Purpose |
|---|---|
| UnaryOperator<T> | Apply a unary operation to an object of type **T** and return the result, which is also of type **T**. Its method is called **apply( )**. |
| BinaryOperator<T> | Apply an operation to two objects of type **T** and return the result, which is also of type **T**. Its method is called **apply( )**. |
| Consumer<T> | Apply an operation on an object of type **T**. Its method is called **accept( )**. |
| Supplier<T> | Return an object of type **T**. Its method is called **get( )**. |
| Function<T, R> | Apply an operation to an object of type **T** and return the result as an object of type **R**. Its method is called **apply( )**. |
| Predicate<T> | Determine if an object of type **T** fulfills some constraint. Return a **boolean** value that indicates the outcome. Its method is called **test( )**. |

The following program shows the **Function** interface in action by using it to rework the earlier example called **BlockLambdaDemo** that demonstrated block lambdas by implementing a factorial example. That example created its own functional interface called **NumericFunc**, but the built-in **Function** interface could have been used, as this version of the program illustrates:

```
// Use the Function built-in functional interface.

// Import the Function interface.
import java.util.function.Function;

class UseFunctionInterfaceDemo {
  public static void main(String[] args)
  {

    // This block lambda computes the factorial of an int value.
    // This time, Function is the functional interface.
    Function<Integer, Integer> factorial = (n) -> {
      int result = 1;
      for(int i=1; i <= n; i++)
        result = i * result;
      return result;
    };

    System.out.println("The factorial of 3 is " + factorial.apply(3));
    System.out.println("The factorial of 5 is " + factorial.apply(5));
  }
}
```

It produces the same output as previous versions of the program

CHAPTER

16

# Modules

JDK 9 introduced a new and important feature called *modules*. Modules give you a way to describe the relationships and dependencies of the code that comprises an application. Modules also let you control which parts of a module are accessible to other modules and which are not. Through the use of modules you can create more reliable, scalable programs.

As a general rule, modules are most helpful to large applications because they help reduce the management complexity often associated with a large software system. However, small programs also benefit from modules because the Java API library has now been organized into modules. Thus, it is now possible to specify which parts of the API are required by your program and which are not. This makes it possible to deploy programs with a smaller run-time footprint, which is especially important when creating code for small devices, such as those intended to be part of the Internet of Things (IoT).

Support for modules is provided both by language elements, including several new keywords, and by enhancements to **javac**, **java**, and other JDK tools. Furthermore, new tools and file formats were introduced. As a result, the JDK and the run-time system were substantially upgraded to support modules.

## Module Basics

In its most fundamental sense, a module is a grouping of packages and resources that can be collectively referred to by the module's name. A module declaration specifies the name of a module and defines the relationship a module and its packages have to other modules.

CHAPTER

# 16 Modules

JDK 9 introduced a new and important feature called *modules*. Modules give you a way to describe the relationships and dependencies of the code that comprises an application. Modules also let you control which parts of a module are accessible to other modules and which are not. Through the use of modules you can create more reliable, scalable programs.

As a general rule, modules are most helpful to large applications because they help reduce the management complexity often associated with a large software system. However, small programs also benefit from modules because the Java API library has now been organized into modules. Thus, it is now possible to specify which parts of the API are required by your program and which are not. This makes it possible to deploy programs with a smaller run-time footprint, which is especially important when creating code for small devices, such as those intended to be part of the Internet of Things (IoT).

Support for modules is provided both by language elements, including several keywords, and by enhancements to **javac**, **java**, and other JDK tools. Furthermore, new tools and file formats were introduced. As a result, the JDK and the run-time system were substantially upgraded to support modules. In short, modules constitute a major addition to, and evolution of, the Java language.

## Module Basics

In its most fundamental sense, a *module* is a grouping of packages and resources that can be collectively referred to by the module's name. A *module declaration* specifies the name of a module and defines the relationship a module and its packages have to other modules.

Module declarations are program statements in a Java source file and are supported by several module-related keywords. They are shown here:

| exports | module | open | opens |
|---|---|---|---|
| provides | requires | to | transitive |
| uses | with | | |

It is important to understand that these keywords are recognized *as keywords* only in the context of a module declaration. Otherwise, they are interpreted as identifiers in other situations. Thus, the keyword **module** could, for example, also be used as a parameter name, although such a use is certainly not recommended. However, making the module-related keywords context-sensitive prevents problems with pre-existing code that may use one or more of them as identifiers.

A module declaration is contained in a file called **module-info.java**. Thus, a module is defined in a Java source file. This file is then compiled by **javac** into a class file and is known as its *module descriptor*. The **module-info.java** file must contain only a module definition. It cannot contain other types of declarations.

A module declaration begins with the keyword **module**. Here is its general form:

```
module moduleName {
   // module definition
}
```

The name of the module is specified by *moduleName,* which must be a valid Java identifier or a sequence of identifiers separated by periods. The module definition is specified within the braces. Although a module definition may be empty (which results in a declaration that simply names the module), typically it specifies one or more clauses that define the characteristics of the module.

## A Simple Module Example

At the foundation of a module's capabilities are two key features. The first is a module's ability to specify that it requires another module. In other words, one module can specify that it *depends* on another. A dependence relationship is specified by use of a **requires** statement. By default, the presence of the required module is checked at both compile time and at run time. The second key feature is a module's ability to control which, if any, of its packages are accessible by another module. This is accomplished by use of the **exports** keyword. The public and protected types within a package are accessible to other modules only if they are explicitly exported. Here we will develop an example that introduces both of these features.

The following example creates a modular application that demonstrates some simple mathematical functions. Although this application is purposely very small, it illustrates the core concepts and procedures required to create, compile, and run module-based code. Furthermore, the general approach shown here also applies to larger, real-world applications. It is strongly recommended that you work through the example on your computer, carefully following each step.

**NOTE** This chapter shows the process of creating, compiling, and running module-based code by use of the command-line tools. This approach has two advantages. First, it works for all Java programmers because no IDE is required. Second, it very clearly shows the fundamentals of the module system, including how it utilizes directories. To follow along, you will need to manually create a number of directories and ensure that each file is placed in its proper directory. As you might expect, when creating real-world, module-based applications, you will likely find a module-aware IDE easier to use because, typically, it will automate much of the process. However, learning the fundamentals of modules using the command-line tools ensures that you have a solid understanding of the topic.

The application defines two modules. The first module is called **appstart**. It contains a package called **appstart.mymodappdemo** that defines the application's entry point in a class called **MyModAppDemo**. Thus, **MyModAppDemo** contains the application's **main( )** method. The second module is called **appfuncs**. It contains a package called **appfuncs.simplefuncs** that includes the class **SimpleMathFuncs**. This class defines three static methods that implement some simple mathematical functions. The entire application will be contained in a directory tree that begins at **mymodapp**.

Before continuing, a few words about module names are appropriate. First, in the examples that follow, the name of a module (such as **appfuncs**) is the prefix of the name of a package (such as **appfuncs.simplefuncs**) that it contains. This is *not* required, but it's used here as a way of clearly indicating to what module a package belongs. In general, when learning about and experimenting with modules, short, simple names, such as those used in this chapter, are helpful, and you can use any sort of convenient names that you like. However, when creating modules suitable for distribution, you must be careful with the names you choose because you will want those names to be unique. At the time of this writing, the suggested way to achieve this is to use the reverse domain name method. In this method, the reverse domain name of the domain that "owns" the project is used as a prefix for the module. For example, a project associated with **hotburgers.com** would use **com.hotburgers** as the module prefix. (The same goes for package names.) Because naming conventions may evolve over time, you will want to check the Java documentation for current recommendations.

Let's now begin. Start by creating the necessary source code directories by following these steps:

1. Create a directory called **mymodapp**. This is the top-level directory for the entire application.
2. Under **mymodapp**, create a subdirectory called **appsrc**. This is the top-level directory for the application's source code.
3. Under **appsrc**, create the subdirectory **appstart**. Under this directory, create a subdirectory also called **appstart**. Under this directory, create the directory **mymodappdemo**. Thus, beginning with **appsrc**, you will have created this tree:

   ```
   appsrc\appstart\appstart\mymodappdemo
   ```
4. Also under **appsrc**, create the subdirectory **appfuncs**. Under this directory, create a subdirectory also called **appfuncs**. Under this directory, create the directory called **simplefuncs**. Thus, beginning with **appsrc**, you will have created this tree:

   ```
   appsrc\appfuncs\appfuncs\simplefuncs
   ```

Your directory tree should look like that shown here.

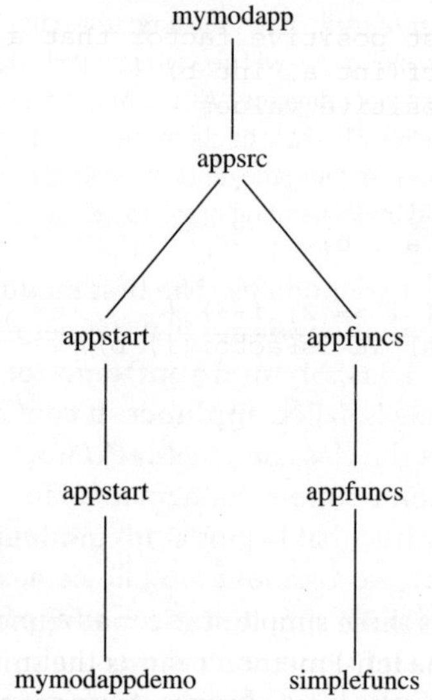


After you have set up these directories, you can create the application's source files.

This example will use four source files. Two are the source files that define the application. The first is **SimpleMathFuncs.java**, shown here. Notice that **SimpleMathFuncs** is packaged in **appfuncs.simplefuncs**.

```
// Some simple math functions.

package appfuncs.simplefuncs;

public class SimpleMathFuncs {

  // Determine if a is a factor of b.
  public static boolean isFactor(int a, int b) {
    if((b%a) == 0) return true;
    return false;
  }

  // Return the smallest positive factor that a and b have in common.
  public static int lcf(int a, int b) {
    // Factor using positive values.
    a = Math.abs(a);
    b = Math.abs(b);

    int min = a < b ? a : b;

    for(int i = 2; i <= min/2; i++) {
      if(isFactor(i, a) && isFactor(i, b))
        return i;
    }
```

```
      return 1;
    }

    // Return the largest positive factor that a and b have in common.
    public static int gcf(int a, int b) {
      // Factor using positive values.
      a = Math.abs(a);
      b = Math.abs(b);

      int min = a < b ? a : b;

      for(int i = min/2; i >= 2; i--) {
        if(isFactor(i, a) && isFactor(i, b))
          return i;
      }

      return 1;
    }
}
```

**SimpleMathFuncs** defines three simple **static** math functions. The first, **isFactor( )**, returns true if **a** is a factor of **b**. The **lcf( )** method returns the smallest factor common to both **a** and **b**. In other words, it returns the least common factor of **a** and **b**. The **gcf( )** method returns the greatest common factor of **a** and **b**. In both cases, 1 is returned if no common factors are found. This file must be put in the following directory:

```
appsrc\appfuncs\appfuncs\simplefuncs
```

This is the **appfuncs.simplefuncs** package directory.

The second source file is **MyModAppDemo.java**, shown next. It uses the methods in **SimpleMathFuncs**. Notice that it is packaged in **appstart.mymodappdemo**. Also note that it imports the **SimpleMathFuncs** class because it depends on **SimpleMathFuncs** for its operation.

```
// Demonstrate a simple module-based application.
package appstart.mymodappdemo;

import appfuncs.simplefuncs.SimpleMathFuncs;

public class MyModAppDemo {
  public static void main(String[] args) {

    if(SimpleMathFuncs.isFactor(2, 10))
      System.out.println("2 is a factor of 10");

    System.out.println("Smallest factor common to both 35 and 105 is " +
                       SimpleMathFuncs.lcf(35, 105));

    System.out.println("Largest factor common to both 35 and 105 is " +
                       SimpleMathFuncs.gcf(35, 105));

  }
}
```

This file must be put in the following directory:

```
appsrc\appstart\appstart\mymodappdemo
```

This is the directory for the **appstart.mymodappdemo** package.

Next, you will need to add **module-info.java** files for each module. These files contain the module definitions. First, add this one, which defines the **appfuncs** module:

```
// Module definition for the functions module.
module appfuncs {
  // Exports the package appfuncs.simplefuncs.
  exports appfuncs.simplefuncs;
}
```

Notice that **appfuncs** exports the package **appfuncs.simplefuncs**, which makes it accessible to other modules. This file must be put into this directory:

```
appsrc\appfuncs
```

Thus, it goes in the **appfuncs** module directory, which is above the package directories.

Finally, the **module-info.java** file for the **appstart** module is shown next. Notice that **appstart** requires the module **appfuncs**.

```
// Module definition for the main application module.
module appstart {
  // Requires the module appfuncs.
  requires appfuncs;
}
```

This file must be put into its module directory:

```
appsrc\appstart
```

Before examining the **requires**, **exports**, and **module** statements more closely, let's first compile and run this example. Be sure that you have correctly created the directories and entered each file into its proper directory, as just explained.

## Compile and Run the First Module Example

Beginning with JDK 9, **javac** has been updated to support modules. Thus, like all other Java programs, module-based programs are compiled using **javac**. The process is easy, with the primary difference being that you will usually explicitly specify a *module path*. A module path tells the compiler where the compiled files will be located. When following along with this example, be sure that you execute the **javac** commands from the **mymodapp** directory in order for the paths to be correct. Recall that **mymodapp** is the top-level directory for the entire module application.

To begin, compile **SimpleMathFuncs.java** using this command:

```
javac -d appmodules\appfuncs
  appsrc\appfuncs\appfuncs\simplefuncs\SimpleMathFuncs.java
```

Remember, this command *must be* executed from the **mymodapp** directory. Notice the use of the **-d** option. This tells **javac** where to put the output **.class** file. For the examples in this chapter, the top of the directory tree for compiled code is **appmodules**. This command will create the output package directories for **appfuncs.simplefuncs** under **appmodules\appfuncs** as needed.

Next, here is the **javac** command that compiles the **module-info.java** file for the **appfuncs** module:

```
javac -d appmodules\appfuncs appsrc\appfuncs\module-info.java
```

This puts the **module-info.class** file into the **appmodules\appfuncs** directory.

Although the preceding two-step process works, it was shown primarily for the sake of discussion. It is usually easier to compile a module's **module-info.java** file and its source files in one command line. Here, the preceding two **javac** commands are combined into one:

```
javac -d appmodules\appfuncs appsrc\appfuncs\module-info.java
  appsrc\appfuncs\appfuncs\simplefuncs\SimpleMathFuncs.java
```

In this case, each compiled file is put in its proper module or package directory.

Now, compile **module-info.java** and **MyModAppDemo.java** for the **appstart** module, using this command:

```
javac --module-path appmodules -d appmodules\appstart
  appsrc\appstart\module-info.java
  appsrc\appstart\appstart\mymodappdemo\MyModAppDemo.java
```

Notice the **--module-path** option. It specifies the module path, which is the path on which the compiler will look for the user-defined modules required by the **module-info.java** file. In this case, it will look for the **appfuncs** module because it is needed by the **appstart** module. Also, notice that it specifies the output directory as **appmodules\appstart**. This means that the **module-info.class** file will be in the **appmodules\appstart** module directory and **MyModAppDemo.class** will be in the **appmodules\appstart\appstart\mymodappdemo** package directory.

Once you have completed the compilation, you can run the application with this **java** command:

```
java --module-path appmodules -m appstart/appstart.mymodappdemo.MyModAppDemo
```

Here, the **--module-path** option specifies the path to the application's modules. As mentioned, **appmodules** is the directory at the top of the compiled modules tree. The **-m** option specifies the class that contains the entry point of the application and, in this case, the name of the class that contains the **main( )** method. When you run the program, you will see the following output:

```
2 is a factor of 10
Smallest factor common to both 35 and 105 is 5
Largest factor common to both 35 and 105 is 7
```

## A Closer Look at requires and exports

The preceding module-based example relies on the two foundational features of the module system: the ability to specify a dependence and the ability to satisfy that dependence. These capabilities are specified through the use of the **requires** and **exports** statements within a **module** declaration. Each merits a closer examination at this time.

Here is the form of the **requires** statement used in the example:

requires *moduleName*;

Here, *moduleName* specifies the name of a module that is required by the module in which the **requires** statement occurs. This means that the required module must be present in order for the current module to compile. In the language of modules, the current module is said to *read* the module specified in the **requires** statement. When more than one module is required, it must be specified in its own **requires** statement. Thus, a module declaration may include several different **requires** statements. In general, the **requires** statement gives you a way to ensure that your program has access to the modules that it needs.

Here is the general form of the **exports** statement used in the example:

exports *packageName*;

Here, *packageName* specifies the name of the package that is exported by the module in which this statement occurs. A module can export as many packages as needed, with each one specified in a separate **exports** statement. Thus, a module may have several **exports** statements.

When a module exports a package, it makes all of the public and protected types in the package accessible to other modules. Furthermore, the public and protected members of those types are also accessible. However, if a package within a module is not exported, then it is private to that module, including all of its public types. For example, even though a class is declared as **public** within a package, if that package is not explicitly exported by an **exports** statement, then that class is not accessible to other modules. It is important to understand that the public and protected types of a package, whether exported or not, are always accessible within that package's module. The **exports** statement simply makes them accessible to outside modules. Thus, any nonexported package is only for the internal use of its module.

The key to understanding **requires** and **exports** is that they work together. If one module depends on another, then it must specify that dependence with **requires**. The module on which another depends must explicitly export (i.e., make accessible) the packages that the dependent module needs. If either side of this dependence relationship is missing, the dependent module will not compile. As it relates to the foregoing example, **MyModAppDemo** uses the functions in **SimpleMathFuncs**. As a result, the **appstart** module declaration contains a **requires** statement that names the **appfuncs** module. The **appfuncs** module declaration exports the **appfuncs.simplefuncs** package, thus making the public types in the **SimpleMathFuncs** class available. Since both sides of the dependence relationship have been fulfilled, the application can compile and run. If either is missing, the compilation will fail.

It is important to emphasize that **requires** and **exports** statements must occur only within a **module** statement. Furthermore, a **module** statement must occur by itself in a file called **module-info.java**.

## java.base and the Platform Modules

As mentioned at the start of this chapter, beginning with JDK 9, the Java API packages have been incorporated into modules. In fact, the modularization of the API is one of the primary benefits realized by the addition of the modules. Because of their special role, the API modules are referred to as *platform modules,* and their names all begin with the prefix **java**. Here are some examples: **java.base**, **java.desktop**, and **java.xml**. By modularizing the API, it becomes possible to deploy an application with only the packages that it requires, rather than the entire Java Runtime Environment (JRE). Because of the size of the full JRE, this is a very important improvement.

The fact that all of the Java API library packages are now in modules gives rise to the following question: How can the **main( )** method in **MyModAppDemo** in the preceding example use **System.out.println( )** without specifying a **requires** statement for the module that contains the **System** class? Obviously, the program will not compile and run unless **System** is present. The same question also applies to the use of the **Math** class in **SimpleMathFuncs**. The answer to this question is found in **java.base**.

Of the platform modules, the most important is **java.base**. It includes and exports those packages fundamental to Java, such as **java.lang**, **java.io**, and **java.util**, among many others. Because of its importance, **java.base** is *automatically accessible* to all modules. Furthermore, all other modules automatically require **java.base**. There is no need to include a **requires java.base** statement in a module declaration. (As a point of interest, it is not wrong to explicitly specify **java.base**, it's just not necessary.) Thus, in much the same way that **java.lang** is automatically available to all programs without the use of an **import** statement, the **java.base** module is automatically accessible to all module-based programs without explicitly requesting it.

Because **java.base** contains the **java.lang** package, and **java.lang** contains the **System** class, **MyModAppDemo** in the preceding example can automatically use **System.out.println( )** without an explicit **requires** statement. The same applies to the use of the **Math** class in **SimpleMathFuncs**, because the **Math** class is also in **java.lang**. As you will see when you begin to create your own module-based applications, many of the API classes you will commonly need are in the packages included in **java.base**. Thus, the automatic inclusion of **java.base** simplifies the creation of module-based code because Java's core packages are automatically accessible.

One last point: Beginning with JDK 9, the documentation for the Java API now tells you the name of the module in which a package is contained. If the module is **java.base**, then you can use the contents of that package directly. Otherwise, your module declaration must include a **requires** clause for the desired module.

## Legacy Code and the Unnamed Module

Another question may have occurred to you when working through the first sample module program. Because Java now supports modules, and the API packages are also contained in modules, why do all of the other programs in the preceding chapters compile and run without error even though they do not use modules? More generally, since there is now over 20 years of Java code in existence and (at the time of this writing) the vast majority of that code does not use modules, how is it possible to compile, run, and maintain that legacy code with a JDK 9 or later compiler? Given Java's original philosophy of "write once, run everywhere," this is a very important question because backward capability must be maintained. As you will see, Java answers this question by providing an elegant, nearly transparent means of ensuring backward compatibility with pre-existing code.

Support for legacy code is provided by two key features. The first is the *unnamed module.* When you use code that is not part of a named module, it automatically becomes part of the unnamed module. The unnamed module has two important attributes. First, all of the packages in the unnamed module are automatically exported. Second, the unnamed module can access any and all other modules. Thus, when a program does not use modules, all API modules in the Java platform are automatically accessible through the unnamed module.

The second key feature that supports legacy code is the automatic use of the class path, rather than the module path. When you compile a program that does not use modules, the class path mechanism is employed, just as it has been since Java's original release. As a result, the program is compiled and run in the same way it was prior to the advent of modules.

Because of the unnamed module and the automatic use of the class path, there was no need to declare any modules for the sample programs shown elsewhere in this book. They run properly whether you compile them with a modern compiler or an earlier one, such as JDK 8. Thus, even though modules are a feature that has significant impact on Java, compatibility with legacy code is maintained. This approach also provides a smooth, nonintrusive, nondisruptive transition path to modules. Thus, it enables you to move a legacy application to modules at your own pace. Furthermore, it allows you to avoid the use of modules when they are not needed.

Before moving on, an important point needs to be made. For the types of sample programs used elsewhere in this book, and for sample programs in general, there is no benefit in using modules. Modularizing them would simply add clutter and complicate them for no reason or benefit. Furthermore, for many simple programs, there is no need to contain them in modules. For the reasons stated at the start of this chapter, modules are often of the greatest benefit when creating commercial programs. Therefore, no examples outside this chapter will use modules. This also allows the examples to be compiled and run in a pre–JDK 9 environment, which is important to readers using an older version of Java. Thus, except for the examples in this chapter, the examples in this book work for both pre-module and post-module JDKs.

## Exporting to a Specific Module

The basic form of the **exports** statement makes a package accessible to any and all other modules. This is often exactly what you want. However, in some specialized development situations, it can be desirable to make a package accessible to only a *specific set* of modules, not *all* other modules. For example, a library developer might want to export a support package to certain other modules within the library, but not make it available for general use. Adding a **to** clause to the **exports** statement provides a means by which this can be accomplished.

In an **exports** statement, the **to** clause specifies a list of one or more modules that have access to the exported package. Furthermore, only those modules named in the **to** clause will have access. In the language of modules, the **to** clause creates what is known as a *qualified export*.

The form of **exports** that includes **to** is shown here:

exports *packageName* to *moduleNames*;

Here, *moduleNames* is a comma-separated list of modules to which the exporting module grants access.

You can try the **to** clause by changing the **module-info.java** file for the **appfuncs** module, as shown here:

```
// Module definition that uses a to clause.
module appfuncs {
  // Exports the package appfuncs.simplefuncs to appstart.
  exports appfuncs.simplefuncs to appstart;
}
```

Now, **simplefuncs** is exported only to **appstart** and to no other modules. After making this change, you can recompile the application by using this **javac** command:

```
javac -d appmodules --module-source-path appsrc
  appsrc\appstart\appstart\mymodappdemo\MyModAppDemo.java
```

After compiling, you can run the application as shown earlier.

This example also uses another module-related feature. Look closely at the preceding **javac** command. First, notice that it specifies the **--module-source-path** option. The module source path specifies the top of the module source tree. The **--module-source-path** option automatically compiles the files in the tree under the specified directory, which is **appsrc** in this example. The **--module-source-path** option must be used with the **-d** option to ensure that the compiled modules are stored in their proper directories under **appmodules**. This form of **javac** is called *multi-module mode* because it enables more than one module to be compiled at a time. The multi-module compilation mode is especially helpful here because the **to** clause refers to a specific module, and the requiring module must have access to the exported package. Thus, in this case, both **appstart** and **appfuncs** are needed to avoid warnings and/or errors during compilation. Multi-module mode avoids this problem because both modules are being compiled at the same time.

The multi-module mode of **javac** has another advantage. It automatically finds and compiles all source files for the application, creating the necessary output directories. Because of the advantages that multi-module compilation mode offers, it will be used for the subsequent examples.

---

**NOTE** As a general rule, qualified export is a special case feature. Most often, your modules will either provide unqualified export of a package or not export the package at all, keeping it inaccessible. As such, qualified export is discussed here primarily for the sake of completeness. Also, qualified export by itself does not prevent the exported package from being misused by malicious code in a module that masquerades as the targeted module. The security techniques required to prevent this from happening are beyond the scope of this book. Consult the Oracle documentation for details on security in this regard, and Java security details in general.

## Using requires transitive

Consider a situation in which there are three modules, A, B, and C, that have the following dependences:

- A requires B.
- B requires C.

Given this situation, it is clear that since A depends on B and B depends on C, A has an indirect dependence on C. As long as A does not directly use any of the contents of C, then you can simply have A require B in its module-info file, and have B export the packages required by A in its module-info file, as shown here:

```
// A's module-info file:
module A {
  requires B;
}

// B's module-info file.
module B {
  exports somepack;
  requires C;
}
```

Here, *somepack* is a placeholder for the package exported by B and used by A. Although this works as long as A does not need to use anything defined in C, a problem occurs if A *does* want to access a type in C. In this case, there are two solutions.

The first solution is to simply add a **requires C** statement to A's file, as shown here:

```
// A's module-info file updated to explicitly require C:
module A {
  requires B;
  requires C; // also require C
}
```

This solution certainly works, but if B will be used by many modules, you must add **requires C** to all module definitions that require B. This is not only tedious, it is also error prone. Fortunately, there is a better solution. You can create an *implied dependence* on C. Implied dependence is also referred to as *implied readability*.

To create an implied dependence, add the **transitive** keyword after **requires** in the clause that requires the module upon which an implied readability is needed. In the case of this example, you would change B's module-info file as shown here:

```
// B's module-info file.
module B {
  exports somepack;
  requires transitive C;
}
```

Here, C is now required as transitive. After making this change, any module that depends on B will also, automatically, depend on C. Thus, A would automatically have access to C.

You can experiment with **requires transitive** by reworking the preceding modular application example so that the **isFactor( )** method is removed from the **SimpleMathFuncs** class in the **appfuncs.simplefuncs** package and put into a new class, module, and package. The new class will be called **SupportFuncs**, the module will be called **appsupport**, and the package will be called **appsupport.supportfuncs**. The **appfuncs** module will then add a dependence on the **appsupport** module by use of **requires transitive**. This will enable both the **appfuncs** and **appstart** modules to access it without **appstart** having to provide its own **requires** statement. This works because **appstart** receives access to it through an **appfuncs** **requires transitive** statement. The following describes the process in detail.

To begin, create the source directories that support the new **appsupport** module. First, create **appsupport** under the **appsrc** directory. This is the module directory for the support functions. Under **appsupport**, create the package directory by adding the **appsupport** subdirectory followed by the **supportfuncs** subdirectory. Thus, the directory tree for **appsupport** should now look like this:

```
appsrc\appsupport\appsupport\supportfuncs
```

Once the directories have been established, create the **SupportFuncs** class. Notice that **SupportFuncs** is part of the **appsupport.supportfuncs** package. Therefore, you must put it in the **appsupport.supportfuncs** package directory.

```
// Support functions.

package appsupport.supportfuncs;

public class SupportFuncs {

  // Determine if a is a factor of b.
  public static boolean isFactor(int a, int b) {
    if((b%a) == 0) return true;
    return false;
  }
}
```

Notice that **isFactor( )** is now part of **SupportFuncs**, rather than **SimpleMathFuncs**.

Next, create the **module-info.java** file for the **appsupport** module and put it in the **appsrc\appsupport** directory.

```
// Module definition for appsupport.
module appsupport {
  exports appsupport.supportfuncs;
}
```

As you can see, it exports the **appsupport.supportfuncs** package.

Because **isFactor( )** is now part of **Supportfuncs**, remove it from **SimpleMathFuncs**. Thus, **SimpleMathFuncs.java** will now look like this:

```
// Some simple math functions, with isFactor() removed.

package appfuncs.simplefuncs;
import appsupport.supportfuncs.SupportFuncs;
```

```
public class SimpleMathFuncs {

  // Return the smallest positive factor that a and b have in common.
  public static int lcf(int a, int b) {
    // Factor using positive values.
    a = Math.abs(a);
    b = Math.abs(b);

    int min = a < b ? a : b;

    for(int i = 2; i <= min/2; i++) {
      if(SupportFuncs.isFactor(i, a) && SupportFuncs.isFactor(i, b))
        return i;
    }

    return 1;
  }

  // Return the largest positive factor that a and b have in common.
  public static int gcf(int a, int b) {
    // Factor using positive values.
    a = Math.abs(a);
    b = Math.abs(b);

    int min = a < b ? a : b;

    for(int i = min/2; i >= 2; i--) {
      if(SupportFuncs.isFactor(i, a) && SupportFuncs.isFactor(i, b))
        return i;
    }

    return 1;
  }
}
```

Notice that now the **SupportFuncs** class is imported and calls to **isFactor( )** are referred to through the class name **SupportFuncs**.

Next, change the **module-info.java** file for **appfuncs** so that in its **requires** statement, **appsupport** is specified as **transitive**, as shown here:

```
// Module definition for appfuncs.
module appfuncs {
  // Exports the package appfuncs.simplefuncs.
  exports appfuncs.simplefuncs;

  // Requires appsupport and makes it transitive.
  requires transitive appsupport;
}
```

Because **appfuncs** requires **appsupport** as **transitive**, there is no need for the **module-info .java** file for **appstart** to also require it. Its dependence on **appsupport** is implied. Thus, no changes to the **module-info.java** file for **appstart** are needed.

Finally, update **MyModAppDemo.java** to reflect these changes. Specifically, it must now import the **SupportFuncs** class and specify it when invoking **isFactor( )**, as shown here:

```
// Updated to use SupportFuncs.
package appstart.mymodappdemo;

import appfuncs.simplefuncs.SimpleMathFuncs;
import appsupport.supportfuncs.SupportFuncs;

public class MyModAppDemo {
  public static void main(String[] args) {

    // Now, isFactor() is referred to via SupportFuncs,
    // not SimpleMathFuncs.
    if(SupportFuncs.isFactor(2, 10))
      System.out.println("2 is a factor of 10");

    System.out.println("Smallest factor common to both 35 and 105 is " +
                       SimpleMathFuncs.lcf(35, 105));

    System.out.println("Largest factor common to both 35 and 105 is " +
                       SimpleMathFuncs.gcf(35, 105));

  }
}
```

Once you have completed all of the preceding steps, you can recompile the entire program using this multi-module compilation command:

```
javac -d appmodules --module-source-path appsrc
   appsrc\appstart\appstart\mymodappdemo\MyModAppDemo.java
```

As explained earlier, the multi-module compilation will automatically create the parallel module subdirectories, under the **appmodules** directory.

You can run the program using this command:

```
java --module-path appmodules -m appstart/appstart.mymodappdemo.MyModAppDemo
```

It will produce the same output as the previous version. However, this time three different modules are required.

To prove that the **transitive** modifier is actually required by the application, remove it from the **module-info.java** file for **appfuncs**. Then, try to compile the program. As you will see, an error will result because **appsupport** is no longer accessible by **appstart**.

Here is another experiment. In the module-info file for **appsupport**, try exporting the **appsupport.supportfuncs** package to only **appfuncs** by use of a qualified export, as shown here:

```
exports appsupport.supportfuncs to appfuncs;
```

Next, attempt to compile the program. As you see, the program will not compile because now the support function **isFactor( )** is not available to **MyModAppDemo**, which is in the **appstart** module. As explained previously, a qualified export restricts access to a package to only those modules specified by the **to** clause.

One final point: because of a special exception in the Java language syntax, in a **requires** statement, if **transitive** is immediately followed by a separator (such as a semicolon), it is interpreted as an identifier (for example, as a module name) rather than a keyword.

# Use Services

In programming, it is often useful to separate *what* must be done from *how* it is done. As you learned in Chapter 9, one way this is accomplished in Java is through the use of interfaces. The interface specifies the *what,* and the implementing class specifies the *how.* This concept can be expanded so that the implementing class is provided by code that is outside your program, through the use of a *plug-in.* Using such an approach, the capabilities of an application can be enhanced, upgraded, or altered by simply changing the plug-in. The core of the application itself remains unchanged. One way that Java supports a pluggable application architecture is through the use of *services* and *service providers.* Because of their importance, especially in large, commercial applications, Java's module system provides support for them.

Before we begin, it is necessary to state that applications that use services and service providers are typically fairly sophisticated. Therefore, you may find that you do not often need the service-based module features. However, because support for services constitutes a rather significant part of the module system, it is important that you have a general understanding of how these features work. Also, a simple example is presented that illustrates the core techniques needed to use them.

## Service and Service Provider Basics

In Java, a *service* is a program unit whose functionality is defined by an interface or abstract class. Thus, a service specifies in a general way some form of program activity. A concrete implementation of a service is supplied by a *service provider.* In other words, a service defines the form of some action, and the service provider supplies that action.

As mentioned, services are often used to support a pluggable architecture. For example, a service might be used to support the translation of one language into another. In this case, the service supports translation in general. The service provider supplies a specific translation, such as German to English or French to Chinese. Because all service providers implement the same interface, different translators can be used to translate different languages without having to change the core of the application. You can simply change the service provider.

Service providers are supported by the **ServiceLoader** class. **ServiceLoader** is a generic class packaged in **java.util**. It is declared like this:

```
class ServiceLoader<S>
```

Here, **S** specifies the service type. Service providers are loaded by the **load( )** method. It has several forms; the one we will use is shown here:

```
public static <S> ServiceLoader<S> load(Class <S> serviceType)
```

Here, *serviceType* specifies the **Class** object for the desired service type. Recall that **Class** is a class that encapsulates information about a class. There are a variety of ways to obtain a

**Class** instance. The way we will use here involves a class literal. Recall that a class literal has this general form:

*className*.class

Here, *className* specifies the name of the class.

When **load( )** is called, it returns a **ServiceLoader** instance for the application. This object supports iteration and can be cycled through by use of a for-each **for** loop. Therefore, to find a specific provider, simply search for it using a loop.

## The Service-Based Keywords

Modules support services through the use of the keywords **provides**, **uses**, and **with**. Essentially, a module specifies that it provides a service with a **provides** statement. A module indicates that it requires a service with a **uses** statement. The specific type of service provider is declared by **with**. When used together, they enable you to specify a module that provides a service, a module that needs that service, and the specific implementation of that service. Furthermore, the module system ensures that the service and service providers are available and will be found.

Here is the general form of **provides**:

provides *serviceType* with *implementationTypes*;

Here, *serviceType* specifies the type of the service, which is often an interface, although abstract classes are also used. A comma-separated list of the implementation types is specified by *implementationTypes*. Therefore, to provide a service, the module indicates both the name of the service and its implementation.

Here is the general form of the **uses** statement:

uses *serviceType*;

Here, *serviceType* specifies the type of the service required.

## A Module-Based Service Example

To demonstrate the use of services, we will add a service to the modular application example that we have been evolving. For simplicity, we will begin with the first version of the application shown at the start of this chapter. To it we will add two new modules. The first is called **userfuncs**. It will define interfaces that support functions that perform binary operations in which each argument is an **int** and the result is an **int**. The second module is called **userfuncsimp**, and it contains concrete implementations of the interfaces.

Begin by creating the necessary source directories:

1. Under the **appsrc** directory, add directories called **userfuncs** and **userfuncsimp**.
2. Under **userfuncs**, add the subdirectory also called **userfuncs**. Under that directory, add the subdirectory **binaryfuncs**. Thus, beginning with **appsrc**, you will have created this tree:

   ```
   appsrc\userfuncs\userfuncs\binaryfuncs
   ```

3. Under **userfuncsimp**, add the subdirectory also called **userfuncsimp**. Under that directory, add the subdirectory **binaryfuncsimp**. Thus, beginning with **appsrc**, you will have created this tree:

   ```
   appsrc\userfuncsimp\userfuncsimp\binaryfuncsimp
   ```

This example expands the original version of the application by providing support for functions beyond those built into the application. Recall that the **SimpleMathFuncs** class supplies three built-in functions: **isFactor( )**, **lcf( )**, and **gcf( )**. Although it would be possible to add more functions to this class, doing so requires modifying and recompiling the application. By implementing services, it becomes possible to "plug in" new functions at run time, without modifying the application, and that is what this example will do. In this case, the service supplies functions that take two **int** arguments and return an **int** result. Of course, other types of functions can be supported if additional interfaces are provided, but support for binary integer functions is sufficient for our purposes and keeps the source code size of the example manageable.

## The Service Interfaces

Two service-related interfaces are needed. One specifies the form of an action, and the other specifies the form of the provider of that action. Both go in the **binaryfuncs** directory, and both are in the **userfuncs.binaryfuncs** package. The first, called **BinaryFunc**, declares the form of a binary function. It is shown here:

```
// This interface defines a function that takes two int
// arguments and returns an int result. Thus, it can
// describe any binary operation on two ints that
// returns an int.

package userfuncs.binaryfuncs;

public interface BinaryFunc {
  // Obtain the name of the function.
  public String getName();

  // This is the function to perform. It will be
  // provided by specific implementations.
  public int func(int a, int b);
}
```

**BinaryFunc** declares the form of an object that can implement a binary integer function. This is specified by the **func( )** method. The name of the function is obtainable from **getName( )**. The name will be used to determine what type of function is implemented. This interface is implemented by a class that supplies a binary function.

The second interface declares the form of the service provider. It is called **BinFuncProvider** and is shown here:

```
// This interface defines the form of a service provider that
// obtains BinaryFunc instances.
package userfuncs.binaryfuncs;
```

```
import userfuncs.binaryfuncs.BinaryFunc;

public interface BinFuncProvider {

  // Obtain a BinaryFunc.
  public BinaryFunc get();
}
```

**BinFuncProvider** declares only one method, **get( )**, which is used to obtain an instance of **BinaryFunc**. This interface must be implemented by a class that wants to provide instances of **BinaryFunc**.

## The Implementation Classes

In this example, two concrete implementations of **BinaryFunc** are supported. The first is **AbsPlus**, which returns the sum of the absolute values of its arguments. The second is **AbsMinus**, which returns the result of subtracting the absolute value of the second argument from the absolute value of the first argument. These are provided by the classes **AbsPlusProvider** and **AbsMinusProvider**. The source code for these classes must be stored in the **binaryfuncsimp** directory, and they are all part of the **userfuncsimp.binaryfuncsimp** package.

The code for **AbsPlus** is shown here:

```
// AbsPlus provides a concrete implementation of
// BinaryFunc. It returns the result of abs(a) + abs(b).
package userfuncsimp.binaryfuncsimp;

import userfuncs.binaryfuncs.BinaryFunc;

public class AbsPlus implements BinaryFunc {

  // Return name of this function.
  public String getName() {
    return "absPlus";
  }

  // Implement the AbsPlus function.
  public int func(int a, int b) { return Math.abs(a) + Math.abs(b); }
}
```

**AbsPlus** implements **func( )** such that it returns the result of adding the absolute values of **a** and **b**. Notice that **getName( )** returns the "absPlus" string. It identifies this function.

The **AbsMinus** class is shown next:

```
// AbsMinus provides a concrete implementation of
// BinaryFunc. It returns the result of abs(a) - abs(b).

package userfuncsimp.binaryfuncsimp;

import userfuncs.binaryfuncs.BinaryFunc;

public class AbsMinus implements BinaryFunc {
```

```
  // Return name of this function.
  public String getName() {
    return "absMinus";
  }

  // Implement the AbsMinus function.
  public int func(int a, int b) { return Math.abs(a) - Math.abs(b); }
}
```

Here, **func( )** is implemented to return the difference between the absolute values of **a** and **b**, and the string "absMinus" is returned by **getName( )**.

To obtain an instance of **AbsPlus**, the **AbsPlusProvider** is used. It implements **BinFuncProvider** and is shown here:

```
// This is a provider for the AbsPlus function.

package userfuncsimp.binaryfuncsimp;

import userfuncs.binaryfuncs.*;

public class AbsPlusProvider implements BinFuncProvider {

  // Provide an AbsPlus object.
  public BinaryFunc get() { return new AbsPlus(); }
}
```

The **get( )** method simply returns a new **AbsPlus( )** object. Although this provider is very simple, it is important to point out that some service providers will be much more complex.

The provider for **AbsMinus** is called **AbsMinusProvider** and is shown next:

```
// This is a provider for the AbsMinus function.

package userfuncsimp.binaryfuncsimp;

import userfuncs.binaryfuncs.*;

public class AbsMinusProvider implements BinFuncProvider {

  // Provide an AbsMinus object.
  public BinaryFunc get() { return new AbsMinus(); }
}
```

Its **get( )** method returns an object of **AbsMinus**.

## The Module Definition Files

Next, two module definition files are needed. The first is for the **userfuncs** module. It is shown here:

```
module userfuncs {
  exports userfuncs.binaryfuncs;
}
```

This code must be contained in a **module-info.java** file that is in the **userfuncs** module directory. Notice that it exports the **userfuncs.binaryfuncs** package. This is the package that defines the **BinaryFunc** and **BinFuncProvider** interfaces.

The second **module-info.java** file is shown next. It defines the module that contains the implementations. It goes in the **userfuncsimp** module directory.

```
module userfuncsimp {
  requires userfuncs;

  provides userfuncs.binaryfuncs.BinFuncProvider with
    userfuncsimp.binaryfuncsimp.AbsPlusProvider,
    userfuncsimp.binaryfuncsimp.AbsMinusProvider;
}
```

This module requires **userfuncs** because that is where **BinaryFunc** and **BinFuncProvider** are contained, and those interfaces are needed by the implementations. The module provides **BinFuncProvider** implementations with the classes **AbsPlusProvider** and **AbsMinusProvider**.

## Demonstrate the Service Providers in MyModAppDemo

To demonstrate the use of the services, the **main( )** method of **MyModAppDemo** is expanded to use **AbsPlus** and **AbsMinus**. It does so by loading them at run time by use of **ServiceLoader.load( )**. Here is the updated code:

```
// A module-based application that demonstrates services
// and service providers.

package appstart.mymodappdemo;

import java.util.ServiceLoader;

import appfuncs.simplefuncs.SimpleMathFuncs;
import userfuncs.binaryfuncs.*;

public class MyModAppDemo {
  public static void main(String[] args) {

    // First, use built-in functions as before.
    if(SimpleMathFuncs.isFactor(2, 10))
      System.out.println("2 is a factor of 10");

    System.out.println("Smallest factor common to both 35 and 105 is " +
                       SimpleMathFuncs.lcf(35, 105));

    System.out.println("Largest factor common to both 35 and 105 is " +
                       SimpleMathFuncs.gcf(35, 105));
```

```
      // Now, use service-based, user-defined operations.

      // Get a service loader for binary functions.
      ServiceLoader<BinFuncProvider> ldr =
        ServiceLoader.load(BinFuncProvider.class);

      BinaryFunc binOp = null;

      // Find the provider for absPlus and obtain the function.
      for(BinFuncProvider bfp : ldr) {
        if(bfp.get().getName().equals("absPlus")) {
          binOp = bfp.get();
          break;
        }
      }

      if(binOp != null)
        System.out.println("Result of absPlus function: " +
                           binOp.func(12, -4));
      else
        System.out.println("absPlus function not found");

      binOp = null;

      // Now, find the provider for absMinus and obtain the function.
      for(BinFuncProvider bfp : ldr) {
        if(bfp.get().getName().equals("absMinus")) {
          binOp = bfp.get();
          break;
        }
      }

      if(binOp != null)
        System.out.println("Result of absMinus function: " +
                           binOp.func(12, -4));
      else
        System.out.println("absMinus function not found");

    }
  }
```

Let's take a close look at how a service is loaded and executed by the preceding code. First, a service loader for services of type **BinFuncProvider** is created with this statement:

```
ServiceLoader<BinFuncProvider> ldr =
  ServiceLoader.load(BinFuncProvider.class);
```

Notice that the type parameter to **ServiceLoader** is **BinFuncProvider**. This is also the type used in the call to **load( )**. This means that providers that implement this interface will be found. Thus, after this statement executes, **BinFuncProvider** classes in the module will be available through **ldr**. In this case, both **AbsPlusProvider** and **AbsMinusProvider** will be available.

Next, a reference of type **BinaryFunc** called **binOp** is declared and initialized to **null**. It will be used to refer to an implementation that supplies a specific type of binary function. Next, the following loop searches **ldr** for one that has the "absPlus" name.

```
// Find the provider for absPlus and obtain the function.
for(BinFuncProvider bfp : ldr) {
  if(bfp.get().getName().equals("absPlus")) {
    binOp = bfp.get();
    break;
  }
}
```

Here, a for-each loop iterates through **ldr**. Inside the loop, the name of the function supplied by the provider is checked. If it matches "absPlus", that function is assigned to **binOp** by calling the provider's **get( )** method.

Finally, if the function is found, as it will be in this example, it is executed by this statement:

```
if(binOp != null)
  System.out.println("Result of absPlus function: " +
                     binOp.func(12, -4));
```

In this case, because **binOp** refers to an instance of **AbsPlus**, the call to **func( )** performs an absolute value addition. A similar sequence is used to find and execute **AbsMinus**.

Because **MyModAppDemo** now uses **BinFuncProvider**, its module definition file must include a **uses** statement that specifies this fact. Recall that **MyModAppDemo** is in the **appstart** module. Therefore, you must change the **module-info.java** file for **appstart** as shown here:

```
// Module definition for the main application module.
// It now uses BinFuncProvider.
module appstart {
  // Requires the modules appfuncs and userfuncs.
  requires appfuncs;
  requires userfuncs;

  // appstart now uses BinFuncProvider.
  uses userfuncs.binaryfuncs.BinFuncProvider;
}
```

## Compile and Run the Module-Based Service Example

Once you have performed all of the preceding steps, you can compile and run the example by executing the following commands:

```
javac  -d appmodules --module-source-path appsrc
  appsrc\userfuncsimp\module-info.java
  appsrc\appstart\appstart\mymodappdemo\MyModAppDemo.java

java --module-path appmodules -m appstart/appstart.mymodappdemo.MyModAppDemo
```

Here is the output:

```
2 is a factor of 10
Smallest factor common to both 35 and 105 is 5
Largest factor common to both 35 and 105 is 7
Result of absPlus function: 16
Result of absMinus function: 8
```

As the output shows, the binary functions were located and executed. It is important to emphasize that if either the **provides** statement in the **userfuncsimp** module or the **uses** statement in the **appstart** module were missing, the application would fail.

One last point: The preceding example was kept very simple in order to clearly illustrate module support for services, but much more sophisticated uses are possible. For example, you might use a service to provide a **sort( )** method that sorts a file. Various sorting algorithms could be supported and made available through the service. The specific sort could then be chosen based on the desired run-time characteristics, the nature and/or size of the data, and whether random access to the data is supported. You might want to try implementing such a service as a way to further experiment with services in modules.

## Module Graphs

A term you are likely to encounter when working with modules is *module graph*. During compilation, the compiler resolves the dependence relationships between modules by creating a module graph that represents the dependences. The process ensures that *all dependences* are resolved, including those that occur indirectly. For example, if module A requires module B, and B requires module C, then the module graph will contain module C even if A does not use it directly.

Module graphs can be depicted visually in a drawing to illustrate the relationship between modules. Here is a simple example. Assume six modules called **A**, **B**, **C**, **D**, **E**, and **F**. Further assume that **A** requires **B** and **C**, **B** requires **D** and **E**, and **C** requires **F**. The following visually depicts this relationship. (Because **java.base** is automatically included, it is not shown in the diagram.)

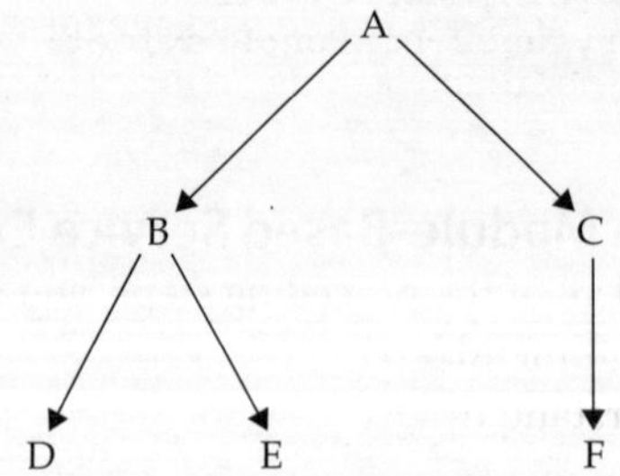


In Java, the arrows point from the dependent module to the required module. Thus, a drawing of a module graph depicts what modules have access to what other modules.

Frankly, only the smallest applications can have their module graphs visually represented because of the complexity typically involved in many commercial applications.

# Three Specialized Module Features

The preceding discussions have described the key features of modules supported by the Java language, and they are the features on which you will typically rely when creating your own modules. However, there are three additional module-related features that can be quite useful in certain circumstances. These are the **open** module, the **opens** statement, and the use of **requires static**. Each of these features is designed to handle a specialized situation, and each constitutes a fairly advanced aspect of the module system. That said, it is important for all Java programmers to have a general understanding of their purpose.

## Open Modules

As you learned earlier in this chapter, by default, the types in a module's packages are accessible only if they are explicitly exported via an **exports** statement. While this is usually what you will want, there can be circumstances in which it is useful to enable run-time access to all packages in the module, whether a package is exported or not. To allow this, you can create an *open module*. An open module is declared by preceding the **module** keyword with the **open** modifier, as shown here:

```
open module moduleName {
  // module definition
}
```

In an open module, types in all its packages are accessible at run time. Understand, however, that only those packages that are explicitly exported are available at compile time. Thus, the **open** modifier affects only run-time accessibility. The primary reason for an open module is to enable the packages in the module to be accessed through reflection. As explained in Chapter 12, reflection is the feature that lets a program analyze code at run time.

## The opens Statement

It is possible for a module to open a specific package for run-time access by other modules and for reflective access rather than opening an entire module. To do so, use the **opens** statement, shown here:

```
opens packageName;
```

Here, *packageName* specifies the package to open. It is also possible to include a **to** clause, which names those modules for which the package is opened.

It is important to understand **opens** does not grant compile-time access. It is used only to open a package for run-time and reflective access. However, you can both export and open a module. One other point: an **opens** statement cannot be used in an open module. Remember, all packages in an open module are already open.

### requires static

As you know, **requires** specifies a dependence that, by default, is enforced both during compilation and at run time. However, it is possible to relax this requirement in such a way that a module is not required at run time. This is accomplished by use of the **static** modifier in a **requires** statement. For example, this specifies that **mymod** is required for compilation, but not at run time:

```
requires static mymod;
```

In this case, the addition of **static** makes **mymod** optional at run time. This can be helpful in a situation in which a program can utilize functionality if it is present, but not require it.

## Introducing jlink and Module JAR Files

As the preceding discussions have shown, modules represent a substantial enhancement to the Java language. The module system also supports enhancements at run time. One of the most important is the ability to create a run-time image that is specifically tailored to your application. To accomplish this, you can use a JDK tool called **jlink**. It combines a group of modules into an optimized run-time image. You can use **jlink** to link modular JAR files, JMOD files, or even modules in their unarchived, "exploded directory" form.

### Linking Files in an Exploded Directory

Let's look first at using **jlink** to create a run-time image from unarchived modules. That is, the files are contained in their raw form in a fully expanded (i.e., exploded) directory. Assuming a Windows environment, the following command links the modules for the first example in this chapter. It must be executed from a directory *directly above* **mymodapp**.

```
jlink --launcher MyModApp=appstart/appstart.mymodappdemo.MyModAppDemo
      --module-path "%JAVA_HOME%"\jmods;mymodapp\appmodules
      --add-modules appstart --output mylinkedmodapp
```

Let's look closely at this command. First, the option **--launcher** tells **jlink** to create a command that starts the application. It specifies the name of the application and the path to the main class. In this case, the main class is **MyModAppDemo**. The **--module-path** option specifies the path to the required modules. The first is the path to the platform modules; the second is the path to the application modules. Notice the use of the environmental variable **JAVA_HOME**. It represents the path to the standard JDK directory. For example, in a standard Windows installation, the path will typically be something similar to **"C:\program files"\java\jdk-17\jmods**, but the use of **JAVA_HOME** is both shorter and able to work no matter in what directory the JDK was installed. The **--add-modules** option specifies the module or modules to add. Notice that only **appstart** is specified. This is because **jlink** automatically resolves all dependencies and includes all required modules. Finally, **--output** specifies the output directory.

After you run the preceding command, a directory called **mylinkedmodapp** will have been created that contains the run-time image. In its **bin** directory, you will find a launcher file called **MyModApp** that you can use to run the application. For example, in Windows, this will be a batch file that executes the program.

## Linking Modular JAR Files

Although linking modules from their exploded directory is convenient, when working on real-world code, you will often be using JAR files. (Recall that JAR stands for *J*ava *AR*chive. It is a file format typically used for application deployment.) In the case of modular code, you will be using *modular JAR files*. A modular JAR file is one that contains a **module-info.class** file. Beginning with JDK 9, the **jar** tool has the ability to create modular JAR files. For example, it can now recognize a module path. Once you have created modular JAR files, you can use **jlink** to link them into a run-time image. To understand the process, let's work through an example. Again assuming the first example in this chapter, here are the **jar** commands that create modular JAR files for the **MyModAppDemo** program. Each must be executed from a directory directly above **mymodapp**. Also, you will need to create a directory called **applib** under **mymodapp**.

```
jar --create --file=mymodapp\applib\appfuncs.jar
     -C mymodapp\appmodules\appfuncs .

jar --create --file=mymodapp\applib\appstart.jar
    --main-class=appstart.mymodappdemo.MyModAppDemo
    -C mymodapp\appmodules\appstart .
```

Here, **--create** tells **jar** to create a new JAR file. The **--file** option specifies the name of the JAR file. The files to include are specified by the **-C** option. The class that contains **main( )** is specified by the **--main-class** option. After running these commands, the JAR files for the application will be in the **applib** directory under **mymodapp**.

Given the modular JAR files just created, here is the command that links them:

```
jlink --launcher MyModApp=appstart
      --module-path "%JAVA_HOME%"\jmods;mymodapp\applib
      --add-modules appstart --output mylinkedmodapp
```

Here, the module path to the JAR files is specified, not the path to the exploded directories. Otherwise, the **jlink** command is the same as before.

As a point of interest, you can use the following command to run the application directly from the JAR files. It must be executed from a directory directly above **mymodapp**.

```
java -p mymodapp\applib -m appstart
```

Here, **-p** specifies the module path, and **-m** specifies the module that contains the program's entry point.

## JMOD Files

The **jlink** tool can also link files that use the newer JMOD format introduced by JDK 9. JMOD files can include things that are not applicable to a JAR file. They are created by the new **jmod** tool. Although most applications will still use module JAR files, JMOD files will be of value in specialized situations. As a point of interest, beginning with JDK 9, the platform modules are contained in JMOD files.

---

**NOTE** **jlink** can also be used by the recently added **jpackage** tool. This tool can create a natively installable application.

## A Brief Word About Layers and Automatic Modules

When learning about modules, you are likely to encounter reference to two additional module-related features. These are *layers* and *automatic modules*. Both are designed for specialized, advanced work with modules or when migrating preexisting applications. Although it is likely that most programmers will not need to make use of these features, a brief description of each is given here in the interest of completeness.

A module layer associates the modules in a module graph with a class loader. Thus, different layers can use different class loaders. Layers enable certain specialized types of applications to be more easily constructed.

An automatic module is created by specifying a nonmodular JAR file on the module path, with its name being automatically derived. (It is also possible to explicitly specify a name for an automatic module in the manifest file.) Automatic modules enable normal modules to have a dependence on code in the automatic module. Automatic modules are provided as an aid in migration from pre-modular code to fully modular code. Thus, they are primarily a transitional feature.

## Final Thoughts on Modules

The preceding discussions have introduced and demonstrated the core elements of Java's module system. These are the features about which every Java programmer should have at least a basic understanding. As you might guess, the module system provides additional features that give you fine-grained control over the creation and use of modules. For example, both **javac** and **java** have many more options related to modules than described in this chapter. Because modules are a significant addition to Java, it is likely that the module system will evolve over time. You will want to watch for enhancements to this innovative aspect of Java.

CHAPTER

# 17 Switch Expressions, Records, and Other Recently Added Features

A key attribute of Java has been its ability to adapt to the increasing demands of the modern computing environment. Over the years, Java has incorporated many new features, each responding to changes in the computing environment or to innovations in computer language design. This ongoing process has enabled Java to remain one of the world's most important and popular computer languages. As explained earlier, this book has been updated for JDK 21, which is a long-term support (LTS) version of Java. JDK 21 and its LTS predecessor JDK 17 have added a number of features to the Java language since the previous LTS version, JDK 11. A few of the smaller additions have been described in the preceding chapters. In this chapter, several major additions are examined. They are

- Records
- Patterns in **instanceof**
- Enhancements to **switch**
- Text blocks
- Sealed classes and interfaces

Here is a brief description of each. Supported by the new keyword **record**, records enable you to create a class that is specifically designed to hold a group of values. A second form of **instanceof** has been added that uses a type pattern. With this form, you can specify a variable that receives an instance of the type being tested if **instanceof** succeeds. The **switch** has been enhanced in a number of ways, the most impacting of which is the ***switch expression***. A **switch** expression enables a **switch** to produce a value. *Text blocks* allow a string literal to occupy more than a single line. It is now possible to specify a *sealed* class or interface. A sealed class can be inherited by only explicitly specified subclasses. A sealed interface can be implemented by only explicitly specified classes or extended by only explicitly specified interfaces. Thus, sealing a class or interface gives you fine-grained control over its inheritance and implementation.

# Records

Beginning with JDK 16, Java supports a special-purpose class called a *record*. A record is designed to provide an efficient, easy-to-use way to hold a group of values. For example, you might use a record to hold a set of coordinates; bank account numbers and balances; the length, width, and height of a shipping container; and so on. Because it holds a group of values, a record is commonly referred to as an *aggregate* type. However, the record is more than simply a means of grouping data, because records also have some of the capabilities of a class. In addition, a record has unique features that simplify its declaration and streamline access to its values. As a result, records make it much easier to work with groups of data. Records are supported by the new context-sensitive keyword **record**.

One of the central motivations for records is the reduction of the effort required to create a class whose primary purpose is to organize two or more values into a single unit. Although it has always been possible to use **class** for this purpose, doing so can entail writing a number of lines of code for constructors, getter methods, and possibly (depending on use) overriding one or more of the methods inherited from **Object**. As you will see, by creating a data aggregate by using **record**, these elements are handled automatically for you, greatly simplifying your code. Another reason for the addition of records is to enable a program to clearly indicate that the intended purpose of a class is to hold a grouping of data, rather than act as a full-featured class. Because of these advantages, records are a much welcomed addition to Java.

## Record Basics

As stated, a record is a narrowly focused, specialized class. It is declared by use of the **record** context-sensitive keyword. As such, **record** is a keyword only in the context of a **record** declaration. Otherwise, it is treated as a user-defined identifier with no special meaning. Thus, the addition of **record** does not impact or break existing code.

The general form of a basic **record** declaration is shown here:

record *recordName*(*component-list*) {
    // *optional body statements*
}

As the general form shows, a **record** declaration has significant differences from a **class** declaration. First, notice that the record name is immediately followed by a comma-separated list of parameter declarations called a *component list*. This list defines the data that the record will hold. Second, notice that the body is optional. This is made possible because the compiler will automatically provide the elements necessary to store the data; construct a record; create *getter methods* to access the data; and override **toString( )**, **equals( )**, and **hashCode( )** inherited from **Object**. As a result, for many uses of a record, no body is required because the **record** declaration itself fully defines the record.

Here is an example of a simple **record** declaration:

```
record Employee(String name, int idNum) {}
```

Here, the record name is **Employee** and it has two components: the string **name** and the integer **idNum**. It specifies no statements in its body, so its body is empty. As the names imply, such a record could be used to store the name and ID number of an employee.

Given the **Employee** declaration just shown, a number of elements are automatically created. First, private final fields for **name** and **idNum** are declared as type **String** and **int**, respectively. Second, public read-only accessor methods (getter methods) that have the same names and types as the record components **name** and **idNum** are provided. Therefore, these getter methods are called **name( )** and **idNum( )**. In general, each record component will have a corresponding private final field and a read-only public getter method automatically created by the compiler.

Another element created automatically by the compiler will be the record's *canonical constructor*. This constructor has a parameter list that contains the same elements, in the same order, as the component list in the record declaration. The values passed to the constructor are automatically assigned to the corresponding fields in the record. In a **record**, the canonical constructor takes the place of the default constructor used by a **class**.

A **record** is instantiated by use of **new**, just the way you create an instance of a **class**. For example, this creates a new **Employee** object, with the name "Doe, John" and ID number 1047:

```
Employee emp = new Employee("Doe, John", 1047);
```

After this declaration executes, the private fields **name** and **idNum** for **emp** will contain the values "Doe, John" and 1047, respectively. Therefore, you can use the following statement to display the information associated with **emp**:

```
System.out.println("The employee ID for " + emp.name() + " is " +
                   emp.idNum());
```

The resulting output is shown here:

```
The employee ID for Doe, John is 1047
```

A key point about a record is that its data is held in private final fields and only getter methods are provided. Thus, the data that a record holds is immutable. In other words, once you construct a record, its contents cannot be changed. However, if a record holds a reference to some object, you can make a change to that object, but you cannot change to what object the reference in the record refers. Thus, in Java terms, records are said to be *shallowly immutable*.

The following program puts the preceding discussion into action. Records are often used as elements in a list. For example, a business might maintain a list of **Employee** records to store an employee's name along with his or her corresponding ID number. The following program shows a simple example of such usage. It creates a small array of **Employee** records. It then cycles through the array, displaying the contents of each record.

```
// A simple Record example.

// Declare an employee record. This automatically creates a
// record class with private, final fields called name and idNum,
// and with read only accessors called name() and idNum().
record Employee(String name, int idNum) {}

class RecordDemo {
  public static void main(String[] args) {
    // Create an array of Employee records.
    Employee[] empList = new Employee[4];
```

```
    // Create a list of employees that uses the Employee record.
    // Notice how each record is constructed. The arguments
    // are automatically assigned to the name and idNum fields in
    // record that is being created.
    empList[0] = new Employee("Doe, John", 1047);
    empList[1] = new Employee("Jones, Robert", 1048);
    empList[2] = new Employee("Smith, Rachel", 1049);
    empList[3] = new Employee("Martin, Dave", 1050);

    // Use the record accessors to display names and IDs.
    for(Employee e: empList)
      System.out.println("The employee ID for " + e.name() + " is " +
                         e.idNum());
  }
}
```

The output is shown here:

```
The employee ID for Doe, John is 1047
The employee ID for Jones, Robert is 1048
The employee ID for Smith, Rachel is 1049
The employee ID for Martin, Dave is 1050
```

Before continuing, it is important to mention some key points related to records. First, a **record** cannot inherit another class. However, all records implicitly inherit **java.lang .Record**, which specifies abstract overrides of the **equals( )**, **hashCode( )**, and **toString( )** methods declared by **Object**. Implicit implementations of these methods are automatically created, based on the record declaration. A **record** type cannot be extended. Thus, all **record** declarations are considered final. Although a **record** cannot extend another class, it can implement one or more interfaces. With the exception of **equals**, you cannot use the names of methods defined by **Object** as names for a **record**'s components. Aside from the fields associated with a **record**'s components, any other fields must be **static**. Finally, a **record** can be generic.

## Create Record Constructors

Although you will often find that the automatically supplied canonical constructor is precisely what you want, you can also declare one or more of your own constructors. You can also define your own implementation of the canonical constructor. You might want to declare a **record** constructor for a number of reasons. For example, the constructor could check that a value is within a required range, verify that a value is in the proper format, ensure that an object implements optional functionality, or confirm that an argument is not **null**. For a **record**, there are two general types of constructors that you can explicitly create: canonical and non-canonical, and there are some differences between the two. The creation of each type is examined here, beginning with defining your own implementation of the canonical constructor.

## Declare a Canonical Constructor

Although the canonical constructor has a specific, predefined form, there are two ways that you can code your own implementation. First, you can explicitly declare the full form of the canonical constructor. Second, you can use what is called a *compact record constructor*. Each approach is examined here, beginning with the full form.

To define your own implementation of a canonical constructor, simply do so as you would with any other constructor, specifying the record's name and its parameter list. It is important to emphasize that for the canonical constructor, the types and parameter names must be the same as those specified by the **record** declaration. This is because the parameter names are linked to the automatically created fields and accessor methods defined by the **record** declaration. Thus, they must agree in both type and name. Furthermore, each component must be fully initialized upon completion of the constructor. The following restrictions also apply: the constructor must be at least as accessible as its **record** declaration Thus, if the access modifier for the **record** is **public**, the constructor must also be specified **public**. A constructor cannot be generic, and it cannot include a **throws** clause (though it is permitted to throw an unchecked exception at run time). It also cannot invoke another constructor defined for the record.

Here is an example of the **Employee** record that explicitly defines the canonical constructor. It uses this constructor to remove any leading or trailing whitespace from a name. This ensures that names are stored in a consistent manner.

```
record Employee(String name, int idNum) {

  // Use a canonical constructor to remove any leading and trailing spaces
  // that might be in the name string. This ensures that names are stored
  // in a consistent manner.
  public Employee(String name, int idNum) {
    // Remove any leading and trailing spaces.
    this.name = name.trim();
    this.idNum = idNum;
  }
}
```

In the constructor, leading and/or trailing whitespace is removed by a call to **trim( )**. Defined by the **String** class, **trim( )** deletes all leading and trailing whitespace from a string and returns the result. (If there are no leading or trailing spaces, the original string is returned unaltered.) The resulting string is assigned to the field **this.name**. Thus, no **Employee** record **name** will contain leading or trailing spaces. Next, the value of **idNum** is assigned to **this.idNum**. Because the identifiers **name** and **idNum** are the same for both fields corresponding to the **Employee** components and for the names used by the canonical constructor's parameters, the field names must be qualified by **this**.

Although there is certainly nothing wrong with creating a canonical constructor as just shown, there is often an easier way: through the use of a *compact constructor*. A compact record constructor is declared by specifying the name of the record, but without parameters. The compact constructor implicitly has parameters that are the same as the record's components, and its components are automatically assigned the values of the arguments passed to the constructor. Within the compact constructor you can, however, alter one or more of the arguments prior to their value being assigned to the record.

The following example converts the previous canonical constructor into its compact form:

```
// Use a compact canonical constructor to remove any leading and
// trailing spaces from the name string.
public Employee {
  // Remove any leading and trailing spaces.
  name = name.trim();
}
```

Here, the result of **trim( )** is called on the **name** parameter (which is implicitly declared by the compact constructor) and the result is assigned back to the **name** parameter. At the end of the compact constructor, the value of **name** is automatically assigned to its corresponding field. The value of the implicit **idNum** parameter is also assigned to its corresponding field at the end of the constructor. Because the parameters are implicitly assigned to their corresponding fields when the constructor ends, there is no need to initialize the fields explicitly. Moreover, it would not be legal to do so.

Here is a reworked version of the previous program that demonstrates the compact canonical constructor:

```
// Use a compact record constructor.

// Declare an employee record.
record Employee(String name, int idNum) {

  // Use a compact canonical constructor to remove any leading and
  // trailing spaces from the name string.
  public Employee {
    // Remove any leading and trailing spaces.
    name = name.trim();
  }
}

class RecordDemo2 {
  public static void main(String[] args) {
    Employee[] empList = new Employee[4];

    // Here, the name has no leading or trailing spaces.
    empList[0] = new Employee("Doe, John", 1047);

    // The next three names have leading and/or trailing spaces.
    empList[1] = new Employee("  Jones, Robert", 1048);
    empList[2] = new Employee("Smith, Rachel    ", 1049);
    empList[3] = new Employee("   Martin, Dave   ", 1050);

    // Use the record accessors to display names and IDs.
    // Notice that all leading and/or trailing spaces have been
    // removed from the name component by the constructor.
    for(Employee e: empList)
      System.out.println("The employee ID for " + e.name() + " is " +
                         e.idNum());
  }
}
```

The output is shown here:

```
The employee ID for Doe, John is 1047
The employee ID for Jones, Robert is 1048
The employee ID for Smith, Rachel is 1049
The employee ID for Martin, Dave is 1050
```

As you can see, the names have been standardized with leading and trailing spaces removed. To prove to yourself that the call to **trim( )** is necessary to achieve this result, simply remove the compact constructor, recompile, and run the program. The leading and trailing spaces will still be in the names.

## Declare a Non-canonical Constructor

Although the canonical constructor will often be sufficient, you can declare other constructors. The key requirement is that any non-canonical constructor must first call another constructor in the record via **this**. The constructor invoked will often be the canonical constructor. Doing this ultimately ensures that all fields are assigned. Declaring a non-canonical constructor enables you to create special-case records. For example, you might use such a constructor to create a record in which one or more of the components is given a default placeholder value.

The following program declares a non-canonical constructor for **Employee** that initializes the name to a known value, but gives the **idNum** field the special value **pendingID** (which is –1) to indicate an ID value is not available when the record is created:

```
// Use a non-canonical constructor in a record.

// Declare an employee record that explicitly declares both
// a canonical and non-canonical constructor.
record Employee(String name, int idNum) {

  // Use a static field in a record.
  static int pendingID = -1;

  // Use a compact canonical constructor to remove any leading and
  // trailing spaces from the name string.
  public Employee {
    // Remove any leading and trailing spaces.
    name = name.trim();
  }

  // This is a non-canonical constructor. Notice that it is
  // not passed an ID number. Instead, it passes pendingID to the
  // canonical constructor to create the record.
  public Employee(String name) {
    this(name, pendingID);
  }
}

class RecordDemo3 {
  public static void main(String[] args) {
    Employee[] empList = new Employee[4];
```

```
        // Create a list of employees that uses the Employee record.
        empList[0] = new Employee("Doe, John", 1047);
        empList[1] = new Employee("Jones, Robert", 1048);
        empList[2] = new Employee("Smith, Rachel", 1049);

        // Here, the ID number is pending.
        empList[3] = new Employee("Martin, Dave");

        // Display names and IDs.
        for(Employee e: empList) {
          System.out.print("The employee ID for " + e.name() + " is ");
          if(e.idNum() == Employee.pendingID) System.out.println("Pending");
          else System.out.println(e.idNum());
        }
    }
}
```

Pay special attention to the way that the record for Martin, Dave is created by use of the non-canonical constructor. That constructor passes the **name** argument to the canonical constructor, but specifies the value **pendingID** as the **idNum** value. This enables a placeholder record to be created without having to specify an ID number. One other point: Notice that the value **pendingID** is declared as a **static** field in **Employee**. As explained earlier, instance fields are not allowed in a **record** declaration, but a **static** field is legal.

Notice that this version of **Employee** declares both a canonical constructor and a non-canonical constructor. This is perfectly valid. A record can define as many different constructors as its needs, as long as all adhere to the rules defined for **record**.

It is important to emphasize that records are immutable. As it relates to this example, it means that when an ID value for Martin, Dave is obtained, the old record must be replaced by a new record that contains the ID number. It is not possible to alter the record to update the ID. The immutability of records is a primary attribute.

## Another Record Constructor Example

Before leaving the topic of record constructors, we will look at one more example. Because a **record** is used to aggregate data, a common use of a **record** constructor is to verify the validity or applicability of an argument. For example, before constructing the record, the constructor may need to determine if a value is out of range, in an improper format, or otherwise unsuitable for use. If an invalid condition is found, the constructor could create a default or error instance. However, often it would be better for the constructor to throw an exception. This way, the user of the **record** would immediately be aware of the error and could take steps to correct it.

In the preceding **Employee** record examples, names have been specified using the common convention of *lastname, firstname*, such as Doe, John. However, there was no mechanism to verify or enforce that this format was being used. The following version of the compact canonical constructor provides a limited check that the name has the format *lastname, firstname*. It does so by confirming that there is one and only one comma in the name and that there is at least one character (other than space) before and after the comma. Although a far more thorough, careful verification would be needed by a real-world program, this minimal check is sufficient to serve as an example of the validation role a record constructor might play.

Here is a version of the **Employee** record in which the compact canonical constructor throws an exception if the **name** component does not meet the minimal criteria required for the *lastname, firstname* format:

```
// Use a compact canonical constructor to remove any leading
// and trailing spaces in the name component. Also perform
// a basic check that the required format of lastname, firstname
// is passed to the name parameter.
public Employee {
  // Remove any leading and trailing spaces.
  name = name.trim();

  // Perform a minimalist check that name follows the
  // lastname, firstname format.
  //
  // First, confirm that name contains only one comma.
  int i = name.indexOf(','); // look for comma separating names.
  int j = name.lastIndexOf(',');
  if(i != j) throw
    new IllegalArgumentException("Multiple commas found.");

  // Next, confirm that a comma is present after
  // at least one leading character, and that at least one
  // character follows the comma.
  if(i < 1 | name.length() == i+1) throw
    new IllegalArgumentException("Required format: last, first");
}
```

When using this constructor, the following statement is still correct:

```
empList[0] = new Employee("Doe, John", 1047);
```

However, the following three are invalid and will result in an exception:

```
// No comma between last and first name.
empList[1] = new Employee("Jones Robert", 1048);

// Extra commas.
empList[1] = new Employee("Jones, ,Robert", 1048);

// Missing last name.
empList[1] = new Employee(", Robert", 1048);
```

As an aside, you might find it interesting to think of ways that you can improve the ability of the constructor to verify that the name uses the proper format. For example, you might want to explore an approach that uses a regular expression. (See Chapter 31.)

## Create Record Getter Methods

Although it is seldom necessary, it is possible to create your own implementation of a getter method. When you declare the getter, the implicit version is no longer supplied. One possible reason you might want to declare your own getter is to throw an exception if some condition is not met. For example, if a record holds a filename and a URL, the getter for the filename might throw a **FileNotFoundException** if the file is not present at the URL. There is a very important requirement, however, that applies to creating your getters: they must adhere to the principle that a record is immutable. Thus, a getter that returns an altered value is semantically questionable (and should be avoided) even though such code would be syntactically correct.

If you do declare a getter implementation, there are a number of rules that apply. A getter must have the same return type and name as the component that it obtains. It must also be explicitly declared public. (Thus, default accessibility is not sufficient for a getter declaration in a **record**.) No **throws** clause is allowed in a getter declaration. Finally, a getter must be non-generic and non-static.

A better alternative to overriding a getter in cases in which you want to obtain a modified value of a component is to declare a separate method with its own name. For example, assuming the **Employee** record, you might want to obtain only the last name from the **name** component. Using the standard getter to do this would entail modifying the value obtained from the component. Doing this is a bad idea because it would violate the immutability aspect of the record. However, you could declare another method, called **lastName( )**, that returns only the last name. The following program demonstrates this approach. It also uses the format-checking constructor from the previous section to ensure that names are stored as *lastname, firstname.*

```
// Use an instance method in a record.

// This version of Employee provides a method called lastName()
// that returns only the last name of the name component.
// It also includes the version of the compact constructor that
// checks for the conventional lastname, firstname format.
record Employee(String name, int idNum) {

  // Use a compact canonical constructor to remove any leading
  // and trailing spaces in the name component. Also perform
  // a basic check that the required format of lastname, firstname.
  // is passed to the name parameter.
  public Employee {
    // Remove any leading and trailing spaces.
    name = name.trim();

    // Perform a minimalist check that name follows the
    // lastname, firstname format.
    //
    // First, confirm that name contains only one comma.
    int i = name.indexOf(','); // look for comma separating names.
    int j = name.lastIndexOf(',');
    if(i != j) throw
      new IllegalArgumentException("Multiple commas found.");

    // Next, confirm that a comma is present after
    // at least one leading character, and that at least one
    // character follows the comma.
    if(i < 1 | name.length() == i+1) throw
      new IllegalArgumentException("Required format: last, first");
  }
```

```
    // An instance method that returns only the last name
    // without the first name.
    String lastName() {
      return name.substring(0, name.trim().indexOf(','));
    }
  }

  class RecordDemo4 {
    public static void main(String[] args) {
      Employee emp = new Employee("Jones, Robert", 1048);

      // Display the name component unmodified.
      System.out.println("Employee full name is " + emp.name());

      // Display only last name.
      System.out.println("Employee last name is " +  emp.lastName());
    }
  }
```

The output is shown here:

```
Employee full name is Jones, Robert
Employee last name is Jones
```

As the output shows, the implicit getter for the **name** component returns the name unaltered. The instance method **lastName( )** obtains only the last name. With this approach, the immutable attribute of the **Employee** record is preserved, while still providing a convenient means of obtaining the last name.

# Pattern Matching with instanceof

The traditional form of the **instanceof** operator was introduced in Chapter 13. As explained there, **instanceof** evaluates to **true** if an object is of a specified type, or can be cast to that type. Beginning with JDK 16, a second form of the **instanceof** operator has been added to Java that supports the new *pattern matching* feature. In general terms, *pattern matching* defines a mechanism that determines if a value fits a general form. As it relates to **instanceof**, pattern matching is used to test the type of a value (which must be a reference type) against a specified type. If the pattern matches, a *pattern variable* will receive a reference to the object matched by the pattern. Beginning with JDK 21 there are two kinds of patterns: *type patterns* and *record patterns*. Type patterns are described here. Record patterns are discussed later in this chapter.

The pattern matching form of **instanceof** is shown here:

*objref* instanceof *type pattern-var*

If **instanceof** succeeds, *pattern-var* will be created and contain a reference to the object that matches the pattern. If it fails, *pattern-var* is never created. This form of **instanceof** succeeds if the object referred to by *objref* can be cast to *type* and the static type of *objref* is not a subtype of *type*.

For example, the following fragment creates a **Number** reference called **myOb** that refers to an **Integer** object. (Recall that **Number** is a superclass of all numeric primitive-type wrappers.) It then uses the **instanceof** operator to confirm that the object referred to by **myOb** is an **Integer**, which it will be in this example. This results in an object called **iObj** of type **Integer** being instantiated that contains the matched value.

```
Number myOb = Integer.valueOf(9);

// Use the pattern matching version of instanceof.
if(myOb instanceof Integer iObj) {
  // iObj is known and in scope here.
  System.out.println("iObj refers to an integer: " + iObj);
}
// iObj does not exist here
```

As the comments indicate, **iObj** is known only within the scope of the **if** clause. It is not known outside of the **if**. It also would not be known within an **else** clause, should one have been included. It is crucial to understand that the pattern variable **iObj** is created only if the pattern matching succeeds.

The primary advantage of the pattern matching form of **instanceof** is that it reduces the amount of code that was typically needed by the traditional form of **instanceof**. For example, consider this functionally equivalent version of the preceding example that uses the traditional approach:

```
// Use a traditional instanceof.
if(myOb instanceof Integer) {
  // Use an explicit cast to obtain iObj.
  Integer iObj = (Integer) myOb;
  System.out.println("iObj refers to an integer: " + iObj);
}
```

With the traditional form, a separate declaration statement and explicit cast are required to create the **iObj** variable. The pattern matching form of **instanceof** streamlines the process.

## Pattern Variables in a Logical AND Expression

An **instanceof** can be used in a logical AND expression. However, you need to remember that the pattern variable is only in scope after it has been created. For example, the following **if** succeeds only when **myOb** refers to an **Integer** and its value is nonnegative. Pay special attention to the expression in the **if**:

```
if((myOb instanceof Integer iObj) && (iObj >= 0)) { // is OK
  // myOb is both an Integer and nonnegative.
  // ...
}
```

The **iObj** pattern variable is created only if the left side of the **&&** (the part that contains the **instanceof** operator) is true. Notice that **iObj** is also used by the right side. This is possible because the short-circuit form of the AND logical operator is used, and the right side is evaluated *only if* the left succeeds. Thus, if the right-side operand is evaluated, **iObj** will be in scope. However, if you tried to write the preceding statement using the **&** operator like this:

```
if((myOb instanceof Integer iObj) & (iObj >= 0)) { // Error!
  // myOb is both an Integer and nonnegative.
  // ...
}
```

a compilation error would occur because **iObj** will not be in scope if the left side fails. Recall that the **&** operator causes both sides of the expression to be evaluated, but **iObj** is only in scope if the left side is true. This error is caught by the compiler. A related situation occurs with this fragment:

```
int count = 10;
if((count < 100) && myOb instanceof Integer iObj) { // is OK
  // myOb is both an Integer and nonnegative, and count is less than 100.

  iObj = count;
  // ...
}
```

This fragment compiles because the **if** block will execute only when both sides of the **&&** are true. Thus, the use of **iObj** in the **if** block is valid. However, a compilation error will result if you tried to use the **&** rather than the **&&**, as shown here:

```
if((count < 100) & myOb instanceof Integer iObj) { // Error!
```

In this case, the compiler cannot know whether or not **iObj** will be in scope in the **if** block because the right side of the **&** will not necessarily be evaluated.

One other point: A logical expression cannot introduce the same pattern variable more than once. For example, in a logical AND, it is an error if both operands create the same pattern variable.

## Pattern Matching in Other Statements

Although a frequent use of the pattern matching form of **instanceof** is in an **if** statement, it is by no means limited to that use. It can also be employed in the conditional portion of the loop statements. As an example, imagine that you are processing a collection of objects, perhaps contained in an array. Furthermore, at the start of the array are several strings, and you want to process those strings, but not any of the remaining objects in the list. The following sequence accomplishes this task with a **for** loop in which the condition uses **instanceof** to confirm that an object in the array is a **String** and to obtain that string for processing within the loop. Thus, pattern matching is used to control the execution of a **for** loop and to obtain the next value for processing.

```
Object[] someObjs = {
  new String("Alpha"),
  new String("Beta"),
  new String("Omega"),
  Integer.valueOf(10)
};
```

```
int i;

// This loop iterates until an element is not a String, or the end
// of the array is reached.
for(i = 0; (someObjs[i] instanceof String str)  && (i < someObjs.length); i++) {
  System.out.println("Processing " + str);
  // ...
}

System.out.println("The first " + i + " entries in the list are strings.");
```

The output from this fragment is shown here:

```
Processing Alpha
Processing Beta
Processing Omega
The first 3 entries in the list are strings.
```

The pattern matching form of **instanceof** can also be useful in a **while** loop. For example, here is the preceding **for** loop, recoded as a **while**:

```
i = 0;
while((someObjs[i] instanceof String str)  && (i < someObjs.length)) {
  System.out.println("Processing " + str);
  i++;
}
```

Although it is technically possible to use the pattern matching **instanceof** in the conditional portion of a **do** loop, such use is severely limited because the pattern variable cannot be used in body of the loop because it will not be in scope until the **instanceof** operator is executed.

# Enhancements to switch

The **switch** statement has been part of Java since the start. It is a crucial element of Java's program control statements and provides for a multiway branch. Moreover, **switch** is so fundamental to programming that it is found in one form or another in other popular programming languages. The traditional form of **switch** was described in Chapter 5. This is the form of **switch** that has always been part of Java. Beginning with JDK 14, **switch** has been substantially enhanced with the addition of four new features, and in JDK 21 a fifth, shown here:

- The **switch** expression
- The **yield** statement
- Support for a list of **case** constants
- The **case** with an arrow
- Pattern matching in **switch**

Each new feature is examined in detail in the discussions that follow, but here is a brief description: The **switch** expression is, essentially, a **switch** that produces a value. Thus, a

**switch** expression can be used on the right side of an assignment, for example. The **yield** statement specifies a value that is produced by a **switch** expression. It is now possible to have more than one **case** constant in a **case** statement through the use of a list of constants. A second form of **case** has been added that uses an arrow (->) instead of a colon. The arrow gives **case** new capabilities.

Collectively, the enhancements to **switch** represent a fairly significant change to the Java language. Not only do they provide new capabilities, but in some situations, they also offer superior alternatives to traditional approaches. Because of this, a solid understanding of the "how" and "why" behind the new **switch** features is important.

One of the best ways to understand the **switch** enhancements is to start with an example that uses a traditional **switch** and then gradually incorporate each new feature. This way, the use and benefit of the enhancements will be clearly apparent. To begin, imagine some device that produces integer codes that indicate various events, and you want to associate a priority level with each event code. Most events will have a normal priority, but a few will have a higher priority. Here is a program that uses a traditional **switch** statement to supply a priority level given an event code:

```
// Use a traditional switch to set a priority level based on which
// event code is matched.
class TraditionalSwitch {

  public static void main(String[] args) {
    int priorityLevel;

    int eventCode = 6010;

    // A traditional switch that supplies a value associated
    // with a case.
    switch(eventCode) {
      case 1000: // In this traditional switch, case stacking is used.
      case 1205:
      case 8900:
        priorityLevel = 1;
        break;
      case 2000:
      case 6010:
      case 9128:
        priorityLevel = 2;
        break;
      case 1002:
      case 7023:
      case 9300:
        priorityLevel = 3;
        break;
      default: // normal priority
        priorityLevel = 0;
    }

    System.out.println("Priority level for event code " + eventCode +
                       " is " + priorityLevel);
  }
}
```

The output is shown here:

```
Priority level for event code 6010 is 2
```

There is certainly nothing wrong with using a traditional **switch** as shown in the program, and this is the way Java code has been written for more than two decades. However, as the following sections will show, in many cases, the traditional **switch** can be improved by use of the enhanced **switch** features.

## Use a List of case Constants

We begin with one of the easiest ways to modernize a traditional **switch**: by use of a list of **case** constants. In the past, when two constants were both handled by the same code sequence, ***case** stacking* was employed, and this is the approach used by the preceding program. For example, here are how the **case**s for 1000, 1205, and 8900 are handled:

```
case 1000: // In this traditional switch, case stacking is used.
case 1205:
case 8900:
  priorityLevel = 1;
  break;
```

The stacking of **case** statements enables all three **case** statements to use the same code sequence to set **priorityLevel** to 1. As explained in Chapter 5, in a traditional-style **switch**, the stacking of **case**s is made possible because execution falls through each **case** until a **break** is encountered. Although this approach works, a more elegant solution can be achieved by use of a ***case** constant list.*

Beginning with JDK 14, you can specify more than one **case** constant in a single **case**. To do so, simply separate each constant with a comma. For example, here is a more compact way to code the **case** for 1000, 1205, and 8900:

```
case 1000, 1205, 8900: // use a case list
  priorityLevel = 1;
  break;
```

Here is the entire **switch**, rewritten to use lists of **case** constants:

```
// This switch uses a list of constants with each case.
switch(eventCode) {
  case 1000, 1205, 8900:
    priorityLevel = 1;
    break;
  case 2000, 6010, 9128:
    priorityLevel = 2;
    break;
  case 1002, 7023, 9300:
    priorityLevel = 3;
    break;
  default: // normal priority
    priorityLevel = 0;
}
```

As you can see, the number of **case** statements has been reduced by six, making the **switch** easier to read and a bit more manageable. Although support for a **case** constant list does not by itself add any fundamentally new functionality to the **switch**, it does help streamline your code. In many situations, it also offers an easy way to improve existing code—especially when extensive **case**-stacking was previously employed. Thus, it is a feature that you can put to work immediately, with minimal code rewriting.

## Introducing the switch Expression and the yield Statement

Of the enhancements to **switch**, the one that will have the most profound impact is the ***switch expression***. A **switch** expression is, essentially, a **switch** that returns a value. Thus, it has all of the capabilities of a traditional **switch** statement, plus the ability to produce a result. This added capability makes the **switch** expression one of the more important additions to Java in recent years.

One way to supply the value of a **switch** expression is with the new **yield** statement. It has this general form:

yield *value*;

Here, *value* is the value produced by the **switch**, and it can be any expression compatible with the type of value required. A key point to understand about **yield** is that it immediately terminates the **switch**. Thus, it works somewhat like **break**, with the added capability of supplying a value. It is important to point out that **yield** is a context-sensitive keyword. This means that outside its use in a **switch** expression, **yield** is simply an identifier with no special meaning. However, if you use a method called **yield( )**, it must be qualified. For example, if **yield( )** is a non-**static** method within its class, you must use **this.yield( )**.

It is very easy to specify a **switch** expression. Simply use the **switch** in a context in which a value is required, such as on the right side of an assignment statement, an argument to a method, or a return value. For example, this line indicates that a **switch** expression is being employed:

```
int x = switch(y) { // ...
```

Here, the **switch** result is being assigned to the **x** variable. A key point about using a **switch** expression is that each **case** (plus **default**) must produce a value (unless it throws an exception). In other words, each path through a **switch** expression must produce a result.

The addition of the **switch** expression simplifies the coding of situations in which each **case** sets the value of some variable. Such situations can occur in a number of different ways. For example, each **case** might set a **boolean** variable that indicates the success or failure of some action taken by the **switch**. Often, however, setting a variable is the *primary purpose* of the **switch**, as is the case with the **switch** used by the preceding program. Its job is to produce the priority level associated with an event code. With a traditional **switch** statement, each **case** statement must individually assign a value to the variable, and this variable becomes the de facto result of the **switch**. This is the approach used by the preceding programs, in which the value of the variable **priorityLevel** is set by each **case**. Although this approach has been used in Java programs for decades, the **switch** expression offers a better solution because the desired value is produced by the **switch** itself.

The following version of the program puts the preceding discussion into action by changing the **switch** statement into a **switch** expression:

```
// Convert a switch statement into a switch expression.
class SwitchExpr {

  public static void main(String[] args) {
    int eventCode = 6010;

    // This is a switch expression. Notice how its value is assigned
    // to the priorityLevel variable. Also notice how the value of the
    // switch is supplied by the yield statement.
    int priorityLevel = switch(eventCode) {
      case 1000, 1205, 8900:
        yield 1;
      case 2000, 6010, 9128:
        yield 2;
      case 1002, 7023, 9300:
        yield 3;
      default: // normal priority
        yield 0;
    };

    System.out.println("Priority level for event code " + eventCode +
                       " is " + priorityLevel);
  }
}
```

Look closely at the **switch** in the program. Notice that it differs in important ways from the one used in the previous examples. Instead of each **case** assigning a value to **priorityLevel** individually, this version assigns the outcome of the **switch** itself to the **priorityLevel** variable. Thus, only one assignment to **priorityLevel** is required, and the length of the **switch** is reduced. Using a **switch** expression also ensures that each **case** yields a value, thus avoiding the possibility of forgetting to give **priorityLevel** a value in one of the **cases**. Notice that the value of the **switch** is produced by the **yield** statement inside each **case**. As explained, **yield** causes immediate termination of the **switch**, so no fall-through from **case** to **case** will occur. Thus, no **break** statement is required, or allowed. One other thing to notice is the semicolon after the closing brace of the **switch**. Because this **switch** is used in an assignment, it must be terminated by a semicolon.

There is an important restriction that applies to a **switch** expression: the **case** statements must handle all of the values that might occur. Thus, a **switch** expression must be *exhaustive*. For example, if its controlling expression is of type **int**, then all **int** values must be handled by the **switch**. This would, of course, constitute a very large number of **case** statements! For this reason, most **switch** expressions will have a **default** statement. The exception to this rule is when an enumeration is used, and each value of the enumeration is matched by a **case**.

## Introducing the Arrow in a case Statement

Although the use of **yield** in the preceding program is a perfectly valid way to specify a value for a **switch** expression, it is not the only way to do so. In many situations, an easier way to supply a value is through the use of a new form of the **case** that substitutes **->** for the colon in a **case**. For example, this line:

```
case 'X': // ...
```

can be rewritten using the arrow like this:

```
case 'X' -> // ...
```

To avoid confusion, in this discussion we will refer to a **case** with an arrow as an *arrow* ***case*** and the traditional, colon-based form as a *colon* ***case***. Although both forms will match the character X, the precise action of each style of **case** statement differs in three very important ways.

First, one arrow **case** *does not* fall through to the next **case**. Thus, there is no need to use **break**. Execution simply terminates at the end of an arrow **case**. Although the fall-through nature of a traditional colon-based **case** has always been part of Java, fall-through has been criticized because it can be a source for bugs, such as when the programmer forgets to add a **break** statement to prevent fall-through when fall-through is not desired. The arrow **case** avoids this situation. Second, the arrow **case** provides a "shorthand" way to supply a value when used in a **switch** expression. For this reason, the arrow **case** is often used in **switch** expressions. Third, the target of an arrow **case** must be either an expression, a block, or throw an exception. It cannot be a statement sequence, as is allowed with a traditional **case**. Thus, the arrow case will have one of these general forms:

case *constant* -> *expression*;
case *constant* -> { *block-of-statements* }
case *constant* -> throw ...

Of course, the first two forms represent the primary uses.

Arguably, the most common use of an arrow **case** is in a **switch** expression, and the most common target of the arrow **case** is an expression. Thus, it is here that we will begin. When the target of an arrow **case** is an expression, the value of that expression becomes the value of the **switch** expression when that **case** is matched. Thus, it provides a very efficient alternative to the **yield** statement in many situations. For example, here is the first **case** in the event code example rewritten to use an arrow **case**:

```
case 1000, 1205, 8900 -> 1;
```

Here, the value of the expression (which is 1) automatically becomes the value produced by the **switch** when this **case** is matched. In other words, the expression becomes the value yielded by the **switch**. Notice that this statement is quite compact, yet clearly expresses the intent to supply a value.

In the following program, the entire **switch** expression has been completely rewritten to use the arrow **case**:

```
// Use the arrow "shorthand" to supply the priority level.
class SwitchExpr2 {

  public static void main(String[] args) {
    int eventCode = 6010;
```

```
    // In this switch expression, notice how the value is supplied
    // by use of an arrow case. Notice that no break statement is
    // required (or allowed) to prevent fall-through.
    int priorityLevel = switch(eventCode) {
      case 1000, 1205, 8900 -> 1;
      case 2000, 6010, 9128 -> 2;
      case 1002, 7023, 9300 -> 3;
      default -> 0; // normal priority
    };

    System.out.println("Priority level for event code " + eventCode +
                       " is " + priorityLevel);
  }
}
```

This produces the same output as before. Looking at the code, it is easy to see why this form of the arrow **case** is so appropriate for many types of **switch** expressions. It is compact and eliminates the need for a separate **yield** statement. Because the arrow **case** does not fall through, there is no need for a **break** statement. Each **case** terminates by yielding the value of its expression. Furthermore, if you compare this final version of the **switch** to the original, traditional **switch** shown at the start of this discussion, it is readily apparent how streamlined and expressive this version is. In combination, the **switch** enhancements offer a truly impressive way to improve the clarity and resiliency of your code.

## A Closer Look at the Arrow case

The arrow **case** provides considerable flexibility. First, when using its expression form, the expression can be of any type. For example, the following is a valid **case** statement:

```
case -1 -> getErrorCode();
```

Here, the result of the call to **getErrorCode( )** becomes the value of the enclosing **switch** expression. Here is another example:

```
case 0 -> normalCompletion = true;
```

In this case, the result of the assignment, which is **true**, becomes the value yielded. The key point is that any valid expression can be used as the target of the arrow **case** as long as it is compatible with the type required by the **switch**.

As mentioned, the target of the -> can also be a block of code. You will need to use a block as the target of an arrow **case** whenever you need more than a single expression. For example, each **case** in this version of the event code program sets the value of a **boolean** variable called **stopNow** to indicate if immediate termination is required and then yields the priority level:

```
// Use blocks with an arrow.
class BlockArrowCase {

  public static void main(String[] args) {
    boolean stopNow;
```

```
    int eventCode = 9300;

    // Use code blocks with an arrow.  Again, notice
    // that no break statement is required (or allowed)
    // to prevent fall through. Because the target of an
    // arrow is a block, yield must be used to supply a value.
    int priorityLevel = switch(eventCode) {
      case 1000, 1205, 8900 -> { // use a block with an arrow
              stopNow = false;
              System.out.println("Alert");
              yield 1;
            }
      case 2000, 6010, 9128 -> {
              stopNow = false;
              System.out.println("Warning");
              yield 2;
            }
      case 1002, 7023, 9300 -> {
              stopNow = true;
              System.out.println("Danger");
              yield 3;
            }
      default ->  {
              stopNow = false;
              System.out.println("Normal.");
              yield 0;
           }
    };

    System.out.println("Priority level for event code " + eventCode +
                       " is " + priorityLevel);
    if(stopNow) System.out.println("Stop required.");
  }
}
```

Here is the output:

```
Danger
Priority level for event code 9300 is 3
Stop required.
```

As this example shows, when using a block, you must use **yield** to supply a value to a **switch** expression. Furthermore, even though block targets are used, each path through the **switch** expression must still provide a value.

Although the preceding program provides a simple illustration of a block target of an arrow **case**, it also raises an interesting question. Notice that each **case** in the **switch** sets the value of two variables. The first is **priorityLevel**, which is the value yielded. The second is **stopNow**. Is there a way for a **switch** expression to yield more than one value? In a direct sense, the answer is "no" because only one value can be produced by the **switch**. However, it is possible to encapsulate two or more values within a class and yield an object of that class. Beginning with JDK 16, Java provides an especially streamlined and efficient way to accomplish this: the **record**. Described later in this chapter, a **record** aggregates two or more values into a single logical unit. As it relates to this example, a **record** could hold both the **priorityLevel** and the **stopNow** values, and this **record** could be yielded by the **switch** as a unit. Thus, a **record** offers a convenient way for a **switch** to yield more than a single value.

Although the arrow **case** is very helpful in a **switch** expression, it is important to emphasize that it is not limited to that use. The arrow **case** can also be used in a **switch** statement, which enables you to write **switch**es in which no **case** fall-through can occur. In this situation, no **yield** statement is required (or allowed), and no value is produced by the **switch**. In essence, it works much like a traditional **switch** but without the fall-through. Here is an example:

```
// Use case arrows with a switch statement
class StatementSwitchWithArrows {

  public static void main(String[] args) {
    int up = 0;
    int down = 0;
    int left = 0;
    int right = 0;

    char direction = 'R';

    // Use arrows with a switch statement.  Notice that
    // no value is produced.
    switch(direction) {
      case 'L' ->  {
                    System.out.println("Turning Left");
                    left++;
                  }
      case 'R' -> {
                  System.out.println("Turning Right");
                  right++;
                }
      case 'U' -> {
                  System.out.println("Moving Up");
                  up++;
                }
      case 'D' -> {
                  System.out.println("Moving Down");
                  down++;
                }
    }
    System.out.println(right);
  }
}
```

In this program, the **switch** is a statement, not an expression. This is because of two reasons. First, no value is produced. Second, it is not exhaustive because no **default** statement is included. (Recall that **switch** expressions must be exhaustive, but not **switch** statements.) Notice, however, that because no fall-through occurs with an arrow **case**, no **break** statement is needed. As a point of interest, because each **case** increases the value of a different variable, it would not be possible to transform this **switch** into an expression. What value would it produce? All four **cases** increment a different variable.

One last point: you cannot mix arrow **cases** with traditional colon **cases** in the same **switch**. You must choose one or the other. For example, this sequence is invalid:

```
// This won't work! You cannot mix a colon case with an arrow case.
switch(direction) {
  case 'L' ->  {
                  System.out.println("Turning Left");
                  left++;
               }
  case 'R' : // Wrong! Can't mix case styles.
              System.out.println("Turning Right");
              right++;
              break;
  case 'U' -> {
                 System.out.println("Moving Up");
                 up++;
              }
  case 'D' -> {
                 System.out.println("Moving Down");
                 down++;
              }
}
```

## Another switch Expression Example

To continue this overview of the **switch** enhancements, another example is presented. It uses a **switch** expression to determine whether a letter is an English-language vowel. It makes use of all of the new **switch** features. Pay special attention to the way Y is handled. In English, Y can be a vowel or a consonant. The program lets you specify which way you want the Y interpreted by the way the **yIsVowel** variable is set. To handle this special case, a block is used as the target of the ->.

```
// Use a switch expression to determine if a character is an English vowel.
// Notice the use of a block as the target of an arrow case for Y.

class Vowels {

  public static void main(String[] args) {

    // If Y is to be counted as a vowel, set this
    // variable to true.
    boolean yIsVowel = true;

    char ch = 'Y';

    boolean isVowel = switch(ch) {
      case 'a', 'e', 'i', 'o', 'u', 'A', 'E', 'I', 'O', 'U' -> true;
      case 'y', 'Y' -> { if(yIsVowel) yield true; else yield false; }
      default -> false;
    };
```

```
      if(isVowel) System.out.println(ch + " is a vowel.");
    }
  }
```

As an experiment, try rewriting this program using a traditional **switch**. As you will find, doing so results in a much longer, less manageable version. The new **switch** enhancements often provide a superior approach.

## Pattern Matching in switch

JDK 21 introduces a convenient way to use pattern matching with **switch**, and it's the last of the enhancements to **switch**. It follows a similar syntax of pattern matching that you saw earlier in the context of the **instanceof** keyword, but within **switch** statements.

By now you are familiar with the power of **switch** statements to simplify code that chooses to perform different functions based on different values of a variable, but what about when the variable can be of a number of different types, enums, null values, and even ranges of values?

Take a look at the following code, which prints a message based on an object that identifies an employee of some kind at a company. The object can come in many shapes and sizes: it can be a Java record representing an employee with name and ID, an implementation of an interface called Employee, a particular implementation of that interface, a Java enum representing the chief executive and chief financial officers of a company, an integer, a string, or something else entirely. Depending on its nature, you want the code to handle the object representing an employee differently. You might naturally think of using **instanceof** checks in a chain of if-else statements to separate out all the different cases. If you did, you would end up with something that looks like this:

```
interface Employee {};
static class RegularEmployee implements Employee {};
enum CSuiteEmployee implements Employee {CEO, CFO}
record EmpId(String name, int id) {}

static void handleId(Object empObject) {
   if (empObject == null) {
      System.out.println("Oops, the Id was null !");
   } else if (empObjectinstanceof Integer idInt) {
      if (idInt == -1 || idInt == 0) {
         System.out.println("A reserved employee Id");
      } else if (idInt < 0) {
         System.out.println("A negative employee Id: " + idInt);
      } else {
         System.out.println("A positive employee Id: " + idInt);
      }
   } else if (empObjectinstanceof String s) {
      System.out.println("A String Id: " + s);
   } else if (empObject instanceof EmpId eid) {
      System.out.println("An Employee Id: [" + eid.id + ", "
                                                + eid.name + "]");
   } else if (empObjectinstanceof Employee e) {
      if (e instanceof CSuiteEmployee cse) {
         switch (cse) {
            case CEO -> System.out.println("It's the boss !");
            case CFO -> System.out.println("There's the money !");
```

```
            }
        } else if (e instanceof RegularEmployee) {
            System.out.println("A regular employee.");
        } else {
            System.out.println("An irregular employee.");
        }
    } else {
        System.out.println("Some other kind of employee: "
                                              + empObject.toString());
    }
}
```

In this example, you can see that the message the code formulates to print out depends upon the type of the employee object. You can also see in the case when the **id** is an **Integer**, the message printed is different for numerical values that are exactly equal to **-1** or **0**, or are negative or positive. The logic of this code to sift through all the possible types of employee is buried in the structure of the **if-else** statements, making it quite difficult to see how the different types and values are treated without deep study. Fortunately, by using pattern matching in **switch** statements, you can simplify this code by using the four new features of **switch**, described as follows.

**You can use null in a case statement.**

Before JDK 21, if you passed a null value into a **switch** statement, it would throw a **NullPointerException** at run time. This meant that you would need to have an explicit **null** check somewhere before your **switch** statement. But the new enhanced **switch** statements can have a **case** statement to deal with **null** values in the **switch** variable, like this:

```
case null -> // handle null value here
```

Note that if you don't provide a **case** statement to handle a **null** case, the **switch** statement still throws a **NullPointerException** in the case of a **null** value, just as before JDK 21.

**You can use pattern matching within case statements.**

This second expansion of the power of the **case** statement allows you to concisely check that the **switch** variable is of a given type and also assign a variable to it that you can use for processing this case. For example:

```
case String s -> System.out.println("It's a String with value: " + s);
```

**You can refine the case statement to deal with specific values.**

This is an important addition to the use of the contextual keyword **when** to the syntax because it allows you to express a **case** label that is conditional on the value of an object reference instead of the fixed values of a literal. For example, you can express a case label for a **String** value that only applies if the **String** has a certain form:

```
case String s when s.startsWith("A") -> System.out.println("It's a String"
                                         + "beginning with the letter A");
```

**You can use Java records and more easily use enum constants in switch statements.**

Prior to JDK 21 you could only use enum constants in **switch** statements where the switch variable was that enum type. This limitation has been relaxed in JDK 21 to allow you to use enum constants in **case** statements when the switch variable is a more general type. You can also use a Java record in a **case** statement and in pattern matching form.

Let's combine all four of these new features to simplify the code you started out with and make it much more concise and readable:

```
// use patterns in switch to simplify processing
// the switch variable, here an object representing
// an id, depending on its type and value.
static void handleId(Object empObject) {
    switch (empObject) {
        case null -> System.out.println("Oops, the Id was null !");
        case Integer i -> {
            switch (i) {
                case -1, 0 -> System.out.println("A reserved employee Id");
                case Integer idInt
                    when idInt < 0 -> System.out.println("A negative employee Id: "
                                                          + idInt);
                case Integer idInt -> System.out.println("A positive employee Id: "
                                                          + idInt);
            }
        }
        case String s -> System.out.println("A String Id " + s);
        case EmpId eid -> System.out.println("An Employee Id: [" + eid.id() + ", "
                                                       + eid.name + "]");
        case Employee e -> {
            switch (e) {
                case CSuiteEmployee.CEO -> System.out.println("It's the boss !");
                case CSuiteEmployee.CFO -> System.out.println("There's the money !");
                case RegularEmployee re -> System.out.println("A regular employee.");
                default -> System.out.println("An irregular employee.");
            }
        }
        default -> System.out.println("Some other kind of Id "
                                           + empObject.toString());
    }
```

Something may have occurred to you as you look at this code: since the **switch** variable can be any reference type, you can write many **case** statements that might be true for a given value of **switch** variable. In our example, we have a **switch** statement testing the kind of **Employee** object passed in. If you had two **case** statements, one pattern matching on the general **Employee** type

```
case Employee e -> …
```

and one on the **RegularEmployee** type

```
case RegularEmployee re -> …
```

and you passed in an object of type **RegularEmployee**, you might notice that both **case** statements would match. But, if so, in the context of your **switch** statement, which **case** would "win"? Only one **case** statement can be executed! To understand how which one is determined, you need to understand the concept of *case label dominance.*

One **case** label is said to *dominate* a second if it includes all the possible situations where the second applies and more. So, in our example, the **case Employee e** label dominates the **case RegularEmployee re case** label, because all **RegularEmployee** objects are also **Employee** objects, since the **RegularEmployee** class implements the **Employee** interface.

Now, Java uses a very simple approach to determine which one of possibly many **case** labels to select for a given value: it simply chooses the *first* **case** label in the order they are written that matches the **switch** variable. You need to understand **case** label dominance because this approach can potentially lead to cases where code could never be reached when one **case** label that dominates another appears before it in the **switch** statement. In fact, this situation will be interpreted by Java as a compilation error.

In our example earlier, in processing employee IDs that we know to be integers represented by the variable **i**, if you reversed the order of the **case** statements,

```
switch (i) {
   case Integer idInt -> System.out.println("An employee Id: " + idInt);
   case Integer idInt  // compilation error !
     when idInt < 0 -> System.out.println("A negative employee Id: ");
   case -1, 0 -> System.out.println("A reserved employee Id");
}
```

you would see that the first case label **Integer idInt** dominates the rest of the **case** labels that follow. All values of the **Integer i** would match the first **case** label, and the other case labels would never be reached in any circumstance. The code will not compile.

So when you write this kind of pattern matching **switch** statement, it is important to remember to put the least dominant **case** labels first. Case labels for a given type that use the contextual keyword **when** to refine the matching values are dominated by those that don't. In our example, **case Integer idInt** dominates **case Integer idInt when idInt < 0** because the first applies to all **Integer** values, including all the negative ones. **case** labels using a pattern for a given type dominate **case** labels using a constant expression for that type. In our example code, the **case -1, 0** label is dominated by the other two **case** labels. In general, provided you remember to put the most specific **case** labels first in order, you should end up with code that compiles without errors.

With this final collection of features that have been added to **switch** expressions and statements, you can see now just how powerful they have become, particularly for concisely handling objects that may come in many shapes and forms.

## Text Blocks

Beginning with JDK 15, Java provides support for *text blocks*. A text block is a new kind of literal that is comprised of a sequence of characters that can occupy more than one line. A text block reduces the tedium programmers often face when creating long string literals because newline characters can be used in a text block without the need for the **\n** escape sequence. Furthermore, tab and double quote characters can also be entered directly, without using an escape sequence, and the indentation of a multiline string can be preserved. Although text blocks may, at first, seem to be a relatively small addition to Java, they may well become one of the most popular features.

## Text Block Fundamentals

A text block is supported by a new delimiter, which is three double-quote characters: """. A text block is created by enclosing a string within a set of these delimiters. Specifically, a text block begins immediately following the newline after the opening """. Thus, the line containing the opening delimiter must end with a newline. The text block begins on the next line. A text block ends at the first character of the closing """. Here is a simple example:

```
"""
Text blocks make
multiple lines easy.
"""
```

This example creates a string in which the line "Text blocks make" is separated from "multiple lines easy." by a newline. It is not necessary to use the **\n** escape sequence to obtain the newline. Thus, the text block automatically preserves the newlines in the text. Again, the text block begins after the newline *following* the opening delimiter and ends at the start of the closing delimiter. Therefore, the newline after the second line is also preserved.

It is important to emphasize that even though a text block uses the """ delimiter, it is of type **String**. Thus, the preceding text block could be assigned to a **String** variable, as shown here:

```
String str = """
Text blocks make
multiple lines easy.
""";
```

When **str** is output using this statement:

```
System.out.println(str);
```

the following is displayed:

```
Text blocks make
multiple lines easy.
```

Notice something else about this example. Because the last line ends with a newline, that newline will also be in the resulting string. If you don't want a trailing newline, then put the closing delimiter at the end of the last line, like this:

```
String str = """
Text blocks make
multiple lines easy."""; // now, no newline at the end
```

## Understanding Leading Whitespace

In the preceding example, the text in the block was placed flush left. However, this is not required. You can have leading whitespace in a text block. There are two primary reasons that you might want leading whitespace. First, it will enable the text to be better aligned with the indentation level of the code around it. Second, it supports one or more levels of indentation within the text block itself.

In general, leading whitespace in a text block is automatically removed. However, the number of leading whitespaces to remove from each line is determined by the number of leading whitespaces in the line with the least indentation. For example, if all lines are flush left, then no whitespace is removed. If all lines are indented two spaces, then two spaces are removed from each line. However, if one line is indented two spaces, the next four spaces, and the third six spaces, then only two spaces are removed from the start of each line. This removes unwanted leading space while preserving the indentation of text within the block. This mechanism is illustrated by the following program:

```
// Demonstrate indentation in a text block.

class TextBlockDemo {

  public static void main(String[] args) {
    String str = """
                 Text blocks support strings that
                 span two or more lines and preserve
                     indentation. They reduce the
                         tedium associated with the
                      entry of long or complicated
                 strings into a program.
                 """;

    System.out.println(str);
  }
}
```

This program produces the following output:

```
Text blocks support strings that
span two or more lines and preserve
    indentation. They reduce the
        tedium associated with the
    entry of long or complicated
strings into a program.
```

As you can see, leading whitespace has been removed up to, but not beyond, the level of the leftmost lines. Thus, the text block can be indented in the program to better fit the indentation level of the code, with the leading whitespace removed when the string is created. However, any whitespace after the indentation level of the block is preserved.

One other key point: The closing """ participates in determining the amount of whitespace to remove because it, too, can set the indentation level. Thus, if the closing delimiter is flush left, no whitespace is removed. Otherwise, whitespace is removed up to the first text character or when the closing delimiter is encountered. For example, consider this sequence:

```
String str = """
    A
        B
    C
"""; // this will determine the start of indent
```

```
String str2 = """
     A
         B
     C
         """; // this has no effect

String str3 = """
     A
         B
     C
   """; // this removes whitespace up to the """

System.out.print(str);
System.out.print(str2);
System.out.print(str3);
```

This sequence displays the following:

```
     A
         B
     C
A
    B
C
  A
      B
  C
```

Pay special attention to the placement of the closing delimiter for **str2**. Because the number of preceding spaces for the lines containing A and C are fewer than that preceding the """, the closing delimiter has no effect on the number of spaces removed.

## Use Double Quotes in a Text Block

Another major advantage to text blocks is the ability to use double quotes without the need for the \" escape sequence. In a text block, double quotes are treated like any other character. For example, consider the following program:

```
// Use double quotes in a text block.

class TextBlockDemo2 {

  public static void main(String[] args) {

    String str = """
                 A text block can use double quotes without
                 the need for escape sequences. For example:

                 He said, "The cat is on the roof."
                 She asked, "How did it get up there?"
                 """;

    System.out.println(str);
  }
}
```

The output is shown here:

```
A text block can use double quotes without
the need for escape sequences. For example:

He said, "The cat is on the roof."
She asked, "How did it get up there?"
```

As you can see, there was no need to use the \" escape sequence. Furthermore, because double quotes are treated as "normal" characters, there is also no need for them to be balanced within a text block. For example

```
"""
""xyz"
"""
```

is perfectly acceptable. Just remember that three double quotes as a unit defines the text block delimiter.

## Escape Sequences in Text Blocks

The escape sequences, such as **\n** or **\t**, can be used in a text block. However, because double quotes, newlines, and tabs can be entered directly, they will not often be needed. That said, with the addition of text blocks, two new escape sequences were added to Java. The first is **\s**, which specifies a space. Thus, it can be used to indicate trailing spaces. The second is *endofline.* Because the \ must be followed by a line terminator, it must be used only at the end of the line. In a text block, the \ prevents a newline character from being included at the end of its line. Thus, the \ is essentially a line continuation indicator. For example:

```
String str = """
             one \
             two
             three \
             four
             """;
System.out.println(str);
```

Because the newline is suppressed after one and three, the output will be as shown here:

```
one two
three four
```

It is important to point out that *endofline* can only be used in a text block. It cannot be used to continue a traditional string literal, for example.

One final point before leaving the topic of text blocks: Because text blocks provide a better, easier way to enter many types of strings into your program, it is anticipated that they will be widely used by the Java programmer community. It is likely that you will begin to encounter them in code that you work on, or use them in code that you create. Just remember, your JDK release must be at least 15 or later.

## Pattern Matching with Records

JDK 21 introduces a convenient way to use pattern matching with records, called ***record patterns***. Given that a record defines the structure of its member variables, or *components*, this feature simplifies the instanceof-then-cast idiom, tailored specifically to records. With record patterns, you can pass a record pattern as an operand of the **instanceof** operator, where a record pattern is of the general form

*recordName(component-list)*

and, most importantly, should the **instanceof** expression match, all the record components become available as local variables. Specifically, the record pattern form of **instanceof** is

*objref* **instanceof** *recordName*(*component-list*)

If the record pattern matches, each record component variable in the list will be automatically assigned the value of the corresponding record component from the matched *objref* object.

Let's work through an example to see firsthand the benefits record patterns can bring to your code. Let's return to processing objects representing employees at a company using a Java record to encode their data.

```
record Employee(String name, Id id){};
record Id(int idNum, Type type) {
    enum Type {FULL_TIME, PART_TIME}
}
```

This time you can see that there is some additional structure to represent different kinds of employees: full or part time. We can use record patterns to make it easy to process this kind of object in code. Now, assume you want to write some code to check if an object passed to you is an instance of this **Employee** record and, if it is, you will want to access some of its data, or record components. Prior to the advent of record patterns, you would use an **instanceof** expression with a type pattern and access the record data in the conditional block using its accessor methods. You can see this approach here:

```
if (obj instanceof Employee employee) {
   System.out.println("The employee ID for " +
                      employee.name() + " is " +
                      employee.id().idNum() + " and the type is " +
                      employee.id().type()
                 );
}
```

While it's clear what this code is doing, it also shows that the variable **employee** is simply being used as a holder to get at what you really are interested in from this record, which are its **name** and **id** components. With the record patterns feature, you can change the operand of **instanceof** to be a record pattern. In the event that the value is indeed a record of the type you specify, the record object is assigned to the variable you provide, and all its components become locally scoped variables that you can access. This holds true when the record components are simple types such as **String** or **Integer** and also for any class type or record whose nested structure matches the operand.

Here is a fuller listing using a record pattern to simplify the processing of the object passed to your code that may or may not be the **Employee** object you want:

```
public static void printObject(Object obj) {
   if (obj instanceof Employee(String empName, Id empId)) {
     System.out.println("The employee ID for " +
                 empName + " is " +
                 empId.idNum() + " and the type is " +
                 empId.type());
     } else if (obj == null) {
        throw new IllegalArgumentException("null not allowed");
     } else {
        System.out.println("Printing: " + obj.toString());
   }
}
```

Notice that the component names in the record pattern, **empName** and **empId**, do not need to match names in the declaration of the record, **name** and **id**, in order for an **Employee** object to match the record pattern. This means you are free to name the components to suit the context of the code you are writing. An object that is **null** will never match a record pattern, even if its variable declaration is of the correct type. In this example, the **null** case is handled explicitly. You can see in the example that when the **obj** variable is indeed an **Employee** object, you don't have to use a variable for the **Employee** object; you can directly use its **name** and **id** components.

In fact, we can apply this pattern once more in our example because record patterns can nest inside each other. You'll notice in our example that while we got rid of the useless variable for the **Employee**, we still have the **empId** variable for the **Id** record, which is used only to get at the **idNum** and **type** values it holds. So, let's decompose this further with another record pattern for the **Id** record as well:

```
public static void printObjectNested(Object obj) {
   if (obj instanceof Employee(String empName, Id(int id, Id.Type type))) {
      // here we can use the empName variable from the Employee object and
      // the id and type variables from the Employee objects Id object directly !
      System.out.println("The employee ID for " +
                  empName + " is " +
                  id + " and the type is " +
                  type);
   } else if (obj == null) {
      throw new IllegalArgumentException("null not allowed");
   } else {
      System.out.println("Printing: " + obj.toString());
   }
}
```

Just as records are simply carriers for the data they hold, record patterns are an attractive way to simplify code so that it gets straight to the point of a record: its data.

## Sealed Classes and Interfaces

Beginning with JDK 17, it is possible to declare a class that can be inherited by only specific subclasses. Such a class is called *sealed*. Prior to the advent of sealed classes, inheritance was an "all or nothing" situation. A class could either be extended by any subclass or marked as

**final**, which prevented its inheritance entirely. Sealed classes fall between these two extremes because they enable you to specify precisely what subclasses a superclass will allow. In similar fashion, it is also possible to declare a sealed interface in which you specify only those classes that implement the interface and/or those interfaces that extend the sealed interface. Together, sealed classes and interfaces give you significantly greater control over inheritance, which can be especially important when designing class libraries.

## Sealed Classes

To declare a sealed class, precede the declaration with **sealed**. Then, after the class name, include a **permits** clause that specifies the allowed subclasses. Both **sealed** and **permits** are context-sensitive keywords that have special meaning only in a class or interface declaration. Outside of a class or interface declaration, **sealed** and **permits** are unrestricted and have no special meaning. Here is a simple example of a sealed class:

```
public sealed class MySealedClass permits Alpha, Beta {
  // ...
}
```

Here, the sealed class is called **MySealedClass**. It allows only two subclasses: **Alpha** and **Beta**. If any other class attempts to inherit **MySealedClass**, a compile-time error will occur.

Here are **Alpha** and **Beta**, the two subclasses of **MySealedClass**:

```
public final class Alpha extends MySealedClass {
  // ...
}

public final class Beta extends MySealedClass {
  // ...
}
```

Notice that each is specified as **final**. In general, a subclass of a sealed class must be declared as either **final**, **sealed**, or **non-sealed**. Let's look at each option. First, in this example, each subclass is declared **final**. This means that the only subclasses of **MySealedClass** are **Alpha** and **Beta**, and no subclasses of either of those can be created. Therefore, the inheritance chain ends with **Alpha** and **Beta**.

To indicate that a subclass is itself sealed, it must be declared **sealed** and its permitted subclasses must be specified. For example, this version of **Alpha** permits **Gamma**:

```
public sealed class Alpha extends MySealedClass permits Gamma {
  // ...
}
```

Of course, the class **Gamma** must then itself be declared either **sealed**, **final**, or **non-sealed**.

At first it might seem a bit surprising, but you can unseal a subclass of a sealed class by declaring it **non-sealed**. This context-sensitive keyword was added by JDK 17. It unlocks the subclass, enabling it to be inherited by any other class. For example, **Beta** could be coded like this:

```
public non-sealed class Beta extends MySealedClass {
  // ...
}
```

Now, any class may inherit **Beta**. However, the only direct subclasses of **MySealedClass** remain **Alpha** and **Beta**. A primary reason for **non-sealed** is to enable a superclass to specify a limited set of direct subclasses that provide a baseline of well-defined functionality but allow those subclasses to be freely extended.

If a class is specified in a **permits** clause for a sealed class, then that class *must* directly extend the sealed class. Otherwise, a compile-time error will result. Thus, a sealed class and its subclasses define a mutually dependent logical unit. Additionally, it is illegal to declare a class that does not extend a sealed class as **non-sealed**.

A key requirement of a sealed class is that every subclass that it permits must be accessible. Furthermore, if a sealed class is contained in a named module, then each subclass must also be in the same named module. In this case, a subclass can be in a different package from the sealed class. If the sealed class is in the unnamed module, then the sealed class and all permitted subclasses must be in the same package.

In the preceding discussion, the superclass **MySealedClass** and its subclasses **Alpha** and **Beta** would have been stored in separate files because they are all public classes. However, it is also possible for a sealed class and its subclasses to be stored in a single file (formally, a compilation unit) as long as the subclasses have default package access. In cases such as this, no **permits** clause is required for a sealed class. For example, here all three classes are in the same file:

```
// Because this is all in one file, MySealedClass does not require
// a permits clause.
public sealed class MySealedClass {
  // ...
}

final class Alpha extends MySealedClass {
  // ...
}

final class Beta extends MySealedClass {
  // ...
}
```

One last point: An abstract class can also be sealed. There is no restriction in this regard.

## Sealed Interfaces

A sealed interface is declared in the same way as a sealed class, by the use of **sealed**. A sealed interface uses its **permits** clause to specify the classes allowed to implement it and/or the interfaces allowed to extend it. Thus, a class that is not part of the **permits** clause cannot implement a sealed interface, and an interface not included in the **permits** clause cannot extend it.

Here is a simple example of a sealed interface that permits only the classes **Alpha** and **Beta** to implement it:

```
public sealed interface MySealedIF permits Alpha, Beta {
  void myMeth();
}
```

A class that implements a sealed interface must itself be specified as either **final**, **sealed**, or **non-sealed**. For example, here **Alpha** is marked **non-sealed** and **Beta** is specified as **final**:

```
public non-sealed class Alpha implements MySealedIF {
  public void myMeth() { System.out.println("In Alpha's myMeth()."); }
  // ...
}

public final class Beta implements MySealedIF {
  public void myMeth() { System.out.println("Inside Beta's myMeth()."); }
  // ...
}
```

Here is a key point: Any class specified in a sealed interface's **permits** clause *must* implement the interface. Thus, a sealed interface and its implementing classes form a logical unit.

A sealed interface can also specify which other interfaces can extend the sealed interface. For example, here, **MySealedIF** specifies that **MyIF** is permitted to extend it:

```
// Notice that MyIF is added to the permits clause.
public sealed interface MySealedIF permits Alpha, Beta, MyIF {
  void myMeth();
}
```

Because **MyIF** is part of the **MySealedIF permits** clause, it must be marked as either **non-sealed** or **sealed** and it must extend **MySealedIF**. For example:

```
public non-sealed interface MyIF extends MySealedIF {
  // ...
}
```

As you might expect, it is possible for a class to inherit a sealed class *and* implement a sealed interface. For example, here **Alpha** inherits **MySealedClass** and implements **MySealedIF**:

```
public non-sealed class Alpha extends MySealedClass implements MySealedIF {
  public void myMeth() { System.out.println("In Alpha's myMeth()."); }
  // ...
}
```

In the preceding examples, each class and interface are declared **public**. Thus, each is in its own file. However, as is the case with sealed classes, it is also possible for a sealed interface and its implementing classes (and extending interfaces) to be stored in a single file as long as the classes and interfaces have default package access. In cases such as this, no **permits** clause is required for a sealed interface. For example, here **MySealedIF** does not include a **permits** clause because **Alpha** and **Beta** are declared in the same file in the unnamed module:

```
public sealed interface MySealedIF {
  void myMeth();
}
```

```
non-sealed class Alpha extends MySealedClass implements MySealedIF {
  public void myMeth() { System.out.println("In Alpha's myMeth()."); }
  // ...
}

final class Beta extends MySealedClass implements MySealedIF {
  public void myMeth() { System.out.println("In Beta's myMeth()."); }
  // ...
}
```

One final point: Sealed classes and interfaces are most applicable to developers of API libraries in which subclasses and subinterfaces must be strictly controlled.

# Future Directions

As discussed in Chapter 1, beginning with JDK 12, Java releases may, and often do, include *preview features*. A preview feature is a new, fully developed enhancement to Java. However, a preview feature is *not yet* formally part of Java. Instead, a feature is previewed to allow programmers time to experiment with the feature and, if desired, communicate their thoughts and opinions prior to the feature being made permanent. This process enables a new feature to be improved or optimized based on actual developer use. As a result, a preview feature is *subject to change*. It can even be withdrawn. This means that a preview feature should not be used for code that you intend to publicly release That said, it is expected that most preview features will ultimately become part of Java, possibly after a period of refinement. Preview features chart the course of Java's future direction.

For example, the new pattern matching in **switch** and record pattern language features were first introduced in preview form in JDK 17 and JDK 19, respectively. They evolved in subsequent releases based on developer feedback, until they have reached their finalized forms, as described earlier in this chapter, in JDK 21. JDK 21 previews additional enhancements to the Java language, such as String Templates (JEP 430) and Unnamed Patterns and Variables (JEP 443), giving an indication of what may turn into finalized language features in a future release of the JDK. Because these are preview features that are subject to change, they are not discussed further in this book.

Java releases may also include *incubator modules*, which preview a new API or tool that is undergoing development. Like a preview feature, an incubator feature is subject to change. Furthermore, an incubator feature can be removed in the future. Thus, there is no guarantee that an incubator module will formally become part of Java in the future. Incubator features give developers an opportunity to experiment with the API or tool, and possibly supply feedback. JDK 21 includes one incubator module, the Vector API (JEP 448).

It is important to emphasize that preview features and incubator modules can be introduced in any Java release. Therefore, you will want to watch for them in each new version of Java. They give you a chance to try a new enhancement before it potentially becomes a formal part of Java. Perhaps more importantly, preview features and incubator modules give you advance information on where Java's development is headed.

# PART II

# The Java Library

CHAPTER

# 18 String Handling

A brief overview of Java's string handling was presented in Chapter 7. In this chapter, it is described in detail. As is the case in most other programming languages, in Java a string is a sequence of characters. But, unlike some other languages that implement strings as character arrays, Java implements strings as objects of type **String**.

Implementing strings as built-in objects allows Java to provide a full complement of features that make string handling convenient. For example, Java has methods to compare two strings, search for a substring, concatenate two strings, and change the case of letters within a string. Also, **String** objects can be constructed a number of ways, making it easy to obtain a string when needed.

Somewhat unexpectedly, when you create a **String** object, you are creating a string that cannot be changed. That is, once a **String** object has been created, you cannot change the characters that comprise that string. At first, this may seem to be a serious restriction. However, such is not the case. You can still perform all types of string operations. The difference is that each time you need an altered version of an existing string, a new **String** object is created that contains the modifications. The original string is left unchanged. This approach is used because fixed, immutable strings can be implemented more efficiently than changeable ones. For those cases in which a modifiable string is desired, Java provides two options: **StringBuffer** and **StringBuilder**. Both hold strings that can be modified after they are created.

The **String**, **StringBuffer**, and **StringBuilder** classes are defined in **java.lang**. Thus, they are available to all programs automatically. All are declared **final**, which means that none of these classes may be subclassed. This allows certain optimizations that increase performance to take place on common string operations. All three implement the **CharSequence** interface.

One last point: To say that the strings within objects of type **String** are unchangeable means that the contents of the **String** instance cannot be changed after it has been created. However, a variable declared as a **String** reference can be changed to point at some other **String** object at any time.

## The String Constructors

The **String** class supports several constructors. To create an empty **String**, call the default constructor. For example,

```
String s = new String();
```

will create an instance of **String** with no characters in it.

Frequently, you will want to create strings that have initial values. The **String** class provides a variety of constructors to handle this. To create a **String** initialized by an array of characters, use the constructor shown here:

String(char[ ] *chars*)

Here is an example:

```
char[] chars = { 'a', 'b', 'c' };
String s = new String(chars);
```

This constructor initializes **s** with the string "abc".

You can specify a subrange of a character array as an initializer using the following constructor:

String(char[ ] *chars*, int *startIndex*, int *numChars*)

Here, *startIndex* specifies the index at which the subrange begins, and *numChars* specifies the number of characters to use. Here is an example:

```
char[] chars = { 'a', 'b', 'c', 'd', 'e', 'f' };
String s = new String(chars, 2, 3);
```

This initializes **s** with the characters **cde**.

You can construct a **String** object that contains the same character sequence as another **String** object using this constructor:

String(String *strObj*)

Here, *strObj* is a **String** object. Consider this example:

```
// Construct one String from another.
class MakeString {
  public static void main(String[] args) {
    char[] c = {'J', 'a', 'v', 'a'};
    String s1 = new String(c);
    String s2 = new String(s1);

    System.out.println(s1);
    System.out.println(s2);
  }
}
```

The output from this program is as follows:

```
Java
Java
```

As you can see, **s1** and **s2** contain the same string.

Even though Java's **char** type uses 16 bits to represent the basic Unicode character set, the typical format for strings on the Internet uses arrays of 8-bit bytes constructed from the ASCII character set. Because 8-bit ASCII strings are common, the **String** class provides constructors that initialize a string when given a **byte** array. Two forms are shown here:

String(byte[ ] *chrs*)
String(byte[ ] *chrs*, int *startIndex*, int *numChars*)



Here, *chrs* specifies the array of bytes. The second form allows you to specify a subrange. In each of these constructors, the byte-to-character conversion is done by using the default character encoding of the platform. The following program illustrates these constructors:

```
// Construct string from subset of char array.
class SubStringCons {
  public static void main(String[] args) {
    byte[] ascii = {65, 66, 67, 68, 69, 70 };

    String s1 = new String(ascii);
    System.out.println(s1);

    String s2 = new String(ascii, 2, 3);
    System.out.println(s2);
  }
}
```

This program generates the following output:

```
ABCDEF
CDE
```

Starting with JDK 18, the default platform encoding is UTF-8, where previous JDKs chose an encoding that was dependent on the locale and operating system. Since UTF-8 has now become so widely adopted, this is usually the one you will want. But if you want to specify the encoding yourself, extended versions of the byte-to-string constructors are also defined in which you can specify the character encoding that determines how bytes are converted to characters. However, you will often want to use the default encoding provided by the platform.

**NOTE** The contents of the array are copied whenever you create a **String** object from an array. If you modify the contents of the array after you have created the string, the **String** will be unchanged.

You can construct a **String** from a **StringBuffer** by using the constructor shown here:

String(StringBuffer *strBufObj*)

You can construct a **String** from a **StringBuilder** by using this constructor:

String(StringBuilder *strBuildObj*)

The following constructor supports the extended Unicode character set:

String(int[ ] *codePoints*, int *startIndex*, int *numChars*)

Here, *codePoints* is an array that contains Unicode code points. The resulting string is constructed from the range that begins at *startIndex* and runs for *numChars*.

There are also constructors that let you specify a **Charset**.

---

**NOTE** A discussion of Unicode code points and how they are handled by Java is found in Chapter 19.

# String Length

The length of a string is the number of characters that it contains. To obtain this value, call the **length( )** method, shown here:

int length( )

The following fragment prints "3", since there are three characters in the string **s**:

```
char[] chars = { 'a', 'b', 'c' };
String s = new String(chars);
System.out.println(s.length());
```

# Special String Operations

Because strings are a common and important part of programming, Java has added special support for several string operations within the syntax of the language. These operations include the automatic creation of new **String** instances from string literals, concatenation of multiple **String** objects by use of the + operator, and the conversion of other data types to a string representation. There are explicit methods available to perform all of these functions, but Java does them automatically as a convenience for the programmer and to add clarity.

## String Literals

The earlier examples showed how to explicitly create a **String** instance from an array of characters by using the **new** operator. However, there is an easier way to do this using a string literal. For each string literal in your program, Java automatically constructs a **String** object. Thus, you can use a string literal to initialize a **String** object. For example, the following code fragment creates two equivalent strings:

```
char[] chars = { 'a', 'b', 'c' };
String s1 = new String(chars);

String s2 = "abc"; // use string literal
```

Because a **String** object is created for every string literal, you can use a string literal any place you can use a **String** object. For example, you can call methods directly on a quoted string as if it were an object reference, as the following statement shows. It calls the **length( )** method on the string "abc". As expected, it prints "3".

```
System.out.println("abc".length());
```

## String Concatenation

In general, Java does not allow operators to be applied to **String** objects. The one exception to this rule is the + operator, which concatenates two strings, producing a **String** object as the result. This allows you to chain together a series of + operations. For example, the following fragment concatenates three strings:

```
String age = "9";
String s = "He is " + age + " years old.";
System.out.println(s);
```

This displays the string "He is 9 years old."

One practical use of string concatenation is found when you are creating very long strings. Instead of letting long strings wrap around within your source code, you can break them into smaller pieces, using the + to concatenate them. Here is an example:

```
// Using concatenation to prevent long lines.
class ConCat {
  public static void main(String[] args) {
    String longStr = "This could have been " +
      "a very long line that would have " +
      "wrapped around.  But string concatenation " +
      "prevents this.";

    System.out.println(longStr);
  }
}
```



## String Concatenation with Other Data Types

You can concatenate strings with other types of data. For example, consider this slightly different version of the earlier example:

```
int age = 9;
String s = "He is " + age + " years old.";
System.out.println(s);
```

In this case, **age** is an **int** rather than another **String**, but the output produced is the same as before. This is because the **int** value in **age** is automatically converted into its string representation within a **String** object. This string is then concatenated as before. The compiler will convert an operand to its string equivalent whenever the other operand of the + is an instance of **String**.

Be careful when you mix other types of operations with string concatenation expressions, however. You might get surprising results. Consider the following:

```
String s = "four: " + 2 + 2;
System.out.println(s);
```

This fragment displays

```
four: 22
```

rather than the

```
four: 4
```

that you probably expected. Here's why: Operator precedence causes the concatenation of "four" with the string equivalent of 2 to take place first. This result is then concatenated with the string equivalent of 2 a second time. To complete the integer addition first, you must use parentheses, like this:

```
String s = "four: " + (2 + 2);
```

Now **s** contains the string "four: 4".

## String Conversion and toString( )

One way to convert data into its string representation is by calling one of the overloaded versions of the string conversion method **valueOf( )** defined by **String**. **valueOf( )** is overloaded for all the primitive types and for type **Object**. For the primitive types, **valueOf( )** returns a string that contains the human-readable equivalent of the value with which it is called. For objects, **valueOf( )** calls the **toString( )** method on the object. We will look more closely at **valueOf( )** later in this chapter. Here, let's examine the **toString( )** method, because it is the means by which you can determine the string representation for objects of classes that you create.

Every class implements **toString( )** because it is defined by **Object**. However, the default implementation of **toString( )** is seldom sufficient. For most important classes that you create, you will want to override **toString( )** and provide your own string representations. Fortunately, this is easy to do. The **toString( )** method has this general form:

String toString( )

To implement **toString( )**, simply return a **String** object that contains the human-readable string that appropriately describes an object of your class.

By overriding **toString( )** for classes that you create, you allow them to be fully integrated into Java's programming environment. For example, they can be used in **print( )** and **println( )** statements and in concatenation expressions. The following program demonstrates this by overriding **toString( )** for the **Box** class:

```
// Override toString() for Box class.
class Box {
  double width;
  double height;
  double depth;

  Box(double w, double h, double d) {
    width = w;
    height = h;
    depth = d;
  }

  public String toString() {
    return "Dimensions are " + width + " by " +
```

```
            depth + " by " + height + ".";
  }
}

class toStringDemo {
  public static void main(String[] args) {
    Box b = new Box(10, 12, 14);
    String s = "Box b: " + b; // concatenate Box object

    System.out.println(b); // convert Box to string
    System.out.println(s);
  }
}
```



The output of this program is shown here:

```
Dimensions are 10.0 by 14.0 by 12.0
Box b: Dimensions are 10.0 by 14.0 by 12.0
```

As you can see, **Box**'s **toString( )** method is automatically invoked when a **Box** object is used in a concatenation expression or in a call to **println( )**.

# Character Extraction

The **String** class provides a number of ways in which characters can be extracted from a **String** object. Several are examined here. Although the characters that comprise a string within a **String** object cannot be indexed as if they were a character array, many of the **String** methods employ an index (or offset) into the string for their operation. Like arrays, the string indexes begin at zero.

## charAt( )

To extract a single character from a **String**, you can refer directly to an individual character via the **charAt( )** method. It has this general form:

char charAt(int *where*)

Here, *where* is the index of the character that you want to obtain. The value of *where* must be nonnegative and specify a location within the string. **charAt( )** returns the character at the specified location. For example,

```
char ch;
ch = "abc".charAt(1);
```

assigns the value **b** to **ch**.

## getChars( )

If you need to extract more than one character at a time, you can use the **getChars( )** method. It has this general form:

void getChars(int *sourceStart*, int *sourceEnd*, char[ ] *target*, int *targetStart*)

Here, *sourceStart* specifies the index of the beginning of the substring, and *sourceEnd* specifies an index that is one past the end of the desired substring. Thus, the substring contains the characters from *sourceStart* through *sourceEnd*–1. The array that will receive the characters is specified by *target.* The index within *target* at which the substring will be copied is passed in *targetStart.* Care must be taken to ensure that the *target* array is large enough to hold the number of characters in the specified substring.

The following program demonstrates **getChars( )**:

```
class getCharsDemo {
  public static void main(String[] args) {
    String s = "This is a demo of the getChars method.";
    int start = 10;
    int end = 14;
    char[] buf = new char[end - start];

    s.getChars(start, end, buf, 0);
    System.out.println(buf);
  }
}
```

Here is the output of this program:

```
demo
```

### getBytes( )

There is an alternative to **getChars( )** that stores the characters in an array of bytes. This method is called **getBytes( )**, and it uses the default character-to-byte conversions provided by the platform. Here is its simplest form:

byte[ ] getBytes( )

Other forms of **getBytes( )** are also available. **getBytes( )** is most useful when you are exporting a **String** value into an environment that does not support 16-bit Unicode characters.

### toCharArray( )

If you want to convert all the characters in a **String** object into a character array, the easiest way is to call **toCharArray( )**. It returns an array of characters for the entire string. It has this general form:

char[ ] toCharArray( )

This function is provided as a convenience, since it is possible to use **getChars( )** to achieve the same result.

## String Comparison

The **String** class includes a number of methods that compare strings or substrings within strings. Several are examined here.

## equals( ) and equalsIgnoreCase( )

To compare two strings for equality, use **equals( )**. It has this general form:

boolean equals(Object *str*)

Here, *str* is the **String** object being compared with the invoking **String** object. It returns **true** if the strings contain the same characters in the same order, and **false** otherwise. The comparison is case-sensitive.

To perform a comparison that ignores case differences, call **equalsIgnoreCase( )**. When it compares two strings, it considers **A-Z** to be the same as **a-z**. It has this general form:

boolean equalsIgnoreCase(String *str*)

Here, *str* is the **String** object being compared with the invoking **String** object. It, too, returns **true** if the strings contain the same characters in the same order, and **false** otherwise.

Here is an example that demonstrates **equals( )** and **equalsIgnoreCase( )**:

```
// Demonstrate equals() and equalsIgnoreCase().
class equalsDemo {
  public static void main(String[] args) {
    String s1 = "Hello";
    String s2 = "Hello";
    String s3 = "Good-bye";
    String s4 = "HELLO";
    System.out.println(s1 + " equals " + s2 + " -> " +
                       s1.equals(s2));
    System.out.println(s1 + " equals " + s3 + " -> " +
                       s1.equals(s3));
    System.out.println(s1 + " equals " + s4 + " -> " +
                       s1.equals(s4));
    System.out.println(s1 + " equalsIgnoreCase " + s4 + " -> " +
                       s1.equalsIgnoreCase(s4));
  }
}
```

The output from the program is shown here:

```
Hello equals Hello -> true
Hello equals Good-bye -> false
Hello equals HELLO -> false
Hello equalsIgnoreCase HELLO -> true
```

## regionMatches( )

The **regionMatches( )** method compares a specific region inside a string with another specific region in another string. There is an overloaded form that allows you to ignore case in such comparisons. Here are the general forms for these two methods:

boolean regionMatches(int *startIndex*, String *str2*,
int *str2StartIndex*, int *numChars*)

boolean regionMatches(boolean *ignoreCase*,
int *startIndex*, String *str2*,
int *str2StartIndex*, int *numChars*)

For both versions, *startIndex* specifies the index at which the region begins within the invoking **String** object. The **String** being compared is specified by *str2*. The index at which the comparison will start within *str2* is specified by *str2StartIndex*. The length of the substring being compared is passed in *numChars*. In the second version, if *ignoreCase* is **true**, the case of the characters is ignored. Otherwise, case is significant.

## startsWith( ) and endsWith( )

**String** defines two methods that are, more or less, specialized forms of **regionMatches( )**. The **startsWith( )** method determines whether a given **String** begins with a specified string. Conversely, **endsWith( )** determines whether the **String** in question ends with a specified string. They have the following general forms:

boolean startsWith(String *str*)
boolean endsWith(String *str*)

Here, *str* is the **String** being tested. If the string matches, **true** is returned. Otherwise, **false** is returned. For example,

```
"Foobar".endsWith("bar")
```

and

```
"Foobar".startsWith("Foo")
```

are both **true**.

A second form of **startsWith( )**, shown here, lets you specify a starting point:

boolean startsWith(String *str*, int *startIndex*)

Here, *startIndex* specifies the index into the invoking string at which point the search will begin. For example,

```
"Foobar".startsWith("bar", 3)
```

returns **true**.

## equals( ) Versus ==

It is important to understand that the **equals( )** method and the == operator perform two different operations. As just explained, the **equals( )** method compares the characters inside a **String** object. The == operator compares two object references to see whether they refer to the same instance. The following program shows how two different **String** objects can contain the same characters, but references to these objects will not compare as equal:

```
// equals() vs ==
class EqualsNotEqualTo {
  public static void main(String[] args) {
```

```
    String s1 = "Hello";
    String s2 = new String(s1);

    System.out.println(s1 + " equals " + s2 + " -> " +
                       s1.equals(s2));
    System.out.println(s1 + " == " + s2 + " -> " + (s1 == s2));
  }
}
```

The variable **s1** refers to the **String** instance created by **"Hello"**. The object referred to by **s2** is created with **s1** as an initializer. Thus, the contents of the two **String** objects are identical, but they are distinct objects. This means that **s1** and **s2** do not refer to the same objects and are, therefore, not ==, as is shown here by the output of the preceding example:



```
Hello equals Hello -> true
Hello == Hello -> false
```

## compareTo( )

Often, it is not enough to simply know whether two strings are identical. For sorting applications, you need to know which is *less than, equal to,* or *greater than* the next. A string is less than another if it comes before the other in dictionary order. A string is greater than another if it comes after the other in dictionary order. The method **compareTo( )** serves this purpose. It is specified by the **Comparable<T>** interface, which **String** implements. It has this general form:

int compareTo(String *str*)

Here, *str* is the **String** being compared with the invoking **String**. The result of the comparison is returned and is interpreted as shown here:

| Value | Meaning |
|---|---|
| Less than zero | The invoking string is less than *str*. |
| Greater than zero | The invoking string is greater than *str*. |
| Zero | The two strings are equal. |

Here is a sample program that sorts an array of strings. The program uses **compareTo( )** to determine sort ordering for a bubble sort:

```
// A bubble sort for Strings.
class SortString {
  static String[] arr = {
    "Now", "is", "the", "time", "for", "all", "good", "men",
    "to", "come", "to", "the", "aid", "of", "their", "country"
  };
  public static void main(String[] args) {
    for(int j = 0; j < arr.length; j++) {
      for(int i = j + 1; i < arr.length; i++) {
        if(arr[i].compareTo(arr[j]) < 0) {
          String t = arr[j];
          arr[j] = arr[i];
```

```
          arr[i] = t;
        }
      }
      System.out.println(arr[j]);
    }
  }
}
```

The output of this program is the list of words:

```
Now
aid
all
come
country
for
good
is
men
of
the
the
their
time
to
to
```

As you can see from the output of this example, **compareTo( )** takes into account uppercase and lowercase letters. The word "Now" came out before all the others because it begins with an uppercase letter, which means it has a lower value in the ASCII character set.

If you want to ignore case differences when comparing two strings, use **compareToIgnoreCase( )**, as shown here:

int compareToIgnoreCase(String *str*)

This method returns the same results as **compareTo( )**, except that case differences are ignored. You might want to try substituting it into the previous program. After doing so, "Now" will no longer be first.

# Searching Strings

The **String** class provides two methods that allow you to search a string for a specified character or substring:

- **indexOf( )** Searches for the first occurrence of a character or substring
- **lastIndexOf( )** Searches for the last occurrence of a character or substring

These two methods are overloaded in several different ways. In all cases, the methods return the index at which the character or substring was found, or –1 on failure.

To search for the first occurrence of a character, use

int indexOf(int *ch*)

To search for the last occurrence of a character, use

int lastIndexOf(int *ch*)

Here, *ch* is the character being sought.

To search for the first or last occurrence of a substring, use

int indexOf(String *str*)
int lastIndexOf(String *str*)

Here, *str* specifies the substring.

You can specify a starting point for the search using these forms:

int indexOf(int *ch*, int *startIndex*)
int lastIndexOf(int *ch*, int *startIndex*)

int indexOf(String *str*, int *startIndex*)
int lastIndexOf(String *str*, int *startIndex*)

Here, *startIndex* specifies the index at which point the search begins. For **indexOf( )**, the search runs from *startIndex* to the end of the string. For **lastIndexOf( )**, the search runs from *startIndex* to zero.

Beginning in JDK21, you can also specify an index range to narrow the search for the first occurrence of a character or substring using these forms:

int indexOf(String *str*, int *startIndex*, int *endIndex*)
int indexOf(int ch, int *startIndex*, int *endIndex*)

Here, *startIndex* and *endIndex* specify the indices at which the search starts and ends, respectively. The first form searches for the substring given by *str*, the second for the character *ch*.

The following example shows how to use the various index methods to search inside of a **String**:

```
// Demonstrate indexOf() and lastIndexOf().
class indexOfDemo {
  public static void main(String[] args) {
    String s = "Now is the time for all good men " +
               "to come to the aid of their country.";

    System.out.println(s);
    System.out.println("indexOf(t) = " +
                       s.indexOf('t'));
    System.out.println("lastIndexOf(t) = " +
                       s.lastIndexOf('t'));
    System.out.println("indexOf(the) = " +
                       s.indexOf("the"));
    System.out.println("lastIndexOf(the) = " +
                       s.lastIndexOf("the"));
    System.out.println("indexOf(t, 10) = " +
                       s.indexOf('t', 10));
    System.out.println("lastIndexOf(t, 60) = " +
                       s.lastIndexOf('t', 60));
```

Part II

```
    System.out.println("indexOf(the, 10) = " +
                       s.indexOf("the", 10));
    System.out.println("lastIndexOf(the, 60) = " +
                       s.lastIndexOf("the", 60));
    System.out.println("indexOf(the, 3, 47) = " +
                       s.indexOf("the", 3, 47));
  }
}
```

Here is the output of this program:

```
Now is the time for all good men to come to the aid of their country.
indexOf(t) = 7
lastIndexOf(t) = 65
indexOf(the) = 7
lastIndexOf(the) = 55
indexOf(t, 10) = 11
lastIndexOf(t, 60) = 55
indexOf(the, 10) = 44
lastIndexOf(the, 60) = 55
indexOf(the, 3, 47) = 7
```

# Modifying a String

Because **String** objects are immutable, whenever you want to modify a **String**, you must either copy it into a **StringBuffer** or **StringBuilder**, or use a **String** method that constructs a new copy of the string with your modifications complete. A sampling of these methods are described here.

## substring( )

You can extract a substring using **substring( )**. It has two forms. The first is

String substring(int *startIndex*)

Here, *startIndex* specifies the index at which the substring will begin. This form returns a copy of the substring that begins at *startIndex* and runs to the end of the invoking string.

The second form of **substring( )** allows you to specify both the beginning and ending index of the substring:

String substring(int *startIndex*, int *endIndex*)

Here, *startIndex* specifies the beginning index, and *endIndex* specifies the stopping point. The string returned contains all the characters from the beginning index, up to, but not including, the ending index.

The following program uses **substring( )** to replace all instances of one substring with another within a string:

```
// Substring replacement.
class StringReplace {
  public static void main(String[] args) {
    String org = "This is a test. This is, too.";
    String search = "is";
```

```
      String sub = "was";
      String result = "";
      int i;

      do { // replace all matching substrings
        System.out.println(org);
        i = org.indexOf(search);
        if(i != -1) {
          result = org.substring(0, i);
          result = result + sub;
          result = result + org.substring(i + search.length());
          org = result;
        }
      } while(i != -1);
    }
  }
```



The output from this program is shown here:

```
This is a test. This is, too.
Thwas is a test. This is, too.
Thwas was a test. This is, too.
Thwas was a test. Thwas is, too.
Thwas was a test. Thwas was, too.
```

## concat( )

You can concatenate two strings using **concat( )**, shown here:

String concat(String *str*)

This method creates a new object that contains the invoking string with the contents of *str* appended to the end. **concat( )** performs the same function as +. For example,

```
String s1 = "one";
String s2 = s1.concat("two");
```

puts the string "onetwo" into **s2**. It generates the same result as the following sequence:

```
String s1 = "one";
String s2 = s1 + "two";
```

## replace( )

The **replace( )** method has two forms. The first replaces all occurrences of one character in the invoking string with another character. It has the following general form:

String replace(char *original*, char *replacement*)

Here, *original* specifies the character to be replaced by the character specified by *replacement*. The resulting string is returned. For example,

```
String s = "Hello".replace('l', 'w');
```

puts the string "Hewwo" into **s**.

The second form of **replace( )** replaces one character sequence with another. It has this general form:

String replace(CharSequence *original*, CharSequence *replacement*)

## trim( ) and strip( )

The **trim( )** method returns a copy of the invoking string from which any leading and trailing spaces have been removed. As it relates to this method, spaces consist of those characters with a value of 32 or less. The **trim( )** method has this general form:

String trim( )

Here is an example:

```
String s = "   Hello World    ".trim();
```

This puts the string "Hello World" into **s**.

The **trim( )** method is quite useful when you process user commands. For example, the following program prompts the user for the name of a state and then displays that state's capital. It uses **trim( )** to remove any leading or trailing spaces that may have inadvertently been entered by the user.

```
// Using trim() to process commands.
import java.io.*;

class UseTrim {
  public static void main(String[] args)
    throws IOException
  {
    // create a BufferedReader using System.in
    BufferedReader br = new BufferedReader(new
      InputStreamReader(System.in, System.console().charset()));
    String str;

    System.out.println("Enter 'stop' to quit.");
    System.out.println("Enter State: ");
    do {
      str = br.readLine();
      str = str.trim(); // remove whitespace

      if(str.equals("Illinois"))
        System.out.println("Capital is Springfield.");
      else if(str.equals("Missouri"))
        System.out.println("Capital is Jefferson City.");
      else if(str.equals("California"))
        System.out.println("Capital is Sacramento.");
      else if(str.equals("Washington"))
        System.out.println("Capital is Olympia.");
      // ...
    } while(!str.equals("stop"));
  }
}
```

Beginning with JDK 11, Java also provides the methods **strip( )**, **stripLeading( )**, and **stripTrailing( )**. The **strip( )** method removes all whitespace characters (as defined by Java) from the beginning and end of the invoking string and returns the result. Such whitespace characters include, among others, spaces, tabs, carriage returns, and line feeds.

The methods **stripLeading( )** and **stripTrailing( )** delete whitespace characters from the start and end, respectively, of the invoking string and return the result. JDK 15 added the methods **stripIndent( )**, which removes extraneous whitespace while retaining meaningful indentation, and **translateEscapes( )**, which replaces escape sequences with their character equivalents.

## Data Conversion Using valueOf( )

The **valueOf( )** method converts data from its internal format into a human-readable form. It is a static method that is overloaded within **String** for all of Java's built-in types so that each type can be converted properly into a string. **valueOf( )** is also overloaded for type **Object**, so an object of any class type you create can also be used as an argument. (Recall that **Object** is a superclass for all classes.) Here are a few of its forms:

static String valueOf(double *num*)
static String valueOf(long *num*)
static String valueOf(Object *ob*)
static String valueOf(char[ ] *chars*)

As discussed earlier, **valueOf( )** can be called when a string representation of some other type of data is needed. You can call this method directly with any data type and get a reasonable **String** representation. All of the simple types are converted to their common **String** representation. Any object that you pass to **valueOf( )** will return the result of a call to the object's **toString( )** method. In fact, you could just call **toString( )** directly and get the same result.

For most arrays, **valueOf( )** returns a rather cryptic string, which indicates that it is an array of some type. For arrays of **char**, however, a **String** object is created that contains the characters in the **char** array. There is a special version of **valueOf( )** that allows you to specify a subset of a **char** array. It has this general form:

static String valueOf(char[ ] *chars*, int *startIndex*, int *numChars*)

Here, *chars* is the array that holds the characters, *startIndex* is the index into the array of characters at which the desired substring begins, and *numChars* specifies the length of the substring.

## Changing the Case of Characters Within a String

The method **toLowerCase( )** converts all the characters in a string from uppercase to lowercase. The **toUpperCase( )** method converts all the characters in a string from lowercase to uppercase. Nonalphabetical characters, such as digits, are unaffected. Here are the simplest forms of these methods:

String toLowerCase( )
String toUpperCase( )

Both methods return a **String** object that contains the uppercase or lowercase equivalent of the invoking **String**. The default locale governs the conversion in both cases.

Here is an example that uses **toLowerCase( )** and **toUpperCase( )**:

```
// Demonstrate toUpperCase() and toLowerCase().

class ChangeCase {
  public static void main(String[] args)
  {
    String s = "This is a test.";

    System.out.println("Original: " + s);

    String upper = s.toUpperCase();
    String lower = s.toLowerCase();

    System.out.println("Uppercase: " + upper);
    System.out.println("Lowercase: " + lower);
  }
}
```

The output produced by the program is shown here:

```
Original: This is a test.
Uppercase: THIS IS A TEST.
Lowercase: this is a test.
```

One other point: Overloaded versions of **toLowerCase( )** and **toUpperCase( )** that let you specify a **Locale** object to govern the conversion are also supplied. Specifying the locale can be quite important in some cases and can help internationalize your application.

## Joining Strings

The **join( )** method is used to concatenate two or more strings, separating each string with a delimiter, such as a space or a comma. It has two forms. Its first is shown here:

static String join(CharSequence *delim*, CharSequence . . . *strs*)

Here, *delim* specifies the delimiter used to separate the character sequences specified by *strs*. Because **String** implements the **CharSequence** interface, *strs* can be a list of strings. (See Chapter 19 for information on **CharSequence**.) The following program demonstrates this version of **join( )**:

```
// Demonstrate the join() method defined by String.
class StringJoinDemo {
  public static void main(String[] args) {

    String result = String.join(" ", "Alpha", "Beta", "Gamma");
    System.out.println(result);

    result = String.join(", ", "John", "ID#: 569",
                         "E-mail: John@HerbSchildt.com");
    System.out.println(result);
  }
}
```

The output is shown here:

```
Alpha Beta Gamma
John, ID#: 569, E-mail: John@HerbSchildt.com
```

In the first call to **join( )**, a space is inserted between each string. In the second call, the delimiter is a comma followed by a space. This illustrates that the delimiter need not be just a single character.

The second form of **join( )** lets you join a list of strings obtained from an object that implements the **Iterable** interface. **Iterable** is implemented by the Collections Framework classes described in Chapter 20, among others. See Chapter 19 for information on **Iterable**.



# Additional String Methods

In addition to those methods discussed earlier, **String** has many other methods. Several are summarized in the following table:

| Method | Description |
|---|---|
| int codePointAt(int *i*) | Returns the Unicode code point at the location specified by *i*. |
| int codePointBefore(int *i*) | Returns the Unicode code point at the location that precedes that specified by *i*. |
| int codePointCount(int *start*, int *end*) | Returns the number of code points in the portion of the invoking **String** that are between *start* and *end*–1. |
| boolean contains(CharSequence *str*) | Returns **true** if the invoking object contains the string specified by *str*. Returns **false** otherwise. |
| boolean contentEquals(CharSequence *str*) | Returns **true** if the invoking string contains the same string as *str*. Otherwise, returns **false**. |
| boolean contentEquals(StringBuffer *str*) | Returns **true** if the invoking string contains the same string as *str*. Otherwise, returns **false**. |
| static String format(String *fmtstr*, Object ... *args*) | Returns a string formatted as specified by *fmtstr*. (See Chapter 20 for details on formatting.) |
| static String format(Locale *loc*, String *fmtstr*, Object ... *args*) | Returns a string formatted as specified by *fmtstr*. Formatting is governed by the locale specified by *loc*. (See Chapter 20 for details on formatting.) |
| String formatted(Object .... *args*) | Returns a string formatted as specified by the invoking string applied to *args*. (See Chapter 21 for details on formatting.) |
| String indent(int *num*) | When *num* is positive, indents each line in the invoking string by *num* spaces. When *num* is negative, each line has *num* leading whitespace characters deleted, if possible. Otherwise, when *num* is negative, leading whitespace is deleted until the first non-whitespace character is encountered. In all cases, including when *num* is zero, each line will end with a newline character. Returns the resulting string. |
| boolean isEmpty( ) | Returns **true** if the invoking string contains no characters and has a length of zero. |

| Method | Description |
|---|---|
| Stream<String> lines( ) | Decomposes a string into individual lines based on carriage return and line feed characters, and returns a **Stream** containing the lines. |
| boolean matches(string *regExp*) | Returns **true** if the invoking string matches the regular expression passed in *regExp*. Otherwise, returns **false**. |
| int offsetByCodePoints(int *start*, int *num*) | Returns the index within the invoking string that is *num* code points beyond the starting index specified by *start*. |
| String replaceFirst(String *regExp*, String *newStr*) | Returns a string in which the first substring that matches the regular expression specified by *regExp* is replaced by *newStr*. |
| String replaceAll(String *regExp*, String *newStr*) | Returns a string in which all substrings that match the regular expression specified by *regExp* are replaced by *newStr*. |
| String[ ] split(String *regExp*) | Decomposes the invoking string into parts and returns an array that contains the result. Each part is delimited by the regular expression passed in *regExp*. |
| String[ ] split(String *regExp*, int *max*) | Decomposes the invoking string into parts and returns an array that contains the result. Each part is delimited by the regular expression passed in *regExp*. The number of pieces is specified by *max*. If *max* is negative, then the invoking string is fully decomposed. Otherwise, if *max* contains a nonzero value, the last entry in the returned array contains the remainder of the invoking string. If *max* is zero, the invoking string is fully decomposed, but no trailing empty strings will be included. |
| String[ ] splitWithDelimiters(String regex, int limit) | Decomposes the invoking string into parts and returns an array that contains the parts and the delimiters that match the regular expression passed in *regExp*. The number of parts returned is specified by *max*. If *max* is negative, then the invoking string is fully decomposed. Otherwise, if *max* contains a nonzero value, the last entry in the returned array contains the remainder of the invoking string. If *max* is zero, the invoking string is fully decomposed. |
| CharSequence subSequence(int *startIndex*, int *stopIndex*) | Returns a substring of the invoking string, beginning at *startIndex* and stopping at *stopIndex*. This method is required by the **CharSequence** interface, which is implemented by **String**. |
| <R> R transform(Function<? super String, ? extends R> *func*) | Executes the function specified by *func* on the invoking string and returns the result. |

Notice that several of these methods work with regular expressions. Regular expressions are described in Chapter 31. One other point: Beginning with JDK 12, **String** implements the **Constable** and **ConstantDesc** interfaces.

# StringBuffer

**StringBuffer** supports a modifiable string. As you know, **String** represents fixed-length, immutable character sequences. In contrast, **StringBuffer** represents growable and writable character sequences. **StringBuffer** may have characters and substrings inserted in the middle or appended to the end. **StringBuffer** will automatically grow to make room for such additions and often has more characters preallocated than are actually needed, to allow room for growth.



## StringBuffer Constructors

**StringBuffer** defines these four constructors:

StringBuffer( )
StringBuffer(int *size*)
StringBuffer(String *str*)
StringBuffer(CharSequence *chars*)

The default constructor (the one with no parameters) reserves room for 16 characters without reallocation. The second version accepts an integer argument that explicitly sets the size of the buffer. The third version accepts a **String** argument that sets the initial contents of the **StringBuffer** object and reserves room for 16 more characters without reallocation. **StringBuffer** allocates room for 16 additional characters when no specific buffer length is requested, because reallocation is a costly process in terms of time. Also, frequent reallocations can fragment memory. By allocating room for a few extra characters, **StringBuffer** reduces the number of reallocations that take place. The fourth constructor creates an object that contains the character sequence contained in *chars* and reserves room for 16 more characters.

## length( ) and capacity( )

The current length of a **StringBuffer** can be found via the **length( )** method, while the total allocated capacity can be found through the **capacity( )** method. They have the following general forms:

int length( )
int capacity( )

Here is an example:

```
// StringBuffer length vs. capacity.
class StringBufferDemo {
  public static void main(String[] args) {
    StringBuffer sb = new StringBuffer("Hello");

    System.out.println("buffer = " + sb);
    System.out.println("length = " + sb.length());
    System.out.println("capacity = " + sb.capacity());
  }
}
```

Here is the output of this program, which shows how **StringBuffer** reserves extra space for additional manipulations:

```
buffer = Hello
length = 5
capacity = 21
```

Since **sb** is initialized with the string "Hello" when it is created, its length is 5. Its capacity is 21 because room for 16 additional characters is automatically added.

## ensureCapacity( )

If you want to preallocate room for a certain number of characters after a **StringBuffer** has been constructed, you can use **ensureCapacity( )** to set the size of the buffer. This is useful if you know in advance that you will be appending a large number of small strings to a **StringBuffer**. **ensureCapacity( )** has this general form:

void ensureCapacity(int *minCapacity*)

Here, *minCapacity* specifies the minimum size of the buffer. (A buffer larger than *minCapacity* may be allocated for reasons of efficiency.)

## setLength( )

To set the length of the string within a **StringBuffer** object, use **setLength( )**. Its general form is shown here:

void setLength(int *len*)

Here, *len* specifies the length of the string. This value must be nonnegative.

When you increase the size of the string, null characters are added to the end. If you call **setLength( )** with a value less than the current value returned by **length( )**, then the characters stored beyond the new length will be lost. The **setCharAtDemo** sample program in the following section uses **setLength( )** to shorten a **StringBuffer**.

## charAt( ) and setCharAt( )

The value of a single character can be obtained from a **StringBuffer** via the **charAt( )** method. You can set the value of a character within a **StringBuffer** using **setCharAt( )**. Their general forms are shown here:

char charAt(int *where*)
void setCharAt(int *where*, char *ch*)

For **charAt( )**, *where* specifies the index of the character being obtained. For **setCharAt( )**, *where* specifies the index of the character being set, and *ch* specifies the new value of that character. For both methods, *where* must be nonnegative and must not specify a location beyond the end of the string.

The following example demonstrates **charAt( )** and **setCharAt( )**:

```
// Demonstrate charAt() and setCharAt().
class setCharAtDemo {
```

```
  public static void main(String[] args) {
    StringBuffer sb = new StringBuffer("Hello");
    System.out.println("buffer before = " + sb);
    System.out.println("charAt(1) before = " + sb.charAt(1));

    sb.setCharAt(1, 'i');
    sb.setLength(2);
    System.out.println("buffer after = " + sb);
    System.out.println("charAt(1) after = " + sb.charAt(1));
  }
}
```

Here is the output generated by this program:

```
buffer before = Hello
charAt(1) before = e
buffer after = Hi
charAt(1) after = i
```



## getChars( )

To copy a substring of a **StringBuffer** into an array, use the **getChars( )** method. It has this general form:

void getChars(int *sourceStart*, int *sourceEnd*, char[ ] *target*, int *targetStart*)

Here, *sourceStart* specifies the index of the beginning of the substring, and *sourceEnd* specifies an index that is one past the end of the desired substring. This means that the substring contains the characters from *sourceStart* through *sourceEnd*–1. The array that will receive the characters is specified by *target*. The index within *target* at which the substring will be copied is passed in *targetStart*. Care must be taken to ensure that the *target* array is large enough to hold the number of characters in the specified substring.

## append( )

The **append( )** method concatenates the string representation of any other type of data to the end of the invoking **StringBuffer** object. It has several overloaded versions. Here are a few of its forms:

StringBuffer append(String *str*)
StringBuffer append(int *num*)
StringBuffer append(Object *obj*)

First, the string representation of each parameter is obtained. Then, the result is appended to the current **StringBuffer** object. The buffer itself is returned by each version of **append( )**. This allows subsequent calls to be chained together, as shown in the following example:

```
// Demonstrate append().
class appendDemo {
  public static void main(String[] args) {
    String s;
    int a = 42;
    StringBuffer sb = new StringBuffer(40);
```

```
    s = sb.append("a = ").append(a).append("!").toString();
    System.out.println(s);
  }
}
```

The output of this example is shown here:

```
a = 42!
```

## insert( )

The **insert( )** method inserts one string into another. It is overloaded to accept values of all the primitive types, plus **Strings**, **Objects**, and **CharSequences**. Like **append( )**, it obtains the string representation of the value it is called with. This string is then inserted into the invoking **StringBuffer** object. These are a few of its forms:

StringBuffer insert(int *index*, String *str*)
StringBuffer insert(int *index*, char *ch*)
StringBuffer insert(int *index*, Object *obj*)

Here, *index* specifies the index at which point the string will be inserted into the invoking **StringBuffer** object.

The following sample program inserts "like" between "I" and "Java":

```
// Demonstrate insert().
class insertDemo {
  public static void main(String[] args) {
    StringBuffer sb = new StringBuffer("I Java!");

    sb.insert(2, "like ");
    System.out.println(sb);
  }
}
```

The output of this example is shown here:

```
I like Java!
```

## reverse( )

You can reverse the characters within a **StringBuffer** object using **reverse( )**, shown here:

StringBuffer reverse( )

This method returns the reverse of the object on which it was called. The following program demonstrates **reverse( )**:

```
// Using reverse() to reverse a StringBuffer.
class ReverseDemo {
  public static void main(String[] args) {
    StringBuffer s = new StringBuffer("abcdef");

    System.out.println(s);
    s.reverse();
```

```
      System.out.println(s);
    }
  }
```

Here is the output produced by the program:

```
abcdef
fedcba
```

## delete( ) and deleteCharAt( )

You can delete characters within a **StringBuffer** by using the methods **delete( )** and **deleteCharAt( )**. These methods are shown here:

StringBuffer delete(int *startIndex*, int *endIndex*)
StringBuffer deleteCharAt(int *loc*)

The **delete( )** method deletes a sequence of characters from the invoking object. Here, *startIndex* specifies the index of the first character to remove, and *endIndex* specifies an index one past the last character to remove. Thus, the substring deleted runs from *startIndex* to *endIndex*–1. The resulting **StringBuffer** object is returned.

The **deleteCharAt( )** method deletes the character at the index specified by *loc*. It returns the resulting **StringBuffer** object.

Here is a program that demonstrates the **delete( )** and **deleteCharAt( )** methods:

```
// Demonstrate delete() and deleteCharAt()
class deleteDemo {
  public static void main(String[] args) {
    StringBuffer sb = new StringBuffer("This is a test.");

    sb.delete(4, 7);
    System.out.println("After delete: " + sb);

    sb.deleteCharAt(0);
    System.out.println("After deleteCharAt: " + sb);
  }
}
```

The following output is produced:

```
After delete: This a test.
After deleteCharAt: his a test.
```

## replace( )

You can replace one set of characters with another set inside a **StringBuffer** object by calling **replace( )**. Its signature is shown here:

StringBuffer replace(int *startIndex*, int *endIndex*, String *str*)

The substring being replaced is specified by the indexes *startIndex* and *endIndex*. Thus, the substring at *startIndex* through *endIndex*–1 is replaced. The replacement string is passed in *str*. The resulting **StringBuffer** object is returned.

Part II

The following program demonstrates **replace( )**:

```
// Demonstrate replace()
class replaceDemo {
  public static void main(String[] args) {
    StringBuffer sb = new StringBuffer("This is a test.");

    sb.replace(5, 7, "was");
    System.out.println("After replace: " + sb);
  }
}
```

Here is the output:

```
After replace: This was a test.
```

## substring( )

You can obtain a portion of a **StringBuffer** by calling **substring( )**. It has the following two forms:

String substring(int *startIndex*)
String substring(int *startIndex*, int *endIndex*)

The first form returns the substring that starts at *startIndex* and runs to the end of the invoking **StringBuffer** object. The second form returns the substring that starts at *startIndex* and runs through *endIndex*–1. These methods work just like those defined for **String** that were described earlier.

## Additional StringBuffer Methods

In addition to those methods just described, **StringBuffer** supplies others. Several are summarized in the following table:

| Method | Description |
|---|---|
| StringBuffer appendCodePoint(int *ch*) | Appends a Unicode code point to the end of the invoking object. A reference to the object is returned. |
| int codePointAt(int *i*) | Returns the Unicode code point at the location specified by *i*. |
| int codePointBefore(int *i*) | Returns the Unicode code point at the location that precedes that specified by *i*. |
| int codePointCount(int *start*, int *end*) | Returns the number of code points in the portion of the invoking **String** that are between *start* and *end*–1. |
| int indexOf(String *str*) | Searches the invoking **StringBuffer** for the first occurrence of *str*. Returns the index of the match, or –1 if no match is found. |
| int indexOf(String *str*, int *startIndex*) | Searches the invoking **StringBuffer** for the first occurrence of *str*, beginning at *startIndex*. Returns the index of the match, or –1 if no match is found. |
| int lastIndexOf(String *str*) | Searches the invoking **StringBuffer** for the last occurrence of *str*. Returns the index of the match, or –1 if no match is found. |

| Method | Description |
|---|---|
| int lastIndexOf(String *str*, int *startIndex*) | Searches the invoking **StringBuffer** for the last occurrence of *str*, beginning at *startIndex*. Returns the index of the match, or –1 if no match is found. |
| int offsetByCodePoints(int *start*, int *num*) | Returns the index within the invoking string that is *num* code points beyond the starting index specified by *start*. |
| StringBuffer repeat(CharSequence cs, int n) | Appends *n* copies of the supplied character sequence cs to the StringBuffer. |
| StringBuffer repeat(int codePoint, int n) | Appends *n* copies of the supplied Unicode code point to the StringBuffer. |
| CharSequence subSequence(int *startIndex*, int *stopIndex*) | Returns a substring of the invoking string, beginning at *startIndex* and stopping at *stopIndex*. This method is required by the **CharSequence** interface, which is implemented by **StringBuffer**. |
| void trimToSize( ) | Requests that the size of the character buffer for the invoking object be reduced to better fit the current contents. |



The following program demonstrates **indexOf( )** and **lastIndexOf( )**:

```
class IndexOfDemo {
  public static void main(String[] args) {
    StringBuffer sb = new StringBuffer("one two one");
    int i;

    i = sb.indexOf("one");
    System.out.println("First index: " + i);

    i = sb.lastIndexOf("one");
    System.out.println("Last index: " + i);
  }
}
```

The output is shown here:

```
First index: 0
Last index: 8
```

## StringBuilder

**StringBuilder** is similar to **StringBuffer**, except for one important difference: it is not synchronized, which means that it is not thread-safe. The advantage of **StringBuilder** is faster performance. However, in cases in which a mutable string will be accessed by multiple threads, and no external synchronization is employed, you must use **StringBuffer** rather than **StringBuilder**.

CHAPTER

# 19 Exploring java.lang

This chapter discusses classes and interfaces defined by **java.lang**. As you know, **java.lang** is automatically imported into all programs. It contains classes and interfaces that are fundamental to virtually all of Java programming. It is Java's most widely used package. Beginning with JDK 9, all of **java.lang** is part of the **java.base** module.

**java.lang** includes the following classes:

| | | | |
|---|---|---|---|
| Boolean | Float | ProcessBuilder | StringBuffer |
| Byte | InheritableThreadLocal | ProcessBuilder.Redirect | StringBuilder |
| Character | Integer | Record | System |
| Character.Subset | Long | Runtime | System.LoggerFinder |
| Character.UnicodeBlock | Math | RuntimePermission | Thread |
| Class | Module | Runtime.Version | ThreadGroup |
| ClassLoader | ModuleLayer | SecurityManager | ThreadLocal |
| ClassValue | ModuleLayer.Controller | Short | Throwable |
| Compiler | Number | StackTraceElement | Void |
| Double | Object | StackWalker | |
| Enum | Package | StrictMath | |
| Enum.EnumDesc | Process | String | |

**java.lang** defines the following interfaces:

| | | |
|---|---|---|
| Appendable | Iterable | StackWalker.StackFrame |
| AutoCloseable | ProcessHandle | System.Logger |
| CharSequence | ProcessHandle.Info | Thread.UncaughtExceptionHandler |
| Cloneable | Readable | |
| Comparable | Runnable | |

Several of the classes contained in **java.lang** contain deprecated methods, many dating back to Java 1.0. Deprecated methods are still provided by Java to support legacy code but are not recommended for new code since they may be removed in a future release. Because of this, in most cases the deprecated methods are not discussed here.

# Primitive Type Wrappers

As mentioned in Part I of this book, Java uses primitive types, such as **int** and **char**, for performance reasons. These data types are not part of the object hierarchy. They are passed by value to methods and cannot be directly passed by reference. Also, there is no way for two methods to refer to the *same instance* of an **int**. At times, you will need to create an object representation for one of these primitive types. For example, there are collection classes discussed in Chapter 20 that deal only with objects; to store a primitive type in one of these classes, you need to wrap the primitive type in a class. To address this need, Java provides classes that correspond to each of the primitive types. In essence, these classes encapsulate, or *wrap*, the primitive types within a class. Thus, they are commonly referred to as *type wrappers*. The type wrappers were introduced in Chapter 12. They are examined in detail here.

Before we begin, an important point needs to be mentioned. Beginning with JDK 16, the primitive type wrapper classes are now documented as *value-based*. As such, various rules and restrictions apply. For example, you should avoid using instances of a value-based class for synchronization. See Chapter 13 for additional information on value-based classes.

## Number

The abstract class **Number** defines a superclass that is implemented by the classes that wrap the numeric types **byte**, **short**, **int**, **long**, **float**, and **double**. **Number** has abstract methods that return the value of the object in each of the different number formats. For example, **doubleValue( )** returns the value as a **double**, **floatValue( )** returns the value as a **float**, and so on. These methods are shown here:

```
byte byteValue( )
double doubleValue( )
float floatValue( )
int intValue( )
long longValue( )
short shortValue( )
```

The values returned by these methods might be rounded, truncated, or result in a "garbage" value due to the effects of a narrowing conversion.

**Number** has concrete subclasses that hold explicit values of each primitive numeric type: **Double**, **Float**, **Byte**, **Short**, **Integer**, and **Long**.

## Double and Float

**Double** and **Float** are wrappers for floating-point values of type **double** and **float**, respectively. The constructors for **Float** are shown here:

Float(double *num*)
Float(float *num*)
Float(String *str*) throws NumberFormatException

**Float** objects can be constructed with values of type **float** or **double**. They can also be constructed from the string representation of a floating-point number. Beginning with JDK 9, these constructors have been deprecated, and beginning with JDK 16, they have been deprecated for removal. The **valueOf( )** method is the strongly recommended alternative.

The constructors for **Double** are shown here:

Double(double *num*)
Double(String *str*) throws NumberFormatException

**Double** objects can be constructed with a **double** value or a string containing a floating-point value. Beginning with JDK 9, these constructors have been deprecated, and beginning with JDK 16, they have been deprecated for removal. The **valueOf( )** method is the strongly recommended alternative.

The commonly used methods defined by **Float** include those shown in Table 19-1. The commonly used methods defined by **Double** include those shown in Table 19-2. Beginning with JDK 12, **Float** and **Double** also implement the **Constable** and **ConstantDesc** interfaces. Both **Float** and **Double** define the following constants:

| | |
|---|---|
| BYTES | The width of a **float** or **double** in bytes |
| MAX_EXPONENT | Maximum exponent |
| MAX_VALUE | Maximum positive value |
| MIN_EXPONENT | Minimum exponent |
| MIN_NORMAL | Minimum positive normal value |
| MIN_VALUE | Minimum positive value |
| NaN | Not a number |
| POSITIVE_INFINITY | Positive infinity |
| PRECISION | The number of bits used to represent this number type |
| NEGATIVE_INFINITY | Negative infinity |
| SIZE | The bit width of the wrapped value |
| TYPE | The **Class** object for **float** or **double** |

The following example creates two **Double** objects—one by using a **double** value and the other by passing a string that can be parsed as a **double**:

```
class DoubleDemo {
  public static void main(String[] args) {
    Double d1 = Double.valueOf(3.14159);
    Double d2 = Double.valueOf("314159E-5");

    System.out.println(d1 + " = " + d2 + " -> " + d1.equals(d2));
  }
}
```

| Method | Description |
|---|---|
| byte byteValue( ) | Returns the value of the invoking object as a **byte**. |
| static int compare(float *num1*, float *num2*) | Compares the values of *num1* and *num2*. Returns 0 if the values are equal. Returns a negative value if *num1* is less than *num2*. Returns a positive value if *num1* is greater than *num2*. |
| int compareTo(Float *f*) | Compares the numerical value of the invoking object with that of *f*. Returns 0 if the values are equal. Returns a negative value if the invoking object has a lower value. Returns a positive value if the invoking object has a greater value. |
| double doubleValue( ) | Returns the value of the invoking object as a **double**. |
| boolean equals(Object *FloatObj*) | Returns **true** if the invoking **Float** object is equivalent to *FloatObj*. Otherwise, it returns **false**. |
| static int floatToIntBits(float *num*) | Returns the IEEE-compatible, single-precision bit pattern that corresponds to *num*. |
| static int floatToRawIntBits(float *num*) | Returns the IEEE-compatible single-precision bit pattern that corresponds to *num*. A NaN value is preserved. |
| float floatValue( ) | Returns the value of the invoking object as a **float**. |
| int hashCode( ) | Returns the hash code for the invoking object. |
| static int hashCode(float *num*) | Returns the hash code for *num*. |
| static float intBitsToFloat(int *num*) | Returns **float** equivalent of the IEEE-compatible, single-precision bit pattern specified by *num*. |
| int intValue( ) | Returns the value of the invoking object as an **int**. |
| static boolean isFinite(float *num*) | Returns **true** if *num* is not **NaN** and is not infinite. |
| boolean isInfinite( ) | Returns **true** if the invoking object contains an infinite value. Otherwise, it returns **false**. |
| static boolean isInfinite(float *num*) | Returns **true** if *num* specifies an infinite value. Otherwise, it returns **false**. |
| boolean isNaN( ) | Returns **true** if the invoking object contains a value that is not a number. Otherwise, it returns **false**. |
| static boolean isNaN(float *num*) | Returns **true** if *num* specifies a value that is not a number. Otherwise, it returns **false**. |
| long longValue( ) | Returns the value of the invoking object as a **long**. |
| static float max(float *val*, float *val2*) | Returns the maximum of *val* and *val2*. |
| static float min(float *val*, float *val2*) | Returns the minimum of *val* and *val2*. |
| static float parseFloat(String *str*) throws NumberFormatException | Returns the **float** equivalent of the number contained in the string specified by *str* using radix 10. |
| short shortValue( ) | Returns the value of the invoking object as a **short**. |

**Table 19-1** Commonly Used Methods Defined by **Float**

| Method | Description |
|---|---|
| static float sum(float *val*, float *val2*) | Returns the result of *val* + *val2*. |
| static String toHexString(float *num*) | Returns a string containing the value of *num* in hexadecimal format. |
| String toString( ) | Returns the string equivalent of the invoking object. |
| static String toString(float *num*) | Returns the string equivalent of the value specified by *num*. |
| static Float valueOf(float *num*) | Returns a **Float** object containing the value passed in *num*. |
| static Float valueOf(String *str*) throws NumberFormatException | Returns the **Float** object that contains the value specified by the string in *str*. |

**Table 19-1** Commonly Used Methods Defined by **Float** *(continued)*



| Method | Description |
|---|---|
| byte byteValue( ) | Returns the value of the invoking object as a **byte**. |
| static int compare(double *num1*, double *num2*) | Compares the values of *num1* and *num2*. Returns 0 if the values are equal. Returns a negative value if *num1* is less than *num2*. Returns a positive value if *num1* is greater than *num2*. |
| int compareTo(Double *d*) | Compares the numerical value of the invoking object with that of *d*. Returns 0 if the values are equal. Returns a negative value if the invoking object has a lower value. Returns a positive value if the invoking object has a greater value. |
| static long doubleToLongBits(double *num*) | Returns the IEEE-compatible, double-precision bit pattern that corresponds to *num*. |
| static long doubleToRawLongBits(double *num*) | Returns the IEEE-compatible double-precision bit pattern that corresponds to *num*. A NaN value is preserved. |
| double doubleValue( ) | Returns the value of the invoking object as a **double**. |
| boolean equals(Object *DoubleObj*) | Returns **true** if the invoking **Double** object is equivalent to *DoubleObj*. Otherwise, it returns **false**. |
| float floatValue( ) | Returns the value of the invoking object as a **float**. |
| int hashcode( ) | Returns the hash code for the invoking object. |
| static int hashCode(double *num*) | Returns the hash code for *num*. |
| int intValue( ) | Returns the value of the invoking object as an **int**. |
| static boolean isFinite(double *num*) | Returns **true** if *num* is not **NaN** and is not infinite. |

**Table 19-2** Commonly Used Methods Defined by **Double**

| Method | Description |
|---|---|
| boolean isInfinite( ) | Returns **true** if the invoking object contains an infinite value. Otherwise, it returns **false**. |
| static boolean isInfinite(double *num*) | Returns **true** if *num* specifies an infinite value. Otherwise, it returns **false**. |
| boolean isNaN( ) | Returns **true** if the invoking object contains a value that is not a number. Otherwise, it returns **false**. |
| static boolean isNaN(double *num*) | Returns **true** if *num* specifies a value that is not a number. Otherwise, it returns **false**. |
| static double longBitsToDouble(long *num*) | Returns **double** equivalent of the IEEE-compatible, double-precision bit pattern specified by *num*. |
| long longValue( ) | Returns the value of the invoking object as a **long**. |
| static double max(double *val*, double *val2*) | Returns the maximum of *val* and *val2*. |
| static double min(double *val*, double *val2*) | Returns the minimum of *val* and *val2*. |
| static double parseDouble(String *str*) throws NumberFormatException | Returns the **double** equivalent of the number contained in the string specified by *str* using radix 10. |
| short shortValue( ) | Returns the value of the invoking object as a **short**. |
| static double sum(double *val*, double *val2*) | Returns the result of *val* + *val2*. |
| static String toHexString(double *num*) | Returns a string containing the value of *num* in hexadecimal format. |
| String toString( ) | Returns the string equivalent of the invoking object. |
| static String toString(double *num*) | Returns the string equivalent of the value specified by *num*. |
| static Double valueOf(double *num*) | Returns a **Double** object containing the value passed in *num*. |
| static Double valueOf(String *str*) throws NumberFormatException | Returns a **Double** object that contains the value specified by the string in *str*. |

**Table 19-2** Commonly Used Methods Defined by **Double** *(continued)*

As you can see from the following output, both versions of **valueOf( )** created identical **Double** instances, as shown by the **equals( )** method returning **true**:

```
3.14159 = 3.14159 -> true
```

## Understanding isInfinite( ) and isNaN( )

**Float** and **Double** provide the methods **isInfinite( )** and **isNaN( )**, which help when manipulating two special **double** and **float** values. These methods test for two unique values: infinity and NaN (not a number). **isInfinite( )** returns **true** if the value being tested is infinitely large or small in magnitude. **isNaN( )** returns **true** if the value being tested is not a number.

The following example creates two **Double** objects; one is infinite, and the other is not a number:

```
// Demonstrate isInfinite() and isNaN()
class InfNaN {
  public static void main(String[] args) {
     Double d1 = Double.valueOf(1/0.);
     Double d2 = Double.valueOf(0/0.);

     System.out.println(d1 + ": " + d1.isInfinite() + ", " + d1.isNaN());
     System.out.println(d2 + ": " + d2.isInfinite() + ", " + d2.isNaN());
  }
}
```

This program generates the following output:

```
Infinity: true, false
NaN: false, true
```



## Byte, Short, Integer, and Long

The **Byte**, **Short**, **Integer**, and **Long** classes are wrappers for **byte**, **short**, **int**, and **long** integer types, respectively. Their constructors are shown here:

Byte(byte *num*)
Byte(String *str*) throws NumberFormatException

Short(short *num*)
Short(String *str*) throws NumberFormatException

Integer(int *num*)
Integer(String *str*) throws NumberFormatException

Long(long *num*)
Long(String *str*) throws NumberFormatException

As you can see, these objects can be constructed from numeric values or from strings that contain valid whole number values. Beginning with JDK 9, these constructors have been deprecated, and beginning with JDK 16, they have been deprecated for removal. The **valueOf( )** method is the strongly recommended alternative.

The commonly used methods defined by these classes are shown in Tables 19-3 through 19-6. As you can see, they define methods for parsing integers from strings and converting strings back into integers. Variants of these methods allow you to specify the *radix*, or numeric base, for conversion. Common radixes are 2 for binary, 8 for octal, 10 for decimal, and 16 for hexadecimal. Beginning with JDK 12, **Integer** and **Long** also implement the **Constable** and **ConstantDesc** interfaces. Beginning with JDK 15, **Byte** and **Short** also implement **Constable**.

| Method | Description |
|---|---|
| byte byteValue( ) | Returns the value of the invoking object as a **byte**. |
| static int compare(byte *num1*, byte *num2*) | Compares the values of *num1* and *num2*. Returns 0 if the values are equal. Returns a negative value if *num1* is less than *num2*. Returns a positive value if *num1* is greater than *num2*. |
| int compareTo(Byte *b*) | Compares the numerical value of the invoking object with that of *b*. Returns 0 if the values are equal. Returns a negative value if the invoking object has a lower value. Returns a positive value if the invoking object has a greater value. |
| static int compareUnsigned(byte *num1*, byte *num2*) | Performs an unsigned comparison of *num1* and *num2*. Returns 0 if the values are equal. Returns a negative value if *num1* is less than *num2*. Returns a positive value if *num1* is greater than *num2*. |
| static Byte decode(String *str*) throws NumberFormatException | Returns a **Byte** object that contains the value specified by the string in *str*. |
| double doubleValue( ) | Returns the value of the invoking object as a **double**. |
| boolean equals(Object *ByteObj*) | Returns **true** if the invoking **Byte** object is equivalent to *ByteObj*. Otherwise, it returns **false**. |
| float floatValue( ) | Returns the value of the invoking object as a **float**. |
| int hashCode( ) | Returns the hash code for the invoking object. |
| static int hashCode(byte *num*) | Returns the hash code for *num*. |
| int intValue( ) | Returns the value of the invoking object as an **int**. |
| long longValue( ) | Returns the value of the invoking object as a **long**. |
| static byte parseByte(String *str*) throws NumberFormatException | Returns the **byte** equivalent of the number contained in the string specified by *str* using radix 10. |
| static byte parseByte(String *str*, int *radix*) throws NumberFormatException | Returns the **byte** equivalent of the number contained in the string specified by *str* using the specified radix. |
| short shortValue( ) | Returns the value of the invoking object as a **short**. |
| String toString( ) | Returns a string that contains the decimal equivalent of the invoking object. |
| static String toString(byte *num*) | Returns a string that contains the decimal equivalent of *num*. |
| static int toUnsignedInt(byte *val*) | Returns the value of *val* as an unsigned integer. |
| static long toUnsignedLong(byte *val*) | Returns the value of *val* as an unsigned long integer. |
| static Byte valueOf(byte *num*) | Returns a **Byte** object containing the value passed in *num*. |
| static Byte valueOf(String *str*) throws NumberFormatException | Returns a **Byte** object that contains the value specified by the string in *str*. |
| static Byte valueOf(String *str*, int *radix*) throws NumberFormatException | Returns a **Byte** object that contains the value specified by the string in *str* using the specified *radix*. |

**Table 19-3** Commonly Used Methods Defined by **Byte**

| Method | Description |
|---|---|
| byte byteValue( ) | Returns the value of the invoking object as a **byte**. |
| static int compare(short *num1*, short *num2* | Compares the values of *num1* and *num2*. Returns 0 if the values are equal. Returns a negative value if *num1* is less than *num2*. Returns a positive value if *num1* is greater than *num2*. |
| int compareTo(Short *s*) | Compares the numerical value of the invoking object with that of *s*. Returns 0 if the values are equal. Returns a negative value if the invoking object has a lower value. Returns a positive value if the invoking object has a greater value. |
| static int compareUnsigned(short *num1*, short *num2*) | Performs an unsigned comparison of *num1* and *num2*. Returns 0 if the values are equal. Returns a negative value if *num1* is less than *num2*. Returns a positive value if *num1* is greater than *num2*. |
| static Short decode(String *str*) throws NumberFormatException | Returns a **Short** object that contains the value specified by the string in *str*. |
| double doubleValue( ) | Returns the value of the invoking object as a **double**. |
| boolean equals(Object *ShortObj*) | Returns **true** if the invoking **Short** object is equivalent to *ShortObj*. Otherwise, it returns **false**. |
| float floatValue( ) | Returns the value of the invoking object as a **float**. |
| int hashCode( ) | Returns the hash code for the invoking object. |
| static int hashCode(short *num*) | Returns the hash code for *num*. |
| int intValue( ) | Returns the value of the invoking object as an **int**. |
| long longValue( ) | Returns the value of the invoking object as a **long**. |
| static short parseShort(String *str*) throws NumberFormatException | Returns the **short** equivalent of the number contained in the string specified by *str* using radix 10. |
| static short parseShort(String *str*, int *radix*) throws NumberFormatException | Returns the **short** equivalent of the number contained in the string specified by *str* using the specified *radix*. |
| static short reverseBytes(short *num*) | Exchanges the high- and low-order bytes of *num* and returns the result. |
| short shortValue( ) | Returns the value of the invoking object as a **short**. |
| String toString( ) | Returns a string that contains the decimal equivalent of the invoking object. |
| static String toString(short *num*) | Returns a string that contains the decimal equivalent of *num*. |
| static int toUnsignedInt(short *val*) | Returns the value of *val* as an unsigned integer. |
| static long toUnsignedLong(short *val*) | Returns the value of *val* as an unsigned long integer. |
| static Short valueOf(short *num*) | Returns a **Short** object containing the value passed in *num*. |
| static Short valueOf(String *str*) throws NumberFormatException | Returns a **Short** object that contains the value specified by the string in *str* using radix 10. |
| static Short valueOf(String *str*, int *radix*) throws NumberFormatException | Returns a **Short** object that contains the value specified by the string in *str* using the specified *radix*. |

**Table 19-4** Commonly Used Methods Defined by **Short**

| Method | Description |
|---|---|
| static int bitCount(int *num*) | Returns the number of set bits in *num*. |
| byte byteValue( ) | Returns the value of the invoking object as a **byte**. |
| static int compare(int *num1*, int *num2*) | Compares the values of *num1* and *num2*. Returns 0 if the values are equal. Returns a negative value if *num1* is less than *num2*. Returns a positive value if *num1* is greater than *num2*. |
| int compareTo(Integer *i*) | Compares the numerical value of the invoking object with that of *i*. Returns 0 if the values are equal. Returns a negative value if the invoking object has a lower value. Returns a positive value if the invoking object has a greater value. |
| static int compareUnsigned(int *num1*, int *num2*) | Performs an unsigned comparison of *num1* and *num2*. Returns 0 if the values are equal. Returns a negative value if *num1* is less than *num2*. Returns a positive value if *num1* is greater than *num2*. |
| static Integer decode(String *str*) throws NumberFormatException | Returns an **Integer** object that contains the value specified by the string in *str*. |
| static int divideUnsigned(int *dividend*, int *divisor*) | Returns the result, as an unsigned value, of the unsigned division of *dividend* by *divisor*. |
| double doubleValue( ) | Returns the value of the invoking object as a **double**. |
| boolean equals(Object *IntegerObj*) | Returns **true** if the invoking **Integer** object is equivalent to *IntegerObj*. Otherwise, it returns **false**. |
| float floatValue( ) | Returns the value of the invoking object as a **float**. |
| static Integer getInteger(String *propertyName*) | Returns the value associated with the environmental property specified by *propertyName*. A **null** is returned on failure. |
| static Integer getInteger(String *propertyName*, int *default*) | Returns the value associated with the environmental property specified by *propertyName*. The value of *default* is returned on failure. |
| static Integer getInteger(String *propertyName*, Integer *default*) | Returns the value associated with the environmental property specified by *propertyName*. The value of *default* is returned on failure. |
| int hashCode( ) | Returns the hash code for the invoking object. |
| static int hashCode(int *num*) | Returns the hash code for *num*. |
| static int highestOneBit(int *num*) | Determines the position of the highest order set bit in *num*. It returns a value in which only this bit is set. If no bit is set to one, then zero is returned. |
| int intValue( ) | Returns the value of the invoking object as an **int**. |
| long longValue( ) | Returns the value of the invoking object as a **long**. |
| static int lowestOneBit(int *num*) | Determines the position of the lowest order set bit in *num*. It returns a value in which only this bit is set. If no bit is set to one, then zero is returned. |
| static int max(int *val*, int *val2*) | Returns the maximum of *val* and *val2*. |
| static int min(int *val*, int *val2*) | Returns the minimum of *val* and *val2*. |
| static int numberOfLeadingZeros(int *num*) | Returns the number of high-order zero bits that precede the first high-order set bit in *num*. If *num* is zero, 32 is returned. |

**Table 19-5** Commonly Used Methods Defined by **Integer**

| Method | Description |
|---|---|
| static int numberOfTrailingZeros(int *num*) | Returns the number of low-order zero bits that precede the first low-order set bit in *num*. If *num* is zero, 32 is returned. |
| static int parseInt(CharSequence *chars*, int *startIdx*, int *stopIdx*, int *radix*) throws NumberFormatException | Returns the integer equivalent of the number contained in the sequence specified by *chars*, between the indices *startIdx* and *stopIdx*-1, using the specified *radix*. |
| static int parseInt(String *str*) throws NumberFormatException | Returns the integer equivalent of the number contained in the string specified by *str* using radix 10. |
| static int parseInt(String *str*, int *radix*) throws NumberFormatException | Returns the integer equivalent of the number contained in the string specified by *str* using the specified *radix*. |
| static int parseUnsignedInt(CharSequence *chars*, int *startIdx*, int *stopIdx*, int *radix*) throws NumberFormatException | Returns the integer equivalent of the unsigned number contained in the sequence specified by *chars*, between the indices *startIdx* and *stopIdx*-1, using the specified *radix*. |
| static int parseUnsignedInt(String *str*) throws NumberFormatException | Returns the unsigned integer equivalent of the number contained in the string specified by *str* using the radix 10. |
| static int parseUnsignedInt(String *str*, int *radix*) throws NumberFormatException | Returns the unsigned integer equivalent of the number contained in the string specified by *str* using the radix specified by *radix*. |
| static int remainderUnsigned(int *dividend*, int *divisor*) | Returns the remainder, as an unsigned value, of the unsigned division of *dividend* by *divisor*. |
| static int reverse(int *num*) | Reverses the order of the bits in *num* and returns the result. |
| static int reverseBytes(int *num*) | Reverses the order of the bytes in *num* and returns the result. |
| static int rotateLeft(int *num*, int *n*) | Returns the result of rotating *num* left *n* positions. |
| static int rotateRight(int *num*, int *n*) | Returns the result of rotating *num* right *n* positions. |
| short shortValue( ) | Returns the value of the invoking object as a **short**. |
| static int signum(int *num*) | Returns –1 if *num* is negative, 0 if it is zero, and 1 if it is positive. |
| static int sum(int *val*, int *val2*) | Returns the result of *val* + *val2*. |
| static String toBinaryString(int *num*) | Returns a string that contains the binary equivalent of *num*. |
| static String toHexString(int *num*) | Returns a string that contains the hexadecimal equivalent of *num*. |
| static String toOctalString(int *num*) | Returns a string that contains the octal equivalent of *num*. |
| String toString( ) | Returns a string that contains the decimal equivalent of the invoking object. |
| static String toString(int *num*) | Returns a string that contains the decimal equivalent of *num*. |
| static String toString(int *num*, int *radix*) | Returns a string that contains the decimal equivalent of *num* using the specified *radix*. |
| static long toUnsignedLong(int *val*) | Returns the value of *val* as an unsigned long integer. |
| static String toUnsignedString(int *val*) | Returns a string that contains the decimal value of *val* as an unsigned integer. |

**Table 19-5** Commonly Used Methods Defined by **Integer** *(continued)*

| Method | Description |
|---|---|
| static String toUnsignedString(int *val*, int *radix*) | Returns a string that contains the value of *val* as an unsigned integer in the radix specified by *radix*. |
| static Integer valueOf(int *num*) | Returns an **Integer** object containing the value passed in *num*. |
| static Integer valueOf(String *str*) throws NumberFormatException | Returns an **Integer** object that contains the value specified by the string in *str*. |
| static Integer valueOf(String *str*, int *radix*) throws NumberFormatException | Returns an **Integer** object that contains the value specified by the string in *str* using the specified *radix*. |

**Table 19-5** Commonly Used Methods Defined by **Integer** *(continued)*

| Method | Description |
|---|---|
| static int bitCount(long *num*) | Returns the number of set bits in *num*. |
| byte byteValue( ) | Returns the value of the invoking object as a **byte**. |
| static int compare(long *num1*, long *num2*) | Compares the values of *num1* and *num2*. Returns 0 if the values are equal. Returns a negative value if *num1* is less than *num2*. Returns a positive value if *num1* is greater than *num2*. |
| int compareTo(Long *l*) | Compares the numerical value of the invoking object with that of *l*. Returns 0 if the values are equal. Returns a negative value if the invoking object has a lower value. Returns a positive value if the invoking object has a greater value. |
| static int compareUnsigned(long *num1*, long *num2*) | Performs an unsigned comparison of *num1* and *num2*. Returns 0 if the values are equal. Returns a negative value if *num1* is less than *num2*. Returns a positive value if *num1* is greater than *num2*. |
| static Long decode(String *str*) throws NumberFormatException | Returns a **Long** object that contains the value specified by the string in *str*. |
| static long divideUnsigned(long *dividend*, long *divisor*) | Returns the result, as an unsigned value, of the unsigned division of *dividend* by *divisor*. |
| double doubleValue( ) | Returns the value of the invoking object as a **double**. |
| boolean equals(Object *LongObj*) | Returns **true** if the invoking **Long** object is equivalent to *LongObj*. Otherwise, it returns **false**. |
| float floatValue( ) | Returns the value of the invoking object as a **float**. |
| static Long getLong(String *propertyName*) | Returns the value associated with the environmental property specified by *propertyName*. A **null** is returned on failure. |
| static Long getLong(String *propertyName*, long *default*) | Returns the value associated with the environmental property specified by *propertyName*. The value of *default* is returned on failure. |
| static Long getLong(String *propertyName*, Long *default*) | Returns the value associated with the environmental property specified by *propertyName*. The value of *default* is returned on failure. |
| int hashCode( ) | Returns the hash code for the invoking object. |
| static int hashCode(long *num*) | Returns the hash code for *num*. |

**Table 19-6** Commonly Used Methods Defined by **Long**

| Method | Description |
|---|---|
| static long highestOneBit(long *num*) | Determines the position of the highest-order set bit in *num*. It returns a value in which only this bit is set. If no bit is set to one, then zero is returned. |
| int intValue( ) | Returns the value of the invoking object as an **int**. |
| long longValue( ) | Returns the value of the invoking object as a **long**. |
| static long lowestOneBit(long *num*) | Determines the position of the lowest-order set bit in *num*. It returns a value in which only this bit is set. If no bit is set to one, then zero is returned. |
| static long max(long *val*, long *val2*) | Returns the maximum of *val* and *val2*. |
| static long min(long *val*, long *val2*) | Returns the minimum of *val* and *val2*. |
| static int numberOfLeadingZeros(long *num*) | Returns the number of high-order zero bits that precede the first high-order set bit in *num*. If *num* is zero, 64 is returned. |
| static int numberOfTrailingZeros(long *num*) | Returns the number of low-order zero bits that precede the first low-order set bit in *num*. If *num* is zero, 64 is returned. |
| static long parseLong(CharSequence *chars*, int *startIdx*, int *stopIdx*, int *radix*) throws NumberFormatException | Returns the **long** equivalent of the number contained in the sequence specified by *chars*, between the indices *startIdx* and *stopIdx*–1, using the specified *radix*. |
| static long parseLong(String *str*) throws NumberFormatException | Returns the **long** equivalent of the number contained in the string specified by *str* using radix 10. |
| static long parseLong(String *str*, int *radix*) throws NumberFormatException | Returns the **long** equivalent of the number contained in the string specified by *str* using the specified *radix*. |
| static long parseUnsignedLong (CharSequence *chars*, int *startIdx*, int *stopIdx*, int *radix*) throws NumberFormatException | Returns the **long** equivalent of the unsigned number contained in the sequence specified by *chars*, between the indices *startIdx* and *stopIdx*–1, using the specified *radix*. |
| static long parseUnsignedLong(String *str*) throws NumberFormatException | Returns the unsigned integer equivalent of the number contained in the string specified by *str* using the radix 10. |
| static long parseUnsignedLong(String *str*, int *radix*) throws NumberFormatException | Returns the unsigned integer equivalent of the number contained in the string specified by *str* using the radix specified by *radix*. |
| static long remainderUnsigned (long *dividend*, long *divisor*) | Returns the remainder, as an unsigned value, of the unsigned division of *dividend* by *divisor*. |
| static long reverse(long *num*) | Reverses the order of the bits in *num* and returns the result. |
| static long reverseBytes(long *num*) | Reverses the order of the bytes in *num* and returns the result. |
| static long rotateLeft(long *num*, int *n*) | Returns the result of rotating *num* left *n* positions. |
| static long rotateRight(long *num*, int *n*) | Returns the result of rotating *num* right *n* positions. |
| short shortValue( ) | Returns the value of the invoking object as a **short**. |
| static int signum(long *num*) | Returns –1 if *num* is negative, 0 if it is zero, and 1 if it is positive. |
| static long sum(long *val*, long *val2*) | Returns the result of *val* + *val2*. |
| static String toBinaryString(long *num*) | Returns a string that contains the binary equivalent of *num*. |

**Table 19-6** Commonly Used Methods Defined by **Long** *(continued)*

Part II

| Method | Description |
|---|---|
| static String toHexString(long *num*) | Returns a string that contains the hexadecimal equivalent of *num*. |
| static String toOctalString(long *num*) | Returns a string that contains the octal equivalent of *num*. |
| String toString( ) | Returns a string that contains the decimal equivalent of the invoking object. |
| static String toString(long *num*) | Returns a string that contains the decimal equivalent of *num*. |
| static String toString(long *num*, int *radix*) | Returns a string that contains the decimal equivalent of *num* using the specified *radix*. |
| static String toUnsignedString(long *val*) | Returns a string that contains the decimal value of *val* as an unsigned integer. |
| static String toUnsignedString(long *val*, int *radix*) | Returns a string that contains the value of *val* as an unsigned integer in the radix specified by *radix*. |
| static Long valueOf(long *num*) | Returns a **Long** object containing the value passed in *num*. |
| static Long valueOf(String *str*) throws NumberFormatException | Returns a **Long** object that contains the value specified by the string in *str*. |
| static Long valueOf(String *str*, int *radix*) throws NumberFormatException | Returns a **Long** object that contains the value specified by the string in *str* using the specified *radix*. |

**Table 19-6** Commonly Used Methods Defined by **Long** *(continued)*

The following constants are defined:

| | |
|---|---|
| BYTES | The width of the integer type in bytes |
| MIN_VALUE | Minimum value |
| MAX_VALUE | Maximum value |
| SIZE | The bit width of the wrapped value |
| TYPE | The **Class** object for **byte, short, int,** or **long** |

## Converting Numbers to and from Strings

One of the most common programming chores is converting the string representation of a number into its internal, binary format. Fortunately, Java provides an easy way to accomplish this. The **Byte**, **Short**, **Integer**, and **Long** classes provide the **parseByte( )**, **parseShort( )**, **parseInt( )**, and **parseLong( )** methods, respectively. These methods return the **byte**, **short**, **int**, or **long** equivalent of the numeric string with which they are called. (Similar methods also exist for the **Float** and **Double** classes.)

The following program demonstrates **parseInt( )**. It sums a list of integers entered by the user. It reads the integers using **readLine( )** and uses **parseInt( )** to convert these strings into their **int** equivalents.

```
/* This program sums a list of numbers entered
   by the user.  It converts the string representation
   of each number into an int using parseInt().
*/
```

```
import java.io.*;

class ParseDemo {
  public static void main(String[] args)
    throws IOException
  {
    // create a BufferedReader using System.in
    BufferedReader br = new BufferedReader(new
      InputStreamReader(System.in, System.console().charset()));
    String str;
    int i;
    int sum=0;

    System.out.println("Enter numbers, 0 to quit.");
    do {
      str = br.readLine();
      try {
        i = Integer.parseInt(str);
      } catch(NumberFormatException e) {
        System.out.println("Invalid format");
        i = 0;
      }
      sum += i;
      System.out.println("Current sum is: " + sum);
    } while(i != 0);
  }
}
```

To convert a whole number into a decimal string, use the versions of **toString( )** defined in the **Byte**, **Short**, **Integer**, or **Long** classes. The **Integer** and **Long** classes also provide the methods **toBinaryString( )**, **toHexString( )**, and **toOctalString( )**, which convert a value into a binary, hexadecimal, or octal string, respectively.

The following program demonstrates binary, hexadecimal, and octal conversion:

```
/* Convert an integer into binary, hexadecimal,
   and octal.
*/

class StringConversions {
  public static void main(String[] args) {
    int num = 19648;
    System.out.println(num + " in binary: " +
                       Integer.toBinaryString(num));

    System.out.println(num + " in octal: " +
                       Integer.toOctalString(num));

    System.out.println(num + " in hexadecimal: " +
                       Integer.toHexString(num));
  }
}
```

The output of this program is shown here:

```
19648 in binary: 100110011000000
19648 in octal: 46300
19648 in hexadecimal: 4cc0
```

## Character

**Character** is a simple wrapper around a **char**. The constructor for **Character** is

Character(char *ch*)

Here, *ch* specifies the character that will be wrapped by the **Character** object being created. Beginning with JDK 9, this constructor has been deprecated, and beginning with JDK 16, it has been deprecated for removal. The **valueOf( )** method is the strongly recommended alternative.

To obtain the **char** value contained in a **Character** object, call **charValue( )**, shown here:

char charValue( )

It returns the character.

The **Character** class defines several constants, including the following:

| | |
|---|---|
| BYTES | The width of a **char** in bytes |
| MAX_RADIX | The largest radix |
| MIN_RADIX | The smallest radix |
| MAX_VALUE | The largest character value |
| MIN_VALUE | The smallest character value |
| TYPE | The **Class** object for **char** |

**Character** includes several static methods that categorize characters and alter their case. A sampling is shown in Table 19-7. The following example demonstrates several of these methods:

```
// Demonstrate several Is... methods.

class IsDemo {
  public static void main(String[] args) {
    char[] a = {'a', 'b', '5', '?', 'A', ' '};

    for(int i=0; i<a.length; i++) {
      if(Character.isDigit(a[i]))
        System.out.println(a[i] + " is a digit.");
      if(Character.isLetter(a[i]))
        System.out.println(a[i] + " is a letter.");
      if(Character.isWhitespace(a[i]))
        System.out.println(a[i] + " is whitespace.");
      if(Character.isUpperCase(a[i]))
        System.out.println(a[i] + " is uppercase.");
      if(Character.isLowerCase(a[i]))
        System.out.println(a[i] + " is lowercase.");
    }
  }
}
```

| Method | Description |
| --- | --- |
| static boolean isDefined(char *ch*) | Returns **true** if *ch* is defined by Unicode. Otherwise, it returns **false**. |
| static boolean isDigit(char *ch*) | Returns **true** if *ch* is a digit. Otherwise, it returns **false**. |
| static boolean isIdentifierIgnorable(char *ch*) | Returns **true** if *ch* should be ignored in an identifier. Otherwise, it returns **false**. |
| static boolean isISOControl(char *ch*) | Returns **true** if *ch* is an ISO control character. Otherwise, it returns **false**. |
| static boolean isJavaIdentifierPart(char *ch*) | Returns **true** if *ch* is allowed as part of a Java identifier (other than the first character). Otherwise, it returns **false**. |
| static boolean isJavaIdentifierStart(char *ch*) | Returns **true** if *ch* is allowed as the first character of a Java identifier. Otherwise, it returns **false**. |
| static boolean isLetter(char *ch*) | Returns **true** if *ch* is a letter. Otherwise, it returns false. |
| static boolean isLetterOrDigit(char *ch*) | Returns **true** if *ch* is a letter or a digit. Otherwise, it returns **false**. |
| static boolean isLowerCase(char *ch*) | Returns **true** if *ch* is a lowercase letter. Otherwise, it returns **false**. |
| static boolean isMirrored(char *ch*) | Returns **true** if *ch* is a mirrored Unicode character. A mirrored character is one that is reversed for text that is displayed right-to-left. |
| static boolean isSpaceChar(char *ch*) | Returns **true** if *ch* is a Unicode space character. Otherwise, it returns **false**. |
| static boolean isTitleCase(char *ch*) | Returns **true** if *ch* is a Unicode titlecase character. Otherwise, it returns **false**. |
| static boolean isUnicodeIdentifierPart(char *ch*) | Returns **true** if *ch* is allowed as part of a Unicode identifier (other than the first character). Otherwise, it returns **false**. |
| static Boolean isUnicodeIdentifierStart(char *ch*) | Returns **true** if *ch* is allowed as the first character of a Unicode identifier. Otherwise, it returns **false**. |
| static boolean isUpperCase(char *ch*) | Returns **true** if *ch* is an uppercase letter. Otherwise, it returns **false**. |
| static boolean isWhitespace(char *ch*) | Returns **true** if *ch* is whitespace. Otherwise, it returns **false**. |
| static char toLowerCase(char *ch*) | Returns lowercase equivalent of *ch*. |
| static char toTitleCase(char *ch*) | Returns titlecase equivalent of *ch*. |
| static char toUpperCase(char *ch*) | Returns uppercase equivalent of *ch*. |

**Table 19-7** Various Character **Methods**

The output from this program is shown here:

```
a is a letter.
a is lowercase.
b is a letter.
b is lowercase.
5 is a digit.
A is a letter.
A is uppercase.
  is whitespace.
```

**Character** defines two methods, **forDigit( )** and **digit( )**, that enable you to convert between integer values and the digits they represent. They are shown here:

static char forDigit(int *num*, int *radix*)
static int digit(char *digit*, int *radix*)

**forDigit( )** returns the digit character associated with the value of *num*. The radix of the conversion is specified by *radix*. **digit( )** returns the integer value associated with the specified character (which is presumably a digit) according to the specified radix. (There is a second form of **digit( )** that takes a code point. See the following section for a discussion of code points.)

Another method defined by **Character** is **compareTo( )**, which has the following form:

int compareTo(Character *c*)

It returns zero if the invoking object and *c* have the same value. It returns a negative value if the invoking object has a lower value. Otherwise, it returns a positive value.

**Character** includes a method called **getDirectionality( )**, which can be used to determine the direction of a character. Several constants are defined that describe directionality. Most programs will not need to use character directionality.

**Character** also overrides **equals( )** and **hashCode( )**, and it provides a number of other methods. Beginning with JDK 15, **Character** also implements the **Constable** interface.

Two other character-related classes are **Character.Subset**, used to describe a subset of Unicode, and **Character.UnicodeBlock**, which contains Unicode character blocks.

## Additions to Character for Unicode Code Point Support

A number of years ago, major additions were made to **Character** that support 32-bit Unicode characters. In the early days of Java, all Unicode characters could be held by 16 bits, which is the size of a **char** (and the size of the value encapsulated within a **Character**), because those values ranged from 0 to FFFF. However, the Unicode character set has been expanded, and more than 16 bits are required. Characters can now range from 0 to 10FFFF.

Here are three important terms. A *code point* is a character in the range 0 to 10FFFF. Characters that have values greater than FFFF are called *supplemental characters*. The *basic multilingual plane (BMP)* are those characters between 0 and FFFF.

The expansion of the Unicode character set caused a fundamental problem for Java. Because a supplemental character has a value greater than a **char** can hold, some means of handling the supplemental characters was needed. Java addressed this problem in two ways. First, Java uses two **char**s to represent a supplemental character. The first **char** is called the *high surrogate*, and the second is called the *low surrogate*. Methods, such as **codePointAt( )**, were provided to translate between code points and supplemental characters.

Second, Java overloaded several preexisting methods in the **Character** class. The overloaded forms use **int** rather than **char** data. Because an **int** is large enough to hold any character as a single value, it can be used to store any character. For example, all of the methods in Table 19-7 have overloaded forms that operate on **int**. Here is a sampling:

static boolean isDigit(int *cp*)
static boolean isLetter(int *cp*)
static int toLowerCase(int *cp*)



In addition to the methods overloaded to accept code points, **Character** adds methods that provide additional support for code points. A sampling is shown in Table 19-8.

## Boolean

**Boolean** is a very thin wrapper around **boolean** values, which is useful mostly when you want to pass a **boolean** variable by reference. It contains the constants **TRUE** and **FALSE**, which define true and false **Boolean** objects. **Boolean** also defines the **TYPE** field, which is the **Class** object for **boolean**. **Boolean** defines these constructors:

Boolean(boolean *boolValue*)
Boolean(String *boolString*)

In the first version, *boolValue* must be either **true** or **false**. In the second version, if *boolString* contains the string "true" (in uppercase or lowercase), then the new **Boolean** object will be **true**. Otherwise, it will be **false**. Beginning with JDK 9, these constructors have been deprecated, and beginning with JDK 16, they have been deprecated for removal. The **valueOf( )** method is the strongly recommended alternative.

Commonly used methods defined by **Boolean** are shown in Table 19-9. Beginning with JDK 15, **Boolean** also implements the **Constable** special-purpose interface.

# Void

The **Void** class has one field, **TYPE**, which holds a reference to the **Class** object for type **void**. You do not create instances of this class.

# Process

The abstract **Process** class encapsulates a *process*—that is, an executing program. It is used primarily as a superclass for the type of objects created by **exec( )** in the **Runtime** class, or by **start( )** in the **ProcessBuilder** class. A sampling of the **Process** methods are shown

| Method | Description |
|---|---|
| static int charCount(int *cp*) | Returns 1 if *cp* can be represented by a single **char**. It returns 2 if two **char**s are needed. |
| static int codePointAt(CharSequence *chars*, int *loc*) | Returns the code point at the location specified by *loc*. |
| static int codePointAt(char[ ] *chars*, int *loc*) | Returns the code point at the location specified by *loc*. |
| static int codePointBefore(CharSequence *chars*, int *loc*) | Returns the code point at the location that precedes that specified by *loc*. |
| static int codePointBefore(char[ ] *chars*, int *loc*) | Returns the code point at the location that precedes that specified by *loc*. |
| static boolean isBmpCodePoint(int *cp*) | Returns **true** if *cp* is part of the basic multilingual plane and **false** otherwise. |
| static boolean isHighSurrogate(char *ch*) | Returns **true** if *ch* contains a valid high surrogate character. |
| static boolean isLowSurrogate(char *ch*) | Returns **true** if *ch* contains a valid low surrogate character. |
| static boolean isSupplementaryCodePoint(int *cp*) | Returns **true** if *cp* contains a supplemental character. |
| static boolean isSurrogatePair(char *highCh*, char *lowCh*) | Returns **true** if *highCh* and *lowCh* form a valid surrogate pair. |
| static boolean isValidCodePoint(int *cp*) | Returns **true** if *cp* contains a valid code point. |
| static char[ ] toChars(int *cp*) | Converts the code point in *cp* into its **char** equivalent, which might require two **chars**. An array holding the result is returned. |
| static int toChars(int *cp*, char[ ] *target*, int *loc*) | Converts the code point in *cp* into its **char** equivalent, storing the result in *target*, beginning at *loc*. Returns 1 if *cp* can be represented by a single **char**. It returns 2 otherwise. |
| static int toCodePoint(char *highCh*, char *lowCh*) | Converts *highCh* and *lowCh* into their equivalent code point. |

**Table 19-8** A Sampling of Methods That Provide Support for 32-Bit Unicode Code Points

in Table 19-10. Beginning with JDK 9, you can obtain a handle to the process in the form of a **ProcessHandle** instance, and you can obtain information about the process encapsulated in a **ProcessHandle.Info** instance. These offer additional control and information about a process. One particularly interesting piece of information is the amount

| Method | Description |
|---|---|
| boolean booleanValue( ) | Returns **boolean** equivalent. |
| static int compare(boolean *b1*, boolean *b2*) | Returns zero if *b1* and *b2* contain the same value. Returns a positive value if *b1* is **true** and *b2* is **false**. Otherwise, returns a negative value. |
| int compareTo(Boolean *b*) | Returns zero if the invoking object and *b* contain the same value. Returns a positive value if the invoking object is **true** and *b* is **false**. Otherwise, returns a negative value. |
| boolean equals(Object *boolObj*) | Returns **true** if the invoking object is equivalent to *boolObj*. Otherwise, it returns **false**. |
| static Boolean getBoolean(String *propertyName*) | Returns **true** if the system property specified by *propertyName* is **true**. Otherwise, it returns **false**. |
| int hashCode( ) | Returns the hash code for the invoking object. |
| static int hashCode(boolean *boolVal*) | Returns the hash code for *boolVal*. |
| static boolean logicalAnd(boolean *op1*, boolean *op2*) | Performs a logical AND of *op1* and *op2* and returns the result. |
| static boolean logicalOr(boolean *op1*, boolean *op2*) | Performs a logical OR of *op1* and *op2* and returns the result. |
| static boolean logicalXor(boolean *op1*, boolean *op2*) | Performs a logical XOR of *op1* and *op2* and returns the result. |
| static boolean parseBoolean(String *str*) | Returns **true** if *str* contains the string "true". Case is not significant. Otherwise, returns **false**. |
| String toString( ) | Returns the string equivalent of the invoking object. |
| static String toString(boolean *boolVal*) | Returns the string equivalent of *boolVal*. |
| static Boolean valueOf(boolean *boolVal*) | Returns the **Boolean** equivalent of *boolVal*. |
| static Boolean valueOf(String *boolString*) | Returns **true** if *boolString* contains the string "true" (in uppercase or lowercase). Otherwise, it returns **false**. |

**Table 19-9** Commonly Used Methods Defined by **Boolean**

of CPU time that a process receives. This is obtained by calling **totalCpuDuration( )** defined by **ProcessHandle.Info**. Another especially helpful piece of information is obtained by calling **isAlive( )** on a **ProcessHandle**. It will return **true** if the process is still executing. Beginning with JDK 17, **Process** also provides the methods **inputReader( )**, **errorReader( )**, and **outputWriter( )**.

| Method | Description |
|---|---|
| Stream<ProcessHandle> children( ) | Returns a stream that contains **ProcessHandle** objects that represent the immediate children of the invoking process. |
| Stream<ProcessHandle> descendants( ) | Returns a stream that contains **ProcessHandle** objects that represent both the immediate children of the invoking process, plus all of their descendants. |
| void destroy( ) | Terminates the process. |
| Process destroyForcibly( ) | Forces termination of the invoking process. Returns a reference to the process. |
| int exitValue( ) | Returns an exit code obtained from a subprocess. |
| InputStream getErrorStream( ) | Returns an input stream that reads input from the process's **err** output stream. |
| InputStream getInputStream( ) | Returns an input stream that reads input from the process's **out** output stream. |
| OutputStream getOutputStream( ) | Returns an output stream that writes output to the process's **in** input stream. |
| ProcessHandle.Info info( ) | Returns information about the process in the form of a **ProcessHandle.Info** object. |
| boolean isAlive( ) | Returns **true** if the invoking process is still active. Otherwise, returns **false**. |
| CompletableFuture<Process> onExit( ) | Returns a **CompletableFuture** for the invoking process, which can be used to perform tasks at termination. |
| long pid( ) | Returns the process ID associated with the invoking process. |
| boolean supportsNormalTermination( ) | Determines if a call to **destroy( )** will result in normal or forced termination. Returns **true** if termination is normal, and **false** otherwise. |
| ProcessHandle toHandle( ) | Returns a handle to the invoking process in the form of a **ProcessHandle** object. |
| int waitFor( ) throws InterruptedException | Returns the exit code returned by the process. This method does not return until the process on which it is called terminates. |
| boolean waitFor(long *waitTime*, TimeUnit *timeUnit*) throws InterruptedException | Waits for the invoking process to end. The amount of time to wait is specified by *waitTime* in the units specified by *timeUnit*. Returns **true** if the process has ended and **false** if the wait time runs out. |

**Table 19-10** A Sampling of the Methods Defined by **Process**

## Runtime

The **Runtime** class encapsulates the run-time environment. You cannot instantiate a **Runtime** object. However, you can get a reference to the current **Runtime** object by calling the static method **Runtime.getRuntime( )**. Once you obtain a reference to the current **Runtime** object, you can call several methods that control the state and behavior of the Java Virtual Machine. Untrusted code typically cannot call any of the **Runtime** methods without raising a **SecurityException**. A sampling of methods defined by **Runtime** are shown in Table 19-11.

| Method | Description |
|---|---|
| void addShutdownHook(Thread *thrd*) | Registers *thrd* as a thread to be run when the Java Virtual Machine terminates. |
| Process exec(String[ ] *comLineArray*) throws IOException | Executes the command line specified by the strings in *comLineArray* as a separate process. An object of type **Process** is returned that describes the new process. |
| Process exec(String[ ] *comLineArray*, String[ ] *environment*) throws IOException | Executes the command line specified by the strings in *comLineArray* as a separate process with the environment specified by *environment*. An object of type **Process** is returned that describes the new process. |
| void exit(int *exitCode*) | Halts execution and returns the value of *exitCode* to the parent process. By convention, 0 indicates normal termination. All other values indicate some form of error. |
| long freeMemory( ) | Returns the approximate number of bytes of free memory available to the Java run-time system. |
| void gc( ) | Initiates garbage collection. |
| static Runtime getRuntime( ) | Returns the current **Runtime** object. |
| void halt(int *code*) | Immediately terminates the Java Virtual Machine. No shutdown hooks are run. The value of *code* is returned to the invoking process. |
| void load(String *libraryFileName*) | Loads the dynamic library whose file is specified by *libraryFileName*, which must specify its complete path. |
| void loadLibrary(String *libraryName*) | Loads the dynamic library whose name is associated with *libraryName*. |
| Boolean removeShutdownHook(Thread *thrd*) | Removes *thrd* from the list of threads to run when the Java Virtual Machine terminates. It returns **true** if successful—that is, if the thread was removed. |
| long totalMemory( ) | Returns the total number of bytes of memory available to the program. |
| static Runtime.Version version( ) | Returns the Java version being used. See **Runtime .Version** for details. |

**Table 19-11** A Sampling of Methods Defined by **Runtime**

**NOTE** JDK 18 deprecates the forms of **exec( )** that take a **String** parameter representing a space-separated **String** of command arguments, preferring instead the equivalent forms that take a **String** array instead. This is due to ambiguities in how to parse parameters—for example those including filenames containing spaces.

Let's look at one of the more interesting uses of the **Runtime** class: executing additional processes.

## Executing Other Programs

In safe environments, you can use Java to execute other heavyweight processes (that is, programs) on your multitasking operating system. Several forms of the **exec( )** method allow you to name the program you want to run as well as its input parameters. The **exec( )** method returns a **Process** object, which can then be used to control how your Java program interacts with this new running process. Because Java can run on a variety of platforms and under a variety of operating systems, **exec( )** is inherently environment-dependent.

The following example uses **exec( )** to launch **notepad**, Windows' simple text editor. Obviously, this example must be run under the Windows operating system.

```
// Demonstrate exec().
class ExecDemo {
  public static void main(String[] args) {
    Runtime r = Runtime.getRuntime();
    Process p = null;

    try {
      p = r.exec(new String[]{"notepad"});
    } catch (Exception e) {
      System.out.println("Error executing notepad.");
    }
  }
}
```

There are several alternative forms of **exec( )**, but the one shown in the example is often sufficient. The **Process** object returned by **exec( )** can be manipulated by **Process**'s methods after the new program starts running. You can kill the subprocess with the **destroy( )** method. The **waitFor( )** method causes your program to wait until the subprocess finishes. The **exitValue( )** method returns the value returned by the subprocess when it is finished. This is typically 0 if no problems occur. Here is the preceding **exec( )** example modified to wait for the running process to exit:

```
// Wait until notepad is terminated.
class ExecDemoFini {
  public static void main(String[] args) {
    Runtime r = Runtime.getRuntime();
    Process p = null;

    try {
      p = r.exec(new String[]{"notepad"});
      p.waitFor();
    } catch (Exception e) {
      System.out.println("Error executing notepad.");
    }
    System.out.println("Notepad returned " + p.exitValue());
  }
}
```

While a subprocess is running, you can write to and read from its standard input and output. The **getOutputStream( )** and **getInputStream( )** methods return the handles to standard **in** and **out** of the subprocess. Alternatively, beginning with JDK 17, you can also use **outputWriter( )** and **inputReader( )** to obtain a writer and reader. (I/O is examined in detail in Chapter 22.)

## Runtime.Version



**Runtime.Version** encapsulates version information (which includes the version number) pertaining to the Java environment. You can obtain an instance of **Runtime.Version** for the current platform by calling **Runtime.version( )**. Originally added by JDK 9, **Runtime.Version** was substantially changed with the release of JDK 10 to better accommodate the faster, time-based release cadence. As discussed earlier in this book, starting with JDK 10, a feature release is anticipated to occur on a strict schedule, with the time between feature releases expected to be six months. **Runtime.Version** is a value-based class. (See Chapter 13 for a description of value-based classes.)

In the past, the JDK version number used the well-known *major.minor* approach. This mechanism did not, however, provide a good fit with the time-based release schedule. As a result, a different meaning was given to the elements of a version number. Today, the first four elements specify *counters,* which occur in the following order: feature release counter, interim release counter, update release counter, and patch release counter. Each number is separated by a period. However, trailing zeros, along with their preceding periods, are removed. Although additional elements may also be included, only the meaning of the first four are predefined.

The feature release counter specifies the number of the release. This counter is updated with each feature release. To smooth the transition from the previous version scheme, the feature release counter began at 10. Thus, the feature release counter for JDK 10 is 10, the one for JDK 11 is 11, and so on.

The interim release counter indicates the number of a release that occurs between feature releases. At the time of this writing, the value of the interim release counter will be zero because interim releases are not expected to be part of the increased release cadence. (It is defined for possible future use.) An interim release will not cause breaking changes to the JDK feature set. The update release counter indicates the number of a release that addresses security and possibly other problems. The patch release counter specifies a number of a release that addresses a serious flaw that must be fixed as soon as possible. With each new feature release, the interim, update, and patch counters are reset to zero.

It is useful to point out that the version number just described is a necessary component of the *version string,* but optional elements may also be included in the string. For example, a version string may include information for a pre-release version. Optional elements follow the version number in the version string.

Beginning with JDK 10, **Runtime.Version** was updated to include the following methods that support the new feature, interim, update, and patch counter values:

```
int feature( )
int interim( )
int update( )
int patch( )
```

Each returns an integer value that represents the indicated value. Here is a short program that demonstrates their use:

```
// Demonstrate Runtime.Version release counters.
class VerDemo {
  public static void main(String[] args) {
    Runtime.Version ver = Runtime.version();

    // Display individual counters.
    System.out.println("Feature release counter: " + ver.feature());
    System.out.println("Interim release counter: " + ver.interim());
    System.out.println("Update release counter: " + ver.update());
    System.out.println("Patch release counter: " + ver.patch());
  }
}
```

As a result of the change to time-based releases, the following methods in **Runtime.Version** have been deprecated: **major( )**, **minor( )**, and **security( )**. Previously, these returned the major version number, the minor version number, and the security update number. These values have been superseded by the feature, interim, and update numbers, as just described.

In addition to the methods just discussed, **Runtime.Version** has methods that obtain various pieces of optional data. For example, you can obtain the build number, if present, by calling **build( )**. Pre-release information, if present, is returned by **pre( )**. Other optional information may also be present and is obtained by calling **optional( )**. You can compare versions by using **compareTo( )** or **compareToIgnoreOptional( )**. You can use **equals( )** and **equalsIgnoreOptional( )** to determine version equality. The **version( )** method returns a list of the version numbers. You can convert a valid version string into a **Runtime.Version** object by calling **parse( )**.

# ProcessBuilder

**ProcessBuilder** provides another way to start and manage processes (that is, programs). As explained earlier, all processes are represented by the **Process** class, and a process can be started by **Runtime.exec( )**. **ProcessBuilder** offers more control over the processes. For example, you can set the current working directory.

**ProcessBuilder** defines these constructors:

ProcessBuilder(List<String> *args*)
ProccessBuilder(String ... *args*)

Here, *args* is a list of arguments that specify the name of the program to be executed along with any required command-line arguments. In the first constructor, the arguments are passed in a **List**. In the second, they are specified through a varargs parameter. Table 19-12 describes the methods defined by **ProcessBuilder**.

In Table 19-12, notice the methods that use the **ProcessBuilder.Redirect** class. This abstract class encapsulates an I/O source or target linked to a subprocess. Among other things, these methods enable you to redirect the source or target of I/O operations.

| Method | Description |
|---|---|
| List<String> command( ) | Returns a reference to a **List** that contains the name of the program and its arguments. Changes to this list affect the invoking object. |
| ProcessBuilder command(List<String> *args*) | Sets the name of the program and its arguments to those specified by *args*. Changes to this list affect the invoking object. Returns a reference to the invoking object. |
| ProcessBuilder command(String ... *args*) | Sets the name of the program and its arguments to those specified by *args*. Returns a reference to the invoking object. |
| File directory( ) | Returns the current working directory of the invoking object. This value will be **null** if the directory is the same as that of the Java program that started the process. |
| ProcessBuilder directory(File *dir*) | Sets the current working directory of the invoking object. Returns a reference to the invoking object. |
| Map<String, String> environment( ) | Returns the environmental variables associated with the invoking object as key/value pairs. |
| ProcessBuilder inheritIO( ) | Causes the invoked process to use the same source and target for the standard I/O streams as the invoking process. |
| ProcessBuilder.Redirect redirectError( ) | Returns the target for standard error as a **ProcessBuilder.Redirect** object. |
| ProcessBuilder redirectError(File *f*) | Sets the target for standard error to the specified file. Returns a reference to the invoking object. |
| ProcessBuilder redirectError( ProcessBuilder.Redirect *target*) | Sets the target for standard error as specified by *target*. Returns a reference to the invoking object. |
| boolean redirectErrorStream( ) | Returns **true** if the standard error stream has been redirected to the standard output stream. Returns **false** if the streams are separate. |
| ProcessBuilder redirectErrorStream(boolean *merge*) | If *merge* is **true**, then the standard error stream is redirected to standard output. If *merge* is **false**, the streams are separated, which is the default state. Returns a reference to the invoking object. |
| ProcessBuilder.Redirect redirectInput( ) | Returns the source for standard input as a **ProcessBuilder.Redirect** object. |
| ProcessBuilder redirectInput(File *f*) | Sets the source for standard input to the specified file. Returns a reference to the invoking object. |
| ProcessBuilder redirectInput( ProcessBuilder.Redirect *source*) | Sets the source for standard input as specified by *source*. Returns a reference to the invoking object. |
| ProcessBuilder.Redirect redirectOutput( ) | Returns the target for standard output as a **ProcessBuilder.Redirect** object. |

**Table 19-12** The Methods Defined by **ProcessBuilder**

| Method | Description |
|---|---|
| ProcessBuilder redirectOutput(File *f*) | Sets the target for standard output to the specified file. Returns a reference to the invoking object. |
| ProcessBuilder redirectOutput( ProcessBuilder.Redirect *target*) | Sets the target for standard output as specified by *target*. Returns a reference to the invoking object. |
| Process start( ) throws IOException | Begins the process specified by the invoking object. In other words, it runs the specified program. |
| static List<Process> startPipeline( List<ProcessBuilder> *pbList*) *throws IOException* | Pipelines the processes in *pbList*. |

**Table 19-12** The Methods Defined by **ProcessBuilder** *(continued)*

For example, you can redirect to a file by calling **to( )**, redirect from a file by calling **from( )**, and append to a file by calling **appendTo( )**. A **File** object linked to the file can be obtained by calling **file( )**. These methods are shown here:

static ProcessBuilder.Redirect to(File *f*)
static ProcessBuilder.Redirect from(File *f*)
static ProcessBuilder.Redirect appendTo(File *f*)
File file( )

Another method supported by **ProcessBuilder.Redirect** is **type( )**, which returns a value of the enumeration type **ProcessBuilder.Redirect.Type**. This enumeration describes the type of the redirection. It defines these values: **APPEND**, **INHERIT**, **PIPE**, **READ**, and **WRITE**. **ProcessBuilder.Redirect** also defines the constants **INHERIT**, **PIPE**, and **DISCARD**.

To create a process using **ProcessBuilder**, simply create an instance of **ProcessBuilder**, specifying the name of the program and any needed arguments. To begin execution of the program, call **start( )** on that instance. Here is an example that executes the Windows text editor **notepad**. Notice that it specifies the name of the file to edit as an argument.

```
class PBDemo {
  public static void main(String[] args) {

    try {
      ProcessBuilder proc =
        new ProcessBuilder("notepad.exe", "testfile");
      proc.start();
    } catch (Exception e) {
      System.out.println("Error executing notepad.");
    }
  }
}
```

# System

The **System** class holds a collection of static methods and variables. The standard input, output, and error output of the Java run time are stored in the **in**, **out**, and **err** variables, respectively. The non-deprecated methods defined by **System** are shown in Table 19-13.

| Method | Description |
|---|---|
| static void arraycopy(Object *source*, int *sourceStart*, Object *target*, int *targetStart*, int *size*) | Copies an array. The array to be copied is passed in *source*, and the index at which point the copy will begin within *source* is passed in *sourceStart*. The array that will receive the copy is passed in *target*, and the index at which point the copy will begin within *target* is passed in *targetStart*. *size* is the number of elements that are copied. |
| static String clearProperty(String *which*) | Deletes the environmental variable specified by *which*. The previous value associated with *which* is returned. |
| static Console console( ) | Returns the console associated with the JVM. **null** is returned if the JVM currently has no console. |
| static long currentTimeMillis( ) | Returns the current time in terms of milliseconds since midnight, January 1, 1970. |
| static void exit(int *exitCode*) | Halts execution and returns the value of *exitCode* to the parent process (usually the operating system). By convention, 0 indicates normal termination. All other values indicate some form of error. |
| static void gc( ) | Initiates garbage collection. |
| static Map<String, String> getenv( ) | Returns a **Map** that contains the current environmental variables and their values. |
| static String getenv(String *which*) | Returns the value associated with the environmental variable passed in *which*. |
| static System.Logger getLogger(String *logName)* | Returns a reference to an object that can be used for program logging. The name of the logger is passed in *logName*. |
| static System.Logger getLogger(String *logName*, ResourceBundle *rb*) | Returns a reference to an object that can be used for program logging. The name of the logger is passed in *logName*. Localization is supported by the resource bundle passed in *rb*. |
| static Properties getProperties( ) | Returns the properties associated with the Java run-time system. (The **Properties** class is described in Chapter 20.) |
| static String getProperty(String *which*) | Returns the property associated with *which*. A **null** object is returned if the desired property is not found. |
| static String getProperty(String *which*, String *default*) | Returns the property associated with *which*. If the desired property is not found, *default* is returned. |
| static int identityHashCode(Object *obj*) | Returns the identity hash code for *obj*. |
| static Channel inheritedChannel( ) throws IOException | Returns the channel inherited by the Java Virtual Machine. Returns **null** if no channel is inherited. |
| static String lineSeparator( ) | Returns a string that contains the line-separator characters. |

**Table 19-13** The Non-Deprecated Methods Defined by **System**

Part II

| Method | Description |
|---|---|
| static void load(String *libraryFileName*) | Loads the dynamic library whose file is specified by *libraryFileName*, which must specify its complete path. |
| static void loadLibrary(String *libraryName*) | Loads the dynamic library whose name is associated with *libraryName*. |
| static String mapLibraryName(String *lib*) | Returns a platform-specific name for the library named *lib*. |
| static long nanoTime( ) | Obtains the most precise timer in the system and returns its value in terms of nanoseconds since some arbitrary starting point. The accuracy of the timer is unknowable. |
| static void setErr(PrintStream *eStream*) | Sets the standard **err** stream to *eStream*. |
| static void setIn(InputStream *iStream*) | Sets the standard **in** stream to *iStream*. |
| static void setOut(PrintStream *oStream*) | Sets the standard **out** stream to *oStream*. |
| static void setProperties(Properties *sysProperties*) | Sets the current system properties as specified by *sysProperties*. |
| static String setProperty(String *which*, String *v*) | Assigns the value *v* to the property named *which*. |

**Table 19-13** The Non-Deprecated Methods Defined by **System** *(continued)*

Many of the methods throw a **SecurityException** if the operation is not permitted by the security manager. Be aware, however, that JDK 17 deprecates for removal the security manager.

Let's look at some common uses of **System**.

## Using currentTimeMillis( ) to Time Program Execution

One use of the **System** class that you might find particularly interesting is to use the **currentTimeMillis( )** method to time how long various parts of your program take to execute. The **currentTimeMillis( )** method returns the current time in terms of milliseconds since midnight, January 1, 1970. To time a section of your program, store this value just before beginning the section in question. Immediately upon completion, call **currentTimeMillis( )** again. The elapsed time will be the ending time minus the starting time. The following program demonstrates this:

```
// Timing program execution.

class Elapsed {
  public static void main(String[] args) {
    long start, end;

    System.out.println("Timing a for loop from 0 to 100,000,000");

    // time a for loop from 0 to 100,000,000
```

```
    start = System.currentTimeMillis(); // get starting time
    for(long i=0; i < 100000000L; i++) ;
    end = System.currentTimeMillis(); // get ending time

    System.out.println("Elapsed time: " + (end-start));
  }
}
```

Here is a sample run (remember that your results probably will differ):

```
Timing a for loop from 0 to 100,000,000
Elapsed time: 10
```

If your system has a timer that offers nanosecond precision, then you could rewrite the preceding program to use **nanoTime( )** rather than **currentTimeMillis( )**. For example, here is the key portion of the program rewritten to use **nanoTime( )**:

```
start = System.nanoTime(); // get starting time
for(long i=0; i < 100000000L; i++) ;
end = System.nanoTime(); // get ending time
```

## Using arraycopy( )

The **arraycopy( )** method can be used to copy quickly an array of any type from one place to another. This is much faster than the equivalent loop written out longhand in Java. Here is an example of two arrays being copied by the **arraycopy( )** method. First, **a** is copied to **b**. Next, all of **a**'s elements are shifted *down* by one. Then, **b** is shifted *up* by one.

```
// Using arraycopy().

class ACDemo {
  static byte[] a = { 65, 66, 67, 68, 69, 70, 71, 72, 73, 74 };
  static byte[] b = { 77, 77, 77, 77, 77, 77, 77, 77, 77, 77 };

  public static void main(String[] args) {
    System.out.println("a = " + new String(a));
    System.out.println("b = " + new String(b));
    System.arraycopy(a, 0, b, 0, a.length);
    System.out.println("a = " + new String(a));
    System.out.println("b = " + new String(b));
    System.arraycopy(a, 0, a, 1, a.length - 1);
    System.arraycopy(b, 1, b, 0, b.length - 1);
    System.out.println("a = " + new String(a));
    System.out.println("b = " + new String(b));
  }
}
```

As you can see from the following output, you can copy using the same source and destination in either direction:

```
a = ABCDEFGHIJ
b = MMMMMMMMMM
a = ABCDEFGHIJ
b = ABCDEFGHIJ
a = AABCDEFGHI
b = BCDEFGHIJJ
```

## Environment Properties

At the time of this writing, the following properties are available:

| | | |
|---|---|---|
| file.separator | java.vendor | java.vm.version |
| java.class.path | java.vendor.url | line.separator |
| java.class.version | java.vendor.version | native.encoding |
| java.compiler | java.version | os.arch |
| java.home | java.version.date | os.name |
| java.io.tmpdir | java.vm.name | os.version |
| java.library.path | java.vm.specification.name | path.separator |
| java.specification.name | java.vm.specification.vendor | user.dir |
| java.specification.vendor | java.vm.specification.version | user.home |
| java.specification.version | java.vm.vendor | user.name |

You can obtain the values of various environment variables by calling the **System.getProperty( )** method. For example, the following program displays the path to the current user directory:

```
class ShowUserDir {
  public static void main(String[] args) {
    System.out.println(System.getProperty("user.dir"));
  }
}
```

# System.Logger and System.LoggerFinder

The **System.Logger** interface and **System.LoggerFinder** class support a program log. A logger can be found by use of **System.getLogger( )**. **System.Logger** provides the interface to the logger.

# Object

As mentioned in Part I, **Object** is a superclass of all other classes. **Object** defines the methods shown in Table 19-14, which are available to every object.

# Using clone( ) and the Cloneable Interface

Most of the methods defined by **Object** are discussed elsewhere in this book. However, one deserves special attention: **clone( )**. The **clone( )** method generates a duplicate copy of the object on which it is called. Only classes that implement the **Cloneable** interface can be cloned.

The **Cloneable** interface defines no members. It is used to indicate that a class allows an exact copy of an object (that is, a *clone*) to be made. If you try to call **clone( )** on a class that does not implement **Cloneable**, a **CloneNotSupportedException** is thrown. When a clone

| Method | Description |
|---|---|
| Object clone( ) throws CloneNotSupportedException | Creates a new object that is the same as the invoking object. |
| boolean equals(Object *object*) | Returns **true** if the invoking object is equivalent to *object*. |
| void finalize( ) throws Throwable | Default **finalize( )** method. It is called before an unused object is recycled. (Deprecated for removal by JDK 18.) |
| final Class<?> getClass( ) | Obtains a **Class** object that describes the invoking object. |
| int hashCode( ) | Returns the hash code associated with the invoking object. |
| final void notify( ) | Notifies a thread waiting on the invoking object. |
| final void notifyAll( ) | Notifies all threads waiting on the invoking object. |
| String toString( ) | Returns a string that describes the object. |
| final void wait( ) throws InterruptedException | Waits on another thread of execution. |
| final void wait(long *milliseconds*) throws InterruptedException | Waits up to the specified number of *milliseconds* on another thread of execution. |
| final void wait(long *milliseconds*, int *nanoseconds*) throws InterruptedException | Waits up to the specified number of *milliseconds* plus *nanoseconds* on another thread of execution. |

**Table 19-14** The Methods Defined by **Object**

is made, the constructor for the object being cloned is *not* called. As implemented by **Object**, a clone is simply an exact copy of the original.

Cloning is a potentially dangerous action, because it can cause unintended side effects. For example, if the object being cloned contains a reference variable called *obRef*, then when the clone is made, *obRef* in the clone will refer to the same object as does *obRef* in the original. If the clone makes a change to the contents of the object referred to by *obRef*, then it will be changed for the original object, too. Here is another example: If an object opens an I/O stream and is then cloned, two objects will be capable of operating on the same stream. Further, if one of these objects closes the stream, the other object might still attempt to write to it, causing an error. In some cases, you will need to override the **clone( )** method defined by **Object** to handle these types of problems.

Because cloning can cause problems, **clone( )** is declared as **protected** inside **Object**. This means that it must either be called from within a method defined by the class that implements **Cloneable**, or it must be explicitly overridden by that class so that it is public. Let's look at an example of each approach.

The following program implements **Cloneable** and defines the method **cloneTest( )**, which calls **clone( )** in **Object**:

```
// Demonstrate the clone() method

class TestClone implements Cloneable {
  int a;
  double b;
```

```
  // This method calls Object's clone().
  TestClone cloneTest() {
    try {
      // call clone in Object.
      return (TestClone) super.clone();
    } catch(CloneNotSupportedException e) {
      System.out.println("Cloning not allowed.");
      return this;
    }
  }
}

class CloneDemo {
  public static void main(String[] args) {
    TestClone x1 = new TestClone();
    TestClone x2;

    x1.a = 10;
    x1.b = 20.98;

    x2 = x1.cloneTest(); // clone x1

    System.out.println("x1: " + x1.a + " " + x1.b);
    System.out.println("x2: " + x2.a + " " + x2.b);
  }
}
```

Here, the method **cloneTest( )** calls **clone( )** in **Object** and returns the result. Notice that the object returned by **clone( )** must be cast into its appropriate type (**TestClone**).

The following example overrides **clone( )** so that it can be called from code outside of its class. To do this, its access specifier must be **public**, as shown here:

```
// Override the clone() method.

class TestClone implements Cloneable {
  int a;
  double b;

  // clone() is now overridden and is public.
  public Object clone() {
    try {
      // call clone in Object.
      return super.clone();
    } catch(CloneNotSupportedException e) {
      System.out.println("Cloning not allowed.");
      return this;
    }
  }
}

class CloneDemo2 {
  public static void main(String[] args) {
    TestClone x1 = new TestClone();
    TestClone x2;
```

```
        x1.a = 10;
        x1.b = 20.98;

        // here, clone() is called directly.
        x2 = (TestClone) x1.clone();

        System.out.println("x1: " + x1.a + " " + x1.b);
        System.out.println("x2: " + x2.a + " " + x2.b);
    }
}
```

The side effects caused by cloning are sometimes difficult to see at first. It is easy to think that a class is safe for cloning when it actually is not. In general, you should not implement **Cloneable** for any class without good reason.



## Class

**Class** encapsulates the run-time state of a class or interface. Objects of type **Class** are created automatically, when classes are loaded. You cannot explicitly declare a **Class** object. Generally, you obtain a **Class** object by calling the **getClass( )** method defined by **Object**. **Class** is a generic class that is declared as shown here:

class Class<T>

Here, **T** is the type of the class or interface represented. A sampling of methods defined by **Class** is shown in Table 19-15. In the table, notice the **getModule( )** method. It is part of the support for the modules feature added by JDK 9. **Class** implements several interfaces, including **Constable** and **TypeDescriptor**.

| Method | Description |
|---|---|
| static Class<?> forName(Module *mod*, String *name*) | Returns a **Class** object corresponding to its complete name and the module in which is resides. |
| static Class<?> forName(String *name*) throws ClassNotFoundException | Returns a **Class** object given its complete name. |
| static Class<?> forName(String *name*, boolean *how*, ClassLoader *ldr*) throws ClassNotFoundException | Returns a **Class** object given its complete name. The object is loaded using the loader specified by *ldr*. If *how* is **true**, the object is initialized; otherwise, it is not. |
| <A extends Annotation> A getAnnotation(Class<A> *annoType*) | Returns an **Annotation** object that contains the annotation associated with *annoType* for the invoking object. |
| Annotation[ ] getAnnotations( ) | Obtains all annotations associated with the invoking object and stores them in an array of **Annotation** objects. Returns a reference to this array. |
| <A extends Annotation> A[ ] getAnnotationsByType( Class<A> *annoType*) | Returns an array of the annotations (including repeated annotations) of *annoType* associated with the invoking object. |

**Table 19-15** A Sampling of Methods Defined by **Class**

| Method | Description |
|---|---|
| Class<?>[ ] getClasses( ) | Returns a **Class** object for each public class and interface that is a member of the class represented by the invoking object. |
| ClassLoader getClassLoader( ) | Returns the **ClassLoader** object that loaded the class or interface. |
| Constructor<T> getConstructor(Class<?> ... *paramTypes*) throws NoSuchMethodException, SecurityException | Returns a **Constructor** object that represents the constructor for the class represented by the invoking object that has the parameter types specified by *paramTypes*. |
| Constructor<?>[ ] getConstructors( ) throws SecurityException | Obtains a **Constructor** object for each public constructor of the class represented by the invoking object and stores them in an array. Returns a reference to this array. |
| Annotation[ ] getDeclaredAnnotations( ) | Obtains an **Annotation** object for all the annotations that are declared by the invoking object and stores them in an array. Returns a reference to this array. (Inherited annotations are ignored.) |
| <A extends Annotation> A[ ] getDeclaredAnnotationsByType( Class<A> *annoType*) | Returns an array of the non-inherited annotations (including repeated annotations) of *annoType* associated with the invoking object. |
| Constructor<?>[ ] getDeclaredConstructors( ) throws SecurityException | Obtains a **Constructor** object for each constructor declared by the class represented by the invoking object and stores them in an array. Returns a reference to this array. (Superclass constructors are ignored.) |
| Field[ ] getDeclaredFields( ) throws SecurityException | Obtains a **Field** object for each field declared by the class or interface represented by the invoking object and stores them in an array. Returns a reference to this array. (Inherited fields are ignored.) |
| Method[ ] getDeclaredMethods( ) throws SecurityException | Obtains a **Method** object for each method declared by the class or interface represented by the invoking object and stores them in an array. Returns a reference to this array. (Inherited methods are ignored.) |
| Field getField(String *fieldName*) throws NoSuchMethodException, SecurityException | Returns a **Field** object that represents the public field specified by *fieldName* for the class or interface represented by the invoking object. |
| Field[ ] getFields( ) throws SecurityException | Obtains a **Field** object for each public field of the class or interface represented by the invoking object and stores them in an array. Returns a reference to this array. |
| Class<?>[ ] getInterfaces( ) | When invoked on an object that represents a class, this method returns an array of the interfaces implemented by that class. When invoked on an object that represents an interface, this method returns an array of interfaces extended by that interface. |
| Method getMethod(String *methName*, Class<?> ... *paramTypes*) throws NoSuchMethodException, SecurityException | Returns a **Method** object that represents the public method specified by *methName* and having the parameter types specified by *paramTypes* in the class or interface represented by the invoking object. |

**Table 19-15** A Sampling of Methods Defined by **Class** *(continued)*

| Method | Description |
|---|---|
| Method[ ] getMethods( ) throws SecurityException | Obtains a **Method** object for each public method of the class or interface represented by the invoking object and stores them in an array. Returns a reference to this array. |
| Module getModule( ) | Returns a **Module** object that represents the module in which the invoking class type resides. |
| String getName( ) | Returns the complete name of the class or interface of the type represented by the invoking object. |
| String getPackageName( ) | Returns the name of the package of which the invoking class type is a part. |
| ProtectionDomain getProtectionDomain( ) | Returns the protection domain associated with the invoking object. |
| Class<? super T> getSuperclass( ) | Returns the superclass of the type represented by the invoking object. The return value is **null** if the represented type is **Object** or not a class. |
| boolean isInterface( ) | Returns **true** if the type represented by the invoking object is an interface. Otherwise, it returns **false**. |
| String toString( ) | Returns the string representation of the type represented by the invoking object or interface. |

**Table 19-15** A Sampling of Methods Defined by **Class** *(continued)*



The methods defined by **Class** are often useful in situations where run-time type information about an object is required. As Table 19-15 shows, methods are provided that allow you to determine additional information about a particular class, such as its public constructors, fields, and methods. Among other things, this is important for the Java Beans functionality, which is discussed later in this book.

The following program demonstrates **getClass( )** (inherited from **Object**) and **getSuperclass( )** (from **Class**):

```
// Demonstrate Run-Time Type Information.

class X {
  int a;
  float b;
}

class Y extends X {
  double c;
}

class RTTI {
  public static void main(String[] args) {
    X x = new X();
    Y y = new Y();
    Class<?> clObj;

    clObj = x.getClass(); // get Class reference
    System.out.println("x is object of type: " +
                       clObj.getName());
```

```
      clObj = y.getClass(); // get Class reference
      System.out.println("y is object of type: " +
                         clObj.getName());
      clObj = clObj.getSuperclass();
      System.out.println("y's superclass is " +
                         clObj.getName());
   }
}
```

The output from this program is shown here:

```
x is object of type: X
y is object of type: Y
y's superclass is X
```

Beginning with JDK 16, **Class** has included methods that support records. These are **getRecordComponents( )**, which obtains information about a record's components, and **isRecord( )**, which returns true if the invoking **Class** represents a record. Beginning with JDK 17, **Class** has included methods that support sealed classes and interfaces. They are **isSealed( )**, which returns true if the invoking **Class** is a sealed, and **getPermittedSubclasses( )**, which obtains an array of **Class** instances of the subclasses or subinterfaces permitted by the invoking **Class**. Records and sealed classes and interfaces are discussed Chapter 17.

Before moving on, it is useful to mention another **Class** capability that you may find interesting. Beginning with JDK 11, **Class** provides three methods that relate to a nest. A *nest* is a group of classes and/or interfaces nested within an outer class or interface. The nest concept enables the JVM to more efficiently handle certain situations involving access between nest members. It is important to state that a nest is *not* a source code mechanism, and it does *not* change the Java language or how it defines accessibility. Nests relate specifically to how the compiler and JVM work. However, it is now possible to obtain a nest's top-level class/interface, which is called the *nest host*, by use of **getNestHost( )**. You can determine if one class/interface is a member of the same nest as another by use of **isNestMateOf( )**. Finally, you can get an array containing a list of the nest members by calling **getNestMembers( )**. You may find these methods useful when using reflection, for example.

## ClassLoader

The abstract class **ClassLoader** defines how classes are loaded. Your application can create subclasses that extend **ClassLoader**, implementing its methods. Doing so allows you to load classes in some way other than the way they are normally loaded by the Java run-time system. However, this is not something that you will normally need to do.

## Math

The **Math** class contains all the floating-point functions that are used for geometry and trigonometry, as well as several general-purpose methods. **Math** defines three well-known **double** constants: **E** (approximately 2.72), **PI** (approximately 3.14), and **TAU** (approximately 6.28).

## Trigonometric Functions

The following methods accept a **double** parameter for an angle in radians and return the result of their respective trigonometric function:

| Method | Description |
|---|---|
| static double sin(double *arg*) | Returns the sine of the angle specified by *arg* in radians |
| static double cos(double *arg*) | Returns the cosine of the angle specified by *arg* in radians |
| static double tan(double *arg*) | Returns the tangent of the angle specified by *arg* in radians |

The next methods take as a parameter the result of a trigonometric function and return, in radians, the angle that would produce that result. They are the inverse of their non-arc companions.

| Method | Description |
|---|---|
| static double asin(double *arg*) | Returns the angle whose sine is specified by *arg* |
| static double acos(double *arg*) | Returns the angle whose cosine is specified by *arg* |
| static double atan(double *arg*) | Returns the angle whose tangent is specified by *arg* |
| static double atan2(double *x*, double *y*) | Returns the angle whose tangent is *x*/*y* |

The next methods compute the hyperbolic sine, cosine, and tangent of an angle:

| Method | Description |
|---|---|
| static double sinh(double *arg*) | Returns the hyperbolic sine of the angle specified by *arg* |
| static double cosh(double *arg*) | Returns the hyperbolic cosine of the angle specified by *arg* |
| static double tanh(double *arg*) | Returns the hyperbolic tangent of the angle specified by *arg* |

## Exponential Functions

**Math** defines the following exponential methods:

| Method | Description |
|---|---|
| static double cbrt(double *arg*) | Returns the cube root of *arg* |
| static double exp(double *arg*) | Returns e to the *arg* |
| static double expm1(double *arg*) | Returns e to the *arg*–1 |
| static double log(double *arg*) | Returns the natural logarithm of *arg* |
| static double log10(double *arg*) | Returns the base 10 logarithm for *arg* |
| static double log1p(double *arg*) | Returns the natural logarithm for *arg* + 1 |
| static double pow(double *y*, double *x*) | Returns *y* raised to the *x*; for example, pow(2.0, 3.0) returns 8.0 |
| static double scalb(double *arg*, int *factor*) | Returns *arg* × $2^{factor}$ |
| static float scalb(float *arg*, int *factor*) | Returns *arg* × $2^{factor}$ |
| static double sqrt(double *arg*) | Returns the square root of *arg* |

Part II

## Rounding Functions

The **Math** class defines several methods that provide various types of rounding operations. They are shown in Table 19-16. Notice the two **ulp( )** methods at the end of the table. In this context, *ulp* stands for *units in the last place.* It indicates the distance between a value and the next higher value. It can be used to help assess the accuracy of a result.

| Method | Description |
|---|---|
| static int abs(int *arg*) | Returns the absolute value of *arg*. |
| static long abs(long *arg*) | Returns the absolute value of *arg*. |
| static float abs(float *arg*) | Returns the absolute value of *arg*. |
| static double abs(double *arg*) | Returns the absolute value of *arg*. |
| static double ceil(double *arg*) | Returns the ceiling of *arg*, that is, the smallest whole number greater than or equal to *arg*. |
| static double floor(double *arg*) | Returns the floor of *arg*, that is, the largest whole number less than or equal to *arg*. |
| static int ceilDiv(int *dividend*, int *divisor*) | Returns the ceiling of the result of *dividend/divisor*. |
| static int ceilDiv(long *dividend*, int *divisor*) | Returns the ceiling of the result of *dividend/divisor*. |
| static long ceilDiv(long *dividend*, long *divisor*) | Returns the ceiling of the result of *dividend/divisor*. |
| static int ceilDivExact(int *dividend*, int *divisor*) | Returns the ceiling of result of *dividend/divisor*. Throws an **ArithmeticException** if an overflow occurs. |
| static long ceilDivExact(long *dividend*, long *divisor*) | Returns the ceiling of the result of *dividend/divisor*. Throws an **ArithmeticException** if an overflow occurs. |
| static int ceilMod(int *dividend*, int *divisor*) | Returns the ceiling of the remainder of *dividend/divisor*. |
| static int ceilMod(long *dividend*, int *divisor*) | Returns the ceiling of the remainder of *dividend/divisor*. |
| static long ceilMod(long *dividend*, long *divisor*) | Returns the ceiling of the remainder of *dividend/divisor*. |
| static int divideExact(int *dividend*, int *divisor*) | Returns the result of *dividend/divisor*. Throws an **ArithmeticException** if an overflow occurs. |
| static long divideExact(long *dividend*, long *divisor*) | Returns the result of *dividend/divisor*. Throws an **ArithmeticException** if an overflow occurs. |
| static double clamp(double *value*, double *min*, double *max*) | If *value* is less than *min*, then return *min*; if greater than *max*, return *max*. Otherwise, return *value*. |

**Table 19-16** The Rounding Methods Defined by **Math**

| Method | Description |
|---|---|
| static float clamp(float *value*, float *min*, float *max*) | If *value* is less than *min*, then return *min*; if greater than *max*, return *max*. Otherwise, return *value*. |
| static int clamp(long *value*, int *min*, int *max*) | If *value* is less than *min*, then return *min*; if greater than *max*, return *max*. Otherwise, return *value*. |
| static long clamp(long *value*, long *min*, long *max*) | If *value* is less than *min*, then return *min*; if greater than *max*, return *max*. Otherwise, return *value*. |
| static int floorDiv(int *dividend*, int *divisor*) | Returns the floor of the result of *dividend/divisor*. |
| static long floorDiv(long *dividend*, int *divisor*) | Returns the floor of the result of *dividend/divisor*. |
| static long floorDiv(long *dividend*, long *divisor*) | Returns the floor of the result of *dividend/divisor*. |
| static int floorDivExact(int *dividend*, int *divisor*) | Returns the floor of the result of *dividend/divisor*. Throws an **ArithmeticException** if an overflow occurs. |
| static long floorDivExact(long *dividend*, long *divisor*) | Returns the floor of the result of *dividend/divisor*. Throws an **ArithmeticException** if an overflow occurs. |
| static int floorMod(int *dividend*, int *divisor*) | Returns the floor of the remainder of *dividend/divisor*. |
| static int floorMod(long *dividend*, int *divisor*) | Returns the floor of the remainder of *dividend/divisor*. |
| static long floorMod(long *dividend*, long *divisor*) | Returns the floor of the remainder of *dividend/divisor*. |
| static int max(int *x*, int *y*) | Returns the maximum of *x* and *y*. |
| static long max(long *x*, long *y*) | Returns the maximum of *x* and *y*. |
| static float max(float *x*, float *y*) | Returns the maximum of *x* and *y*. |
| static double max(double *x*, double *y*) | Returns the maximum of *x* and *y*. |
| static int min(int *x*, int *y*) | Returns the minimum of *x* and *y*. |
| static long min(long *x*, long *y*) | Returns the minimum of *x* and *y*. |
| static float min(float *x*, float *y*) | Returns the minimum of *x* and *y*. |
| static double min(double *x*, double *y*) | Returns the minimum of *x* and *y*. |
| static double nextAfter(double *arg*, double *toward*) | Beginning with the value of *arg*, returns the next value in the direction of *toward*. If *arg* == *toward*, then *toward* is returned. |
| static float nextAfter(float *arg*, double *toward*) | Beginning with the value of *arg*, returns the next value in the direction of *toward*. If *arg* == *toward*, then *toward* is returned. |
| static double nextDown(double *val*) | Returns the next value lower than *val*. |

**Table 19-16** The Rounding Methods Defined by **Math** *(continued)*

| Method | Description |
|---|---|
| static float nextDown(float *val*) | Returns the next value lower than *val*. |
| static double nextUp(double *arg*) | Returns the next value in the positive direction from *arg*. |
| static float nextUp(float *arg*) | Returns the next value in the positive direction from *arg*. |
| static double rint(double *arg*) | Returns the integer nearest in value to *arg*. |
| static int round(float *arg*) | Returns *arg* rounded up to the nearest **int**. |
| static long round(double *arg*) | Returns *arg* rounded up to the nearest **long**. |
| static float ulp(float *arg*) | Returns the ulp for *arg*. |
| static double ulp(double *arg*) | Returns the ulp for *arg*. |

**Table 19-16** The Rounding Methods Defined by **Math** *(continued)*

## Miscellaneous Math Methods

In addition to the methods just shown, **Math** defines several other methods, which are shown in Table 19-17. Notice that several of the methods use the suffix **Exact**. They throw an **ArithmeticException** if overflow occurs. Thus, these methods give you an easy way to watch various operations for overflow.

| Method | Description |
|---|---|
| static int absExact(int *arg*) | Returns the absolute value of *arg*. |
| static long absExact(long *arg*) | Returns the absolute value of *arg*. |
| static int addExact(int *arg1*, int *arg2*) | Returns *arg1* + *arg2*. Throws an **ArithmeticException** if overflow occurs. |
| static long addExact(long *arg1*, long *arg2* | Returns *arg1* + *arg2*. Throws an **ArithmeticException** if overflow occurs. |
| static double copySign(double *arg*, double *signarg*) | Returns *arg* with same sign as that of *signarg*. |
| static float copySign(float *arg*, float *signarg*) | Returns *arg* with same sign as that of *signarg*. |
| static int decrementExact(int *arg*) | Returns *arg* – 1. Throws an **ArithmeticException** if overflow occurs. |
| static long decrementExact(long *arg*) | Returns *arg* – 1. Throws an **ArithmeticException** if overflow occurs. |
| static double fma(double *arg1*, double *arg2*, double *arg3*) | Adds *arg3* to the product of *arg1* and *arg2* and returns the rounded result. The name is short for fused multiply add. |
| static float fma(float *arg1*, float *arg2*, float *arg3*) | Adds *arg3* to the product of *arg1* and *arg2* and returns the rounded result. The name is short for fused multiply add. |
| static int getExponent(double *arg*) | Returns the base-2 exponent used by the binary representation of *arg*. |
| static int getExponent(float *arg*) | Returns the base-2 exponent used by the binary representation of *arg*. |
| static hypot(double *side1*, double *side2*) | Returns the length of the hypotenuse of a right triangle given the length of the two opposing sides. |

**Table 19-17** Other Methods Defined by **Math**

| Method | Description |
|---|---|
| static double IEEEremainder(double *dividend*, double *divisor*) | Returns the remainder of *dividend / divisor*. |
| static int incrementExact(int *arg*) | Returns *arg* + 1. Throws an **ArithmeticException** if overflow occurs. |
| static long incrementExact(long *arg*) | Returns *arg* + 1. Throws an **ArithmeticException** if overflow occurs. |
| static int multiplyExact(int *arg1*, int *arg2*) | Returns *arg1* * *arg2*. Throws an **ArithmeticException** if overflow occurs. |
| static long multiplyExact(long *arg1*, int *arg2*) | Returns *arg1* * *arg2*. Throws an **ArithmeticException** if overflow occurs. |
| static long multiplyExact(long *arg1*, long *arg2*) | Returns *arg1* * *arg2*. Throws an **ArithmeticException** if overflow occurs. |
| static long multiplyFull(int *arg1*, int *arg2*) | Returns *arg1* * *arg2* as a **long** value. |
| static long multiplyHigh(long *arg1*, long *arg2*) | Returns a **long** value that contains the most significant bits of *arg1* * *arg2*. |
| static int negateExact(int *arg*) | Returns –*arg*. Throws an **ArithmeticException** if overflow occurs. |
| static long negateExact(long *arg*) | Returns –*arg*. Throws an **ArithmeticException** if overflow occurs. |
| static double random( ) | Returns a pseudorandom number between 0 and 1. |
| static float signum(double *arg*) | Determines the sign of a value. It returns 0 if *arg* is 0, 1 if *arg* is greater than 0, and –1 if *arg* is less than 0. |
| static float signum(float *arg*) | Determines the sign of a value. It returns 0 if *arg* is 0, 1 if *arg* is greater than 0, and –1 if *arg* is less than 0. |
| static int subtractExact(int *arg1*, int *arg2*) | Returns *arg1* – *arg2*. Throws an **ArithmeticException** if overflow occurs. |
| static long subtractExact(long *arg1*, long *arg2*) | Returns *arg1* – *arg2*. Throws an **ArithmeticException** if overflow occurs. |
| static double toDegrees(double *angle*) | Converts radians to degrees. The angle passed must be specified in radians. The result in degrees is returned. |
| static int toIntExact(long *arg*) | Returns *arg* as an int. Throws an **ArithmeticException** if overflow occurs. |
| static double toRadians(double *angle*) | Converts degrees to radians. The *angle* passed must be specified in degrees. The result in radians is returned. |
| static long unsignedMultiplyHigh(int *arg1*, int *arg2*) | Returns *arg1* * *arg2* as an unsigned 64-bit long. |

**Table 19-17** Other Methods Defined by **Math** *(continued)*

The following program demonstrates **toRadians( )** and **toDegrees( )**:

```
// Demonstrate toDegrees() and toRadians().
class Angles {
  public static void main(String[] args) {
    double theta = 120.0;

    System.out.println(theta + " degrees is " +
                       Math.toRadians(theta) + " radians.");

    theta = 1.312;
    System.out.println(theta + " radians is " +
                       Math.toDegrees(theta) + " degrees.");
  }
}
```

The output is shown here:

```
120.0 degrees is 2.0943951023931953 radians.
1.312 radians is 75.17206272116401 degrees.
```

## StrictMath

The **StrictMath** class defines a complete set of mathematical methods that parallel those in **Math**. The difference is that the **StrictMath** version is guaranteed to generate precisely identical results across all Java implementations, whereas the methods in **Math** are given more latitude in order to improve performance. It is important to point out that beginning with JDK 17, all math computations are now strict.

## Compiler

The **Compiler** class supports the creation of Java environments in which Java bytecode is compiled into executable code rather than interpreted. It is not for normal programming use and has been deprecated for removal.

## Thread, ThreadGroup, and Runnable

The **Runnable** interface and the **Thread** and **ThreadGroup** classes support multithreaded programming. Each is examined next.

**NOTE** An overview of the techniques used to manage threads, implement the **Runnable** interface, and create multithreaded programs is presented in Chapter 11.

### The Runnable Interface

The **Runnable** interface must be implemented by any class that will initiate a separate thread of execution. **Runnable** only defines one abstract method, called **run( )**, which is the entry point to the thread. It is defined like this:

void run( )

Threads that you create must implement this method.

### Thread

**Thread** creates a new thread of execution. It implements **Runnable** and defines a number of constructors. Several are shown here:

Thread( )
Thread(Runnable *threadOb*)
Thread(Runnable *threadOb*, String *threadName*)
Thread(String *threadName*)
Thread(ThreadGroup *groupOb*, Runnable *threadOb*)
Thread(ThreadGroup *groupOb*, Runnable *threadOb*, String *threadName*)
Thread(ThreadGroup *groupOb*, String *threadName*)

*threadOb* is an instance of a class that implements the **Runnable** interface and defines where execution of the thread will begin. The name of the thread is specified by *threadName*. When a name is not specified, one is created by the Java Virtual Machine. *groupOb* specifies the thread group to which the new thread will belong. When no thread group is specified, by default the new thread belongs to the same group as the parent thread.

The following constants are defined by **Thread**:

MAX_PRIORITY
MIN_PRIORITY
NORM_PRIORITY

As expected, these constants specify the maximum, minimum, and default thread priorities, respectively.

The non-deprecated methods defined by **Thread** are shown in Table 19-18. **Thread** also includes the deprecated methods **stop( )**, **suspend( )**, and **resume( )**. However, as explained in Chapter 11, these were deprecated because they were inherently unstable. Also deprecated are **countStackFrames( )**, because it calls **suspend( )**, and **destroy( )**, because it can cause deadlock. Furthermore, beginning with JDK 11, **destroy( )** and one version of **stop( )** have now been removed from **Thread**. Also, JDK 17 deprecated **checkAccess( )** for removal.



| Method | Description |
|---|---|
| static int activeCount( ) | Returns the approximate number of active threads in the group to which the thread belongs. |
| static Thread currentThread( ) | Returns a **Thread** object that encapsulates the thread that calls this method. |
| static void dumpStack( ) | Displays the call stack for the thread. |
| static int enumerate(Thread[ ] *threads*) | Puts copies of all **Thread** objects in the current thread's group into *threads*. The number of threads is returned. |
| static Map<Thread, StackTraceElement[ ]> getAllStackTraces( ) | Returns a **Map** that contains the stack traces for all live platform threads. In the map, each entry consists of a key, which is the **Thread** object, and its value, which is an array of **StackTraceElement**. |
| ClassLoader getContextClassLoader( ) | Returns the context class loader that is used to load classes and resources for this thread. |
| static Thread.UncaughtExceptionHandler getDefaultUncaughtExceptionHandler( ) | Returns the default uncaught exception handler. |
| final String getName( ) | Returns the thread's name. |
| final int getPriority( ) | Returns the thread's priority setting. |
| StackTraceElement[ ] getStackTrace( ) | Returns an array containing the stack trace for the invoking thread. |
| Thread.State getState( ) | Returns the invoking thread's state. |
| final ThreadGroup getThreadGroup( ) | Returns the **ThreadGroup** object of which the invoking thread is a member. |

**Table 19-18** The Non-Deprecated Methods Defined by **Thread**

| Method | Description |
|---|---|
| Thread.UncaughtExceptionHandler getUncaughtExceptionHandler( ) | Returns the invoking thread's uncaught exception handler. |
| static boolean holdsLock(Object *ob*) | Returns **true** if the invoking thread owns the lock on *ob*. Returns **false** otherwise. |
| void interrupt( ) | Interrupts the thread. |
| static boolean interrupted( ) | Returns **true** if the currently executing thread has been interrupted. Otherwise, it returns **false**. |
| final boolean isAlive( ) | Returns **true** if the thread is still active. Otherwise, it returns **false**. |
| final boolean isDaemon( ) | Returns **true** if the thread is a daemon thread. Otherwise, it returns **false**. |
| boolean isInterrupted( ) | Returns **true** if the invoking thread has been interrupted. Otherwise, it returns **false**. |
| public final boolean isVirtual( ) | Returns **true** if the thread is virtual, that is, if it is scheduled by the JVM rather than the operating system. |
| final void join( ) throws InterruptedException | Waits until the thread terminates. |
| final boolean join(Duration duration) throws InterruptedException | Waits for the time defined by the *duration* object for the thread to terminate, returning **true** if the thread terminated. |
| final void join(long *milliseconds*) throws InterruptedException | Waits up to the specified number of milliseconds for the thread on which it is called to terminate. |
| final void join(long *milliseconds*, int *nanoseconds*) throws InterruptedException | Waits up to the specified number of milliseconds plus nanoseconds for the thread on which it is called to terminate. |
| static Thread.Builder.OfPlatform ofPlatform() | Returns a builder for creating platform threads, i.e., those scheduled by the operating system. |
| static Thread.Builder.OfVirtual ofVirtual() | Returns a builder for creating virtual threads, i.e., threads scheduled by Java not the operating system. |
| static void onSpinWait( ) | Called to signify that execution is currently inside a wait loop, possibly enabling a runtime optimization. |
| void run( ) | Begins execution of a thread. |
| void setContextClassLoader(ClassLoader *cl*) | Sets the context class loader that will be used by the invoking thread to *cl*. |
| final void setDaemon(boolean *state*) | Flags the thread as a daemon thread. |
| static void setDefaultUncaughtExceptionHandler( Thread.UncaughtExceptionHandler *e*) | Sets the default uncaught exception handler to *e*. |

**Table 19-18** The Non-Deprecated Methods Defined by **Thread** *(continued)*

| Method | Description |
|---|---|
| final void setName(String *threadName*) | Sets the name of the thread to that specified by *threadName*. |
| final void setPriority(int *priority*) | Sets the priority of the thread to that specified by *priority*. |
| void setUncaughtExceptionHandler( Thread.UncaughtExceptionHandler *e*) | Sets the invoking thread's default uncaught exception handler to *e*. |
| static void sleep(Duration duration) throws InterruptedException | Suspects execution of the thread for the time period specified by the duration object. |
| static void sleep(long *milliseconds*) throws InterruptedException | Suspends execution of the thread for the specified number of milliseconds. |
| static void sleep(long *milliseconds*, int *nanoseconds*) throws InterruptedException | Suspends execution of the thread for the specified number of milliseconds plus nanoseconds. |
| static Thread startVirtualThread( Runnable task) | Creates a virtual thread and schedules it to execute the given *task* object. |
| final long threadId() | Returns the unique identifier for this thread. |
| void start( ) | Starts execution of the thread. |
| String toString( ) | Returns the string equivalent of a thread. |
| static void yield( ) | The calling thread offers to yield the CPU to another thread. |

**Table 19-18** The Non-Deprecated Methods Defined by **Thread** *(continued)*

## ThreadGroup

**ThreadGroup** creates a group of threads. It defines these two constructors:

ThreadGroup(String *groupName*)
ThreadGroup(ThreadGroup *parentOb*, String *groupName*)

For both forms, *groupName* specifies the name of the thread group. The first version creates a new group that has the current thread as its parent. In the second form, the parent is specified by *parentOb*. The non-deprecated methods defined by **ThreadGroup** are shown in Table 19-19.

| Method | Description |
|---|---|
| int activeCount( ) | Returns the approximate number of active threads in the invoking group (including those in subgroups). |
| int activeGroupCount( ) | Returns the approximate number of active groups (including subgroups) for which the invoking thread is a parent. |

**Table 19-19** The Non-Deprecated Methods Defined by **ThreadGroup**

| Method | Description |
|---|---|
| int enumerate(Thread[ ] *group*) | Puts the active threads that comprise the invoking thread group (including those in subgroups) into the *group* array. |
| int enumerate(Thread[ ] *group*, boolean *all*) | Puts the active threads that comprise the invoking thread group into the *group* array. If *all* is **true**, then threads in all subgroups of the thread are also put into *group*. |
| int enumerate(ThreadGroup[ ] *group*) | Puts the active subgroups (including subgroups of subgroups, and so on) of the invoking thread group into the *group* array. |
| int enumerate(ThreadGroup[ ] *group*, boolean *all*) | Puts the active subgroups of the invoking thread group into the *group* array. If *all* is **true**, then all active subgroups of the subgroups (and so on) are also put into *group*. |
| final int getMaxPriority( ) | Returns the maximum priority setting for the group. |
| final String getName( ) | Returns the name of the group. |
| final ThreadGroup getParent( ) | Returns **null** if the invoking **ThreadGroup** object has no parent. Otherwise, it returns the parent of the invoking object. |
| final void interrupt( ) | Invokes the **interrupt( )** method of all threads in the group and any subgroups. |
| void list( ) | Displays information about the group. |
| final boolean parentOf(ThreadGroup *group*) | Returns **true** if the invoking thread is the parent of *group* (or *group* itself). Otherwise, it returns **false**. |
| final void setMaxPriority(int *priority*) | Sets the maximum priority of the invoking group to *priority*. |
| String toString( ) | Returns the string equivalent of the group. |
| void uncaughtException(Thread *thread*, Throwable *e*) | This method is called when an exception goes uncaught. |

**Table 19-19** The Non-Deprecated Methods Defined by **ThreadGroup** *(continued)*

Thread groups offer a convenient way to manage groups of threads as a unit. This is particularly valuable in situations in which you want to suspend and resume a number of related threads. For example, imagine a program in which one set of threads is used for printing a document, another set is used to display the document on the screen, and another set saves the document to a disk file. If printing is aborted, you will want an easy way to stop all threads related to printing. Thread groups offer this convenience. The following program, which creates two thread groups of two threads each, illustrates this usage:

```
// Demonstrate thread groups.
class NewThread extends Thread {
  boolean suspendFlag;

  NewThread(String threadname, ThreadGroup tgOb) {
    super(tgOb, threadname);
    System.out.println("New thread: " + this);
    suspendFlag = false;
  }
```

```
  // This is the entry point for thread.
  public void run() {
    try {
      for(int i = 5; i > 0; i--) {
        System.out.println(getName() + ": " + i);
        Thread.sleep(1000);
        synchronized(this) {
          while(suspendFlag) {
            wait();
          }
        }
      }
    } catch (Exception e) {
      System.out.println("Exception in " + getName());
    }
      System.out.println(getName() + " exiting.");
    }

    synchronized void mysuspend() {
      suspendFlag = true;
    }

    synchronized void myresume() {
      suspendFlag = false;
      notify();
    }
  }

class ThreadGroupDemo {
  public static void main(String[] args) {
    ThreadGroup groupA = new ThreadGroup("Group A");
    ThreadGroup groupB = new ThreadGroup("Group B");

    NewThread ob1 = new NewThread("One", groupA);
    NewThread ob2 = new NewThread("Two", groupA);
    NewThread ob3 = new NewThread("Three", groupB);
    NewThread ob4 = new NewThread("Four", groupB);

    ob1.start();
    ob2.start();
    ob3.start();
    ob4.start();

    System.out.println("\nHere is output from list():");
    groupA.list();
    groupB.list();
    System.out.println();

    System.out.println("Suspending Group A");
    Thread[] tga = new Thread[groupA.activeCount()];
    groupA.enumerate(tga); // get threads in group
    for(int i = 0; i < tga.length; i++) {
      ((NewThread)tga[i]).mysuspend(); // suspend each thread
    }
```

```
    try {
      Thread.sleep(4000);
    } catch (InterruptedException e) {
      System.out.println("Main thread interrupted.");
    }

    System.out.println("Resuming Group A");
    for(int i = 0; i < tga.length; i++) {
      ((NewThread)tga[i]).myresume(); // resume threads in group
    }

    // wait for threads to finish
    try {
      System.out.println("Waiting for threads to finish.");
      ob1.join();
      ob2.join();
      ob3.join();
      ob4.join();
    } catch (Exception e) {
      System.out.println("Exception in Main thread");
    }

    System.out.println("Main thread exiting.");
  }
}
```

Sample output from this program is shown here (the precise output you see may differ):

```
New thread: Thread[One,5,Group A]
New thread: Thread[Two,5,Group A]
New thread: Thread[Three,5,Group B]
New thread: Thread[Four,5,Group B]
Here is output from list():
java.lang.ThreadGroup[name=Group A,maxpri=10]
  Thread[One,5,Group A]
  Thread[Two,5,Group A]
java.lang.ThreadGroup[name=Group B,maxpri=10]
  Thread[Three,5,Group B]
  Thread[Four,5,Group B]
Suspending Group A
Three: 5
Four: 5
Three: 4
Four: 4
Three: 3
Four: 3
Three: 2
Four: 2
Resuming Group A
Waiting for threads to finish.
One: 5
Two: 5
Three: 1
Four: 1
```

```
One: 4
Two: 4
Three exiting.
Four exiting.
One: 3
Two: 3
One: 2
Two: 2
One: 1
Two: 1
One exiting.
Two exiting.
Main thread exiting.
```

Inside the program, notice that thread group A is suspended for four seconds. As the output confirms, this causes threads One and Two to pause, but threads Three and Four continue running. After the four seconds, threads One and Two are resumed. Notice how thread group A is suspended and resumed. First, the threads in group A are obtained by calling **enumerate( )** on group A. Then, each thread is suspended by iterating through the resulting array. To resume the threads in A, the list is again traversed and each thread is resumed.

## ThreadLocal and InheritableThreadLocal

Java defines two additional thread-related classes in **java.lang**:

- **ThreadLocal** Used to create thread local variables. Each thread will have its own copy of a thread local variable.
- **InheritableThreadLocal** Creates thread local variables that may be inherited.

## Package

**Package** encapsulates information about a package. The methods defined by **Package** are shown in Table 19-20. The following program demonstrates **Package**, displaying the packages about which the program currently is aware:

```
// Demonstrate Package
class PkgTest {
  public static void main(String[] args) {
    Package[] pkgs;

    pkgs = Package.getPackages();

    for(int i=0; i < pkgs.length; i++)
      System.out.println(
              pkgs[i].getName() + " " +
              pkgs[i].getImplementationTitle() + " " +
              pkgs[i].getImplementationVendor() + " " +
              pkgs[i].getImplementationVersion()
      );
  }
}
```

| Method | Description |
|---|---|
| <A extends Annotation> A getAnnotation(Class<A> *annoType*) | Returns an **Annotation** object that contains the annotation associated with *annoType* for the invoking object. |
| Annotation[ ] getAnnotations( ) | Returns all annotations associated with the invoking object in an array of **Annotation** objects. Returns a reference to this array. |
| <A extends Annotation> A[ ] getAnnotationsByType( Class<A> *annoType*) | Returns an array of the annotations (including repeated annotations) of *annoType* associated with the invoking object. |
| <A extends Annotation> A getDeclaredAnnotation( Class<A> *annoType*) | Returns an **Annotation** object that contains the non-inherited annotation associated with *annoType*. |
| Annotation[ ] getDeclaredAnnotations( ) | Returns an **Annotation** object for all the annotations that are declared by the invoking object. (Inherited annotations are ignored.) |
| <A extends Annotation> A[ ] getDeclaredAnnotationsByType( Class<A> *annoType*) | Returns an array of the non-inherited annotations (including repeated annotations) of *annoType* associated with the invoking object. |
| String getImplementationTitle( ) | Returns the title of the invoking package. |
| String getImplementationVendor( ) | Returns the name of the implementor of the invoking package. |
| String getImplementationVersion( ) | Returns the version number of the invoking package. |
| String getName( ) | Returns the name of the invoking package. |
| static Package[ ] getPackages( ) | Returns all packages about which the invoking program is currently aware. |
| String getSpecificationTitle( ) | Returns the title of the invoking package's specification. |
| String getSpecificationVendor( ) | Returns the name of the owner of the specification for the invoking package. |
| String getSpecificationVersion( ) | Returns the invoking package's specification version number. |
| int hashCode( ) | Returns the hash code for the invoking package. |
| boolean isAnnotationPresent( Class<? extends Annotation> *anno*) | Returns **true** if the annotation described by *anno* is associated with the invoking object. Returns **false** otherwise. |
| boolean isCompatibleWith(String *verNum*) throws NumberFormatException | Returns **true** if *verNum* is less than or equal to the invoking package's version number. |
| boolean isSealed( ) | Returns **true** if the invoking package is sealed. Returns **false** otherwise. |
| boolean isSealed(URL *url*) | Returns **true** if the invoking package is sealed relative to *url*. Returns **false** otherwise. |
| String toString( ) | Returns the string equivalent of the invoking package. |

**Table 19-20** The Methods Defined by **Package**

# Module

Added by JDK 9, the **Module** class encapsulates a module. Using a **Module** instance you can add various access rights to a module, determine access rights, or obtain information about a module. For example, to export a package to a specified module, call **addExports( )**; to open a package to a specified module, call **addOpens( )**; to read another module, call **addReads( )**; and to add a service requirement, call **addUses( )**. You can determine if a module can access another by calling **canRead( )**. To determine if a module uses a service, call **canUse( )**. Although these methods will be most useful in specialized situations, **Module** defines several others that may be of more general interest.

For example, you can obtain the name of a module by calling **getName( )**. If called from within a named module, the name is returned. If called from the unnamed module, **null** is returned. You can obtain a **Set** of the packages in a module by calling **getPackages( )**. A module descriptor, in the form of a **ModuleDescriptor** instance, is returned by **getDescriptor( )**. (**ModuleDescriptor** is a class declared in **java.lang.module**.) You can determine if a package is exported or opened by the invoking module by calling **isExported( )** or **isOpen( )**. Use **isNamed( )** to determine if a module is named or unnamed. Other methods include **getAnnotation( )**, **getDeclaredAnnotations( )**, **getLayer( )**, **getClassLoader( )**, and **getResourceAsStream( )**. The **toString( )** method is also overridden for **Module**.

Assuming the modules defined by the examples in Chapter 16, you can easily experiment with the **Module** class. For example, try adding the following lines to the **MyModAppDemo** class:

```
Module myMod = MyModAppDemo.class.getModule();
System.out.println("Module is " + myMod.getName());

System.out.print("Packages: ");
for(String pkg : myMod.getPackages()) System.out.println(pkg + " ");
```

Here, the methods **getName( )** and **getPackages( )** are used. Notice that a **Module** instance is obtained by calling **getModule( )** on the **Class** instance for **MyModAppDemo**. When run, these lines produce the following output:

```
Module is appstart
Packages: appstart.mymodappdemo
```

# ModuleLayer

**ModuleLayer**, added by JDK 9, encapsulates a module layer. The nested class **ModuleLayer .Controller**, also added by JDK 9, is the controller for a module layer. In general, these classes are for specialized applications.

# RuntimePermission

**RuntimePermission** relates to Java's security mechanism.

## Throwable

The **Throwable** class supports Java's exception-handling system and is the class from which all exception classes are derived. It is discussed in Chapter 10.

## SecurityManager

**SecurityManager** has been deprecated for removal by JDK 17. Consult the Java documentation for the latest details.

## StackTraceElement

The **StackTraceElement** class describes a single *stack frame,* which is an individual element of a stack trace when an exception occurs. Each stack frame represents an *execution point,* which includes such things as the name of the class, the name of the method, the name of the file, and the source-code line number. Beginning with JDK 9, module information is also included. **StackTraceElement** defines two constructors, but typically you won't need to use them because an array of **StackTraceElement**s is returned by various methods, such as the **getStackTrace( )** method of the **Throwable** and **Thread** classes.

The methods supported by **StackTraceElement** are shown in Table 19-21. These methods give you programmatic access to a stack trace.

| Method | Description |
|---|---|
| boolean equals(Object *ob*) | Returns **true** if the invoking **StackTraceElement** is the same as the one passed in *ob*. Otherwise, it returns **false**. |
| String getClassLoaderName( ) | Returns the name of the class loader used to load the class in which the execution point described by the invoking **StackTraceElement** occurred. If the object does not include class loader information, **null** is returned. |
| String getClassName( ) | Returns the name of the class in which the execution point described by the invoking **StackTraceElement** occurred. |
| String getFileName( ) | Returns the name of the file in which the source code of the execution point described by the invoking **StackTraceElement** is stored. |
| int getLineNumber( ) | Returns the source-code line number at which the execution point described by the invoking **StackTraceElement** occurred. In some situations, the line number will not be available, in which case a negative value is returned. |
| String getMethodName( ) | Returns the name of the method in which the execution point described by the invoking **StackTraceElement** occurred. |
| String getModuleName( ) | Returns the name of the module in which the execution point described by the invoking **StackTraceElement** occurred. If the object does not include module information, **null** is returned. |

**Table 19-21** The Methods Defined by **StackTraceElement**

| Method | Description |
|---|---|
| String getModuleVersion( ) | Returns the version of the module in which the execution point described by the invoking **StackTraceElement** occurred. If the object does not include module information, **null** is returned. |
| int hashCode( ) | Returns the hash code for the invoking **StackTraceElement**. |
| boolean isNativeMethod( ) | Returns **true** if the execution point described by the invoking **StackTraceElement** occurred in a native method. Otherwise, it returns **false**. |
| String toString( ) | Returns the **String** equivalent of the invoking sequence. |

**Table 19-21** The Methods Defined by **StackTraceElement** *(continued)*



## StackWalker and StackWalker.StackFrame

Added by JDK 9, the **StackWalker** class and the **StackWalker.StackFrame** interface support stack walking operations. A **StackWalker** instance is obtained by use of the static **getInstance( )** method defined by **StackWalker**. Stack walking is initiated by calling the **walk( )** method of **StackWalker**. Each stack frame is encapsulated as a **StackWalker.StackFrame** object. The **StackWalker.Option** enumeration was also added.

## Enum

As described in Chapter 12, an enumeration is a list of named constants. (Recall that an enumeration is created by using the keyword **enum**.) All enumerations automatically inherit **Enum**. **Enum** is a generic class that is declared as shown here:

```
class Enum<E extends Enum<E>>
```

Here, **E** stands for the enumeration type. **Enum** has no public constructors.

**Enum** defines several commonly used methods, which are shown in Table 19-22. Beginning with JDK 12, **Enum** also implements the **Constable** interface, which specifies the **describeConstable( )** method. JDK 12 also added the **Enum.EnumDesc** class.

| Method | Description |
|---|---|
| protected final Object clone( ) throws CloneNotSupportedException | Invoking this method causes a **CloneNotSupportedException** to be thrown. This prevents enumerations from being cloned. |
| final int compareTo(E *e*) | Compares the ordinal value of two constants of the same enumeration. Returns a negative value if the invoking constant has an ordinal value less than *e*'s, zero if the two ordinal values are the same, and a positive value if the invoking constant has an ordinal value greater than *e*'s. |

**Table 19-22** Commonly Used Methods Defined by **Enum**

| Method | Description |
|---|---|
| final boolean equals(Object *obj*) | Returns **true** if *obj* and the invoking object refer to the same constant. |
| final Class<E> getDeclaringClass( ) | Returns the type of enumeration of which the invoking constant is a member. |
| final int hashCode( ) | Returns the hash code for the invoking object. |
| final String name( ) | Returns the unaltered name of the invoking constant. |
| final int ordinal( ) | Returns a value that indicates an enumeration constant's position in the list of constants. |
| String toString( ) | Returns the name of the invoking constant. This name may differ from the one used in the enumeration's declaration. |
| static <T extends Enum<T>> T valueOf(Class<T> *e-type*, String *name*) | Returns the constant associated with *name* in the enumeration type specified by *e-type*. |

**Table 19-22** Commonly Used Methods Defined by **Enum** *(continued)*

# Record

Added by JDK 16, **Record** is the superclass for all records. In other words, all records automatically inherit **Record**. It defines no methods of its own, but overrides **equals( )**, **hashCode( )**, and **toString( )**, which are inherited from **Object**. Records are discussed in Chapter 17.

# ClassValue

**ClassValue** can be used to associate a value with a type. It is a generic class defined like this:

```
Class ClassValue<T>
```

It is designed for highly specialized uses, not for normal programming.

# The CharSequence Interface

The **CharSequence** interface defines methods that grant read-only access to a sequence of characters. These methods are shown in Table 19-23. This interface is implemented by **String**, **StringBuffer**, and **StringBuilder**, among others.

| Method | Description |
|---|---|
| char charAt(int *idx*) | Returns the character at the index specified by *idx*. |
| static int compare(CharSequence *seqA*, CharSequence *seqB*) | Compares *seqA* to *seqB*. Returns 0 if the sequences are the same. Returns a negative value if *seqA* is less than *seqB*. Returns a positive value if *seqA* is greater than *seqB*. |

**Table 19-23** The Methods Defined by **CharSequence**

| Method | Description |
|---|---|
| default IntStream chars( ) | Returns a stream (in the form of an **IntStream**) to the characters in the invoking object. |
| default IntStream codePoints( ) | Returns a stream (in the form of an **IntStream**) to the code points in the invoking object. |
| default boolean isEmpty( ) | Returns **true** if the invoking sequence contains no characters. Otherwise, returns **false**. |
| int length( ) | Returns the number of characters in the invoking sequence. |
| CharSequence subSequence(int *startIdx*, int *stopIdx*) | Returns a subset of the invoking sequence beginning at *startIdx* and ending at *stopIdx*–1. |
| String toString( ) | Returns the **String** equivalent of the invoking sequence. |

**Table 19-23** The Methods Defined by **CharSequence** *(continued)*



## The Comparable Interface

Objects of classes that implement **Comparable** can be ordered. In other words, classes that implement **Comparable** contain objects that can be compared in some meaningful manner. **Comparable** is generic and is declared like this:

interface Comparable<T>

Here, **T** represents the type of objects being compared.

The **Comparable** interface declares one method that is used to determine what Java calls the *natural ordering* of instances of a class. The signature of the method is shown here:

int compareTo(T *obj*)

This method compares the invoking object with *obj*. It returns 0 if the values are equal. A negative value is returned if the invoking object has a lower value. Otherwise, a positive value is returned.

This interface is implemented by several of the classes already reviewed in this book, such as **Byte**, **Character**, **Double**, **Float**, **Long**, **Short**, **String**, **Integer**, and **Enum**.

## The Appendable Interface

An object of a class that implements **Appendable** can have a character or character sequences appended to it. **Appendable** defines these three methods:

Appendable append(char *ch*) throws IOException
Appendable append(CharSequence *chars*) throws IOException
Appendable append(CharSequence *chars*, int *begin*, int *end*) throws IOException

In the first form, the character *ch* is appended to the invoking object. In the second form, the character sequence *chars* is appended to the invoking object. The third form allows you to indicate a portion (the characters running from *begin* through *end*–1) of the sequence specified by *chars*. In all cases, a reference to the invoking object is returned.

## The Iterable Interface

**Iterable** must be implemented by any class whose objects will be used by the for-each version of the **for** loop. In other words, in order for an object to be used within a for-each style **for** loop, its class must implement **Iterable**. **Iterable** is a generic interface that has this declaration:

```
interface Iterable<T>
```

Here, **T** is the type of the object being iterated. It defines one abstract method, **iterator( )**, which is shown here:

```
Iterator<T> iterator( )
```

It returns an iterator to the elements contained in the invoking object.

**Iterable** also defines two default methods. The first is called **forEach( )**:

```
default void forEach(Consumer<? super T> action)
```

For each element being iterated, **forEach( )** executes the code specified by *action*. (**Consumer** is a functional interface defined in **java.util.function**. See Chapter 21.)

The second default method is **spliterator( )**, shown next:

```
default Spliterator<T> spliterator( )
```

It returns a **Spliterator** to the sequence being iterated. (See Chapters 20 and 30 for details on spliterators.)

---

**NOTE** Iterators are described in detail in Chapter 20.

## The Readable Interface

The **Readable** interface indicates that an object can be used as a source for characters. It defines one method called **read( )**, which is shown here:

```
int read(CharBuffer buf) throws IOException
```

This method reads characters into *buf*. It returns the number of characters read, or –1 if an EOF is encountered.

## The AutoCloseable Interface

**AutoCloseable** provides support for the **try**-with-resources statement, which implements what is sometimes referred to as *automatic resource management* (ARM). The **try**-with-resources statement automates the process of releasing a resource (such as a stream) when it is no longer needed. (See Chapter 13 for details.) Only objects of classes that implement **AutoCloseable** can be used with **try**-with-resources. The **AutoCloseable** interface defines only the **close( )** method, which is shown here:

```
void close( ) throws Exception
```

This method closes the invoking object, releasing any resources that it may hold. It is automatically called at the end of a **try**-with-resources statement, thus eliminating the need to explicitly invoke **close( )**. **AutoCloseable** is implemented by several classes, including all of the I/O classes that open a stream that can be closed.

# The Thread.UncaughtExceptionHandler Interface

The static **Thread.UncaughtExceptionHandler** interface is implemented by classes that want to handle uncaught exceptions. It is implemented by **ThreadGroup**. It declares only one method, which is shown here:

void uncaughtException(Thread *thrd*, Throwable *exc*)

Here, *thrd* is a reference to the thread that generated the exception and *exc* is a reference to the exception.



# The java.lang Subpackages

Java defines several subpackages of **java.lang**. Except as otherwise noted, these packages are in the **java.base** module.

- java.lang.annotation
- java.lang.constant
- java.lang.instrument
- java.lang.invoke
- java.lang.management
- java.lang.module
- java.lang.ref
- java.lang.reflect

Each is briefly described here.

## java.lang.annotation

Java's annotation facility is supported by **java.lang.annotation**. It defines the **Annotation** interface, the **ElementType** and **RetentionPolicy** enumerations, and several predefined annotations. Annotations are described in Chapter 12.

## java.lang.constant

**java.lang.constant** is a specialized package that supports descriptors for constants. It is typically used by applications that access bytecode, and it was added by JDK 12.

## java.lang.instrument

**java.lang.instrument** defines features that can be used to add instrumentation to various aspects of program execution. It defines the **Instrumentation** and **ClassFileTransformer** interfaces, and the **ClassDefinition** class. This package is in the **java.instrument** module.

## java.lang.invoke

**java.lang.invoke** supports dynamic language features. It includes classes such as **CallSite**, **MethodHandle**, and **MethodType**.

## java.lang.management

The **java.lang.management** package provides management support for the JVM and the execution environment. Using the features in **java.lang.management**, you can observe and manage various aspects of program execution. This package is in the **java.management** module.

## java.lang.module

The **java.lang.module** package supports modules. It includes classes such as **ModuleDescriptor** and **ModuleReference**, and the interfaces **ModuleFinder** and **ModuleReader**.

## java.lang.ref

You learned earlier that the garbage collection facilities in Java automatically determine when no references exist to an object. The object is then assumed to be no longer needed and its memory is reclaimed. The classes in the **java.lang.ref** package provide more flexible control over the garbage collection process.

## java.lang.reflect

*Reflection* is the ability of a program to analyze code at run time. The **java.lang.reflect** package provides the ability to obtain information about the fields, constructors, methods, and modifiers of a class. Among other reasons, you need this information to build software tools that enable you to work with Java Beans components. The tools use reflection to determine dynamically the characteristics of a component. Reflection was introduced in Chapter 12 and is also examined in Chapter 31.

**java.lang.reflect** defines several classes, including **Method**, **Field**, and **Constructor**. It also defines several interfaces, including **AnnotatedElement**, **Member**, and **Type**. In addition, the **java.lang.reflect** package includes the **Array** class, which enables you to create and access arrays dynamically.

CHAPTER

# 20 java.util Part 1: The Collections Framework

This chapter begins our examination of **java.util**. This important package contains a large assortment of classes and interfaces that support a broad range of functionality. For example, **java.util** has classes that generate pseudorandom numbers, manage date and time, support events, manipulate sets of bits, tokenize strings, and handle formatted data. The **java.util** package also contains one of Java's most powerful subsystems: the *Collections Framework*. The Collections Framework is a sophisticated hierarchy of interfaces and classes that provide state-of-the-art technology for managing groups of objects. It merits close attention by all programmers. Beginning with JDK 9, **java.util** is part of the **java.base** module.

Because **java.util** contains a wide array of functionality, it is quite large. Here is a list of its top-level classes:

| | | |
|---|---|---|
| AbstractCollection | Formatter | PropertyPermission |
| AbstractList | GregorianCalendar | PropertyResourceBundle |
| AbstractMap | HashMap | Random |
| AbstractQueue | HashSet | ResourceBundle |
| AbstractSequentialList | Hashtable | Scanner |
| AbstractSet | HexFormat | ServiceLoader |
| ArrayDeque | IdentityHashMap | SimpleTimeZone |
| ArrayList | IntSummaryStatistics | Spliterators |
| Arrays | LinkedHashMap | SplitableRandom |
| Base64 | LinkedHashSet | Stack |
| BitSet | LinkedList | StringJoiner |
| Calendar | ListResourceBundle | StringTokenizer |
| Collections | Locale | Timer |
| Currency | LongSummaryStatistics | TimerTask |
| Date | Objects | TimeZone |

| | | |
|---|---|---|
| Dictionary | Observable (deprecated by JDK 9) | TreeMap |
| DoubleSummaryStatistics | Optional | TreeSet |
| EnumMap | OptionalDouble | UUID |
| EnumSet | OptionalInt | Vector |
| EventListenerProxy | OptionalLong | WeakHashMap |
| EventObject | PriorityQueue | |
| FormattableFlags | Properties | |

The interfaces defined by **java.util** are shown next:

| | | |
|---|---|---|
| Collection | NavigableMap | SequencedSet |
| Comparator | NavigableSet | ServiceLoader.Provider |
| Deque | Observer (deprecated by JDK 9.) | Set |
| Enumeration | PrimitiveIterator | SortedMap |
| EventListener | PrimitiveIterator.OfDouble | SortedSet |
| Formattable | PrimitiveIterator.OfInt | Spliterator |
| Iterator | PrimitiveIterator.OfLong | Spliterator.OfDouble |
| List | Queue | Spliterator.OfInt |
| ListIterator | RandomAccess | Spliterator.OfLong |
| Map | SequencedCollection | Spliterator.OfPrimitive |
| Map.Entry | SequencedMap | |

Because of its size, the description of **java.util** is broken into two chapters. This chapter examines those members of **java.util** that are part of the Collections Framework. Chapter 21 discusses its other classes and interfaces.

## Collections Overview

The Java Collections Framework standardizes the way in which groups of objects are handled by your programs. Collections were not part of the original Java release but were added by J2SE 1.2. Prior to the Collections Framework, Java provided ad hoc classes such as **Dictionary**, **Vector**, **Stack**, and **Properties** to store and manipulate groups of objects. Although these classes were quite useful, they lacked a central, unifying theme. The way that you used **Vector** was different from the way that you used **Properties**, for example. Also, this early, ad hoc approach was not designed to be easily extended or adapted. Collections were an answer to these (and other) problems.

The Collections Framework was designed to meet several goals. First, the framework had to be high-performance. The implementations for the fundamental collections (dynamic arrays, linked lists, trees, and hash tables) are highly efficient. You seldom, if ever, need to code one of these "data engines" manually. Second, the framework had to allow different types of collections to work in a similar manner and with a high degree of interoperability.

Third, extending and/or adapting a collection had to be easy. Toward this end, the entire Collections Framework is built upon a set of standard interfaces. Several standard implementations (such as **LinkedList**, **HashSet**, and **TreeSet**) of these interfaces are provided that you may use as-is. You may also implement your own collection, if you choose. Various special-purpose implementations are created for your convenience, and some partial implementations are provided that make creating your own collection class easier. Finally, mechanisms were added that allow the integration of standard arrays into the Collections Framework.

*Algorithms* are another important part of the collection mechanism. Algorithms operate on collections and are defined as static methods within the **Collections** class. Thus, they are available for all collections. Each collection class need not implement its own versions. The algorithms provide a standard means of manipulating collections.

Another item closely associated with the Collections Framework is the **Iterator** interface. An *iterator* offers a general-purpose, standardized way of accessing the elements within a collection, one at a time. Thus, an iterator provides a means of *enumerating the contents of a collection*. Because each collection provides an iterator, the elements of any collection class can be accessed through the methods defined by **Iterator**. Thus, with only small changes, the code that cycles through a set can also be used to cycle through a list, for example.

JDK 8 added another type of iterator called a *spliterator*. In brief, spliterators are iterators that provide support for parallel iteration. The interfaces that support spliterators are **Spliterator** and several nested interfaces that support primitive types. Also available are iterator interfaces designed for use with primitive types, such as **PrimitiveIterator** and **PrimitiveIterator.OfDouble**.

In addition to collections, the framework defines several map interfaces and classes. *Maps* store key/value pairs. Although maps are part of the Collections Framework, they are not "collections" in the strict use of the term. You can, however, obtain a *collection-view* of a map. Such a view contains the elements from the map stored in a collection. Thus, you can process the contents of a map as a collection, if you choose.

JDK 21 further expands on the utility of the Collections Framework by formalizing the idea of the order in which you process elements in collections and maps, known as the *encounter order*. This order is important when you are looping through or iterating over the elements of such a collection. This idea is encapsulated in the form of the new **SequencedCollection**, **SequencedSet**, and **SequencedMap** interfaces and is implemented in those collections that have an inherent ordering in their elements.

The collection mechanism was retrofitted to some of the original classes defined by **java.util** so that they too could be integrated into the new system. It is important to understand that although the addition of collections altered the architecture of many of the original utility classes, it did not cause the deprecation of any. Collections simply provide a better way of doing several things.

**NOTE** If you are familiar with C++, then you will find it helpful to know that the Java collections technology is similar in spirit to the Standard Template Library (STL) defined by C++. What C++ calls a container, Java calls a collection. However, there are significant differences between the Collections Framework and the STL. It is important to not jump to conclusions.

# The Collection Interfaces

The Collections Framework defines several core interfaces. This section provides an overview of each interface. Beginning with the collection interfaces is necessary because they determine the fundamental nature of the collection classes. Put differently, the concrete classes simply provide different implementations of the standard interfaces. The interfaces that underpin collections are summarized in the following table:

| Interface | Description |
|---|---|
| Collection | Enables you to work with groups of objects; it is at the top of the collections hierarchy. |
| Deque | Extends **Queue** and **SequencedCollection** to handle a double-ended queue. |
| List | A kind of sequenced collection that holds and manipulates lists of objects. |
| NavigableSet | Extends **SortedSet** to handle retrieval of elements based on closest-match searches. |
| Queue | Extends **Collection** to handle special types of lists in which elements are removed only from the head. |
| SequencedCollection | Extends **Collection** to define collections that hold elements in a defined encounter order. |
| SequencedSet | Extends **SequencedCollection** and **Set** to define collections that are sequenced and whose elements are unique. |
| Set | Extends **Collection** to handle sets, which must contain unique elements. |
| SortedSet | Extends **Set** and **SequencedSet** to handle sets whose elements are sorted into an order defined by a means of comparison. |

In addition to the collection interfaces, collections also use the **Comparator**, **RandomAccess**, **Iterator**, **ListIterator**, and **Spliterator** interfaces, which are described in depth later in this chapter. Briefly, **Comparator** defines how two objects are compared; **Iterator**, **ListIterator**, and **Spliterator** enumerate the objects within a collection. By implementing **RandomAccess**, a list indicates that it supports efficient, random access to its elements.

To provide the greatest flexibility in their use, the collection interfaces allow some methods to be optional. The optional methods enable you to modify the contents of a collection. Collections that support these methods are called *modifiable.* Collections that do not allow their contents to be changed are called *unmodifiable.* If an attempt is made to use one of these methods on an unmodifiable collection, an **UnsupportedOperationException** is thrown. All the built-in collections are modifiable.

The following sections examine the collection interfaces.

## The Collection Interface

The **Collection** interface is the foundation upon which the Collections Framework is built because it must be implemented by any class that defines a collection. **Collection** is a generic interface that has this declaration:

```
interface Collection<E>
```

Here, **E** specifies the type of objects that the collection will hold. **Collection** extends the **Iterable** interface. This means that all collections can be cycled through by use of the for-each style **for** loop. (Recall that only classes that implement **Iterable** can be cycled through by the **for**.)

**Collection** declares the core methods that all collections will have. These methods are summarized in Table 20-1. Because all collections implement **Collection**, familiarity with its methods is necessary for a clear understanding of the framework. Several of these methods can throw an **UnsupportedOperationException**. As explained, this occurs if a collection cannot be modified. A **ClassCastException** is generated when one object is incompatible with another, such as when an attempt is made to add an incompatible object to a collection. A **NullPointerException** is thrown if an attempt is made to store a **null** object and **null** elements are not allowed in the collection. An **IllegalArgumentException** is thrown if an invalid argument is used. An **IllegalStateException** is thrown if an attempt is made to add an element to a fixed-length collection that is full.

Objects are added to a collection by calling **add( )**. Notice that **add( )** takes an argument of type **E**, which means that objects added to a collection must be compatible with the type



| Method | Description |
|---|---|
| boolean add(E *obj*) | Adds *obj* to the invoking collection. Returns **true** if *obj* was added to the collection. Returns **false** if *obj* is already a member of the collection and the collection does not allow duplicates. |
| boolean addAll(Collection<? extends E> *c*) | Adds all the elements of *c* to the invoking collection. Returns **true** if the collection changed (i.e., the elements were added). Otherwise, returns **false**. |
| void clear( ) | Removes all elements from the invoking collection. |
| boolean contains(Object *obj*) | Returns **true** if *obj* is an element of the invoking collection. Otherwise, returns **false**. |
| boolean containsAll(Collection<?> *c*) | Returns **true** if the invoking collection contains all elements of *c*. Otherwise, returns **false**. |
| boolean equals(Object *obj*) | Returns **true** if the invoking collection and *obj* are equal. Otherwise, returns **false**. |
| int hashCode( ) | Returns the hash code for the invoking collection. |
| boolean isEmpty( ) | Returns **true** if the invoking collection is empty. Otherwise, returns **false**. |
| Iterator<E> iterator( ) | Returns an iterator for the invoking collection. |
| default Stream<E> parallelStream( ) | Returns a stream that uses the invoking collection as its source for elements. If possible, the stream supports parallel operations. |
| boolean remove(Object *obj*) | Removes one instance of *obj* from the invoking collection. Returns **true** if the element was removed. Otherwise, returns **false**. |

**Table 20-1** The Methods Declared by **Collection**

| Method | Description |
|---|---|
| boolean removeAll(Collection<?> *c*) | Removes all elements of *c* from the invoking collection. Returns **true** if the collection changed (i.e., elements were removed). Otherwise, returns **false**. |
| default boolean removeIf( Predicate<? super E> *predicate*) | Removes from the invoking collection those elements that satisfy the condition specified by *predicate.* |
| boolean retainAll(Collection<?> *c*) | Removes all elements from the invoking collection except those in *c*. Returns **true** if the collection changed (i.e., elements were removed). Otherwise, returns **false**. |
| int size( ) | Returns the number of elements held in the invoking collection. |
| default Spliterator<E> spliterator( ) | Returns a spliterator to the invoking collections. |
| default Stream<E> stream( ) | Returns a stream that uses the invoking collection as its source for elements. The stream is sequential. |
| default <T> T[ ] toArray( IntFunction<T[ ]> *arrayGen*) | Returns an array of the elements from the invoking collection. The returned array is created by the function specified by *arrayGen*. An **ArrayStoreException** is thrown if any collection element has a type that is not compatible with the array type. |
| Object[ ] toArray( ) | Returns an array of the elements from the invoking collection. |
| <T> T[ ] toArray(T[ ] *array*) | Returns an array of the elements from the invoking collection. If the size of *array* equals the number of elements, these are returned in *array*. If the size of *array* is less than the number of elements, a new array of the necessary size is allocated and returned. If the size of *array* is greater than the number of elements, the array element following the last collection element is set to **null**. An **ArrayStoreException** is thrown if any collection element has a type that is not compatible with the array type. |

**Table 20-1** The Methods Declared by **Collection** *(continued)*

of data expected by the collection. You can add the entire contents of one collection to another by calling **addAll( )**.

You can remove an object by using **remove( )**. To remove a group of objects, call **removeAll( )**. You can remove all elements except those of a specified group by calling **retainAll( )**. To remove an element only if it satisifies some condition, you can use **removeIf( )**. To empty a collection, call **clear( )**.

You can determine whether a collection contains a specific object by calling **contains( )**. To determine whether one collection contains all the members of another, call **containsAll( )**. You can determine when a collection is empty by calling **isEmpty( )**. The number of elements currently held in a collection can be determined by calling **size( )**.

The **toArray( )** methods return an array that contains the elements stored in the collection. The first returns an array of **Object**. The second returns an array of elements that have the same type as the array specified as a parameter. Normally, the second form is more convenient because it returns the desired array type. Beginning with JDK 11, a third form has been added that lets you specify a function that obtains the array. These methods are more important than they might at first seem. Often, processing the contents of a collection by using array-like syntax is advantageous. By providing a pathway between collections and arrays, you can have the best of both worlds.

Two collections can be compared for equality by calling **equals( )**. The precise meaning of "equality" may differ from collection to collection. For example, you can implement **equals( )** so that it compares the values of elements stored in the collection. Alternatively, **equals( )** can compare references to those elements.

Another important method is **iterator( )**, which returns an iterator to a collection. The **spliterator( )** method returns a spliterator to the collection. Iterators are frequently used when working with collections. Finally, the **stream( )** and **parallelStream( )** methods return a **Stream** that uses the collection as a source of elements. (See Chapter 30 for a detailed discussion of the **Stream** interface.)



## The SequencedCollection Interface

Introduced in JDK 21, the **SequencedCollection** interface extends **Collection** and defines a special kind of collection that has an *encounter order*. This is a short way of saying that a **SequencedCollection** has a well-defined order in which you can process the elements, from one end of the collection to the other, such as when you use a **for** loop or an **Iterator**. **SequencedCollection** is a generic interface that has the declaration

interface SequencedCollection<E>

where **E** specifies the type of the objects this **SequencedCollection** will hold.

In addition to the methods of the **Collection** interface, **SequencedCollection** defines several methods that allow access and modifications to the first and last objects it holds as well as provide a reversed version of the collection, wherein the encounter order is backwards relative to the original collection. The methods of the **SequencedCollection** interface are shown in Table 20-2.

| Method | Description |
|---|---|
| default void addFirst(E *obj*) | Adds *obj* as the first element of the collection. (Optional) |
| default void addLast(E *obj*) | Adds *obj* as the last element of the collection. (Optional) |
| default E getFirst() | Returns the first element of the collection. |
| default E getLast() | Returns the last element of the collection. |
| default E removeFirst() | Removes and returns the first element of the collection or throws a **NoSuchElementException** if the collection is empty. (Optional) |
| default E removeLast() | Removes and returns the last element of the collection or throws a **NoSuchElementException** if the collection is empty. (Optional) |
| SequencedCollection<E> reversed() | Returns a **SequencedCollection** containing all the same elements, but in reverse order. |

**Table 20-2** The API Methods of **SequencedCollection**

Just as with the methods on its parent interface, the methods that add and remove objects from a **SequencedCollection**, such as **addFirst( )**, are optional. That means that if the collection represented as a **SequencedCollection** is not able to be modified (we shall see later that there are such "read-only" implementations of collections), these methods will throw an **UnsupportedOperationException**. Similarly, either of the **SequencedCollection** methods that remove objects from the collection, such as **removeLast( )**, are called when the collection doesn't contain any objects; the result will be a **NoSuchElementException**. The **reversed( )** method is very convenient if you want to loop or iterate backwards over a **SequencedCollection**. However, depending on the collection class implementing interface **SequencedCollection**, the reversed **SequencedCollection** obtained by calling this method may or may not change if you later modify the original collection on which you called **reversed( )**.

## The List Interface

The **List** interface extends **SequencedCollection** and declares the behavior of a collection that allows precise control over where in the sequence of objects an element can be placed. Elements can be inserted or accessed by their position in the list, using a zero-based index. A list may contain duplicate elements. **List** is a generic interface that has this declaration:

```
interface List<E>
```

Here, **E** specifies the type of objects that the list will hold.

In addition to the methods defined by **SequencedCollection, List** defines some of its own, which are summarized in Table 20-3. Note again that several of these methods will throw an **UnsupportedOperationException** if the list cannot be modified, and a **ClassCastException** is generated when one object is incompatible with another, such as when an attempt is made to add an incompatible object to a list. Also, several methods will throw an **IndexOutOfBoundsException** if an invalid index is used. A **NullPointerException** is thrown if an attempt is made to store a **null** object and **null** elements are not allowed in the list. An **IllegalArgumentException** is thrown if an invalid argument is used.

To the versions of **add( )** and **addAll( )** defined by **Collection, List** adds the methods **add(int, E)** and **addAll(int, Collection)**. These methods insert elements at the specified index. Also, the semantics of **add(E)** and **addAll(Collection)** defined by **Collection** are changed by **List** so that they add elements to the end of the list. You can modify each element in the collection by using **replaceAll( )**.

To obtain the object stored at a specific location, call **get( )** with the index of the object. To assign a value to an element in the list, call **set( )**, specifying the index of the object to be changed. To find the index of an object, use **indexOf( )** or **lastIndexOf( )**.

You can obtain a sublist of a list by calling **subList( )**, specifying the beginning and ending indexes of the sublist. As you can imagine, **subList( )** makes list processing quite convenient. One way to sort a list is with the **sort( )** method defined by **List**.

Beginning with JDK 9, **List** includes the **of( )** factory method, which has a number of overloads. Each version returns an unmodifiable, value-based collection that is comprised of the arguments that it is passed. The primary purpose of **of( )** is to provide a convenient,

| Method | Description |
|---|---|
| void add(int *index*, E *obj*) | Inserts *obj* into the invoking list at the index passed in *index*. Any preexisting elements at or beyond the point of insertion are shifted up. Thus, no elements are overwritten. |
| boolean addAll(int *index*, Collection<? extends E> *c*) | Inserts all elements of *c* into the invoking list at the index passed in *index*. Any preexisting elements at or beyond the point of insertion are shifted up. Thus, no elements are overwritten. Returns **true** if the invoking list changes and returns **false** otherwise. |
| static <E> List<E> copyOf(Collection<? extends E> *from*) | Returns a list that contains the same elements as that specified by *from*. The returned list is unmodifiable and value-based. Null values are not allowed. |
| E get(int *index*) | Returns the object stored at the specified index within the invoking collection. |
| int indexOf(Object *obj*) | Returns the index of the first instance of *obj* in the invoking list. If *obj* is not an element of the list, –1 is returned. |
| int lastIndexOf(Object *obj*) | Returns the index of the last instance of *obj* in the invoking list. If *obj* is not an element of the list, –1 is returned. |
| ListIterator<E> listIterator( ) | Returns an iterator to the start of the invoking list. |
| ListIterator<E> listIterator(int *index*) | Returns an iterator to the invoking list that begins at the specified *index*. |
| static <E> List<E> of( *parameter-list* ) | Creates an unmodifiable value-based list containing the elements specified in *parameter-list*. Null elements are not allowed. Many overloaded versions are provided. See the discussion in the text for details. |
| E remove(int *index*) | Removes the element at position *index* from the invoking list and returns the deleted element. The resulting list is compacted. That is, the indexes of subsequent elements are decremented by one. |
| default void replaceAll(UnaryOperator<E> *opToApply*) | Updates each element in the list with the value obtained from the *opToApply* function. |
| E set(int *index*, E *obj*) | Assigns *obj* to the location specified by *index* within the invoking list. Returns the old value. |
| default void sort(Comparator<? super E> *comp*) | Sorts the list using the comparator specified by *comp*. |
| List<E> subList(int *start*, int *end*) | Returns a list that includes elements from *start* to *end*–1 in the invoking list. Elements in the returned list are also referenced by the invoking object. |

**Table 20-3** The Methods Declared by **List**

efficient way to create a small **List** collection. There are 12 overloads of **of( )**. One takes no arguments and creates an empty list. It is shown here:

static <E> List<E> of( )

Ten overloads take from 1 to 10 arguments and create a list that contains the specified elements. They are shown here:

static <E> List<E> of(E *obj1*)
static <E> List<E> of(E *obj1*, E *obj2*)
static <E> List<E> of(E *obj*, E *obj2*, E *obj3*)
...
static <E> List<E> of(E *ob1*, E *obj2*, E *obj3*, E *obj4*, E *obj5*,
E *obj6*, E *obj7*, E *obj8*, E *obj9*, E *obj10*)

The final **of( )** overload specifies a varargs parameter that takes an arbitrary number of elements or an array of elements. It is shown here:

static <E> List<E> of(E ... *objs*)

For all versions, **null** elements are not allowed. In all cases, the **List** implementation is unspecified.

## The Set Interface

The **Set** interface defines a set. It extends **Collection** and specifies the behavior of a collection that does not allow duplicate elements. Therefore, the **add( )** method returns **false** if an attempt is made to add duplicate elements to a set. With two exceptions, it does not specify any additional methods of its own. **Set** is a generic interface that has this declaration:

interface Set<E>

Here, **E** specifies the type of objects that the set will hold.

Beginning with JDK 9, **Set** includes the **of( )** factory method, which has a number of overloads. Each version returns an unmodifiable, value-based collection that is comprised of the arguments that it is passed. The primary purpose of **of( )** is to provide a convenient, efficient way to create a small **Set** collection. There are 12 overloads of **of( )**. One takes no arguments and creates an empty set. It is shown here:

static <E> Set<E> of( )

Ten overloads take from 1 to 10 arguments and create a list that contains the specified elements. They are shown here:

static <E> Set<E> of(E *obj1*)
static <E> Set<E> of(E *obj1*, E *obj2*)
static <E> Set<E> of(E *obj*, E *obj2*, E *obj3*)
...
static <E> Set<E> of(E *ob1*, E *obj2*, E *obj3*, E *obj4*, E *obj5*,
E *obj6*, E *obj7*, E *obj8*, E *obj9*, E *obj10*)

The final **of( )** overload specifies a varargs parameter that takes an arbitrary number of elements or an array of elements. It is shown here:

static <E> Set<E> of(E ... *objs*)

For all versions, **null** elements are not allowed. In all cases, the **Set** implementation is unspecified.

Beginning with JDK 10, **Set** includes the static **copyOf( )** method shown here:

static <E> Set<E> copyOf(Collection <? extends E> *from*)

It returns a set that contains the same elements as *from*. Null values are not allowed. The returned set is unmodifiable and value-based.



## The SequencedSet Interface

The **SequencedSet** interface, introduced in JDK 21, extends both **Set** and **SequencedCollection** and so inherits the behaviors of both of those types of collections. In other words, a **SequencedSet** is a special kind of collection with unique elements and with a well-defined order in which you can process the elements from one end of the collection to the other. **SequencedSet** is a generic interface that has this declaration:

interface SequencedSet<E>

Here, **E** specifies the type of objects this **SequencedSet** will hold.

The **SequencedSet** interface defines only one method over those it inherits. It overrides the **reversed()** method it inherits from **SequencedCollection**. It is shown here:

SequencedSet<E> reversed()

You can see that instead of returning just a **SequencedCollection**, it returns the more special **SequencedSet**, which, after all, it should: a special set with an order that has been reversed is still a special set with an order!

## The SortedSet Interface

The **SortedSet** interface extends **SequencedSet** and declares the behavior of a set that has a well-defined algorithm it uses to order its elements in ascending order. **SortedSet** is a generic interface that has this declaration:

interface SortedSet<E>

Here, **E** specifies the type of objects that the set will hold.

In addition to those methods provided by **Set**, the **SortedSet** interface declares the methods summarized in Table 20-4. Several methods throw a **NoSuchElementException** when no items are contained in the invoking set. A **ClassCastException** is thrown when an object is incompatible with the elements in a set. A **NullPointerException** is thrown if an attempt is made to use a **null** object and **null** is not allowed in the set. An **IllegalArgumentException** is thrown if an invalid argument is used.

**SortedSet** defines several methods that make set processing more convenient. To obtain the first object in the set, call **getFirst( )**. To get the last element, use **getLast( )**. You can obtain a subset of a sorted set by calling **subSet( )**, specifying the first and last object in

| Method | Description |
|---|---|
| Comparator<? super E> comparator( ) | Returns the invoking sorted set's comparator. If the natural ordering is used for this set, **null** is returned. |
| E getFirst() / E first() | Returns the first element in the invoking sorted set. |
| SortedSet<E> headSet(E *end*) | Returns a **SortedSet** containing those elements less than *end* that are contained in the invoking sorted set. Elements in the returned sorted set are also referenced by the invoking sorted set. |
| default E void removeFirst( ) | Removes and returns the first element in the sorted set. |
| default E void removeLast( ) | Removes and returns the first element in the sorted set. |
| E getLast( ) / E last( ) | Returns the last element in the invoking sorted set. |
| SortedSet<E> subSet(E *start*, E *end*) | Returns a **SortedSet** that includes those elements between *start* and *end*–1. Elements in the returned collection are also referenced by the invoking object. |
| SortedSet<E> tailSet(E *start*) | Returns a **SortedSet** that contains those elements greater than or equal to *start* that are contained in the sorted set. Elements in the returned set are also referenced by the invoking object. |

**Table 20-4** Useful Methods Declared by **SortedSet**

the set. If you need the subset that starts with the first element in the set, use **headSet( )**. If you want the subset that ends the set, use **tailSet( )**.

Because **SortedSet** inherits from **SequencedSet**, it also inherits its parent interface's methods to add elements from the start and end of the collection, namely the methods **addFirst( )** and **addLast( )**. But in a **SortedSet**, the order of the elements is always defined by its **Comparator**. So it doesn't make sense to try to add or remove elements. For this reason, those methods throw an **UnsupportedOperationException**.

**NOTE** **Note on *sequenced* versus *sorted*:** In the collections framework, the idea of being *sequenced* is used to mean that the elements in a collection are arranged in a given order that does not change unless the collection is modified. This could be simply the order in which the elements were first added. The idea of a collection being *sorted* is stronger than sequenced: it means the collection is not only sequenced but is sequenced according to a given algorithm defined by its **Comparator**. If more elements are added to a sorted collection, they are put into position according to the comparator.

## The NavigableSet Interface

The **NavigableSet** interface extends **SortedSet** and declares the behavior of a collection that supports the retrieval of elements based on the closest match to a given value or values. **NavigableSet** is a generic interface that has this declaration:

```
interface NavigableSet<E>
```

Here, **E** specifies the type of objects that the set will hold. In addition to the methods that it inherits from **SortedSet**, **NavigableSet** adds those summarized in Table 20-5.

| Method | Description |
|---|---|
| E ceiling(E *obj*) | Searches the set for the smallest element *e* such that *e* >= *obj*. If such an element is found, it is returned. Otherwise, **null** is returned. |
| Iterator<E> descendingIterator( ) | Returns an iterator that moves from the greatest to least. In other words, it returns a reverse iterator. |
| NavigableSet<E> descendingSet( ) | Returns a **NavigableSet** that is the reverse of the invoking set. The resulting set is backed by the invoking set. |
| E floor(E *obj*) | Searches the set for the largest element *e* such that *e* <= *obj*. If such an element is found, it is returned. Otherwise, **null** is returned. |
| NavigableSet<E> headSet(E *upperBound*, boolean *incl*) | Returns a **NavigableSet** that includes all elements from the invoking set that are less than *upperBound*. If *incl* is **true**, then an element equal to *upperBound* is included. The resulting set is backed by the invoking set. |
| E higher(E *obj*) | Searches the set for the smallest element *e* such that *e* > *obj*. If such an element is found, it is returned. Otherwise, **null** is returned. |
| E lower(E *obj*) | Searches the set for the largest element *e* such that *e* < *obj*. If such an element is found, it is returned. Otherwise, **null** is returned. |
| E pollFirst( ) | Returns the first element, removing the element in the process. Because the set is sorted, this is the element with the least value. **null** is returned if the set is empty. |
| E pollLast( ) | Returns the last element, removing the element in the process. Because the set is sorted, this is the element with the greatest value. **null** is returned if the set is empty. |
| NavigableSet<E> subSet(E *lowerBound*, boolean *lowIncl*, E *upperBound*, boolean *highIncl*) | Returns a **NavigableSet** that includes all elements from the invoking set that are greater than *lowerBound* and less than *upperBound*. If *lowIncl* is **true**, then an element equal to *lowerBound* is included. If *highIncl* is **true**, then an element equal to *upperBound* is included. The resulting set is backed by the invoking set. |
| NavigableSet<E> tailSet(E *lowerBound*, boolean *incl*) | Returns a **NavigableSet** that includes all elements from the invoking set that are greater than *lowerBound*. If *incl* is **true**, then an element equal to *lowerBound* is included. The resulting set is backed by the invoking set. |

**Table 20-5** The Methods Declared by **NavigableSet**

A **ClassCastException** is thrown when an object is incompatible with the elements in the set. A **NullPointerException** is thrown if an attempt is made to use a **null** object and **null** is not allowed in the set. An **IllegalArgumentException** is thrown if an invalid argument is used.

## The Queue Interface

The **Queue** interface extends **Collection** and declares the behavior of a queue, which is often a first-in, first-out list. However, there are types of queues in which the ordering is based upon other criteria. **Queue** is a generic interface that has this declaration:

```
interface Queue<E>
```

Here, **E** specifies the type of objects that the queue will hold. The methods declared by **Queue** are shown in Table 20-6.

| Method | Description |
|---|---|
| E element( ) | Returns the element at the head of the queue. The element is not removed. It throws **NoSuchElementException** if the queue is empty. |
| boolean offer(E *obj*) | Attempts to add *obj* to the queue. Returns **true** if *obj* was added and **false** otherwise. |
| E peek( ) | Returns the element at the head of the queue. It returns **null** if the queue is empty. The element is not removed. |
| E poll( ) | Returns the element at the head of the queue, removing the element in the process. It returns **null** if the queue is empty. |
| E remove( ) | Removes the element at the head of the queue, returning the element in the process. It throws **NoSuchElementException** if the queue is empty. |

**Table 20-6** The Methods Declared by **Queue**

Several methods throw a **ClassCastException** when an object is incompatible with the elements in the queue. A **NullPointerException** is thrown if an attempt is made to store a **null** object and **null** elements are not allowed in the queue. An **IllegalArgumentException** is thrown if an invalid argument is used. An **IllegalStateException** is thrown if an attempt is made to add an element to a fixed-length queue that is full. A **NoSuchElementException** is thrown if an attempt is made to remove an element from an empty queue.

Despite its simplicity, **Queue** offers several points of interest. First, elements can only be removed from the head of the queue. Second, there are two methods that obtain and remove elements: **poll( )** and **remove( )**. The difference between them is that **poll( )** returns **null** if the queue is empty, but **remove( )** throws an exception. Third, there are two methods, **element( )** and **peek( )**, that obtain but don't remove the element at the head of the queue. They differ only in that **element( )** throws an exception if the queue is empty, but **peek( )** returns **null**. Finally, notice that **offer( )** only attempts to add an element to a queue. Because some queues have a fixed length and might be full, **offer( )** can fail.

## The Deque Interface

The **Deque** interface extends **Queue** and **SequencedCollection** and so declares the behavior of a double-ended queue. Double-ended queues can function as standard, first-in, first-out queues or as last-in, first-out stacks. **Deque** is a generic interface that has this declaration:

```
interface Deque<E>
```

Here, **E** specifies the type of objects that the deque will hold. In addition to the methods that it inherits from **Queue** and **SequencedCollection**, **Deque** adds those methods summarized in Table 20-7. Several methods throw a **ClassCastException** when an object is incompatible with the elements in the deque. A **NullPointerException** is thrown if an attempt is made to store a **null** object and **null** elements are not allowed in the deque. An **IllegalArgumentException** is thrown if an invalid argument is used. An **IllegalStateException** is thrown if an attempt is made to add an element to a fixed-length deque that is full. A **NoSuchElementException** is thrown if an attempt is made to remove an element from an empty deque.

| Method | Description |
|---|---|
| Iterator<E> descendingIterator( ) | Returns an iterator that moves from the tail to the head of the deque. In other words, it returns a reverse iterator. |
| boolean offerFirst(E *obj*) | Attempts to add *obj* to the head of the deque. Returns **true** if *obj* was added and **false** otherwise. Therefore, this method returns **false** when an attempt is made to add *obj* to a full, capacity-restricted deque. |
| boolean offerLast(E *obj*) | Attempts to add *obj* to the tail of the deque. Returns **true** if *obj* was added and **false** otherwise. |
| E peekFirst( ) | Returns the element at the head of the deque. It returns **null** if the deque is empty. The object is not removed. |
| E peekLast( ) | Returns the element at the tail of the deque. It returns **null** if the deque is empty. The object is not removed. |
| E pollFirst( ) | Returns the element at the head of the deque, removing the element in the process. It returns **null** if the deque is empty. |
| E pollLast( ) | Returns the element at the tail of the deque, removing the element in the process. It returns **null** if the deque is empty. |
| E pop( ) | Returns the element at the head of the deque, removing it in the process. It throws **NoSuchElementException** if the deque is empty. |
| void push(E *obj*) | Adds *obj* to the head of the deque. Throws an **IllegalStateException** if a capacity-restricted deque is out of space. |
| boolean removeFirstOccurrence(Object *obj*) | Removes the first occurrence of *obj* from the deque. Returns **true** if successful and **false** if the deque did not contain *obj*. |
| boolean removeLastOccurrence(Object *obj*) | Removes the last occurrence of *obj* from the deque. Returns **true** if successful and **false** if the deque did not contain *obj*. |

**Table 20-7** The Methods Declared by **Deque**

Notice that **Deque** includes the methods **push( )** and **pop( )**. These methods enable a **Deque** to function as a stack. Also, notice the **descendingIterator**( ) method. It returns an iterator that returns elements in reverse order. In other words, it returns an iterator that moves from the end of the collection to the start. The **reversed( )** method **Deque** since JDK 21, by virtue of its inheritance from **SequencedCollection**, serves a similar purpose, except it returns a **Deque** object instead of an **Iterator**. For traversing elements in large **Deque** collections, using the **Iterator** obtained by calling **descendingIterator()** may be more efficient. A **Deque** implementation can be *capacity-restricted*, which means that only a limited number of elements can be added to the deque. When this is the case, an attempt to add an element to the deque can fail. **Deque** allows you to handle such a failure in two ways. First, methods such as **addFirst( )** and **addLast( )** throw an **IllegalStateException** if a capacity-restricted deque is full. Second, methods such as **offerFirst( )** and **offerLast( )** return **false** if the element cannot be added.

# The Collection Classes

Now that you are familiar with the collection interfaces, you are ready to examine the standard classes that implement them. Some of the classes provide full implementations that can be used as-is. Others are abstract, providing skeletal implementations that are used as starting points for creating concrete collections. As a general rule, the collection classes are not synchronized, but as you will see later in this chapter, it is possible to obtain synchronized versions.

The core collection classes are summarized in the following table:

| Class | Description |
|---|---|
| AbstractCollection | Implements most of the **Collection** interface |
| AbstractList | Extends **AbstractCollection** and implements most of the **List** interface |
| AbstractQueue | Extends **AbstractCollection** and implements parts of the **Queue** interface |
| AbstractSequentialList | Extends **AbstractList** for use by a collection that uses sequential rather than random access of its elements |
| LinkedList | Implements a linked list by extending **AbstractSequentialList** |
| ArrayList | Implements a dynamic array by extending **AbstractList** |
| ArrayDeque | Implements a dynamic double-ended queue by extending **AbstractCollection** and implementing the **Deque** interface |
| AbstractSet | Extends **AbstractCollection** and implements most of the **Set** interface |
| EnumSet | Extends **AbstractSet** for use with **enum** elements |
| HashSet | Extends **AbstractSet** for use with a hash table |
| LinkedHashSet | Extends **HashSet** with a well-defined encounter order |
| PriorityQueue | Extends **AbstractQueue** to support a priority-based queue |
| TreeSet | Implements a set stored in a tree. Extends **AbstractSet** |

The following sections examine the concrete collection classes and illustrate their use.

**NOTE** In addition to the collection classes, several legacy classes, such as **Vector**, **Stack**, and **Hashtable**, have been reengineered to support collections. These are examined later in this chapter.

## The ArrayList Class

The **ArrayList** class extends **AbstractList** and implements the **List** interface. **ArrayList** is a generic class that has this declaration:

```
class ArrayList<E>
```

Here, **E** specifies the type of objects that the list will hold.

**ArrayList** supports dynamic arrays that can grow as needed. In Java, standard arrays are of a fixed length. After arrays are created, they cannot grow or shrink, which means that you must know in advance how many elements an array will hold. But, sometimes, you may not know until run time precisely how large an array you need. To handle this situation, the Collections Framework defines **ArrayList**. In essence, an **ArrayList** is a variable-length array of object references. That is, an **ArrayList** can dynamically increase or decrease in size. Array lists are created with an initial size. When this size is exceeded, the collection is automatically enlarged. When objects are removed, the array can be shrunk.

**NOTE** Dynamic arrays are also supported by the legacy class **Vector**, which is described later in this chapter.

**ArrayList** has the constructors shown here:

ArrayList( )
ArrayList(Collection<? extends E> *c*)
ArrayList(int *capacity*)

The first constructor builds an empty array list. The second constructor builds an array list that is initialized with the elements of the collection c. The third constructor builds an array list that has the specified initial *capacity*. The capacity is the size of the underlying array that is used to store the elements. The capacity grows automatically as elements are added to an array list.

The following program shows a simple use of **ArrayList**. An array list is created for objects of type **String**, and then several strings are added to it. (Recall that a quoted string is translated into a **String** object.) The list is then displayed. Some of the elements are removed and the list is displayed again.

```
// Demonstrate ArrayList.
import java.util.*;

class ArrayListDemo {
  public static void main(String[] args) {
    // Create an array list.
    List<String> al = new ArrayList<>();

    System.out.println("Initial size of al: " +
                       al.size());

    // Add elements to the array list.

    al.add("B");
    al.add("X");
    al.add(1, "C");
    al.addFirst("A");
    al.add("D");
    al.add("Y");
    al.add("Z");
    System.out.println("Size of al after additions: " +
                       al.size());

    // Display the array list.
    System.out.println("Contents of al: " + al);

    // Remove elements from the array list.
    al.remove("Y");
    al.remove(3);
    al.removeLast();

    System.out.println("Size of al after deletions: " +
                       al.size());
    System.out.println("Contents of al, in reverse order: " + al.reversed());
  }
}
```

Part II

The output from this program is shown here:

```
Initial size of al: 0
Size of al after additions: 7
Contents of al: [A, B, C, X, D, Y, Z]
Size of al after deletions: 4
Contents of al, in reverse order: [D, C, B, A]
```

Notice that **al** starts out empty and grows as elements are added to it. When elements are removed, its size is reduced.

In the preceding example, the contents of a collection are displayed using the default conversion provided by **toString( )**, which was inherited from **AbstractCollection**. Although it is sufficient for short, sample programs, you seldom use this method to display the contents of a real-world collection. Usually, you provide your own output routines. But, for the next few examples, the default output created by **toString( )** is sufficient.

Although the capacity of an **ArrayList** object increases automatically as objects are stored in it, you can increase the capacity of an **ArrayList** object manually by calling **ensureCapacity( )**. You might want to do this if you know in advance that you will be storing many more items in the collection than it can currently hold. By increasing its capacity once, at the start, you can prevent several reallocations later. Because reallocations are costly in terms of time, preventing unnecessary ones improves performance. The signature for **ensureCapacity( )** is shown here:

void ensureCapacity(int *cap*)

Here, *cap* specifies the new minimum capacity of the collection.

Conversely, if you want to reduce the size of the array that underlies an **ArrayList** object so that it is precisely as large as the number of items that it is currently holding, call **trimToSize( )**, shown here:

void trimToSize( )

Finally, you can see that, through the methods of the **List** interface it implements, the **ArrayList** provides a variety of ways to add and remove elements precisely at the position you need and even produce a list in reverse order with the **reversed( )** method.

## Obtaining an Array from an ArrayList

When working with **ArrayList**, you will sometimes want to obtain an actual array that contains the contents of the list. You can do this by calling **toArray( )**, which is defined by **Collection**. Several reasons exist why you might want to convert a collection into an array, such as:

- To obtain faster processing times for certain operations
- To pass an array to a method that is not overloaded to accept a collection
- To integrate collection-based code with legacy code that does not understand collections

Whatever the reason, converting an **ArrayList** to an array is a trivial matter.

As explained earlier, there are three versions of **toArray( )**, which are shown again here for your convenience:

object[ ] toArray( )
<T> T[ ] toArray(T[ ] *array*)
default <T> T[ ] toArray(IntFunction<T[ ]> *arrayGen*)

The first returns an array of **Object**. The second and third forms return an array of elements that have the same type as **T**. Here, we will use the second form because of its convenience. The following program shows it in action:

```
// Convert an ArrayList into an array.
import java.util.*;

class ArrayListToArray {
  public static void main(String[] args) {
    // Create an array list.
    ArrayList<Integer> al = new ArrayList<Integer>();

    // Add elements to the array list.
    al.add(1);
    al.add(2);
    al.add(3);
    al.add(4);

    System.out.println("Contents of al: " + al);

    // Get the array.
    Integer[] ia = new Integer[al.size()];
    ia = al.toArray(ia);

    int sum = 0;

    // Sum the array.
    for(int i : ia) sum += i;

    System.out.println("Sum is: " + sum);
  }
}
```

The output from the program is shown here:

```
Contents of al: [1, 2, 3, 4]
Sum is: 10
```

The program begins by creating a collection of integers. Next, **toArray( )** is called, and it obtains an array of **Integers**. Then, the contents of that array are summed by use of a for-each style **for** loop.

There is something else of interest in this program. As you know, collections can store only references, not values of primitive types. However, autoboxing makes it possible to pass values of type **int** to **add( )** without having to manually wrap them within an **Integer**, as the program shows. Autoboxing causes them to be automatically wrapped. In this way, autoboxing significantly improves the ease with which collections can be used to store primitive values.

Part II

## The LinkedList Class

The **LinkedList** class extends **AbstractSequentialList** and implements the **List**, **Deque**, and **Queue** interfaces. It provides a linked-list data structure. **LinkedList** is a generic class that has this declaration:

class LinkedList<E>

Here, **E** specifies the type of objects that the list will hold. **LinkedList** has the two constructors shown here:

LinkedList( )
LinkedList(Collection<? extends E> *c*)

The first constructor builds an empty linked list. The second constructor builds a linked list that is initialized with the elements of the collection *c*.

Because **LinkedList** implements the **Deque** interface, you have access to the methods defined by **Deque**. For example, to add elements to the start of a list, you can use **addFirst( )** or **offerFirst( )**. To add elements to the end of the list, use **addLast( )** or **offerLast( )**. To obtain the first element, you can use **getFirst( )** or **peekFirst( )**. To obtain the last element, use **getLast( )** or **peekLast( )**. To remove the first element, use **removeFirst( )** or **pollFirst( )**. To remove the last element, use **removeLast( )** or **pollLast( )**.

The following program illustrates **LinkedList**:

```
// Demonstrate LinkedList.
import java.util.*;

class LinkedListDemo {
  public static void main(String[] args) {
    // Create a linked list.
    LinkedList<String> ll = new LinkedList<String>();

    // Add elements to the linked list.
    ll.add("F");
    ll.add("B");
    ll.add("D");
    ll.add("E");
    ll.add("C");
    ll.addLast("Z");
    ll.addFirst("A");

    ll.add(1, "A2");

    System.out.println("Original contents of ll: " + ll);

    // Remove elements from the linked list.
    ll.remove("F");
    ll.remove(2);

    System.out.println("Contents of ll after deletion: "
                       + ll);
```

```
    // Remove first and last elements.
    ll.removeFirst();
    ll.removeLast();

    System.out.println("ll after deleting first and last: "
                       + ll);

    // Get and set a value.

    String val = ll.get(2);
    ll.set(2, val + " Changed");

    System.out.println("ll after change: " + ll);
  }
}
```



The output from this program is shown here:

```
Original contents of ll: [A, A2, F, B, D, E, C, Z]
Contents of ll after deletion: [A, A2, D, E, C, Z]
ll after deleting first and last: [A2, D, E, C]
ll after change: [A2, D, E Changed, C]
```

Because **LinkedList** implements the **List** interface, calls to **add(E)** append items to the end of the list, as do calls to **addLast( )**. To insert items at a specific location, use the **add(int, E)** form of **add( )**, as illustrated by the call to **add(1, "A2")** in the example.

Notice how the third element in **ll** is changed by employing calls to **get( )** and **set( )**. To obtain the current value of an element, pass **get( )** the index at which the element is stored. To assign a new value to that index, pass **set( )** the index and its new value.

## The HashSet Class

**HashSet** extends **AbstractSet** and implements the **Set** interface. It creates a collection that uses a hash table for storage. **HashSet** is a generic class that has this declaration:

class HashSet<E>

Here, **E** specifies the type of objects that the set will hold.

As most readers likely know, a hash table stores information by using a mechanism called hashing. In *hashing*, the informational content of a key is used to determine a unique value, called its *hash code*. The hash code is then used as the index at which the data associated with the key is stored. The transformation of the key into its hash code is performed automatically—you never see the hash code itself. Also, your code can't directly index the hash table. The advantage of hashing is that it allows the execution time of **add( )**, **contains( )**, **remove( )**, and **size( )** to remain constant even for large sets.

The following constructors are defined:

HashSet( )
HashSet(Collection<? extends E> *c*)
HashSet(int *capacity*)
HashSet(int *capacity*, float *fillRatio*)

The first form constructs a default hash set. The second form initializes the hash set by using the elements of *c*. The third form initializes the capacity of the hash set to *capacity*. (The default capacity is 16.) The fourth form initializes both the capacity and the fill ratio (also called *load factor*) of the hash set from its arguments. The fill ratio must be between 0.0 and 1.0, and it determines how full the hash set can be before it is resized upward. Specifically, when the number of elements is greater than the capacity of the hash set multiplied by its fill ratio, the hash set is expanded. For constructors that do not take a fill ratio, 0.75 is used.

**HashSet** defines only one additional method, **newHashSet( )**, added in JDK 19, beyond those provided by its superclasses and interfaces.

It is important to note that **HashSet** does not guarantee the order of its elements, because the process of hashing doesn't usually lend itself to the creation of sorted sets. If you need sorted storage, then another collection, such as **TreeSet**, is a better choice.

Here is an example that demonstrates **HashSet**:

```
// Demonstrate HashSet.
import java.util.*;

class HashSetDemo {
  public static void main(String[] args) {
    // Create a hash set.
    HashSet<String> hs = new HashSet<String>();

    // Add elements to the hash set.
    hs.add("Beta");
    hs.add("Alpha");
    hs.add("Eta");
    hs.add("Gamma");
    hs.add("Epsilon");
    hs.add("Omega");

    System.out.println(hs);
  }
}
```

The following is the output from this program:

```
[Gamma, Eta, Alpha, Epsilon, Omega, Beta]
```

As explained, the elements are not stored in sorted order, and the precise output may vary.

## The LinkedHashSet Class

The **LinkedHashSet** class extends **HashSet** and adds only one method of its own, **newLinkedHashSet( )**, beginning in JDK 19. It is a generic class that has this declaration:

class LinkedHashSet<E>

Here, **E** specifies the type of objects that the set will hold. Its constructors parallel those in **HashSet**.

**LinkedHashSet** maintains a linked list of the entries in the set, in the order in which they were inserted. This allows insertion-order iteration over the set. That is, when you're cycling through a **LinkedHashSet** using an iterator, the elements will be returned in the order in which they were inserted. This is also the order in which they are contained in the string returned by **toString( )** when called on a **LinkedHashSet** object. To see the effect of **LinkedHashSet**, try substituting **LinkedHashSet** for **HashSet** in the preceding program. The output will be

```
[Beta, Alpha, Eta, Gamma, Epsilon, Omega]
```

which is the order in which the elements were inserted.

Since JDK 21, **LinkedHashSet** implements the methods of the new **SequencedSet** interface, which allows easy addition and removal of elements at the start and end.



## The TreeSet Class

**TreeSet** extends **AbstractSet** and implements the **NavigableSet** interface. It creates a collection that uses a tree for storage. Objects are stored in sorted, ascending order. Access and retrieval times are quite fast, which makes **TreeSet** an excellent choice when storing large amounts of sorted information that must be found quickly.

**TreeSet** is a generic class that has this declaration:

class TreeSet<E>

Here, **E** specifies the type of objects that the set will hold.

**TreeSet** has the following constructors:

TreeSet( )
TreeSet(Collection<? extends E> *c*)
TreeSet(Comparator<? super E> *comp*)
TreeSet(SortedSet<E> *ss*)

The first form constructs an empty tree set that will be sorted in ascending order according to the natural order of its elements. The second form builds a tree set that contains the elements of *c*. The third form constructs an empty tree set that will be sorted according to the comparator specified by *comp*. (Comparators are described later in this chapter.) The fourth form builds a tree set that contains the elements of *ss*.

Here is an example that demonstrates a **TreeSet**:

```
// Demonstrate TreeSet.
import java.util.*;

class TreeSetDemo {
  public static void main(String[] args) {
    // Create a tree set.
    TreeSet<String> ts = new TreeSet<String>();

    // Add elements to the tree set.
    ts.add("C");
    ts.add("A");
    ts.add("B");
    ts.add("E");
    ts.add("F");
    ts.add("D");
```

```
        System.out.println(ts);
    }
}
```

The output from this program is shown here:

```
[A, B, C, D, E, F]
```

As explained, because **TreeSet** stores its elements in a tree, they are automatically arranged in sorted order, as the output confirms.

Because **TreeSet** implements the **NavigableSet** interface, you can use the methods defined by **NavigableSet** to retrieve elements of a **TreeSet**. For example, assuming the preceding program, the following statement uses **subSet( )** to obtain a subset of **ts** that contains the elements between **C** (inclusive) and **F** (exclusive). It then displays the resulting set.

```
System.out.println(ts.subSet("C", "F"));
```

The output from this statement is shown here:

```
[C, D, E]
```

You might want to experiment with the other methods defined by **NavigableSet**.

## The PriorityQueue Class

**PriorityQueue** extends **AbstractQueue** and implements the **Queue** interface. It creates a queue that is prioritized based on the queue's comparator. **PriorityQueue** is a generic class that has this declaration:

class PriorityQueue<E>

Here, **E** specifies the type of objects stored in the queue. **PriorityQueue**s are dynamic, growing as necessary.

**PriorityQueue** defines the seven constructors shown here:

PriorityQueue( )
PriorityQueue(int *capacity*)
PriorityQueue(Comparator<? super E> *comp*)
PriorityQueue(int *capacity*, Comparator<? super E> *comp*)
PriorityQueue(Collection<? extends E> *c*)
PriorityQueue(PriorityQueue<? extends E> *c*)
PriorityQueue(SortedSet<? extends E> *c*)

The first constructor builds an empty queue. Its starting capacity is 11. The second constructor builds a queue that has the specified initial capacity. The third constructor specifies a comparator, and the fourth builds a queue with the specified capacity and comparator. The last three constructors create queues that are initialized with the elements of the collection passed in *c*. In all cases, the capacity grows automatically as elements are added.

If no comparator is specified when a **PriorityQueue** is constructed, then the default comparator for the type of data stored in the queue is used. The default comparator will order the queue in ascending order. Thus, the head of the queue will be the smallest value. However, by providing a custom comparator, you can specify a different ordering scheme. For example, when storing items that include a time stamp, you could prioritize the queue such that the oldest items are first in the queue.

You can obtain a reference to the comparator used by a **PriorityQueue** by calling its **comparator( )** method, shown here:

Comparator<? super E> comparator( )

It returns the comparator. If natural ordering is used for the invoking queue, **null** is returned.

One word of caution: Although you can iterate through a **PriorityQueue** using an iterator, the order of that iteration is undefined. To properly use a **PriorityQueue**, you must call methods such as **offer( )** and **poll( )**, which are defined by the **Queue** interface.



## The ArrayDeque Class

The **ArrayDeque** class extends **AbstractCollection** and implements the **Deque** interface. It adds no methods of its own. **ArrayDeque** creates a dynamic array and has no capacity restrictions. (The **Deque** interface supports implementations that restrict capacity but does not require such restrictions.) **ArrayDeque** is a generic class that has this declaration:

class ArrayDeque<E>

Here, **E** specifies the type of objects stored in the collection.

**ArrayDeque** defines the following constructors:

ArrayDeque( )
ArrayDeque(int *size*)
ArrayDeque(Collection<? extends E> *c*)

The first constructor builds an empty deque. Its starting capacity is 16. The second constructor builds a deque that has the specified initial capacity. The third constructor creates a deque that is initialized with the elements of the collection passed in *c*. In all cases, the capacity grows as needed to handle the elements added to the deque.

The following program demonstrates **ArrayDeque** by using it to create a stack:

```
// Demonstrate ArrayDeque.
import java.util.*;

class ArrayDequeDemo {
  public static void main(String[] args) {
    // Create an array deque.
    ArrayDeque<String> adq = new ArrayDeque<String>();

    // Use an ArrayDeque like a stack.
    adq.push("A");
    adq.push("B");
    adq.push("D");
    adq.push("E");
    adq.push("F");
```

```
    System.out.print("Popping the stack: ");

    while(adq.peek() != null)
      System.out.print(adq.pop() + " ");

    System.out.println();
  }
}
```

The output is shown here:

```
Popping the stack: F E D B A
```

## The EnumSet Class

**EnumSet** extends **AbstractSet** and implements **Set**. It is specifically for use with elements of an **enum** type. It is a generic class that has this declaration:

class EnumSet<E extends Enum<E>>

Here, **E** specifies the elements. Notice that **E** must extend **Enum<E>**, which enforces the requirement that the elements must be of the specified **enum** type.

**EnumSet** defines no constructors. Instead, it uses the factory methods shown in Table 20-8 to create objects. All methods can throw **NullPointerException**. The **copyOf( )** and **range( )** methods can also throw **IllegalArgumentException**. Notice that the **of( )** method is overloaded a number of times. This is in the interest of efficiency. Passing a known number of arguments can be faster than using a vararg parameter when the number of arguments is small.

# Accessing a Collection via an Iterator

Often, you will want to cycle through the elements in a collection. For example, you might want to display each element. One way to do this is to employ an *iterator*, which is an object that implements either the **Iterator** or the **ListIterator** interface. **Iterator** enables you to cycle through a collection, obtaining or removing elements. **ListIterator** extends **Iterator** to allow bidirectional traversal of a list, and the modification of elements. **Iterator** and **ListIterator** are generic interfaces, which are declared as shown here:

interface Iterator<E>
interface ListIterator<E>

Here, **E** specifies the type of objects being iterated. The **Iterator** interface declares the methods shown in Table 20-9. The methods declared by **ListIterator** (along with those inherited from **Iterator**) are shown in Table 20-10. In both cases, operations that modify the underlying collection are optional. For example, **remove( )** will throw **UnsupportedOperationException** when used with a read-only collection. Various other exceptions are possible.

---

**NOTE** You can also use a **Spliterator** to cycle through a collection. **Spliterator** works differently than does **Iterator**, and it is described later in this chapter.

| Method | Description |
|---|---|
| static <E extends Enum<E>> EnumSet<E> allOf(Class<E> *t*) | Creates an **EnumSet** that contains the elements in the enumeration specified by *t* |
| static <E extends Enum<E>> EnumSet<E> complementOf(EnumSet<E> *e*) | Creates an **EnumSet** that is comprised of those elements not stored in *e* |
| static <E extends Enum<E>> EnumSet<E> copyOf(EnumSet<E> *c*) | Creates an **EnumSet** from the elements stored in *c* |
| static <E extends Enum<E>> EnumSet<E> copyOf(Collection<E> *c*) | Creates an **EnumSet** from the elements stored in *c* |
| static <E extends Enum<E>> EnumSet<E> noneOf(Class<E> *t*) | Creates an **EnumSet** that contains the elements that are not in the enumeration specified by *t*, which is an empty set by definition |
| static <E extends Enum<E>> EnumSet<E> of(E *v*, E ... *varargs*) | Creates an **EnumSet** that contains *v* and zero or more additional enumeration values |
| static <E extends Enum<E>> EnumSet<E> of(E *v*) | Creates an **EnumSet** that contains *v* |
| static <E extends Enum<E>> EnumSet<E> of(E *v1*, E *v2*) | Creates an **EnumSet** that contains *v1* and *v2* |
| static <E extends Enum<E>> EnumSet<E> of(E *v1*, E *v2*, E *v3*) | Creates an **EnumSet** that contains *v1* through *v3* |
| static <E extends Enum<E>> EnumSet<E> of(E *v1*, E *v2*, E *v3*, E *v4*) | Creates an **EnumSet** that contains *v1* through *v4* |
| static <E extends Enum<E>> EnumSet<E> of(E *v1*, E *v2*, E *v3*, E *v4*, E *v5*) | Creates an **EnumSet** that contains *v1* through *v5* |
| static <E extends Enum<E>> EnumSet<E> range(E *start*, E *end*) | Creates an **EnumSet** that contains the elements in the range specified by *start* and *end* |

**Table 20-8** The Methods Declared by **EnumSet**

| Method | Description |
|---|---|
| default void forEachRemaining( Consumer<? super E> *action*) | The action specified by *action* is executed on each unprocessed element in the collection. |
| boolean hasNext( ) | Returns **true** if there are more elements. Otherwise, returns **false**. |
| E next( ) | Returns the next element. Throws **NoSuchElementException** if there is not a next element. |
| default void remove( ) | Removes the current element. Throws **IllegalStateException** if an attempt is made to call **remove( )** that is not preceded by a call to **next( )**. The default version throws an **UnsupportedOperationException**. |

**Table 20-9** The Methods Declared by **Iterator**

| Method | Description |
|---|---|
| void add(E *obj*) | Inserts *obj* into the list in front of the element that will be returned by the next call to **next( )**. |
| default void forEachRemaining( Consumer<? super E> *action*) | The action specified by *action* is executed on each unprocessed element in the collection. |
| boolean hasNext( ) | Returns **true** if there is a next element. Otherwise, returns **false**. |
| boolean hasPrevious( ) | Returns **true** if there is a previous element. Otherwise, returns **false**. |
| E next( ) | Returns the next element. A **NoSuchElementException** is thrown if there is not a next element. |
| int nextIndex( ) | Returns the index of the next element. If there is not a next element, returns the size of the list. |
| E previous( ) | Returns the previous element. A **NoSuchElementException** is thrown if there is not a previous element. |
| int previousIndex( ) | Returns the index of the previous element. If there is not a previous element, returns –1. |
| void remove( ) | Removes the current element from the list. An **IllegalStateException** is thrown if **remove( )** is called before **next( )** or **previous( )** is invoked. |
| void set(E *obj*) | Assigns *obj* to the current element. This is the element last returned by a call to either **next( )** or **previous( )**. |

**Table 20-10** The Methods Provided by **ListIterator**

## Using an Iterator

Before you can access a collection through an iterator, you must obtain one. Each of the collection classes provides an **iterator( )** method that returns an iterator to the start of the collection. By using this iterator object, you can access each element in the collection, one element at a time. In general, to use an iterator to cycle through the contents of a collection, follow these steps:

1. Obtain an iterator to the start of the collection by calling the collection's **iterator( )** method.
2. Set up a loop that makes a call to **hasNext( )**. Have the loop iterate as long as **hasNext( )** returns **true**.
3. Within the loop, obtain each element by calling **next( )**.

For collections that implement **List**, you can also obtain an iterator by calling **listIterator( )**. As explained, a list iterator gives you the ability to access the collection in either the forward or backward direction and lets you modify an element. Otherwise, **ListIterator** is used just like **Iterator**.

The following example implements these steps, demonstrating both the **Iterator** and **ListIterator** interfaces. It uses an **ArrayList** object, but the general principles apply to any type of collection. Of course, **ListIterator** is available only to those collections that implement the **List** interface.

```
// Demonstrate iterators.
import java.util.*;

class IteratorDemo {
  public static void main(String[] args) {
    // Create an array list.
    ArrayList<String> al = new ArrayList<String>();

    // Add elements to the array list.
    al.add("C");
    al.add("A");
    al.add("E");
    al.add("B");
    al.add("D");
    al.add("F");

    // Use iterator to display contents of al.
    System.out.print("Original contents of al: ");
    Iterator<String> itr = al.iterator();
    while(itr.hasNext()) {
      String element = itr.next();
      System.out.print(element + " ");
    }
    System.out.println();

    // Modify objects being iterated.
    ListIterator<String> litr = al.listIterator();
    while(litr.hasNext()) {
      String element = litr.next();
      litr.set(element + "+");
    }

    System.out.print("Modified contents of al: ");
    itr = al.iterator();
    while(itr.hasNext()) {
      String element = itr.next();
      System.out.print(element + " ");
    }
    System.out.println();

    // Now, display the list backwards.
    System.out.print("Modified list backwards: ");
    while(litr.hasPrevious()) {
      String element = litr.previous();
      System.out.print(element + " ");
    }
    System.out.println();
  }
}
```

The output is shown here:

```
Original contents of al: C A E B D F
Modified contents of al: C+ A+ E+ B+ D+ F+
Modified list backwards: F+ D+ B+ E+ A+ C+
```

Pay special attention to how the list is displayed in reverse. After the list is modified, **litr** points to the end of the list. (Remember, **litr.hasNext( )** returns **false** when the end of the list has been reached.) To traverse the list in reverse, the program continues to use **litr**, but this time it checks to see whether it has a previous element. As long as it does, that element is obtained and displayed.

## The For-Each Alternative to Iterators

If you won't be modifying the contents of a collection or obtaining elements in reverse order, then the for-each version of the **for** loop is often a more convenient alternative to cycling through a collection than is using an iterator. Recall that the **for** can cycle through any collection of objects that implement the **Iterable** interface. Because all of the collection classes implement this interface, they can all be operated upon by the **for**.

The following example uses a **for** loop to sum the contents of a collection:

```
// Use the for-each for loop to cycle through a collection.
import java.util.*;

class ForEachDemo {
  public static void main(String[] args) {
    // Create an array list for integers.
    ArrayList<Integer> vals = new ArrayList<Integer>();

    // Add values to the array list.
    vals.add(1);
    vals.add(2);
    vals.add(3);
    vals.add(4);
    vals.add(5);

    // Use for loop to display the values.
    System.out.print("Contents of vals: ");
    for(int v : vals)
      System.out.print(v + " ");

    System.out.println();

    // Now, sum the values by using a for loop.
    int sum = 0;
    for(int v : vals)
      sum += v;

    System.out.println("Sum of values: " + sum);
  }
}
```

The output from the program is shown here:

```
Contents of vals: 1 2 3 4 5
Sum of values: 15
```

As you can see, the **for** loop is substantially shorter and simpler to use than the iterator-based approach. One limitation is that you can't modify the contents of the collection during the **for** loop. In addition, you can also only cycle forward through a collection, though for those collections that implement **SequencedCollection**, like **List** and **SortedSet**, you can easily use **reversed( )** to produce an **Iterator** with which you can use a **for** loop to cycle backwards through your collection.



## Spliterators

JDK 8 added another type of iterator called a *spliterator* that is defined by the **Spliterator** interface. A spliterator cycles through a sequence of elements, and in this regard, it is similar to the iterators just described. However, the techniques required to use it differ. Furthermore, it offers substantially more functionality than does either **Iterator** or **ListIterator**. Perhaps the most important aspect of **Spliterator** is its ability to provide support for parallel iteration of portions of the sequence. Thus, **Spliterator** supports parallel programming. (See Chapter 29 for information on concurrency and parallel programming.) However, you can use **Spliterator** even if you won't be using parallel execution. One reason you might want to do so is because it offers a streamlined approach that combines the *hasNext* and *next* operations into one method.

**Spliterator** is a generic interface that is declared like this:

interface Spliterator<T>

Here, **T** is the type of elements being iterated. **Spliterator** declares the methods shown in Table 20-11.

Using **Spliterator** for basic iteration tasks is quite easy: simply call **tryAdvance( )** until it returns **false**. If you will be applying the same action to each element in the sequence, **forEachRemaining( )** offers a streamlined alternative. In both cases, the action that will occur with each iteration is defined by what the **Consumer** object does with each element. **Consumer** is a functional interface that applies an action to an object. It is a generic functional interface declared in **java.util.function**. (See Chapter 21 for information on **java.util.function**.) **Consumer** specifies only one abstract method, **accept( )**, which is shown here:

void accept(T *objRef*)

In the case of **tryAdvance( )**, each iteration passes the next element in the sequence to *objRef*. Often, the easiest way to implement **Consumer** is by use of a lambda expression.

The following program provides a simple example of **Spliterator**. Notice that the program demonstrates both **tryAdvance( )** and **forEachRemaining( )**. Also notice how these methods combine the actions of **Iterator**'s **next( )** and **hasNext( )** methods into a single call.

```
// A simple Spliterator demonstration.
import java.util.*;

class SpliteratorDemo {
```

| Method | Description |
|---|---|
| int characteristics( ) | Returns the characteristics of the invoking spliterator, encoded into an integer. |
| long estimateSize( ) | Estimates the number of elements left to iterate and returns the result. Returns **Long.MAX_VALUE** if the count cannot be obtained for any reason. |
| default void forEachRemaining( Consumer<? super T> *action*) | Applies *action* to each unprocessed element in the data source. |
| default Comparator<? super T> getComparator( ) | Returns the comparator used by the invoking spliterator or **null** if natural ordering is used. If the sequence is unordered, **IllegalStateException** is thrown. |
| default long getExactSizeIfKnown( ) | If the invoking spliterator is sized, returns the number of elements left to iterate. Returns –1 otherwise. |
| default boolean hasCharacteristics(int *val*) | Returns **true** if the invoking spliterator has the characteristics passed in *val*. Returns **false** otherwise. |
| boolean tryAdvance( Consumer<? super T> *action*) | Executes *action* on the next element in the iteration. Returns **true** if there is a next element. Returns **false** if no elements remain. |
| Spliterator<T> trySplit( ) | If possible, splits the invoking spliterator, returning a reference to a new spliterator for the partition. Otherwise, returns **null**. Thus, if successful, the original spliterator iterates over one portion of the sequence and the returned spliterator iterates over the other portion. |

**Table 20-11** The Methods Declared by **Spliterator**

```
  public static void main(String[] args) {
    // Create an array list for doubles.
    ArrayList<Double> vals = new ArrayList<>();

    // Add values to the array list.
    vals.add(1.0);
    vals.add(2.0);
    vals.add(3.0);
    vals.add(4.0);
    vals.add(5.0);

    // Use tryAdvance() to display contents of vals.
    System.out.print("Contents of vals:\n");
    Spliterator<Double> spltitr = vals.spliterator();
    while(spltitr.tryAdvance((n) -> System.out.println(n)));
    System.out.println();

    // Create new list that contains square roots.
    spltitr = vals.spliterator();
    ArrayList<Double> sqrs = new ArrayList<>();
    while(spltitr.tryAdvance((n) -> sqrs.add(Math.sqrt(n))));
```

```
    // Use forEachRemaining() to display contents of sqrs.
    System.out.print("Contents of sqrs:\n");
    spltitr = sqrs.spliterator();
    spltitr.forEachRemaining((n) -> System.out.println(n));
    System.out.println();
  }
}
```

The output is shown here:

```
Contents of vals:
1.0
2.0
3.0
4.0
5.0

Contents of sqrs:
1.0
1.4142135623730951
1.7320508075688772
2.0
2.23606797749979
```

Although this program demonstrates the mechanics of using **Spliterator**, it does not reveal its full power. As mentioned, **Spliterator**'s maximum benefit is found in situations that involve parallel processing.

In Table 20-10, notice the methods **characteristics( )** and **hasCharacteristics( )**. Each **Spliterator** has a set of attributes, called *characteristics*, associated with it. These are defined by static **int** fields in **Spliterator**, such as **SORTED**, **DISTINCT**, **SIZED**, and **IMMUTABLE**, to name a few. You can obtain the characteristics by calling **characteristics( )**. You can determine if a characteristic is present by calling **hasCharacteristics( )**. Often, you won't need to access a **Spliterator**'s characteristics, but in some cases, they can aid in creating efficient, resilient code.

**NOTE** For a further discussion of **Spliterator**, see Chapter 30, where it is used in the context of the stream API. For a discussion of lambda expressions, see Chapter 15. See Chapter 29 for a discussion of parallel programming and concurrency.

There are several nested subinterfaces of **Spliterator** designed for use with the primitive types **double**, **int**, and **long**. These are called **Spliterator.OfDouble**, **Spliterator.OfInt**, and **Spliterator.OfLong**. There is also a generalized version called **Spliterator.OfPrimitive( )**, which offers additional flexibility and serves as a superinterface of the aforementioned ones.

## Storing User-Defined Classes in Collections

For the sake of simplicity, the foregoing examples have stored built-in objects, such as **String** and **Integer**, in a collection. Of course, collections are not limited to the storage of built-in objects. Quite the contrary. The power of collections is that they can store any type of object, including objects of classes that you create. For example, consider the following example, which uses a **LinkedList** to store mailing addresses:

```
// A simple mailing list example.
import java.util.*;

class Address {
  private String name;
  private String street;
  private String city;
  private String state;
  private String code;

  Address(String n, String s, String c,
          String st, String cd) {

    name = n;
    street = s;
    city = c;
    state = st;
    code = cd;
  }

  public String toString() {
    return name + "\n" + street + "\n" +
           city + " " + state + " " + code;
  }
}

class MailList {
  public static void main(String[] args) {
    LinkedList<Address> ml = new LinkedList<Address>();

    // Add elements to the linked list.
    ml.add(new Address("J.W. West", "11 Oak Ave",
                       "Urbana", "IL", "61801"));
    ml.add(new Address("Ralph Baker", "1142 Maple Lane",
                       "Mahomet", "IL", "61853"));
    ml.add(new Address("Tom Carlton", "867 Elm St",
                       "Champaign", "IL", "61820"));

    // Display the mailing list.
    for(Address element : ml)
      System.out.println(element + "\n");

    System.out.println();
  }
}
```

The output from the program is shown here:

```
J.W. West
11 Oak Ave
Urbana IL 61801

Ralph Baker
1142 Maple Lane
Mahomet IL 61853

Tom Carlton
867 Elm St
Champaign IL 61820
```



Aside from storing a user-defined class in a collection, another important thing to notice about the preceding program is that it is quite short. When you consider that it sets up a linked list that can store, retrieve, and process mailing addresses in about 50 lines of code, the power of the Collections Framework begins to become apparent. As most readers know, if all of this functionality had to be coded manually, the program would be several times longer. Collections offer off-the-shelf solutions to a wide variety of programming problems. You should use them whenever the situation presents itself.

## The RandomAccess Interface

The **RandomAccess** interface contains no members. However, by implementing this interface, a collection signals that it supports efficient random access to its elements. Although a collection might support random access, it might not do so efficiently. By checking for the **RandomAccess** interface, client code can determine at run time whether a collection is suitable for certain types of random access operations—especially as they apply to large collections. (You can use **instanceof** to determine if a class implements an interface.) **RandomAccess** is implemented by **ArrayList** and by the legacy **Vector** class, among others.

## Working with Maps

A *map* is an object that stores associations between keys and values, or *key/value pairs*. Given a key, you can find its value. Both keys and values are objects. The keys must be unique, but the values may be duplicated. Some maps can accept a **null** key and **null** values, and others cannot.

There is one key point about maps that is important to mention at the outset: they don't implement the **Iterable** interface. This means that you *cannot* cycle through a map using a for-each style **for** loop. Furthermore, you can't obtain an iterator to a map. However, as you will soon see, you can obtain a collection-view of a map, which does allow the use of either the **for** loop or an iterator.

## The Map Interfaces

Because the map interfaces define the character and nature of maps, this discussion of maps begins with them. The following interfaces support maps:

| Interface | Description |
|---|---|
| Map | Maps unique keys to values. |
| Map.Entry | Describes an element (a key/value pair) in a map. This is a nested interface of **Map**. |
| NavigableMap | Extends **SortedMap** to handle the retrieval of entries based on closest-match searches. |
| SequencedMap | Defines a special kind of **Map** whose **Map.Entry** objects have a well-defined encounter order. |
| SortedMap | Extends **SequencedMap** so that the keys are maintained in ascending order. |

Each interface is examined next, in turn.

### The Map Interface

The **Map** interface maps unique keys to values. A *key* is an object that you use to retrieve a value at a later date. Given a key and a value, you can store the value in a **Map** object. After the value is stored, you can retrieve it by using its key. **Map** is generic and is declared as shown here:

```
interface Map<K, V>
```

Here, **K** specifies the type of keys, and **V** specifies the type of values.

The methods declared by **Map** are summarized in Table 20-12. Several methods throw a **ClassCastException** when an object is incompatible with the elements in a map. A **NullPointerException** is thrown if an attempt is made to use a **null** object and **null** is not allowed in the map. An **UnsupportedOperationException** is thrown when an attempt is made to change an unmodifiable map. An **IllegalArgumentException** is thrown if an invalid argument is used.

Maps revolve around two basic operations: **get( )** and **put( )**. To put a value into a map, use **put( )**, specifying the key and the value. To obtain a value, call **get( )**, passing the key as an argument. The value is returned.

As mentioned earlier, although part of the Collections Framework, maps are not, themselves, collections because they do not implement the **Collection** interface. However, you can obtain a collection-view of a map. To do this, you can use the **entrySet( )** method. It returns a **Set** that contains the elements in the map. To obtain a collection-view of the keys, use **keySet( )**. To get a collection-view of the values, use **values( )**. For all three collection-views, the collection is backed by the map. Changing one affects the other. Collection-views are the means by which maps are integrated into the larger Collections Framework.

Beginning with JDK 9, **Map** includes the **of( )** factory method, which has a number of overloads. Each version returns an unmodifiable, value-based map that is comprised of the arguments that it is passed. The primary purpose of **of( )** is to provide a convenient, efficient

| Method | Description |
|---|---|
| void clear( ) | Removes all key/value pairs from the invoking map. |
| default V compute(K *k*, BiFunction<? super K, ? super V, ? extends V> *func*) | Calls *func* to construct a new value. If *func* returns non-**null**, the new key/value pair is added to the map, any preexisting pairing is removed, and the new value is returned. If *func* returns **null**, any preexisting pairing is removed, and **null** is returned. |
| default V computeIfAbsent(K *k*, Function<? super K, ? extends V> *func*) | Returns the value associated with the key *k*. Otherwise, the value is constructed through a call to *func* and the pairing is entered into the map and the constructed value is returned. If no value can be constructed, **null** is returned. |
| default V computeIfPresent(K *k*, BiFunction<? super K, ? super V, ? extends V> *func*) | If *k* is in the map, a new value is constructed through a call to *func* and the new value replaces the old value in the map. In this case, the new value is returned. If the value returned by *func* is **null**, the existing key and value are removed from the map and **null** is returned. |
| boolean containsKey(Object *k*) | Returns **true** if the invoking map contains *k* as a key. Otherwise, returns **false**. |
| boolean containsValue(Object *v*) | Returns **true** if the map contains *v* as a value. Otherwise, returns **false**. |
| static <K, V> Map<K, V> copyOf(Map<? extends K, ? extends V> *from*) | Returns a map that contains the same key/value pairs as that specified by *from*. The returned map is unmodifiable and value-based. Null keys or values are not allowed. |
| static <K, V> Map.Entry<K, V> entry(K *k*, V *v*) | Returns an unmodifiable value-based map entry comprised of the specified key and value. A **null** key or value is not allowed. |
| Set<Map.Entry<K, V>> entrySet( ) | Returns a **Set** that contains the entries in the map. The set contains objects of type **Map.Entry**. Thus, this method provides a set-view of the invoking map. |
| boolean equals(Object *obj*) | Returns **true** if *obj* is a **Map** and contains the same entries. Otherwise, returns **false**. |
| default void forEach(BiConsumer< ? super K, ? super V> *action*) | Executes *action* on each element in the invoking map. A **ConcurrentModificationException** will be thrown if an element is removed during the process. |
| V get(Object *k*) | Returns the value associated with the key *k*. Returns **null** if the key is not found. |
| default V getOrDefault(Object *k*, V *defVal*) | Returns the value associated with *k* if it is in the map. Otherwise, *defVal* is returned. |
| int hashCode( ) | Returns the hash code for the invoking map. |
| boolean isEmpty( ) | Returns **true** if the invoking map is empty. Otherwise, returns **false**. |

**Table 20-12** The Methods Declared by **Map**

| Method | Description |
|---|---|
| Set<K> keySet( ) | Returns a **Set** that contains the keys in the invoking map. This method provides a set-view of the keys in the invoking map. |
| default V merge(K *k*, V *v*, BiFunction<? super V, ? super V, ? extends V> *func*) | If *k* is not in the map, the pairing *k,v* is added to the map. In this case, *v* is returned. Otherwise, *func* returns a new value based on the old value, the key is updated to use this value, and **merge( )** returns this value. If the value returned by *func* is **null**, the existing key and value are removed from the map and **null** is returned. |
| static <K, V> Map<K, V> of( *parameter-list* ) | Creates an unmodifiable value-based map containing the entries specified in *parameter-list*. Null keys or values are not allowed. Many overloaded versions are provided. See the discussion in the text for details. |
| static <K, V> Map<K, V> ofEntries(Map.Entry<? extends K, ? extends V> ... *entries*) | Returns an unmodifiable value-based map that contains the key/value mappings described by the entries passed in *entries*. Null keys or values are not allowed. |
| V put(K *k*, V *v*) | Puts an entry in the invoking map, overwriting any previous value associated with the key. The key and value are *k* and *v*, respectively. Returns **null** if the key did not already exist. Otherwise, the previous value linked to the key is returned. |
| void putAll(Map<? extends K, ? extends V> *m*) | Puts all the entries from *m* into this map. |
| default V putIfAbsent(K *k*, V *v*) | Inserts the key/value pair into the invoking map if this pairing is not already present or if the existing value is **null**. Returns the old value. The **null** value is returned when no previous mapping exists or the value is **null**. |
| V remove(Object *k*) | Removes the entry whose key equals *k*. |
| default boolean remove(Object *k*, Object *v*) | If the key/value pair specified by *k* and *v* is in the invoking map, it is removed and **true** is returned. Otherwise, **false** is returned. |
| default boolean replace(K *k*, V *oldV*, V *newV*) | If the key/value pair specified by *k* and *oldV* is in the invoking map, the value is replaced by *newV* and **true** is returned. Otherwise **false** is returned. |
| default V replace(K *k*, V *v*) | If the key specified by *k* is in the invoking map, its value is set to *v* and the previous value is returned. Otherwise, **null** is returned. |
| default void replaceAll(BiFunction< ? super K, ? super V, ? extends V> *func*) | Executes *func* on each element of the invoking map, replacing the element with the result returned by *func*. A **ConcurrentModificationException** will be thrown if an element is removed during the process. |

**Table 20-12** The Methods Declared by **Map** *(continued)*

| Method | Description |
|---|---|
| int size( ) | Returns the number of key/value pairs in the map. |
| Collection<V> values( ) | Returns a collection containing the values in the map. This method provides a collection-view of the values in the map. |

**Table 20-12** The Methods Declared by **Map** *(continued)*



way to create a small **Map**. There are 11 overloads of **of( )**. One takes no arguments and creates an empty map. It is shown here:

static <K, V> Map<K, V> of( )

Ten overloads take from 1 to 10 arguments and create a list that contains the specified elements. They are shown here:

static <K, V> Map<K, V> of(K *k1,* V *v1*)
static <K, V> Map<K, V> of(K *k1,* V *v1,* K *k2,* V *v2*)
static <K, V> Map<K, V> of(K *k1,* V *v1,* K *k2,* V *v2,* K *k3,* V *v3*)
...
static <K, V> Map<K, V> of(K *k1,* V *v1,* K *k2,* V *v2,* K *k3,* V *v3,* K *k4,* V *v4,*
K *k5,* V *v5,* K *k6,* V *v6,* K *k7,* V *v7,* K *k8,* V *v8,*
K *k9,* V *v9,* K *k10,* V *v10*)

For all versions, **null** keys and/or values are not allowed. In all cases, the **Map** implementation is unspecified.

## The SequencedMap Interface

Introduced in JDK 21, the **SequencedMap** interface extends **Map** to define a special kind of map whose entries (key value pairs) have a well-defined encounter order. This is a short way of saying that **SequencedMap** objects have a well-defined order in which you can process the entries, such as when you use a **for** loop or an **Iterator**. **SequencedMap** is a generic interface that has this declaration:

interface SequencedMap<E>

Here, **E** specifies the type of objects this **SequencedMap** will hold.

In addition to the methods of the **Map** interface, **SequencedMap** defines several methods that allow access and modifications to its first and last entries as well as provide a reversed version of the itself, wherein the encounter order of the entries is reversed. The methods of the **SequencedMap** interface are shown in Table 20-13.

You can think of a **SequencedMap** as being similar to a **SequencedCollection**, but instead of applying to its elements, the encounter order of a **SequencedMap** applies to its entries. This allows for convenient manipulation of the addition of entries to the **SequencedMap** at the beginning or the end of the map using methods like **putFirst( )** and **pollLast( )**. You can use the sequenced collection representations of the keys, values, and entries as obtained when you call **sequencedKeySet( )**, **sequencedValues( )**, and **sequencedEntrySet( )**, respectively. Finally together with the **reversed( )** method, which returns a map containing the same entries but in

| Method | Description |
|---|---|
| Map.Entry<K, V> firstEntry() | Returns the first key value pair in this map, or **null** if there aren't any. |
| Map.Entry<K, V> lastEntry() | Returns the last key value pair in this map, or **null** if there aren't any. |
| Map.Entry<K, V> pollFirstEntry() | Removes and returns the first key value pair in this map, or **null** if there aren't any. |
| Map.Entry<K, V> pollLastEntry() | Removes and returns the last key value pair in this map, or **null** if there aren't any. |
| V putFirst(K k, V v) | Inserts the key value pair as the first entry in the map. If the key is already present in an entry in the map with a different value, that value is either replaced with the one passed in or an **UnsupportedOperationException** is thrown. |
| V putLast(K k, V v) | Inserts the key value pair as the last entry in the map. If the key is already present in an entry in the map with a different value, that value is either replaced with the one passed in or an **UnsupportedOperationException** is thrown. |
| SequencedMap<K, V> reversed() | Returns a **SequencedMap** whose entries are the same, but in reverse order. |
| SequencedSet<E> sequencedKeySet() | Returns a **SequencedSet** containing the keys of this map's entries, in the same order. |
| SequencedCollection<E> sequencedValues() | Returns a **SequencedCollection** containing the value of this map's entries, in the same order. |
| SequencedSet<Map.Entry<K, V>> sequencedEntrySet() | Returns a **SequencedSet** containing the entries this map contains, in the same order. |

**Table 20-13** The Methods Declared by **SequencedMap**

backwards encounter order, you can use **Iterators** and **for** loops to conveniently traverse all aspects of the **SequencedMap**'s contents in any direction you like.

## The SortedMap Interface

The **SortedMap** interface extends **SequencedMap**. It ensures that the entries are maintained in ascending order based on a well-defined sorting algorithm used to order the map's keys. Note this is a stronger type of ordering than that defined by **SequencedMap**. A **SequencedMap**'s entries may be ordered simply in the order they were added, even in the case, for example, where its keys are integers with no particular numerical ordering applied. In sorting its keys with a particular **Comparator** object, a **SortedMap** always has a well-defined encounter order. **SortedMap** is generic and is declared as shown here:

```
interface SortedMap<K, V>
```

Here, **K** specifies the type of keys, and **V** specifies the type of values.

| Method | Description |
|---|---|
| Comparator<? super K> comparator( ) | Returns the invoking sorted map's comparator. If natural ordering is used for the invoking map, **null** is returned. |
| K firstKey( ) | Returns the first key in the invoking map. |
| SortedMap<K, V> headMap(K *end*) | Returns a sorted map for those map entries with keys that are less than *end*. |
| K lastKey( ) | Returns the last key in the invoking map. |
| SortedMap<K, V> subMap(K *start*, K *end*) | Returns a map containing those entries with keys that are greater than or equal to *start* and less than *end*. |
| SortedMap<K, V> tailMap(K *start*) | Returns a map containing those entries with keys that are greater than or equal to *start*. |

**Table 20-14** The Methods Declared by **SortedMap**



The methods added by **SortedMap** are summarized in Table 20-14. Several methods throw a **NoSuchElementException** when no items are in the invoking map. A **ClassCastException** is thrown when an object is incompatible with the elements in a map. A **NullPointerException** is thrown if an attempt is made to use a **null** object when **null** is not allowed in the map. An **IllegalArgumentException** is thrown if an invalid argument is used.

Sorted maps allow very efficient manipulations of *submaps* (in other words, subsets of a map). To obtain a submap, use **headMap( )**, **tailMap( )**, or **subMap( )**. The submap returned by these methods is backed by the invoking map. Changing one changes the other. To get the first key in the set, call **firstKey( )**. To get the last key, use **lastKey( )**.

## The NavigableMap Interface

The **NavigableMap** interface extends **SortedMap** and declares the behavior of a map that supports the retrieval of entries based on the closest match to a given key or keys. **NavigableMap** is a generic interface that has this declaration:

```
interface NavigableMap<K,V>
```

Here, **K** specifies the type of the keys, and **V** specifies the type of the values associated with the keys. In addition to the methods that it inherits from **SortedMap**, **NavigableMap** adds those summarized in Table 20-15. Several methods throw a **ClassCastException** when an object is incompatible with the keys in the map. A **NullPointerException** is thrown if an attempt is made to use a **null** object and **null** keys are not allowed in the set. An **IllegalArgumentException** is thrown if an invalid argument is used.

## The Map.Entry Interface

The **Map.Entry** interface enables you to work with a map entry. For example, recall that the **entrySet( )** method declared by the **Map** interface returns a **Set** containing the map entries. Each of these set elements is a **Map.Entry** object. **Map.Entry** is generic and is declared like this:

```
interface Map.Entry<K, V>
```

Here, **K** specifies the type of keys, and **V** specifies the type of values. Table 20-16 summarizes the non-static methods declared by **Map.Entry**. It also has three static methods. The first is

| Method | Description |
|---|---|
| Map.Entry<K,V> ceilingEntry(K *obj*) | Searches the map for the smallest key *k* such that *k* >= *obj*. If such a key is found, its entry is returned. Otherwise, **null** is returned. |
| K ceilingKey(K *obj*) | Searches the map for the smallest key *k* such that *k* >= *obj*. If such a key is found, it is returned. Otherwise, **null** is returned. |
| NavigableSet<K> descendingKeySet( ) | Returns a **NavigableSet** that contains the keys in the invoking map in reverse order. Thus, it returns a reverse set-view of the keys. The resulting set is backed by the map. |
| NavigableMap<K,V> descendingMap( ) | Returns a **NavigableMap** that is the reverse of the invoking map. The resulting map is backed by the invoking map. |
| Map.Entry<K,V> firstEntry( ) | Returns the first entry in the map. This is the entry with the least key. |
| Map.Entry<K,V> floorEntry(K *obj*) | Searches the map for the largest key *k* such that *k* <= *obj*. If such a key is found, its entry is returned. Otherwise, **null** is returned. |
| K floorKey(K *obj*) | Searches the map for the largest key *k* such that *k* <= *obj*. If such a key is found, it is returned. Otherwise, **null** is returned. |
| NavigableMap<K,V> headMap(K *upperBound*, boolean *incl*) | Returns a **NavigableMap** that includes all entries from the invoking map that have keys that are less than *upperBound*. If *incl* is **true**, then an element equal to *upperBound* is included. The resulting map is backed by the invoking map. |
| Map.Entry<K,V> higherEntry(K *obj*) | Searches the set for the largest key *k* such that *k* > *obj*. If such a key is found, its entry is returned. Otherwise, **null** is returned. |
| K higherKey(K *obj*) | Searches the set for the largest key *k* such that *k* > *obj*. If such a key is found, it is returned. Otherwise, **null** is returned. |
| Map.Entry<K,V> lastEntry( ) | Returns the last entry in the map. This is the entry with the largest key. |
| Map.Entry<K,V> lowerEntry(K obj) | Searches the set for the largest key *k* such that *k* < *obj*. If such a key is found, its entry is returned. Otherwise, **null** is returned. |
| K lowerKey(K *obj*) | Searches the set for the largest key *k* such that *k* < *obj*. If such a key is found, it is returned. Otherwise, **null** is returned. |

**Table 20-15** The Methods Declared by **NavigableMap**

| Method | Description |
|---|---|
| NavigableSet<K> navigableKeySet( ) | Returns a **NavigableSet** that contains the keys in the invoking map. The resulting set is backed by the invoking map. |
| Map.Entry<K,V> pollFirstEntry( ) | Returns the first entry, removing the entry in the process. Because the map is sorted, this is the entry with the least key value. **null** is returned if the map is empty. |
| Map.Entry<K,V> pollLastEntry( ) | Returns the last entry, removing the entry in the process. Because the map is sorted, this is the entry with the greatest key value. **null** is returned if the map is empty. |
| NavigableMap<K,V> subMap(K *lowerBound*, boolean *lowIncl*, K *upperBound* boolean *highIncl*) | Returns a **NavigableMap** that includes all entries from the invoking map that have keys that are greater than *lowerBound* and less than *upperBound*. If *lowIncl* is **true**, then an element equal to *lowerBound* is included. If *highIncl* is **true**, then an element equal to *highIncl* is included. The resulting map is backed by the invoking map. |
| NavigableMap<K,V> tailMap(K *lowerBound*, boolean *incl*) | Returns a **NavigableMap** that includes all entries from the invoking map that have keys that are greater than *lowerBound*. If *incl* is **true**, then an element equal to *lowerBound* is included. The resulting map is backed by the invoking map. |

**Table 20-15** The Methods Declared by **NavigableMap** *(continued)*

**comparingByKey( )**, which returns a **Comparator** that compares entries by key. The second is **comparingByValue( )**, which returns a **Comparator** that compares entries by value. The third is **copyOf( )**, added by JDK 17. It returns an unmodifiable value-based object that is a copy of the invoking object but is not a part of a map.

| Method | Description |
|---|---|
| boolean equals(Object *obj*) | Returns **true** if *obj* is a **Map.Entry** whose key and value are equal to that of the invoking object. |
| K getKey( ) | Returns the key for this map entry. |
| V getValue( ) | Returns the value for this map entry. |
| int hashCode( ) | Returns the hash code for this map entry. |
| V setValue(V *v*) | Sets the value for this map entry to *v*. A **ClassCastException** is thrown if *v* is not the correct type for the map. An **IllegalArgumentException** is thrown if there is a problem with *v*. A **NullPointerException** is thrown if *v* is **null** and the map does not permit **null** keys. An **UnsupportedOperationException** is thrown if the map cannot be changed. |

**Table 20-16** The Non-Static Methods Declared by **Map.Entry**

## The Map Classes

Several classes provide implementations of the map interfaces. The classes that can be used for maps are summarized here:

| Class | Description |
|---|---|
| AbstractMap | Implements most of the **Map** interface |
| EnumMap | Extends **AbstractMap** for use with **enum** keys |
| HashMap | Extends **AbstractMap** using a hash table to implement the **Map** methods |
| TreeMap | Extends **AbstractMap** using a tree implementation to be a **SortedMap** |
| WeakHashMap | Extends **AbstractMap** to use a hash table with weak keys that may be garbage-collected |
| LinkedHashMap | Extends **HashMap** so that this is also a **SequencedMap** implementation |
| IdentityHashMap | Extends **AbstractMap** and uses reference equality when comparing documents |

Notice that **AbstractMap** is a superclass for all concrete map implementations.

**WeakHashMap** implements a map that uses "weak keys," which allows an element in a map to be garbage-collected when its key is otherwise unused. This class is not discussed further here. The other map classes are described next.

### The HashMap Class

The **HashMap** class extends **AbstractMap** and implements the **Map** interface. It uses a hash table to store the map. This allows the execution time of **get( )** and **put( )** to remain constant even for large sets. **HashMap** is a generic class that has this declaration:

```
class HashMap<K, V>
```

Here, **K** specifies the type of keys, and **V** specifies the type of values.

The following constructors are defined:

HashMap( )
HashMap(Map<? extends K, ? extends V> *m*)
HashMap(int *capacity*)
HashMap(int *capacity*, float *fillRatio*)

The first form constructs a default hash map. The second form initializes the hash map by using the elements of *m*. The third form initializes the capacity of the hash map to *capacity*. The fourth form initializes both the capacity and fill ratio of the hash map by using its arguments. The meaning of capacity and fill ratio is the same as for **HashSet**, described earlier. The default capacity is 16. The default fill ratio is 0.75.

**HashMap** implements **Map** and extends **AbstractMap**. It adds just one method of its own: the **newHashMap( )** method, added in JDK 19.

You should note that a hash map does not guarantee the order of its elements. Therefore, the order in which elements are added to a hash map is not necessarily the order in which they are read by an iterator.

The following program illustrates **HashMap**. It maps names to account balances. Notice how a set-view is obtained and used.

```
import java.util.*;

class HashMapDemo {
  public static void main(String[] args) {

    // Create a hash map.
    HashMap<String, Double> hm = new HashMap<String, Double>();

    // Put elements to the map
    hm.put("John Doe", 3434.34);
    hm.put("Tom Smith", 123.22);
    hm.put("Jane Baker", 1378.00);
    hm.put("Tod Hall", 99.22);
    hm.put("Ralph Smith", -19.08);

    // Get a set of the entries.
    Set<Map.Entry<String, Double>> set = hm.entrySet();

    // Display the set.
    for(Map.Entry<String, Double> me : set) {
      System.out.print(me.getKey() + ": ");
      System.out.println(me.getValue());
    }

    System.out.println();

    // Deposit 1000 into John Doe's account.
    double balance = hm.get("John Doe");
    hm.put("John Doe", balance + 1000);

    System.out.println("John Doe's new balance: " +
      hm.get("John Doe"));
  }
}
```

Output from this program is shown here (the precise order may vary):

```
Ralph Smith: -19.08
Tom Smith: 123.22
John Doe: 3434.34
Tod Hall: 99.22
Jane Baker: 1378.0

John Doe's new balance: 4434.34
```

The program begins by creating a hash map and then adds the mapping of names to balances. Next, the contents of the map are displayed by using a set-view, obtained by calling **entrySet( )**. The keys and values are displayed by calling the **getKey( )** and **getValue( )** methods that are defined by **Map.Entry**. Pay close attention to how the deposit is made into

John Doe's account. The **put( )** method automatically replaces any preexisting value that is associated with the specified key with the new value. Thus, after John Doe's account is updated, the hash map will still contain just one "John Doe" account.

## The TreeMap Class

The **TreeMap** class extends **AbstractMap** and implements the **NavigableMap** interface. It creates maps stored in a tree structure. A **TreeMap** provides an efficient means of storing key/value pairs in sorted order and allows rapid retrieval. You should note that, unlike a hash map, a tree map guarantees that its elements will be sorted in ascending key order. **TreeMap** is a generic class that has this declaration:

class TreeMap<K, V>

Here, **K** specifies the type of keys, and **V** specifies the type of values.

The following **TreeMap** constructors are defined:

TreeMap( )
TreeMap(Comparator<? super K> *comp*)
TreeMap(Map<? extends K, ? extends V> *m*)
TreeMap(SortedMap<K, ? extends V> *sm*)

The first form constructs an empty tree map that will be sorted by using the natural order of its keys. The second form constructs an empty tree-based map that will be sorted by using the **Comparator** *comp*. (Comparators are discussed later in this chapter.) The third form initializes a tree map with the entries from *m*, which will be sorted by using the natural order of the keys. The fourth form initializes a tree map with the entries from *sm*, which will be sorted in the same order as *sm*.

**TreeMap** has no map methods beyond those specified by the **NavigableMap** interface and the **AbstractMap** class.

The following program reworks the preceding example so that it uses **TreeMap**:

```
import java.util.*;

class TreeMapDemo {
  public static void main(String[] args) {

    // Create a tree map.
    TreeMap<String, Double> tm = new TreeMap<String, Double>();

    // Put elements to the map.
    tm.put("John Doe", 3434.34);
    tm.put("Tom Smith", 123.22);
    tm.put("Jane Baker", 1378.00);
    tm.put("Tod Hall", 99.22);
    tm.put("Ralph Smith", -19.08);

    // Get a set of the entries.
    Set<Map.Entry<String, Double>> set = tm.entrySet();

    // Display the elements.
    for(Map.Entry<String, Double> me : set) {
```

```
      System.out.print(me.getKey() + ": ");
      System.out.println(me.getValue());
    }
    System.out.println();

    // Deposit 1000 into John Doe's account.
    double balance = tm.get("John Doe");
    tm.put("John Doe", balance + 1000);

    System.out.println("John Doe's new balance: " +
      tm.get("John Doe"));
  }
}
```



The following is the output from this program:

```
Jane Baker: 1378.0
John Doe: 3434.34
Ralph Smith: -19.08
Todd Hall: 99.22
Tom Smith: 123.22

John Doe's current balance: 4434.34
```

Notice that **TreeMap** sorts the keys. However, in this case, they are sorted by first name instead of last name. You can alter this behavior by specifying a comparator when the map is created, as described shortly.

## The LinkedHashMap Class

**LinkedHashMap** extends **HashMap**. It maintains a linked list of the entries in the map, in the order in which they were inserted. This allows insertion-order iteration over the map. That is, when iterating through a collection-view of a **LinkedHashMap**, the elements will be returned in the order in which they were inserted. You can also create a **LinkedHashMap** that returns its elements in the order in which they were last accessed. This ordering of entries by insertion order, or last access order, is a difference between the preceding TreeMap, which sorts its entries using a Comparator, and this LinkedHashMap. The difference is reflected in the class hierarchy by TreeMap implementing SortedMap and LinkedHashMap the less imposing SequencedMap interface. **LinkedHashMap** is a generic class that has this declaration:

class LinkedHashMap<K, V>

Here, **K** specifies the type of keys, and **V** specifies the type of values.

**LinkedHashMap** defines the following constructors:

LinkedHashMap( )
LinkedHashMap(Map<? extends K, ? extends V> *m*)
LinkedHashMap(int *capacity*)
LinkedHashMap(int *capacity*, float *fillRatio*)
LinkedHashMap(int *capacity*, float *fillRatio*, boolean *Order*)

The first form constructs a default **LinkedHashMap**. The second form initializes the **LinkedHashMap** with the elements from *m*. The third form initializes the capacity.

The fourth form initializes both capacity and fill ratio. The meaning of capacity and fill ratio are the same as for **HashMap**. The default capacity is 16. The default ratio is 0.75. The last form allows you to specify whether the elements will be stored in the linked list by insertion order or by order of last access. If *Order* is **true**, then access order is used. If *Order* is **false**, then insertion order is used.

By implementing the **SequencedMap** interface, **LinkedHashMap** implements the methods that allow you to access, add, and remove entries at the start and end of its ordered collection of entries that we saw earlier when we examined the **SequencedMap** interface and also to produce a version of itself with the entries in reverse order, using the **reversed( )** method. We can see this in action by looking at some code similar to the **TreeMap** example but using a **LinkedHashMap** instead.

```
// Using a LinkedHashMap
import java.util.*;

public class LinkedHashMapDemo {

  public static void main(String[] args) {

    // Create a tree map.
    SequencedMap<String, Double> sm = new LinkedHashMap<>();

    // Put elements to the map.
    tm.put("Carla Dupres", 2749.50);
    tm.putFirst("David Garcia", 314.15);
    tm.putLast("Bella Yip", 1289.41);
    tm.putFirst("Elizabeth Johnson", 72.96);
    tm.put("Adam Smith", -34.99);

    // Display the elements.
    for(Map.Entry<String, Double> me : tm.entrySet()) {
      System.out.print(me.getKey() + ": ");
      System.out.println(me.getValue());
    }
  }

}
```

You will notice that this code is using a **LinkedHashMap** implementation of a **SequencedMap** type. It's using the **putFirst( )** and **putLast( )** to carefully insert the entries into particular positions, which consist, as in the **TreeMap** example, of a name and a **Double** representing an amount of money representing the balance in a bank account. The output of the program is shown here:

```
Elizabeth Johnson: 72.96
David Garcia: 314.15
Carla Dupres: 2749.5
Bella Yip: 1289.41
Adam Smith: -34.99
```

You can see that the order in which the entries are printed out as the code loops through them derives from the position in which the entries were inserted into the map. This is what you would expect since the code uses the default constructor to create an empty map whose encounter order is its insertion order. This is unlike the **TreeMap** example since the encounter order is reverse alphabetical.

### The IdentityHashMap Class

**IdentityHashMap** extends **AbstractMap** and implements the **Map** interface. It is similar to **HashMap** except that it uses reference equality when comparing elements. **IdentityHashMap** is a generic class that has this declaration:

```
class IdentityHashMap<K, V>
```

Here, **K** specifies the type of key, and **V** specifies the type of value. The API documentation explicitly states that **IdentityHashMap** is not for general use.



### The EnumMap Class

**EnumMap** extends **AbstractMap** and implements **Map**. It is specifically for use with keys of an **enum** type. It is a generic class that has this declaration:

```
class EnumMap<K extends Enum<K>, V>
```

Here, **K** specifies the type of key, and **V** specifies the type of value. Notice that **K** must extend **Enum<K>**, which enforces the requirement that the keys must be of an **enum** type.

**EnumMap** defines the following constructors:

EnumMap(Class<K> *kType*)
EnumMap(Map<K, ? extends V> *m*)
EnumMap(EnumMap<K, ? extends V> *em*)

The first constructor creates an empty **EnumMap** of type *kType*. The second creates an **EnumMap** map that contains the same entries as *m*. The third creates an **EnumMap** initialized with the values in *em*.

**EnumMap** defines no methods of its own.

## Comparators

Both **TreeSet** and **TreeMap** store elements in sorted order. However, it is the comparator that defines precisely what "sorted order" means. By default, these classes store their elements by using what Java refers to as "natural ordering," which is usually the ordering that you would expect (A before B, 1 before 2, and so forth). If you want to order elements a different way, then specify a **Comparator** when you construct the set or map. Doing so gives you the ability to govern precisely how elements are stored within sorted collections and maps.

**Comparator** is a generic interface that has this declaration:

```
interface Comparator<T>
```

Here, **T** specifies the type of objects being compared.

Prior to JDK 8, the **Comparator** interface defined only two methods: **compare( )** and **equals( )**. The **compare( )** method, shown here, compares two elements for order:

int compare(T *obj1*, T *obj2*)

*obj1* and *obj2* are the objects to be compared. Normally, this method returns zero if the objects are equal. It returns a positive value if *obj1* is greater than *obj2*. Otherwise, a negative value is returned. The method can throw a **ClassCastException** if the types of the objects are not compatible for comparison. By implementing **compare( )**, you can alter the way that objects are ordered. For example, to sort in reverse order, you can create a comparator that reverses the outcome of a comparison.

The **equals( )** method, shown here, tests whether an object equals the invoking comparator:

boolean equals(object *obj*)

Here, *obj* is the object to be tested for equality. The method returns **true** if *obj* and the invoking object are both **Comparator** objects and use the same ordering. Otherwise, it returns **false**. Overriding **equals( )** is not necessary, and most simple comparators will not do so.

For many years, the preceding two methods were the only methods defined by **Comparator**. With the release of JDK 8, the situation dramatically changed. JDK 8 added significant new functionality to **Comparator** through the use of default and static interface methods. Each is described here.

You can obtain a comparator that reverses the ordering of the comparator on which it is called by using **reversed( )**, shown here:

default Comparator<T> reversed( )

It returns the reverse comparator. For example, assuming a comparator that uses natural ordering for the characters A through Z, a reverse order comparator would put B before A, C before B, and so on.

A method related to **reversed( )** is **reverseOrder( )**, shown next:

static <T extends Comparable<? super T>> Comparator<T> reverseOrder( )

It returns a comparator that reverses the natural order of the elements. Conversely, you can obtain a comparator that uses natural ordering by calling the static method **naturalOrder( )**, shown next:

static <T extends Comparable<? super T>> Comparator<T> naturalOrder( )

If you want a comparator that can handle **null** values, use **nullsFirst( )** or **nullsLast( )**, shown here:

static <T> Comparator<T> nullsFirst(Comparator<? super T> *comp*)
static <T> Comparator<T> nullsLast(Comparator<? super T> *comp*)

The **nullsFirst( )** method returns a comparator that views **null** values as less than other values. The **nullsLast( )** method returns a comparator that views **null** values as greater than other values. In both cases, if the two values being compared are non-**null**, *comp* performs the comparison. If *comp* is passed **null**, then all non-**null** values are viewed as equivalent.

Another default method is **thenComparing( )**. It returns a comparator that performs a second comparison when the outcome of the first comparison indicates that the objects being compared are equal. Thus, it can be used to create a "compare by X then compare by Y" sequence. For example, when comparing cities, the first comparison might compare names, with the second comparison comparing states. (Therefore, Springfield, Illinois, would come before Springfield, Missouri, assuming normal, alphabetical order.) The **thenComparing( )** method has three forms. The first, shown here, lets you specify the second comparator by passing an instance of **Comparator**:

default Comparator<T> thenComparing(Comparator<? super T> *thenByComp*)

Here, *thenByComp* specifies the comparator that is called if the first comparison returns equal.

The next versions of **thenComparing( )** let you specify the standard functional interface **Function** (defined by **java.util.function**). They are shown here:

default <U extends Comparable<? super U> Comparator<T><br>
  thenComparing(Function<? super T, ? extends U> *getKey*)

default <U> Comparator<T><br>
  thenComparing(Function<? super T, ? extends U> *getKey*,<br>
    Comparator<? super U> *keyComp*)

In both, *getKey* refers to function that obtains the next comparison key, which is used if the first comparison returns equal. In the second version, *keyComp* specifies the comparator used to compare keys. (Here, and in subsequent uses, **U** specifies the type of the key.)

**Comparator** also adds the following specialized versions of "then comparing" methods for the primitive types:

default Comparator<T><br>
  thenComparingDouble(ToDoubleFunction<? super T> *getKey*)

default Comparator<T><br>
  thenComparingInt(ToIntFunction<? super T> *getKey*)

default Comparator<T><br>
  thenComparingLong(ToLongFunction<? super T> *getKey*)

In all methods, *getKey* refers to a function that obtains the next comparison key

Finally, **Comparator** has a method called **comparing( )**. It returns a comparator that obtains its comparison key from a function passed to the method. There are two versions of **comparing( )**, shown here:

static <T, U extends Comparable<? super U>> Comparator<T><br>
  comparing(Function<? super T, ? extends U> *getKey*)

static <T, U> Comparator<T><br>
  comparing(Function<? super T, ? extends U> *getKey*,<br>
    Comparator<? super U> *keyComp*)

In both, *getKey* refers to a function that obtains the next comparison key. In the second version, *keyComp* specifies the comparator used to compare keys. **Comparator** also adds the following specialized versions of these methods for the primitive types:

static <T> Comparator<T>
    comparingDouble(ToDoubleFunction<? super T> *getKey*)

static <T> Comparator<T>
    comparingInt(ToIntFunction<? super T> *getKey*)

static <T> Comparator<T>
    comparingLong(ToLongFunction<? super T> *getKey*)

In all methods, *getKey* refers to a function that obtains the next comparison key.

## Using a Comparator

The following is an example that demonstrates the power of a custom comparator. It implements the **compare( )** method for strings that operates in reverse of normal. Thus, it causes a tree set to be sorted in reverse order.

```
// Use a custom comparator.
import java.util.*;

// A reverse comparator for strings.
class MyComp implements Comparator<String> {
  public int compare(String aStr, String bStr) {

    // Reverse the comparison.
    return bStr.compareTo(aStr);
  }

  // No need to override equals or the default methods.
}

class CompDemo {
  public static void main(String[] args) {
    // Create a tree set.
    TreeSet<String> ts = new TreeSet<String>(new MyComp());

    // Add elements to the tree set.
    ts.add("C");
    ts.add("A");
    ts.add("B");
    ts.add("E");
    ts.add("F");
    ts.add("D");

    // Display the elements.
    for(String element : ts)
      System.out.print(element + " ");

    System.out.println();
  }
}
```

As the following output shows, the tree is now sorted in reverse order:

```
F E D C B A
```

Look closely at the **MyComp** class, which implements **Comparator** by implementing **compare( )**. (As explained earlier, overriding **equals( )** is neither necessary nor common. It is also not necessary to override the default methods.) Inside **compare( )**, the **String** method **compareTo( )** compares the two strings. However, **bStr**—not **aStr**—invokes **compareTo( )**. This causes the outcome of the comparison to be reversed.

Although the way in which the reverse order comparator is implemented by the preceding program is perfectly adequate, there is another way to approach a solution. It is now possible to simply call **reversed( )** on a natural-order comparator. It will return an equivalent comparator, except that it runs in reverse. For example, assuming the preceding program, you can rewrite **MyComp** as a natural-order comparator, as shown here:



```
class MyComp implements Comparator<String> {
  public int compare(String aStr, String bStr) {
    return aStr.compareTo(bStr);
  }
}
```

Next, you can use the following sequence to create a **TreeSet** that orders its string elements in reverse:

```
MyComp mc = new MyComp(); // Create a comparator

// Pass a reverse order version of MyComp to TreeSet.
TreeSet<String> ts = new TreeSet<String>(mc.reversed());
```

If you plug this new code into the preceding program, it will produce the same results as before. In this case, there is no advantage gained by using **reversed( )**. However, in cases in which you need to create both a natural-order comparator and a reversed comparator, then using **reversed( )** gives you an easy way to obtain the reverse-order comparator without having to code it explicitly.

It is not actually necessary to create the **MyComp** class in the preceding examples because a lambda expression can be easily used instead. For example, you can remove the **MyComp** class entirely and create the string comparator by using this statement:

```
// Use a lambda expression to implement Comparator<String>.
Comparator<String> mc = (aStr, bStr) -> aStr.compareTo(bStr);
```

One other point: in this simple example, it would also be possible to specify a reverse comparator via a lambda expression directly in the call to the **TreeSet( )** constructor, as shown here:

```
// Pass a reversed comparator to TreeSet() via a
// lambda expression.
TreeSet<String> ts = new TreeSet<String>(
                          (aStr, bStr) -> bStr.compareTo(aStr));
```

By making these changes, the program is substantially shortened, as its final version shown here illustrates:

```
// Use a lambda expression to create a reverse comparator.
import java.util.*;

class CompDemo2 {
  public static void main(String[] args) {

    // Pass a reverse comparator to TreeSet() via a
    // lambda expression.
    TreeSet<String> ts = new TreeSet<String>(
                          (aStr, bStr) -> bStr.compareTo(aStr));

    // Add elements to the tree set.
    ts.add("C");
    ts.add("A");
    ts.add("B");
    ts.add("E");
    ts.add("F");
    ts.add("D");

    // Display the elements.
    for(String element : ts)
      System.out.print(element + " ");

    System.out.println();
  }
}
```

For a more practical example that uses a custom comparator, the following program is an updated version of the **TreeMap** program shown earlier that stores account balances. In the previous version, the accounts were sorted by name, but the sorting began with the first name. The following program sorts the accounts by last name. To do so, it uses a comparator that compares the last name of each account. This results in the map being sorted by last name.

```
// Use a comparator to sort accounts by last name.
import java.util.*;

// Compare last whole words in two strings.
class TComp implements Comparator<String> {
  public int compare(String aStr, String bStr) {
    int i, j, k;

    // Find index of beginning of last name.
    i = aStr.lastIndexOf(' ');
    j = bStr.lastIndexOf(' ');

    k = aStr.substring(i).compareToIgnoreCase (bStr.substring(j));
    if(k==0) // last names match, check entire name
      return aStr.compareToIgnoreCase (bStr);
    else
      return k;
  }
```

```
    // No need to override equals.
}

class TreeMapDemo2 {
  public static void main(String[] args) {
    // Create a tree map.
    TreeMap<String, Double> tm = new TreeMap<String, Double>(new TComp());

    // Put elements to the map.
    tm.put("John Doe", 3434.34);
    tm.put("Tom Smith", 123.22);
    tm.put("Jane Baker", 1378.00);
    tm.put("Tod Hall", 99.22);
    tm.put("Ralph Smith", -19.08);

    // Get a set of the entries.
    Set<Map.Entry<String, Double>> set = tm.entrySet();

    // Display the elements.
    for(Map.Entry<String, Double> me : set) {
      System.out.print(me.getKey() + ": ");
      System.out.println(me.getValue());
    }
    System.out.println();

    // Deposit 1000 into John Doe's account.
    double balance =  tm.get("John Doe");
    tm.put("John Doe", balance + 1000);

    System.out.println("John Doe's new balance: " +
      tm.get("John Doe"));
  }
}
```

Here is the output; notice that the accounts are now sorted by last name:

```
Jane Baker: 1378.0
John Doe: 3434.34
Todd Hall: 99.22
Ralph Smith: -19.08
Tom Smith: 123.22

John Doe's new balance: 4434.34
```

The comparator class **TComp** compares two strings that hold first and last names. It does so by first comparing last names. To do this, it finds the index of the last space in each string and then compares the substrings of each element that begin at that point. In cases where last names are equivalent, the first names are then compared. This yields a tree map that is sorted by last name, and within last name by first name. You can see this because Ralph Smith comes before Tom Smith in the output.

There is another way that you could code the preceding program so the map is sorted by last name and then by first name. This approach uses the **thenComparing( )** method.

Recall that **thenComparing( )** lets you specify a second comparator that will be used if the invoking comparator returns equal. This approach is put into action by the following program, which reworks the preceding example to use **thenComparing( )**:

```
// Use thenComparing() to sort by last, then first name.
import java.util.*;

// A comparator that compares last names.
class CompLastNames implements Comparator<String> {
  public int compare(String aStr, String bStr) {
    int i, j;

    // Find index of beginning of last name.
    i = aStr.lastIndexOf(' ');
    j = bStr.lastIndexOf(' ');

    return aStr.substring(i).compareToIgnoreCase(bStr.substring(j));
  }
}

// Sort by entire name when last names are equal.
class CompThenByFirstName implements Comparator<String> {
  public int compare(String aStr, String bStr) {
    int i, j;

    return aStr.compareToIgnoreCase(bStr);
  }
}

class TreeMapDemo2A {
  public static void main(String[] args) {
    // Use thenComparing() to create a comparator that compares
    // last names, then compares entire name when last names match.
    CompLastNames compLN = new CompLastNames();
    Comparator<String> compLastThenFirst =
                         compLN.thenComparing(new CompThenByFirstName());

    // Create a tree map.
    TreeMap<String, Double> tm =
                         new TreeMap<String, Double>(compLastThenFirst);

    // Put elements to the map.
    tm.put("John Doe", 3434.34);
    tm.put("Tom Smith", 123.22);
    tm.put("Jane Baker", 1378.00);
    tm.put("Tod Hall", 99.22);
    tm.put("Ralph Smith", -19.08);

    // Get a set of the entries.
    Set<Map.Entry<String, Double>> set = tm.entrySet();
```

```
    // Display the elements.
    for(Map.Entry<String, Double> me : set) {
      System.out.print(me.getKey() + ": ");
      System.out.println(me.getValue());
    }
    System.out.println();

    // Deposit 1000 into John Doe's account.
    double balance =  tm.get("John Doe");
    tm.put("John Doe", balance + 1000);

    System.out.println("John Doe's new balance: " +
      tm.get("John Doe"));
  }
}
```



This version produces the same output as before. It differs only in how it accomplishes its job. To begin, notice that a comparator called **CompLastNames** is created. This comparator compares only the last names. A second comparator, called **CompThenByFirstName**, compares the entire name, starting with the first name. Next, the **TreeMap** is created by the following sequence:

```
CompLastNames compLN = new CompLastNames();
Comparator<String> compLastThenFirst =
                     compLN.thenComparing(new CompThenByFirstName());
```

Here, the primary comparator is **compLN**. It is an instance of **CompLastNames**. On it is called **thenComparing( )**, passing in an instance of **CompThenByFirstName**. The result is assigned to the comparator called **compLastThenFirst**. This comparator is used to construct the **TreeMap**, as shown here:

```
TreeMap<String, Double> tm =
                     new TreeMap<String, Double>(compLastThenFirst);
```

Now, whenever the last names of the items being compared are equal, the entire name, beginning with the first name, is used to order the two. This means that names are ordered based on last name, and within last names, by first names.

One last point: in the interest of clarity, this example explicitly creates two comparator classes called **CompLastNames** and **ThenByFirstNames**, but lambda expressions could have been used instead. You might want to try this on your own. Just follow the same general approach described for the **CompDemo2** example shown earlier.

# The Collection Algorithms

The Collections Framework defines several algorithms that can be applied to collections and maps. These algorithms are defined as static methods within the **Collections** class. They are summarized in Table 20-17.

| Method | Description |
|---|---|
| static <T> boolean<br>addAll(Collection <? super T> *c*,<br>T... *elements*) | Inserts the elements specified by *elements* into the collection specified by *c*. Returns **true** if the elements were added and **false** otherwise. |
| static <T> Queue<T> asLifoQueue(Deque<T> *c*) | Returns a last-in, first-out view of *c*. |
| static <T><br>int binarySearch(List<? extends T> *list*,<br>T *value*,<br>Comparator<? super T> *c*) | Searches for *value* in *list* ordered according to *c*. Returns the position of value in *list*, or a negative value if *value* is not found. |
| static <T><br>int binarySearch(List<? extends<br>Comparable<? super T>> *list*,<br>T *value*) | Searches for *value* in *list*. The list must be sorted. Returns the position of *value* in *list*, or a negative value if *value* is not found. |
| static <E> Collection<E><br>checkedCollection(Collection<E> *c*,<br>Class<E> *t*) | Returns a run-time type-safe view of a collection. An attempt to insert an incompatible element will cause a **ClassCastException**. |
| static <E> List<E><br>checkedList(List<E> *c*, Class<E> *t*) | Returns a run-time type-safe view of a **List**. An attempt to insert an incompatible element will cause a **ClassCastException**. |
| static <K, V> Map<K, V><br>checkedMap(Map<K, V> *c*,<br>Class<K> *keyT*,<br>Class<V> *valueT*) | Returns a run-time type-safe view of a **Map**. An attempt to insert an incompatible element will cause a **ClassCastException**. |
| static <K, V> NavigableMap<K, V><br>checkedNavigableMap(<br>NavigableMap<K, V> *nm*,<br>Class<E> *keyT*,<br>Class<V> *valueT*) | Returns a run-time type-safe view of a **NavigableMap**. An attempt to insert an incompatible element will cause a **ClassCastException**. |
| static <E> NavigableSet<E><br>checkedNavigableSet(NavigableSet<E> *ns*,<br>Class<E> *t*) | Returns a run-time type-safe view of a **NavigableSet**. An attempt to insert an incompatible element will cause a **ClassCastException**. |
| static <E> Queue<E><br>checkedQueue(Queue<E> *q*,<br>Class<E> *t*) | Returns a run-time type-safe view of a **Queue**. An attempt to insert an incompatible element will cause a **ClassCastException**. |
| static <E> List<E><br>checkedSet(Set<E> *c*, Class<E> *t*) | Returns a run-time type-safe view of a **Set**. An attempt to insert an incompatible element will cause a **ClassCastException**. |
| static <K, V> SortedMap<K, V><br>checkedSortedMap(SortedMap<K, V> *c*,<br>Class<K> *keyT*,<br>Class<V> *valueT*) | Returns a run-time type-safe view of a **SortedMap**. An attempt to insert an incompatible element will cause a **ClassCastException**. |

**Table 20-17** The Algorithms Defined by **Collections**

| Method | Description |
|---|---|
| static <E> SortedSet<E> checkedSortedSet(SortedSet<E> *c*, Class<E> *t*) | Returns a run-time type-safe view of a **SortedSet**. An attempt to insert an incompatible element will cause a **ClassCastException**. |
| static <T> void copy(List<? super T> *list1*, List<? extends T> *list2*) | Copies the elements of *list2* to *list1*. |
| static boolean disjoint(Collection<?> *a*, Collection<?> *b*) | Compares the elements in *a* to elements in *b*. Returns **true** if the two collections contain no common elements (i.e., the collections contain disjoint sets of elements). Otherwise, returns **false**. |
| static <T> Enumeration<T> emptyEnumeration( ) | Returns an empty enumeration, which is an enumeration with no elements. |
| static <T> Iterator<T> emptyIterator( ) | Returns an empty iterator, which is an iterator with no elements. |
| static <T> List<T> emptyList( ) | Returns an immutable, empty **List** object of the inferred type. |
| static <T> ListIterator<T> emptyListIterator( ) | Returns an empty list iterator, which is a list iterator that has no elements. |
| static <K, V> Map<K, V> emptyMap( ) | Returns an immutable, empty **Map** object of the inferred type. |
| static <K, V> NavigableMap<K, V> emptyNavigableMap( ) | Returns an immutable, empty **NavigableMap** object of the inferred type. |
| static <E> NavigableSet<E> emptyNavigableSet( ) | Returns an immutable, empty **NavigableSet** object of the inferred type. |
| static <T> Set<T> emptySet( ) | Returns an immutable, empty **Set** object of the inferred type. |
| static <K, V> SortedMap<K, V> emptySortedMap( ) | Returns an immutable, empty **SortedMap** object of the inferred type. |
| static <E> SortedSet<E> emptySortedSet( ) | Returns an immutable, empty **SortedSet** object of the inferred type. |
| static <T> Enumeration<T> enumeration(Collection<T> *c*) | Returns an enumeration over *c*. (See "The Enumeration Interface," later in this chapter.) |
| static <T> void fill(List<? super T> *list*, T *obj*) | Assigns *obj* to each element of *list*. |
| static int frequency(Collection<?> *c*, object *obj*) | Counts the number of occurrences of *obj* in *c* and returns the result. |
| static int indexOfSubList(List<?> *list*, List<?> *subList*) | Searches *list* for the first occurrence of *subList*. Returns the index of the first match, or –1 if no match is found. |
| static int lastIndexOfSubList(List<?> *list*, List<?> *subList*) | Searches *list* for the last occurrence of *subList*. Returns the index of the last match, or –1 if no match is found. |

**Table 20-17** The Algorithms Defined by **Collections** *(continued)*

| Method | Description |
|---|---|
| static <T> ArrayList<T> list(Enumeration<T> *enum*) | Returns an **ArrayList** that contains the elements of *enum*. |
| static <T> T max(Collection<? extends T> *c*, Comparator<? super T> *comp*) | Returns the maximum element in *c* as determined by *comp*. |
| static <T extends Object & Comparable<? super T>> T max(Collection<? extends T> *c*) | Returns the maximum element in *c* as determined by natural ordering. The collection need not be sorted. |
| static <T> T min(Collection<? extends T> *c*, Comparator<? super T> *comp*) | Returns the minimum element in *c* as determined by *comp*. The collection need not be sorted. |
| static <T extends Object & Comparable<? super T>> T min(Collection<? extends T> *c*) | Returns the minimum element in *c* as determined by natural ordering. |
| static <T> List<T> nCopies(int *num*, T *obj*) | Returns *num* copies of *obj* contained in an immutable list. *num* must be greater than or equal to zero. |
| static <E> SequencedSet<E> newSequencedSetFromMap(SequencedMap<E,Boolean> *m*) | Creates and returns a sequenced set backed by the map specified by *m*, which must be empty at the time this method is called. |
| static <E> Set<E> newSetFromMap(Map<E, Boolean> *m*) | Creates and returns a set backed by the map specified by *m*, which must be empty at the time this method is called. |
| static <T> boolean replaceAll(List<T> *list*, T *old*, T *new*) | Replaces all occurrences of *old* with *new* in *list*. Returns **true** if at least one replacement occurred. Returns **false** otherwise. |
| static void reverse(List<T> *list*) | Reverses the sequence in *list*. |
| static <T> Comparator<T> reverseOrder(Comparator<T> *comp*) | Returns a reverse comparator based on the one passed in *comp*. That is, the returned comparator reverses the outcome of a comparison that uses *comp*. |
| static <T> Comparator<T> reverseOrder( ) | Returns a reverse comparator, which is a comparator that reverses the outcome of a comparison between two elements. |
| static void rotate(List<T> *list*, int *n*) | Rotates *list* by *n* places to the right. To rotate left, use a negative value for *n*. |
| static void shuffle(List<T> *list*, Random *r*) | Shuffles (i.e., randomizes) the elements in *list* by using *r* as a source of random numbers. |
| static void shuffle(List<?> list, RandomGenerator *rnd*) | Shuffles the elements in the *list* into a random order using the randomizer specified by *rnd*. |
| static void shuffle(List<T> *list*) | Shuffles (i.e., randomizes) the elements in *list*. |
| static <T> Set<T> singleton(T *obj*) | Returns *obj* as an immutable set. This is an easy way to convert a single object into a set. |

**Table 20-17** The Algorithms Defined by **Collections** *(continued)*

| Method | Description |
|---|---|
| static <T> List<T> singletonList(T *obj*) | Returns *obj* as an immutable list. This is an easy way to convert a single object into a list. |
| static <K, V> Map<K, V> singletonMap(K *k*, V *v*) | Returns the key/value pair *k/v* as an immutable map. This is an easy way to convert a single key/value pair into a map. |
| static <T> void sort(List<T> *list*, Comparator<? super T> *comp*) | Sorts the elements of *list* as determined by *comp*. |
| static <T extends Comparable<? super T>> void sort(List<T> *list*) | Sorts the elements of *list* as determined by their natural ordering. |
| static void swap(List<?> *list*, int *idx1*, int *idx2*) | Exchanges the elements in *list* at the indices specified by *idx1* and *idx2*. |
| static <T> Collection<T> synchronizedCollection(Collection<T> *c*) | Returns a thread-safe collection backed by *c*. |
| static <T> List<T> synchronizedList(List<T> *list*) | Returns a thread-safe list backed by *list*. |
| static <K, V> Map<K, V> synchronizedMap(Map<K, V> *m*) | Returns a thread-safe map backed by *m*. |
| static <K, V> NavigableMap<K, V> synchronizedNavigableMap( NavigableMap<K, V> *nm*) | Returns a synchronized navigable map backed by *nm*. |
| static <T> NavigableSet<T> synchronizedNavigableSet( NavigableSet<T> *ns*) | Returns a synchronized navigable set backed by *ns*. |
| static <T> Set<T> synchronizedSet(Set<T> *s*) | Returns a thread-safe set backed by *s*. |
| static <K, V> SortedMap<K, V> synchronizedSortedMap(SortedMap<K, V> *sm*) | Returns a thread-safe sorted map backed by *sm*. |
| static <T> SortedSet<T> synchronizedSortedSet(SortedSet<T> *ss*) | Returns a thread-safe sorted set backed by *ss*. |
| static <T> Collection<T> unmodifiableCollection( Collection<? extends T> *c*) | Returns an unmodifiable collection backed by *c*. |
| static <T> List<T> unmodifiableList(List<? extends T> *list*) | Returns an unmodifiable list backed by *list*. |
| static <K, V> Map<K, V> unmodifiableMap(Map<? extends K, ? extends V> *m*) | Returns an unmodifiable map backed by *m*. |
| static <K, V> NavigableMap<K, V> unmodifiableNavigableMap( NavigableMap<K, ? extends V> *nm*) | Returns an unmodifiable navigable map backed by *nm*. |

**Table 20-17** The Algorithms Defined by **Collections** *(continued)*

| Method | Description |
|---|---|
| static <T> NavigableSet<T><br>unmodifiableNavigableSet(<br>NavigableSet<T> *ns*) | Returns an unmodifiable navigable set backed by *ns*. |
| static <T> SequencedCollection<T><br>unmodifiableSequencedCollection(<br>SequencedCollection<? extends T> *c*) | Returns an unmodifiable sequenced collection backed by *c*. |
| static <K, V> SequencedMap<K,V><br>unmodifiableSequencedMap(<br>SequencedMap<? extends K,? extends V> *m*) | Returns an unmodifiable sequenced map backed by *m*. |
| static <T> SequencedSet<T><br>unmodifiableSequencedSet(<br>SequencedSet<? extends T> *s*) | Returns an unmodifiable sequenced set backed by *s*. |
| static <T> Set<T><br>unmodifiableSet(Set<? extends T> *s*) | Returns an unmodifiable set backed by *s*. |
| static <K, V> SortedMap<K, V><br>unmodifiableSortedMap(SortedMap<K,<br>? extends V> *sm*) | Returns an unmodifiable sorted map backed by *sm*. |
| static <T> SortedSet<T><br>unmodifiableSortedSet(SortedSet<T> *ss*) | Returns an unmodifiable sorted set backed by *ss*. |

**Table 20-17** The Algorithms Defined by **Collections** *(continued)*

Several of the methods can throw a **ClassCastException**, which occurs when an attempt is made to compare incompatible types, or an **UnsupportedOperationException**, which occurs when an attempt is made to modify an unmodifiable collection. Other exceptions are possible, depending on the method.

One thing to pay special attention to is the set of **checked** methods, such as **checkedCollection( )**, which returns what the API documentation refers to as a "dynamically typesafe view" of a collection. This view is a reference to the collection that monitors insertions into the collection for type compatibility at run time. An attempt to insert an incompatible element will cause a **ClassCastException**. Using such a view is especially helpful during debugging because it ensures that the collection always contains valid elements. Related methods include **checkedSet( )**, **checkedList( )**, **checkedMap( )**, and so on. They obtain a type-safe view for the indicated collection.

Notice that several methods, such as **synchronizedList( )** and **synchronizedSet( )**, are used to obtain synchronized (*thread-safe*) copies of the various collections. As a general rule, the standard collections implementations are not synchronized. You must use the synchronization algorithms to provide synchronization. One other point: iterators to synchronized collections must be used within **synchronized** blocks.

The set of methods that begins with **unmodifiable** returns views of the various collections that cannot be modified. These will be useful when you want to grant some process read—but not write—capabilities on a collection.

**Collections** defines three static variables: **EMPTY_SET, EMPTY_LIST,** and **EMPTY_MAP**. All are immutable.

The following program demonstrates some of the algorithms. It creates and initializes a linked list. The **reverseOrder( )** method returns a **Comparator** that reverses the comparison of **Integer** objects. The list elements are sorted according to this comparator and then are displayed. Next, the list is randomized by calling **shuffle( )**, and then its minimum and maximum values are displayed.

```
// Demonstrate various algorithms.
import java.util.*;

class AlgorithmsDemo {
  public static void main(String[] args) {

    // Create and initialize linked list.
    LinkedList<Integer> ll = new LinkedList<Integer>();
    ll.add(-8);
    ll.add(20);
    ll.add(-20);
    ll.add(8);

    // Create a reverse order comparator.
    Comparator<Integer> r = Collections.reverseOrder();

    // Sort list by using the comparator.
    Collections.sort(ll, r);

    System.out.print("List sorted in reverse: ");
    for(int i : ll)
      System.out.print(i+ " ");

    System.out.println();

    // Shuffle list.
    Collections.shuffle(ll);

    // Display randomized list.
    System.out.print("List shuffled: ");
    for(int i : ll)
      System.out.print(i + " ");

    System.out.println();
    System.out.println("Minimum: " + Collections.min(ll));
    System.out.println("Maximum: " + Collections.max(ll));
  }
}
```

Output from this program is shown here:

```
List sorted in reverse: 20 8 -8 -20
List shuffled: 20 -20 8 -8
Minimum: -20
Maximum: 20
```

Notice that **min( )** and **max( )** operate on the list after it has been shuffled. Neither requires a sorted list for its operation.

# Arrays

The **Arrays** class provides various static utility methods that are useful when working with arrays. These methods help bridge the gap between collections and arrays. Each method defined by **Arrays** is examined in this section.

The **asList( )** method returns a **List** that is backed by a specified array. In other words, both the list and the array refer to the same location. It has the following signature:

static <T> List asList(T... *array*)

Here, *array* is the array that contains the data.

The **binarySearch( )** method uses a binary search to find a specified value. This method must be applied to sorted arrays. Here are some of its forms. (Additional forms let you search a subrange):

static int binarySearch(byte[ ] *array*, byte *value*)
static int binarySearch(char[ ] *array*, char *value*)
static int binarySearch(double[ ] *array*, double *value*)
static int binarySearch(float[ ] *array*, float *value*)
static int binarySearch(int[ ] *array*, int *value*)
static int binarySearch(long[ ] *array*, long *value*)
static int binarySearch(short[ ] *array*, short *value*)
static int binarySearch(Object[ ] *array*, Object *value*)
static <T> int binarySearch(T[ ] *array*, T *value*, Comparator<? super T> *c*)

Here, *array* is the array to be searched, and *value* is the value to be located. The last two forms throw a **ClassCastException** if *array* contains elements that cannot be compared (for example, **Double** and **StringBuffer**) or if *value* is not compatible with the types in *array*. In the last form, the **Comparator** *c* is used to determine the order of the elements in *array*. In all cases, if *value* exists in *array*, the index of the element is returned. Otherwise, a negative value is returned.

The **copyOf( )** method returns a copy of an array and has the following forms:

static boolean[ ] copyOf(boolean[ ] *source*, int *len*)
static byte[ ] copyOf(byte[ ] *source*, int *len*)
static char[ ] copyOf(char[ ] *source*, int *len*)
static double[ ] copyOf(double[ ] *source*, int *len*)
static float[ ] copyOf(float[ ] *source*, int *len*)
static int[ ] copyOf(int[ ] *source*, int *len*)
static long[ ] copyOf(long[ ] *source*, int *len*)
static short[ ] copyOf(short[ ] *source*, int *len*)
static <T> T[ ] copyOf(T[ ] *source*, int *len*)
static <T,U> T[ ] copyOf(U[ ] *source*, int *len*, Class<? extends T[ ]> *resultT*)

The original array is specified by *source*, and the length of the copy is specified by *len*. If the copy is longer than *source*, then the copy is padded with zeros (for numeric arrays), **null**s (for object arrays), or **false** (for boolean arrays). If the copy is shorter than *source*, then the copy is truncated. In the last form, the type of *resultT* becomes the type of the array returned. If *len* is negative, a **NegativeArraySizeException** is thrown. If *source* is **null**, a **NullPointerException** is thrown. If *resultT* is incompatible with the type of *source*, an **ArrayStoreException** is thrown.

The **copyOfRange( )** method returns a copy of a range within an array and has the following forms:

static boolean[ ] copyOfRange(boolean[ ] *source*, int *start*, int *end*)
static byte[ ] copyOfRange(byte[ ] *source*, int *start*, int *end*)
static char[ ] copyOfRange(char[ ] *source*, int *start*, int *end*)
static double[ ] copyOfRange(double[ ] *source*, int *start*, int *end*)
static float[ ] copyOfRange(float[ ] *source*, int *start*, int *end*)
static int[ ] copyOfRange(int[ ] *source*, int *start*, int *end*)
static long[ ] copyOfRange(long[ ] *source*, int *start*, int *end*)
static short[ ] copyOfRange(short[ ] *source*, int *start*, int *end*)
static <T> T[ ] copyOfRange(T[ ] *source*, int *start*, int *end*)
static <T,U> T[ ] copyOfRange(U[ ] *source*, int *start*, int *end*,
Class<? extends T[ ]> *resultT*)

The original array is specified by *source*. The range to copy is specified by the indices passed via *start* and *end*. The range runs from *start* to *end* – 1. If the range is longer than *source*, then the copy is padded with zeros (for numeric arrays), **null**s (for object arrays), or **false** (for boolean arrays). In the last form, the type of *resultT* becomes the type of the array returned. If *start* is negative or greater than the length of *source*, an **ArrayIndexOutOfBoundsException** is thrown. If *start* is greater than *end*, an **IllegalArgumentException** is thrown. If *source* is **null**, a **NullPointerException** is thrown. If *resultT* is incompatible with the type of *source*, an **ArrayStoreException** is thrown.

The **equals( )** method returns **true** if two arrays are equivalent. Otherwise, it returns **false**. Here are a number of its forms. Several more versions are available that let you specify a range, a generic array type, and/or a comparator.

static boolean equals(boolean[ ] *array1*, boolean[ ] *array2*)
static boolean equals(byte[ ] *array1*, byte[ ] *array2*)
static boolean equals(char[ ] *array1*, char[ ] *array2*)
static boolean equals(double[ ] *array1*, double[ ] *array2*)
static boolean equals(float[ ] *array1*, float[ ] *array2*)
static boolean equals(int[ ] *array1*, int[ ] *array2*)
static boolean equals(long[ ] *array1*, long[ ] *array2*)
static boolean equals(short[ ] *array1*, short[ ] *array2*)
static boolean equals(Object[ ] *array1*, Object[ ] *array2*)

Here, *array1* and *array2* are the two arrays that are compared for equality.

The **deepEquals( )** method can be used to determine if two arrays, which might contain nested arrays, are equal. It has this declaration:

static boolean deepEquals(Object[ ] *a*, Object[ ] *b*)

It returns **true** if the arrays passed in *a* and *b* contain the same elements. If *a* and *b* contain nested arrays, then the contents of those nested arrays are also checked. It returns **false** if the arrays, or any nested arrays, differ.

The **fill( )** method assigns a value to all elements in an array. In other words, it fills an array with a specified value. The **fill( )** method has two versions. The first version, which has the following forms, fills an entire array:

static void fill(boolean[ ] *array*, boolean *value*)
static void fill(byte[ ] *array*, byte *value*)
static void fill(char[ ] *array*, char *value*)
static void fill(double[ ] *array*, double *value*)
static void fill(float[ ] *array*, float *value*)
static void fill(int[ ] *array*, int *value*)
static void fill(long[ ] *array*, long *value*)
static void fill(short[ ] *array*, short *value*)
static void fill(Object[ ] *array*, Object *value*)

Here, *value* is assigned to all elements in *array*. The second version of the **fill( )** method assigns a value to a subset of an array.

The **sort( )** method sorts an array so that it is arranged in ascending order. The **sort( )** method has two versions. The first version, shown here, sorts the entire array:

static void sort(byte[ ] *array*)
static void sort(char[ ] *array*)
static void sort(double[ ] *array*)
static void sort(float[ ] *array*)
static void sort(int[ ] *array*)
static void sort(long[ ] *array*)
static void sort(short[ ] *array*)
static void sort(Object[ ] *array*)
static <T> void sort(T[ ] *array*, Comparator<? super T> *c*)

Here, *array* is the array to be sorted. In the last form, *c* is a **Comparator** that is used to order the elements of *array*. The last two forms can throw a **ClassCastException** if elements of the array being sorted are not comparable. The second version of **sort( )** enables you to specify a range within an array that you want to sort.

One quite powerful method in **Arrays** is **parallelSort( )** because it sorts, into ascending order, portions of an array in parallel and then merges the results. This approach can greatly speed up sorting times. Like **sort( )**, there are two basic types of **parallelSort( )**, each with several overloads. The first type sorts the entire array. It is shown here:

static void parallelSort(byte[ ] *array*)
static void parallelSort(char[ ] *array*)
static void parallelSort(double[ ] *array*)
static void parallelSort(float[ ] *array*)
static void parallelSort(int[ ] *array*)
static void parallelSort(long[ ] *array*)
static void parallelSort(short[ ] *array*)
static <T extends Comparable<? super T>> void parallelSort(T[ ] *array*)
static <T> void parallelSort(T[ ] *array*, Comparator<? super T> *c*)

Here, *array* is the array to be sorted. In the last form, *c* is a comparator that is used to order the elements in the array. The last two forms can throw a **ClassCastException** if the elements of the array being sorted are not comparable. The second version of **parallelSort( )** enables you to specify a range within the array that you want to sort.

**Arrays** supports spliterators by including the **spliterator( )** method. It has two basic forms. The first type returns a spliterator to an entire array. It is shown here:

static Spliterator.OfDouble spliterator(double[ ] *array*)
static Spliterator.OfInt spliterator(int[ ] *array*)
static Spliterator.OfLong spliterator(long[ ] *array*)
static <T> Spliterator spliterator(T[ ] *array*)

Here, *array* is the array that the spliterator will cycle through. The second version of **spliterator( )** enables you to specify a range to iterate within the array.

**Arrays** supports the **Stream** interface by including the **stream( )** method. It has two forms. The first is shown here:

static DoubleStream stream(double[ ] *array*)
static IntStream stream(int[ ] *array*)
static LongStream stream(long[ ] *array*)
static <T> Stream stream(T[ ] *array*)

Here, *array* is the array to which the stream will refer. The second version of **stream( )** enables you to specify a range within the array.

Another two methods are related: **setAll( )** and **parallelSetAll( )**. Both assign values to all of the elements, but **parallelSetAll( )** works in parallel. Here is an example of each:

static void setAll(double[ ] *array*,
                IntToDoubleFunction<? extends T> *genVal*)

static void parallelSetAll(double[ ] *array*,
                IntToDoubleFunction<? extends T> *genVal*)

Several overloads exist for each of these that handle types **int**, **long**, and generic.

One of the more intriguing methods defined by **Arrays** is called **parallelPrefix( )**, and it modifies an array so that each element contains the cumulative result of an operation applied to all previous elements. For example, if the operation is multiplication, then on return, the array elements will contain the values associated with the running product of the original values. It has several overloads. Here is one example:

static void parallelPrefix(double[ ] *array*, DoubleBinaryOperator *func*)

Here, *array* is the array being acted upon, and *func* specifies the operation applied. (**DoubleBinaryOperator** is a functional interface defined in **java.util.function**.) Many other versions are provided, including those that operate on types **int**, **long**, and generic, and those that let you specify a range within the array on which to operate.

JDK 9 added three comparison methods to **Arrays**. They are **compare( )**, **compareUnsigned( )**, and **mismatch( )**. Each has several overloads, and each has versions that let you define a range to compare. Here is a brief description of each. The **compare( )** method compares two arrays. It returns zero if they are the same, a positive value if the first array is greater than the second, and negative if the first array is less than the second.

To perform an unsigned comparison of two arrays that hold integer values, use **compareUnsigned( )**. To find the location of the first mismatch between two arrays, use **mismatch( )**. It returns the index of the mismatch, or –1 if the arrays are equivalent.

**Arrays** also provides **toString( )** and **hashCode( )** for the various types of arrays. In addition, **deepToString( )** and **deepHashCode( )** are provided, which operate effectively on arrays that contain nested arrays.

The following program illustrates how to use some of the methods of the **Arrays** class:

```
// Demonstrate Arrays
import java.util.*;

class ArraysDemo {
  public static void main(String[] args) {

    // Allocate and initialize array.
    int[] array = new int[10];
    for(int i = 0; i < 10; i++)
      array[i] = -3 * i;

    // Display, sort, and display the array.
    System.out.print("Original contents: ");
    display(array);
    Arrays.sort(array);
    System.out.print("Sorted: ");
    display(array);

    // Fill and display the array.
    Arrays.fill(array, 2, 6, -1);
    System.out.print("After fill(): ");
    display(array);

    // Sort and display the array.
    Arrays.sort(array);
    System.out.print("After sorting again: ");
    display(array);

    // Binary search for -9.
    System.out.print("The value -9 is at location ");
    int index =
      Arrays.binarySearch(array, -9);

    System.out.println(index);
  }

  static void display(int[] array) {
    for(int i: array)
      System.out.print(i + " ");

    System.out.println();
  }
}
```

The following is the output from this program:

```
Original contents: 0 -3 -6 -9 -12 -15 -18 -21 -24 -27
Sorted: -27 -24 -21 -18 -15 -12 -9 -6 -3 0
After fill(): -27 -24 -1 -1 -1 -1 -9 -6 -3 0
After sorting again: -27 -24 -9 -6 -3 -1 -1 -1 -1 0
The value -9 is at location 2
```

# The Legacy Classes and Interfaces

As explained at the start of this chapter, early versions of **java.util** did not include the Collections Framework. Instead, it defined several classes and an interface that provided an ad hoc method of storing objects. When collections were added (by J2SE 1.2), several of the original classes were reengineered to support the collection interfaces. Thus, they are now technically part of the Collections Framework. However, where a modern collection duplicates the functionality of a legacy class, you will usually want to use the newer collection class.

One other point: none of the modern collection classes described in this chapter are synchronized, but all the legacy classes are synchronized. This distinction may be important in some situations. Of course, you can easily synchronize collections by using one of the algorithms provided by **Collections**.

The legacy classes defined by **java.util** are shown here:

| Dictionary | Hashtable | Properties | Stack | Vector |
|---|---|---|---|---|

There is one legacy interface called **Enumeration**. The following sections examine **Enumeration** and each of the legacy classes, in turn.

## The Enumeration Interface

The **Enumeration** interface defines the methods by which you can *enumerate* (obtain one at a time) the elements in a collection of objects. This legacy interface has been superseded by **Iterator**. Although not deprecated, **Enumeration** is considered obsolete for new code. However, it is used by several methods defined by the legacy classes (such as **Vector** and **Properties**) and is used by several other API classes. It was retrofitted for generics by JDK 5. It has this declaration:

interface Enumeration<E>

Here, **E** specifies the type of element being enumerated.

**Enumeration** specifies the following two abstract methods:

boolean hasMoreElements( )
E nextElement( )

When implemented, **hasMoreElements( )** must return **true** while there are still more elements to extract, and **false** when all the elements have been enumerated. **nextElement( )**

returns the next object in the enumeration. That is, each call to **nextElement( )** obtains the next object in the enumeration. It throws **NoSuchElementException** when the enumeration is complete.

JDK 9 added a default method to **Enumeration** called **asIterator( )**. It is shown here:

default Iterator<E> asIterator( )

It returns an iterator to the elements in the enumeration. As such, it provides an easy way to convert an old-style **Enumeration** into a modern **Iterator**. Furthermore, if a portion of the elements in the enumeration have already been read prior to calling **asIterator( )**, the returned iterator accesses only the remaining elements.

## Vector

**Vector** implements a dynamic array. It is similar to **ArrayList**, but with two differences: **Vector** is synchronized, and it contains many legacy methods that duplicate the functionality of methods defined by the Collections Framework. With the advent of collections, **Vector** was reengineered to extend **AbstractList** and to implement the **List** interface. With the release of JDK 5, it was retrofitted for generics and reengineered to implement **Iterable**. This means that **Vector** is fully compatible with collections, and a **Vector** can have its contents iterated by the enhanced **for** loop.

**Vector** is declared like this:

class Vector<E>

Here, **E** specifies the type of element that will be stored.

Here are the **Vector** constructors:

Vector( )
Vector(int *size*)
Vector(int *size*, int *incr*)
Vector(Collection<? extends E> *c*)

The first form creates a default vector, which has an initial size of 10. The second form creates a vector whose initial capacity is specified by *size*. The third form creates a vector whose initial capacity is specified by *size* and whose increment is specified by *incr*. The increment specifies the number of elements to allocate each time that a vector is resized upward. The fourth form creates a vector that contains the elements of collection *c*.

All vectors start with an initial capacity. After this initial capacity is reached, the next time that you attempt to store an object in the vector, the vector automatically allocates space for that object plus extra room for additional objects. By allocating more than just the required memory, the vector reduces the number of allocations that must take place as the vector grows. This reduction is important, because allocations are costly in terms of time. The amount of extra space allocated during each reallocation is determined by the increment that you specify when you create the vector. If you don't specify an increment, the vector's size is doubled by each allocation cycle.

**Vector** defines these protected data members:

int capacityIncrement;
int elementCount;
Object[ ] elementData;

The increment value is stored in **capacityIncrement**. The number of elements currently in the vector is stored in **elementCount**. The array that holds the vector is stored in **elementData**.

In addition to the collections methods specified by **List**, **Vector** defines several legacy methods, which are summarized in Table 20-18.



| Method | Description |
|---|---|
| void addElement(E *element*) | The object specified by *element* is added to the vector. |
| int capacity( ) | Returns the capacity of the vector. |
| Object clone( ) | Returns a duplicate of the invoking vector. |
| boolean contains(Object *element*) | Returns **true** if *element* is contained by the vector, and returns **false** if it is not. |
| void copyInto(Object[ ] *array*) | The elements contained in the invoking vector are copied into the array specified by *array*. |
| E elementAt(int *index*) | Returns the element at the location specified by *index*. |
| Enumeration<E> elements( ) | Returns an enumeration of the elements in the vector. |
| void ensureCapacity(int *size*) | Sets the minimum capacity of the vector to *size*. |
| E firstElement( ) | Returns the first element in the vector. |
| int indexOf(Object *element*) | Returns the index of the first occurrence of *element*. If the object is not in the vector, –1 is returned. |
| int indexOf(Object *element*, int *start*) | Returns the index of the first occurrence of *element* at or after *start*. If the object is not in that portion of the vector, –1 is returned. |
| void insertElementAt(E *element*, int *index*) | Adds *element* to the vector at the location specified by *index*. |
| boolean isEmpty( ) | Returns **true** if the vector is empty, and returns **false** if it contains one or more elements. |
| E lastElement( ) | Returns the last element in the vector. |
| int lastIndexOf(Object *element*) | Returns the index of the last occurrence of *element*. If the object is not in the vector, –1 is returned. |
| int lastIndexOf(Object *element*, int *start*) | Returns the index of the last occurrence of *element* before *start*. If the object is not in that portion of the vector, –1 is returned. |
| void removeAllElements( ) | Empties the vector. After this method executes, the size of the vector is zero. |

**Table 20-18** The Legacy Methods Defined by **Vector**

| Method | Description |
|---|---|
| boolean removeElement(Object *element*) | Removes *element* from the vector. If more than one instance of the specified object exists in the vector, then it is the first one that is removed. Returns **true** if successful and **false** if the object is not found. |
| void removeElementAt(int *index*) | Removes the element at the location specified by *index*. |
| void setElementAt(E *element*, int *index*) | The location specified by *index* is assigned *element*. |
| void setSize(int *size*) | Sets the number of elements in the vector to *size*. If the new size is less than the old size, elements are lost. If the new size is larger than the old size, **null** elements are added. |
| int size( ) | Returns the number of elements currently in the vector. |
| String toString( ) | Returns the string equivalent of the vector. |
| void trimToSize( ) | Sets the vector's capacity equal to the number of elements that it currently holds. |

**Table 20-18** The Legacy Methods Defined by **Vector** *(continued)*

Because **Vector** implements **List**, you can use a vector just like you use an **ArrayList** instance. You can also manipulate one using its legacy methods. For example, after you instantiate a **Vector**, you can add an element to it by calling **addElement( )**. To obtain the element at a specific location, call **elementAt( )**. To obtain the first element in the vector, call **firstElement( )**. To retrieve the last element, call **lastElement( )**. You can obtain the index of an element by using **indexOf( )** and **lastIndexOf( )**. To remove an element, call **removeElement( )** or **removeElementAt( )**.

The following program uses a vector to store various types of numeric objects. It demonstrates several of the legacy methods defined by **Vector**. It also demonstrates the **Enumeration** interface.

```
// Demonstrate various Vector operations.
import java.util.*;

class VectorDemo {
  public static void main(String[] args) {

    // initial size is 3, increment is 2
    Vector<Integer> v = new Vector<Integer>(3, 2);

    System.out.println("Initial size: " + v.size());
    System.out.println("Initial capacity: " +
                       v.capacity());

    v.addElement(1);
    v.addElement(2);
    v.addElement(3);
    v.addElement(4);
```

```
    System.out.println("Capacity after four additions: " +
                       v.capacity());

    v.addElement(5);
    System.out.println("Current capacity: " +
                       v.capacity());

    v.addElement(6);
    v.addElement(7);

    System.out.println("Current capacity: " +
                       v.capacity());

    v.addElement(9);
    v.addElement(10);

    System.out.println("Current capacity: " +
                       v.capacity());

    v.addElement(11);
    v.addElement(12);

    System.out.println("First element: " + v.firstElement());
    System.out.println("Last element: " + v.lastElement());

    if(v.contains(3))
      System.out.println("Vector contains 3.");

    // Enumerate the elements in the vector.
    Enumeration<Integer> vEnum = v.elements();

    System.out.println("\nElements in vector:");
    while(vEnum.hasMoreElements())
      System.out.print(vEnum.nextElement() + " ");
    System.out.println();
  }
}
```

The output from this program is shown here:

```
Initial size: 0
Initial capacity: 3
Capacity after four additions: 5
Current capacity: 5
Current capacity: 7
Current capacity: 9
First element: 1
Last element: 12
Vector contains 3.

Elements in vector:
1 2 3 4 5 6 7 9 10 11 12
```

Part II

Instead of relying on an enumeration to cycle through the objects (as the preceding program does), you can use an iterator. For example, the following iterator-based code can be substituted into the program:

```
// Use an iterator to display contents.
Iterator<Integer> vItr = v.iterator();

System.out.println("\nElements in vector:");
while(vItr.hasNext())
  System.out.print(vItr.next() + " ");
System.out.println();
```

You can also use a for-each **for** loop to cycle through a **Vector**, as the following version of the preceding code shows:

```
// Use an enhanced for loop to display contents
System.out.println("\nElements in vector:");
for(int i : v)
  System.out.print(i + " ");

System.out.println();
```

Because the **Enumeration** interface is not recommended for new code, you will usually use an iterator or a for-each **for** loop to enumerate the contents of a vector. Of course, legacy code will employ **Enumeration**. Fortunately, enumerations and iterators work in nearly the same manner.

## Stack

**Stack** is a subclass of **Vector** that implements a standard last-in, first-out stack. **Stack** only defines the default constructor, which creates an empty stack. With the release of JDK 5, **Stack** was retrofitted for generics and is declared as shown here:

class Stack<E>

Here, **E** specifies the type of element stored in the stack.

**Stack** includes all the methods defined by **Vector** and adds several of its own, shown in Table 20-19.

| Method | Description |
|---|---|
| boolean empty( ) | Returns **true** if the stack is empty, and returns **false** if the stack contains elements. |
| E peek( ) | Returns the element on the top of the stack, but does not remove it. |
| E pop( ) | Returns the element on the top of the stack, removing it in the process. |
| E push(E *element*) | Pushes *element* onto the stack. *element* is also returned. |
| int search(Object *element*) | Searches for *element* in the stack. If found, its offset from the top of the stack is returned. Otherwise, –1 is returned. |

**Table 20-19** The Methods Defined by **Stack**

To put an object on the top of the stack, call **push( )**. To remove and return the top element, call **pop( )**. You can use **peek( )** to return, but not remove, the top object. An **EmptyStackException** is thrown if you call **pop( )** or **peek( )** when the invoking stack is empty. The **empty( )** method returns **true** if nothing is on the stack. The **search( )** method determines whether an object exists on the stack and returns the number of pops that are required to bring it to the top of the stack. Here is an example that creates a stack, pushes several **Integer** objects onto it, and then pops them off again:

```
// Demonstrate the Stack class.
import java.util.*;

class StackDemo {
  static void showpush(Stack<Integer> st, int a) {
    st.push(a);
    System.out.println("push(" + a + ")");
    System.out.println("stack: " + st);
  }

  static void showpop(Stack<Integer> st) {
    System.out.print("pop -> ");
    Integer a = st.pop();
    System.out.println(a);
    System.out.println("stack: " + st);
  }

  public static void main(String[] args) {
    Stack<Integer> st = new Stack<Integer>();

    System.out.println("stack: " + st);
    showpush(st, 42);
    showpush(st, 66);
    showpush(st, 99);
    showpop(st);
    showpop(st);
    showpop(st);

    try {
      showpop(st);
    } catch (EmptyStackException e) {
      System.out.println("empty stack");
    }
  }
}
```

The following is the output produced by the program; notice how the exception handler for **EmptyStackException** is used so that you can gracefully handle a stack underflow:

```
stack: [ ]
push(42)
stack: [42]
push(66)
stack: [42, 66]
push(99)
stack: [42, 66, 99]
```

Part II

```
pop -> 99
stack: [42, 66]
pop -> 66
stack: [42]
pop -> 42
stack: [ ]
pop -> empty stack
```

One other point: although **Stack** is not deprecated, **ArrayDeque** is a better choice.

## Dictionary

**Dictionary** is an abstract class that represents a key/value storage repository and operates much like **Map**. Given a key and value, you can store the value in a **Dictionary** object. Once the value is stored, you can retrieve it by using its key. Thus, like a map, a dictionary can be thought of as a list of key/value pairs. Although not currently deprecated, **Dictionary** is classified as obsolete, because it is fully superseded by **Map**. However, **Dictionary** is still in use and thus is discussed here.

With the advent of JDK 5, **Dictionary** was made generic. It is declared as shown here:

class Dictionary<K, V>

Here, **K** specifies the type of keys, and **V** specifies the type of values. The abstract methods defined by **Dictionary** are listed in Table 20-20.

To add a key and a value, use the **put( )** method. Use **get( )** to retrieve the value of a given key. The keys and values can each be returned as an **Enumeration** by the **keys( )** and **elements( )** methods, respectively. The **size( )** method returns the number of key/value pairs stored in a dictionary, and **isEmpty( )** returns **true** when the dictionary is empty. You can use the **remove( )** method to delete a key/value pair.

**REMEMBER** The **Dictionary** class is obsolete. You should implement the **Map** interface to obtain key/value storage functionality.

| Method | Purpose |
|---|---|
| Enumeration<V> elements( ) | Returns an enumeration of the values contained in the dictionary. |
| V get(Object *key*) | Returns the object that contains the value associated with *key*. If *key* is not in the dictionary, a **null** object is returned. |
| boolean isEmpty( ) | Returns **true** if the dictionary is empty, and returns **false** if it contains at least one key. |
| Enumeration<K> keys( ) | Returns an enumeration of the keys contained in the dictionary. |
| V put(K *key*, V *value*) | Inserts a key and its value into the dictionary. Returns **null** if *key* is not already in the dictionary; returns the previous value associated with *key* if *key* is already in the dictionary. |
| V remove(Object *key*) | Removes *key* and its value. Returns the value associated with *key*. If *key* is not in the dictionary, a **null** is returned. |
| int size( ) | Returns the number of entries in the dictionary. |

**Table 20-20** The Abstract Methods Defined by **Dictionary**

## Hashtable

**Hashtable** was part of the original **java.util** and is a concrete implementation of a **Dictionary**. However, with the advent of collections, **Hashtable** was reengineered to also implement the **Map** interface. Thus, **Hashtable** is integrated into the Collections Framework. It is similar to **HashMap**, but is synchronized.

Like **HashMap**, **Hashtable** stores key/value pairs in a hash table. However, neither keys nor values can be **null**. When using a **Hashtable**, you specify an object that is used as a key, and the value that you want linked to that key. The key is then hashed, and the resulting hash code is used as the index at which the value is stored within the table.

**Hashtable** was made generic by JDK 5. It is declared like this:

class Hashtable<K, V>

Here, **K** specifies the type of keys, and **V** specifies the type of values.

A hash table can only store keys that override the **hashCode( )** and **equals( )** methods that are defined by **Object**. The **hashCode( )** method must compute and return the hash code for the object. Of course, **equals( )** compares two objects. Fortunately, many of Java's built-in classes already implement the **hashCode( )** method. For example, a common type of **Hashtable** uses a **String** object as the key. **String** implements both **hashCode( )** and **equals( )**.

The **Hashtable** constructors are shown here:

Hashtable( )
Hashtable(int *size*)
Hashtable(int *size*, float *fillRatio*)
Hashtable(Map<? extends K, ? extends V> *m*)

The first version is the default constructor. The second version creates a hash table that has an initial size specified by *size*. (The default size is 11.) The third version creates a hash table that has an initial size specified by *size* and a fill ratio specified by *fillRatio*. This ratio (also referred to as a *load factor*) must be between 0.0 and 1.0, and it determines how full the hash table can be before it is resized upward. Specifically, when the number of elements is greater than the capacity of the hash table multiplied by its fill ratio, the hash table is expanded. If you do not specify a fill ratio, then 0.75 is used. Finally, the fourth version creates a hash table that is initialized with the elements in *m*. The default load factor of 0.75 is used.

In addition to the methods defined by the **Map** interface, which **Hashtable** now implements, **Hashtable** defines the legacy methods listed in Table 20-21. Several methods throw **NullPointerException** if an attempt is made to use a **null** key or value.

The following example reworks the bank account program, shown earlier, so that it uses a **Hashtable** to store the names of bank depositors and their current balances:

```
// Demonstrate a Hashtable.
import java.util.*;

class HTDemo {
  public static void main(String[] args) {
    Hashtable<String, Double> balance =
      new Hashtable<String, Double>();
```

| Method | Description |
|---|---|
| void clear( ) | Resets and empties the hash table. |
| Object clone( ) | Returns a duplicate of the invoking object. |
| boolean contains(Object *value*) | Returns **true** if some value equal to *value* exists within the hash table. Returns **false** if the value isn't found. |
| boolean containsKey(Object *key*) | Returns **true** if some key equal to *key* exists within the hash table. Returns **false** if the key isn't found. |
| boolean containsValue(Object *value*) | Returns **true** if some value equal to *value* exists within the hash table. Returns **false** if the value isn't found. |
| Enumeration<V> elements( ) | Returns an enumeration of the values contained in the hash table. |
| V get(Object *key*) | Returns the object that contains the value associated with *key*. If *key* is not in the hash table, a **null** object is returned. |
| boolean isEmpty( ) | Returns **true** if the hash table is empty; returns **false** if it contains at least one key. |
| Enumeration<K> keys( ) | Returns an enumeration of the keys contained in the hash table. |
| V put(K *key*, V *value*) | Inserts a key and a value into the hash table. Returns **null** if *key* isn't already in the hash table; returns the previous value associated with *key* if *key* is already in the hash table. |
| void rehash( ) | Increases the size of the hash table and rehashes all of its keys. |
| V remove(Object *key*) | Removes *key* and its value. Returns the value associated with *key*. If *key* is not in the hash table, a **null** object is returned. |
| int size( ) | Returns the number of entries in the hash table. |
| String toString( ) | Returns the string equivalent of a hash table. |

**Table 20-21** The Legacy Methods Defined by **Hashtable**

```
Enumeration<String> names;
String str;
double bal;

balance.put("John Doe", 3434.34);
balance.put("Tom Smith", 123.22);
balance.put("Jane Baker", 1378.00);
balance.put("Tod Hall", 99.22);
balance.put("Ralph Smith", -19.08);

// Show all balances in hashtable.
names = balance.keys();
while(names.hasMoreElements()) {
  str = names.nextElement();
  System.out.println(str + ": " +
                     balance.get(str));
}

System.out.println();
```

```
    // Deposit 1,000 into John Doe's account.
    bal = balance.get("John Doe");
    balance.put("John Doe", bal+1000);
    System.out.println("John Doe's new balance: " +
                       balance.get("John Doe"));
  }
}
```

The output from this program is shown here:

```
Todd Hall: 99.22
Ralph Smith: -19.08
John Doe: 3434.34
Jane Baker: 1378.0
Tom Smith: 123.22

John Doe's new balance: 4434.34
```



One important point: Like the map classes, **Hashtable** does not directly support iterators. Thus, the preceding program uses an enumeration to display the contents of **balance**. However, you can obtain set-views of the hash table, which permits the use of iterators. To do so, you simply use one of the collection-view methods defined by **Map**, such as **entrySet( )** or **keySet( )**. For example, you can obtain a set-view of the keys and cycle through them using either an iterator or an enhanced **for** loop. Here is a reworked version of the program that shows this technique:

```
// Use iterators with a Hashtable.
import java.util.*;

class HTDemo2 {
  public static void main(String[] args) {
    Hashtable<String, Double> balance =
      new Hashtable<String, Double>();

    String str;
    double bal;

    balance.put("John Doe", 3434.34);
    balance.put("Tom Smith", 123.22);
    balance.put("Jane Baker", 1378.00);
    balance.put("Tod Hall", 99.22);
    balance.put("Ralph Smith", -19.08);

    // Show all balances in hashtable.
    // First, get a set view of the keys.
    Set<String> set = balance.keySet();

    // Get an iterator.
    Iterator<String> itr = set.iterator();
    while(itr.hasNext()) {
      str = itr.next();
      System.out.println(str + ": " +
                         balance.get(str));
```

```
    }

    System.out.println();

    // Deposit 1,000 into John Doe's account.
    bal = balance.get("John Doe");
    balance.put("John Doe", bal+1000);
    System.out.println("John Doe's new balance: " +
                       balance.get("John Doe"));
  }
}
```

## Properties

**Properties** is a subclass of **Hashtable**. It is used to maintain lists of values in which the key is a **String** and the value is also a **String**. The **Properties** class is used by some other Java classes. For example, it is the type of object returned by **System.getProperties( )** when obtaining environmental values. Although the **Properties** class, itself, is not generic, several of its methods are.

**Properties** defines the following protected volatile instance variable:

Properties defaults;

This variable holds a default property list associated with a **Properties** object. **Properties** defines these constructors:

Properties( )
Properties(Properties *propDefault*)
Properties(int *capacity*)

The first version creates a **Properties** object that has no default values. The second creates an object that uses *propDefault* for its default values. In both cases, the property list is empty. The third constructor lets you specify an initial capacity for the property list. In all cases, the list will grow as needed.

In addition to the methods that **Properties** inherits from **Hashtable, Properties** defines the methods listed in Table 20-22. **Properties** also contains one deprecated method: **save( )**. This was replaced by **store( )** because **save( )** did not handle errors correctly.

| Method | Description |
|---|---|
| String getProperty(String *key*) | Returns the value associated with *key*. A **null** object is returned if *key* is neither in the list nor in the default property list. |
| String getProperty(String *key*, String *defaultProperty*) | Returns the value associated with *key*. *defaultProperty* is returned if *key* is neither in the list nor in the default property list. |
| void list(PrintStream *streamOut*) | Sends the property list to the output stream linked to *streamOut*. |
| void list(PrintWriter *streamOut*) | Sends the property list to the output stream linked to *streamOut*. |

**Table 20-22** The Methods Defined by **Properties**

| Method | Description |
|---|---|
| void load(InputStream *streamIn*) throws IOException | Inputs a property list from the input stream linked to *streamIn.* |
| void load(Reader *streamIn*) throws IOException | Inputs a property list from the input stream linked to *streamIn.* |
| void loadFromXML(InputStream *streamIn*) throws IOException, InvalidPropertiesFormatException | Inputs a property list from an XML document linked to *streamIn.* |
| Enumeration<?> propertyNames( ) | Returns an enumeration of the keys. This includes those keys found in the default property list, too. |
| Object setProperty(String *key*, String *value*) | Associates *value* with *key*. Returns the previous value associated with *key*, or returns **null** if no such association exists. |
| void store(OutputStream *streamOut*, String *description*) throws IOException | After writing the string specified by *description*, the property list is written to the output stream *streamOut.* |
| void store(Writer *streamOut*, String *description*) throws IOException | After writing the string specified by *description*, the property list is written to the output stream *streamOut.* |
| void storeToXML(OutputStream *streamOut*, String *description*) throws IOException | The property list and the string specified by *description* are written as an XML document to *streamOut.* |
| void storeToXML(OutputStream *streamOut*, String *description*, String *enc*) | The property list and the string specified by *description* are written as an XML document to *streamOut* using the specified character encoding. |
| void storeToXML(OutputStream *streamOut*, String *description*, Charset *cs*) | The property list and the string specified by *description* are written as an XML document to *streamOut* using the specified encoding. |
| Set<String> stringPropertyNames( ) | Returns a set of keys. |

**Table 20-22** The Methods Defined by **Properties** *(continued)*

Part II

One useful capability of the **Properties** class is that you can specify a default property that will be returned if no value is associated with a certain key. For example, a default value can be specified along with the key in the **getProperty( )** method—such as **getProperty ("name" ,"default value")**. If the "name" value is not found, then "default value" is returned. When you construct a **Properties** object, you can pass another instance of **Properties** to be used as the default properties for the new instance. In this case, if you call **getProperty("foo")** on a given **Properties** object, and "foo" does not exist, Java looks for "foo" in the default **Properties** object. This allows for arbitrary nesting of levels of default properties.

The following example demonstrates **Properties**. It creates a property list in which the keys are the names of states and the values are the names of their capitals. Notice that the attempt to find the capital for Florida includes a default value.

```
// Demonstrate a Property list.
import java.util.*;
```

```
class PropDemo {
  public static void main(String[] args) {
    Properties capitals = new Properties();

    capitals.setProperty("Illinois", "Springfield");
    capitals.setProperty("Missouri", "Jefferson City");
    capitals.setProperty("Washington", "Olympia");
    capitals.setProperty("California", "Sacramento");
    capitals.setProperty("Indiana", "Indianapolis");

    // Get a set-view of the keys.
    Set<?> states = capitals.keySet();

    // Show all of the states and capitals.
    for(Object name : states)
      System.out.println("The capital of " +
                         name + " is " +
                         capitals.getProperty((String)name)
                         + ".");

    System.out.println();

    // Look for state not in list -- specify default.
    String str = capitals.getProperty("Florida", "Not Found");
    System.out.println("The capital of Florida is " + str + ".");
  }
}
```

The output from this program is shown here:

```
The capital of Missouri is Jefferson City.
The capital of Illinois is Springfield.
The capital of Indiana is Indianapolis.
The capital of California is Sacramento.
The capital of Washington is Olympia.

The capital of Florida is Not Found.
```

Since Florida is not in the list, the default value is used.

Although it is perfectly valid to use a default value when you call **getProperty( )**, as the preceding example shows, there is a better way of handling default values for most applications of property lists. For greater flexibility, specify a default property list when constructing a **Properties** object. The default list will be searched if the desired key is not found in the main list. For example, the following is a slightly reworked version of the preceding program, with a default list of states specified. Now, when Florida is sought, it will be found in the default list:

```
// Use a default property list.
import java.util.*;
```

```
class PropDemoDef {
  public static void main(String[] args) {
    Properties defList = new Properties();
    defList.setProperty("Florida", "Tallahassee");
    defList.setProperty("Wisconsin", "Madison");

    Properties capitals = new Properties(defList);

    capitals.setProperty("Illinois", "Springfield");
    capitals.setProperty("Missouri", "Jefferson City");
    capitals.setProperty("Washington", "Olympia");
    capitals.setProperty("California", "Sacramento");
    capitals.setProperty("Indiana", "Indianapolis");

    // Get a set-view of the keys.
    Set<?> states = capitals.keySet();

    // Show all of the states and capitals.
    for(Object name : states)
      System.out.println("The capital of " +
                         name + " is " +
                         capitals.getProperty((String)name)
                         + ".");

    System.out.println();

    // Florida will now be found in the default list.
    String str = capitals.getProperty("Florida");
    System.out.println("The capital of Florida is "
                       + str + ".");
  }
}
```



## Using store( ) and load( )

One of the most useful aspects of **Properties** is that the information contained in a **Properties** object can be easily stored to or loaded from disk with the **store( )** and **load( )** methods. At any time, you can write a **Properties** object to a stream or read it back. This makes property lists especially convenient for implementing simple databases. For example, the following program uses a property list to create a simple computerized telephone book that stores names and phone numbers. To find a person's number, you enter his or her name. The program uses the **store( )** and **load( )** methods to store and retrieve the list. When the program executes, it first tries to load the list from a file called **phonebook.dat**. If this file exists, the list is loaded. You can then add to the list. If you do, the new list is saved when you terminate the program. Notice how little code is required to implement a small, but functional, computerized phone book.

```
/* A simple telephone number database that uses
   a property list. */
import java.io.*;
import java.util.*;
```

```
class Phonebook {
  public static void main(String[] args)
    throws IOException
  {
    Properties ht = new Properties();
    BufferedReader br = new BufferedReader(new
      InputStreamReader(System.in, System.console().charset()));
    String name, number;
    FileInputStream fin = null;
    boolean changed = false;

    // Try to open phonebook.dat file.
    try {
      fin = new FileInputStream("phonebook.dat");
    } catch(FileNotFoundException e) {
      // ignore missing file
    }

    /* If phonebook file already exists,
       load existing telephone numbers. */
    try {
      if(fin != null) {
        ht.load(fin);
        fin.close();
      }
    } catch(IOException e) {
      System.out.println("Error reading file.");
    }

    // Let user enter new names and numbers.
    do {
      System.out.println("Enter new name" +
                         " ('quit' to stop): ");
      name = br.readLine();
      if(name.equals("quit")) continue;

      System.out.println("Enter number: ");
      number = br.readLine();

      ht.setProperty(name, number);
      changed = true;
    } while(!name.equals("quit"));

    // If phone book data has changed, save it.
    if(changed) {
      FileOutputStream fout = new FileOutputStream("phonebook.dat");

      ht.store(fout, "Telephone Book");
      fout.close();
    }
```

```
      // Look up numbers given a name.
      do {
        System.out.println("Enter name to find" +
                           " ('quit' to quit): ");
        name = br.readLine();
        if(name.equals("quit")) continue;

        number = (String) ht.get(name);
        System.out.println(number);
      } while(!name.equals("quit"));
    }
  }
```



## Parting Thoughts on Collections

The Collections Framework gives you, the programmer, a powerful set of well-engineered solutions to some of programming's most common tasks. Consider using a collection the next time you need to store and retrieve information. Remember, collections need not be reserved for only the "large jobs," such as corporate databases, mailing lists, or inventory systems. They are also effective when applied to smaller jobs. For example, a **TreeMap** might make an excellent collection to hold the directory structure of a set of files. A **TreeSet** could be quite useful for storing project-management information. Frankly, the types of problems that will benefit from a collections-based solution are limited only by your imagination. One last point: In Chapter 30, the stream API is discussed. Because streams are integrated with collections, consider using a stream when operating on a collection.

CHAPTER

# 21 java.util Part 2: More Utility Classes

This chapter continues our discussion of **java.util** by examining those classes and interfaces that are not part of the Collections Framework. These include classes that support timers, work with dates, compute random numbers, and bundle resources. Also covered are the **Formatter** and **Scanner** classes, which make it easy to write and read formatted data, and the **Optional** class, which simplifies handling situations in which a value may be absent. Finally, the subpackages of **java.util** are summarized at the end of this chapter. Of particular interest is **java.util.function**, which defines several standard functional interfaces. One last point: the **Observer** interface and the **Observable** class packaged in **java.util**. have been deprecated since JDK 9. For this reason they are not discussed here.

## StringTokenizer

The processing of text often consists of parsing a formatted input string. *Parsing* is the division of text into a set of discrete parts, or *tokens*, which in a certain sequence can convey a semantic meaning. The **StringTokenizer** class provides the first step in this parsing process, often called the *lexer* (lexical analyzer) or *scanner*. **StringTokenizer** implements the **Enumeration** interface. Therefore, given an input string, you can enumerate the individual tokens contained in it using **StringTokenizer**. Before we begin, it is important to point out that **StringTokenizer** is described here primarily for the benefit of those programmers working with legacy code. For new code, regular expressions, discussed in Chapter 31, offer a more modern alternative.

To use **StringTokenizer**, you specify an input string and a string that contains delimiters. *Delimiters* are characters that separate tokens. Each character in the delimiters string is considered a valid delimiter—for example, ",;:" sets the delimiters to a comma, semicolon, and colon. The default set of delimiters consists of the whitespace characters: space, tab, form feed, newline, and carriage return.

The **StringTokenizer** constructors are shown here:

StringTokenizer(String *str*)
StringTokenizer(String *str*, String *delimiters*)
StringTokenizer(String *str*, String *delimiters*, boolean *delimAsToken*)

In all versions, *str* is the string that will be tokenized. In the first version, the default delimiters are used. In the second and third versions, *delimiters* is a string that specifies the delimiters. In the third version, if *delimAsToken* is **true**, then the delimiters are also returned as tokens when the string is parsed. Otherwise, the delimiters are not returned. Delimiters are not returned as tokens by the first two forms.

Once you have created a **StringTokenizer** object, the **nextToken( )** method is used to extract consecutive tokens. The **hasMoreTokens( )** method returns **true** while there are more tokens to be extracted. Since **StringTokenizer** implements **Enumeration**, the **hasMoreElements( )** and **nextElement( )** methods are also implemented, and they act the same as **hasMoreTokens( )** and **nextToken( )**, respectively. The **StringTokenizer** methods are shown in Table 21-1.

Here is an example that creates a **StringTokenizer** to parse "key=value" pairs. Consecutive sets of "key=value" pairs are separated by a semicolon.

```
// Demonstrate StringTokenizer.
import java.util.StringTokenizer;

class STDemo {
  static String in = "title=Java: The Complete Reference;" +
    "author=Schildt;" +
    "publisher=McGraw Hill;" +
    "copyright=2022";

  public static void main(String[] args) {
    StringTokenizer st = new StringTokenizer(in, "=;");

    while(st.hasMoreTokens()) {
      String key = st.nextToken();
      String val = st.nextToken();
      System.out.println(key + "\t" + val);
    }
  }
}
```

| Method | Description |
|---|---|
| int countTokens( ) | Using the current set of delimiters, the method determines the number of tokens left to be parsed and returns the result. |
| boolean hasMoreElements( ) | Returns **true** if one or more tokens remain in the string and returns **false** if there are none. |
| boolean hasMoreTokens( ) | Returns **true** if one or more tokens remain in the string and returns **false** if there are none. |
| Object nextElement( ) | Returns the next token as an **Object**. |
| String nextToken( ) | Returns the next token as a **String**. |
| String nextToken(String *delimiters*) | Returns the next token as a **String** and sets the delimiters string to that specified by *delimiters*. |

**Table 21-1** The Methods Defined by **StringTokenizer**

The output from this program is shown here:

```
title  Java: The Complete Reference
author  Schildt
publisher  McGraw Hill
copyright  2022
```

# BitSet

A **BitSet** class creates a special type of array that holds bit values in the form of **boolean** values. This array can increase in size as needed. This makes it similar to a vector of bits. The **BitSet** constructors are shown here:

BitSet( )
BitSet(int *size*)

The first version creates a default object. The second version allows you to specify its initial size (that is, the number of bits that it can hold). All bits are initialized to **false**.

**BitSet** defines the methods listed in Table 21-2.



| Method | Description |
|---|---|
| void and(BitSet *bitSet*) | ANDs the contents of the invoking **BitSet** object with those specified by *bitSet*. The result is placed into the invoking object. |
| void andNot(BitSet *bitSet*) | For each set bit in *bitSet*, the corresponding bit in the invoking **BitSet** is cleared. |
| int cardinality( ) | Returns the number of set bits in the invoking object. |
| void clear( ) | Zeros all bits. |
| void clear(int *index*) | Zeros the bit specified by *index*. |
| void clear(int *startIndex*, int *endIndex*) | Zeros the bits from *startIndex* to *endIndex*–1. |
| Object clone( ) | Duplicates the invoking **BitSet** object. |
| boolean equals(Object *bitSet*) | Returns **true** if the invoking bit set is equivalent to the one passed in *bitSet*. Otherwise, the method returns **false**. |
| void flip(int *index*) | Reverses the bit specified by *index*. |
| void flip(int *startIndex*, int *endIndex*) | Reverses the bits from *startIndex* to *endIndex*–1. |
| boolean get(int *index*) | Returns the current state of the bit at the specified index. |
| BitSet get(int *startIndex*, int *endIndex*) | Returns a **BitSet** that consists of the bits from *startIndex* to *endIndex*–1. The invoking object is not changed. |
| int hashCode( ) | Returns the hash code for the invoking object. |
| boolean intersects(BitSet *bitSet*) | Returns **true** if at least one pair of corresponding bits within the invoking object and *bitSet* are set. |

**Table 21-2** The Methods Defined by **BitSet**

| Method | Description |
|---|---|
| boolean isEmpty( ) | Returns **true** if all bits in the invoking object are cleared. |
| int length( ) | Returns the number of bits required to hold the contents of the invoking **BitSet**. This value is determined by the location of the last set bit. |
| int nextClearBit(int *startIndex*) | Returns the index of the next cleared bit (that is, the next **false** bit), starting from the index specified by *startIndex*. |
| int nextSetBit(int *startIndex*) | Returns the index of the next set bit (that is, the next **true** bit), starting from the index specified by *startIndex*. If no bit is set, –1 is returned. |
| void or(BitSet *bitSet*) | ORs the contents of the invoking **BitSet** object with that specified by *bitSet*. The result is placed into the invoking object. |
| int previousClearBit(int *startIndex*) | Returns the index of the next cleared bit (that is, the next **false** bit) at or prior to the index specified by *startIndex*. If no cleared bit is found, –1 is returned. |
| int previousSetBit(int *startIndex*) | Returns the index of the next set bit (that is, the next **true** bit) at or prior to the index specified by *startIndex*. If no set bit is found, –1 is returned. |
| void set(int *index*) | Sets the bit specified by *index*. |
| void set(int *index*, boolean *v*) | Sets the bit specified by *index* to the value passed in *v*. **true** sets the bit; **false** clears the bit. |
| void set(int *startIndex*, int *endIndex*) | Sets the bits from *startIndex* to *endIndex*–1. |
| void set(int *startIndex*, int *endIndex*, boolean *v*) | Sets the bits from *startIndex* to *endIndex*–1 to the value passed in *v*. **true** sets the bits; **false** clears the bits. |
| int size( ) | Returns the number of bits in the invoking **BitSet** object. |
| IntStream stream( ) | Returns a stream that contains the bit positions, from low to high, that have set bits. |
| byte[ ] toByteArray( ) | Returns a **byte** array that contains the invoking **BitSet** object. |
| long[ ] toLongArray( ) | Returns a **long** array that contains the invoking **BitSet** object. |
| String toString( ) | Returns the string equivalent of the invoking **BitSet** object. |
| static BitSet valueOf(byte[ ] *v*) | Returns a **BitSet** that contains the bits in *v*. |
| static BitSet valueOf(ByteBuffer *v*) | Returns a **BitSet** that contains the bits in *v*. |
| static BitSet valueOf(long[ ] *v*) | Returns a **BitSet** that contains the bits in *v*. |
| static BitSet valueOf(LongBuffer *v*) | Returns a **BitSet** that contains the bits in *v*. |
| void xor(BitSet *bitSet*) | XORs the contents of the invoking **BitSet** object with that specified by *bitSet*. The result is placed into the invoking object. |

**Table 21-2** The Methods Defined by **BitSet** *(continued)*

Here is an example that demonstrates **BitSet**:

```
// BitSet Demonstration.
import java.util.BitSet;

class BitSetDemo {
  public static void main(String[] args) {
    BitSet bits1 = new BitSet(16);
    BitSet bits2 = new BitSet(16);

    // set some bits
    for(int i=0; i<16; i++) {
      if((i%2) == 0) bits1.set(i);
      if((i%5) != 0) bits2.set(i);
    }

    System.out.println("Initial pattern in bits1: ");
    System.out.println(bits1);
    System.out.println("\nInitial pattern in bits2: ");
    System.out.println(bits2);

    // AND bits
    bits2.and(bits1);
    System.out.println("\nbits2 AND bits1: ");
    System.out.println(bits2);

    // OR bits
    bits2.or(bits1);
    System.out.println("\nbits2 OR bits1: ");
    System.out.println(bits2);

    // XOR bits
    bits2.xor(bits1);
    System.out.println("\nbits2 XOR bits1: ");
    System.out.println(bits2);
  }
}
```

The output from this program is shown here. When **toString( )** converts a **BitSet** object to its string equivalent, each set bit is represented by its bit position. Cleared bits are not shown.

```
Initial pattern in bits1:
{0, 2, 4, 6, 8, 10, 12, 14}

Initial pattern in bits2:
{1, 2, 3, 4, 6, 7, 8, 9, 11, 12, 13, 14}

bits2 AND bits1:
{2, 4, 6, 8, 12, 14}

bits2 OR bits1:
{0, 2, 4, 6, 8, 10, 12, 14}

bits2 XOR bits1:
{}
```

## Optional, OptionalDouble, OptionalInt, and OptionalLong

Beginning with JDK 8, the classes called **Optional**, **OptionalDouble**, **OptionalInt**, and **OptionalLong** offer a way to handle situations in which a value may or may not be present. In the past, you would normally use the value **null** to indicate that no value is present. However, this can lead to null pointer exceptions if an attempt is made to dereference a null reference. As a result, frequent checks for a **null** value were necessary to avoid generating an exception. These classes provide a better way to handle such situations. One other point: These classes are value-based. (See Chapter 13 for a description of value-based classes.)

The first and most general of these classes is **Optional**. For this reason, it is the primary focus of this discussion. It is shown here:

```
class Optional<T>
```

Here, **T** specifies the type of value stored. It is important to understand that an **Optional** instance can either contain a value of type **T** or be empty. In other words, an **Optional** object does not necessarily contain a value. **Optional** does not define any constructors, but it does define several methods that let you work with **Optional** objects. For example, you can determine if a value is present, obtain the value if it is present, obtain a default value when no value is present, and construct an **Optional** value. The **Optional** methods are shown in Table 21-3.

| Method | Description |
|---|---|
| static <T> Optional<T> empty( ) | Returns an object for which **isPresent( )** returns **false**. |
| boolean equals(Object *optional*) | Returns **true** if the invoking object equals *optional*. Otherwise, returns **false**. |
| Optional<T> filter(<br>Predicate<? super T> *condition*) | Returns an **Optional** instance that contains the same value as the invoking object if that value satisfies *condition*. Otherwise, an empty object is returned. |
| U Optional<U> flatMap(<br>Function<? super T,<br>Optional<U>> *mapFunc*) | Applies the mapping function specified by *mapFunc* to the invoking object if that object contains a value and returns the result. Returns an empty object otherwise. |
| T get( ) | Returns the value in the invoking object. However, if no value is present, **NoSuchElementException** is thrown. |
| int hashCode( ) | Returns a hash code for the value in invoking object. Returns 0 if there is no value. |
| void ifPresent(<br>Consumer<? super T> *func*) | Calls *func* if a value is present in the invoking object, passing the object to *func*. If no value is present, no action occurs. |
| void ifPresentOrElse(<br>Consumer<? super T> *func*,<br>Runnable *onEmpty*) | Calls *func* if a value is present in the invoking object, passing the object to *func*. If no value is present, *onEmpty* will be executed. |

**Table 21-3** The Methods Defined by **Optional**

| Method | Description |
|---|---|
| boolean isEmpty( ) | Returns **true** if the invoking object does not contain a value. Returns **false** if a value is present. |
| boolean isPresent( ) | Returns **true** if the invoking object contains a value. Returns **false** if no value is present. |
| U Optional<U> map( Function<? super T, ? extends U>> *mapFunc*) | Applies the mapping function specified by *mapFunc* to the invoking object if that object contains a value and returns the result. Returns an empty object otherwise. |
| static <T> Optional<T> of(T *val*) | Creates an **Optional** instance that contains *val* and returns the result. The value of *val* must not be **null**. |
| static <T> Optional<T> ofNullable(T *val*) | Creates an **Optional** instance that contains *val* and returns the result. However, if *val* is **null**, then an empty **Optional** instance is returned. |
| Optional<T> or(Supplier<? extends Optional<? extends T>> *func*) | If no value is present in the invoking object, calls *func* to construct and return an **Optional** instance that contains a value. Otherwise, returns an **Optional** instance that contains the invoking object's value. |
| T orElse(T *defVal*) | If the invoking object contains a value, the value is returned. Otherwise, the value specified by *defVal* is returned. |
| T orElseGet( Supplier<? extends T> *getFunc*) | If the invoking object contains a value, the value is returned. Otherwise, the value obtained from *getFunc* is returned. |
| T orElseThrow( ) | Returns the value in the invoking object. However, if no value is present, **NoSuchElementException** is thrown. |
| <X extends Throwable> T orElseThrow( Supplier<? extends X> *excFunc*) throws X extends Throwable | Returns the value in the invoking object. However, if no value is present, the exception generated by *excFunc* is thrown. |
| Stream<T> stream( ) | Returns a stream that contains the invoking object's value. If no value is present, the stream will contain no values. |
| String toString( ) | Returns a string corresponding to the invoking object. |

**Table 21-3** The Methods Defined by **Optional** *(continued)*

The best way to understand **Optional** is to work through an example that uses its core methods. At the foundation of **Optional** are **isPresent( )** and **get( )**. You can determine if a value is present by calling **isPresent( )**. If a value is available, it will return **true**. Otherwise, **false** is returned. If a value is present in an **Optional** instance, you can obtain it by calling **get( )**. However, if you call **get( )** on an object that does not contain a value, **NoSuchElementException** is thrown. For this reason, you should always first confirm that a value is present before calling **get( )** on an **Optional** object. Beginning with JDK 10, the parameterless version of **orElseThrow( )** can be used instead of **get( )**, and its name adds clarity to the operation. However, the examples in this book will use **get( )** so that the code will compile for readers using earlier versions of Java.

Of course, having to call two methods to retrieve a value adds overhead to each access. Fortunately, **Optional** defines methods that combine the check for a value with the retrieval of the value. One such method is **orElse( )**. If the object on which it is called contains a value, the value is returned. Otherwise, a default value is returned.

**Optional** does not define any constructors. Instead, you will use one of its methods to create an instance. For example, you can create an **Optional** instance with a specified value by using **of( )**. You can create an instance of **Optional** that does not contain a value by using **empty( )**.

The following program demonstrates these methods:

```
// Demonstrate several Optional<T> methods

import java.util.*;

class OptionalDemo {
  public static void main(String[] args) {

    Optional<String> noVal = Optional.empty();

    Optional<String> hasVal = Optional.of("ABCDEFG");

    if(noVal.isPresent()) System.out.println("This won't be displayed");
    else System.out.println("noVal has no value");

    if(hasVal.isPresent()) System.out.println("The string in hasVal is: " +
                                              hasVal.get());

    String defStr = noVal.orElse("Default String");
    System.out.println(defStr);
  }
}
```

The output is shown here:

```
noVal has no value
The string in hasVal is: ABCDEFG
Default String
```

As the output shows, a value can be obtained from an **Optional** object only if one is present. This basic mechanism enables **Optional** to prevent null pointer exceptions.

The **OptionalDouble**, **OptionalInt**, and **OptionalLong** classes work much like **Optional**, except that they are designed expressly for use on **double**, **int**, and **long** values, respectively. As such, they specify the methods **getAsDouble( )**, **getAsInt( )**, and **getAsLong( )**, respectively, rather than **get( )**. Also, they do not support the **filter( )**, **ofNullable( )**, **map( )**, **flatMap( )**, and **or( )** methods.

# Date

The **Date** class encapsulates the current date and time. Before beginning our examination of **Date**, it is important to point out that it has changed substantially from its original version defined by Java 1.0. When Java 1.1 was released, many of the functions carried out by the original **Date** class were moved into the **Calendar** and **DateFormat** classes, and as a result, many of the original 1.0 **Date** methods were deprecated. Since the deprecated 1.0 methods should not be used for new code, they are not described here.

| Method | Description |
|---|---|
| boolean after(Date *date*) | Returns **true** if the invoking **Date** object contains a date that is later than the one specified by *date*. Otherwise, it returns **false**. |
| boolean before(Date *date*) | Returns **true** if the invoking **Date** object contains a date that is earlier than the one specified by *date*. Otherwise, it returns **false**. |
| Object clone( ) | Duplicates the invoking **Date** object. |
| int compareTo(Date *date*) | Compares the value of the invoking object with that of *date*. Returns 0 if the values are equal. Returns a negative value if the invoking object is earlier than *date*. Returns a positive value if the invoking object is later than *date*. |
| boolean equals(Object *date*) | Returns **true** if the invoking **Date** object contains the same time and date as the one specified by *date*. Otherwise, it returns **false**. |
| static Date from(Instant t) | Returns a **Date** object corresponding to the **Instant** object passed in *t*. |
| long getTime( ) | Returns the number of milliseconds that have elapsed since January 1, 1970. |
| int hashCode( ) | Returns a hash code for the invoking object. |
| void setTime(long *time*) | Sets the time and date as specified by *time*, which represents an elapsed time in milliseconds from midnight, January 1, 1970. |
| Instant toInstant( ) | Returns an **Instant** object corresponding to the invoking **Date** object. |
| String toString( ) | Converts the invoking **Date** object into a string and returns the result. |

**Table 21-4** The Nondeprecated Methods Defined by **Date**

**Date** supports the following non-deprecated constructors:

Date( )
Date(long *millisec*)

The first constructor initializes the object with the current date and time. The second constructor accepts one argument that equals the number of milliseconds that have elapsed since midnight, January 1, 1970. The non-deprecated methods defined by **Date** are shown in Table 21-4. **Date** also implements the **Comparable** interface.

As you can see by examining Table 21-4, the non-deprecated **Date** features do not allow you to obtain the individual components of the date or time. As the following program demonstrates, you can only obtain the date and time in terms of milliseconds, in its default string representation as returned by **toString( )**, or as an **Instant** object. To obtain more-detailed information about the date and time, you will use the **Calendar** class.

```
// Show date and time using only Date methods.
import java.util.Date;

class DateDemo {
  public static void main(String[] args) {
    // Instantiate a Date object
    Date date = new Date();
```

Part II

```
    // display time and date using toString()
    System.out.println(date);

    // Display number of milliseconds since midnight, January 1, 1970 GMT
    long msec = date.getTime();
    System.out.println("Milliseconds since Jan. 1, 1970 GMT = " + msec);
  }
}
```

Sample output is shown here:

```
Sat Jan 01 10:52:44 CST 2022
Milliseconds since Jan. 1, 1970 GMT = 1641056951341
```

# Calendar

The abstract **Calendar** class provides a set of methods that allows you to convert a time in milliseconds to a number of useful components. Some examples of the type of information that can be provided are year, month, day, hour, minute, and second. It is intended that subclasses of **Calendar** will provide the specific functionality to interpret time information according to their own rules. This is one aspect of the Java class library that enables you to write programs that can operate in international environments. An example of such a subclass is **GregorianCalendar**.

**NOTE** Another date and time API is found in **java.time**. See Chapter 31.

**Calendar** provides no public constructors. **Calendar** defines several protected instance variables. **areFieldsSet** is a **boolean** that indicates if the time components have been set. **fields** is an array of **int**s that holds the components of the time. **isSet** is a **boolean** array that indicates if a specific time component has been set. **time** is a **long** that holds the current time for this object. **isTimeSet** is a **boolean** that indicates if the current time has been set.

A sampling of methods defined by **Calendar** are shown in Table 21-5.

| Method | Description |
|---|---|
| abstract void add(int *which*, int *val*) | Adds *val* to the time or date component specified by *which*. To subtract, add a negative value. *which* must be one of the fields defined by **Calendar**, such as **Calendar.HOUR**. |
| boolean after(Object *calendarObj*) | Returns **true** if the invoking **Calendar** object contains a date that is later than the one specified by *calendarObj*. Otherwise, it returns **false**. |
| boolean before(Object *calendarObj*) | Returns **true** if the invoking **Calendar** object contains a date that is earlier than the one specified by *calendarObj*. Otherwise, it returns **false**. |

**Table 21-5** A Sampling of the Methods Defined by **Calendar**

| Method | Description |
|---|---|
| final void clear( ) | Zeros all time components in the invoking object. |
| final void clear(int *which*) | Zeros the time component specified by *which* in the invoking object. |
| Object clone( ) | Returns a duplicate of the invoking object. |
| boolean equals(Object *calendarObj*) | Returns **true** if the invoking **Calendar** object contains a date that is equal to the one specified by *calendarObj*. Otherwise, it returns **false**. |
| int get(int *calendarField*) | Returns the value of one component of the invoking object. The component is indicated by *calendarField*. Examples of the components that can be requested are **Calendar.YEAR**, **Calendar.MONTH**, **Calendar.MINUTE**, and so forth. |
| static Locale[ ] getAvailableLocales( ) | Returns an array of **Locale** objects that contains the locales for which calendars are available. |
| static Calendar getInstance( ) | Returns a **Calendar** object for the default locale and time zone. |
| static Calendar getInstance(TimeZone *tz*) | Returns a **Calendar** object for the time zone specified by *tz*. The default locale is used. |
| static Calendar getInstance(Locale *locale*) | Returns a **Calendar** object for the locale specified by *locale*. The default time zone is used. |
| static Calendar getInstance(TimeZone *tz*, Locale *locale*) | Returns a **Calendar** object for the time zone specified by *tz* and the locale specified by *locale*. |
| final Date getTime( ) | Returns a **Date** object equivalent to the time of the invoking object. |
| TimeZone getTimeZone( ) | Returns the time zone for the invoking object. |
| final boolean isSet(int *which*) | Returns **true** if the specified time component is set. Otherwise, it returns **false**. |
| void set(int *which*, int *val*)<br><br>final void set(int *year*, int *month*, int *dayOfMonth*) | Sets the date or time component specified by *which* to the value specified by *val* in the invoking object. *which* must be one of the fields defined by **Calendar**, such as **Calendar.HOUR**.<br><br>Sets various date and time components of the invoking object. |
| final void set(int *year*, int *month*, int *dayOfMonth*, int *hours*, int *minutes*) | Sets various date and time components of the invoking object. |
| final void set(int *year*, int *month*, int *dayOfMonth*, int *hours*, int *minutes*, int *seconds*) | Sets various date and time components of the invoking object. |

**Table 21-5** A Sampling of the Methods Defined by **Calendar** *(continued)*

| Method | Description |
|---|---|
| final void setTime(Date *d*) | Sets various date and time components of the invoking object. This information is obtained from the **Date** object *d*. |
| void setTimeZone(TimeZone *tz*) | Sets the time zone for the invoking object to that specified by *tz*. |
| final Instant toInstant( ) | Returns an **Instant** object corresponding to the invoking **Calendar** instance. |

**Table 21-5** A Sampling of the Methods Defined by **Calendar** *(continued)*

**Calendar** defines the following **int** constants, which are used when you get or set components of the calendar.

| | | |
|---|---|---|
| ALL_STYLES | HOUR_OF_DAY | PM |
| AM | JANUARY | SATURDAY |
| AM_PM | JULY | SECOND |
| APRIL | JUNE | SEPTEMBER |
| AUGUST | LONG | SHORT |
| DATE | LONG_FORMAT | SHORT_FORMAT |
| DAY_OF_MONTH | LONG_STANDALONE | SHORT_STANDALONE |
| DAY_OF_WEEK | MARCH | SUNDAY |
| DAY_OF_WEEK_IN_MONTH | MAY | THURSDAY |
| DAY_OF_YEAR | MILLISECOND | TUESDAY |
| DECEMBER | MINUTE | UNDECIMBER |
| DST_OFFSET | MONDAY | WEDNESDAY |
| ERA | MONTH | WEEK_OF_MONTH |
| FEBRUARY | NARROW_FORMAT | WEEK_OF_YEAR |
| FIELD_COUNT | NARROW_STANDALONE | YEAR |
| FRIDAY | NOVEMBER | ZONE_OFFSET |
| HOUR | OCTOBER | |

The following program demonstrates several **Calendar** methods:

```
// Demonstrate Calendar
import java.util.Calendar;

class CalendarDemo {
  public static void main(String[] args) {
    String[] months = {
             "Jan", "Feb", "Mar", "Apr",
             "May", "Jun", "Jul", "Aug",
             "Sep", "Oct", "Nov", "Dec"};
```

```
        // Create a calendar initialized with the
        // current date and time in the default
        // locale and timezone.
        Calendar calendar = Calendar.getInstance();

        // Display current time and date information.
        System.out.print("Date: ");
        System.out.print(months[calendar.get(Calendar.MONTH)]);
        System.out.print(" " + calendar.get(Calendar.DATE) + " ");
        System.out.println(calendar.get(Calendar.YEAR));

        System.out.print("Time: ");
        System.out.print(calendar.get(Calendar.HOUR) + ":");
        System.out.print(calendar.get(Calendar.MINUTE) + ":");
        System.out.println(calendar.get(Calendar.SECOND));

        // Set the time and date information and display it.
        calendar.set(Calendar.HOUR, 10);
        calendar.set(Calendar.MINUTE, 29);
        calendar.set(Calendar.SECOND, 22);
        System.out.print("Updated time: ");
        System.out.print(calendar.get(Calendar.HOUR) + ":");
        System.out.print(calendar.get(Calendar.MINUTE) + ":");
        System.out.println(calendar.get(Calendar.SECOND));
    }
}
```

Sample output is shown here:

```
Date: Jan 1 2022
Time: 11:29:39
Updated time: 10:29:22
```

## GregorianCalendar

**GregorianCalendar** is a concrete implementation of a **Calendar** that implements the normal Gregorian calendar with which you are familiar. The **getInstance( )** method of **Calendar** will typically return a **GregorianCalendar** initialized with the current date and time in the default locale and time zone.

**GregorianCalendar** defines two fields: **AD** and **BC**. These represent the two eras defined by the Gregorian calendar.

There are also several constructors for **GregorianCalendar** objects. The default, **GregorianCalendar( )**, initializes the object with the current date and time in the default locale and time zone. Three more constructors offer increasing levels of specificity:

GregorianCalendar(int *year*, int *month*, int *dayOfMonth*)
GregorianCalendar(int *year*, int *month*, int *dayOfMonth*, int *hours*,
int *minutes*)
GregorianCalendar(int *year*, int *month*, int *dayOfMonth*, int *hours*,
int *minutes*, int *seconds*)

All three versions set the day, month, and year. Here, *year* specifies the year. The month is specified by *month*, with zero indicating January. The day of the month is specified by *dayOfMonth*. The first version sets the time to midnight. The second version also sets the hours and the minutes. The third version adds seconds.

You can also construct a **GregorianCalendar** object by specifying the locale and/or time zone. The following constructors create objects initialized with the current date and time using the specified time zone and/or locale:

GregorianCalendar(Locale *locale*)
GregorianCalendar(TimeZone *timeZone*)
GregorianCalendar(TimeZone *timeZone*, Locale *locale*)

**GregorianCalendar** provides an implementation of all the abstract methods in **Calendar**. It also provides some additional methods. Perhaps the most interesting is **isLeapYear( )**, which tests if the year is a leap year. Its form is

boolean isLeapYear(int *year*)

This method returns **true** if *year* is a leap year and **false** otherwise. Two other methods of interest are **from( )** and **toZonedDateTime( )**, which support the date and time API added by JDK 8 and packaged in **java.time**.

The following program demonstrates **GregorianCalendar**:

```
// Demonstrate GregorianCalendar
import java.util.*;

class GregorianCalendarDemo {
  public static void main(String[] args) {
    String[] months = {
             "Jan", "Feb", "Mar", "Apr",
             "May", "Jun", "Jul", "Aug",
             "Sep", "Oct", "Nov", "Dec"};
    int year;

    // Create a Gregorian calendar initialized
    // with the current date and time in the
    // default locale and timezone.
    GregorianCalendar gcalendar = new GregorianCalendar();

    // Display current time and date information.
    System.out.print("Date: ");
    System.out.print(months[gcalendar.get(Calendar.MONTH)]);
    System.out.print(" " + gcalendar.get(Calendar.DATE) + " ");
    System.out.println(year = gcalendar.get(Calendar.YEAR));

    System.out.print("Time: ");
    System.out.print(gcalendar.get(Calendar.HOUR) + ":");
    System.out.print(gcalendar.get(Calendar.MINUTE) + ":");
    System.out.println(gcalendar.get(Calendar.SECOND));

    // Test if the current year is a leap year
    if(gcalendar.isLeapYear(year)) {
      System.out.println("The current year is a leap year");
    }
```

```
      else {
        System.out.println("The current year is not a leap year");
      }
    }
  }
```

Sample output is shown here:

```
Date: Jan 1 2022
Time: 1:45:5
The current year is not a leap year
```



# TimeZone

Another time-related class is **TimeZone**. The abstract **TimeZone** class allows you to work with time zone offsets from Greenwich Mean Time (GMT), also referred to as Coordinated Universal Time (UTC). It also computes daylight saving time. **TimeZone** only supplies the default constructor.

A sampling of methods defined by **TimeZone** is given in Table 21-6.

| Method | Description |
|---|---|
| Object clone( ) | Returns a **TimeZone**-specific version of **clone( )**. |
| static String[ ] getAvailableIDs( ) | Returns an array of **String** objects representing the names of all time zones. |
| static String[ ] getAvailableIDs(int *timeDelta*) | Returns an array of **String** objects representing the names of all time zones that are *timeDelta* offset from GMT. |
| static TimeZone getDefault( ) | Returns a **TimeZone** object that represents the default time zone used on the host computer. |
| String getID( ) | Returns the name of the invoking **TimeZone** object. |
| abstract int getOffset(int *era*, int *year*, int *month*, int *dayOfMonth*, int *dayOfWeek*, int *millisec*) | Returns the offset that should be added to GMT to compute local time. This value is adjusted for daylight saving time. The parameters to the method represent date and time components. |
| abstract int getRawOffset( ) | Returns the raw offset (in milliseconds) that should be added to GMT to compute local time. This value is not adjusted for daylight saving time. |
| static TimeZone getTimeZone(String *tzName*) | Returns the **TimeZone** object for the time zone named *tzName*. |
| abstract boolean inDaylightTime(Date *d*) | Returns **true** if the date represented by *d* is in daylight saving time in the invoking object. Otherwise, it returns **false**. |

**Table 21-6** A Sampling of the Methods Defined by **TimeZone**

| Method | Description |
|---|---|
| static void setDefault(TimeZone *tz*) | Sets the default time zone to be used on this host. *tz* is a reference to the **TimeZone** object to be used. |
| void setID(String *tzName*) | Sets the name of the time zone (that is, its ID) to that specified by *tzName*. |
| abstract void setRawOffset(int *millis*) | Sets the offset in milliseconds from GMT. |
| ZoneId toZoneId( ) | Converts the invoking object into a **ZoneId** and returns the result. **ZoneId** is packaged in **java.time**. |
| abstract boolean useDaylightTime( ) | Returns **true** if the invoking object uses daylight saving time. Otherwise, it returns **false**. |

**Table 21-6** A Sampling of the Methods Defined by **TimeZone** *(continued)*

## SimpleTimeZone

The **SimpleTimeZone** class is a convenient subclass of **TimeZone**. It implements **TimeZone**'s abstract methods and allows you to work with time zones for a Gregorian calendar. It also computes daylight saving time.

**SimpleTimeZone** defines four constructors. One is

SimpleTimeZone(int *timeDelta*, String *tzName*)

This constructor creates a **SimpleTimeZone** object. The offset relative to Greenwich Mean Time (GMT) is *timeDelta*. The time zone is named *tzName*.

The second **SimpleTimeZone** constructor is

SimpleTimeZone(int *timeDelta*, String *tzId*, int *dstMonth0*,
int *dstDayInMonth0*, int *dstDay0*, int *time0*,
int *dstMonth1*, int *dstDayInMonth1*, int *dstDay1*,
int *time1*)

Here, the offset relative to GMT is specified in *timeDelta*. The time zone name is passed in *tzId*. The start of daylight saving time is indicated by the parameters *dstMonth0*, *dstDayInMonth0*, *dstDay0*, and *time0*. The end of daylight saving time is indicated by the parameters *dstMonth1*, *dstDayInMonth1*, *dstDay1*, and *time1*.

The third **SimpleTimeZone** constructor is

SimpleTimeZone(int *timeDelta*, String *tzId*, int *dstMonth0*,
int *dstDayInMonth0*, int *dstDay0*, int *time0*,
int *dstMonth1*, int *dstDayInMonth1*,
int *dstDay1*, int *time1*, int *dstDelta*)

Here, *dstDelta* is the number of milliseconds saved during daylight saving time.

The fourth **SimpleTimeZone** constructor is

SimpleTimeZone(int *timeDelta*, String *tzId*, int *dstMonth0*,
int *dstDayInMonth0*, int *dstDay0*, int *time0*,
int *time0mode*, int *dstMonth1*, int *dstDayInMonth1*,
int *dstDay1*, int *time1*, int *time1mode*, int *dstDelta*)

Here, *time0mode* specifies the mode of the starting time, and *time1mode* specifies the mode of the ending time. Valid mode values include:

| STANDARD_TIME | WALL_TIME | UTC_TIME |
|---|---|---|

The time mode indicates how the time values are interpreted. The default mode used by the other constructors is **WALL_TIME**.

# Locale

The **Locale** class is instantiated to produce objects that describe a geographical or cultural region. It is one of several classes that provide you with the ability to write programs that can execute in different international environments. For example, the formats used to display dates, times, and numbers are different in various regions.

Internationalization is a large topic that is beyond the scope of this book. However, many programs will only need to deal with its basics, which include setting the current locale.

The **Locale** class defines the following constants that are useful for dealing with several common locales:

| CANADA | GERMAN | KOREAN |
|---|---|---|
| CANADA_FRENCH | GERMANY | PRC |
| CHINA | ITALIAN | SIMPLIFIED_CHINESE |
| CHINESE | ITALY | TAIWAN |
| ENGLISH | JAPAN | TRADITIONAL_CHINESE |
| FRANCE | JAPANESE | UK |
| FRENCH | KOREA | US |

For example, the expression **Locale.CANADA** represents the **Locale** object for Canada.

The constructors for **Locale** are

Locale(String *language*)
Locale(String *language*, String *country*)
Locale(String *language*, String *country*, String *variant*)

These constructors build a **Locale** object to represent a specific *language* and, in the case of the last two, *country*. These values must contain standard language and country codes. Auxiliary variant information can be provided in *variant*.

**Locale** defines several methods. One of the most important is **setDefault( )**, shown here:

static void setDefault(Locale *localeObj*)

This sets the default locale used by the JVM to that specified by *localeObj*.

Some other interesting methods are the following:

final String getDisplayCountry( )
final String getDisplayLanguage( )
final String getDisplayName( )

These return human-readable strings that can be used to display the name of the country, the name of the language, and the complete description of the locale.

The default locale can be obtained using **getDefault( )**, shown here:

static Locale getDefault( )

JDK 7 added significant upgrades to the **Locale** class that support Internet Engineering Task Force (IETF) BCP 47, which defines tags for identifying languages, and Unicode Technical Standard (UTS) 35, which defines the Locale Data Markup Language (LDML). Support for BCP 47 and UTS 35 caused several features to be added to **Locale**, including several new methods and the **Locale.Builder** class. Among others, new methods include **getScript( )**, which obtains the locale's script, and **toLanguageTag( )**, which obtains a string that contains the locale's language tag. The **Locale.Builder** class constructs **Locale** instances. It ensures that a locale specification is well-formed as defined by BCP 47. (The **Locale** constructors do not provide such a check.) Several new methods were also added to **Locale** by JDK 8. Among these are methods that support filtering, extensions, and lookups. JDK 9 added a method called **getISOCountries( )**, which returns a collection of country codes for a given **Locale.IsoCountryCode** enumeration value.

**Calendar** and **GregorianCalendar** are examples of classes that operate in a locale-sensitive manner. **DateFormat** and **SimpleDateFormat** also depend on the locale.

## Random

The **Random** class is a generator of pseudorandom numbers. These are called *pseudorandom* numbers because they are simply uniformly distributed sequences. Beginning with JDK 17, **Random** implements the new **RandomGenerator** interface, which provides a standardized interface for random value generators.

**Random** defines the following constructors:

Random( )
Random(long *seed*)

The first version creates a number generator that uses a reasonably unique seed. The second form allows you to specify a seed value manually.

If you initialize a **Random** object with a seed, you define the starting point for the random sequence. If you use the same seed to initialize another **Random** object, you will extract the same random sequence. If you want to generate different sequences, specify different seed values. One way to do this is to use the current time to seed a **Random** object. This approach reduces the possibility of getting repeated sequences.

The core public methods provided by **Random** are shown in Table 21-7. These are the methods that have been available in **Random** for several years (many since Java 1.0) and are widely used.

As you can see, there are seven types of random numbers that you can extract from a **Random** object. Random Boolean values are available from **nextBoolean( )**. Random bytes can be obtained by calling **nextBytes( )**. Integers can be extracted via the **nextInt( )** method. Long integers can be obtained with **nextLong( )**. The **nextFloat( )** and **nextDouble( )** methods return **float** and **double** values, respectively, between 0.0 and 1.0. Finally, **nextGaussian( )** returns a **double** value centered at 0.0 with a standard deviation of 1.0. This is what is known as a *bell curve*.

| Method | Description |
|---|---|
| boolean nextBoolean( ) | Returns the next **boolean** random number |
| void nextBytes(byte[ ] *vals*) | Fills *vals* with randomly generated values |
| double nextDouble( ) | Returns the next **double** random number |
| float nextFloat( ) | Returns the next **float** random number |
| double nextGaussian( ) | Returns the next Gaussian random number |
| int nextInt( ) | Returns the next **int** random number |
| int nextInt(int *n*) | Returns the next **int** random number within the range zero to *n* |
| long nextLong( ) | Returns the next **long** random number. |
| void setSeed(long *newSeed*) | Sets the seed value (that is, the starting point for the random number generator) to that specified by *newSeed* |

**Table 21-7** The Core Methods Defined by **Random**



Here is an example that demonstrates the sequence produced by **nextGaussian( )**. It obtains 100 random Gaussian values and averages these values. The program also counts the number of values that fall within two standard deviations, plus or minus, using increments of 0.5 for each category. The result is graphically displayed sideways on the screen.

```
// Demonstrate random Gaussian values.
import java.util.Random;
class RandDemo {
  public static void main(String[] args) {
    Random r = new Random();
    double val;
    double sum = 0;
    int[] bell = new int[10];

    for(int i=0; i<100; i++) {
      val = r.nextGaussian();
      sum += val;
      double t = -2;

      for(int x=0; x<10; x++, t += 0.5)
        if(val < t) {
          bell[x]++;
          break;
        }
    }
    System.out.println("Average of values: " +
                        (sum/100));

    // display bell curve, sideways
    for(int i=0; i<10; i++) {
      for(int x=bell[i]; x>0; x--)
        System.out.print("*");
      System.out.println();
    }
  }
}
```

Here is a sample program run. As you can see, a bell-like distribution of numbers is obtained.

```
Average of values: 0.0702235271133344
**
*******
******
***************
******************
*****************
*************
**********
********
***
```

It is useful to point out that JDK 8 added three methods to **Random** that support the stream API (see Chapter 30). They are called **doubles( )**, **ints( )**, and **longs( )**, and each returns a reference to a stream that contains a sequence of pseudorandom values of the specified type. Each method defines several overloads. Here are their simplest forms:

DoubleStream doubles( )

IntStream ints( )

LongStream longs( )

The **doubles( )** method returns a stream that contains pseudorandom **double** values. (The range of these values will be less than 1.0 but greater than or equal to 0.0.) The **ints( )** method returns a stream that contains pseudorandom **int** values. The **longs( )** method returns a stream that contains pseudorandom **long** values. For these three methods, the stream returned is effectively infinite. Several overloads of each method are provided that let you specify the size of the stream, an origin, and an upper bound.

## Timer and TimerTask

An interesting and useful feature offered by **java.util** is the ability to schedule a task for execution at some future time. The classes that support this are **Timer** and **TimerTask**. Using these classes, you can create a thread that runs in the background, waiting for a specific time. When the time arrives, the task linked to that thread is executed. Various options allow you to schedule a task for repeated execution and to schedule a task to run on a specific date. Although it was always possible to manually create a task that would be executed at a specific time using the **Thread** class, **Timer** and **TimerTask** greatly simplify this process.

**Timer** and **TimerTask** work together. **Timer** is the class that you will use to schedule a task for execution. The task being scheduled must be an instance of **TimerTask**. Thus, to schedule a task, you will first create a **TimerTask** object and then schedule it for execution using an instance of **Timer**.

**TimerTask** implements the **Runnable** interface; thus, it can be used to create a thread of execution. Its constructor is shown here:

protected TimerTask( )

| Method | Description |
|---|---|
| boolean cancel( ) | Terminates the task. Returns **true** if an execution of the task is prevented. Otherwise, returns **false**. |
| abstract void run( ) | Contains the code for the timer task. |
| long scheduledExecutionTime( ) | Returns the time at which the last execution of the task was scheduled to have occurred. |

**Table 21-8** The Methods Defined by **TimerTask**



**TimerTask** defines the methods shown in Table 21-8. Notice that **run( )** is abstract, which means that it must be overridden. The **run( )** method, defined by the **Runnable** interface, contains the code that will be executed. Thus, the easiest way to create a timer task is to extend **TimerTask** and override **run( )**.

Once a task has been created, it is scheduled for execution by an object of type **Timer**. The constructors for **Timer** are shown here:

Timer( )
Timer(boolean *DThread*)
Timer(String *tName*)
Timer(String *tName*, boolean *DThread*)

The first version creates a **Timer** object that runs as a normal thread. The second uses a daemon thread if *DThread* is **true**. A daemon thread will execute only as long as the rest of the program continues to execute. The third and fourth constructors allow you to specify a name for the **Timer** thread. The methods defined by **Timer** are shown in Table 21-9.

Once a **Timer** has been created, you will schedule a task by calling **schedule( )** on the **Timer** that you created. As Table 21-9 shows, there are several forms of **schedule( )** that allow you to schedule tasks in a variety of ways.

If you create a non-daemon task, then you will want to call **cancel( )** to end the task when your program ends. If you don't do this, then your program may "hang" for a period of time.

The following program demonstrates **Timer** and **TimerTask**. It defines a timer task whose **run( )** method displays the message "Timer task executed." This task is scheduled to run once every half second after an initial delay of one second.

```
// Demonstrate Timer and TimerTask.

import java.util.*;

class MyTimerTask extends TimerTask {
  public void run() {
    System.out.println("Timer task executed.");
  }
}

class TTest {
  public static void main(String[] args) {
    MyTimerTask myTask = new MyTimerTask();
    Timer myTimer = new Timer();
```

| Method | Description |
|---|---|
| void cancel( ) | Cancels the timer thread. |
| int purge( ) | Deletes canceled tasks from the timer's queue. |
| void schedule(TimerTask *TTask*, long *wait*) | *TTask* is scheduled for execution after the period passed in *wait* has elapsed. The *wait* parameter is specified in milliseconds. |
| void schedule(TimerTask *TTask*, long *wait*, long *repeat*) | *TTask* is scheduled for execution after the period passed in *wait* has elapsed. The task is then executed repeatedly at the interval specified by *repeat*. Both *wait* and *repeat* are specified in milliseconds. |
| void schedule(TimerTask *TTask*, Date *targetTime*) | *TTask* is scheduled for execution at the time specified by *targetTime*. |
| void schedule(TimerTask *TTask*, Date *targetTime*, long *repeat*) | *TTask* is scheduled for execution at the time specified by *targetTime*. The task is then executed repeatedly at the interval passed in *repeat*. The *repeat* parameter is specified in milliseconds. |
| void scheduleAtFixedRate( TimerTask *TTask*, long *wait*, long *repeat*) | *TTask* is scheduled for execution after the period passed in *wait* has elapsed. The task is then executed repeatedly at the interval specified by *repeat*. Both *wait* and *repeat* are specified in milliseconds. The time of each repetition is relative to the first execution, not the preceding execution. Thus, the overall rate of execution is fixed. |
| void scheduleAtFixedRate( TimerTask *TTask*, Date *targetTime*, long *repeat*) | *TTask* is scheduled for execution at the time specified by *targetTime*. The task is then executed repeatedly at the interval passed in *repeat*. The *repeat* parameter is specified in milliseconds. The time of each repetition is relative to the first execution, not the preceding execution. Thus, the overall rate of execution is fixed. |

**Table 21-9** The Methods Defined by **Timer**

```
    /* Set an initial delay of 1 second,
       then repeat every half second.
    */
    myTimer.schedule(myTask, 1000, 500);

    try {
      Thread.sleep(5000);
    } catch (InterruptedException exc) {}

    myTimer.cancel();
  }
}
```

| Method | Description |
|---|---|
| static Set<Currency> getAvailableCurrencies( ) | Returns a set of the supported currencies. |
| String getCurrencyCode( ) | Returns the code (as defined by ISO 4217) that describes the invoking currency. |
| int getDefaultFractionDigits( ) | Returns the number of digits after the decimal point that are normally used by the invoking currency. For example, there are two fractional digits normally used for dollars. |
| String getDisplayName( ) | Returns the name of the invoking currency for the default locale. |
| String getDisplayName(Locale *loc*) | Returns the name of the invoking currency for the specified locale. |
| static Currency getInstance(Locale *localeObj*) | Returns a **Currency** object for the locale specified by *localeObj*. |
| static Currency getInstance(String *code*) | Returns a **Currency** object associated with the currency code passed in *code*. |
| int getNumericCode( ) | Returns the numeric code (as defined by ISO 4217) for the invoking currency. |
| String getNumericCodeAsString( ) | Returns in string form the numeric code (as defined by ISO 4217) for the invoking currency. |
| String getSymbol( ) | Returns the currency symbol (such as $) for the invoking object. |
| String getSymbol(Locale *localeObj*) | Returns the currency symbol (such as $) for the locale passed in *localeObj*. |
| String toString( ) | Returns the currency code for the invoking object. |

**Table 21-10** The Methods Defined by **Currency**

# Currency

The **Currency** class encapsulates information about a currency. It defines no constructors. The methods supported by **Currency** are shown in Table 21-10. The following program demonstrates **Currency**:

```
// Demonstrate Currency.
import java.util.*;

class CurDemo {
  public static void main(String[] args) {
    Currency c;

    c = Currency.getInstance(Locale.US);

    System.out.println("Symbol: " + c.getSymbol());
    System.out.println("Default fractional digits: " +
                       c.getDefaultFractionDigits());
  }
}
```

The output is shown here:

```
Symbol: $
Default fractional digits: 2
```

# Formatter

At the core of Java's support for creating formatted output is the **Formatter** class. It provides *format conversions* that let you display numbers, strings, and time and date in virtually any format you like. It operates in a manner similar to the C/C++ **printf( )** function, which means that if you are familiar with C/C++, then learning to use **Formatter** will be very easy. It also further streamlines the conversion of C/C++ code to Java. If you are not familiar with C/C++, it is still quite easy to format data.

**NOTE** Although Java's **Formatter** class operates in a manner very similar to the C/C++ **printf( )** function, there are some differences, and some new features. Therefore, if you have a C/C++ background, a careful reading is advised.

## The Formatter Constructors

Before you can use **Formatter** to format output, you must create a **Formatter** object. In general, **Formatter** works by converting the binary form of data used by a program into formatted text. It stores the formatted text in a buffer, the contents of which can be obtained by your program whenever they are needed. It is possible to let **Formatter** supply this buffer automatically, or you can specify the buffer explicitly when a **Formatter** object is created. It is also possible to have **Formatter** output its buffer to a file.

The **Formatter** class defines many constructors, which enable you to construct a **Formatter** in a variety of ways. Here is a sampling:

Formatter( )

Formatter(Appendable *buf*)

Formatter(Appendable *buf*, Locale *loc*)

Formatter(String *filename*)
throws FileNotFoundException

Formatter(String *filename*, String *charset*)
throws FileNotFoundException, UnsupportedEncodingException

Formatter(File *outF*)
throws FileNotFoundException

Formatter(OutputStream *outStrm*)

Here, *buf* specifies a buffer for the formatted output. If *buf* is null, then **Formatter** automatically allocates a **StringBuilder** to hold the formatted output. The *loc* parameter specifies a locale. If no locale is specified, the default locale is used. The *filename* parameter specifies the name of a file that will receive the formatted output. The *charset* parameter specifies the character set. If no character set is specified, then the

| Method | Description |
|---|---|
| void close( ) | Closes the invoking **Formatter**. This causes any resources used by the object to be released. After a **Formatter** has been closed, it cannot be reused. An attempt to use a closed **Formatter** results in a **FormatterClosedException**. |
| void flush( ) | Flushes the format buffer. This causes any output currently in the buffer to be written to the destination. This applies mostly to a **Formatter** tied to a file. |
| Formatter format(String *fmtString*, Object ... *args*) | Formats the arguments passed via *args* according to the format specifiers contained in *fmtString*. Returns the invoking object. |
| Formatter format(Locale *loc*, String *fmtString*, Object ... *args*) | Formats the arguments passed via *args* according to the format specifiers contained in *fmtString*. The locale specified by *loc* is used for this format. Returns the invoking object. |
| IOException ioException( ) | If the underlying object that is the destination for output throws an **IOException**, then this exception is returned. Otherwise, **null** is returned. |
| Locale locale( ) | Returns the invoking object's locale. |
| Appendable out( ) | Returns a reference to the underlying object that is the destination for output. |
| String toString( ) | Returns a **String** containing the formatted output. |

**Table 21-11** The Methods Defined by **Formatter**



default character set is used. The *outF* parameter specifies a reference to an open file that will receive output. The *outStrm* parameter specifies a reference to an output stream that will receive output. When using a file, output is also written to the file.

Perhaps the most widely used constructor is the first, which has no parameters. It automatically uses the default locale and allocates a **StringBuilder** to hold the formatted output.

## The Formatter Methods

**Formatter** defines the methods shown in Table 21-11.

## Formatting Basics

After you have created a **Formatter**, you can use it to create a formatted string. To do so, use the **format( )** method. The version we will use is shown here:

Formatter format(String *fmtString*, Object ... *args*)

The *fmtSring* consists of two types of items. The first type is composed of characters that are simply copied to the output buffer. The second type contains *format specifiers* that define the way the subsequent arguments are displayed.

In its simplest form, a format specifier begins with a percent sign followed by the format *conversion specifier*. All format conversion specifiers consist of a single character. For example, the format specifier for floating-point data is **%f**. In general, there must be the same number of arguments as there are format specifiers, and the format specifiers and the arguments are matched in order from left to right. For example, consider this fragment:

```
Formatter fmt = new Formatter();
fmt.format("Formatting %s is easy %d %f", "with Java", 10, 98.6);
```

This sequence creates a **Formatter** that contains the following string:

```
Formatting with Java is easy 10 98.600000
```

In this example, the format specifiers, **%s**, **%d**, and **%f**, are replaced with the arguments that follow the format string. Thus, **%s** is replaced by "with Java", **%d** is replaced by 10, and **%f** is replaced by 98.6. All other characters are simply used as-is. As you might guess, the format specifier **%s** specifies a string, and **%d** specifies an integer value. As mentioned earlier, the **%f** specifies a floating-point value.

The **format( )** method accepts a wide variety of format specifiers, which are shown in Table 21-12. Notice that many specifiers have both upper- and lowercase forms. When an

| Format Specifier | Conversion Applied |
|---|---|
| %a<br>%A | Floating-point hexadecimal |
| %b<br>%B | Boolean |
| %c<br>%C | Character |
| %d | Decimal integer |
| %h<br>%H | Hash code of the argument |
| %e<br>%E | Scientific notation |
| %f | Decimal floating-point |
| %g<br>%G | Uses **%e** or **%f**, based on the value being formatted and the precision |
| %o | Octal integer |
| %n | Inserts a newline character |
| %s<br>%S | String |
| %t<br>%T | Time and date |
| %x<br>%X | Integer hexadecimal |
| %% | Inserts a % sign |

**Table 21-12** The Format Specifiers

uppercase specifier is used, then letters are shown in uppercase. Otherwise, the upper- and lowercase specifiers perform the same conversion. It is important to understand that Java type-checks each format specifier against its corresponding argument. If the argument doesn't match, an **IllegalFormatException** is thrown.

Once you have formatted a string, you can obtain it by calling **toString( )**. For example, continuing with the preceding example, the following statement obtains the formatted string contained in **fmt**:

```
String str = fmt.toString();
```

Of course, if you simply want to display the formatted string, there is no reason to first assign it to a **String** object. When a **Formatter** object is passed to **println( )**, for example, its **toString( )** method is automatically called.

Here is a short program that puts together all of the pieces, showing how to create and display a formatted string:

```
// A very simple example that uses Formatter.
import java.util.*;

class FormatDemo {
  public static void main(String[] args) {
    Formatter fmt = new Formatter();

    fmt.format("Formatting %s is easy %d %f", "with Java", 10, 98.6);

    System.out.println(fmt);
    fmt.close();
  }
}
```

One other point: You can obtain a reference to the underlying output buffer by calling **out( )**. It returns a reference to an **Appendable** object.

Now that you know the general mechanism used to create a formatted string, the remainder of this section discusses in detail each conversion. It also describes various options, such as justification, minimum field width, and precision.

## Formatting Strings and Characters

To format an individual character, use **%c**. This causes the matching character argument to be output, unmodified. To format a string, use **%s**.

## Formatting Numbers

To format an integer in decimal format, use **%d**. To format a floating-point value in decimal format, use **%f**. To format a floating-point value in scientific notation, use **%e**. Numbers represented in scientific notation take this general form:

*x.dddddd*e+/–yy

The **%g** format specifier causes **Formatter** to use either **%f** or **%e**, based on the value being formatted and the precision, which is 6 by default. The following program demonstrates the effect of the **%f** and **%e** format specifiers:

```
// Demonstrate the %f and %e format specifiers.
import java.util.*;

class FormatDemo2 {
  public static void main(String[] args) {
    Formatter fmt = new Formatter();

    for(double i=1.23; i < 1.0e+6; i *= 100) {
      fmt.format("%f %e ", i, i);
      System.out.println(fmt);
    }
    fmt.close();

  }
}
```

It produces the following output:

```
1.230000 1.230000e+00
1.230000 1.230000e+00 123.000000 1.230000e+02
1.230000 1.230000e+00 123.000000 1.230000e+02 12300.000000 1.230000e+04
```

You can display integers in octal or hexadecimal format by using **%o** and **%x**, respectively. For example, the fragment

```
fmt.format("Hex: %x, Octal: %o", 196, 196);
```

produces this output:

```
Hex: c4, Octal: 304
```

You can display floating-point values in hexadecimal format by using **%a**. The format produced by **%a** appears a bit strange at first glance. This is because its representation uses a form similar to scientific notation that consists of a hexadecimal significand and a decimal exponent of powers of 2. Here is the general format:

0x1.*sig*p*exp*

Here, *sig* contains the fractional portion of the significand and *exp* contains the exponent. The **p** indicates the start of the exponent. For example, the call

```
fmt.format("%a", 512.0);
```

produces this output:

```
0x1.0p9
```

## Formatting Time and Date

One of the more powerful conversion specifiers is **%t**. It lets you format time and date information. The **%t** specifier works a bit differently than the others because it requires the use of a suffix to describe the portion and precise format of the time or date desired. The suffixes are shown in Table 21-13. For example, to display minutes, you would use **%tM**, where **M** indicates minutes in a two-character field. The argument corresponding to the **%t** specifier must be of type **Calendar**, **Date**, **Long**, **long**, or **TemporalAccessor**.

| Suffix | Replaced By |
|---|---|
| a | Abbreviated weekday name |
| A | Full weekday name |
| b | Abbreviated month name |
| B | Full month name |
| c | Standard date and time string formatted as<br>*day month date hh::mm:ss tzone year* |
| C | First two digits of year |
| d | Day of month as a decimal (01–31) |
| D | month/day/year |
| e | Day of month as a decimal (1–31) |
| F | year-month-day |
| h | Abbreviated month name |
| H | Hour (00 to 23) |
| I | Hour (01 to 12) |
| j | Day of year as a decimal (001 to 366) |
| k | Hour (0 to 23) |
| l | Hour (1 to 12) |
| L | Millisecond (000 to 999) |
| m | Month as decimal (01 to 13) |
| M | Minute as decimal (00 to 59) |
| N | Nanosecond (000000000 to 999999999) |
| p | Locale's equivalent of AM or PM in lowercase |
| Q | Milliseconds from 1/1/1970 |
| r | *hh:mm:ss* (12-hour format) |
| R | *hh:mm* (24-hour format) |
| S | Seconds (00 to 60) |
| s | Seconds from 1/1/1970 UTC |

**Table 21-13** The Time and Date Format Suffixes

| Suffix | Replaced By |
|---|---|
| T | *hh:mm:ss* (24-hour format) |
| y | Year in decimal without century (00 to 99) |
| Y | Year in decimal including century (0001 to 9999) |
| z | Offset from UTC |
| Z | Time zone name |

**Table 21-13** The Time and Date Format Suffixes *(continued)*

Here is a program that demonstrates several of the formats:

```
// Formatting time and date.
import java.util.*;

class TimeDateFormat {
  public static void main(String[] args) {
    Formatter fmt = new Formatter();
    Calendar cal = Calendar.getInstance();

    // Display standard 12-hour time format.
    fmt.format("%tr", cal);
    System.out.println(fmt);
    fmt.close();

    // Display complete time and date information.
    fmt = new Formatter();
    fmt.format("%tc", cal);
    System.out.println(fmt);
    fmt.close();

    // Display just hour and minute.
    fmt = new Formatter();
    fmt.format("%tl:%tM", cal, cal);
    System.out.println(fmt);
    fmt.close();

    // Display month by name and number.
    fmt = new Formatter();
    fmt.format("%tB %tb %tm", cal, cal, cal);
    System.out.println(fmt);
    fmt.close();
  }
}
```

Sample output is shown here:

```
03:15:34 PM
Sat Jan 01 15:15:34 CST 2022
3:15
January Jan 01
```

## The %n and %% Specifiers

The **%n** and**%%** format specifiers differ from the others in that they do not match an argument. Instead, they are simply escape sequences that insert a character into the output sequence. The **%n** inserts a newline. The **%%** inserts a percent sign. Neither of these characters can be entered directly into the format string. Of course, you can also use the standard escape sequence **\n** to embed a newline character.

Here is an example that demonstrates the **%n** and **%%** format specifiers:

```
// Demonstrate the %n and %% format specifiers.
import java.util.*;

class FormatDemo3 {
  public static void main(String[] args) {
    Formatter fmt = new Formatter();

    fmt.format("Copying file%nTransfer is %d%% complete", 88);
    System.out.println(fmt);
    fmt.close();
  }
}
```

It displays the following output:

```
Copying file
Transfer is 88% complete
```

## Specifying a Minimum Field Width

An integer placed between the **%** sign and the format conversion code acts as a *minimum field-width specifier*. This pads the output with spaces to ensure that it reaches a certain minimum length. If the string or number is longer than that minimum, it will still be printed in full. The default padding is done with spaces. If you want to pad with 0's, place a 0 before the field-width specifier. For example, **%05d** will pad a number of less than five digits with 0's so that its total length is five. The field-width specifier can be used with all format specifiers except **%n**.

The following program demonstrates the minimum field-width specifier by applying it to the **%f** conversion:

```
// Demonstrate a field-width specifier.
import java.util.*;

class FormatDemo4 {
  public static void main(String[] args) {
    Formatter fmt = new Formatter();

    fmt.format("|%f|%n|%12f|%n|%012f|",
               10.12345, 10.12345, 10.12345);
```

```
      System.out.println(fmt);
      fmt.close();
    }
}
```

This program produces the following output:

```
|10.123450|
|   10.123450|
|00010.123450|
```

The first line displays the number 10.12345 in its default width. The second line displays that value in a 12-character field. The third line displays the value in a 12-character field, padded with leading zeros.

The minimum field-width modifier is often used to produce tables in which the columns line up. For example, the next program produces a table of squares and cubes for the numbers between 1 and 10:

```
// Create a table of squares and cubes.
import java.util.*;

class FieldWidthDemo {
  public static void main(String[] args) {
    Formatter fmt;

    for(int i=1; i <= 10; i++) {
      fmt = new Formatter();
      fmt.format("%4d %4d %4d", i, i*i, i*i*i);
      System.out.println(fmt);
      fmt.close();
    }
  }
}
```

Its output is shown here:

```
   1    1    1
   2    4    8
   3    9   27
   4   16   64
   5   25  125
   6   36  216
   7   49  343
   8   64  512
   9   81  729
  10  100 1000
```

## Specifying Precision

A *precision specifier* can be applied to the **%f**, **%e**, **%g**, and **%s** format specifiers, among others. It follows the minimum field-width specifier (if there is one) and consists of a period followed by an integer. Its exact meaning depends upon the type of data to which it is applied.

When you apply the precision specifier to floating-point data using the **%f** or **%e** specifiers, it determines the number of decimal places displayed. For example, **%10.4f** displays a number at least ten characters wide with four decimal places. When using **%g**, the precision determines the number of significant digits. The default precision is 6.

Applied to strings, the precision specifier specifies the maximum field length. For example, **%5.7s** displays a string of at least five and not exceeding seven characters long. If the string is longer than the maximum field width, the end characters will be truncated.

The following program illustrates the precision specifier:

```
// Demonstrate the precision modifier.
import java.util.*;

class PrecisionDemo {
  public static void main(String[] args) {
    Formatter fmt = new Formatter();

    // Format 4 decimal places.
    fmt.format("%.4f", 123.1234567);
    System.out.println(fmt);
    fmt.close();

    // Format to 2 decimal places in a 16 character field
    fmt = new Formatter();
    fmt.format("%16.2e", 123.1234567);
    System.out.println(fmt);
    fmt.close();

    // Display at most 15 characters in a string.
    fmt = new Formatter();
    fmt.format("%.15s", "Formatting with Java is now easy.");
    System.out.println(fmt);
    fmt.close();
  }
}
```

It produces the following output:

```
123.1235
        1.23e+02
Formatting with
```

## Using the Format Flags

**Formatter** recognizes a set of format *flags* that lets you control various aspects of a conversion. All format flags are single characters, and a format flag follows the % in a format specification. The flags are shown here:

| Flag | Effect |
|---|---|
| – | Left justification. |
| # | Alternate conversion format. |
| 0 | Output is padded with zeros rather than spaces. |
| *space* | Positive numeric output is preceded by a space. |
| + | Positive numeric output is preceded by a + sign. |
| , | Numeric values include grouping separators. |
| ( | Negative numeric values are enclosed within parentheses. |

Not all flags apply to all format specifiers. The following sections explain each in detail.

## Justifying Output

By default, all output is right-justified. That is, if the field width is larger than the data printed, the data will be placed on the right edge of the field. You can force output to be left-justified by placing a minus sign directly after the %. For instance, **%–10.2f** left-justifies a floating-point number with two decimal places in a 10-character field. For example, consider this program:

```
// Demonstrate left justification.
import java.util.*;

class LeftJustify {
  public static void main(String[] args) {
    Formatter fmt = new Formatter();

    // Right justify by default
    fmt.format("|%10.2f|", 123.123);
    System.out.println(fmt);
    fmt.close();

    // Now, left justify.
    fmt = new Formatter();
    fmt.format("|%-10.2f|", 123.123);
    System.out.println(fmt);
    fmt.close();
  }
}
```

It produces the following output:

```
|    123.12|
|123.12    |
```

As you can see, the second line is left-justified within a 10-character field.

## The Space, +, 0, and ( Flags

To cause a + sign to be shown before positive numeric values, add the + flag. For example,

```
fmt.format("%+d", 100);
```

creates this string:

```
+100
```

When creating columns of numbers, it is sometimes useful to output a space before positive values so that positive and negative values line up. To do this, add the space flag. For example:

```
// Demonstrate the space format specifiers.
import java.util.*;

class FormatDemo5 {
  public static void main(String[] args) {
    Formatter fmt = new Formatter();

    fmt.format("% d", -100);
    System.out.println(fmt);
    fmt.close();

    fmt = new Formatter();
    fmt.format("% d", 100);
    System.out.println(fmt);
    fmt.close();

    fmt = new Formatter();
    fmt.format("% d", -200);
    System.out.println(fmt);
    fmt.close();

    fmt = new Formatter();
    fmt.format("% d", 200);
    System.out.println(fmt);
    fmt.close();
  }
}
```

The output is shown here:

```
-100
 100
-200
 200
```

Notice that the positive values have a leading space, which causes the digits in the column to line up properly.

To show negative numeric output inside parentheses, rather than with a leading –, use the ( flag. For example,

```
fmt.format("%(d", -100);
```

creates this string:

```
(100)
```

The 0 flag causes output to be padded with zeros rather than spaces.

## The Comma Flag

When displaying large numbers, it is often useful to add grouping separators, which in English are commas. For example, the value 1234567 is more easily read when formatted as 1,234,567. To add grouping specifiers, use the comma (,) flag. For example,

```
fmt.format("%,.2f", 4356783497.34);
```

creates this string:

```
4,356,783,497.34
```

## The # Flag

The # can be applied to **%o**, **%x**, **%e**, and **%f**. For **%e** and **%f**, the # ensures that there will be a decimal point even if there are no decimal digits. If you precede the **%x** format specifier with a #, the hexadecimal number will be printed with a **0x** prefix. Preceding the **%o** specifier with # causes the number to be printed with a leading zero.

## The Uppercase Option

As mentioned earlier, several of the format specifiers have uppercase versions that cause the conversion to use uppercase where appropriate. The following table describes the effect.

| Specifier | Effect |
|---|---|
| %A | Causes the hexadecimal digits *a* through *f* to be displayed in uppercase as *A* through *F*. Also, the prefix **0x** is displayed as **0X**, and the **p** will be displayed as **P**. |
| %B | Uppercases the values **true** and **false**. |
| %E | Causes the *e* symbol that indicates the exponent to be displayed in uppercase. |
| %G | Causes the *e* symbol that indicates the exponent to be displayed in uppercase. |
| %H | Causes the hexadecimal digits *a* through *f* to be displayed in uppercase as *A* through *F*. |
| %S | Uppercases the corresponding string. |
| %X | Causes the hexadecimal digits *a* through *f* to be displayed in uppercase as *A* through *F*. Also, the optional prefix **0x** is displayed as **0X**, if present. |

For example, the call

```
fmt.format("%X", 250);
```

creates this string:

```
FA
```

The call

```
fmt.format("%E", 123.1234);
```

creates this string:

```
1.231234E+02
```

## Using an Argument Index

**Formatter** includes a very useful feature that lets you specify the argument to which a format specifier applies. Normally, format specifiers and arguments are matched in order, from left to right. That is, the first format specifier matches the first argument, the second format specifier matches the second argument, and so on. However, by using an *argument index*, you can explicitly control which argument a format specifier matches.

An argument index immediately follows the **%** in a format specifier. It has the following format:

*n*$

Here, *n* is the index of the desired argument, beginning with 1. For example, consider this example:

```
fmt.format("%3$d %1$d %2$d", 10, 20, 30);
```

It produces this string:

```
30 10 20
```

In this example, the first format specifier matches 30, the second matches 10, and the third matches 20. Thus, the arguments are used in an order other than strictly left to right.

One advantage of argument indexes is that they enable you to reuse an argument without having to specify it twice. For example, consider this line:

```
fmt.format("%d in hex is %1$x", 255);
```

It produces the following string:

```
255 in hex is ff
```

As you can see, the argument 255 is used by both format specifiers.

There is a convenient shorthand called a *relative index* that enables you to reuse the argument matched by the preceding format specifier. Simply specify < for the argument index. For example, the following call to **format( )** produces the same results as the previous example:

```
fmt.format("%d in hex is %<x", 255);
```

Relative indexes are especially useful when creating custom time and date formats. Consider the following example:

```
// Use relative indexes to simplify the
// creation of a custom time and date format.
import java.util.*;

class FormatDemo6 {
  public static void main(String[] args) {
    Formatter fmt = new Formatter();
    Calendar cal = Calendar.getInstance();

    fmt.format("Today is day %te of %<tB, %<tY", cal);
    System.out.println(fmt);
    fmt.close();
  }
}
```

Here is sample output:

```
Today is day 1 of January, 2022
```

Because of relative indexing, the argument **cal** need only be passed once, rather than three times.

## Closing a Formatter

In general, you should close a **Formatter** when you are done using it. Doing so frees any resources that it was using. This is especially important when formatting to a file, but it can be important in other cases, too. As the previous examples have shown, one way to close a **Formatter** is to explicitly call **close( )**. However, **Formatter** also implements the **AutoCloseable** interface. This means that it supports the **try**-with-resources statement. Using this approach, the **Formatter** is automatically closed when it is no longer needed.

The **try**-with-resources statement is described in Chapter 13, in connection with files, because files are some of the most commonly used resources that must be closed. However, the same basic techniques apply here. For example, here is the first **Formatter** example reworked to use automatic resource management:

```
// Use automatic resource management with Formatter.
import java.util.*;

class FormatDemo {
  public static void main(String[] args) {

    try (Formatter fmt = new Formatter())
    {
      fmt.format("Formatting %s is easy %d %f", "with Java",
                 10, 98.6);
      System.out.println(fmt);
    }
  }
}
```

The output is the same as before.

## The Java printf( ) Connection

Although there is nothing technically wrong with using **Formatter** directly (as the preceding examples have done) when creating output that will be displayed on the console, there is a more convenient alternative: the **printf( )** method. The **printf( )** method automatically uses **Formatter** to create a formatted string. It then displays that string on **System.out**, which is the console by default. The **printf( )** method is defined by both **PrintStream** and **PrintWriter**. The **printf( )** method is described in Chapter 22.



# Scanner

**Scanner** is the complement of **Formatter**. It reads formatted input and converts it into its binary form. **Scanner** can be used to read input from the console, a file, a string, or any source that implements the **Readable** interface or **ReadableByteChannel**. For example, you can use **Scanner** to read a number from the keyboard and assign its value to a variable. As you will see, given its power, **Scanner** is surprisingly easy to use.

## The Scanner Constructors

**Scanner** defines many constructors. A sampling is shown in Table 21-14. In general, a **Scanner** can be created for a **String**, an **InputStream**, a **File**, a **Path**, or any object that implements the **Readable** or **ReadableByteChannel** interface. Here are some examples.

The following sequence creates a **Scanner** that reads the file **Test.txt**:

```
FileReader fin = new FileReader("Test.txt");
Scanner src = new Scanner(fin);
```

This works because **FileReader** implements the **Readable** interface. Thus, the call to the constructor resolves to **Scanner(Readable)**.

This next line creates a **Scanner** that reads from standard input, which is the keyboard by default:

```
Scanner conin = new Scanner(System.in);
```

This works because **System.in** is an object of type **InputStream**. Thus, the call to the constructor maps to **Scanner(InputStream)**.

The next sequence creates a **Scanner** that reads from a string:

```
String instr = "10 99.88 scanning is easy.";
Scanner conin = new Scanner(instr);
```

## Scanning Basics

Once you have created a **Scanner**, it is a simple matter to use it to read formatted input. In general, a **Scanner** reads *tokens* from the underlying source that you specified when the **Scanner** was created. As it relates to **Scanner**, a token is a portion of input that is delineated by a set of delimiters, which is whitespace by default. A token is read by matching it with a particular *regular expression*, which defines the format of the data. Although **Scanner** allows

| Method | Description |
|---|---|
| Scanner(File *from*) throws FileNotFoundException | Creates a **Scanner** that uses the file specified by *from* as a source for input |
| Scanner(File *from*, String *charset*) throws FileNotFoundException | Creates a **Scanner** that uses the file specified by *from* with the encoding specified by *charset* as a source for input |
| Scanner(InputStream *from*) | Creates a **Scanner** that uses the stream specified by *from* as a source for input |
| Scanner(InputStream *from*, String *charset*) | Creates a **Scanner** that uses the stream specified by *from* with the encoding specified by *charset* as a source for input |
| Scanner(Path *from*) throws IOException | Creates a **Scanner** that uses the file specified by *from* as a source for input |
| Scanner(Path *from*, String *charset*) throws IOException | Creates a **Scanner** that uses the file specified by *from* with the encoding specified by *charset* as a source for input |
| Scanner(Readable *from*) | Creates a **Scanner** that uses the **Readable** object specified by *from* as a source for input |
| Scanner (ReadableByteChannel *from*) | Creates a **Scanner** that uses the **ReadableByteChannel** specified by *from* as a source for input |
| Scanner(ReadableByteChannel *from*, String *charset*) | Creates a **Scanner** that uses the **ReadableByteChannel** specified by *from* with the encoding specified by *charset* as a source for input |
| Scanner(String *from*) | Creates a **Scanner** that uses the string specified by *from* as a source for input |

**Table 21-14** A Sampling of **Scanner** Constructors

you to define the specific type of expression that its next input operation will match, it includes many predefined patterns, which match the primitive types, such as **int** and **double**, and strings. Thus, often you won't need to specify a pattern to match.

In general, to use **Scanner**, follow this procedure:

1. Determine if a specific type of input is available by calling one of **Scanner**'s **hasNext***X* methods, where *X* is the type of data desired.
2. If input is available, read it by calling one of **Scanner**'s **next***X* methods.
3. Repeat the process until input is exhausted.
4. Close the **Scanner** by calling **close( )**.

As the preceding indicates, **Scanner** defines two sets of methods that enable you to read input. The first set is the **hasNext***X* methods, which are shown in Table 21-15. These methods determine if the specified type of input is available. For example, calling **hasNextInt( )** returns **true** only if the next token to be read is an integer. If the desired data is available, then you read it by calling one of **Scanner**'s **next***X* methods, which are shown in Table 21-16.

| Method | Description |
|---|---|
| boolean hasNext( ) | Returns **true** if another token of any type is available to be read. Returns **false** otherwise. |
| boolean hasNext(Pattern *pattern*) | Returns **true** if a token that matches the pattern passed in *pattern* is available to be read. Returns **false** otherwise. |
| boolean hasNext(String *pattern*) | Returns **true** if a token that matches the pattern passed in *pattern* is available to be read. Returns **false** otherwise. |
| boolean hasNextBigDecimal( ) | Returns **true** if a value that can be stored in a **BigDecimal** object is available to be read. Returns **false** otherwise. |
| boolean hasNextBigInteger( ) | Returns **true** if a value that can be stored in a **BigInteger** object is available to be read. Returns **false** otherwise. The default radix is used. (Unless changed, the default radix is 10.) |
| boolean hasNextBigInteger(int *radix*) | Returns **true** if a value in the specified radix that can be stored in a **BigInteger** object is available to be read. Returns **false** otherwise. |
| boolean hasNextBoolean( ) | Returns **true** if a **boolean** value is available to be read. Returns **false** otherwise. |
| boolean hasNextByte( ) | Returns **true** if a **byte** value is available to be read. Returns **false** otherwise. The default radix is used. (Unless changed, the default radix is 10.) |
| boolean hasNextByte(int *radix*) | Returns **true** if a **byte** value in the specified radix is available to be read. Returns **false** otherwise. |
| boolean hasNextDouble( ) | Returns **true** if a **double** value is available to be read. Returns **false** otherwise. |
| boolean hasNextFloat( ) | Returns **true** if a **float** value is available to be read. Returns **false** otherwise. |
| boolean hasNextInt( ) | Returns **true** if an **int** value is available to be read. Returns **false** otherwise. The default radix is used. (Unless changed, the default radix is 10.) |
| boolean hasNextInt(int *radix*) | Returns **true** if an **int** value in the specified radix is available to be read. Returns **false** otherwise. |
| boolean hasNextLine( ) | Returns **true** if a line of input is available. |
| boolean hasNextLong( ) | Returns **true** if a **long** value is available to be read. Returns **false** otherwise. The default radix is used. (Unless changed, the default radix is 10.) |
| boolean hasNextLong(int *radix*) | Returns **true** if a **long** value in the specified radix is available to be read. Returns **false** otherwise. |
| boolean hasNextShort( ) | Returns **true** if a **short** value is available to be read. Returns **false** otherwise. The default radix is used. (Unless changed, the default radix is 10.) |
| boolean hasNextShort(int *radix*) | Returns **true** if a **short** value in the specified radix is available to be read. Returns **false** otherwise. |

**Table 21-15** The **Scanner hasNext** Methods

| Method | Description |
|---|---|
| String next( ) | Returns the next token of any type from the input source. |
| String next(Pattern *pattern*) | Returns the next token that matches the pattern passed in *pattern* from the input source. |
| String next(String *pattern*) | Returns the next token that matches the pattern passed in *pattern* from the input source. |
| BigDecimal nextBigDecimal( ) | Returns the next token as a **BigDecimal** object. |
| BigInteger nextBigInteger( ) | Returns the next token as a **BigInteger** object. The default radix is used. (Unless changed, the default radix is 10.) |
| BigInteger nextBigInteger(int *radix*) | Returns the next token (using the specified radix) as a **BigInteger** object. |
| boolean nextBoolean( ) | Returns the next token as a **boolean** value. |
| byte nextByte( ) | Returns the next token as a **byte** value. The default radix is used. (Unless changed, the default radix is 10.) |
| byte nextByte(int *radix*) | Returns the next token (using the specified radix) as a **byte** value. |
| double nextDouble( ) | Returns the next token as a **double** value. |
| float nextFloat( ) | Returns the next token as a **float** value. |
| int nextInt( ) | Returns the next token as an **int** value. The default radix is used. (Unless changed, the default radix is 10.) |
| int nextInt(int *radix*) | Returns the next token (using the specified radix) as an **int** value. |
| String nextLine( ) | Returns the next line of input as a string. |
| long nextLong( ) | Returns the next token as a **long** value. The default radix is used. (Unless changed, the default radix is 10.) |
| long nextLong(int *radix*) | Returns the next token (using the specified radix) as a **long** value. |
| short nextShort( ) | Returns the next token as a **short** value. The default radix is used. (Unless changed, the default radix is 10.) |
| short nextShort(int *radix*) | Returns the next token (using the specified radix) as a **short** value. |

**Table 21-16** The **Scanner next** Methods

For example, to read the next integer, call **nextInt( )**. The following sequence shows how to read a list of integers from the keyboard:

```
Scanner conin = new Scanner(System.in);
int i;

// Read a list of integers.
while(conin.hasNextInt()) {
  i = conin.nextInt();
  // ...
}
```

The **while** loop stops as soon as the next token is not an integer. Thus, the loop stops reading integers as soon as a non-integer is encountered in the input stream.

If a **next** method cannot find the type of data it is looking for, it throws an **InputMismatchException**. A **NoSuchElementException** is thrown if no more input is available. For this reason, it is best to first confirm that the desired type of data is available by calling a **hasNext** method before calling its corresponding **next** method.

## Some Scanner Examples

**Scanner** makes what could be a tedious task into an easy one. To understand why, let's look at some examples. The following program averages a list of numbers entered at the keyboard:

```
// Use Scanner to compute an average of the values.
import java.util.*;

class AvgNums {
  public static void main(String[] args) {
    Scanner conin = new Scanner(System.in);

    int count = 0;
    double sum = 0.0;

    System.out.println("Enter numbers to average.");

    // Read and sum numbers.
    while(conin.hasNext()) {
      if(conin.hasNextDouble()) {
        sum += conin.nextDouble();
        count++;
      }
      else {
        String str = conin.next();
        if(str.equals("done")) break;
        else {
          System.out.println("Data format error.");
          return;
        }
      }
    }

    conin.close();
    System.out.println("Average is " + sum / count);
  }
}
```

The program reads numbers from the keyboard, summing them in the process, until the user enters the string "done". It then stops input and displays the average of the numbers. Here is a sample run:

```
Enter numbers to average.
1.2
2
3.4
4
done
Average is 2.65
```

The program reads numbers until it encounters a token that does not represent a valid **double** value. When this occurs, it confirms that the token is the string "done". If it is, the program terminates normally. Otherwise, it displays an error.

Notice that the numbers are read by calling **nextDouble( )**. This method reads any number that can be converted into a **double** value, including an integer value, such as 2, and a floating-point value, like 3.4. Thus, a number read by **nextDouble( )** need not specify a decimal point. This same general principle applies to all **next** methods. They will match and read any data format that can represent the type of value being requested.

One thing that is especially nice about **Scanner** is that the same technique used to read from one source can be used to read from another. For example, here is the preceding program reworked to average a list of numbers contained in a text file:

```
// Use Scanner to compute an average of the values in a file.
import java.util.*;
import java.io.*;

class AvgFile {
  public static void main(String[] args)
    throws IOException {

    int count = 0;
    double sum = 0.0;

    // Write output to a file.
    FileWriter fout = new FileWriter("test.txt");
    fout.write("2 3.4 5 6 7.4 9.1 10.5 done");
    fout.close();

    FileReader fin = new FileReader("Test.txt");

    Scanner src = new Scanner(fin);

    // Read and sum numbers.
    while(src.hasNext()) {
      if(src.hasNextDouble()) {
        sum += src.nextDouble();
        count++;
      }
```

```
        else {
          String str = src.next();
          if(str.equals("done")) break;
          else {
            System.out.println("File format error.");
            return;
          }
        }
      }

      src.close();
      System.out.println("Average is " + sum / count);
    }
  }
```



Here is the output:

```
Average is 6.2
```

The preceding program illustrates another important feature of **Scanner**. Notice that the file reader referred to by **fin** is not closed directly. Rather, it is closed automatically when **src** calls **close( )**. When you close a **Scanner**, the **Readable** associated with it is also closed (if that **Readable** implements the **Closeable** interface). Therefore, in this case, the file referred to by **fin** is automatically closed when **src** is closed.

**Scanner** also implements the **AutoCloseable** interface. This means that it can be managed by a **try**-with-resources block. As explained in Chapter 13, when **try**-with-resources is used, the scanner is automatically closed when the block ends. For example, **src** in the preceding program could have been managed like this:

```
try (Scanner src = new Scanner(fin))
{
  // Read and sum numbers.
  while(src.hasNext()) {
    if(src.hasNextDouble()) {
      sum += src.nextDouble();
      count++;
    }
    else {
      String str = src.next();
      if(str.equals("done")) break;
      else {
        System.out.println("File format error.");
        return;
      }
    }
  }
}
```

To clearly demonstrate the closing of a **Scanner**, the following examples will call **close( )** explicitly, but you should feel free to use **try**-with-resources in your own code when appropriate.

One other point: To keep this and the other examples in this section compact, I/O exceptions are simply thrown out of **main( )**. However, your real-world code will normally handle I/O exceptions itself.

You can use **Scanner** to read input that contains several different types of data—even if the order of that data is unknown in advance. You must simply check what type of data is available before reading it. For example, consider this program:

```
// Use Scanner to read various types of data from a file.
import java.util.*;
import java.io.*;

class ScanMixed {
  public static void main(String[] args)
    throws IOException {

    int i;
    double d;
    boolean b;
    String str;

    // Write output to a file.
    FileWriter fout = new FileWriter("test.txt");
    fout.write("Testing Scanner 10 12.2 one true two false");
    fout.close();

    FileReader fin = new FileReader("Test.txt");

    Scanner src = new Scanner(fin);

    // Read to end.
    while(src.hasNext()) {
      if(src.hasNextInt()) {
        i = src.nextInt();
        System.out.println("int: " + i);
      }
      else if(src.hasNextDouble()) {
        d = src.nextDouble();
        System.out.println("double: " + d);
      }
      else if(src.hasNextBoolean()) {
        b = src.nextBoolean();
        System.out.println("boolean: " + b);
      }
      else {
        str = src.next();
        System.out.println("String: " + str);
      }
    }

    src.close();
  }
}
```

Here is the output:

```
String: Testing
String: Scanner
int: 10
double: 12.2
String: one
boolean: true
String: two
boolean: false
```

When reading mixed data types, as the preceding program does, you need to be a bit careful about the order in which you call the **next** methods. For example, if the loop reversed the order of the calls to **nextInt( )** and **nextDouble( )**, both numeric values would have been read as **doubles**, because **nextDouble( )** matches any numeric string that can be represented as a **double**.



## Setting Delimiters

**Scanner** defines where a token starts and ends based on a set of *delimiters*. The default delimiters are the whitespace characters, and this is the delimiter set that the preceding examples have used. However, it is possible to change the delimiters by calling the **useDelimiter( )** method, shown here:

Scanner useDelimiter(String *pattern*)

Scanner useDelimiter(Pattern *pattern*)

Here, *pattern* is a regular expression that specifies the delimiter set.

Here is the program that reworks the average program shown earlier so that it reads a list of numbers that are separated by commas, and any number of spaces:

```
// Use Scanner to compute an average a list of
// comma-separated values.
import java.util.*;
import java.io.*;

class SetDelimiters {
  public static void main(String[] args)
    throws IOException {

    int count = 0;
    double sum = 0.0;

    // Write output to a file.
    FileWriter fout = new FileWriter("test.txt");

    // Now, store values in comma-separated list.
    fout.write("2, 3.4,     5,6, 7.4, 9.1, 10.5, done");
    fout.close();

    FileReader fin = new FileReader("Test.txt");

    Scanner src = new Scanner(fin);
```

```
    // Set delimiters to space and comma.
    src.useDelimiter(", *");

    // Read and sum numbers.
    while(src.hasNext()) {
      if(src.hasNextDouble()) {
        sum += src.nextDouble();
        count++;
      }
      else {
        String str = src.next();
        if(str.equals("done")) break;
        else {
          System.out.println("File format error.");
          return;
        }
      }
    }

    src.close();
    System.out.println("Average is " + sum / count);
  }
}
```

In this version, the numbers written to **test.txt** are separated by commas and spaces. The use of the delimiter pattern **", * "** tells **Scanner** to match a comma and zero or more spaces as delimiters. The output is the same as before.

You can obtain the current delimiter pattern by calling **delimiter( )**, shown here:

Pattern delimiter( )

## Other Scanner Features

**Scanner** defines several other methods in addition to those already discussed. One that is particularly useful in some circumstances is **findInLine( )**. Its general forms are shown here:

String findInLine(Pattern *pattern*)
String findInLine(String *pattern*)

This method searches for the specified pattern within the next line of text. If the pattern is found, the matching token is consumed and returned. Otherwise, **null** is returned. It operates independently of any delimiter set. This method is useful if you want to locate a specific pattern. For example, the following program locates the Age field in the input string and then displays the age:

```
// Demonstrate findInLine().
import java.util.*;

class FindInLineDemo {
  public static void main(String[] args) {
    String instr = "Name: Tom Age: 28 ID: 77";

    Scanner conin = new Scanner(instr);
```

```
    // Find and display age.
    conin.findInLine("Age:"); // find Age

    if(conin.hasNext())
      System.out.println(conin.next());
    else
      System.out.println("Error!");

    conin.close();
  }
}
```



The output is **28**. In the program, **findInLine( )** is used to find an occurrence of the pattern "Age". Once found, the next token is read, which is the age.

Related to **findInLine( )** is **findWithinHorizon( )**. It is shown here:

String findWithinHorizon(Pattern *pattern*, int *count*)

String findWithinHorizon(String *pattern*, int *count*)

This method attempts to find an occurrence of the specified pattern within the next *count* characters. If successful, it returns the matching pattern. Otherwise, it returns **null**. If *count* is zero, then all input is searched until either a match is found or the end of input is encountered.

You can bypass a pattern using **skip( )**, shown here:

Scanner skip(Pattern *pattern*)

Scanner skip(String *pattern*)

If *pattern* is matched, **skip( )** simply advances beyond it and returns a reference to the invoking object. If pattern is not found, **skip( )** throws **NoSuchElementException**.

Other **Scanner** methods include **radix( )**, which returns the default radix used by the **Scanner**; **useRadix( )**, which sets the radix; **reset( )**, which resets the scanner; and **close( )**, which closes the scanner. JDK 9 added the methods **tokens( )**, which returns all tokens in the form of a **Stream<String>**, and **findAll( )**, which returns tokens that match the specified pattern in the form of a **Stream<MatchResult>**.

## The ResourceBundle, ListResourceBundle, and PropertyResourceBundle Classes

The **java.util** package includes three classes that aid in the internationalization of your program. The first is the abstract class **ResourceBundle**. It defines methods that enable you to manage a collection of locale-sensitive resources, such as the strings that are used to label the user interface elements in your program. You can define two or more sets of translated strings that support various languages, such as English, German, and Chinese, with each translation set residing in its own bundle. You can then load the bundle appropriate to the current locale and use the strings to construct the program's user interface.

Resource bundles are identified by their *family name* (also called their *base name*). To the family name can be added a *language code* that specifies the language. In this case, if a requested locale matches the language code, then that version of the resource bundle is used. For example, a resource bundle with a family name of **SampleRB** could have a German version called **SampleRB_de** and a Russian version called **SampleRB_ru**. (Notice that an underscore links the family name to the language code.) Therefore, if the locale is **Locale.GERMAN**, **SampleRB_de** will be used.

It is also possible to indicate specific variants of a language that relate to a specific country by specifying a *country code* after the language code, such as **AU** for Australia or **IN** for India. A country code is also preceded by an underscore when linked to the resource bundle name. Other variations are also supported. A resource bundle that has only the family name is the default bundle. It is used when no language-specific bundles are applicable.

**NOTE** The language codes are defined by ISO standard 639 and the country codes by ISO standard 3166.

The methods defined by **ResourceBundle** are summarized in Table 21-17. One important point: **null** keys are not allowed, and several of the methods will throw a **NullPointerException** if **null** is passed as the key. Notice the nested class **ResourceBundle.Control**. It is used to control the resource-bundle loading process.

| Method | Description |
|---|---|
| static final void clearCache( ) | Deletes all resource bundles from the cache that were loaded by the class loader. Beginning with JDK 9, this method deletes all resource bundles from the cache that were loaded by the module from which this method is called. |
| static final void clearCache(ClassLoader *ldr*) | Deletes all resource bundles from the cache that were loaded by *ldr*. |
| boolean containsKey(String *k*) | Returns **true** if *k* is a key within the invoking resource bundle (or its parent). |
| String getBaseBundleName( ) | Returns the resource bundle's base name if available. Returns **null** otherwise. |
| static final ResourceBundle getBundle(String *familyName*) | Loads the resource bundle with a family name of *familyName* using the default locale. Throws **MissingResourceException** if no resource bundle matching the name is available. |
| static ResourceBundle getBundle( String *familyName*, Module *mod*) | Loads the resource bundle with a family name of *familyName* for the module specified by *mod*. The default locale is used. Throws **MissingResourceException** if no resource bundle matching the name is available. |
| static final ResourceBundle getBundle(String *familyName*, Locale *loc*) | Loads the resource bundle with a family name of *familyName* using the specified locale. Throws **MissingResourceException** if no resource bundle matching the name is available. |

**Table 21-17** The Methods Defined by **ResourceBundle**

| Method | Description |
|---|---|
| static ResourceBundle getBundle(<br>String *familyName*,<br>Locale *loc*,<br>Module *mod*) | Loads the resource bundle with a family name of *familyName* using the locale passed in *loc* for the module specified by *mod*. Throws **MissingResourceException** if no resource bundle matching the name is available. |
| static ResourceBundle<br>getBundle(String *familyName*,<br>Locale *loc*,<br>ClassLoader *ldr*) | Loads the resource bundle with a family name of *familyName* using the specified locale and the specified class loader. Throws **MissingResourceException** if no resource bundle matching the name is available. |
| static final ResourceBundle<br>getBundle(String *familyName*,<br>ResourceBundle.Control *cntl*) | Loads the resource bundle with a family name of *familyName* using the default locale. The loading process is under the control of *cntl*. Throws **MissingResourceException** if no resource bundle matching the name is available. |
| static final ResourceBundle<br>getBundle(String *familyName*,<br>Locale *loc*,<br>ResourceBundle.Control *cntl*) | Loads the resource bundle with a family name of *familyName* using the specified locale. The loading process is under the control of *cntl*. Throws **MissingResourceException** if no resource bundle matching the name is available. |
| static ResourceBundle<br>getBundle(String *familyName*,<br>Locale *loc*,<br>ClassLoader *ldr*,<br>ResourceBundle.Control *cntl*) | Loads the resource bundle with a family name of *familyName* using the specified locale and the specified class loader. The loading process is under the control of *cntl*. Throws **MissingResourceException** if no resource bundle matching the name is available. |
| abstract Enumeration<String> getKeys( ) | Returns the resource bundle keys as an enumeration of strings. Any parent's keys are also obtained. |
| Locale getLocale( ) | Returns the locale supported by the resource bundle. |
| final Object getObject(String *k*) | Returns the object associated with the key passed via *k*. Throws **MissingResourceException** if *k* is not in the resource bundle. |
| final String getString(String *k*) | Returns the string associated with the key passed via *k*. Throws **MissingResourceException** if *k* is not in the resource bundle. Throws **ClassCastException** if the object associated with *k* is not a string. |
| final String[ ] getStringArray(String *k*) | Returns the string array associated with the key passed via *k*. Throws **MissingResourceException** if *k* is not in the resource bundle. Throws **MissingResourceException** if the object associated with *k* is not a string array. |
| protected abstract Object<br>handleGetObject(String *k*) | Returns the object associated with the key passed via *k*. Returns **null** if *k* is not in the resource bundle. |
| protected Set<String> handleKeySet( ) | Returns the resource bundle keys as a set of strings. No parent's keys are obtained. |

**Table 21-17** The Methods Defined by **ResourceBundle** *(continued)*

| Method | Description |
|---|---|
| Set<String> keySet( ) | Returns the resource bundle keys as a set of strings. Any parent keys are also obtained. |
| protected void setParent(ResourceBundle *parent*) | Sets *parent* as the parent bundle for the resource bundle. When a key is looked up, the parent will be searched if the key is not found in the invoking resource object. |

**Table 21-17** The Methods Defined by **ResourceBundle** *(continued)*

**NOTE** Notice that JDK 9 added methods to **ResourceBundle** that support modules. Furthermore, the addition of modules raises several issues related to the use of resource bundles that are beyond the scope of this discussion. Consult the API documentation for details on how modules affect the use of **ResourceBundle**.

There are two subclasses of **ResourceBundle**. The first is **PropertyResourceBundle**, which manages resources by using property files. **PropertyResourceBundle** adds no methods of its own. The second is the abstract class **ListResourceBundle**, which manages resources in an array of key/value pairs. **ListResourceBundle** adds the method **getContents( )**, which all subclasses must implement. It is shown here:

protected abstract Object[ ][ ] getContents( )

It returns a two-dimensional array that contains key/value pairs that represent resources. The keys must be strings. The values are typically strings but can be other types of objects.

Here is an example that demonstrates using a resource bundle in an unnamed module. The resource bundle has the family name **SampleRB**. Two resource bundle classes of this family are created by extending **ListResourceBundle**. The first is called **SampleRB**, and it is the default bundle (which uses English). It is shown here:

```
import java.util.*;
public class SampleRB extends ListResourceBundle {
  protected Object[][] getContents() {
    Object[][] resources = new Object[3][2];

    resources[0][0] = "title";
    resources[0][1] = "My Program";

    resources[1][0] = "StopText";
    resources[1][1] = "Stop";

    resources[2][0] = "StartText";
    resources[2][1] = "Start";

    return resources;
  }
}
```

The second resource bundle, shown next, is called **SampleRB_de**. It contains the German translation.

```
import java.util.*;

// German version.
public class SampleRB_de extends ListResourceBundle {
  protected Object[][] getContents() {
    Object[][] resources = new Object[3][2];

    resources[0][0] = "title";
    resources[0][1] = "Mein Programm";

    resources[1][0] = "StopText";
    resources[1][1] = "Anschlag";

    resources[2][0] = "StartText";
    resources[2][1] = "Anfang";

    return resources;
  }
}
```

The following program demonstrates these two resource bundles by displaying the string associated with each key for both the default (English) version and the German version:

```
// Demonstrate a resource bundle.
import java.util.*;

class LRBDemo {
  public static void main(String[] args) {
    // Load the default bundle.
    ResourceBundle rd = ResourceBundle.getBundle("SampleRB");

    System.out.println("English version: ");
    System.out.println("String for Title key : " +
                       rd.getString("title"));

    System.out.println("String for StopText key: " +
                       rd.getString("StopText"));

    System.out.println("String for StartText key: " +
                       rd.getString("StartText"));

    // Load the German bundle.
    rd = ResourceBundle.getBundle("SampleRB", Locale.GERMAN);

    System.out.println("\nGerman version: ");
    System.out.println("String for Title key : " +
                       rd.getString("title"));

    System.out.println("String for StopText key: " +
                       rd.getString("StopText"));
```

```
        System.out.println("String for StartText key: " +
                           rd.getString("StartText"));
    }
}
```

The output from the program is shown here:

```
English version:
String for Title key : My Program
String for StopText key: Stop
String for StartText key: Start

German version:
String for Title key : Mein Programm
String for StopText key: Anschlag
String for StartText key: Anfang
```

## Miscellaneous Utility Classes and Interfaces

In addition to the classes already discussed, **java.util** includes the following classes:

| | |
|---|---|
| Base64 | Supports Base64 encoding. **Encoder** and **Decoder** nested classes are also defined. |
| DoubleSummaryStatistics | Supports the compilation of **double** values. The following statistics are available: average, minimum, maximum, count, and sum. |
| EventListenerProxy | Extends the **EventListener** class to allow additional parameters. See Chapter 25 for a discussion of event listeners. |
| EventObject | The superclass for all event classes. Events are discussed in Chapter 25. |
| FormattableFlags | Defines formatting flags that are used with the **Formattable** interface. |
| HexFormat | Provides various conversions to and from hexadecimal strings and digits. It is a value-based class. |
| IntSummaryStatistics | Supports the compilation of **int** values. The following statistics are available: average, minimum, maximum, count, and sum. |
| Objects | Various methods that operate on objects. |
| PropertyPermission | Manages property permissions. |
| ServiceLoader | Provides a means of finding service providers. |
| StringJoiner | Supports the concatenation of **CharSequence**s, which may include a separator, a prefix, and a suffix. |
| UUID | Encapsulates and manages Universally Unique Identifiers (UUIDs). |

The following interfaces are also packaged in **java.util**:

| | |
|---|---|
| EventListener | Indicates that a class is an event listener. Events are discussed in Chapter 25. |
| Formattable | Enables a class to provide custom formatting. |

# The java.util Subpackages

Java defines the following subpackages of **java.util**:

- java.util.concurrent
- java.util.concurrent.atomic
- java.util.concurrent.locks
- java.util.function
- java.util.jar
- java.util.logging
- java.util.prefs
- java.util.random
- java.util.regex
- java.util.spi
- java.util.stream
- java.util.zip

Except as otherwise noted, all are part of the **java.base** module. Each is briefly examined here.

## java.util.concurrent, java.util.concurrent.atomic, and java.util.concurrent.locks

The **java.util.concurrent** package along with its two subpackages, **java.util.concurrent .atomic** and **java.util.concurrent.locks**, support concurrent programming. These packages provide a high-performance alternative to using Java's built-in synchronization features when thread-safe operation is required. The **java.util.concurrent** package also provides the Fork/ Join Framework. These packages are examined in detail in Chapter 29.

## java.util.function

The **java.util.function** package defines several predefined functional interfaces that you can use when creating lambda expressions or method references. They are also widely used throughout the Java API. The functional interfaces defined by **java.util.function** are shown in Table 21-18 along with a synopsis of their abstract methods. Be aware that some of these interfaces also define default or static methods that supply additional functionality. You will want to explore them fully on your own. (For a discussion of the use of functional interfaces, see Chapter 15.)

## java.util.jar

The **java.util.jar** package provides the ability to read and write Java Archive (JAR) files.

Part II

| Interface | Abstract Method |
|---|---|
| BiConsumer<T, U> | void accept(T *tVal*, U *uVal*)<br>**Description**: Acts on *tVal* and *uVal*. |
| BiFunction<T, U, R> | R apply(T *tVal*, U *uVal*)<br>**Description**: Acts on *tVal* and *uVal* and returns the result. |
| BinaryOperator<T> | T apply(T *val1*, T *val2*)<br>**Description**: Acts on two objects of the same type and returns the result, which is also of the same type. |
| BiPredicate<T, U> | boolean test(T *tVal*, U *uVal*)<br>**Description**: Returns **true** if *tVal* and *uVal* satisfy the condition defined by **test( )** and **false** otherwise. |
| BooleanSupplier | boolean getAsBoolean( )<br>**Description**: Returns a **boolean** value. |
| Consumer<T> | void accept(T *val*)<br>**Description**: Acts on *val*. |
| DoubleBinaryOperator | double applyAsDouble(double *val1*, double *val2*)<br>**Description**: Acts on two **double** values and returns a **double** result. |
| DoubleConsumer | void accept(double *val*)<br>**Description**: Acts on *val*. |
| DoubleFunction<R> | R apply(double *val*)<br>**Description**: Acts on a **double** value and returns the result. |
| DoublePredicate | boolean test(double *val*)<br>**Description**: Returns **true** if *val* satisfies the condition defined by **test( )** and **false** otherwise. |
| DoubleSupplier | double getAsDouble( )<br>**Description**: Returns a **double** result. |
| DoubleToIntFunction | int applyAsInt(double *val*)<br>**Description**: Acts on a **double** value and returns the result as an **int**. |
| DoubleToLongFunction | long applyAsLong(double *val*)<br>**Description**: Acts on a **double** value and returns the result as a **long**. |
| DoubleUnaryOperator | double applyAsDouble(double *val*)<br>**Description**: Acts on a **double** and returns a **double** result. |
| Function<T, R> | R apply(T *val*)<br>**Description**: Acts on *val* and returns the result. |
| IntBinaryOperator | int applyAsInt(int *val1*, int *val2*)<br>**Description**: Acts on two **int** values and returns an **int** result. |

**Table 21-18** Functional Interfaces Defined by **java.util.function** and Their Abstract Methods

| Interface | Abstract Method |
|---|---|
| IntConsumer | int accept(int *val*)<br>**Description**: Acts on *val*. |
| IntFunction<R> | R apply(int *val*)<br>**Description**: Acts on an **int** value and returns the result. |
| IntPredicate | boolean test(int *val*)<br>**Description**: Returns **true** if *val* satisfies the condition defined by **test( )** and **false** otherwise. |
| IntSupplier | int getAsInt( )<br>**Description**: Returns an **int** result. |
| IntToDoubleFunction | double applyAsDouble(int *val*)<br>**Description**: Acts on an **int** value and returns the result as a **double**. |
| IntToLongFunction | long applyAsLong(int *val*)<br>**Description**: Acts on an **int** value and returns the result as a **long**. |
| IntUnaryOperator | int applyAsInt(int *val*)<br>**Description**: Acts on an **int** and returns an **int** result. |
| LongBinaryOperator | long applyAsLong(long *val1*, long *val2*)<br>**Description**: Acts on two **long** values and returns a **long** result. |
| LongConsumer | void accept(long *val*)<br>**Description**: Acts on *val*. |
| LongFunction<R> | R apply(long *val*)<br>**Description**: Acts on a **long** value and returns the result. |
| LongPredicate | boolean test(long *val*)<br>**Description**: Returns **true** if *val* satisfies the condition defined by **test( )** and **false** otherwise. |
| LongSupplier | long getAsLong( )<br>**Description**: Returns a **long** result. |
| LongToDoubleFunction | double applyAsDouble(long *val*)<br>**Description**: Acts on a **long** value and returns the result as a **double**. |
| LongToIntFunction | int applyAsInt(long *val*)<br>**Description**: Acts on a **long** value and returns the result as an **int**. |
| LongUnaryOperator | long applyAsLong(long *val*)<br>**Description**: Acts on a **long** and returns a **long** result. |
| ObjDoubleConsumer<T> | void accept(T *val1*, double *val2*)<br>**Description**: Acts on *val1* and the **double** value *val2*. |

**Table 21-18** Functional Interfaces Defined by **java.util.function** and Their Abstract Methods *(continued)*

| Interface | Abstract Method |
|---|---|
| ObjIntConsumer<T> | void accept(T *val1*, int *val2*)<br>**Description**: Acts on *val1* and the **int** value *val2*. |
| ObjLongConsumer<T> | void accept(T *val1*, long *val2*)<br>**Description**: Acts on *val1* and the **long** value *val2*. |
| Predicate<T> | boolean test(T *val*)<br>**Description**: Returns **true** if *val* satisfies the condition defined by **test( )** and **false** otherwise. |
| Supplier<T> | T get( )<br>**Description**: Returns an object of type **T**. |
| ToDoubleBiFunction<T, U> | double applyAsDouble(T *tVal*, U *uVal*)<br>**Description**: Acts on *tVal* and *uVal* and returns the result as a **double**. |
| ToDoubleFunction<T> | double applyAsDouble(T *val*)<br>**Description**: Acts on *val* and returns the result as a **double**. |
| ToIntBiFunction<T, U> | int applyAsInt(T *tVal*, U *uVal*)<br>**Description**: Acts on *tVal* and *uVal* and returns the result as an **int**. |
| ToIntFunction<T> | int applyAsInt(T *val*)<br>**Description**: Acts on *val* and returns the result as an **int**. |
| ToLongBiFunction<T, U> | long applyAsLong(T *tVal*, U *uVal*)<br>**Description**: Acts on *tVal* and *uVal* and returns the result as a **long**. |
| ToLongFunction<T> | long applyAsLong(T *val*)<br>**Description**: Acts on *val* and returns the result as a **long**. |
| UnaryOperator<T> | T apply(T *val*)<br>**Description**: Acts on *val* and returns the result |

**Table 21-18** Functional Interfaces Defined by **java.util.function** and Their Abstract Methods *(continued)*

## java.util.logging

The **java.util.logging** package provides support for program activity logs, which can be used to record program actions, and to help find and debug problems. This package is in the **java.logging** module.

## java.util.prefs

The **java.util.prefs** package provides support for user preferences. It is typically used to support program configuration. This package is in the **java.prefs** module.

## java.util.random

The **java.util.random** package provides extensive support for random number generators. (Added by JDK 17.)

## java.util.regex

The **java.util.regex** package provides support for regular expression handling. It is described in detail in Chapter 31.

## java.util.spi

The **java.util.spi** package provides support for service providers.

## java.util.stream

The **java.util.stream** package contains Java's stream API. A discussion of the stream API is found in Chapter 30.

## java.util.zip

The **java.util.zip** package provides the ability to read and write files in the popular ZIP and GZIP formats. Both ZIP and GZIP input and output streams are available.

CHAPTER

# 22 Input/Output: Exploring java.io

This chapter explores **java.io**, which provides support for I/O operations. Chapter 13 presented an overview of Java's I/O system, including basic techniques for reading and writing files, handling I/O exceptions, and closing a file. Here, we will examine the Java I/O system in greater detail.

As all programmers learn early on, most programs cannot accomplish their goals without accessing external data. Data is retrieved from an *input* source. The results of a program are sent to an *output* destination. In Java, these sources or destinations are defined very broadly. For example, a network connection, memory buffer, or disk file can be manipulated by the Java I/O classes. Although physically different, these devices are all handled by the same abstraction: the *stream*. An I/O stream, as explained in Chapter 13, is a logical entity that either produces or consumes information. An I/O stream is linked to a physical device by the Java I/O system. All I/O streams behave in the same manner, even if the actual physical devices they are linked to differ.

**NOTE** The stream-based I/O system packaged in **java.io** and described in this chapter has been part of Java since its original release and is widely used. However, beginning with version 1.4, a second I/O system was added to Java. It is called NIO (which was originally an acronym for New I/O). NIO is packaged in **java.nio** and its subpackages. The NIO system is described in Chapter 23.

**NOTE** It is important not to confuse the I/O streams used by the I/O system discussed here with the stream API added by JDK 8. Although conceptually related, they are two different things. Therefore, when the term stream is used in this chapter, it refers to an I/O stream.

## The I/O Classes and Interfaces

The I/O classes defined by **java.io** are listed here:

| | | |
|---|---|---|
| BufferedInputStream | FileWriter | PipedInputStream |
| BufferedOutputStream | FilterInputStream | PipedOutputStream |
| BufferedReader | FilterOutputStream | PipedReader |
| BufferedWriter | FilterReader | PipedWriter |
| ByteArrayInputStream | FilterWriter | PrintStream |
| ByteArrayOutputStream | InputStream | PrintWriter |
| CharArrayReader | InputStreamReader | PushbackInputStream |
| CharArrayWriter | LineNumberReader | PushbackReader |
| Console | ObjectInputFilter.Config | RandomAccessFile |
| DataInputStream | ObjectInputStream | Reader |
| DataOutputStream | ObjectInputStream.GetField | SequenceInputStream |
| File | ObjectOutputStream | SerializablePermission |
| FileDescriptor | ObjectOutputStream.PutField | StreamTokenizer |
| FileInputStream | ObjectStreamClass | StringReader |
| FileOutputStream | ObjectStreamField | StringWriter |
| FilePermission | OutputStream | Writer |
| FileReader | OutputStreamWriter | |

The **java.io** package also contains two deprecated classes that are not shown in the preceding table: **LineNumberInputStream** and **StringBufferInputStream**. These classes should not be used for new code.

The following interfaces are defined by **java.io**:

| | | |
|---|---|---|
| Closeable | FilenameFilter | ObjectInputValidation |
| DataInput | Flushable | ObjectOutput |
| DataOutput | ObjectInput | ObjectStreamConstants |
| Externalizable | ObjectInputFilter | Serializable |
| FileFilter | ObjectInputFilter.FilterInfo | |

As you can see, there are many classes and interfaces in the **java.io** package. These include byte and character streams, and object serialization (the storage and retrieval of objects). This chapter examines several commonly used I/O components. We begin our discussion with one of the most distinctive I/O classes: **File**.

## File

Although most of the classes defined by **java.io** operate on streams, the **File** class does not. It deals directly with files and the file system. That is, the **File** class does not specify how information is retrieved from or stored in files; it describes the properties of a file itself. A **File** object is used to obtain or manipulate the information associated with a disk file, such as the permissions, time, date, and directory path, and to navigate subdirectory hierarchies.

**NOTE** The **Path** interface and **Files** class, which are part of the NIO system, offer a powerful alternative to **File** in many cases. See Chapter 23 for details.



Files are a primary source and destination for data within many programs. Although there are severe restrictions on their use within untrusted code for security reasons, files are still a central resource for storing persistent and shared information. A directory in Java is treated simply as a **File** with one additional property—a list of filenames that can be examined by the **list( )** method.

The following constructors can be used to create **File** objects:

File(String *directoryPath*)
File(String *directoryPath*, String *filename*)
File(File *dirObj*, String *filename*)
File(URI *uriObj*)

Here, *directoryPath* is the path name of the file; *filename* is the name of the file or subdirectory; *dirObj* is a **File** object that specifies a directory; and *uriObj* is a **URI** object that describes a file.

The following example creates three files: **f1**, **f2**, and **f3**. The first **File** object is constructed with a directory path as the only argument. The second includes two arguments—the path and the filename. The third includes the file path assigned to **f1** and a filename; **f3** refers to the same file as **f2**.

```
File f1 = new File("/");
File f2 = new File("/","autoexec.bat");
File f3 = new File(f1,"autoexec.bat");
```

**NOTE** Java does the right thing with path separators between UNIX and Windows conventions. If you use a forward slash (/) on a Windows version of Java, the path will still resolve correctly. Remember, if you are using the Windows convention of a backslash character (\), you will need to use its escape sequence (\\) within a string.

**File** defines many methods that obtain the standard properties of a **File** object. For example, **getName( )** returns the name of the file; **getParent( )** returns the name of the parent directory; and **exists( )** returns **true** if the file exists, **false** if it does not. The following example demonstrates several of the **File** methods. It assumes that a directory called **java** exists off the root directory and that it contains a file called **COPYRIGHT**.

```
// Demonstrate File.
import java.io.File;
```

```
class FileDemo {
  static void p(String s) {
    System.out.println(s);
  }

  public static void main(String[] args) {
    File f1 = new File("/java/COPYRIGHT");

    p("File Name: " + f1.getName());
    p("Path: " + f1.getPath());
    p("Abs Path: " + f1.getAbsolutePath());
    p("Parent: " + f1.getParent());
    p(f1.exists() ? "exists" : "does not exist");
    p(f1.canWrite() ? "is writeable" : "is not writeable");
    p(f1.canRead() ? "is readable" : "is not readable");
    p("is " + (f1.isDirectory() ? "" : "not" + " a directory"));
    p(f1.isFile() ? "is normal file" : "might be a named pipe");
    p(f1.isAbsolute() ? "is absolute" : "is not absolute");
    p("File last modified: " + f1.lastModified());
    p("File size: " + f1.length() + " Bytes");
  }
}
```

This program will produce output similar to this:

```
File Name: COPYRIGHT
Path: \java\COPYRIGHT
Abs Path: C:\java\COPYRIGHT
Parent: \java
exists
is writeable
is readable
is not a directory
is normal file
is not absolute
File last modified: 1282832030047
File size: 695 Bytes
```

Most of the **File** methods are self-explanatory. **isFile( )** and **isAbsolute( )** are not. **isFile( )** returns **true** if called on a file and **false** if called on a directory. Also, **isFile( )** returns **false** for some special files, such as device drivers and named pipes, so this method can be used to make sure the file will behave as a file. The **isAbsolute( )** method returns **true** if the file has an absolute path and **false** if its path is relative.

**File** includes two useful utility methods of special interest. The first is **renameTo( )**, shown here:

boolean renameTo(File *newName*)

Here, the filename specified by *newName* becomes the new name of the file. It will return **true** upon success and **false** if the file cannot be renamed (if you attempt to rename a file so that it uses an existing filename, for example).

The second utility method is **delete( )**, which deletes the disk file represented by the path of the invoking **File** object. It is shown here:

boolean delete( )

You can also use **delete( )** to delete a directory if the directory is empty. **delete( )** returns **true** if it deletes the file and **false** if the file cannot be removed.

Here are some other **File** methods that you will find helpful:

| Method | Description |
|---|---|
| void deleteOnExit( ) | Removes the file associated with the invoking object when the Java Virtual Machine terminates. |
| long getFreeSpace( ) | Returns the number of free bytes of storage available on the partition associated with the invoking object. |
| long getTotalSpace( ) | Returns the storage capacity of the partition associated with the invoking object. |
| long getUsableSpace( ) | Returns the number of usable free bytes of storage available on the partition associated with the invoking object. |
| boolean isHidden( ) | Returns **true** if the invoking file is hidden. Returns **false** otherwise. |
| boolean setLastModified(long *millisec*) | Sets the time stamp on the invoking file to that specified by *millisec*, which is the number of milliseconds from January 1, 1970, Coordinated Universal Time (UTC). |
| boolean setReadOnly( ) | Sets the invoking file to read-only. |



Methods also exist to mark files as readable, writable, and executable. Because **File** implements the **Comparable** interface, the method **compareTo( )** is also supported.

A method of special interest is called **toPath( )**, which is shown here:

Path toPath( )

**toPath( )** returns a **Path** object that represents the file encapsulated by the invoking **File** object. (In other words, **toPath( )** converts a **File** into a **Path**.) **Path** is packaged in **java.nio.file** and is part of NIO. Thus, **toPath( )** forms a bridge between the older **File** class and the newer **Path** interface. (See Chapter 23 for a discussion of **Path**.)

## Directories

A directory is a **File** that contains a list of other files and directories. When you create a **File** object that is a directory, the **isDirectory( )** method will return **true**. In this case, you can call **list( )** on that object to extract the list of other files and directories inside. It has two forms. The first is shown here:

String[ ] list( )

The list of files is returned in an array of **String** objects.

The program shown here illustrates how to use **list( )** to examine the contents of a directory:

```
// Using directories.
import java.io.File;

class DirList {
  public static void main(String[] args) {
    String dirname = "/java";
    File f1 = new File(dirname);

    if (f1.isDirectory()) {
      System.out.println("Directory of " + dirname);
      String[] s = f1.list();

      for (int i=0; i < s.length; i++) {
        File f = new File(dirname + "/" + s[i]);
        if (f.isDirectory()) {
          System.out.println(s[i] + " is a directory");
        } else {
          System.out.println(s[i] + " is a file");
        }
      }
    } else {
      System.out.println(dirname + " is not a directory");
    }
  }
}
```

Here is sample output from the program. (Of course, the output you see will be different, based on what is in the directory.)

```
Directory of /java
bin is a directory
lib is a directory
demo is a directory
COPYRIGHT is a file
README is a file
index.html is a file
include is a directory
src.zip is a file
src is a directory
```

## Using FilenameFilter

You will often want to limit the number of files returned by the **list( )** method to include only those files that match a certain filename pattern, or *filter*. To do this, you must use a second form of **list( )**, shown here:

String[ ] list(FilenameFilter *FFObj*)

In this form, *FFObj* is an object of a class that implements the **FilenameFilter** interface.

**FilenameFilter** defines only a single method, **accept( )**, which is called once for each file in a list. Its general form is given here:

boolean accept(File *directory*, String *filename*)

The **accept( )** method returns **true** for files in the directory specified by *directory* that should be included in the list (that is, those that match the *filename* argument) and returns **false** for those files that should be excluded.

The **OnlyExt** class, shown next, implements **FilenameFilter**. It will be used to modify the preceding program to restrict the visibility of the filenames returned by **list( )** to files with names that end in the file extension specified when the object is constructed.

```
import java.io.*;

public class OnlyExt implements FilenameFilter {
  String ext;

  public OnlyExt(String ext) {
    this.ext = "." + ext;
  }

  public boolean accept(File dir, String name) {
    return name.endsWith(ext);
  }
}
```

The modified directory listing program is shown here. Now it will only display files that use the **.html** extension.

```
// Directory of .HTML files.
import java.io.*;

class DirListOnly {
  public static void main(String[] args) {
    String dirname = "/java";
    File f1 = new File(dirname);
    FilenameFilter only = new OnlyExt("html");
    String[] s = f1.list(only);

    for (int i=0; i < s.length; i++) {
      System.out.println(s[i]);
    }
  }
}
```

## The listFiles( ) Alternative

There is a variation to the **list( )** method, called **listFiles( )**, that you might find useful. The signatures for **listFiles( )** are shown here:

File[ ] listFiles( )
File[ ] listFiles(FilenameFilter *FFObj*)
File[ ] listFiles(FileFilter *FObj*)

These methods return the file list as an array of **File** objects instead of strings. The first method returns all files, and the second returns those files that satisfy the specified **FilenameFilter**. Aside from returning an array of **File** objects, these two versions of **listFiles( )** work like their equivalent **list( )** methods.

The third version of **listFiles( )** returns those files with path names that satisfy the specified **FileFilter**. **FileFilter** defines only a single method, **accept( )**, which is called once for each file in a list. Its general form is given here:

```
boolean accept(File path)
```

The **accept( )** method returns **true** for files that should be included in the list (that is, those that match the *path* argument) and **false** for those that should be excluded.

## Creating Directories

Another two useful **File** utility methods are **mkdir( )** and **mkdirs( )**. The **mkdir( )** method creates a directory, returning **true** on success and **false** on failure. Failure can occur for various reasons, such as the path specified in the **File** object already exists or the directory cannot be created because the entire path does not exist yet. To create a directory for which no path exists, use the **mkdirs( )** method. It creates both a directory and all the parents of the directory.

# The AutoCloseable, Closeable, and Flushable Interfaces

There are three interfaces that are quite important to the stream classes. Two are **Closeable** and **Flushable**. They are defined in **java.io**. The third, **AutoCloseable**, is packaged in **java.lang**.

**AutoCloseable** provides support for the **try**-with-resources statement, which automates the process of closing a resource. (See Chapter 13.) Only objects of classes that implement **AutoCloseable** can be managed by **try**-with-resources. **AutoCloseable** is discussed in Chapter 18, but it is reviewed here for convenience. The **AutoCloseable** interface defines only the **close( )** method:

```
void close( ) throws Exception
```

This method closes the invoking object, releasing any resources that it may hold. It is called automatically at the end of a **try**-with-resources statement, thus eliminating the need to explicitly call **close( )**. Because this interface is implemented by all of the I/O classes that open a stream, all such streams can be automatically closed by a **try**-with-resources statement. Automatically closing a stream ensures that it is properly closed when it is no longer needed, thus preventing memory leaks and other problems.

The **Closeable** interface also defines the **close( )** method. Objects of a class that implement **Closeable** can be closed. **Closeable** extends **AutoCloseable**. Therefore, any class that implements **Closeable** also implements **AutoCloseable**.

Objects of a class that implements **Flushable** can force buffered output to be written to the stream to which the object is attached. It defines the **flush( )** method, shown here:

```
void flush( ) throws IOException
```

Flushing a stream typically causes buffered output to be physically written to the underlying device. This interface is implemented by all of the I/O classes that write to a stream.

# I/O Exceptions

Two exceptions play an important role in I/O handling. The first is **IOException**. As it relates to most of the I/O classes described in this chapter, if an I/O error occurs, an **IOException** is thrown. In many cases, if a file cannot be opened, a **FileNotFoundException** is thrown. **FileNotFoundException** is a subclass of **IOException**, so both can be caught with a single **catch** that catches **IOException**. For brevity, this is the approach used by most of the sample code in this chapter. However, in your own applications, you might find it useful to **catch** each exception separately.

Another exception class that is sometimes important when performing I/O is **SecurityException**. As explained in Chapter 13, in situations in which a security manager is present, several of the file classes will throw a **SecurityException** if a security violation occurs when attempting to open a file. By default, applications run via **java** do not use a security manager. For that reason, the I/O examples in this book do not need to watch for a possible **SecurityException**. However, other applications could generate a **SecurityException**. In such a case, you will need to handle this exception. Be aware, however, that the security manager was deprecated for removal by JDK 17.



# Two Ways to Close a Stream

In general, a stream must be closed when it is no longer needed. Failure to do so can lead to memory leaks and resource starvation. The techniques used to close a stream were described in Chapter 13, but because of their importance, they warrant a brief review here before the stream classes are examined.

There are two basic ways in which you can close a stream. The first is to explicitly call **close( )** on the stream. This is the traditional approach that has been used since the original release of Java. With this approach, **close( )** is typically called within a **finally** block. Thus, a simplified skeleton for the traditional approach is shown here:

```
try {
  // open and access file
} catch( I/O-exception) {
  // ...
} finally {
  // close the file
}
```

This general technique (or variation thereof) is common in code that predates JDK 7.

The second approach to closing a stream is to automate the process by using the **try**-with-resources statement that was added by JDK 7. The **try**-with-resources statement is an enhanced form of **try** that has the following form:

```
try (resource-specification) {
  // use the resource
}
```

Typically, *resource-specification* is a statement or statements that declares and initializes a resource, such as a file or other stream-related resource. It consists of a variable declaration in which the variable is initialized with a reference to the object being managed. When the

**try** block ends, the resource is automatically released. In the case of a file, this means that the file is automatically closed. Thus, there is no need to call **close( )** explicitly. Beginning with JDK 9, it is also possible for the resource specification of the **try** to consist of a variable that has been declared and initialized earlier in the program. However, that variable must be effectively **final**, which means that it has not been assigned a new value after being given its initial value.

Here are three key points about the **try**-with-resources statement:

- Resources managed by **try**-with-resources must be objects of classes that implement **AutoCloseable**.
- A resource declared in the **try** is implicitly **final**. A resource declared outside the **try** must be effectively **final**.
- You can manage more than one resource by separating each declaration by a semicolon.

Also, remember that the scope of a resource declared inside the **try** is limited to the **try**-with-resources statement.

The principal advantage of **try**-with-resources is that the resource (in this case, a stream) is closed automatically when the **try** block ends. Thus, it is not possible to forget to close the stream, for example. The **try**-with-resources approach also typically results in shorter, clearer, easier-to-maintain source code.

Because of its advantages, **try**-with-resources is expected to be used extensively in new code. As a result, most of the code in this chapter (and in this book) will use it. However, because a large amount of older code still exists, it is important for all programmers to also be familiar with the traditional approach to closing a stream. For example, you will quite likely have to work on legacy code that uses the traditional approach or in an environment that uses an older version of Java. There may also be times when the automated approach is not appropriate because of other aspects of your code. For this reason, a few I/O examples in this book will demonstrate the traditional approach so you can see it in action.

One last point: The examples that use **try**-with-resources must be compiled by a modern version of Java. They won't work with an older compiler. The examples that use the traditional approach can be compiled by older versions of Java.

**REMEMBER** Because **try**-with-resources streamlines the process of releasing a resource and eliminates the possibility of accidentally forgetting to release a resource, it is the approach recommended for new code when its use is appropriate.

## The Stream Classes

Java's stream-based I/O is built upon four abstract classes: **InputStream**, **OutputStream**, **Reader**, and **Writer**. These classes were briefly discussed in Chapter 13. They are used to create several concrete stream subclasses. Although your programs perform their I/O operations through concrete subclasses, the top-level classes define the basic functionality common to all stream classes.

**InputStream** and **OutputStream** are designed for byte streams. **Reader** and **Writer** are designed for character streams. The byte stream classes and the character stream classes form separate hierarchies. In general, you should use the character stream classes when working with characters or strings and use the byte stream classes when working with bytes or other binary objects.

In the remainder of this chapter, both the byte- and character-oriented streams are examined.

# The Byte Streams



The byte stream classes provide a rich environment for handling byte-oriented I/O. A byte stream can be used with any type of object, including binary data. This versatility makes byte streams important to many types of programs. Since the byte stream classes are topped by **InputStream** and **OutputStream**, our discussion begins with them.

## InputStream

**InputStream** is an abstract class that defines Java's model of streaming byte input. It implements the **AutoCloseable** and **Closeable** interfaces. Most of the methods in this class will throw an **IOException** when an I/O error occurs. (The exceptions are **mark( )** and **markSupported( )**.) Table 22-1 shows the methods in **InputStream**.

---

NOTE Most of the methods described in Table 22-1 are implemented by the subclasses of **InputStream**. The **mark( )** and **reset( )** methods are exceptions; notice their use, or lack thereof, by each subclass in the discussions that follow.

## OutputStream

**OutputStream** is an abstract class that defines streaming byte output. It implements the **AutoCloseable**, **Closeable**, and **Flushable** interfaces. Most of the methods defined by this class return **void** and throw an **IOException** in the case of I/O errors. Table 22-2 shows the methods in **OutputStream**.

## FileInputStream

The **FileInputStream** class creates an **InputStream** that you can use to read bytes from a file. Two commonly used constructors are shown here:

FileInputStream(String *filePath*)
FileInputStream(File *fileObj*)

Either can throw a **FileNotFoundException**. Here, *filePath* is the full path name of a file, and *fileObj* is a **File** object that describes the file.

The following example creates two **FileInputStreams** that use the same file and each of the two constructors:

```
FileInputStream f0 = new FileInputStream("/autoexec.bat")
File f = new File("/autoexec.bat");
FileInputStream f1 = new FileInputStream(f);
```

Although the first constructor is probably more commonly used, the second allows you to closely examine the file using the **File** methods, before attaching it to an input stream.

| Method | Description |
|---|---|
| int available( ) | Returns the number of bytes of input currently available for reading. |
| void close( ) | Closes the input source. Further read attempts will generate an **IOException**. |
| void mark(int *numBytes*) | Places a mark at the current point in the input stream that will remain valid until *numBytes* bytes are read. |
| boolean markSupported( ) | Returns **true** if **mark( )** / **reset( )** are supported by the invoking stream. |
| static InputStream nullInputStream( ) | Returns an open, but null input stream, which is a stream that contains no data. Thus, the stream is always at the end of the stream and no input can be obtained. The stream can, however, be closed. |
| int read( ) | Returns an integer representation of the next available byte of input. –1 is returned when an attempt is made to read at the end of the stream. |
| int read(byte[ ] *buffer*) | Attempts to read up to *buffer.length* bytes into *buffer* and returns the actual number of bytes that were successfully read. –1 is returned when an attempt is made to read at the end of the stream. |
| int read(byte[ ] *buffer*, int *offset*, int *numBytes*) | Attempts to read up to *numBytes* bytes into *buffer* starting at *buffer*[*offset*], returning the number of bytes successfully read. –1 is returned when an attempt is made to read at the end of the stream. |
| byte[ ] readAllBytes( ) | Beginning at the current position, reads to the end of the stream, returning a byte array that holds the input. |
| byte[ ] readNBytes(int *numBytes*) | Attempts to read *numBytes* bytes, returning the result in a byte array. If the end of the stream is reached before *numBytes* bytes have been read, then the returned array will contain less than *numBytes* bytes. |
| int readNBytes(byte[ ] *buffer*, int *offset*, int *numBytes*) | Attempts to read up to *numBytes* bytes into *buffer* starting at *buffer*[*offset*], returning the number of bytes successfully read. |
| void reset( ) | Resets the input pointer to the previously set mark. |
| long skip(long *numBytes*) | Ignores (that is, skips) *numBytes* bytes of input, returning the number of bytes actually ignored. |
| void skipNBytes(long *numBytes*) | Ignores (that is, skips) *numBytes* of input. Throws **EOFException** if the end of the stream is reached before *numBytes* are skipped, or **IOException** if an I/O error occurs. |
| long transferTo(OutputStream *strm*) | Copies the bytes in the invoking stream into *strm*, returning the number of bytes copied. |

**Table 22-1** The Methods Defined by **InputStream**

When a **FileInputStream** is created, it is also opened for reading. **FileInputStream** overrides several of the methods in the abstract class **InputStream**. The **mark( )** and **reset( )** methods are not overridden, and any attempt to use **reset( )** on a **FileInputStream** will generate an **IOException**.

| Method | Description |
|---|---|
| void close( ) | Closes the output stream. Further write attempts will generate an **IOException**. |
| void flush( ) | Finalizes the output state so that any buffers are cleared. That is, it flushes the output buffers. |
| static OutputStream nullOutputStream( ) | Returns an open, but null output stream, which is a stream to which no output is actually written. Thus, its output methods can be called but don't actually produce output. The stream can, however, be closed. |
| void write(int *b*) | Writes a single byte to an output stream. Note that the parameter is an **int**, which allows you to call **write( )** with an expression without having to cast it back to **byte**. |
| void write(byte[ ] *buffer*) | Writes a complete array of bytes to an output stream. |
| void write(byte[ ] *buffer*, int *offset*, int *numBytes*) | Writes a subrange of *numBytes* bytes from the array *buffer*, beginning at *buffer*[*offset*]. |

**Table 22-2** The Methods Defined by **OutputStream**



The next example shows how to read a single byte, an array of bytes, and a subrange of an array of bytes. It also illustrates how to use **available( )** to determine the number of bytes remaining and how to use the **skip( )** method to skip over unwanted bytes. The program reads its own source file, which must be in the current directory. Notice that it uses the **try**-with-resources statement to automatically close the file when it is no longer needed.

```
// Demonstrate FileInputStream.

import java.io.*;

class FileInputStreamDemo {
  public static void main(String[] args) {
    int size;

    // Use try-with-resources to close the stream.
    try ( FileInputStream f =
           new FileInputStream("FileInputStreamDemo.java") ) {

      System.out.println("Total Available Bytes: " +
                         (size = f.available()));

      int n = size/40;
      System.out.println("First " + n +
                         " bytes of the file one read() at a time");
      for (int i=0; i < n; i++) {
        System.out.print((char) f.read());
      }

      System.out.println("\nStill Available: " + f.available());
```

```
      System.out.println("Reading the next " + n +
                         " with one read(b[])");
      byte[] b = new byte[n];
      if (f.read(b) != n) {
        System.err.println("couldn't read " + n + " bytes.");
      }

      System.out.println(new String(b, 0, n));
      System.out.println("\nStill Available: " + (size = f.available()));
      System.out.println("Skipping half of remaining bytes with skip()");
      f.skip(size/2);
      System.out.println("Still Available: " + f.available());

      System.out.println("Reading " + n/2 + " into the end of array");
      if (f.read(b, n/2, n/2) != n/2) {
        System.err.println("couldn't read " + n/2 + " bytes.");
      }

      System.out.println(new String(b, 0, b.length));
      System.out.println("\nStill Available: " + f.available());
    } catch(IOException e) {
      System.out.println("I/O Error: " + e);
    }
  }
}
```

Here is the output produced by this program:

```
Total Available Bytes: 1714
First 42 bytes of the file one read() at a time
// Demonstrate FileInputStream.

impor
Still Available: 1672
Reading the next 42 with one read(b[])
t java.io.*;

class FileInputStreamD

Still Available: 1630
Skipping half of remaining bytes with skip()
Still Available: 815
Reading 21 into the end of array
t java.io.*;

c n) {
    Syst

Still Available: 794
```

This somewhat contrived example demonstrates how to read three ways, to skip input, and to inspect the amount of data available on a stream.

**NOTE** The preceding example and the other examples in this chapter handle any I/O exceptions that might occur as described in Chapter 13. See Chapter 13 for details and alternatives.

## FileOutputStream

**FileOutputStream** creates an **OutputStream** that you can use to write bytes to a file. It implements the **AutoCloseable**, **Closeable**, and **Flushable** interfaces. Four of its constructors are shown here:

FileOutputStream(String *filePath*)
FileOutputStream(File *fileObj*)
FileOutputStream(String *filePath*, boolean *append*)
FileOutputStream(File *fileObj*, boolean *append*)



They can throw a **FileNotFoundException**. Here, *filePath* is the full path name of a file, and *fileObj* is a **File** object that describes the file. If *append* is **true**, the file is opened in append mode.

Creation of a **FileOutputStream** is not dependent on the file already existing. **FileOutputStream** will create the file before opening it for output when you create the object. In the case where you attempt to open a read-only file, an exception will be thrown.

The following example creates a sample buffer of bytes by first making a **String** and then using the **getBytes( )** method to extract the byte array equivalent. It then creates three files. The first, **file1.txt**, will contain every other byte from the sample. The second, **file2.txt**, will contain the entire set of bytes. The third and last, **file3.txt**, will contain only the last quarter.

```
// Demonstrate FileOutputStream.
// This program uses the traditional approach to closing a file.

import java.io.*;

class FileOutputStreamDemo {
  public static void main(String[] args) {
    String source = "Now is the time for all good men\n"
      + " to come to the aid of their country\n"
      + " and pay their due taxes.";
    byte[] buf = source.getBytes();
    FileOutputStream f0 = null;
    FileOutputStream f1 = null;
    FileOutputStream f2 = null;

    try {
      f0 = new FileOutputStream("file1.txt");
      f1 = new FileOutputStream("file2.txt");
      f2 = new FileOutputStream("file3.txt");

      // write to first file
      for (int i=0; i < buf.length; i += 2) f0.write(buf[i]);

      // write to second file
      f1.write(buf);

      // write to third file
      f2.write(buf, buf.length-buf.length/4, buf.length/4);
    } catch(IOException e) {
      System.out.println("An I/O Error Occurred");
    } finally {
```

```
        try {
          if(f0 != null) f0.close();
        } catch(IOException e) {
          System.out.println("Error Closing file1.txt");
        }
        try {
          if(f1 != null) f1.close();
        } catch(IOException e) {
          System.out.println("Error Closing file2.txt");
        }
        try {
          if(f2 != null) f2.close();
        } catch(IOException e) {
          System.out.println("Error Closing file3.txt");
        }
      }
    }
  }
```

Here are the contents of each file after running this program. First, **file1.txt**:

```
Nwi h iefralgo e
t oet h i ftercuty n a hi u ae.
```

Next, **file2.txt**:

```
Now is the time for all good men
 to come to the aid of their country
 and pay their due taxes.
```

Finally, **file3.txt**:

```
nd pay their due taxes.
```

As the comment at the top of the program states, the preceding program shows an example that uses the traditional approach to closing a file when it is no longer needed. This approach is required by all versions of Java prior to JDK 7 and is widely used in legacy code. As you can see, quite a bit of rather awkward code is required to explicitly call **close( )** because each call could generate an **IOException** if the close operation fails. This program can be substantially improved by using the **try**-with-resources statement. For comparison, here is the revised version. Notice that it is much shorter and streamlined:

```
// Demonstrate FileOutputStream.
// This version uses try-with-resources.

import java.io.*;

class FileOutputStreamDemo {
  public static void main(String[] args) {
    String source = "Now is the time for all good men\n"
      + " to come to the aid of their country\n"
      + " and pay their due taxes.";
    byte[] buf = source.getBytes();
```

```
    // Use try-with-resources to close the files.
    try (FileOutputStream f0 = new FileOutputStream("file1.txt");
         FileOutputStream f1 = new FileOutputStream("file2.txt");
         FileOutputStream f2 = new FileOutputStream("file3.txt") )
    {

      // write to first file
      for (int i=0; i < buf.length; i += 2) f0.write(buf[i]);

      // write to second file
      f1.write(buf);

      // write to third file
      f2.write(buf, buf.length-buf.length/4, buf.length/4);
    } catch(IOException e) {
      System.out.println("An I/O Error Occurred");
    }
  }
}
```



## ByteArrayInputStream

**ByteArrayInputStream** is an implementation of an input stream that uses a byte array as the source. This class has two constructors, each of which requires a byte array to provide the data source:

ByteArrayInputStream(byte[ ] *array*)
ByteArrayInputStream(byte[ ] *array*, int *start*, int *numBytes*)

Here, *array* is the input source. The second constructor creates an **InputStream** from a subset of the byte array that begins with the character at the index specified by *start* and is *numBytes* long.

The **close( )** method has no effect on a **ByteArrayInputStream**. Therefore, it is not necessary to call **close( )** on a **ByteArrayInputStream**, but doing so is not an error.

The following example creates a pair of **ByteArrayInputStreams**, initializing them with the byte representation of the alphabet:

```
// Demonstrate ByteArrayInputStream.
import java.io.*;

class ByteArrayInputStreamDemo {
  public static void main(String[] args) {
    String tmp = "abcdefghijklmnopqrstuvwxyz";
    byte[] b = tmp.getBytes();

    ByteArrayInputStream input1 = new ByteArrayInputStream(b);
    ByteArrayInputStream input2 = new ByteArrayInputStream(b,0,3);
  }
}
```

The **input1** object contains the entire lowercase alphabet, whereas **input2** contains only the first three letters.

A **ByteArrayInputStream** implements both **mark( )** and **reset( )**. However, if **mark( )** has not been called, then **reset( )** sets the stream pointer to the start of the stream—which, in this case, is the start of the byte array passed to the constructor. The next example shows how to use the **reset( )** method to read the same input twice. In this case, the program reads and prints the letters "abc" once in lowercase and then again in uppercase.

```
import java.io.*;

class ByteArrayInputStreamReset {
  public static void main(String[] args) {
    String tmp = "abc";
    byte[] b = tmp.getBytes();
    ByteArrayInputStream in = new ByteArrayInputStream(b);

    for (int i=0; i<2; i++) {
      int c;
      while ((c = in.read()) != -1) {
        if (i == 0) {
          System.out.print((char) c);
        } else {
          System.out.print(Character.toUpperCase((char) c));
        }
      }
      System.out.println();
      in.reset();
    }
  }
}
```

This example first reads each character from the stream and prints it as-is in lowercase. It then resets the stream and begins reading again, this time converting each character to uppercase before printing. Here's the output:

```
abc
ABC
```

## ByteArrayOutputStream

**ByteArrayOutputStream** is an implementation of an output stream that uses a byte array as the destination. **ByteArrayOutputStream** has two constructors, shown here:

ByteArrayOutputStream( )
ByteArrayOutputStream(int *numBytes*)

In the first form, a buffer of 32 bytes is created. In the second, a buffer is created with a size equal to that specified by *numBytes*. The buffer is held in the protected **buf** field of **ByteArrayOutputStream**. The buffer size will be increased automatically, if needed. The number of bytes held by the buffer is contained in the protected **count** field of **ByteArrayOutputStream**.

The **close( )** method has no effect on a **ByteArrayOutputStream**. Therefore, it is not necessary to call **close( )** on a **ByteArrayOutputStream**, but doing so is not an error.

The following example demonstrates **ByteArrayOutputStream**:

```
// Demonstrate ByteArrayOutputStream.

import java.io.*;

class ByteArrayOutputStreamDemo {
  public static void main(String[] args) {
    ByteArrayOutputStream f = new ByteArrayOutputStream();
    String s = "This should end up in the array";
    byte[] buf = s.getBytes();

    try {
      f.write(buf);
    } catch(IOException e) {
      System.out.println("Error Writing to Buffer");
      return;
    }

    System.out.println("Buffer as a string");
    System.out.println(f.toString());
    System.out.println("Into array");
    byte[] b = f.toByteArray();
    for (int i=0; i<b.length; i++) System.out.print((char) b[i]);

    System.out.println("\nTo an OutputStream()");

    // Use try-with-resources to manage the file stream.
    try ( FileOutputStream f2 = new FileOutputStream("test.txt") )
    {
      f.writeTo(f2);
    } catch(IOException e) {
      System.out.println("I/O Error: " + e);
      return;
    }

    System.out.println("Doing a reset");
    f.reset();

    for (int i=0; i\<3; i++) f.write('X');

    System.out.println(f.toString());
  }
}
```

When you run the program, you will create the following output. Notice how after the call to **reset( )**, the three X's end up at the beginning.

```
Buffer as a string
This should end up in the array
Into array
This should end up in the array
```

```
To an OutputStream()
Doing a reset
XXX
```

This example uses the **writeTo( )** convenience method to write the contents of **f** to **test.txt**. Examining the contents of the **test.txt** file created in the preceding example shows the result we expected:

```
This should end up in the array
```

## Filtered Byte Streams

*Filtered streams* are simply wrappers around underlying input or output streams that transparently provide some extended level of functionality. These streams are typically accessed by methods that are expecting a generic stream, which is a superclass of the filtered streams. Typical extensions are buffering, character translation, and raw data translation. The filtered byte streams are **FilterInputStream** and **FilterOutputStream**. Their constructors are shown here:

FilterOutputStream(OutputStream *os*)
FilterInputStream(InputStream *is*)

The methods provided in these classes are identical to those in **InputStream** and **OutputStream**.

## Buffered Byte Streams

For the byte-oriented streams, a *buffered stream* extends a filtered stream class by attaching a memory buffer to the I/O stream. This buffer allows Java to do I/O operations on more than a byte at a time, thereby improving performance. Because the buffer is available, skipping, marking, and resetting of the stream become possible. The buffered byte stream classes are **BufferedInputStream** and **BufferedOutputStream**. **PushbackInputStream** also implements a buffered stream.

### BufferedInputStream

Buffering I/O is a very common performance optimization. Java's **BufferedInputStream** class allows you to "wrap" any **InputStream** into a buffered stream to improve performance.

**BufferedInputStream** has two constructors:

BufferedInputStream(InputStream *inputStream*)
BufferedInputStream(InputStream *inputStream*, int *bufSize*)

The first form creates a buffered stream using a default buffer size. In the second, the size of the buffer is passed in *bufSize*. Use of sizes that are multiples of a memory page, a disk block, and so on, can have a significant positive impact on performance. This is, however, implementation-dependent. An optimal buffer size is generally dependent on the host operating system, the amount of memory available, and how the machine is configured. To make good use of buffering doesn't necessarily require quite this degree of sophistication. A good guess for a size is around 8192 bytes, and attaching even a rather small buffer to an

I/O stream is always a good idea. That way, the low-level system can read blocks of data from the disk or network and store the results in your buffer. Thus, even if you are reading the data a byte at a time out of the **InputStream**, you will be manipulating fast memory most of the time.

Buffering an input stream also provides the foundation required to support moving backward in the stream of the available buffer. Beyond the **read( )** and **skip( )** methods implemented in any **InputStream**, **BufferedInputStream** also supports the **mark( )** and **reset( )** methods. This support is reflected by **BufferedInputStream.markSupported( )** returning **true**.

The following example contrives a situation where we can use **mark( )** to remember where we are in an input stream and later use **reset( )** to get back there. This example is parsing a stream for the HTML entity reference for the copyright symbol. Such a reference begins with an ampersand (&) and ends with a semicolon (;) without any intervening whitespace. The sample input has two ampersands to show the case where the **reset( )** happens and where it does not.



```
// Use buffered input.

import java.io.*;

class BufferedInputStreamDemo {
  public static void main(String[] args) {
    String s = "This is a &copy; copyright symbol " +
      "but this is &copy not.\n";
    byte[] buf = s.getBytes();

    ByteArrayInputStream in = new ByteArrayInputStream(buf);
    int c;
    boolean marked = false;

    // Use try-with-resources to manage the file.
    try ( BufferedInputStream f = new BufferedInputStream(in) )
    {
      while ((c = f.read()) != -1) {
        switch(c) {
        case '&':
          if (!marked) {
            f.mark(32);
            marked = true;
          } else {
            marked = false;
          }
          break;
        case ';':
          if (marked) {
            marked = false;
            System.out.print("(c)");
          } else
            System.out.print((char) c);
          break;
```

```
          case ' ':
            if (marked) {
              marked = false;
              f.reset();
              System.out.print("&");
            } else
              System.out.print((char) c);
            break;
          default:
            if (!marked)
              System.out.print((char) c);
            break;
          }
        }
      } catch(IOException e) {
        System.out.println("I/O Error: " + e);
      }
    }
}
```

Notice that this example uses **mark(32)**, which preserves the mark for the next 32 bytes read (which is enough for all entity references). Here is the output produced by this program:

```
This is a (c) copyright symbol but this is &copy not.
```

## BufferedOutputStream

A **BufferedOutputStream** is similar to any **OutputStream** with the exception that the **flush( )** method is used to ensure that data buffers are written to the stream being buffered. Since the point of a **BufferedOutputStream** is to improve performance by reducing the number of times the system actually writes data, you may need to call **flush( )** to cause any data that is in the buffer to be immediately written.

Unlike buffered input, buffering output does not provide additional functionality. Buffers for output in Java are there to increase performance. Here are the two available constructors:

BufferedOutputStream(OutputStream *outputStream*)
BufferedOutputStream(OutputStream *outputStream*, int *bufSize*)

The first form creates a buffered stream using the default buffer size. In the second form, the size of the buffer is passed in *bufSize*.

## PushbackInputStream

One of the novel uses of buffering is the implementation of pushback. *Pushback* is used on an input stream to allow a byte to be read and then returned (that is, "pushed back") to the stream. The **PushbackInputStream** class implements this idea. It provides a mechanism to "peek" at what is coming from an input stream without disrupting it.

**PushbackInputStream** has the following constructors:

PushbackInputStream(InputStream *inputStream*)
PushbackInputStream(InputStream *inputStream*, int *numBytes*)

The first form creates a stream object that allows one byte to be returned to the input stream. The second form creates a stream that has a pushback buffer that is *numBytes* long. This allows multiple bytes to be returned to the input stream.

Beyond the familiar methods of **InputStream**, **PushbackInputStream** provides **unread( )**, shown here:

void unread(int *b*)
void unread(byte[ ] *buffer*)
void unread(byte *buffer*, int *offset*, int *numBytes*)

The first form pushes back the low-order byte of *b*. This will be the next byte returned by a subsequent call to **read( )**. The second form pushes back the bytes in *buffer*. The third form pushes back *numBytes* bytes beginning at *offset* from *buffer*. An **IOException** will be thrown if there is an attempt to push back a byte when the pushback buffer is full.

Here is an example that shows how a programming language parser might use a **PushbackInputStream** and **unread( )** to deal with the difference between the = = operator for comparison and the = operator for assignment:

```
// Demonstrate unread().

import java.io.*;

class PushbackInputStreamDemo {
  public static void main(String[] args) {
    String s = "if (a == 4) a = 0;\n";
    byte[] buf = s.getBytes();
    ByteArrayInputStream in = new ByteArrayInputStream(buf);
    int c;

    try ( PushbackInputStream f = new PushbackInputStream(in) )
    {
      while ((c = f.read()) != -1) {
        switch(c) {
        case '=':
          if ((c = f.read()) == '=')
            System.out.print(".eq.");
          else {
            System.out.print("<-");
            f.unread(c);
          }
          break;
        default:
          System.out.print((char) c);
          break;
        }
      }
    } catch(IOException e) {
      System.out.println("I/O Error: " + e);
    }
  }
}
```

Here is the output for this example. Notice that == was replaced by "**.eq.**" and = was replaced by "<–".

```
if (a .eq. 4) a <- 0;
```

---

**CAUTION** **PushbackInputStream** has the side effect of invalidating the **mark( )** or **reset( )** method of the **InputStream** used to create it. Use **markSupported( )** to check any stream on which you are going to use **mark( )/reset( )**.

## SequenceInputStream

The **SequenceInputStream** class allows you to concatenate multiple **InputStreams**. The construction of a **SequenceInputStream** is different from any other **InputStream**. A **SequenceInputStream** constructor uses either a pair of **InputStreams** or an **Enumeration** of **InputStreams** as its argument:

SequenceInputStream(InputStream *first*, InputStream *second*)
SequenceInputStream(Enumeration <? extends InputStream> *streamEnum*)

Operationally, the class fulfills read requests from the first **InputStream** until it runs out and then switches over to the second one. In the case of an **Enumeration**, it will continue through all of the **InputStreams** until the end of the last one is reached. When the end of each file is reached, its associated stream is closed. Closing the stream created by **SequenceInputStream** causes all unclosed streams to be closed.

Here is a simple example that uses a **SequenceInputStream** to output the contents of two files. For demonstration purposes, this program uses the traditional technique used to close a file. As an exercise, you might want to try changing it to use the **try**-with-resources statement.

```
// Demonstrate sequenced input.
// This program uses the traditional approach to closing a file.

import java.io.*;
import java.util.*;

class InputStreamEnumerator implements Enumeration<FileInputStream> {
  private Enumeration<String> files;

  public InputStreamEnumerator(Vector<String> files) {
    this.files = files.elements();
  }

  public boolean hasMoreElements() {
    return files.hasMoreElements();
  }

  public FileInputStream nextElement() {
    try {
      return new FileInputStream(files.nextElement().toString());
```

```
    } catch (IOException e) {
      return null;
    }
  }
}

class SequenceInputStreamDemo {
  public static void main(String[] args) {
    int c;
    Vector<String> files = new Vector<String>();

    files.addElement("file1.txt");
    files.addElement("file2.txt");
    files.addElement("file3.txt");
    InputStreamEnumerator ise = new InputStreamEnumerator(files);
    InputStream input = new SequenceInputStream(ise);

    try {
      while ((c = input.read()) != -1)
        System.out.print((char) c);
    } catch(NullPointerException e) {
      System.out.println("Error Opening File.");
    } catch(IOException e) {
      System.out.println("I/O Error: " + e);
    } finally {
      try {
        input.close();
      } catch(IOException e) {
        System.out.println("Error Closing SequenceInputStream");
      }
    }
  }
}
```

This example creates a **Vector** and then adds three filenames to it. It passes that vector of names to the **InputStreamEnumerator** class, which is designed to provide a wrapper on the vector where the elements returned are not the filenames but, rather, open **FileInputStream**s on those names. The **SequenceInputStream** opens each file in turn, and this example prints the contents of the files.

Notice in **nextElement( )** that if a file cannot be opened, **null** is returned. This results in a **NullPointerException**, which is caught in **main( )**.

## PrintStream

The **PrintStream** class provides all of the output capabilities we have been using from the **System** file handle, **System.out**, since the beginning of the book. This makes **PrintStream** one of Java's most often used classes. It implements the **Appendable**, **AutoCloseable**, **Closeable**, and **Flushable** interfaces.

**PrintStream** defines several constructors. The ones shown next have been specified from the start:

PrintStream(OutputStream *outputStream*)
PrintStream(OutputStream *outputStream*, boolean *autoFlushingOn*)

PrintStream(OutputStream *outputStream*, boolean *autoFlushingOn* String *charSet*)
throws UnsupportedEncodingException

Here, *outputStream* specifies an open **OutputStream** that will receive output. The *autoFlushingOn* parameter controls whether the output buffer is automatically flushed every time a newline (**\n**) character or a byte array is written or when **println( )** is called. If *autoFlushingOn* is **true**, flushing automatically takes place. If it is **false**, flushing is not automatic. The first constructor does not automatically flush. You can specify a character encoding by passing its name in *charSet*.

The next set of constructors gives you an easy way to construct a **PrintStream** that writes its output to a file:

PrintStream(File *outputFile*) throws FileNotFoundException
PrintStream(File *outputFile*, String *charSet*)
throws FileNotFoundException, UnsupportedEncodingException
PrintStream(String *outputFileName*) throws FileNotFoundException
PrintStream(String *outputFileName*, String *charSet*) throws FileNotFoundException,
UnsupportedEncodingException

These allow a **PrintStream** to be created from a **File** object or by specifying the name of a file. In either case, the file is automatically created. Any preexisting file by the same name is destroyed. Once created, the **PrintStream** object directs all output to the specified file. You can specify a character encoding by passing its name in *charSet*. There are also constructors that let you specify a **Charset** parameter.

---

**NOTE** If a security manager is present, some **PrintStream** constructors will throw a **SecurityException** if a security violation occurs. Be aware that the **SecurityManager** was deprecated for removal by JDK 17.

**PrintStream** supports the **print( )** and **println( )** methods for all types, including **Object**. If an argument is not a primitive type, the **PrintStream** methods will call the object's **toString( )** method and then display the result. **PrintStream** also supports a number of **write( )** methods, and provides methods that handle errors.

A number of years ago a very useful method called **printf( )** was added to **PrintStream**. It allows you to specify the precise format of the data to be written. The **printf( )** method formats as described by the **Formatter** class discussed in Chapter 21. It then writes this data to the invoking stream. Although formatting can be done manually, by using **Formatter** directly, **printf( )** streamlines the process. It also parallels the C/C++ **printf( )** function, which makes it easy to convert existing C/C++ code into Java. Frankly, **printf( )** was a much welcome addition to the Java API because it greatly simplified the output of formatted data to the console.

The **printf( )** method has the following general forms:

PrintStream printf(String *fmtString*, Object ... *args*)
PrintStream printf(Locale *loc*, String *fmtString*, Object ... *args*)

The first version writes *args* to standard output in the format specified by *fmtString*, using the default locale. The second lets you specify a locale. Both return the invoking **PrintStream**.

In general, **printf( )** works in a manner similar to the **format( )** method specified by **Formatter**. The *fmtString* consists of two types of items. The first type is composed of characters that are simply copied to the output buffer. The second type contains format specifiers that define the way the subsequent arguments, specified by *args*, are displayed. For complete information on formatting output, including a description of the format specifiers, see the **Formatter** class in Chapter 20.

Because **System.out** is a **PrintStream**, you can call **printf( )** on **System.out**. Thus, **printf( )** can be used in place of **println( )** when writing to the console whenever formatted output is desired. For example, the following program uses **printf( )** to output numeric values in various formats. In the past, such formatting required a bit of work. With the addition of **printf( )**, this is now an easy task.



```
// Demonstrate printf().

class PrintfDemo {
  public static void main(String[] args) {
    System.out.println("Here are some numeric values " +
                       "in different formats.\n");

    System.out.printf("Various integer formats: ");
    System.out.printf("%d %(d %+d %05d\n", 3, -3, 3, 3);

    System.out.println();
    System.out.printf("Default floating-point format: %f\n",
                       1234567.123);
    System.out.printf("Floating-point with commas: %,f\n",
                       1234567.123);
    System.out.printf("Negative floating-point default: %,f\n",
                       -1234567.123);
    System.out.printf("Negative floating-point option: %,(f\n",
                       -1234567.123);

    System.out.println();

    System.out.printf("Line up positive and negative values:\n");
    System.out.printf("% ,.2f\n% ,.2f\n",
                       1234567.123, -1234567.123);
  }
}
```

The output is shown here:

```
Here are some numeric values in different formats.

Various integer formats: 3 (3) +3 00003

Default floating-point format: 1234567.123000
Floating-point with commas: 1,234,567.123000
Negative floating-point default: -1,234,567.123000
Negative floating-point option: (1,234,567.123000)
```

```
Line up positive and negative values:
  1,234,567.12
 -1,234,567.12
```

**PrintStream** also defines the **format( )** method. It has these general forms:

PrintStream format(String *fmtString*, Object ... *args*)
PrintStream format(Locale *loc*, String *fmtString*, Object ... *args*)

It works exactly like **printf( )**.

## DataOutputStream and DataInputStream

**DataOutputStream** and **DataInputStream** enable you to write or read primitive data to or from a stream. They implement the **DataOutput** and **DataInput** interfaces, respectively. These interfaces define methods that convert primitive values to or from a sequence of bytes. These streams make it easy to store binary data, such as integers or floating-point values, in a file. Each is examined here.

**DataOutputStream** extends **FilterOutputStream**, which extends **OutputStream**. In addition to implementing **DataOutput**, **DataOutputStream** also implements **AutoCloseable**, **Closeable**, and **Flushable**. **DataOutputStream** defines the following constructor:

DataOutputStream(OutputStream *outputStream*)

Here, *outputStream* specifies the output stream to which data will be written. When a **DataOutputStream** is closed (by calling **close( )**), the underlying stream specified by *outputStream* is also closed automatically.

**DataOutputStream** supports all of the methods defined by its superclasses. However, it is the methods defined by the **DataOutput** interface, which it implements, that make it interesting. **DataOutput** defines methods that convert values of a primitive type into a byte sequence and then writes it to the underlying stream. Here is a sampling of these methods:

final void writeDouble(double *value*) throws IOException
final void writeBoolean(boolean *value*) throws IOException
final void writeInt(int *value*) throws IOException

Here, *value* is the value written to the stream.

**DataInputStream** is the complement of **DataOuputStream**. It extends **FilterInputStream**, which extends **InputStream**. In addition to implementing the **DataInput** interface, **DataInputStream** also implements **AutoCloseable** and **Closeable**. Here is its only constructor:

DataInputStream(InputStream *inputStream*)

Here, *inputStream* specifies the input stream from which data will be read. When a **DataInputStream** is closed (by calling **close( )**), the underlying stream specified by *inputStream* is also closed automatically.

Like **DataOutputStream**, **DataInputStream** supports all of the methods of its superclasses, but it is the methods defined by the **DataInput** interface that make it unique. These methods read a sequence of bytes and convert them into values of a primitive type. Here is a sampling of these methods:

final double readDouble( ) throws IOException
final boolean readBoolean( ) throws IOException
final int readInt( ) throws IOException

The following program demonstrates the use of **DataOutputStream** and **DataInputStream**:

```
// Demonstrate DataInputStream and DataOutputStream.

import java.io.*;

class DataIODemo {
  public static void main(String[] args) throws IOException {

    // First, write the data.
    try ( DataOutputStream dout =
            new DataOutputStream(new FileOutputStream("Test.dat")) )
    {
      dout.writeDouble(98.6);
      dout.writeInt(1000);
      dout.writeBoolean(true);

    } catch(FileNotFoundException e) {
      System.out.println("Cannot Open Output File");
      return;
    } catch(IOException e) {
      System.out.println("I/O Error: " + e);
    }

    // Now, read the data back.
    try ( DataInputStream din =
            new DataInputStream(new FileInputStream("Test.dat")) )
    {

      double d = din.readDouble();
      int i = din.readInt();
      boolean b = din.readBoolean();

      System.out.println("Here are the values: " +
                          d + " " + i + " " + b);
    } catch(FileNotFoundException e) {
      System.out.println("Cannot Open Input File");
      return;
    } catch(IOException e) {
      System.out.println("I/O Error: " + e);
    }
  }
}
```

The output is shown here:

```
Here are the values: 98.6 1000 true
```

## RandomAccessFile

**RandomAccessFile** encapsulates a random-access file. It is not derived from **InputStream** or **OutputStream**. Instead, it implements the interfaces **DataInput** and **DataOutput**, which define the basic I/O methods. It also implements the **AutoCloseable** and **Closeable** interfaces. **RandomAccessFile** is special because it supports positioning requests—that is, you can position the file pointer within the file. It has these two constructors:

RandomAccessFile(File *fileObj*, String *access*)
 throws FileNotFoundException

RandomAccessFile(String *filename*, String *access*)
 throws FileNotFoundException

In the first form, *fileObj* specifies the file to open as a **File** object. In the second form, the name of the file is passed in *filename*. In both cases, *access* determines what type of file access is permitted. If it is "r", then the file can be read, but not written. If it is "rw", then the file is opened in read-write mode. If it is "rws", the file is opened for read-write operations and every change to the file's data or metadata will be immediately written to the physical device. If it is "rwd", the file is opened for read-write operations and every change to the file's data will be immediately written to the physical device.

The method **seek( )**, shown here, is used to set the current position of the file pointer within the file:

void seek(long *newPos*) throws IOException

Here, *newPos* specifies the new position, in bytes, of the file pointer from the beginning of the file. After a call to **seek( )**, the next read or write operation will occur at the new file position.

**RandomAccessFile** implements the standard input and output methods, which you can use to read and write to random access files. It also includes some additional methods. One is **setLength( )**. It has this signature:

void setLength(long *len*) throws IOException

This method sets the length of the invoking file to that specified by *len*. This method can be used to lengthen or shorten a file. If the file is lengthened, the added portion is undefined.

# The Character Streams

While the byte stream classes provide sufficient functionality to handle any type of I/O operation, they cannot work directly with Unicode characters. Since one of the main purposes of Java is to support the "write once, run anywhere" philosophy, it was necessary to include direct I/O support for characters. In this section, several of the character I/O classes are discussed. As explained earlier, at the top of the character stream hierarchies are the **Reader** and **Writer** abstract classes. We will begin with them.

| Method | Description |
|---|---|
| abstract void close( ) | Closes the input source. Further read attempts will generate an **IOException**. |
| void mark(int *numChars*) | Places a mark at the current point in the input stream that will remain valid until *numChars* characters are read. |
| boolean markSupported( ) | Returns **true** if **mark( )**/**reset( )** are supported on this stream. |
| static Reader nullReader( ) | Returns an open, but null reader, which is a reader that contains no data. Thus, the reader is always at the end of the stream and no input can be obtained. The reader can, however, be closed. |
| int read( ) | Returns an integer representation of the next available character from the invoking input stream. –1 is returned when an attempt is made to read at the end of the stream. |
| int read(char[ ] *buffer*) | Attempts to read up to *buffer.length* characters into *buffer* and returns the actual number of characters that were successfully read. –1 is returned when an attempt is made to read at the end of the stream. |
| int read(CharBuffer *buffer*) | Attempts to read characters into *buffer* and returns the actual number of characters that were successfully read. –1 is returned when an attempt is made to read at the end of the stream. |
| abstract int read(char[ ] *buffer*, int *offset*, int *numChars*) | Attempts to read up to *numChars* characters into *buffer* starting at *buffer*[*offset*], returning the number of characters successfully read. –1 is returned when an attempt is made to read at the end of the stream. |
| boolean ready( ) | Returns **true** if the next input request will not wait. Otherwise, it returns **false**. |
| void reset( ) | Resets the input pointer to the previously set mark. |
| long skip(long *numChars*) | Skips over *numChars* characters of input, returning the number of characters actually skipped. |
| long transferTo(Writer *writer*) | Copies the contents of the invoking reader to *writer*, returning the number of characters copied. |

**Table 22-3** The Methods Defined by **Reader**

## Reader

**Reader** is an abstract class that defines Java's model of streaming character input. It implements the **AutoCloseable**, **Closeable**, and **Readable** interfaces. All of the methods in this class (except for **markSupported( )**) will throw an **IOException** on error conditions. Table 22-3 provides a synopsis of the methods in **Reader**.

## Writer

**Writer** is an abstract class that defines streaming character output. It implements the **AutoCloseable**, **Closeable**, **Flushable**, and **Appendable** interfaces. All of the methods in this class throw an **IOException** in the case of errors. Table 22-4 shows a synopsis of the methods in **Writer**.

| Method | Description |
|---|---|
| Writer append(char *ch*) | Appends *ch* to the end of the invoking output stream. Returns a reference to the invoking stream. |
| Writer append(CharSequence *chars*) | Appends *chars* to the end of the invoking output stream. Returns a reference to the invoking stream. |
| Writer append(CharSequence *chars*, int *begin*, int *end*) | Appends the subrange of *chars* specified by *begin* and *end*–1 to the end of the invoking output stream. Returns a reference to the invoking stream. |
| abstract void close( ) | Closes the output stream. Further write attempts will generate an **IOException**. |
| abstract void flush( ) | Finalizes the output state so that any buffers are cleared. That is, it flushes the output buffers. |
| static Writer nullWriter( ) | Returns an open, but null writer, which is a writer to which no output is actually written. Thus, its output methods can be called but don't actually produce output. The writer can, however, be closed. |
| void write(int *ch*) | Writes a single character to the invoking output stream. Note that the parameter is an **int**, which allows you to call **write** with an expression without having to cast it back to **char**. However, only the low-order 16 bits are written. |
| void write(char[ ] *buffer*) | Writes a complete array of characters to the invoking output stream. |
| abstract void write(char[ ] *buffer*, int *offset*, int *numChars*) | Writes a subrange of *numChars* characters from the array *buffer*, beginning at *buffer*[*offset*] to the invoking output stream. |
| void write(String *str*) | Writes *str* to the invoking output stream. |
| void write(String *str*, int *offset*, int *numChars*) | Writes a subrange of *numChars* characters from the string *str*, beginning at the specified *offset*. |

**Table 22-4** The Methods Defined by **Writer**

## FileReader

The **FileReader** class creates a **Reader** that you can use to read the contents of a file. Two commonly used constructors are shown here:

FileReader(String *filePath*)
FileReader(File *fileObj*)

Either can throw a **FileNotFoundException**. Here, *filePath* is the full path name of a file, and *fileObj* is a **File** object that describes the file.

The following example shows how to read lines from a file and display them on the standard output device. It reads its own source file, which must be in the current directory.

```
// Demonstrate FileReader.

import java.io.*;

class FileReaderDemo {
  public static void main(String[] args) {

    try ( FileReader fr = new FileReader("FileReaderDemo.java") )
    {
      int c;

      // Read and display the file.
      while((c = fr.read()) != -1) System.out.print((char) c);

    } catch(IOException e) {
      System.out.println("I/O Error: " + e);
    }
  }
}
```

## FileWriter

**FileWriter** creates a **Writer** that you can use to write to a file. Four commonly used constructors are shown here:

FileWriter(String *filePath*)
FileWriter(String *filePath*, boolean *append*)
FileWriter(File *fileObj*)
FileWriter(File *fileObj*, boolean *append*)

They can all throw an **IOException**. Here, *filePath* is the full path name of a file, and *fileObj* is a **File** object that describes the file. If *append* is **true**, then output is appended to the end of the file.

Creation of a **FileWriter** is not dependent on the file already existing. **FileWriter** will create the file before opening it for output when you create the object. In the case where you attempt to open a read-only file, an **IOException** will be thrown.

The following example is a character stream version of an example shown earlier when **FileOutputStream** was discussed. This version creates a sample buffer of characters by first making a **String** and then using the **getChars( )** method to extract the character array equivalent. It then creates three files. The first, **file1.txt**, will contain every other character from the sample. The second, **file2.txt**, will contain the entire set of characters. Finally, the third, **file3.txt**, will contain only the last quarter.

```
// Demonstrate FileWriter.

import java.io.*;
```

```
class FileWriterDemo {
  public static void main(String[] args) throws IOException {
    String source = "Now is the time for all good men\n"
      + " to come to the aid of their country\n"
      + " and pay their due taxes.";
    char[] buffer = new char[source.length()];
    source.getChars(0, source.length(), buffer, 0);

    try ( FileWriter f0 = new FileWriter("file1.txt");
          FileWriter f1 = new FileWriter("file2.txt");
          FileWriter f2 = new FileWriter("file3.txt") )
    {
      // write to first file
      for (int i=0; i < buffer.length; i += 2) {
        f0.write(buffer[i]);
      }

      // write to second file
      f1.write(buffer);

      // write to third file
      f2.write(buffer,buffer.length-buffer.length/4,buffer.length/4);

    } catch(IOException e) {
      System.out.println("An I/O Error Occurred");
    }
  }
}
```

## CharArrayReader

**CharArrayReader** is an implementation of an input stream that uses a character array as the source. This class has two constructors, each of which requires a character array to provide the data source:

CharArrayReader(char[ ] *array*)
CharArrayReader(char[ ] *array*, int *start*, int *numChars*)

Here, *array* is the input source. The second constructor creates a **Reader** from a subset of your character array that begins with the character at the index specified by *start* and is *numChars* long.

The **close( )** method implemented by **CharArrayReader** does not throw any exceptions. This is because it cannot fail.

The following example uses a pair of **CharArrayReaders**:

```
// Demonstrate CharArrayReader.

import java.io.*;

public class CharArrayReaderDemo {
  public static void main(String[] args) {
    String tmp = "abcdefghijklmnopqrstuvwxyz";
    int length = tmp.length();
    char[] c = new char[length];
```

```
    tmp.getChars(0, length, c, 0);
    int i;

    try (CharArrayReader input1 = new CharArrayReader(c) )
    {
      System.out.println("input1 is:");
      while((i = input1.read()) != -1) {
        System.out.print((char)i);
      }
      System.out.println();
    } catch(IOException e) {
      System.out.println("I/O Error: " + e);
    }

    try ( CharArrayReader input2 = new CharArrayReader(c, 0, 5) )
    {
      System.out.println("input2 is:");
      while((i = input2.read()) != -1) {
        System.out.print((char)i);
      }
      System.out.println();
    } catch(IOException e) {
      System.out.println("I/O Error: " + e);
    }
  }
}
```

The **input1** object is constructed using the entire lowercase alphabet, whereas **input2** contains only the first five letters. Here is the output:

```
input1 is:
abcdefghijklmnopqrstuvwxyz
input2 is:
abcde
```

## CharArrayWriter

**CharArrayWriter** is an implementation of an output stream that uses an array as the destination. **CharArrayWriter** has two constructors, shown here:

CharArrayWriter( )
CharArrayWriter(int *numChars*)

In the first form, a buffer with a default size is created. In the second, a buffer is created with a size equal to that specified by *numChars*. The buffer is held in the **buf** field of **CharArrayWriter**. The buffer size will be increased automatically, if needed. The number of characters held by the buffer is contained in the **count** field of **CharArrayWriter**. Both **buf** and **count** are protected fields.

The **close( )** method has no effect on a **CharArrayWriter**.

The following example demonstrates **CharArrayWriter** by reworking the sample program shown earlier for **ByteArrayOutputStream**. It produces the same output as the previous version.

Part II

```
// Demonstrate CharArrayWriter.

import java.io.*;

class CharArrayWriterDemo {
  public static void main(String[] args) throws IOException {
    CharArrayWriter f = new CharArrayWriter();
    String s = "This should end up in the array";
    char[] buf = new char[s.length()];

    s.getChars(0, s.length(), buf, 0);

    try {
      f.write(buf);
    } catch(IOException e) {
      System.out.println("Error Writing to Buffer");
      return;
    }

    System.out.println("Buffer as a string");
    System.out.println(f.toString());
    System.out.println("Into array");

    char[] c = f.toCharArray();
    for (int i=0; i<c.length; i++) {
      System.out.print(c[i]);
    }

    System.out.println("\nTo a FileWriter()");

    // Use try-with-resources to manage the file stream.
    try ( FileWriter f2 = new FileWriter("test.txt") )
    {
      f.writeTo(f2);
    } catch(IOException e) {
      System.out.println("I/O Error: " + e);
    }

    System.out.println("Doing a reset");
    f.reset();

    for (int i=0; i<3; i++) f.write('X');

    System.out.println(f.toString());
  }
}
```

## BufferedReader

**BufferedReader** improves performance by buffering input. It has two constructors:

BufferedReader(Reader *inputStream*)
BufferedReader(Reader *inputStream*, int *bufSize*)

The first form creates a buffered character stream using a default buffer size. In the second, the size of the buffer is passed in *bufSize*.

Closing a **BufferedReader** also causes the underlying stream specified by *inputStream* to be closed.

As is the case with the byte-oriented stream, buffering an input character stream also provides the foundation required to support moving backward in the stream within the available buffer. To support this, **BufferedReader** implements the **mark( )** and **reset( )** methods, and **BufferedReader.markSupported( )** returns **true**. A relatively recent addition to **BufferedReader** is called **lines( )**. It returns a **Stream** reference to the sequence of lines read by the reader. (**Stream** is part of the stream API discussed in Chapter 30.)

The following example reworks the **BufferedInputStream** example, shown earlier, so that it uses a **BufferedReader** character stream rather than a buffered byte stream. As before, it uses the **mark( )** and **reset( )** methods to parse a stream for the HTML entity reference for the copyright symbol. Such a reference begins with an ampersand (&) and ends with a semicolon (;) without any intervening whitespace. The sample input has two ampersands to show the case where the **reset( )** happens and where it does not. Output is the same as that shown earlier.



```
// Use buffered input.

import java.io.*;

class BufferedReaderDemo {
  public static void main(String[] args) throws IOException {
    String s = "This is a &copy; copyright symbol " +
      "but this is &copy not.\n";
    char[] buf = new char[s.length()];
    s.getChars(0, s.length(), buf, 0);

    CharArrayReader in = new CharArrayReader(buf);
    int c;
    boolean marked = false;

    try ( BufferedReader f = new BufferedReader(in) )
    {

      while ((c = f.read()) != -1) {
        switch(c) {
        case '&':
          if (!marked) {
            f.mark(32);
            marked = true;
          } else {
            marked = false;
          }
          break;
        case ';':
          if (marked) {
            marked = false;
            System.out.print("(c)");
          } else
            System.out.print((char) c);
          break;
```

```
        case ' ':
          if (marked) {
            marked = false;
            f.reset();
            System.out.print("&");
          } else
            System.out.print((char) c);
          break;
        default:
          if (!marked)
            System.out.print((char) c);
          break;
        }
      }
    } catch(IOException e) {
      System.out.println("I/O Error: " + e);
    }
  }
}
```

## BufferedWriter

A **BufferedWriter** is a **Writer** that buffers output. Using a **BufferedWriter** can improve performance by reducing the number of times data is actually physically written to the output device.

A **BufferedWriter** has these two constructors:

BufferedWriter(Writer *outputStream*)
BufferedWriter(Writer *outputStream*, int *bufSize*)

The first form creates a buffered stream using a buffer with a default size. In the second, the size of the buffer is passed in *bufSize*.

## PushbackReader

The **PushbackReader** class allows one or more characters to be returned to the input stream. This allows you to look ahead in the input stream. Here are its two constructors:

PushbackReader(Reader *inputStream*)
PushbackReader(Reader *inputStream*, int *bufSize*)

The first form creates a buffered stream that allows one character to be pushed back. In the second, the size of the pushback buffer is passed in *bufSize*.

Closing a **PushbackReader** also closes the underlying stream specified by *inputStream*.

**PushbackReader** provides **unread( )**, which returns one or more characters to the invoking input stream. It has the three forms shown here:

void unread(int *ch*) throws IOException
void unread(char[ ] *buffer*) throws IOException
void unread(char[ ] *buffer*, int *offset*, int *numChars*) throws IOException

The first form pushes back the character passed in *ch*. This will be the next character returned by a subsequent call to **read( )**. The second form returns the characters in *buffer*. The third form pushes back *numChars* characters beginning at *offset* from *buffer*. An **IOException** will be thrown if there is an attempt to return a character when the pushback buffer is full.

The following program reworks the earlier **PushbackInputStream** example by replacing **PushbackInputStream** with **PushbackReader**. As before, it shows how a programming language parser can use a pushback stream to deal with the difference between the == operator for comparison and the = operator for assignment.

```
// Demonstrate unread().

import java.io.*;

class PushbackReaderDemo {
  public static void main(String[] args) {
    String s = "if (a == 4) a = 0;\n";
    char[] buf = new char[s.length()];
    s.getChars(0, s.length(), buf, 0);
    CharArrayReader in = new CharArrayReader(buf);

    int c;

    try ( PushbackReader f = new PushbackReader(in) )
    {
      while ((c = f.read()) != -1) {
        switch(c) {
        case '=':
          if ((c = f.read()) == '=')
            System.out.print(".eq.");
          else {
            System.out.print("<-");
            f.unread(c);
          }
          break;
        default:
          System.out.print((char) c);
          break;
        }
      }
    } catch(IOException e) {
      System.out.println("I/O Error: " + e);
    }
  }
}
```

## PrintWriter

**PrintWriter** is essentially a character-oriented version of **PrintStream**. It implements the **Appendable, AutoCloseable, Closeable,** and **Flushable** interfaces. **PrintWriter** has several constructors. The following have been supplied by **PrintWriter** from the start:

PrintWriter(OutputStream *outputStream*)
PrintWriter(OutputStream *outputStream*, boolean *autoFlushingOn*)
PrintWriter(Writer *outputStream*)
PrintWriter(Writer *outputStream*, boolean *autoFlushingOn*)

Here, *outputStream* specifies an open **OutputStream** that will receive output. The *autoFlushingOn* parameter controls whether the output buffer is automatically flushed every time **println( )**, **printf( )**, or **format( )** is called. If *autoFlushingOn* is **true**, flushing automatically takes place. If **false**, flushing is not automatic. Constructors that do not specify the *autoFlushingOn* parameter do not automatically flush.

The next set of constructors gives you an easy way to construct a **PrintWriter** that writes its output to a file.

PrintWriter(File *outputFile*) throws FileNotFoundException
PrintWriter(File *outputFile*, String *charSet*)
 throws FileNotFoundException, UnsupportedEncodingException
PrintWriter(String *outputFileName*) throws FileNotFoundException
PrintWriter(String *outputFileName*, String *charSet*)
 throws FileNotFoundException, UnsupportedEncodingException

These allow a **PrintWriter** to be created from a **File** object or by specifying the name of a file. In either case, the file is automatically created. Any preexisting file by the same name is destroyed. Once created, the **PrintWriter** object directs all output to the specified file. You can specify a character encoding by passing its name in *charSet*. There are also constructors that let you specify a **Charset** parameter.

**PrintWriter** supports the **print( )** and **println( )** methods for all types, including **Object**. If an argument is not a primitive type, the **PrintWriter** methods will call the object's **toString( )** method and then output the result.

**PrintWriter** also supports the **printf( )** method. It works the same way it does in the **PrintStream** class described earlier: It allows you to specify the precise format of the data. Here is how **printf( )** is declared in **PrintWriter**:

PrintWriter printf(String *fmtString*, Object ... *args*)
PrintWriter printf(Locale *loc*, String *fmtString*, Object ...*args*)

The first version writes *args* to standard output in the format specified by *fmtString*, using the default locale. The second lets you specify a locale. Both return the invoking **PrintWriter**.

The **format( )** method is also supported. It has these general forms:

PrintWriter format(String *fmtString*, Object ... *args*)
PrintWriter format(Locale *loc*, String *fmtString*, Object ... *args*)

It works exactly like **printf( )**.

## The Console Class

The **Console** class is used to read from and write to the console, if one exists. It implements the **Flushable** interface. **Console** is primarily a convenience class because most of its functionality is available through **System.in** and **System.out**. However, its use can simplify some types of console interactions, especially when reading strings from the console.

**Console** supplies no constructors. Instead, a **Console** object is obtained by calling **System.console( )**, which is shown here:

static Console console( )

If a console is available, then a reference to it is returned. Otherwise, **null** is returned. A console will not be available in all cases. Thus, if **null** is returned, no console I/O is possible.

**Console** defines the methods shown in Table 22-5. Notice that the input methods, such as **readLine( )**, throw **IOError** if an input error occurs. **IOError** is a subclass of **Error**. It indicates an I/O failure that is beyond the control of your program. Thus, you will not normally catch an **IOError**. Frankly, if an **IOError** is thrown while accessing the console, it usually means there has been a catastrophic system failure.

Also notice the **readPassword( )** methods. These methods let your application read a password without echoing what is typed. After reading passwords, you should "zero-out" both the array that holds the string entered by the user and the array that holds the password that the string is tested against. This reduces the chance that a malicious program will be able to obtain a password by scanning memory.



| Method | Description |
|---|---|
| Charset charset( ) | Obtains the **Charset** associated with the console and returns the result. (Added by JDK 17.) |
| void flush( ) | Causes buffered output to be written physically to the console. |
| Console format(String *fmtString*, Object...*args*) | Writes *args* to the console using the format specified by *fmtString*. |
| Console printf(String *fmtString*, Object...*args*) | Writes *args* to the console using the format specified by *fmtString*. |
| Reader reader( ) | Returns a reference to a **Reader** connected to the console. |
| String readLine( ) | Reads and returns a string entered at the keyboard. Input stops when the user presses ENTER. If the end of the console input stream has been reached, **null** is returned. An **IOError** is thrown on failure. |
| String readLine(String *fmtString*, Object...*args*) | Displays a prompting string formatted as specified by *fmtString* and *args*, and then reads and returns a string entered at the keyboard. Input stops when the user presses ENTER. If the end of the console input stream has been reached, **null** is returned. An **IOError** is thrown on failure. |
| char[ ] readPassword( ) | Reads a string entered at the keyboard. Input stops when the user presses ENTER. The string is not displayed. If the end of the console input stream has been reached, **null** is returned. An **IOError** is thrown on failure. |
| char[ ] readPassword(String *fmtString*, Object... *args*) | Displays a prompting string formatted as specified by *fmtString* and *args*, and then reads a string entered at the keyboard. Input stops when the user presses ENTER. The string is not displayed. If the end of the console input stream has been reached, **null** is returned. An **IOError** is thrown on failure. |
| PrintWriter writer( ) | Returns a reference to a **Writer** connected to the console. |

**Table 22-5** The Methods Defined by **Console**

Here is an example that demonstrates the **Console** class:

```
// Demonstrate Console.
import java.io.*;

class ConsoleDemo {
  public static void main(String[] args) {
    String str;
    Console con;

    // Obtain a reference to the console.
    con = System.console();
    // If no console available, exit.
    if(con == null) return;

    // Read a string and then display it.
    str = con.readLine("Enter a string: ");
    con.printf("Here is your string: %s\n", str);
  }
}
```

Here is sample output:

```
Enter a string: This is a test.
Here is your string: This is a test.
```

# Serialization

*Serialization* is the process of writing the state of an object to a byte stream. This is useful when you want to save the state of your program to a persistent storage area, such as a file. At a later time, you may restore these objects by using the process of deserialization.

Serialization is also needed to implement *Remote Method Invocation (RMI)*. RMI allows a Java object on one machine to invoke a method of a Java object on a different machine. An object may be supplied as an argument to that remote method. The sending machine serializes the object and transmits it. The receiving machine deserializes it. (More information about RMI appears in Chapter 31.)

Assume that an object to be serialized has references to other objects, which, in turn, have references to still more objects. This set of objects and the relationships among them form a directed graph. There may also be circular references within this object graph. That is, object X may contain a reference to object Y, and object Y may contain a reference back to object X. Objects may also contain references to themselves. The object serialization and deserialization facilities have been designed to work correctly in these scenarios. If you attempt to serialize an object at the top of an object graph, all of the other referenced objects are recursively located and serialized. Similarly, during the process of deserialization, all of these objects and their references are correctly restored. It is important to note that serialization and deserialization can impact security, especially as it relates to the deserialization of items that you do not trust (i.e., *untrusted data*). Because the topic of security is outside the scope of this book, consult the Java documentation for the latest information about this and about security in general.

An overview of the interfaces and classes that support serialization follows.

## Serializable

Only an object that implements the **Serializable** interface can be saved and restored by the serialization facilities. The **Serializable** interface defines no members. It is simply used to indicate that a class may be serialized. If a class is serializable, all of its subclasses are also serializable.

In general, all instance variables are saved by serialization. However, variables that are declared as **transient** are not saved by the serialization facilities. Also, **static** variables are not saved. (It is also possible to explicitly specify which variables will be saved by using a **serialPersistentFields** array.)



## Externalizable

The Java facilities for serialization and deserialization have been designed so that much of the work to save and restore the state of an object occurs automatically. However, there are cases in which the programmer may need to have control over these processes. For example, it may be desirable to use compression or encryption techniques. The **Externalizable** interface is designed for these situations.

The **Externalizable** interface defines these two methods:

void readExternal(ObjectInput *inStream*)
  throws IOException, ClassNotFoundException
void writeExternal(ObjectOutput *outStream*)
  throws IOException

In these methods, *inStream* is the byte stream from which the object is to be read, and *outStream* is the byte stream to which the object is to be written.

## ObjectOutput

The **ObjectOutput** interface extends the **DataOutput** and **AutoCloseable** interfaces and supports object serialization. It defines the methods shown in Table 22-6. Note especially the

| Method | Description |
|---|---|
| void close( ) | Closes the invoking stream. Further write attempts will generate an **IOException**. |
| void flush( ) | Finalizes the output state so any buffers are cleared. That is, it flushes the output buffers. |
| void write(byte[ ] *buffer*) | Writes an array of bytes to the invoking stream. |
| void write(byte[ ] *buffer*, int *offset*, int *numBytes*) | Writes a subrange of *numBytes* bytes from the array *buffer*, beginning at *buffer*[*offset*]. |
| void write(int *b*) | Writes a single byte to the invoking stream. The byte written is the low-order byte of *b*. |
| void writeObject(Object *obj*) | Writes object *obj* to the invoking stream. |

**Table 22-6** The Methods Defined by **ObjectOutput**

**writeObject( )** method. This is called to serialize an object. All of these methods will throw an **IOException** on error conditions.

## ObjectOutputStream

The **ObjectOutputStream** class extends the **OutputStream** class and implements the **ObjectOutput** interface. It is responsible for writing objects to a stream. One constructor of this class is shown here:

ObjectOutputStream(OutputStream *outStream*) throws IOException

The argument *outStream* is the output stream to which serialized objects will be written. Closing an **ObjectOutputStream** automatically closes the underlying stream specified by *outStream*.

Several commonly used methods in this class are shown in Table 22-7. They will throw an **IOException** on error conditions. There is also a nested class in **ObjectOuputStream**

| Method | Description |
|---|---|
| void close( ) | Closes the invoking stream. Further write attempts will generate an **IOException**. The underlying stream is also closed. |
| void flush( ) | Finalizes the output state so any buffers are cleared. That is, it flushes the output buffers. |
| void write(byte[ ] *buffer*) | Writes an array of bytes to the invoking stream. |
| void write(byte[ ] *buffer*, int *offset*, int *numBytes*) | Writes a subrange of *numBytes* bytes from the array *buffer*, beginning at *buffer*[*offset*]. |
| void write(int *b*) | Writes a single **byte** to the invoking stream. The byte written is the low-order byte of *b*. |
| void writeBoolean(boolean *b*) | Writes a **boolean** to the invoking stream. |
| void writeByte(int *b*) | Writes a **byte** to the invoking stream. The byte written is the low-order byte of *b*. |
| void writeBytes(String *str*) | Writes the bytes representing *str* to the invoking stream. |
| void writeChar(int *c*) | Writes a **char** to the invoking stream. |
| void writeChars(String *str*) | Writes the characters in *str* to the invoking stream. |
| void writeDouble(double *d*) | Writes a **double** to the invoking stream. |
| void writeFloat(float *f*) | Writes a **float** to the invoking stream. |
| void writeInt(int *i*) | Writes an **int** to the invoking stream. |
| void writeLong(long *l*) | Writes a **long** to the invoking stream. |
| final void writeObject(Object *obj*) | Writes *obj* to the invoking stream. |
| void writeShort(int *i*) | Writes a **short** to the invoking stream. |

**Table 22-7** A Sampling of Commonly Used Methods Defined by **ObjectOutputStream**

| Method | Description |
|---|---|
| int available( ) | Returns the number of bytes that are now available in the input buffer. |
| void close( ) | Closes the invoking stream. Further read attempts will generate an **IOException**. |
| int read( ) | Returns an integer representation of the next available byte of input. –1 is returned when an attempt is made to read at the end of the stream. |
| int read(byte[ ] *buffer*) | Attempts to read up to *buffer.length* bytes into *buffer*, returning the number of bytes that were successfully read. –1 is returned when an attempt is made to read at the end of the stream. |
| int read(byte[ ] *buffer*, int *offset*, int *numBytes*) | Attempts to read up to *numBytes* bytes into *buffer* starting at *buffer*[*offset*], returning the number of bytes that were successfully read. –1 is returned when an attempt is made to read at the end of the stream. |
| Object readObject( ) | Reads an object from the invoking stream. |
| long skip(long *numBytes*) | Ignores (that is, skips) *numBytes* bytes in the invoking stream, returning the number of bytes actually ignored. |

**Table 22-8** The Methods Defined by **ObjectInput**

called **PutField**. It facilitates the writing of persistent fields, and its use is beyond the scope of this book.

## ObjectInput

The **ObjectInput** interface extends the **DataInput** and **AutoCloseable** interfaces and defines the methods shown in Table 22-8. It supports object serialization. Note especially the **readObject( )** method. This is called to deserialize an object. All of these methods will throw an **IOException** on error conditions. The **readObject( )** method can also throw **ClassNotFoundException**.

## ObjectInputStream

The **ObjectInputStream** class extends the **InputStream** class and implements the **ObjectInput** interface. **ObjectInputStream** is responsible for reading objects from a stream. One constructor of this class is shown here:

ObjectInputStream(InputStream *inStream*) throws IOException

The argument *inStream* is the input stream from which serialized objects should be read. Closing an **ObjectInputStream** automatically closes the underlying stream specified by *inStream*.

Several commonly used methods in this class are shown in Table 22-9. They will throw an **IOException** on error conditions. The **readObject( )** method can also throw **ClassNotFoundException**. There is also a nested class in **ObjectInputStream** called

| Method | Description |
|---|---|
| int available( ) | Returns the number of bytes that are now available in the input buffer. |
| void close( ) | Closes the invoking stream. Further read attempts will generate an **IOException**. The underlying stream is also closed. |
| int read( ) | Returns an integer representation of the next available byte of input. –1 is returned when an attempt is made to read at the end of the stream. |
| int read(byte[ ] *buffer*, int *offset*, int *numBytes*) | Attempts to read up to *numBytes* bytes into *buffer* starting at *buffer*[*offset*], returning the number of bytes successfully read. –1 is returned when an attempt is made to read at the end of the stream. |
| Boolean readBoolean( ) | Reads and returns a **boolean** from the invoking stream. |
| byte readByte( ) | Reads and returns a **byte** from the invoking stream. |
| char readChar( ) | Reads and returns a **char** from the invoking stream. |
| double readDouble( ) | Reads and returns a **double** from the invoking stream. |
| float readFloat( ) | Reads and returns a **float** from the invoking stream. |
| void readFully(byte[ ] *buffer*) | Reads *buffer.length* bytes into *buffer*. Returns only when all bytes have been read. |
| void readFully(byte[ ] *buffer*, int *offset*, int *numBytes*) | Reads *numBytes* bytes into *buffer* starting at *buffer*[*offset*]. Returns only when *numBytes* have been read. |
| int readInt( ) | Reads and returns an **int** from the invoking stream. |
| long readLong( ) | Reads and returns a **long** from the invoking stream. |
| final Object readObject( ) | Reads and returns an object from the invoking stream. |
| short readShort( ) | Reads and returns a **short** from the invoking stream. |
| int readUnsignedByte( ) | Reads and returns an unsigned **byte** from the invoking stream. |
| int readUnsignedShort( ) | Reads and returns an unsigned **short** from the invoking stream. |

**Table 22-9** Commonly Used Methods Defined by **ObjectInputStream**

**GetField**. It facilitates the reading of persistent fields, and its use is beyond the scope of this book.

Beginning with JDK 9, **ObjectInputStream** includes the methods **getObjectInputFilter( )** and **setObjectInputFilter( )**. These support the filtering of object input streams through the use of **ObjectInputFilter**, **ObjectInputFilter.FilterInfo**, **ObjectInputFilter.Config**, and **ObjectInputFilter.Status**, which were all added by JDK 9. Filtering gives you a measure of control over deserialization.

## A Serialization Example

The following program illustrates the basic mechanism of object serialization and deserialization. It begins by instantiating an object of class **MyClass**. This object has three instance variables that are of types **String**, **int**, and **double**. This is the information we want to save and restore.

A **FileOutputStream** is created that refers to a file named "serial", and an **ObjectOutputStream** is created for that file stream. The **writeObject( )** method of **ObjectOutputStream** is then used to serialize our object. The object output stream is flushed and closed.

A **FileInputStream** is then created that refers to the file named "serial", and an **ObjectInputStream** is created for that file stream. The **readObject( )** method of **ObjectInputStream** is then used to deserialize our object. The object input stream is then closed.

Note that **MyClass** is defined to implement the **Serializable** interface. If this is not done, a **NotSerializableException** is thrown. Try experimenting with this program by declaring some of the **MyClass** instance variables to be **transient**. That data is then not saved during serialization.

```
// A serialization demo.

import java.io.*;

public class SerializationDemo {
  public static void main(String[] args) {

    // Object serialization

    try ( ObjectOutputStream objOStrm =
            new ObjectOutputStream(new FileOutputStream("serial")) )
    {
      MyClass object1 = new MyClass("Hello", -7, 2.7e10);
      System.out.println("object1: " + object1);

      objOStrm.writeObject(object1);
    }
    catch(IOException e) {
      System.out.println("Exception during serialization: " + e);
    }

    // Object deserialization

    try ( ObjectInputStream objIStrm =
            new ObjectInputStream(new FileInputStream("serial")) )
    {
      MyClass object2 = (MyClass)objIStrm.readObject();
      System.out.println("object2: " + object2);
    }
    catch(Exception e) {
      System.out.println("Exception during deserialization: " + e);
    }
  }
}
```

```
class MyClass implements Serializable {
  String s;
  int i;
  double d;

  public MyClass(String s, int i, double d) {
    this.s = s;
    this.i = i;
    this.d = d;
  }

  public String toString() {
    return "s=" + s + "; i=" + i + "; d=" + d;
  }
}
```

This program demonstrates that the instance variables of **object1** and **object2** are identical. The output is shown here:

```
object1: s=Hello; i=-7; d=2.7E10
object2: s=Hello; i=-7; d=2.7E10
```

For classes that you intend to serialize, you will normally want them to define the **static**, **final**, **long** constant **serialVersionUID** as a private member. Although Java will automatically define this value (as is the case for **MyClass** in the preceding example), for real-world applications, it is far better for you to define this value explicitly.

The preceding example demonstrated the basic mechanism used to write and read serialized data. Another key feature related to serialization is the *deserialization filter*. A deserialization filter gives you a degree of control over the deserialization process. Although deserialization filters can be quite sophisticated, it is easy to add a simple one to an **ObjectInputStream**. The following example illustrates the general steps involved.

Assuming the **SerializationDemo** program, this sequence adds a deserialization filter to the code that reads a **MyClass** object. It ensures that **objIStrm** will deserialize only a **MyClass** object. An attempt to deserialize any other class will cause an exception at runtime.

```
// Object deserialization with a filter.
try ( ObjectInputStream objIStrm =
        new ObjectInputStream(new FileInputStream("serial")) )
{
  // Create and add a simple deserialization filter.
  ObjectInputFilter myfilter =
                      ObjectInputFilter.Config.createFilter("MyClass;!*");
  objIStrm.setObjectInputFilter(myfilter);

  MyClass object2 = (MyClass)objIStrm.readObject();
  System.out.println("object2: " + object2);
}
catch(Exception e) {
  System.out.println("Exception during deserialization: " + e);
}
```

The key lines are

```
ObjectInputFilter myfilter =
                    ObjectInputFilter.Config.createFilter("MyClass;!*");
objIStrm.setObjectInputFilter(myfilter);
```

An **ObjectInputFilter** is created by calling the static **createFilter( )** method defined by the **ObjectInputFilter.Config** nested class. This method lets you specify a string pattern that helps validate input. For example, you can specify one or more class names for which serialization will be allowed, with each name separated by a semicolon. In this case, **MyClass** is specified. The pattern **!*** specifies that all other classes are to be rejected. As a result, only instances of **MyClass** are allowed to be deserialized. In general, putting a **!** before a class causes the class to be rejected. The * is a wildcard character that matches all class names. Once the filter has been created, it is associated with **objIStrm** by a call to **setObjectInputFilter( )**. After this call, the stream filter will be active on the input stream.

The preceding example specifies a filter specific to **objIStrm**. Thus, another **ObjectInputStream** will not have the same filter. You can, however, define a filter that will be used by all **ObjectInputStreams**. This is called a *JVM-wide* filter. It is set by calling the **setSerialFilter( )** method in **ObjectInputFilter.Config**. For example, after this sequence, all **ObjectInputStreams** will use the specified filter:

```
ObjectInputFilter.Config.setSerialFilter(myfilter);
```

It is important to understand that whether a JVM-wide filter or a stream-specific filter is used, you must set it before reading from the stream. Furthermore, when a JVM-wide filter is used, it must be set before an **ObjectInputStream** is created. Also, a filter can only be set once.

When using a filter, you can also check various resource limits. The limits are specified by the **maxdepth, maxrefs, maxbytes,** and **maxarray** patterns, which must include a = followed by a value. For example, the **maxbytes** limit specifies the maximum length of the input stream. Here is the preceding filter, rewritten to include a maximum input stream length of 80 bytes:

```
ObjectInputFilter myfilter =
      ObjectInputFilter.Config.createFilter("MyClass;!*;maxbytes=80");
```

Now, any **ObjectInputStream** that supplies more than 80 bytes will be rejected.

In addition to the examples just shown, there are several other filter pattern options available. Check the Java documentation for additional information on deserialization filters. One last point: There are documentation comments that pertain to serialization. (See Appendix A, where documentation comments are discussed.)

---

**REMEMBER** There are significant security issues surrounding serialization and deserialization. It is important to consult the latest Java documentation in this regard.

## Stream Benefits

The streaming interface to I/O in Java provides a clean abstraction for a complex and often cumbersome task. The composition of the filtered stream classes allows you to dynamically build the custom streaming interface to suit your data transfer requirements. Java programs written to adhere to the abstract, high-level **InputStream**, **OutputStream**, **Reader**, and **Writer** classes should continue to function properly in the future, even if concrete stream classes evolve. As you will see in Chapter 24, this model works very well when we switch from a file system-based set of streams to the network and socket streams. Finally, serialization of objects plays an important role in many types of Java programs. Java's serialization I/O classes provide a portable solution to this sometimes tricky task.

CHAPTER

# 23 Exploring NIO

Beginning with version 1.4, Java has provided a second I/O system called NIO (which is short for *New I/O*). It supports a buffer-oriented, channel-based approach to I/O operations. With the release of JDK 7, the NIO system was greatly expanded, providing enhanced support for file-handling and file system features. In fact, so significant were the changes that the term *NIO.2* is often used. Because of the capabilities supported by the NIO file classes, NIO has become an important approach to file handling. This chapter explores several of the key features of the NIO system.

## The NIO Classes

The NIO classes are contained in the packages shown here. Beginning with JDK 9, all are in the **java.base** module.

| Package | Purpose |
|---|---|
| java.nio | Top-level package for the NIO system. Encapsulates various types of buffers that contain data operated upon by the NIO system. |
| java.nio.channels | Supports channels, which are essentially open I/O connections. |
| java.nio.channels.spi | Supports service providers for channels. |
| java.nio.charset | Encapsulates character sets. Also supports encoders and decoders that convert characters to bytes and bytes to characters, respectively. |
| java.nio.charset.spi | Supports service providers for character sets. |
| java.nio.file | Provides support for files. |
| java.nio.file.attribute | Provides support for file attributes. |
| java.nio.file.spi | Supports service providers for file systems. |

Before we begin, it is important to emphasize that the NIO subsystem does not replace the stream-based I/O classes found in **java.io**, which are discussed in Chapter 22, and good working knowledge of the stream-based I/O in **java.io** is helpful to understanding NIO.

**NOTE** This chapter assumes that you have read the overview of I/O given in Chapter 13 and the discussion of stream-based I/O supplied in Chapter 22.

# NIO Fundamentals

The NIO system is built on two foundational items: buffers and channels. A *buffer* holds data. A *channel* represents an open connection to an I/O device, such as a file or a socket. In general, to use the NIO system, you obtain a channel to an I/O device and a buffer to hold data. You then operate on the buffer, inputting or outputting data as needed. The following sections examine buffers and channels in more detail.

## Buffers

Buffers are defined in the **java.nio** package. All buffers are subclasses of the **Buffer** class, which defines the core functionality common to all buffers: current position, limit, and capacity. The *current position* is the index within the buffer at which the next read or write operation will take place. The current position is advanced by most read or write operations. The *limit* is the index value one past the last valid location in the buffer. The *capacity* is the number of elements that the buffer can hold. Often the limit equals the capacity of the buffer. **Buffer** also supports mark and reset. **Buffer** defines several methods, which are shown in Table 23-1.

| Method | Description |
|---|---|
| abstract Object array( ) | If the invoking buffer is backed by an array, returns a reference to the array. Otherwise, an **UnsupportedOperationException** is thrown. If the array is read-only, a **ReadOnlyBufferException** is thrown. |
| abstract int arrayOffset( ) | If the invoking buffer is backed by an array, returns the index of the first element. Otherwise, an **UnsupportedOperationException** is thrown. If the array is read-only, a **ReadOnlyBufferException** is thrown. |
| final int capacity( ) | Returns the number of elements that the invoking buffer is capable of holding. |
| final Buffer clear( ) | Clears the invoking buffer and returns a reference to the buffer. |
| abstract Buffer duplicate( ) | Returns a buffer that is identical to the invoking buffer. Thus, both buffers will contain and refer to the same elements. |
| final Buffer flip( ) | Sets the invoking buffer's limit to the current position and resets the current position to 0. Returns a reference to the buffer. |
| abstract boolean hasArray( ) | Returns **true** if the invoking buffer is backed by a read/write array and **false** otherwise. |

**Table 23-1** The Methods Defined by **Buffer**

| Method | Description |
|---|---|
| final boolean hasRemaining( ) | Returns **true** if there are elements remaining in the invoking buffer. Returns **false** otherwise. |
| abstract boolean isDirect( ) | Returns **true** if the invoking buffer is direct, which means I/O operations act directly upon it. Returns **false** otherwise. |
| abstract boolean isReadOnly( ) | Returns **true** if the invoking buffer is read-only. Returns **false** otherwise. |
| final int limit( ) | Returns the invoking buffer's limit. |
| final Buffer limit(int *n*) | Sets the invoking buffer's limit to *n*. Returns a reference to the buffer. |
| final Buffer mark( ) | Sets the mark and returns a reference to the invoking buffer. |
| final int position( ) | Returns the current position. |
| final Buffer position(int *n*) | Sets the invoking buffer's current position to *n*. Returns a reference to the buffer. |
| int remaining( ) | Returns the number of elements available before the limit is reached. In other words, it returns the limit minus the current position. |
| final Buffer reset( ) | Resets the current position of the invoking buffer to the previously set mark. Returns a reference to the buffer. |
| final Buffer rewind( ) | Sets the position of the invoking buffer to 0. Returns a reference to the buffer. |
| abstract Buffer slice( ) | Returns a buffer that consists of the elements in the invoking buffer, beginning at the invoking buffer's current position. Thus, for the slice, both buffers will contain and refer to the same elements. |
| abstract Buffer slice(int *startIdx*, int *size*) | Returns a buffer that consists of *size* elements in the invoking buffer, beginning at *startIdx*. Thus, for the slice, both buffers will contain and refer to the same elements. |

**Table 23-1** The Methods Defined by **Buffer** *(continued)*

From **Buffer**, the following specific buffer classes are derived, which hold the type of data that their names imply:

| ByteBuffer | CharBuffer | DoubleBuffer | FloatBuffer |
|---|---|---|---|
| IntBuffer | LongBuffer | MappedByteBuffer | ShortBuffer |

**MappedByteBuffer** is a subclass of **ByteBuffer** and is used to map a file to a buffer.

All of the aforementioned buffers provide various **get( )** and **put( )** methods, which allow you to get data from a buffer or put data into a buffer. (Of course, if a buffer is read-only, then **put( )** operations are not available.) Table 23-2 shows the **get( )** and **put( )** methods defined by **ByteBuffer**. The other buffer classes have similar methods. All buffer classes also support methods that perform various buffer operations. For example, you can allocate a buffer manually using **allocate( )**. You can wrap an array inside a buffer using **wrap( )**. You can create a subsequence of a buffer using **slice( )**.

| Method | Description |
|---|---|
| abstract byte get( ) | Returns the byte at the current position. |
| ByteBuffer get(byte[ ] *vals*) | Copies the invoking buffer into the array referred to by *vals*. Returns a reference to the buffer. If there are not *vals*.**length** elements remaining in the buffer, a **BufferUnderflowException** is thrown. |
| ByteBuffer get(byte[ ] *vals*, int *start*, int *num*) | Copies *num* elements from the invoking buffer into the array referred to by *vals*, beginning at the index specified by *start*. Returns a reference to the buffer. If there are not *num* elements remaining in the buffer, a **BufferUnderflowException** is thrown. |
| abstract byte get(int *idx*) | Returns the byte at the index specified by *idx* within the invoking buffer. |
| ByteBuffer get(int *bufferStartIdx*, byte[] *vals*) | Copies all elements from the invoking buffer into the array referred to by *vals*, beginning at the index specified by *bufferStartIdx*. Returns a reference to the buffer. The *vals* array must be large enough to hold the elements. Otherwise, an **IndexOutOfBoundsException** will be thrown. |
| ByteBuffer get(int *bufferStartIdx*, byte[] *vals*, int *arrayStartIdx*, int *num*) | Beginning at the buffer index *bufferStartIdx*, copies *num* elements from the invoking buffer into the array referred to by *vals*, beginning at the array index specified by *arrayStartIdx*. Returns a reference to the buffer. The *vals* array must be large enough to hold the elements. Otherwise, an **IndexOutOfBoundsException** will be thrown. |
| abstract ByteBuffer put(byte *b*) | Copies *b* into the invoking buffer at the current position. Returns a reference to the buffer. If the buffer is full, a **BufferOverflowException** is thrown. |
| final ByteBuffer put(byte[ ] *vals* ) | Copies all elements of *vals* into the invoking buffer, beginning at the current position. Returns a reference to the buffer. If the buffer cannot hold all of the elements, a **BufferOverflowException** is thrown. |
| ByteBuffer put(byte[ ] *vals*, int *start*, int *num*) | Copies *num* elements from *vals*, beginning at *start*, into the invoking buffer. Returns a reference to the buffer. If the buffer cannot hold all of the elements, a **BufferOverflowException** is thrown. |
| ByteBuffer put(ByteBuffer *bb*) | Copies the elements in *bb* to the invoking buffer, beginning at the current position. If the buffer cannot hold all of the elements, a **BufferOverflowException** is thrown. Returns a reference to the buffer. |

**Table 23-2** The **get( )** and **put( )** Methods Defined for **ByteBuffer**

| Method | Description |
|---|---|
| abstract ByteBuffer put(int *idx*, byte *b*) | Copies *b* into the invoking buffer at the location specified by *idx*. Returns a reference to the buffer. |
| ByteBuffer put(int *bufferStartIdx*, byte[] *vals*) | Copies all elements from the array referred to by *vals* into the invoking buffer, beginning at the index specified by *bufferStartIdx*. Returns a reference to the buffer. |
| ByteBuffer put(int *bufferStartIdx*, byte[] *vals*, int *arrayStartIdx*, int *num*) | Beginning at *arrayStartIdx*, copies *num* elements from the array referred to by *vals* into the invoking buffer, beginning at the index specified by *bufferStartIdx*. Returns a reference to the buffer. |
| ByteBuffer put(int *toBufferStartIdx*, ByteBuffer *bb*, int *fromBufferStartIdx*, int *num*) | Beginning at *fromBufferStartIdx*, copies *num* elements from the buffer referred to by *bb* into the invoking buffer, beginning at the index specified by *toBufferStartIdx*. Returns a reference to the buffer. |

**Table 23-2** The **get( )** and **put( )** Methods Defined for **ByteBuffer** *(continued)*

## Channels

Channels are defined in **java.nio.channels**. A channel represents an open connection to an I/O source or destination. Channels implement the **Channel** interface. It extends **Closeable**, and it extends **AutoCloseable**. By implementing **AutoCloseable**, channels can be managed with a **try**-with-resources statement. When used in a **try**-with-resources block, a channel is closed automatically when it is no longer needed. (See Chapter 13 for a discussion of **try**-with-resources.)

One way to obtain a channel is by calling **getChannel( )** on an object that supports channels. For example, **getChannel( )** is supported by the following I/O classes:

| | | |
|---|---|---|
| DatagramSocket | FileInputStream | FileOutputStream |
| RandomAccessFile | ServerSocket | Socket |

The specific type of channel returned depends upon the type of object **getChannel( )** is called on. For example, when called on a **FileInputStream**, **FileOutputStream**, or **RandomAccessFile**, **getChannel( )** returns a channel of type **FileChannel**. When called on a **Socket**, **getChannel( )** returns a **SocketChannel**.

Another way to obtain a channel is to use one of the **static** methods defined by the **Files** class. For example, using **Files**, you can obtain a byte channel by calling **newByteChannel( )**. It returns a **SeekableByteChannel**, which is an interface implemented by **FileChannel**. (The **Files** class is examined in detail later in this chapter.)

Part II

Channels such as **FileChannel** and **SocketChannel** support various **read( )** and **write( )** methods that enable you to perform I/O operations through the channel. For example, here are a few of the **read( )** and **write( )** methods defined for **FileChannel**:

| Method | Description |
|---|---|
| abstract int read(ByteBuffer *bb*) throws IOException | Reads bytes from the invoking channel into *bb* until the buffer is full or there is no more input. Returns the number of bytes actually read. Returns –1 when an attempt is made to read at the end of the file. |
| abstract int read(ByteBuffer *bb*, long *start*) throws IOException | Beginning at the file location specified by *start*, reads bytes from the invoking channel into *bb* until the buffer is full or there is no more input. The current position is unchanged. Returns the number of bytes actually read or –1 if *start* is beyond the end of the file. |
| abstract int write(ByteBuffer *bb*) throws IOException | Writes the contents of *bb* to the invoking channel, starting at the current position. Returns the number of bytes written. |
| abstract int write(ByteBuffer *bb*, long *start*) throws IOException | Beginning at the file location specified by *start*, writes the contents of *bb* to the invoking channel. The current position is unchanged. Returns the number of bytes written. |

All channels support additional methods that give you access to and control over the channel. For example, **FileChannel** supports methods to get or set the current position, transfer information between file channels, obtain the current size of the channel, and lock the channel, among others. **FileChannel** provides a **static** method called **open( )**, which opens a file and returns a channel to it. This provides another way to obtain a channel. **FileChannel** also provides the **map( )** method, which lets you map a file to a buffer.

## Charsets and Selectors

Two other entities used by NIO are charsets and selectors. A *charset* defines the way that bytes are mapped to characters. You can encode a sequence of characters into bytes using an *encoder*. You can decode a sequence of bytes into characters using a *decoder*. Charsets, encoders, and decoders are supported by classes defined in the **java.nio.charset** package. Because default encoders and decoders are provided, you will not often need to work explicitly with charsets.

A *selector* supports key-based, non-blocking, multiplexed I/O. In other words, selectors enable you to perform I/O through multiple channels. Selectors are supported by classes defined in the **java.nio.channels** package. Selectors are most applicable to socket-backed channels.

We will not use charsets or selectors in this chapter, but you might find them useful in your own applications.

# Enhancements Added by NIO.2

Beginning with JDK 7, the NIO system was substantially expanded and enhanced. In addition to support for the **try**-with-resources statement (which provides automatic resource management), the improvements included three new packages (**java.nio.file**, **java.nio.file.attribute**, and

**java.nio.file.spi**); several new classes, interfaces, and methods; and direct support for stream-based I/O. The additions have greatly expanded the ways in which NIO can be used, especially with files. Several of the key additions are described in the following sections.

## The Path Interface

Perhaps the single most important addition to the NIO system was the **Path** interface because it encapsulates a path to a file. As you will see, **Path** is the glue that binds together many of the NIO.2 file-based features. It describes a file's location within the directory structure. **Path** is packaged in **java.nio.file**, and it inherits the following interfaces: **Watchable**, **Iterable<Path>**, and **Comparable<Path>**. **Watchable** describes an object that can be monitored for changes. The **Iterable** and **Comparable** interfaces were described earlier in this book.

**Path** declares a number of methods that operate on the path. A sampling is shown in Table 23-3. Pay special attention to the **getName( )** method. It is used to obtain an element in a path. It works using an index. At index zero is the part of the path nearest the root, which is the leftmost element in a path. Subsequent indexes specify elements to the right of the root. The number of elements in a path can be obtained by calling **getNameCount( )**. If you want to obtain a string representation of the entire path, simply call **toString( )**. Notice that you can resolve a relative path into an absolute path by using the **resolve( )** method.

Beginning with JDK 11, an important new **static** factory method called **of( )** was added to **Path**. It returns a **Path** instance from either a path name or a URI. Thus, **of( )** gives you a way to construct a new **Path** instance.

One other point: When updating legacy code that uses the **File** class defined by **java.io**, it is possible to convert a **File** instance into a **Path** instance by calling **toPath( )** on the **File** object. Furthermore, it is possible to obtain a **File** instance by calling the **toFile( )** method defined by **Path**.

| Method | Description |
|---|---|
| default boolean endsWith(String *path*) | Returns **true** if the invoking **Path** ends with the path specified by *path*. Otherwise, returns **false**. |
| boolean endsWith(Path *path*) | Returns **true** if the invoking **Path** ends with the path specified by *path*. Otherwise, returns **false**. |
| Path getFileName( ) | Returns the filename associated with the invoking **Path**. |
| Path getName(int *idx*) | Returns a **Path** object that contains the name of the path element specified by *idx* within the invoking object. The leftmost element is at index 0. This is the element nearest the root. The rightmost element is at **getNameCount( )** – 1. |
| int getNameCount( ) | Returns the number of elements beyond the root directory in the invoking **Path**. |
| Path getParent( ) | Returns a **Path** that contains the entire path except for the name of the file specified by the invoking **Path**. |
| Path getRoot( ) | Returns the root of the invoking **Path**. |
| boolean isAbsolute( ) | Returns **true** if the invoking **Path** is absolute. Otherwise, returns **false**. |

**Table 23-3** A Sampling of Methods Specified by **Path**

| Method | Description |
|---|---|
| static Path of(String *pathname*, String ... *parts*) | Returns a **Path** that encapsulates the specified path. If the *parts* varargs parameter is not used, then the path must be specified in its entirety by *pathname*. Otherwise, the arguments passed via *parts* are added to *pathname* (usually with an appropriate separator) to form the entire path. In either case, if the path specified is syntactically invalid, an **InvalidPathException** will occur. |
| static Path of(URI uri) | The path corresponding to *uri* is returned. |
| Path resolve(Path *path*) | If *path* is absolute, *path* is returned. Otherwise, if *path* does not contain a root, *path* is prefixed by the root specified by the invoking **Path** and the result is returned. If *path* is empty, the invoking **Path** is returned. Otherwise, the behavior is unspecified. |
| default Path resolve(String *path*) | If *path* is absolute, *path* is returned. Otherwise, if *path* does not contain a root, *path* is prefixed by the root specified by the invoking **Path** and the result is returned. If *path* is empty, the invoking **Path** is returned. Otherwise, the behavior is unspecified. |
| default boolean startsWith(String *path*) | Returns **true** if the invoking **Path** starts with the path specified by *path*. Otherwise, returns **false**. |
| boolean startsWith(Path *path*) | Returns **true** if the invoking **Path** starts with the path specified by *path*. Otherwise, returns **false**. |
| Path toAbsolutePath( ) | Returns the invoking **Path** as an absolute path. |
| String toString( ) | Returns a string representation of the invoking **Path**. |

**Table 23-3** A Sampling of Methods Specified by **Path** *(continued)*

## The Files Class

Many of the actions that you perform on a file are provided by **static** methods within the **Files** class. The file to be acted upon is specified by its **Path**. Thus, the **Files** methods use a **Path** to specify the file that is being operated upon. **Files** contains a wide array of functionality. For example, it has methods that let you open or create a file that has the specified path. You can obtain information about a **Path**, such as whether it is executable, hidden, or read-only. **Files** also supplies methods that let you copy or move files. A sampling is shown in Table 23-4. In addition to **IOException**, several other exceptions are possible. **Files** also includes these four methods: **list( )**, **walk( )**, **lines( )**, and **find( )**. All return a **Stream** object. These methods help integrate NIO with the stream API described in Chapter 30. **Files** also includes the methods **readString( )** and **writeString( )**, which returns a **String** containing the characters in a file or writes a **CharSequence** (such as a **String**) to a file.

| Method | Description |
|---|---|
| static Path copy(Path *src*, Path *dest*, CopyOption ... *how*) throws IOException | Copies the file specified by *src* to the location specified by *dest*. The *how* parameter specifies how the copy will take place. |
| static Path createDirectory(Path *path*, FileAttribute<?> ... *attribs*) throws IOException | Creates the directory whose path is specified by *path*. The directory attributes are specified by *attribs*. |
| static Path createFile(Path *path*, FileAttribute<?> ... *attribs*) throws IOException | Creates the file whose path is specified by *path*. The file attributes are specified by *attribs*. |
| static void delete(Path *path*) throws IOException | Deletes the file whose path is specified by *path*. |
| static boolean exists(Path *path*, LinkOption ... *opts*) | Returns **true** if the file specified by *path* exists and **false** otherwise. If *opts* is not specified, then symbolic links are followed. To prevent the following of symbolic links, pass **NOFOLLOW_LINKS** to *opts*. |
| static boolean isDirectory(Path *path*, LinkOption ... *opts*) | Returns **true** if *path* specifies a directory and **false** otherwise. If *opts* is not specified, then symbolic links are followed. To prevent the following of symbolic links, pass **NOFOLLOW_LINKS** to *opts*. |
| static boolean isExecutable(Path *path*) | Returns **true** if the file specified by *path* is executable and **false** otherwise. |
| static boolean isHidden(Path *path*) throws IOException | Returns **true** if the file specified by *path* is hidden and **false** otherwise. |
| static boolean isReadable(Path *path*) | Returns **true** if the file specified by *path* can be read from and **false** otherwise. |
| static boolean isRegularFile(Path *path*, LinkOption ... *opts*) | Returns **true** if *path* specifies a file and **false** otherwise. If *opts* is not specified, then symbolic links are followed. To prevent the following of symbolic links, pass **NOFOLLOW_LINKS** to *opts*. |
| static boolean isWritable(Path *path*) | Returns **true** if the file specified by *path* can be written to and **false** otherwise. |
| static Path move(Path *src*, Path *dest*, CopyOption ... *how*) throws IOException | Moves the file specified by *src* to the location specified by *dest*. The *how* parameter specifies how the move will take place. |
| static SeekableByteChannel newByteChannel(Path *path*, OpenOption ... *how*) throws IOException | Opens the file specified by *path*, as specified by *how*. Returns a **SeekableByteChannel** to the file. This is a byte channel whose current position can be changed. **SeekableByteChannel** is implemented by **FileChannel**. |
| static DirectoryStream<Path> newDirectoryStream(Path *path*) throws IOException | Opens the directory specified by *path*. Returns a **DirectoryStream** linked to the directory. |

**Table 23-4** A Sampling of Methods Defined by **Files**

| Method | Description |
|---|---|
| static InputStream newInputStream(Path *path*, OpenOption ... *how*) throws IOException | Opens the file specified by *path*, as specified by *how*. Returns an **InputStream** linked to the file. |
| static OutputStream newOutputStream(Path *path*, OpenOption ... *how*) throws IOException | Opens the file specified by the invoking object, as specified by *how*. Returns an **OutputStream** linked to the file. |
| static boolean notExists(Path *path*, LinkOption ... *opts*) | Returns **true** if the file specified by *path* does *not* exist and **false** otherwise. If *opts* is not specified, then symbolic links are followed. To prevent the following of symbolic links, pass **NOFOLLOW_LINKS** to *opts*. |
| static <A extends BasicFileAttributes> A readAttributes(Path *path*, Class<A> *attribType*, LinkOption ... *opts*) throws IOException | Obtains the attributes associated with the file specified by *path*. The type of attributes to obtain is passed in *attribType*. If *opts* is not specified, then symbolic links are followed. To prevent the following of symbolic links, pass **NOFOLLOW_LINKS** to *opts*. |
| static long size(Path *path*) throws IOException | Returns the size of the file specified by *path*. |

**Table 23-4** A Sampling of Methods Defined by **Files** *(continued)*

Notice that several of the methods in Table 23-4 take an argument of type **OpenOption**. This is an interface that describes how to open a file. It is implemented by the **StandardOpenOption** enumeration that has the values shown in Table 23-5.

## The Paths Class

Because **Path** is an interface, not a class, you can't create an instance of **Path** directly through the use of a constructor. Instead, you obtain a **Path** by a calling a method that returns one. Prior to JDK 11, you would typically do this by using the **get( )** method defined by the **Paths** class. There are two forms of **get( )**. The first is shown here:

static Path get(String *pathname*, String ... *parts*)

It returns a **Path** that encapsulates the specified path. The path can be specified in two ways. First, if *parts* is not used, then the path must be specified in its entirety by *pathname*. Alternatively, you can pass the path in pieces, with the first part passed in *pathname* and the subsequent elements specified by the *parts* varargs parameter. In either case, if the path specified is syntactically invalid, **get( )** will throw an **InvalidPathException**.

The second form of **get( )** creates a **Path** from a **URI**. It is shown here:

static Path get(URI *uri*)

The **Path** corresponding to *uri* is returned.

Although the **Paths.get( )** method just described has been in use since JDK 7 and, at the time of this writing, is still available for use, it is no longer recommended. Instead, the Java

| Value | Meaning |
|---|---|
| APPEND | Causes output to be written to the end of the file. |
| CREATE | Creates the file if it does not already exist. |
| CREATE_NEW | Creates the file only if it does not already exist. |
| DELETE_ON_CLOSE | Deletes the file when it is closed. |
| DSYNC | Causes changes to the file to be immediately written to the physical file. Normally, changes to a file are buffered by the file system in the interest of efficiency, being written to the file only as needed. |
| READ | Opens the file for input operations. |
| SPARSE | Indicates to the file system that the file is sparse, meaning that it may not be completely filled with data. If the file system does not support sparse files, this option is ignored. |
| SYNC | Causes changes to the file or its metadata to be immediately written to the physical file. Normally, changes to a file are buffered by the file system in the interest of efficiency, being written to the file only as needed. |
| TRUNCATE_EXISTING | Causes a preexisting file opened for output to be reduced to zero length. |
| WRITE | Opens the file for output operations. |

**Table 23-5** The Standard Open Options



API documentation now recommends the use of the new **Path.of( )** method, which was added by JDK 11. Because of this, **Path.of( )** is now the preferred approach. Of course, if you are using a compiler that predates JDK 11, then you must continue to use **Paths.get( )**.

It is important to understand that obtaining a **Path** to a file does not open or create a file. It simply creates an object that encapsulates the file's directory path.

## The File Attribute Interfaces

Associated with a file is a set of attributes. These attributes include such things as the file's time of creation, the time of its last modification, whether the file is a directory, and its size. NIO organizes file attributes into several different interfaces. Attributes are represented by a hierarchy of interfaces defined in **java.nio.file.attribute**. At the top is **BasicFileAttributes**. It encapsulates the set of attributes that are commonly found in a variety of file systems. The methods defined by **BasicFileAttributes** are shown in Table 23-6.

From **BasicFileAttributes** two interfaces are derived: **DosFileAttributes** and **PosixFileAttributes**. **DosFileAttributes** describes those attributes related to the FAT file system as first defined by DOS. It defines the methods shown here:

| Method | Description |
|---|---|
| boolean isArchive( ) | Returns **true** if the file is flagged for archiving and **false** otherwise. |
| boolean isHidden( ) | Returns **true** if the file is hidden and **false** otherwise. |
| boolean isReadOnly( ) | Returns **true** if the file is read-only and **false** otherwise. |
| boolean isSystem( ) | Returns **true** if the file is flagged as a system file and **false** otherwise. |

| Method | Description |
|---|---|
| FileTime creationTime( ) | Returns the time at which the file was created. If creation time is not provided by the file system, then an implementation-dependent value is returned. |
| Object fileKey( ) | Returns the file key. If not supported, **null** is returned. |
| boolean isDirectory( ) | Returns **true** if the file represents a directory. |
| boolean isOther( ) | Returns **true** if the file is not a file, symbolic link, or a directory. |
| boolean isRegularFile( ) | Returns **true** if the file is a normal file, rather than a directory or symbolic link. |
| boolean isSymbolicLink( ) | Returns **true** if the file is a symbolic link. |
| FileTime lastAccessTime( ) | Returns the time at which the file was last accessed. If the time of last access is not provided by the file system, then an implementation-dependent value is returned. |
| FileTime lastModifiedTime( ) | Returns the time at which the file was last modified. If the time of last modification is not provided by the file system, then an implementation-dependent value is returned. |
| long size( ) | Returns the size of the file. |

**Table 23-6** The Methods Defined by **BasicFileAttributes**

**PosixFileAttributes** encapsulates attributes defined by the POSIX standards. (POSIX stands for *Portable Operating System Interface.*) It defines the methods shown here:

| Method | Description |
|---|---|
| GroupPrincipal group( ) | Returns the file's group owner |
| UserPrincipal owner( ) | Returns the file's owner |
| Set<PosixFilePermission> permissions( ) | Returns the file's permissions |

There are various ways to access a file's attributes. First, you can obtain an object that encapsulates a file's attributes by calling **readAttributes( )**, which is a **static** method defined by **Files**. One of its forms is shown here:

static <A extends BasicFileAttributes>
    A readAttributes(Path *path*, Class<A> *attrType*, LinkOption... *opts*)
        throws IOException

This method returns a reference to an object that specifies the attributes associated with the file passed in *path*. The specific type of attributes is specified as a **Class** object in the *attrType* parameter. For example, to obtain the basic file attributes, pass **BasicFileAttributes.class** to *attrType*. For DOS attributes, use **DosFileAttributes.class**, and for POSIX attributes, use **PosixFileAttributes.class**. Optional link options are passed via *opts*. If not specified, symbolic links are followed. The method returns a reference to requested attributes. If the requested attribute type is not available, **UnsupportedOperationException** is thrown. Using the object returned, you can access the file's attributes.

A second way to gain access to a file's attributes is to call **getFileAttributeView( )** defined by **Files**. NIO defines several attribute view interfaces, including **AttributeView**, **BasicFileAttributeView**, **DosFileAttributeView**, and **PosixFileAttributeView**, among others. Although we won't be using attribute views in this chapter, they are a feature that you may find helpful in some situations.

In some cases, you won't need to use the file attribute interfaces directly because the **Files** class offers **static** convenience methods that access several of the attributes. For example, **Files** includes methods such as **isHidden( )** and **isWritable( )**.

It is important to understand that not all file systems support all possible attributes. For example, the DOS file attributes apply to the older FAT file system as first defined by DOS. The attributes that will apply to a wide variety of file systems are described by **BasicFileAttributes**. For this reason, these attributes are used in the examples in this chapter.



## The FileSystem, FileSystems, and FileStore Classes

You can easily access the file system through the **FileSystem** and **FileSystems** classes packaged in **java.nio.file**. In fact, by using the **newFileSystem( )** method defined by **FileSystems**, it is even possible to obtain a new file system. The **FileStore** class encapsulates the file storage system. Although these classes are not used directly in this chapter, you may find them helpful in your own applications.

# Using the NIO System

This section illustrates how to apply the NIO system to a variety of tasks. Before beginning, it is important to emphasize that beginning with JDK 7, the NIO subsystem was greatly expanded. As a result, its uses have also been greatly expanded. As mentioned, the enhanced version is sometimes referred to as NIO.2. Because the features added by NIO.2 are so substantial, they have changed the way that much NIO-based code is written and have increased the types of tasks to which NIO can be applied. Because of its importance, the remaining discussion and examples in this chapter utilize NIO.2 features and, therefore, require a modern version of Java.

In the past, the primary purpose of NIO was channel-based I/O, and this is still a very important use. However, you can now use NIO for stream-based I/O and for performing file-system operations. As a result, the discussion of using NIO is divided into three parts:

- Using NIO for channel-based I/O
- Using NIO for stream-based I/O
- Using NIO for path and file system operations

Because the most common I/O device is the disk file, the rest of this chapter uses disk files in the examples. Because all file channel operations are byte-based, the type of buffers that we will be using are of type **ByteBuffer**.

Before you can open a file for access via the NIO system, you must obtain a **Path** that describes the file. In the past, one way to do this was to call the **Paths.get( )** factory method. However, as explained earlier, beginning with JDK 11, the preferred approach is to use

**Path.of( )** rather than **Paths.get( )**. Because of this, the examples use **Path.of( )**. If you are using a version of Java prior to JDK 11, simply substitute **Paths.get( )** for **Path.of( )** in the programs. The form of **of( )** used in the examples is shown here:

static Path of(String *pathname*, String ... *parts*)

Recall that the path can be specified in two ways. It can be passed in pieces, with the first part passed in *pathname* and the subsequent elements specified by the *parts* varargs parameter. Alternatively, the entire path can be specified in *pathname* and *parts* is not used. This is the approach used by the examples.

## Use NIO for Channel-Based I/O

An important use of NIO is to access a file via a channel and buffers. The following sections demonstrate some techniques that use a channel to read from and write to a file.

### Reading a File via a Channel

There are several ways to read data from a file using a channel. Perhaps the most common way is to manually allocate a buffer and then perform an explicit read operation that loads that buffer with data from the file. It is with this approach that we begin.

Before you can read from a file, you must open it. To do this, first create a **Path** that describes the file. Then use this **Path** to open the file. There are various ways to open the file depending on how it will be used. In this example, the file will be opened for byte-based input via explicit input operations. Therefore, this example will open the file and establish a channel to it by calling **Files.newByteChannel( )**. The version of **newByteChannel( )** that we will use has this general form:

static SeekableByteChannel newByteChannel(Path *path*, OpenOption ... *how*)
throws IOException

It returns a **SeekableByteChannel** object, which encapsulates the channel for file operations. The **Path** that describes the file is passed in *path*. The *how* parameter specifies how the file will be opened. Because it is a varargs parameter, you can specify zero or more comma-separated arguments. (The valid values were discussed earlier and shown in Table 23-5.) If no arguments are specified, the file is opened for input operations. **SeekableByteChannel** is an interface that describes a channel that can be used for file operations. It is implemented by the **FileChannel** class. When the default file system is used, the returned object can be cast to **FileChannel**. You must close the channel after you have finished with it. Since all channels, including **FileChannel**, implement **AutoCloseable**, you can use a **try**-with-resources statement to close the file automatically instead of calling **close( )** explicitly. This approach is used in the examples.

Next, you must obtain a buffer that will be used by the channel either by wrapping an existing array or by allocating the buffer dynamically. The examples use allocation, but the choice is yours. Because file channels operate on byte buffers, we will use the **allocate( )** method defined by **ByteBuffer** to obtain the buffer. It has this general form:

static ByteBuffer allocate(int *cap*)

Here, *cap* specifies the capacity of the buffer. A reference to the buffer is returned.

After you have created the buffer, call **read( )** on the channel, passing a reference to the buffer. The version of **read( )** that we will use is shown next:

int read(ByteBuffer *buf*) throws IOException

Each time it is called, **read( )** fills the buffer specified by *buf* with data from the file. The reads are sequential, meaning that each call to **read( )** reads the next buffer's worth of bytes from the file. The **read( )** method returns the number of bytes actually read. It returns –1 when there is an attempt to read at the end of the file.

The following program puts the preceding discussion into action by reading a file called **test.txt** through a channel using explicit input operations:



```
// Use Channel I/O to read a file.

import java.io.*;
import java.nio.*;
import java.nio.channels.*;
import java.nio.file.*;

public class ExplicitChannelRead {
  public static void main(String[] args) {
    int count;
    Path filepath = null;

    // First, obtain a path to the file.
    try {
      filepath = Path.of("test.txt");
    } catch(InvalidPathException e) {
      System.out.println("Path Error " + e);
      return;
    }

    // Next, obtain a channel to that file within a try-with-resources block.
    try ( SeekableByteChannel fChan = Files.newByteChannel(filepath) )
    {

      // Allocate a buffer.
      ByteBuffer mBuf = ByteBuffer.allocate(128);

      do {
        // Read a buffer.
        count = fChan.read(mBuf);

        // Stop when end of file is reached.
        if(count != -1) {

          // Rewind the buffer so that it can be read.
          mBuf.rewind();

          // Read bytes from the buffer and show
          // them on the screen as characters.
          for(int i=0; i < count; i++)
```

```
            System.out.print((char)mBuf.get());
          }
        } while(count != -1);

        System.out.println();
      } catch (IOException e) {
        System.out.println("I/O Error " + e);
      }
    }
  }
```

Here is how the program works. First, a **Path** object is obtained that contains the relative path to a file called **test.txt**. A reference to this object is assigned to **filepath**. Next, a channel connected to the file is obtained by calling **newByteChannel( )**, passing in **filepath**. Because no open option is specified, the file is opened for reading. Notice that this channel is the object managed by the **try**-with-resources statement. Thus, the channel is automatically closed when the block ends. The program then calls the **allocate( )** method of **ByteBuffer** to allocate a buffer that will hold the contents of the file when it is read. A reference to this buffer is stored in **mBuf**. The contents of the file are then read, one buffer at a time, into **mBuf** through a call to **read( )**. The number of bytes read is stored in **count**. Next, the buffer is rewound through a call to **rewind( )**. This call is necessary because the current position is at the end of the buffer after the call to **read( )**. It must be reset to the start of the buffer in order for the bytes in **mBuf** to be read by calling **get( )**. (Recall that **get( )** is defined by **ByteBuffer**.) Because **mBuf** is a byte buffer, the values returned by **get( )** are bytes. They are cast to **char** so the file can be displayed as text. (Alternatively, it is possible to create a buffer that encodes the bytes into characters and then read that buffer.) When the end of the file has been reached, the value returned by **read( )** will be –1. When this occurs, the program ends, and the channel is automatically closed.

As a point of interest, notice that the program obtains the **Path** within one **try** block and then uses another **try** block to obtain and manage a channel linked to that path. Although there is nothing wrong, per se, with this approach, in many cases, it can be streamlined so that only one **try** block is needed. In this approach, the calls to **Path.of( )** and **newByteChannel( )** are sequenced together. For example, here is a reworked version of the program that uses this approach:

```
// A more compact way to open a channel.

import java.io.*;
import java.nio.*;
import java.nio.channels.*;
import java.nio.file.*;

public class ExplicitChannelRead {
  public static void main(String[] args) {
    int count;

    // Here, the channel is opened on the Path returned by Path.of().
    // There is no need for the filepath variable.
    try ( SeekableByteChannel fChan =
            Files.newByteChannel(Path.of("test.txt")) )
    {
```

```
            // Allocate a buffer.
            ByteBuffer mBuf = ByteBuffer.allocate(128);

            do {
              // Read a buffer.
              count = fChan.read(mBuf);

              // Stop when end of file is reached.
              if(count != -1) {

                // Rewind the buffer so that it can be read.
                mBuf.rewind();

                // Read bytes from the buffer and show
                // them on the screen as characters.
                for(int i=0; i < count; i++)
                  System.out.print((char)mBuf.get());
              }
            } while(count != -1);

            System.out.println();
          } catch(InvalidPathException e) {
            System.out.println("Path Error " + e);
          } catch (IOException e) {
            System.out.println("I/O Error " + e);
          }
        }
      }
```

In this version, the variable **filepath** is not needed and both exceptions are handled by the same **try** statement. Because this approach is more compact, it is the approach used in the rest of the examples in this chapter. Of course, in your own code, you may encounter situations in which the creation of a **Path** object needs to be separate from the acquisition of a channel. In these cases, the previous approach can be used.

Another way to read a file is to map it to a buffer. The advantage is that the buffer automatically contains the contents of the file. No explicit read operation is necessary. To map and read the contents of a file, follow this general procedure. First, obtain a **Path** object that encapsulates the file as previously described. Next, obtain a channel to that file by calling **Files.newByteChannel( )**, passing in the **Path** and casting the returned object to **FileChannel**. As explained, **newByteChannel( )** returns a **SeekableByteChannel**. When using the default file system, this object can be cast to **FileChannel**. Then, map the channel to a buffer by calling **map( )** on the channel. The **map( )** method is defined by **FileChannel**. This is why the cast to **FileChannel** is needed. The **map( )** function is shown here:

MappedByteBuffer map(FileChannel.MapMode *how*,
long *pos*, long *size*) throws IOException

The **map( )** method causes the data in the file to be mapped into a buffer in memory. The value in *how* determines what type of operations are allowed. It must be one of these values:

| MapMode.READ_ONLY | MapMode.READ_WRITE | MapMode.PRIVATE |
|---|---|---|

For reading a file, use **MapMode.READ_ONLY**. To read and write, use **MapMode.READ_WRITE**. **MapMode.PRIVATE** causes a private copy of the file to be made, and changes to the buffer do not affect the underlying file. The location within the file to begin mapping is specified by *pos*, and the number of bytes to map are specified by *size*. A reference to this buffer is returned as a **MappedByteBuffer**, which is a subclass of **ByteBuffer**. Once the file has been mapped to a buffer, you can read the file from that buffer. Here is an example that illustrates this approach:

```
// Use a mapped file to read a file.

import java.io.*;
import java.nio.*;
import java.nio.channels.*;
import java.nio.file.*;

public class MappedChannelRead {
  public static void main(String[] args) {

    // Obtain a channel to a file within a try-with-resources block.
    try ( FileChannel fChan =
          (FileChannel) Files.newByteChannel(Path.of("test.txt")) )
    {

      // Get the size of the file.
      long fSize = fChan.size();

      // Now, map the file into a buffer.
      MappedByteBuffer mBuf = fChan.map(FileChannel.MapMode.READ_ONLY, 0, fSize);

      // Read and display bytes from buffer.
      for(int i=0; i < fSize; i++)
        System.out.print((char)mBuf.get());

      System.out.println();

    } catch(InvalidPathException e) {
      System.out.println("Path Error " + e);
    } catch (IOException e) {
      System.out.println("I/O Error " + e);
    }
  }
}
```

In the program, a **Path** to the file is created and then opened via **newByteChannel( )**. The channel is cast to **FileChannel** and stored in **fChan**. Next, the size of the file is obtained by calling **size( )** on the channel. Then, the entire file is mapped into memory by calling **map( )** on **fChan** and a reference to the buffer is stored in **mBuf**. Notice that **mBuf** is declared as a reference to a **MappedByteBuffer**. The bytes in **mBuf** are read by calling **get( )**.

## Writing to a File via a Channel

As is the case when reading from a file, there are also several ways to write data to a file using a channel. We will begin with one of the most common. In this approach, you manually allocate a buffer, write data to that buffer, and then perform an explicit write operation to write that data to a file.

Before you can write to a file, you must open it. To do this, first obtain a **Path** that describes the file and then use this **Path** to open the file. In this example, the file will be opened for byte-based output via explicit output operations. Therefore, this example will open the file and establish a channel to it by calling **Files.newByteChannel( )**. As shown in the previous section, the **newByteChannel( )** method that we will use has this general form:

static SeekableByteChannel newByteChannel(Path *path*, OpenOption ... *how*)
    throws IOException

It returns a **SeekableByteChannel** object, which encapsulates the channel for file operations. To open a file for output, the *how* parameter must specify **StandardOpenOption.WRITE**. If you want to create the file if it does not already exist, then you must also specify **StandardOpenOption.CREATE**. (Other options, which are shown in Table 23-5, are also available.) As explained in the previous section, **SeekableByteChannel** is an interface that describes a channel that can be used for file operations. It is implemented by the **FileChannel** class. When the default file system is used, the return object can be cast to **FileChannel**. You must close the channel after you have finished with it.

Here is one way to write to a file through a channel using explicit calls to **write( )**. First, obtain a **Path** to the file and then open it with a call to **newByteChannel( )**, casting the result to **FileChannel**. Next, allocate a byte buffer and write data to that buffer. Before the data is written to the file, call **rewind( )** on the buffer to set its current position to zero. (Each output operation on the buffer increases the current position. Thus, it must be reset prior to writing to the file.) Then, call **write( )** on the channel, passing in the buffer. The following program demonstrates this procedure. It writes the alphabet to a file called **test.txt**.

```
// Write to a file using NIO.

import java.io.*;
import java.nio.*;
import java.nio.channels.*;
import java.nio.file.*;

public class ExplicitChannelWrite {
  public static void main(String[] args) {

    // Obtain a channel to a file within a try-with-resources block.
    try ( FileChannel fChan = (FileChannel)
            Files.newByteChannel(Path.of("test.txt"),
                                 StandardOpenOption.WRITE,
                                 StandardOpenOption.CREATE) )
    {
      // Create a buffer.
      ByteBuffer mBuf = ByteBuffer.allocate(26);

      // Write some bytes to the buffer.
      for(int i=0; i<26; i++)
        mBuf.put((byte)('A' + i));

      // Reset the buffer so that it can be written.
      mBuf.rewind();
```

```
      // Write the buffer to the output file.
      fChan.write(mBuf);

    } catch(InvalidPathException e) {
      System.out.println("Path Error " + e);
    } catch (IOException e) {
      System.out.println("I/O Error: " + e);
      System.exit(1);
    }
  }
}
```

It is useful to emphasize an important aspect of this program. As mentioned, after data is written to **mBuf**, but before it is written to the file, a call to **rewind( )** on **mBuf** is made. This is necessary in order to reset the current position to zero after data has been written to **mBuf**. Remember, each call to **put( )** on **mBuf** advances the current position. Therefore, it is necessary for the current position to be reset to the start of the buffer before calling **write( )**. If this is not done, **write( )** will think that there is no data in the buffer.

Another way to handle the resetting of the buffer between input and output operations is to call **flip( )** instead of **rewind( )**. The **flip( )** method sets the value of the current position to zero and the limit to the previous current position. In the preceding example, because the capacity of the buffer equals its limit, **flip( )** could have been used instead of **rewind( )**. However, the two methods are not interchangeable in all cases.

In general, you must reset the buffer between read and write operations. For example, assuming the preceding example, the following loop will write the alphabet to the file three times. Pay special attention to the calls to **rewind( )**.

```
for(int h=0; h<3; h++) {
  // Write some bytes to the buffer.
  for(int i=0; i<26; i++)
    mBuf.put((byte)('A' + i));

  // Rewind the buffer so that it can be written.
  mBuf.rewind();

  // Write the buffer to the output file.
  fChan.write(mBuf);

  // Rewind the buffer so that it can be written to again.
  mBuf.rewind();
}
```

Notice that **rewind( )** is called between each read and write operation.

One other thing about the program warrants mentioning: When the buffer is written to the file, the first 26 bytes in the file will contain the output. If the file **test.txt** was preexisting, then after the program executes, the first 26 bytes of **test.txt** will contain the alphabet, but the remainder of the file will remain unchanged.

Another way to write to a file is to map it to a buffer. The advantage to this approach is that the data written to the buffer will automatically be written to the file. No explicit write operation is necessary. To map and write the contents of a file, we will use this general procedure. First, obtain a **Path** object that encapsulates the file and then create a channel to that file by calling **Files.newByteChannel( )**, passing in the **Path**. Cast the reference returned by **newByteChannel( )** to **FileChannel**. Next, map the channel to a buffer by calling **map( )** on the channel. The **map( )** method was described in detail in the previous section. It is summarized here for your convenience. Here is its general form:

MappedByteBuffer map(FileChannel.MapMode *how*,
long *pos*, long *size*) throws IOException

The **map( )** method causes the data in the file to be mapped into a buffer in memory. The value in *how* determines what type of operations are allowed. For writing to a file, *how* must be **MapMode.READ_WRITE**. The location within the file to begin mapping is specified by *pos*, and the number of bytes to map are specified by *size*. A reference to this buffer is returned. Once the file has been mapped to a buffer, you can write data to that buffer, and it will automatically be written to the file. Therefore, no explicit write operations to the channel are necessary.

Here is the preceding program reworked so that a mapped file is used. Notice that in the call to **newByteChannel( )**, the open option **StandardOpenOption.READ** has been added. This is because a mapped buffer can either be read-only or read/write. Thus, to write to the mapped buffer, the channel must be opened as read/write.

```
// Write to a mapped file.

import java.io.*;
import java.nio.*;
import java.nio.channels.*;
import java.nio.file.*;

public class MappedChannelWrite {
  public static void main(String[] args) {

    // Obtain a channel to a file within a try-with-resources block.
    try ( FileChannel fChan = (FileChannel)
          Files.newByteChannel(Path.of("test.txt"),
                   StandardOpenOption.WRITE,
                   StandardOpenOption.READ,
                   StandardOpenOption.CREATE) )
    {

      // Then, map the file into a buffer.
      MappedByteBuffer mBuf = fChan.map(FileChannel.MapMode.READ_WRITE, 0, 26);

      // Write some bytes to the buffer.
      for(int i=0; i<26; i++)
        mBuf.put((byte)('A' + i));

    } catch(InvalidPathException e) {
      System.out.println("Path Error " + e);
    } catch (IOException e) {
      System.out.println("I/O Error " + e);
    }
  }
}
```

As you can see, there are no explicit write operations to the channel itself. Because **mBuf** is mapped to the file, changes to **mBuf** are automatically reflected in the underlying file.

## Copying a File Using NIO

NIO simplifies several types of file operations. Although we can't examine them all, an example will give you an idea of what is available. The following program copies a file using a call to a single NIO method: **copy( )**, which is a **static** method defined by **Files**. It has several forms. Here is the one we will be using:

static Path copy(Path *src*, Path *dest*, CopyOption ... *how*) throws IOException

The file specified by *src* is copied to the file specified by *dest*. How the copy is performed is specified by *how*. Because it is a varargs parameter, it can be missing. If specified, it can be one or more of these values, which are valid for all file systems:

| | |
|---|---|
| StandardCopyOption.COPY_ATTRIBUTES | Request that the file's attributes be copied. |
| LinkOption.NOFOLLOW_LINKS | Do not follow symbolic links. |
| StandardCopyOption.REPLACE_EXISTING | Overwrite a preexisting file. |

Other options may be supported, depending on the implementation.

The following program demonstrates **copy( )**. The source and destination files are specified on the command line, with the source file specified first. Notice how short the program is. You might want to compare this version of the file copy program to the one found in Chapter 13. As you will find, the part of the program that actually copies the file is substantially shorter in the NIO version shown here.

```
// Copy a file using NIO.
import java.io.*;
import java.nio.*;
import java.nio.channels.*;
import java.nio.file.*;

public class NIOCopy {

  public static void main(String[] args) {

    if(args.length != 2) {
      System.out.println("Usage: Copy from to");
      return;
    }

    try {
      Path source = Path.of(args[0]);
      Path target = Path.of(args[1]);

      // Copy the file.
      Files.copy(source, target, StandardCopyOption.REPLACE_EXISTING);

    } catch(InvalidPathException e) {
      System.out.println("Path Error " + e);
    } catch (IOException e) {
      System.out.println("I/O Error " + e);
    }
  }
}
```

## Use NIO for Stream-Based I/O

Beginning with NIO.2, you can use NIO to open an I/O stream. Once you have a **Path**, open a file by calling **newInputStream( )** or **newOutputStream( )**, which are **static** methods defined by **Files**. These methods return a stream connected to the specified file. In either case, the stream can then be operated on in the way described in Chapter 21, and the same techniques apply. The advantage of using **Path** to open a file is that all of the features defined by NIO are available for your use.

To open a file for stream-based input, use **Files.newInputStream( )**. It is shown here:

static InputStream newInputStream(Path *path*, OpenOption ... *how*)
    throws IOException

Here, *path* specifies the file to open and *how* specifies how the file will be opened. It can be one or more of the values defined by **StandardOpenOption**, described earlier. (Of course, only those options that relate to an input stream will apply.) If no options are specified, then the file is opened as if **StandardOpenOption.READ** were passed.

Once opened, you can use any of the methods defined by **InputStream**. For example, you can use **read( )** to read bytes from the file.

The following program demonstrates the use of NIO-based stream I/O. It reworks the **ShowFile** program from Chapter 13 so that it uses NIO features to open the file and obtain a stream. As you can see, it is very similar to the original, except for the use of **Path** and **newInputStream( )**.

```
/* Display a text file using stream-based, NIO code.
   To use this program, specify the name
   of the file that you want to see.
   For example, to see a file called TEST.TXT,
   use the following command line.

   java ShowFile TEST.TXT
*/

import java.io.*;
import java.nio.file.*;

class ShowFile {
  public static void main(String[] args)
  {
    int i;

    // First, confirm that a filename has been specified.
    if(args.length != 1) {
      System.out.println("Usage: ShowFile filename");
      return;
    }

    // Open the file and obtain a stream linked to it.
    try ( InputStream fin = Files.newInputStream(Path.of(args[0])) )
    {
      do {
```

```
          i = fin.read();
          if(i != -1) System.out.print((char) i);
        } while(i != -1);

      } catch(InvalidPathException e) {
        System.out.println("Path Error " + e);
      } catch(IOException e) {
        System.out.println("I/O Error " + e);
      }
    }
  }
```

Because the stream returned by **newInputStream( )** is a normal stream, it can be used like any other stream. For example, you can wrap the stream inside a buffered stream, such as a **BufferedInputStream**, to provide buffering, as shown here:

```
new BufferedInputStream(Files.newInputStream(Path.of(args[0])))
```

Now, all reads will be automatically buffered.

To open a file for output, use **Files.newOutputStream( )**. It is shown here:

static OutputStream newOutputStream(Path *path*, OpenOption ... *how*)
throws IOException

Here, *path* specifies the file to open and *how* specifies how the file will be opened. It must be one or more of the values defined by **StandardOpenOption**, described earlier. (Of course, only those options that relate to an output stream will apply.) If no options are specified, then the file is opened as if **StandardOpenOption.WRITE**, **StandardOpenOption.CREATE**, and **StandardOpenOption.TRUNCATE_EXISTING** were passed.

The methodology for using **newOutputStream( )** is similar to that shown previously for **newInputStream( )**. Once opened, you can use any of the methods defined by **OutputStream**. For example, you can use **write( )** to write bytes to the file. You can also wrap the stream inside a **BufferedOutputStream** to buffer the stream.

The following program shows **newOutputStream( )** in action. It writes the alphabet to a file called **test.txt**. Notice the use of buffered I/O.

```
// Demonstrate NIO-based, stream output.

import java.io.*;
import java.nio.file.*;

class NIOStreamWrite {
  public static void main(String[] args)
  {
    // Open the file and obtain a stream linked to it.
    try ( OutputStream fout =
          new BufferedOutputStream(
                Files.newOutputStream(Path.of("test.txt"))) )
    {
      // Write some bytes to the stream.
      for(int i=0; i < 26; i++)
        fout.write((byte)('A' + i));
```

```
    } catch(InvalidPathException e) {
      System.out.println("Path Error " + e);
    } catch(IOException e) {
      System.out.println("I/O Error: " + e);
    }
  }
}
```

## Use NIO for Path and File System Operations

At the beginning of Chapter 22, the **File** class in the **java.io** package was examined. As explained there, the **File** class deals with the file system and with the various attributes associated with a file, such as whether a file is read-only, hidden, and so on. It was also used to obtain information about a file's path. Although the **File** class is still perfectly acceptable, the interfaces and classes defined by NIO.2 offer a better way to perform these functions. The benefits include support for symbolic links, better support for directory tree traversal, and improved handling of metadata, among others. The following sections show samples of two common file system operations: obtaining information about a path and file and getting the contents of a directory.



**REMEMBER** If you want to change code that uses **java.io.File** to the **Path** interface, you can use the **toPath( )** method to obtain a **Path** instance from a **File** instance.

### Obtain Information About a Path and a File

Information about a path can be obtained by using methods defined by **Path**. Some attributes associated with the file described by a **Path** (such as whether or not the file is hidden) are obtained by using methods defined by **Files**. The **Path** methods used here are **getName( )**, **getParent( )**, and **toAbsolutePath( )**. Those provided by **Files** are **isExecutable( )**, **isHidden( )**, **isReadable( )**, **isWritable( )**, and **exists( )**. These are summarized in Tables 23-3 and 23-4, shown earlier.

**CAUTION** Methods such as **isExecutable( )**, **isReadable( )**, **isWritable( )**, and **exists( )** must be used with care because the state of the file system may change after the call, in which case a program malfunction could occur. Such a situation could have security implications.

Other file attributes are obtained by requesting a list of attributes by calling **Files.readAttributes( )**. In the program, this method is called to obtain the **BasicFileAttributes** associated with a file, but the general approach applies to other types of attributes.

The following program demonstrates several of the **Path** and **Files** methods, along with several methods provided by **BasicFileAttributes**. This program assumes that a file called **test.txt** exists in a directory called **examples**, which must be a subdirectory of the current directory.

```
// Obtain information about a path and a file.
import java.io.*;
import java.nio.file.*;
import java.nio.file.attribute.*;
```

```
class PathDemo {
  public static void main(String[] args) {
    Path filepath = Path.of("examples\\test.txt");

    System.out.println("File Name: " + filepath.getName(1));
    System.out.println("Path: " + filepath);
    System.out.println("Absolute Path: " + filepath.toAbsolutePath());
    System.out.println("Parent: " + filepath.getParent());

    if(Files.exists(filepath))
      System.out.println("File exists");
    else
      System.out.println("File does not exist");

    try {
      if(Files.isHidden(filepath))
        System.out.println("File is hidden");
      else
        System.out.println("File is not hidden");
    } catch(IOException e) {
        System.out.println("I/O Error: " + e);
    }

    Files.isWritable(filepath);
    System.out.println("File is writable");


    Files.isReadable(filepath);
    System.out.println("File is readable");

    try {
      BasicFileAttributes attribs =
        Files.readAttributes(filepath, BasicFileAttributes.class);

      if(attribs.isDirectory())
        System.out.println("The file is a directory");
      else
        System.out.println("The file is not a directory");

      if(attribs.isRegularFile())
        System.out.println("The file is a normal file");
      else
        System.out.println("The file is not a normal file");

      if(attribs.isSymbolicLink())
        System.out.println("The file is a symbolic link");
      else
        System.out.println("The file is not a symbolic link");

      System.out.println("File last modified: " + attribs.lastModifiedTime());
      System.out.println("File size: " + attribs.size() + " Bytes");
    } catch(IOException e) {
      System.out.println("Error reading attributes: " + e);
    }
  }
}
```

If you execute this program from a directory called **MyDir**, which has a subdirectory called **examples**, and the **examples** directory contains the **test.txt** file, then you will see output similar to that shown here. (Of course, the information you see will differ.)

```
File Name: test.txt
Path: examples\test.txt
Absolute Path: C:\MyDir\examples\test.txt
Parent: examples
File exists
File is not hidden
File is writable
File is readable
The file is not a directory
The file is a normal file
The file is not a symbolic link
File last modified: 2017-01-01T18:20:46.380445Z
File size: 18 Bytes
```

If you are using a computer that supports the FAT file system (i.e., the DOS file system), then you might want to try using the methods defined by **DosFileAttributes**. If you are using a POSIX-compatible system, then try using **PosixFileAttributes**.



## List the Contents of a Directory

If a path describes a directory, then you can read the contents of that directory by using **static** methods defined by **Files**. To do this, you first obtain a directory stream by calling **newDirectoryStream( )**, passing in a **Path** that describes the directory. One form of **newDirectoryStream( )** is shown here:

static DirectoryStream<Path> newDirectoryStream(Path *dirPath*)
throws IOException

Here, *dirPath* encapsulates the path to the directory. The method returns a **DirectoryStream<Path>** object that can be used to obtain the contents of the directory. It will throw an **IOException** if an I/O error occurs and a **NotDirectoryException** (which is a subclass of **IOException**) if the specified path is not a directory. A **SecurityException** is also possible if access to the directory is not permitted.

**DirectoryStream<Path>** implements **AutoCloseable**, so it can be managed by a **try**-with-resources statement. It also implements **Iterable<Path>**. This means that you can obtain the contents of the directory by iterating over the **DirectoryStream** object. When iterating, each directory entry is represented by a **Path** instance. An easy way to iterate over a **DirectoryStream** is to use a for-each style **for** loop. It is important to understand, however, that the iterator implemented by **DirectoryStream<Path>** can be obtained only once for each instance. Thus, the **iterator( )** method can be called only once, and a for-each loop can be executed only once.

The following program displays the contents of a directory called **MyDir**:

```
// Display a directory.

import java.io.*;
import java.nio.file.*;
import java.nio.file.attribute.*;
```

```
class DirList {
  public static void main(String[] args) {
    String dirname = "\\MyDir";

    // Obtain and manage a directory stream within a try block.
    try ( DirectoryStream<Path> dirstrm =
            Files.newDirectoryStream(Path.of(dirname)) )
    {
      System.out.println("Directory of " + dirname);

      // Because DirectoryStream implements Iterable, we
      // can use a "foreach" loop to display the directory.
      for(Path entry : dirstrm) {
        BasicFileAttributes attribs =
            Files.readAttributes(entry, BasicFileAttributes.class);

        if(attribs.isDirectory())
          System.out.print("<DIR> ");
        else
          System.out.print("      ");

        System.out.println(entry.getName(1));
      }
    } catch(InvalidPathException e) {
      System.out.println("Path Error " + e);
    } catch(NotDirectoryException e) {
      System.out.println(dirname + " is not a directory.");
    } catch (IOException e) {
      System.out.println("I/O Error: " + e);
    }
  }
}
```

Here is sample output from the program:

```
Directory of \MyDir
      DirList.class
      DirList.java
<DIR> examples
      Test.txt
```

You can filter the contents of a directory in two ways. The easiest is to use this version of **newDirectoryStream( )**:

static DirectoryStream<Path> newDirectoryStream(Path *dirPath*, String *wildcard*)
throws IOException

In this version, only files that match the wildcard filename specified by *wildcard* will be obtained. For *wildcard*, you can specify either a complete filename or a *glob*. A *glob* is a string that defines a general pattern that will match one or more files using the familiar * and **?**

wildcard characters. These match zero or more of any character and any one character, respectively. The following are also recognized within a glob:

| ** | Matches zero or more of any character across directories. |
|---|---|
| [*chars*] | Matches any one character in *chars*. A * or ? within *chars* will be treated as a normal character, not a wildcard. A range can be specified by use of a hyphen, such as [x-z]. |
| {*globlist*} | Matches any one of the globs specified in a comma-separated list of globs in *globlist*. |



You can specify a * or **?** character using * and \?. To specify a \, use \\. You can experiment with a glob by substituting this call to **newDirectoryStream( )** into the previous program:

```
Files.newDirectoryStream(Path.of(dirname), "{Path,Dir}*.{java,class}")
```

This obtains a directory stream that contains only those files whose names begin with either "Path" or "Dir" and use either the "java" or "class" extension. Thus, it would match names like **DirList.java** and **PathDemo.java**, but not **MyPathDemo.java**, for example.

Another way to filter a directory is to use this version of **newDirectoryStream( )**:

static DirectoryStream<Path> newDirectoryStream(Path *dirPath*,
DirectoryStream.Filter<? super Path> *filefilter*)
throws IOException

Here, **DirectoryStream.Filter** is an interface that specifies the following method:

boolean accept(T *entry*) throws IOException

In this case, **T** will be **Path**. If you want to include *entry* in the list, return **true**. Otherwise, return **false**. This form of **newDirectoryStream( )** offers the advantage of being able to filter a directory based on something other than a filename. For example, you can filter based on size, creation date, modification date, or attribute, to name a few.

The following program demonstrates the process. It will list only those files that are writable.

```
// Display a directory of only those files that are writable.

import java.io.*;
import java.nio.file.*;
import java.nio.file.attribute.*;

class DirList {
  public static void main(String[] args) {
    String dirname = "\\MyDir";

    // Create a filter that returns true only for writable files.
    DirectoryStream.Filter<Path> how = new DirectoryStream.Filter<Path>() {
      public boolean accept(Path filename) throws IOException {
        if(Files.isWritable(filename)) return true;
```

```
          return false;
        }
      };

      // Obtain and manage a directory stream of writable files.
      try (DirectoryStream<Path> dirstrm =
               Files.newDirectoryStream(Path.of(dirname), how) )
      {
        System.out.println("Directory of " + dirname);

        for(Path entry : dirstrm) {
          BasicFileAttributes attribs =
            Files.readAttributes(entry, BasicFileAttributes.class);

          if(attribs.isDirectory())
            System.out.print("<DIR> ");
          else
            System.out.print("      ");

          System.out.println(entry.getName(1));
        }
      } catch(InvalidPathException e) {
        System.out.println("Path Error " + e);
      } catch(NotDirectoryException e) {
        System.out.println(dirname + " is not a directory.");
      } catch (IOException e) {
        System.out.println("I/O Error: " + e);
      }
    }
}
```

## Use walkFileTree( ) to List a Directory Tree

The preceding examples have obtained the contents of only a single directory. However, sometimes you will want to obtain a list of the files in a directory tree. In the past, this was quite a chore, but NIO.2 makes it easy because now you can use the **walkFileTree( )** method defined by **Files** to process a directory tree. It has two forms. The one used in this chapter is shown here:

static Path walkFileTree(Path *root*, FileVisitor<? super Path> *fv*)
    throws IOException

The path to the starting point of the directory walk is passed in *root*. An instance of **FileVisitor** is passed in *fv*. The implementation of **FileVisitor** determines how the directory tree is traversed, and it gives you access to the directory information. If an I/O error occurs, an **IOException** is thrown. A **SecurityException** is also possible.

**FileVisitor** is an interface that defines how files are visited when a directory tree is traversed. It is a generic interface that is declared like this:

interface FileVisitor<T>

For use in **walkFileTree( )**, **T** will be **Path** (or any type derived from **Path**). **FileVisitor** defines the following methods:

| Method | Description |
|---|---|
| FileVisitResult postVisitDirectory(T *dir*, IOException *exc*) throws IOException | Called after a directory has been visited. The directory is passed in *dir*, and any **IOException** is passed in *exc*. If *exc* is **null**, no exception occurred. The result is returned. |
| FileVisitResult preVisitDirectory(T *dir*, BasicFileAttributes *attribs*) throws IOException | Called before a directory is visited. The directory is passed in *dir*, and the attributes associated with the directory are passed in *attribs*. The result is returned. To examine the directory, return **FileVisitResult.CONTINUE**. |
| FileVisitResult visitFile(T *file*, BasicFileAttributes *attribs*) throws IOException | Called when a file is visited. The file is passed in *file*, and the attributes associated with the file are passed in *attribs*. The result is returned. |
| FileVisitResult visitFileFailed(T *file*, IOException *exc*) throws IOException | Called when an attempt to visit a file fails. The file that failed is passed in *file*, and the **IOException** is passed in *exc*. The result is returned. |

Notice that each method returns a **FileVisitResult**. This enumeration defines the following values:

| CONTINUE | SKIP_SIBLINGS | SKIP_SUBTREE | TERMINATE |
|---|---|---|---|

In general, to continue traversing the directory and subdirectories, a method should return **CONTINUE**. For **preVisitDirectory( )**, return **SKIP_SIBLINGS** to bypass the directory and its siblings and prevent **postVisitDirectory( )** from being called. To bypass just the directory and subdirectories, return **SKIP_SUBTREE**. To stop the directory traversal, return **TERMINATE**.

Although it is certainly possible to create your own visitor class that implements these methods defined by **FileVisitor**, you won't normally do so because a simple implementation is provided by **SimpleFileVisitor**. You can just override the default implementation of the method or methods in which you are interested. Here is a short example that illustrates the process. It displays all files in the directory tree that has **\MyDir** as its root. Notice how short this program is.

```
// A simple example that uses walkFileTree( ) to display a directory tree.
import java.io.*;
import java.nio.file.*;
import java.nio.file.attribute.*;


// Create a custom version of SimpleFileVisitor that overrides
// the visitFile( ) method.
class MyFileVisitor extends SimpleFileVisitor<Path> {
  public FileVisitResult visitFile(Path path, BasicFileAttributes attribs)
```

```
    throws IOException
  {
    System.out.println(path);
    return FileVisitResult.CONTINUE;
  }
}

class DirTreeList {
  public static void main(String[] args) {
    String dirname = "\\MyDir";

    System.out.println("Directory tree starting with " + dirname + ":\n");

    try {
      Files.walkFileTree(Path.of(dirname), new MyFileVisitor());
    } catch (IOException exc) {
      System.out.println("I/O Error");
    }
  }
}
```

Here is sample output produced by the program when used on the same **MyDir** directory shown earlier. In this example, the subdirectory called **examples** contains one file called **MyProgram.java**.

```
Directory tree starting with \MyDir:

\MyDir\DirList.class
\MyDir\DirList.java
\MyDir\examples\MyProgram.java
\MyDir\Test.txt
```

In the program, the class **MyFileVisitor** extends **SimpleFileVisitor**, overriding only the **visitFile( )** method. In this example, **visitFile( )** simply displays the files, but more sophisticated functionality is easy to achieve. For example, you could filter the files or perform actions on the files, such as copying them to a backup device. For the sake of clarity, a named class was used to override **visitFile( )**, but you could also use an anonymous inner class.

One last point: It is possible to watch a directory for changes by using **java.nio.file.WatchService**.

# CHAPTER 24 Networking

Since its beginning, Java has been associated with Internet programming. There are a number of reasons for this, not the least of which is its ability to generate secure, cross-platform, portable code. However, one of the most important reasons that Java became the premier language for network programming is the classes defined in the **java.net** package. They provide a convenient means by which programmers of all skill levels can access network resources. Beginning with JDK 11, Java has also provided enhanced networking support for HTTP clients in the **java.net.http** package in a module by the same name. Called the HTTP Client API, it further solidifies Java's networking capabilities.

This chapter explores the **java.net** package. It concludes by introducing the **java.http.net** package. It is important to emphasize that networking is a very large and at times complicated topic. It is not possible for this book to discuss all of the capabilities contained in these two packages. Instead, this chapter focuses on several of their core classes and interfaces.

## Networking Basics

Before we begin, it will be useful to review some key networking concepts and terms. At the core of Java's networking support is the concept of a *socket*. A socket identifies an endpoint in a network. The socket paradigm was part of the 4.2BSD Berkeley UNIX release in the early 1980s. Because of this, the term *Berkeley socket* is also used. Sockets are at the foundation of modern networking because a socket allows a single computer to serve many different clients at once, as well as to serve many different types of information. This is accomplished through the use of a *port*, which is a numbered socket on a particular machine. A server process is said to "listen" to a port until a client connects to it. A server is allowed to accept multiple clients connected to the same port number, although each session is unique. To manage multiple client connections, a server process must be multithreaded or have some other means of multiplexing the simultaneous I/O.

Socket communication takes place via a protocol. *Internet Protocol (IP)* is a low-level routing protocol that breaks data into small packets and sends them to an address across a network, which does not guarantee to deliver said packets to the destination. *Transmission Control Protocol (TCP)* is a higher-level protocol that manages to robustly string together these packets, sorting and retransmitting them as necessary to reliably transmit data. A third protocol, *User Datagram Protocol (UDP),* sits next to TCP and can be used directly to support fast, connectionless, unreliable transport of packets.

Once a connection has been established, a higher-level protocol ensues, which is dependent on which port you are using. TCP/IP reserves the lower 1024 ports for specific protocols. A few might be familiar to you. For example, port number 21 is for FTP; 23 is for Telnet; 25 is for e-mail; 43 is for whois; 80 is for HTTP; 119 is for netnews. It is up to each protocol to determine how a client should interact with the port.

For example, HTTP is the protocol that web browsers and servers use to transfer hypertext pages and images. It is a quite simple protocol for a basic page-browsing web server. Here's how it works. When a client requests a file from an HTTP server, an action known as a *hit,* it simply sends the name of the file in a special format to a predefined port and reads back the contents of the file. The server also responds with a status code to tell the client whether or not the request can be fulfilled and why.

A key component of the Internet is the *address*. Every computer on the Internet has one. An Internet address is a number that uniquely identifies each computer on the Net. Originally, all Internet addresses consisted of 32-bit values, organized as four 8-bit values. This address type was specified by IPv4 (Internet Protocol, version 4). However, a newer addressing scheme, called IPv6 (Internet Protocol, version 6) has come into play. IPv6 uses a 128-bit value to represent an address, organized into eight 16-bit chunks. Although there are several reasons for and advantages to IPv6, the main one is that it supports a much larger address space than does IPv4. Fortunately, when using Java, you won't normally need to worry about whether IPv4 or IPv6 addresses are used because Java handles the details for you.

Just as the numbers of an IP address describe a network hierarchy, the name of an Internet address, called its *domain name,* describes a machine's location in a name space. For example, **www.HerbSchildt.com** is in the *COM* top-level domain (used by U.S. commercial sites); it is called *HerbSchildt,* and *www* identifies the server for web requests. An Internet domain name is mapped to an IP address by the *Domain Naming Service (DNS).* This enables users to work with domain names, but the Internet operates on IP addresses.

# The java.net Networking Classes and Interfaces

The **java.net** package contains Java's original networking features, which have been available since version 1.0. It supports TCP/IP both by extending the already established stream I/O interface introduced in Chapter 22 and by adding the features required to build I/O objects across the network. Java supports both the TCP and UDP protocol families. TCP is used for reliable stream-based I/O across the network. UDP supports a simpler, hence faster, point-to-point datagram-oriented model. The classes contained in the **java.net** package are shown here:

| | | |
|---|---|---|
| Authenticator | InetAddress | SocketAddress |
| CacheRequest | InetSocketAddress | SocketImpl |
| CacheResponse | InterfaceAddress | SocketPermission |
| ContentHandler | JarURLConnection | StandardSocketOption |
| CookieHandler | MulticastSocket | UnixDomainSocketAddress |

| CookieManager | NetPermission | URI |
|---|---|---|
| DatagramPacket | NetworkInterface | URL |
| DatagramSocket | PasswordAuthentication | URLClassLoader |
| DatagramSocketImpl | Proxy | URLConnection |
| HttpCookie | ProxySelector | URLDecoder |
| HttpURLConnection | ResponseCache | URLEncoder |
| IDN | SecureCacheResponse | URLPermission |
| Inet4Address | ServerSocket | URLStreamHandler |
| Inet6Address | Socket | |



The **java.net** package's interfaces are listed here:

| ContentHandlerFactory | FileNameMap | SocketOptions |
|---|---|---|
| CookiePolicy | ProtocolFamily | URLStreamHandlerFactory |
| CookieStore | SocketImplFactory | |
| DatagramSocketImplFactory | SocketOption | |

Beginning with JDK 9, **java.net** is part of the **java.base** module. In the sections that follow, we will examine the main networking classes and show several examples that apply to them. Once you understand these core networking classes, you will be able to easily explore the others on your own.

# InetAddress

The **InetAddress** class is used to encapsulate both the numerical IP address and the domain name for that address. You interact with this class by using the name of an IP host, which is more convenient and understandable than its IP address. The **InetAddress** class hides the number inside. **InetAddress** can handle both IPv4 and IPv6 addresses.

## Factory Methods

The **InetAddress** class has no visible constructors. To create an **InetAddress** object, you have to use one of the available factory methods. As explained earlier in this book, *factory methods* are merely a convention whereby static methods in a class return an instance of that class. This is done in lieu of overloading a constructor with various parameter lists when having unique method names makes the results much clearer. Three commonly used **InetAddress** factory methods are shown here:

```
static InetAddress getLocalHost( )
  throws UnknownHostException

static InetAddress getByName(String hostName)
  throws UnknownHostException

static InetAddress[ ] getAllByName(String hostName)
  throws UnknownHostException
```

The **getLocalHost( )** method simply returns the **InetAddress** object that represents the local host. The **getByName( )** method returns an **InetAddress** for a host name passed to it. If these methods are unable to resolve the host name, they throw an **UnknownHostException**.

On the Internet, it is common for a single name to be used to represent several machines. In the world of web servers, this is one way to provide some degree of scaling. The **getAllByName( )** factory method returns an array of **InetAddress**es that represent all of the addresses that a particular name resolves to. It will also throw an **UnknownHostException** if it can't resolve the name to at least one address.

**InetAddress** also includes the factory method **getByAddress( ),** which takes an IP address and returns an **InetAddress** object. Either an IPv4 or an IPv6 address can be used.

The following example prints the addresses and names of the local machine and two Internet websites:

```
// Demonstrate InetAddress.
import java.net.*;

class InetAddressTest
{
  public static void main(String[] args) throws UnknownHostException {
    InetAddress Address = InetAddress.getLocalHost();
    System.out.println(Address);

    Address = InetAddress.getByName("www.HerbSchildt.com");
    System.out.println(Address);

    InetAddress[] SW = InetAddress.getAllByName("www.nba.com");
    for (int i=0; i<SW.length; i++)
      System.out.println(SW[i]);
  }
}
```

Here is the output produced by this program. (Of course, the output you see may be slightly different.)

```
default/166.203.115.212
www.HerbSchildt.com/216.92.65.4
www.nba.com/23.67.86.30
www.nba.com/2600:1407:2800:3a4:0:0:0:1f51
www.nba.com/2600:1407:2800:3ad:0:0:0:1f51
```

## Instance Methods

The **InetAddress** class has several other methods, which can be used on the objects returned by the methods just discussed. Here is a sampling:

| | |
|---|---|
| boolean equals(Object *other*) | Returns **true** if this object has the same Internet address as *other*. |
| byte[ ] getAddress( ) | Returns a byte array that represents the object's IP address in network byte order. |

| | |
|---|---|
| String getHostAddress( ) | Returns a string that represents the host address associated with the **InetAddress** object. |
| String getHostName( ) | Returns a string that represents the host name associated with the **InetAddress** object. |
| boolean isMulticastAddress( ) | Returns **true** if this address is a multicast address. Otherwise, it returns **false.** |
| String toString( ) | Returns a string that lists the host name and the IP address for convenience. |



Internet addresses are looked up in a series of hierarchically cached servers. That means that your local computer might know a particular name-to-IP-address mapping automatically, such as for itself and nearby servers. For other names, it may ask a local DNS server for IP address information. If that server doesn't have a particular address, it can go to a remote site and ask for it. This can continue all the way up to the root server. This process might take a long time, so it is wise to structure your code so that you cache IP address information locally rather than look it up repeatedly.

**NOTE** Starting with JDK 18, you can provide your own algorithm for looking up Internet addresses, for example, if you want to optimize the lookup for the specific environment where your application is deployed. To provide this specialized functionality, you would implement the **java.net.spi.InetAddressResolver** interface.

## Inet4Address and Inet6Address

Java includes support for both IPv4 and IPv6 addresses. Because of this, two subclasses of **InetAddress** were created: **Inet4Address** and **Inet6Address**. **Inet4Address** represents a traditional-style IPv4 address. **Inet6Address** encapsulates a newer IPv6 address. Because they are subclasses of **InetAddress,** an **InetAddress** reference can refer to either. This is one way that Java was able to add IPv6 functionality without breaking existing code or adding many more classes. For the most part, you can simply use **InetAddress** when working with IP addresses because it can accommodate both styles.

## TCP/IP Client Sockets

TCP/IP sockets are used to implement reliable, bidirectional, persistent, point-to-point, stream-based connections between hosts on the Internet. A socket can be used to connect Java's I/O system to other programs that may reside either on the local machine or on any other machine on the Internet, subject to security constraints.

There are two kinds of TCP sockets in Java. One is for servers, and the other is for clients. The **ServerSocket** class is designed to be a "listener," which waits for clients to connect before doing anything. Thus, **ServerSocket** is for servers. The **Socket** class is for clients. It is designed to connect to server sockets and initiate protocol exchanges. Because client sockets are the most commonly used by Java applications, they are examined here.

The creation of a **Socket** object implicitly establishes a connection between the client and server. There are no methods or constructors that explicitly expose the details of establishing that connection. Here are two constructors used to create client sockets:

| | |
|---|---|
| Socket(String *hostName*, int *port*) throws UnknownHostException, IOException | Creates a socket connected to the named host and port |
| Socket(InetAddress *ipAddress*, int *port*) throws IOException | Creates a socket using a preexisting **InetAddress** object and a port |

**Socket** defines several instance methods. For example, a **Socket** can be examined at any time for the address and port information associated with it, by use of the following methods:

| | |
|---|---|
| InetAddress getInetAddress( ) | Returns the **InetAddress** associated with the **Socket** object. It returns **null** if the socket is not connected. |
| int getPort( ) | Returns the remote port to which the invoking **Socket** object is connected. It returns 0 if the socket is not connected. |
| int getLocalPort( ) | Returns the local port to which the invoking **Socket** object is bound. It returns –1 if the socket is not bound. |

You can gain access to the input and output streams associated with a **Socket** by use of the **getInputStream( )** and **getOuptutStream( )** methods, as shown here. Each can throw an **IOException** if the socket has been invalidated by a loss of connection. These streams are used exactly like the I/O streams described in Chapter 22 to send and receive data.

| | |
|---|---|
| InputStream getInputStream( ) throws IOException | Returns the **InputStream** associated with the invoking socket |
| OutputStream getOutputStream( ) throws IOException | Returns the **OutputStream** associated with the invoking socket |

Several other methods are available, including **connect( ),** which allows you to specify a new connection; **isConnected( ),** which returns true if the socket is connected to a server; **isBound( ),** which returns true if the socket is bound to an address; and **isClosed( ),** which returns true if the socket is closed. To close a socket, call **close( )**. Closing a socket also closes the I/O streams associated with the socket. **Socket** also implements **AutoCloseable,** which means that you can use a **try**-with-resources block to manage a socket.

The following program provides a simple **Socket** example. It opens a connection to a "whois" port (port 43) on the InterNIC server, sends the command-line argument down the socket, and then prints the data that is returned. InterNIC will try to look up the argument as a registered Internet domain name, and then send back the IP address and contact information for that site.

```
// Demonstrate Sockets.
import java.net.*;
import java.io.*;

class Whois {
  public static void main(String[] args) throws Exception {
    int c;

    // Create a socket connected to internic.net, port 43.
    Socket s = new Socket("whois.internic.net", 43);

    // Obtain input and output streams.
    InputStream in = s.getInputStream();
    OutputStream out = s.getOutputStream();

    // Construct a request string.

    String str = (args.length == 0 ? "MHProfessional.com" : args[0]) + "\n";
    // Convert to bytes.
    byte[] buf = str.getBytes();

    // Send request.
    out.write(buf);

    // Read and display response.
    while ((c = in.read()) != -1) {
      System.out.print((char) c);
    }
    s.close();
  }
}
```

Here is how the program works. First, a **Socket** is constructed that specifies the host name "whois.internic.net" and the port number 43. **Internic.net** is the InterNIC website that handles whois requests. Port 43 is the whois port. Next, both input and output streams are opened on the socket. Then, a string is constructed that contains the name of the website you want to obtain information about. In this case, if no website is specified on the command line, then "MHProfessional.com" is used. The string is converted into a **byte** array and then sent out of the socket. The response is read by inputting from the socket, and the results are displayed. Finally, the socket is closed, which also closes the I/O streams.

In the preceding example, the socket was closed manually by calling **close( )**. If you are using a modern version of Java, you can use a **try**-with-resources block to automatically close the socket. For example, here is another way to write the **main( )** method of the previous program:

```
// Use try-with-resources to close a socket.
public static void main(String[] args) throws Exception {
  int c;

  // Create a socket connected to internic.net, port 43. Manage this
  // socket with a try-with-resources block.
  try ( Socket s = new Socket("whois.internic.net", 43) ) {
```

```
      // Obtain input and output streams.
      InputStream in = s.getInputStream();
      OutputStream out = s.getOutputStream();

      // Construct a request string.
      String str = (args.length == 0 ? "MHProfessional.com" : args[0]) + "\n";
      // Convert to bytes.
      byte[] buf = str.getBytes();

      // Send request.
      out.write(buf);

      // Read and display response.
      while ((c = in.read()) != -1) {
        System.out.print((char) c);
      }
    }
    // The socket is now closed.
  }
```

In this version, the socket is automatically closed when the **try** block ends.

So the examples will work with earlier versions of Java and to clearly illustrate when a network resource can be closed, subsequent examples will continue to call **close( )** explicitly. However, in your own code, you should consider using automatic resource management since it offers a more streamlined approach. One other point: In this version, exceptions are still thrown out of **main( )**, but they could be handled by adding **catch** clauses to the end of the **try**-with-resources block.

---

**NOTE** For simplicity, the examples in this chapter simply throw all exceptions out of **main( )**. This allows the logic of the network code to be clearly illustrated. However, in real-world code, you will normally need to handle the exceptions in an appropriate way.

# URL

The preceding example was rather obscure because the modern Internet is not about the older protocols such as whois, finger, and FTP. It is about WWW, the World Wide Web. The Web is a loose collection of higher-level protocols and file formats, all unified in a web browser. One of the most important aspects of the Web is that Tim Berners-Lee devised a scalable way to locate all of the resources of the Net. Once you can reliably name anything and everything, it becomes a very powerful paradigm. The Uniform Resource Locator (URL) does exactly that.

The URL provides a reasonably intelligible form to uniquely identify or address information on the Internet. URLs are ubiquitous; every browser uses them to identify information on the Web. Within Java's network class library, the **URL** class provides a simple, concise API to access information across the Internet using URLs.

All URLs share the same basic format, although some variation is allowed. Here are two examples: **http://www.HerbSchildt.com/** and **http://www.HerbSchildt.com:80/index.htm**.

A URL specification is based on four components. The first is the protocol to use, separated from the rest of the locator by a colon (:). Common protocols are HTTP, FTP, and file, although these days almost everything is being done via HTTP (in fact, most browsers will proceed correctly if you leave off the "http://" from your URL specification). The second component is the host name or IP address of the host to use; this is delimited on the left by double slashes (//) and on the right by a slash (/) or optionally a colon (:). The third component, the port number, is an optional parameter, delimited on the left from the host name by a colon (:) and on the right by a slash (/). (It defaults to port 80, the predefined HTTP port; thus, ":80" is redundant.) The fourth part is the actual file path. Most HTTP servers will append a file named **index.html** or **index.htm** to URLs that refer directly to a directory resource. Thus, **http://www.HerbSchildt.com/** is the same as **http://www.HerbSchildt.com/index.htm**.

Java's **URL** class has several constructors, but as of JDK 21 they have been deprecated because they did not validate the arguments as securely as is possible. Instead, to create a **URL** object, you should use the constructors of the **URI** class, each of which can throw a **URISyntaxException** if the parameters passed in do not follow the rules of what a legal **URI** is. Creating a **URL** from a **URI** object is easy: you can simply call its **toURL()** method. One commonly used constructor specifies the **URI** with a string that is identical to what you see displayed in a browser:

URI(String *urlSpecifier*) throws URISyntaxException

Another commonly used form of the constructor allows you to break up the **URI** into its component parts:

URI(String scheme, String host, String path, String fragment) throws URISyntaxException

For example,

URL url = new URI("https", "en.wikipedia.org", "/wiki/Java", null).toURL();

produces the URL whose string representation is

https://en.wikipedia.org/wiki/Java

The following example creates a URL to a page on **wikipedia.org** and then examines its properties:

```
// Demonstrate URL.
import java.net.*;
class URLDemo {
  public static void main(String[] args) throws URISyntaxException,
    MalformedURLException {
    URL hp = new URI("https://en.wikipedia.org:443/wiki/Java").toURL();

    System.out.println("Protocol: " + hp.getProtocol());
    System.out.println("Port: " + hp.getPort());

    System.out.println("Host: " + hp.getHost());
    System.out.println("File: " + hp.getFile());
    System.out.println("Ext:" + hp.toExternalForm());
  }
}
```

When you run this, you will get the following output:

```
Protocol: https
Port: 443
Host: en.wikipedia.org
File: /wiki/Java
Ext:https://en.wikipedia.org/wiki/Java
```

Given a **URL** object, you can retrieve the data associated with it. To access the actual bits or content information of a **URL,** create a **URLConnection** object from it, using its **openConnection( )** method, like this:

```
urlc = url.openConnection()
```

**openConnection( )** has the following general form:

URLConnection openConnection( ) throws IOException

It returns a **URLConnection** object associated with the invoking **URL** object. Notice that it may throw an **IOException.**

## URLConnection

**URLConnection** is a general-purpose class for accessing the attributes of a remote resource. Once you make a connection to a remote server, you can use **URLConnection** to inspect the properties of the remote object before actually transporting it locally. These attributes are exposed by the HTTP protocol specification and, as such, only make sense for **URL** objects that are using the HTTP protocol.

**URLConnection** defines several methods. Here is a sampling:

| | |
|---|---|
| int getContentLength( ) | Returns the size in bytes of the content associated with the resource. If the length is unavailable, –1 is returned. |
| long getContentLengthLong( ) | Returns the size in bytes of the content associated with the resource. If the length is unavailable, –1 is returned. |
| String getContentType( ) | Returns the type of content found in the resource. This is the value of the **content-type** header field. Returns **null** if the content type is not available. |
| long getDate( ) | Returns the time and date of the response represented in terms of milliseconds since January 1, 1970 GMT. |
| long getExpiration( ) | Returns the expiration time and date of the resource represented in terms of milliseconds since January 1, 1970 GMT. Zero is returned if the expiration date is unavailable. |

| | |
|---|---|
| String getHeaderField(int *idx*) | Returns the value of the header field at index *idx*. (Header field indexes begin at 0.) Returns **null** if the value of *idx* exceeds the number of fields. |
| String getHeaderField(String *fieldName*) | Returns the value of header field whose name is specified by *fieldName*. Returns **null** if the specified name is not found. |
| String getHeaderFieldKey(int *idx*) | Returns the header field key at index *idx*. (Header field indexes begin at 0.) Returns **null** if the value of *idx* exceeds the number of fields. |
| Map<String, List<String>> getHeaderFields( ) | Returns a map that contains all of the header fields and values. |
| long getLastModified( ) | Returns the time and date, represented in terms of milliseconds since January 1, 1970 GMT, of the last modification of the resource. Zero is returned if the last-modified date is unavailable. |
| InputStream getInputStream( ) throws IOException | Returns an **InputStream** that is linked to the resource. This stream can be used to obtain the content of the resource. |

Notice that **URLConnection** defines several methods that handle header information. A header consists of pairs of keys and values represented as strings. By using **getHeaderField( )**, you can obtain the value associated with a header key. By calling **getHeaderFields( )**, you can obtain a map that contains all of the headers. Several standard header fields are available directly through methods such as **getDate( )** and **getContentType( )**.

The following example creates a **URLConnection** using the **openConnection( )** method of a **URL** object and then uses it to examine the document's properties and content:

```
// Demonstrate URLConnection.
import java.net.*;
import java.io.*;
import java.util.Date;

class UCDemo
{
  public static void main(String[] args) throws Exception {
    int c;
    URL hp = new URI("http://www.internic.net").toURL();
    URLConnection hpCon = hp.openConnection();

    // get date
    long d = hpCon.getDate();
    if(d==0)
      System.out.println("No date information.");
    else
      System.out.println("Date: " + new Date(d));
```

```
    // get content type
    System.out.println("Content-Type: " + hpCon.getContentType());

    // get expiration date
    d = hpCon.getExpiration();
    if(d==0)
      System.out.println("No expiration information.");
    else
      System.out.println("Expires: " + new Date(d));

    // get last-modified date
    d = hpCon.getLastModified();
    if(d==0)
      System.out.println("No last-modified information.");
    else
      System.out.println("Last-Modified: " + new Date(d));

    // get content length
    long len = hpCon.getContentLengthLong();
    if(len == -1)
      System.out.println("Content length unavailable.");
    else
      System.out.println("Content-Length: " + len);

    if(len != 0) {
      System.out.println("=== Content ===");
      InputStream input = hpCon.getInputStream();
      while (((c = input.read()) != -1)) {
        System.out.print((char) c);
      }
      input.close();

    } else {
      System.out.println("No content available.");
    }
  }
}
```

The program establishes an HTTP connection to **www.internic.net** over port 80. It then displays several header values and retrieves the content. You might find it interesting to try this example, observing the results, and then for comparison purposes try different websites of your own choosing.

## HttpURLConnection

Java provides a subclass of **URLConnection** that provides support for HTTP connections. This class is called **HttpURLConnection.** You obtain an **HttpURLConnection** in the same way just shown, by calling **openConnection( )** on a **URL** object, but you must cast the result to **HttpURLConnection.** (Of course, you must make sure that you are actually opening an HTTP connection.) Once you have obtained a reference to an **HttpURLConnection** object, you can use any of the methods inherited from **URLConnection.** You can also use any of the several methods defined by **HttpURLConnection.** Here is a sampling:

| | |
|---|---|
| static boolean getFollowRedirects( ) | Returns **true** if redirects are automatically followed and **false** otherwise. This feature is on by default. |
| String getRequestMethod( ) | Returns a string representing how URL requests are made. The default is GET. Other options, such as POST, are available. |
| int getResponseCode( ) throws IOException | Returns the HTTP response code. –1 is returned if no response code can be obtained. An **IOException** is thrown if the connection fails. |
| String getResponseMessage( ) throws IOException | Returns the response message associated with the response code. Returns **null** if no message is available. An **IOException** is thrown if the connection fails. |
| static void setFollowRedirects(boolean *how*) | If *how* is **true,** then redirects are automatically followed. If *how* is **false,** redirects are not automatically followed. By default, redirects are automatically followed. |
| void setRequestMethod(String *how*) throws ProtocolException | Sets the method by which HTTP requests are made to that specified by *how*. The default method is GET, but other options, such as POST, are available. If *how* is invalid, a **ProtocolException** is thrown. |



The following program demonstrates **HttpURLConnection.** It first establishes a connection to **www.google.com**. Then it displays the request method, the response code, and the response message. Finally, it displays the keys and values in the response header.

```
// Demonstrate HttpURLConnection.
import java.net.*;
import java.io.*;
import java.util.*;

class HttpURLDemo
{

public static void main(String[] args) throws Exception {
  URL hp = new URI("http://www.google.com").toURL();

  HttpURLConnection hpCon = (HttpURLConnection) hp.openConnection();

  // Display request method.
  System.out.println("Request method is " +
                     hpCon.getRequestMethod());

  // Display response code.
  System.out.println("Response code is " +
                     hpCon.getResponseCode());

  // Display response message
  System.out.println("Response Message is " +
                     hpCon.getResponseMessage());
```

```
    // Get a list of the header fields and a set
    // of the header keys.
    Map<String, List<String>> hdrMap = hpCon.getHeaderFields();
    Set<String> hdrField = hdrMap.keySet();

    System.out.println("\nHere is the header:");

     // Display all header keys and values.
     for(String k : hdrField) {
       System.out.println("Key: " + k +
                          "  Value: " + hdrMap.get(k));
     }
   }
}
```

Here is a small portion of the output produced by the program. (Of course, the exact response returned by **www.google.com** will vary over time.)

```
Request method is GET
Response code is 200
Response Message is OK

Here is the header:
Key: Transfer-Encoding  Value: [chunked]
Key: null  Value: [HTTP/1.1 200 OK]
Key: Server  Value: [gws]
```

Notice how the header keys and values are displayed. First, a map of the header keys and values is obtained by calling **getHeaderFields( )** (which is inherited from **URLConnection**). Next, a set of the header keys is retrieved by calling **keySet( )** on the map. Then, the key set is cycled through by using a for-each style **for** loop. The value associated with each key is obtained by calling **get( )** on the map.

## The URI Class

The **URI** class that you have already encountered in creating **URL** objects encapsulates a *Uniform Resource Identifier (URI)*. URIs are similar to URLs. In fact, URLs constitute a subset of URIs. A URI represents a standard way to identify a resource. A URL also describes how to access the resource.

## Cookies

The **java.net** package includes classes and interfaces that help manage cookies and can be used to create a stateful (as opposed to stateless) HTTP session. The classes are **CookieHandler, CookieManager,** and **HttpCookie.** The interfaces are **CookiePolicy** and **CookieStore.** The creation of a stateful HTTP session is beyond the scope of this book.

**NOTE** For information about using cookies with servlets, see Chapter 36.

## TCP/IP Server Sockets

As mentioned earlier, Java has a different socket class that must be used for creating server applications. The **ServerSocket** class is used to create servers that listen for either local or remote client programs to connect to them on published ports. **ServerSocket**s are quite different from normal **Socket**s. When you create a **ServerSocket**, it will register itself with the system as having an interest in client connections. The constructors for **ServerSocket** reflect the port number that you want to accept connections on and, optionally, how long you want the queue for said port to be. The queue length tells the system how many client connections it can leave pending before it should simply refuse connections. The default is 50. The constructors might throw an **IOException** under adverse conditions. Here are three of its constructors:

| | |
|---|---|
| ServerSocket(int *port*) throws IOException | Creates a server socket on the specified port with a queue length of 50. |
| ServerSocket(int *port,* int *maxQueue*) throws IOException | Creates a server socket on the specified port with a maximum queue length of *maxQueue*. |
| ServerSocket(int *port,* int *maxQueue,* InetAddress *localAddress*) throws IOException | Creates a server socket on the specified port with a maximum queue length of *maxQueue*. On a multihomed host, *localAddress* specifies the IP address to which this socket binds. |

**ServerSocket** has a method called **accept( ),** which is a blocking call that will wait for a client to initiate communications and then return with a normal **Socket** that is then used for communication with the client.

## Datagrams

TCP/IP-style networking is appropriate for most networking needs. It provides a serialized, predictable, reliable stream of packet data. This is not without its cost, however. TCP includes many complicated algorithms for dealing with congestion control on crowded networks, as well as pessimistic expectations about packet loss. This leads to a somewhat inefficient way to transport data. Datagrams provide an alternative.

*Datagrams* are bundles of information passed between machines. They are somewhat like a hard throw from a well-trained but blindfolded catcher to the third baseman. Once the datagram has been released to its intended target, there is no assurance that it will arrive or even that someone will be there to catch it. Likewise, when the datagram is received, there is no assurance that it hasn't been damaged in transit or that whoever sent it is still there to receive a response.

Java implements datagrams on top of the UDP protocol by using two classes: the **DatagramPacket** object is the data container, while the **DatagramSocket** is the mechanism used to send or receive the **DatagramPacket**s. Each is examined here.

## DatagramSocket

**DatagramSocket** defines four public constructors. They are shown here:

DatagramSocket( ) throws SocketException

DatagramSocket(int *port*) throws SocketException

DatagramSocket(int *port*, InetAddress *ipAddress*) throws SocketException

DatagramSocket(SocketAddress *address*) throws SocketException

The first creates a **DatagramSocket** bound to any unused port on the local computer. The second creates a **DatagramSocket** bound to the port specified by *port*. The third constructs a **DatagramSocket** bound to the specified port and **InetAddress**. The fourth constructs a **DatagramSocket** bound to the specified **SocketAddress**. **SocketAddress** is an abstract class that is implemented by the concrete class **InetSocketAddress**. **InetSocketAddress** encapsulates an IP address with a port number. All can throw a **SocketException** if an error occurs while creating the socket.

**DatagramSocket** defines many methods. Two of the most important are **send( )** and **receive( )**, which are shown here:

void send(DatagramPacket *packet*) throws IOException

void receive(DatagramPacket *packet*) throws IOException

The **send( )** method sends a packet to the port specified by *packet*. The **receive( )** method waits for a packet to be received and returns the result.

**DatagramSocket** also defines the **close( )**method, which closes the socket. **DatagramSocket** also implements **AutoCloseable**, which means that a **DatagramSocket** can be managed by a **try**-with-resources block.

Other methods give you access to various attributes associated with a **DatagramSocket**. Here is a sampling:

| | |
|---|---|
| InetAddress getInetAddress( ) | If the socket is connected, then the address is returned. Otherwise, **null** is returned. |
| int getLocalPort( ) | Returns the number of the local port. |
| int getPort( ) | Returns the number of the port connected to the socket. It returns –1 if the socket is not connected to a port. |
| boolean isBound( ) | Returns **true** if the socket is bound to an address. Returns **false** otherwise. |
| boolean isConnected( ) | Returns **true** if the socket is connected to a server. Returns **false** otherwise. |
| void setSoTimeout(int *millis*) throws SocketException | Sets the time-out period to the number of milliseconds passed in *millis*. |

## DatagramPacket

**DatagramPacket** defines several constructors. Four are shown here:

DatagramPacket(byte[ ] *data*, int *size*)
DatagramPacket(byte[ ] *data*, int *offset*, int *size*)
DatagramPacket(byte[ ] *data*, int *size*, InetAddress *ipAddress*, int *port*)
DatagramPacket(byte[ ] *data*, int *offset*, int *size*, InetAddress *ipAddress*, int *port*)

The first constructor specifies a buffer that will receive data and the size of a packet. It is used for receiving data over a **DatagramSocket.** The second form allows you to specify an offset into the buffer at which data will be stored. The third form specifies a target address and port, which are used by a **DatagramSocket** to determine where the data in the packet will be sent. The fourth form transmits packets beginning at the specified offset into the data. Think of the first two forms as building an "in box," and the second two forms as stuffing and addressing an envelope.

**DatagramPacket** defines several methods, including those shown here, that give access to the address and port number of a packet, as well as the raw data and its length:

| Method | Description |
|---|---|
| InetAddress getAddress( ) | Returns the address of the source (for datagrams being received) or destination (for datagrams being sent). |
| byte[ ] getData( ) | Returns the byte array of data contained in the datagram. Mostly used to retrieve data from the datagram after it has been received. |
| int getLength( ) | Returns the length of the valid data contained in the byte array that would be returned from the **getData( )** method. This may not equal the length of the whole byte array. |
| int getOffset( ) | Returns the starting index of the data. |
| int getPort( ) | Returns the port number. |
| void setAddress(InetAddress *ipAddress*) | Sets the address to which a packet will be sent. The address is specified by *ipAddress*. |
| void setData(byte[ ] *data*) | Sets the data to *data*, the offset to zero, and the length to number of bytes in *data*. |
| void setData(byte[ ] *data*, int *idx*, int *size*) | Sets the data to *data*, the offset to *idx*, and the length to *size*. |
| void setLength(int *size*) | Sets the length of the packet to *size*. |
| void setPort(int *port*) | Sets the port to *port*. |

## A Datagram Example

The following example implements a very simple networked communications client and server. Messages are typed into the window at the server and written across the network to the client side, where they are displayed.

```
// Demonstrate datagrams.
import java.net.*;
```

```
class WriteServer {
  public static int serverPort = 998;
  public static int clientPort = 999;
  public static int buffer_size = 1024;
  public static DatagramSocket ds;
  public static byte[] buffer = new byte[buffer_size];

  public static void TheServer() throws Exception {
    int pos=0;
    while (true) {
      int c = System.in.read();
      switch (c) {
        case -1:
          System.out.println("Server Quits.");
          ds.close();
          return;
        case '\r':
          break;
        case '\n':
          ds.send(new DatagramPacket(buffer,pos,
             InetAddress.getLocalHost(),clientPort));
          pos=0;
          break;
        default:
          buffer[pos++] = (byte) c;
      }
    }
  }

  public static void TheClient() throws Exception {
    while(true) {
      DatagramPacket p = new DatagramPacket(buffer, buffer.length);
      ds.receive(p);
      System.out.println(new String(p.getData(), 0, p.getLength()));
    }
  }

  public static void main(String[] args) throws Exception {
    if(args.length == 1) {
      ds = new DatagramSocket(serverPort);
      TheServer();
    } else {
      ds = new DatagramSocket(clientPort);
      TheClient();
    }
  }
}
```

This sample program is restricted by the **DatagramSocket** constructor to running between two ports on the local machine. To use the program, run

```
java WriteServer
```

in one window; this will be the client. Then run

```
java WriteServer 1
```

This will be the server. Anything that is typed in the server window will be sent to the client window after a newline is received.

**NOTE** The use of datagrams may not be allowed on your computer. (For example, a firewall may prevent their use.) If this is the case, the preceding example cannot be used. Also, the port numbers used in the program work on the author's system but may have to be adjusted for your environment.

# Introducing java.net.http

The preceding material introduced Java's traditional support for networking provided by **java.net**. This API is available in all versions of Java and is widely used. Thus, knowledge of Java's traditional approach to networking is important for all programmers. However, beginning with JDK 11, a new networking package called **java.net.http**, in the module **java.net.http**, has been added. It provides enhanced, updated networking support for HTTP clients. This new API is generally referred to as the *HTTP Client API.*

For many types of HTTP networking, the capabilities defined by the API in **java.net.http** can provide superior solutions. In addition to offering a streamlined, easy-to-use API, other advantages include support for asynchronous communication, HTTP/2, and flow control. In general, the HTTP Client API is designed as a superior alternative to the functionality provided by **HttpURLConnection**. It also supports the WebSocket protocol for bidirectional communication.

The following discussion explores several key features of the HTTP Client API. Be aware that it contains much more than described here. If you will be writing sophisticated network-based code, then it is a package that you will want to examine in detail. Our purpose here is to introduce some of the fundamentals associated with this important module.



## Three Key Elements

The focus of the following discussion is centered on three core HTTP Client API elements:

| | |
|---|---|
| HttpClient | Encapsulates an HTTP client. It provides the means by which you send a request and obtain a response. |
| HttpRequest | Encapsulates a request. |
| HttpResponse | Encapsulates a response. |

These work together to support the request/response features of HTTP. Here is the general procedure. First, create an instance of **HttpClient**. Then, construct an **HttpRequest** and send it by calling **send( )** on the **HttpClient**. The response is returned by **send( )**. From the response, you can obtain the headers and response body. Before working through an example, we will begin with an overview of these fundamental aspects of the API.

### HttpClient

**HttpClient** encapsulates the HTTP request/response mechanism. It supports both synchronous and asynchronous communication. Here, we will be using only synchronous communication, but you might want to experiment with asynchronous communication on your own. Once you have an **HttpClient** object, you can use it to send requests and obtain responses. Thus, it is at the foundation of the HTTP Client API.

**HttpClient** is an abstract class, and instances are not created via a public constructor. Rather, you will use a factory method to build one. **HttpClient** supports *builders* with the **HttpClient.Builder** interface, which provides several methods that let you configure the **HttpClient**. To obtain an **HttpClient** builder, use the **newBuilder( )** static method. It returns a builder that lets you configure the **HttpClient** that it will create. Next, call **build( )** on the builder. It creates and returns the **HttpClient** instance. For example, this creates an **HttpClient** that uses the default settings:

```
HttpClient myHC = HttpClient.newBuilder().build();
```

**HttpClient.Builder** defines a number of methods that let you configure the builder. Here is one example. By default, redirects are not followed. You can change this by calling **followRedirects( )**, passing in the new redirect setting, which must be a value in the **HttpClient.Redirect** enumeration. It defines the following values: **ALWAYS**, **NEVER**, and **NORMAL**. The first two are self explanatory. The **NORMAL** setting causes redirects to be followed unless a redirect is from an HTTPS site to an HTTP site. For example, this creates a builder in which the redirect policy is **NORMAL**. It then uses that builder to construct an **HttpClient**.

```
HttpClient.Builder myBuilder =
  HttpClient.newBuilder().followRedirects(HttpClient.Redirect.NORMAL);
HttpClient.myHC = myBuilder.build();
```

Among others, builder configuration settings include authentication, proxy, HTTP version, and priority. Therefore, you can build an HTTP client to fit virtually any need.

In cases in which the default configuration is sufficient, you can obtain a default **HttpClient** directly by calling the **newHttpClient( )** method. It is shown here:

static HttpClient newHttpClient( )

An **HttpClient** with a default configuration is returned. For example, this creates a new default **HttpClient**:

```
HttpClient myHC = HttpClient.newHttpClient();
```

Because a default client is sufficient for the purposes of this book, this is the approach used by the examples that follow.

Once you have an **HttpClient** instance, you can send a synchronous request by calling its **send( )** method, shown here:

<T> HttpResponse <T> send(HttpRequest *req*,
HttpResponse.BodyHandler<T> *handler*)
throws IOException, InterruptedException

Here, *req* encapsulates the request and *handler* specifies how the response body is handled. As you will shortly see, often, you can use one of the predefined body handlers provided by the **HttpResponse.BodyHandlers** class. An **HttpResponse** object is returned. Thus, **send( )** provides the basic mechanism for HTTP communication.

## HttpRequest

The HTTP Client API encapsulates requests in the **HttpRequest** abstract class. To create an **HttpRequest** object, you will use a builder. To obtain a builder, call **HttpRequest**'s **newBuilder( )** method. Here are two of its forms:

static HttpRequest.Builder newBuilder( )

static HttpRequest.Builder newBuilder(URI *uri*)

The first form creates a default builder. The second lets you specify the URI of the resource. There is also a third form lets you obtain a builder that can create an **HttpRequest** object that will be similar to a specified **HttpRequest** object.

**HttpRequest.Builder** lets you specify various aspects of the request, such as what request method to use. (The default is GET.) You can also set header information, the URI, and the HTTP version, among others. Aside from the URI, often the default settings are sufficient. You can obtain a string representation of the request method by calling **method( )** on the **HttpRequest** object.

To actually construct a request, call **build( )** on the builder instance. It is shown here:

HttpRequest build( )

Once you have an **HttpRequest** instance, you can use it in a call to **HttpClient**'s **send( )** method, as shown in the previous section.

## HttpResponse

The HTTP Client API encapsulates a response in an implementation of the **HttpResponse** interface. It is a generic interface declared like this:

HttpResponse<T>

Here, **T** specifies the type of body. Because the body type is generic, it enables the body to be handled in a variety of ways. This gives you a wide degree of flexibility in how your response code is written.

When a request is sent, an **HttpResponse** instance is returned that contains the response. **HttpResponse** defines several methods that give you access to the information in the response. Arguably, the most important is **body( )**, shown here:

T body( )

A reference to the body is returned. The specific type of reference is determined by the type of **T**, which is specified by the body handler specified by the **send( )** method.

You can obtain the status code associated with the response by calling **statusCode( )**, shown here:

int statusCode( )

The HTTP status code is returned. A value of 200 indicates success.

Another method in **HttpResponse** is **headers( )**, which obtains the response headers. It is shown here:

HttpHeaders headers( )

The headers associated with the response are encapsulated in an instance of the **HttpHeaders** class. It contains various methods that give you access to the headers. The one used by the example that follows is **map( )**, shown here:

Map<String, List<String>> map( )

It returns a map that contains all of the header fields and values.

One of the advantages of the HTTP Client API is that responses can be handled automatically and in a variety of ways. Responses are handled by implementations of the **HttpResponse.BodyHandler** interface. A number of predefined body handler factory methods are provided in the **HttpResponse.BodyHandlers** class. Here are three examples:

| | |
|---|---|
| static HttpResponse.BodyHandler<Path> ofFile(Path *filename*) | Writes the body of the response to the file specified by *filename*. After the response is obtained, **HttpResponse.body( )** will return a **Path** to the file. |
| static HttpResponse.BodyHandler<InputStream> ofInputStream( ) | Opens an **InputStream** to the response body. After the response is obtained, **HttpResponse.body( )** will return a reference to the **InputStream**. |
| static HttpResponse.BodyHandler<String> ofString( ) | The body of the response is put in a string. After the response is obtained, **HttpResponse.body( )** returns the string. |

Other predefined handlers obtain the response body as a byte array, a stream of lines, a download file, and a **Flow.Publisher**. A non-flow-controlled consumer is also supported. Before moving on, it is important to point out that the stream returned by **ofInputStream( )** should be read in its entirety. Doing so enables associated resources to be freed. If the entire body cannot be read for some reason, call **close( )** to close the stream, which may also close the HTTP connection. In general, it is best to simply read the entire stream.

## A Simple HTTP Client Example

The following example puts into action the features of the HTTP Client API just described. It demonstrates the sending of a request, displaying the body of the response, and obtaining a list of the response headers. You should compare it to parallel sections of code in the preceding **UCDemo** and **HttpURLDemo** programs shown earlier. Notice that it uses **ofInputStream( )** to obtain an input stream linked to the response body.

```
// Demonstrate HttpClient.
import java.net.*;
import java.net.http.*;
import java.io.*;
import java.util.*;

class HttpClientDemo
{
  public static void main(String[] args) throws Exception {
```

```
    // Obtain a client that uses the default settings.
    HttpClient myHC = HttpClient.newHttpClient();

    // Create a request.
    HttpRequest myReq = HttpRequest.newBuilder(
                          new URI("http://www.google.com/")).build();

    // Send the request and get the response. Here, an InputStream is
    // used for the body.
    HttpResponse<InputStream> myResp = myHC.send(myReq,
                          HttpResponse.BodyHandlers.ofInputStream());

    // Display response code and response method.
    System.out.println("Response code is " + myResp.statusCode());
    System.out.println("Request method is " + myReq.method());

    // Get headers from the response.
    HttpHeaders hdrs = myResp.headers();

    // Get a map of the headers.
    Map<String, List<String>> hdrMap = hdrs.map();
    Set<String> hdrField = hdrMap.keySet();

    System.out.println("\nHere is the header:");

    // Display all header keys and values.
    for(String k : hdrField) {
      System.out.println("Key: " + k +
                         "  Value: " + hdrMap.get(k));
    }

    // Display the body.
    System.out.println("\nHere is the body: ");

    InputStream input = myResp.body();
    int c;
    // Read and display the entire body.
    while((c = input.read()) != -1) {
      System.out.print((char) c);
    }
  }
}
```

The program first creates an **HttpClient** and then uses that client to send a request to **www.google.com** (of course, you can substitute any website you like). The body handler uses an input stream by way of **ofInputStream( )**. Next, the response status code and the request method are displayed. Then, the header is displayed, followed by the body. Because **ofInputStream( )** was specified in the **send( )** method, the **body( )** method will return an **InputStream**. This stream is then used to read and display the body.

Part II

The preceding program used an input stream to handle the body for comparison purposes with the **UCDemo** program shown earlier, which uses a parallel approach. However, other options are available. For example, you can use **ofString( )** to handle the body as a string. With this approach, when the response is obtained, the body will be in a **String** instance. To try this, first substitute the line that calls **send( )** with the following:

```
HttpResponse<InputStream> myResp = myHC.send(myReq,
                    HttpResponse.BodyHandlers.ofString());
```

Next, replace the code that uses an input stream to read and display the body with the following line:

```
System.out.println(myResp.body());
```

Because the body of the response is already stored in a string, it can be output directly. You might want to experiment with other body handlers. Of particular interest is **ofLines( )**, which lets you access the body as a stream of lines. One of the benefits of the HTPP Client API is that there are built-in body handlers for a variety of situations.

## Things to Explore in java.net.http

The preceding introduction described a number of key features in the HTTP Client API in **java.net.http**, but there are several more that you will want to explore. One of the most important is the **WebSocket** class, which supports bidirectional communication. Another is the asynchronous capability supported by the API. In general, if network programming is in your future, you will want to thoroughly explore **java.net.http**. It is an important addition to Java's networking APIs.

CHAPTER

# 25 Event Handling

This chapter examines an important aspect of Java: the event. Event handling is fundamental to Java programming because it is integral to the creation of many kinds of applications. For example, any program that uses a graphical user interface, such as a Java application written for Windows, is event driven. Thus, you cannot write these types of programs without a solid command of event handling. Events are supported by a number of packages, including **java.util**, **java.awt**, and **java.awt.event**. Beginning with JDK 9, **java.awt** and **java.awt.event** are part of the **java.desktop** module, and **java.util** is part of the **java.base** module.

Many events to which your program will respond are generated when the user interacts with a GUI-based program. These are the types of events examined in this chapter. They are passed to your program in a variety of ways, with the specific method dependent upon the actual event. There are several types of events, including those generated by the mouse, the keyboard, and various GUI controls, such as a push button, scroll bar, or check box.

This chapter begins with an overview of Java's event handling mechanism. It then examines a number of event classes and interfaces used by the Abstract Window Toolkit (AWT). The AWT was Java's first GUI framework, and it offers a simple way to present the basics of event handling. Next, the chapter develops several examples that demonstrate the fundamentals of event processing. This chapter also introduces key concepts related to GUI programming and explains how to use adapter classes, inner classes, and anonymous inner classes to streamline event handling code. The examples provided in the remainder of this book make frequent use of these techniques.

**NOTE** This chapter focuses on events related to GUI-based programs. However, events are also occasionally used for purposes not directly related to GUI-based programs. In all cases, the same basic event handling techniques apply.

## Two Event Handling Mechanisms

Before beginning our discussion of event handling, an important historical point must be made: The way in which events are handled changed significantly between the original version of Java (1.0) and all subsequent versions of Java, beginning with version 1.1.

Although the 1.0 method of event handling is still supported, it is not recommended for new programs. Also, many of the methods that support the old 1.0 event model have been deprecated. The modern approach is the way that events should be handled by all new programs and thus is the method employed by programs in this book.

# The Delegation Event Model

The modern approach to handling events is based on the *delegation event model,* which defines standard and consistent mechanisms to generate and process events. Its concept is quite simple: a *source* generates an event and sends it to one or more *listeners.* In this scheme, the listener simply waits until it receives an event. Once an event is received, the listener processes the event and then returns. The advantage of this design is that the application logic that processes events is cleanly separated from the user interface logic that generates those events. A user interface element is able to "delegate" the processing of an event to a separate piece of code.

In the delegation event model, listeners must register with a source in order to receive an event notification. This provides an important benefit: notifications are sent only to listeners that want to receive them. This is a more efficient way to handle events than the design used by the original Java 1.0 approach, in which an event was propagated up the containment hierarchy until it was handled by a component. This required components to receive events that they did not process, and it wasted valuable time. The delegation event model eliminates this overhead.

The following sections define events and describe the roles of sources and listeners.

## Events

In the delegation model, an *event* is an object that describes a state change in a source. Among other causes, an event can be generated as a consequence of a person interacting with the elements in a graphical user interface. Some of the activities that cause events to be generated are pressing a button, entering a character via the keyboard, selecting an item in a list, and clicking the mouse. Many other user operations could also be cited as examples.

Events may also occur that are not directly caused by interactions with a user interface. For example, an event may be generated when a timer expires, a counter exceeds a value, a software or hardware failure occurs, or an operation is completed. You are free to define events that are appropriate for your application.

## Event Sources

A *source* is an object that generates an event. This occurs when the internal state of that object changes in some way. Sources may generate more than one type of event.

A source must register listeners in order for the listeners to receive notifications about a specific type of event. Each type of event has its own registration method. Here is the general form:

public void add*Type*Listener (*Type*Listener *el*)

Here, *Type* is the name of the event, and *el* is a reference to the event listener. For example, the method that registers a keyboard event listener is called **addKeyListener( )**. The method that registers a mouse motion listener is called **addMouseMotionListener( )**. When an event occurs, all registered listeners are notified and receive a copy of the event object. This is known as *multicasting* the event. In all cases, notifications are sent only to listeners that register to receive them.

Some sources may allow only one listener to register. The general form of such a method is this:

```
public void addTypeListener(TypeListener el)
  throws java.util.TooManyListenersException
```

Here, *Type* is the name of the event, and *el* is a reference to the event listener. When such an event occurs, the registered listener is notified. This is known as *unicasting* the event.

A source must also provide a method that allows a listener to unregister an interest in a specific type of event. The general form of such a method is this:

```
public void removeTypeListener(TypeListener el)
```

Here, *Type* is the name of the event, and *el* is a reference to the event listener. For example, to remove a keyboard listener, you would call **removeKeyListener( )**.

The methods that add or remove listeners are provided by the source that generates events. For example, **Component**, which is a top-level class defined by the AWT, provides methods to add and remove keyboard and mouse event listeners.

### Event Listeners

A *listener* is an object that is notified when an event occurs. It has two major requirements. First, it must have been registered with one or more sources to receive notifications about specific types of events. Second, it must implement methods to receive and process these notifications. In other words, the listener must supply the event handlers.

The methods that receive and process events are defined in a set of interfaces, such as those found in **java.awt.event**. For example, the **MouseMotionListener** interface defines two methods to receive notifications when the mouse is dragged or moved. Any object may handle one or both of these events if it provides an implementation of this interface. Other listener interfaces are discussed later in this and other chapters.

Here is one more key point about events: An event handler must return quickly. For the most part, a GUI program should not enter a "mode" of operation in which it maintains control for an extended period. Instead, it must perform specific actions in response to events and then return control to the run-time system. Failure to do this can cause your program to appear sluggish or even non-responsive. If your program needs to perform a repetitive task, such as scrolling a banner, it must do so by starting a separate thread. In short, when your program receives an event, it must process it immediately, and then return.

## Event Classes

The classes that represent events are at the core of Java's event handling mechanism. Thus, a discussion of event handling must begin with the event classes. It is important to understand, however, that Java defines several types of events and that not all event classes can be discussed in this chapter. Arguably, the most widely used events at the time of this writing are those defined by the AWT and those defined by Swing. This chapter focuses on the AWT events. (Most of these events also apply to Swing.) Several Swing-specific events are described in Chapter 32, when Swing is covered.

At the root of the Java event class hierarchy is **EventObject**, which is in **java.util**. It is the superclass for all events. Its one constructor is shown here:

EventObject(Object *src*)

Here, *src* is the object that generates this event.

**EventObject** defines two methods: **getSource( )** and **toString( )**. The **getSource( )** method returns the source of the event. Its general form is shown here:

Object getSource( )

As expected, **toString( )** returns the string equivalent of the event.

The class **AWTEvent**, defined within the **java.awt** package, is a subclass of **EventObject**. It is the superclass (either directly or indirectly) of all AWT-based events used by the delegation event model. Its **getID( )** method can be used to determine the type of the event. The signature of this method is shown here:

int getID( )

Typically, you won't use the features defined by **AWTEvent** directly. Rather, you will use its subclasses. At this point, it is important to know only that all of the other classes discussed in this section are subclasses of **AWTEvent**.

To summarize:

- **EventObject** is a superclass of all events.
- **AWTEvent** is a superclass of all AWT events that are handled by the delegation event model.

The package **java.awt.event** defines many types of events that are generated by various user interface elements. Table 25-1 shows several commonly used event classes and provides a brief description of when they are generated. Commonly used constructors and methods in each class are described in the following sections.

## The ActionEvent Class

An **ActionEvent** is generated when a button is pressed, a list item is double-clicked, or a menu item is selected. The **ActionEvent** class defines four integer constants that can be used to identify any modifiers associated with an action event: **ALT_MASK**, **CTRL_MASK**, **META_MASK**, and **SHIFT_MASK**. In addition, there is an integer constant, **ACTION_PERFORMED**, that can be used to identify action events.

**ActionEvent** has these three constructors:

ActionEvent(Object *src*, int *type*, String *cmd*)
ActionEvent(Object *src*, int *type*, String *cmd*, int *modifiers*)
ActionEvent(Object *src*, int *type*, String *cmd*, long *when*, int *modifiers*)

| Event Class | Description |
|---|---|
| ActionEvent | Generated when a button is pressed, a list item is double-clicked, or a menu item is selected. |
| AdjustmentEvent | Generated when a scroll bar is manipulated. |
| ComponentEvent | Generated when a component is hidden, moved, resized, or becomes visible. |
| ContainerEvent | Generated when a component is added to or removed from a container. |
| FocusEvent | Generated when a component gains or loses keyboard focus. |
| InputEvent | Abstract superclass for all component input event classes. |
| ItemEvent | Generated when a check box or list item is clicked; also occurs when a choice selection is made or a checkable menu item is selected or deselected. |
| KeyEvent | Generated when input is received from the keyboard. |
| MouseEvent | Generated when the mouse is dragged, moved, clicked, pressed, or released; also generated when the mouse enters or exits a component. |
| MouseWheelEvent | Generated when the mouse wheel is moved. |
| TextEvent | Generated when the value of a text area or text field is changed. |
| WindowEvent | Generated when a window is activated, closed, deactivated, deiconified, iconified, opened, or quit. |

**Table 25-1** Commonly Used Event Classes in **java.awt.event**



Here, *src* is a reference to the object that generated this event. The type of the event is specified by *type,* and its command string is *cmd.* The argument *modifiers* indicates which modifier keys (ALT, CTRL, META, and/or SHIFT) were pressed when the event was generated. The *when* parameter specifies when the event occurred.

You can obtain the command name for the invoking **ActionEvent** object by using the **getActionCommand( )** method, shown here:

```
String getActionCommand( )
```

For example, when a button is pressed, an action event is generated that has a command name equal to the label on that button.

The **getModifiers( )** method returns a value that indicates which modifier keys (ALT, CTRL, META, and/or SHIFT) were pressed when the event was generated. Its form is shown here:

```
int getModifiers( )
```

The method **getWhen( )** returns the time at which the event took place. This is called the event's *timestamp.* The **getWhen( )** method is shown here:

```
long getWhen( )
```

## The AdjustmentEvent Class

An **AdjustmentEvent** is generated by a scroll bar. There are five types of adjustment events. The **AdjustmentEvent** class defines integer constants that can be used to identify them. The constants and their meanings are shown here:

| | |
|---|---|
| BLOCK_DECREMENT | The user clicked inside the scroll bar to decrease its value. |
| BLOCK_INCREMENT | The user clicked inside the scroll bar to increase its value. |
| TRACK | The slider was dragged. |
| UNIT_DECREMENT | The button at the end of the scroll bar was clicked to decrease its value. |
| UNIT_INCREMENT | The button at the end of the scroll bar was clicked to increase its value. |

In addition, there is an integer constant, **ADJUSTMENT_VALUE_CHANGED**, that indicates that a change has occurred.

Here is one **AdjustmentEvent** constructor:

AdjustmentEvent(Adjustable *src*, int *id*, int *type*, int *val*)

Here, *src* is a reference to the object that generated this event. The *id* specifies the event. The type of the adjustment is specified by *type,* and its associated value is *val.*

The **getAdjustable( )** method returns the object that generated the event. Its form is shown here:

Adjustable getAdjustable( )

The type of the adjustment event may be obtained by the **getAdjustmentType( )** method. It returns one of the constants defined by **AdjustmentEvent**. The general form is shown here:

int getAdjustmentType( )

The amount of the adjustment can be obtained from the **getValue( )** method, shown here:

int getValue( )

For example, when a scroll bar is manipulated, this method returns the value represented by that change.

## The ComponentEvent Class

A **ComponentEvent** is generated when the size, position, or visibility of a component is changed. There are four types of component events. The **ComponentEvent** class defines integer constants that can be used to identify them. The constants and their meanings are shown here:

| | |
|---|---|
| COMPONENT_HIDDEN | The component was hidden. |
| COMPONENT_MOVED | The component was moved. |
| COMPONENT_RESIZED | The component was resized. |
| COMPONENT_SHOWN | The component became visible. |

**ComponentEvent** has this constructor:

ComponentEvent(Component *src*, int *type*)

Here, *src* is a reference to the object that generated this event. The type of the event is specified by *type*.

**ComponentEvent** is the superclass either directly or indirectly of **ContainerEvent**, **FocusEvent**, **KeyEvent**, **MouseEvent**, and **WindowEvent**, among others.

The **getComponent( )** method returns the component that generated the event. It is shown here:

Component getComponent( )



## The ContainerEvent Class

A **ContainerEvent** is generated when a component is added to or removed from a container. There are two types of container events. The **ContainerEvent** class defines **int** constants that can be used to identify these events: **COMPONENT_ADDED** and **COMPONENT_REMOVED**. They indicate that a component has been added to or removed from the container.

**ContainerEvent** is a subclass of **ComponentEvent** and has this constructor:

ContainerEvent(Component *src*, int *type*, Component *comp*)

Here, *src* is a reference to the container that generated this event. The type of the event is specified by *type*, and the component that has been added to or removed from the container is *comp*.

You can obtain a reference to the container that generated this event by using the **getContainer** ( ) method, shown here:

Container getContainer( )

The **getChild( )** method returns a reference to the component that was added to or removed from the container. Its general form is shown here:

Component getChild( )

## The FocusEvent Class

A **FocusEvent** is generated when a component gains or loses input focus. These events are identified by the integer constants **FOCUS_GAINED** and **FOCUS_LOST**.

**FocusEvent** is a subclass of **ComponentEvent** and has these constructors:

FocusEvent(Component *src*, int *type*)
FocusEvent(Component *src*, int *type*, boolean *temporaryFlag*)
FocusEvent(Component *src*, int *type*, boolean *temporaryFlag*, Component *other*)
FocusEvent(Component *src*, int *type*, boolean *temporaryFlag*, Component *other*,
FocusEvent.Cause *what*)

Here, *src* is a reference to the component that generated this event. The type of the event is specified by *type*. The argument *temporaryFlag* is set to **true** if the focus event is temporary. Otherwise, it is set to **false**. (A temporary focus event occurs as a result of another user interface operation. For example, assume that the focus is in a text field. If the user moves the mouse to adjust a scroll bar, the focus is temporarily lost.)

The other component involved in the focus change, called the *opposite component,* is passed in *other.* Therefore, if a **FOCUS_GAINED** event occurred, *other* will refer to the component that lost focus. Conversely, if a **FOCUS_LOST** event occurred, *other* will refer to the component that gains focus.

The fourth constructor was added by JDK 9. Its *what* parameter specifies why the event was generated. It is specified as a **FocusEvent.Cause** enumeration value that identifies the cause of the focus event. The **FocusEvent.Cause** enumeration was also added by JDK 9.

You can determine the other component by calling **getOppositeComponent( )**, shown here:

Component getOppositeComponent( )

The opposite component is returned.

The **isTemporary( )** method indicates if this focus change is temporary. Its form is shown here:

boolean isTemporary( )

The method returns **true** if the change is temporary. Otherwise, it returns **false.**

Beginning with JDK 9, you can obtain the cause of the event by calling **getCause( )**, shown here:

final FocusEvent.Cause getCause( )

The cause is returned in the form of a **FocusEvent.Cause** enumeration value.

## The InputEvent Class

The abstract class **InputEvent** is a subclass of **ComponentEvent** and is the superclass for component input events. Its subclasses are **KeyEvent** and **MouseEvent**.

**InputEvent** defines several integer constants that represent any modifiers, such as the control key being pressed, that might be associated with the event. Originally, the **InputEvent** class defined the following eight values to represent the modifiers, and these modifiers may still be found in older legacy code:

| | | |
|---|---|---|
| ALT_MASK | BUTTON2_MASK | META_MASK |
| ALT_GRAPH_MASK | BUTTON3_MASK | SHIFT_MASK |
| BUTTON1_MASK | CTRL_MASK | |

However, because of possible conflicts between the modifiers used by keyboard events and mouse events, and other issues, the following extended modifier values were added:

| | | |
|---|---|---|
| ALT_DOWN_MASK | BUTTON2_DOWN_MASK | META_DOWN_MASK |
| ALT_GRAPH_DOWN_MASK | BUTTON3_DOWN_MASK | SHIFT_DOWN_MASK |
| BUTTON1_DOWN_MASK | CTRL_DOWN_MASK | |

When writing new code, you should use the new, extended modifiers rather than the original modifiers. Furthermore, the original modifiers have been deprecated since JDK 9.

To test if a modifier was pressed at the time an event is generated, use the **isAltDown( )**, **isAltGraphDown( )**, **isControlDown( )**, **isMetaDown( )**, and **isShiftDown( )** methods. The forms of these methods are shown here:

```
boolean isAltDown( )
boolean isAltGraphDown( )
boolean isControlDown( )
boolean isMetaDown( )
boolean isShiftDown( )
```

It is possible to obtain a value that contains all of the original modifier flags by calling the **getModifiers( )** method. It is shown here:

```
int getModifiers( )
```

Although you may still encounter **getModifiers( )** in legacy code, it is important to point out that because the original modifier flags have been deprecated by JDK 9, this method has also been deprecated by JDK 9. Instead, you should obtain the extended modifiers by calling **getModifiersEx( )**, which is shown here:

```
int getModifiersEx( )
```

## The ItemEvent Class

An **ItemEvent** is generated when a check box or a list item is clicked or when a checkable menu item is selected or deselected. (Check boxes and list boxes are described later in this book.) There are two types of item events, which are identified by the following integer constants:

| | |
|---|---|
| DESELECTED | The user deselected an item. |
| SELECTED | The user selected an item. |

In addition, **ItemEvent** defines the integer constant, **ITEM_STATE_CHANGED**, that signifies a change of state.

**ItemEvent** has this constructor:

ItemEvent(ItemSelectable *src*, int *type*, Object *entry*, int *state*)

Here, *src* is a reference to the component that generated this event. For example, this might be a list or choice element. The type of the event is specified by *type*. The specific item that generated the item event is passed in *entry*. The current state of that item is in *state*.

The **getItem( )** method can be used to obtain a reference to the item that changed. Its signature is shown here:

```
Object getItem( )
```

The **getItemSelectable( )** method can be used to obtain a reference to the **ItemSelectable** object that generated an event. Its general form is shown here:

```
ItemSelectable getItemSelectable( )
```

Lists and choices are examples of user interface elements that implement the **ItemSelectable** interface.

The **getStateChange( )** method returns the state change (that is, **SELECTED** or **DESELECTED**) for the event. It is shown here:

```
int getStateChange( )
```

## The KeyEvent Class

A **KeyEvent** is generated when keyboard input occurs. There are three types of key events, which are identified by these integer constants: **KEY_PRESSED**, **KEY_RELEASED**, and **KEY_TYPED**. The first two events are generated when any key is pressed or released. The last event occurs only when a character is generated. Remember, not all keypresses result in characters. For example, pressing SHIFT does not generate a character.

There are many other integer constants that are defined by **KeyEvent**. For example, **VK_0** through **VK_9** and **VK_A** through **VK_Z** define the ASCII equivalents of the numbers and letters. Here are some others:

| | | | |
|---|---|---|---|
| VK_ALT | VK_DOWN | VK_LEFT | VK_RIGHT |
| VK_CANCEL | VK_ENTER | VK_PAGE_DOWN | VK_SHIFT |
| VK_CONTROL | VK_ESCAPE | VK_PAGE_UP | VK_UP |

The **VK** constants specify *virtual key codes* and are independent of any modifiers, such as CONTROL, SHIFT, or ALT.

**KeyEvent** is a subclass of **InputEvent**. Here is one of its constructors:

KeyEvent(Component *src*, int *type*, long *when*, int *modifiers*, int *code*, char *ch*)

Here, *src* is a reference to the component that generated the event. The type of the event is specified by *type.* The system time at which the key was pressed is passed in *when.* The *modifiers* argument indicates which modifiers were pressed when this key event occurred. The virtual key code, such as **VK_UP**, **VK_A**, and so forth, is passed in *code.* The character equivalent (if one exists) is passed in *ch.* If no valid character exists, then *ch* contains **CHAR_UNDEFINED**. For **KEY_TYPED** events, *code* will contain **VK_UNDEFINED**.

The **KeyEvent** class defines several methods, but probably the most commonly used ones are **getKeyChar( )**, which returns the character that was entered, and **getKeyCode( )**, which returns the key code. Their general forms are shown here:

```
char getKeyChar( )
int getKeyCode( )
```

If no valid character is available, then **getKeyChar( )** returns **CHAR_UNDEFINED**. When a **KEY_TYPED** event occurs, **getKeyCode( )** returns **VK_UNDEFINED**.

## The MouseEvent Class

There are eight types of mouse events. The **MouseEvent** class defines the following integer constants that can be used to identify them:

| | |
|---|---|
| MOUSE_CLICKED | The user clicked the mouse. |
| MOUSE_DRAGGED | The user dragged the mouse. |
| MOUSE_ENTERED | The mouse entered a component. |
| MOUSE_EXITED | The mouse exited from a component. |
| MOUSE_MOVED | The mouse moved. |
| MOUSE_PRESSED | The mouse was pressed. |
| MOUSE_RELEASED | The mouse was released. |
| MOUSE_WHEEL | The mouse wheel was moved. |



**MouseEvent** is a subclass of **InputEvent**. Here is one of its constructors:

MouseEvent(Component *src*, int *type*, long *when*, int *modifiers*,
int *x*, int *y*, int *clicks*, boolean *triggersPopup*)

Here, *src* is a reference to the component that generated the event. The type of the event is specified by *type*. The system time at which the mouse event occurred is passed in *when*. The *modifiers* argument indicates which modifiers were pressed when a mouse event occurred. The coordinates of the mouse are passed in *x* and *y*. The click count is passed in *clicks*. The *triggersPopup* flag indicates if this event causes a pop-up menu to appear on this platform.

Two commonly used methods in this class are **getX( )** and **getY( )**. These return the X and Y coordinates of the mouse within the component when the event occurred. Their forms are shown here:

int getX( )
int getY( )

Alternatively, you can use the **getPoint( )** method to obtain the coordinates of the mouse. It is shown here:

Point getPoint( )

It returns a **Point** object that contains the X,Y coordinates in its integer members: **x** and **y**.

The **translatePoint( )** method changes the location of the event. Its form is shown here:

void translatePoint(int *x*, int *y*)

Here, the arguments *x* and *y* are added to the coordinates of the event.

The **getClickCount( )** method obtains the number of mouse clicks for this event. Its signature is shown here:

int getClickCount( )

The **isPopupTrigger( )** method tests if this event causes a pop-up menu to appear on this platform. Its form is shown here:

boolean isPopupTrigger( )

Also available is the **getButton( )** method, shown here:

int getButton( )

It returns a value that represents the button that caused the event. For most cases, the return value will be one of these constants defined by **MouseEvent**:

| NOBUTTON | BUTTON1 | BUTTON2 | BUTTON3 |
|---|---|---|---|

The **NOBUTTON** value indicates that no button was pressed or released.

Also available are three methods that obtain the coordinates of the mouse relative to the screen rather than the component. They are shown here:

Point getLocationOnScreen( )

int getXOnScreen( )

int getYOnScreen( )

The **getLocationOnScreen( )** method returns a **Point** object that contains both the X and Y coordinates. The other two methods return the indicated coordinate.

## The MouseWheelEvent Class

The **MouseWheelEvent** class encapsulates a mouse wheel event. It is a subclass of **MouseEvent**. Not all mice have wheels. If a mouse has a wheel, it is typically located between the left and right buttons. Mouse wheels are used for scrolling. **MouseWheelEvent** defines these two integer constants:

| WHEEL_BLOCK_SCROLL | A page-up or page-down scroll event occurred. |
|---|---|
| WHEEL_UNIT_SCROLL | A line-up or line-down scroll event occurred. |

Here is one of the constructors defined by **MouseWheelEvent**:

MouseWheelEvent(Component *src*, int *type*, long *when*, int *modifiers*,
int *x*, int *y*, int *clicks*, boolean *triggersPopup*,
int *scrollHow*, int *amount*, int *count*)

Here, *src* is a reference to the object that generated the event. The type of the event is specified by *type.* The system time at which the mouse event occurred is passed in *when.* The *modifiers* argument indicates which modifiers were pressed when the event occurred. The coordinates of the mouse are passed in *x* and *y.* The number of clicks is passed in *clicks.* The *triggersPopup* flag indicates if this event causes a pop-up menu to appear on this platform. The *scrollHow* value must be either **WHEEL_UNIT_SCROLL** or **WHEEL_BLOCK_SCROLL**. The number of units to scroll is passed in *amount.* The *count* parameter indicates the number of rotational units that the wheel moved.

**MouseWheelEvent** defines methods that give you access to the wheel event. To obtain the number of rotational units, call **getWheelRotation( )**, shown here:

int getWheelRotation( )

It returns the number of rotational units. If the value is positive, the wheel moved counterclockwise. If the value is negative, the wheel moved clockwise. Also available is a method called **getPreciseWheelRotation( )**, which supports high-resolution wheels. It works like **getWheelRotation( )** but returns a **double**.

To obtain the type of scroll, call **getScrollType( )**, shown next:

int getScrollType( )

It returns either **WHEEL_UNIT_SCROLL** or **WHEEL_BLOCK_SCROLL**.

If the scroll type is **WHEEL_UNIT_SCROLL**, you can obtain the number of units to scroll by calling **getScrollAmount( )**. It is shown here:

int getScrollAmount( )



## The TextEvent Class

Instances of this class describe text events. These are generated by text fields and text areas when characters are entered by a user or program. **TextEvent** defines the integer constant **TEXT_VALUE_CHANGED**.

The one constructor for this class is shown here:

TextEvent(Object *src*, int *type*)

Here, *src* is a reference to the object that generated this event. The type of the event is specified by *type*.

The **TextEvent** object does not include the characters currently in the text component that generated the event. Instead, your program must use other methods associated with the text component to retrieve that information. This operation differs from other event objects discussed in this section. Think of a text event notification as a signal to a listener that it should retrieve information from a specific text component.

## The WindowEvent Class

There are ten types of window events. The **WindowEvent** class defines integer constants that can be used to identify them. The constants and their meanings are shown here:

| | |
|---|---|
| WINDOW_ACTIVATED | The window was activated. |
| WINDOW_CLOSED | The window has been closed. |
| WINDOW_CLOSING | The user requested that the window be closed. |
| WINDOW_DEACTIVATED | The window was deactivated. |
| WINDOW_DEICONIFIED | The window was deiconified. |
| WINDOW_GAINED_FOCUS | The window gained input focus. |
| WINDOW_ICONIFIED | The window was iconified. |
| WINDOW_LOST_FOCUS | The window lost input focus. |
| WINDOW_OPENED | The window was opened. |
| WINDOW_STATE_CHANGED | The state of the window changed. |

**WindowEvent** is a subclass of **ComponentEvent**. It defines several constructors. The first is

WindowEvent(Window *src*, int *type*)

Here, *src* is a reference to the object that generated this event. The type of the event is *type*.

The next three constructors offer more detailed control:

WindowEvent(Window *src*, int *type*, Window *other*)
WindowEvent(Window *src*, int *type*, int *fromState*, int *toState*)
WindowEvent(Window *src*, int *type*, Window *other*, int *fromState*, int *toState*)

Here, *other* specifies the opposite window when a focus or activation event occurs. The *fromState* specifies the prior state of the window, and *toState* specifies the new state that the window will have when a window state change occurs.

A commonly used method in this class is **getWindow( )**. It returns the **Window** object that generated the event. Its general form is shown here:

Window getWindow( )

**WindowEvent** also defines methods that return the opposite window (when a focus or activation event has occurred), the previous window state, and the current window state. These methods are shown here:

Window getOppositeWindow( )
int getOldState( )
int getNewState( )

## Sources of Events

Table 25-2 lists some of the user interface components that can generate the events described in the previous section. In addition to these graphical user interface elements, any class derived from **Component**, such as **Frame**, can generate events. For example, you can receive

| Event Source | Description |
|---|---|
| Button | Generates action events when the button is pressed. |
| Check box | Generates item events when the check box is selected or deselected. |
| Choice | Generates item events when the choice is changed. |
| List | Generates action events when an item is double-clicked; generates item events when an item is selected or deselected. |
| Menu item | Generates action events when a menu item is selected; generates item events when a checkable menu item is selected or deselected. |
| Scroll bar | Generates adjustment events when the scroll bar is manipulated. |
| Text components | Generates text events when the user enters a character. |
| Window | Generates window events when a window is activated, closed, deactivated, deiconified, iconified, opened, or quit. |

**Table 25-2** Event Source Examples

key and mouse events from an instance of **Frame**. In this chapter, we will be handling only mouse and keyboard events, but subsequent chapters will be handling events from a variety of sources.

# Event Listener Interfaces

As explained, the delegation event model has two parts: sources and listeners. As it relates to this chapter, listeners are created by implementing one or more of the interfaces defined by the **java.awt.event** package. When an event occurs, the event source invokes the appropriate method defined by the listener and provides an event object as its argument. Table 25-3 lists several commonly used listener interfaces and provides a brief description of the methods that they define. The following sections examine the specific methods that are contained in each interface.



## The ActionListener Interface

This interface defines the **actionPerformed( )** method that is invoked when an action event occurs. Its general form is shown here:

void actionPerformed(ActionEvent *ae*)

| Interface | Description |
|---|---|
| ActionListener | Defines one method to receive action events. |
| AdjustmentListener | Defines one method to receive adjustment events. |
| ComponentListener | Defines four methods to recognize when a component is hidden, moved, resized, or shown. |
| ContainerListener | Defines two methods to recognize when a component is added to or removed from a container. |
| FocusListener | Defines two methods to recognize when a component gains or loses keyboard focus. |
| ItemListener | Defines one method to recognize when the state of an item changes. |
| KeyListener | Defines three methods to recognize when a key is pressed, released, or typed. |
| MouseListener | Defines five methods to recognize when the mouse is clicked, enters a component, exits a component, is pressed, or is released. |
| MouseMotionListener | Defines two methods to recognize when the mouse is dragged or moved. |
| MouseWheelListener | Defines one method to recognize when the mouse wheel is moved. |
| TextListener | Defines one method to recognize when a text value changes. |
| WindowFocusListener | Defines two methods to recognize when a window gains or loses input focus. |
| WindowListener | Defines seven methods to recognize when a window is activated, closed, deactivated, deiconified, iconified, opened, or quit. |

**Table 25-3** Commonly Used Event Listener Interfaces

## The AdjustmentListener Interface

This interface defines the **adjustmentValueChanged( )** method that is invoked when an adjustment event occurs. Its general form is shown here:

void adjustmentValueChanged(AdjustmentEvent *ae*)

## The ComponentListener Interface

This interface defines four methods that are invoked when a component is resized, moved, shown, or hidden. Their general forms are shown here:

void componentResized(ComponentEvent *ce*)
void componentMoved(ComponentEvent *ce*)
void componentShown(ComponentEvent *ce*)
void componentHidden(ComponentEvent *ce*)

## The ContainerListener Interface

This interface contains two methods. When a component is added to a container, **componentAdded( )** is invoked. When a component is removed from a container, **componentRemoved( )** is invoked. Their general forms are shown here:

void componentAdded(ContainerEvent *ce*)
void componentRemoved(ContainerEvent *ce*)

## The FocusListener Interface

This interface defines two methods. When a component obtains keyboard focus, **focusGained( )** is invoked. When a component loses keyboard focus, **focusLost( )** is called. Their general forms are shown here:

void focusGained(FocusEvent *fe*)
void focusLost(FocusEvent *fe*)

## The ItemListener Interface

This interface defines the **itemStateChanged( )** method that is invoked when the state of an item changes. Its general form is shown here:

void itemStateChanged(ItemEvent *ie*)

## The KeyListener Interface

This interface defines three methods. The **keyPressed( )** and **keyReleased( )** methods are invoked when a key is pressed and released, respectively. The **keyTyped( )** method is invoked when a character has been entered.

For example, if a user presses and releases the A key, three events are generated in sequence: key pressed, typed, and released. If a user presses and releases the HOME key, two key events are generated in sequence: key pressed and released.

The general forms of these methods are shown here:

void keyPressed(KeyEvent *ke*)
void keyReleased(KeyEvent *ke*)
void keyTyped(KeyEvent *ke*)

## The MouseListener Interface

This interface defines five methods. If the mouse is pressed and released at the same point, **mouseClicked( )** is invoked. When the mouse enters a component, the **mouseEntered( )** method is called. When it leaves, **mouseExited( )** is called. The **mousePressed( )** and **mouseReleased( )** methods are invoked when the mouse is pressed and released, respectively.

The general forms of these methods are shown here:

void mouseClicked(MouseEvent *me*)
void mouseEntered(MouseEvent *me*)
void mouseExited(MouseEvent *me*)
void mousePressed(MouseEvent *me*)
void mouseReleased(MouseEvent *me*)

## The MouseMotionListener Interface

This interface defines two methods. The **mouseDragged( )** method is called multiple times as the mouse is dragged. The **mouseMoved( )** method is called multiple times as the mouse is moved. Their general forms are shown here:

void mouseDragged(MouseEvent *me*)
void mouseMoved(MouseEvent *me*)

## The MouseWheelListener Interface

This interface defines the **mouseWheelMoved( )** method that is invoked when the mouse wheel is moved. Its general form is shown here:

void mouseWheelMoved(MouseWheelEvent *mwe*)

## The TextListener Interface

This interface defines the **textValueChanged( )** method that is invoked when a change occurs in a text area or text field. Its general form is shown here:

void textValueChanged(TextEvent *te*)

## The WindowFocusListener Interface

This interface defines two methods: **windowGainedFocus( )** and **windowLostFocus( )**. These are called when a window gains or loses input focus. Their general forms are shown here:

void windowGainedFocus(WindowEvent *we*)
void windowLostFocus(WindowEvent *we*)

### The WindowListener Interface

This interface defines seven methods. The **windowActivated( )** and **windowDeactivated( )** methods are invoked when a window is activated or deactivated, respectively. If a window is iconified, the **windowIconified( )** method is called. When a window is deiconified, the **windowDeiconified( )** method is called. When a window is opened or closed, the **windowOpened( )** or **windowClosed( )** method is called, respectively. The **windowClosing( )** method is called when a window is being closed. The general forms of these methods are

void windowActivated(WindowEvent *we*)
void windowClosed(WindowEvent *we*)
void windowClosing(WindowEvent *we*)
void windowDeactivated(WindowEvent *we*)
void windowDeiconified(WindowEvent *we*)
void windowIconified(WindowEvent *we*)
void windowOpened(WindowEvent *we*)

## Using the Delegation Event Model

Now that you have learned the theory behind the delegation event model and have had an overview of its various components, it is time to see it in practice. Using the delegation event model is actually quite easy. Just follow these two steps:

1. Implement the appropriate interface in the listener so that it can receive the type of event desired.
2. Implement code to register and unregister (if necessary) the listener as a recipient for the event notifications.

Remember that a source may generate several types of events. Each event must be registered separately. Also, an object may register to receive several types of events, but it must implement all of the interfaces that are required to receive these events. In all cases, an event handler must return quickly. As explained earlier, an event handler must not retain control for an extended period of time.

To see how the delegation model works in practice, we will look at examples that handle two common event generators: the mouse and keyboard.

### Some Key AWT GUI Concepts

To demonstrate the fundamentals of event handling, we will use several simple, GUI-based programs. As stated earlier, most events to which your program will respond will be generated by user interaction with GUI programs. Although the GUI programs shown in this chapter are very simple, it is still necessary to explain a few key concepts because GUI-based programs differ from the console-based programs found in many other parts of this book.

Before we begin, it is important to point out that all modern versions of Java support two GUI frameworks: the AWT and Swing. The AWT was Java's first GUI framework, and for very limited GUI programs, it is the easiest to use. Swing, which is built on the foundation of the

AWT, was Java's second GUI framework and is its most popular and widely used. (A third Java GUI called JavaFX was provided with several recent versions of Java. However, beginning JDK 11, it is no longer part of the JDK.) Both the AWT and Swing are discussed later in this book. However, to demonstrate the fundamentals of event handling, simple AWT-based GUI programs are an appropriate choice and are used here.

There are four key AWT features used by the following programs. First, all create a top-level window by extending the **Frame** class. **Frame** defines what one would think of as a "normal" window. For example, it has minimize, maximize, and close boxes. It can be resized, covered, and redisplayed. Second, all override the **paint( )** method to display output in the window. This method is called by the run-time system to display output in the window. For example, it is called when a window is first shown and after a window has been hidden and then uncovered. Third, when your program needs output displayed, it does not call **paint( )** directly. Instead, you call **repaint( )**. In essence, **repaint( )** tells the AWT to call **paint( )**. You will see how the process works in the examples that follow. Finally, when the top-level **Frame** window for an application is closed—for example, by clicking its close box—the program must explicitly exit, often through a call to **System.exit( )**. Clicking the close box, by itself, does not cause the program to terminate. Therefore, it is necessary for an AWT-based GUI program to handle a window-close event.



## Handling Mouse Events

To handle mouse events, you must implement the **MouseListener** and the **MouseMotionListener** interfaces. (You may also want to implement **MouseWheelListener**, but we won't be doing so here.) The following program demonstrates the process. It displays the current coordinates of the mouse in the program's window. Each time a button is pressed, the phrase "Button Down" is displayed at the location of the mouse pointer. Each time the button is released, the phrase "Button Released" is shown. If a button is clicked, a message stating this fact is displayed at the current mouse location.

As the mouse enters or exits the window, a message is displayed that indicates what happened. When the user drags the mouse, a * is shown, which tracks with the mouse pointer as it is dragged. Notice that the two variables, **mouseX** and **mouseY**, store the location of the mouse when a mouse pressed, released, or dragged event occurs. These coordinates are then used by **paint( )** to display output at the point of these occurrences.

```
// Demonstrate several mouse event handlers
import java.awt.*;
import java.awt.event.*;

public class MouseEventsDemo extends Frame
  implements MouseListener, MouseMotionListener {

  String msg = "";
  int mouseX = 0, mouseY = 0; // coordinates of mouse

  public MouseEventsDemo() {
     addMouseListener(this);
     addMouseMotionListener(this);
     addWindowListener(new MyWindowAdapter());
  }
```

```
    // Handle mouse clicked.
    public void mouseClicked(MouseEvent me) {
      msg = msg + " -- click received";
      repaint();
    }

    // Handle mouse entered.
    public void mouseEntered(MouseEvent me) {
      mouseX = 100;
      mouseY = 100;
      msg = "Mouse entered.";
      repaint();
    }

    // Handle mouse exited.
    public void mouseExited(MouseEvent me) {
      mouseX = 100;
      mouseY = 100;
      msg = "Mouse exited.";
      repaint();
    }

    // Handle button pressed.
    public void mousePressed(MouseEvent me) {
      // save coordinates
      mouseX = me.getX();
      mouseY = me.getY();
      msg = "Button down";
      repaint();
    }

    // Handle button released.
    public void mouseReleased(MouseEvent me) {
      // save coordinates
      mouseX = me.getX();
      mouseY = me.getY();
      msg = "Button Released";
      repaint();
    }

    // Handle mouse dragged.
    public void mouseDragged(MouseEvent me) {
      // save coordinates
      mouseX = me.getX();
      mouseY = me.getY();
      msg = "*" + " mouse at " + mouseX + ", " + mouseY;
      repaint();
    }

    // Handle mouse moved.
    public void mouseMoved(MouseEvent me) {
      msg = "Moving mouse at " + me.getX() + ", " + me.getY();
      repaint();
    }
```

```
  // Display msg in the window at current X,Y location.
  public void paint(Graphics g) {
    g.drawString(msg, mouseX, mouseY);
  }

  public static void main(String[] args) {
    MouseEventsDemo appwin = new MouseEventsDemo();

    appwin.setSize(new Dimension(300, 300));
    appwin.setTitle("MouseEventsDemo");
    appwin.setVisible(true);
  }
}

// When the close box in the frame is clicked,
// close the window and exit the program.
class MyWindowAdapter extends WindowAdapter {
  public void windowClosing(WindowEvent we) {
    System.exit(0);
  }
}
```

Sample output from this program is shown here:

Let's look closely at this example. First, notice that **MouseEventsDemo** extends **Frame**. Thus, it forms the top-level window for the application. Next, notice that it implements both the **MouseListener** and **MouseMotionListener** interfaces. These two interfaces contain methods that receive and process various types of mouse events. Notice that **MouseEventsDemo** is both the source and the listener for these events. This works because **Frame** supplies the **addMouseListener( )** and **addMouseMotionListener( )** methods. Being both the source and the listener for events is not uncommon for simple GUI programs.

Inside the **MouseEventsDemo** constructor, the program registers itself as a listener for mouse events. This is done by calling **addMouseListener( )** and **addMouseMotionListener( )**. They are shown here:

void addMouseListener(MouseListener *ml*)
void addMouseMotionListener(MouseMotionListener *mml*)

Here, *ml* is a reference to the object receiving mouse events, and *mml* is a reference to the object receiving mouse motion events. In this program, the same object is used for both. **MouseEventsDemo** then implements all of the methods defined by the **MouseListener** and **MouseMotionListener** interfaces. These are the event handlers for the various mouse events. Each method handles its event and then returns.

Notice that the **MouseEventsDemo** constructor also adds a **WindowListener**. This is needed to enable the program to respond to a window close event when the user clicks the close box. This listener uses an *adapter class* to implement the **WindowListener** interface. Adapter classes supply empty implementations of a listener interface, enabling you to override only the method or methods in which you are interested. They are described in detail later in this chapter, but one is used here to greatly simplify the code needed to close the program. In this case, the **windowClosing( )** method is overridden. This method is called by the AWT when the window is closed. Here, it calls **System.exit( )** to end the program.

Now notice the mouse event handlers. Each time a mouse event occurs, **msg** is assigned a string that describes what happened and then **repaint( )** is called. In this case, **repaint( )** ultimately causes the AWT to call **paint( )** to display output. (This process is examined in greater detail in Chapter 26.) Notice that **paint( )** has a parameter of type **Graphics**. This class describes the *graphics context* of the program. It is required for output. The program uses the **drawString( )** method provided by **Graphics** to actually display a string in the window at the specified X, Y location. The form used in the program is shown here:

void drawString(String *message*, int *x*, int *y*)

Here, *message* is the string to be output beginning at *x*, *y*. In a Java window, the upper-left corner is location 0,0. As mentioned, **mouseX** and **mouseY** keep track of the location of the mouse. These values are passed to **drawString( )** as the location at which output is displayed.

Finally, the program is started by creating a **MouseEventsDemo** instance and then setting the size of the window, its title, and making the window visible. These features are described in greater detail in Chapter 26.

## Handling Keyboard Events

To handle keyboard events, you use the same general architecture as that shown in the mouse event example in the preceding section. The difference, of course, is that you will be implementing the **KeyListener** interface.

Before looking at an example, it is useful to review how key events are generated. When a key is pressed, a **KEY_PRESSED** event is generated. This results in a call to the **keyPressed( )** event handler. When the key is released, a **KEY_RELEASED** event is generated and the **keyReleased( )** handler is executed. If a character is generated by the keystroke, then a **KEY_TYPED** event is sent and the **keyTyped( )** handler is invoked. Thus, each time the user presses a key, at least two and often three events are generated. If all you care about are actual characters, then you can ignore the information passed by the key press and release events. However, if your program needs to handle special keys, such as the arrow or function keys, then it must watch for them through the **keyPressed( )** handler.

The following program demonstrates keyboard input. It echoes keystrokes to the window and shows the pressed/released status of each key.

```
// Demonstrate the key event handlers.
import java.awt.*;
import java.awt.event.*;

public class SimpleKey extends Frame
  implements KeyListener {

  String msg = "";
  String keyState = "";

  public SimpleKey() {
    addKeyListener(this);
    addWindowListener(new MyWindowAdapter());
  }

  // Handle a key press.
  public void keyPressed(KeyEvent ke) {
    keyState = "Key Down";
    repaint();
  }

  // Handle a key release.
  public void keyReleased(KeyEvent ke) {
    keyState = "Key Up";
    repaint();
  }

  // Handle key typed.
  public void keyTyped(KeyEvent ke) {
    msg += ke.getKeyChar();
    repaint();
  }

  // Display keystrokes.
  public void paint(Graphics g) {
    g.drawString(msg, 20, 100);
    g.drawString(keyState, 20, 50);
  }

  public static void main(String[] args) {
    SimpleKey appwin = new SimpleKey();

    appwin.setSize(new Dimension(200, 150));
    appwin.setTitle("SimpleKey");
    appwin.setVisible(true);
  }
}

// When the close box in the frame is clicked,
// close the window and exit the program.
class MyWindowAdapter extends WindowAdapter {
  public void windowClosing(WindowEvent we) {
    System.exit(0);
  }
}
```

Sample output is shown here:

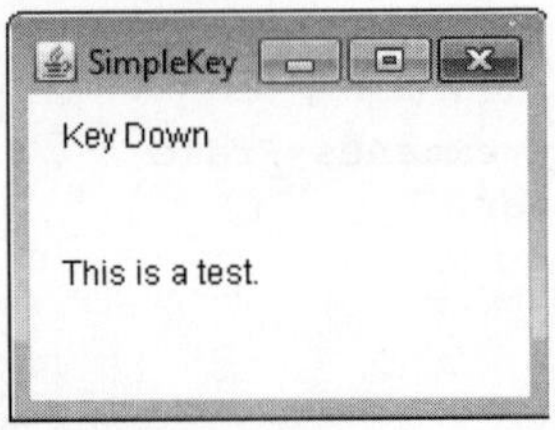


If you want to handle the special keys, such as the arrow or function keys, you need to respond to them within the **keyPressed( )** handler. They are not available through **keyTyped( )**. To identify the keys, you use their virtual key codes. For example, the next program outputs the name of a few of the special keys:

```
// Demonstrate some virtual key codes.
import java.awt.*;
import java.awt.event.*;

public class KeyEventsDemo extends Frame
  implements KeyListener {

  String msg = "";
  String keyState = "";

  public KeyEventsDemo() {
    addKeyListener(this);
    addWindowListener(new MyWindowAdapter());
  }

  // Handle a key press.
  public void keyPressed(KeyEvent ke) {
    keyState = "Key Down";

    int key = ke.getKeyCode();
    switch(key) {
      case KeyEvent.VK_F1:
        msg += "<F1>";
        break;
      case KeyEvent.VK_F2:
        msg += "<F2>";
        break;
      case KeyEvent.VK_F3:
        msg += "<F3>";
        break;
      case KeyEvent.VK_PAGE_DOWN:
        msg += "<PgDn>";
        break;
```

```
      case KeyEvent.VK_PAGE_UP:
        msg += "<PgUp>";
        break;
      case KeyEvent.VK_LEFT:
        msg += "<Left Arrow>";
        break;
      case KeyEvent.VK_RIGHT:
        msg += "<Right Arrow>";
        break;
    }

    repaint();
  }

  // Handle a key release.
  public void keyReleased(KeyEvent ke) {
    keyState = "Key Up";
    repaint();
  }

  // Handle key typed.
  public void keyTyped(KeyEvent ke) {
    msg += ke.getKeyChar();
    repaint();
  }

  // Display keystrokes.
  public void paint(Graphics g) {
    g.drawString(msg, 20, 100);
    g.drawString(keyState, 20, 50);
  }

  public static void main(String[] args) {
    KeyEventsDemo appwin = new KeyEventsDemo();

    appwin.setSize(new Dimension(200, 150));
    appwin.setTitle("KeyEventsDemo");
    appwin.setVisible(true);
  }
}

// When the close box in the frame is clicked,
// close the window and exit the program.
class MyWindowAdapter extends WindowAdapter {
  public void windowClosing(WindowEvent we) {
    System.exit(0);
  }
}
```

Sample output is shown here:

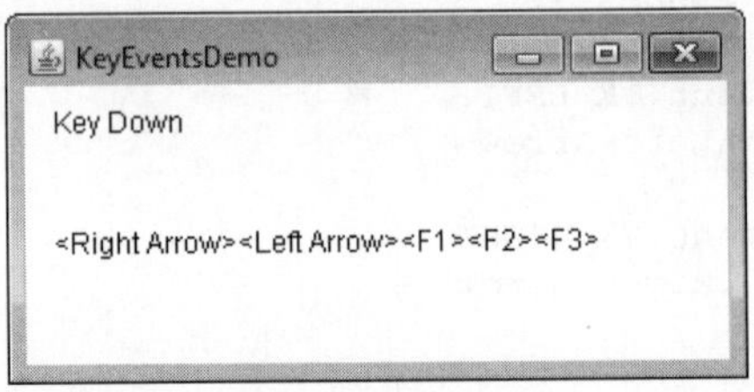


The procedures shown in the preceding keyboard and mouse event examples can be generalized to any type of event handling, including those events generated by controls. In later chapters, you will see many examples that handle other types of events, but they will all follow the same basic structure as the programs just described.

# Adapter Classes

Java provides a special feature, called an *adapter class,* that can simplify the creation of event handlers in certain situations. An adapter class provides an empty implementation of all methods in an event listener interface. Adapter classes are useful when you want to receive and process only some of the events that are handled by a particular event listener interface. You can define a new class to act as an event listener by extending one of the adapter classes and implementing only those events in which you are interested.

For example, the **MouseMotionAdapter** class has two methods, **mouseDragged( )** and **mouseMoved( )**, which are the methods defined by the **MouseMotionListener** interface. If you were interested in only mouse drag events, then you could simply extend **MouseMotionAdapter** and override **mouseDragged( )**. The empty implementation of **mouseMoved( )** would handle the mouse motion events for you.

Table 25-4 lists several commonly used adapter classes in **java.awt.event** and notes the interface that each implements.

You have already seen one adapter class in action in the preceding examples: **WindowAdapter**. Recall that the **WindowListener** interface defines seven methods, but only one, **windowClosing( )**, was needed by the programs. The use of the adapter prevented the need to provide empty implementations of the other unused methods, thus avoiding clutter in the examples. As you would expect, the other adapter classes can be employed in a similar fashion.

The following program provides another example of an adapter. It uses **MouseAdapter** to respond to mouse click and mouse drag events. As shown in Table 25-4, **MouseAdapter** implements all of the mouse listener interfaces. Thus, you can use it to handle all types of mouse events. Of course, you need override only those methods that are used by your program. In the following example, **MyMouseAdapter** extends **MouseAdapter** and overrides the **mouseClicked( )** and **mouseDragged( )** methods. All other mouse events are silently ignored. Notice that the **MyMouseAdapter** constructor is passed a reference to the

| Adapter Class | Listener Interface |
|---|---|
| ComponentAdapter | ComponentListener |
| ContainerAdapter | ContainerListener |
| FocusAdapter | FocusListener |
| KeyAdapter | KeyListener |
| MouseAdapter | MouseListener, MouseMotionListener, and MouseWheelListener |
| MouseMotionAdapter | MouseMotionListener |
| WindowAdapter | WindowListener, WindowFocusListener, and WindowStateListener |

**Table 25-4** Commonly Used Listener Interfaces Implemented by Adapter Classes



**AdapterDemo** instance. This reference is saved and then used to assign a string to **msg** and to invoke **repaint( )** on the object that receives the event notification. As before, a **WindowAdapter** is used to handle a window closing event.

```
// Demonstrate adapter classes.
import java.awt.*;
import java.awt.event.*;

public class AdapterDemo extends Frame {
  String msg = "";

  public AdapterDemo() {
     addMouseListener(new MyMouseAdapter(this));
     addMouseMotionListener(new MyMouseAdapter(this));
     addWindowListener(new MyWindowAdapter());
  }

  // Display the mouse information.
  public void paint(Graphics g) {
    g.drawString(msg, 20, 80);
  }

  public static void main(String[] args) {
    AdapterDemo appwin = new AdapterDemo();

    appwin.setSize(new Dimension(200, 150));
    appwin.setTitle("AdapterDemo");
    appwin.setVisible(true);
  }
}

// Handle only mouse click and drag events.
class MyMouseAdapter extends MouseAdapter {
  AdapterDemo adapterDemo;
```

```
  public MyMouseAdapter(AdapterDemo adapterDemo) {
    this.adapterDemo = adapterDemo;
  }

  // Handle mouse clicked.
  public void mouseClicked(MouseEvent me) {
    adapterDemo.msg = "Mouse clicked";
    adapterDemo.repaint();
  }

  // Handle mouse dragged.
  public void mouseDragged(MouseEvent me) {
    adapterDemo.msg = "Mouse dragged";
    adapterDemo.repaint();
  }
}

// When the close box in the frame is clicked,
// close the window and exit the program.
class MyWindowAdapter extends WindowAdapter {
  public void windowClosing(WindowEvent we) {
    System.exit(0);
  }
}
```

As you can see by looking at the program, not having to implement all of the methods defined by the **MouseMotionListener**, **MouseListener**, and **MouseWheelListener** interfaces saves you a considerable amount of effort and prevents your code from becoming cluttered with empty methods. As an exercise, you might want to try rewriting one of the keyboard input examples shown earlier so that it uses a **KeyAdapter**.

# Inner Classes

In Chapter 7, the basics of inner classes were explained. Here, you will see why they are important. Recall that an *inner class* is a class defined within another class, or even within an expression. This section illustrates how inner classes can be used to simplify the code when using event adapter classes.

To understand the benefit provided by inner classes, consider the program shown in the following listing. It *does not* use an inner class. Its goal is to display the string "Mouse Pressed" when the mouse is pressed. Similar to the approach used by the preceding example, a reference to the **MousePressedDemo** instance is passed to the **MyMouseAdapter** constructor and saved. This reference is used to assign a string to **msg** and invoke **repaint( )** on the object that received the event.

```
// This program does NOT use an inner class.
import java.awt.*;
import java.awt.event.*;

public class MousePressedDemo extends Frame {
  String msg = "";
```

```
  public MousePressedDemo() {
    addMouseListener(new MyMouseAdapter(this));
    addWindowListener(new MyWindowAdapter());
  }

  public void paint(Graphics g) {
    g.drawString(msg, 20, 100);
  }

  public static void main(String[] args) {
    MousePressedDemo appwin = new MousePressedDemo();

    appwin.setSize(new Dimension(200, 150));
    appwin.setTitle("MousePressedDemo");
    appwin.setVisible(true);
  }
}

class MyMouseAdapter extends MouseAdapter {
  MousePressedDemo mousePressedDemo;

  public MyMouseAdapter(MousePressedDemo mousePressedDemo) {
    this.mousePressedDemo = mousePressedDemo;
  }

  // Handle a mouse pressed.
  public void mousePressed(MouseEvent me) {
    mousePressedDemo.msg = "Mouse Pressed.";
    mousePressedDemo.repaint();
  }
}

// When the close box in the frame is clicked,
// close the window and exit the program.
class MyWindowAdapter extends WindowAdapter {
  public void windowClosing(WindowEvent we) {
    System.exit(0);
  }
}
```

The following listing shows how the preceding program can be improved by using an inner class. Here, **InnerClassDemo** is the top-level class, and **MyMouseAdapter** is an inner class. Because **MyMouseAdapter** is defined within the scope of **InnerClassDemo**, it has access to all of the variables and methods within the scope of that class. Therefore, the **mousePressed( )** method can call the **repaint( )** method directly. It no longer needs to do this via a stored reference. The same applies to assigning a value to **msg**. Thus, it is no longer necessary to pass **MyMouseAdapter( )** a reference to the invoking object. Also notice that **MyWindowAdapter** has been made into an inner class.

```
// Inner class demo.
import java.awt.*;
import java.awt.event.*;
```

```
public class InnerClassDemo extends Frame {
  String msg = "";

  public InnerClassDemo() {
    addMouseListener(new MyMouseAdapter());
    addWindowListener(new MyWindowAdapter());
  }

  // Inner class to handle mouse pressed events.
  class MyMouseAdapter extends MouseAdapter {
    public void mousePressed(MouseEvent me) {
      msg = "Mouse Pressed.";
      repaint();
    }
  }

  // Inner class to handle window close events.
  class MyWindowAdapter extends WindowAdapter {
    public void windowClosing(WindowEvent we) {
      System.exit(0);
    }
  }

  public void paint(Graphics g) {
    g.drawString(msg, 20, 80);
  }

  public static void main(String[] args) {
    InnerClassDemo appwin = new InnerClassDemo();

    appwin.setSize(new Dimension(200, 150));
    appwin.setTitle("InnerClassDemo");
    appwin.setVisible(true);
  }
}
```

## Anonymous Inner Classes

An *anonymous* inner class is one that is not assigned a name. This section illustrates how an anonymous inner class can facilitate the writing of event handlers. Consider the program shown in the following listing. As before, its goal is to display the string "Mouse Pressed" when the mouse is pressed.

```
// Anonymous inner class demo.
import java.awt.*;
import java.awt.event.*;

public class AnonymousInnerClassDemo extends Frame {
  String msg = "";

  public AnonymousInnerClassDemo() {
```

```
    // Anonymous inner class to handle mouse pressed events.
    addMouseListener(new MouseAdapter() {
      public void mousePressed(MouseEvent me) {
        msg = "Mouse Pressed.";
        repaint();
      }
    });

    // Anonymous inner class to handle window close events.
    addWindowListener(new WindowAdapter() {
      public void windowClosing(WindowEvent we) {
        System.exit(0);
      }
    });
  }

  public void paint(Graphics g) {
    g.drawString(msg, 20, 80);
  }

  public static void main(String[] args) {
    AnonymousInnerClassDemo appwin =
                  new AnonymousInnerClassDemo();

    appwin.setSize(new Dimension(200, 150));
    appwin.setTitle("AnonymousInnerClassDemo");
    appwin.setVisible(true);
  }
}
```

There is one top-level class in this program: **AnonymousInnerClassDemo**. Its constructor calls the **addMouseListener( )** method. Its argument is an expression that defines and instantiates an anonymous inner class. Let's analyze this expression carefully.

The syntax **new MouseAdapter(){...}** indicates to the compiler that the code between the braces defines an anonymous inner class. Furthermore, that class extends **MouseAdapter**. This new class is not named, but it is automatically instantiated when this expression is executed. This syntax can be generalized and is the same when creating other anonymous classes, such as when an anonymous **WindowAdapter** is created by the program.

Because this anonymous inner class is defined within the scope of **AnonymousInnerClassDemo**, it has access to all of the variables and methods within the scope of that class. Therefore, it can call the **repaint( )** method and access **msg** directly.

As just illustrated, both named and anonymous inner classes solve some annoying problems in a simple yet effective way. They also allow you to create more efficient code.

Part II

CHAPTER

# 26 Introducing the AWT: Working with Windows, Graphics, and Text

The Abstract Window Toolkit (AWT) was Java's first GUI framework, and it has been part of Java since version 1.0. It contains numerous classes and methods that allow you to create windows and simple controls. The AWT was introduced in Chapter 25, where it was used in several short examples that demonstrated event handling. This chapter begins a more detailed examination. Here, you will learn how to manage windows, work with fonts, output text, and utilize graphics. Chapter 27 describes various AWT controls, layout managers, and menus. It also explains further aspects of Java's event handling mechanism. Chapter 28 introduces the AWT's imaging subsystem.

It is important to state at the outset that you will seldom create GUIs based solely on the AWT because more powerful GUI frameworks (such as Swing, described later in this book) have been developed for Java. Despite this fact, the AWT remains an important part of Java. To understand why, consider the following.

At the time of this writing, the framework that is most widely used is Swing. Because Swing provides a richer, more flexible GUI framework than does the AWT, it is easy to jump to the conclusion that the AWT is no longer relevant—that it has been fully superseded by Swing. This assumption is, however, false. Instead, an understanding of the AWT is still important because the AWT underpins Swing, with many AWT classes being used either directly or indirectly by Swing. As a result, a solid knowledge of the AWT is still required to use Swing effectively. Also, for some types of small programs that make only minimal use of a GUI, using the AWT may still be appropriate. Therefore, even though the AWT constitutes Java's oldest GUI framework, a basic working knowledge of its fundamentals is still important today.

One last point before beginning: The AWT is quite large and a full description would easily fill an entire book. Therefore, it is not possible to describe in detail every AWT class, method, or instance variable. However, this and the following chapters explain the basic techniques needed to use the AWT. From there, you will be able to explore other parts of the AWT on your own. You will also be ready to move on to Swing.

**NOTE** If you have not yet read Chapter 25, please do so now. It provides an overview of event handling, which is used by many of the examples in this chapter.

## AWT Classes

The AWT classes are contained in the **java.awt** package. It is one of Java's largest packages. Fortunately, because it is logically organized in a top-down, hierarchical fashion, it is easier to understand and use than you might at first believe. Beginning with JDK 9, **java.awt** is part of the **java.desktop** module. Table 26-1 lists some of the many AWT classes.

Although the basic structure of the AWT has been the same since Java 1.0, some of the original methods were deprecated and replaced by new ones. For backward-compatibility, Java still supports all the original 1.0 methods. However, because these methods are not for use with new code, this book does not describe them.

| Class | Description |
|---|---|
| AWTEvent | Encapsulates AWT events. |
| AWTEventMulticaster | Dispatches events to multiple listeners. |
| BorderLayout | The border layout manager. Border layouts use five components: North, South, East, West, and Center. |
| Button | Creates a push button control. |
| Canvas | A blank, semantics-free window. |
| CardLayout | The card layout manager. Card layouts emulate index cards. Only the one on top is showing. |
| Checkbox | Creates a check box control. |
| CheckboxGroup | Creates a group of check box controls. |
| CheckboxMenuItem | Creates an on/off menu item. |
| Choice | Creates a pop-up list. |
| Color | Manages colors in a portable, platform-independent fashion. |
| Component | An abstract superclass for various AWT components. |
| Container | A subclass of **Component** that can hold other components. |
| Cursor | Encapsulates a bitmapped cursor. |
| Dialog | Creates a dialog window. |
| Dimension | Specifies the dimensions of an object. The width is stored in **width**, and the height is stored in **height**. |
| EventQueue | Queues events. |
| FileDialog | Creates a window from which a file can be selected. |

**Table 26-1** A Sampling of AWT Classes

| Class | Description |
|---|---|
| FlowLayout | The flow layout manager. Flow layout positions components left to right, top to bottom. |
| Font | Encapsulates a type font. |
| FontMetrics | Encapsulates various information related to a font. This information helps you display text in a window. |
| Frame | Creates a standard window that has a title bar, resize corners, and a menu bar. |
| Graphics | Encapsulates the graphics context. This context is used by the various output methods to display output in a window. |
| GraphicsDevice | Describes a graphics device such as a screen or printer. |
| GraphicsEnvironment | Describes the collection of available **Font** and **GraphicsDevice** objects. |
| GridBagConstraints | Defines various constraints relating to the **GridBagLayout** class. |
| GridBagLayout | The grid bag layout manager. Grid bag layout displays components subject to the constraints specified by **GridBagConstraints**. |
| GridLayout | The grid layout manager. Grid layout displays components in a two-dimensional grid. |
| Image | Encapsulates graphical images. |
| Insets | Encapsulates the borders of a container. |
| Label | Creates a label that displays a string. |
| List | Creates a list from which the user can choose. Similar to the standard Windows list box. |
| MediaTracker | Manages media objects. |
| Menu | Creates a pull-down menu. |
| MenuBar | Creates a menu bar. |
| MenuComponent | An abstract class implemented by various menu classes. |
| MenuItem | Creates a menu item. |
| MenuShortcut | Encapsulates a keyboard shortcut for a menu item. |
| Panel | The simplest concrete subclass of **Container**. |
| Point | Encapsulates a Cartesian coordinate pair, stored in **x** and **y**. |
| Polygon | Encapsulates a polygon. |
| PopupMenu | Encapsulates a pop-up menu. |
| PrintJob | An abstract class that represents a print job. |
| Rectangle | Encapsulates a rectangle. |
| Robot | Supports automated testing of AWT-based applications. |
| Scrollbar | Creates a scroll bar control. |
| ScrollPane | A container that provides horizontal and/or vertical scroll bars for another component. |

**Table 26-1** A Sampling of AWT Classes *(continued)*

| Class | Description |
|---|---|
| SystemColor | Contains the colors of GUI widgets such as windows, scroll bars, text, and others. |
| TextArea | Creates a multiline edit control. |
| TextComponent | A superclass for **TextArea** and **TextField**. |
| TextField | Creates a single-line edit control. |
| Toolkit | Abstract class implemented by the AWT. |
| Window | Creates a window with no frame, no menu bar, and no title. |

**Table 26-1** A Sampling of AWT Classes *(continued)*

# Window Fundamentals

The AWT defines windows according to a class hierarchy that adds functionality and specificity with each level. Arguably the two most important window-related classes are **Frame** and **Panel**. **Frame** encapsulates a top-level window and it is typically used to create what would be thought of as a standard application window. **Panel** provides a container to which other components can be added. (**Panel** is also a superclass for **Applet**, which has been deprecated since JDK 9.) Much of the functionality of **Frame** and **Panel** is derived from their parent classes. Thus, a description of the class hierarchies relating to these two classes is fundamental to their understanding. Figure 26-1 shows the class hierarchy for **Panel** and **Frame**. Let's look at each of these classes now.

## Component

At the top of the AWT hierarchy is the **Component** class. **Component** is an abstract class that encapsulates all of the attributes of a visual component. Except for menus, all user interface elements that are displayed on the screen and that interact with the user are

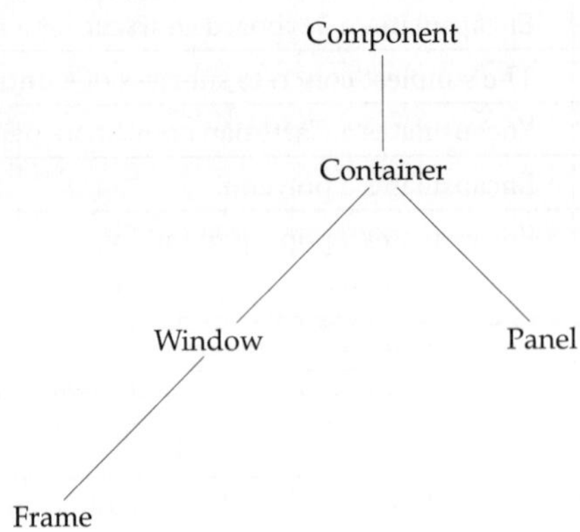


**Figure 26-1** The class hierarchy for **Panel** and **Frame**

subclasses of **Component**. It defines over a hundred public methods that are responsible for managing events, such as mouse and keyboard input, positioning and sizing the window, and repainting. A **Component** object is responsible for remembering the current foreground and background colors and the currently selected text font.

### Container

The **Container** class is a subclass of **Component**. It has additional methods that allow other **Component** objects to be nested within it. Other **Container** objects can be stored inside of a **Container** (since they are themselves instances of **Component**). This makes for a multileveled containment system. A container is responsible for laying out (that is, positioning) any components that it contains. It does this through the use of various layout managers, which you will learn about in Chapter 27.



### Panel

The **Panel** class is a concrete subclass of **Container**. A **Panel** may be thought of as a recursively nestable, concrete screen component. Other components can be added to a **Panel** object by its **add( )** method (inherited from **Container**). Once these components have been added, you can position and resize them manually using the **setLocation( )**, **setSize( )**, **setPreferredSize( )**, and **setBounds( )** methods defined by **Component**.

### Window

The **Window** class creates a top-level window. A *top-level window* is not contained within any other object; it sits directly on the desktop. Generally, you won't create **Window** objects directly. Instead, you will use a subclass of **Window** called **Frame**, described next.

### Frame

**Frame** encapsulates what is commonly thought of as a "window." It is a subclass of **Window** and has a title bar, menu bar, borders, and resizing corners. The precise look of a **Frame** will differ among environments.

### Canvas

Although it is not part of the hierarchy for **Panel** or **Frame**, there is one other class that you will find valuable: **Canvas**. Derived from **Component**, **Canvas** encapsulates a blank window upon which you can draw. You will see an example of **Canvas** later in this book.

## Working with Frame Windows

Typically, the type of AWT-based application window you will most often create is derived from **Frame**. As mentioned, it creates a standard-style, top-level window that has all of the features normally associated with an application window, such as a close box and title

Here are two of **Frame**'s constructors:

Frame( ) throws HeadlessException
Frame(String *title*) throws HeadlessException

The first form creates a standard window that does not contain a title. The second form creates a window with the title specified by *title*. Notice that you cannot specify the dimensions of the window. Instead, you must set the size of the window after it has been created. A **HeadlessException** is thrown if an attempt is made to create a **Frame** instance in an environment that does not support user interaction.

There are several key methods you will use when working with **Frame** windows. They are examined here.

## Setting the Window's Dimensions

The **setSize( )** method is used to set the dimensions of the window. It is shown here:

void setSize(int *newWidth*, int *newHeight*)
void setSize(Dimension *newSize*)

The new size of the window is specified by *newWidth* and *newHeight*, or by the **width** and **height** fields of the **Dimension** object passed in *newSize*. The dimensions are specified in terms of pixels.

The **getSize( )** method is used to obtain the current size of a window. One of its forms is shown here:

Dimension getSize( )

This method returns the current size of the window contained within the **width** and **height** fields of a **Dimension** object.

## Hiding and Showing a Window

After a frame window has been created, it will not be visible until you call **setVisible( )**. Its signature is shown here:

void setVisible(boolean *visibleFlag*)

The component is visible if the argument to this method is **true**. Otherwise, it is hidden.

## Setting a Window's Title

You can change the title in a frame window using **setTitle( )**, which has this general form:

void setTitle(String *newTitle*)

Here, *newTitle* is the new title for the window.

## Closing a Frame Window

When using a frame window, your program must remove that window from the screen when it is closed. If it is not the top-level window of your application, this is done by calling **setVisible(false)**. For the main application window, you can simply terminate the program by calling **System.exit( )** as the examples in Chapter 24 did. To intercept a window-close event, you must implement the **windowClosing( )** method of the **WindowListener** interface. (See Chapter 25 for details on the **WindowListener** interface.)

## The paint( ) Method

As you saw in Chapter 25, output to a window typically occurs when the **paint( )** method is called by the run-time system. This method is defined by **Component** and overridden by **Container** and **Window**. Thus, it is available to instances of **Frame**.

The **paint( )** method is called each time an AWT-based application's output must be redrawn. This situation can occur for several reasons. For example, the program's window may be overwritten by another window and then uncovered. Or the window may be minimized and then restored. **paint( )** is also called when the window is first displayed. Whatever the cause, whenever the window must redraw its output, **paint( )** is called. This implies that your program must have some way to retain its output so that it can be redisplayed each time **paint( )** executes.

The **paint( )** method is shown here:

void paint(Graphics *context*)

The **paint( )** method has one parameter of type **Graphics**. This parameter will contain the graphics context, which describes the graphics environment in which the program is running. This context is used whenever output to the window is required.

## Displaying a String

To output a string to a **Frame**, use **drawString( )**, which is a member of the **Graphics** class. It was introduced in Chapter 25, and we will be making extensive use of it here and in the next chapter. This is the form we will use:

void drawString(String *message*, int *x*, int *y*)

Here, *message* is the string to be output beginning at *x,y*. In a Java window, the upper-left corner is location 0,0. The **drawString( )** method will not recognize newline characters. If you want to start a line of text on another line, you must do so manually, specifying the precise X,Y location where you want the line to begin. (As you will see in the next chapter, there are techniques that make this process easy.)

## Setting the Foreground and Background Colors

You can set both the foreground and background colors used by a **Frame**. To set the background color, use **setBackground( )**. To set the foreground color (the color in which text is shown, for example), use **setForeground( )**. These methods are defined by **Component**, and they have the following general forms:

void setBackground(Color *newColor*)
void setForeground(Color *newColor*)

Here, *newColor* specifies the new color. The class **Color** defines the constants shown here that can be used to specify colors. (Uppercase versions of these constants are also provided.)

| Color.black | Color.magenta |
|---|---|
| Color.blue | Color.orange |
| Color.cyan | Color.pink |
| Color.darkGray | Color.red |
| Color.gray | Color.white |
| Color.green | Color.yellow |
| Color.lightGray | |

For example, the following sets the background color to green and the foreground color to red:

```
setBackground(Color.green);
setForeground(Color.red);
```

You can also create custom colors. A good place to initially set the foreground and background colors is in the constructor for the frame. Of course, you can change these colors as often as necessary during the execution of your program.

You can obtain the current settings for the background and foreground colors by calling **getBackground( )** and **getForeground( )**, respectively. They are also defined by **Component** and are shown here:

Color getBackground( )
Color getForeground( )

## Requesting Repainting

As a general rule, an application writes to its window only when its **paint( )** method is called by the AWT. This raises an interesting question: How can the program itself cause its window to be updated to display new output? For example, if a program displays a moving banner, what mechanism does it use to update the window each time the banner scrolls? Remember, one of the fundamental architectural constraints imposed on a GUI program is that it must quickly return control to the run-time system. It cannot create a loop inside **paint( )** that repeatedly scrolls the banner, for example. This would prevent control from passing back to the AWT. Given this constraint, it may seem that output to your window will be difficult at best. Fortunately, this is not the case. Whenever your program needs to update the information displayed in its window, it simply calls **repaint( )**.

The **repaint( )** method is defined by **Component**. As it relates to **Frame**, this method causes the AWT run-time system to execute a call to the **update( )** method (also defined by **Component**). However, the default implementation of **update( )** calls **paint( )**. Thus, to output to a window, simply store the output and then call **repaint( )**. The AWT will then execute a call to **paint( )**, which can display the stored information. For example, if part of your program needs to output a string, it can store this string in a **String** variable and then call **repaint( )**. Inside **paint( )**, you will output the string using **drawString( )**.

The **repaint( )** method has four forms. Let's look at each one in turn. The simplest version of **repaint( )** is shown here:

void repaint( )

This version causes the entire window to be repainted. The following version specifies a region that will be repainted:

void repaint(int *left*, int *top*, int *width*, int *height*)

Here, the coordinates of the upper-left corner of the region are specified by *left* and *top*, and the width and height of the region are passed in *width* and *height*. These dimensions are specified in pixels. You save time by specifying a region to repaint. Window updates are costly in terms of time. If you need to update only a small portion of the window, it is more efficient to repaint only that region.

Calling **repaint( )** is essentially a request that a window be repainted sometime soon. However, if your system is slow or busy, **update( )** might not be called immediately. Multiple requests for repainting that occur within a short time can be collapsed by the AWT in a manner such that **update( )** is only called sporadically. This can be a problem in many situations, including animation, in which a consistent update time is necessary. One solution to this problem is to use the following forms of **repaint( )**:

void repaint(long *maxDelay*)
void repaint(long *maxDelay*, int *x*, int *y*, int *width*, int *height*)

Here, *maxDelay* specifies the maximum number of milliseconds that can elapse before **update( )** is called.

**NOTE** It is possible for a method other than **paint( )** or **update( )** to output to a window. To do so, it must obtain a graphics context by calling **getGraphics( )** (defined by **Component**) and then use this context to output to the window. However, for most applications, it is better and easier to route window output through **paint( )** and to call **repaint( )** when the contents of the window change.

## Creating a Frame-Based Application

While it is possible to simply create a window by creating an instance of **Frame**, you will seldom do so, because you would not be able to do much with it. For example, you would not be able to receive or process events that occur within it or easily output information to it. Therefore, to create a **Frame**-based application, you will normally create a subclass of **Frame**. Among other reasons, doing so lets you override **paint( )** and provide event handling.

As the event handling examples in Chapter 25 illustrated, creating a new **Frame**-based application is actually quite easy. In general, you create a subclass of **Frame**, override **paint( )** to supply your output to the window, and implement the necessary event listeners. In all cases, you will need to implement the **windowClosing( )** method of the **WindowListener** interface. In a top-level frame, you will typically call **System.exit( )** to terminate the program. To simply remove a secondary frame from the screen, you can call **setVisible(false)** when the window is closed.

Once you have defined a **Frame** subclass, you can create an instance of that class. This causes a frame window to come into existence, but it will not be initially visible. You make it visible by calling **setVisible(true)**. When created, the window is given a default height and width. You can set the size of the window explicitly by calling the **setSize( )** method. For a top-level frame, you will want to define its title.

## Introducing Graphics

The AWT includes several methods that support graphics. All graphics are drawn relative to a window. This can be the main window of an application or a child window. (These methods are also supported by Swing-based windows.) The origin of each window is at the top-left corner and is 0,0. Coordinates are specified in pixels. All output to a window takes place through a *graphics context.*

A graphics context is encapsulated by the **Graphics** class. Here are two ways in which a graphics context can be obtained:

- It is passed to a method, such as **paint( )** or **update( )**, as an argument.
- It is returned by the **getGraphics( )** method of **Component**.

Among other things, the **Graphics** class defines a number of methods that draw various types of objects, such as lines, rectangles, and arcs. In several cases, objects can be drawn edge-only or filled. Objects are drawn and filled in the currently selected color, which is black by default. When a graphics object is drawn that exceeds the dimensions of the window, output is automatically clipped. A sampling of the drawing methods supported by **Graphics** is presented here.

**NOTE** A number of years ago, the graphics capabilities of Java were expanded by the inclusion of several new classes. One of these is **Graphics2D**, which extends **Graphics**. **Graphics2D** supports several enhancements to the basic capabilities provided by **Graphics**. To gain access to this extended functionality, you must cast the graphics context obtained from a method, such as **paint( )**, to **Graphics2D**. Although the basic graphics functions supported by **Graphics** are adequate for the purposes of this book, **Graphics2D** is a class that you may want to explore fully on your own.

### Drawing Lines

Lines are drawn by means of the **drawLine( )** method, shown here:

void drawLine(int *startX*, int *startY*, int *endX*, int *endY*)

**drawLine( )** displays a line in the current drawing color that begins at *startX, startY* and ends at *endX, endY.*

### Drawing Rectangles

The **drawRect( )** and **fillRect( )** methods display an outlined and filled rectangle, respectively. They are shown here:

void drawRect(int *left*, int *top*, int *width*, int *height*)
void fillRect(int *left*, int *top*, int *width*, int *height*)

The upper-left corner of the rectangle is at *left, top*. The dimensions of the rectangle are specified by *width* and *height*.

To draw a rounded rectangle, use **drawRoundRect( )** or **fillRoundRect( )**, both shown here:

void drawRoundRect(int *left*, int *top*, int *width*, int *height*,
int *xDiam*, int *yDiam*)

void fillRoundRect(int *left*, int *top*, int *width*, int *height*,
int *xDiam*, int *yDiam*)

A rounded rectangle has rounded corners. The upper-left corner of the rectangle is at *left, top*. The dimensions of the rectangle are specified by *width* and *height*. The diameter of the rounding arc along the X axis is specified by *xDiam*. The diameter of the rounding arc along the Y axis is specified by *yDiam*.



## Drawing Ellipses and Circles

To draw an ellipse, use **drawOval( )**. To fill an ellipse, use **fillOval( )**. These methods are shown here:

void drawOval(int *left*, int *top*, int *width*, int *height*)
void fillOval(int *left*, int *top*, int *width*, int *height*)

The ellipse is drawn within a bounding rectangle whose upper-left corner is specified by *left, top* and whose width and height are specified by *width* and *height*. To draw a circle, specify a square as the bounding rectangle.

## Drawing Arcs

Arcs can be drawn with **drawArc( )** and **fillArc( )**, shown here:

void drawArc(int *left*, int *top*, int *width*, int *height*, int *startAngle*,
int *sweepAngle*)

void fillArc(int *left*, int *top*, int *width*, int *height*, int *startAngle*,
int *sweepAngle*)

The arc is bounded by the rectangle whose upper-left corner is specified by *left, top* and whose width and height are specified by *width* and *height*. The arc is drawn from *startAngle* through the angular distance specified by *sweepAngle*. Angles are specified in degrees. Zero degrees is on the horizontal, at the three o'clock position. The arc is drawn counterclockwise if *sweepAngle* is positive, and clockwise if *sweepAngle* is negative. Therefore, to draw an arc from twelve o'clock to six o'clock, the start angle would be 90 and the sweep angle 180.

## Drawing Polygons

It is possible to draw arbitrarily shaped figures using **drawPolygon( )** and **fillPolygon( )**, shown here:

void drawPolygon(int[ ] *x*, int[ ] *y*, int *numPoints*)
void fillPolygon(int[ ] *x*, int[ ] *y*, int *numPoints*)

The polygon's endpoints are specified by the coordinate pairs contained within the *x* and *y* arrays. The number of points defined by these arrays is specified by *numPoints*. There are alternative forms of these methods in which the polygon is specified by a **Polygon** object.

## Demonstrating the Drawing Methods

The following program demonstrates the drawing methods just described.

```
// Draw graphics elements.
import java.awt.event.*;
import java.awt.*;

public class GraphicsDemo extends Frame {

  public GraphicsDemo() {
    // Anonymous inner class to handle window close events.
    addWindowListener(new WindowAdapter() {
      public void windowClosing(WindowEvent we) {
        System.exit(0);
      }
    });
  }

  public void paint(Graphics g) {

    // Draw lines.
    g.drawLine(20, 40, 100, 90);
    g.drawLine(20, 90, 100, 40);
    g.drawLine(40, 45, 250, 80);

    // Draw rectangles.
    g.drawRect(20, 150, 60, 50);
    g.fillRect(110, 150, 60, 50);
    g.drawRoundRect(200, 150, 60, 50, 15, 15);
    g.fillRoundRect(290, 150, 60, 50, 30, 40);

    // Draw ellipses and circles.
    g.drawOval(20, 250, 50, 50);
    g.fillOval(100, 250, 75, 50);
    g.drawOval(200, 260, 100, 40);

    // Draw arcs.
    g.drawArc(20, 350, 70, 70, 0, 180);
    g.fillArc(70, 350, 70, 70, 0, 75);

    // Draw a polygon.
    int[] xpoints = {20, 200, 20, 200, 20};
    int[] ypoints = {450, 450, 650, 650, 450};
    int num = 5;

    g.drawPolygon(xpoints, ypoints, num);
  }

  public static void main(String[] args) {
    GraphicsDemo appwin = new GraphicsDemo();
```

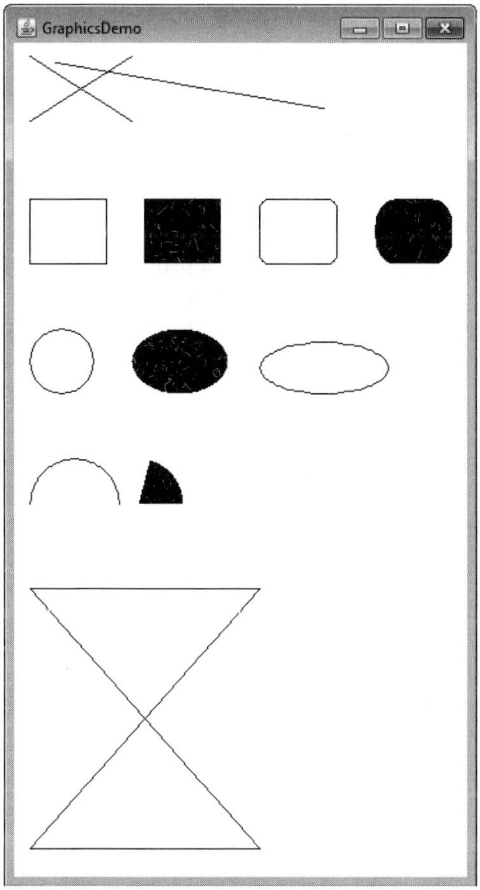


**Figure 26-2** Sample output from the **GraphicsDemo** program

```
    appwin.setSize(new Dimension(370, 700));
    appwin.setTitle("GraphicsDemo");
    appwin.setVisible(true);
  }
}
```

Sample output is shown in Figure 26-2.

## Sizing Graphics

Often, you will want to size a graphics object to fit the current size of the frame in which it is drawn. To do so, first obtain the current dimensions of the frame by calling **getSize( )**. It returns the dimensions as integer values stored in the **width** and **height** fields of a **Dimension** instance. However, the dimensions returned by **getSize( )** reflect the overall size of the frame, including border and title bar. To obtain the dimensions of the paintable area, you will need to reduce the size obtained from **getSize( )** by the dimensions of the border/title bar. The values that describe the size of the border/title region are called *insets*. The inset values are obtained by calling **getInsets( )**, shown here:

Insets getInsets( )

It returns an **Insets** object that encapsulates the insets dimensions as four **int** values called **left**, **right**, **top**, and **bottom**. Therefore, the coordinate of the top-left corner of the paintable area is **left**, **top**. The coordinate of the bottom-right corner is **width–right**, **height–bottom**. Once you have both the size and insets, you can scale your graphical output accordingly.

To demonstrate this technique, here is a program whose frame starts with dimensions 200×200 pixels. It grows by 25 in both width and height each time the mouse is clicked until the size is larger than 500×500. At that point, the next click will return it to 200×200, and the process starts over. Within the paintable area, an X is drawn so that it fills the region.

```
// Resizing output to fit the current size of a window.
import java.awt.*;
import java.awt.event.*;

public class ResizeMe extends Frame {
  final int inc = 25;
  int max = 500;
  int min = 200;
  Dimension d;

  public ResizeMe() {
    // Anonymous inner class to handle mouse release events.
    addMouseListener(new MouseAdapter() {
      public void mouseReleased(MouseEvent me) {
        int w = (d.width + inc) > max?min :(d.width + inc);
        int h = (d.height + inc) > max?min :(d.height + inc);
        setSize(new Dimension(w, h));
      }
    });

    // Anonymous inner class to handle window close events.
    addWindowListener(new WindowAdapter() {
      public void windowClosing(WindowEvent we) {
        System.exit(0);
      }
    });
  }

  public void paint(Graphics g) {
    Insets i = getInsets();
    d = getSize();

    g.drawLine(i.left, i.top, d.width-i.right, d.height-i.bottom);
    g.drawLine(i.left, d.height-i.bottom, d.width-i.right, i.top);
  }

  public static void main(String[] args) {
    ResizeMe appwin = new ResizeMe();
```

```
        appwin.setSize(new Dimension(200, 200));
        appwin.setTitle("ResizeMe");
        appwin.setVisible(true);
    }
}
```

# Working with Color

Java supports color in a portable, device-independent fashion. The AWT color system allows you to specify any color you want. It then finds the best match for that color, given the limits of the display hardware currently executing your program. Thus, your code does not need to be concerned with the differences in the way color is supported by various hardware devices. Color is encapsulated by the **Color** class.

As you saw earlier, **Color** defines several constants (for example, **Color.black**) to specify a number of common colors. You can also create your own colors, using one of the **Color** constructors. Three commonly used forms are shown here:

Color(int *red*, int *green*, int *blue*)
Color(int *rgbValue*)
Color(float *red*, float *green*, float *blue*)

The first constructor takes three integers that specify the color as a mix of red, green, and blue. These values must be between 0 and 255, as in this example:

```
new Color(255, 100, 100); // light red
```

The second color constructor takes a single integer that contains the mix of red, green, and blue packed into an integer. The integer is organized with red in bits 16 to 23, green in bits 8 to 15, and blue in bits 0 to 7. Here is an example of this constructor:

```
int newRed = (0xff000000 | (0xc0 << 16) | (0x00 << 8) | 0x00);
Color darkRed = new Color(newRed);
```

The third constructor, **Color(float, float, float)**, takes three **float** values (between 0.0 and 1.0) that specify the relative mix of red, green, and blue.

Once you have created a color, you can use it to set the foreground and/or background color by using the **setForeground( )** and **setBackground( )** methods as mentioned earlier. You can also select it as the current drawing color.

## Color Methods

The **Color** class defines several methods that help manipulate colors. Several are examined here.

### Using Hue, Saturation, and Brightness

The *hue-saturation-brightness (HSB)* color model is an alternative to red-green-blue (RGB) for specifying particular colors. Figuratively, *hue* is a wheel of color. The hue can be specified with a number between 0.0 and 1.0, which is used to obtain an angle into the color wheel. (The principal colors are approximately red, orange, yellow, green, blue, indigo, and violet.) *Saturation* is another scale ranging from 0.0 to 1.0, representing light pastels to intense hues. *Brightness* values also range from 0.0 to 1.0, where 1 is bright white and 0 is black. **Color** supplies two methods that let you convert between RGB and HSB. They are shown here:

static int HSBtoRGB(float *hue*, float *saturation*, float *brightness*)
static float[ ] RGBtoHSB(int *red*, int *green*, int *blue*, float[ ] *values*)

**HSBtoRGB( )** returns a packed RGB value compatible with the **Color(int)** constructor. **RGBtoHSB( )** returns a **float** array of HSB values corresponding to RGB integers. If *values* is not **null**, then this array is given the HSB values and returned. Otherwise, a new array is created and the HSB values are returned in it. In either case, the array contains the hue at index 0, saturation at index 1, and brightness at index 2.

### getRed( ), getGreen( ), getBlue( )

You can obtain the red, green, and blue components of a color independently using **getRed( )**, **getGreen( )**, and **getBlue( )**, shown here:

int getRed( )
int getGreen( )
int getBlue( )

Each of these methods returns the RGB color component found in the invoking **Color** object in the lower 8 bits of an integer.

### getRGB( )

To obtain a packed, RGB representation of a color, use **getRGB( )**, shown here:

int getRGB( )

The return value is organized as described earlier.

## Setting the Current Graphics Color

By default, graphics objects are drawn in the current foreground color. You can change this color by calling the **Graphics** method **setColor( )**:

void setColor(Color *newColor*)

Here, *newColor* specifies the new drawing color.

You can obtain the current color by calling **getColor( )**, shown here:

Color getColor( )

## A Color Demonstration Program

The following program constructs several colors and draws various objects using these colors:

```
// Demonstrate color.
import java.awt.*;
import java.awt.event.*;
```

```
public class ColorDemo extends Frame {

  public ColorDemo() {
    addWindowListener(new WindowAdapter() {
      public void windowClosing(WindowEvent we) {
        System.exit(0);
      }
    });
  }

  // Draw in different colors.
  public void paint(Graphics g) {
    Color c1 = new Color(255, 100, 100);
    Color c2 = new Color(100, 255, 100);
    Color c3 = new Color(100, 100, 255);

    g.setColor(c1);
    g.drawLine(20, 40, 100, 100);
    g.drawLine(20, 100, 100, 20);

    g.setColor(c2);
    g.drawLine(40, 45, 250, 180);
    g.drawLine(75, 90, 400, 400);

    g.setColor(c3);
    g.drawLine(20, 150, 400, 40);
    g.drawLine(25, 290, 80, 19);

    g.setColor(Color.red);
    g.drawOval(20, 40, 50, 50);
    g.fillOval(70, 90, 140, 100);

    g.setColor(Color.blue);
    g.drawOval(190, 40, 90, 60);
    g.drawRect(40, 40, 55, 50);

    g.setColor(Color.cyan);
    g.fillRect(100, 40, 60, 70);
    g.drawRoundRect(190, 40, 60, 60, 15, 15);
  }

  public static void main(String[] args) {
    ColorDemo appwin = new ColorDemo();

    appwin.setSize(new Dimension(340, 260));
    appwin.setTitle("ColorDemo");
    appwin.setVisible(true);
  }
}
```

## Setting the Paint Mode

The *paint mode* determines how objects are drawn in a window. By default, new output to a window overwrites any preexisting contents. However, it is possible to have new objects XORed onto the window by using **setXORMode( )**, as follows:

void setXORMode(Color *xorColor*)

Here, *xorColor* specifies the color that will be XORed to the window when an object is drawn. The advantage of XOR mode is that the new object is always guaranteed to be visible no matter what color the object is drawn over.

To return to overwrite mode, call **setPaintMode( )**, shown here:

void setPaintMode( )

In general, you will want to use overwrite mode for normal output, and XOR mode for special purposes. For example, the following program displays cross hairs that track the mouse pointer. The cross hairs are XORed onto the window and are always visible, no matter what the underlying color is.

```
// Demonstrate XOR mode.
import java.awt.*;
import java.awt.event.*;

public class XOR extends Frame {
  int chsX=100, chsY=100;

  public XOR() {
    addMouseMotionListener(new MouseMotionAdapter() {
      public void mouseMoved(MouseEvent me) {
        int x = me.getX();
        int y = me.getY();
        chsX = x-10;
        chsY = y-10;
        repaint();
      }
    });

    addWindowListener(new WindowAdapter() {
      public void windowClosing(WindowEvent we) {
        System.exit(0);
      }
    });
  }

  // Demonstrate XOR mode.
  public void paint(Graphics g) {
    g.setColor(Color.green);
    g.fillRect(20, 40, 60, 70);

    g.setColor(Color.blue);
    g.fillRect(110, 40, 60, 70);
```

```
    g.setColor(Color.black);
    g.fillRect(200, 40, 60, 70);

    g.setColor(Color.red);
    g.fillRect(60, 120, 160, 110);

    // XOR cross hairs
    g.setXORMode(Color.black);
    g.drawLine(chsX-10, chsY, chsX+10, chsY);
    g.drawLine(chsX, chsY-10, chsX, chsY+10);
    g.setPaintMode();
  }

  public static void main(String[] args) {
    XOR appwin = new XOR();

    appwin.setSize(new Dimension(300, 260));
    appwin.setTitle("XOR Demo");
    appwin.setVisible(true);
  }

}
```

Sample output from this program is shown here:

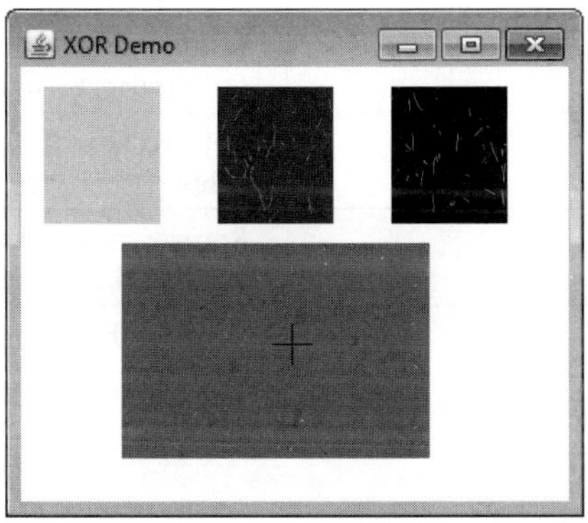


## Working with Fonts

The AWT supports multiple type fonts. Years ago, fonts emerged from the domain of traditional typesetting to become an important part of computer-generated documents and displays. The AWT provides flexibility by abstracting font-manipulation operations and allowing for dynamic selection of fonts.

Fonts have a family name, a logical font name, and a face name. The *family name* is the general name of the font, such as Courier. The *logical name* specifies a name, such as Monospaced, that is linked to an actual font at runtime. The *face name* specifies a specific font, such as Courier Italic.

| Method | Description |
|---|---|
| static Font decode(String *str*) | Returns a font given its name. |
| boolean equals(Object *FontObj*) | Returns **true** if the invoking object contains the same font as that specified by *FontObj*. Otherwise, it returns **false**. |
| String getFamily( ) | Returns the name of the font family to which the invoking font belongs. |
| static Font getFont(String *property*) | Returns the font associated with the system property specified by *property*. **null** is returned if *property* does not exist. |
| static Font getFont(String *property*, Font *defaultFont*) | Returns the font associated with the system property specified by *property*. The font specified by *defaultFont* is returned if *property* does not exist. |
| String getFontName() | Returns the face name of the invoking font. |
| String getName( ) | Returns the logical name of the invoking font. |
| int getSize( ) | Returns the size, in points, of the invoking font. |
| int getStyle( ) | Returns the style values of the invoking font. |
| int hashCode( ) | Returns the hash code associated with the invoking object. |
| boolean isBold( ) | Returns **true** if the font includes the **BOLD** style value. Otherwise, **false** is returned. |
| boolean isItalic( ) | Returns **true** if the font includes the **ITALIC** style value. Otherwise, **false** is returned. |
| boolean isPlain( ) | Returns **true** if the font includes the **PLAIN** style value. Otherwise, **false** is returned. |
| String toString( ) | Returns the string equivalent of the invoking font. |

**Table 26-2** A Sampling of Methods Defined by **Font**

Fonts are encapsulated by the **Font** class. Several of the methods defined by **Font** are listed in Table 26-2.

The **Font** class defines these protected variables:

| Variable | Meaning |
|---|---|
| String name | Name of the font |
| float pointSize | Size of the font in points |
| int size | Size of the font in points |
| int style | Font style |

Several static fields are also defined.

## Determining the Available Fonts

When working with fonts, often you need to know which fonts are available on your machine. To obtain this information, you can use the **getAvailableFontFamilyNames( )** method defined by the **GraphicsEnvironment** class. It is shown here:

String[ ] getAvailableFontFamilyNames( )

This method returns an array of strings that contains the names of the available font families.

In addition, the **getAllFonts( )** method is defined by the **GraphicsEnvironment** class. It is shown here:

Font[ ] getAllFonts( )

This method returns an array of **Font** objects for all of the available fonts.

Since these methods are members of **GraphicsEnvironment**, you need a **GraphicsEnvironment** reference to call them. You can obtain this reference by using the **getLocalGraphicsEnvironment( )** static method, which is defined by **GraphicsEnvironment**. It is shown here:

static GraphicsEnvironment getLocalGraphicsEnvironment( )

Here is a program that shows how to obtain the names of the available font families:

```
// Display Fonts.
import java.awt.event.*;
import java.awt.*;

public class ShowFonts extends Frame {
  String msg = "First five fonts: ";
  GraphicsEnvironment ge;

  public ShowFonts() {
    addWindowListener(new WindowAdapter() {
      public void windowClosing(WindowEvent we) {
        System.exit(0);
      }
    });

    // Get the graphics environment.
    ge = GraphicsEnvironment.getLocalGraphicsEnvironment();

    // Obtain a list of the fonts.
    String[] fontList = ge.getAvailableFontFamilyNames();

    // Create a string of the first 5 fonts.
    for(int i=0; (i < 5) && (i < fontList.length); i++)
      msg += fontList[i] + " ";
  }

  // Display the fonts.
  public void paint(Graphics g) {
    g.drawString(msg, 10, 60);
  }
```

Part II

```
  public static void main(String[] args) {
    ShowFonts appwin = new ShowFonts();

    appwin.setSize(new Dimension(500, 100));
    appwin.setTitle("ShowFonts");
    appwin.setVisible(true);
  }
}
```

Sample output from this program is shown next. However, when you run this program, you may see a different set of fonts than the one shown in this illustration.

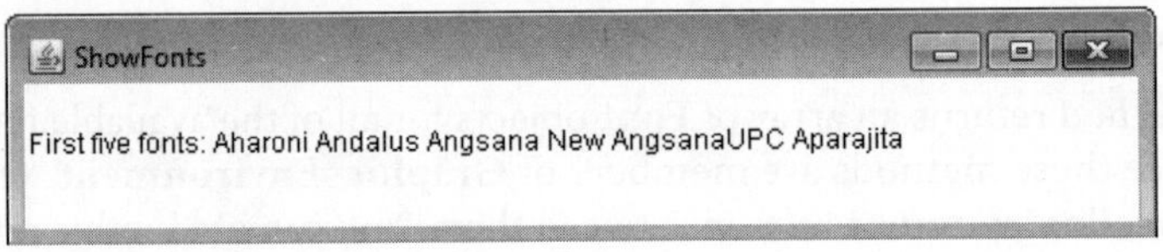


## Creating and Selecting a Font

To create a new font, construct a **Font** object that describes that font. One **Font** constructor has this general form:

Font(String *fontName*, int *fontStyle*, int *pointSize*)

Here, *fontName* specifies the name of the desired font. The name can be specified using either the family or face name. All Java environments will support the following fonts: Dialog, DialogInput, SansSerif, Serif, and Monospaced. Dialog is the font used by your system's dialog boxes. Dialog is also the default if you don't explicitly set a font. You can also use any other fonts supported by your particular environment, but be careful—these other fonts may not be universally available.

The style of the font is specified by *fontStyle*. It may consist of one or more of these three constants: **Font.PLAIN**, **Font.BOLD**, and **Font.ITALIC**. To combine styles, OR them together. For example, **Font.BOLD | Font.ITALIC** specifies a bold, italics style.

The size, in points, of the font is specified by *pointSize*.

To use a font that you have created, you must select it using **setFont( )**, which is defined by **Component**. It has this general form:

void setFont(Font *fontObj*)

Here, *fontObj* is the object that contains the desired font.

The following program outputs a sample of each standard font. Each time you click the mouse within its window, a new font is selected and its name is displayed.

```
// Display fonts.
import java.awt.*;
import java.awt.event.*;

public class SampleFonts extends Frame {
  int next = 0;
  Font f;
  String msg;
```

```
  public SampleFonts() {
    f = new Font("Dialog", Font.PLAIN, 12);
    msg = "Dialog";
    setFont(f);

    addMouseListener(new MyMouseAdapter(this));

    addWindowListener(new WindowAdapter() {
      public void windowClosing(WindowEvent we) {
        System.exit(0);
      }
    });
  }

  public void paint(Graphics g) {
    g.drawString(msg, 10, 60);
  }

  public static void main(String[] args) {
    SampleFonts appwin = new SampleFonts();

    appwin.setSize(new Dimension(200, 100));
    appwin.setTitle("SampleFonts");
    appwin.setVisible(true);
  }
}

class MyMouseAdapter extends MouseAdapter {
  SampleFonts sampleFonts;

  public MyMouseAdapter(SampleFonts sampleFonts) {
    this.sampleFonts = sampleFonts;
  }

  public void mousePressed(MouseEvent me) {
    // Switch fonts with each mouse click.
    sampleFonts.next++;

    switch(sampleFonts.next) {
      case 0:
        sampleFonts.f = new Font("Dialog", Font.PLAIN, 12);
        sampleFonts.msg = "Dialog";
        break;
      case 1:
        sampleFonts.f = new Font("DialogInput", Font.PLAIN, 12);
        sampleFonts.msg = "DialogInput";
        break;
      case 2:
        sampleFonts.f = new Font("SansSerif", Font.PLAIN, 12);
        sampleFonts.msg = "SansSerif";
        break;
      case 3:
        sampleFonts.f = new Font("Serif", Font.PLAIN, 12);
```

```
        sampleFonts.msg = "Serif";
        break;
      case 4:
        sampleFonts.f = new Font("Monospaced", Font.PLAIN, 12);
        sampleFonts.msg = "Monospaced";
        break;
    }

    if(sampleFonts.next == 4) sampleFonts.next = -1;
    sampleFonts.setFont(sampleFonts.f);
    sampleFonts.repaint();
  }
}
```

Sample output from this program is shown here:

## Obtaining Font Information

Suppose you want to obtain information about the currently selected font. To do this, you must first get the current font by calling **getFont( )**. This method is defined by the **Graphics** class, as shown here:

Font getFont( )

Once you have obtained the currently selected font, you can retrieve information about it using various methods defined by **Font**. For example, this program displays the name, family, size, and style of the currently selected font:

```
// Display font info.
import java.awt.event.*;
import java.awt.*;

public class FontInfo extends Frame {

  public FontInfo() {
    addWindowListener(new WindowAdapter() {
      public void windowClosing(WindowEvent we) {
        System.exit(0);
      }
    });
  }

  public void paint(Graphics g) {
    Font f = g.getFont();
    String fontName = f.getName();
    String fontFamily = f.getFamily();
    int fontSize = f.getSize();
    int fontStyle = f.getStyle();
```

```
    String msg = "Family: " + fontName;

    msg += ", Font: " + fontFamily;
    msg += ", Size: " + fontSize + ", Style: ";

    if((fontStyle & Font.BOLD) == Font.BOLD)
      msg += "Bold ";
    if((fontStyle & Font.ITALIC) == Font.ITALIC)
      msg += "Italic ";
    if((fontStyle & Font.PLAIN) == Font.PLAIN)
      msg += "Plain ";

    g.drawString(msg, 10, 60);
  }

  public static void main(String[] args) {
    FontInfo appwin = new FontInfo();

    appwin.setSize(new Dimension(300, 100));
    appwin.setTitle("FontInfo");
    appwin.setVisible(true);
  }
}
```



# Managing Text Output Using FontMetrics

As just explained, Java supports a number of fonts. For most fonts, characters are not all the same dimension—most fonts are proportional. Also, the height of each character, the length of *descenders* (the hanging parts of letters, such as *y*), and the amount of space between horizontal lines vary from font to font. Further, the point size of a font can be changed. That these (and other) attributes are variable would not be of too much consequence except that Java demands that you, the programmer, manually manage virtually all text output.

Given that the size of each font may differ and that fonts may be changed while your program is executing, there must be some way to determine the dimensions and various other attributes of the currently selected font. For example, to write one line of text after another implies that you have some way of knowing how tall the font is and how many pixels are needed between lines. To fill this need, the AWT includes the **FontMetrics** class, which encapsulates various information about a font. Let's begin by defining the common terminology used when describing fonts:

| | |
|---|---|
| Height | The top-to-bottom size of a line of text |
| Baseline | The line that the bottoms of characters are aligned to (not counting descent) |
| Ascent | The distance from the baseline to the top of a character |
| Descent | The distance from the baseline to the bottom of a character |
| Leading | The distance between the bottom of one line of text and the top of the next |

As you know, we have used the **drawString( )** method in many of the previous examples. It paints a string in the current font and color, beginning at a specified location. However, this location is at the left edge of the baseline of the characters, not at the upper-left corner as is usual with other drawing methods. It is a common error to draw a string at the same coordinate that you would draw a box. For example, if you were to draw a rectangle at the top, left location, you would see a full rectangle. If you were to draw the string "Typesetting" at this location, you would only see the tails (or descenders) of the *y, p,* and *g.* As you will see, by using font metrics, you can determine the proper placement of each string that you display.

**FontMetrics** defines several methods that help you manage text output. A number of commonly used ones are listed in Table 26-3. These methods help you properly display text in a window.

Perhaps the most common use of **FontMetrics** is to determine the spacing between lines of text. The second most common use is to determine the length of a string that is being displayed. Here, you will see how to accomplish these tasks.

In general, to display multiple lines of text, your program must manually keep track of the current output position. Each time a newline is desired, the Y coordinate must be advanced to the beginning of the next line. Each time a string is displayed, the X coordinate must be set to the point at which the string ends. This allows the next string to be written so that it begins at the end of the preceding one.

| Method | Description |
|---|---|
| int bytesWidth(byte[ ] *b*, int *start*, int *numBytes*) | Returns the width of *numBytes* characters held in array *b*, beginning at *start.* |
| int charsWidth(char[ ] *c*, int *start*, int *numChars*) | Returns the width of *numChars* characters held in array *c*, beginning at *start.* |
| int charWidth(char *c*) | Returns the width of *c*. |
| int charWidth(int *c*) | Returns the width of *c*. |
| int getAscent( ) | Returns the ascent of the font. |
| int getDescent( ) | Returns the descent of the font. |
| Font getFont( ) | Returns the font. |
| int getHeight( ) | Returns the height of a line of text. This value can be used to output multiple lines of text in a window. |
| int getLeading( ) | Returns the space between lines of text. |
| int getMaxAdvance( ) | Returns an estimate of the width of the widest character. –1 is returned if this value is not available. |
| int getMaxAscent( ) | Returns the maximum ascent. |
| int getMaxDescent( ) | Returns the maximum descent. |
| int[ ] getWidths( ) | Returns the widths of the first 256 characters. |
| int stringWidth(String *str*) | Returns the width of the string specified by *str*. |
| String toString( ) | Returns the string equivalent of the invoking object. |

**Table 26-3** A Sampling of Methods Defined by **FontMetrics**

To determine the spacing between lines, you can use the value returned by **getLeading( )**. To determine the total height of the font, add the value returned by **getAscent( )** to the value returned by **getDescent( )**. You can then use these values to position each line of text you output. However, in many cases, you will not need to use these individual values. Often, all that you will need to know is the total height of a line, which is the sum of the leading space and the font's ascent and descent values. The easiest way to obtain this value is to call **getHeight( )**. In many cases, you can simply increment the Y coordinate by this value each time you want to advance to the next line when outputting text.

To start output at the end of previous output on the same line, you must know the length, in pixels, of each string that you display. To obtain this value, call **stringWidth( )**. You can use this value to advance the X coordinate each time you display a line.

The following program shows how to output multiple lines of text in a window. It also displays multiple sentences on the same line. Notice the variables **curX** and **curY**. They keep track of the current text output position.

```
// Demonstrate multiline output.
import java.awt.event.*;
import java.awt.*;

public class MultiLine extends Frame {
  int curX=20, curY=40; // current position

  public MultiLine() {
    Font f = new Font("SansSerif", Font.PLAIN, 12);
    setFont(f);

    addWindowListener(new WindowAdapter() {
      public void windowClosing(WindowEvent we) {
        System.exit(0);
      }
    });
  }

  public void paint(Graphics g) {
    FontMetrics fm = g.getFontMetrics();

    nextLine("This is on line one.", g);
    nextLine("This is on line two.", g);
    sameLine(" This is on same line.", g);
    sameLine(" This, too.", g);
    nextLine("This is on line three.", g);

    curX = 20; curY = 40; // reset the coordinates for each repaint
  }

  // Advance to next line.
  void nextLine(String s, Graphics g) {
    FontMetrics fm = g.getFontMetrics();
```

```
    curY += fm.getHeight(); // advance to next line
    curX = 20;
    g.drawString(s, curX, curY);
    curX += fm.stringWidth(s); // advance to end of line
  }

  // Display on same line.
  void sameLine(String s, Graphics g) {
    FontMetrics fm = g.getFontMetrics();

    g.drawString(s, curX, curY);
    curX += fm.stringWidth(s); // advance to end of line
  }

  public static void main(String[] args) {
    MultiLine appwin = new MultiLine();

    appwin.setSize(new Dimension(300, 120));
    appwin.setTitle("MultiLine");
    appwin.setVisible(true);
  }
}
```

Sample output from this program is shown here:

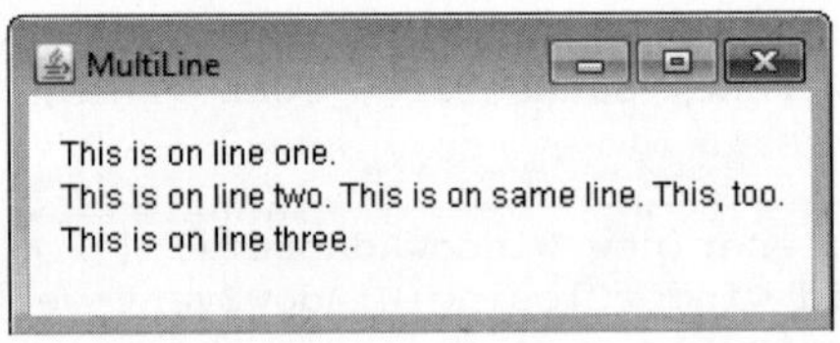

CHAPTER

# 27 Using AWT Controls, Layout Managers, and Menus

This chapter continues our overview of the Abstract Window Toolkit (AWT). It begins with a look at several of the AWT's controls and layout managers. It then discusses menus and the menu bar. The chapter also includes a discussion of the dialog box.

*Controls* are components that allow a user to interact with your application in various ways—for example, a commonly used control is the push button. A *layout manager* automatically positions components within a container. Thus, the appearance of a window is determined by a combination of the controls that it contains and the layout manager used to position them.

In addition to the controls, a frame window can also include a standard-style *menu bar*. Each entry in a menu bar activates a drop-down menu of options from which the user can choose. This constitutes the *main menu* of an application. As a general rule, a menu bar is positioned at the top of a window. Although different in appearance, menu bars are handled in much the same way as are the other controls.

While it is possible to manually position components within a window, doing so is quite tedious. The layout manager automates this task. For the first part of this chapter, which introduces various controls, a simple layout manager will be used that displays components in a container using line-by-line, top-to-bottom organization. Once the controls have been covered, several other layout managers will be examined. There, you will see ways to better manage the positioning of controls.

Before continuing, it is important to emphasize that today you will seldom create GUIs based solely on the AWT because more powerful GUI frameworks have been developed for Java. However, the material presented here remains important for the following reasons. First, much of the information and many of the techniques related to controls and event handling are generalizable to Swing. (As mentioned in the previous chapter, Swing is built upon the AWT.) Second, the layout managers described here are also used by Swing. Third, for some small applications, the AWT components might be the appropriate choice. Finally, you may encounter legacy code that uses the AWT. Therefore, a basic understanding of the AWT is important for all Java programmers.

## AWT Control Fundamentals

The AWT supports the following types of controls:

- Labels
- Push buttons
- Check boxes
- Choice lists
- Lists
- Scroll bars
- Text editing

All AWT controls are subclasses of **Component**. Although the set of controls provided by the AWT is not particularly rich, it is sufficient for simple applications, such as short utility programs intended for your own use. It is also quite useful for introducing the basic concepts and techniques related to handling events in controls. It is important to point out, however, that Swing provides a substantially larger, more sophisticated set of controls better suited for creating commercial applications.

### Adding and Removing Controls

To include a control in a window, you must add it to the window. To do this, you must first create an instance of the desired control and then add it to a window by calling **add( )**, which is defined by **Container**. The **add( )** method has several forms. The following form is the one that is used for the first part of this chapter:

Component add(Component *compRef*)

Here, *compRef* is a reference to an instance of the control that you want to add. A reference to the object is returned. Once a control has been added, it will automatically be visible whenever its parent window is displayed.

Sometimes you will want to remove a control from a window when the control is no longer needed. To do this, call **remove( )**. This method is also defined by **Container**. Here is one of its forms:

void remove(Component *compRef*)

Here, *compRef* is a reference to the control you want to remove. You can remove all controls by calling **removeAll( )**.

### Responding to Controls

Except for labels, which are passive, all other controls generate events when they are accessed by the user. For example, when the user clicks on a push button, an event is sent that identifies the push button. In general, your program simply implements the appropriate interface and then registers an event listener for each control that you need to monitor. As explained in Chapter 25, once a listener has been installed, events are automatically sent to it. In the sections that follow, the appropriate interface for each control is specified.

## The HeadlessException

Most of the AWT controls described in this chapter have constructors that can throw a **HeadlessException** when an attempt is made to instantiate a GUI component in a non-interactive environment (such as one in which no display, mouse, or keyboard is present). You can use this exception to write code that can adapt to non-interactive environments. (Of course, this is not always possible.) This exception is not handled by the programs in this chapter because an interactive environment is required to demonstrate the AWT controls.



# Labels

The easiest control to use is a label. A *label* is an object of type **Label**, and it contains a string, which it displays. Labels are passive controls that do not support any interaction with the user. **Label** defines the following constructors:

Label( ) throws HeadlessException
Label(String *str*) throws HeadlessException
Label(String *str*, int *how*) throws HeadlessException

The first version creates a blank label. The second version creates a label that contains the string specified by *str*. This string is left-justified. The third version creates a label that contains the string specified by *str* using the alignment specified by *how*. The value of *how* must be one of these three constants: **Label.LEFT**, **Label.RIGHT**, or **Label.CENTER**.

You can set or change the text in a label by using the **setText( )** method. You can obtain the current label by calling **getText( )**. These methods are shown here:

void setText(String *str*)
String getText( )

For **setText( )**, *str* specifies the new label. For **getText( )**, the current label is returned.

You can set the alignment of the string within the label by calling **setAlignment( )**. To obtain the current alignment, call **getAlignment( )**. The methods are as follows:

void setAlignment(int *how*)
int getAlignment( )

Here, *how* must be one of the alignment constants shown earlier.

The following example creates three labels and adds them to a **Frame**.

```
// Demonstrate Labels.
import java.awt.*;
import java.awt.event.*;

public class LabelDemo extends Frame {
  public LabelDemo() {
```

```
    // Use a flow layout.
    setLayout(new FlowLayout());

    Label one = new Label("One");
    Label two = new Label("Two");
    Label three = new Label("Three");

    // Add labels to frame.
    add(one);
    add(two);
    add(three);

    addWindowListener(new WindowAdapter() {
      public void windowClosing(WindowEvent we) {
        System.exit(0);
      }
    });
  }

  public static void main(String[] args) {
    LabelDemo appwin = new LabelDemo();

    appwin.setSize(new Dimension(300, 100));
    appwin.setTitle("LabelDemo");
    appwin.setVisible(true);
  }
}
```

Here is sample output from the **LabelDemo** program:

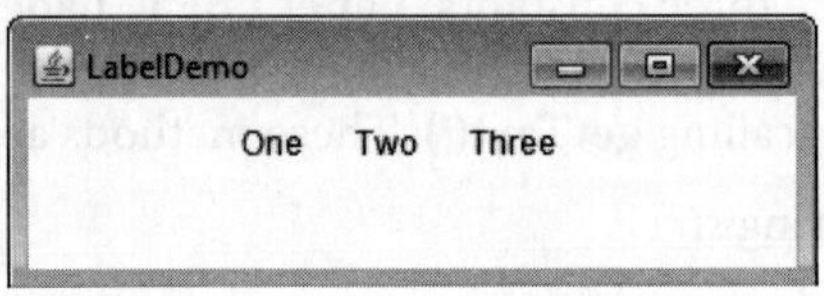


Notice that the labels are organized in the window left-to-right. This is handled automatically by the **FlowLayout** layout manager, which is one of the layout managers provided by the AWT. Here it is used in its default configuration, which lays out components line-by-line, left-to-right, top-to-bottom, and centered. As you will see later in this chapter, it supports several options, but for now, its default behavior is sufficient. Notice that **FlowLayout** is selected as the layout manager by use of **setLayout( )**. This method sets the layout manager associated with the container, which in this case is the enclosing frame. Although **FlowLayout** is very convenient and sufficient for our purposes at this time, it does not give you detailed control over the placement of components within a window. Later in this chapter, when the topic of layout managers is examined in detail, you will see how to gain more control over the organization of your windows.

# Using Buttons

Perhaps the most widely used control is the push button. A *push button* is a component that contains a label and generates an event when it is pressed. Push buttons are objects of type **Button**. **Button** defines these two constructors:

Button( ) throws HeadlessException
Button(String *str*) throws HeadlessException

The first version creates an empty button. The second creates a button that contains *str* as a label.

After a button has been created, you can set its label by calling **setLabel( )**. You can retrieve its label by calling **getLabel( )**. These methods are as follows:

void setLabel(String *str*)
String getLabel( )

Here, *str* becomes the new label for the button.



## Handling Buttons

Each time a button is pressed, an action event is generated. This is sent to any listeners that previously registered an interest in receiving action event notifications from that component. Each listener implements the **ActionListener** interface. That interface defines the **actionPerformed( )** method, which is called when an event occurs. An **ActionEvent** object is supplied as the argument to this method. It contains both a reference to the button that generated the event and a reference to the *action command string* associated with the button. By default, the action command string is the label of the button. Either the button reference or the action command string can be used to identify the button. (You will soon see examples of each approach.)

Here is an example that creates three buttons labeled "Yes", "No", and "Undecided". Each time one is pressed, a message is displayed that reports which button has been pressed. In this version, the action command of the button (which, by default, is its label) is used to determine which button has been pressed. The label is obtained by calling the **getActionCommand( )** method on the **ActionEvent** object passed to **actionPerformed( )**.

```
// Demonstrate Buttons.
import java.awt.*;
import java.awt.event.*;

public class ButtonDemo extends Frame implements ActionListener {
  String msg = "";
  Button yes, no, maybe;

  public ButtonDemo() {

    // Use a flow layout.
    setLayout(new FlowLayout());
```

```
    // Create some buttons.
    yes = new Button("Yes");
    no = new Button("No");
    maybe = new Button("Undecided");

    // Add them to the frame.
    add(yes);
    add(no);
    add(maybe);

    // Add action listeners for the buttons.
    yes.addActionListener(this);
    no.addActionListener(this);
    maybe.addActionListener(this);

    addWindowListener(new WindowAdapter() {
      public void windowClosing(WindowEvent we) {
        System.exit(0);
      }
    });
  }

  // Handle button action events.
  public void actionPerformed(ActionEvent ae) {
    String str = ae.getActionCommand();
    if(str.equals("Yes")) {
      msg = "You pressed Yes.";
    }
    else if(str.equals("No")) {
      msg = "You pressed No.";
    }
    else {
      msg = "You pressed Undecided.";
    }

    repaint();
  }

  public void paint(Graphics g) {
    g.drawString(msg, 20, 100);
  }

  public static void main(String[] args) {
    ButtonDemo appwin = new ButtonDemo();

    appwin.setSize(new Dimension(250, 150));
    appwin.setTitle("ButtonDemo");
    appwin.setVisible(true);
  }
}
```

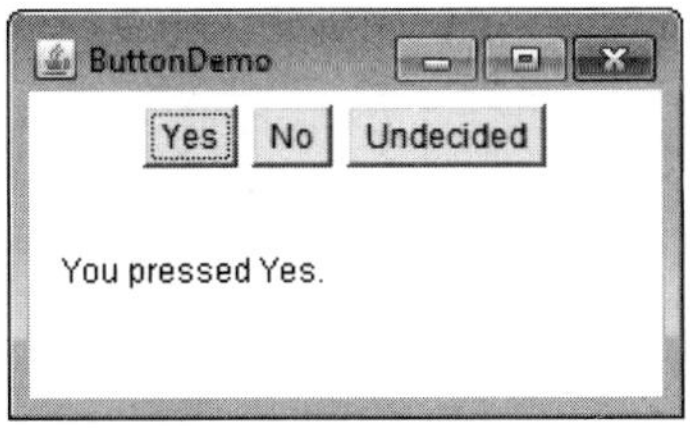


**Figure 27-1** Sample output from the **ButtonDemo** program



Sample output from the **ButtonDemo** program is shown in Figure 27-1.

As mentioned, in addition to comparing button action command strings, you can also determine which button has been pressed by comparing the object obtained from the **getSource( )** method to the button objects that you added to the window. To do this, you must keep a list of the objects when they are added. The following program shows this approach:

```
// Recognize Button objects.
import java.awt.*;
import java.awt.event.*;

public class ButtonList extends Frame implements ActionListener {
  String msg = "";
  Button[] bList = new Button[3];

  public ButtonList() {

    // Use a flow layout.
    setLayout(new FlowLayout());

    // Create some buttons.
    Button yes = new Button("Yes");
    Button no = new Button("No");
    Button maybe = new Button("Undecided");

    // Store references to buttons as added.
    bList[0] = (Button) add(yes);
    bList[1] = (Button) add(no);
    bList[2] = (Button) add(maybe);

    // Register to receive action events.
    for(int i = 0; i < 3; i++) {
      bList[i].addActionListener(this);
    }

    addWindowListener(new WindowAdapter() {
      public void windowClosing(WindowEvent we) {
        System.exit(0);
      }
    });
  }
```

```
  // Handle button action events.
  public void actionPerformed(ActionEvent ae) {
    for(int i = 0; i < 3; i++) {
      if(ae.getSource() == bList[i]) {
        msg = "You pressed " + bList[i].getLabel();
      }
    }
    repaint();
  }

  public void paint(Graphics g) {
     g.drawString(msg, 20, 100);
  }

  public static void main(String[] args) {
    ButtonList appwin = new ButtonList();

    appwin.setSize(new Dimension(250, 150));
    appwin.setTitle("ButtonList");
    appwin.setVisible(true);
  }
}
```

In this version, the program stores each button reference in an array when the buttons are added to the frame. (Recall that the **add( )** method returns a reference to the button when it is added.) Inside **actionPerformed( )**, this array is then used to determine which button has been pressed.

For simple programs, it is usually easier to recognize buttons by their labels. However, in situations in which you will be changing the label inside a button during the execution of your program, or using buttons that have the same label, it may be easier to determine which button has been pushed by using its object reference. It is also possible to set the action command string associated with a button to something other than its label by calling **setActionCommand( )**. This method changes the action command string but does not affect the string used to label the button. Thus, setting the action command enables the action command and the label of a button to differ.

In some cases, you can handle the action events generated by a button (or some other type of control) by use of an anonymous inner class (as described in Chapter 25) or a lambda expression (discussed in Chapter 15). For example, assuming the previous programs, here is a set of action event handlers that use lambda expressions:

```
// Use lambda expressions to handle action events.
yes.addActionListener((ae) -> {
  msg = "You pressed " + ae.getActionCommand();
  repaint();
});

no.addActionListener((ae) -> {
  msg = "You pressed " + ae.getActionCommand();
  repaint();
});
```

```
maybe.addActionListener((ae) -> {
  msg = "You pressed " + ae.getActionCommand();
  repaint();
});
```

This code works because **ActionListener** defines a functional interface, which is an interface with exactly one abstract method. Thus, it can be used by a lambda expression. In general, you can use a lambda expression to handle an AWT event when its listener defines a functional interface. For example, **ItemListener** is also a functional interface. Of course, whether you use the traditional approach, an anonymous inner class, or a lambda expression will be determined by the precise nature of your application.



## Applying Check Boxes

A *check box* is a control that is used to turn an option on or off. It consists of a small box that can either contain a check mark or not. There is a label associated with each check box that describes what option the box represents. You change the state of a check box by clicking on it. Check boxes can be used individually or as part of a group. Check boxes are objects of the **Checkbox** class.

**Checkbox** supports these constructors:

Checkbox( ) throws HeadlessException
Checkbox(String *str*) throws HeadlessException
Checkbox(String *str*, boolean *on*) throws HeadlessException
Checkbox(String *str*, boolean *on*, CheckboxGroup *cbGroup*) throws HeadlessException
Checkbox(String *str*, CheckboxGroup *cbGroup*, boolean *on*) throws HeadlessException

The first form creates a check box whose label is initially blank. The state of the check box is unchecked. The second form creates a check box whose label is specified by *str*. The state of the check box is unchecked. The third form allows you to set the initial state of the check box. If *on* is **true**, the check box is initially checked; otherwise, it is cleared. The fourth and fifth forms create a check box whose label is specified by *str* and whose group is specified by *cbGroup*. If this check box is not part of a group, then *cbGroup* must be **null**. (Check box groups are described in the next section.) The value of *on* determines the initial state of the check box.

To retrieve the current state of a check box, call **getState( )**. To set its state, call **setState( )**. You can obtain the current label associated with a check box by calling **getLabel( )**. To set the label, call **setLabel( )**. These methods are as follows:

boolean getState( )
void setState(boolean *on*)
String getLabel( )
void setLabel(String *str*)

Here, if *on* is **true**, the box is checked. If it is **false**, the box is cleared. The string passed in *str* becomes the new label associated with the invoking check box.

## Handling Check Boxes

Each time a check box is selected or deselected, an item event is generated. This is sent to any listeners that previously registered an interest in receiving item event notifications from that component. Each listener implements the **ItemListener** interface. That interface defines the **itemStateChanged( )** method. An **ItemEvent** object is supplied as the argument to this method. It contains information about the event (for example, whether it was a selection or deselection).

The following program creates four check boxes. The initial state of the first box is checked. The status of each check box is displayed. Each time you change the state of a check box, the status display is updated.

```
// Demonstrate check boxes.
import java.awt.*;
import java.awt.event.*;

public class CheckboxDemo extends Frame implements ItemListener {
  String msg = "";
  Checkbox windows, android, linux, mac;

  public CheckboxDemo() {

    // Use a flow layout.
    setLayout(new FlowLayout());

    // Create check boxes.
    windows = new Checkbox("Windows", true);
    android = new Checkbox("Android");
    linux = new Checkbox("Linux");
    mac = new Checkbox("Mac OS");

    // Add the check boxes to the frame.
    add(windows);
    add(android);
    add(linux);
    add(mac);

    // Add item listeners.
    windows.addItemListener(this);
    android.addItemListener(this);
    linux.addItemListener(this);
    mac.addItemListener(this);

    addWindowListener(new WindowAdapter() {
      public void windowClosing(WindowEvent we) {
        System.exit(0);
      }
    });
  }

  public void itemStateChanged(ItemEvent ie) {
    repaint();
  }
```

**Figure 27-2** Sample output from the **CheckboxDemo** program

```
  // Display current state of the check boxes.
  public void paint(Graphics g) {
    msg = "Current state: ";
    g.drawString(msg, 20, 120);
    msg = "    Windows: " + windows.getState();
    g.drawString(msg, 20, 140);
    msg = "    Android: " + android.getState();
    g.drawString(msg, 20, 160);
    msg = "    Linux: " + linux.getState();
    g.drawString(msg, 20, 180);
    msg = "    Mac OS: " + mac.getState();
    g.drawString(msg, 20, 200);
  }

  public static void main(String[] args) {
    CheckboxDemo appwin = new CheckboxDemo();

    appwin.setSize(new Dimension(240, 220));
    appwin.setTitle("CheckboxDemo");
    appwin.setVisible(true);
  }
}
```

Sample output is shown in Figure 27-2.

# CheckboxGroup

It is possible to create a set of mutually exclusive check boxes in which one and only one check box in the group can be checked at any one time. These check boxes are often called *radio buttons,* because they act like the station selector on a car radio—only one station can be selected at any one time. To create a set of mutually exclusive check boxes, you must first define the group to which they will belong and then specify that group when you construct the check boxes. Check box groups are objects of type **CheckboxGroup**. Only the default constructor is defined, which creates an empty group.

You can determine which check box in a group is currently selected by calling **getSelectedCheckbox( )**. You can set a check box by calling **setSelectedCheckbox( )**. These methods are as follows:

Checkbox getSelectedCheckbox( )
void setSelectedCheckbox(Checkbox *which*)

Here, *which* is the check box that you want to be selected. The previously selected check box will be turned off.

Here is a program that uses check boxes that are part of a group:

```
// Demonstrate check box group.
import java.awt.*;
import java.awt.event.*;

public class CBGroup extends Frame implements ItemListener {
  String msg = "";
  Checkbox windows, android, linux, mac;
  CheckboxGroup cbg;

  public CBGroup() {

    // Use a flow layout.
    setLayout(new FlowLayout());

    // Create a check box group.
    cbg = new CheckboxGroup();

    // Create the check boxes and include them
    // in the group.
    windows = new Checkbox("Windows", cbg, true);
    android = new Checkbox("Android", cbg, false);
    linux = new Checkbox("Linux", cbg, false);
    mac = new Checkbox("Mac OS", cbg, false);

    // Add the check boxes to the frame.
    add(windows);
    add(android);
    add(linux);
    add(mac);

    // Add item listeners.
    windows.addItemListener(this);
    android.addItemListener(this);
    linux.addItemListener(this);
    mac.addItemListener(this);

    addWindowListener(new WindowAdapter() {
      public void windowClosing(WindowEvent we) {
        System.exit(0);
      }
    });
  }
```

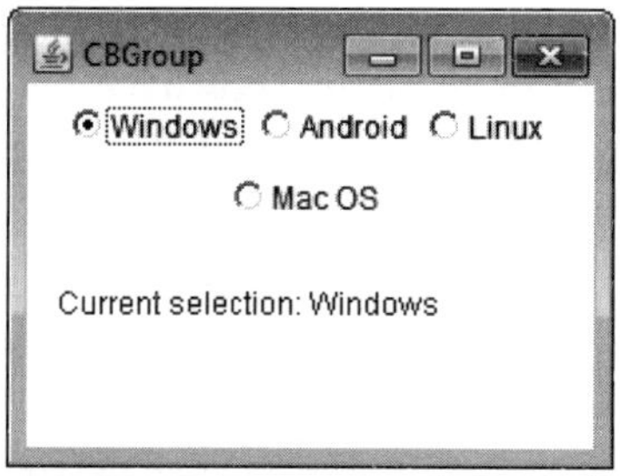


**Figure 27-3** Sample output from the **CBGroup** program



```
  public void itemStateChanged(ItemEvent ie) {
    repaint();
  }

  // Display current state of the check boxes.
  public void paint(Graphics g) {
    msg = "Current selection: ";
    msg += cbg.getSelectedCheckbox().getLabel();
    g.drawString(msg, 20, 120);
  }

  public static void main(String[] args) {
    CBGroup appwin = new CBGroup();

    appwin.setSize(new Dimension(240, 180));
    appwin.setTitle("CBGroup");
    appwin.setVisible(true);
  }
}
```

Sample output generated by the **CBGroup** program is shown in Figure 27-3. Notice that the check boxes are now circular in shape.

# Choice Controls

The **Choice** class is used to create a *pop up list* of items from which the user may choose. Thus, a **Choice** control is a form of menu. When inactive, a **Choice** component takes up only enough space to show the currently selected item. When the user clicks on it, the whole list of choices pops up, and a new selection can be made. Each item in the list is a string that appears as a left-justified label in the order it is added to the **Choice** object. **Choice** defines only the default constructor, which creates an empty list.

To add a selection to the list, call **add( )**. It has this general form:

void add(String *name*)

Here, *name* is the name of the item being added. Items are added to the list in the order in which calls to **add( )** occur.

To determine which item is currently selected, you may call either **getSelectedItem( )** or **getSelectedIndex( )**. These methods are shown here:

String getSelectedItem( )
int getSelectedIndex( )

The **getSelectedItem( )** method returns a string containing the name of the item. **getSelectedIndex( )** returns the index of the item. The first item is at index 0. By default, the first item added to the list is selected.

To obtain the number of items in the list, call **getItemCount( )**. You can set the currently selected item using the **select( )** method with either a zero-based integer index or a string that will match a name in the list. These methods are shown here:

int getItemCount( )
void select(int *index*)
void select(String *name*)

Given an index, you can obtain the name associated with the item at that index by calling **getItem( )**, which has this general form:

String getItem(int *index*)

Here, *index* specifies the index of the desired item.

## Handling Choice Lists

Each time a choice is selected, an item event is generated. This is sent to any listeners that previously registered an interest in receiving item event notifications from that component. Each listener implements the **ItemListener** interface. That interface defines the **itemStateChanged( )** method. An **ItemEvent** object is supplied as the argument to this method.

Here is an example that creates two **Choice** menus. One selects the operating system. The other selects the browser.

```
// Demonstrate Choice lists.
import java.awt.*;
import java.awt.event.*;

public class ChoiceDemo extends Frame implements ItemListener {
  Choice os, browser;
  String msg = "";

  public ChoiceDemo() {

    // Use a flow layout.
    setLayout(new FlowLayout());

    // Create choice lists.
    os = new Choice();
    browser = new Choice();
```

```
    // Add items to os list.
    os.add("Windows");
    os.add("Android");
    os.add("Linux");
    os.add("Mac OS");

    // Add items to browser list.
    browser.add("Edge");
    browser.add("Firefox");
    browser.add("Chrome");

    // Add choice lists to window.
    add(os);
    add(browser);

    // Add item listeners.
    os.addItemListener(this);
    browser.addItemListener(this);

    addWindowListener(new WindowAdapter() {
      public void windowClosing(WindowEvent we) {
        System.exit(0);
      }
    });
  }

  public void itemStateChanged(ItemEvent ie) {
    repaint();
  }

  // Display current selections.
  public void paint(Graphics g) {
    msg = "Current OS: ";
    msg += os.getSelectedItem();
    g.drawString(msg, 20, 120);
    msg = "Current Browser: ";
    msg += browser.getSelectedItem();
    g.drawString(msg, 20, 140);
  }

  public static void main(String[] args) {
    ChoiceDemo appwin = new ChoiceDemo();

    appwin.setSize(new Dimension(240, 180));
    appwin.setTitle("ChoiceDemo");
    appwin.setVisible(true);
  }
}
```

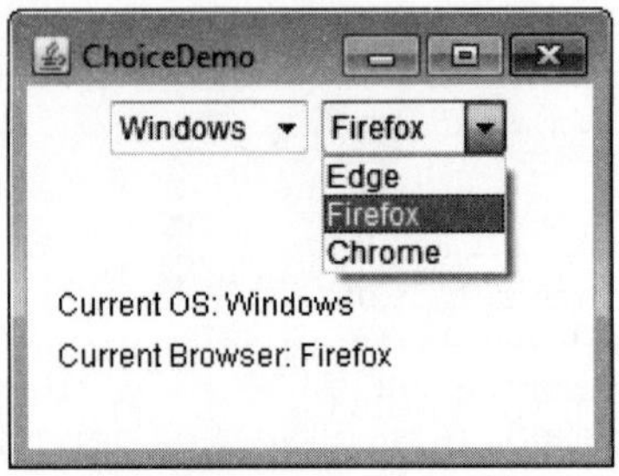


**Figure 27-4** Sample output from the **ChoiceDemo** program

Sample output is shown in Figure 27-4.

## Using Lists

The **List** class provides a compact, multiple-choice, scrolling selection list. Unlike the **Choice** object, which shows only the single selected item in the menu, a **List** object can be constructed to show any number of choices in the visible window. It can also be created to allow multiple selections. **List** provides these constructors:

List( ) throws HeadlessException
List(int *numRows*) throws HeadlessException
List(int *numRows*, boolean *multipleSelect*) throws HeadlessException

The first version creates a **List** control that allows only one item to be selected at any one time. In the second form, the value of *numRows* specifies the number of entries in the list that will always be visible (others can be scrolled into view as needed). In the third form, if *multipleSelect* is **true**, then the user may select two or more items at a time. If it is **false**, then only one item may be selected.

To add a selection to the list, call **add( )**. It has the following two forms:

void add(String *name*)
void add(String *name*, int *index*)

Here, *name* is the name of the item added to the list. The first form adds items to the end of the list. The second form adds the item at the index specified by *index*. Indexing begins at zero. You can specify –1 to add the item to the end of the list.

For lists that allow only single selection, you can determine which item is currently selected by calling either **getSelectedItem( )** or **getSelectedIndex( )**. These methods are shown here:

String getSelectedItem( )
int getSelectedIndex( )

The **getSelectedItem( )** method returns a string containing the name of the item. If more than one item is selected, or if no selection has yet been made, **null** is returned. **getSelectedIndex( )** returns the index of the item. The first item is at index 0. If more than one item is selected, or if no selection has yet been made, –1 is returned.

For lists that allow multiple selection, you must use either **getSelectedItems( )** or **getSelectedIndexes( )**, shown here, to determine the current selections:

String[ ] getSelectedItems( )
int[ ] getSelectedIndexes( )

**getSelectedItems( )** returns an array containing the names of the currently selected items. **getSelectedIndexes( )** returns an array containing the indexes of the currently selected items.

To obtain the number of items in the list, call **getItemCount( )**. You can set the currently selected item by using the **select( )** method with a zero-based integer index. These methods are shown here:

int getItemCount( )
void select(int *index*)

Given an index, you can obtain the name associated with the item at that index by calling **getItem( )**, which has this general form:

String getItem(int *index*)

Here, *index* specifies the index of the desired item.

## Handling Lists

To process list events, you will need to implement the **ActionListener** interface. Each time a **List** item is double-clicked, an **ActionEvent** object is generated. Its **getActionCommand( )** method can be used to retrieve the name of the newly selected item. Also, each time an item is selected or deselected with a single click, an **ItemEvent** object is generated. Its **getStateChange( )** method can be used to determine whether a selection or deselection triggered this event. **getItemSelectable( )** returns a reference to the object that triggered this event.

Here is an example that converts the **Choice** controls in the preceding section into **List** components, one multiple choice and the other single choice:

```
// Demonstrate Lists.
import java.awt.*;
import java.awt.event.*;

public class ListDemo extends Frame implements ActionListener {
  List os, browser;
  String msg = "";

  public ListDemo() {

    // Use a flow layout.
    setLayout(new FlowLayout());

    // Create a multi-selection list.
    os = new List(4, true);

    // Create a single-selection list.
    browser = new List(4);

    // Add items to os list.
    os.add("Windows");
```

Part II

```
    os.add("Android");
    os.add("Linux");
    os.add("Mac OS");

    // Add items to browser list.
    browser.add("Edge");
    browser.add("Firefox");
    browser.add("Chrome");

    // Make initial selections.
    browser.select(1);
    os.select(0);

    // Add lists to the frame.
    add(os);
    add(browser);

    // Add action listeners.
    os.addActionListener(this);
    browser.addActionListener(this);

    addWindowListener(new WindowAdapter() {
      public void windowClosing(WindowEvent we) {
        System.exit(0);
      }
    });
  }

  public void actionPerformed(ActionEvent ae) {
    repaint();
  }

  // Display current selections.
  public void paint(Graphics g) {
    int[] idx;

    msg = "Current OS: ";
    idx = os.getSelectedIndexes();
    for(int i=0; i<idx.length; i++)
      msg += os.getItem(idx[i]) + "  ";
    g.drawString(msg, 20, 120);
    msg = "Current Browser: ";
    msg += browser.getSelectedItem();
    g.drawString(msg, 20, 140);
  }

  public static void main(String[] args) {
    ListDemo appwin = new ListDemo();

    appwin.setSize(new Dimension(300, 180));
    appwin.setTitle("ListDemo");
    appwin.setVisible(true);
  }
}
```

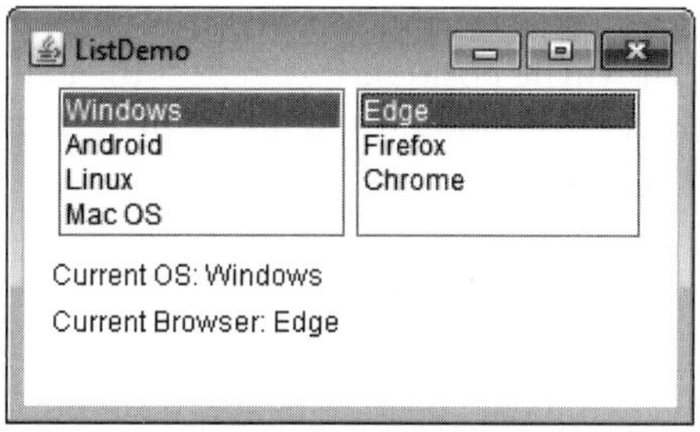


**Figure 27-5** Sample output from the **ListDemo** program



Sample output generated by the **ListDemo** program is shown in Figure 27-5.

# Managing Scroll Bars

*Scroll bars* are used to select continuous values between a specified minimum and maximum. Scroll bars may be oriented horizontally or vertically. A scroll bar is actually a composite of several individual parts. Each end has an arrow that you can click to move the current value of the scroll bar one unit in the direction of the arrow. The current value of the scroll bar relative to its minimum and maximum values is indicated by the *slider box* (or *thumb*) for the scroll bar. The slider box can be dragged by the user to a new position. The scroll bar will then reflect this value. In the background space on either side of the thumb, the user can click to cause the thumb to jump in that direction by some increment larger than 1. Typically, this action translates into some form of page up and page down. Scroll bars are encapsulated by the **Scrollbar** class.

**Scrollbar** defines the following constructors:

Scrollbar( ) throws HeadlessException
Scrollbar(int *style*) throws HeadlessException
Scrollbar(int *style*, int *initialValue*, int *thumbSize*, int *min*, int *max*)
    throws HeadlessException

The first form creates a vertical scroll bar. The second and third forms allow you to specify the orientation of the scroll bar. If *style* is **Scrollbar.VERTICAL**, a vertical scroll bar is created. If *style* is **Scrollbar.HORIZONTAL**, the scroll bar is horizontal. In the third form of the constructor, the initial value of the scroll bar is passed in *initialValue*. The number of units represented by the height of the thumb is passed in *thumbSize*. The minimum and maximum values for the scroll bar are specified by *min* and *max*.

If you construct a scroll bar by using one of the first two constructors, then you need to set its parameters by using **setValues( )**, shown here, before it can be used:

void setValues(int *initialValue*, int *thumbSize*, int *min*, int *max*)

The parameters have the same meaning as they have in the third constructor just described.

To obtain the current value of the scroll bar, call **getValue( )**. It returns the current setting. To set the current value, call **setValue( )**. These methods are as follows:

int getValue( )
void setValue(int *newValue*)

Here, *newValue* specifies the new value for the scroll bar. When you set a value, the slider box inside the scroll bar will be positioned to reflect the new value.

You can also retrieve the minimum and maximum values via **getMinimum( )** and **getMaximum( )**, shown here:

int getMinimum( )
int getMaximum( )

They return the requested quantity.

By default, 1 is the increment added to or subtracted from the scroll bar each time it is scrolled up or down one line. You can change this increment by calling **setUnitIncrement( )**. By default, page-up and page-down increments are 10. You can change this value by calling **setBlockIncrement( )**. These methods are shown here:

void setUnitIncrement(int *newIncr*)
void setBlockIncrement(int *newIncr*)

## Handling Scroll Bars

To process scroll bar events, you need to implement the **AdjustmentListener** interface. Each time a user interacts with a scroll bar, an **AdjustmentEvent** object is generated. Its **getAdjustmentType( )** method can be used to determine the type of the adjustment. The types of adjustment events are as follows:

| | |
|---|---|
| BLOCK_DECREMENT | A page-down event has been generated. |
| BLOCK_INCREMENT | A page-up event has been generated. |
| TRACK | An absolute tracking event has been generated. |
| UNIT_DECREMENT | The line-down button in a scroll bar has been pressed. |
| UNIT_INCREMENT | The line-up button in a scroll bar has been pressed. |

The following example creates both a vertical and a horizontal scroll bar. The current settings of the scroll bars are displayed. If you drag the mouse while inside the window, the coordinates of each drag event are used to update the scroll bars. An asterisk is displayed at the current drag position. Notice the use of **setPreferredSize( )** to set the size of the scroll bars.

```
// Demonstrate scroll bars.
import java.awt.*;
import java.awt.event.*;

public class SBDemo extends Frame
  implements AdjustmentListener {

  String msg = "";
  Scrollbar vertSB, horzSB;

  public SBDemo() {

    // Use a flow layout.
    setLayout(new FlowLayout());
```

```
    // Create scroll bars and set preferred size.
    vertSB = new Scrollbar(Scrollbar.VERTICAL,
                           0, 1, 0, 200);
    vertSB.setPreferredSize(new Dimension(20, 100));

    horzSB = new Scrollbar(Scrollbar.HORIZONTAL,
                           0, 1, 0, 100);
    horzSB.setPreferredSize(new Dimension(100, 20));

    // Add the scroll bars to the frame.
    add(vertSB);
    add(horzSB);

    // Add AdjustmentListeners for the scroll bars.
    vertSB.addAdjustmentListener(this);
    horzSB.addAdjustmentListener(this);

    // Add MouseMotionListener.
    addMouseMotionListener(new MouseAdapter() {
      // Update scroll bars to reflect mouse dragging.
      public void mouseDragged(MouseEvent me) {
        int x = me.getX();
        int y = me.getY();
        vertSB.setValue(y);
        horzSB.setValue(x);
        repaint();
      }
    });

    addWindowListener(new WindowAdapter() {
      public void windowClosing(WindowEvent we) {
        System.exit(0);
      }
    });
  }

  public void adjustmentValueChanged(AdjustmentEvent ae) {
    repaint();
  }

  // Display current value of scroll bars.
  public void paint(Graphics g) {
     msg = "Vertical: " + vertSB.getValue();
     msg += ", Horizontal: " + horzSB.getValue();
     g.drawString(msg, 20, 160);

     // show current mouse drag position
     g.drawString("*", horzSB.getValue(),
                  vertSB.getValue());
  }

  public static void main(String[] args) {
    SBDemo appwin = new SBDemo();
```

Part II

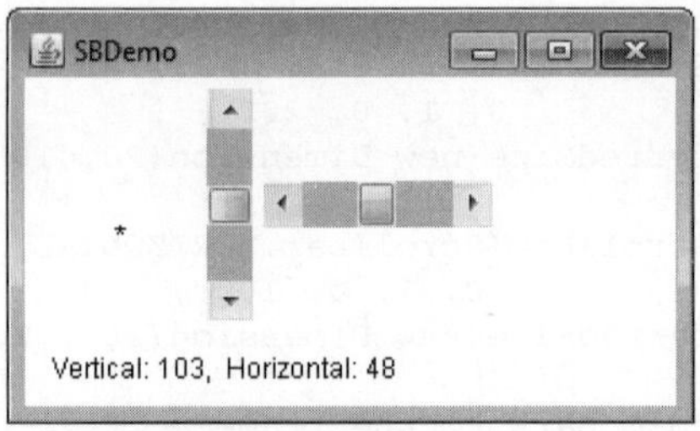


**Figure 27-6** Sample output from the **SBDemo** program

```
    appwin.setSize(new Dimension(300, 180));
    appwin.setTitle("SBDemo");
    appwin.setVisible(true);
  }
}
```

Sample output from the **SBDemo** program is shown in Figure 27-6.

## Using a TextField

The **TextField** class implements a single-line text-entry area, usually called an *edit control.* Text fields allow the user to enter strings and to edit the text using the arrow keys, cut and paste keys, and mouse selections. **TextField** is a subclass of **TextComponent**. **TextField** defines the following constructors:

TextField( ) throws HeadlessException
TextField(int *numChars*) throws HeadlessException
TextField(String *str*) throws HeadlessException
TextField(String *str*, int *numChars*) throws HeadlessException

The first version creates a default text field. The second form creates a text field that is *numChars* characters wide. The third form initializes the text field with the string contained in *str*. The fourth form initializes a text field and sets its width.

**TextField** (and its superclass **TextComponent**) provides several methods that allow you to utilize a text field. To obtain the string currently contained in the text field, call **getText( )**. To set the text, call **setText( )**. These methods are as follows:

String getText( )
void setText(String *str*)

Here, *str* is the new string.

The user can select a portion of the text in a text field. Also, you can select a portion of text under program control by using **select( )**. Your program can obtain the currently selected text by calling **getSelectedText( )**. These methods are shown here:

String getSelectedText( )
void select(int *startIndex*, int *endIndex*)

**getSelectedText( )** returns the selected text. The **select( )** method selects the characters beginning at *startIndex* and ending at *endIndex* –1.

You can control whether the contents of a text field may be modified by the user by calling **setEditable( )**. You can determine editability by calling **isEditable( )**. These methods are shown here:

boolean isEditable( )
void setEditable(boolean *canEdit*)

**isEditable( )** returns **true** if the text may be changed and **false** if not. In **setEditable( )**, if *canEdit* is **true**, the text may be changed. If it is **false**, the text cannot be altered.

There may be times when you will want the user to enter text that is not displayed, such as a password. You can disable the echoing of the characters as they are typed by calling **setEchoChar( )**. This method specifies a single character that the **TextField** will display when characters are entered (thus, the actual characters typed will not be shown). You can check a text field to see if it is in this mode with the **echoCharIsSet( )** method. You can retrieve the echo character by calling the **getEchoChar( )** method. These methods are as follows:

void setEchoChar(char *ch*)
boolean echoCharIsSet( )
char getEchoChar( )

Here, *ch* specifies the character to be echoed. If *ch* is zero, then normal echoing is restored.

## Handling a TextField

Since text fields perform their own editing functions, your program generally will not respond to individual key events that occur within a text field. However, you may want to respond when the user presses ENTER. When this occurs, an action event is generated.

Here is an example that creates the classic user name and password screen:

```
// Demonstrate text field.
import java.awt.*;
import java.awt.event.*;

public class TextFieldDemo extends Frame
  implements ActionListener {

  TextField name, pass;

  public TextFieldDemo() {

    // Use a flow layout.
    setLayout(new FlowLayout());

    // Create controls.
    Label namep = new Label("Name: ", Label.RIGHT);
    Label passp = new Label("Password: ", Label.RIGHT);
    name = new TextField(12);
    pass = new TextField(8);
    pass.setEchoChar('?');
```

Part II

```
    // Add the controls to the frame.
    add(namep);
    add(name);
    add(passp);
    add(pass);

    // Add action event handlers.
    name.addActionListener(this);
    pass.addActionListener(this);

    addWindowListener(new WindowAdapter() {
      public void windowClosing(WindowEvent we) {
        System.exit(0);
      }
    });
  }

  // User pressed Enter.
  public void actionPerformed(ActionEvent ae) {
    repaint();
  }

  public void paint(Graphics g) {
     g.drawString("Name: " + name.getText(), 20, 100);
     g.drawString("Selected text in name: "
                  + name.getSelectedText(), 20, 120);
     g.drawString("Password: " + pass.getText(), 20, 140);
  }

  public static void main(String[] args) {
    TextFieldDemo appwin = new TextFieldDemo();

    appwin.setSize(new Dimension(380, 180));
    appwin.setTitle("TextFieldDemo");
    appwin.setVisible(true);
  }
}
```

Sample output from the **TextFieldDemo** program is shown in Figure 27-7. (Of course, a real application would need to handle security concerns related to passwords. Consult the Java documentation for the latest information related to security.)

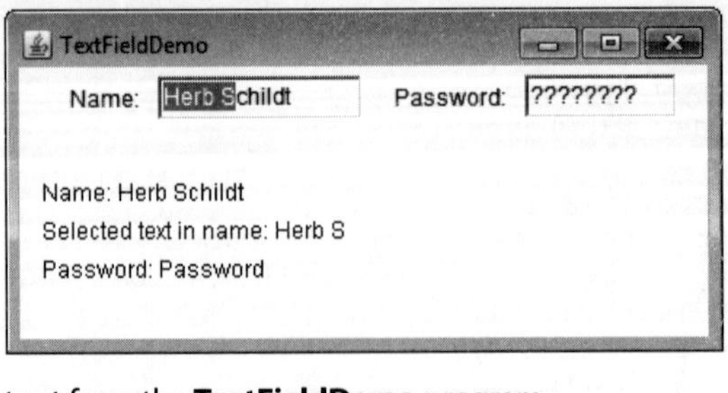


**Figure 27-7** Sample output from the **TextFieldDemo** program

## Using a TextArea

Sometimes a single line of text input is not enough for a given task. To handle these situations, the AWT includes a simple multiline editor called **TextArea**. Following are the constructors for **TextArea**:

TextArea( ) throws HeadlessException
TextArea(int *numLines*, int *numChars*) throws HeadlessException
TextArea(String *str*) throws HeadlessException
TextArea(String *str*, int *numLines*, int *numChars*) throws HeadlessException
TextArea(String *str*, int *numLines*, int *numChars*, int *sBars*) throws HeadlessException

Here, *numLines* specifies the height, in lines, of the text area, and *numChars* specifies its width, in characters. Initial text can be specified by *str*. In the fifth form, you can specify the scroll bars that you want the control to have. *sBars* must be one of these values:

| SCROLLBARS_BOTH | SCROLLBARS_NONE |
|---|---|
| SCROLLBARS_HORIZONTAL_ONLY | SCROLLBARS_VERTICAL_ONLY |

**TextArea** is a subclass of **TextComponent**. Therefore, it supports the **getText( )**, **setText( )**, **getSelectedText( )**, **select( )**, **isEditable( )**, and **setEditable( )** methods described in the preceding section.

**TextArea** adds the following editing methods:

void append(String *str*)
void insert(String *str*, int *index*)
void replaceRange(String *str*, int *startIndex*, int *endIndex*)

The **append( )** method appends the string specified by *str* to the end of the current text. **insert( )** inserts the string passed in *str* at the specified index. To replace text, call **replaceRange( )**. It replaces the characters from *startIndex* to *endIndex*–1, with the replacement text passed in *str*.

Text areas are almost self-contained controls. Your program incurs virtually no management overhead. Normally, your program simply obtains the current text when it is needed. You can, however, listen for **TextEvents**, if you choose.

The following program creates a **TextArea** control:

```
// Demonstrate TextArea.
import java.awt.*;
import java.awt.event.*;

public class TextAreaDemo extends Frame {

  public TextAreaDemo() {

    // Use a flow layout.
    setLayout(new FlowLayout());
```

```
    String val =
      "JDK 17 is the latest version of one of the most\n" +
      "widely-used computer languages for Internet programming.\n" +
      "Building on a rich heritage, Java has advanced both\n" +
      "the art and science of computer language design.\n\n" +
      "One of the reasons for Java's ongoing success is its\n" +
      "constant, steady rate of evolution. Java has never stood\n" +
      "still. Instead, Java has consistently adapted to the\n" +
      "rapidly changing landscape of the networked world.\n" +
      "Moreover, Java has often led the way, charting the\n" +
      "course for others to follow.";

    TextArea text = new TextArea(val, 10, 30);
    add(text);

    addWindowListener(new WindowAdapter() {
      public void windowClosing(WindowEvent we) {
        System.exit(0);
      }
    });
  }

  public static void main(String[] args) {
    TextAreaDemo appwin = new TextAreaDemo();

    appwin.setSize(new Dimension(300, 220));
    appwin.setTitle("TextAreaDemo");
    appwin.setVisible(true);
  }
}
```

Here is sample output from the **TextAreaDemo** program:

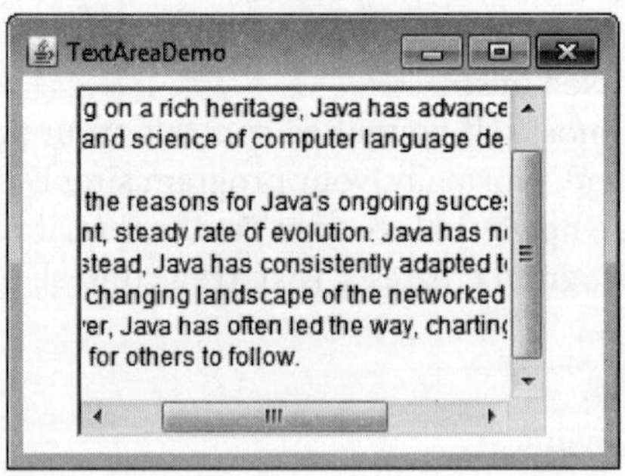


## Understanding Layout Managers

All of the components that we have shown so far have been positioned by the **FlowLayout** layout manager. As we mentioned at the beginning of this chapter, a layout manager automatically arranges your controls within a window by using some type of algorithm.

While it is possible to lay out Java controls by hand, you generally won't want to, for two main reasons. First, it is very tedious to manually lay out a large number of components. Second, sometimes the width and height information is not yet available when you need to arrange some control, because the native toolkit components haven't been realized. This is a chicken-and-egg situation; it is pretty confusing to figure out when it is okay to use the size of a given component to position it relative to another.

Each **Container** object has a layout manager associated with it. A layout manager is an instance of any class that implements the **LayoutManager** interface. The layout manager is set by the **setLayout( )** method. If no call to **setLayout( )** is made, then the default layout manager is used. Whenever a container is resized (or sized for the first time), the layout manager is used to position each of the components within it.

The **setLayout( )** method has the following general form:

void setLayout(LayoutManager *layoutObj*)

Here, *layoutObj* is a reference to the desired layout manager. If you wish to disable the layout manager and position components manually, pass **null** for *layoutObj*. If you do this, you will need to determine the shape and position of each component manually, using the **setBounds( )** method defined by **Component**. Normally, you will want to use a layout manager.

Each layout manager keeps track of a list of components that are stored by their names. The layout manager is notified each time you add a component to a container. Whenever the container needs to be resized, the layout manager is consulted via its **minimumLayoutSize( )** and **preferredLayoutSize( )** methods. Each component that is being managed by a layout manager contains the **getPreferredSize( )** and **getMinimumSize( )** methods. These return the preferred and minimum size required to display each component. The layout manager will honor these requests if at all possible, while maintaining the integrity of the layout policy. You may override these methods for controls that you subclass. Default values are provided otherwise.

Java has several predefined **LayoutManager** classes, several of which are described next. You can use the layout manager that best fits your application.

## FlowLayout

You have already seen **FlowLayout** in action. It is the layout manager that the preceding examples have used. **FlowLayout** implements a simple layout style, which is similar to how words flow in a text editor. The direction of the layout is governed by the container's component orientation property, which, by default, is left to right, top to bottom. Therefore, by default, components are laid out line-by-line beginning at the upper-left corner. In all cases, when a line is filled, layout advances to the next line. A small space is left between each component, above and below, as well as left and right. Here are the constructors for **FlowLayout**:

FlowLayout( )
FlowLayout(int *how*)
FlowLayout(int *how*, int *horz*, int *vert*)

The first form creates the default layout, which centers components and leaves five pixels of space between each component. The second form lets you specify how each line is aligned. Valid values for *how* are as follows:

FlowLayout.LEFT
FlowLayout.CENTER
FlowLayout.RIGHT
FlowLayout.LEADING
FlowLayout.TRAILING

These values specify left, center, right, leading edge, and trailing edge alignment, respectively. The third constructor allows you to specify the horizontal and vertical space left between components in *horz* and *vert*, respectively.

You can see the effect of specifying an alignment with **FlowLayout** by substituting this line in the **CheckboxDemo** program shown earlier:

```
setLayout(new FlowLayout(FlowLayout.LEFT));
```

After making this change, the output will look like that shown here. Compare this with the original output, shown in Figure 27-2.

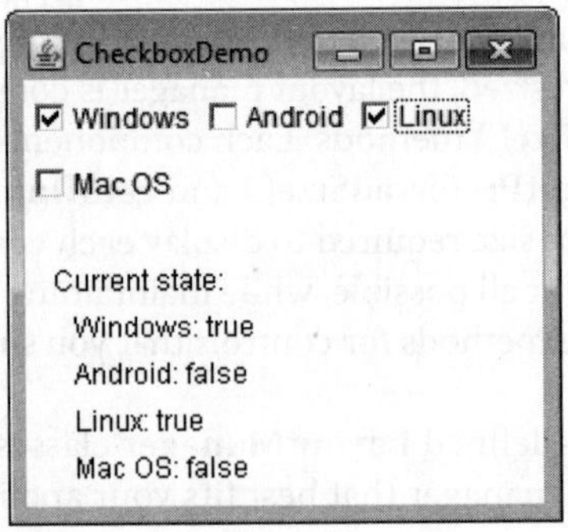


## BorderLayout

The **BorderLayout** class implements a layout style that has four narrow, fixed-width components at the edges and one large area in the center. The four sides are referred to as north, south, east, and west. The middle area is called the center. **BorderLayout** is the default layout manager for **Frame**. Here are the constructors defined by **BorderLayout**:

BorderLayout( )
BorderLayout(int *horz*, int *vert*)

The first form creates a default border layout. The second allows you to specify the horizontal and vertical space left between components in *horz* and *vert*, respectively.

**BorderLayout** defines the following commonly used constants that specify the regions:

| | |
|---|---|
| BorderLayout.CENTER | BorderLayout.SOUTH |
| BorderLayout.EAST | BorderLayout.WEST |
| BorderLayout.NORTH | |

When adding components, you will use these constants with the following form of **add( )**, which is defined by **Container**:

void add(Component *compRef*, Object *region*)

Here, *compRef* is a reference to the component to be added, and *region* specifies where the component will be added.

Here is an example of a **BorderLayout** with a component in each layout area:

```
// Demonstrate BorderLayout.
import java.awt.*;
import java.awt.event.*;

public class BorderLayoutDemo extends Frame {
  public BorderLayoutDemo() {

   // Here, BorderLayout is used by default.

    add(new Button("This is across the top."),
        BorderLayout.NORTH);
    add(new Label("The footer message might go here."),
        BorderLayout.SOUTH);
    add(new Button("Right"), BorderLayout.EAST);
    add(new Button("Left"), BorderLayout.WEST);

    String msg = "The reasonable man adapts " +
      "himself to the world;\n" +
      "the unreasonable one persists in " +
      "trying to adapt the world to himself.\n" +
      "Therefore all progress depends " +
      "on the unreasonable man.\n\n" +
      "         - George Bernard Shaw\n\n";

    add(new TextArea(msg), BorderLayout.CENTER);

    addWindowListener(new WindowAdapter() {
      public void windowClosing(WindowEvent we) {
        System.exit(0);
      }
    });
  }

  public static void main(String[] args) {
    BorderLayoutDemo appwin = new BorderLayoutDemo();

    appwin.setSize(new Dimension(300, 220));
    appwin.setTitle("BorderLayoutDemo");
    appwin.setVisible(true);
  }
}
```

Part II

Sample output from the **BorderLayoutDemo** program is shown here:

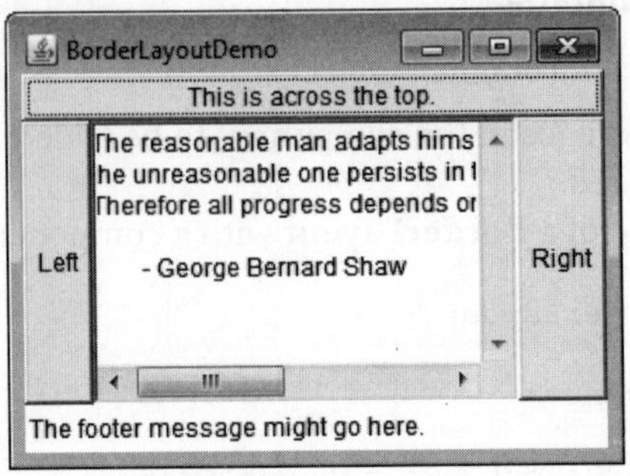


## Using Insets

Sometimes you will want to leave a small amount of space between the container that holds your components and the window that contains it. To do this, override the **getInsets( )** method that is defined by **Container**. This method returns an **Insets** object that contains the top, bottom, left, and right inset to be used when the container is displayed. These values are used by the layout manager to inset the components when it lays out the window. The constructor for **Insets** is shown here:

Insets(int *top*, int *left*, int *bottom*, int *right*)

The values passed in *top, left, bottom,* and *right* specify the amount of space between the container and its enclosing window.

The **getInsets( )** method has this general form:

Insets getInsets( )

When overriding this method, you must return a new **Insets** object that contains the inset spacing you desire.

Here is the preceding **BorderLayout** example modified so that it insets its components. The background color has been set to cyan to help make the insets more visible.

```
// Demonstrate BorderLayout with insets.
import java.awt.*;
import java.awt.event.*;

public class InsetsDemo extends Frame {

  public InsetsDemo() {
    // Here, BorderLayout is used by default.

    // set background color so insets can be easily seen
    setBackground(Color.cyan);

    setLayout(new BorderLayout());
```

```
    add(new Button("This is across the top."),
        BorderLayout.NORTH);
    add(new Label("The footer message might go here."),
        BorderLayout.SOUTH);
    add(new Button("Right"), BorderLayout.EAST);
    add(new Button("Left"), BorderLayout.WEST);

    String msg = "The reasonable man adapts " +
      "himself to the world;\n" +
      "the unreasonable one persists in " +
      "trying to adapt the world to himself.\n" +
      "Therefore all progress depends " +
      "on the unreasonable man.\n\n" +
      "        - George Bernard Shaw\n\n";

    add(new TextArea(msg), BorderLayout.CENTER);

    addWindowListener(new WindowAdapter() {
      public void windowClosing(WindowEvent we) {
        System.exit(0);
      }
    });
  }

  // Override getInsets to add inset values.
  public Insets getInsets() {
    return new Insets(40, 20, 10, 20);
  }

  public static void main(String[] args) {
    InsetsDemo appwin = new InsetsDemo();

    appwin.setSize(new Dimension(300, 220));
    appwin.setTitle("InsetsDemo");
    appwin.setVisible(true);
  }
}
```



Sample output from the **InsetsDemo** program is shown here:

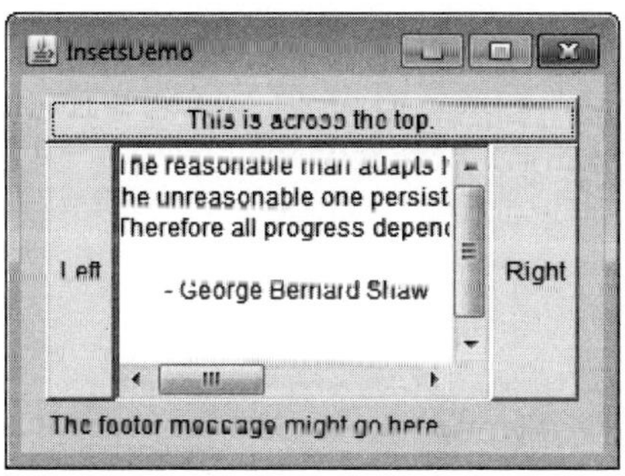

## GridLayout

**GridLayout** lays out components in a two-dimensional grid. When you instantiate a **GridLayout**, you define the number of rows and columns. The constructors supported by **GridLayout** are shown here:

GridLayout( )
GridLayout(int *numRows*, int *numColumns*)
GridLayout(int *numRows*, int *numColumns*, int *horz*, int *vert*)

The first form creates a single-column grid layout. The second form creates a grid layout with the specified number of rows and columns. The third form allows you to specify the horizontal and vertical space left between components in *horz* and *vert*, respectively. Either *numRows* or *numColumns* can be zero. Specifying *numRows* as zero allows for unlimited-length columns. Specifying *numColumns* as zero allows for unlimited-length rows.

Here is a sample program that creates a 4×4 grid and fills it in with 15 buttons, each labeled with its index:

```
// Demonstrate GridLayout
import java.awt.*;
import java.awt.event.*;

public class GridLayoutDemo extends Frame {
  static final int n = 4;

  public GridLayoutDemo() {

    // Use GridLayout.
    setLayout(new GridLayout(n, n));

    setFont(new Font("SansSerif", Font.BOLD, 24));

    for(int i = 0; i < n; i++) {
      for(int j = 0; j < n; j++) {
        int k = i * n + j;
        if(k > 0)
          add(new Button("" + k));
      }
    }

    addWindowListener(new WindowAdapter() {
      public void windowClosing(WindowEvent we) {
        System.exit(0);
      }
    });
  }

  public static void main(String[] args) {
    GridLayoutDemo appwin = new GridLayoutDemo();
```

```
    appwin.setSize(new Dimension(300, 220));
    appwin.setTitle("GridLayoutDemo");
    appwin.setVisible(true);
  }
}
```

Following is sample output generated by the **GridLayoutDemo** program:

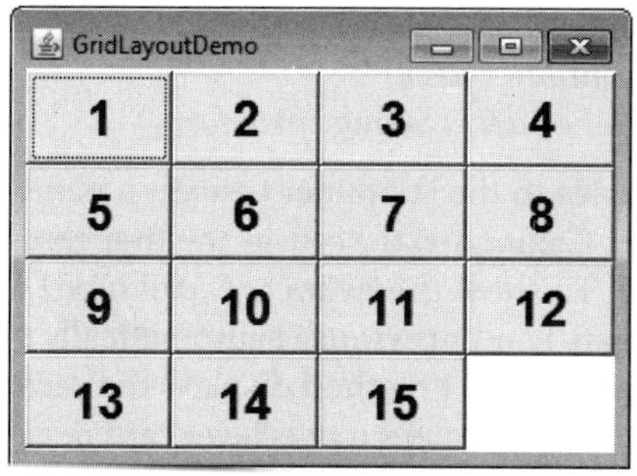




**TIP** You might try using this example as the starting point for a 15-square puzzle.

## CardLayout

The **CardLayout** class is unique among the other layout managers in that it stores several different layouts. Each layout can be thought of as being on a separate index card in a deck that can be shuffled so that any card is on top at a given time. This can be useful for user interfaces with optional components that can be dynamically enabled and disabled upon user input. You can prepare the other layouts and have them hidden, ready to be activated when needed.

**CardLayout** provides these two constructors:

CardLayout( )
CardLayout(int *horz*, int *vert*)

The first form creates a default card layout. The second form allows you to specify the horizontal and vertical space left between components in *horz* and *vert*, respectively.

Use of a card layout requires a bit more work than the other layouts. The cards are typically held in an object of type **Panel**. This panel must have **CardLayout** selected as its layout manager. The cards that form the deck are also typically objects of type **Panel**. Thus, you must create a panel that contains the deck and a panel for each card in the deck. Next, you add to the appropriate panel the components that form each card. You then add these panels to the panel for which **CardLayout** is the layout manager. Finally, you add this panel to the window. Once these steps are complete, you must provide some way for the user to select between cards. One common approach is to include one push button for each card in the deck.

When card panels are added to a panel, they are usually given a name. One way to do this is to use this form of **add( )** when adding cards to a panel:

void add(Component *panelRef*, Object *name*)

Here, *name* is a string that specifies the name of the card whose panel is specified by *panelRef.*

After you have created a deck, your program activates a card by calling one of the following methods defined by **CardLayout**:

void first(Container *deck*)
void last(Container *deck*)
void next(Container *deck*)
void previous(Container *deck*)
void show(Container *deck*, String *cardName*)

Here, *deck* is a reference to the container (usually a panel) that holds the cards, and *cardName* is the name of a card. Calling **first( )** causes the first card in the deck to be shown. To show the last card, call **last( )**. To show the next card, call **next( )**. To show the previous card, call **previous( )**. Both **next( )** and **previous( )** automatically cycle back to the top or bottom of the deck, respectively. The **show( )** method displays the card whose name is passed in *cardName.*

The following example creates a two-level card deck that allows the user to select an operating system. Windows-based operating systems are displayed in one card. Mac OS, Android, and Linux are displayed in the other card.

```
// Demonstrate CardLayout.
import java.awt.*;
import java.awt.event.*;

public class CardLayoutDemo extends Frame {

  Checkbox windows10, windows7, windows8, android, linux, mac;
  Panel osCards;
  CardLayout cardLO;
  Button win, other;

  public CardLayoutDemo() {

    // Use a flow layout for the main frame.
    setLayout(new FlowLayout());

    win = new Button("Windows");
    other = new Button("Other");
    add(win);
    add(other);

    // Set osCards panel to use CardLayout.
    cardLO = new CardLayout();
    osCards = new Panel();
    osCards.setLayout(cardLO);

    windows7 = new Checkbox("Windows 7", true);
    windows8 = new Checkbox("Windows 8");
```

```
    windows10 = new Checkbox("Windows 10");
    android = new Checkbox("Android");
    linux = new Checkbox("Linux");
    mac = new Checkbox("Mac OS");

    // Add Windows check boxes to a panel.
    Panel winPan = new Panel();
    winPan.add(windows7);
    winPan.add(windows8);
    winPan.add(windows10);

    // Add other OS check boxes to a panel.
    Panel otherPan = new Panel();
    otherPan.add(android);
    otherPan.add(linux);
    otherPan.add(mac);

    // Add panels to card deck panel.
    osCards.add(winPan, "Windows");
    osCards.add(otherPan, "Other");

    // Add cards to main frame panel.
    add(osCards);

    // Use lambda expressions to handle button events.
    win.addActionListener((ae) -> cardLO.show(osCards, "Windows"));
    other.addActionListener((ae) -> cardLO.show(osCards, "Other"));

    // Register for mouse pressed events.
    addMouseListener(new MouseAdapter() {
      // Cycle through panels.
      public void mousePressed(MouseEvent me) {
        cardLO.next(osCards);
      }
    });

    addWindowListener(new WindowAdapter() {
      public void windowClosing(WindowEvent we) {
        System.exit(0);
      }
    });
  }

  public static void main(String[] args) {
    CardLayoutDemo appwin = new CardLayoutDemo();

    appwin.setSize(new Dimension(300, 220));
    appwin.setTitle("CardLayoutDemo");
    appwin.setVisible(true);
  }
}
```

Here is sample output generated by the **CardLayoutDemo** program. Each card is activated by pushing its button. You can also cycle through the cards by clicking the mouse.

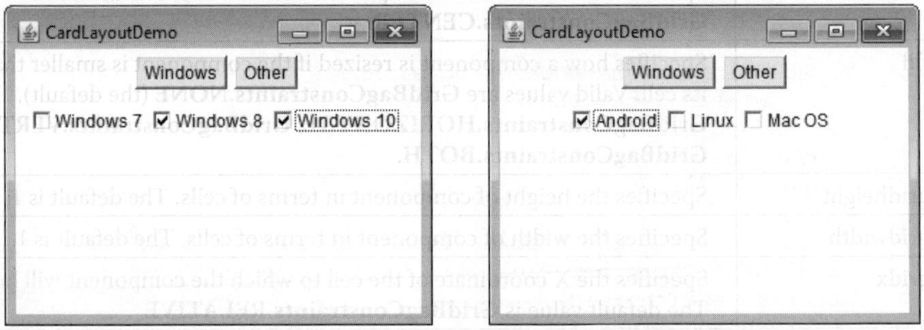


## GridBagLayout

Although the preceding layouts are perfectly acceptable for many uses, some situations will require that you take a bit more control over how the components are arranged. A good way to do this is to use a grid bag layout, which is specified by the **GridBagLayout** class. What makes the grid bag useful is that you can specify the relative placement of components by specifying their positions within cells inside a grid. The key to the grid bag is that each component can be a different size, and each row in the grid can have a different number of columns. This is why the layout is called a *grid bag*. It's a collection of small grids joined together.

The location and size of each component in a grid bag are determined by a set of constraints linked to it. The constraints are contained in an object of type **GridBagConstraints**. Constraints include the height and width of a cell, and the placement of a component, its alignment, and its anchor point within the cell.

The general procedure for using a grid bag is to first create a new **GridBagLayout** object and to make it the current layout manager. Then, set the constraints that apply to each component that will be added to the grid bag. Finally, add the components to the layout manager. Although **GridBagLayout** is a bit more complicated than the other layout managers, it is still quite easy to use once you understand how it works.

**GridBagLayout** defines only one constructor, which is shown here:

GridBagLayout( )

**GridBagLayout** defines several methods, of which many are protected and not for general use. There is one method, however, that you must use: **setConstraints( )**. It is shown here:

void setConstraints(Component *comp*, GridBagConstraints *cons*)

Here, *comp* is the component for which the constraints specified by *cons* apply. This method sets the constraints that apply to each component in the grid bag.

The key to successfully using **GridBagLayout** is the proper setting of the constraints, which are stored in a **GridBagConstraints** object. **GridBagConstraints** defines several fields that you can set to govern the size, placement, and spacing of a component. These are shown in Table 27-1. Several are described in greater detail in the following discussion.

| Field | Purpose |
|---|---|
| int anchor | Specifies the location of a component within a cell. The default is **GridBagConstraints.CENTER**. |
| int fill | Specifies how a component is resized if the component is smaller than its cell. Valid values are **GridBagConstraints.NONE** (the default), **GridBagConstraints.HORIZONTAL**, **GridBagConstraints.VERTICAL**, and **GridBagConstraints.BOTH**. |
| int gridheight | Specifies the height of component in terms of cells. The default is 1. |
| int gridwidth | Specifies the width of component in terms of cells. The default is 1. |
| int gridx | Specifies the X coordinate of the cell to which the component will be added. The default value is **GridBagConstraints.RELATIVE**. |
| int gridy | Specifies the Y coordinate of the cell to which the component will be added. The default value is **GridBagConstraints.RELATIVE**. |
| Insets insets | Specifies the insets. Default insets are all zero. |
| int ipadx | Specifies extra horizontal space that surrounds a component within a cell. The default is 0. |
| int ipady | Specifies extra vertical space that surrounds a component within a cell. The default is 0. |
| double weightx | Specifies a weight value that determines the horizontal spacing between cells and the edges of the container that holds them. The default value is 0.0. The greater the weight, the more space that is allocated. If all values are 0.0, extra space is distributed evenly between the edges of the window. |
| double weighty | Specifies a weight value that determines the vertical spacing between cells and the edges of the container that holds them. The default value is 0.0. The greater the weight, the more space that is allocated. If all values are 0.0, extra space is distributed evenly between the edges of the window. |

**Table 27-1** Constraint Fields Defined by **GridBagConstraints**

**GridBagConstraints** also defines several static fields that contain standard constraint values, such as **GridBagConstraints.CENTER** and **GridBagConstraints.VERTICAL**.

When a component is smaller than its cell, you can use the **anchor** field to specify where within the cell the component's top-left corner will be located. There are three types of values that you can give to **anchor**. The first are absolute:

| | |
|---|---|
| GridBagConstraints.CENTER | GridBagConstraints.SOUTH |
| GridBagConstraints.EAST | GridBagConstraints.SOUTHEAST |
| GridBagConstraints.NORTH | GridBagConstraints.SOUTHWEST |
| GridBagConstraints.NORTHEAST | GridBagConstraints.WEST |
| GridBagConstraints.NORTHWEST | |

As their names imply, these values cause the component to be placed at the specific locations.

The second type of values that can be given to **anchor** is relative, which means the values are relative to the container's orientation, which might differ for non-Western languages. The relative values are shown here:

| | |
|---|---|
| GridBagConstraints.FIRST_LINE_END | GridBagConstraints.LINE_END |
| GridBagConstraints.FIRST_LINE_START | GridBagConstraints.LINE_START |
| GridBagConstraints.LAST_LINE_END | GridBagConstraints.PAGE_END |
| GridBagConstraints.LAST_LINE_START | GridBagConstraints.PAGE_START |

Their names describe the placement.

The third type of values that can be given to **anchor** allows you to position components relative to the baseline of the row. These values are shown here:

| | |
|---|---|
| GridBagConstraints.BASELINE | GridBagConstraints.BASELINE_LEADING |
| GridBagConstraints.BASELINE_TRAILING | GridBagConstraints.ABOVE_BASELINE |
| GridBagConstraints.ABOVE_BASELINE_LEADING | GridBagConstraints.ABOVE_BASELINE_TRAILING |
| GridBagConstraints.BELOW_BASELINE | GridBagConstraints.BELOW_BASELINE_LEADING |
| GridBagConstraints. BELOW_BASELINE_TRAILING | |

The horizontal position can be either centered, against the leading edge (LEADING), or against the trailing edge (TRAILING).

The **weightx** and **weighty** fields are both quite important and quite confusing at first glance. In general, their values determine how much of the extra space within a container is allocated to each row and column. By default, both these values are zero. When all values within a row or a column are zero, extra space is distributed evenly between the edges of the window. By increasing the weight, you increase that row or column's allocation of space proportional to the other rows or columns. The best way to understand how these values work is to experiment with them a bit.

The **gridwidth** variable lets you specify the width of a cell in terms of cell units. The default is 1. To specify that a component use the remaining space in a row, use **GridBagConstraints.REMAINDER**. To specify that a component use the next-to-last cell in a row, use **GridBagConstraints.RELATIVE**. The **gridheight** constraint works the same way, but in the vertical direction.

You can specify a padding value that will be used to increase the minimum size of a cell. To pad horizontally, assign a value to **ipadx**. To pad vertically, assign a value to **ipady**.

Here is an example that uses **GridBagLayout** to demonstrate several of the points just discussed:

```
// Use GridBagLayout.
import java.awt.*;
import java.awt.event.*;
```

```
public class GridBagDemo extends Frame
  implements ItemListener {

  String msg = "";
  Checkbox windows, android, linux, mac;

  public GridBagDemo() {

    // Use a GridBagLayout
    GridBagLayout gbag = new GridBagLayout();
    GridBagConstraints gbc = new GridBagConstraints();
    setLayout(gbag);

    // Define check boxes.
    windows = new Checkbox("Windows ", true);
    android = new Checkbox("Android");
    linux = new Checkbox("Linux");
    mac = new Checkbox("Mac OS");

    // Define the grid bag.

    // Use default row weight of 0 for first row.
    gbc.weightx = 1.0; // use a column weight of 1
    gbc.ipadx = 200; // pad by 200 units
    gbc.insets = new Insets(0, 6, 0, 0); // inset slightly from left

    gbc.anchor = GridBagConstraints.NORTHEAST;

    gbc.gridwidth = GridBagConstraints.RELATIVE;
    gbag.setConstraints(windows, gbc);

    gbc.gridwidth = GridBagConstraints.REMAINDER;
    gbag.setConstraints(android, gbc);

    // Give second row a weight of 1.
    gbc.weighty = 1.0;

    gbc.gridwidth = GridBagConstraints.RELATIVE;
    gbag.setConstraints(linux, gbc);

    gbc.gridwidth = GridBagConstraints.REMAINDER;
    gbag.setConstraints(mac, gbc);

    // Add the components.
    add(windows);
    add(android);
    add(linux);
    add(mac);

    // Register to receive item events.
    windows.addItemListener(this);
    android.addItemListener(this);
    linux.addItemListener(this);
    mac.addItemListener(this);
```

```
    addWindowListener(new WindowAdapter() {
      public void windowClosing(WindowEvent we) {
        System.exit(0);
      }
    });
  }

  // Repaint when status of a check box changes.
  public void itemStateChanged(ItemEvent ie) {
    repaint();
  }

  // Display current state of the check boxes.
  public void paint(Graphics g) {
    msg = "Current state: ";
    g.drawString(msg, 20, 100);
    msg = "  Windows: " + windows.getState();
    g.drawString(msg, 30, 120);
    msg = "  Android: " + android.getState();
    g.drawString(msg, 30, 140);
    msg = "  Linux: " + linux.getState();
    g.drawString(msg, 30, 160);
    msg = "  Mac OS: " + mac.getState();
    g.drawString(msg, 30, 180);
  }

  public static void main(String[] args) {
    GridBagDemo appwin = new GridBagDemo();

    appwin.setSize(new Dimension(250, 200));
    appwin.setTitle("GridBagDemo");
    appwin.setVisible(true);
  }
}
```

Sample output produced by the program is shown here.

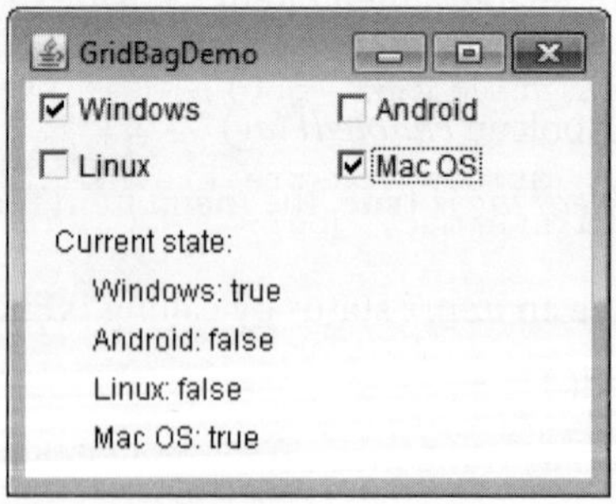


In this layout, the operating system check boxes are positioned in a 2×2 grid. Each cell has a horizontal padding of 200. Each component is inset slightly (by 6 units) from the left. The column weight is set to 1, which causes any extra horizontal space to be distributed evenly between the columns. The first row uses a default weight of 0; the second has a weight of 1. This means that any extra vertical space is added to the second row.

**GridBagLayout** is a powerful layout manager. It is worth taking some time to experiment with and explore. Once you understand what the various settings do, you can use **GridBagLayout** to position components with a high degree of precision.

## Menu Bars and Menus

A top-level window can have a menu bar associated with it. A menu bar displays a list of top-level menu choices. Each choice is associated with a drop-down menu. This concept is implemented in the AWT by the following classes: **MenuBar**, **Menu**, and **MenuItem**. In general, a menu bar contains one or more **Menu** objects. Each **Menu** object contains a list of **MenuItem** objects. Each **MenuItem** object represents something that can be selected by the user. Since **Menu** is a subclass of **MenuItem**, a hierarchy of nested submenus can be created. It is also possible to include checkable menu items. These are menu options of type **CheckboxMenuItem** and will have a check mark next to them when they are selected.

To create a menu bar, first create an instance of **MenuBar**. This class defines only the default constructor. Next, create instances of **Menu** that will define the selections displayed on the bar. Following are the constructors for **Menu**:

Menu( ) throws HeadlessException
Menu(String *optionName*) throws HeadlessException
Menu(String *optionName*, boolean *removable*) throws HeadlessException

Here, *optionName* specifies the name of the menu selection. If *removable* is **true**, the menu can be removed and allowed to float free. Otherwise, it will remain attached to the menu bar. (Removable menus are implementation-dependent.) The first form creates an empty menu.

Individual menu items are of type **MenuItem**. It defines these constructors:

MenuItem( ) throws HeadlessException
MenuItem(String *itemName*) throws HeadlessException
MenuItem(String *itemName*, MenuShortcut *keyAccel*) throws HeadlessException

Here, *itemName* is the name shown in the menu, and *keyAccel* is the menu shortcut for this item.

You can disable or enable a menu item by using the **setEnabled( )** method. Its form is shown here:

void setEnabled(boolean *enabledFlag*)

If the argument *enabledFlag* is **true**, the menu item is enabled. If **false**, the menu item is disabled.

You can determine an item's status by calling **isEnabled( )**. This method is shown here:

boolean isEnabled( )

**isEnabled( )** returns **true** if the menu item on which it is called is enabled. Otherwise, it returns **false**.

You can change the name of a menu item by calling **setLabel( )**. You can retrieve the current name by using **getLabel( )**. These methods are as follows:

void setLabel(String *newName*)
String getLabel( )

Here, *newName* becomes the new name of the invoking menu item. **getLabel( )** returns the current name.

You can create a checkable menu item by using a subclass of **MenuItem** called **CheckboxMenuItem**. It has these constructors:

CheckboxMenuItem( ) throws HeadlessException
CheckboxMenuItem(String *itemName*) throws HeadlessException
CheckboxMenuItem(String *itemName*, boolean *on*) throws HeadlessException

Here, *itemName* is the name shown in the menu. Checkable items operate as toggles. Each time one is selected, its state changes. In the first two forms, the checkable entry is unchecked. In the third form, if *on* is **true**, the checkable entry is initially checked. Otherwise, it is cleared.

You can obtain the status of a checkable item by calling **getState( )**. You can set it to a known state by using **setState( )**. These methods are shown here:

boolean getState( )
void setState(boolean *checked*)

If the item is checked, **getState( )** returns **true**. Otherwise, it returns **false**. To check an item, pass **true** to **setState( )**. To clear an item, pass **false**.

Once you have created a menu item, you must add the item to a **Menu** object by using **add( )**, which has the following general form:

MenuItem add(MenuItem *item*)

Here, *item* is the item being added. Items are added to a menu in the order in which the calls to **add( )** take place. The *item* is returned.

Once you have added all items to a **Menu** object, you can add that object to the menu bar by using this version of **add( )** defined by **MenuBar**:

Menu add(Menu *menu*)

Here, *menu* is the menu being added. The *menu* is returned.

Menus generate events only when an item of type **MenuItem** or **CheckboxMenuItem** is selected. They do not generate events when a menu bar is accessed to display a drop-down menu, for example. Each time a menu item is selected, an **ActionEvent** object is generated. By default, the action command string is the name of the menu item. However, you can specify a different action command string by calling **setActionCommand( )** on the menu item. Each time a check box menu item is checked or unchecked, an **ItemEvent** object is generated. Thus, you must implement the **ActionListener** and/or **ItemListener** interfaces in order to handle these menu events.

The **getItem( )** method of **ItemEvent** returns a reference to the item that generated this event. The general form of this method is shown here:

Object getItem( )

Following is an example that adds a series of nested menus to a pop-up window. The item selected is displayed in the window. The state of the two check box menu items is also displayed.

```
// Illustrate menus.
import java.awt.*;
import java.awt.event.*;

class MenuDemo extends Frame {
  String msg = "";
  CheckboxMenuItem debug, test;

  public MenuDemo() {

    // Create menu bar and add it to frame.
    MenuBar mbar = new MenuBar();
    setMenuBar(mbar);

    // Create the menu items.
    Menu file = new Menu("File");
    MenuItem item1, item2, item3, item4, item5;
    file.add(item1 = new MenuItem("New..."));
    file.add(item2 = new MenuItem("Open..."));
    file.add(item3 = new MenuItem("Close"));
    file.add(item4 = new MenuItem("-"));
    file.add(item5 = new MenuItem("Quit..."));
    mbar.add(file);

    Menu edit = new Menu("Edit");
    MenuItem item6, item7, item8, item9;
    edit.add(item6 = new MenuItem("Cut"));
    edit.add(item7 = new MenuItem("Copy"));
    edit.add(item8 = new MenuItem("Paste"));
    edit.add(item9 = new MenuItem("-"));

    Menu sub = new Menu("Special");
    MenuItem item10, item11, item12;
    sub.add(item10 = new MenuItem("First"));
    sub.add(item11 = new MenuItem("Second"));
    sub.add(item12 = new MenuItem("Third"));
    edit.add(sub);

    // These are checkable menu items.
    debug = new CheckboxMenuItem("Debug");
    edit.add(debug);
    test = new CheckboxMenuItem("Testing");
    edit.add(test);

    mbar.add(edit);

    // Create an object to handle action and item events.
    MyMenuHandler handler = new MyMenuHandler();

    // Register to receive those events.
    item1.addActionListener(handler);
    item2.addActionListener(handler);
    item3.addActionListener(handler);
```

Part II

```
    item4.addActionListener(handler);
    item6.addActionListener(handler);
    item7.addActionListener(handler);
    item8.addActionListener(handler);
    item9.addActionListener(handler);
    item10.addActionListener(handler);
    item11.addActionListener(handler);
    item12.addActionListener(handler);
    debug.addItemListener(handler);
    test.addItemListener(handler);

    // Use a lambda expression to handle the Quit selection.
    item5.addActionListener((ae) -> System.exit(0));

    addWindowListener(new WindowAdapter() {
      public void windowClosing(WindowEvent we) {
        System.exit(0);
      }
    });
  }

  public void paint(Graphics g) {
    g.drawString(msg, 10, 220);

   if(debug.getState())
      g.drawString("Debug is on.", 10, 240);
    else
      g.drawString("Debug is off.", 10, 240);

    if(test.getState())
      g.drawString("Testing is on.", 10, 260);
    else
      g.drawString("Testing is off.", 10, 260);
  }

  public static void main(String[] args) {
    MenuDemo appwin = new MenuDemo();

    appwin.setSize(new Dimension(250, 300));
    appwin.setTitle("MenuDemo");
    appwin.setVisible(true);
  }

  // An inner class for handling action and item events
  // for the menu.
  class MyMenuHandler implements ActionListener, ItemListener {

    // Handle action events.
    public void actionPerformed(ActionEvent ae) {
        msg = "You selected ";
        String arg = ae.getActionCommand();
```

```
        if(arg.equals("New..."))
          msg += "New.";
        else if(arg.equals("Open..."))
          msg += "Open.";
        else if(arg.equals("Close"))
          msg += "Close.";
        else if(arg.equals("Edit"))
          msg += "Edit.";
        else if(arg.equals("Cut"))
          msg += "Cut.";
        else if(arg.equals("Copy"))
          msg += "Copy.";
        else if(arg.equals("Paste"))
          msg += "Paste.";
        else if(arg.equals("First"))
          msg += "First.";
        else if(arg.equals("Second"))
          msg += "Second.";
        else if(arg.equals("Third"))
          msg += "Third.";
        else if(arg.equals("Debug"))
          msg += "Debug.";
        else if(arg.equals("Testing"))
          msg += "Testing.";

        repaint();
      }

      // Handle item events.
      public void itemStateChanged(ItemEvent ie) {
        repaint();
      }
    }
}
```



Sample output from the **MenuDemo** program is shown in Figure 27-8.

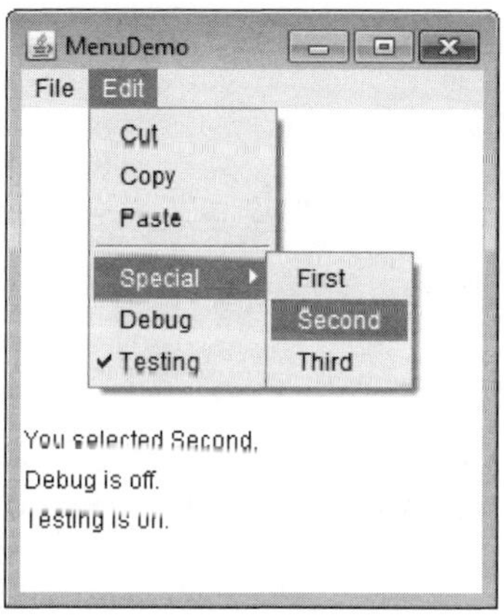


**Figure 27-8** Sample output from the **MenuDemo** program

There is one other menu-related class that you might find interesting: **PopupMenu**. It works just like **Menu** but produces a menu that can be displayed at a specific location. **PopupMenu** provides a flexible, useful alternative for some types of menuing situations.

## Dialog Boxes

Often, you will want to use a *dialog box* to hold a set of related controls. Dialog boxes are primarily used to obtain user input and are often child windows of a top-level window. Dialog boxes don't have menu bars, but in other respects, they function like frame windows. (You can add controls to them, for example, in the same way that you add controls to a frame window.) Dialog boxes may be modal or modeless. In general terms, when a *modal* dialog box is active, you cannot access other windows in your program (except for child windows of the dialog window) until you have closed the dialog box. When a *modeless* dialog box is active, input focus can be directed to another window in your program. Thus, other parts of your program remain active and accessible. Beginning with JDK 6, modal dialog boxes can be created with three different types of modality, as specified by the **Dialog.ModalityType** enumeration. The default is **APPLICATION_MODAL**, which prevents the use of other top-level windows in the application. This is the traditional type of modality. Other types are **DOCUMENT_MODAL** and **TOOLKIT_MODAL**. The **MODELESS** type is also included.

In the AWT, dialog boxes are of type **Dialog**. Two commonly used constructors are shown here:

Dialog(Frame *parentWindow*, boolean *mode*)
Dialog(Frame *parentWindow*, String *title*, boolean *mode*)

Here, *parentWindow* is the owner of the dialog box. If *mode* is **true**, the dialog box uses the default modality. Otherwise, it is modeless. The title of the dialog box can be passed in *title*. Generally, you will subclass **Dialog**, adding the functionality required by your application.

Following is a modified version of the preceding menu program that displays a modeless dialog box when the New option is chosen. Notice that when the dialog box is closed, **dispose( )** is called. This method is defined by **Window**, and it frees all system resources associated with the dialog box window.

```
// Illustrate a dialog box.
import java.awt.*;
import java.awt.event.*;

class DialogDemo extends Frame {
  String msg = "";
  CheckboxMenuItem debug, test;
  SampleDialog myDialog;

  public DialogDemo() {

    // Create the dialog box.
    myDialog  = new SampleDialog(this, "New Dialog Box");
```

```
// Create menu bar and add it to frame.
MenuBar mbar = new MenuBar();
setMenuBar(mbar);

// Create the menu items.
Menu file = new Menu("File");
MenuItem item1, item2, item3, item4, item5;
file.add(item1 = new MenuItem("New..."));
file.add(item2 = new MenuItem("Open..."));
file.add(item3 = new MenuItem("Close"));
file.add(item4 = new MenuItem("-"));
file.add(item5 = new MenuItem("Quit..."));
mbar.add(file);

Menu edit = new Menu("Edit");
MenuItem item6, item7, item8, item9;
edit.add(item6 = new MenuItem("Cut"));
edit.add(item7 = new MenuItem("Copy"));
edit.add(item8 = new MenuItem("Paste"));
edit.add(item9 = new MenuItem("-"));

Menu sub = new Menu("Special");
MenuItem item10, item11, item12;
sub.add(item10 = new MenuItem("First"));
sub.add(item11 = new MenuItem("Second"));
sub.add(item12 = new MenuItem("Third"));
edit.add(sub);

// These are checkable menu items.
debug = new CheckboxMenuItem("Debug");
edit.add(debug);
test = new CheckboxMenuItem("Testing");
edit.add(test);

mbar.add(edit);

// Create an object to handle action and item events.
MyMenuHandler handler = new MyMenuHandler();

// Register to receive those events.
item1.addActionListener(handler);
item2.addActionListener(handler);
item3.addActionListener(handler);
item4.addActionListener(handler);
item6.addActionListener(handler);
item7.addActionListener(handler);
item8.addActionListener(handler);
item9.addActionListener(handler);
item10.addActionListener(handler);
item11.addActionListener(handler);
item12.addActionListener(handler);
debug.addItemListener(handler);
test.addItemListener(handler);
```

Part II

```
    // Use a lambda expression to handle the Quit selection.
    item5.addActionListener((ae) -> System.exit(0));

    addWindowListener(new WindowAdapter() {
      public void windowClosing(WindowEvent we) {
        System.exit(0);
      }
    });
  }

  public void paint(Graphics g) {
    g.drawString(msg, 10, 220);

   if(debug.getState())
      g.drawString("Debug is on.", 10, 240);
    else
      g.drawString("Debug is off.", 10, 240);

    if(test.getState())
      g.drawString("Testing is on.", 10, 260);
    else
      g.drawString("Testing is off.", 10, 260);
  }

  public static void main(String[] args) {
    DialogDemo appwin = new DialogDemo();

    appwin.setSize(new Dimension(250, 300));
    appwin.setTitle("DialogDemo");
    appwin.setVisible(true);
  }

  // An inner class for handling action and item events
  // for the menu.
  class MyMenuHandler implements ActionListener, ItemListener {

    // Handle action events.
    public void actionPerformed(ActionEvent ae) {
        msg = "You selected ";
        String arg = ae.getActionCommand();

      if(arg.equals("New...")) {
         msg += "New.";
         myDialog.setVisible(true);
       }
        else if(arg.equals("Open..."))
          msg += "Open.";
        else if(arg.equals("Close"))
          msg += "Close.";
        else if(arg.equals("Edit"))
          msg += "Edit.";
```

```
        else if(arg.equals("Cut"))
          msg += "Cut.";
        else if(arg.equals("Copy"))
          msg += "Copy.";
        else if(arg.equals("Paste"))
          msg += "Paste.";
        else if(arg.equals("First"))
          msg += "First.";
        else if(arg.equals("Second"))
          msg += "Second.";
        else if(arg.equals("Third"))
          msg += "Third.";
        else if(arg.equals("Debug"))
          msg += "Debug.";
        else if(arg.equals("Testing"))
          msg += "Testing.";

        repaint();
      }

      // Handle item events.
      public void itemStateChanged(ItemEvent ie) {
        repaint();
      }
    }
  }

// Create a subclass of Dialog.
class SampleDialog extends Dialog {
  SampleDialog(Frame parent, String title) {
    super(parent, title, false);
    setLayout(new FlowLayout());
    setSize(300, 200);

    add(new Label("Press this button:"));

    Button b;
    add(b = new Button("Cancel"));
    b.addActionListener((ae) -> dispose());

    addWindowListener(new WindowAdapter() {
      public void windowClosing(WindowEvent we) {
        dispose();
      }
    });
  }

  public void paint(Graphics g) {
    g.drawString("This is in the dialog box", 20, 80);
  }
}
```

Here is sample output from the **DialogDemo** program:

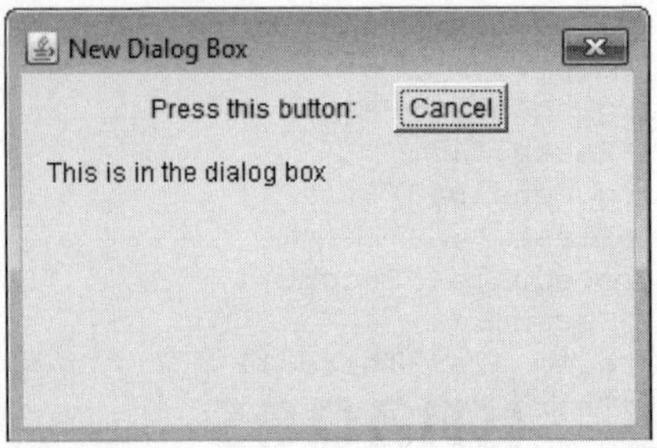


**TIP** On your own, try defining dialog boxes for the other options presented by the menus.

# A Word About Overriding paint( )

Before concluding our examination of AWT controls, a short word about overriding **paint( )** is in order. Although not relevant to the simple AWT examples shown in this book, when overriding **paint( )**, there are times when it is necessary to call the superclass implementation of **paint( )**. Therefore, for some programs, you will need to use this **paint( )** skeleton:

```
public void paint(Graphics g) {

  // code to repaint this window

  // Call superclass paint()
  super.paint(g);
}
```

In Java, there are two general types of components: heavyweight and lightweight. A heavyweight component has its own native window, which is called its *peer*. A lightweight component is implemented completely in Java code and uses the window provided by an ancestor. The AWT controls described and used in this chapter are all heavyweight. However, if a container holds any lightweight components (that is, has lightweight child components), your override of **paint( )** for that container must call **super.paint( )**. By calling **super.paint( )**, you ensure that any lightweight child components, such as lightweight controls, get properly painted. If you are unsure of a child component's type, you can call **isLightweight( )**, defined by **Component**, to find out. It returns **true** if the component is lightweight, and **false** otherwise.

CHAPTER

# 28 Images

This chapter examines the **Image** class and the **java.awt.image** package. Together, they provide support for *imaging* (the display and manipulation of graphical images). An *image* is simply a rectangular graphical object. Images are a key component of web design. In fact, the inclusion of the **<img>** tag in the Mosaic browser at NCSA (National Center for Supercomputer Applications) was a catalyst that helped the Web begin to grow explosively in 1993. This tag was used to include an image *inline* with the flow of hypertext. Java expands upon this basic concept, allowing images to be managed under program control. Because of its importance, Java provides extensive support for imaging.

Images are supported by the **Image** class, which is part of the **java.awt** package. Images are manipulated using the classes found in the **java.awt.image** package. There are a large number of imaging classes and interfaces defined by **java.awt.image**, and it is not possible to examine them all. Instead, we will focus on those that form the foundation of imaging. Here are the **java.awt.image** classes discussed in this chapter:

| | |
|---|---|
| CropImageFilter | MemoryImageSource |
| FilteredImageSource | PixelGrabber |
| ImageFilter | RGBImageFilter |

The interfaces that we will use are **ImageConsumer** and **ImageProducer**.

## File Formats

Originally, web images could only be in GIF format. The GIF image format was created by CompuServe in 1987 to make it possible for images to be viewed while online, so it was well suited to the Internet. GIF images can have only up to 256 colors each. This limitation caused the major browser vendors to add support for JPEG images in 1995. The JPEG format was created by a group of photographic experts to store full-color-spectrum, continuous-tone images. These images, when properly created, can be of much higher fidelity as well as more highly compressed than a GIF encoding of the same source image. Another file format is

PNG. It, too, is an alternative to GIF. In almost all cases, you will never care or notice which format is being used in your programs. The Java image classes abstract the differences behind a clean interface.

## Image Fundamentals: Creating, Loading, and Displaying

There are three common operations that occur when you work with images: creating an image, loading an image, and displaying an image. In Java, the **Image** class is used to refer to images in memory and to images that must be loaded from external sources. Thus, Java provides ways for you to create a new image object and ways to load one. It also provides a means by which an image can be displayed. Let's look at each.

### Creating an Image Object

You might expect that you create a memory image using something like the following:

```
Image test = new Image(200, 100); // Error -- won't work
```

Not so. Because images must eventually be painted on a window to be seen, the **Image** class doesn't have enough information about its environment to create the proper data format for the screen. Therefore, the **Component** class in **java.awt** has a factory method called **createImage( )** that is used to create **Image** objects. (Remember that all of the AWT components are subclasses of **Component**, so all support this method.)

The **createImage( )** method has the following two forms:

Image createImage(ImageProducer *imgProd*)
Image createImage(int *width*, int *height*)

The first form returns an image produced by *imgProd*, which is an object of a class that implements the **ImageProducer** interface. (We will look at image producers later.) The second form returns a blank (that is, empty) image that has the specified width and height. Here is an example:

```
Canvas c = new Canvas();
Image test = c.createImage(200, 100);
```

This creates an instance of **Canvas** and then calls the **createImage( )** method to actually make an **Image** object. At this point, the image is blank. Later, you will see how to write data to it.

### Loading an Image

Another way to obtain an image is to load one, either from a file on the local file system or from a URL. Here, we will use the local file system. The easiest way to load an image is to use one of the static methods defined by the **ImageIO** class. **ImageIO** provides extensive support for reading and writing images. It is packaged in **javax.imageio**, and beginning with JDK 9, **javax.imageio** is part of the **java.desktop** module. The method that loads an image is called **read( )**. The form we will use is shown here:

static BufferedImage read(File *imageFile*) throws IOException

**Figure 28-1** Sample output from **SimpleImageLoad**

Here, *imageFile* specifies the file that contains the image. It returns a reference to the image in the form of a **BufferedImage**, which is a subclass of **Image** that includes a buffer. Null is returned if the file does not contain a valid image.

## Displaying an Image

Once you have an image, you can display it by using **drawImage( )**, which is a member of the **Graphics** class. It has several forms. The one we will be using is shown here:

boolean drawImage(Image *imgObj*, int *left*, int *top*, ImageObserver *imgOb*)

This displays the image passed in *imgObj* with its upper-left corner specified by *left* and *top*. *imgOb* is a reference to a class that implements the **ImageObserver** interface. This interface is implemented by all AWT (and Swing) components. An *image observer* is an object that can monitor an image while it loads. When no image observer is needed, *imgOb* can be **null**.

Using **read( )** and **drawImage( )**, it is actually quite easy to load and display an image. Here is a program that loads and displays a single image. The file **Lilies.jpg** is loaded, but you can substitute any image you like (just make sure it is available in the same directory as the program). Sample output is shown in Figure 28-1.

```
// Load and display an image.
import java.awt.*;
import java.awt.event.*;
import javax.imageio.*;
import java.io.*;

public class SimpleImageLoad extends Frame {
  Image img;

  public SimpleImageLoad() {
```

```
    try {
      File imageFile = new File("Lilies.jpg");

      // Load the image.
      img = ImageIO.read(imageFile);
    } catch (IOException exc) {
      System.out.println("Cannot load image file.");
      System.exit(0);
    }

    addWindowListener(new WindowAdapter() {
      public void windowClosing(WindowEvent we) {
        System.exit(0);
      }
    });
  }

  public void paint(Graphics g) {
    g.drawImage(img, getInsets().left, getInsets().top, null);
  }

  public static void main(String[] args) {
    SimpleImageLoad appwin = new SimpleImageLoad();

    appwin.setSize(new Dimension(400, 365));
    appwin.setTitle("SimpleImageLoad");
    appwin.setVisible(true);
  }
}
```

## Double Buffering

Not only are images useful for storing pictures, as we've just shown, but you can also use them as offscreen drawing surfaces. This allows you to render any image, including text and graphics, to an offscreen buffer that you can display at a later time. The advantage to doing this is that the image is seen only when it is complete. Drawing a complicated image could take several milliseconds or more, which can be seen by the user as flashing or flickering. This flashing is distracting and causes the user to perceive your rendering as slower than it actually is. Use of an offscreen image to reduce flicker is called *double buffering*, because the screen is considered a buffer for pixels, and the offscreen image is the second buffer, where you can prepare pixels for display.

Earlier in this chapter, you saw how to create a blank **Image** object. Now you will see how to draw on that image rather than the screen. As you recall from earlier chapters, you need a **Graphics** object in order to use any of Java's rendering methods. Conveniently, the **Graphics** object that you can use to draw on an **Image** is available via the **getGraphics( )** method. Here is a code fragment that creates a new image, obtains its graphics context, and fills the entire image with red pixels:

```
Canvas c = new Canvas();
Image test = c.createImage(200, 100);
```

```
Graphics gc = test.getGraphics();
gc.setColor(Color.red);
gc.fillRect(0, 0, 200, 100);
```

Once you have constructed and filled an offscreen image, it will still not be visible. To actually display the image, call **drawImage( )**. Here is an example that draws a time-consuming image to demonstrate the difference that double buffering can make in perceived drawing time:

```
// Demonstrate the use of an off-screen buffer.
import java.awt.*;
import java.awt.event.*;

public class DoubleBuffer extends Frame {
  int gap = 3;
  int mx, my;
  boolean flicker = true;
  Image buffer = null;
  int w = 400, h = 400;

  public DoubleBuffer() {
    addMouseMotionListener(new MouseMotionAdapter() {
      public void mouseDragged(MouseEvent me) {
        mx = me.getX();
        my = me.getY();
        flicker = false;
        repaint();
      }
      public void mouseMoved(MouseEvent me) {
        mx = me.getX();
        my = me.getY();
        flicker = true;
        repaint();
      }
    });

    addWindowListener(new WindowAdapter() {
      public void windowClosing(WindowEvent we) {
        System.exit(0);
      }
    });
  }

  public void paint(Graphics g) {
    Graphics screengc = null;

    if (!flicker) {
      screengc = g;
      g = buffer.getGraphics();
    }

    g.setColor(Color.blue);
    g.fillRect(0, 0, w, h);
```

```
    g.setColor(Color.red);
    for (int i=0; i<w; i+=gap)
      g.drawLine(i, 0, w-i, h);
    for (int i=0; i<h; i+=gap)
      g.drawLine(0, i, w, h-i);

    g.setColor(Color.black);
    g.drawString("Press mouse button to double buffer", 10, h/2);

    g.setColor(Color.yellow);
    g.fillOval(mx - gap, my - gap, gap*2+1, gap*2+1);

    if (!flicker) {
      screengc.drawImage(buffer, 0, 0, null);
    }
  }

  public void update(Graphics g) {
    paint(g);
  }

  public static void main(String[] args) {
    DoubleBuffer appwin = new DoubleBuffer();

    appwin.setSize(new Dimension(400, 400));
    appwin.setTitle("DoubleBuffer");
    appwin.setVisible(true);

    // Create an off-screen buffer.
    appwin.buffer = appwin.createImage(appwin.w, appwin.h);
  }
}
```

This simple program has a complicated **paint( )** method. It fills the background with blue and then draws a red moiré pattern on top of that. It paints some black text on top of that and then paints a yellow circle centered at the coordinates **mx**, **my**. The **mouseMoved( )** and **mouseDragged( )** methods are overridden to track the mouse position. These methods are identical, except for the setting of the **flicker** Boolean variable. **mouseMoved( )** sets **flicker** to **true**, and **mouseDragged( )** sets it to **false**. This has the effect of calling **repaint( )** with **flicker** set to **true** when the mouse is moved (but no button is pressed) and set to **false** when the mouse is dragged with any button pressed.

When **paint( )** gets called with **flicker** set to **true**, we see each drawing operation as it is executed on the screen. In the case where a mouse button is pressed and **paint( )** is called with **flicker** set to **false**, we see quite a different picture. The **paint( )** method swaps the **Graphics** reference **g** with the graphics context that refers to the offscreen canvas, **buffer**, which we created in **main( )**. Then all of the drawing operations are invisible. At the end of **paint( )**, we simply call **drawImage( )** to show the results of these drawing methods all at once.

Sample output is shown in Figure 28-2. The left snapshot is what the screen looks like with the mouse button not pressed. As you can see, the image was in the middle of repainting

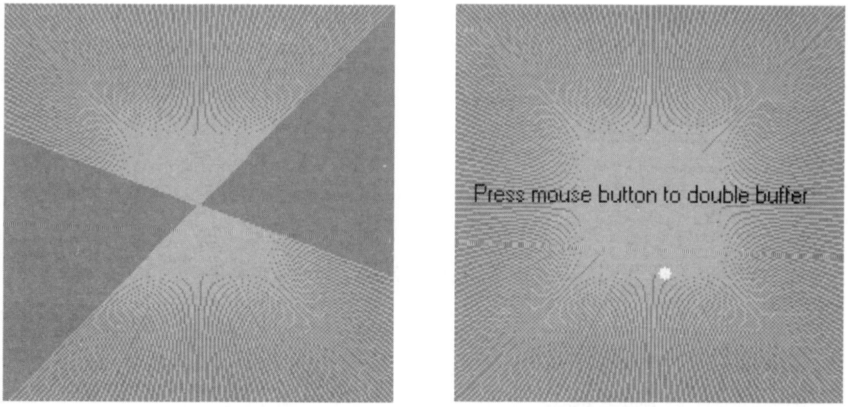


**Figure 28-2** Output from **DoubleBuffer** without (left) and with (right) double buffering



when this snapshot was taken. The right snapshot shows how, when a mouse button is pressed, the image is always complete and clean due to double buffering.

# ImageProducer

**ImageProducer** is an interface for objects that want to produce data for images. An object that implements the **ImageProducer** interface will supply integer or byte arrays that represent image data and produce **Image** objects. As you saw earlier, one form of the **createImage( )** method takes an **ImageProducer** object as its argument. There are two image producers contained in **java.awt.image**: **MemoryImageSource** and **FilteredImageSource**. Here, we will examine **MemoryImageSource** and create a new **Image** object from generated data.

## MemoryImageSource

**MemoryImageSource** is a class that creates a new **Image** from an array of data. It defines several constructors. Here is the one we will be using:

MemoryImageSource(int *width*, int *height*, int[ ] *pixel*, int *offset*,
int *scanLineWidth*)

The **MemoryImageSource** object is constructed out of the array of integers specified by *pixel*, in the default RGB color model to produce data for an **Image** object. In the default color model, a pixel is an integer with Alpha, Red, Green, and Blue (0xAARRGGBB). The Alpha value represents a degree of transparency for the pixel. Fully transparent is 0, and fully opaque is 255. The width and height of the resulting image are passed in *width* and *height*. The starting point in the pixel array to begin reading data is passed in *offset*. The width of a scan line (which is often the same as the width of the image) is passed in *scanLineWidth*.

The following short example generates a **MemoryImageSource** object using a variation on a simple algorithm (a bitwise-exclusive-OR of the x and y address of each pixel) from the book *Beyond Photography: The Digital Darkroom* by Gerard J. Holzmann (Prentice Hall, 1988).

```
// Create an image in memory.
import java.awt.*;
import java.awt.image.*;
import java.awt.event.*;

public class MemoryImageGenerator extends Frame {
  Image img;
  int w = 512;
  int h = 512;

  public MemoryImageGenerator() {
    int[] pixels = new int[w * h];
    int i = 0;

    for(int y=0; y<h; y++) {
      for(int x=0; x<w; x++) {
        int r = (x^y)&0xff;
        int g = (x*2^y*2)&0xff;
        int b = (x*4^y*4)&0xff;
        pixels[i++] = (255 << 24) | (r << 16) | (g << 8) | b;
      }
    }
    img = createImage(new MemoryImageSource(w, h, pixels, 0, w));

    addWindowListener(new WindowAdapter() {
      public void windowClosing(WindowEvent we) {
        System.exit(0);
      }
    });
  }

  public void paint(Graphics g) {
    g.drawImage(img, getInsets().left, getInsets().top, null);
  }

  public static void main(String[] args) {
    MemoryImageGenerator appwin = new MemoryImageGenerator();

    appwin.setSize(new Dimension(400, 400));
    appwin.setTitle("MemoryImageGenerator");
    appwin.setVisible(true);
  }
}
```

The data for the new **MemoryImageSource** is created in the constructor. An array of integers is created to hold the pixel values; the data is generated in the nested **for** loops where the **r**, **g**, and **b** values get shifted into a pixel in the **pixels** array. Finally, **createImage( )** is called with a new instance of a **MemoryImageSource** created from the raw pixel data as its parameter. Figure 28-3 shows the image.

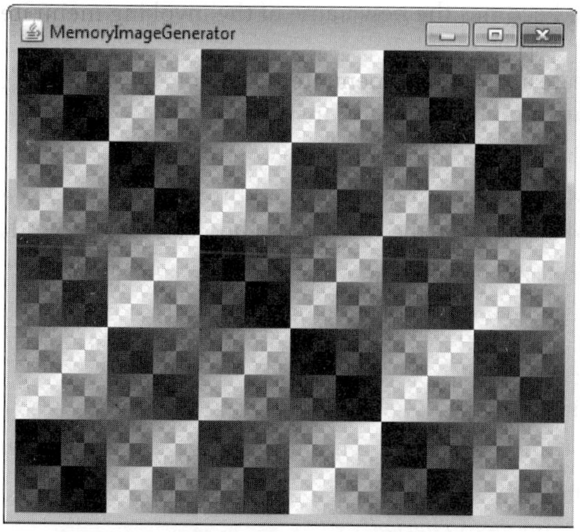


**Figure 28-3** Sample output from **MemoryImageGenerator**

# ImageConsumer

**ImageConsumer** is an interface for objects that want to take pixel data from images and supply it as another kind of data. This, obviously, is the opposite of **ImageProducer**, described earlier. An object that implements the **ImageConsumer** interface is going to create **int** or **byte** arrays that represent pixels from an **Image** object. We will examine the **PixelGrabber** class, which is a simple implementation of the **ImageConsumer** interface.

## PixelGrabber

The **PixelGrabber** class is defined within **java.lang.image**. It is the inverse of the **MemoryImageSource** class. Rather than constructing an image from an array of pixel values, it takes an existing image and *grabs* the pixel array from it. To use **PixelGrabber**, you first create an array of **int**s big enough to hold the pixel data, and then you create a **PixelGrabber** instance passing in the rectangle that you want to grab. Finally, you call **grabPixels( )** on that instance.

The **PixelGrabber** constructor that is used in this chapter is shown here:

PixelGrabber(Image *imgObj*, int *left*, int *top*, int *width*, int *height*, int[ ] *pixel*, int *offset*, int *scanLineWidth*)

Here, *imgObj* is the object whose pixels are being grabbed. The values of *left* and *top* specify the upper-left corner of the rectangle, and *width* and *height* specify the dimensions of the rectangle from which the pixels will be obtained. The pixels will be stored in *pixel* beginning at *offset*. The width of a scan line (which is often the same as the width of the image) is passed in *scanLineWidth*.

**grabPixels( )** is defined like this:

boolean grabPixels( )
  throws InterruptedException

boolean grabPixels(long *milliseconds*)
  throws InterruptedException

Both methods return **true** if successful and **false** otherwise. In the second form, *milliseconds* specifies how long the method will wait for the pixels. Both throw **InterruptedException** if execution is interrupted by another thread.

Here is an example that grabs the pixels from an image and then creates a histogram of pixel brightness. The *histogram* is simply a count of pixels that are a certain brightness for all brightness settings between 0 and 255. After the program paints the image, it draws the histogram over the top.

```
// Demonstrate PixelGraber.
import java.awt.* ;
import java.awt.event.*;
import java.awt.image.* ;
import javax.imageio.*;
import java.io.*;

public class HistoGrab extends Frame {
  Dimension d;
  Image img;
  int iw, ih;
  int[] pixels;
  int[] hist = new int[256];
  int max_hist = 0;
  Insets ins;

  public HistoGrab() {

    try {
      File imageFile = new File("Lilies.jpg");

      // Load the image.
      img = ImageIO.read(imageFile);

      iw = img.getWidth(null);
      ih = img.getHeight(null);
      pixels = new int[iw * ih];
      PixelGrabber pg = new PixelGrabber(img, 0, 0, iw, ih,
                                         pixels, 0, iw);
      pg.grabPixels();
    } catch (InterruptedException e) {
      System.out.println("Interrupted");
      return;
    } catch (IOException exc) {
```

```
      System.out.println("Cannot load image file.");
      System.exit(0);
    }

    for (int i=0; i<iw*ih; i++) {
      int p = pixels[i];
      int r = 0xff & (p >> 16);
      int g = 0xff & (p >> 8);
      int b = 0xff & (p);
      int y = (int) (.33 * r + .56 * g + .11 * b);
      hist[y]++;
    }
    for (int i=0; i<256; i++) {
      if (hist[i] > max_hist)
        max_hist = hist[i];
    }

    addWindowListener(new WindowAdapter() {
      public void windowClosing(WindowEvent we) {
        System.exit(0);
      }
    });
  }

  public void paint(Graphics g) {
    // Get the border/header insets.
    ins = getInsets();

    g.drawImage(img, ins.left, ins.top, null);

    int x = (iw - 256) / 2;
    int lasty = ih - ih * hist[0] / max_hist;

    for (int i=0; i<256; i++, x++) {
      int y = ih - ih * hist[i] / max_hist;
      g.setColor(new Color(i, i, i));
      g.fillRect(x+ins.left, y+ins.top, 1, ih-y);
      g.setColor(Color.red);
      g.drawLine((x-1)+ins.left,lasty+ins.top,x+ins.left,y+ins.top);
      lasty = y;
    }
  }

  public static void main(String[] args) {
    HistoGrab appwin = new HistoGrab();

    appwin.setSize(new Dimension(400, 380));
    appwin.setTitle("HistoGrab");
    appwin.setVisible(true);
  }
}
```

Figure 28-4 shows a sample image and its histogram.

**Figure 28-4** Sample output from **HistoGrab**

# ImageFilter

Given the **ImageProducer** and **ImageConsumer** interface pair—and their concrete classes **MemoryImageSource** and **PixelGrabber**—you can create an arbitrary set of translation filters that takes a source of pixels, modifies them, and passes them on to an arbitrary consumer. This mechanism is analogous to the way concrete classes are created from the abstract I/O classes **InputStream**, **OutputStream**, **Reader**, and **Writer** (described in Chapter 22). This stream model for images is completed by the introduction of the **ImageFilter** class. Some subclasses of **ImageFilter** in the **java.awt.image** package are **AreaAveragingScaleFilter**, **CropImageFilter**, **ReplicateScaleFilter**, and **RGBImageFilter**. There is also an implementation of **ImageProducer** called **FilteredImageSource**, which takes an arbitrary **ImageFilter** and wraps it around an **ImageProducer** to filter the pixels it produces. An instance of **FilteredImageSource** can be used as an **ImageProducer** in calls to **createImage( )**, in much the same way that **BufferedInputStream**s can be used as **InputStream**s.

In this chapter, we examine two filters: **CropImageFilter** and **RGBImageFilter**.

## CropImageFilter

**CropImageFilter** filters an image source to extract a rectangular region. One situation in which this filter is valuable is where you want to use several small images from a single, larger source image. Loading twenty 2K images takes much longer than loading a single 40K image that has many frames of an animation tiled into it. If every subimage is the same size, then you can easily extract these images by using **CropImageFilter** to disassemble the block once your program starts. Here is an example that creates 16 images taken from a single image. The tiles are then scrambled by swapping a random pair from the 16 images 32 times.

```
// Demonstrate CropImageFilter.
import java.awt.*;
import java.awt.image.*;
import java.awt.event.*;
import javax.imageio.*;
import java.io.*;

public class TileImage extends Frame {
  Image img;
  Image[] cell = new Image[4*4];
  int iw, ih;
  int tw, th;

  public TileImage() {
    try {
      File imageFile = new File("Lilies.jpg");

      // Load the image.
      img = ImageIO.read(imageFile);

      iw = img.getWidth(null);
      ih = img.getHeight(null);
      tw = iw / 4;
      th = ih / 4;

      CropImageFilter f;
      FilteredImageSource fis;

      for (int y=0; y<4; y++) {
        for (int x=0; x<4; x++) {
          f = new CropImageFilter(tw*x, th*y, tw, th);
          fis = new FilteredImageSource(img.getSource(), f);
          int i = y*4+x;
          cell[i] = createImage(fis);
        }
      }

      for (int i=0; i<32; i++) {
        int si = (int)(Math.random() * 16);
        int di = (int)(Math.random() * 16);
        Image tmp = cell[si];
        cell[si] = cell[di];
        cell[di] = tmp;
      }
    } catch (IOException exc) {
      System.out.println("Cannot load image file.");
      System.exit(0);
    }

    addWindowListener(new WindowAdapter() {
      public void windowClosing(WindowEvent we) {
        System.exit(0);
      }
    });
  }
```

Part II

```
  public void paint(Graphics g) {
    for (int y=0; y<4; y++) {
      for (int x=0; x<4; x++) {
        g.drawImage(cell[y*4+x], x * tw + getInsets().left,
                    y * th + getInsets().top, null);
      }
    }
  }

  public static void main(String[] args) {
    TileImage appwin = new TileImage();

    appwin.setSize(new Dimension(420, 420));
    appwin.setTitle("TileImage");
    appwin.setVisible(true);
  }
}
```

Figure 28-5 shows the flowers image scrambled by **TileImage**.

## RGBImageFilter

The **RGBImageFilter** is used to convert one image to another, pixel by pixel, transforming the colors along the way. This filter could be used to brighten an image, to increase its contrast, or even to convert it to grayscale.

To demonstrate **RGBImageFilter**, we have developed a somewhat complicated example that employs a dynamic plug-in strategy for image-processing filters. We've created an interface for generalized image filtering so that a program can simply load these filters at run time without having to know about all of the **ImageFilter**s in advance. This example consists of the

**Figure 28-5** Sample output from **TileImage**

main class called **ImageFilterDemo**, the interface called **PlugInFilter**, and a utility class called **LoadedImage**. Also included are three filters—**Grayscale**, **Invert**, and **Contrast**—that simply manipulate the color space of the source image using **RGBImageFilter**s, and two more classes—**Blur** and **Sharpen**—that do more complicated "convolution" filters that change pixel data based on the pixels surrounding each pixel of source data. **Blur** and **Sharpen** are subclasses of an abstract helper class called **Convolver**. Let's look at each part of our example.

## ImageFilterDemo.java

The **ImageFilterDemo** class is the main class for the sample image filters. It employs the default **BorderLayout**, with a **Panel** at the *South* position to hold the buttons that will represent each filter. A **Label** object occupies the *North* slot for informational messages about filter progress. The *Center* is where the image (which is encapsulated in the **LoadedImage Canvas** subclass, described later) is put.

The **actionPerformed( )** method is interesting because it uses the label from a button as the name of a filter class that it loads. This method is robust and takes appropriate action if the button does not correspond to a proper class that implements **PlugInFilter**.

```
// Demonstrate image filters.
import java.awt.*;
import java.awt.event.*;
import javax.imageio.*;
import java.io.*;
import java.lang.reflect.*;

public class ImageFilterDemo extends Frame implements ActionListener {
  Image img;
  PlugInFilter pif;
  Image fimg;
  Image curImg;
  LoadedImage lim;
  Label lab;
  Button reset;

  // Names of the filters.
  String[] filters = { "Grayscale", "Invert", "Contrast",
                       "Blur", "Sharpen" };

  public ImageFilterDemo() {
    Panel p = new Panel();
    add(p, BorderLayout.SOUTH);

    // Create Reset button.
    reset = new Button("Reset");
    reset.addActionListener(this);
    p.add(reset);

    // Add the filter buttons.
    for(String fstr: filters) {
      Button b = new Button(fstr);
      b.addActionListener(this);
      p.add(b);
    }
```

```
    // Create the top label.
    lab = new Label("");
    add(lab, BorderLayout.NORTH);

    // Load the image.
    try {
      File imageFile = new File("Lilies.jpg");

      // Load the image.
      img = ImageIO.read(imageFile);
    } catch (IOException exc) {
      System.out.println("Cannot load image file.");
      System.exit(0);
    }

    // Get a LoadedImage and add it to the center.
    lim = new LoadedImage(img);
    add(lim, BorderLayout.CENTER);

    addWindowListener(new WindowAdapter() {
      public void windowClosing(WindowEvent we) {
        System.exit(0);
      }
    });
  }

  public void actionPerformed(ActionEvent ae) {
    String a = "";

    try {
      a = ae.getActionCommand();
      if (a.equals("Reset")) {
        lim.set(img);
        lab.setText("Normal");
      }
      else {
        // Get the selected filter.
        pif = (PlugInFilter)
                (Class.forName(a)).getConstructor().newInstance();
        fimg = pif.filter(this, img);
        lim.set(fimg);
        lab.setText("Filtered: " + a);
      }
      repaint();
    } catch (ClassNotFoundException e) {
      lab.setText(a + " not found");
      lim.set(img);
      repaint();
    } catch (InstantiationException e) {
      lab.setText("couldn't new " + a);
    } catch (IllegalAccessException e) {
```

```
      lab.setText("no access: " + a);
    } catch (NoSuchMethodException | InvocationTargetException e) {
      lab.setText("Filter creation error: " + e);
    }
  }

  public static void main(String[] args) {
    ImageFilterDemo appwin = new ImageFilterDemo();

    appwin.setSize(new Dimension(420, 420));
    appwin.setTitle("ImageFilterDemo");
    appwin.setVisible(true);
  }
}
```



Figure 28-6 shows what the program looks like when it is first loaded.

## PlugInFilter.java

**PlugInFilter** is a simple interface used to abstract image filtering. It has only one method, **filter( )**, which takes the frame and the source image and returns a new image that has been filtered in some way.

```
interface PlugInFilter {
  java.awt.Image filter(java.awt.Frame f, java.awt.Image in);
}
```

**Figure 28-6** Sample normal output from **ImageFilterDemo**

## LoadedImage.java

**LoadedImage** is a convenient subclass of **Canvas**. It behaves properly under layout manager control because it overrides the **getPreferredSize( )** and **getMinimumSize( )** methods. Also, it has a method called **set( )** that can be used to set a new **Image** to be displayed in this **Canvas**. That is how the filtered image is displayed after the plug-in is finished.

```
import java.awt.*;

public class LoadedImage extends Canvas {
  Image img;

  public LoadedImage(Image i) {
    set(i);
  }

  void set(Image i) {
    img = i;
    repaint();
  }

  public void paint(Graphics g) {
    if (img == null) {
      g.drawString("no image", 10, 30);
    } else {
      g.drawImage(img, 0, 0, this);
    }
  }

  public Dimension getPreferredSize()  {
    return new Dimension(img.getWidth(this), img.getHeight(this));
  }

  public Dimension getMinimumSize()  {
    return getPreferredSize();
  }
}
```

## Grayscale.java

The **Grayscale** filter is a subclass of **RGBImageFilter**, which means that **Grayscale** can use itself as the **ImageFilter** parameter to **FilteredImageSource**'s constructor. Then all it needs to do is override **filterRGB( )** to change the incoming color values. It takes the red, green, and blue values and computes the brightness of the pixel, using the NTSC (National Television Standards Committee) color-to-brightness conversion factor. It then simply returns a gray pixel that is the same brightness as the color source.

```
// Grayscale filter.
import java.awt.*;
import java.awt.image.*;

class Grayscale extends RGBImageFilter implements PlugInFilter {
  public Grayscale() {}
```

```
  public Image filter(Frame f, Image in) {
    return f.createImage(new FilteredImageSource(in.getSource(), this));
  }

  public int filterRGB(int x, int y, int rgb) {
    int r = (rgb >> 16) & 0xff;
    int g = (rgb >> 8) & 0xff;
    int b = rgb & 0xff;
    int k = (int) (.56 * g + .33 * r + .11 * b);
    return (0xff000000 | k << 16 | k << 8 | k);
  }
}
```



## Invert.java

The **Invert** filter is also quite simple. It takes apart the red, green, and blue values and then inverts them by subtracting them from 255. These inverted values are packed back into a pixel value and returned.

```
// Invert colors filter.
import java.awt.*;
import java.awt.image.*;

class Invert extends RGBImageFilter implements PlugInFilter {
  public Invert() { }

  public Image filter(Frame f, Image in) {
    return f.createImage(new FilteredImageSource(in.getSource(), this));
  }

  public int filterRGB(int x, int y, int rgb) {
    int r = 0xff - (rgb >> 16) & 0xff;
    int g = 0xff - (rgb >> 8) & 0xff;
    int b = 0xff - rgb & 0xff;
    return (0xff000000 | r << 16 | g << 8 | b);
  }
}
```

Figure 28-7 shows the image after it has been run through the **Invert** filter.

## Contrast.java

The **Contrast** filter is very similar to **Grayscale**, except its override of **filterRGB( )** is slightly more complicated. The algorithm it uses for contrast enhancement takes the red, green, and blue values separately and boosts them by 1.2 times if they are already brighter than 128. If they are below 128, then they are divided by 1.2. The boosted values are properly clamped at 255 by the **multclamp( )** method.

```
// Contrast filter.
import java.awt.*;
import java.awt.image.*;
```

**Figure 28-7** Using the **Invert** filter with **ImageFilterDemo**

```
public class Contrast extends RGBImageFilter implements PlugInFilter {

  public Image filter(Frame f, Image in) {
    return f.createImage(new FilteredImageSource(in.getSource(), this));
  }

  private int multclamp(int in, double factor) {
    in = (int) (in * factor);
    return in > 255 ? 255 : in;
  }

  double gain = 1.2;
  private int cont(int in) {
    return (in < 128) ? (int)(in/gain) : multclamp(in, gain);
  }

  public int filterRGB(int x, int y, int rgb) {
    int r = cont((rgb >> 16) & 0xff);
    int g = cont((rgb >> 8) & 0xff);
    int b = cont(rgb & 0xff);
    return (0xff000000 | r << 16 | g << 8 | b);
  }
}
```

Figure 28-8 shows the image after **Contrast** is pressed.

**Figure 28-8** Using the **Contrast** filter with **ImageFilterDemo**

## Convolver.java

The abstract class **Convolver** handles the basics of a convolution filter by implementing the **ImageConsumer** interface to move the source pixels into an array called **imgpixels**. It also creates a second array called **newimgpixels** for the filtered data. Convolution filters sample a small rectangle of pixels around each pixel in an image, called the *convolution kernel*. This area, 3×3 pixels in this demo, is used to decide how to change the center pixel in the area.

**NOTE** The reason that the filter can't modify the **imgpixels** array in place is that the next pixel on a scan line would try to use the original value for the previous pixel, which would have just been filtered away.

The two concrete subclasses, shown in the next section, simply implement the **convolve( )** method, using **imgpixels** for source data and **newimgpixels** to store the result.

```
// Convolution filter.
import java.awt.*;
import java.awt.image.*;

abstract class Convolver implements ImageConsumer, PlugInFilter {
  int width, height;
  int[] imgpixels, newimgpixels;
  boolean imageReady = false;

  abstract void convolve();  // filter goes here...

  public Image filter(Frame f, Image in) {
    imageReady = false;
```

```
    in.getSource().startProduction(this);
    waitForImage();
    newimgpixels = new int[width*height];

    try {
      convolve();
    } catch (Exception e) {
      System.out.println("Convolver failed: " + e);
      e.printStackTrace();
    }

    return f.createImage(
      new MemoryImageSource(width, height, newimgpixels, 0, width));
  }

  synchronized void waitForImage() {
    try {
      while(!imageReady)
        wait();
    } catch (Exception e) {
      System.out.println("Interrupted");
    }
  }

  public void setProperties(java.util.Hashtable<?,?> dummy) { }
  public void setColorModel(ColorModel dummy) { }
  public void setHints(int dummy) { }

  public synchronized void imageComplete(int dummy) {
    imageReady = true;
    notifyAll();
  }

  public void setDimensions(int x, int y) {
    width = x;
    height = y;
    imgpixels = new int[x*y];
  }

  public void setPixels(int x1, int y1, int w, int h,
    ColorModel model, byte[] pixels, int off, int scansize) {
    int pix, x, y, x2, y2, sx, sy;

    x2 = x1+w;
    y2 = y1+h;
    sy = off;
    for(y=y1; y<y2; y++) {
      sx = sy;
      for(x=x1; x<x2; x++) {
        pix = model.getRGB(pixels[sx++]);
        if((pix & 0xff000000) == 0)
            pix = 0x00ffffff;
```

```
        imgpixels[y*width+x] = pix;
      }
      sy += scansize;
    }
  }

  public void setPixels(int x1, int y1, int w, int h,
    ColorModel model, int[] pixels, int off, int scansize) {
    int pix, x, y, x2, y2, sx, sy;

    x2 = x1+w;
    y2 = y1+h;
    sy = off;
    for(y=y1; y<y2; y++) {
      sx = sy;
      for(x=x1; x<x2; x++) {
        pix = model.getRGB(pixels[sx++]);
        if((pix & 0xff000000) == 0)
            pix = 0x00ffffff;
        imgpixels[y*width+x] = pix;
      }
      sy += scansize;
    }
  }
}
```



**NOTE** A built-in convolution filter called **ConvolveOp** is provided by **java.awt.image**. You may want to explore its capabilities on your own.

## Blur.java

The **Blur** filter is a subclass of **Convolver** and simply runs through every pixel in the source image array, **imgpixels**, and computes the average of the 3×3 box surrounding it. The corresponding output pixel in **newimgpixels** is that average value.

```
public class Blur extends Convolver {
  public void convolve() {
    for(int y=1; y<height-1; y++) {
      for(int x=1; x<width-1; x++) {
        int rs = 0;
        int gs = 0;
        int bs = 0;

        for(int k=-1; k<=1; k++) {
          for(int j=-1; j<=1; j++) {
            int rgb = imgpixels[(y+k)*width+x+j];
            int r = (rgb >> 16) & 0xff;
            int g = (rgb >> 8) & 0xff;
            int b = rgb & 0xff;
            rs += r;
            gs += g;
```

```
                bs += b;
            }
        }

        rs /= 9;
        gs /= 9;
        bs /= 9;

        newimgpixels[y*width+x] = (0xff000000 |
                                   rs << 16 | gs << 8 | bs);
      }
    }
  }
}
```

Figure 28-9 shows the image after **Blur**.

## Sharpen.java

The **Sharpen** filter is also a subclass of **Convolver** and is (more or less) the inverse of **Blur**. It runs through every pixel in the source image array, **imgpixels**, and computes the average of the 3×3 box surrounding it, not counting the center. The corresponding output pixel in **newimgpixels** has the difference between the center pixel and the surrounding average added to it. This basically says that if a pixel is 30 brighter than its surroundings, make it

**Figure 28-9** Using the **Blur** filter with **ImageFilterDemo**

another 30 brighter. If, however, it is 10 darker, then make it another 10 darker. This tends to accentuate edges while leaving smooth areas unchanged.

```
public class Sharpen extends Convolver {

  private final int clamp(int c) {
    return (c > 255 ? 255 : (c < 0 ? 0 : c));
  }

  public void convolve() {
    int r0=0, g0=0, b0=0;

    for(int y=1; y<height-1; y++) {
      for(int x=1; x<width-1; x++) {
        int rs = 0;
        int gs = 0;
        int bs = 0;

        for(int k=-1; k<=1; k++) {
          for(int j=-1; j<=1; j++) {
            int rgb = imgpixels[(y+k)*width+x+j];
            int r = (rgb >> 16) & 0xff;
            int g = (rgb >> 8) & 0xff;
            int b = rgb & 0xff;
            if (j == 0 && k == 0) {
              r0 = r;
              g0 = g;
              b0 = b;
            } else {
              rs += r;
              gs += g;
              bs += b;
            }
          }
        }

        rs >>= 3;
        gs >>= 3;
        bs >>= 3;
        newimgpixels[y*width+x] = (0xff000000 |
                                   clamp(r0+r0-rs) << 16 |
                                   clamp(g0+g0-gs) << 8 |
                                   clamp(b0+b0-bs));
      }
    }
  }
}
```

**Figure 28-10** Using the **Sharpen** filter with **ImageFilterDemo**

Figure 28-10 shows the image after **Sharpen**.

## Additional Imaging Classes

In addition to the imaging classes described in this chapter, **java.awt.image** supplies several others that offer enhanced control over the imaging process and that support advanced imaging techniques. Also available is the imaging package called **javax.imageio**. It supports reading and writing images, and has plug-ins that handle various image formats. If sophisticated graphical output is of special interest to you, then you will want to explore the additional classes found in **java.awt.image** and **javax.imageio**.

CHAPTER

# 29 The Concurrency Utilities

From the start, Java has provided built-in support for multithreading and synchronization. For example, new threads can be created by implementing **Runnable** or by extending **Thread**; synchronization is available by use of the **synchronized** keyword; and interthread communication is supported by the **wait( )** and **notify( )** methods that are defined by **Object**. In general, this built-in support for multithreading was one of Java's most important innovations and is still one of its major strengths.

However, as conceptually pure as Java's original support for multithreading is, it is not ideal for all applications—especially those that make intensive use of multiple threads. For example, the original multithreading support does not provide several high-level features, such as semaphores, thread pools, and execution managers, that facilitate the creation of intensively concurrent programs.

It is important to explain at the outset that many Java programs make use of multithreading and are, therefore, "concurrent." However, as it is used in this chapter, the term *concurrent program* refers to a program that makes *extensive, integral* use of concurrently executing threads. An example of such a program is one that uses separate threads to simultaneously compute the partial results of a larger computation. Another example is a program that coordinates the activities of several threads, each of which seeks access to information in a database. In this case, read-only accesses might be handled differently from those that require read/write capabilities.

To begin to handle the needs of a concurrent program, JDK 5 added the *concurrency utilities,* also commonly referred to as the *concurrent API.* The original set of concurrency utilities supplied many features that had long been wanted by programmers who develop concurrent applications. For example, it offered synchronizers (such as the semaphore), thread pools, execution managers, locks, several concurrent collections, and a streamlined way to use threads to obtain computational results.

Although the original concurrent API was impressive in its own right, it was significantly expanded by JDK 7. The most important addition was the *Fork/Join Framework.* The Fork/Join Framework facilitates the creation of programs that make use of multiple processors (such as those found in multicore systems). Thus, it streamlines the development of programs in which two or more pieces execute with true simultaneity (that is, true parallel execution), not just time-slicing. As you can easily imagine, parallel execution can dramatically increase the speed of certain operations. Because multicore systems are now commonplace, the inclusion of the Fork/Join Framework was as timely as it was powerful. The Fork/Join Framework was further enhanced by JDK 8.

Furthermore, both JDK 8 and JDK 9 added features related to other parts of the concurrent API. Thus, over the years, the concurrent API has evolved and expanded to meet the needs of the contemporary computing environment.

The original concurrent API was quite large, and the additions made over the years have increased its size substantially. As you might expect, many of the issues surrounding the concurrency utilities are quite complex. It is beyond the scope of this book to discuss all of its facets. The preceding notwithstanding, it is important for all programmers to have a general, working knowledge of key aspects of the concurrent API. Even in programs that are not intensively parallel, features such as synchronizers, callable threads, and executors are applicable to a wide variety of situations. Perhaps most importantly, because of the rise of multicore computers, solutions involving the Fork/Join Framework are becoming more common. For these reasons, this chapter presents an overview of several core features defined by the concurrency utilities and shows a number of examples that demonstrate their use. It concludes with an introduction to the Fork/Join Framework.

# The Concurrent API Packages

The concurrency utilities are contained in the **java.util.concurrent** package and in its two subpackages: **java.util.concurrent.atomic** and **java.util.concurrent.locks**. Beginning with JDK 9, all are in the **java.base** module. A brief overview of their contents is given here.

## java.util.concurrent

**java.util.concurrent** defines the core features that support alternatives to the built-in approaches to synchronization and interthread communication. These include

- Synchronizers
- Executors
- Concurrent collections
- The Fork/Join Framework

*Synchronizers* offer high-level ways of synchronizing the interactions between multiple threads. The synchronizer classes defined by **java.util.concurrent** are

| | |
|---|---|
| Semaphore | Implements the classic semaphore |
| CountDownLatch | Waits until a specified number of events have occurred |
| CyclicBarrier | Enables a group of threads to wait at a predefined execution point |
| Exchanger | Exchanges data between two threads |
| Phaser | Synchronizes threads that advance through multiple phases of an operation |

Notice that each synchronizer provides a solution to a specific type of synchronization problem. This enables each synchronizer to be optimized for its intended use. In the early days of Java, these types of synchronization objects had to be crafted by hand. The concurrent API standardized them and made them available to all Java programmers.

*Executors* manage thread execution. At the top of the executor hierarchy is the **Executor** interface, which is used to initiate a thread. **ExecutorService** extends **Executor** and provides methods that manage execution. There are three implementations of **ExecutorService**: **ThreadPoolExecutor**, **ScheduledThreadPoolExecutor**, and **ForkJoinPool**. In addition, **java.util.concurrent** also defines the **Executors** utility class, which includes a number of static methods that simplify the creation of various executors.

Related to executors are the **Future** and **Callable** interfaces. A **Future** contains a value that is returned by a thread after it executes. Thus, its value becomes defined "in the future," when the thread terminates. **Callable** defines a thread that returns a value.

**java.util.concurrent** defines several concurrent collection classes, including **ConcurrentHashMap**, **ConcurrentLinkedQueue**, and **CopyOnWriteArrayList**. These offer concurrent alternatives to their related classes defined by the Collections Framework.

The *Fork/Join Framework* supports parallel programming. Its main classes are **ForkJoinTask**, **ForkJoinPool**, **RecursiveTask**, and **RecursiveAction**.

To better handle thread timing, **java.util.concurrent** defines the **TimeUnit** enumeration.

Beginning with JDK 9, **java.util.concurrent** also includes a subsystem that offers a means by which the flow of data can be controlled. It is based on the **Flow** class and these nested interfaces: **Flow.Subscriber**, **Flow.Publisher**, **Flow.Processor**, and **Flow.Subscription**. Although a detailed discussion of the **Flow** subsystem is outside the focus of this chapter, here is a brief description. **Flow** and its nested interfaces support the *reactive streams* specification. This specification defines a means by which a consumer of data can prevent the producer of the data from overrunning the consumer's ability to process the data. In this approach, data is produced by a *publisher* and consumed by a *subscriber*. Control is achieved by implementing a form of *back pressure*.

## java.util.concurrent.atomic

**java.util.concurrent.atomic** facilitates the use of variables in a concurrent environment. It provides a means of efficiently updating the value of a variable without the use of locks. This is accomplished through the use of classes, such as **AtomicInteger** and **AtomicLong**, and methods, such as **compareAndSet( )**, **decrementAndGet( )**, and **getAndSet( )**. These methods execute as a single, non-interruptible operation.

## java.util.concurrent.locks

**java.util.concurrent.locks** provides an alternative to the use of synchronized methods. At the core of this alternative is the **Lock** interface, which defines the basic mechanism used to acquire and relinquish access to an object. The key methods are **lock( )**, **tryLock( )**, and **unlock( )**. The advantage to using these methods is greater control over synchronization.

The remainder of this chapter takes a closer look at the constituents of the concurrent API.

Part II

# Using Synchronization Objects

Synchronization objects are supported by the **Semaphore**, **CountDownLatch**, **CyclicBarrier**, **Exchanger**, and **Phaser** classes. Collectively, they enable you to handle several formerly difficult synchronization situations with ease. They are also applicable to a wide range of programs—even those that contain only limited concurrency. Because the synchronization objects will be of interest to nearly all Java programs, each is examined here in some detail.

## Semaphore

The synchronization object that many readers will immediately recognize is **Semaphore**, which implements a classic semaphore. A semaphore controls access to a shared resource through the use of a counter. If the counter is greater than zero, then access is allowed. If it is zero, then access is denied. What the counter is counting are *permits* that allow access to the shared resource. Thus, to access the resource, a thread must be granted a permit from the semaphore.

In general, to use a semaphore, the thread that wants access to the shared resource tries to acquire a permit. If the semaphore's count is greater than zero, then the thread acquires a permit, which causes the semaphore's count to be decremented. Otherwise, the thread will be blocked until a permit can be acquired. When the thread no longer needs access to the shared resource, it releases the permit, which causes the semaphore's count to be incremented. If there is another thread waiting for a permit, then that thread will acquire a permit at that time. Java's **Semaphore** class implements this mechanism.

**Semaphore** has the two constructors shown here:

Semaphore(int *num*)
Semaphore(int *num*, boolean *how*)

Here, *num* specifies the initial permit count. Thus, *num* specifies the number of threads that can access a shared resource at any one time. If *num* is one, then only one thread can access the resource at any one time. By default, waiting threads are granted a permit in an undefined order. By setting *how* to **true**, you can ensure that waiting threads are granted a permit in the order in which they requested access.

To acquire a permit, call the **acquire( )** method, which has these two forms:

void acquire( ) throws InterruptedException
void acquire(int *num*) throws InterruptedException

The first form acquires one permit. The second form acquires *num* permits. Most often, the first form is used. If the permit cannot be granted at the time of the call, then the invoking thread suspends until the permit is available.

To release a permit, call **release( )**, which has these two forms:

void release( )
void release(int *num*)

The first form releases one permit. The second form releases the number of permits specified by *num*.

To use a semaphore to control access to a resource, each thread that wants to use that resource must first call **acquire( )** before accessing the resource. When the thread is done with the resource, it must call **release( )**. Here is an example that illustrates the use of a semaphore:

```
// A simple semaphore example.

import java.util.concurrent.*;

class SemDemo {

  public static void main(String[] args) {
    Semaphore sem = new Semaphore(1);

    new Thread(new IncThread(sem, "A")).start();
    new Thread(new DecThread(sem, "B")).start();

  }
}

// A shared resource.
class Shared {
  static int count = 0;
}

// A thread of execution that increments count.
class IncThread implements Runnable {
  String name;
  Semaphore sem;

  IncThread(Semaphore s, String n) {
    sem = s;
    name = n;
  }

  public void run() {

    System.out.println("Starting " + name);

    try {
      // First, get a permit.
      System.out.println(name + " is waiting for a permit.");
      sem.acquire();
      System.out.println(name + " gets a permit.");

      // Now, access shared resource.
      for(int i=0; i < 5; i++) {
        Shared.count++;
        System.out.println(name + ": " + Shared.count);

        // Now, allow a context switch -- if possible.
        Thread.sleep(10);
      }
```

```
      } catch (InterruptedException exc) {
        System.out.println(exc);
      }

      // Release the permit.
      System.out.println(name + " releases the permit.");
      sem.release();
    }
  }

  // A thread of execution that decrements count.
  class DecThread implements Runnable {
    String name;
    Semaphore sem;

    DecThread(Semaphore s, String n) {
      sem = s;
      name = n;
    }

    public void run() {

      System.out.println("Starting " + name);

      try {
        // First, get a permit.
        System.out.println(name + " is waiting for a permit.");
        sem.acquire();
        System.out.println(name + " gets a permit.");

        // Now, access shared resource.
        for(int i=0; i < 5; i++) {
          Shared.count--;
          System.out.println(name + ": " + Shared.count);

          // Now, allow a context switch -- if possible.
          Thread.sleep(10);
        }
      } catch (InterruptedException exc) {
        System.out.println(exc);
      }

      // Release the permit.
      System.out.println(name + " releases the permit.");
      sem.release();
    }
  }
```

The output from the program is shown here. (The precise order in which the threads execute may vary.)

```
Starting A
A is waiting for a permit.
A gets a permit.
```

```
A: 1
Starting B
B is waiting for a permit.
A: 2
A: 3
A: 4
A: 5
A releases the permit.
B gets a permit.
B: 4
B: 3
B: 2
B: 1
B: 0
B releases the permit.
```



The program uses a semaphore to control access to the **count** variable, which is a static variable within the **Shared** class. **Shared.count** is incremented five times by the **run( )** method of **IncThread** and decremented five times by **DecThread**. To prevent these two threads from accessing **Shared.count** at the same time, access is allowed only after a permit is acquired from the controlling semaphore. After access is complete, the permit is released. In this way, only one thread at a time will access **Shared.count**, as the output shows.

In both **IncThread** and **DecThread**, notice the call to **sleep( )** within **run( )**. It is used to "prove" that accesses to **Shared.count** are synchronized by the semaphore. In **run( )**, the call to **sleep( )** causes the invoking thread to pause between each access to **Shared.count**. This would normally enable the second thread to run. However, because of the semaphore, the second thread must wait until the first has released the permit, which happens only after all accesses by the first thread are complete. Thus, **Shared.count** is incremented five times by **IncThread** and decremented five times by **DecThread**. The increments and decrements are *not* intermixed.

Without the use of the semaphore, accesses to **Shared.count** by both threads would have occurred simultaneously, and the increments and decrements would be intermixed. To confirm this, try commenting out the calls to **acquire( )** and **release( )**. When you run the program, you will see that access to **Shared.count** is no longer synchronized, and each thread accesses it as soon as it gets a timeslice.

Although many uses of a semaphore are as straightforward as that shown in the preceding program, more intriguing uses are also possible. Here is an example. The following program reworks the producer/consumer program shown in Chapter 11 so that it uses two semaphores to regulate the producer and consumer threads, ensuring that each call to **put( )** is followed by a corresponding call to **get( )**:

```
// An implementation of a producer and consumer
// that use semaphores to control synchronization.

import java.util.concurrent.Semaphore;

class Q {
  int n;
```

```
  // Start with consumer semaphore unavailable.
  static Semaphore semCon = new Semaphore(0);
  static Semaphore semProd = new Semaphore(1);

  void get() {
    try {
      semCon.acquire();
    } catch(InterruptedException e) {
      System.out.println("InterruptedException caught");
    }

    System.out.println("Got: " + n);
    semProd.release();
  }

  void put(int n) {
    try {
      semProd.acquire();
    } catch(InterruptedException e) {
      System.out.println("InterruptedException caught");
    }

    this.n = n;
    System.out.println("Put: " + n);
    semCon.release();
  }
}

class Producer implements Runnable {
  Q q;

  Producer(Q q) {
    this.q = q;
  }

  public void run() {
    for(int i=0; i < 20; i++) q.put(i);
  }
}

class Consumer implements Runnable {
  Q q;

  Consumer(Q q) {
    this.q = q;
  }

  public void run() {
    for(int i=0; i < 20; i++) q.get();
  }
}
```

```
class ProdCon {
  public static void main(String[] args) {
    Q q = new Q();
    new Thread(new Consumer(q), "Consumer").start();
    new Thread(new Producer(q), "Producer").start();
  }
}
```

A portion of the output is shown here:

```
Put: 0
Got: 0
Put: 1
Got: 1
Put: 2
Got: 2
Put: 3
Got: 3
Put: 4
Got: 4
Put: 5
Got: 5
.
.
.
```

As you can see, the calls to **put( )** and **get( )** are synchronized. That is, each call to **put( )** is followed by a call to **get( )** and no values are missed. Without the semaphores, multiple calls to **put( )** would have occurred without matching calls to **get( )**, resulting in values being missed. (To prove this, remove the semaphore code and observe the results.)

The sequencing of **put( )** and **get( )** calls is handled by two semaphores: **semProd** and **semCon**. Before **put( )** can produce a value, it must acquire a permit from **semProd**. After it has set the value, it releases **semCon**. Before **get( )** can consume a value, it must acquire a permit from **semCon**. After it consumes the value, it releases **semProd**. This "give and take" mechanism ensures that each call to **put( )** must be followed by a call to **get( )**.

Notice that **semCon** is initialized with no available permits. This ensures that **put( )** executes first. The ability to set the initial synchronization state is one of the more powerful aspects of a semaphore.

## CountDownLatch

Sometimes you will want a thread to wait until one or more events have occurred. To handle such a situation, the concurrent API supplies **CountDownLatch**. A **CountDownLatch** is initially created with a count of the number of events that must occur before the latch is released. Each time an event happens, the count is decremented. When the count reaches zero, the latch opens.

**CountDownLatch** has the following constructor:

CountDownLatch(int *num*)

Here, *num* specifies the number of events that must occur in order for the latch to open.

To wait on the latch, a thread calls **await( )**, which has the forms shown here:

void await( ) throws InterruptedException
boolean await(long *wait*, TimeUnit *tu*) throws InterruptedException

The first form waits until the count associated with the invoking **CountDownLatch** reaches zero. The second form waits only for the period of time specified by *wait*. The units represented by *wait* are specified by *tu*, which is an object of the **TimeUnit** enumeration. (**TimeUnit** is described later in this chapter.) It returns **false** if the time limit is reached and **true** if the countdown reaches zero.

To signal an event, call the **countDown( )** method, shown next:

void countDown( )

Each call to **countDown( )** decrements the count associated with the invoking object.

The following program demonstrates **CountDownLatch**. It creates a latch that requires five events to occur before it opens.

```
// An example of CountDownLatch.

import java.util.concurrent.CountDownLatch;

class CDLDemo {
  public static void main(String[] args) {
    CountDownLatch cdl = new CountDownLatch(5);

    System.out.println("Starting");

    new Thread(new MyThread(cdl)).start();

    try {
      cdl.await();
    } catch (InterruptedException exc) {
      System.out.println(exc);
    }

    System.out.println("Done");
  }
}

class MyThread implements Runnable {
  CountDownLatch latch;

  MyThread(CountDownLatch c) {
    latch = c;
  }

  public void run() {
    for(int i = 0; i<5; i++) {
      System.out.println(i);
      latch.countDown(); // decrement count
    }
  }
}
```

The output produced by the program is shown here:

```
Starting
0
1
2
3
4
Done
```

Inside **main( )**, a **CountDownLatch** called **cdl** is created with an initial count of five. Next, an instance of **MyThread** is created, which begins execution of a new thread. Notice that **cdl** is passed as a parameter to **MyThread**'s constructor and stored in the **latch** instance variable. Then, the main thread calls **await( )** on **cdl**, which causes execution of the main thread to pause until **cdl**'s count has been decremented five times.

Inside the **run( )** method of **MyThread**, a loop is created that iterates five times. With each iteration, the **countDown( )** method is called on **latch**, which refers to **cdl** in **main( )**. After the fifth iteration, the latch opens, which allows the main thread to resume.

**CountDownLatch** is a powerful yet easy-to-use synchronization object that is appropriate whenever a thread must wait for one or more events to occur.



## CyclicBarrier

A situation not uncommon in concurrent programming occurs when a set of two or more threads must wait at a predetermined execution point until all threads in the set have reached that point. To handle such a situation, the concurrent API supplies the **CyclicBarrier** class. It enables you to define a synchronization object that suspends until the specified number of threads has reached the barrier point.

**CyclicBarrier** has the following two constructors:

CyclicBarrier(int *numThreads*)
CyclicBarrier(int *numThreads*, Runnable *action*)

Here, *numThreads* specifies the number of threads that must reach the barrier before execution continues. In the second form, *action* specifies a thread that will be executed when the barrier is reached.

Here is the general procedure that you will follow to use **CyclicBarrier**. First, create a **CyclicBarrier** object, specifying the number of threads that you will be waiting for. Next, when each thread reaches the barrier, have it call **await( )** on that object. This will pause execution of the thread until all of the other threads also call **await( )**. Once the specified number of threads has reached the barrier, **await( )** will return and execution will resume. Also, if you have specified an action, then that thread is executed.

The **await( )** method has the following two forms:

int await( ) throws InterruptedException, BrokenBarrierException

int await(long *wait*, TimeUnit *tu*)
throws InterruptedException, BrokenBarrierException, TimeoutException

The first form waits until all the threads have reached the barrier point. The second form waits only for the period of time specified by *wait.* The units represented by *wait* are specified by *tu.* Both forms return a value that indicates the order that the threads arrive at the barrier point. The first thread returns a value equal to the number of threads waited upon minus one. The last thread returns zero.

Here is an example that illustrates **CyclicBarrier**. It waits until a set of three threads has reached the barrier. When that occurs, the thread specified by **BarAction** executes.

```
// An example of CyclicBarrier.

import java.util.concurrent.*;

class BarDemo {
  public static void main(String[] args) {
    CyclicBarrier cb = new CyclicBarrier(3, new BarAction() );

    System.out.println("Starting");

    new Thread(new MyThread(cb, "A")).start();
    new Thread(new MyThread(cb, "B")).start();
    new Thread(new MyThread(cb, "C")).start();

  }
}

// A thread of execution that uses a CyclicBarrier.

class MyThread implements Runnable {
  CyclicBarrier cbar;
  String name;

  MyThread(CyclicBarrier c, String n) {
    cbar = c;
    name = n;
  }

  public void run() {

    System.out.println(name);

    try {
      cbar.await();
    } catch (BrokenBarrierException exc) {
      System.out.println(exc);
    } catch (InterruptedException exc) {
      System.out.println(exc);
    }
  }
}

// An object of this class is called when the
// CyclicBarrier ends.
```

```
class BarAction implements Runnable {
  public void run() {
    System.out.println("Barrier Reached!");
  }
}
```

The output is shown here. (The precise order in which the threads execute may vary.)

```
Starting
A
B
C
Barrier Reached!
```



A **CyclicBarrier** can be reused because it will release waiting threads each time the specified number of threads calls **await( )**. For example, suppose you change **main( )** in the preceding program so that it looks like this:

```
public static void main(String[] args) {
  CyclicBarrier cb = new CyclicBarrier(3, new BarAction() );

  System.out.println("Starting");

  new Thread(new MyThread(cb, "A")).start();
  new Thread(new MyThread(cb, "B")).start();
  new Thread(new MyThread(cb, "C")).start();
  new Thread(new MyThread(cb, "X")).start();
  new Thread(new MyThread(cb, "Y")).start();
  new Thread(new MyThread(cb, "Z")).start();

}
```

In that case, the following output will be produced. (The precise order in which the threads execute may vary.)

```
Starting
A
B
C
Barrier Reached!
X
Y
Z
Barrier Reached!
```

As the preceding example shows, the **CyclicBarrier** offers a streamlined solution to what was previously a complicated problem.

## Exchanger

Perhaps the most interesting of the synchronization classes is **Exchanger**. It is designed to simplify the exchange of data between two threads. The operation of an **Exchanger** is astoundingly simple: it simply waits until two separate threads call its **exchange( )** method.

When that occurs, it exchanges the data supplied by the threads. This mechanism is both elegant and easy to use. Uses for **Exchanger** are easy to imagine. For example, one thread might prepare a buffer for receiving information over a network connection. Another thread might fill that buffer with the information from the connection. The two threads work together so that each time a new buffer is needed, an exchange is made.

**Exchanger** is a generic class that is declared as shown here:

Exchanger<V>

Here, **V** specifies the type of the data being exchanged.

The only method defined by **Exchanger** is **exchange( )**, which has the two forms shown here:

V exchange(V *objRef*) throws InterruptedException
V exchange(V *objRef*, long *wait*, TimeUnit *tu*)
  throws InterruptedException, TimeoutException

Here, *objRef* is a reference to the data to exchange. The data received from the other thread is returned. The second form of **exchange( )** allows a time-out period to be specified. The key point about **exchange( )** is that it won't succeed until it has been called on the same **Exchanger** object by two separate threads. Thus, **exchange( )** synchronizes the exchange of the data.

Here is an example that demonstrates **Exchanger**. It creates two threads. One thread creates an empty buffer that will receive the data put into it by the second thread. In this case, the data is a string. Thus, the first thread exchanges an empty string for a full one.

```
// An example of Exchanger.

import java.util.concurrent.Exchanger;

class ExgrDemo {
  public static void main(String[] args) {
    Exchanger<String> exgr = new Exchanger<String>();

    new Thread(new UseString(exgr)).start();
    new Thread(new MakeString(exgr)).start();
  }
}

// A Thread that constructs a string.
class MakeString implements Runnable {
  Exchanger<String> ex;
  String str;

  MakeString(Exchanger<String> c) {
    ex = c;
    str = new String();

  }
```

```
  public void run() {
    char ch = 'A';

    for(int i = 0; i < 3; i++) {

      // Fill Buffer
      for(int j = 0; j < 5; j++)
        str += ch++;

      try {
        // Exchange a full buffer for an empty one.
        str = ex.exchange(str);
      } catch(InterruptedException exc) {
        System.out.println(exc);
      }
    }
  }
}

// A Thread that uses a string.
class UseString implements Runnable {
  Exchanger<String> ex;
  String str;
  UseString(Exchanger<String> c) {
    ex = c;
  }

  public void run() {

    for(int i=0; i < 3; i++) {
      try {
        // Exchange an empty buffer for a full one.
        str = ex.exchange(new String());
        System.out.println("Got: " + str);
      } catch(InterruptedException exc) {
        System.out.println(exc);
      }
    }
  }
}
```

Here is the output produced by the program:

```
Got: ABCDE
Got: FGHIJ
Got: KLMNO
```

In the program, the **main( )** method creates an **Exchanger** for strings. This object is then used to synchronize the exchange of strings between the **MakeString** and **UseString** classes. The **MakeString** class fills a string with data. The **UseString** exchanges an empty string for a full one. It then displays the contents of the newly constructed string. The exchange of empty and full buffers is synchronized by the **exchange( )** method, which is called by both classes' **run( )** method.

## Phaser

Another synchronization class is called **Phaser**. Its primary purpose is to enable the synchronization of threads that represent one or more phases of activity. For example, you might have a set of threads that implement three phases of an order-processing application. In the first phase, separate threads are used to validate customer information, check inventory, and confirm pricing. When that phase is complete, the second phase has two threads that compute shipping costs and all applicable tax. After that, a final phase confirms payment and determines estimated shipping time. In the past, to synchronize the multiple threads that comprise this scenario would require a bit of work on your part. With the inclusion of **Phaser**, the process is now much easier.

To begin, it helps to know that a **Phaser** works a bit like a **CyclicBarrier**, described earlier, except that it supports multiple phases. As a result, **Phaser** lets you define a synchronization object that waits until a specific phase has completed. It then advances to the next phase, again waiting until that phase concludes. It is important to understand that **Phaser** can also be used to synchronize only a single phase. In this regard, it acts much like a **CyclicBarrier**. However, its primary use is to synchronize multiple phases.

**Phaser** defines four constructors. Here are the two used in this section:

Phaser( )

Phaser(int *numParties*)

The first creates a phaser that has a registration count of zero. The second sets the registration count to *numParties*. The term *party* is often applied to the objects that register with a phaser. Although typically there is a one-to-one correspondence between the number of registrants and the number of threads being synchronized, this is not required. In both cases, the current phase is zero. That is, when a **Phaser** is created, it is initially at phase zero.

In general, here is how you use **Phaser**. First, create a new instance of **Phaser**. Next, register one or more parties with the phaser, either by calling **register( )** or by specifying the number of parties in the constructor. For each registered party, have the phaser wait until all registered parties complete a phase. A party signals this by calling one of a variety of methods supplied by **Phaser**, such as **arrive( )** or **arriveAndAwaitAdvance( )**. After all parties have arrived, the phase is complete, and the phaser can move on to the next phase (if there is one) or terminate. The following sections explain the process in detail.

To register parties after a **Phaser** has been constructed, call **register( )**. It is shown here:

int register()

It returns the phase number of the phase to which it is registered.

To signal that a party has completed a phase, it must call **arrive( )** or some variation of **arrive( )**. When the number of arrivals equals the number of registered parties, the phase is completed and the **Phaser** moves on to the next phase (if there is one). The **arrive( )** method has this general form:

int arrive( )

This method signals that a party (normally a thread of execution) has completed some task (or portion of a task). It returns the current phase number. If the phaser has been terminated, then it returns a negative value. The **arrive( )** method does not suspend execution of the calling thread. This means that it does not wait for the phase to be completed. This method should be called only by a registered party.

If you want to indicate the completion of a phase and then wait until all other registrants have also completed that phase, use **arriveAndAwaitAdvance( )**. It is shown here:

int arriveAndAwaitAdvance( )

It waits until all parties have arrived. It returns the next phase number or a negative value if the phaser has been terminated. This method should be called only by a registered party.

A thread can arrive and then deregister itself by calling **arriveAndDeregister( )**. It is shown here:

int arriveAndDeregister( )

It returns the current phase number or a negative value if the phaser has been terminated. It does not wait until the phase is complete. This method should be called only by a registered party.

To obtain the current phase number, call **getPhase( )**, which is shown here:

final int getPhase( )

When a **Phaser** is created, the first phase will be 0, the second phase 1, the third phase 2, and so on. A negative value is returned if the invoking **Phaser** has been terminated.

Here is an example that shows **Phaser** in action. It creates three threads, each of which have three phases. It uses a **Phaser** to synchronize each phase.

```
// An example of Phaser.

import java.util.concurrent.*;

class PhaserDemo {
  public static void main(String[] args) {
    Phaser phsr = new Phaser(1);
    int curPhase;

    System.out.println("Starting");

    new Thread(new MyThread(phsr, "A")).start();
    new Thread(new MyThread(phsr, "B")).start();
    new Thread(new MyThread(phsr, "C")).start();

    // Wait for all threads to complete phase one.
    curPhase = phsr.getPhase();
    phsr.arriveAndAwaitAdvance();
    System.out.println("Phase " + curPhase + " Complete");

    // Wait for all threads to complete phase two.
    curPhase =  phsr.getPhase();
    phsr.arriveAndAwaitAdvance();
    System.out.println("Phase " + curPhase + " Complete");

    curPhase =  phsr.getPhase();
    phsr.arriveAndAwaitAdvance();
    System.out.println("Phase " + curPhase + " Complete");
```

Part II

```
    // Deregister the main thread.
    phsr.arriveAndDeregister();

    if(phsr.isTerminated())
      System.out.println("The Phaser is terminated");
  }
}

// A thread of execution that uses a Phaser.
class MyThread implements Runnable {
  Phaser phsr;
  String name;

  MyThread(Phaser p, String n) {
    phsr = p;
    name = n;
    phsr.register();
  }

  public void run() {

    System.out.println("Thread " + name + " Beginning Phase One");
    phsr.arriveAndAwaitAdvance(); // Signal arrival.

    // Pause a bit to prevent jumbled output. This is for illustration
    // only. It is not required for the proper operation of the phaser.
    try {
      Thread.sleep(100);
    } catch(InterruptedException e) {
      System.out.println(e);
    }

    System.out.println("Thread " + name + " Beginning Phase Two");
    phsr.arriveAndAwaitAdvance(); // Signal arrival.

    // Pause a bit to prevent jumbled output. This is for illustration
    // only. It is not required for the proper operation of the phaser.
    try {
      Thread.sleep(100);
    } catch(InterruptedException e) {
      System.out.println(e);
    }

    System.out.println("Thread " + name + " Beginning Phase Three");
    phsr.arriveAndDeregister(); // Signal arrival and deregister.
  }
}
```

Sample output is shown here. (Your output may vary.)

```
Starting
Thread A Beginning Phase One
Thread C Beginning Phase One
Thread B Beginning Phase One
```

```
Phase 0 Complete
Thread B Beginning Phase Two
Thread C Beginning Phase Two
Thread A Beginning Phase Two
Phase 1 Complete
Thread C Beginning Phase Three
Thread B Beginning Phase Three
Thread A Beginning Phase Three
Phase 2 Complete
The Phaser is terminated
```



Let's look closely at the key sections of the program. First, in **main( )**, a **Phaser** called **phsr** is created with an initial party count of 1 (which corresponds to the main thread). Then three threads are started by creating three **MyThread** objects. Notice that **MyThread** is passed a reference to **phsr** (the phaser). The **MyThread** objects use this phaser to synchronize their activities. Next, **main( )** calls **getPhase( )** to obtain the current phase number (which is initially zero) and then calls **arriveAndAwaitAdvance( )**. This causes **main( )** to suspend until phase zero has completed. This won't happen until all **MyThread**s also call **arriveAndAwaitAdvance( )**. When this occurs, **main( )** will resume execution, at which point it displays that phase zero has completed, and it moves on to the next phase. This process repeats until all three phases have finished. Then, **main( )** calls **arriveAndDeregister( )**. At that point, all three **MyThread**s have also deregistered. Since this results in there being no registered parties when the phaser advances to the next phase, the phaser is terminated.

Now look at **MyThread**. First, notice that the constructor is passed a reference to the phaser that it will use and then registers with the new thread as a party on that phaser. Thus, each new **MyThread** becomes a party registered with the passed-in phaser. Also notice that each thread has three phases. In this example, each phase consists of a placeholder that simply displays the name of the thread and what it is doing. Obviously, in real-world code, the thread would be performing more meaningful actions. Between the first two phases, the thread calls **arriveAndAwaitAdvance( )**. Thus, each thread waits until all threads have completed the phase (and the main thread is ready). After all threads have arrived (including the main thread), the phaser moves on to the next phase. After the third phase, each thread deregisters itself with a call to **arriveAndDeregister( )**. As the comments in **MyThread** explain, the calls to **sleep( )** are used for the purposes of illustration to ensure that the output is not jumbled because of the multithreading. They are not needed to make the phaser work properly. If you remove them, the output may look a bit jumbled, but the phases will still be synchronized correctly.

One other point. Although the preceding example used three threads that were all of the same type, this is not a requirement. Each party that uses a phaser can be unique, with each performing some separate task.

It is possible to take control of precisely what happens when a phase advance occurs. To do this, you must override the **onAdvance( )** method. This method is called by the run time when a **Phaser** advances from one phase to the next. It is shown here:

protected boolean onAdvance(int *phase*, int *numParties*)

Here, *phase* will contain the current phase number prior to being incremented and *numParties* will contain the number of registered parties. To terminate the phaser, **onAdvance( )** must return **true**. To keep the phaser alive, **onAdvance( )** must return **false**.

The default version of **onAdvance( )** returns **true** (thus terminating the phaser) when there are no registered parties. As a general rule, your override should also follow this practice.

One reason to override **onAdvance( )** is to enable a phaser to execute a specific number of phases and then stop. The following example gives you the flavor of this usage. It creates a class called **MyPhaser** that extends **Phaser** so that it will run a specified number of phases. It does this by overriding the **onAdvance( )** method. The **MyPhaser** constructor accepts one argument, which specifies the number of phases to execute. Notice that **MyPhaser** automatically registers one party. This behavior is useful in this example, but the needs of your own applications may differ.

```
// Extend Phaser and override onAdvance() so that only a specific
// number of phases are executed.

import java.util.concurrent.*;

// Extend MyPhaser to allow only a specific number of phases
// to be executed.
class MyPhaser extends Phaser {
  int numPhases;

  MyPhaser(int parties, int phaseCount) {
    super(parties);
    numPhases = phaseCount - 1;
  }

  // Override onAdvance() to execute the specified
  // number of phases.
  protected boolean onAdvance(int p, int regParties) {
    // This println() statement is for illustration only.
    // Normally, onAdvance() will not display output.
    System.out.println("Phase " + p + " completed.\n");

    // If all phases have completed, return true
    if(p == numPhases || regParties == 0) return true;

    // Otherwise, return false.
    return false;
  }
}

class PhaserDemo2 {
  public static void main(String[] args) {

    MyPhaser phsr = new MyPhaser(1, 4);

    System.out.println("Starting\n");

    new Thread(new MyThread(phsr, "A")).start();
    new Thread(new MyThread(phsr, "B")).start();
    new Thread(new MyThread(phsr, "C")).start();
```

```
      // Wait for the specified number of phases to complete.
      while(!phsr.isTerminated()) {
        phsr.arriveAndAwaitAdvance();
      }

      System.out.println("The Phaser is terminated");
    }
  }

  // A thread of execution that uses a Phaser.
  class MyThread implements Runnable {
    Phaser phsr;
    String name;

    MyThread(Phaser p, String n) {
      phsr = p;
      name = n;
      phsr.register();
    }

    public void run() {

      while(!phsr.isTerminated()) {
        System.out.println("Thread " + name + " Beginning Phase " +
                           phsr.getPhase());

        phsr.arriveAndAwaitAdvance();

        // Pause a bit to prevent jumbled output. This is for illustration
        // only. It is not required for the proper operation of the phaser.
        try {
          Thread.sleep(100);
        } catch(InterruptedException e) {
          System.out.println(e);
        }
      }
    }
  }
```

The output from the program is shown here:

```
Starting

Thread B Beginning Phase 0
Thread A Beginning Phase 0
Thread C Beginning Phase 0
Phase 0 completed.

Thread A Beginning Phase 1
Thread B Beginning Phase 1
Thread C Beginning Phase 1
Phase 1 completed.
```

```
Thread C Beginning Phase 2
Thread B Beginning Phase 2
Thread A Beginning Phase 2
Phase 2 completed.

Thread C Beginning Phase 3
Thread B Beginning Phase 3
Thread A Beginning Phase 3
Phase 3 completed.

The Phaser is terminated
```

Inside **main( )**, one instance of **Phaser** is created. It is passed 4 as an argument, which means that it will execute four phases and then stop. Next, three threads are created and then the following loop is entered:

```
// Wait for the specified number of phases to complete.
while(!phsr.isTerminated()) {
  phsr.arriveAndAwaitAdvance();
}
```

This loop simply calls **arriveAndAwaitAdvance( )** until the phaser is terminated. The phaser won't terminate until the specified number of phases have been executed. In this case, the loop continues to execute until four phases have run. Next, notice that the threads also call **arriveAndAwaitAdvance( )** within a loop that runs until the phaser is terminated. This means that they will execute until the specified number of phases has been completed.

Now, look closely at the code for **onAdvance( )**. Each time **onAdvance( )** is called, it is passed the current phase and the number of registered parties. If the current phase equals the specified phase, or if the number of registered parties is zero, **onAdvance( )** returns **true**, thus stopping the phaser. This is accomplished with this line of code:

```
// If all phases have completed, return true
if(p == numPhases || regParties == 0) return true;
```

As you can see, very little code is needed to accommodate the desired outcome.

Before moving on, it is useful to point out that you don't necessarily need to explicitly extend **Phaser** as the previous example does to simply override **onAdvance( )**. In some cases, more compact code can be created by using an anonymous inner class to override **onAdvance( )**.

**Phaser** has additional capabilities that may be of use in your applications. You can wait for a specific phase by calling **awaitAdvance( )**, which is shown here:

int awaitAdvance(int *phase*)

Here, *phase* indicates the phase number on which **awaitAdvance( )** will wait until a transition to the next phase takes place. It will return immediately if the argument passed to *phase* is not equal to the current phase. It will also return immediately if the phaser is terminated. However, if *phase* is passed the current phase, then it will wait until the phase increments. This method should be called only by a registered party. There is also an interruptible version of this method called **awaitAdvanceInterruptibly( )**.

To register more than one party, call **bulkRegister( )**. To obtain the number of registered parties, call **getRegisteredParties( )**. You can also obtain the number of arrived parties and unarrived parties by calling **getArrivedParties( )** and **getUnarrivedParties( )**, respectively. To force the phaser to enter a terminated state, call **forceTermination( )**.

**Phaser** also lets you create a tree of phasers. This is supported by two additional constructors, which let you specify the parent, and the **getParent( )** method.

## Using an Executor



The concurrent API supplies a feature called an *executor* that initiates and controls the execution of threads. As such, an executor offers an alternative to managing threads through the **Thread** class.

At the core of an executor is the **Executor** interface. It defines the following method:

void execute(Runnable *thread*)

The thread specified by *thread* is executed. Thus, **execute( )** starts the specified thread.

The **ExecutorService** interface extends **Executor** by adding methods that help manage and control the execution of threads. For example, **ExecutorService** defines **shutdown( )**, shown here, which stops the invoking **ExecutorService**:

void shutdown( )

**ExecutorService** also defines methods that execute threads that return results, that execute a set of threads, and that determine the shutdown status. We will look at several of these methods a little later.

Also defined is the interface **ScheduledExecutorService**, which extends **ExecutorService** to support the scheduling of threads.

The concurrent API defines three predefined executor classes: **ThreadPoolExecutor**, **ScheduledThreadPoolExecutor**, and **ForkJoinPool**. **ThreadPoolExecutor** implements the **Executor** and **ExecutorService** interfaces and provides support for a managed pool of threads. **ScheduledThreadPoolExecutor** also implements the **ScheduledExecutorService** interface to allow a pool of threads to be scheduled. **ForkJoinPool** implements the **Executor** and **ExecutorService** interfaces and is used by the Fork/Join Framework. It is described later in this chapter.

A thread pool provides a set of threads that is used to execute various tasks. Instead of each task using its own thread, the threads in the pool are used. This reduces the overhead associated with creating many separate threads. Although you can use **ThreadPoolExecutor** and **ScheduledThreadPoolExecutor** directly, most often you will want to obtain an executor by calling one of the static factory methods defined by the **Executors** utility class. Here are some examples:

static ExecutorService newCachedThreadPool( )
static ExecutorService newFixedThreadPool(int *numThreads*)
static ScheduledExecutorService newScheduledThreadPool(int *numThreads*)

**newCachedThreadPool( )** creates a thread pool that adds threads as needed but reuses threads if possible. **newFixedThreadPool( )** creates a thread pool that consists of a specified number of threads. **newScheduledThreadPool( )** creates a thread pool that supports thread scheduling. Each returns a reference to an **ExecutorService** that can be used to manage the pool.

## A Simple Executor Example

Before going any further, a simple example that uses an executor will be of value. The following program creates a fixed thread pool that contains two threads. It then uses that pool to execute four tasks. Thus, four tasks share the two threads that are in the pool. After the tasks finish, the pool is shut down and the program ends.

```
// A simple example that uses an Executor.

import java.util.concurrent.*;

class SimpExec {
  public static void main(String[] args) {
    CountDownLatch cdl = new CountDownLatch(5);
    CountDownLatch cdl2 = new CountDownLatch(5);
    CountDownLatch cdl3 = new CountDownLatch(5);
    CountDownLatch cdl4 = new CountDownLatch(5);
    ExecutorService es = Executors.newFixedThreadPool(2);

    System.out.println("Starting");

    // Start the threads.
    es.execute(new MyThread(cdl, "A"));
    es.execute(new MyThread(cdl2, "B"));
    es.execute(new MyThread(cdl3, "C"));
    es.execute(new MyThread(cdl4, "D"));

    try {
      cdl.await();
      cdl2.await();
      cdl3.await();
      cdl4.await();
    } catch (InterruptedException exc) {
      System.out.println(exc);
    }

    es.shutdown();
    System.out.println("Done");
  }
}

class MyThread implements Runnable {
  String name;
  CountDownLatch latch;

  MyThread(CountDownLatch c, String n) {
    latch = c;
    name = n;

  }
```

```
    public void run() {

      for(int i = 0; i < 5; i++) {
        System.out.println(name + ": " + i);
        latch.countDown();
      }
    }
  }
```

The output from the program is shown here. (The precise order in which the threads execute may vary.)

```
Starting
A: 0
A: 1
A: 2
A: 3
A: 4
C: 0
C: 1
C: 2
C: 3
C: 4
D: 0
D: 1
D: 2
D: 3
D: 4
B: 0
B: 1
B: 2
B: 3
B: 4
Done
```

As the output shows, even though the thread pool contains only two threads, all four tasks are still executed. However, only two can run at the same time. The others must wait until one of the pooled threads is available for use.

The call to **shutdown( )** is important. If it were not present in the program, then the program would not terminate because the executor would remain active. To try this for yourself, simply comment out the call to **shutdown( )** and observe the result.

## Using Callable and Future

One of the most interesting features of the concurrent API is the **Callable** interface. This interface represents a thread that returns a value. An application can use **Callable** objects to compute results that are then returned to the invoking thread. This is a powerful mechanism because it facilitates the coding of many types of numerical computations in which partial results are computed simultaneously. It can also be used to run a thread that returns a status code that indicates the successful completion of the thread.

**Callable** is a generic interface that is defined like this:

interface Callable<V>

Here, **V** indicates the type of data returned by the task. **Callable** defines only one method, **call( )**, which is shown here:

V call( ) throws Exception

Inside **call( )**, you define the task that you want performed. After that task completes, you return the result. If the result cannot be computed, **call( )** must throw an exception.

A **Callable** task is executed by an **ExecutorService**, by calling its **submit( )** method. There are three forms of **submit( )**, but only one is used to execute a **Callable**. It is shown here:

<T> Future<T> submit(Callable<T> *task*)

Here, *task* is the **Callable** object that will be executed in its own thread. The result is returned through an object of type **Future.**

**Future** is a generic interface that represents the value that will be returned by a **Callable** object. Because this value is obtained at some future time, the name **Future** is appropriate. **Future** is defined like this:

interface Future<V>

Here, **V** specifies the type of the result.

To obtain the returned value, you will call **Future**'s **get( )** method, which has these two forms:

V get( )
throws InterruptedException, ExecutionException

V get(long *wait*, TimeUnit *tu*)
throws InterruptedException, ExecutionException, TimeoutException

The first form waits for the result indefinitely. The second form allows you to specify a timeout period in *wait.* The units of *wait* are passed in *tu,* which is an object of the **TimeUnit** enumeration, described later in this chapter.

The following program illustrates **Callable** and **Future** by creating three tasks that perform three different computations. The first returns the summation of a value, the second computes the length of the hypotenuse of a right triangle given the length of its sides, and the third computes the factorial of a value. All three computations occur simultaneously.

```
// An example that uses a Callable.

import java.util.concurrent.*;

class CallableDemo {
  public static void main(String[] args) {
    ExecutorService es = Executors.newFixedThreadPool(3);
    Future<Integer> f;
    Future<Double> f2;
    Future<Integer> f3;

    System.out.println("Starting");
```

```
    f = es.submit(new Sum(10));
    f2 = es.submit(new Hypot(3, 4));
    f3 = es.submit(new Factorial(5));

    try {
      System.out.println(f.get());
      System.out.println(f2.get());
      System.out.println(f3.get());
    } catch (InterruptedException exc) {
      System.out.println(exc);
    }
    catch (ExecutionException exc) {
      System.out.println(exc);
    }

    es.shutdown();
    System.out.println("Done");
  }
}

// Following are three computational threads.

class Sum implements Callable<Integer> {
  int stop;

  Sum(int v) { stop = v; }

  public Integer call() {
    int sum = 0;
    for(int i = 1; i <= stop; i++) {
      sum += i;
    }
    return sum;
  }
}

class Hypot implements Callable<Double> {
  double side1, side2;

  Hypot(double s1, double s2) {
    side1 = s1;
    side2 = s2;
  }

  public Double call() {
    return Math.sqrt((side1*side1) + (side2*side2));
  }
}

class Factorial implements Callable<Integer> {
  int stop;

  Factorial(int v) { stop = v; }
```

```
    public Integer call() {
      int fact = 1;
      for(int i = 2; i <= stop; i++) {
        fact *= i;
      }
      return fact;
    }
}
```

The output is shown here:

```
Starting
55
5.0
120
Done
```

## The TimeUnit Enumeration

The concurrent API defines several methods that take an argument of type **TimeUnit**, which indicates a time-out period. **TimeUnit** is an enumeration that is used to specify the *granularity* (or resolution) of the timing. **TimeUnit** is defined within **java.util.concurrent**. It can be one of the following values:

DAYS
HOURS
MINUTES
SECONDS
MICROSECONDS
MILLISECONDS
NANOSECONDS

Although **TimeUnit** lets you specify any of these values in calls to methods that take a timing argument, there is no guarantee that the system is capable of the specified resolution.

Here is an example that uses **TimeUnit**. The **CallableDemo** class, shown in the previous section, is modified as shown next to use the second form of **get( )** that takes a **TimeUnit** argument.

```
try {
  System.out.println(f.get(10, TimeUnit.MILLISECONDS));
  System.out.println(f2.get(10, TimeUnit.MILLISECONDS));
  System.out.println(f3.get(10, TimeUnit.MILLISECONDS));
} catch (InterruptedException exc) {
  System.out.println(exc);
}
catch (ExecutionException exc) {
  System.out.println(exc);
} catch (TimeoutException exc) {
  System.out.println(exc);
}
```

In this version, no call to **get( )** will wait more than 10 milliseconds.

The **TimeUnit** enumeration defines various methods that convert between units. Those originally defined by **TimeUnit** are shown here:

long convert(long *tval*, TimeUnit *tu*)
long toMicros(long *tval*)
long toMillis(long *tval*)
long toNanos(long *tval*)
long toSeconds(long *tval*)
long toDays(long *tval*)
long toHours(long *tval*)
long toMinutes(long *tval*)

The **convert( )** method converts *tval* into the specified unit and returns the result. The **to** methods perform the indicated conversion and return the result. To these methods, JDK 9 added the methods **toChronoUnit( )** and **of( )**, which convert between **java.time.temporal.ChronoUnits** and **TimeUnits**. JDK 11 added another version of **convert( )** that converts a **java.time.Duration** object into a **long**.

**TimeUnit** also defines the following timing methods:

void sleep(long *delay*) throws InterruptedExecution
void timedJoin(Thread *thrd*, long *delay*) throws InterruptedExecution
void timedWait(Object *obj*, long *delay*) throws InterruptedExecution

Here, **sleep( )** pauses execution for the specified delay period, which is specified in terms of the invoking enumeration constant. It translates into a call to **Thread.sleep( )**. The **timedJoin( )** method is a specialized version of **Thread.join( )** in which *thrd* pauses for the time period specified by *delay*, which is described in terms of the invoking time unit. The **timedWait( )** method is a specialized version of **Object.wait( )** in which *obj* is waited on for the period of time specified by *delay*, which is described in terms of the invoking time unit.

## The Concurrent Collections

As explained, the concurrent API defines several collection classes that have been engineered for concurrent operation. They include:

ArrayBlockingQueue
ConcurrentHashMap
ConcurrentLinkedDeque
ConcurrentLinkedQueue
ConcurrentSkipListMap
ConcurrentSkipListSet
CopyOnWriteArrayList
CopyOnWriteArraySet
DelayQueue
LinkedBlockingDeque
LinkedBlockingQueue
LinkedTransferQueue
PriorityBlockingQueue
SynchronousQueue

These offer concurrent alternatives to their related classes defined by the Collections Framework. These collections work much like the other collections except that they provide concurrency support. Programmers familiar with the Collections Framework will have no trouble using these concurrent collections.

## Locks

The **java.util.concurrent.locks** package provides support for *locks,* which are objects that offer an alternative to using **synchronized** to control access to a shared resource. In general, here is how a lock works. Before accessing a shared resource, the lock that protects that resource is acquired. When access to the resource is complete, the lock is released. If a second thread attempts to acquire the lock when it is in use by another thread, the second thread will suspend until the lock is released. In this way, conflicting access to a shared resource is prevented.

Locks are particularly useful when multiple threads need to access the value of shared data. For example, an inventory application might have a thread that first confirms that an item is in stock and then decreases the number of items on hand as each sale occurs. If two or more of these threads are running, then without some form of synchronization, it would be possible for one thread to be in the middle of a transaction when the second thread begins its transaction. The result could be that both threads would assume that adequate inventory exists, even if there is only sufficient inventory on hand to satisfy one sale. In this type of situation, a lock offers a convenient means of handling the needed synchronization.

The **Lock** interface defines a lock. The methods defined by **Lock** are shown in Table 29-1. In general, to acquire a lock, call **lock( )**. If the lock is unavailable, **lock( )** will wait. To release a lock, call **unlock( )**. To see if a lock is available, and to acquire it if it is, call **tryLock( )**. This

| Method | Description |
|---|---|
| void lock( ) | Waits until the invoking lock can be acquired. |
| void lockInterruptibly( ) throws InterruptedException | Waits until the invoking lock can be acquired, unless interrupted. |
| Condition newCondition( ) | Returns a **Condition** object that is associated with the invoking lock. |
| boolean tryLock( ) | Attempts to acquire the lock. This method will not wait if the lock is unavailable. Instead, it returns **true** if the lock has been acquired and **false** if the lock is currently in use by another thread. |
| boolean tryLock(long *wait,* TimeUnit *tu*) throws InterruptedException | Attempts to acquire the lock. If the lock is unavailable, this method will wait no longer than the period specified by *wait,* which is in *tu* units. It returns **true** if the lock has been acquired and **false** if the lock cannot be acquired within the specified period. |
| void unlock( ) | Releases the lock. |

**Table 29-1** The **Lock** Methods

method will not wait for the lock if it is unavailable. Instead, it returns **true** if the lock is acquired and **false** otherwise. The **newCondition( )** method returns a **Condition** object associated with the lock. Using a **Condition**, you gain detailed control of the lock through methods such as **await( )** and **signal( )**, which provide functionality similar to **Object.wait( )** and **Object.notify( )**.

**java.util.concurrent.locks** supplies an implementation of **Lock** called **ReentrantLock**. **ReentrantLock** implements a *reentrant lock,* which is a lock that can be repeatedly entered by the thread that currently holds the lock. Of course, in the case of a thread reentering a lock, all calls to **lock( )** must be offset by an equal number of calls to **unlock( )**. Otherwise, a thread seeking to acquire the lock will suspend until the lock is not in use.

The following program demonstrates the use of a lock. It creates two threads that access a shared resource called **Shared.count**. Before a thread can access **Shared.count**, it must obtain a lock. After obtaining the lock, **Shared.count** is incremented and then, before releasing the lock, the thread sleeps. This causes the second thread to attempt to obtain the lock. However, because the lock is still held by the first thread, the second thread must wait until the first thread stops sleeping and releases the lock. The output shows that access to **Shared.count** is, indeed, synchronized by the lock.

```
// A simple lock example.

import java.util.concurrent.locks.*;

class LockDemo {

  public static void main(String[] args) {
    ReentrantLock lock = new ReentrantLock();

    new Thread(new LockThread(lock, "A")).start();
    new Thread(new LockThread(lock, "B")).start();
  }
}

// A shared resource.
class Shared {
  static int count = 0;
}

// A thread of execution that increments count.
class LockThread implements Runnable {
  String name;
  ReentrantLock lock;

  LockThread(ReentrantLock lk, String n) {
    lock = lk;
    name = n;
  }

  public void run() {

    System.out.println("Starting " + name);
```

Part II

```
      try {
        // First, lock count.
        System.out.println(name + " is waiting to lock count.");
        lock.lock();
        System.out.println(name + " is locking count.");

        Shared.count++;
        System.out.println(name + ": " + Shared.count);

        // Now, allow a context switch -- if possible.
        System.out.println(name + " is sleeping.");
        Thread.sleep(1000);
      } catch (InterruptedException exc) {
        System.out.println(exc);
      } finally {
        // Unlock
        System.out.println(name + " is unlocking count.");
        lock.unlock();
      }
    }
  }
```

The output is shown here. (The precise order in which the threads execute may vary.)

```
Starting A
A is waiting to lock count.
A is locking count.
A: 1
A is sleeping.
Starting B
B is waiting to lock count.
A is unlocking count.
B is locking count.
B: 2
B is sleeping.
B is unlocking count.
```

**java.util.concurrent.locks** also defines the **ReadWriteLock** interface. This interface specifies a lock that maintains separate locks for read and write access. This enables multiple locks to be granted for readers of a resource as long as the resource is not being written. **ReentrantReadWriteLock** provides an implementation of **ReadWriteLock**.

**NOTE** There is a specialized lock called **StampedLock**. It does not implement the **Lock** or **ReadWriteLock** interfaces. It does, however, provide a mechanism that enables aspects of it to be used like a **Lock** or **ReadWriteLock**.

## Atomic Operations

**java.util.concurrent.atomic** offers an alternative to the other synchronization features when reading or writing the value of some types of variables. This package offers methods that get, set, or compare the value of a variable in one uninterruptible (that is, atomic) operation. This means that no lock or other synchronization mechanism is required.

Atomic operations are accomplished through the use of classes, such as **AtomicInteger** and **AtomicLong**, and methods, such as **get( )**, **set( )**, **compareAndSet( )**, **decrementAndGet( )**, and **getAndSet( )**, which perform the action indicated by their names.

Here is an example that demonstrates how access to a shared integer can be synchronized by the use of **AtomicInteger**:

```
// A simple example of Atomic.

import java.util.concurrent.atomic.*;

class AtomicDemo {

  public static void main(String[] args) {
    new Thread(new AtomThread("A")).start();
    new Thread(new AtomThread("B")).start();
    new Thread(new AtomThread("C")).start();
  }
}

class Shared {
  static AtomicInteger ai = new AtomicInteger(0);
}

// A thread of execution that increments count.
class AtomThread implements Runnable {
  String name;

  AtomThread(String n) {
    name = n;
  }

public void run() {

  System.out.println("Starting " + name);

  for(int i=1; i <= 3; i++)
    System.out.println(name + " got: " +
           Shared.ai.getAndSet(i));
  }
}
```

In the program, a static **AtomicInteger** named **ai** is created by **Shared**. Then, three threads of type **AtomThread** are created. Inside **run( )**, **Shared.ai** is modified by calling **getAndSet( )**. This method returns the previous value and then sets the value to the one passed as an argument. The use of **AtomicInteger** prevents two threads from writing to **ai** at the same time.

In general, the atomic operations offer a convenient (and possibly more efficient) alternative to the other synchronization mechanisms when only a single variable is involved. Among other features, **java.util.concurrent.atomic** also provides four classes that support lock-free cumulative operations. These are **DoubleAccumulator**, **DoubleAdder**, **LongAccumulator**, and **LongAdder**. The accumulator classes support a series of user-specified operations. The adder classes maintain a cumulative sum.

## Parallel Programming via the Fork/Join Framework

In recent years, an important trend has emerged in software development: *parallel programming*. Parallel programming is the name commonly given to the techniques that take advantage of computers that contain two or more processors (multicore). As most readers will know, multicore computers have become commonplace. The advantage that multi-processor environments offer is the ability to significantly increase program performance. As a result, a mechanism was needed that gives Java programmers a simple, yet effective way to make use of multiple processors in a clean, scalable manner. To answer this need, several new classes and interfaces that support parallel programming were incorporated into the concurrent API when JDK 7 was released. They are commonly referred to as the *Fork/Join Framework*. The Fork/Join Framework is defined in the **java.util.concurrent** package.

The Fork/Join Framework enhances multithreaded programming in two important ways. First, it simplifies the creation and use of multiple threads. Second, it automatically makes use of multiple processors. In other words, by using the Fork/Join Framework, you enable your applications to automatically scale to make use of the number of available processors. These two features make the Fork/Join Framework the recommended approach to multithreading when parallel processing is desired.

Before continuing, it is important to point out the distinction between traditional multithreading and parallel programming. In the past, most computers had a single CPU and multithreading was primarily used to take advantage of idle time, such as when a program is waiting for user input. Using this approach, one thread can execute while another is waiting. In other words, on a single-CPU system, multithreading is used to allow two or more tasks to share the CPU. This type of multithreading is typically supported by an object of type **Thread** (as described in Chapter 11). Although this type of multithreading will always remain quite useful, it was not optimized for situations in which two or more CPUs are available (multicore computers).

When multiple CPUs are present, a second type of multithreading capability that supports true parallel execution is required. With two or more CPUs, it is possible to execute portions of a program simultaneously, with each part executing on its own CPU. This can be used to significantly speed up the execution of some types of operations, such as sorting, transforming, and searching a large array. In many cases, these types of operations can be broken down into smaller pieces (each acting on a portion of the array), and each piece can be run on its own CPU. As you can imagine, the gain in efficiency can be enormous. Simply put: Parallel programming will be part of nearly every programmer's future because it offers a way to dramatically improve program performance.

### The Main Fork/Join Classes

The Fork/Join Framework is packaged in **java.util.concurrent**. At the core of the Fork/Join Framework are the following four classes:

| | |
|---|---|
| ForkJoinTask<V> | An abstract class that defines a task |
| ForkJoinPool | Manages the execution of **ForkJoinTasks** |
| RecursiveAction | A subclass of **ForkJoinTask<V>** for tasks that do not return values |
| RecursiveTask<V> | A subclass of **ForkJoinTask<V>** for tasks that return values |

Here is how they relate. A **ForkJoinPool** manages the execution of **ForkJoinTasks**. **ForkJoinTask** is an abstract class that is extended by the abstract classes **RecursiveAction** and **RecursiveTask**. Typically, your code will extend these classes to create a task. Before we look at the process in detail, an overview of the key aspects of each class will be helpful.

**NOTE** The class **CountedCompleter** also extends **ForkJoinTask**. However, a discussion of **CountedCompleter** is beyond the scope of this book.



## ForkJoinTask<V>

**ForkJoinTask<V>** is an abstract class that defines a task that can be managed by a **ForkJoinPool**. The type parameter **V** specifies the result type of the task. **ForkJoinTask** differs from **Thread** in that **ForkJoinTask** represents lightweight abstraction of a task, rather than a thread of execution. **ForkJoinTasks** are executed by threads managed by a thread pool of type **ForkJoinPool**. This mechanism allows a large number of tasks to be managed by a small number of actual threads. Thus, **ForkJoinTasks** are very efficient when compared to threads.

**ForkJoinTask** defines many methods. At the core are **fork( )** and **join( )**, shown here:

final ForkJoinTask<V> fork( )

final V join( )

The **fork( )** method submits the invoking task for asynchronous execution of the invoking task. This means that the thread that calls **fork( )** continues to run. The **fork( )** method returns **this** after the task is scheduled for execution. Prior to JDK 8, **fork( )** could be executed only from within the computational portion of another **ForkJoinTask**, which is running within a **ForkJoinPool**. (You will see how to create the computational portion of a task shortly.) However, with modern versions of Java, if **fork( )** is not called while executing within a **ForkJoinPool**, then a common pool is automatically used. The **join( )** method waits until the task on which it is called terminates. The result of the task is returned. Thus, through the use of **fork( )** and **join( )**, you can start one or more new tasks and then wait for them to finish.

Another important **ForkJoinTask** method is **invoke( )**. It combines the fork and join operations into a single call because it begins a task and then waits for it to end. It is shown here:

final V invoke( )

The result of the invoking task is returned.

You can invoke more than one task at a time by using **invokeAll( )**. Two of its forms are shown here:

static void invokeAll(ForkJoinTask<?> *taskA*, ForkJoinTask<?> *taskB*)

static void invokeAll(ForkJoinTask<?> ... *taskList*)

In the first case, *taskA* and *taskB* are executed. In the second case, all specified tasks are executed. In both cases, the calling thread waits until all of the specified tasks have terminated. Like **fork( )**, originally the **invoke( )** and **invokeAll( )** methods could be executed only from within the computational portion of another **ForkJoinTask**, which is running within a **ForkJoinPool**. The inclusion of the common pool by JDK 8 relaxed this requirement.

## RecursiveAction

A subclass of **ForkJoinTask** is **RecursiveAction**. This class encapsulates a task that does not return a result. Typically, your code will extend **RecursiveAction** to create a task that has a **void** return type. **RecursiveAction** specifies four methods, but only one is usually of interest: the abstract method called **compute( )**. When you extend **RecursiveAction** to create a concrete class, you will put the code that defines the task inside **compute( )**. The **compute( )** method represents the *computational* portion of the task.

The **compute( )** method is defined by **RecursiveAction** like this:

protected abstract void compute( )

Notice that **compute( )** is **protected** and **abstract**. This means that it must be implemented by a subclass (unless that subclass is also abstract).

In general, **RecursiveAction** is used to implement a recursive, divide-and-conquer strategy for tasks that don't return results. (See "The Divide-and-Conquer Strategy" later in this chapter.)

## RecursiveTask<V>

Another subclass of **ForkJoinTask** is **RecursiveTask<V>**. This class encapsulates a task that returns a result. The result type is specified by **V**. Typically, your code will extend **RecursiveTask<V>** to create a task that returns a value. Like **RecursiveAction**, its abstract **compute( )** method is often of the greatest interest because it represents the computational portion of the task. When you extend **RecursiveTask<V>** to create a concrete class, put the code that represents the task inside **compute( )**. This code must also return the result of the task.

The **compute( )** method is defined by **RecursiveTask<V>** like this:

protected abstract V compute( )

Notice that **compute( )** is **protected** and **abstract**. This means that it must be implemented by a subclass. When implemented, it must return the result of the task.

In general, **RecursiveTask** is used to implement a recursive, divide-and-conquer strategy for tasks that return results. (See "The Divide-and-Conquer Strategy" later in this chapter.)

## ForkJoinPool

The execution of **ForkJoinTask**s takes place within a **ForkJoinPool**, which also manages the execution of the tasks. Therefore, in order to execute a **ForkJoinTask**, you must first have a **ForkJoinPool**. There are two ways to acquire a **ForkJoinPool**. First, you can explicitly create one by using a **ForkJoinPool** constructor. Second, you can use what is referred to as the *common pool.* The common pool (which was added by JDK 8) is a static **ForkJoinPool** that is automatically available for your use. Each method is introduced here, beginning with manually constructing a pool.

**ForkJoinPool** defines several constructors. Here are two commonly used ones:

ForkJoinPool( )

ForkJoinPool(int *pLevel*)

The first creates a default pool that supports a level of parallelism equal to the number of processors available in the system. The second lets you specify the level of parallelism. Its value must be greater than zero and not more than the limits of the implementation. The level of parallelism determines the number of threads that can execute concurrently. As a result, the level of parallelism effectively determines the number of tasks that can be executed simultaneously. (Of course, the number of tasks that can execute simultaneously cannot exceed the number of processors.) It is important to understand that the level of parallelism *does not,* however, limit the number of tasks that can be managed by the pool. A **ForkJoinPool** can manage many more tasks than its level of parallelism. Also, the level of parallelism is only a target. It is not a guarantee.

After you have created an instance of **ForkJoinPool**, you can start a task in a number of different ways. The first task started is often thought of as the main task. Frequently, the main task begins subtasks that are also managed by the pool. One common way to begin a main task is to call **invoke( )** on the **ForkJoinPool**. It is shown here:

<T> T invoke(ForkJoinTask<T> *task*)

This method begins the task specified by *task*, and it returns the result of the task. This means that the calling code waits until **invoke( )** returns.

To start a task without waiting for its completion, you can use **execute( )**. Here is one of its forms:

void execute(ForkJoinTask<?> *task*)

In this case, *task* is started, but the calling code does not wait for its completion. Rather, the calling code continues execution asynchronously.

For modern versions of Java, it is not necessary to explicitly construct a **ForkJoinPool** because a common pool is available for your use. In general, if you are not using a pool that you explicitly created, then the common pool will automatically be used. Although it won't always be necessary, you can obtain a reference to the common pool by calling **commonPool( )**, which is defined by **ForkJoinPool**. It is shown here:

static ForkJoinPool commonPool( )

A reference to the common pool is returned. The common pool provides a default level of parallelism. It can be set by use of a system property. (See the API documentation for details.) Typically, the default common pool is a good choice for many applications. Of course, you can always construct your own pool.

There are two basic ways to start a task using the common pool. First, you can obtain a reference to the pool by calling **commonPool( )** and then use that reference to call **invoke( )** or **execute( )**, as just described. Second, you can call **ForkJoinTask** methods such as **fork( )** and **invoke( )** on the task from outside its computational portion. In this case, the common pool will automatically be used. In other words, **fork( )** and **invoke( )** will start a task using the common pool if the task is not already running within a **ForkJoinPool**.

**ForkJoinPool** manages the execution of its threads using an approach called *work-stealing*. Each worker thread maintains a queue of tasks. If one worker thread's queue is empty, it will take a task from another worker thread. This adds to overall efficiency and helps maintain a balanced load. (Because of demands on CPU time by other processes in the system, even two worker threads with identical tasks in their respective queues may not complete at the same time.)

One other point: **ForkJoinPool** uses daemon threads. A daemon thread is automatically terminated when all user threads have terminated. Thus, there is no need to explicitly shut down a **ForkJoinPool**. However, with the exception of the common pool, it is possible to do so by calling **shutdown( )**. The **shutdown( )** method has no effect on the common pool.

## The Divide-and-Conquer Strategy

As a general rule, users of the Fork/Join Framework will employ a *divide-and-conquer* strategy that is based on recursion. This is why the two subclasses of **ForkJoinTask** are called **RecursiveAction** and **RecursiveTask**. It is anticipated that you will extend one of these classes when creating your own fork/join task.

The divide-and-conquer strategy is based on recursively dividing a task into smaller subtasks until the size of a subtask is small enough to be handled sequentially. For example, a task that applies a transform to each element in an array of *N* integers can be broken down into two subtasks in which each transforms half the elements in the array. That is, one subtask transforms the elements 0 to *N*/2, and the other transforms the elements *N*/2 to *N*. In turn, each subtask can be reduced to another set of subtasks, each transforming half of the remaining elements. This process of dividing the array will continue until a threshold is reached in which a sequential solution is faster than creating another division.

The advantage of the divide-and-conquer strategy is that the processing can occur in parallel. Therefore, instead of cycling through an entire array using a single thread, pieces of the array can be processed simultaneously. Of course, the divide-and-conquer approach works in many cases in which an array (or collection) is not present, but the most common uses involve some type of array, collection, or grouping of data.

One of the keys to best employing the divide-and-conquer strategy is correctly selecting the threshold at which sequential processing (rather than further division) is used. Typically, an optimal threshold is obtained through profiling the execution characteristics. However, very significant speed-ups will still occur even when a less-than-optimal threshold is used. It is, however, best to avoid overly large or overly small thresholds. At the time of this writing, the Java API documentation for **ForkJoinTask<T>** states that, as a rule of thumb, a task should perform somewhere between 100 and 10,000 computational steps.

It is also important to understand that the optimal threshold value is also affected by how much time the computation takes. If each computational step is fairly long, then smaller thresholds might be better. Conversely, if each computational step is quite short, then larger thresholds could yield better results. For applications that are to be run on a known system, with a known number of processors, you can use the number of processors to make informed decisions about the threshold value. However, for applications that will be running on a variety of systems, the capabilities of which are not known in advance, you can make no assumptions about the execution environment.

One other point: Although multiple processors may be available on a system, other tasks (and the operating system itself) will be competing with your application for CPU time. Thus, it is important not to assume that your program will have unrestricted access to all CPUs. Furthermore, different runs of the same program may display different run-time characteristics because of varying task loads.

## A Simple First Fork/Join Example

At this point, a simple example that demonstrates the Fork/Join Framework and the divide-and-conquer strategy will be helpful. Following is a program that transforms the elements in an array of **double** into their square roots. It does so via a subclass of **RecursiveAction**. Notice that it creates its own **ForkJoinPool**.

```
// A simple example of the basic divide-and-conquer strategy.
// In this case, RecursiveAction is used.
import java.util.concurrent.*;
import java.util.*;

// A ForkJoinTask (via RecursiveAction) that transforms
// the elements in an array of doubles into their square roots.
class SqrtTransform extends RecursiveAction {
  // The threshold value is arbitrarily set at 1,000 in this example.
  // In real-world code, its optimal value can be determined by
  // profiling and experimentation.
  final int seqThreshold = 1000;

  // Array to be accessed.
  double[] data;

  // Determines what part of data to process.
  int start, end;

  SqrtTransform(double[] vals, int s, int e ) {
    data = vals;
    start = s;
    end = e;
  }

  // This is the method in which parallel computation will occur.
  protected void compute() {

    // If number of elements is below the sequential threshold,
    // then process sequentially.
    if((end - start) < seqThreshold) {
      // Transform each element into its square root.
      for(int i = start; i < end; i++) {
        data[i] = Math.sqrt(data[i]);
      }
    }
    else {
      // Otherwise, continue to break the data into smaller pieces.

      // Find the midpoint.
      int middle = (start + end) / 2;
```

```
        // Invoke new tasks, using the subdivided data.
        invokeAll(new SqrtTransform(data, start, middle),
                  new SqrtTransform(data, middle, end));
      }
    }
  }

  // Demonstrate parallel execution.
  class ForkJoinDemo {
    public static void main(String[] args) {
      // Create a task pool.
      ForkJoinPool fjp = new ForkJoinPool();

      double[] nums = new double[100000];

      // Give nums some values.
      for(int i = 0; i < nums.length; i++)
        nums[i] = (double) i;

      System.out.println("A portion of the original sequence:");

      for(int i=0; i < 10; i++)
        System.out.print(nums[i] + " ");
      System.out.println("\n");

      SqrtTransform task = new SqrtTransform(nums, 0, nums.length);

      // Start the main ForkJoinTask.
      fjp.invoke(task);

      System.out.println("A portion of the transformed sequence" +
                         " (to four decimal places):");
      for(int i=0; i < 10; i++)
        System.out.format("%.4f ", nums[i]);
      System.out.println();
    }
  }
```

The output from the program is shown here:

```
A portion of the original sequence:
0.0 1.0 2.0 3.0 4.0 5.0 6.0 7.0 8.0 9.0

A portion of the transformed sequence (to four decimal places):
0.0000 1.0000 1.4142 1.7321 2.0000 2.2361 2.4495 2.6458 2.8284 3.0000
```

As you can see, the values of the array elements have been transformed into their square roots.

Let's look closely at how this program works. First, notice that **SqrtTransform** is a class that extends **RecursiveAction**. As explained, **RecursiveAction** extends **ForkJoinTask** for tasks that do not return results. Next, notice the **final** variable **seqThreshold**. This is the value that determines when sequential processing will take place. This value is set (somewhat arbitrarily) to 1000. Next, notice that a reference to the array to be processed is stored in

**data** and that the fields **start** and **end** are used to indicate the boundaries of the elements to be accessed.

The main action of the program takes place in **compute( )**. It begins by checking if the number of elements to be processed is below the sequential processing threshold. If it is, then those elements are processed (by computing their square root in this example). If the sequential processing threshold has not been reached, then two new tasks are started by calling **invokeAll( )**. In this case, each subtask processes half the elements. As explained earlier, **invokeAll( )** waits until both tasks return. After all of the recursive calls unwind, each element in the array will have been modified, with much of the action taking place in parallel (if multiple processors are available).



As mentioned, today it is not necessary to explicitly construct a **ForkJoinPool** because a common pool is available for your use. Furthermore, using the common pool is a simple matter. For example, you can obtain a reference to the common pool by calling the static **commonPool( )** method defined by **ForkJoinPool**. Therefore, the preceding program could be rewritten to use the common pool by replacing the call to the **ForkJoinPool** constructor with a call to **commonPool( )**, as shown here:

```
ForkJoinPool fjp = ForkJoinPool.commonPool();
```

Alternatively, there is no need to explicitly obtain a reference to the common pool because calling the **ForkJoinTask** methods **invoke( )** or **fork( )** on a task that is not already part of a pool will cause it to execute within the common pool automatically. For example, in the preceding program, you can eliminate the **fjp** variable entirely and start the task using this line:

```
task.invoke();
```

As this discussion shows, the common pool can be easier to use than creating your own pool. Furthermore, in many cases, the common pool is the preferable approach.

## Understanding the Impact of the Level of Parallelism

Before moving on, it is important to understand the impact that the level of parallelism has on the performance of a fork/join task and how the parallelism and the threshold interact. The program shown in this section lets you experiment with different degrees of parallelism and threshold values. Assuming that you are using a multicore computer, you can interactively observe the effect of these values.

In the preceding example, the default level of parallelism was used. However, you can specify the level of parallelism that you want. One way is to specify it when you create a **ForkJoinPool** using this constructor:

ForkJoinPool(int *pLevel*)

Here, *pLevel* specifies the level of parallelism, which must be greater than zero and less than the implementation defined limit.

The following program creates a fork/join task that transforms an array of **doubles**. The transformation is arbitrary, but it is designed to consume several CPU cycles. This was done to ensure that the effects of changing the threshold or the level of parallelism would be more clearly displayed. To use the program, specify the threshold value and the level of parallelism on the command line. The program then runs the tasks. It also displays the amount of time it takes the tasks to run. To do this, it uses **System.nanoTime( )**, which returns the value of the JVM's high-resolution timer.

```
// A simple program that lets you experiment with the effects of
// changing the threshold and parallelism of a ForkJoinTask.
import java.util.concurrent.*;

// A ForkJoinTask (via RecursiveAction) that performs a
// a transform on the elements of an array of doubles.
class Transform extends RecursiveAction {

  // Sequential threshold, which is set by the constructor.
  int seqThreshold;

  // Array to be accessed.
  double[] data;

  // Determines what part of data to process.
  int start, end;

  Transform(double[] vals, int s, int e, int t ) {
    data = vals;
    start = s;
    end = e;
    seqThreshold = t;
  }

  // This is the method in which parallel computation will occur.
  protected void compute() {

    // If number of elements is below the sequential threshold,
    // then process sequentially.
    if((end - start) < seqThreshold) {
      // The following code assigns an element at an even index the
      // square root of its original value. An element at an odd
      // index is assigned its cube root. This code is designed
      // to simply consume CPU time so that the effects of concurrent
      // execution are more readily observable.
      for(int i = start; i < end; i++) {
        if((data[i] % 2) == 0)
          data[i] = Math.sqrt(data[i]);
        else
          data[i] = Math.cbrt(data[i]);
      }
    }
    else {
      // Otherwise, continue to break the data into smaller pieces.
```

```
            // Find the midpoint.
            int middle = (start + end) / 2;

            // Invoke new tasks, using the subdivided data.
            invokeAll(new Transform(data, start, middle, seqThreshold),
                      new Transform(data, middle, end, seqThreshold));
        }
    }
}

// Demonstrate parallel execution.
class FJExperiment {

  public static void main(String[] args) {
    int pLevel;
    int threshold;

    if(args.length != 2) {
      System.out.println("Usage: FJExperiment parallelism threshold ");
      return;
    }

    pLevel = Integer.parseInt(args[0]);
    threshold = Integer.parseInt(args[1]);

    // These variables are used to time the task.
    long beginT, endT;

    // Create a task pool. Notice that the parallelism level is set.
    ForkJoinPool fjp = new ForkJoinPool(pLevel);

    double[] nums = new double[1000000];

    for(int i = 0; i < nums.length; i++)
      nums[i] = (double) i;

    Transform task = new Transform(nums, 0, nums.length, threshold);

    // Starting timing.
    beginT = System.nanoTime();

    // Start the main ForkJoinTask.
    fjp.invoke(task);

    // End timing.
    endT = System.nanoTime();

    System.out.println("Level of parallelism: " + pLevel);
    System.out.println("Sequential threshold: " + threshold);
    System.out.println("Elapsed time: " + (endT - beginT) + " ns");
    System.out.println();
  }
}
```

Part II

To use the program, specify the level of parallelism followed by the threshold limit. You should try experimenting with different values for each, observing the results. Remember, to be effective, you must run the code on a computer with at least two processors. Also, understand that two different runs may (almost certainly will) produce different results because of the effect of other processes in the system consuming CPU time.

To give you an idea of the difference that parallelism makes, try this experiment. First, execute the program like this:

```
java FJExperiment 1 1000
```

This requests one level of parallelism (essentially sequential execution) with a threshold of 1000. Here is a sample run produced on a dual-core computer:

```
Level of parallelism: 1
Sequential threshold: 1000
Elapsed time: 259677487 ns
```

Now, specify two levels of parallelism, like this:

```
java FJExperiment 2 1000
```

Here is sample output from this run produced by the same dual-core computer:

```
Level of parallelism: 2
Sequential threshold: 1000
Elapsed time: 169254472 ns
```

As is evident, adding parallelism substantially decreases execution time, thus increasing the speed of the program. You should experiment with varying the threshold and parallelism on your own computer. The results may surprise you.

Here are two other methods that you might find useful when experimenting with the execution characteristics of a fork/join program. First, you can obtain the level of parallelism by calling **getParallelism( )**, which is defined by **ForkJoinPool**. It is shown here:

int getParallelism( )

It returns the parallelism level currently in effect. Recall that for pools that you create, by default, this value will equal the number of available processors. (To obtain the parallelism level for the common pool, you can also use **getCommonPoolParallelism( )**.) Second, you can obtain the number of processors available in the system by calling **availableProcessors( )**, which is defined by the **Runtime** class. It is shown here:

int availableProcessors( )

The value returned may change from one call to the next because of other system demands.

## An Example that Uses RecursiveTask<V>

The two preceding examples are based on **RecursiveAction**, which means that they concurrently execute tasks that do not return results. To create a task that returns a result, use **RecursiveTask**. In general, solutions are designed in the same manner as just shown.

The key difference is that the **compute( )** method returns a result. Thus, you must aggregate the results so that when the first invocation finishes, it returns the overall result. Another difference is that you will typically start a subtask by calling **fork( )** and **join( )** explicitly (rather than implicitly by calling **invokeAll( )**, for example).

The following program demonstrates **RecursiveTask**. It creates a task called **Sum** that returns the summation of the values in an array of **double**. In this example, the array consists of 5000 elements. However, every other value is negative. Thus, the first values in the array are 0, –1, 2, –3, 4, and so on. (Notice that this example creates its own pool. You might try changing it to use the common pool as an exercise.)

```
// A simple example that uses RecursiveTask<V>.
import java.util.concurrent.*;

// A RecursiveTask that computes the summation of an array of doubles.
class Sum extends RecursiveTask<Double> {

  // The sequential threshold value.
  final int seqThresHold = 500;

  // Array to be accessed.
  double[] data;

  // Determines what part of data to process.
  int start, end;

  Sum(double[] vals, int s, int e ) {
    data = vals;
    start = s;
    end = e;
  }

  // Find the summation of an array of doubles.
  protected Double compute() {
    double sum = 0;

    // If number of elements is below the sequential threshold,
    // then process sequentially.
    if((end - start) < seqThresHold) {
      // Sum the elements.
      for(int i = start; i < end; i++) sum += data[i];
    }
    else {
      // Otherwise, continue to break the data into smaller pieces.

      // Find the midpoint.
      int middle = (start + end) / 2;

      // Invoke new tasks, using the subdivided data.
      Sum subTaskA = new Sum(data, start, middle);
      Sum subTaskB = new Sum(data, middle, end);
```

Part II

```
      // Start each subtask by forking.
      subTaskA.fork();
      subTaskB.fork();

      // Wait for the subtasks to return, and aggregate the results.
      sum = subTaskA.join() + subTaskB.join();
    }
    // Return the final sum.
    return sum;
  }
}

// Demonstrate parallel execution.
class RecurTaskDemo {
  public static void main(String[] args) {
    // Create a task pool.
    ForkJoinPool fjp = new ForkJoinPool();

    double[] nums = new double[5000];

    // Initialize nums with values that alternate between
    // positive and negative.
    for(int i=0; i < nums.length; i++)
      nums[i] = (double) (((i%2) == 0) ? i : -i) ;

    Sum task = new Sum(nums, 0, nums.length);

    // Start the ForkJoinTasks.  Notice that, in this case,
    // invoke() returns a result.
    double summation = fjp.invoke(task);

    System.out.println("Summation " + summation);
  }
}
```

Here's the output from the program:

```
Summation -2500.0
```

There are a couple of interesting items in this program. First, notice that the two subtasks are executed by calling **fork( )**, as shown here:

```
subTaskA.fork();
subTaskB.fork();
```

In this case, **fork( )** is used because it starts a task but does not wait for it to finish. (Thus, it asynchronously runs the task.) The result of each task is obtained by calling **join( )**, as shown here:

```
sum = subTaskA.join() + subTaskB.join();
```

This statement waits until each task ends. It then adds the results of each and assigns the total to **sum**. Thus, the summation of each subtask is added to the running total. Finally,

**compute( )** ends by returning **sum**, which will be the final total when the first invocation returns.

There are other ways to approach the handling of the asynchronous execution of the subtasks. For example, the following sequence uses **fork( )** to start **subTaskA** and uses **invoke( )** to start and wait for **subTaskB**:

```
subTaskA.fork();
sum = subTaskB.invoke() + subTaskA.join();
```

Another alternative is to have **subTaskB** call **compute( )** directly, as shown here:

```
subTaskA.fork();
sum = subTaskB.compute() + subTaskA.join();
```



## Executing a Task Asynchronously

The preceding programs have called **invoke( )** on a **ForkJoinPool** to initiate a task. This approach is commonly used when the calling thread must wait until the task has completed (which is often the case) because **invoke( )** does not return until the task has terminated. However, you can start a task asynchronously. In this approach, the calling thread continues to execute. Thus, both the calling thread and the task execute simultaneously. To start a task asynchronously, use **execute( )**, which is also defined by **ForkJoinPool**. It has the two forms shown here:

void execute(ForkJoinTask<?> *task*)

void execute(Runnable *task*)

In both forms, *task* specifies the task to run. Notice that the second form lets you specify a **Runnable** rather than a **ForkJoinTask** task. Thus, it forms a bridge between Java's traditional approach to multithreading and the Fork/Join Framework. It is important to remember that the threads used by a **ForkJoinPool** are daemons. Thus, they will end when the main thread ends. As a result, you may need to keep the main thread alive until the tasks have finished.

## Cancelling a Task

A task can be cancelled by calling **cancel( )**, which is defined by **ForkJoinTask**. It has this general form:

boolean cancel(boolean *interruptOK*)

It returns **true** if the task on which it was called is cancelled. It returns **false** if the task has ended or can't be cancelled. At this time, the *interruptOK* parameter is not used by the default implementation. In general, **cancel( )** is intended to be called from code outside the task because a task can easily cancel itself by returning.

You can determine if a task has been cancelled by calling **isCancelled( )**, as shown here:

final boolean isCancelled( )

It returns **true** if the invoking task has been cancelled prior to completion and **false** otherwise.

## Determining a Task's Completion Status

In addition to **isCancelled( )**, which was just described, **ForkJoinTask** includes two other methods that you can use to determine a task's completion status. The first is **isCompletedNormally( )**, which is shown here:

```
final boolean isCompletedNormally( )
```

It returns **true** if the invoking task completed normally, that is, if it did not throw an exception and it was not cancelled via a call to **cancel( )**. It returns **false** otherwise.

The second is **isCompletedAbnormally( )**, which is shown here:

```
final boolean isCompletedAbnormally( )
```

It returns **true** if the invoking task completed because it was cancelled or because it threw an exception. It returns **false** otherwise.

## Restarting a Task

Normally, you cannot rerun a task. In other words, once a task completes, it cannot be restarted. However, you can reinitialize the state of the task (after it has completed) so it can be run again. This is done by calling **reinitialize( )**, as shown here:

```
void reinitialize( )
```

This method resets the state of the invoking task. However, any modification made to any persistent data that is operated upon by the task will not be undone. For example, if the task modifies an array, then those modifications are not undone by calling **reinitialize( )**.

## Things to Explore

The preceding discussion presented the fundamentals of the Fork/Join Framework and described several commonly used methods. However, Fork/Join is a rich framework that includes additional capabilities that give you extended control over concurrency. Although it is far beyond the scope of this book to examine all of the issues and nuances surrounding parallel programming and the Fork/Join Framework, a sampling of the other features are mentioned here.

### A Sampling of Other ForkJoinTask Features

In some cases, you will want to ensure that methods such as **invokeAll( )** and **fork( )** are called only from within a **ForkJoinTask**. This is usually a simple matter, but occasionally, you may have code that can be executed from either inside or outside a task. You can determine if your code is executing inside a task by calling **inForkJoinPool( )**.

You can convert a **Runnable** or **Callable** object into a **ForkJoinTask** by using the **adapt( )** method defined by **ForkJoinTask**. It has three forms: one for converting a **Callable**, one for a **Runnable** that does not return a result, and one for a **Runnable** that does return a result. In the case of a **Callable**, the **call( )** method is run. In the case of **Runnable**, the **run( )** method is run.

You can obtain an approximate count of the number of tasks that are in the queue of the invoking thread by calling **getQueuedTaskCount( )**. You can obtain an approximate count of how many tasks the invoking thread has in its queue that are in excess of the number of other threads in the pool that might "steal" them, by calling **getSurplusQueuedTaskCount( )**. Remember, in the Fork/Join Framework, work-stealing is one way in which a high level of efficiency is obtained. Although this process is automatic, in some cases, the information may prove helpful in optimizing throughput.

**ForkJoinTask** defines the following variants of **join( )** and **invoke( )** that begin with the prefix **quietly**. They are shown here:

| | |
|---|---|
| final void quietlyJoin( ) | Joins a task, but does not return a result or throw an exception |
| final void quietlyInvoke( ) | Invokes a task, but does not return a result or throw an exception |

In essence, these methods are similar to their non-quiet counterparts except they don't return values or throw exceptions.

You can attempt to "un-invoke" (in other words, unschedule) a task by calling **tryUnfork( )**.

Several methods, such as **getForkJoinTaskTag( )** and **setForkJoinTaskTag( )**, support tags. Tags are short integer values that are linked with a task. They may be useful in specialized applications.



**ForkJoinTask** implements **Serializable**. Thus, it can be serialized. However, serialization is not used during execution.

## A Sampling of Other ForkJoinPool Features

One method that is quite useful when tuning fork/join applications is **ForkJoinPool**'s override of **toString( )**. It displays a "user-friendly" synopsis of the state of the pool. To see it in action, use this sequence to start and then wait for the task in the **FJExperiment** class of the task experimenter program shown earlier:

```
// Asynchronously start the main ForkJoinTask.
fjp.execute(task);

// Display the state of the pool while waiting.
while(!task.isDone()) {
  System.out.println(fjp);
}
```

When you run the program, you will see a series of messages on the screen that describe the state of the pool. Here is an example of one. Of course, your output may vary, based on the number of processors, threshold values, task load, and so on.

```
java.util.concurrent.ForkJoinPool@141d683[Running, parallelism = 2,
size = 2, active = 0, running = 2, steals = 0, tasks = 0, submissions = 1]
```

You can determine if a pool is currently idle by calling **isQuiescent( )**. It returns **true** if the pool has no active threads and **false** otherwise.

You can obtain the number of worker threads currently in the pool by calling **getPoolSize( )**. You can obtain an approximate count of the active threads in the pool by calling **getActiveThreadCount( )**.

To shut down a pool, call **shutdown( )**. Currently active tasks will still be executed, but no new tasks can be started. To stop a pool immediately, call **shutdownNow( )**. In this case, an attempt is made to cancel currently active tasks. (It is important to point out, however, that neither of these methods affects the common pool.) You can determine if a pool is shut down by calling **isShutdown( )**. It returns **true** if the pool has been shut down and **false** otherwise. To determine if the pool has been shut down and all tasks have been completed, call **isTerminated( )**.

### Some Fork/Join Tips

Here are a few tips to help you avoid some of the more troublesome pitfalls associated with using the Fork/Join Framework. First, avoid using a sequential threshold that is too low. In general, erring on the high side is better than erring on the low side. If the threshold is too low, more time can be consumed generating and switching tasks than in processing the tasks. Second, usually it is best to use the default level of parallelism. If you specify a smaller number, it may significantly reduce the benefits of using the Fork/Join Framework.

In general, a **ForkJoinTask** should not use synchronized methods or synchronized blocks of code. Also, you will not normally want to have the **compute( )** method use other types of synchronization, such as a semaphore. (The **Phaser** can, however, be used when appropriate because it is compatible with the fork/join mechanism.) Remember, the main idea behind a **ForkJoinTask** is the divide-and-conquer strategy. Such an approach does not normally lend itself to situations in which outside synchronization is needed. Also, avoid situations in which substantial blocking will occur through I/O. Therefore, in general, a **ForkJoinTask** will not perform I/O. Simply put, to best utilize the Fork/Join Framework, a task should perform a computation that can run without outside blocking or synchronization.

One last point: Except under unusual circumstances, do not make assumptions about the execution environment that your code will run in. This means you should not assume that some specific number of processors will be available, or that the execution characteristics of your program won't be affected by other processes running at the same time.

## The Concurrency Utilities Versus Java's Traditional Approach

Given the power and flexibility found in the concurrency utilities, it is natural to ask the following question: Do they replace Java's traditional approach to multithreading and synchronization? The answer is a resounding no! The original support for multithreading and the built-in synchronization features are still the mechanisms that should be employed for many, many Java programs. For example, **synchronized**, **wait( )**, and **notify( )** offer elegant solutions to a wide range of problems. However, when extra control is needed, the concurrency utilities are available to handle the chore. Furthermore, the Fork/Join Framework offers a powerful way to integrate parallel programming techniques into your more sophisticated applications.

CHAPTER

# 30 The Stream API

Over the years, Java has been engaged in a process of ongoing evolution, with each release adding features that expand the richness and power of the language. Two such features of special importance are lambda expressions and the stream API. Lambda expressions were described in Chapter 15. The stream API is described here. As you will see, the stream API is designed with lambda expressions in mind. Moreover, the stream API provides some of the most significant demonstrations of the power that lambdas bring to Java.

Although its design compatibility with lambda expressions is impressive, the key aspect of the stream API is its ability to perform very sophisticated operations that search, filter, map, or otherwise manipulate data. For example, using the stream API, you can construct sequences of actions that resemble, in concept, the type of database queries for which you might use SQL. Furthermore, in many cases, such actions can be performed in parallel, thus providing a high level of efficiency, especially when large data sets are involved. Put simply, the stream API provides a powerful means of handling data in an efficient, yet easy to use way.

Before we continue, an important point needs to be made: The stream API uses some of Java's most advanced features. To fully understand and utilize it requires a solid understanding of generics and lambda expressions. The basic concepts of parallel execution and a working knowledge of the Collections Framework are also needed. (See Chapters 14, 15, 20, and 29.)

## Stream Basics

Let's begin by defining the term *stream* as it applies to the stream API: a stream is a conduit for data. Thus, a stream represents a sequence of objects. A stream operates on a data source, such as an array or a collection. A stream, itself, never provides storage for the data. It simply moves data, possibly filtering, sorting, or otherwise operating on that data in the process. As a general rule, however, a stream operation by itself does not modify the data source. For example, sorting a stream does not change the order of the source. Rather, sorting a stream results in the creation of a new stream that produces the sorted result.

**NOTE** It is necessary to state that the term *stream* as used here differs from the use of *stream* when the I/O classes were described earlier in this book. Although an I/O stream can act conceptually much like one of the streams defined by **java.util.stream**, they are not the same. Thus, throughout this chapter, when the term *stream* is used, it refers to objects based on one of the stream types described here.

## Stream Interfaces

The stream API defines several stream interfaces, which are packaged in **java.util.stream** and contained in the **java.base** module. At the foundation is **BaseStream**, which defines the basic functionality available in all streams. **BaseStream** is a generic interface declared like this:

```
interface BaseStream<T, S extends BaseStream<T, S>>
```

Here, **T** specifies the type of the elements in the stream, and **S** specifies the type of stream that extends **BaseStream**. **BaseStream** extends the **AutoCloseable** interface; thus, a stream can be managed in a **try**-with-resources statement. In general, however, only those streams whose data source requires closing (such as those connected to a file) will need to be closed. In most cases, such as those in which the data source is a collection, there is no need to close the stream. The methods declared by **BaseStream** are shown in Table 30-1.

| Method | Description |
|---|---|
| void close( ) | Closes the invoking stream, calling any registered close handlers. (As explained in the text, few streams need to be closed.) |
| boolean isParallel( ) | Returns **true** if the invoking stream is parallel. Returns **false** if the stream is sequential. |
| Iterator<T> iterator( ) | Obtains an iterator to the stream and returns a reference to it. (Terminal operation.) |
| S onClose(Runnable *handler*) | Returns a new stream with the close handler specified by *handler*. This handler will be called when the stream is closed. (Intermediate operation.) |
| S parallel( ) | Returns a parallel stream based on the invoking stream. If the invoking stream is already parallel, then that stream is returned. (Intermediate operation.) |
| S sequential( ) | Returns a sequential stream based on the invoking stream. If the invoking stream is already sequential, then that stream is returned. (Intermediate operation.) |
| Spliterator<T> spliterator( ) | Obtains a spliterator to the stream and returns a reference to it. (Terminal operation.) |
| S unordered( ) | Returns an unordered stream based on the invoking stream. If the invoking stream is already unordered, then that stream is returned. (Intermediate operation.) |

**Table 30-1** The Methods Declared by **BaseStream**

From **BaseStream** are derived several types of stream interfaces. The most general of these is **Stream**. It is declared as shown here:

interface Stream<T>

Here, **T** specifies the type of the elements in the stream. Because it is generic, **Stream** is used for all reference types. In addition to the methods that it inherits from **BaseStream**, the **Stream** interface adds several of its own, a sampling of which is shown in Table 30-2.

| Method | Description |
|---|---|
| <R, A> R collect(Collector<? super T, A, R> *collectorFunc*) | Collects elements into a container, which is changeable, and returns the container. This is called a mutable reduction operation. Here, **R** specifies the type of the resulting container and **T** specifies the element type of the invoking stream. **A** specifies the internal accumulated type. The *collectorFunc* specifies how the collection process works. (Terminal operation.) |
| long count( ) | Counts the number of elements in the stream and returns the result. (Terminal operation.) |
| Stream<T> filter(Predicate<? super T> *pred*) | Produces a stream that contains those elements from the invoking stream that satisfy the predicate specified by *pred*. (Intermediate operation.) |
| void forEach(Consumer<? super T> *action*) | For each element in the invoking stream, the code specified by *action* is executed. (Terminal operation.) |
| <R> Stream<R> map(Function<? super T, ? extends R> *mapFunc*) | Applies *mapFunc* to the elements from the invoking stream, yielding a new stream that contains those elements. (Intermediate operation.) |
| DoubleStream mapToDouble( ToDoubleFunction<? super T> *mapFunc*) | Applies *mapFunc* to the elements from the invoking stream, yielding a new **DoubleStream** that contains those elements. (Intermediate operation.) |
| IntStream mapToInt( ToIntFunction<? super T> *mapFunc*) | Applies *mapFunc* to the elements from the invoking stream, yielding a new **IntStream** that contains those elements. (Intermediate operation.) |
| LongStream mapToLong( ToLongFunction<? super T> *mapFunc*) | Applies *mapFunc* to the elements from the invoking stream, yielding a new **LongStream** that contains those elements. (Intermediate operation.) |
| Optional<T> max( Comparator<? super T> *comp*) | Using the ordering specified by *comp*, finds and returns the maximum element in the invoking stream. (Terminal operation.) |
| Optional<T> min(Comparator<? super T> *comp*) | Using the ordering specified by *comp*, finds and returns the minimum element in the invoking stream. (Terminal operation.) |

**Table 30-2** A Sampling of Methods Declared by **Stream**

| Method | Description |
|---|---|
| T reduce(T *identityVal*, BinaryOperator<T> *accumulator*) | Returns a result based on the elements in the invoking stream. This is called a reduction operation. (Terminal operation.) |
| Stream<T> sorted( ) | Produces a new stream that contains the elements of the invoking stream sorted in natural order. (Intermediate operation.) |
| Object[] toArray( ) | Creates an array from the elements in the invoking stream. (Terminal operation.) |
| default List<T> toList( ) | Creates an unmodifiable **List** from the elements in the invoking stream (Terminal operation.) |

**Table 30-2** A Sampling of Methods Declared by **Stream** *(continued)*

In both tables, notice that many of the methods are notated as being either *terminal* or *intermediate*. The difference between the two is very important. A *terminal* operation consumes the stream. It is used to produce a result, such as finding the minimum value in the stream, or to execute some action, as is the case with the **forEach( )** method. Once a stream has been consumed, it cannot be reused. *Intermediate* operations produce another stream. Thus, intermediate operations can be used to create a *pipeline* that performs a sequence of actions. One other point: intermediate operations do not take place immediately. Instead, the specified action is performed when a terminal operation is executed on the new stream created by an intermediate operation. This mechanism is referred to as *lazy behavior*, and the intermediate operations are referred to as *lazy*. The use of lazy behavior enables the stream API to perform more efficiently.

Another key aspect of streams is that some intermediate operations are *stateless* and some are *stateful*. In a stateless operation, each element is processed independently of the others. In a stateful operation, the processing of an element may depend on aspects of the other elements. For example, sorting is a stateful operation because an element's order depends on the values of the other elements. Thus, the **sorted( )** method is stateful. However, filtering elements based on a stateless predicate is stateless because each element is handled individually. Thus, **filter( )** can (and should be) stateless. The difference between stateless and stateful operations is especially important when parallel processing of a stream is desired because a stateful operation may require more than one pass to complete.

Because **Stream** operates on object references, it can't operate directly on primitive types. To handle primitive type streams, the stream API defines the following interfaces:

DoubleStream

IntStream

LongStream

These streams all extend **BaseStream** and have capabilities similar to **Stream** except that they operate on primitive types rather than reference types. They also provide some convenience methods, such as **boxed( )**, that facilitate their use. Because streams of objects are the most common, **Stream** is the primary focus of this chapter, but the primitive type streams can be used in much the same way.

## How to Obtain a Stream

You can obtain a stream in a number of ways. Perhaps the most common is when a stream is obtained for a collection. Beginning with JDK 8, the **Collection** interface was expanded to include two methods that obtain a stream from a collection. The first is **stream( )**, shown here:

default Stream<E> stream( )

Its default implementation returns a sequential stream. The second method is **parallelStream( )**, shown next:

default Stream<E> parallelStream( )

Its default implementation returns a parallel stream, if possible. (If a parallel stream cannot be obtained, a sequential stream may be returned instead.) Parallel streams support parallel execution of stream operations. Because **Collection** is implemented by every collection, these methods can be used to obtain a stream from any collection class, such as **ArrayList** or **HashSet**.

A stream can also be obtained from an array by use of the static **stream( )** method, which was added to the **Arrays** class. One of its forms is shown here:

static <T> Stream<T> stream(T[ ] *array*)

This method returns a sequential stream to the elements in *array*. For example, given an array called **addresses** of type **Address**, the following obtains a stream to it:

```
Stream<Address> addrStrm = Arrays.stream(addresses);
```

Several overloads of the **stream( )** method are also defined, such as those that handle arrays of the primitive types. They return a stream of type **IntStream**, **DoubleStream**, or **LongStream**.

Streams can be obtained in a variety of other ways. For example, many stream operations return a new stream, and a stream to an I/O source can be obtained by calling **lines( )** on a **BufferedReader**. However a stream is obtained, it can be used in the same way as any other stream.

## A Simple Stream Example

Before going any further, let's work through an example that uses streams. The following program creates an **ArrayList** called **myList** that holds a collection of integers (which are automatically boxed into the **Integer** reference type). Next, it obtains a stream that uses **myList** as a source. It then demonstrates various stream operations.

```
// Demonstrate several stream operations.

import java.util.*;
import java.util.stream.*;
```

```
class StreamDemo {

  public static void main(String[] args) {

    // Create a list of Integer values.
    ArrayList<Integer> myList = new ArrayList<>( );
    myList.add(7);
    myList.add(18);
    myList.add(10);
    myList.add(24);
    myList.add(17);
    myList.add(5);

    System.out.println("Original list: " + myList);

    // Obtain a Stream to the array list.
    Stream<Integer> myStream = myList.stream();

    // Obtain the minimum and maximum value by use of min(),
    // max(), isPresent(), and get().
    Optional<Integer> minVal = myStream.min(Integer::compare);
    if(minVal.isPresent()) System.out.println("Minimum value: " +
                                               minVal.get());

    // Must obtain a new stream because previous call to min()
    // is a terminal operation that consumed the stream.
    myStream = myList.stream();
    Optional<Integer> maxVal = myStream.max(Integer::compare);
    if(maxVal.isPresent()) System.out.println("Maximum value: " +
                                               maxVal.get());

    // Sort the stream by use of sorted().
    Stream<Integer> sortedStream = myList.stream().sorted();

    // Display the sorted stream by use of forEach().
    System.out.print("Sorted stream: ");
    sortedStream.forEach((n) -> System.out.print(n + " "));
    System.out.println();

    // Display only the odd values by use of filter().
    Stream<Integer> oddVals =
         myList.stream().sorted().filter((n) -> (n % 2) == 1);
    System.out.print("Odd values: ");
    oddVals.forEach((n) -> System.out.print(n + " "));
    System.out.println();

    // Display only the odd values that are greater than 5. Notice that
    // two filter operations are pipelined.
    oddVals = myList.stream().filter( (n) -> (n % 2) == 1)
                             .filter((n) -> n > 5);
    System.out.print("Odd values greater than 5: ");
```

```
    oddVals.forEach((n) -> System.out.print(n + " ") );
    System.out.println();
  }
}
```

The output is shown here:

```
Original list: [7, 18, 10, 24, 17, 5]
Minimum value: 5
Maximum value: 24
Sorted stream: 5 7 10 17 18 24
Odd values: 5 7 17
Odd values greater than 5: 7 17
```



Let's look closely at each stream operation. After creating an **ArrayList**, the program obtains a stream for the list by calling **stream( )**, as shown here:

```
Stream<Integer> myStream = myList.stream();
```

As explained, the **Collection** interface defines the **stream( )** method, which obtains a stream from the invoking collection. Because **Collection** is implemented by every collection class, **stream( )** can be used to obtain a stream for any type of collection, including the **ArrayList** used here. In this case, a reference to the stream is assigned to **myStream**.

Next, the program obtains the minimum value in the stream (which is, of course, also the minimum value in the data source) and displays it, as shown here:

```
Optional<Integer> minVal = myStream.min(Integer::compare);
if(minVal.isPresent()) System.out.println("Minimum value: " +
                                          minVal.get());
```

Recall from Table 30-2 that **min( )** is declared like this:

Optional<T> min(Comparator<? super T> *comp*)

First, notice that the type of **min( )**'s parameter is a **Comparator**. This comparator is used to compare two elements in the stream. In the example, **min( )** is passed a method reference to **Integer**'s **compare( )** method, which is used to implement a **Comparator** capable of comparing two **Integers**. Next, notice that the return type of **min( )** is **Optional**. The **Optional** class is described in Chapter 21, but briefly, here is how it works: **Optional** is a generic class packaged in **java.util** and declared like this:

class Optional<T>

Here, **T** specifies the element type. An **Optional** instance can either contain a value of type **T** or be empty. You can use **isPresent( )** to determine if a value is present. Assuming that a value is available, it can be obtained by calling **get( )**, or if you are using JDK 10 or later, **orElseThrow( )**. Here, **get( )** is used. In this example, the object returned will hold the minimum value of the stream as an **Integer** object.

One other point about the preceding line: **min( )** is a terminal operation that consumes the stream. Thus, **myStream** cannot be used again after **min( )** executes.

The next lines obtain and display the maximum value in the stream:

```
myStream = myList.stream();
Optional<Integer> maxVal = myStream.max(Integer::compare);
if(maxVal.isPresent()) System.out.println("Maximum value: " +
                                          maxVal.get());
```

First, **myStream** is once again assigned the stream returned by **myList.stream( )**. As just explained, this is necessary because the previous call to **min( )** consumed the previous stream. Thus, a new one is needed. Next, the **max( )** method is called to obtain the maximum value. Like **min( )**, **max( )** returns an **Optional** object. Its value is obtained by calling **get( )**.

The program then obtains a sorted stream through the use of this line:

```
Stream<Integer> sortedStream = myList.stream().sorted();
```

Here, the **sorted( )** method is called on the stream returned by **myList.stream( )**. Because **sorted( )** is an intermediate operation, its result is a new stream, and this is the stream assigned to **sortedStream**. The contents of the sorted stream are displayed by use of **forEach( )**:

```
sortedStream.forEach((n) -> System.out.print(n + " "));
```

Here, the **forEach( )** method executes an operation on each element in the stream. In this case, it simply calls **System.out.print( )** for each element in **sortedStream**. This is accomplished by use of a lambda expression. The **forEach( )** method has this general form:

void forEach(Consumer<? super T> *action*)

**Consumer** is a generic functional interface declared in **java.util.function**. Its abstract method is **accept( )**, shown here:

void accept(T *objRef*)

The lambda expression in the call to **forEach( )** provides the implementation of **accept( )**. The **forEach( )** method is a terminal operation. Thus, after it completes, the stream has been consumed.

Next, a sorted stream is filtered by **filter( )** so that it contains only odd values:

```
Stream<Integer> oddVals =
        myList.stream().sorted().filter((n) -> (n % 2) == 1);
```

The **filter( )** method filters a stream based on a predicate. It returns a new stream that contains only those elements that satisfy the predicate. It is shown here:

Stream<T> filter(Predicate<? super T> *pred*)

**Predicate** is a generic functional interface defined in **java.util.function**. Its abstract method is **test( )**, which is shown here:

boolean test(T *objRef*)

It returns **true** if the object referred to by *objRef* satisfies the predicate, and **false** otherwise. The lambda expression passed to **filter( )** implements this method. Because **filter( )** is an intermediate operation, it returns a new stream that contains filtered values, which, in this case, are the odd numbers. These elements are then displayed via **forEach( )** as before.

Because **filter( )**, or any other intermediate operation, returns a new stream, it is possible to filter a filtered stream a second time. This is demonstrated by the following line, which produces a stream that contains only those odd values greater than 5:

```
oddVals = myList.stream().filter((n) -> (n % 2) == 1)
                         .filter((n) -> n > 5);
```

Notice that lambda expressions are passed to both filters.



## Reduction Operations

Consider the **min( )** and **max( )** methods in the preceding sample program. Both are terminal operations that return a result based on the elements in the stream. In the language of the stream API, they represent *reduction operations* because each reduces a stream to a single value—in this case, the minimum and maximum. The stream API refers to these as *special case* reductions because they perform a specific function. In addition to **min( )** and **max( )**, other special case reductions are also available, such as **count( )**, which counts the number of elements in a stream. However, the stream API generalizes this concept by providing the **reduce( )** method. By using **reduce( )**, you can return a value from a stream based on any arbitrary criteria. By definition, all reduction operations are terminal operations.

**Stream** defines three versions of **reduce( )**. The two we will use first are shown here:

Optional<T> reduce(BinaryOperator<T> *accumulator*)

T reduce(T *identityVal*, BinaryOperator<T> *accumulator*)

The first form returns an object of type **Optional**, which contains the result. The second form returns an object of type **T** (which is the element type of the stream). In both forms, *accumulator* is a function that operates on two values and produces a result. In the second form, *identityVal* is a value such that an accumulator operation involving *identityVal* and any element of the stream yields that element, unchanged. For example, if the operation is addition, then the identity value will be 0 because 0+x is x. For multiplication, the value will be 1, because 1*x is x.

**BinaryOperator** is a functional interface declared in **java.util.function** that extends the **BiFunction** functional interface. **BiFunction** defines this abstract method:

R apply(T *val*, U *val2*)

Here, **R** specifies the result type, **T** is the type of the first operand, and **U** is the type of second operand. Thus, **apply( )** applies a function to its two operands (*val* and *val2*) and returns the result. When **BinaryOperator** extends **BiFunction**, it specifies the same type for all the type parameters. Thus, as it relates to **BinaryOperator**, **apply( )** looks like this:

T apply(T *val*, T *val2*)

Furthermore, as it relates to **reduce( )**, *val* will contain the previous result and *val2* will contain the next element. In its first invocation, *val* will contain either the identity value or the first element, depending on which version of **reduce( )** is used.

It is important to understand that the accumulator operation must satisfy three constraints. It must be

- Stateless
- Non-interfering
- Associative

As explained earlier, *stateless* means that the operation does not rely on any state information. Thus, each element is processed independently. *Non-interfering* means that the data source is not modified by the operation. Finally, the operation must be *associative*. Here, the term *associative* is used in its normal, arithmetic sense, which means that, given an associative operator used in a sequence of operations, it does not matter which pair of operands is processed first. For example,

(10 * 2) * 7

yields the same result as

10 * (2 * 7)

Associativity is of particular importance to the use of reduction operations on parallel streams, discussed in the next section.

The following program demonstrates the versions of **reduce( )** just described:

```
// Demonstrate the reduce() method.

import java.util.*;
import java.util.stream.*;

class StreamDemo2 {

  public static void main(String[] args) {

    // Create a list of Integer values.
    ArrayList<Integer> myList = new ArrayList<>( );

    myList.add(7);
    myList.add(18);
    myList.add(10);
    myList.add(24);
    myList.add(17);
    myList.add(5);

    // Two ways to obtain the integer product of the elements
    // in myList by use of reduce().
    Optional<Integer> productObj = myList.stream().reduce((a,b) -> a*b);
    if(productObj.isPresent())
      System.out.println("Product as Optional: " + productObj.get());
```

```
        int product = myList.stream().reduce(1, (a,b) -> a*b);
        System.out.println("Product as int: " + product);
    }
}
```

As the output here shows, both uses of **reduce( )** produce the same result:

```
Product as Optional: 2570400
Product as int: 2570400
```



In the program, the first version of **reduce( )** uses the lambda expression to produce a product of two values. In this case, because the stream contains **Integer** values, the **Integer** objects are automatically unboxed for the multiplication and reboxed to return the result. The two values represent the current value of the running result and the next element in the stream. The final result is returned in an object of type **Optional**. The value is obtained by calling **get( )** on the returned object.

In the second version, the identity value is explicitly specified, which for multiplication is 1. Notice that the result is returned as an object of the element type, which is **Integer** in this case.

Although simple reduction operations such as multiplication are useful for examples, reductions are not limited in this regard. For example, assuming the preceding program, the following obtains the product of only the even values:

```
int evenProduct = myList.stream().reduce(1, (a,b) -> {
                      if(b%2 == 0) return a*b; else return a;
                  });
```

Pay special attention to the lambda expression. If **b** is even, then **a*b** is returned. Otherwise, **a** is returned. This works because **a** holds the current result and **b** holds the next element, as explained earlier.

## Using Parallel Streams

Before exploring any more of the stream API, it will be helpful to discuss parallel streams. As has been pointed out previously in this book, the parallel execution of code via multicore processors can result in a substantial increase in performance. Because of this, parallel programming has become an important part of the modern programmer's job. However, parallel programming can be complex and error-prone. One of the benefits that the stream library offers is the ability to easily—and reliably—parallel process certain operations.

Parallel processing of a stream is quite simple to request: just use a parallel stream. As mentioned earlier, one way to obtain a parallel stream is to use the **parallelStream( )** method defined by **Collection**. Another way to obtain a parallel stream is to call the **parallel( )** method on a sequential stream. The **parallel( )** method is defined by **BaseStream**, as shown here:

S parallel()

It returns a parallel stream based on the sequential stream that invokes it. (If it is called on a stream that is already parallel, then the invoking stream is returned.) Understand, of course, that even with a parallel stream, parallelism will be achieved only if the environment supports it.

Once a parallel stream has been obtained, operations on the stream can occur in parallel, assuming that parallelism is supported by the environment. For example, the first **reduce( )** operation in the preceding program can be parallelized by substituting **parallelStream( )** for the call to **stream( )**:

```
Optional<Integer> productObj = myList.parallelStream().reduce((a,b) -> a*b);
```

The results will be the same, but the multiplications can occur in different threads.

As a general rule, any operation applied to a parallel stream must be stateless. It should also be non-interfering and associative. This ensures that the results obtained by executing operations on a parallel stream are the same as those obtained from executing the same operations on a sequential stream.

When using parallel streams, you might find the following version of **reduce( )** especially helpful. It gives you a way to specify how partial results are combined:

<U> U reduce(U *identityVal*, BiFunction<U, ? super T, U> *accumulator*
BinaryOperator<U> *combiner*)

In this version, *combiner* defines the function that combines two values that have been produced by the *accumulator* function. Assuming the preceding program, the following statement computes the product of the elements in **myList** by use of a parallel stream:

```
int parallelProduct = myList.parallelStream().reduce(1, (a,b) -> a*b,
                                                        (a,b) -> a*b);
```

As you can see, in this example, both the accumulator and combiner perform the same function. However, there are cases in which the actions of the accumulator must differ from those of the combiner. For example, consider the following program. Here, **myList** contains a list of **double** values. It then uses the combiner version of **reduce( )** to compute the product of the *square roots* of each element in the list.

```
// Demonstrate the use of a combiner with reduce()

import java.util.*;
import java.util.stream.*;

class StreamDemo3 {

  public static void main(String[] args) {

    // This is now a list of double values.
    ArrayList<Double> myList = new ArrayList<>( );

    myList.add(7.0);
    myList.add(18.0);
    myList.add(10.0);
    myList.add(24.0);
    myList.add(17.0);
    myList.add(5.0);
```

```
        double productOfSqrRoots = myList.parallelStream().reduce(
                                        1.0,
                                        (a,b) -> a * Math.sqrt(b),
                                        (a,b) -> a * b
                                   );

        System.out.println("Product of square roots: " + productOfSqrRoots);
    }
}
```



Notice that the accumulator function multiplies the square roots of two elements, but the combiner multiplies the partial results. Thus, the two functions differ. Moreover, for this computation to work correctly, they *must* differ. For example, if you tried to obtain the product of the square roots of the elements by using the following statement, an error would result:

```
// This won't work.
double productOfSqrRoots2 = myList.parallelStream().reduce(
                                1.0,
                                (a,b) -> a * Math.sqrt(b));
```

In this version of **reduce( )**, the accumulator and the combiner function are one and the same. This results in an error because when two partial results are combined, their square roots are multiplied together rather than the partial results themselves.

As a point of interest, if the stream in the preceding call to **reduce( )** had been changed to a sequential stream, then the operation would yield the correct answer because there would have been no need to combine two partial results. The problem occurs when a parallel stream is used.

You can switch a parallel stream to sequential by calling the **sequential( )** method, which is specified by **BaseStream**. It is shown here:

S sequential( )

In general, a stream can be switched between parallel and sequential on an as-needed basis.

There is one other aspect of a stream to keep in mind when using parallel execution: the order of the elements. Streams can be either ordered or unordered. In general, if the data source is ordered, then the stream will also be ordered. However, when using a parallel stream, a performance boost can sometimes be obtained by allowing a stream to be unordered. When a parallel stream is unordered, each partition of the stream can be operated on independently, without having to coordinate with the others. In cases in which the order of the operations does not matter, it is possible to specify unordered behavior by calling the **unordered( )** method, shown here:

S unordered( )

One other point: the **forEach( )** method may not preserve the ordering of a parallel stream. If you want to perform an operation on each element in a parallel stream while preserving the order, consider using **forEachOrdered( )**. It is used just like **forEach( )**.

## Mapping

Often it is useful to map the elements of one stream to another. For example, a stream that contains a database of name, telephone, and e-mail address information might map only the name and e-mail address portions to another stream. As another example, you might want to apply some transformation to the elements in a stream. To do this, you could map the transformed elements to a new stream. Because mapping operations are quite common, the stream API provides built-in support for them. The most general mapping method is **map( )**. It is shown here:

<R> Stream<R> map(Function<? super T, ? extends R> *mapFunc*)

Here, **R** specifies the type of elements of the new stream; **T** is the type of elements of the invoking stream; and *mapFunc* is an instance of **Function**, which does the mapping. The map function must be stateless and non-interfering. Since a new stream is returned, **map( )** is an intermediate method.

**Function** is a functional interface declared in **java.util.function**. It is declared as shown here:

Function<T, R>

As it relates to **map( )**, **T** is the element type and **R** is the result of the mapping. **Function** has the abstract method shown here:

R apply(T *val*)

Here, *val* is a reference to the object being mapped. The mapped result is returned.

The following is a simple example of **map( )**. It provides a variation on the previous sample program. As before, the program computes the product of the square roots of the values in an **ArrayList**. In this version, however, the square roots of the elements are first mapped to a new stream. Then, **reduce( )** is employed to compute the product.

```
// Map one stream to another.

import java.util.*;
import java.util.stream.*;

class StreamDemo4 {

  public static void main(String[] args) {

    // A list of double values.
    ArrayList<Double> myList = new ArrayList<>( );

    myList.add(7.0);
    myList.add(18.0);
    myList.add(10.0);
    myList.add(24.0);
    myList.add(17.0);
    myList.add(5.0);
```

```
    // Map the square root of the elements in myList to a new stream.
    Stream<Double> sqrtRootStrm = myList.stream().map((a) -> Math.sqrt(a));

    // Find the product of the square roots.
    double productOfSqrRoots = sqrtRootStrm.reduce(1.0, (a,b) -> a*b);

    System.out.println("Product of square roots is " + productOfSqrRoots);
  }
}
```



The output is the same as before. The difference between this version and the previous is simply that the transformation (i.e., the computation of the square roots) occurs during mapping, rather than during the reduction. Because of this, it is possible to use the two-parameter form of **reduce( )** to compute the product because it is no longer necessary to provide a separate combiner function.

Here is an example that uses **map( )** to create a new stream that contains only selected fields from the original stream. In this case, the original stream contains objects of type **NamePhoneEmail**, which contains names, phone numbers, and e-mail addresses. The program then maps only the names and phone numbers to a new stream of **NamePhone** objects. The e-mail addresses are discarded.

```
// Use map() to create a new stream that contains only
// selected aspects of the original stream.

import java.util.*;
import java.util.stream.*;

class NamePhoneEmail {
  String name;
  String phonenum;
  String email;

  NamePhoneEmail(String n, String p, String e) {
    name = n;
    phonenum = p;
    email = e;
  }
}

class NamePhone {
  String name;
  String phonenum;

  NamePhone(String n, String p) {
    name = n;
    phonenum = p;
  }
}
```

```
class StreamDemo5 {

  public static void main(String[] args) {

    // A list of names, phone numbers, and e-mail addresses.
    ArrayList<NamePhoneEmail> myList = new ArrayList<>( );

    myList.add(new NamePhoneEmail("Larry", "555-5555",
                                  "Larry@HerbSchildt.com"));
    myList.add(new NamePhoneEmail("James", "555-4444",
                                  "James@HerbSchildt.com"));
    myList.add(new NamePhoneEmail("Mary", "555-3333",
                                  "Mary@HerbSchildt.com"));

    System.out.println("Original values in myList: ");
    myList.stream().forEach( (a) -> {
      System.out.println(a.name + " " + a.phonenum + " " + a.email);
    });
    System.out.println();

    // Map just the names and phone numbers to a new stream.
    Stream<NamePhone> nameAndPhone = myList.stream().map(
                                 (a) -> new NamePhone(a.name,a.phonenum)
                               );

    System.out.println("List of names and phone numbers: ");
    nameAndPhone.forEach( (a) -> {
      System.out.println(a.name + " " + a.phonenum);
    });
  }
}
```

The output, shown here, verifies the mapping:

```
Original values in myList:
Larry 555-5555 Larry@HerbSchildt.com
James 555-4444 James@HerbSchildt.com
Mary 555-3333 Mary@HerbSchildt.com

List of names and phone numbers:
Larry 555-5555
James 555-4444
Mary 555-3333
```

Because you can pipeline more than one intermediate operation together, you can easily create very powerful actions. For example, the following statement uses **filter( )** and then **map( )** to produce a new stream that contains only the name and phone number of the elements with the name "James":

```
Stream<NamePhone> nameAndPhone = myList.stream().
                              filter((a) -> a.name.equals("James")).
                              map((a) -> new NamePhone(a.name,a.phonenum));
```

This type of filter operation is very common when creating database-style queries. As you gain experience with the stream API, you will find that such chains of operations can be used to create very sophisticated queries, merges, and selections on a data stream.

In addition to the version just described, three other versions of **map( )** are provided. They return a primitive stream, as shown here:

IntStream mapToInt(ToIntFunction<? super T> *mapFunc*)

LongStream mapToLong(ToLongFunction<? super T> *mapFunc*)

DoubleStream mapToDouble(ToDoubleFunction<? super T> *mapFunc*)

Each *mapFunc* must implement the abstract method defined by the specified interface, returning a value of the indicated type. For example, **ToDoubleFunction** specifies the **applyAsDouble(T *val* )** method, which must return the value of its parameter as a **double**.

Here is an example that uses a primitive stream. It first creates an **ArrayList** of **Double** values. It then uses **stream( )** followed by **mapToInt( )** to create an **IntStream** that contains the ceiling of each value.

```
// Map a Stream to an IntStream.

import java.util.*;
import java.util.stream.*;

class StreamDemo6 {

  public static void main(String[] args) {

    // A list of double values.
    ArrayList<Double> myList = new ArrayList<>( );

    myList.add(1.1);
    myList.add(3.6);
    myList.add(9.2);
    myList.add(4.7);
    myList.add(12.1);
    myList.add(5.0);

    System.out.print("Original values in myList: ");
    myList.stream().forEach( (a) -> {
      System.out.print(a + " ");
    });
    System.out.println();

    // Map the ceiling of the elements in myList to an IntStream.
    IntStream cStrm = myList.stream().mapToInt((a) -> (int) Math.ceil(a));

    System.out.print("The ceilings of the values in myList: ");
    cStrm.forEach( (a) -> {
      System.out.print(a + " ");
    });

  }
}
```

Part II

The output is shown here:

```
Original values in myList: 1.1 3.6 9.2 4.7 12.1 5.0
The ceilings of the values in myList: 2 4 10 5 13 5
```

The stream produced by **mapToInt( )** contains the ceiling values of the original elements in **myList**.

Before leaving the topic of mapping, it is necessary to point out that the stream API also provides methods that support *flat maps*. These are **flatMap( )**, **flatMapToInt( )**, **flatMapToLong( )**, and **flatMapToDouble( )**. The flat map methods are designed to handle situations in which each element in the original stream is mapped to more than one element in the resulting stream. Beginning with JDK 16, **Stream** also supplies these additional flat map related methods: **mapMulti( )**, **mapMultiToInt( )**, **mapMultiToLong( )**, and **mapMulltiToDouble( )**.

## Collecting

As the preceding examples have shown, it is possible (indeed, common) to obtain a stream from a collection. Sometimes it is desirable to obtain the opposite: to obtain a collection from a stream. To perform such an action, you will generally use the **collect( )** method. It has two forms. The one we will use first is shown here:

<R, A> R collect(Collector<? super T, A, R> *collectorFunc*)

Here, **R** specifies the type of the result, and **T** specifies the element type of the invoking stream. The internal accumulated type is specified by **A**. The *collectorFunc* specifies how the collection process works. The **collect( )** method is a terminal operation.

The **Collector** interface is declared in **java.util.stream**, as shown here:

interface Collector<T, A, R>

**T**, **A**, and **R** have the same meanings as just described. **Collector** specifies several methods, but for the purposes of this chapter, we won't need to implement them. Instead, we will use two of the predefined collectors that are provided by the **Collectors** class, which is packaged in **java.util.stream**.

The **Collectors** class defines a number of static collector methods that you can use as-is. The two we will use are **toList( )** and **toSet( )**, shown here:

static <T> Collector<T, ?, List<T>> toList( )

static <T> Collector<T, ?, Set<T>> toSet( )

The **toList( )** method returns a collector that can be used to collect elements into a **List**. The **toSet( )** method returns a collector that can be used to collect elements into a **Set**. For example, to collect elements into a **List**, you can call **collect( )** like this:

```
collect(Collectors.toList())
```

The following program puts the preceding discussion into action. It reworks the example in the previous section so that it collects the names and phone numbers into a **List** and a **Set**.

```
// Use collect() to create a List and a Set from a stream.

import java.util.*;
import java.util.stream.*;

class NamePhoneEmail {
  String name;
  String phonenum;
  String email;

  NamePhoneEmail(String n, String p, String e) {
    name = n;
    phonenum = p;
    email = e;
  }
}

class NamePhone {
  String name;
  String phonenum;

  NamePhone(String n, String p) {
    name = n;
    phonenum = p;
  }
}

class StreamDemo7 {

  public static void main(String[] args) {

    // A list of names, phone numbers, and e-mail addresses.
    ArrayList<NamePhoneEmail> myList = new ArrayList<>( );

    myList.add(new NamePhoneEmail("Larry", "555-5555",
                                  "Larry@HerbSchildt.com"));
    myList.add(new NamePhoneEmail("James", "555-4444",
                                  "James@HerbSchildt.com"));
    myList.add(new NamePhoneEmail("Mary", "555-3333",
                                  "Mary@HerbSchildt.com"));

    // Map just the names and phone numbers to a new stream.
    Stream<NamePhone> nameAndPhone = myList.stream().map(
                                     (a) -> new NamePhone(a.name,a.phonenum)
                                    );

    // Use collect to create a List of the names and phone numbers.
    List<NamePhone> npList = nameAndPhone.collect(Collectors.toList());
```

```
    System.out.println("Names and phone numbers in a List:");
    for(NamePhone e : npList)
      System.out.println(e.name + ": " + e.phonenum);

    // Obtain another mapping of the names and phone numbers.
    nameAndPhone = myList.stream().map(
                                (a) -> new NamePhone(a.name,a.phonenum)
                               );

    // Now, create a Set by use of collect().
    Set<NamePhone> npSet = nameAndPhone.collect(Collectors.toSet());

    System.out.println("\nNames and phone numbers in a Set:");
    for(NamePhone e : npSet)
     System.out.println(e.name + ": " + e.phonenum);
  }
}
```

The output is shown here:

```
Names and phone numbers in a List:
Larry: 555-5555
James: 555-4444
Mary: 555-3333

Names and phone numbers in a Set:
James: 555-4444
Larry: 555-5555
Mary: 555-3333
```

In the program, the following line collects the name and phone numbers into a **List** by using **toList( )**:

```
List<NamePhone> npList = nameAndPhone.collect(Collectors.toList());
```

After this line executes, the collection referred to by **npList** can be used like any other **List** collection. For example, it can be cycled through by using a for-each **for** loop, as shown in the next line:

```
for(NamePhone e : npList)
  System.out.println(e.name + ": " + e.phonenum);
```

The creation of a **Set** via **collect(Collectors.toSet( ))** works in the same way. The ability to move data from a collection to a stream, and then back to a collection again, is a very powerful attribute of the stream API. It gives you the ability to operate on a collection through a stream, but then repackage it as a collection. Furthermore, the stream operations can, if appropriate, occur in parallel.

The version of **collect( )** used by the previous example is quite convenient, and often the one you want, but there is a second version that gives you more control over the collection process. It is shown here:

<R> R collect(Supplier<R> *target*, BiConsumer<R, ? super T> *accumulator*,
BiConsumer <R, R> *combiner*)

Here, *target* specifies how the object that holds the result is created. For example, to use a **LinkedList** as the result collection, you would specify its constructor. The *accumulator* function adds an element to the result and *combiner* combines two partial results. Thus, these functions work similarly to the way they do in **reduce( )**. For both, they must be stateless and non-interfering. They must also be associative.

Note that the *target* parameter is of type **Supplier**. It is a functional interface declared in **java.util.function**. It specifies only the **get( )** method, which has no parameters and, in this case, returns an object of type **R**. Thus, as it relates to **collect( )**, **get( )** returns a reference to a mutable storage object, such as a collection.

Note also that the types of *accumulator* and *combiner* are **BiConsumer**. This is a functional interface defined in **java.util.function**. It specifies the abstract method **accept( )** that is shown here:

void accept(T *obj*, U *obj2*)

This method performs some type of operation on *obj* and *obj2*. As it relates to *accumulator*, *obj* specifies the target collection, and *obj2* specifies the element to add to that collection. As it relates to *combiner*, *obj* and *obj2* specify two collections that will be combined.

Using the version of **collect( )** just described, you could use a **LinkedList** as the target in the preceding program, as shown here:

```
LinkedList<NamePhone> npList = nameAndPhone.collect(
                                 () -> new LinkedList<>(),
                                 (list, element) -> list.add(element),
                                 (listA,listB ) -> listA.addAll(listB));
```

Notice that the first argument to **collect( )** is a lambda expression that returns a new **LinkedList**. The second argument uses the standard collection method **add( )** to add an element to the list. The third element uses **addAll( )** to combine two linked lists. As a point of interest, you can use any method defined by **LinkedList** to add an element to the list. For example, you could use **addFirst( )** to add elements to the start of the list, as shown here:

```
(list, element) -> list.addFirst(element)
```

As you may have guessed, it is not always necessary to specify a lambda expression for the arguments to **collect( )**. Often, method and/or constructor references will suffice. For example, again assuming the preceding program, this statement creates a **HashSet** that contains all of the elements in the **nameAndPhone** stream:

```
HashSet<NamePhone> npSet = nameAndPhone.collect(HashSet::new,
                                                HashSet::add,
                                                HashSet::addAll);
```

Notice that the first argument specifies the **HashSet** constructor reference. The second and third specify method references to **HashSet**'s **add( )** and **addAll( )** methods.

One last point: In the language of the stream API, the **collect( )** method performs what is called a *mutable reduction*. This is because the result of the reduction is a mutable (i.e., changeable) storage object, such as a collection. If you want to obtain an unmodifiable collection from a stream, then beginning with JDK 16, you can use the **toList( )** method in **Stream**. It returns an unmodifiable **List**.

## Iterators and Streams

Although a stream is not a data storage object, you can still use an iterator to cycle through its elements in much the same way as you would use an iterator to cycle through the elements of a collection. The stream API supports two types of iterators. The first is the traditional **Iterator**. The second is **Spliterator**, which was added by JDK 8. It provides significant advantages in certain situations when used with parallel streams.

### Use an Iterator with a Stream

As just mentioned, you can use an iterator with a stream in just the same way that you do with a collection. Iterators are discussed in Chapter 20, but a brief review will be useful here. Iterators are objects that implement the **Iterator** interface declared in **java.util**. Its two key methods are **hasNext( )** and **next( )**. If there is another element to iterate, **hasNext( )** returns **true**, and **false** otherwise. The **next( )** method returns the next element in the iteration.

---

**NOTE** There are additional iterator types that handle the primitive streams: **PrimitiveIterator**, **PrimitiveIterator.OfDouble**, **PrimitiveIterator.OfLong**, and **PrimitiveIterator.OfInt**. These iterators all extend the **Iterator** interface and work in the same general way as those based directly on **Iterator**.

To obtain an iterator to a stream, call **iterator( )** on the stream. The version used by **Stream** is shown here:

Iterator<T> iterator( )

Here, **T** specifies the element type. (The primitive streams return iterators of the appropriate primitive type.)

The following program shows how to iterate through the elements of a stream. In this case, the strings in an **ArrayList** are iterated, but the process is the same for any type of stream.

```
// Use an iterator with a stream.

import java.util.*;
import java.util.stream.*;

class StreamDemo8 {
  public static void main(String[] args) {

    // Create a list of Strings.
    ArrayList<String> myList = new ArrayList<>( );
    myList.add("Alpha");
    myList.add("Beta");
    myList.add("Gamma");
    myList.add("Delta");
    myList.add("Phi");
    myList.add("Omega");

    // Obtain a Stream to the array list.
    Stream<String> myStream = myList.stream();
```

```
    // Obtain an iterator to the stream.
    Iterator<String> itr = myStream.iterator();

    // Iterate the elements in the stream.
    while(itr.hasNext())
      System.out.println(itr.next());
  }
}
```

The output is shown here:

```
Alpha
Beta
Gamma
Delta
Phi
Omega
```



## Use Spliterator

**Spliterator** offers an alternative to **Iterator**, especially when parallel processing is involved. In general, **Spliterator** is more sophisticated than **Iterator**, and a discussion of **Spliterator** is found in Chapter 20. However, it will be useful to review its key features here. **Spliterator** defines several methods, but we only need to use three. The first is **tryAdvance( )**. It performs an action on the next element and then advances the iterator. It is shown here:

boolean tryAdvance(Consumer<? super T> *action*)

Here, *action* specifies the action that is executed on the next element in the iteration. **tryAdvance( )** returns **true** if there is a next element. It returns **false** if no elements remain. As discussed earlier in this chapter, **Consumer** declares one method called **accept( )** that receives an element of type **T** as an argument and returns **void**.

Because **tryAdvance( )** returns **false** when there are no more elements to process, it makes the iteration loop construct very simple, for example:

```
while(splitItr.tryAdvance( // perform action here );
```

As long as **tryAdvance( )** returns **true**, the action is applied to the next element. When **tryAdvance( )** returns **false**, the iteration is complete. Notice how **tryAdvance( )** consolidates the purposes of **hasNext( )** and **next( )** provided by **Iterator** into a single method. This improves the efficiency of the iteration process.

The following version of the preceding program substitutes a **Spliterator** for the **Iterator**:

```
// Use a Spliterator.

import java.util.*;
import java.util.stream.*;

class StreamDemo9 {
```

```
  public static void main(String[] args) {

    // Create a list of Strings.
    ArrayList<String> myList = new ArrayList<>( );
    myList.add("Alpha");
    myList.add("Beta");
    myList.add("Gamma");
    myList.add("Delta");
    myList.add("Phi");
    myList.add("Omega");

    // Obtain a Stream to the array list.
    Stream<String> myStream = myList.stream();

    // Obtain a Spliterator.
    Spliterator<String> splitItr = myStream.spliterator();

    // Iterate the elements of the stream.
    while(splitItr.tryAdvance((n) -> System.out.println(n)));
  }
}
```

The output is the same as before.

In some cases, you might want to perform some action on each element collectively, rather than one at a time. To handle this type of situation, **Spliterator** provides the **forEachRemaining( )** method, shown here:

default void forEachRemaining(Consumer<? super T> *action*)

This method applies *action* to each unprocessed element and then returns. For example, assuming the preceding program, the following displays the strings remaining in the stream:

```
splitItr.forEachRemaining((n) -> System.out.println(n));
```

Notice how this method eliminates the need to provide a loop to cycle through the elements one at a time. This is another advantage of **Spliterator**.

One other **Spliterator** method of particular interest is **trySplit( )**. It splits the elements being iterated in two, returning a new **Spliterator** to one of the partitions. The other partition remains accessible by the original **Spliterator**. It is shown here:

Spliterator<T> trySplit( )

If it is not possible to split the invoking **Spliterator**, **null** is returned. Otherwise, a reference to the partition is returned. For example, here is another version of the preceding program that demonstrates **trySplit( )**:

```
// Demonstrate trySplit().

import java.util.*;
import java.util.stream.*;
```

```
class StreamDemo10 {

  public static void main(String[] args) {

    // Create a list of Strings.
    ArrayList<String> myList = new ArrayList<>( );
    myList.add("Alpha");
    myList.add("Beta");
    myList.add("Gamma");
    myList.add("Delta");
    myList.add("Phi");
    myList.add("Omega");

    // Obtain a Stream to the array list.
    Stream<String> myStream = myList.stream();

    // Obtain a Spliterator.
    Spliterator<String> splitItr = myStream.spliterator();

    // Now, split the first iterator.
    Spliterator<String> splitItr2 = splitItr.trySplit();

     // If splitItr could be split, use splitItr2 first.
    if(splitItr2 != null) {
      System.out.println("Output from splitItr2: ");
      splitItr2.forEachRemaining((n) -> System.out.println(n));
    }

    // Now, use the splitItr.
    System.out.println("\nOutput from splitItr: ");
    splitItr.forEachRemaining((n) -> System.out.println(n));
  }
}
```

The output is shown here:

```
Output from splitItr2:
Alpha
Beta
Gamma

Output from splitItr:
Delta
Phi
Omega
```

Although splitting the **Spliterator** in this simple illustration is of no practical value, splitting can be of *great value* for parallel processing over large data sets. However, in many cases, it is better to use one of the other **Stream** methods in conjunction with a parallel stream, rather than manually handling these details with **Spliterator**. **Spliterator** is primarily for the cases in which none of the predefined methods seems appropriate.

## More to Explore in the Stream API

This chapter has discussed several key aspects of the stream API and introduced the techniques required to use them, but the stream API has much more to offer. To begin, here are a few of the other methods provided by **Stream** that you will find helpful:

- To determine if one or more elements in a stream satisfy a specified predicate, use **allMatch( )**, **anyMatch( )**, or **noneMatch( )**.
- To obtain the number of elements in the stream, call **count( )**.
- To obtain a stream that contains only unique elements, use **distinct( )**.
- To create a stream that contains a specified set of elements, use **of( )**.

One last point: The stream API is a powerful aspect of Java. You will want to explore all of the capabilities that **java.util.stream** has to offer.

# CHAPTER 31 Regular Expressions and Other Packages

When Java was originally released, it included a set of eight packages, called the *core API*. Each subsequent release added to the API. Today, the Java API contains a very large number of packages. Many of the packages support areas of specialization that are beyond the scope of this book. However, several packages warrant an introduction here. Four are **java.util.regex**, **java.lang.reflect**, **java.rmi**, and **java.text**. They support regular expression processing, reflection, Remote Method Invocation (RMI), and text formatting, respectively. The chapter ends by introducing the date and time API in **java.time** and its subpackages.

The *regular expression* package lets you perform sophisticated pattern matching operations. This chapter provides an introduction to this package along with extensive examples. *Reflection* is the ability of software to analyze itself. It is an essential part of the Java Beans technology that is covered in Chapter 35. *Remote Method Invocation (RMI)* allows you to build Java applications that are distributed among several machines. This chapter provides a simple client/server example that uses RMI. The *text formatting* capabilities of **java.text** have many uses. The one examined here formats date and time strings. The date and time API supplies an up-to-date approach to handling date and time.

## Regular Expression Processing

The **java.util.regex** package supports regular expression processing. Beginning with JDK 9, **java.util.regex** is in the **java.base** module. As the term is used here, a *regular expression* is a string of characters that describes a character sequence. This general description, called a *pattern*, can then be used to find matches in other character sequences. Regular expressions can specify wildcard characters, sets of characters, and various quantifiers. Thus, you can specify a regular expression that represents a general form that can match several different specific character sequences.

There are two classes that support regular expression processing: **Pattern** and **Matcher**. These classes work together. Use **Pattern** to define a regular expression. Match the pattern against another sequence using **Matcher**.

## Pattern

The **Pattern** class defines no constructors. Instead, a pattern is created by calling the **compile( )** factory method. One of its forms is shown here:

```
static Pattern compile(String pattern)
```

Here, *pattern* is the regular expression that you want to use. The **compile( )** method transforms the string in *pattern* into a pattern that can be used for pattern matching by the **Matcher** class. It returns a **Pattern** object that contains the pattern.

Once you have created a **Pattern** object, you will use it to create a **Matcher**. This is done by calling the **matcher( )** method defined by **Pattern**. It is shown here:

```
Matcher matcher(CharSequence str)
```

Here *str* is the character sequence that the pattern will be matched against. This is called the *input sequence.* **CharSequence** is an interface that defines a read-only set of characters. It is implemented by the **String** class, among others. Thus, you can pass a string to **matcher( )**.

## Matcher

The **Matcher** class has no constructors. Instead, you create a **Matcher** by calling the **matcher( )** factory method defined by **Pattern**, as just explained. Once you have created a **Matcher**, you will use its methods to perform various pattern matching operations. Several are described here.

The simplest pattern matching method is **matches( )**, which determines whether the character sequence matches the pattern. It is shown here:

```
boolean matches( )
```

It returns **true** if the sequence and the pattern match, and **false** otherwise. Understand that the entire sequence must match the pattern, not just a subsequence of it.

To determine if a subsequence of the input sequence matches the pattern, use **find( )**. One version is shown here:

```
boolean find( )
```

It returns **true** if there is a matching subsequence and **false** otherwise. This method can be called repeatedly, allowing it to find all matching subsequences. Each call to **find( )** begins where the previous one left off.

You can obtain a string containing the last matching sequence by calling **group( )**. One of its forms is shown here:

```
String group( )
```

The matching string is returned. If no match exists, then an **IllegalStateException** is thrown.

You can obtain the index within the input sequence of the current match by calling **start( )**. The index one past the end of the current match is obtained by calling **end( )**. The forms used in this chapter are shown here:

```
int start( )
int end( )
```

Both throw **IllegalStateException** if no match exists.

You can replace all occurrences of a matching sequence with another sequence by calling **replaceAll( )**. One version is shown here:

String replaceAll(String *newStr*)

Here, *newStr* specifies the new character sequence that will replace the ones that match the pattern. The updated input sequence is returned as a string.

## Regular Expression Syntax

Before we demonstrate **Pattern** and **Matcher**, it is necessary to explain how to construct a regular expression. Although no rule is complicated by itself, there are a large number of them, and a complete discussion is beyond the scope of this chapter. However, a few of the more commonly used constructs are described here.

In general, a regular expression is comprised of normal characters, character classes (sets of characters), wildcard characters, and quantifiers. A normal character is matched as-is. Thus, if a pattern consists of "xy", then the only input sequence that will match it is "xy". Characters such as newline and tab are specified using the standard escape sequences, which begin with a \. For example, a newline is specified by **\n**. In the language of regular expressions, a normal character is also called a *literal*.

A character class is a set of characters. A character class is specified by putting the characters in the class between brackets. For example, the class [wxyz] matches w, x, y, or z. To specify an inverted set, precede the characters with a ^. For example, [^wxyz] matches any character except w, x, y, or z. You can specify a range of characters using a hyphen. For example, to specify a character class that will match the digits 1 through 9, use [1-9].

The wildcard character is the **.** (dot), and it matches any character. Thus, a pattern that consists of "." will match these (and other) input sequences: "A", "a", "x", and so on.

A quantifier determines how many times an expression is matched. The basic quantifiers are shown here:

| | |
|---|---|
| + | Match one or more |
| * | Match zero or more |
| ? | Match zero or one |

For example, the pattern "x+" will match "x", "xx", and "xxx", among others. As you will see, variations are supported that affect how matching is performed.

One other point: In general, if you specify an invalid expression, a **PatternSyntaxException** will be thrown.

## Demonstrating Pattern Matching

The best way to understand how regular expression pattern matching operates is to work through some examples. The first, shown here, looks for a match with a literal pattern:

```
// A simple pattern matching demo.
import java.util.regex.*;
```

```
class RegExpr {
  public static void main(String[] args) {
    Pattern pat;
    Matcher mat;
    boolean found;

    pat = Pattern.compile("Java");
    mat = pat.matcher("Java");
    found = mat.matches(); // check for a match

    System.out.println("Testing Java against Java.");
    if(found) System.out.println("Matches");
    else System.out.println("No Match");

    System.out.println();

    System.out.println("Testing Java against Java SE.");
    mat = pat.matcher("Java SE"); // create a new matcher

    found = mat.matches(); // check for a match

    if(found) System.out.println("Matches");
    else System.out.println("No Match");
  }
}
```

The output from the program is shown here:

```
Testing Java against Java.
Matches

Testing Java against Java SE.
No Match
```

Let's look closely at this program. The program begins by creating the pattern that contains the sequence "Java". Next, a **Matcher** is created for that pattern that has the input sequence "Java". Then, the **matches( )** method is called to determine if the input sequence matches the pattern. Because the sequence and the pattern are the same, **matches( )** returns **true**. Next, a new **Matcher** is created with the input sequence "Java SE" and **matches( )** is called again. In this case, the pattern and the input sequence differ, and no match is found. Remember, the **matches( )** function returns **true** only when the input sequence precisely matches the pattern. It will not return **true** just because a subsequence matches.

You can use **find( )** to determine if the input sequence contains a subsequence that matches the pattern. Consider the following program:

```
// Use find() to find a subsequence.
import java.util.regex.*;

class RegExpr2 {
  public static void main(String[] args) {
    Pattern pat = Pattern.compile("Java");
    Matcher mat = pat.matcher("Java SE");
```

```
    System.out.println("Looking for Java in Java SE.");

    if(mat.find()) System.out.println("subsequence found");
    else System.out.println("No Match");
  }
}
```

The output is shown here:

```
Looking for Java in Java SE.
subsequence found
```

In this case, **find( )** finds the subsequence "Java".

The **find( )** method can be used to search the input sequence for repeated occurrences of the pattern because each call to **find( )** picks up where the previous one left off. For example, the following program finds two occurrences of the pattern "test":

```
// Use find() to find multiple subsequences.
import java.util.regex.*;

class RegExpr3 {
  public static void main(String[] args) {
    Pattern pat = Pattern.compile("test");
    Matcher mat = pat.matcher("test 1 2 3 test");

    while(mat.find()) {
      System.out.println("test found at index " +
                         mat.start());
    }
  }
}
```

The output is shown here:

```
test found at index 0
test found at index 11
```

As the output shows, two matches were found. The program uses the **start( )** method to obtain the index of each match.

## Using Wildcards and Quantifiers

Although the preceding programs show the general technique for using **Pattern** and **Matcher**, they don't show their power. The real benefit of regular expression processing is not seen until wildcards and quantifiers are used. To begin, consider the following example that uses the + quantifier to match any arbitrarily long sequence of Ws:

```
// Use a quantifier.
import java.util.regex.*;

class RegExpr4 {
  public static void main(String[] args) {
    Pattern pat = Pattern.compile("W+");
    Matcher mat = pat.matcher("W WW WWW");
```

Part II

```
    while(mat.find())
      System.out.println("Match: " + mat.group());
  }
}
```

The output from the program is shown here:

```
Match: W
Match: WW
Match: WWW
```

As the output shows, the regular expression pattern "W+" matches any arbitrarily long sequence of Ws.

The next program uses a wildcard to create a pattern that will match any sequence that begins with *e* and ends with *d*. To do this, it uses the dot wildcard character along with the + quantifier.

```
// Use wildcard and quantifier.
import java.util.regex.*;

class RegExpr5 {
  public static void main(String[] args) {
    Pattern pat = Pattern.compile("e.+d");
    Matcher mat = pat.matcher("extend cup end table");

    while(mat.find())
      System.out.println("Match: " + mat.group());
  }
}
```

You might be surprised by the output produced by the program, which is shown here:

```
Match: extend cup end
```

Only one match is found, and it is the longest sequence that begins with *e* and ends with *d*. You might have expected two matches: "extend" and "end". The reason that the longer sequence is found is that the pattern "e.+d" matches the longest sequence that fits the pattern. This is called *greedy behavior*. You can specify *reluctant behavior* by adding the **?** to the pattern, as shown in this version of the program. It causes the shortest matching pattern to be obtained.

```
// Use a reluctant quantifier.
import java.util.regex.*;

class RegExpr6 {
  public static void main(String[] args) {
    // Use reluctant matching behavior.
    Pattern pat = Pattern.compile("e.+?d");
    Matcher mat = pat.matcher("extend cup end table");
```

```
    while(mat.find())
      System.out.println("Match: " + mat.group());
  }
}
```

The output from the program is shown here:

```
Match: extend
Match: end
```

As the output shows, the pattern "e.+?d" will match the shortest sequence that begins with *e* and ends with *d*. Thus, two matches are found.

In general, to convert a greedy quantifier into a reluctant quantifier, add a **?**. You can also specify *possessive* behavior by appending a **+**. For example, you might want to try the pattern **"e.?+d"** and observe the result. You can also specify a number of times to match by using {***min, limit***}, which matches *min* times, up to *limit* times. Also supported are {***min***} and {***min,***} which match *min* times, and *min* times but possibly more, respectively.



## Working with Classes of Characters

Sometimes you will want to match any sequence that contains one or more characters, in any order, that are part of a set of characters. For example, to match whole words, you want to match any sequence of the letters of the alphabet. One of the easiest ways to do this is to use a character class, which defines a set of characters. Recall that a character class is created by putting the characters you want to match between brackets. For example, to match the lowercase characters a through z, use **[a-z]**. The following program demonstrates this technique:

```
// Use a character class.
import java.util.regex.*;

class RegExpr7 {
  public static void main(String[] args) {
    // Match lowercase words.
    Pattern pat = Pattern.compile("[a-z]+");
    Matcher mat = pat.matcher("this is a test.");

    while(mat.find())
      System.out.println("Match: " + mat.group());
  }
}
```

The output is shown here:

```
Match: this
Match: is
Match: a
Match: test
```

## Using replaceAll( )

The **replaceAll( )** method supplied by **Matcher** lets you perform powerful search-and-replace operations that use regular expressions. For example, the following program replaces all occurrences of sequences that begin with "Jon" with "Eric":

```
// Use replaceAll().
import java.util.regex.*;

class RegExpr8 {
  public static void main(String[] args) {
    String str = "Jon Jonathan Frank Ken Todd";

    Pattern pat = Pattern.compile("Jon.*? ");
    Matcher mat = pat.matcher(str);

    System.out.println("Original sequence: " + str);

    str = mat.replaceAll("Eric ");

    System.out.println("Modified sequence: " + str);

  }
}
```

The output is shown here:

```
Original sequence: Jon Jonathan Frank Ken Todd
Modified sequence: Eric Eric Frank Ken Todd
```

Because the regular expression "Jon.*? " matches any string that begins with Jon followed by zero or more characters, ending in a space, it can be used to match and replace both Jon and Jonathan with the name Eric. Such a substitution is not easily accomplished without pattern-matching capabilities.

## Using split( )

You can reduce an input sequence into its individual tokens by using the **split( )** method defined by **Pattern**. One form of the **split( )** method is shown here:

String[ ] split(CharSequence *str*)

It processes the input sequence passed in *str*, reducing it into tokens based on the delimiters specified by the pattern.

For example, the following program finds tokens that are separated by spaces, commas, periods, and exclamation points:

```
// Use split().
import java.util.regex.*;

class RegExpr9 {
  public static void main(String[] args) {
```

```
    // Match lowercase words.
    Pattern pat = Pattern.compile("[ ,.!]");

    String[] strs = pat.split("one two,alpha9 12!done.");

    for(int i=0; i < strs.length; i++)
      System.out.println("Next token: " + strs[i]);

  }
}
```

The output is shown here:

```
Next token: one
Next token: two
Next token: alpha9
Next token: 12
Next token: done
```

As the output shows, the input sequence is reduced to its individual tokens. Notice that the delimiters are not included.

## Two Pattern-Matching Options

Although the pattern-matching techniques described in the foregoing offer the greatest flexibility and power, there are two alternatives you might find useful in some circumstances. If you only need to perform a one-time pattern match, you can use the **matches( )** method defined by **Pattern**. It is shown here:

static boolean matches(String *pattern*, CharSequence *str*)

It returns **true** if *pattern* matches *str* and **false** otherwise. This method automatically compiles *pattern* and then looks for a match. If you will be using the same pattern repeatedly, then using **matches( )** is less efficient than compiling the pattern and using the pattern-matching methods defined by **Matcher**, as described previously.

You can also perform a pattern match by using the **matches( )** method implemented by **String**. It is shown here:

boolean matches(String *pattern*)

If the invoking string matches the regular expression in *pattern*, then **matches( )** returns **true**. Otherwise, it returns **false**.

## Exploring Regular Expressions

The overview of regular expressions presented in this section only hints at their power. Since text parsing, manipulation, and tokenization are a large part of programming, you will likely find Java's regular expression subsystem a powerful tool that you can use to your advantage. It is, therefore, wise to explore the capabilities of regular expressions. Experiment with several different types of patterns and input sequences. Once you understand how regular expression pattern matching works, you will find it useful in many of your programming endeavors.

| Class | Primary Function |
|---|---|
| AccessibleObject | Allows you to bypass the default access control checks |
| Array | Allows you to dynamically create and manipulate arrays |
| Constructor | Provides information about a constructor |
| Executable | An abstract superclass extended by **Method** and **Constructor** |
| Field | Provides information about a field |
| Method | Provides information about a method |
| Modifier | Provides information about class and member access modifiers |
| Parameter | Provides information about parameters |
| Proxy | Supports dynamic proxy classes |
| RecordComponent | Provides information about a record |
| ReflectPermission | Allows reflection of private or protected members of a class |

**Table 31-1** Classes Defined in **java.lang.reflect**

## Reflection

Reflection is the ability of software to analyze itself. This is provided by the **java.lang.reflect** package and elements in **Class**. Beginning with JDK 9, **java.lang.reflect** is part of the **java.base** module. Reflection is an important capability, especially when using components called Java Beans. It allows you to analyze a software component and describe its capabilities dynamically, at run time rather than at compile time. For example, by using reflection, you can determine what methods, constructors, and fields a class supports. Reflection was introduced in Chapter 12. It is examined further here.

The package **java.lang.reflect** includes several interfaces. Of special interest is **Member**, which defines methods that allow you to get information about a field, constructor, or method of a class. There are also 11 classes in this package. These are listed in Table 31-1.

The following application illustrates a simple use of the Java reflection capabilities. It prints the constructors, fields, and methods of the class **java.awt.Dimension**. The program begins by using the **forName( )** method of **Class** to get a class object for **java.awt.Dimension**. Once this is obtained, **getConstructors( )**, **getFields( )**, and **getMethods( )** are used to analyze this class object. They return arrays of **Constructor**, **Field**, and **Method** objects that provide the information about the object. The **Constructor**, **Field**, and **Method** classes define several methods that can be used to obtain information about an object. You will want to explore these on your own. However, each supports the **toString( )** method. Therefore, using **Constructor**, **Field**, and **Method** objects as arguments to the **println( )** method is straightforward, as shown in the program.

```
// Demonstrate reflection.
import java.lang.reflect.*;
public class ReflectionDemo1 {
  public static void main(String[] args) {
    try {
      Class<?> c = Class.forName("java.awt.Dimension");
      System.out.println("Constructors:");
```

```
      Constructor<?>[] constructors = c.getConstructors();
      for(int i = 0; i < constructors.length; i++) {
        System.out.println(" " + constructors[i]);
      }

      System.out.println("Fields:");
      Field[] fields = c.getFields();
      for(int i = 0; i < fields.length; i++) {
        System.out.println(" " + fields[i]);
      }

      System.out.println("Methods:");
      Method[] methods = c.getMethods();
      for(int i = 0; i < methods.length; i++) {
        System.out.println(" " + methods[i]);
      }
    }
    catch(Exception e) {
      System.out.println("Exception: " + e);
    }
  }
}
```

Here is the output from this program. (The output you see when you run the program may differ slightly from that shown.)

```
Constructors:
 public java.awt.Dimension(int,int)
 public java.awt.Dimension()
 public java.awt.Dimension(java.awt.Dimension)
Fields:
 public int java.awt.Dimension.width
 public int java.awt.Dimension.height
Methods:
 public int java.awt.Dimension.hashCode()
 public boolean java.awt.Dimension.equals(java.lang.Object)
 public java.lang.String java.awt.Dimension.toString()
 public java.awt.Dimension java.awt.Dimension.getSize()
 public void java.awt.Dimension.setSize(double,double)
 public void java.awt.Dimension.setSize(java.awt.Dimension)
 public void java.awt.Dimension.setSize(int,int)
 public double java.awt.Dimension.getHeight()
 public double java.awt.Dimension.getWidth()
 public java.lang.Object java.awt.geom.Dimension2D.clone()
 public void java.awt.geom.
             Dimension2D.setSize(java.awt.geom.Dimension2D)
 public final native java.lang.Class java.lang.Object.getClass()
 public final native void java.lang.Object.wait(long)
   throws java.lang.InterruptedException
 public final void java.lang.Object.wait()
   throws java.lang.InterruptedException
 public final void java.lang.Object.wait(long,int)
   throws java.lang.InterruptedException
 public final native void java.lang.Object.notify()
 public final native void java.lang.Object.notifyAll()
```

Part II

| Method | Description |
|---|---|
| static boolean isAbstract(int *val*) | Returns **true** if *val* has the **abstract** flag set and **false** otherwise |
| static boolean isFinal(int *val*) | Returns **true** if *val* has the **final** flag set and **false** otherwise |
| static boolean isInterface(int *val*) | Returns **true** if *val* has the **interface** flag set and **false** otherwise |
| static boolean isNative(int *val*) | Returns **true** if *val* has the **native** flag set and **false** otherwise |
| static boolean isPrivate(int *val*) | Returns **true** if *val* has the **private** flag set and **false** otherwise |
| static boolean isProtected(int *val*) | Returns **true** if *val* has the **protected** flag set and **false** otherwise |
| static boolean isPublic(int *val*) | Returns **true** if *val* has the **public** flag set and **false** otherwise |
| static boolean isStatic(int *val*) | Returns **true** if *val* has the **static** flag set and **false** otherwise |
| static boolean isStrict(int *val*) | Returns **true** if *val* has the **strict** flag set and **false** otherwise |
| static boolean isSynchronized(int *val*) | Returns **true** if *val* has the **synchronized** flag set and **false** otherwise |
| static boolean isTransient(int *val*) | Returns **true** if *val* has the **transient** flag set and **false** otherwise |
| static boolean isVolatile(int *val*) | Returns **true** if *val* has the **volatile** flag set and **false** otherwise |

**Table 31-2** The "is" Methods Defined by **Modifier** That Determine Modifiers

The next example uses Java's reflection capabilities to obtain the public methods of a class. The program begins by instantiating class **A**. The **getClass( )** method is applied to this object reference, and it returns the **Class** object for class **A**. The **getDeclaredMethods( )** method returns an array of **Method** objects that describe only the methods declared by this class. Methods inherited from superclasses such as **Object** are not included.

Each element of the **methods** array is then processed. The **getModifiers( )** method returns an **int** containing flags that describe which modifiers apply for this element. The **Modifier** class provides a set of **is*X*** methods, shown in Table 31-2, that can be used to examine this value. For example, the static method **isPublic( )** returns **true** if its argument includes the **public** modifier. Otherwise, it returns **false**. In the following program, if the method supports public access, its name is obtained by the **getName( )** method and is then printed.

```
// Show public methods.
import java.lang.reflect.*;
public class ReflectionDemo2 {
  public static void main(String[] args) {
```

```
    try {
      A a = new A();
      Class<?> c = a.getClass();
      System.out.println("Public Methods:");
      Method[] methods = c.getDeclaredMethods();
      for(int i = 0; i < methods.length; i++) {
        int modifiers = methods[i].getModifiers();
        if(Modifier.isPublic(modifiers)) {
          System.out.println(" " + methods[i].getName());
        }
      }
    }
    catch(Exception e) {
      System.out.println("Exception: " + e);
    }
  }
}

class A {
  public void a1() {
  }
  public void a2() {
  }
  protected void a3() {
  }
  private void a4() {
  }
}
```

Here is the output from this program:

```
Public Methods:
 a1
 a2
```

**Modifier** also includes a set of static methods that return the type of modifiers that can be applied to a specific type of program element. These methods are

static int classModifiers( )

static int constructorModifiers( )

static int fieldModifiers( )

static int interfaceModifiers( )

static int methodModifiers( )

static int parameterModifiers( )

For example, **methodModifiers( )** returns the modifiers that can be applied to a method. Each method returns flags, packed into an **int**, that indicate which modifiers are legal. The modifier values are defined by constants in **Modifier**, which include **PROTECTED, PUBLIC, PRIVATE, STATIC, FINAL**, and so on.

# Remote Method Invocation

Remote Method Invocation (RMI) allows a Java object that executes on one machine to invoke a method of a Java object that executes on another machine. This is an important feature, because it allows you to build distributed applications. While a complete discussion of RMI is outside the scope of this book, the following simplified example describes the basic principles involved. RMI is supported by the **java.rmi** package. Beginning with JDK 9, it is part of the **java.rmi** module.

## A Simple Client/Server Application Using RMI

This section provides step-by-step directions for building a simple client/server application by using RMI. The server receives a request from a client, processes it, and returns a result. In this example, the request specifies two numbers. The server adds these together and returns the sum.

### Step One: Enter and Compile the Source Code

This application uses four source files. The first file, **AddServerIntf.java**, defines the remote interface that is provided by the server. It contains one method that accepts two **double** arguments and returns their sum. All remote interfaces must extend the **Remote** interface, which is part of **java.rmi**. **Remote** defines no members. Its purpose is simply to indicate that an interface uses remote methods. All remote methods can throw a **RemoteException**.

```
import java.rmi.*;

public interface AddServerIntf extends Remote {
  double add(double d1, double d2) throws RemoteException;
}
```

The second source file, **AddServerImpl.java**, implements the remote interface. The implementation of the **add( )** method is straightforward. Remote objects typically extend **UnicastRemoteObject**, which provides functionality that is needed to make objects available from remote machines.

```
import java.rmi.*;
import java.rmi.server.*;

public class AddServerImpl extends UnicastRemoteObject
  implements AddServerIntf {

  public AddServerImpl() throws RemoteException {
  }
  public double add(double d1, double d2) throws RemoteException {
    return d1 + d2;
  }
}
```

The third source file, **AddServer.java**, contains the main program for the server machine. Its primary function is to update the RMI registry on that machine. This is done by using the **rebind( )** method of the **Naming** class (found in **java.rmi**). That method associates a name with an object reference. The first argument to the **rebind( )** method is a string that names the server as "AddServer". Its second argument is a reference to an instance of **AddServerImpl**.

```
import java.net.*;
import java.rmi.*;

public class AddServer {
  public static void main(String[] args) {

    try {
      AddServerImpl addServerImpl = new AddServerImpl();
      Naming.rebind("AddServer", addServerImpl);
    }
    catch(Exception e) {
      System.out.println("Exception: " + e);
    }
  }
}
```

The fourth source file, **AddClient.java**, implements the client side of this distributed application. **AddClient.java** requires three command-line arguments. The first is the IP address or name of the server machine. The second and third arguments are the two numbers that are to be summed.

The application begins by forming a string that follows the URL syntax. This URL uses the **rmi** protocol. The string includes the IP address or name of the server and the string "AddServer". The program then invokes the **lookup( )** method of the **Naming** class. This method accepts one argument, the **rmi** URL, and returns a reference to an object of type **AddServerIntf**. All remote method invocations can then be directed to this object.

The program continues by displaying its arguments and then invokes the remote **add( )** method. The sum is returned from this method and is then printed.

```
import java.rmi.*;

public class AddClient {
  public static void main(String[] args) {
    try {
      String addServerURL = "rmi://" + args[0] + "/AddServer";
      AddServerIntf addServerIntf =
                     (AddServerIntf)Naming.lookup(addServerURL);
      System.out.println("The first number is: " + args[1]);
      double d1 = Double.valueOf(args[1]).doubleValue();
      System.out.println("The second number is: " + args[2]);

      double d2 = Double.valueOf(args[2]).doubleValue();
      System.out.println("The sum is: " + addServerIntf.add(d1, d2));
    }
    catch(Exception e) {
      System.out.println("Exception: " + e);
    }
  }
}
```

After you enter all the code, use **javac** to compile the four source files that you created.

## Step Two: Manually Generate a Stub if Required

In the context of RMI, a *stub* is a Java object that resides on the client machine. Its function is to present the same interfaces as the remote server. Remote method calls initiated by the client are actually directed to the stub. The stub works with the other parts of the RMI system to formulate a request that is sent to the remote machine.

A remote method may accept arguments that are simple types or objects. In the latter case, the object may have references to other objects. All of this information must be sent to the remote machine. That is, an object passed as an argument to a remote method call must be serialized and sent to the remote machine. Recall from Chapter 21 that the serialization facilities also recursively process all referenced objects.

If a response must be returned to the client, the process works in reverse. Note that the serialization and deserialization facilities are also used if objects are returned to a client.

Prior to Java 5, stubs needed to be built manually by using **rmic**. This step **is not required** for modern versions of Java. However, if you are working in a very old legacy environment, then you can use the **rmic** compiler, as shown here, to build a stub:

```
rmic AddServerImpl
```

This command generates the file **AddServerImpl_Stub.class**. When using **rmic**, be sure that **CLASSPATH** is set to include the current directory.

## Step Three: Install Files on the Client and Server Machines

Copy **AddClient.class, AddServerImpl_Stub.class** (if needed), and **AddServerIntf.class** to a directory on the client machine. Copy **AddServerIntf.class, AddServerImpl.class, AddServerImpl_Stub.class** (if needed), and **AddServer.class** to a directory on the server machine.

## Step Four: Start the RMI Registry on the Server Machine

The JDK provides a program called **rmiregistry**, which executes on the server machine. It maps names to object references. First, check that the **CLASSPATH** environment variable includes the directory in which your files are located. Then, start the RMI Registry from the command line, as shown here:

```
start rmiregistry
```

When this command returns, you should see that a new window has been created. You need to leave this window open until you are done experimenting with the RMI example.

## Step Five: Start the Server

The server code is started from the command line, as shown here:

```
java AddServer
```

Recall that the **AddServer** code instantiates **AddServerImpl** and registers that object with the name "AddServer".

### Step Six: Start the Client

The **AddClient** software requires three arguments: the name or IP address of the server machine and the two numbers that are to be summed together. You may invoke it from the command line by using one of the two formats shown here:

```
java AddClient server1 8 9
java AddClient 11.12.13.14 8 9
```

In the first line, the name of the server is provided. The second line uses its IP address (11.12.13.14).

You can try this example without actually having a remote server. To do so, simply install all of the programs on the same machine, start **rmiregistry**, start **AddServer**, and then execute **AddClient** using this command line:

```
java AddClient 127.0.0.1 8 9
```

Here, the address 127.0.0.1 is the "loop back" address for the local machine. Using this address allows you to exercise the entire RMI mechanism without actually having to install the server on a remote computer. (If you are using a firewall, then this approach may not work.)

In either case, sample output from this program is shown here:

```
The first number is: 8
The second number is: 9
The sum is: 17.0
```



## Formatting Date and Time with java.text

The package **java.text** allows you to format, parse, search, and manipulate text. Beginning with JDK 9, **java.text** is part of the **java.base** module. This section examines two of **java.text**'s most commonly used classes: those that format date and time information. However, it is important to state at the outset that the new date and time API described later in this chapter offers a modern approach to handling date and time that also supports formatting. Of course, legacy code will continue to use the classes shown here for some time.

### DateFormat Class

**DateFormat** is an abstract class that provides the ability to format and parse dates and times. The **getDateInstance( )** method returns an instance of **DateFormat** that can format date information. It is available in these forms:

static final DateFormat getDateInstance( )
static final DateFormat getDateInstance(int *style*)
static final DateFormat getDateInstance(int *style*, Locale *locale*)

Here, *style* is one of the following values: **DEFAULT, SHORT, MEDIUM, LONG,** or **FULL**. These are **int** constants defined by **DateFormat**. They cause different details about the date to be presented. The parameter *locale* specifies the locale (refer to Chapter 20 for details on **Locale**). If the *style* and/or *locale* is not specified, defaults are used.

One of the most commonly used methods in this class is **format( )**. It has several overloaded forms, one of which is shown here:

final String format(Date *d*)

The argument is a **Date** object that is to be displayed. The method returns a string containing the formatted information.

The following listing illustrates how to format date information. It begins by creating a **Date** object. This captures the current date and time information. Then it outputs the date information by using different styles and locales.

```
// Demonstrate date formats.
import java.text.*;
import java.util.*;

public class DateFormatDemo {
  public static void main(String[] args) {
    Date date = new Date();
    DateFormat df;

    df = DateFormat.getDateInstance(DateFormat.SHORT, Locale.JAPAN);
    System.out.println("Japan: " + df.format(date));

    df = DateFormat.getDateInstance(DateFormat.MEDIUM, Locale.KOREA);
    System.out.println("Korea: " + df.format(date));

    df = DateFormat.getDateInstance(DateFormat.LONG, Locale.UK);
    System.out.println("United Kingdom: " + df.format(date));

    df = DateFormat.getDateInstance(DateFormat.FULL, Locale.US);
    System.out.println("United States: " + df.format(date));
  }
}
```

Sample output from this program is shown here:

```
Japan: 2021/06/30
Korea: 2021. 6. 30.
United Kingdom: 30 June 2021
United States: Wednesday, June 30, 2021
```

The **getTimeInstance( )** method returns an instance of **DateFormat** that can format time information. It is available in these versions:

static final DateFormat getTimeInstance( )
static final DateFormat getTimeInstance(int *style*)
static final DateFormat getTimeInstance(int *style*, Locale *locale*)

Here, *style* is one of the following values: **DEFAULT**, **SHORT**, **MEDIUM**, **LONG**, or **FULL**. These are **int** constants defined by **DateFormat**. They cause different details about the time to be presented. The parameter *locale* specifies the locale. If the *style* and/or *locale* is not specified, defaults are used.

The following listing illustrates how to format time information. It begins by creating a **Date** object. This captures the current date and time information. Then it outputs the time information by using different styles and locales.

```
// Demonstrate time formats.
import java.text.*;
import java.util.*;
public class TimeFormatDemo {
  public static void main(String[] args) {
    Date date = new Date();
    DateFormat df;

    df = DateFormat.getTimeInstance(DateFormat.SHORT, Locale.JAPAN);
    System.out.println("Japan: " + df.format(date));

    df = DateFormat.getTimeInstance(DateFormat.LONG, Locale.UK);
    System.out.println("United Kingdom: " + df.format(date));

    df = DateFormat.getTimeInstance(DateFormat.FULL, Locale.CANADA);
    System.out.println("Canada: " + df.format(date));
  }
}
```

Sample output from this program is shown here:

```
Japan: 13:03
United Kingdom: 13:03:31 GMT-05:00
Canada: 1:03:31 PM Central Daylight Time
```

The **DateFormat** class also has a **getDateTimeInstance( )** method that can format both date and time information. You may wish to experiment with it on your own.

## SimpleDateFormat Class

**SimpleDateFormat** is a concrete subclass of **DateFormat**. It allows you to define your own formatting patterns that are used to display date and time information.

One of its constructors is shown here:

SimpleDateFormat(String *formatString*)

The argument *formatString* describes how date and time information is displayed. An example of its use is given here:

```
SimpleDateFormat sdf = SimpleDateFormat("dd MMM yyyy hh.mm:ss zzz");
```

The symbols used in the formatting string determine the information that is displayed. Table 31-3 lists these symbols and gives a description of each.

| Symbol | Description |
|---|---|
| a | AM or PM |
| d | Day of month (1–31) |
| h | Hour in AM/PM (1–12) |
| k | Hour in day (1–24) |
| m | Minute in hour (0–59) |
| s | Second in minute (0–59) |
| u | Day of week, with Monday being 1 |
| w | Week of year (1–52) |
| y | Year |
| z | Time zone |
| D | Day of year (1–366) |
| E | Day of week (for example, Thursday) |
| F | Day of week in month |
| G | Era (for example, AD or BC) |
| H | Hour in day (0–23) |
| K | Hour in AM/PM (0–11) |
| L | Month |
| M | Month |
| S | Millisecond in second |
| W | Week of month (1–5) |
| X | Time zone in ISO 8601 format |
| Y | Week year |
| Z | Time zone in RFC 822 format |

**Table 31-3** Formatting String Symbols for **SimpleDateFormat**

In most cases, the number of times a symbol is repeated determines how that data is presented. Text information is displayed in an abbreviated form if the pattern letter is repeated less than four times. Otherwise, the unabbreviated form is used. For example, a zzzz pattern can display Pacific Daylight Time, and a zzz pattern can display PDT.

For numbers, the number of times a pattern letter is repeated determines how many digits are presented. For example, hh:mm:ss can present 01:51:15, but h:m:s displays the same time value as 1:51:15.

Finally, M or MM causes the month to be displayed as one or two digits. However, three or more repetitions of M cause the month to be displayed as a text string.

The following program shows how this class is used:

```
// Demonstrate SimpleDateFormat.
import java.text.*;
import java.util.*;

public class SimpleDateFormatDemo {
  public static void main(String[] args) {
    Date date = new Date();
    SimpleDateFormat sdf;
    sdf = new SimpleDateFormat("hh:mm:ss");
    System.out.println(sdf.format(date));
    sdf = new SimpleDateFormat("dd MMM yyyy hh:mm:ss zzz");
    System.out.println(sdf.format(date));
    sdf = new SimpleDateFormat("E MMM dd yyyy");
    System.out.println(sdf.format(date));
  }
}
```

Sample output from this program is shown here:

```
01:30:51
30 Jun 2021 01:30:51 CDT
Wed Jun 30 2021
```

## The java.time Time and Date API

In Chapter 20, Java's long-standing approach to handling date and time through the use of classes such as **Calendar** and **GregorianCalendar** was discussed. It is expected that this traditional approach will remain in widespread use for some time and is, therefore, something that all Java programmers need to be familiar with. Since JDK 8, Java has included another approach to handling time and date. This approach is defined in the following packages:

| Package | Description |
|---|---|
| java.time | Provides top-level classes that support time and date |
| java.time.chrono | Supports alternative, non-Gregorian calendars |
| java.time.format | Supports time and date formatting |
| java.time.temporal | Supports extended date and time functionality |
| java.time.zone | Supports time zones |

These packages define a large number of classes, interfaces, and enumerations that provide extensive, finely grained support for time and date operations. Because of the number of elements that comprise the new time and date API, it can seem fairly intimidating at first. However, it is well organized and logically structured. Its size reflects the detail of control and flexibility that it provides. Although it is far beyond the scope of this book to examine each element in this extensive API, we will look at several of its main classes. As you will see, these classes are sufficient for many uses. Beginning with JDK 9, these packages are in the **java.base** module.

## Time and Date Fundamentals

In **java.time** are defined several top-level classes that give you easy access to the time and date. Three of these are **LocalDate**, **LocalTime**, and **LocalDateTime**. As their names suggest, they encapsulate the local date, time, and date and time. Using these classes, it is easy to obtain the current date and time, format the date and time, and compare dates and times, among other operations. These classes are value-based, as are many others in **java.time**. (See Chapter 13 for information on value-based classes.)

**LocalDate** encapsulates a date that uses the default Gregorian calendar as specified by ISO 8601. **LocalTime** encapsulates a time, as specified by ISO 8601. **LocalDateTime** encapsulates both date and time. These classes contain a large number of methods that give you access to the date and time components, allow you to compare dates and times, add or subtract date or time components, and so on. Because a common naming convention for methods is employed, once you know how to use one of these classes, the others are easy to master.

**LocalDate**, **LocalTime**, and **LocalDateTime** do not define public constructors. Rather, to obtain an instance, you will use a factory method. One very convenient method is **now( )**, which is defined for all three classes. It returns the current date and/or time of the system. Each class defines several versions, but we will use its simplest form. Here is the version we will use as defined by **LocalDate**:

static LocalDate now( )

The version for **LocalTime** is shown here:

static LocalTime now( )

The version for **LocalDateTime** is shown here:

static LocalDateTime now( )

As you can see, in each case, an appropriate object is returned. The object returned by **now( )** can be displayed in its default, human-readable form by use of a **println( )** statement, for example. However, it is also possible to take full control over the formatting of date and time.

The following program uses **LocalDate** and **LocalTime** to obtain the current date and time and then displays them. Notice how **now( )** is called to retrieve the current date and time.

```
// A simple example of LocalDate and LocalTime.
import java.time.*;

class DateTimeDemo {
  public static void main(String[] args) {

    LocalDate curDate = LocalDate.now();
    System.out.println(curDate);
```

```
    LocalTime curTime = LocalTime.now();
    System.out.println(curTime);
  }
}
```

Sample output is shown here:

```
2021-06-30
14:57:29.621839100
```

The output reflects the default format that is given to the date and time. (The next section shows how to specify a different format.)

Because the preceding program displays both the current date and the current time, it could have been more easily written using the **LocalDateTime** class. In this approach, only a single instance needs to be created and only a single call to **now( )** is required, as shown here:

```
LocalDateTime curDateTime = LocalDateTime.now();
System.out.println(curDateTime);
```

Using this approach, the default output includes both date and time. Here is a sample:

```
2021-06-30T14:58:56.498907300
```

One other point: from a **LocalDateTime** instance, it is possible to obtain a reference to the date or time component by using the **toLocalDate( )** and **toLocalTime( )** methods, shown here:

LocalDate toLocalDate( )

LocalTime toLocalTime( )

Each returns a reference to the indicated element.

## Formatting Date and Time

Although the default formats shown in the preceding examples will be adequate for some uses, often you will want to specify a different format. Fortunately, this is easy to do because **LocalDate**, **LocalTime**, and **LocalDateTime** all provide the **format( )** method, shown here:

String format(DateTimeFormatter *fmtr*)

Here, *fmtr* specifies the instance of **DateTimeFormatter** that will provide the format.

**DateTimeFormatter** is packaged in **java.time.format**. To obtain a **DateTimeFormatter** instance, you will typically use one of its factory methods. Three are shown here:

static DateTimeFormatter ofLocalizedDate(FormatStyle *fmtDate*)

static DateTimeFormatter ofLocalizedTime(FormatStyle *fmtTime*)

static DateTimeFormatter ofLocalizedDateTime(FormatStyle *fmtDate*,
FormatStyle *fmtTime*)

Of course, the type of **DateTimeFormatter** that you create will be based on the type of object it will be operating on. For example, if you want to format the date in a **LocalDate** instance, then use **ofLocalizedDate( )**. The specific format is specified by the **FormatStyle** parameter.

**FormatStyle** is an enumeration that is packaged in **java.time.format**. It defines the following constants:

FULL

LONG

MEDIUM

SHORT

These specify the level of detail that will be displayed. (Thus, this form of **DateTimeFormatter** works similarly to **java.text.DateFormat**, described earlier in this chapter.)

Here is an example that uses **DateTimeFormatter** to display the current date and time:

```
// Demonstrate DateTimeFormatter.
import java.time.*;
import java.time.format.*;

class DateTimeDemo2 {
  public static void main(String[] args) {

    LocalDate curDate = LocalDate.now();
    System.out.println(curDate.format(
           DateTimeFormatter.ofLocalizedDate(FormatStyle.FULL)));

    LocalTime curTime = LocalTime.now();
    System.out.println(curTime.format(
           DateTimeFormatter.ofLocalizedTime(FormatStyle.SHORT)));
  }
}
```

Sample output is shown here:

```
Wednesday, June 30, 2021
2:16 PM
```

In some situations, you may want a format different from the ones you can specify by use of **FormatStyle**. One way to accomplish this is to use a predefined formatter, such as **ISO_DATE** or **ISO_TIME**, provided by **DateTimeFormatter**. Another way is to create a custom format by specifying a pattern. To do this, you can use the **ofPattern( )** factory method of **DateTimeFormatter**. One version is shown here:

static DateTimeFormatter ofPattern(String *fmtPattern*)

Here, *fmtPattern* specifies a string that contains the date and time pattern that you want. It returns a **DateTimeFormatter** that will format according to that pattern. The default locale is used.

In general, a pattern consists of format specifiers, called *pattern letters*. A pattern letter will be replaced by the date or time component that it specifies. The full list of pattern letters is shown in the API documentation for **ofPattern( )**. Here is a sampling. Note that the pattern letters are case-sensitive.

| | |
|---|---|
| a | AM/PM indicator |
| d | Day in month |
| E | Day in week |
| h | Hour, 12-hour clock |
| H | Hour, 24-hour clock |
| M | Month |
| m | Minutes |
| s | Seconds |
| y | Year |

In general, the precise output that you see will be determined by how many times a pattern letter is repeated. (Thus, **DateTimeFormatter** works a bit like **java.text.SimpleDateFormat**, described earlier in this chapter.) For example, assuming that the month is April, the patterns:

```
M MM MMM MMMM
```

produce the following formatted output:

```
4 04 Apr April
```

Frankly, experimentation is the best way to understand what each pattern letter does and how various repetitions affect the output.

When you want to output a pattern letter as text, enclose the text between single quotation marks. In general, it is a good idea to enclose all non-pattern characters within single quotation marks to avoid problems if the set of pattern letters changes in subsequent versions of Java.

The following program demonstrates the use of a date and time pattern:

```
// Create a custom date and time format.
import java.time.*;
import java.time.format.*;

class DateTimeDemo3 {
  public static void main(String[] args) {

    LocalDateTime curDateTime = LocalDateTime.now();
    System.out.println(curDateTime.format(
                 DateTimeFormatter.ofPattern("MMMM d',' yyyy h':'mm a")));
  }
}
```

Part II

Sample output is shown here:

```
June 30, 2021 2:22 PM
```

One other point about creating custom date and time output: **LocalDate, LocalTime,** and **LocalDateTime** define methods that let you obtain various date and time components. For example, **getHour( )** returns the hour as an **int**; **getMonth( )** returns the month in the form of a **Month** enumeration value; and **getYear( )** returns the year as an **int**. Using these, and other methods, you can manually construct output. You can also use these values for other purposes, such as when creating specialized timers.

## Parsing Date and Time Strings

**LocalDate**, **LocalTime**, and **LocalDateTime** provide the ability to parse date and/or time strings. To do this, call **parse( )** on an instance of one of those classes. It has two forms. The first uses the default formatter that parses the date and/or time formatted in the standard ISO fashion, such as 03:31 for time and 2021-08-02 for date. The form of this version of **parse( )** for **LocalDateTime** is shown here. (Its form for the other classes is similar except for the type of object returned.)

static LocalDateTime parse(CharSequence *dateTimeStr*)

Here, *dateTimeStr* is a string that contains the date and time in the proper format. If the format is invalid, an exception will be thrown.

If you want to parse a date and/or time string that is in a format other than ISO format, you can use a second form of **parse( )** that lets you specify your own formatter. The version specified by **LocalDateTime** is shown next. (The other classes provide a similar form except for the return type.)

static LocalDateTime parse(CharSequence *dateTimeStr*,
DateTimeFormatter *dateTimeFmtr*)

Here, *dateTimeFmtr* specifies the formatter that you want to use.

Here is a simple example that parses a date and time string by use of a custom formatter:

```
// Parse a date and time.
import java.time.*;
import java.time.format.*;

class DateTimeDemo4 {
  public static void main(String[] args) {

    // Obtain a LocalDateTime object by parsing a date and time string.
    LocalDateTime curDateTime =
         LocalDateTime.parse("June 30, 2021 12:01 AM",
                  DateTimeFormatter.ofPattern("MMMM d',' yyyy hh':'mm a"));

     // Now, display the parsed date and time.
    System.out.println(curDateTime.format(
              DateTimeFormatter.ofPattern("MMMM d',' yyyy h':'mm a")));
  }
}
```

Sample output is shown here:

```
June 30, 2021 12:01 AM
```

## Other Things to Explore in java.time

Although you will want to explore all of the date and time packages, a good place to start is with **java.time**. It contains a great deal of functionality that you may find useful. Begin by examining the methods defined by **LocalDate**, **LocalTime**, and **LocalDateTime**. Each has methods that let you add or subtract dates and/or times, adjust dates and/or times by a given component, compare dates and/or times, and create instances based on date and/or time components, among others. Other classes in **java.time** that you may find of particular interest include **Instant**, **Duration**, and **Period**. **Instant** encapsulates an instant in time. **Duration** encapsulates a length of time. **Period** encapsulates a length of date. You will also want to explore the new **InstantSource** interface added by JDK 17, which is implemented by the **Clock** class.

PART

# III

# Introducing GUI Programming with Swing

CHAPTER

# 32 Introducing Swing

In Part II, you saw how to build very simple user interfaces with the AWT classes. Although the AWT is still a crucial part of Java, its component set is no longer widely used to create graphical user interfaces. Today, programmers typically use Swing for this purpose. Swing is a framework that provides more powerful and flexible GUI components than does the AWT. As a result, it is the GUI that has been widely used by Java programmers for more than two decades.

Coverage of Swing is divided between three chapters. This chapter introduces Swing. It begins by describing Swing's core concepts. It then presents a simple example that shows the general form of a Swing program. This is followed by an example that uses event handling. The chapter concludes by explaining how painting is accomplished in Swing. The next chapter presents several commonly used Swing components. The third chapter introduces Swing-based menus. It is important to understand that the number of classes and interfaces in the Swing packages is quite large, and they can't all be covered in this book. (In fact, full coverage of Swing requires an entire book of its own.) However, these three chapters will give you a basic understanding of this important topic.

**NOTE** For a comprehensive introduction to Swing, see my book *Swing: A Beginner's Guide* published by McGraw Hill (2007).

## The Origins of Swing

Swing did not exist in the early days of Java. Rather, it was a response to deficiencies present in Java's original GUI subsystem: the Abstract Window Toolkit. The AWT defines a basic set of controls, windows, and dialog boxes that support a usable, but limited graphical interface. One reason for the limited nature of the AWT is that it translates its various visual components into their corresponding, platform-specific equivalents, or *peers*. This means that the look and feel of a component is defined by the platform, not by Java. Because the AWT components use native code resources, they are referred to as *heavyweight*.

The use of native peers led to several problems. First, because of variations between operating systems, a component might look, or even act, differently on different platforms. This potential variability threatened the overarching philosophy of Java: write once, run anywhere. Second, the look and feel of each component was fixed (because it is defined by the platform) and could not be (easily) changed. Third, the use of heavyweight components caused some frustrating restrictions. For example, a heavyweight component was always opaque.

Not long after Java's original release, it became apparent that the limitations and restrictions present in the AWT were sufficiently serious that a better approach was needed. The solution was Swing. Introduced in 1997, Swing was included as part of the Java Foundation Classes (JFC). Swing was initially available for use with Java 1.1 as a separate library. However, beginning with Java 1.2, Swing (and the rest of the JFC) was fully integrated into Java.

## Swing Is Built on the AWT

Before moving on, it is necessary to make one important point: although Swing eliminates a number of the limitations inherent in the AWT, Swing *does not* replace it. Instead, Swing is built on the foundation of the AWT. This is why the AWT is still a crucial part of Java. Swing also uses the same event handling mechanism as the AWT. Therefore, a basic understanding of the AWT and of event handling is required to use Swing. (The AWT is covered in Chapters 26 and 27. Event handling is described in Chapter 25.)

## Two Key Swing Features

As just explained, Swing was created to address the limitations present in the AWT. It does this through two key features: lightweight components and a pluggable look and feel. Together they provide an elegant, yet easy-to-use solution to the problems of the AWT. More than anything else, it is these two features that define the essence of Swing. Each is examined here.

### Swing Components Are Lightweight

With very few exceptions, Swing components are *lightweight*. This means that they are written entirely in Java and do not map directly to platform-specific peers. Thus, lightweight components are more efficient and more flexible. Furthermore, because lightweight components do not translate into native peers, the look and feel of each component is determined by Swing, not by the underlying operating system. As a result, each component will work in a consistent manner across all platforms.

### Swing Supports a Pluggable Look and Feel

Swing supports a *pluggable look and feel* (PLAF). Because each Swing component is rendered by Java code rather than by native peers, the look and feel of a component is under the control of Swing. This fact means that it is possible to separate the look and feel of a component from the logic of the component, and this is what Swing does. Separating out the look and feel provides a significant advantage: it becomes possible to change the way that a component is rendered without affecting any of its other aspects. In other words, it is possible to "plug in" a new look and feel for any given component without creating any side effects in the code that uses that component. Moreover, it becomes possible to define entire sets of look-and-feels that represent different GUI styles. To use a specific style, its look and feel is simply "plugged in." Once this is done, all components are automatically rendered using that style.

Pluggable look-and-feels offer several important advantages. It is possible to define a look and feel that is consistent across all platforms. Conversely, it is possible to create a look and feel that acts like a specific platform. It is also possible to design a custom look and feel. Finally, the look and feel can be changed dynamically at run time.

Java provides look-and-feels, such as metal and Nimbus, that are available to all Swing users. The metal look and feel is also called the *Java look and feel*. It is platform-independent and available in all Java execution environments. It is also the default look and feel. This book uses the default Java look and feel (metal) because it is platform independent.

## The MVC Connection

In general, a visual component is a composite of three distinct aspects:

- The way that the component looks when rendered on the screen
- The way that the component reacts to the user
- The state information associated with the component

No matter what architecture is used to implement a component, it must implicitly contain these three parts. Over the years, one component architecture has proven itself to be exceptionally effective: *Model-View-Controller*, or MVC for short.

The MVC architecture is successful because each piece of the design corresponds to an aspect of a component. In MVC terminology, the *model* corresponds to the state information associated with the component. For example, in the case of a check box, the model contains a field that indicates if the box is checked or unchecked. The *view* determines how the component is displayed on the screen, including any aspects of the view that are affected by the current state of the model. The *controller* determines how the component reacts to the user. For example, when the user clicks a check box, the controller reacts by changing the model to reflect the user's choice (checked or unchecked). This then results in the view being updated. By separating a component into a model, a view, and a controller, the specific implementation of each can be changed without affecting the other two. For instance, different view implementations can render the same component in different ways without affecting the model or the controller.

Although the MVC architecture and the principles behind it are conceptually sound, the high level of separation between the view and the controller is not beneficial for Swing components. Instead, Swing uses a modified version of MVC that combines the view and the controller into a single logical entity called the *UI delegate*. For this reason, Swing's approach is called either the *Model-Delegate* architecture or the *Separable Model* architecture. Therefore, although Swing's component architecture is based on MVC, it does not use a classical implementation of it.

Swing's pluggable look and feel is made possible by its Model-Delegate architecture. Because the view (look) and controller (feel) are separate from the model, the look and feel can be changed without affecting how the component is used within a program. Conversely, it is possible to customize the model without affecting the way that the component appears on the screen or responds to user input.

To support the Model-Delegate architecture, most Swing components contain two objects. The first represents the model. The second represents the UI delegate. Models are defined by interfaces. For example, the model for a button is defined by the **ButtonModel** interface. UI delegates are classes that inherit **ComponentUI**. For example, the UI delegate for a button is **ButtonUI**. Normally, your programs will not interact directly with the UI delegate.

## Components and Containers

A Swing GUI consists of two key items: *components* and *containers*. However, this distinction is mostly conceptual because all containers are also components. The difference between the two is found in their intended purpose: As the term is commonly used, a *component* is an independent visual control, such as a push button or slider. A container holds a group of components. Thus, a container is a special type of component that is designed to hold other components. Furthermore, in order for a component to be displayed, it must be held within a container. Thus, all Swing GUIs will have at least one container. Because containers are components, a container can also hold other containers. This enables Swing to define what is called a *containment hierarchy*, at the top of which must be a *top-level container*.

Let's look a bit more closely at components and containers.

### Components

In general, Swing components are derived from the **JComponent** class. (The only exceptions to this are the four top-level containers, described in the next section.) **JComponent** provides the functionality that is common to all components. For example, **JComponent** supports the pluggable look and feel. **JComponent** inherits the AWT classes **Container** and **Component**. Thus, a Swing component is built on and compatible with an AWT component.

All of Swing's components are represented by classes defined within the package **javax.swing**. The following table shows the class names for Swing components (including those used as containers).

| | | | |
|---|---|---|---|
| JApplet (Deprecated) | JButton | JCheckBox | JCheckBoxMenuItem |
| JColorChooser | JComboBox | JComponent | JDesktopPane |
| JDialog | JEditorPane | JFileChooser | JFormattedTextField |
| JFrame | JInternalFrame | JLabel | JLayer |

| JLayeredPane | JList | JMenu | JMenuBar |
|---|---|---|---|
| JMenuItem | JOptionPane | JPanel | JPasswordField |
| JPopupMenu | JProgressBar | JRadioButton | JRadioButtonMenuItem |
| JRootPane | JScrollBar | JScrollPane | JSeparator |
| JSlider | JSpinner | JSplitPane | JTabbedPane |
| JTable | JTextArea | JTextField | JTextPane |
| JTogglebutton | JToolBar | JToolTip | JTree |
| JViewport | JWindow | | |

Notice that all component classes begin with the letter **J**. For example, the class for a label is **JLabel**; the class for a push button is **JButton**; and the class for a scroll bar is **JScrollBar**.

## Containers

Swing defines two types of containers. The first are top-level containers: **JFrame**, **JApplet**, **JWindow**, and **JDialog**. These containers do not inherit **JComponent**. They do, however, inherit the AWT classes **Component** and **Container**. Unlike Swing's other components, which are lightweight, the top-level containers are heavyweight. This makes the top-level containers a special case in the Swing component library.

As the name implies, a top-level container must be at the top of a containment hierarchy. A top-level container is not contained within any other container. Furthermore, every containment hierarchy must begin with a top-level container. The one most commonly used for applications is **JFrame**. In the past, the one used for applets was **JApplet**. As explained in Chapter 1, beginning with JDK 9, applets have been deprecated, and they are now deprecated for removal. As a result, **JApplet** is also deprecated for removal. Furthermore, beginning with JDK 11, applet support has been removed.

The second type of containers supported by Swing are lightweight containers. Lightweight containers *do* inherit **JComponent**. An example of a lightweight container is **JPanel**, which is a general-purpose container. Lightweight containers are often used to organize and manage groups of related components because a lightweight container can be contained within another container. Thus, you can use lightweight containers such as **JPanel** to create subgroups of related controls that are contained within an outer container.

## The Top-Level Container Panes

Each top-level container defines a set of *panes*. At the top of the hierarchy is an instance of **JRootPane**. **JRootPane** is a lightweight container whose purpose is to manage the other panes. It also helps manage the optional menu bar. The panes that comprise the root pane are called the *glass pane*, the *content pane*, and the *layered pane*.

The glass pane is the top-level pane. It sits above and completely covers all other panes. By default, it is a transparent instance of **JPanel**. The glass pane enables you to manage mouse events that affect the entire container (rather than an individual control) or to paint over any other component, for example. In most cases, you won't need to use the glass pane directly, but it is there if you need it.

The layered pane is an instance of **JLayeredPane**. The layered pane allows components to be given a depth value. This value determines which component overlays another. (Thus, the layered pane lets you specify a Z-order for a component, although this is not something that you will usually need to do.) The layered pane holds the content pane and the (optional) menu bar.

Although the glass pane and the layered panes are integral to the operation of a top-level container and serve important purposes, much of what they provide occurs behind the scene. The pane with which your application will interact the most is the content pane, because this is the pane to which you will add visual components. In other words, when you add a component, such as a button, to a top-level container, you will add it to the content pane. By default, the content pane is an opaque instance of **JPanel**.

## The Swing Packages

Swing is a very large subsystem and makes use of many packages. At the time of this writing, these are the packages defined by Swing.

| | | |
|---|---|---|
| javax.swing | javax.swing.plaf.basic | javax.swing.text |
| javax.swing.border | javax.swing.plaf.metal | javax.swing.text.html |
| javax.swing.colorchooser | javax.swing.plaf.multi | javax.swing.text.html.parser |
| javax.swing.event | javax.swing.plaf.nimbus | javax.swing.text.rtf |
| javax.swing.filechooser | javax.swing.plaf.synth | javax.swing.tree |
| javax.swing.plaf | javax.swing.table | javax.swing.undo |

Beginning the JDK 9, the Swing packages are part of the **java.desktop** module.

The main package is **javax.swing**. This package must be imported into any program that uses Swing. It contains the classes that implement the basic Swing components, such as push buttons, labels, and check boxes.

## A Simple Swing Application

Swing programs differ from both the console-based programs and the AWT-based programs shown earlier in this book. For example, they use a different set of components and a different container hierarchy than does the AWT. Swing programs also have special requirements that relate to threading. The best way to understand the structure of a Swing program is to work through an example. Before we begin, it is necessary to point out that in the past there were two types of Java programs in which Swing was typically used. The first is a desktop application. This type of Swing application is widely used, and it's the type of Swing program described here. The second is the applet. Because applets are now deprecated and not suitable for use in new code, they are not discussed in this book.

Although quite short, the following program shows one way to write a Swing application. In the process, it demonstrates several key features of Swing. It uses two Swing components: **JFrame** and **JLabel**. **JFrame** is the top-level container that is commonly used for Swing applications. **JLabel** is the Swing component that creates a label, which is a component that displays information. The label is Swing's simplest component because it is passive. That is, a label does not respond to user input. It just displays output. The program uses a **JFrame** container to hold an instance of a **JLabel**. The label displays a short text message.

```
// A simple Swing application.

import javax.swing.*;

class SwingDemo {

  SwingDemo() {

    // Create a new JFrame container.
    JFrame jfrm = new JFrame("A Simple Swing Application");

    // Give the frame an initial size.
    jfrm.setSize(275, 100);

    // Terminate the program when the user closes the application.
    jfrm.setDefaultCloseOperation(JFrame.EXIT_ON_CLOSE);

    // Create a text-based label.
    JLabel jlab = new JLabel(" Swing means powerful GUIs.");

    // Add the label to the content pane.
    jfrm.add(jlab);

    // Display the frame.
    jfrm.setVisible(true);
  }

  public static void main(String[] args) {
    // Create the frame on the event dispatching thread.
    SwingUtilities.invokeLater(new Runnable() {
      public void run() {
        new SwingDemo();
      }
    });
  }
}
```

Swing programs are compiled and run in the same way as other Java applications. Thus, to compile this program, you can use this command line:

```
javac SwingDemo.java
```

To run the program, use this command line:

```
java SwingDemo
```

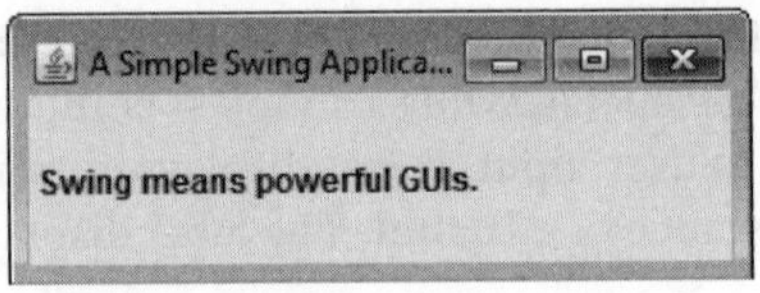


**Figure 32-1** The window produced by the **SwingDemo** program

When the program is run, it will produce a window similar to that shown in Figure 32-1.

Because the **SwingDemo** program illustrates several core Swing concepts, we will examine it carefully, line by line. The program begins by importing **javax.swing**. As mentioned, this package contains the components and models defined by Swing. For example, **javax.swing** defines classes that implement labels, buttons, text controls, and menus. It will be included in all programs that use Swing.

Next, the program declares the **SwingDemo** class and a constructor for that class. The constructor is where most of the action of the program occurs. It begins by creating a **JFrame**, using this line of code:

```
JFrame jfrm = new JFrame("A Simple Swing Application");
```

This creates a container called **jfrm** that defines a rectangular window complete with a title bar; close, minimize, maximize, and restore buttons; and a system menu. Thus, it creates a standard, top-level window. The title of the window is passed to the constructor.

Next, the window is sized using this statement:

```
jfrm.setSize(275, 100);
```

The **setSize( )** method (which is inherited by **JFrame** from the AWT class **Component**) sets the dimensions of the window, which are specified in pixels. Its general form is shown here:

void setSize(int *width*, int *height*)

In this example, the width of the window is set to 275 and the height is set to 100.

By default, when a top-level window is closed (such as when the user clicks the close box), the window is removed from the screen, but the application is not terminated. While this default behavior is useful in some situations, it is not what is needed for most applications. Instead, you will usually want the entire application to terminate when its top-level window is closed. There are a couple of ways to achieve this. The easiest way is to call **setDefaultCloseOperation( )**, as the program does:

```
jfrm.setDefaultCloseOperation(JFrame.EXIT_ON_CLOSE);
```

After this call executes, closing the window causes the entire application to terminate. The general form of **setDefaultCloseOperation( )** is shown here:

void setDefaultCloseOperation(int *what*)

The value passed in *what* determines what happens when the window is closed. There are several other options in addition to **JFrame.EXIT_ON_CLOSE**. They are shown here:

DISPOSE_ON_CLOSE

HIDE_ON_CLOSE

DO_NOTHING_ON_CLOSE

Their names reflect their actions. These constants are declared in **WindowConstants**, which is an interface declared in **javax.swing** that is implemented by **JFrame**.

The next line of code creates a Swing **JLabel** component:

```
JLabel jlab = new JLabel(" Swing means powerful GUIs.");
```

**JLabel** is the simplest and easiest-to-use component because it does not accept user input. It simply displays information, which can consist of text, an icon, or a combination of the two. The label created by the program contains only text, which is passed to its constructor.

The next line of code adds the label to the content pane of the frame:

```
jfrm.add(jlab);
```

As explained earlier, all top-level containers have a content pane in which components are stored. Thus, to add a component to a frame, you must add it to the frame's content pane. This is accomplished by calling **add( )** on the **JFrame** reference (**jfrm** in this case). The general form of **add( )** is shown here:

Component add(Component *comp*)

The **add( )** method is inherited by **JFrame** from the AWT class **Container.**

By default, the content pane associated with a **JFrame** uses a border layout. The version of **add( )** just shown adds the label to the center location. Other versions of **add( )** enable you to specify one of the border regions. When a component is added to the center, its size is adjusted automatically to fit the size of the center.

Before continuing, an important historical point needs to be made. Prior to JDK 5, when adding a component to the content pane, you could not invoke the **add( )** method directly on a **JFrame** instance. Instead, you needed to call **add( )** on the content pane of the **JFrame** object. The content pane can be obtained by calling **getContentPane( )** on a **JFrame** instance. The **getContentPane( )** method is shown here:

Container getContentPane( )

It returns a **Container** reference to the content pane. The **add( )** method was then called on that reference to add a component to a content pane. Thus, in the past, you had to use the following statement to add **jlab** to **jfrm**:

```
jfrm.getContentPane().add(jlab); // old-style
```

Here, **getContentPane( )** first obtains a reference to content pane, and then **add( )** adds the component to the container linked to this pane. This same procedure was also required to invoke **remove( )** to remove a component and **setLayout( )** to set the layout manager for the content pane. This is why you will see explicit calls to **getContentPane( )** frequently throughout pre-5.0 legacy code. Today, the use of **getContentPane( )** is no longer necessary. You can simply call **add( )**, **remove( )**, and **setLayout( )** directly on **JFrame** because these methods have been changed so that they operate on the content pane automatically.

The last statement in the **SwingDemo** constructor causes the window to become visible:

```
jfrm.setVisible(true);
```

The **setVisible( )** method is inherited from the AWT **Component** class. If its argument is **true**, the window will be displayed. Otherwise, it will be hidden. By default, a **JFrame** is invisible, so **setVisible(true)** must be called to show it.

Inside **main( )**, a **SwingDemo** object is created, which causes the window and the label to be displayed. Notice that the **SwingDemo** constructor is invoked using these lines of code:

```
SwingUtilities.invokeLater(new Runnable() {
  public void run() {
    new SwingDemo();
  }
});
```

This sequence causes a **SwingDemo** object to be created on the *event dispatching thread* rather than on the main thread of the application. Here's why: In general, Swing programs are event-driven. For example, when a user interacts with a component, an event is generated. An event is passed to the application by calling an event handler defined by the application. However, the handler is executed on the event dispatching thread provided by Swing and not on the main thread of the application. Thus, although event handlers are defined by your program, they are called on a thread that was not created by your program.

To avoid problems (including the potential for deadlock), all Swing GUI components must be created and updated from the event dispatching thread, not the main thread of the application. However, **main( )** is executed on the main thread. Thus, **main( )** cannot directly instantiate a **SwingDemo** object. Instead, it must create a **Runnable** object that executes on the event dispatching thread and have this object create the GUI.

To enable the GUI code to be created on the event dispatching thread, you must use one of two methods that are defined by the **SwingUtilities** class. These methods are **invokeLater( )** and **invokeAndWait( )**. They are shown here:

static void invokeLater(Runnable *obj*)

static void invokeAndWait(Runnable *obj*)
  throws InterruptedException, InvocationTargetException

Here, *obj* is a **Runnable** object that will have its **run( )** method called by the event dispatching thread. The difference between the two methods is that **invokeLater( )** returns immediately, but **invokeAndWait( )** waits until **obj.run( )** returns. You can use one of these methods to call a method that constructs the GUI for your Swing application, or whenever you need to modify the state of the GUI from code not executed by the event dispatching thread. You will normally want to use **invokeLater( )**, as the preceding program does. However, when the

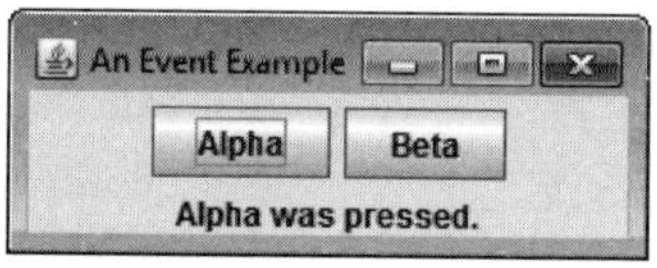


**Figure 32-2** Output from the **EventDemo** program

initial GUI for an applet is constructed, **invokeAndWait( )** is required. Thus, you will see its use in legacy applet code.

# Event Handling

The preceding example showed the basic form of a Swing program, but it left out one important part: event handling. Because **JLabel** does not take input from the user, it does not generate events, so no event handling was needed. However, the other Swing components *do* respond to user input and the events generated by those interactions need to be handled. Events can also be generated in ways not directly related to user input. For example, an event is generated when a timer goes off. Whatever the case, event handling is a large part of any Swing-based application.

The event handling mechanism used by Swing is the same as that used by the AWT. This approach is called the *delegation event model,* and it is described in Chapter 25. In many cases, Swing uses the same events as does the AWT, and these events are packaged in **java.awt.event**. Events specific to Swing are stored in **javax.swing.event**.

Although events are handled in Swing in the same way as they are with the AWT, it is still useful to work through a simple example. The following program handles the event generated by a Swing push button. Sample output is shown in Figure 32-2.

```
// Handle an event in a Swing program.

import java.awt.*;
import java.awt.event.*;
import javax.swing.*;

class EventDemo {

  JLabel jlab;

  EventDemo() {

    // Create a new JFrame container.
    JFrame jfrm = new JFrame("An Event Example");

    // Specify FlowLayout for the layout manager.
    jfrm.setLayout(new FlowLayout());

    // Give the frame an initial size.
    jfrm.setSize(220, 90);
```

Part III

```
    // Terminate the program when the user closes the application.
    jfrm.setDefaultCloseOperation(JFrame.EXIT_ON_CLOSE);

    // Make two buttons.
    JButton jbtnAlpha = new JButton("Alpha");
    JButton jbtnBeta = new JButton("Beta");

    // Add action listener for Alpha.
    jbtnAlpha.addActionListener(new ActionListener() {
      public void actionPerformed(ActionEvent ae) {
        jlab.setText("Alpha was pressed.");
      }
    });

    // Add action listener for Beta.
    jbtnBeta.addActionListener(new ActionListener() {
      public void actionPerformed(ActionEvent ae) {
        jlab.setText("Beta was pressed.");
      }
    });

    // Add the buttons to the content pane.
    jfrm.add(jbtnAlpha);
    jfrm.add(jbtnBeta);

    // Create a text-based label.
    jlab = new JLabel("Press a button.");

    // Add the label to the content pane.
    jfrm.add(jlab);

    // Display the frame.
    jfrm.setVisible(true);
  }

  public static void main(String[] args) {
    // Create the frame on the event dispatching thread.
    SwingUtilities.invokeLater(new Runnable() {
      public void run() {
        new EventDemo();
      }
    });
  }
}
```

First, notice that the program now imports both the **java.awt** and **java.awt.event** packages. The **java.awt** package is needed because it contains the **FlowLayout** class, which supports the standard flow layout manager used to lay out components in a frame. (See Chapter 27 for coverage of layout managers.) The **java.awt.event** package is needed because it defines the **ActionListener** interface and the **ActionEvent** class.

The **EventDemo** constructor begins by creating a **JFrame** called **jfrm**. It then sets the layout manager for the content pane of **jfrm** to **FlowLayout**. By default, the content pane uses **BorderLayout** as its layout manager. However, for this example, **FlowLayout** is more convenient.

After setting the size and default close operation, **EventDemo( )** creates two push buttons, as shown here:

```
JButton jbtnAlpha = new JButton("Alpha");
JButton jbtnBeta = new JButton("Beta");
```

The first button will contain the text "Alpha" and the second will contain the text "Beta". Swing push buttons are instances of **JButton**. **JButton** supplies several constructors. The one used here is

JButton(String *msg*)

The *msg* parameter specifies the string that will be displayed inside the button.

When a push button is pressed, it generates an **ActionEvent.** Thus, **JButton** provides the **addActionListener( )** method, which is used to add an action listener. (**JButton** also provides **removeActionListener( )** to remove a listener, but this method is not used by the program.) As explained in Chapter 25, the **ActionListener** interface defines only one method: **actionPerformed( )**. It is shown again here for your convenience:

void actionPerformed(ActionEvent *ae*)

This method is called when a button is pressed. In other words, it is the event handler that is called when a button press event has occurred.

Next, event listeners for the button's action events are added by the code shown here:

```
// Add action listener for Alpha.
jbtnAlpha.addActionListener(new ActionListener() {
  public void actionPerformed(ActionEvent ae) {
    jlab.setText("Alpha was pressed.");
  }
});

// Add action listener for Beta.
jbtnBeta.addActionListener(new ActionListener() {
  public void actionPerformed(ActionEvent ae) {
    jlab.setText("Beta was pressed.");
  }
});
```

Here, anonymous inner classes are used to provide the event handlers for the two buttons. Each time a button is pressed, the string displayed in **jlab** is changed to reflect which button was pressed.

Beginning with JDK 8, lambda expressions can also be used to implement some types of event handlers. For example, the event handler for the Alpha button could be written like this:

```
jbtnAlpha.addActionListener( (ae) -> jlab.setText("Alpha was pressed."));
```

Part III

As you can see, this code is shorter. Of course, the approach you choose will be determined by the situation and your own preferences.

Next, the buttons are added to the content pane of **jfrm**:

```
jfrm.add(jbtnAlpha);
jfrm.add(jbtnBeta);
```

Finally, **jlab** is added to the content pane and the window is made visible. When you run the program, each time you press a button, a message is displayed in the label that indicates which button was pressed.

One last point: Remember that all event handlers, such as **actionPerformed( )**, are called on the event dispatching thread. Therefore, an event handler must return quickly in order to avoid slowing down the application. If your application needs to do something time consuming as the result of an event, it must use a separate thread.

# Painting in Swing

Although the Swing component set is quite powerful, you are not limited to using it because Swing also lets you write directly into the display area of a frame, panel, or one of Swing's other components, such as **JLabel.** Although many (perhaps most) uses of Swing will *not* involve drawing directly to the surface of a component, it is available for those applications that need this capability. To write output directly to the surface of a component, you will use one or more drawing methods defined by the AWT, such as **drawLine( )** or **drawRect( )**. Thus, most of the techniques and methods described in Chapter 26 also apply to Swing. However, there are also some very important differences, and the process is discussed in detail in this section.

## Painting Fundamentals

Swing's approach to painting is built on the original AWT-based mechanism, but Swing's implementation offers more fine-grained control. Before examining the specifics of Swing-based painting, it is useful to review the AWT-based mechanism that underlies it.

The AWT class **Component** defines a method called **paint( )** that is used to draw output directly to the surface of a component. For the most part, **paint( )** is not called by your program. (In fact, only in the most unusual cases should it ever be called by your program.) Rather, **paint( )** is called by the run-time system whenever a component must be rendered. This situation can occur for several reasons. For example, the window in which the component is displayed can be overwritten by another window and then uncovered. Or, the window might be minimized and then restored. The **paint( )** method is also called when a program begins running. When writing AWT-based code, an application will override **paint( )** when it needs to write output directly to the surface of the component.

Because **JComponent** inherits **Component**, all Swing's lightweight components inherit the **paint( )** method. However, you *will not* override it to paint directly to the surface of a component. The reason is that Swing uses a bit more sophisticated approach to painting that involves three distinct methods: **paintComponent( )**, **paintBorder( )**, and **paintChildren( )**.

These methods paint the indicated portion of a component and divide the painting process into its three distinct, logical actions. In a lightweight component, the original AWT method **paint( )** simply executes calls to these methods, in the order just shown.

To paint to the surface of a Swing component, you will create a subclass of the component and then override its **paintComponent( )** method. This is the method that paints the interior of the component. You will not normally override the other two painting methods. When overriding **paintComponent( )**, the first thing you must do is call **super.paintComponent( )** so that the superclass portion of the painting process takes place. (The only time this is not required is when you are taking complete, manual control over how a component is displayed.) After that, write the output that you want to display. The **paintComponent( )** method is shown here:

protected void paintComponent(Graphics *g*)

The parameter *g* is the graphics context to which output is written.

To cause a component to be painted under program control, call **repaint( )**. It works in Swing just as it does for the AWT. The **repaint( )** method is defined by **Component**. Calling it causes the system to call **paint( )** as soon as it is possible to do so. Because painting is a time-consuming operation, this mechanism allows the run-time system to defer painting momentarily until some higher-priority task has completed, for example. Of course, in Swing the call to **paint( )** results in a call to **paintComponent( )**. Therefore, to output to the surface of a component, your program will store the output until **paintComponent( )** is called. Inside the overridden **paintComponent( )**, you will draw the stored output.



## Compute the Paintable Area

When drawing to the surface of a component, you must be careful to restrict your output to the area that is inside the border. Although Swing automatically clips any output that will exceed the boundaries of a component, it is still possible to paint into the border, which will then get overwritten when the border is drawn. To avoid this, you must compute the *paintable area* of the component. This is the area defined by the current size of the component minus the space used by the border. Therefore, before you paint to a component, you must obtain the width of the border and then adjust your drawing accordingly.

To obtain the border width, call **getInsets( )**, shown here:

Insets getInsets( )

This method is defined by **Container** and overridden by **JComponent**. It returns an **Insets** object that contains the dimensions of the border. The inset values can be obtained by using these fields:

int top;

int bottom;

int left;

int right;

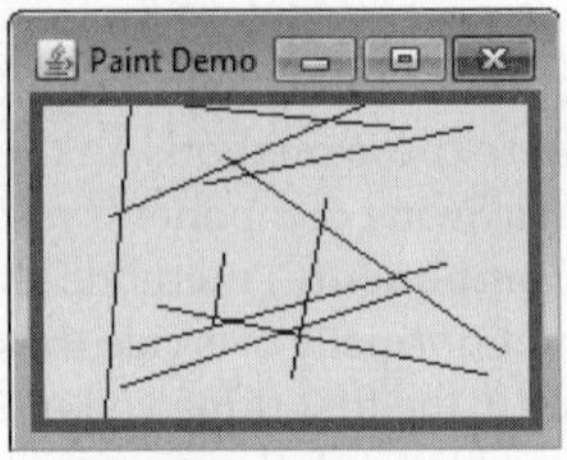


**Figure 32-3** Sample output from the **PaintPanel** program

These values are then used to compute the drawing area given the width and the height of the component. You can obtain the width and height of the component by calling **getWidth( )** and **getHeight( )** on the component. They are shown here:

int getWidth( )

int getHeight( )

By subtracting the value of the insets, you can compute the usable width and height of the component.

## A Paint Example

Here is a program that puts into action the preceding discussion. It creates a class called **PaintPanel** that extends **JPanel**. The program then uses an object of that class to display lines whose endpoints have been generated randomly. Sample output is shown in Figure 32-3.

```
// Paint lines to a panel.

import java.awt.*;
import java.awt.event.*;
import javax.swing.*;
import java.util.*;

// This class extends JPanel. It overrides
// the paintComponent() method so that random
// lines are plotted in the panel.
class PaintPanel extends JPanel {
  Insets ins; // holds the panel's insets

  Random rand; // used to generate random numbers

    // Construct a panel.
    PaintPanel() {

      // Put a border around the panel.
      setBorder(
        BorderFactory.createLineBorder(Color.RED, 5));

      rand = new Random();
    }
```

```
    // Override the paintComponent() method.
    protected void paintComponent(Graphics g) {
      // Always call the superclass method first.
      super.paintComponent(g);

      int x, y, x2, y2;

      // Get the height and width of the component.
      int height = getHeight();
      int width = getWidth();

      // Get the insets.
      ins = getInsets();

      // Draw ten lines whose endpoints are randomly generated.
      for(int i=0; i < 10; i++) {
        // Obtain random coordinates that define
        // the endpoints of each line.
        x = rand.nextInt(width-ins.left);
        y = rand.nextInt(height-ins.bottom);
        x2 = rand.nextInt(width-ins.left);
        y2 = rand.nextInt(height-ins.bottom);

        // Draw the line.
        g.drawLine(x, y, x2, y2);
      }
    }
}

// Demonstrate painting directly onto a panel.
class PaintDemo {

   JLabel jlab;
   PaintPanel pp;

   PaintDemo() {

     // Create a new JFrame container.
     JFrame jfrm = new JFrame("Paint Demo");

     // Give the frame an initial size.
     jfrm.setSize(200, 150);

     // Terminate the program when the user closes the application.
     jfrm.setDefaultCloseOperation(JFrame.EXIT_ON_CLOSE);

     // Create the panel that will be painted.
     pp = new PaintPanel();

     // Add the panel to the content pane. Because the default
     // border layout is used, the panel will automatically be
     // sized to fit the center region.
     jfrm.add(pp);
```

```
    // Display the frame.
    jfrm.setVisible(true);
  }

  public static void main(String[] args) {
    // Create the frame on the event dispatching thread.
    SwingUtilities.invokeLater(new Runnable() {
      public void run() {
        new PaintDemo();
      }
    });
  }
}
```

Let's examine this program closely. The **PaintPanel** class extends **JPanel**. **JPanel** is one of Swing's lightweight containers, which means that it is a component that can be added to the content pane of a **JFrame**. To handle painting, **PaintPanel** overrides the **paintComponent( )** method. This enables **PaintPanel** to write directly to the surface of the component when painting takes place. The size of the panel is not specified because the program uses the default border layout and the panel is added to the center. This results in the panel being sized to fill the center. If you change the size of the window, the size of the panel will be adjusted accordingly.

Notice that the constructor also specifies a 5-pixel-wide, red border. This is accomplished by setting the border by using the **setBorder( )** method, shown here:

void setBorder(Border *border*)

**Border** is the Swing interface that encapsulates a border. You can obtain a border by calling one of the factory methods defined by the **BorderFactory** class. The one used in the program is **createLineBorder( )**, which creates a simple line border. It is shown here:

static Border createLineBorder(Color *clr*, int *width*)

Here, *clr* specifies the color of the border and *width* specifies its width in pixels.

Inside the override of **paintComponent( )**, notice that it first calls **super .paintComponent( )**. As explained, this is necessary to ensure that the component is properly drawn. Next, the width and height of the panel are obtained along with the insets. These values are used to ensure the lines lie within the drawing area of the panel. The drawing area is the overall width and height of a component less the border width. The computations are designed to work with differently sized **PaintPanel**s and borders. To prove this, try changing the size of the window. The lines will still all lie within the borders of the panel.

The **PaintDemo** class creates a **PaintPanel** and then adds the panel to the content pane. When the application is first displayed, the overridden **paintComponent( )** method is called, and the lines are drawn. Each time you resize or hide and restore the window, a new set of lines are drawn. In all cases, the lines fall within the paintable area.

CHAPTER

# 33 Exploring Swing

The previous chapter described several of the core concepts relating to Swing and showed the general form of a Swing application. This chapter continues the discussion of Swing by presenting an overview of several Swing components, such as buttons, check boxes, trees, and tables. The Swing components provide rich functionality and allow a high level of customization. Because of space limitations, it is not possible to describe all of their features and attributes. Rather, the purpose of this overview is to give you a feel for the capabilities of the Swing component set.

The Swing component classes described in this chapter are shown here:

| | | | |
|---|---|---|---|
| JButton | JCheckBox | JComboBox | JLabel |
| JList | JRadioButton | JScrollPane | JTabbedPane |
| JTable | JTextField | JToggleButton | JTree |

These components are all lightweight, which means that they are all derived from **JComponent**.

Also discussed is the **ButtonGroup** class, which encapsulates a mutually exclusive set of Swing buttons, and **ImageIcon**, which encapsulates a graphics image. Both are defined by Swing and packaged in **javax.swing**.

## JLabel and ImageIcon

**JLabel** is Swing's easiest-to-use component. It creates a label and was introduced in the preceding chapter. Here, we will look at **JLabel** a bit more closely. **JLabel** can be used to display text and/or an icon. It is a passive component in that it does not respond to user input. **JLabel** defines several constructors. Here are three of them:

JLabel(Icon *icon*)
JLabel(String *str*)
JLabel(String *str*, Icon *icon*, int *align*)

Here, *str* and *icon* are the text and icon used for the label. The *align* argument specifies the horizontal alignment of the text and/or icon within the dimensions of the label. It must be one of the following values: **LEFT, RIGHT, CENTER, LEADING,** or **TRAILING**. These constants are defined in the **SwingConstants** interface, along with several others used by the Swing classes.

Notice that icons are specified by objects of type **Icon**, which is an interface defined by Swing. The easiest way to obtain an icon is to use the **ImageIcon** class. **ImageIcon** implements **Icon** and encapsulates an image. Thus, an object of type **ImageIcon** can be passed as an argument to the **Icon** parameter of **JLabel**'s constructor. There are several ways to provide the image, including reading it from a file or downloading it from a URL. Here is the **ImageIcon** constructor used by the example in this section:

ImageIcon(String *filename*)

It obtains the image in the file named *filename*.

The icon and text associated with the label can be obtained by the following methods:

Icon getIcon( )
String getText( )

The icon and text associated with a label can be set by these methods:

void setIcon(Icon *icon*)
void setText(String *str*)

Here, *icon* and *str* are the icon and text, respectively. Therefore, using **setText( )**, it is possible to change the text inside a label during program execution.

The following program illustrates how to create and display a label containing both an icon and a string. It begins by creating an **ImageIcon** object for the file **hourglass.png**, which depicts an hourglass. This is used as the second argument to the **JLabel** constructor. The first and last arguments for the **JLabel** constructor are the label text and the alignment. Finally, the label is added to the content pane.

```
import java.awt.*;
import javax.swing.*;

public class JLabelDemo {

  public JLabelDemo() {

    // Set up the JFrame.
    JFrame jfrm = new JFrame("JLabelDemo");
    jfrm.setLayout(new FlowLayout());
    jfrm.setDefaultCloseOperation(JFrame.EXIT_ON_CLOSE);
    jfrm.setSize(260, 210);

    // Create an icon.
    ImageIcon ii = new ImageIcon("hourglass.png");

    // Create a label.
    JLabel jl = new JLabel("Hourglass", ii, JLabel.CENTER);
```

```
    // Add the label to the content pane.
    jfrm.add(jl);

    // Display the frame.
    jfrm.setVisible(true);
  }

  public static void main(String[] args) {
    // Create the frame on the event dispatching thread.

    SwingUtilities.invokeLater(
      new Runnable() {
        public void run() {
          new JLabelDemo();
        }
      }
    );

  }
}
```

Output from the label example is shown here:

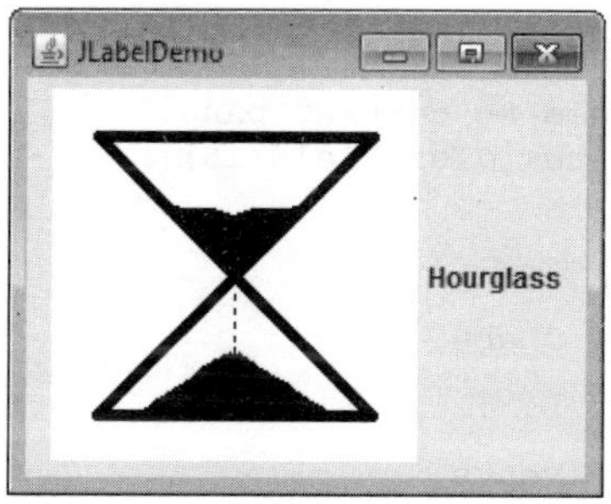




## JTextField

**JTextField** is the simplest Swing text component. It is also probably its most widely used text component. **JTextField** allows you to edit one line of text. It is derived from **JTextComponent**, which provides the basic functionality common to Swing text components. **JTextField** uses the **Document** interface for its model. Three of **JTextField's** constructors are shown here:

JTextField(int *cols*)
JTextField(String *str*, int *cols*)
JTextField(String *str*)

Here, *str* is the string to be initially presented, and *cols* is the number of columns in the text field. If no string is specified, the text field is initially empty. If the number of columns is not specified, the text field is sized to fit the specified string.

**JTextField** generates events in response to user interaction. For example, an **ActionEvent** is fired when the user presses ENTER. A **CaretEvent** is fired each time the caret (i.e., the cursor) changes position. (**CaretEvent** is packaged in **javax.swing.event**.) Other events are also possible. In many cases, your program will not need to handle these events. Instead, you will simply obtain the string currently in the text field when it is needed. To obtain the text currently in the text field, call **getText( )**.

The following example illustrates **JTextField**. It creates a **JTextField** and adds it to the content pane. When the user presses ENTER, an action event is generated. This is handled by displaying the text in a label.

```
// Demonstrate JTextField.
import java.awt.*;
import java.awt.event.*;
import javax.swing.*;

public class JTextFieldDemo {

  public JTextFieldDemo() {

    // Set up the JFrame.
    JFrame jfrm = new JFrame("JTextFieldDemo");
    jfrm.setLayout(new FlowLayout());
    jfrm.setDefaultCloseOperation(JFrame.EXIT_ON_CLOSE);
    jfrm.setSize(260, 120);

    // Add a text field to content pane.
    JTextField jtf = new JTextField(15);
    jfrm.add(jtf);

    // Add a label.
    JLabel jlab = new JLabel();
    jfrm.add(jlab);

    // Handle action events.
    jtf.addActionListener(new ActionListener() {
      public void actionPerformed(ActionEvent ae) {
        // Show text when user presses ENTER.
        jlab.setText(jtf.getText());
      }
    });

    // Display the frame.
    jfrm.setVisible(true);
  }

  public static void main(String[] args) {
    // Create the frame on the event dispatching thread.
    SwingUtilities.invokeLater(
      new Runnable() {
        public void run() {
          new JTextFieldDemo();
        }
      }
    );
```

```
  }
}
```

Output from the text field example is shown here:

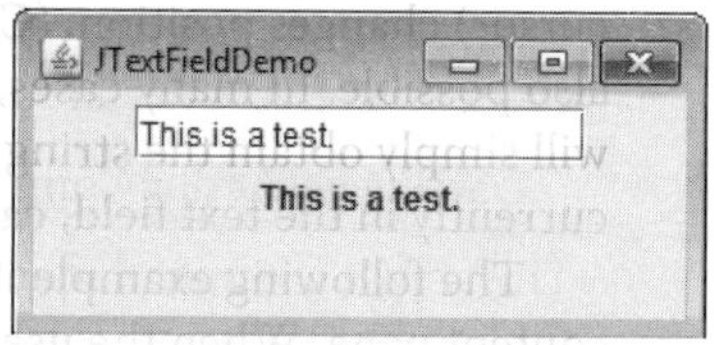


# The Swing Buttons

Swing defines four types of buttons: **JButton**, **JToggleButton**, **JCheckBox**, and **JRadioButton**. All are subclasses of the **AbstractButton** class, which extends **JComponent**. Thus, all buttons share a set of common traits.

**AbstractButton** contains many methods that allow you to control the behavior of buttons. For example, you can define different icons that are displayed for the button when it is disabled, pressed, or selected. Another icon can be used as a *rollover* icon, which is displayed when the mouse is positioned over a button. The following methods set these icons:

void setDisabledIcon(Icon *di*)
void setPressedIcon(Icon *pi*)
void setSelectedIcon(Icon *si*)
void setRolloverIcon(Icon *ri*)

Here, *di*, *pi*, *si*, and *ri* are the icons to be used for the indicated purpose.

The text associated with a button can be read and written via the following methods:

String getText( )
void setText(String *str*)

Here, *str* is the text to be associated with the button.

The model used by all buttons is defined by the **ButtonModel** interface. A button generates an action event when it is pressed. Other events are possible. Each of the concrete button classes is examined next.

## JButton

The **JButton** class provides the functionality of a push button. You have already seen a simple form of it in the preceding chapter. **JButton** allows an icon, a string, or both to be associated with the push button. Three of its constructors are shown here:

JButton(Icon *icon*)
JButton(String *str*)
JButton(String *str*, Icon *icon*)

Here, *str* and *icon* are the string and icon used for the button.

When the button is pressed, an **ActionEvent** is generated. Using the **ActionEvent** object passed to the **actionPerformed( )** method of the registered **ActionListener**, you can obtain the *action command* string associated with the button. By default, this is the string displayed inside the button. However, you can set the action command by calling **setActionCommand( )**

on the button. You can obtain the action command by calling **getActionCommand( )** on the event object. It is declared like this:

String getActionCommand( )

The action command identifies the button. Thus, when using two or more buttons within the same application, the action command gives you an easy way to determine which button was pressed.

In the preceding chapter, you saw an example of a text-based button. The following demonstrates an icon-based button. It displays four push buttons and a label. Each button displays an icon that represents a timepiece. When a button is pressed, the name of that timepiece is displayed in the label.

```
// Demonstrate an icon-based JButton.
import java.awt.*;
import java.awt.event.*;
import javax.swing.*;

public class JButtonDemo implements ActionListener {
  JLabel jlab;

  public JButtonDemo() {

    // Set up the JFrame.
    JFrame jfrm = new JFrame("JButtonDemo");
    jfrm.setLayout(new FlowLayout());
    jfrm.setDefaultCloseOperation(JFrame.EXIT_ON_CLOSE);
    jfrm.setSize(500, 450);

    // Add buttons to content pane.
    ImageIcon hourglass = new ImageIcon("hourglass.png");
    JButton jb = new JButton(hourglass);
    jb.setActionCommand("Hourglass");
    jb.addActionListener(this);
    jfrm.add(jb);

    ImageIcon analog = new ImageIcon("analog.png");
    jb = new JButton(analog);
    jb.setActionCommand("Analog Clock");
    jb.addActionListener(this);
    jfrm.add(jb);

    ImageIcon digital = new ImageIcon("digital.png");
    jb = new JButton(digital);
    jb.setActionCommand("Digital Clock");
    jb.addActionListener(this);
    jfrm.add(jb);

    ImageIcon stopwatch = new ImageIcon("stopwatch.png");
    jb = new JButton(stopwatch);
    jb.setActionCommand("Stopwatch");
    jb.addActionListener(this);
    jfrm.add(jb);
```

```
    // Create and add the label to content pane.
    jlab = new JLabel("Choose a Timepiece");
    jfrm.add(jlab);

    // Display the frame.
    jfrm.setVisible(true);
  }

  // Handle button events.
  public void actionPerformed(ActionEvent ae) {
    jlab.setText("You selected " + ae.getActionCommand());
  }

  public static void main(String[] args) {
    // Create the frame on the event dispatching thread.

    SwingUtilities.invokeLater(
      new Runnable() {
        public void run() {
          new JButtonDemo();
        }
      }
    );

  }
}
```



Output from the button example is shown here:

## JToggleButton

A useful variation on the push button is called a *toggle button*. A toggle button looks just like a push button, but it acts differently because it has two states: pushed and released. That is, when you press a toggle button, it stays pressed rather than popping back up as a regular push button does. When you press the toggle button a second time, it releases (pops up). Therefore, each time a toggle button is pushed, it toggles between its two states.

Toggle buttons are objects of the **JToggleButton** class. **JToggleButton** implements **AbstractButton**. In addition to creating standard toggle buttons, **JToggleButton** is a superclass for two other Swing components that also represent two-state controls. These are **JCheckBox** and **JRadioButton**, which are described later in this chapter. Thus, **JToggleButton** defines the basic functionality of all two-state components.

**JToggleButton** defines several constructors. The one used by the example in this section is shown here:

JToggleButton(String *str*)

This creates a toggle button that contains the text passed in *str*. By default, the button is in the off position. Other constructors enable you to create toggle buttons that contain images, or images and text.

**JToggleButton** uses a model defined by a nested class called **JToggleButton.ToggleButtonModel**. Normally, you won't need to interact directly with the model to use a standard toggle button.

Like **JButton**, **JToggleButton** generates an action event each time it is pressed. Unlike **JButton**, however, **JToggleButton** also generates an item event. This event is used by those components that support the concept of selection. When a **JToggleButton** is pressed in, it is selected. When it is popped out, it is deselected.

To handle item events, you must implement the **ItemListener** interface. Recall from Chapter 25 that each time an item event is generated, it is passed to the **itemStateChanged( )** method defined by **ItemListener**. Inside **itemStateChanged( )**, the **getItem( )** method can be called on the **ItemEvent** object to obtain a reference to the **JToggleButton** instance that generated the event. It is shown here:

Object getItem( )

A reference to the button is returned. You will need to cast this reference to **JToggleButton**.

The easiest way to determine a toggle button's state is by calling the **isSelected( )** method (inherited from **AbstractButton**) on the button that generated the event. It is shown here:

boolean isSelected( )

It returns **true** if the button is selected and **false** otherwise.

Here is an example that uses a toggle button. Notice how the item listener works. It simply calls **isSelected( )** to determine the button's state.

```
// Demonstrate JToggleButton.
import java.awt.*;
import java.awt.event.*;
import javax.swing.*;

public class JToggleButtonDemo {

  public JToggleButtonDemo() {
```

```
    // Set up the JFrame.
    JFrame jfrm = new JFrame("JToggleButtonDemo");
    jfrm.setLayout(new FlowLayout());
    jfrm.setDefaultCloseOperation(JFrame.EXIT_ON_CLOSE);
    jfrm.setSize(200, 100);

    // Create a label.
    JLabel jlab = new JLabel("Button is off.");

    // Make a toggle button.
    JToggleButton jtbn =  new JToggleButton("On/Off");

    // Add an item listener for the toggle button.
    jtbn.addItemListener(new ItemListener() {
      public void itemStateChanged(ItemEvent ie) {
        if(jtbn.isSelected())
          jlab.setText("Button is on.");
        else
          jlab.setText("Button is off.");
      }
    });

    // Add the toggle button and label to the content pane.
    jfrm.add(jtbn);
    jfrm.add(jlab);

    // Display the frame.
    jfrm.setVisible(true);
  }

  public static void main(String[] args) {
    // Create the frame on the event dispatching thread.

    SwingUtilities.invokeLater(
      new Runnable() {
        public void run() {
          new JToggleButtonDemo();
        }
      }
    );

  }
}
```

The output from the toggle button example is shown here:

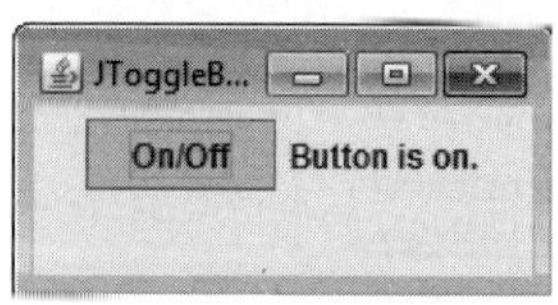

## Check Boxes

The **JCheckBox** class provides the functionality of a check box. Its immediate superclass is **JToggleButton**, which provides support for two-state buttons, as just described. **JCheckBox** defines several constructors. The one used here is

JCheckBox(String *str*)

It creates a check box that has the text specified by *str* as a label. Other constructors let you specify the initial selection state of the button and specify an icon.

When the user selects or deselects a check box, an **ItemEvent** is generated. You can obtain a reference to the **JCheckBox** that generated the event by calling **getItem( )** on the **ItemEvent** passed to the **itemStateChanged( )** method defined by **ItemListener**. The easiest way to determine the selected state of a check box is to call **isSelected( )** on the **JCheckBox** instance.

The following example illustrates check boxes. It displays four check boxes and a label. When the user clicks a check box, an **ItemEvent** is generated. Inside the **itemStateChanged( )** method, **getItem( )** is called to obtain a reference to the **JCheckBox** object that generated the event. Next, a call to **isSelected( )** determines if the box was selected or cleared. The **getText( )** method gets the text for that check box and uses it to set the text inside the label.

```
// Demonstrate JCheckbox.
import java.awt.*;
import java.awt.event.*;
import javax.swing.*;

public class JCheckBoxDemo implements ItemListener {
  JLabel jlab;

  public JCheckBoxDemo() {

    // Set up the JFrame.
    JFrame jfrm = new JFrame("JCheckBoxDemo");
    jfrm.setLayout(new FlowLayout());
    jfrm.setDefaultCloseOperation(JFrame.EXIT_ON_CLOSE);
    jfrm.setSize(250, 100);

    // Add check boxes to the content pane.
    JCheckBox cb = new JCheckBox("C");
    cb.addItemListener(this);
    jfrm.add(cb);

    cb = new JCheckBox("C++");
    cb.addItemListener(this);
    jfrm.add(cb);

    cb = new JCheckBox("Java");
    cb.addItemListener(this);
    jfrm.add(cb);
```

```
    cb = new JCheckBox("Perl");
    cb.addItemListener(this);
    jfrm.add(cb);

    // Create the label and add it to the content pane.
    jlab = new JLabel("Select languages");
    jfrm.add(jlab);

    // Display the frame.
    jfrm.setVisible(true);
  }

  // Handle item events for the check boxes.
  public void itemStateChanged(ItemEvent ie) {
    JCheckBox cb = (JCheckBox)ie.getItem();

    if(cb.isSelected())
      jlab.setText(cb.getText() + " is selected");
    else
      jlab.setText(cb.getText() + " is cleared");
  }

  public static void main(String[] args) {
    // Create the frame on the event dispatching thread.

    SwingUtilities.invokeLater(
      new Runnable() {
        public void run() {
          new JCheckBoxDemo();
        }
      }
    );

  }
}
```

Output from this example is shown here:

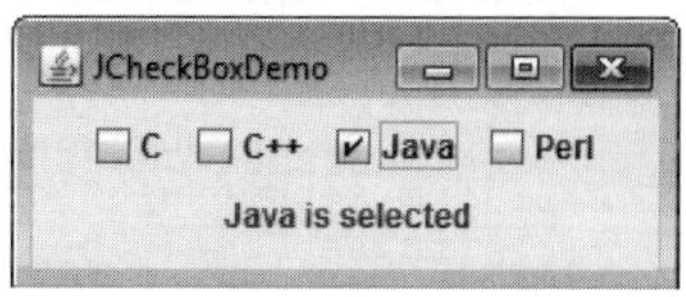


## Radio Buttons

Radio buttons are a group of mutually exclusive buttons, in which only one button can be selected at any one time. They are supported by the **JRadioButton** class, which extends **JToggleButton**. **JRadioButton** provides several constructors. The one used in the example is shown here:

JRadioButton(String *str*)

Here, *str* is the label for the button. Other constructors let you specify the initial selection state of the button and specify an icon.

In order for their mutually exclusive nature to be activated, radio buttons must be configured into a group. Only one of the buttons in the group can be selected at any time. For example, if a user presses a radio button that is in a group, any previously selected button in that group is automatically deselected. A button group is created by the **ButtonGroup** class. Its default constructor is invoked for this purpose. Elements are then added to the button group via the following method:

void add(AbstractButton *ab*)

Here, *ab* is a reference to the button to be added to the group.

A **JRadioButton** generates action events, item events, and change events each time the button selection changes. Most often, it is the action event that is handled, which means that you will normally implement the **ActionListener** interface. Recall that the only method defined by **ActionListener** is **actionPerformed( )**. Inside this method, you can use a number of different ways to determine which button was selected. First, you can check its action command by calling **getActionCommand( )**. By default, the action command is the same as the button label, but you can set the action command to something else by calling **setActionCommand( )** on the radio button. Second, you can call **getSource( )** on the **ActionEvent** object and check that reference against the buttons. Third, you can check each radio button to find out which one is currently selected by calling **isSelected( )** on each button. Finally, each button could use its own action event handler implemented as either an anonymous inner class or a lambda expression. Remember, each time an action event occurs, it means that the button being selected has changed and that one and only one button will be selected.

The following example illustrates how to use radio buttons. Three radio buttons are created. The buttons are then added to a button group. As explained, this is necessary to cause their mutually exclusive behavior. Pressing a radio button generates an action event, which is handled by **actionPerformed( )**. Within that handler, the **getActionCommand( )** method gets the text that is associated with the radio button and uses it to set the text within a label.

```
// Demonstrate JRadioButton
import java.awt.*;
import java.awt.event.*;
import javax.swing.*;

public class JRadioButtonDemo implements ActionListener {
  JLabel jlab;

  public JRadioButtonDemo() {

    // Set up the JFrame.
    JFrame jfrm = new JFrame("JRadioButtonDemo");
    jfrm.setLayout(new FlowLayout());
    jfrm.setDefaultCloseOperation(JFrame.EXIT_ON_CLOSE);
    jfrm.setSize(250, 100);
```

```
    // Create radio buttons and add them to content pane.
    JRadioButton b1 = new JRadioButton("A");
    b1.addActionListener(this);
    jfrm.add(b1);

    JRadioButton b2 = new JRadioButton("B");
    b2.addActionListener(this);
    jfrm.add(b2);

    JRadioButton b3 = new JRadioButton("C");
    b3.addActionListener(this);
    jfrm.add(b3);

    // Define a button group.
    ButtonGroup bg = new ButtonGroup();
    bg.add(b1);
    bg.add(b2);
    bg.add(b3);

    // Create a label and add it to the content pane.
    jlab = new JLabel("Select One");
    jfrm.add(jlab);

    // Display the frame.
    jfrm.setVisible(true);
  }

  // Handle button selection.
  public void actionPerformed(ActionEvent ae) {
    jlab.setText("You selected " + ae.getActionCommand());
  }

  public static void main(String[] args) {
    // Create the frame on the event dispatching thread.

    SwingUtilities.invokeLater(
      new Runnable() {
        public void run() {
          new JRadioButtonDemo();
        }
      }
    );

  }
}
```

Output from the radio button example is shown here:

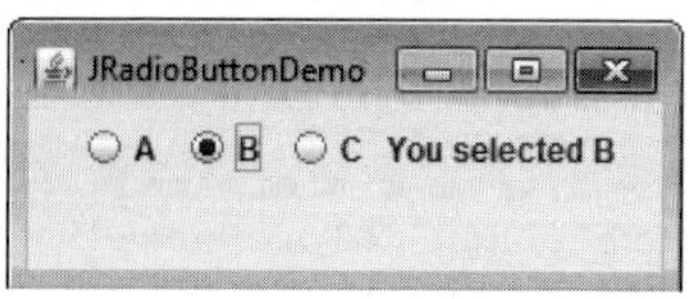

## JTabbedPane

**JTabbedPane** encapsulates a *tabbed pane.* It manages a set of components by linking them with tabs. Selecting a tab causes the component associated with that tab to come to the forefront. Tabbed panes are very common in the modern GUI, and you have no doubt used them many times. Given the complex nature of a tabbed pane, they are surprisingly easy to create and use.

**JTabbedPane** defines three constructors. We will use its default constructor, which creates an empty control with the tabs positioned across the top of the pane. The other two constructors let you specify the location of the tabs, which can be along any of the four sides. **JTabbedPane** uses the **SingleSelectionModel** model.

Tabs are added by calling **addTab( )**. Here is one of its forms:

void addTab(String *name*, Component *comp*)

Here, *name* is the name for the tab, and *comp* is the component that should be added to the tab. Often, the component added to a tab is a **JPanel** that contains a group of related components. This technique allows a tab to hold a set of components.

The general procedure to use a tabbed pane is outlined here:

1. Create an instance of **JTabbedPane**.
2. Add each tab by calling **addTab( )**.
3. Add the tabbed pane to the content pane.

The following example illustrates a tabbed pane. The first tab is titled "Cities" and contains four buttons. Each button displays the name of a city. The second tab is titled "Colors" and contains three check boxes. Each check box displays the name of a color. The third tab is titled "Flavors" and contains one combo box. This enables the user to select one of three flavors.

```
// Demonstrate JTabbedPane.
import javax.swing.*;
import java.awt.*;

public class JTabbedPaneDemo {

  public JTabbedPaneDemo() {

    // Set up the JFrame.
    JFrame jfrm = new JFrame("JTabbedPaneDemo");
    jfrm.setLayout(new FlowLayout());
    jfrm.setDefaultCloseOperation(JFrame.EXIT_ON_CLOSE);
    jfrm.setSize(400, 200);

    // Create the tabbed pane.
    JTabbedPane jtp = new JTabbedPane();
    jtp.addTab("Cities", new CitiesPanel());
    jtp.addTab("Colors", new ColorsPanel());
    jtp.addTab("Flavors", new FlavorsPanel());
    jfrm.add(jtp);
```

```
    // Display the frame.
    jfrm.setVisible(true);
  }

  public static void main(String[] args) {
    // Create the frame on the event dispatching thread.

    SwingUtilities.invokeLater(
      new Runnable() {
        public void run() {
          new JTabbedPaneDemo();
        }
      }
    );

  }
}

// Make the panels that will be added to the tabbed pane.
class CitiesPanel extends JPanel {

  public CitiesPanel() {
    JButton b1 = new JButton("New York");
    add(b1);
    JButton b2 = new JButton("London");
    add(b2);
    JButton b3 = new JButton("Hong Kong");
    add(b3);
    JButton b4 = new JButton("Tokyo");
    add(b4);
  }
}

class ColorsPanel extends JPanel {

  public ColorsPanel() {
    JCheckBox cb1 = new JCheckBox("Red");
    add(cb1);
    JCheckBox cb2 = new JCheckBox("Green");
    add(cb2);
    JCheckBox cb3 = new JCheckBox("Blue");
    add(cb3);
  }
}

class FlavorsPanel extends JPanel {

  public FlavorsPanel() {
    JComboBox<String> jcb = new JComboBox<String>();
    jcb.addItem("Vanilla");
    jcb.addItem("Chocolate");
```

```
      jcb.addItem("Strawberry");
      add(jcb);
    }
  }
```

Output from the tabbed pane example is shown in the following three illustrations:

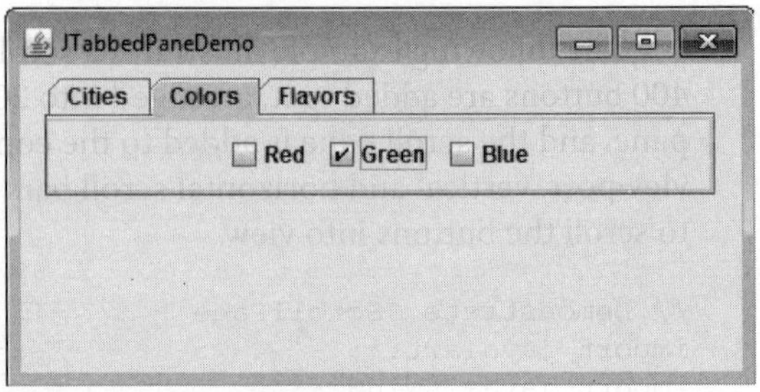


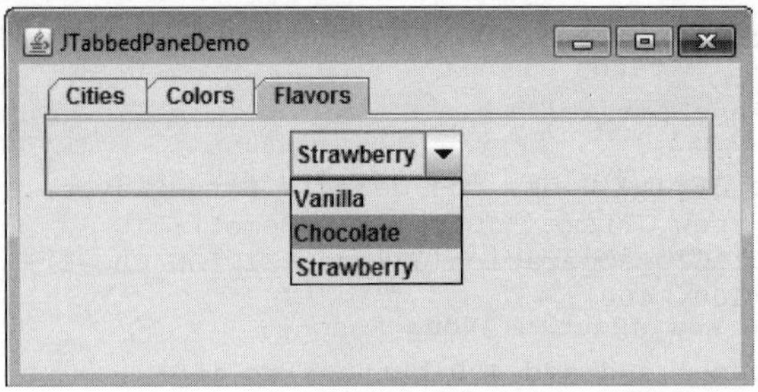


## JScrollPane

**JScrollPane** is a lightweight container that automatically handles the scrolling of another component. The component being scrolled can be either an individual component, such as a table, or a group of components contained within another lightweight container, such as a **JPanel**. In either case, if the object being scrolled is larger than the viewable area, horizontal and/or vertical scroll bars are automatically provided, and the component can be scrolled through the pane. Because **JScrollPane** automates scrolling, it usually eliminates the need to manage individual scroll bars.

The viewable area of a scroll pane is called the *viewport*. It is a window in which the component being scrolled is displayed. Thus, the viewport displays the visible portion of the component being scrolled. The scroll bars scroll the component through the viewport. In its default behavior, a **JScrollPane** will dynamically add or remove a scroll bar as needed. For example, if the component is taller than the viewport, a vertical scroll bar is added. If the component will completely fit within the viewport, the scroll bars are removed.

**JScrollPane** defines several constructors. The one used in this chapter is shown here:

JScrollPane(Component *comp*)

The component to be scrolled is specified by *comp*. Scroll bars are automatically displayed when the content of the pane exceeds the dimensions of the viewport.

Here are the steps to follow to use a scroll pane:

1. Create the component to be scrolled.
2. Create an instance of **JScrollPane**, passing to it the object to scroll.
3. Add the scroll pane to the content pane.

The following example illustrates a scroll pane. First, a **JPanel** object is created, and 400 buttons are added to it, arranged into 20 columns. This panel is then added to a scroll pane, and the scroll pane is added to the content pane. Because the panel is larger than the viewport, vertical and horizontal scroll bars appear automatically. You can use the scroll bars to scroll the buttons into view.

```
// Demonstrate JScrollPane.
import java.awt.*;
import javax.swing.*;

public class JScrollPaneDemo {

  public JScrollPaneDemo() {

    // Set up the JFrame.  Use the default BorderLayot.
    JFrame jfrm = new JFrame("JScrollPaneDemo");
    jfrm.setDefaultCloseOperation(JFrame.EXIT_ON_CLOSE);
    jfrm.setSize(400, 400);

    // Create a panel and add 400 buttons to it.
    JPanel jp = new JPanel();
    jp.setLayout(new GridLayout(20, 20));

    int b = 0;
    for(int i = 0; i < 20; i++) {
      for(int j = 0; j < 20; j++) {
        jp.add(new JButton("Button " + b));
        ++b;
      }
    }

    // Create the scroll pane.
    JScrollPane jsp = new JScrollPane(jp);

    // Add the scroll pane to the content pane.
    // Because the default border layout is used,
    // the scroll pane will be added to the center.
    jfrm.add(jsp, BorderLayout.CENTER);

    // Display the frame.
    jfrm.setVisible(true);
  }
```

Part III

```
  public static void main(String[] args) {
    // Create the frame on the event dispatching thread.
    SwingUtilities.invokeLater(
      new Runnable() {
        public void run() {
          new JScrollPaneDemo();
        }
      }
    );
  }
}
```

Output from the scroll pane example is shown here:

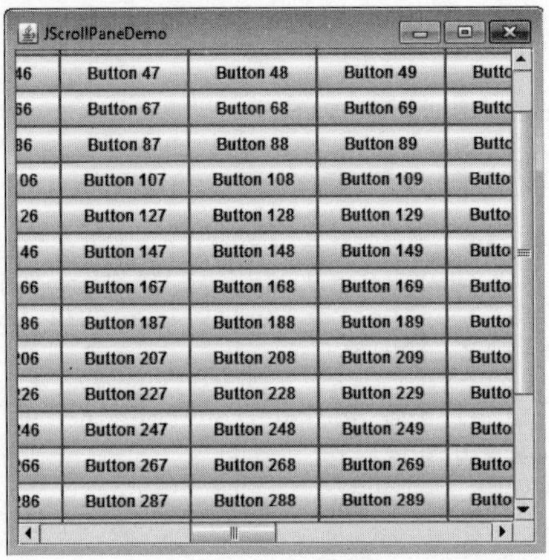


# JList

In Swing, the basic list class is called **JList**. It supports the selection of one or more items from a list. Although the list often consists of strings, it is possible to create a list of just about any object that can be displayed. **JList** is so widely used in Java that it is highly unlikely that you have not seen one before.

In the past, the items in a **JList** were represented as **Object** references. However, beginning with JDK 7, **JList** was made generic and is now declared like this:

class JList<E>

Here, **E** represents the type of the items in the list.

**JList** provides several constructors. The one used here is

JList(E[ ] *items*)

This creates a **JList** that contains the items in the array specified by *items*.

**JList** is based on two models. The first is **ListModel**. This interface defines how access to the list data is achieved. The second model is the **ListSelectionModel** interface, which defines methods that determine what list item or items are selected.

Although a **JList** will work properly by itself, most of the time you will wrap a **JList** inside a **JScrollPane**. This way, long lists will automatically be scrollable, which simplifies GUI design. It also makes it easy to change the number of entries in a list without having to change the size of the **JList** component.

A **JList** generates a **ListSelectionEvent** when the user makes or changes a selection. This event is also generated when the user deselects an item. It is handled by implementing **ListSelectionListener**. This listener specifies only one method, called **valueChanged( )**, which is shown here:

void valueChanged(ListSelectionEvent *le*)

Here, *le* is a reference to the event. Although **ListSelectionEvent** does provide some methods of its own, normally you will interrogate the **JList** object itself to determine what has occurred. Both **ListSelectionEvent** and **ListSelectionListener** are packaged in **javax.swing.event**.

By default, a **JList** allows the user to select multiple ranges of items within the list, but you can change this behavior by calling **setSelectionMode( )**, which is defined by **JList**. It is shown here:

void setSelectionMode(int *mode*)

Here, *mode* specifies the selection mode. It must be one of these values defined by **ListSelectionModel**:

SINGLE_SELECTION

SINGLE_INTERVAL_SELECTION

MULTIPLE_INTERVAL_SELECTION

The default, multiple-interval selection lets the user select multiple ranges of items within a list. With single-interval selection, the user can select one range of items. With single selection, the user can select only a single item. Of course, a single item can be selected in the other two modes, too. It's just that they also allow a range to be selected.

You can obtain the index of the first item selected, which will also be the index of the only selected item when using single-selection mode, by calling **getSelectedIndex( )**, shown here:

int getSelectedIndex( )

Indexing begins at zero. So, if the first item is selected, this method will return 0. If no item is selected, –1 is returned.

Instead of obtaining the index of a selection, you can obtain the value associated with the selection by calling **getSelectedValue( )**:

E getSelectedValue( )

It returns a reference to the first selected value. If no value has been selected, it returns **null**.

Part III

The following program demonstrates a simple **JList**, which holds a list of cities. Each time a city is selected in the list, a **ListSelectionEvent** is generated, which is handled by the **valueChanged( )** method defined by **ListSelectionListener**. It responds by obtaining the index of the selected item and displaying the name of the selected city in a label.

```
// Demonstrate JList.
import javax.swing.*;
import javax.swing.event.*;
import java.awt.*;
import java.awt.event.*;

public class JListDemo {

  // Create an array of cities.
  String[] cities = { "New York", "Chicago", "Houston",
                      "Denver", "Los Angeles", "Seattle",
                      "London", "Paris", "New Delhi",
                      "Hong Kong", "Tokyo", "Sydney" };

  public JListDemo() {

    // Set up the JFrame.
    JFrame jfrm = new JFrame("JListDemo");
    jfrm.setLayout(new FlowLayout());
    jfrm.setDefaultCloseOperation(JFrame.EXIT_ON_CLOSE);
    jfrm.setSize(200, 200);

    // Create a JList.
    JList<String> jlst = new JList<String>(cities);

    // Set the list selection mode to single-selection.
    jlst.setSelectionMode(ListSelectionModel.SINGLE_SELECTION);

    // Add the list to a scroll pane.
    JScrollPane jscrlp = new JScrollPane(jlst);

    // Set the preferred size of the scroll pane.
    jscrlp.setPreferredSize(new Dimension(120, 90));

    // Make a label that displays the selection.
    JLabel jlab = new JLabel("Choose a City");

    // Add selection listener for the list.
    jlst.addListSelectionListener(new ListSelectionListener() {
      public void valueChanged(ListSelectionEvent le) {
        // Get the index of the changed item.
        int idx = jlst.getSelectedIndex();

        // Display selection, if item was selected.
        if(idx != -1)
          jlab.setText("Current selection: " + cities[idx]);
```

```
        else // Otherwise, reprompt.
          jlab.setText("Choose a City");
      }
    });

    // Add the list and label to the content pane.
    jfrm.add(jscrlp);
    jfrm.add(jlab);

    // Display the frame.
    jfrm.setVisible(true);
  }

  public static void main(String[] args) {
    // Create the frame on the event dispatching thread.

    SwingUtilities.invokeLater(
      new Runnable() {
        public void run() {
          new JListDemo();
        }
      }
    );

  }
}
```



Output from the list example is shown here:

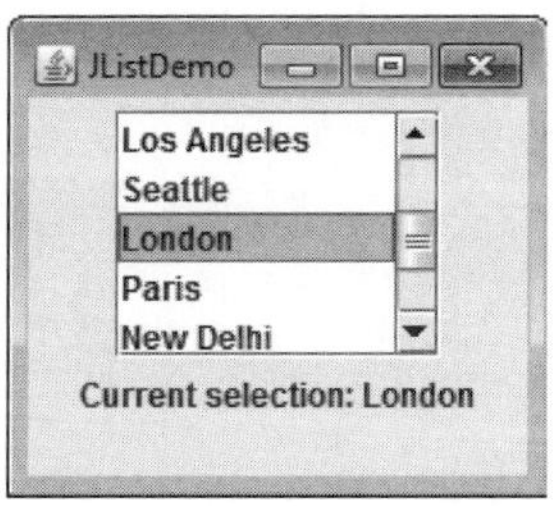


# JComboBox

Swing provides a *combo box* (a combination of a text field and a drop-down list) through the **JComboBox** class. A combo box normally displays one entry, but it will also display a drop-down list that allows a user to select a different entry. You can also create a combo box that lets the user enter a selection into the text field.

In the past, the items in a **JComboBox** were represented as **Object** references. However, beginning with JDK 7, **JComboBox** was made generic and is now declared like this:

class JComboBox<E>

Here, **E** represents the type of the items in the combo box.

The **JComboBox** constructor used by the example is shown here:

JComboBox(E[ ] *items*)

Here, *items* is an array that initializes the combo box. Other constructors are available.

**JComboBox** uses the **ComboBoxModel**. Mutable combo boxes (those whose entries can be changed) use the **MutableComboBoxModel**.

In addition to passing an array of items to be displayed in the drop-down list, items can be dynamically added to the list of choices via the **addItem( )** method, shown here:

void addItem(E *obj*)

Here, *obj* is the object to be added to the combo box. This method must be used only with mutable combo boxes.

**JComboBox** generates an action event when the user selects an item from the list. **JComboBox** also generates an item event when the state of selection changes, which occurs when an item is selected or deselected. Thus, changing a selection means that two item events will occur: one for the deselected item and another for the selected item. Often, it is sufficient to simply listen for action events, but both event types are available for your use.

One way to obtain the item selected in the list is to call **getSelectedItem( )** on the combo box. It is shown here:

Object getSelectedItem( )

You will need to cast the returned value into the type of object stored in the list.

The following example demonstrates the combo box. The combo box contains entries for "Hourglass", "Analog", "Digital", and "Stopwatch". When a timepiece is selected, an icon-based label is updated to display it. You can see how little code is required to use this powerful component.

```
// Demonstrate JComboBox.
import java.awt.*;
import java.awt.event.*;
import javax.swing.*;

public class JComboBoxDemo {

  String[] timepieces = { "Hourglass", "Analog", "Digital", "Stopwatch" };

  public JComboBoxDemo() {

    // Set up the JFrame.
    JFrame jfrm = new JFrame("JCombBoxDemo");
    jfrm.setLayout(new FlowLayout());
    jfrm.setDefaultCloseOperation(JFrame.EXIT_ON_CLOSE);
    jfrm.setSize(400, 250);

    // Instantiate a combo box and add it to the content pane.
    JComboBox<String> jcb = new JComboBox<String>(timepieces);
    jfrm.add(jcb);
```

```
    // Create a label and add it to the content pane.
    JLabel jlab = new JLabel(new ImageIcon("hourglass.png"));
    jfrm.add(jlab);

    // Handle selections.
    jcb.addActionListener(new ActionListener() {
      public void actionPerformed(ActionEvent ae) {
        String s = (String) jcb.getSelectedItem();
        jlab.setIcon(new ImageIcon(s + ".png"));
      }
    });

    // Display the frame.
    jfrm.setVisible(true);
  }

  public static void main(String[] args) {
    // Create the frame on the event dispatching thread.

    SwingUtilities.invokeLater(
      new Runnable() {
        public void run() {
          new JComboBoxDemo();
        }
      }
    );

  }
}
```

Output from the combo box example is shown here:

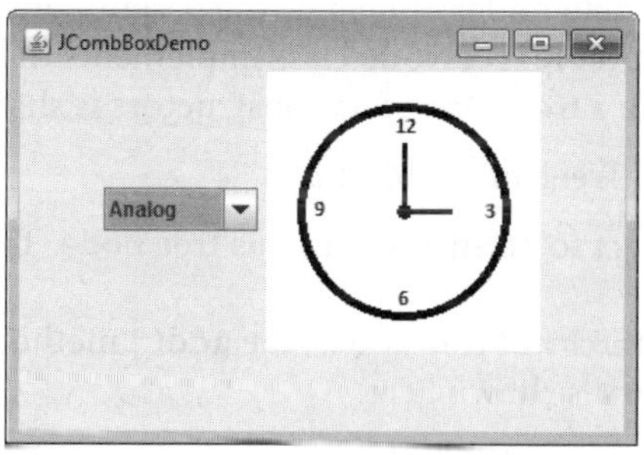


# Trees

A *tree* is a component that presents a hierarchical view of data. The user has the ability to expand or collapse individual subtrees in this display. Trees are implemented in Swing by the **JTree** class. A sampling of its constructors is shown here:

JTree(Object[ ] *obj*)
JTree(Vector<?> *v*)
JTree(TreeNode *tn*)

In the first form, the tree is constructed from the elements in the array *obj*. The second form constructs the tree from the elements of vector *v*. In the third form, the tree whose root node is specified by *tn* specifies the tree.

Although **JTree** is packaged in **javax.swing**, its support classes and interfaces are packaged in **javax.swing.tree**. This is because the number of classes and interfaces needed to support **JTree** is quite large.

**JTree** relies on two models: **TreeModel** and **TreeSelectionModel**. A **JTree** generates a variety of events, but three relate specifically to trees: **TreeExpansionEvent**, **TreeSelectionEvent**, and **TreeModelEvent**. **TreeExpansionEvent** events occur when a node is expanded or collapsed. A **TreeSelectionEvent** is generated when the user selects or deselects a node within the tree. A **TreeModelEvent** is fired when the data or structure of the tree changes. The listeners for these events are **TreeExpansionListener**, **TreeSelectionListener**, and **TreeModelListener**, respectively. The tree event classes and listener interfaces are packaged in **javax.swing.event**.

The event handled by the sample program shown in this section is **TreeSelectionEvent**. To listen for this event, implement **TreeSelectionListener**. It defines only one method, called **valueChanged( )**, which receives the **TreeSelectionEvent** object. You can obtain the path to the selected object by calling **getPath( )**, shown here, on the event object:

TreePath getPath( )

It returns a **TreePath** object that describes the path to the changed node. The **TreePath** class encapsulates information about a path to a particular node in a tree. It provides several constructors and methods. In this book, only the **toString( )** method is used. It returns a string that describes the path.

The **TreeNode** interface declares methods that obtain information about a tree node. For example, it is possible to obtain a reference to the parent node or an enumeration of the child nodes. The **MutableTreeNode** interface extends **TreeNode**. It declares methods that can insert and remove child nodes or change the parent node.

The **DefaultMutableTreeNode** class implements the **MutableTreeNode** interface. It represents a node in a tree. One of its constructors is shown here:

DefaultMutableTreeNode(Object *obj*)

Here, *obj* is the object to be enclosed in this tree node. The new tree node doesn't have a parent or children.

To create a hierarchy of tree nodes, the **add( )** method of **DefaultMutableTreeNode** can be used. Its signature is shown here:

void add(MutableTreeNode *child*)

Here, *child* is a mutable tree node that is to be added as a child to the current node.

**JTree** does not provide any scrolling capabilities of its own. Instead, a **JTree** is typically placed within a **JScrollPane**. This way, a large tree can be scrolled through a smaller viewport.

Here are the steps to follow to use a tree:

1. Create an instance of **JTree**.
2. Create a **JScrollPane** and specify the tree as the object to be scrolled.
3. Add the scroll pane to the content pane.

The following example illustrates how to create a tree and handle selections. The program creates a **DefaultMutableTreeNode** instance labeled "Options". This is the top node of the tree hierarchy. Additional tree nodes are then created, and the **add( )** method is called to connect these nodes to the tree. A reference to the top node in the tree is provided as the argument to the **JTree** constructor. The tree is then provided as the argument to the **JScrollPane** constructor. This scroll pane is then added to the content pane. Next, a label is created and added to the content pane. The tree selection is displayed in this label. To receive selection events from the tree, a **TreeSelectionListener** is registered for the tree. Inside the **valueChanged( )** method, the path to the current selection is obtained and displayed.

```
// Demonstrate JTree.
import java.awt.*;
import javax.swing.event.*;
import javax.swing.*;
import javax.swing.tree.*;

public class JTreeDemo {

  public JTreeDemo() {

    // Set up the JFrame. Use default BorderLayout.
    JFrame jfrm = new JFrame("JTreeDemo");
    jfrm.setDefaultCloseOperation(JFrame.EXIT_ON_CLOSE);
    jfrm.setSize(200, 250);

    // Create top node of tree.
    DefaultMutableTreeNode top = new DefaultMutableTreeNode("Options");

    // Create subtree of "A".
    DefaultMutableTreeNode a = new DefaultMutableTreeNode("A");
    top.add(a);
    DefaultMutableTreeNode a1 = new DefaultMutableTreeNode("A1");
    a.add(a1);
    DefaultMutableTreeNode a2 = new DefaultMutableTreeNode("A2");
    a.add(a2);

    // Create subtree of "B".
    DefaultMutableTreeNode b = new DefaultMutableTreeNode("B");
    top.add(b);
    DefaultMutableTreeNode b1 = new DefaultMutableTreeNode("B1");
    b.add(b1);
    DefaultMutableTreeNode b2 = new DefaultMutableTreeNode("B2");
    b.add(b2);
    DefaultMutableTreeNode b3 = new DefaultMutableTreeNode("B3");
    b.add(b3);

    // Create the tree.
    JTree tree = new JTree(top);
```

Part III

```
    // Add the tree to a scroll pane.
    JScrollPane jsp = new JScrollPane(tree);

    // Add the scroll pane to the content pane.
    jfrm.add(jsp);

    // Add the label to the content pane.
    JLabel jlab = new JLabel();
    jfrm.add(jlab, BorderLayout.SOUTH);

    // Handle tree selection events.
    tree.addTreeSelectionListener(new TreeSelectionListener() {
      public void valueChanged(TreeSelectionEvent tse) {
        jlab.setText("Selection is " + tse.getPath());
      }
    });

    // Display the frame.
    jfrm.setVisible(true);
  }

  public static void main(String[] args) {
    // Create the frame on the event dispatching thread.

    SwingUtilities.invokeLater(
      new Runnable() {
        public void run() {
          new JTreeDemo();
        }
      }
    );

  }
}
```

Output from the tree example is shown here:

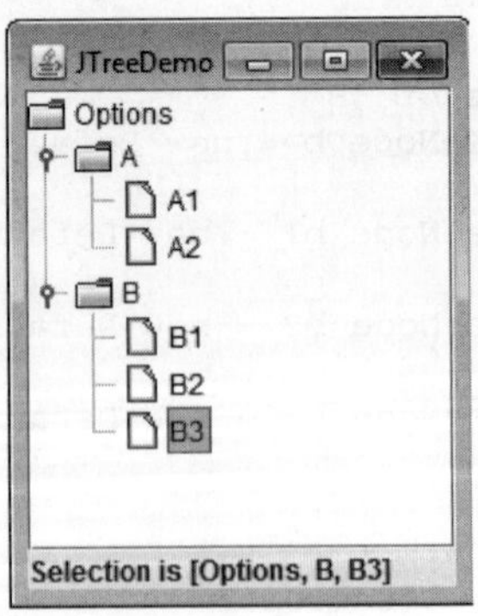


The string presented in the text field describes the path from the top tree node to the selected node.

# JTable

**JTable** is a component that displays rows and columns of data. You can drag the cursor on column boundaries to resize columns. You can also drag a column to a new position. Depending on its configuration, it is also possible to select a row, column, or cell within the table, and to change the data within a cell. **JTable** is a sophisticated component that offers many more options and features than can be discussed here. (It is perhaps Swing's most complicated component.) However, in its default configuration, **JTable** still offers substantial functionality that is easy to use—especially if you simply want to use the table to present data in a tabular format. The brief overview presented here will give you a general understanding of this powerful component.

Like **JTree**, **JTable** has many classes and interfaces associated with it. These are packaged in **javax.swing.table**.

At its core, **JTable** is conceptually simple. It is a component that consists of one or more columns of information. At the top of each column is a heading. In addition to describing the data in a column, the heading also provides the mechanism by which the user can change the size of a column or change the location of a column within the table. **JTable** does not provide any scrolling capabilities of its own. Instead, you will normally wrap a **JTable** inside a **JScrollPane**.

**JTable** supplies several constructors. The one used here is

JTable(Object[ ][ ] *data*, Object[ ] *colHeads*)

Here, *data* is a two-dimensional array of the information to be presented, and *colHeads* is a one-dimensional array with the column headings.

**JTable** relies on three models. The first is the table model, which is defined by the **TableModel** interface. This model defines those things related to displaying data in a two-dimensional format. The second is the table column model, which is represented by **TableColumnModel**. **JTable** is defined in terms of columns, and it is **TableColumnModel** that specifies the characteristics of a column. These two models are packaged in **javax.swing.table**. The third model determines how items are selected, and it is specified by the **ListSelectionModel**, which was described when **JList** was discussed.

A **JTable** can generate several different events. The two most fundamental to a table's operation are **ListSelectionEvent** and **TableModelEvent**. A **ListSelectionEvent** is generated when the user selects something in the table. By default, **JTable** allows you to select one or more complete rows, but you can change this behavior to allow one or more columns, or one or more individual cells to be selected. A **TableModelEvent** is fired when that table's data changes in some way. Handling these events requires a bit more work than it does to handle the events generated by the previously described components and is beyond the scope of this book. However, if you simply want to use **JTable** to display data (as the following example does), then you don't need to handle any events.

Here are the steps required to set up a simple **JTable** that can be used to display data:

1. Create an instance of **JTable**.
2. Create a **JScrollPane** object, specifying the table as the object to scroll.
3. Add the scroll pane to the content pane.

The following example illustrates how to create and use a simple table. A one-dimensional array of strings called **colHeads** is created for the column headings. A two-dimensional array of strings called **data** is created for the table cells. You can see that each element in the array is an array of three strings. These arrays are passed to the **JTable** constructor. The table is added to a scroll pane, and then the scroll pane is added to the content pane. The table displays the data in the **data** array. The default table configuration also allows the contents of a cell to be edited. Changes affect the underlying array, which is **data** in this case.

```
// Demonstrate JTable.
import java.awt.*;
import javax.swing.*;

public class JTableDemo {

  // Initialize column headings.
  String[] colHeads = { "Name", "Extension", "ID#" };

  // Initialize data.
  Object[][] data = {
    { "Gail", "4567", "865" },
    { "Ken", "7566", "555" },
    { "Viviane", "5634", "587" },
    { "Melanie", "7345", "922" },
    { "Anne", "1237", "333" },
    { "John", "5656", "314" },
    { "Matt", "5672", "217" },
    { "Claire", "6741", "444" },
    { "Erwin", "9023", "519" },
    { "Ellen", "1134", "532" },
    { "Jennifer", "5689", "112" },
    { "Ed", "9030", "133" },
    { "Helen", "6751", "145" }
  };

  public JTableDemo() {

    // Set up the JFrame. Use default BorderLayout.
    JFrame jfrm = new JFrame("JTableDemo");
    jfrm.setDefaultCloseOperation(JFrame.EXIT_ON_CLOSE);
    jfrm.setSize(300, 300);

    // Create the table.
    JTable table = new JTable(data, colHeads);

    // Add the table to a scroll pane.
    JScrollPane jsp = new JScrollPane(table);
```

```
    // Add the scroll pane to the content pane.
    jfrm.add(jsp);

    // Display the frame.
    jfrm.setVisible(true);
  }

  public static void main(String[] args) {
    // Create the frame on the event dispatching thread.

    SwingUtilities.invokeLater(
      new Runnable() {
        public void run() {
          new JTableDemo();
        }
      }
    );

  }
}
```

Output from this example is shown here:

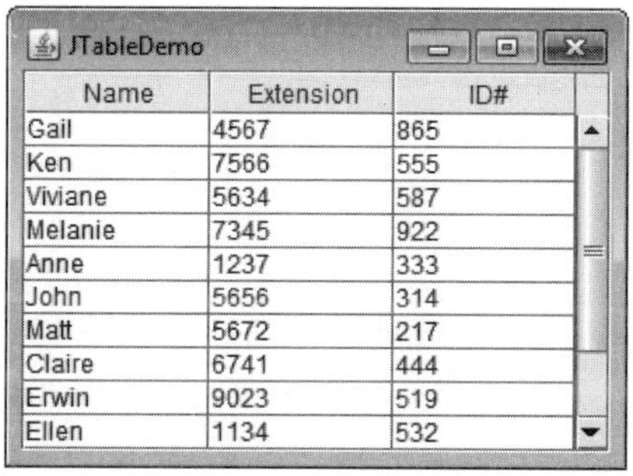

CHAPTER

# 34 Introducing Swing Menus

This chapter introduces another fundamental aspect of the Swing GUI environment: the menu. Menus form an integral part of many applications because they present the program's functionality to the user. Because of their importance, Swing provides extensive support for menus. They are an area in which Swing's power is readily apparent.

The Swing menu system supports several key elements, including

- The menu bar, which is the main menu for an application.
- The standard menu, which can contain either items to be selected or other menus (submenus).
- The popup menu, which is usually activated by right-clicking the mouse.
- The toolbar, which provides rapid access to program functionality, often paralleling menu items.
- The action, which enables two or more different components to be managed by a single object. Actions are commonly used with menus and toolbars.

Swing menus also support accelerator keys, which enable menu items to be selected without having to activate the menu, and mnemonics, which allow a menu item to be selected by the keyboard once the menu options are displayed.

## Menu Basics

The Swing menu system is supported by a group of related classes. The ones used in this chapter are shown in Table 34-1, and they represent the core of the menu system. Although they may seem a bit confusing at first, Swing menus are quite easy to use. Swing allows a high degree of customization, if desired; however, you will normally use the menu classes as-is because they support all of the most needed options. For example, you can easily add images and keyboard shortcuts to a menu.

| Class | Description |
|---|---|
| JMenuBar | An object that holds the top-level menu for the application. |
| JMenu | A standard menu. A menu consists of one or more **JMenuItem**s. |
| JMenuItem | An object that populates menus. |
| JCheckBoxMenuItem | A check box menu item. |
| JRadioButtonMenuItem | A radio button menu item. |
| JSeparator | The visual separator between menu items. |
| JPopupMenu | A menu that is typically activated by right-clicking the mouse. |

**Table 34-1** The Core Swing Menu Classes

Here is a brief overview of how the classes fit together. To create the top-level menu for an application, you first create a **JMenuBar** object. This class is, loosely speaking, a container for menus. To the **JMenuBar** instance, you will add instances of **JMenu**. Each **JMenu** object defines a menu. That is, each **JMenu** object contains one or more selectable items. The items displayed by a **JMenu** are objects of **JMenuItem**. Thus, a **JMenuItem** defines a selection that can be chosen by the user.

As an alternative or adjunct to menus that descend from the menu bar, you can also create stand-alone, popup menus. To create a popup menu, first create an object of type **JPopupMenu**. Then, add **JMenuItem**s to it. A popup menu is normally activated by clicking the right mouse button when the mouse is over a component for which a popup menu has been defined.

In addition to "standard" menu items, you can also include check boxes and radio buttons in a menu. A check box menu item is created by **JCheckBoxMenuItem**. A radio button menu item is created by **JRadioButtonMenuItem**. Both of these classes extend **JMenuItem**. They can be used in standard menus and popup menus.

**JToolBar** creates a stand-alone component that is related to the menu. It is often used to provide fast access to functionality contained within the menus of the application. For example, a toolbar might provide fast access to the formatting commands supported by a word processor.

**JSeparator** is a convenience class that creates a separator line in a menu.

One key point to understand about Swing menus is that each menu item extends **AbstractButton**. Recall that **AbstractButton** is also the superclass of all of Swing's button components, such as **JButton**. Thus, all menu items are, essentially, buttons. Obviously, they won't actually look like buttons when used in a menu, but they will, in many ways, act like buttons. For example, selecting a menu item generates an action event in the same way that pressing a button does.

Another key point is that **JMenuItem** is a superclass of **JMenu**. This allows the creation of submenus, which are, essentially, menus within menus. To create a submenu, you first create and populate a **JMenu** object and then add it to another **JMenu** object. You will see this process in action in the following section.

As mentioned in passing previously, when a menu item is selected, an action event is generated. The action command string associated with that action event will, by default, be the name of the selection. Thus, you can determine which item was selected by examining the action command. Of course, you can also use separate anonymous inner classes or lambda expressions to handle each menu item's action events. In this case, the menu selection is already known, and there is no need to examine the action command string to determine which item was selected.

Menus can also generate other types of events. For example, each time that a menu is activated, selected, or canceled, a **MenuEvent** is generated that can be listened for via a **MenuListener**. Other menu-related events include **MenuKeyEvent**, **MenuDragMouseEvent**, and **PopupMenuEvent**. In many cases, however, you need only watch for action events, and in this chapter, we will use only action events.

# An Overview of JMenuBar, JMenu, and JMenuItem

Before you can create a menu, you need to know something about the three core menu classes: **JMenuBar**, **JMenu**, and **JMenuItem**. These form the minimum set of classes needed to construct a main menu for an application. **JMenu** and **JMenuItem** are also used by popup menus. Thus, these classes form the foundation of the menu system.

## JMenuBar

As mentioned, **JMenuBar** is essentially a container for menus. Like all components, it inherits **JComponent** (which inherits **Container** and **Component**). It has only one constructor, which is the default constructor. Therefore, initially the menu bar will be empty, and you will need to populate it with menus prior to use. Each application has one and only one menu bar.

**JMenuBar** defines several methods, but often you will only need to use one: **add( )**. The **add( )** method adds a **JMenu** to the menu bar. It is shown here:

JMenu add(JMenu *menu*)

Here, *menu* is a **JMenu** instance that is added to the menu bar. A reference to the menu is returned. Menus are positioned in the bar from left to right, in the order in which they are added. If you want to add a menu at a specific location, then use this version of **add( )**, which is inherited from **Container**:

Component add(Component *menu*, int *idx*)

Here, *menu* is added at the index specified by *idx*. Indexing begins at 0, with 0 being the left-most menu.

In some cases, you might want to remove a menu that is no longer needed. You can do this by calling **remove( )**, which is inherited from **Container**. It has these two forms:

void remove(Component *menu*)

void remove(int *idx*)

Here, *menu* is a reference to the menu to remove, and *idx* is the index of the menu to remove. Indexing begins at zero.

Another method that is sometimes useful is **getMenuCount( )**, shown here:

int getMenuCount( )

It returns the number of elements contained within the menu bar.

**JMenuBar** defines some other methods that you might find helpful in specialized applications. For example, you can obtain an array of references to the menus in the bar by calling **getSubElements( )**. You can determine if a menu is selected by calling **isSelected( )**.

Once a menu bar has been created and populated, it is added to a **JFrame** by calling **setJMenuBar( )** on the **JFrame** instance. (Menu bars *are not* added to the content pane.) The **setJMenuBar( )** method is shown here:

void setJMenuBar(JMenuBar *mb*)

Here, *mb* is a reference to the menu bar. The menu bar will be displayed in a position determined by the look and feel. Usually, this is at the top of the window.

## JMenu

**JMenu** encapsulates a menu, which is populated with **JMenuItems**. As mentioned, it is derived from **JMenuItem**. This means that one **JMenu** can be a selection in another **JMenu**. This enables one menu to be a submenu of another. **JMenu** defines a number of constructors. For example, here is the one used in the examples in this chapter:

JMenu(String *name*)

This constructor creates a menu that has the title specified by *name*. Of course, you don't have to give a menu a name. To create an unnamed menu, you can use the default constructor:

JMenu( )

Other constructors are also supported. In each case, the menu is empty until menu items are added to it.

**JMenu** defines many methods. Here is a brief description of some commonly used ones. To add an item to the menu, use the **add( )** method, which has a number of forms, including the two shown here:

JMenuItem add(JMenuItem *item*)

Component add(Component *item*, int *idx*)

Here, *item* is the menu item to add. The first form adds the item to the end of the menu. The second form adds the item at the index specified by *idx*. As expected, indexing starts at zero. Both forms return a reference to the item added. As a point of interest, you can also use **insert( )** to add menu items to a menu.

You can add a separator (an object of type **JSeparator**) to a menu by calling **addSeparator( )**, shown here:

void addSeparator( )

The separator is added onto the end of the menu. You can insert a separator into a menu by calling **insertSeparator( )**, shown next:

void insertSeparator(int *idx*)

Here, *idx* specifies the zero-based index at which the separator will be added.

You can remove an item from a menu by calling **remove( )**. Two of its forms are shown here:

void remove(JMenuItem *menu*)

void remove(int *idx*)

In this case, *menu* is a reference to the item to remove and *idx* is the index of the item to remove.

You can obtain the number of items in the menu by calling **getMenuComponentCount( )**, shown here:

int getMenuComponentCount( )

You can get an array of the items in the menu by calling **getMenuComponents( )**, shown next:

Component[ ] getMenuComponents( )

An array containing the components is returned.

## JMenuItem

**JMenuItem** encapsulates an element in a menu. This element can be a selection linked to some program action, such as Save or Close, or it can cause a submenu to be displayed. As mentioned, **JMenuItem** is derived from **AbstractButton**, and every item in a menu can be thought of as a special kind of button. Therefore, when a menu item is selected, an action event is generated. (This is similar to the way a **JButton** fires an action event when it is pressed.) **JMenuItem** defines many constructors. The ones used in this chapter are shown here:



JMenuItem(String *name*)

JMenuItem(Icon *image*)

JMenuItem(String *name*, Icon *image*)

JMenuItem(String *name*, int *mnem*)

JMenuItem(Action *action*)

The first constructor creates a menu item with the name specified by *name*. The second creates a menu item that displays the image specified by *image*. The third creates a menu item with the name specified by *name* and the image specified by *image*. The fourth creates a menu item with the name specified by *name* and uses the keyboard mnemonic specified by *mnem*. This mnemonic enables you to select an item from the menu by pressing the specified key. The last constructor creates a menu item using the information specified in *action*. A default constructor is also supported.

Because menu items inherit **AbstractButton**, you have access to the functionality provided by **AbstractButton**. One such method that is often useful with menus is **setEnabled( )**, which you can use to enable or disable a menu item. It is shown here:

void setEnabled(boolean *enable*)

If *enable* is **true**, the menu item is enabled. If *enable* is **false**, the item is disabled and cannot be selected.

## Create a Main Menu

Traditionally, the most commonly used menu is the *main menu.* This is the menu defined by the menu bar, and it is the menu that defines all (or nearly all) of the functionality of an application. Fortunately, Swing makes creating and managing the main menu easy. This section shows you how to construct a basic main menu. Subsequent sections will show you how to add options to it.

Constructing the main menu requires several steps. First, create the **JMenuBar** object that will hold the menus. Next, construct each menu that will be in the menu bar. In general, a menu is constructed by first creating a **JMenu** object and then adding **JMenuItems** to it. After the menus have been created, add them to the menu bar. The menu bar, itself, must then be added to the frame by calling **setJMenuBar( )**. Finally, for each menu item, you must add an action listener that handles the action event fired when the menu item is selected.

A good way to understand the process of creating and managing menus is to work through an example. Here is a program that creates a simple menu bar that contains three menus. The first is a standard File menu that contains Open, Close, Save, and Exit selections. The second menu is called Options, and it contains two submenus called Colors and Priority. The third menu is called Help, and it has one item: About. When a menu item is selected, the name of the selection is displayed in a label in the content pane. Sample output is shown in Figure 34-1.

```
// Demonstrate a simple main menu.

import java.awt.*;
import java.awt.event.*;
import javax.swing.*;

class MenuDemo implements ActionListener {

  JLabel jlab;

  MenuDemo() {
    // Create a new JFrame container.
    JFrame jfrm = new JFrame("Menu Demo");
```

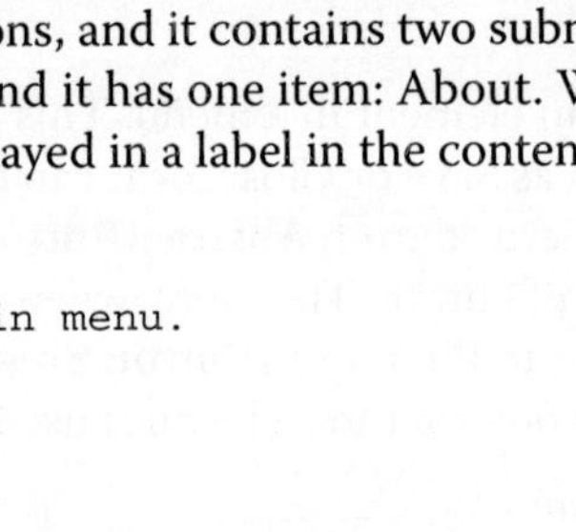


**Figure 34-1** Sample output from the **MenuDemo** program

```
// Specify FlowLayout for the layout manager.
jfrm.setLayout(new FlowLayout());

// Give the frame an initial size.
jfrm.setSize(220, 200);

// Terminate the program when the user closes the application.
jfrm.setDefaultCloseOperation(JFrame.EXIT_ON_CLOSE);

// Create a label that will display the menu selection.
jlab = new JLabel();

// Create the menu bar.
JMenuBar jmb = new JMenuBar();

// Create the File menu.
JMenu jmFile = new JMenu("File");
JMenuItem jmiOpen = new JMenuItem("Open");
JMenuItem jmiClose = new JMenuItem("Close");
JMenuItem jmiSave = new JMenuItem("Save");
JMenuItem jmiExit = new JMenuItem("Exit");
jmFile.add(jmiOpen);
jmFile.add(jmiClose);
jmFile.add(jmiSave);
jmFile.addSeparator();
jmFile.add(jmiExit);
jmb.add(jmFile);

// Create the Options menu.
JMenu jmOptions = new JMenu("Options");

// Create the Colors submenu.
JMenu jmColors = new JMenu("Colors");
JMenuItem jmiRed = new JMenuItem("Red");
JMenuItem jmiGreen = new JMenuItem("Green");
JMenuItem jmiBlue = new JMenuItem("Blue");
jmColors.add(jmiRed);
jmColors.add(jmiGreen);
jmColors.add(jmiBlue);
jmOptions.add(jmColors);

// Create the Priority submenu.
JMenu jmPriority = new JMenu("Priority");
JMenuItem jmiHigh = new JMenuItem("High");
JMenuItem jmiLow = new JMenuItem("Low");
jmPriority.add(jmiHigh);
jmPriority.add(jmiLow);
jmOptions.add(jmPriority);

// Create the Reset menu item.
JMenuItem jmiReset = new JMenuItem("Reset");
jmOptions.addSeparator();
jmOptions.add(jmiReset);
```

Part III

```
    // Finally, add the entire options menu to
    // the menu bar
    jmb.add(jmOptions);

    // Create the Help menu.
    JMenu jmHelp = new JMenu("Help");
    JMenuItem jmiAbout = new JMenuItem("About");
    jmHelp.add(jmiAbout);
    jmb.add(jmHelp);

    // Add action listeners for the menu items.
    jmiOpen.addActionListener(this);
    jmiClose.addActionListener(this);
    jmiSave.addActionListener(this);
    jmiExit.addActionListener(this);
    jmiRed.addActionListener(this);
    jmiGreen.addActionListener(this);
    jmiBlue.addActionListener(this);
    jmiHigh.addActionListener(this);
    jmiLow.addActionListener(this);
    jmiReset.addActionListener(this);
    jmiAbout.addActionListener(this);

    // Add the label to the content pane.
    jfrm.add(jlab);

    // Add the menu bar to the frame.
    jfrm.setJMenuBar(jmb);

    // Display the frame.
    jfrm.setVisible(true);
  }

  // Handle menu item action events.
  public void actionPerformed(ActionEvent ae) {
    // Get the action command from the menu selection.
    String comStr = ae.getActionCommand();

    // If user chooses Exit, then exit the program.
    if(comStr.equals("Exit")) System.exit(0);

    // Otherwise, display the selection.
    jlab.setText(comStr + " Selected");
  }

  public static void main(String[] args) {
    // Create the frame on the event dispatching thread.
    SwingUtilities.invokeLater(new Runnable() {
      public void run() {
        new MenuDemo();
      }
    });
  }
}
```

Let's examine, in detail, how the menus in this program are created, beginning with the **MenuDemo** constructor. It starts by creating a **JFrame** and setting its layout manager, size, and default close operation. (These operations are described in Chapter 32.) A **JLabel** is then constructed. It will be used to display a menu selection. Next, the menu bar is constructed and a reference to it is assigned to **jmb** by this statement:

```
// Create the menu bar.
JMenuBar jmb = new JMenuBar();
```

Then, the File menu **jmFile** and its menu entries are created by this sequence:

```
// Create the File menu.
JMenu jmFile = new JMenu("File");
JMenuItem jmiOpen = new JMenuItem("Open");
JMenuItem jmiClose = new JMenuItem("Close");
JMenuItem jmiSave = new JMenuItem("Save");
JMenuItem jmiExit = new JMenuItem("Exit");
```

The names Open, Close, Save, and Exit will be shown as selections in the menu. Next, the menu entries are added to the file menu by this sequence:

```
jmFile.add(jmiOpen);
jmFile.add(jmiClose);
jmFile.add(jmiSave);
jmFile.addSeparator();
jmFile.add(jmiExit);
```

Finally, the File menu is added to the menu bar with this line:

```
jmb.add(jmFile);
```

Once the preceding code sequence completes, the menu bar will contain one entry: File. The File menu will contain four selections in this order: Open, Close, Save, and Exit. However, notice that a separator has been added before Exit. This visually separates Exit from the preceding three selections.

The Options menu is constructed using the same basic process as the File menu. However, the Options menu consists of two submenus, Colors and Priority, and a Reset entry. The submenus are first constructed individually and then added to the Options menu. The Reset item is added last. Then, the Options menu is added to the menu bar. The Help menu is constructed using the same process.

Notice that **MenuDemo** implements the **ActionListener** interface, and action events generated by a menu selection are handled by the **actionPerformed( )** method defined by **MenuDemo**. Therefore, the program adds **this** as the action listener for the menu items. Notice that no listeners are added to the Colors and Priority items because they are not actually selections. They simply activate submenus.

Finally, the menu bar is added to the frame by the following line:

```
jfrm.setJMenuBar(jmb);
```

As mentioned, menu bars are not added to the content pane. They are added directly to the **JFrame**.

The **actionPerformed( )** method handles the action events generated by the menu. It obtains the action command string associated with the selection by calling **getActionCommand( )** on the event. It stores a reference to this string in **comStr**. Then, it tests the action command against "Exit", as shown here:

```
if(comStr.equals("Exit")) System.exit(0);
```

If the action command is "Exit", then the program terminates by calling **System.exit( )**. This method causes the immediate termination of a program and passes its argument as a status code to the calling process, which is usually the operating system. By convention, a status code of zero means normal termination. Anything else indicates that the program terminated abnormally. For all other menu selections, the choice is displayed.

At this point, you might want to experiment a bit with the **MenuDemo** program. Try adding another menu or adding additional items to an existing menu. It is important that you understand the basic menu concepts before moving on because this program will evolve throughout the course of this chapter.

## Add Mnemonics and Accelerators to Menu Items

The menu created in the preceding example is functional, but it is possible to make it better. In real applications, a menu usually includes support for keyboard shortcuts because they give an experienced user the ability to select menu items rapidly. Keyboard shortcuts come in two forms: mnemonics and accelerators. As it applies to menus, a *mnemonic* defines a key that lets you select an item from an active menu by typing the key. Thus, a mnemonic allows you to use the keyboard to select an item from a menu that is already being displayed. An *accelerator* is a key that lets you select a menu item without having to first activate the menu.

A mnemonic can be specified for both **JMenuItem** and **JMenu** objects. There are two ways to set the mnemonic for **JMenuItem**. First, it can be specified when an object is constructed using this constructor:

JMenuItem(String *name*, int *mnem*)

In this case, the name is passed in *name* and the mnemonic is passed in *mnen*. Second, you can set the mnemonic by calling **setMnemonic( )**. To specify a mnemonic for **JMenu**, you must call **setMnemonic( )**. This method is inherited by both classes from **AbstractButton** and is shown next:

void setMnemonic(int *mnem*)

Here, *mnem* specifies the mnemonic. It should be one of the constants defined in **java.awt.event.KeyEvent**, such as **KeyEvent.VK_F** or **KeyEvent.VK_Z**. (There is another version of **setMnemonic( )** that takes a **char** argument, but it is considered obsolete.) Mnemonics are not case sensitive, so in the case of **VK_A**, typing either *a* or *A* will work.

By default, the first matching letter in the menu item will be underscored. In cases in which you want to underscore a letter other than the first match, specify the index of the letter as an argument to **setDisplayedMnemonicIndex( )**, which is inherited by both **JMenu** and **JMenuItem** from **AbstractButton**. It is shown here:

void setDisplayedMnemonicIndex(int *idx*)

The index of the letter to underscore is specified by *idx*.

An accelerator can be associated with a **JMenuItem** object. It is specified by calling **setAccelerator( )**, shown next:

void setAccelerator(KeyStroke *ks*)

Here, *ks* is the key combination that is pressed to select the menu item. **KeyStroke** is a class that contains several factory methods that construct various types of keystroke accelerators. The following are three examples:

static KeyStroke getKeyStroke(char *ch*)

static KeyStroke getKeyStroke(Character *ch*, int *modifier*)

static KeyStroke getKeyStroke(int *ch*, int *modifier*)

Here, *ch* specifies the accelerator character. In the first version, the character is specified as a **char** value. In the second, it is specified as an object of type **Character**. In the third, it is a value of type **KeyEvent**, previously described. The value of *modifier* must be one or more of the following constants, defined in the **java.awt.event.InputEvent** class:

| | |
|---|---|
| InputEvent.ALT_DOWN_MASK | InputEvent.ALT_GRAPH_DOWN_MASK |
| InputEvent.CTRL_DOWN_MASK | InputEvent.META_DOWN_MASK |
| InputEvent.SHIFT_DOWN_MASK | |

Therefore, if you pass **VK_A** for the key character and **InputEvent.CTRL_DOWN_MASK** for the modifier, the accelerator key combination is CTRL-A.

The following sequence adds both mnemonics and accelerators to the File menu created by the **MenuDemo** program in the previous section. After making this change, you can select the File menu by typing ALT-F. Then, you can use the mnemonic O, C, S, or E to select an option. Alternatively, you can directly select a File menu option by pressing CTRL-O, CTRL-C, CTRL-S, or CTRL-E. Figure 34-2 shows how this menu looks when activated.

```
// Create the File menu with mnemonics and accelerators.
JMenu jmFile = new JMenu("File");
jmFile.setMnemonic(KeyEvent.VK_F);

JMenuItem jmiOpen = new JMenuItem("Open",
                                   KeyEvent.VK_O);
jmiOpen.setAccelerator(
```

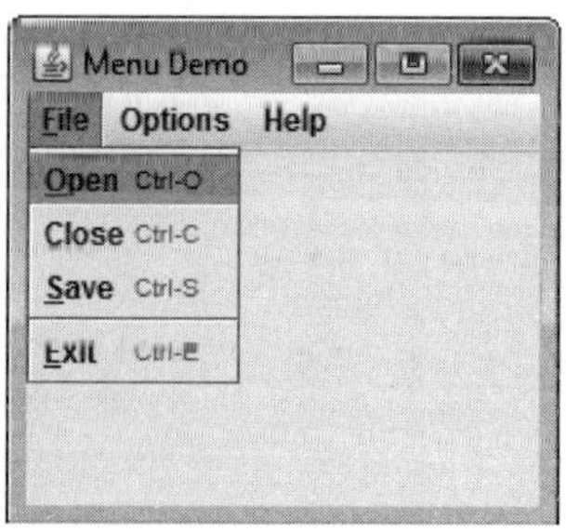


**Figure 34-2** The File menu after adding mnemonics and accelerators

```
        KeyStroke.getKeyStroke(KeyEvent.VK_O,
                               InputEvent.CTRL_DOWN_MASK));

JMenuItem jmiClose = new JMenuItem("Close",
                               KeyEvent.VK_C);
jmiClose.setAccelerator(
        KeyStroke.getKeyStroke(KeyEvent.VK_C,
                               InputEvent.CTRL_DOWN_MASK));

JMenuItem jmiSave = new JMenuItem("Save",
                               KeyEvent.VK_S);
jmiSave.setAccelerator(
        KeyStroke.getKeyStroke(KeyEvent.VK_S,
                               InputEvent.CTRL_DOWN_MASK));

JMenuItem jmiExit = new JMenuItem("Exit",
                               KeyEvent.VK_E);
jmiExit.setAccelerator(
        KeyStroke.getKeyStroke(KeyEvent.VK_E,
                               InputEvent.CTRL_DOWN_MASK));
```

## Add Images and Tooltips to Menu Items

You can add images to menu items or use images instead of text. The easiest way to add an image is to specify it when the menu item is being constructed using one of these constructors:

JMenuItem(Icon *image*)

JMenuItem(String *name*, Icon *image*)

The first creates a menu item that displays the image specified by *image*. The second creates a menu item with the name specified by *name* and the image specified by *image*. For example, here, the About menu item is associated with an image when it is created:

```
ImageIcon icon = new ImageIcon("AboutIcon.gif");
JMenuItem jmiAbout = new JMenuItem("About", icon);
```

After this addition, the icon specified by **icon** will be displayed next to the text "About" when the Help menu is displayed. This is shown in Figure 34-3. You can also add an icon to a menu item after the item has been created by calling **setIcon( )**, which is inherited from

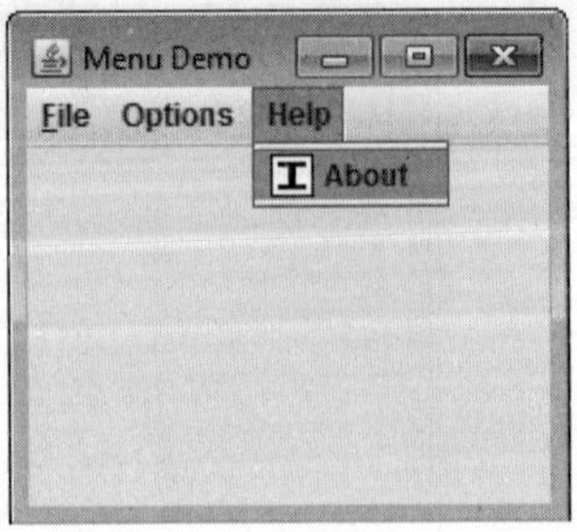


**Figure 34-3** The About item with the addition of an icon

**AbstractButton**. You can specify the horizontal alignment of the image relative to the text by calling **setHorizontalTextPosition( )**.

You can specify a disabled icon, which is shown when the menu item is disabled, by calling **setDisabledIcon( )**. Normally, when a menu item is disabled, the default icon is shown in gray. If a disabled icon is specified, then that icon is displayed when the menu item is disabled.

A *tooltip* is a small message that describes an item. It is automatically displayed if the mouse remains over the item for a moment. You can add a tooltip to a menu item by calling **setToolTipText( )** on the item, specifying the text you want displayed. It is shown here:

void setToolTipText(String *msg*)

In this case, *msg* is the string that will be displayed when the tooltip is activated. For example, this creates a tooltip for the About item:

```
jmiAbout.setToolTipText("Info about the MenuDemo program.");
```

As a point of interest, **setToolTipText( )** is inherited by **JMenuItem** from **JComponent**. This means you can add a tooltip to other types of components, such as a push button. You might want to try this on your own.



## Use JRadioButtonMenuItem and JCheckBoxMenuItem

Although the type of menu items used by the preceding examples are, as a general rule, the most commonly used, Swing defines two others: check boxes and radio buttons. These items can streamline a GUI by allowing a menu to provide functionality that would otherwise require additional, stand-alone components. Also, sometimes, including check boxes or radio buttons in a menu simply seems the most natural place for a specific set of features. Whatever your reason, Swing makes it easy to use check boxes and radio buttons in menus, and both are examined here.

To add a check box to a menu, create a **JCheckBoxMenuItem**. It defines several constructors. This is the one used in this chapter:

JCheckBoxMenuItem(String *name*)

Here, *name* specifies the name of the item. The initial state of the check box is unchecked. If you want to specify the initial state, you can use this constructor:

JCheckBoxMenuItem(String *name*, boolean *state*)

In this case, if *state* is **true**, the box is initially checked. Otherwise, it is cleared. **JCheckBoxMenuItem** also provides constructors that let you specify an icon. Here is one example:

JCheckBoxMenuItem(String *name*, Icon *icon*)

In this case, *name* specifies the name of the item, and the image associated with the item is passed in *icon*. The item is initially unchecked. Other constructors are also supported.

Check boxes in menus work like stand-alone check boxes. For example, they generate action events and item events when their state changes. Check boxes are especially useful in menus when you have options that can be selected and you want to display their selected/deselected status.

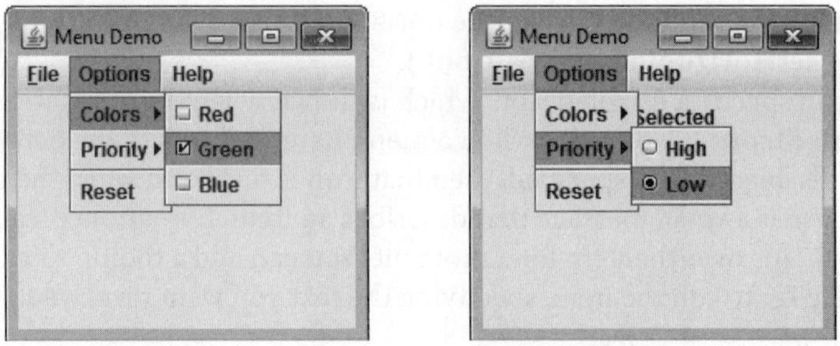


(a) (b)

**Figure 34-4** The effects of check box (a) and radio button (b) menu items

A radio button can be added to a menu by creating an object of type **JRadioButtonMenuItem**. **JRadioButtonMenuItem** inherits **JMenuItem**. It provides a rich assortment of constructors. The ones used in this chapter are shown here:

JRadioButtonMenuItem(String *name*)

JRadioButtonMenuItem(String *name*, boolean *state*)

The first constructor creates an unselected radio button menu item that is associated with the name passed in *name*. The second lets you specify the initial state of the button. If *state* is **true**, the button is initially selected. Otherwise, it is deselected. Other constructors let you specify an icon. Here is one example:

JRadioButtonMenuItem(String *name*, Icon *icon*, boolean *state*)

This creates a radio button menu item that is associated with the name passed in *name* and the image passed in *icon*. If *state* is **true**, the button is initially selected. Otherwise, it is deselected. Several other constructors are supported.

A **JRadioButtonMenuItem** works like a stand-alone radio button, generating item and action events. Like stand-alone radio buttons, menu-based radio buttons must be put into a button group in order for them to exhibit mutually exclusive selection behavior.

Because both **JCheckBoxMenuItem** and **JRadioButtonMenuItem** inherit **JMenuItem**, each has all of the functionality provided by **JMenuItem**. Aside from having the extra capabilities of check boxes and radio buttons, they act like and are used like other menu items.

To try check box and radio button menu items, first remove the code that creates the Options menu in the **MenuDemo** sample program. Then substitute the following code sequence, which uses check boxes for the Colors submenu and radio buttons for the Priority submenu. After making the substitution, the Options menu will look like those shown in Figure 34-4.

```
// Create the Options menu.
JMenu jmOptions = new JMenu("Options");

// Create the Colors submenu.
JMenu jmColors = new JMenu("Colors");
```

```
// Use check boxes for colors. This allows
// the user to select more than one color.
JCheckBoxMenuItem jmiRed = new JCheckBoxMenuItem("Red");
JCheckBoxMenuItem jmiGreen = new JCheckBoxMenuItem("Green");
JCheckBoxMenuItem jmiBlue = new JCheckBoxMenuItem("Blue");

jmColors.add(jmiRed);
jmColors.add(jmiGreen);
jmColors.add(jmiBlue);
jmOptions.add(jmColors);

// Create the Priority submenu.
JMenu jmPriority = new JMenu("Priority");

// Use radio buttons for the priority setting.
// This lets the menu show which priority is used
// but also ensures that one and only one priority
// can be selected at any one time. Notice that
// the High radio button is initially selected.
JRadioButtonMenuItem jmiHigh =
  new JRadioButtonMenuItem("High", true);
JRadioButtonMenuItem jmiLow =
  new JRadioButtonMenuItem("Low");

jmPriority.add(jmiHigh);
jmPriority.add(jmiLow);
jmOptions.add(jmPriority);

// Create button group for the radio button menu items.
ButtonGroup bg = new ButtonGroup();
bg.add(jmiHigh);
bg.add(jmiLow);

// Create the Reset menu item.
JMenuItem jmiReset = new JMenuItem("Reset");
jmOptions.addSeparator();
jmOptions.add(jmiReset);

// Finally, add the entire options menu to
// the menu bar
jmb.add(jmOptions);
```

## Create a Popup Menu

A popular alternative or addition to the menu bar is the popup menu. Typically, a popup menu is activated by clicking the right mouse button when over a component. Popup menus are supported in Swing by the **JPopupMenu** class. **JPopupMenu** has two constructors. In this chapter, only the default constructor is used:

JPopupMenu( )

It creates a default popup menu. The other constructor lets you specify a title for the menu. Whether this title is displayed is subject to the look and feel.

Part III

In general, popup menus are constructed like regular menus. First, create a **JPopupMenu** object, and then add menu items to it. Menu item selections are also handled in the same way: by listening for action events. The main difference between a popup menu and regular menu is the activation process.

Activating a popup menu requires three steps:

1. You must register a listener for mouse events.
2. Inside the mouse event handler, you must watch for the popup trigger.
3. When a popup trigger is received, you must show the popup menu by calling **show( )**.

Let's examine each of these steps closely.

A popup menu is normally activated by clicking the right mouse button when the mouse pointer is over a component for which a popup menu is defined. Thus, the *popup trigger* is usually caused by right-clicking the mouse on a popup menu–enabled component. To listen for the popup trigger, implement the **MouseListener** interface and then register the listener by calling the **addMouseListener( )** method. As described in Chapter 25, **MouseListener** defines the methods shown here:

void mouseClicked(MouseEvent *me*)

void mouseEntered(MouseEvent *me*)

void mouseExited(MouseEvent *me*)

void mousePressed(MouseEvent *me*)

void mouseReleased(MouseEvent *me*)

Of these, two are very important relative to the popup menu: **mousePressed( )** and **mouseReleased( )**. Depending on the installed look and feel, either of these two events can trigger a popup menu. For this reason, it is often easier to use a **MouseAdapter** to implement the **MouseListener** interface and simply override **mousePressed( )** and **mouseReleased( )**.

The **MouseEvent** class defines several methods, but only four are commonly needed when activating a popup menu. They are shown here:

int getX( )

int getY( )

boolean isPopupTrigger( )

Component getComponent( )

The current X,Y location of the mouse relative to the source of the event is found by calling **getX( )** and **getY( )**. These are used to specify the upper-left corner of the popup menu when it is displayed. The **isPopupTrigger( )** method returns **true** if the mouse event represents a popup trigger and **false** otherwise. You will use this method to determine when to pop up the menu. To obtain a reference to the component that generated the mouse event, call **getComponent( )**.

To actually display the popup menu, call the **show( )** method defined by **JPopupMenu**, shown next:

void show(Component *invoker*, int *upperX*, int *upperY*)

Here, *invoker* is the component relative to which the menu will be displayed. The values of *upperX* and *upperY* define the X,Y location of the upper-left corner of the menu, relative to *invoker*. A common way to obtain the invoker is to call **getComponent( )** on the event object passed to the mouse event handler.

The preceding theory can be put into practice by adding a popup Edit menu to the **MenuDemo** program shown at the start of this chapter. This menu will have three items called Cut, Copy, and Paste. Begin by adding the following instance variable to **MenuDemo**:

```
JPopupMenu jpu;
```

The **jpu** variable will hold a reference to the popup menu.

Next, add the following code sequence to the **MenuDemo** constructor:

```
// Create an Edit popup menu.
jpu = new JPopupMenu();

// Create the popup menu items.
JMenuItem jmiCut = new JMenuItem("Cut");
JMenuItem jmiCopy = new JMenuItem("Copy");
JMenuItem jmiPaste = new JMenuItem("Paste");

// Add the menu items to the popup menu.
jpu.add(jmiCut);
jpu.add(jmiCopy);
jpu.add(jmiPaste);

// Add a listener for the popup trigger.
jfrm.addMouseListener(new MouseAdapter() {
  public void mousePressed(MouseEvent me) {
    if(me.isPopupTrigger())
      jpu.show(me.getComponent(), me.getX(), me.getY());
  }
  public void mouseReleased(MouseEvent me) {
    if(me.isPopupTrigger())
      jpu.show(me.getComponent(), me.getX(), me.getY());
  }
});
```

This sequence begins by constructing an instance of **JPopupMenu** and storing it in **jpu**. Then, it creates the three menu items, Cut, Copy, and Paste, in the usual way, and adds them to **jpu**. This finishes the construction of the popup Edit menu. Popup menus are not added to the menu bar or any other object.

Next, a **MouseListener** is added by creating an anonymous inner class. This class is based on the **MouseAdapter** class, which means that the listener need only override those

Part III

methods that are relevant to the popup menu: **mousePressed( )** and **mouseReleased( )**. The adapter provides default implementations of the other **MouseListener** methods. Notice that the mouse listener is added to **jfrm**. This means that a right button click inside any part of the content pane will trigger the popup menu.

The **mousePressed( )** and **mouseReleased( )** methods call **isPopupTrigger( )** to determine if the mouse event is a popup trigger event. If it is, the popup menu is displayed by calling **show( )**. The invoker is obtained by calling **getComponent( )** on the mouse event. In this case, the invoker will be the content pane. The X,Y coordinates of the upper-left corner are obtained by calling **getX( )** and **getY( )**. This makes the menu pop up with its upper-left corner directly under the mouse pointer.

Finally, you also need to add these action listeners to the program. They handle the action events fired when the user selects an item from the popup menu.

```
jmiCut.addActionListener(this);
jmiCopy.addActionListener(this);
jmiPaste.addActionListener(this);
```

After you have made these additions, the popup menu can be activated by clicking the right mouse button anywhere inside the content pane of the application. Figure 34-5 shows the result.

One other point about the preceding example. Because the invoker of the popup menu is always **jfrm**, in this case, you could pass it explicitly rather than calling **getComponent( )**. To do so, you must make **jfrm** into an instance variable of the **MenuDemo** class (rather than a local variable) so that it is accessible to the inner class. Then you can use this call to **show( )** to display the popup menu:

```
jpu.show(jfrm, me.getX(), me.getY());
```

Although this works in this example, the advantage of using **getComponent( )** is that the popup menu will automatically pop up relative to the invoking component. Thus, the same code could be used to display any popup menu relative to its invoking object.

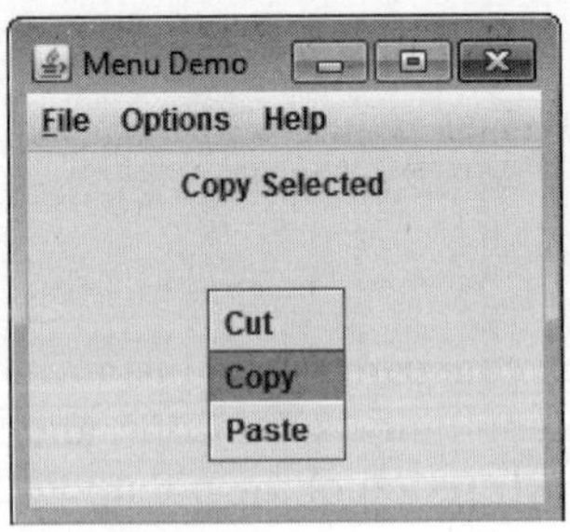


**Figure 34-5** A popup Edit menu

## Create a Toolbar

A toolbar is a component that can serve as both an alternative and as an adjunct to a menu. A toolbar contains a list of buttons (or other components) that give the user immediate access to various program options. For example, a toolbar might contain buttons that select various font options, such as bold, italics, highlight, and underline. These options can be selected without needing to drop through a menu. Typically, toolbar buttons show icons rather than text, although either or both are allowed. Furthermore, tooltips are often associated with icon-based toolbar buttons. Toolbars can be positioned on any side of a window by dragging the toolbar, or they can be dragged out of the window entirely, in which case they become free floating.

In Swing, toolbars are instances of the **JToolBar** class. Its constructors enable you to create a toolbar with or without a title. You can also specify the layout of the toolbar, which will be either horizontal or vertical. The **JToolBar** constructors are shown here:

JToolBar( )

JToolBar(String *title*)

JToolBar(int *how*)

JToolBar(String *title*, int *how*)



The first constructor creates a horizontal toolbar with no title. The second creates a horizontal toolbar with the title specified by *title*. The title will show only when the toolbar is dragged out of its window. The third creates a toolbar that is oriented as specified by *how*. The value of *how* must be either **JToolBar.VERTICAL** or **JToolBar.HORIZONTAL**. The fourth constructor creates a toolbar that has the title specified by *title* and is oriented as specified by *how*.

A toolbar is typically used with a window that uses a border layout. There are two reasons for this. First, it allows the toolbar to be initially positioned along one of the four border positions. Frequently, the top position is used. Second, it allows the toolbar to be dragged to any side of the window.

In addition to dragging the toolbar to different locations within a window, you can also drag it out of the window. Doing so creates an *undocked* toolbar. If you specify a title when you create the toolbar, then that title will be shown when the toolbar is undocked.

You add buttons (or other components) to a toolbar in much the same way that you add them to a menu bar. Simply call **add( )**. The components are shown in the toolbar in the order in which they are added.

Once you have created a toolbar, you *do not* add it to the menu bar (if one exists). Instead, you add it to the window container. As mentioned, typically you will add a toolbar to the top (that is, north) position of a border layout, using a horizontal orientation. The component that will be affected is added to the center of the border layout. Using this approach causes the program to begin running with the toolbar in the expected location. However, you can drag the toolbar to any of the other positions. Of course, you can also drag the toolbar out of the window.

To illustrate the toolbar, we will add one to the **MenuDemo** program. The toolbar will present three debugging options: set a breakpoint, clear a breakpoint, and resume program execution. Three steps are needed to add the toolbar.

First, remove this line from the program:

```
jfrm.setLayout(new FlowLayout());
```

By removing this line, the **JFrame** automatically uses a border layout.

Second, because **BorderLayout** is being used, change the line that adds the label **jlab** to the frame, as shown next:

```
jfrm.add(jlab, BorderLayout.CENTER);
```

This line explicitly adds **jlab** to the center of the border layout. (Explicitly specifying the center position is technically not necessary because, by default, components are added to the center when a border layout is used. However, explicitly specifying the center makes it clear to anyone reading the code that a border layout is being used and that **jlab** goes in the center.)

Next, add the following code, which creates the Debug toolbar:

```
// Create a Debug toolbar.
JToolBar jtb = new JToolBar("Debug");

// Load the images.
ImageIcon set = new ImageIcon("setBP.gif");
ImageIcon clear = new ImageIcon("clearBP.gif");
ImageIcon resume = new ImageIcon("resume.gif");

// Create the toolbar buttons.
JButton jbtnSet = new JButton(set);
jbtnSet.setActionCommand("Set Breakpoint");
jbtnSet.setToolTipText("Set Breakpoint");

JButton jbtnClear = new JButton(clear);
jbtnClear.setActionCommand("Clear Breakpoint");
jbtnClear.setToolTipText("Clear Breakpoint");

JButton jbtnResume = new JButton(resume);
jbtnResume.setActionCommand("Resume");
jbtnResume.setToolTipText("Resume");

// Add the buttons to the toolbar.
jtb.add(jbtnSet);
jtb.add(jbtnClear);
jtb.add(jbtnResume);

// Add the toolbar to the north position of
// the content pane.
jfrm.add(jtb, BorderLayout.NORTH);
```

Let's look at this code closely. First, a **JToolBar** is created and given the title "Debug". Then, a set of **ImageIcon** objects are created that hold the images for the toolbar buttons. Next, three toolbar buttons are created. Notice that each has an image, but no text. Also, each is explicitly given an action command and a tooltip. The action commands are set because the buttons are not given names when they are constructed. Tooltips are especially useful when applied to icon-based toolbar components because sometimes it's hard to design images that are intuitive to all users. The buttons are then added to the toolbar, and the toolbar is added to the north side of the border layout of the frame.

Finally, add the action listeners for the toolbar, as shown here:

```
// Add the toolbar action listeners.
jbtnSet.addActionListener(this);
jbtnClear.addActionListener(this);
jbtnResume.addActionListener(this);
```

Each time the user presses a toolbar button, an action event is fired, and it is handled in the same way as the other menu-related events. Figure 34-6 shows the toolbar in action.

## Use Actions



Often, a toolbar and a menu item contain items in common. For example, the same functions provided by the Debug toolbar in the preceding example might also be offered through a menu selection. In such a case, selecting an option (such as setting a breakpoint) causes the same action to occur, independently of whether the menu or the toolbar was used. Also, both the toolbar button and the menu item would (most likely) use the same icon. Furthermore, when a toolbar button is disabled, the corresponding menu item would also need to be disabled. Such a situation would normally lead to a fair amount of duplicated, interdependent code, which is less than optimal. Fortunately, Swing provides a solution: the *action.*

An action is an instance of the **Action** interface. **Action** extends the **ActionListener** interface and provides a means of combining state information with the **actionPerformed( )** event handler. This combination allows one action to manage two or more components. For example, an action lets you centralize the control and handling of a toolbar button and a menu item. Instead of having to duplicate code, your program need only create an action that automatically handles both components.

Because **Action** extends **ActionListener**, an action must provide an implementation of the **actionPerformed( )** method. This handler will process the action events generated by the objects linked to the action.

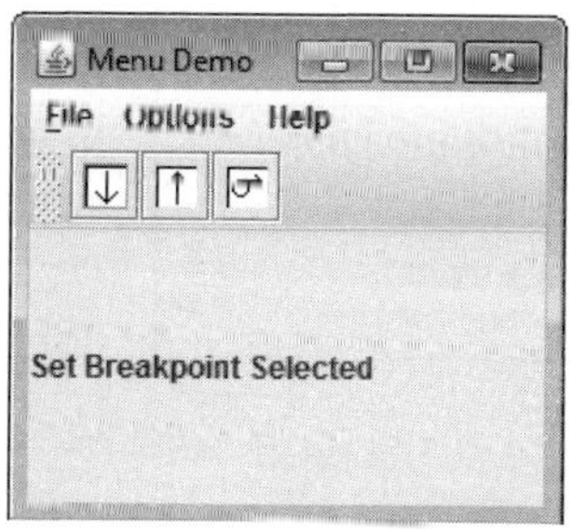


**Figure 34-6** The Debug toolbar in action

In addition to the inherited **actionPerformed( )** method, **Action** defines several methods of its own. One of particular interest is **putValue( )**. It sets the value of the various properties associated with an action and is shown here:

void putValue(String *key*, Object *val*)

It assigns *val* to the property specified by *key* that represents the desired property. Although not used by the example that follows, it is helpful to note that **Action** also supplies the **getValue( )** method that obtains a specified property. It is shown here:

Object getValue(String *key*)

It returns a reference to the property specified by *key*.

The key values used by **putValue( )** and **getValue( )** include those shown here:

| Key Value | Description |
|---|---|
| static final String ACCELERATOR_KEY | Represents the accelerator property. Accelerators are specified as **KeyStroke** objects. |
| static final String ACTION_COMMAND_KEY | Represents the action command property. An action command is specified as a string. |
| static final String DISPLAYED_MNEMONIC_INDEX_KEY | Represents the index of the character displayed as the mnemonic. This is an **Integer** value. |
| static final String LARGE_ICON_KEY | Represents the large icon associated with the action. The icon is specified as an object of type **Icon**. |
| static final String LONG_DESCRIPTION | Represents a long description of the action. This description is specified as a string. |
| static final String MNEMONIC_KEY | Represents the mnemonic property. A mnemonic is specified as a **KeyEvent** constant. |
| static final String NAME | Represents the name of the action (which also becomes the name of the button or menu item to which the action is linked). The name is specified as a string. |
| static final String SELECTED_KEY | Represents the selection status. If set, the item is selected. The state is represented by a **Boolean** value. |
| static final String SHORT_DESCRIPTION | Represents the tooltip text associated with the action. The tooltip text is specified as a string. |
| static final String SMALL_ICON | Represents the icon associated with the action. The icon is specified as an object of type **Icon**. |

For example, to set the mnemonic to the letter *X*, use this call to **putValue( )**:

```
actionOb.putValue(MNEMONIC_KEY, KeyEvent.VK_X);
```

One **Action** property that is not accessible through **putValue( )** and **getValue( )** is the enabled/disabled status. For this, you use the **setEnabled( )** and **isEnabled( )** methods. They are shown here:

void setEnabled(boolean *enabled*)

boolean isEnabled( )

For **setEnabled( )**, if *enabled* is **true**, the action is enabled. Otherwise, it is disabled. If the action is enabled, **isEnabled( )** returns **true**. Otherwise, it returns **false**.

Although you can implement all of the **Action** interface yourself, you won't usually need to. Instead, Swing provides a partial implementation called **AbstractAction** that you can extend. By extending **AbstractAction**, you need implement only one method: **actionPerformed( )**. The other **Action** methods are provided for you. **AbstractAction** provides three constructors. The one used in this chapter is shown here:

AbstractAction(String *name*, Icon *image*)

It constructs an **AbstractAction** that has the name specified by *name* and the icon specified by *image*.

Once you have created an action, it can be added to a **JToolBar** and used to construct a **JMenuItem**. To add an action to a **JToolBar**, use this version of **add( )**:

JButton add(Action *actObj*)

Here, *actObj* is the action that is being added to the toolbar. The properties defined by *actObj* are used to create a toolbar button. To create a menu item from an action, use this **JMenuItem** constructor:

JMenuItem(Action *actObj*)

Here, *actObj* is the action used to construct a menu item according to its properties.

**NOTE** In addition to **JToolBar** and **JMenuItem**, actions are also supported by several other Swing components, such as **JPopupMenu**, **JButton**, **JRadioButton**, and **JCheckBox**. **JRadioButtonMenuItem** and **JCheckBoxMenuItem** also support actions.

To illustrate the benefit of actions, we will use them to manage the Debug toolbar created in the previous section. We will also add a Debug submenu under the Options main menu. The Debug submenu will contain the same selections as the Debug toolbar: Set Breakpoint, Clear Breakpoint, and Resume. The same actions that support these items in the toolbar will also support these items in the menu. Therefore, instead of having to create duplicate code to handle both the toolbar and menu, both are handled by the actions.

Begin by creating an inner class called **DebugAction** that extends **AbstractAction**, as shown here:

```
// A class to create an action for the Debug menu
// and toolbar.
class DebugAction extends AbstractAction {
  public DebugAction(String name, Icon image, int mnem,
                     int accel, String tTip) {
    super(name, image);
    putValue(ACCELERATOR_KEY,
             KeyStroke.getKeyStroke(accel,
                                    InputEvent.CTRL_DOWN_MASK));
    putValue(MNEMONIC_KEY, mnem);
    putValue(SHORT_DESCRIPTION, tTip);
  }

  // Handle events for both the toolbar and the
  // Debug menu.
  public void actionPerformed(ActionEvent ae) {
    String comStr = ae.getActionCommand();

    jlab.setText(comStr + " Selected");

    // Toggle the enabled status of the
    // Set and Clear Breakpoint options.
    if(comStr.equals("Set Breakpoint")) {
      clearAct.setEnabled(true);
      setAct.setEnabled(false);
    } else if(comStr.equals("Clear Breakpoint")) {
      clearAct.setEnabled(false);
      setAct.setEnabled(true);
    }
  }
}
```

**DebugAction** extends **AbstractAction**. It creates an action class that will be used to define the properties associated with the Debug menu and toolbar. Its constructor has five parameters that let you specify the following items:

- Name
- Icon
- Mnemonic
- Accelerator
- Tooltip

The first two are passed to **AbstractAction**'s constructor via **super**. The other three properties are set through calls to **putValue( )**.

The **actionPerformed( )** method of **DebugAction** handles events for the action. This means that when an instance of **DebugAction** is used to create a toolbar button and a menu item, events generated by either of those components are handled by the **actionPerformed( )** method in **DebugAction**. Notice that this handler displays the selection in **jlab**. In addition, if the Set Breakpoint option is selected, then the Clear Breakpoint option is enabled and the Set Breakpoint option is disabled. If the Clear Breakpoint option is selected, then the Set Breakpoint option is enabled and the Clear Breakpoint option is disabled. This illustrates how an action can be used to enable or disable a component. When an action is disabled, it is disabled for all uses of that action. In this case, if Set Breakpoint is disabled, then it is disabled both in the toolbar and in the menu.

Next, add these **DebugAction** instance variables to **MenuDemo**:

```
DebugAction setAct;
DebugAction clearAct;
DebugAction resumeAct;
```

Next, create three **ImageIcons** that represent the Debug options, as shown here:

```
// Load the images for the actions.
ImageIcon setIcon = new ImageIcon("setBP.gif");
ImageIcon clearIcon = new ImageIcon("clearBP.gif");
ImageIcon resumeIcon = new ImageIcon("resume.gif");
```

Now, create the actions that manage the Debug options, as shown here:

```
// Create actions.
setAct =
  new DebugAction("Set Breakpoint",
                  setIcon,
                  KeyEvent.VK_S,
                  KeyEvent.VK_B,
                  "Set a break point.");

clearAct =
  new DebugAction("Clear Breakpoint",
                  clearIcon,
                  KeyEvent.VK_C,
                  KeyEvent.VK_L,
                  "Clear a break point.");

resumeAct =
  new DebugAction("Resume",
                  resumeIcon,
                  KeyEvent.VK_R,
                  KeyEvent.VK_R,
                  "Resume execution after breakpoint.");

// Initially disable the Clear Breakpoint option.
clearAct.setEnabled(false);
```

Notice that the accelerator for Set Breakpoint is B and the accelerator for Clear Breakpoint is L. The reason these keys are used rather than S and C is that these keys are already allocated by the File menu for Save and Close. However, they can still be used as mnemonics because each mnemonic is localized to its own menu. Also notice that the action that represents Clear Breakpoint is initially disabled. It will be enabled only after a breakpoint has been set.

Next, use the actions to create buttons for the toolbar and then add those buttons to the toolbar, as shown here:

```
// Create the toolbar buttons by using the actions.
JButton jbtnSet = new JButton(setAct);
JButton jbtnClear = new JButton(clearAct);
JButton jbtnResume = new JButton(resumeAct);

// Create a Debug toolbar.
JToolBar jtb = new JToolBar("Breakpoints");

// Add the buttons to the toolbar.
jtb.add(jbtnSet);
jtb.add(jbtnClear);
jtb.add(jbtnResume);

// Add the toolbar to the north position of
// the content pane.
jfrm.add(jtb, BorderLayout.NORTH);
```

Finally, create the Debug menu, as shown next:

```
// Now, create a Debug menu that goes under the Options
// menu bar item. Use the actions to create the items.
JMenu jmDebug = new JMenu("Debug");
JMenuItem jmiSetBP = new JMenuItem(setAct);
JMenuItem jmiClearBP = new JMenuItem(clearAct);
JMenuItem jmiResume = new JMenuItem(resumeAct);
jmDebug.add(jmiSetBP);
jmDebug.add(jmiClearBP);
jmDebug.add(jmiResume);
jmOptions.add(jmDebug);
```

After making these changes and additions, the actions that you created will be used to manage both the Debug menu and the toolbar. Thus, changing a property in the action (such as disabling it) will affect all uses of that action. The program will now look as shown in Figure 34-7.

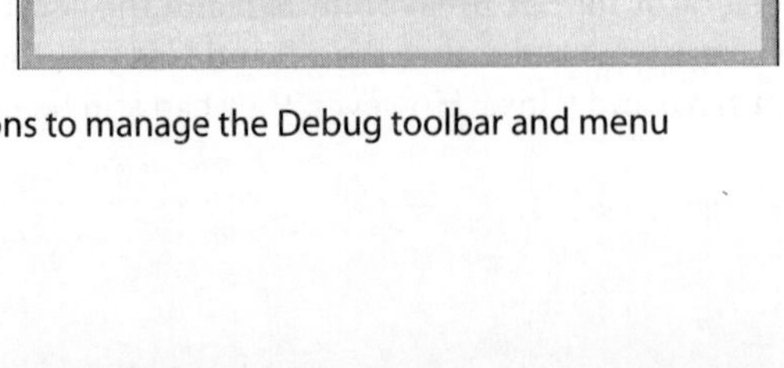


**Figure 34-7** Using actions to manage the Debug toolbar and menu

## Put the Entire MenuDemo Program Together

Throughout the course of this discussion, many changes and additions have been made to the **MenuDemo** program shown at the start of the chapter. Before concluding, it will be helpful to assemble all the pieces. Doing so not only eliminates any ambiguity about the way the pieces fit together, but it also gives you a complete menu demonstration program that you can experiment with.

The following version of **MenuDemo** includes all of the additions and enhancements described in this chapter. For clarity, the program has been reorganized, with separate methods being used to construct the various menus and toolbar. Notice that several of the menu-related variables, such as **jmb**, **jmFile**, and **jtb**, have been made into instance variables.

```
// The complete MenuDemo program.

import java.awt.*;
import java.awt.event.*;
import javax.swing.*;

class MenuDemo implements ActionListener {

  JLabel jlab;

  JMenuBar jmb;

  JToolBar jtb;

  JPopupMenu jpu;

  DebugAction setAct;
  DebugAction clearAct;
  DebugAction resumeAct;

  MenuDemo() {
    // Create a new JFrame container.
    JFrame jfrm = new JFrame("Complete Menu Demo");

    // Use default border layout.

    // Give the frame an initial size.
    jfrm.setSize(360, 200);

    // Terminate the program when the user closes the application.
    jfrm.setDefaultCloseOperation(JFrame.EXIT_ON_CLOSE);

    // Create a label that will display the menu selection.
    jlab = new JLabel();

    // Create the menu bar.
    jmb = new JMenuBar();

    // Make the File menu.
    makeFileMenu();
```

```
    // Construct the Debug actions.
    makeActions();

    // Make the toolbar.
    makeToolBar();

    // Make the Options menu.
    makeOptionsMenu();

    // Make the Help menu.
    makeHelpMenu();

    // Make the Edit popup menu.
    makeEditPUMenu();

    // Add a listener for the popup trigger.
    jfrm.addMouseListener(new MouseAdapter() {
      public void mousePressed(MouseEvent me) {
        if(me.isPopupTrigger())
          jpu.show(me.getComponent(), me.getX(), me.getY());
      }
      public void mouseReleased(MouseEvent me) {
        if(me.isPopupTrigger())
          jpu.show(me.getComponent(), me.getX(), me.getY());
      }
    });

    // Add the label to the center of the content pane.
    jfrm.add(jlab, SwingConstants.CENTER);

    // Add the toolbar to the north position of
    // the content pane.
    jfrm.add(jtb, BorderLayout.NORTH);

    // Add the menu bar to the frame.
    jfrm.setJMenuBar(jmb);

    // Display the frame.
    jfrm.setVisible(true);
  }

  // Handle menu item action events.
  // This does NOT handle events generated
  // by the Debug options.
  public void actionPerformed(ActionEvent ae) {
    // Get the action command from the menu selection.
    String comStr = ae.getActionCommand();

    // If user chooses Exit, then exit the program.
    if(comStr.equals("Exit")) System.exit(0);

    // Otherwise, display the selection.
    jlab.setText(comStr + " Selected");
  }
```

```
// An action class for the Debug menu
// and toolbar.
class DebugAction extends AbstractAction {
  public DebugAction(String name, Icon image, int mnem,
                     int accel, String tTip) {
    super(name, image);
    putValue(ACCELERATOR_KEY,
             KeyStroke.getKeyStroke(accel,
                                    InputEvent.CTRL_DOWN_MASK));
    putValue(MNEMONIC_KEY, mnem);
    putValue(SHORT_DESCRIPTION, tTip);
  }

  // Handle events for both the toolbar and the
  // Debug menu.
  public void actionPerformed(ActionEvent ae) {
    String comStr = ae.getActionCommand();

    jlab.setText(comStr + " Selected");

    // Toggle the enabled status of the
    // Set and Clear Breakpoint options.
    if(comStr.equals("Set Breakpoint")) {
      clearAct.setEnabled(true);
      setAct.setEnabled(false);
    } else if(comStr.equals("Clear Breakpoint")) {
      clearAct.setEnabled(false);
      setAct.setEnabled(true);
    }
  }
}

// Create the File menu with mnemonics and accelerators.
void makeFileMenu() {
  JMenu jmFile = new JMenu("File");
  jmFile.setMnemonic(KeyEvent.VK_F);

  JMenuItem jmiOpen = new JMenuItem("Open",
                                    KeyEvent.VK_O);
  jmiOpen.setAccelerator(
          KeyStroke.getKeyStroke(KeyEvent.VK_O,
                                 InputEvent.CTRL_DOWN_MASK));

  JMenuItem jmiClose = new JMenuItem("Close",
                                     KeyEvent.VK_C);
  jmiClose.setAccelerator(
          KeyStroke.getKeyStroke(KeyEvent.VK_C,
                                 InputEvent.CTRL_DOWN_MASK));

  JMenuItem jmiSave = new JMenuItem("Save",
                                    KeyEvent.VK_S);
  jmiSave.setAccelerator(
          KeyStroke.getKeyStroke(KeyEvent.VK_S,
                                 InputEvent.CTRL_DOWN_MASK));
```

Part III

```
    JMenuItem jmiExit = new JMenuItem("Exit",
                                      KeyEvent.VK_E);
    jmiExit.setAccelerator(
              KeyStroke.getKeyStroke(KeyEvent.VK_E,
                                     InputEvent.CTRL_DOWN_MASK));

    jmFile.add(jmiOpen);
    jmFile.add(jmiClose);
    jmFile.add(jmiSave);
    jmFile.addSeparator();
    jmFile.add(jmiExit);
    jmb.add(jmFile);

    // Add the action listeners for the File menu.
    jmiOpen.addActionListener(this);
    jmiClose.addActionListener(this);
    jmiSave.addActionListener(this);
    jmiExit.addActionListener(this);
  }

  // Create the Options menu.
  void makeOptionsMenu() {
    JMenu jmOptions = new JMenu("Options");

    // Create the Colors submenu.
    JMenu jmColors = new JMenu("Colors");

    // Use check boxes for colors. This allows
    // the user to select more than one color.
    JCheckBoxMenuItem jmiRed = new JCheckBoxMenuItem("Red");
    JCheckBoxMenuItem jmiGreen = new JCheckBoxMenuItem("Green");
    JCheckBoxMenuItem jmiBlue = new JCheckBoxMenuItem("Blue");

    // Add the items to the Colors menu.
    jmColors.add(jmiRed);
    jmColors.add(jmiGreen);
    jmColors.add(jmiBlue);
    jmOptions.add(jmColors);

    // Create the Priority submenu.
    JMenu jmPriority = new JMenu("Priority");

    // Use radio buttons for the priority setting.
    // This lets the menu show which priority is used
    // but also ensures that one and only one priority
    // can be selected at any one time. Notice that
    // the High radio button is initially selected.
    JRadioButtonMenuItem jmiHigh =
      new JRadioButtonMenuItem("High", true);
    JRadioButtonMenuItem jmiLow =
      new JRadioButtonMenuItem("Low");

    // Add the items to the Priority menu.
    jmPriority.add(jmiHigh);
```

```
    jmPriority.add(jmiLow);
    jmOptions.add(jmPriority);

    // Create a button group for the radio button
    //  menu items.
    ButtonGroup bg = new ButtonGroup();
    bg.add(jmiHigh);
    bg.add(jmiLow);

    // Now, create a Debug submenu that goes under
    // the Options menu bar item. Use actions to
    // create the items.
    JMenu jmDebug = new JMenu("Debug");
    JMenuItem jmiSetBP = new JMenuItem(setAct);
    JMenuItem jmiClearBP = new JMenuItem(clearAct);
    JMenuItem jmiResume = new JMenuItem(resumeAct);

    // Add the items to the Debug menu.
    jmDebug.add(jmiSetBP);
    jmDebug.add(jmiClearBP);
    jmDebug.add(jmiResume);
    jmOptions.add(jmDebug);

    // Create the Reset menu item.
    JMenuItem jmiReset = new JMenuItem("Reset");
    jmOptions.addSeparator();
    jmOptions.add(jmiReset);

    // Finally, add the entire options menu to
    // the menu bar
    jmb.add(jmOptions);

    // Add the action listeners for the Options menu,
    // except for those supported by the Debug menu.
    jmiRed.addActionListener(this);
    jmiGreen.addActionListener(this);
    jmiBlue.addActionListener(this);
    jmiHigh.addActionListener(this);
    jmiLow.addActionListener(this);
    jmiReset.addActionListener(this);
  }

  // Create the Help menu
  void makeHelpMenu() {
    JMenu jmHelp = new JMenu("Help");

    // Add an icon to the About menu item.
    ImageIcon icon = new ImageIcon("AboutIcon.gif");

    JMenuItem jmiAbout = new JMenuItem("About", icon);
    jmiAbout.setToolTipText("Info about the MenuDemo program.");
    jmHelp.add(jmiAbout);
    jmb.add(jmHelp);
```

```
    // Add action listener for About.
    jmiAbout.addActionListener(this);
  }

  // Construct the actions needed by the Debug menu
  // and toolbar.
  void makeActions() {
    // Load the images for the actions.
    ImageIcon setIcon = new ImageIcon("setBP.gif");
    ImageIcon clearIcon = new ImageIcon("clearBP.gif");
    ImageIcon resumeIcon = new ImageIcon("resume.gif");

    // Create actions.
    setAct =
      new DebugAction("Set Breakpoint",
                      setIcon,
                      KeyEvent.VK_S,
                      KeyEvent.VK_B,
                      "Set a break point.");

    clearAct =
      new DebugAction("Clear Breakpoint",
                      clearIcon,
                      KeyEvent.VK_C,
                      KeyEvent.VK_L,
                      "Clear a break point.");

    resumeAct =
      new DebugAction("Resume",
                      resumeIcon,
                      KeyEvent.VK_R,
                      KeyEvent.VK_R,
                      "Resume execution after breakpoint.");

    // Initially disable the Clear Breakpoint option.
    clearAct.setEnabled(false);
  }

  // Create the Debug toolbar.
  void makeToolBar() {
    // Create the toolbar buttons by using the actions.
    JButton jbtnSet = new JButton(setAct);
    JButton jbtnClear = new JButton(clearAct);
    JButton jbtnResume = new JButton(resumeAct);

    // Create the Debug toolbar.
    jtb = new JToolBar("Breakpoints");

    // Add the buttons to the toolbar.
    jtb.add(jbtnSet);
    jtb.add(jbtnClear);
    jtb.add(jbtnResume);
  }
```

```
  // Create the Edit popup menu.
  void makeEditPUMenu() {
    jpu = new JPopupMenu();

    // Create the popup menu items
    JMenuItem jmiCut = new JMenuItem("Cut");
    JMenuItem jmiCopy = new JMenuItem("Copy");
    JMenuItem jmiPaste = new JMenuItem("Paste");

    // Add the menu items to the popup menu.
    jpu.add(jmiCut);
    jpu.add(jmiCopy);
    jpu.add(jmiPaste);

    // Add the Edit popup menu action listeners.
    jmiCut.addActionListener(this);
    jmiCopy.addActionListener(this);
    jmiPaste.addActionListener(this);
  }

  public static void main(String[] args) {
    // Create the frame on the event dispatching thread.
    SwingUtilities.invokeLater(new Runnable() {
      public void run() {
        new MenuDemo();
      }
    });
  }
}
```



# Continuing Your Exploration of Swing

Swing defines a very large GUI toolkit. It has many more features that you will want to explore on your own. For example, it supplies dialog classes, such as **JOptionPane** and **JDialog**, that you can use to streamline the construction of dialog windows. It also provides additional controls beyond those introduced in Chapter 33. Two you will want to explore are **JSpinner** (which creates a spin control) and **JFormattedTextField** (which supports formatted text). You will also want to experiment with defining your own models for the various components. Frankly, the best way to become familiar with Swing's capabilities is to experiment with it.

PART

# IV Applying Java

CHAPTER

# 35 Java Beans

This chapter provides an overview of creating Java Beans. Beans are important because they allow you to build complex systems from software components. These components may be provided by you or supplied by one or more different vendors. Java Beans use an architecture called *JavaBeans* that specifies how these building blocks can operate together.

To better understand the value of Beans, consider the following: Hardware designers have a wide variety of components that can be integrated together to construct a system. Resistors, capacitors, and inductors are examples of simple building blocks. Integrated circuits provide more advanced functionality. All of these different parts can be reused. It is not necessary or possible to rebuild these capabilities each time a new system is needed. Also, the same pieces can be used in different types of circuits. This is possible because the behavior of these components is understood and documented.

The software industry also sought the benefits of reusability and interoperability of a component-based approach. To realize these benefits, a component architecture is needed that allows programs to be assembled from software building blocks, perhaps provided by different vendors. It must also be possible for a designer to select a component, understand its capabilities, and incorporate it into an application. When a new version of a component becomes available, it should be easy to incorporate this functionality into existing code. JavaBeans provides just such an architecture.

## What Is a Java Bean?

A *Java Bean* is a software component that has been designed to be reusable in a variety of different environments. There is no restriction on the capability of a Bean. It may perform a simple function, such as obtaining an inventory value, or a complex function, such as forecasting the performance of a stock portfolio. A Bean may be visible to an end user. One example of this is a button on a graphical user interface. A Bean may also be invisible to a user. Software to decode a stream of multimedia information in real time is an example of this type of building block. Finally, a Bean may be designed to work autonomously on a user's workstation or to work in cooperation with a set of other distributed components.

Software to generate a pie chart from a set of data points is an example of a Bean that can execute locally. However, a Bean that provides real-time price information from a stock or commodities exchange would need to work in cooperation with other distributed software to obtain its data.

# Advantages of Beans

The following list enumerates some of the benefits that JavaBeans technology provides for a component developer:

- A Bean obtains all the benefits of Java's "write-once, run-anywhere" paradigm.
- The properties, events, and methods of a Bean that are exposed to another application can be controlled.
- Auxiliary software can be provided to help configure a Bean. This software is only needed when the design-time parameters for that component are being set. It does not need to be included in the run-time environment.
- The state of a Bean can be saved in persistent storage and restored at a later time.
- A Bean may register to receive events from other objects and can generate events that are sent to other objects.

# Introspection

At the core of Bean programming is *introspection.* This is the process of analyzing a Bean to determine its capabilities. This is an essential feature of the JavaBeans API because it allows another application, such as a design tool, to obtain information about a component. Without introspection, the JavaBeans technology could not operate.

There are two ways in which the developer of a Bean can indicate which of its properties, events, and methods should be exposed. With the first method, simple naming conventions are used. These allow the introspection mechanisms to infer information about a Bean. In the second way, an additional class that extends the **BeanInfo** interface is provided that explicitly supplies this information. Both approaches are examined here.

## Design Patterns for Properties

A *property* is a subset of a Bean's state. The values assigned to the properties determine the behavior and appearance of that component. A property is set through a *setter* method. A property is obtained by a *getter* method. There are two types of properties: simple and indexed.

### Simple Properties

A simple property has a single value. It can be identified by the following design patterns, where **N** is the name of the property and **T** is its type:

```
public T getN( )
public void setN(T arg)
```

A read/write property has both of these methods to access its values. A read-only property has only a get method. A write-only property has only a set method.

Here are three simple read/write properties along with their getter and setter methods:

```
private double depth, height, width;

public double getDepth( ) {
  return depth;
}
public void setDepth(double d) {
  depth = d;
}

public double getHeight( ) {
  return height;
}
public void setHeight(double h) {
  height = h;
}

public double getWidth( ) {
  return width;
}
public void setWidth(double w) {
  width = w;
}
```

**NOTE** For a **boolean** property, a method of the form **is***PropertyName*( ) can also be used as an accessor.

## Indexed Properties

An indexed property consists of multiple values. It can be identified by the following design patterns, where **N** is the name of the property and **T** is its type:

> public T getN(int *index*);
> public void setN(int *index*, T *value*);
> public T[ ] getN( );
> public void setN(T[ ] *values*);

Here is an indexed property called **data** along with its getter and setter methods:

```
private double[] data;

public double getData(int index) {
  return data[index];
}
public void setData(int index, double value) {
  data[index] = value;
}
public double[ ] getData( ) {
  return data;
}
public void setData(double[ ] values) {
  data = new double[values.length];
  System.arraycopy(values, 0, data, 0, values.length);
}
```

## Design Patterns for Events

Beans use the delegation event model that was discussed earlier in this book. Beans can generate events and send them to other objects. These can be identified by the following design patterns, where **T** is the type of the event:

public void addTListener(TListener *eventListener*)
public void addTListener(TListener *eventListener*)
throws java.util.TooManyListenersException
public void removeTListener(TListener *eventListener*)

These methods are used to add or remove a listener for the specified event. The version of **addTListener( )** that does not throw an exception can be used to *multicast* an event, which means that more than one listener can register for the event notification. The version that throws **TooManyListenersException** *unicasts* the event, which means that the number of listeners can be restricted to one. In either case, **removeTListener( )** is used to remove the listener. For example, assuming an event interface type called **TemperatureListener**, a Bean that monitors temperature might supply the following methods:

```
public void addTemperatureListener(TemperatureListener tl) {
  ...
}
public void removeTemperatureListener(TemperatureListener tl) {
  ...
}
```

## Methods and Design Patterns

Design patterns are not used for naming nonproperty methods. The introspection mechanism finds all of the public methods of a Bean. Protected and private methods are not presented.

## Using the BeanInfo Interface

As the preceding discussion shows, design patterns *implicitly* determine what information is available to the user of a Bean. The **BeanInfo** interface enables you to *explicitly* control what information is available. The **BeanInfo** interface defines several methods, including these:

PropertyDescriptor[ ] getPropertyDescriptors( )
EventSetDescriptor[ ] getEventSetDescriptors( )
MethodDescriptor[ ] getMethodDescriptors( )

They return arrays of objects that provide information about the properties, events, and methods of a Bean. The classes **PropertyDescriptor**, **EventSetDescriptor**, and **MethodDescriptor** are defined within the **java.beans** package, and they describe the indicated elements. By implementing these methods, a developer can designate exactly what is presented to a user, bypassing introspection based on design patterns.

When creating a class that implements **BeanInfo**, you must call that class *bname*BeanInfo, where *bname* is the name of the Bean. For example, if the Bean is called **MyBean**, then the information class must be called **MyBeanBeanInfo**.

To simplify the use of **BeanInfo**, JavaBeans supplies the **SimpleBeanInfo** class. It provides default implementations of the **BeanInfo** interface, including the three methods just shown. You can extend this class and override one or more of the methods to explicitly control what aspects of a Bean are exposed. If you don't override a method, then design-pattern introspection will be used. For example, if you don't override **getPropertyDescriptors( )**, then design patterns are used to discover a Bean's properties. You will see **SimpleBeanInfo** in action later in this chapter.

## Bound and Constrained Properties

A Bean that has a *bound* property generates an event when the property is changed. The event is of type **PropertyChangeEvent** and is sent to objects that previously registered an interest in receiving such notifications. A class that handles this event must implement the **PropertyChangeListener** interface.

A Bean that has a *constrained* property generates an event when an attempt is made to change its value. It also generates an event of type **PropertyChangeEvent**. It, too, is sent to objects that previously registered an interest in receiving such notifications. However, those other objects have the ability to veto the proposed change by throwing a **PropertyVetoException**. This capability allows a Bean to operate differently according to its run-time environment. A class that handles this event must implement the **VetoableChangeListener** interface.

## Persistence

*Persistence* is the ability to save the current state of a Bean, including the values of a Bean's properties and instance variables, to nonvolatile storage and to retrieve them at a later time. The object serialization capabilities provided by the Java class libraries are used to provide persistence for Beans.

The easiest way to serialize a Bean is to have it implement the **java.io.Serializable** interface, which is simply a marker interface. Implementing **java.io.Serializable** makes serialization automatic. Your Bean need take no other action. Automatic serialization can also be inherited. Therefore, if any superclass of a Bean implements **java.io.Serializable**, then automatic serialization is obtained.

When using automatic serialization, you can prevent a field from being saved through the use of the **transient** keyword. Thus, data members of a Bean specified as **transient** will not be serialized.

If a Bean does not implement **java.io.Serializable**, you must provide serialization yourself, such as by implementing **java.io.Externalizable**. Otherwise, containers cannot save the configuration of your component.

## Customizers

A Bean developer can provide a *customizer* that helps another developer configure the Bean. A customizer can provide a step-by-step guide through the process that must be followed to use the component in a specific context. Online documentation can also be provided. A Bean developer has great flexibility to develop a customizer that can differentiate his or her product in the marketplace.

| Interface | Description |
|---|---|
| BeanInfo | This interface allows a designer to specify information about the properties, events, and methods of a Bean. |
| Customizer | This interface allows a designer to provide a graphical user interface through which a Bean may be configured. |
| DesignMode | Methods in this interface determine if a Bean is executing in design mode. |
| ExceptionListener | A method in this interface is invoked when an exception has occurred. |
| PropertyChangeListener | A method in this interface is invoked when a bound property is changed. |
| PropertyEditor | Objects that implement this interface allow designers to change and display property values. |
| VetoableChangeListener | A method in this interface is invoked when a constrained property is changed. |
| Visibility | Methods in this interface allow a Bean to execute in environments where a graphical user interface is not available. |

**Table 35-1** The Non-Deprecated Interfaces in **java.beans**

# The JavaBeans API

The JavaBeans functionality is provided by a set of classes and interfaces in the **java.beans** package. Beginning with JDK 9, this package is in the **java.desktop** module. This section provides a brief overview of its contents. Table 35-1 lists the non-deprecated interfaces in **java.beans** and provides a brief description of their functionality. Table 35-2 lists the classes in **java.beans**.

| Class | Description |
|---|---|
| BeanDescriptor | This class provides information about a Bean. It also allows you to associate a customizer with a Bean. |
| Beans | This class is used to obtain information about a Bean. |
| DefaultPersistenceDelegate | A concrete subclass of **PersistenceDelegate**. |
| Encoder | Encodes the state of a set of Beans. Can be used to write this information to a stream. |
| EventHandler | Supports dynamic event listener creation. |
| EventSetDescriptor | Instances of this class describe an event that can be generated by a Bean. |
| Expression | Encapsulates a call to a method that returns a result. |
| FeatureDescriptor | This is the superclass of the **PropertyDescriptor**, **EventSetDescriptor**, and **MethodDescriptor** classes, among others. |

**Table 35-2** The Classes in **java.beans**

| Class | Description |
|---|---|
| IndexedPropertyChangeEvent | A subclass of **PropertyChangeEvent** that represents a change to an indexed property. |
| IndexedPropertyDescriptor | Instances of this class describe an indexed property of a Bean. |
| IntrospectionException | An exception of this type is generated if a problem occurs when analyzing a Bean. |
| Introspector | This class analyzes a Bean and constructs a **BeanInfo** object that describes the component. |
| MethodDescriptor | Instances of this class describe a method of a Bean. |
| ParameterDescriptor | Instances of this class describe a method parameter. |
| PersistenceDelegate | Handles the state information of an object. |
| PropertyChangeEvent | This event is generated when bound or constrained properties are changed. It is sent to objects that registered an interest in these events and that implement either the **PropertyChangeListener** or **VetoableChangeListener** interface. |
| PropertyChangeListenerProxy | Extends **EventListenerProxy** and implements **PropertyChangeListener**. |
| PropertyChangeSupport | Beans that support bound properties can use this class to notify **PropertyChangeListener** objects. |
| PropertyDescriptor | Instances of this class describe a property of a Bean. |
| PropertyEditorManager | This class locates a **PropertyEditor** object for a given type. |
| PropertyEditorSupport | This class provides functionality that can be used when writing property editors. |
| PropertyVetoException | An exception of this type is generated if a change to a constrained property is vetoed. |
| SimpleBeanInfo | This class provides functionality that can be used when writing **BeanInfo** classes. |
| Statement | Encapsulates a call to a method. |
| VetoableChangeListenerProxy | Extends **EventListenerProxy** and implements **VetoableChangeListener**. |
| VetoableChangeSupport | Beans that support constrained properties can use this class to notify **VetoableChangeListener** objects. |
| XMLDecoder | Used to read a Bean from an XML document. |
| XMLEncoder | Used to write a Bean to an XML document. |

**Table 35-2** The Classes in **java.beans** *(continued)*

Although it is beyond the scope of this chapter to discuss all of the classes, four are of particular interest: **Introspector**, **PropertyDescriptor**, **EventSetDescriptor**, and **MethodDescriptor**. Each is briefly examined here.

Part IV

## Introspector

The **Introspector** class provides several static methods that support introspection. Of most interest is **getBeanInfo( )**. This method returns a **BeanInfo** object that can be used to obtain information about the Bean. The **getBeanInfo( )** method has several forms, including the one shown here:

static BeanInfo getBeanInfo(Class<?> *bean*) throws IntrospectionException

The returned object contains information about the Bean specified by *bean.*

## PropertyDescriptor

The **PropertyDescriptor** class describes the characteristics of a Bean property. It supports several methods that manage and describe properties. For example, you can determine if a property is bound by calling **isBound( )**. To determine if a property is constrained, call **isConstrained( )**. You can obtain the name of a property by calling **getName( )**.

## EventSetDescriptor

The **EventSetDescriptor** class represents a set of Bean events. It supports several methods that obtain the methods that a Bean uses to add or remove event listeners, and to otherwise manage events. For example, to obtain the method used to add listeners, call **getAddListenerMethod( )**. To obtain the method used to remove listeners, call **getRemoveListenerMethod( )**. To obtain the type of a listener, call **getListenerType( )**. You can obtain the name of an event set by calling **getName( )**.

## MethodDescriptor

The **MethodDescriptor** class represents a Bean method. To obtain the name of the method, call **getName( )**. You can obtain information about the method by calling **getMethod( )**, shown here:

Method getMethod( )

An object of type **Method** that describes the method is returned.

# A Bean Example

This chapter concludes with an example that illustrates various aspects of Bean programming, including introspection and using a **BeanInfo** class. It also makes use of the **Introspector**, **PropertyDescriptor**, and **EventSetDescriptor** classes. The example uses three classes. The first is a Bean called **Colors**, shown here:

```
// A simple Bean.
import java.awt.*;
import java.awt.event.*;
import java.io.Serializable;

public class Colors extends Canvas implements Serializable {
  transient private Color color; // not persistent
  private boolean rectangular; // is persistent
```

```
  public Colors() {
    addMouseListener(new MouseAdapter() {
      public void mousePressed(MouseEvent me) {
        change();
      }
    });
    rectangular = false;
    setSize(200, 100);
    change();
  }

  public boolean getRectangular() {
    return rectangular;
  }

  public void setRectangular(boolean flag) {
    this.rectangular = flag;
    repaint();
  }

  public void change() {
    color = randomColor();
    repaint();
  }

  private Color randomColor() {
    int r = (int)(255*Math.random());
    int g = (int)(255*Math.random());
    int b = (int)(255*Math.random());
    return new Color(r, g, b);
  }

  public void paint(Graphics g) {
    Dimension d = getSize();
    int h = d.height;
    int w = d.width;
    g.setColor(color);
    if(rectangular) {
      g.fillRect(0, 0, w-1, h-1);
    }
    else {
      g.fillOval(0, 0, w-1, h-1);
    }
  }
}
```

The **Colors** Bean displays a colored object within a frame. The color of the component is determined by the private **Color** variable **color**, and its shape is determined by the private **boolean** variable **rectangular**. The constructor defines an anonymous inner class that extends **MouseAdapter** and overrides its **mousePressed( )** method. The **change( )** method is invoked in response to mouse presses. It selects a random color and then repaints the component. The **getRectangular( )** and **setRectangular( )** methods provide access to the one property of this Bean. The **change( )** method calls **randomColor( )** to choose a color and then calls **repaint( )** to make the change visible. Notice that the **paint( )** method uses the **rectangular** and **color** variables to determine how to present the Bean.

The next class is **ColorsBeanInfo**. It is a subclass of **SimpleBeanInfo** that provides explicit information about **Colors**. It overrides **getPropertyDescriptors( )** in order to designate which properties are presented to a Bean user. In this case, the only property exposed is **rectangular**. The method creates and returns a **PropertyDescriptor** object for the **rectangular** property. The **PropertyDescriptor** constructor that is used is shown here:

PropertyDescriptor(String *property*, Class<?> *beanCls*)
  throws IntrospectionException

Here, the first argument is the name of the property, and the second argument is the class of the Bean.

```
// A Bean information class.
import java.beans.*;
public class ColorsBeanInfo extends SimpleBeanInfo {
  public PropertyDescriptor[] getPropertyDescriptors() {
    try {
      PropertyDescriptor rectangular = new
         PropertyDescriptor("rectangular", Colors.class);
      PropertyDescriptor[] pd = {rectangular};
      return pd;
    }
    catch(Exception e) {
      System.out.println("Exception caught. " + e);
    }
    return null;
  }
}
```

The final class is called **IntrospectorDemo**. It uses introspection to display the properties and events that are available within the **Colors** Bean.

```
// Show properties and events.
import java.awt.*;
import java.beans.*;

public class IntrospectorDemo {
  public static void main(String[] args) {
    try {
      Class<?> c = Class.forName("Colors");
      BeanInfo beanInfo = Introspector.getBeanInfo(c);

      System.out.println("Properties:");
      PropertyDescriptor[] propertyDescriptor =
        beanInfo.getPropertyDescriptors();
      for(int i = 0; i < propertyDescriptor.length; i++) {
        System.out.println("\t" + propertyDescriptor[i].getName());
      }
```

```
      System.out.println("Events:");
      EventSetDescriptor[] eventSetDescriptor =
        beanInfo.getEventSetDescriptors();
      for(int i = 0; i < eventSetDescriptor.length; i++) {
        System.out.println("\t" + eventSetDescriptor[i].getName());
      }
    }
    catch(Exception e) {
      System.out.println("Exception caught. " + e);
    }
  }
}
```

The output from this program is the following:

```
Properties:
        rectangular
Events:
        mouseWheel
        mouse
        mouseMotion
        component
        hierarchyBounds
        focus
        hierarchy
        propertyChange
        inputMethod
        key
```

Notice two things in the output. First, because **ColorsBeanInfo** overrides **getPropertyDescriptors( )** such that the only property returned is **rectangular**, only the **rectangular** property is displayed. However, because **getEventSetDescriptors( )** is not overridden by **ColorsBeanInfo**, design-pattern introspection is used, and all events are found, including those in **Colors**' superclass, **Canvas**. Remember, if you don't override one of the "get" methods defined by **SimpleBeanInfo**, then the default, design-pattern introspection is used. To observe the difference that **ColorsBeanInfo** makes, erase its class file and then run **IntrospectorDemo** again. This time it will report more properties.

CHAPTER

# 36 Introducing Servlets

This chapter presents an introduction to *servlets.* Servlets are small programs that execute on the server side of a web connection. The topic of servlets is quite large, and it is beyond the scope of this chapter to cover it all. Instead, we will focus on the core concepts, interfaces, and classes, and develop several examples.

## Background

In order to understand the advantages of servlets, you must have a basic understanding of how web browsers and servers cooperate to provide content to a user. Consider a request for a static web page. A user enters a Uniform Resource Locator (URL) into a browser. The browser generates an HTTP request to the appropriate web server. The web server maps this request to a specific file. That file is returned in an HTTP response to the browser. The HTTP header in the response indicates the type of the content. The Multipurpose Internet Mail Extensions (MIME) are used for this purpose. For example, ordinary ASCII text has a MIME type of text/plain. The Hypertext Markup Language (HTML) source code of a web page has a MIME type of text/html.

Now consider dynamic content. Assume that an online store uses a database to store information about its business. This would include items for sale, prices, availability, orders, and so forth. It wishes to make this information accessible to customers via web pages. The contents of those web pages must be dynamically generated to reflect the latest information in the database.

In the early days of the Web, a server could dynamically construct a page by creating a separate process to handle each client request. The process would open connections to one or more databases in order to obtain the necessary information. It communicated with the web server via an interface known as the Common Gateway Interface (CGI). CGI allowed the separate process to read data from the HTTP request and write data to the HTTP response. A variety of different languages were used to build CGI programs. These included C, C++, and Perl.

However, CGI suffered serious performance problems. It was expensive in terms of processor and memory resources to create a separate process for each client request. It was also expensive to open and close database connections for each client request. In addition, the CGI programs were not platform-independent. Therefore, other techniques were introduced. Among these are servlets.

Servlets offer several advantages in comparison with CGI. First, performance is significantly better. Servlets execute within the address space of a web server. It is not necessary to create a separate process to handle each client request. Second, servlets are platform-independent because they are written in Java. Third, it is possible to enforce a set of restrictions to protect the resources on a server machine. Finally, the full functionality of the Java class libraries is available to a servlet. It can communicate with other software via the sockets and RMI mechanisms that you have seen already.

## The Life Cycle of a Servlet

Three methods are central to the life cycle of a servlet. These are **init( )**, **service( )**, and **destroy( )**. They are implemented by every servlet and are invoked at specific times by the server. Let us consider a typical user scenario to understand when these methods are called.

First, assume that a user enters a Uniform Resource Locator (URL) to a web browser. The browser then generates an HTTP request for this URL. This request is then sent to the appropriate server.

Second, this HTTP request is received by the web server. The server maps this request to a particular servlet. The servlet is dynamically retrieved and loaded into the address space of the server.

Third, the server invokes the **init( )** method of the servlet. This method is invoked only when the servlet is first loaded into memory. It is possible to pass initialization parameters to the servlet so it may configure itself.

Fourth, the server invokes the **service( )** method of the servlet. This method is called to process the HTTP request. You will see that it is possible for the servlet to read data that has been provided in the HTTP request. It may also formulate an HTTP response for the client.

The servlet remains in the server's address space and is available to process any other HTTP requests received from clients. The **service( )** method is called for each HTTP request.

Finally, the server may decide to unload the servlet from its memory. The algorithms by which this determination is made are specific to each server. The server calls the **destroy( )** method to relinquish any resources such as file handles that are allocated for the servlet. Important data may be saved to a persistent store. The memory allocated for the servlet and its objects can then be garbage collected.

## Servlet Development Options

To experiment with servlets, you will need access to a servlet container/server. Two popular ones are Glassfish and Apache Tomcat. The one used in this chapter is Tomcat. Apache Tomcat is an open-source product maintained by the Apache Software Foundation.

Although IDEs such as NetBeans and Eclipse are very useful and can streamline the creation of servlets, they are not used in this chapter. The way you develop and deploy servlets differs among IDEs, and it is simply not possible for this book to address each environment. Furthermore, many readers will be using the command-line tools rather than an IDE. Therefore, if you are using an IDE, you must refer to the instructions for that environment for information concerning the development and deployment of servlets. For this reason, the instructions given here and elsewhere in this chapter assume that only the command-line tools are employed. Thus, they will work for nearly any reader.

As stated, this chapter uses Tomcat in the examples. It provides a simple, yet effective way to experiment with servlets using only the command line tools. It is also widely available in various programming environments. Furthermore, since only command-line tools are used, you don't need to download and install an IDE just to experiment with servlets. Understand, however, that even if you are developing in an environment that uses a different servlet container, the concepts presented here still apply. It is just that the mechanics of preparing a servlet for testing will be slightly different.

**REMEMBER** The instructions for developing and deploying servlets in this chapter are based on Tomcat and use only command-line tools. If you are using an IDE and/or a different servlet container/server, consult the documentation for your environment.

## Using Tomcat

Tomcat contains the class libraries, documentation, and run-time support that you will need to create and test servlets. Several versions of Tomcat are available, and at the time of this writing, the latest released version is 10.0.11. The instructions that follow will also use 10.0.11. This version of Tomcat is used here because it is a modern version of Tomcat and will work for a very wide range of readers. You can download Tomcat from **tomcat.apache.org**. You should choose a version appropriate to your environment.

Once you have installed the correct version of Tomcat for your operating system, you will find everything you need for these examples under directly, the default location is:

```
<install-dir>/apache-tomcat-10.1.11
```

where <install-dir> is the name of the directory where you chose to install Tomcat. This is the location assumed by the examples in this book. If you load Tomcat in a different location (or use a different version of Tomcat), you will need to make appropriate changes to the examples. You may need to set the environmental variable **JAVA_HOME** to the top-level directory in which the Java Development Kit is installed.

**NOTE** All of the directories shown in this section assume Tomcat 10.0.11. If you install a different version of Tomcat, then you will need to adjust the directory names and paths to match those used by the version you installed.

Once installed, you start Tomcat by running **catalina.sh start** from the **bin** directly under the **<install-dir>/apache-tomcat-10.1.11** directory. To stop Tomcat, execute **catalina.sh stop**, also in the **bin** directory.

The classes and interfaces needed to build servlets are contained in **servlet-api.jar**, which is in the following directory:

```
<install-dir>/apache-tomcat-10.1.11/lib
```

Part IV

To make **servlet-api.jar** accessible, update your **CLASSPATH** environment variable so that it includes

```
<install-dir>/apache-tomcat-10.1.11/lib/servlet-api.jar
```

Alternatively, you can specify this file when you compile the servlets. For example, the following command compiles the first servlet example:

```
javac HelloServlet.java -classpath "<install-dir>/apache-tomcat-10.1.11/lib/
servlet-api.jar"
```

Once you have compiled a servlet, you must enable Tomcat to find it. For our purposes, this means putting it into a directory under Tomcat's **webapps** directory and entering its name into a **web.xml** file. To keep things simple, the examples in this chapter use the directory and **web.xml** file that Tomcat supplies for its own sample servlets. This way, you won't have to create any files or directories just to experiment with the sample servlets. Here is the procedure that you will follow.

First, copy the servlet's class file into the following directory:

```
<install-dir>/apache-tomcat-10.1.11/webapps/examples/WEB-INF/classes
```

Next, add the servlet's name and mapping to the **web.xml** file in the following directory:

```
<install-dir>/apache-tomcat-10.1.11/webapps/examples/WEB-INF
```

For instance, assuming the first example, called **HelloServlet**, you will add the following lines in the section that defines the servlets:

```
<servlet>
  <servlet-name>HelloServlet</servlet-name>
  <servlet-class>HelloServlet</servlet-class>
</servlet>
```

Next, you will add the following lines to the section that defines the servlet mappings:

```
<servlet-mapping>
  <servlet-name>HelloServlet</servlet-name>
  <url-pattern>/servlets/servlet/HelloServlet</url-pattern>
</servlet-mapping>
```

Follow this same general procedure for all of the examples.

## A Simple Servlet

To become familiar with the key servlet concepts, we will begin by building and testing a simple servlet. The basic steps are the following:

1. Create and compile the servlet source code. Then, copy the servlet's class file to the proper directory, and add the servlet's name and mappings to the proper **web.xml** file.
2. Start Tomcat.
3. Start a web browser and request the servlet.

Let us examine each of these steps in detail.

## Create and Compile the Servlet Source Code

To begin, create a file named **HelloServlet.java** that contains the following program:

```
import java.io.*;
import jakarta.servlet.*;

public class HelloServlet extends GenericServlet {

  public void service(ServletRequest request,
    ServletResponse response)
  throws ServletException, IOException {
    response.setContentType("text/html");
    PrintWriter pw = response.getWriter();
    pw.println("<B>Hello!");
    pw.close();
  }
}
```

Let's look closely at this program. First, note that it imports the **jakarta.servlet** package. This package contains the classes and interfaces required to build servlets. You will learn more about these later in this chapter. Next, the program defines **HelloServlet** as a subclass of **GenericServlet**. The **GenericServlet** class provides functionality that simplifies the creation of a servlet. For example, it provides versions of **init( )** and **destroy( )**, which may be used as is. You need supply only the **service( )** method.

Inside **HelloServlet**, the **service( )** method (which is inherited from **GenericServlet**) is overridden. This method handles requests from a client. Notice that the first argument is a **ServletRequest** object. This enables the servlet to read data that is provided via the client request. The second argument is a **ServletResponse** object. This enables the servlet to formulate a response for the client.

The call to **setContentType( )** establishes the MIME type of the HTTP response. In this program, the MIME type is text/html. This indicates that the browser should interpret the content as HTML source code.

Next, the **getWriter( )** method obtains a **PrintWriter**. Anything written to this stream is sent to the client as part of the HTTP response. Then **println( )** is used to write some simple HTML source code as the HTTP response.

Compile this source code and place the **HelloServlet.class** file in the proper Tomcat directory as described in the previous section. Also, add **HelloServlet** to the **web.xml** file, as described earlier.

## Start Tomcat

Start Tomcat as explained earlier. Tomcat must be running before you try to execute a servlet.

## Start a Web Browser and Request the Servlet

Start a web browser and enter the URL shown here:

```
http://localhost:8080/examples/servlets/servlet/HelloServlet
```

Alternatively, you may enter the URL shown here:

```
http://127.0.0.1:8080/examples/servlets/servlet/HelloServlet
```

This can be done because 127.0.0.1 is defined as the IP address of the local machine.

You will observe the output of the servlet in the browser display area. It will contain the string **Hello!** in bold type.

## The Servlet API

Two packages contain the classes and interfaces that are required to build the servlets described in this chapter. These are **jakarta.servlet** and **jakarta.servlet.http**. They constitute the core of the Servlet API. Keep in mind that these packages are not part of the Java core packages. Therefore, they are not included with Java SE. Instead, they are provided by the servlet implementation, which is Tomcat in this case.

The Servlet API has been in a process of ongoing development and enhancement. The servlet specification supported by Tomcat 10.0.11 is version 5.0, and is the version used in this edition of this book. However, because this chapter discusses the core of the Servlet API, the information presented here applies to most versions of the servlet specification (and Tomcat), except as noted.

Before continuing, an important point needs to be made. Prior to servlet specification 5, the Servlet API packages began with **javax**, not **jakarta**. Therefore, if you are using a version of Tomcat earlier than 10 (or a servlet implementation based on a specification prior to 5), then you will need to change all references in the sample programs from **jakarta** to **javax**. For example, **jakarta.servlet** would become **javax.servlet**.

**REMEMBER** For servlet implementations based on servlet specifications prior to 5, the API will be in **javax**, not **jakarta**, packages.

## The jakarta.servlet Package

The **jakarta.servlet** package contains a number of interfaces and classes that establish the framework in which servlets operate. The following table summarizes several key interfaces that are provided in this package. The most significant of these is **Servlet**. All servlets must implement this interface or extend a class that implements the interface. The **ServletRequest** and **ServletResponse** interfaces are also very important.

| Interface | Description |
|---|---|
| Servlet | Declares life cycle methods for a servlet |
| ServletConfig | Allows servlets to get initialization parameters |
| ServletContext | Enables servlets to log events and access information about their environment |
| ServletRequest | Used to read data from a client request |
| ServletResponse | Used to write data to a client response |

The following table summarizes the core classes that are provided in the **jakarta.servlet** package:

| Class | Description |
|---|---|
| GenericServlet | Implements the **Servlet** and **ServletConfig** interfaces |
| ServletInputStream | Encapsulates an input stream for reading requests from a client |
| ServletOutputStream | Encapsulates an output stream for writing responses to a client |
| ServletException | Indicates a servlet error occurred |
| UnavailableException | Indicates a servlet is unavailable |

Let us examine these interfaces and classes in more detail.

## The Servlet Interface

All servlets must implement the **Servlet** interface. It declares the **init( )**, **service( )**, and **destroy( )** methods that are called by the server during the life cycle of a servlet. A method is also provided that allows a servlet to obtain any initialization parameters. The methods defined by **Servlet** are shown in Table 36-1.

The **init( )**, **service( )**, and **destroy( )** methods are the life cycle methods of the servlet. These are invoked by the server. The **getServletConfig( )** method is called by the servlet to obtain initialization parameters. A servlet developer overrides the **getServletInfo( )** method to provide a string with useful information (for example, the version number). This method is also invoked by the server.

| Method | Description |
|---|---|
| void destroy( ) | Called when the servlet is unloaded. |
| ServletConfig getServletConfig( ) | Returns a **ServletConfig** object that contains any initialization parameters. |
| String getServletInfo( ) | Returns a string describing the servlet. |
| void init(ServletConfig *sc*) throws ServletException | Called when the servlet is initialized. Initialization parameters for the servlet can be obtained from *sc*. A **ServletException** should be thrown if the servlet cannot be initialized. |
| void service(ServletRequest *req*, ServletResponse *res*) throws ServletException, IOException | Called to process a request from a client. The request from the client can be read from *req*. The response to the client can be written to *res*. An exception is generated if a servlet or I/O problem occurs. |

**Table 36-1** The Methods Defined by **Servlet**

## The ServletConfig Interface

The **ServletConfig** interface allows a servlet to obtain configuration data when it is loaded. The methods declared by this interface are summarized here:

| Method | Description |
|---|---|
| ServletContext getServletContext( ) | Returns the context for this servlet |
| String getInitParameter(String *param*) | Returns the value of the initialization parameter named *param* |
| Enumeration<String> getInitParameterNames( ) | Returns an enumeration of all initialization parameter names |
| String getServletName( ) | Returns the name of the invoking servlet |

## The ServletContext Interface

The **ServletContext** interface enables servlets to obtain information about their environment. Several of its methods are summarized in Table 36-2.

## The ServletRequest Interface

The **ServletRequest** interface enables a servlet to obtain information about a client request. Several of its methods are summarized in Table 36-3.

## The ServletResponse Interface

The **ServletResponse** interface enables a servlet to formulate a response for a client. Several of its methods are summarized in Table 36-4.

| Method | Description |
|---|---|
| Object getAttribute(String *attr*) | Returns the value of the server attribute named *attr* |
| String getMimeType(String *file*) | Returns the MIME type of *file* |
| String getRealPath(String *vpath*) | Returns the real (i.e., absolute) path that corresponds to the relative path *vpath* |
| String getServerInfo( ) | Returns information about the server |
| void log(String *s*) | Writes *s* to the servlet log |
| void log(String *s*, Throwable *e*) | Writes *s* and the stack trace for *e* to the servlet log |
| void setAttribute(String *attr*, Object *val*) | Sets the attribute specified by *attr* to the value passed in *val* |

**Table 36-2** Various Methods Defined by **ServletContext**

| Method | Description |
|---|---|
| Object getAttribute(String *attr*) | Returns the value of the attribute named *attr*. |
| String getCharacterEncoding( ) | Returns the character encoding of the request. |
| int getContentLength( ) | Returns the size of the request. The value –1 is returned if the size is unavailable. |
| String getContentType( ) | Returns the type of the request. A **null** value is returned if the type cannot be determined. |
| ServletInputStream getInputStream( ) throws IOException | Returns a **ServletInputStream** that can be used to read binary data from the request. An **IllegalStateException** is thrown if **getReader( )** has been previously invoked on this object. |
| String getParameter(String *pname*) | Returns the value of the parameter named *pname*. |
| Enumeration<String> getParameterNames( ) | Returns an enumeration of the parameter names for this request. |
| String[ ] getParameterValues(String *name*) | Returns an array containing values associated with the parameter specified by *name*. |
| String getProtocol( ) | Returns a description of the protocol. |
| BufferedReader getReader( ) throws IOException | Returns a buffered reader that can be used to read text from the request. An **IllegalStateException** is thrown if **getInputStream( )** has been previously invoked on this object. |
| String getRemoteAddr( ) | Returns the string equivalent of the client IP address. |
| String getRemoteHost( ) | Returns the string equivalent of the client host name. |
| String getScheme( ) | Returns the transmission scheme of the URL used for the request (for example, "http", "ftp"). |
| String getServerName( ) | Returns the name of the server. |
| int getServerPort( ) | Returns the port number. |

**Table 36-3** Various Methods Defined by **ServletRequest**

| Method | Description |
|---|---|
| String getCharacterEncoding( ) | Returns the character encoding for the response. |
| ServletOutputStream getOutputStream( ) throws IOException | Returns a **ServletOutputStream** that can be used to write binary data to the response. An **IllegalStateException** is thrown if **getWriter( )** has been previously invoked on this object. |
| PrintWriter getWriter( ) throws IOException | Returns a **PrintWriter** that can be used to write character data to the response. An **IllegalStateException** is thrown if **getOutputStream( )** has been previously invoked on this object. |
| void setContentLength(int *size*) | Sets the content length for the response to *size*. |
| void setContentType(String *type*) | Sets the content type for the response to *type*. |

**Table 36-4** Various Methods Defined by **ServletResponse**

## The GenericServlet Class

The **GenericServlet** class provides implementations of the basic life cycle methods for a servlet. **GenericServlet** implements the **Servlet** and **ServletConfig** interfaces. In addition, a method to append a string to the server log file is available. The signatures of this method are shown here:

void log(String *s*)
void log(String *s*, Throwable *e*)

Here, *s* is the string to be appended to the log, and *e* is an exception that occurred.

## The ServletInputStream Class

The **ServletInputStream** class extends **InputStream**. It is implemented by the servlet container and provides an input stream that a servlet developer can use to read the data from a client request. In addition to the input methods inherited from **InputStream**, a method is provided to read bytes from the stream. It is shown here:

int readLine(byte[ ] *buffer*, int *offset*, int *size*) throws IOException

Here, *buffer* is the array into which *size* bytes are placed starting at *offset*. The method returns the actual number of bytes read or –1 if an end-of-stream condition is encountered.

## The ServletOutputStream Class

The **ServletOutputStream** class extends **OutputStream**. It is implemented by the servlet container and provides an output stream that a servlet developer can use to write data to a client response. In addition to the output methods provided by **OutputStream**, it also defines the **print( )** and **println( )** methods, which output data to the stream.

## The Servlet Exception Classes

**jakarta.servlet** defines two exceptions. The first is **ServletException**, which indicates that a servlet problem has occurred. The second is **UnavailableException**, which extends **ServletException**. It indicates that a servlet is unavailable.

# Reading Servlet Parameters

The **ServletRequest** interface includes methods that allow you to read the names and values of parameters that are included in a client request. We will develop a servlet that illustrates their use. The example contains two files. A web page is defined in **PostParameters.html**, and a servlet is defined in **PostParametersServlet.java**.

The HTML source code for **PostParameters.html** is shown in the following listing. It defines a table that contains two labels and two text fields. One of the labels is Employee and the other is Phone. There is also a submit button. Notice that the action parameter of the form tag specifies a URL. The URL identifies the servlet to process the HTTP POST request.

```
<html>
<body>
```

```
<center>
<form name="Form1"
  method="post"
  action="http://localhost:8080/examples/servlets/
          servlet/PostParametersServlet">
<table>
<tr>
  <td><B>Employee</td>
  <td><input type=textbox name="e" size="25" value=""></td>
</tr>
<tr>
  <td><B>Phone</td>
  <td><input type=textbox name="p" size="25" value=""></td>
</tr>
</table>
<input type=submit value="Submit">
</body>
</html>
```

The source code for **PostParametersServlet.java** is shown in the following listing. The **service( )** method is overridden to process client requests. The **getParameterNames( )** method returns an enumeration of the parameter names. These are processed in a loop. You can see that the parameter name and value are output to the client. The parameter value is obtained via the **getParameter( )** method.

```
import java.io.*;
import java.util.*;
import jakarta.servlet.*;

public class PostParametersServlet
extends GenericServlet {

  public void service(ServletRequest request,
    ServletResponse response)
  throws ServletException, IOException {

    // Get print writer.
    PrintWriter pw = response.getWriter();

    // Get enumeration of parameter names.
    Enumeration<String> e = request.getParameterNames();

    // Display parameter names and values.
    while(e.hasMoreElements()) {
      String pname = e.nextElement();
      pw.print(pname + " = ");
      String pvalue = request.getParameter(pname);
      pw.println(pvalue);
   }
   pw.close();
 }
}
```

Compile the servlet. Next, copy it to the appropriate directory and update the **web.xml** file as previously described. Then, perform these steps to test this example:

1. Start Tomcat (if it is not already running).
2. Display the web page in a browser.
3. Enter an employee name and phone number in the text fields.
4. Submit the web page.

After following these steps, the browser will display a response that is dynamically generated by the servlet.

# The jakarta.servlet.http Package

The preceding examples have used the classes and interfaces defined in **jakarta.servlet**, such as **ServletRequest**, **ServletResponse**, and **GenericServlet**, to illustrate the basic functionality of servlets. However, when working with HTTP, you will normally use the interfaces and classes in **jakarta.servlet.http**. As you will see, its functionality makes it easy to build servlets that work with HTTP requests and responses.

The following table summarizes the interfaces used in this chapter:

| Interface | Description |
|---|---|
| HttpServletRequest | Enables servlets to read data from an HTTP request |
| HttpServletResponse | Enables servlets to write data to an HTTP response |
| HttpSession | Allows session data to be read and written |

The following table summarizes the classes used in this chapter. The most important of these is **HttpServlet**. Servlet developers typically extend this class in order to process HTTP requests.

| Class | Description |
|---|---|
| Cookie | Allows state information to be stored on a client machine |
| HttpServlet | Provides methods to handle HTTP requests and responses |

## The HttpServletRequest Interface

The **HttpServletRequest** interface enables a servlet to obtain information about a client request. Several of its methods are shown in Table 36-5.

## The HttpServletResponse Interface

The **HttpServletResponse** interface enables a servlet to formulate an HTTP response to a client. Several constants are defined. These correspond to the different status codes that can be assigned to an HTTP response. For example, **SC_OK** indicates that the HTTP request

| Method | Description |
|---|---|
| String getAuthType( ) | Returns authentication scheme. |
| Cookie[ ] getCookies( ) | Returns an array of the cookies in this request. |
| long getDateHeader(String *field*) | Returns the value of the date header field named *field*. |
| String getHeader(String *field*) | Returns the value of the header field named *field*. |
| Enumeration<String> getHeaderNames( ) | Returns an enumeration of the header names. |
| int getIntHeader(String *field*) | Returns the **int** equivalent of the header field named *field*. |
| String getMethod( ) | Returns the HTTP method for this request. |
| String getPathInfo( ) | Returns any path information that is located after the servlet path and before a query string of the URL. |
| String getPathTranslated( ) | Returns any path information that is located after the servlet path and before a query string of the URL after translating it to a real path. |
| String getQueryString( ) | Returns any query string in the URL. |
| String getRemoteUser( ) | Returns the name of the user who issued this request. |
| String getRequestedSessionId( ) | Returns the ID of the session. |
| String getRequestURI( ) | Returns the URI. |
| StringBuffer getRequestURL( ) | Returns the URL. |
| String getServletPath( ) | Returns that part of the URL that identifies the servlet. |
| HttpSession getSession( ) | Returns the session for this request. If a session does not exist, one is created and then returned. |
| HttpSession getSession(boolean *new*) | If *new* is **true** and no session exists, creates and returns a session for this request. Otherwise, returns the existing session for this request. |
| boolean isRequestedSessionIdFromCookie( ) | Returns **true** if a cookie contains the session ID. Otherwise, returns **false**. |
| boolean isRequestedSessionIdFromURL( ) | Returns **true** if the URL contains the session ID. Otherwise, returns **false**. |
| boolean isRequestedSessionIdValid( ) | Returns **true** if the requested session ID is valid in the current session context. |

**Table 36-5** Various Methods Defined by **HttpServletRequest**

succeeded, and **SC_NOT_FOUND** indicates that the requested resource is not available. Several methods of this interface are summarized in Table 36-6.

## The HttpSession Interface

The **HttpSession** interface enables a servlet to read and write the state information that is associated with an HTTP session. Several of its methods are summarized in Table 36-7. All of these methods throw an **IllegalStateException** if the session has already been invalidated.

| Method | Description |
|---|---|
| void addCookie(Cookie *cookie*) | Adds *cookie* to the HTTP response. |
| boolean containsHeader(String *field*) | Returns **true** if the HTTP response header contains a field named *field*. |
| String encodeURL(String *url*) | Determines if the session ID must be encoded in the URL identified as *url*. If so, returns the modified version of *url*. Otherwise, returns *url*. All URLs generated by a servlet should be processed by this method. |
| String encodeRedirectURL(String *url*) | Determines if the session ID must be encoded in the URL identified as *url*. If so, returns the modified version of *url*. Otherwise, returns *url*. All URLs passed to **sendRedirect( )** should be processed by this method. |
| void sendError(int *c*) throws IOException | Sends the error code *c* to the client. |
| void sendError(int *c*, String *s*) throws IOException | Sends the error code *c* and message *s* to the client. |
| void sendRedirect(String *url*) throws IOException | Redirects the client to *url*. |
| void setDateHeader(String *field*, long *msec*) | Adds *field* to the header with date value equal to *msec* (milliseconds since midnight, January 1, 1970, GMT). |
| void setHeader(String *field*, String *value*) | Adds *field* to the header with value equal to *value*. |
| void setIntHeader(String *field*, int *value*) | Adds *field* to the header with value equal to *value*. |
| void setStatus(int *code*) | Sets the status code for this response to *code*. |

**Table 36-6** Various Methods Defined by **HttpServletResponse**

## The Cookie Class

The **Cookie** class encapsulates a cookie. A *cookie* is stored on a client and contains state information. Cookies are valuable for tracking user activities. For example, assume that a user visits an online store. A cookie can save the user's name, address, and other information. The user does not need to enter this data each time he or she visits the store.

A servlet can write a cookie to a user's machine via the **addCookie( )** method of the **HttpServletResponse** interface. The data for that cookie is then included in the header of the HTTP response that is sent to the browser.

The names and values of cookies are stored on the user's machine. Some of the information that can be saved for each cookie includes the following:

- The name of the cookie
- The value of the cookie
- The expiration date of the cookie
- The domain and path of the cookie

| Method | Description |
|---|---|
| Object getAttribute(String *attr*) | Returns the value associated with the name passed in *attr*. Returns **null** if *attr* is not found. |
| Enumeration<String> getAttributeNames( ) | Returns an enumeration of the attribute names associated with the session. |
| long getCreationTime( ) | Returns the creation time (in milliseconds since midnight, January 1, 1970, GMT) of the invoking session. |
| String getId( ) | Returns the session ID. |
| long getLastAccessedTime( ) | Returns the time (in milliseconds since midnight, January 1, 1970, GMT) when the client last made a request on the invoking session. |
| void invalidate( ) | Invalidates this session and removes it from the context. |
| boolean isNew( ) | Returns **true** if the server created the session and it has not yet been accessed by the client. |
| void removeAttribute(String *attr*) | Removes the attribute specified by *attr* from the session. |
| void setAttribute(String *attr*, Object *val*) | Associates the value passed in *val* with the attribute name passed in *attr*. |

**Table 36-7** Various Methods Defined by **HttpSession**

The expiration date determines when this cookie is deleted from the user's machine. If an expiration date is not explicitly assigned to a cookie, it is deleted when the current browser session ends.

The domain and path of the cookie determine when it is included in the header of an HTTP request. If the user enters a URL whose domain and path match these values, the cookie is then supplied to the web server. Otherwise, it is not.

There is one constructor for **Cookie**. It has the signature shown here:

Cookie(String *name*, String *value*)

Here, the name and value of the cookie are supplied as arguments to the constructor. The methods of the **Cookie** class are summarized in Table 36-8.

## The HttpServlet Class

The **HttpServlet** class extends **GenericServlet**. It is commonly used when developing servlets that receive and process HTTP requests. The methods defined by the **HttpServlet** class are summarized in Table 36-9.

| Method | Description |
|---|---|
| Object clone( ) | Returns a copy of this object. |
| String getComment( ) | Returns the comment. |
| String getDomain( ) | Returns the domain. |
| int getMaxAge( ) | Returns the maximum age (in seconds). |
| String getName( ) | Returns the name. |
| String getPath( ) | Returns the path. |
| boolean getSecure( ) | Returns **true** if the cookie is secure. Otherwise, returns **false**. |
| String getValue( ) | Returns the value. |
| int getVersion( ) | Returns the version. |
| boolean isHttpOnly() | Returns **true** if the cookie has the **HttpOnly** attribute. |
| void setComment(String *c*) | Sets the comment to *c*. |
| void setDomain(String *d*) | Sets the domain to *d*. |
| void setHttpOnly(boolean *httpOnly*) | If *httpOnly* is **true**, then the **HttpOnly** attribute is added to the cookie. If *httpOnly* is **false**, the **HttpOnly** attribute is removed. |
| void setMaxAge(int *secs*) | Sets the maximum age of the cookie to *secs*. This is the number of seconds after which the cookie is deleted. |
| void setPath(String *p*) | Sets the path to *p*. |
| void setSecure(boolean *secure*) | Sets the security flag to *secure*. |
| void setValue(String *v*) | Sets the value to *v*. |
| void setVersion(int *v*) | Sets the version to *v*. |

**Table 36-8** The Methods Defined by **Cookie**

| Method | Description |
|---|---|
| void doDelete(HttpServletRequest *req*, HttpServletResponse *res*) throws IOException, ServletException | Handles an HTTP DELETE request. |
| void doGet(HttpServletRequest *req*, HttpServletResponse *res*) throws IOException, ServletException | Handles an HTTP GET request. |
| void doHead(HttpServletRequest *req*, HttpServletResponse *res*) throws IOException, ServletException | Handles an HTTP HEAD request. |
| void doOptions(HttpServletRequest *req*, HttpServletResponse *res*) throws IOException, ServletException | Handles an HTTP OPTIONS request. |

**Table 36-9** The Methods Defined by **HttpServlet**

| Method | Description |
|---|---|
| void doPost(HttpServletRequest *req*,<br>HttpServletResponse *res*)<br>throws IOException, ServletException | Handles an HTTP POST request. |
| void doPut(HttpServletRequest *req*,<br>HttpServletResponse *res*)<br>throws IOException, ServletException | Handles an HTTP PUT request. |
| void doTrace(HttpServletRequest *req*,<br>HttpServletResponse *res*)<br>throws IOException, ServletException | Handles an HTTP TRACE request. |
| long<br>getLastModified(HttpServletRequest *req*) | Returns the time (in milliseconds since midnight, January 1, 1970, GMT) when the requested resource was last modified. |
| void service(HttpServletRequest *req*,<br>HttpServletResponse *res*)<br>throws IOException, ServletException | Called by the server when an HTTP request arrives for this servlet. The arguments provide access to the HTTP request and response, respectively. |

**Table 36-9** The Methods Defined by **HttpServlet** *(continued)*

# Handling HTTP Requests and Responses

The **HttpServlet** class provides specialized methods that handle the various types of HTTP requests. A servlet developer typically overrides one of these methods. These methods are **doDelete( )**, **doGet( )**, **doHead( )**, **doOptions( )**, **doPost( )**, **doPut( )**, and **doTrace( )**. A complete description of the different types of HTTP requests is beyond the scope of this book. However, the GET and POST requests are commonly used when handling form input. Therefore, this section presents examples of these cases.



## Handling HTTP GET Requests

Here we will develop a servlet that handles an HTTP GET request. The servlet is invoked when a form on a web page is submitted. The example contains two files. A web page is defined in **ColorGet.html**, and a servlet is defined in **ColorGetServlet.java**. The HTML source code for **ColorGet.html** is shown in the following listing. It defines a form that contains a select element and a submit button. Notice that the action parameter of the form tag specifies a URL. The URL identifies a servlet to process the HTTP GET request.

```
<html>
<body>
<center>
<form name="Form1"
  action="http://localhost:8080/examples/servlets/servlet/ColorGetServlet">
<B>Color:</B>
<select name="color" size="1">
<option value="Red">Red</option>
<option value="Green">Green</option>
```

```
<option value="Blue">Blue</option>
</select>
<br><br>
<input type=submit value="Submit">
</form>
</body>
</html>
```

The source code for **ColorGetServlet.java** is shown in the following listing. The **doGet( )** method is overridden to process any HTTP GET requests that are sent to this servlet. It uses the **getParameter( )** method of **HttpServletRequest** to obtain the selection that was made by the user. A response is then formulated.

```
import java.io.*;
import jakarta.servlet.*;
import jakarta.servlet.http.*;

public class ColorGetServlet extends HttpServlet {

  public void doGet(HttpServletRequest request,
    HttpServletResponse response)
  throws ServletException, IOException {

    String color = request.getParameter("color");
    response.setContentType("text/html");
    PrintWriter pw = response.getWriter();
    pw.println("<B>The selected color is: ");
    pw.println(color);
    pw.close();
  }
}
```

Compile the servlet. Next, copy it to the appropriate directory and update the **web.xml** file as previously described. Then, perform these steps to test this example:

1. Start Tomcat, if it is not already running.
2. Display the web page in a browser.
3. Select a color.
4. Submit the web page.

After completing these steps, the browser will display the response that is dynamically generated by the servlet.

One other point: Parameters for an HTTP GET request are included as part of the URL that is sent to the web server. Assume that the user selects the red option and submits the form. The URL sent from the browser to the server is

```
http://localhost:8080/examples/servlets/servlet/ColorGetServlet?color=Red
```

The characters to the right of the question mark are known as the *query string*.

## Handling HTTP POST Requests

Here we will develop a servlet that handles an HTTP POST request. The servlet is invoked when a form on a web page is submitted. The example contains two files. A web page is defined in **ColorPost.html**, and a servlet is defined in **ColorPostServlet.java**.

The HTML source code for **ColorPost.html** is shown in the following listing. It is identical to **ColorGet.html** except that the method parameter for the form tag explicitly specifies that the POST method should be used, and the action parameter for the form tag specifies a different servlet.

```
<html>
<body>
<center>
<form name="Form1"
  method="post"
  action="http://localhost:8080/examples/servlets/servlet/ColorPostServlet">
<B>Color:</B>
<select name="color" size="1">
<option value="Red">Red</option>
<option value="Green">Green</option>
<option value="Blue">Blue</option>
</select>
<br><br>
<input type=submit value="Submit">
</form>
</body>
</html>
```

The source code for **ColorPostServlet.java** is shown in the following listing. The **doPost( )** method is overridden to process any HTTP POST requests that are sent to this servlet. It uses the **getParameter( )** method of **HttpServletRequest** to obtain the selection that was made by the user. A response is then formulated.

```
import java.io.*;
import jakarta.servlet.*;
import jakarta.servlet.http.*;

public class ColorPostServlet extends HttpServlet {

  public void doPost(HttpServletRequest request,
    HttpServletResponse response)
  throws ServletException, IOException {

    String color = request.getParameter("color");
    response.setContentType("text/html");
    PrintWriter pw = response.getWriter();
    pw.println("<B>The selected color is: ");
    pw.println(color);
    pw.close();
  }
}
```

Compile the servlet and perform the same steps as described in the previous section to test it.

Part IV

**NOTE** Parameters for an HTTP POST request are not included as part of the URL that is sent to the web server. In this example, the URL sent from the browser to the server is `http://localhost:8080/examples/servlets/servlet/ColorPostServlet`. The parameter names and values are sent in the body of the HTTP request.

# Using Cookies

Now, let's develop a servlet that illustrates how to use cookies. The servlet is invoked when a form on a web page is submitted. The example contains three files, as summarized here:

| File | Description |
|---|---|
| AddCookie.html | Allows a user to specify a value for the cookie named **MyCookie** |
| AddCookieServlet.java | Processes the submission of **AddCookie.html** |
| GetCookiesServlet.java | Displays cookie values |

The HTML source code for **AddCookie.html** is shown in the following listing. This page contains a text field in which a value can be entered. There is also a submit button on the page. When this button is pressed, the value in the text field is sent to **AddCookieServlet** via an HTTP POST request.

```
<html>
<body>
<center>
<form name="Form1"
  method="post"
  action="http://localhost:8080/examples/servlets/servlet/AddCookieServlet">
<B>Enter a value for MyCookie:</B>
<input type=textbox name="data" size=25 value="">
<input type=submit value="Submit">
</form>
</body>
</html>
```

The source code for **AddCookieServlet.java** is shown in the following listing. It gets the value of the parameter named "data". It then creates a **Cookie** object that has the name "MyCookie" and contains the value of the "data" parameter. The cookie is then added to the header of the HTTP response via the **addCookie( )** method. A feedback message is then written to the browser.

```
import java.io.*;
import jakarta.servlet.*;
import jakarta.servlet.http.*;

public class AddCookieServlet extends HttpServlet {

  public void doPost(HttpServletRequest request,
    HttpServletResponse response)
  throws ServletException, IOException {
```

```
    // Get parameter from HTTP request.
    String data = request.getParameter("data");

    // Create cookie.
    Cookie cookie = new Cookie("MyCookie", data);

    // Add cookie to HTTP response.
    response.addCookie(cookie);

    // Write output to browser.
    response.setContentType("text/html");
    PrintWriter pw = response.getWriter();
    pw.println("<B>MyCookie has been set to");
    pw.println(data);
    pw.close();
  }
}
```

The source code for **GetCookiesServlet.java** is shown in the following listing. It invokes the **getCookies( )** method to read any cookies that are included in the HTTP GET request. The names and values of these cookies are then written to the HTTP response. Observe that the **getName( )** and **getValue( )** methods are called to obtain this information.

```
import java.io.*;
import jakarta.servlet.*;
import jakarta.servlet.http.*;

public class GetCookiesServlet extends HttpServlet {

  public void doGet(HttpServletRequest request,
    HttpServletResponse response)
  throws ServletException, IOException {

    // Get cookies from header of HTTP request.
    Cookie[] cookies = request.getCookies();

    // Display these cookies.
    response.setContentType("text/html");
    PrintWriter pw = response.getWriter();
    pw.println("<B>");
    for(int i = 0; i < cookies.length; i++) {
      String name = cookies[i].getName();
      String value = cookies[i].getValue();
      pw.println("name = " + name +
        "; value = " + value);
    }
    pw.close();
  }
}
```

Part IV

Compile the servlets. Next, copy them to the appropriate directory and update the **web.xml** file as previously described. Then, perform these steps to test this example:

1. Start Tomcat, if it is not already running.
2. Display **AddCookie.html** in a browser.
3. Enter a value for **MyCookie**.
4. Submit the web page.

After completing these steps, you will observe that a feedback message is displayed by the browser.

Next, request the following URL via the browser:

```
http://localhost:8080/examples/servlets/servlet/GetCookiesServlet
```

Observe that the name and value of the cookie are displayed in the browser.

In this example, an expiration date is not explicitly assigned to the cookie via the **setMaxAge( )** method of **Cookie**. Therefore, the cookie expires when the browser session ends. You can experiment by using **setMaxAge( )** and observe that the cookie is then saved on the client machine.

## Session Tracking

HTTP is a stateless protocol. Each request is independent of the previous one. However, in some applications, it is necessary to save state information so that information can be collected from several interactions between a browser and a server. Sessions provide such a mechanism.

A session can be created via the **getSession( )** method of **HttpServletRequest**. An **HttpSession** object is returned. This object can store a set of bindings that associate names with objects. The **setAttribute( )**, **getAttribute( )**, **getAttributeNames( )**, and **removeAttribute( )** methods of **HttpSession** manage these bindings. Session state is shared by all servlets that are associated with a client.

The following servlet illustrates how to use session state. The **getSession( )** method gets the current session. A new session is created if one does not already exist. The **getAttribute( )** method is called to obtain the object that is bound to the name "date". That object is a **Date** object that encapsulates the date and time when this page was last accessed. (Of course, there is no such binding when the page is first accessed.) A **Date** object encapsulating the current date and time is then created. The **setAttribute( )** method is called to bind the name "date" to this object.

```
import java.io.*;
import java.util.*;
import jakarta.servlet.*;
import jakarta.servlet.http.*;

public class DateServlet extends HttpServlet {
```

```
  public void doGet(HttpServletRequest request,
     HttpServletResponse response)
  throws ServletException, IOException {

     // Get the HttpSession object.
     HttpSession hs = request.getSession(true);

     // Get writer.
     response.setContentType("text/html");
     PrintWriter pw = response.getWriter();
     pw.print("<B>");

     // Display date/time of last access.
     Date date = (Date)hs.getAttribute("date");
     if(date != null) {
       pw.print("Last access: " + date + "<br>");
     }

     // Display current date/time.
     date = new Date();
     hs.setAttribute("date", date);
     pw.println("Current date: " + date);
  }
}
```

When you first request this servlet, the browser displays one line with the current date and time information. On subsequent invocations, two lines are displayed. The first line shows the date and time when the servlet was last accessed. The second line shows the current date and time.

# PART V

# Appendixes

# APPENDIX A

# Using Java's Documentation Comments

As explained in Part I, Java supports three types of comments. The first two are the // and the /* */. The third type is called a *documentation comment.* It begins with the character sequence /**. It ends with */. Documentation comments allow you to embed information about your program into the program itself. You can then use the **javadoc** utility program (supplied with the JDK) to extract the information and put it into an HTML file. Documentation comments make it convenient to document your programs. You have almost certainly seen documentation that uses such comments because that is the way the Java API library was documented. Beginning with JDK 9, **javadoc** includes support for modules.

## The javadoc Tags

The **javadoc** utility recognizes several tags, including those shown here:

| Tag | Meaning |
|---|---|
| @author | Identifies the author |
| {@code} | Displays information as-is, without processing HTML styles, in code font |
| @deprecated | Specifies that a program element is deprecated |
| {@docRoot} | Specifies the path to the root directory of the current documentation |
| @end | Specifies the end of a region of code to be used in a fragment of code specified by a **@snippet** tag |
| @exception | Identifies an exception thrown by a method or constructor |
| @hidden | Prevents an element from appearing in the documentation |
| {@index} | Specifies a term for indexing |
| {@inheritDoc} | Inherits a comment from the immediate superclass |
| {@link} | Inserts an in-line link to another topic |
| {@linkplain} | Inserts an in-line link to another topic, but the link is displayed in a plain-text font |
| {@literal} | Displays information as-is, without processing HTML styles |

| Tag | Meaning |
|---|---|
| @param | Documents a parameter |
| @provides | Documents a service provided by a module |
| @return | Documents a method's return value |
| @see | Specifies a link to another topic |
| @serial | Documents a default serializable field |
| @serialData | Documents the data written by the **writeObject( )** or **writeExternal( )** methods |
| @serialField | Documents an **ObjectStreamField** component |
| @since | States the release when a specific change was introduced |
| {@snippet} | Documents a fragment of code |
| @start | Specifies the start of a region of code to be used in a fragment of code specified by a **@snippet** tag |
| {@summary} | Documents a summary of an item |
| {@systemProperty} | States that a name is a system property |
| @throws | Same as **@exception** |
| @uses | Documents a service needed by a module |
| {@value} | Displays the value of a constant, which must be a **static** field |
| @version | Specifies the version of a program element |

Document tags that begin with an "at" sign (@) are called *block* tags (also called *stand-alone* tags), and they must be used at the beginning of their own line. Tags that begin with a brace, such as {**@code**}, are called *inline* tags, and they can be used within a larger description. You may also use other, standard HTML tags in a documentation comment. However, some tags, such as headings, should not be used because they disrupt the look of the HTML file produced by **javadoc**.

As it relates to documenting source code, you can use documentation comments to document classes, interfaces, fields, constructors, methods, packages, and modules. In all cases, the documentation comment must immediately precede the item being documented. Some tags, such as **@see**, **@since**, and **@deprecated**, can be used to document any element. Other tags apply only to the relevant elements. A brief synopsis of each tag follows.

**NOTE** As one would expect, the capabilities of **javadoc** and the documentation comment tags have evolved over time, often in response to new Java features. You will want to refer to the **javadoc** documentation for information on the latest **javadoc** features.

## @author

The **@author** tag documents the author of a program element. It has the following syntax:

@author *description*

Here, *description* will usually be the name of the author. You will need to specify the **-author** option when executing **javadoc** in order for the **@author** field to be included in the HTML documentation.

## {@code}

The **{@code}** tag enables you to embed text, such as a snippet of code, into a comment. That text is then displayed as-is in code font, without any further processing, such as HTML rendering. It has the following syntax:

{@code *code-snippet*}

## @deprecated

The **@deprecated** tag specifies that a program element is deprecated. It is recommended that you include **@see** or **{@link}** tags to inform the programmer about available alternatives. The syntax is the following:

@deprecated *description*

Here, *description* is the message that describes the deprecation. The **@deprecated** tag can be used in documentation for fields, methods, constructors, classes, modules, and interfaces.

## {@docRoot}

**{@docRoot}** specifies the path to the root directory of the current documentation.

## @end

The **@end** tag specifies the end of a region of code that begins with a corresponding **@start** tag.

The syntax of **@end** is

@end *name="region name"*

where the optional name attribute gives the name of the region that is ending. If omitted, the **@end** tag ends the region that is currently in scope.

See **@start**.

## @exception

The **@exception** tag describes an exception to a method. Today, **@throws** is the preferred alternative, but **@exception** is still supported. It has the following syntax:

@exception *exception-name explanation*

Here, the fully qualified name of the exception is specified by *exception-name*, and *explanation* is a string that describes how the exception can occur. The **@exception** tag can only be used in documentation for a method or constructor.

## @hidden

The **@hidden** tag prevents an element from appearing in the documentation.

## {@index}

The **{@index}** tag specifies an item that will be indexed, and thus found when using the search feature. It has the following syntax:

{ @index *term usage-str* }

Here, *term* is the item (which can be a quoted string) to be indexed. *usage-str* is optional. Thus, in the following **@throws** tag, **{@index}** causes the term "error" to be added to the index:

```
@throws IOException On input {@index error}.
```

Note that the word "error" is still displayed as part of the description. It's just that now it is also indexed. If you include the optional *usage-str*, then that description will be shown in the index and in the search box to indicate how the term is used. For example, **{@index error Serious execution failure}** will show "Serious execution failure" under "error" in the index and in the search box.

## {@inheritDoc}

This tag inherits a comment from the immediate superclass.

## {@link}

The **{@link}** tag provides an in-line link to additional information. It has the following syntax:

{@link *mod-name/pkg-name.class-name#member-name text*}

Here, *mod-name/pkg-name.class-name#member-name* specifies the name of a class or method to which a link is added, and *text* is the string that is displayed.

The *text* field is optional. If it's not included, *member* is displayed as the link. Notice that the module name (if present) is separated from the package name with a /. For example,

{@link java.base/java.io.Writer#write}

defines a link to the **write( )** method of **Writer** in **java.io**, in the module **java.base**.

## {@linkplain}

Inserts an in-line link to another topic. The link is displayed in plain-text font. Otherwise, it is similar to **{@link}**.

## {@literal}

The **{@literal}** tag enables you to embed text into a comment. That text is then displayed as-is, without any further processing, such as HTML rendering. It has the following syntax:

{@literal *description*}

Here, *description* is the text that is embedded.

## @param

The **@param** tag documents a parameter. It has the following syntax:

@param *parameter-name explanation*

Here, *parameter-name* specifies the name of a parameter. The meaning of that parameter is described by *explanation.* The **@param** tag can be used only in documentation for a method or constructor, or a generic class or interface.

## @provides

The **@provides** tag documents a service provided by a module. It has the following syntax:

@provides *type explanation*

Here, *type* specifies a service provider type and *explanation* describes the service provider.

## @return

The **@return** tag describes the return value of a method. It has two forms. The first is the block tag show here:

@return *explanation*

Here, *explanation* describes the type and meaning of the value returned by a method. Thus, the tag can be used only in documentation for a method. JDK 16 added an inline tag version:

{@return *explanation*}

This form must be at the top of the method's documentation comment.

## @see

The **@see** tag provides a reference to additional information. Two commonly used forms are shown here:

@see *anchor*
@see *mod-name/pkg-name.class-name#member-name text*

In the first form, *anchor* is a link to an absolute or relative URL. In the second form, *mod-name/pkg-name.class-name#member-name* specifies the name of the item, and *text* is the text displayed for that item. The text parameter is optional, and if not used, then the item specified by *mod-name/pkg-name.class-name#member-name* is displayed. The member name, too, is optional. Thus, you can specify a reference to a module, package, class, or interface in addition to a reference to a specific method or field. The name can be fully qualified or partially qualified. However, the dot that precedes the member name (if it exists) must be replaced by a hash character. There is a third form of **@see** that lets you simply specify a text-based description.

## @serial

The **@serial** tag defines the comment for a default serializable field. Here is its basic form:

@serial *description*

Here, *description* is the comment for that field. Two other forms, shown here, let you indicate if a class or package will be part of the Serialized Form documentation page.

@serial include
@serial exclude

## @serialData

The **@serialData** tag documents the data written by the **writeObject( )** and **writeExternal( )** methods. It has the following syntax:

@serialData *description*

Here, *description* is the comment for that data.

## @serialField

For a class that implements **Serializable**, the **@serialField** tag provides comments for an **ObjectStreamField** component. It has the following syntax:

@serialField *name type description*

Here, *name* is the name of the field, *type* is its type, and *description* is the comment for that field.

## @since

The **@since** tag states that an element was introduced in a specific release. It has the following syntax:

@since *release*

Here, *release* is a string that designates the release or version in which this feature became available.

## {@snippet}

The **@snippet** tag documents source code to be included in the javadoc. Snippets can be *inline* for documenting code provided directly in the javadoc comment, in which case the following syntax applies:

```
{@snippet : {
        source code to be documented
    }
}
```

Alternatively, snippets can be *external*, in which case either the **file** or **class** attribute is used to indicate the source of the code to be documented, together with a **region** attribute to indicate which part of the code in the source to document:

{@snippet class=*classname* | file=*path to file* region=*region name*}

Here, the path to the file is a relative path from the file being documented.

## @start

The **@start** tag specifies the beginning of a region of code that will be referenced in a **@snippet** tag. The syntax of the **@start** tag is

@start *name="region name"*

where the name attribute indicates the name of the region that can be referenced by a **@snippet** tag.

## {@summary}

The **{@summary}** tag explicitly specifies the summary text that will be used for an item. It must be the first tag in the documentation for the item. It has the following syntax:

@summary *explanation*

Here, *explanation* provides a summary of the tagged item, which can span multiple lines. Without the use of **{@summary}**, the first line in an item's documentation comment is used as the summary.

## {@systemProperty}

The **{@systemProperty}** tag lets you indicate a system property. It has this general form:

{@systemProperty *propName*}

Here, *propName* is the name of the property.

## @throws

The **@throws** tag has the same meaning as the **@exception** tag, but it's now the preferred form.

## @uses

The **@uses** tag documents a service provider needed by a module. It has the following syntax:

@uses *type explanation*

Here, *type* specifies a service provider type and *explanation* describes the service.

## {@value}

**{@value}** has two forms. The first displays the value of the constant that it precedes, which must be a **static** field. It has this form:

{@value}

The second form displays the value of a specified **static** field. It has this form:

{@value *pkg.class#field*}

Here, *pkg.class#field* specifies the name of the **static** field.

### @version

The **@version** tag specifies the version of a program element. It has the following syntax:

@version *info*

Here, *info* is a string that contains version information, typically a version number, such as 2.2. You will need to specify the **-version** option when executing **javadoc** in order for the **@version** field to be included in the HTML documentation.

## The General Form of a Documentation Comment

After the beginning /**, the first line or lines become the main description of your class, interface, field, constructor, method, or module. After that, you can include one or more of the various @ tags. Each @ tag must start at the beginning of a new line or follow one or more asterisks (*) that are at the start of a line. Multiple tags of the same type should be grouped together. For example, if you have three **@see** tags, put them one after the other. Inline tags (those that begin with a brace) can be used within any description.

Here is an example of a documentation comment for a class:

```
/**
 * This class draws a bar chart.
 * @author Herbert Schildt
 * @version 3.2
*/
```

## What javadoc Outputs

The **javadoc** program takes as input your Java program's source file and outputs several HTML files that contain the program's documentation. Information about each class will be in its own HTML file. **javadoc** will also output an index and a hierarchy tree. Other HTML files can be generated. Beginning with JDK 9, a search box feature is also included.

## An Example that Uses Documentation Comments

Following is a sample program that uses documentation comments. Notice the way each comment immediately precedes the item that it describes. After being processed by **javadoc**, the documentation about the **SquareNum** class will be found in **SquareNum.html**.

```
import java.io.*;
/**
 * This class demonstrates documentation comments.
 * @author Herbert Schildt
 * @version 1.2
*/
```

```
public class SquareNum {
  /**
   * This method returns the square of num.
   * This is a multiline description. You can use
   * as many lines as you like.
   * @param num The value to be squared.
   * @return num squared.
  */
  public double square(double num) {
    return num * num;
  }

  /**
   * This method inputs a number from the user. It uses
   * {@snippet file="SquareNum.java" name="input code"}
   * to get the input, so the user
   * will need to hit return.
   * @return The value input as a double.
   * @throws IOException On input error.
   * @see IOException
  */
  public double getNumber() throws IOException {
    // create a BufferedReader using System.in
    InputStreamReader isr = new InputStreamReader(System.in);
    BufferedReader inData = new BufferedReader(isr);
    String str;
    // @start name="input code"

    str = inData.readLine();
    return Double.valueOf(str);
    // @end
  }
  /**
   * This method demonstrates square().
   * @param args Unused.
   * @throws IOException On input error.
   * @see IOException
  */

  public static void main(String[] args)
    throws IOException
  {
    SquareNum ob = new SquareNum();
    double val;

    System.out.println("Enter value to be squared: ");
    val = ob.getNumber();
    val = ob.square(val);

    System.out.println("Squared value is " + val);
  }
}
```

APPENDIX

# B Introducing JShell

Beginning with JDK 9, Java has included a tool called JShell. It provides an interactive environment that enables you to quickly and easily experiment with Java code. JShell implements what is referred to as *read-evaluate-print loop* (REPL) execution. Using this mechanism, you are prompted to enter a fragment of code. This fragment is then read and evaluated. Next, JShell displays output related to the code, such as the output produced by a **println( )** statement, the result of an expression, or the current value of a variable. JShell then prompts for the next piece of code, and the process continues (i.e., loops). In the language of JShell, each code sequence you enter is called a *snippet*.

A key point to understand about JShell is that you do not need to enter a complete Java program to use it. Each snippet you enter is simply evaluated as you enter it. This is possible because JShell handles many of the details associated with a Java program for you automatically. This lets you concentrate on a specific feature without having to write a complete program, which makes JShell especially helpful when you are first learning Java.

As you might expect, JShell can also be useful to experienced programmers. Because JShell stores state information, it is possible to enter multiline code sequences and run them inside JShell. This makes JShell quite useful when you need to prototype a concept because it lets you interactively experiment with your code without having to develop and compile a complete program.

This appendix introduces JShell and explores several of its key features, with the primary focus being on those features most useful to beginning Java programmers.

## JShell Basics

JShell is a command-line tool. Thus, it runs in a command-prompt window. To start a JShell session, execute **jshell** from the command line. After doing so, you will see the JShell prompt:

```
jshell>
```

When this prompt is displayed, you can enter a code snippet or a JShell command.

In its simplest form, JShell lets you enter an individual statement and immediately see the result. To begin, think back to the first sample Java program in this book. It is shown again here:

```
class Example {
  // Your program begins with a call to main().
  public static void main(String[] args) {
    System.out.println("This is a simple Java program.");
  }
}
```

In this program, only the **println( )** statement actually performs an action, which is displaying its message on the screen. The rest of the code simply provides the required class and method declarations. In JShell, it is not necessary to explicitly specify the class or method in order to execute the **println( )** statement. JShell can execute it directly on its own. To see how, enter the following line at the JShell prompt:

```
System.out.println("This is a simple Java program.");
```

Then, press ENTER. This output is displayed:

```
This is a simple Java program.

jshell>
```

As you can see, the call to **println( )** is evaluated and its string argument is output. Then, the prompt is redisplayed.

Before moving on, it is useful to explain why JShell can execute a single statement, such as the call to **println( )**, when the Java compiler, **javac**, requires a complete program. JShell is able to evaluate a single statement because JShell automatically provides the necessary program framework for you, behind the scenes. This consists of a *synthetic class* and a *synthetic method*. Thus, in this case, the **println( )** statement is embedded in a synthetic method that is part of a synthetic class. As a result, the preceding code is still part of a valid Java program even though you don't see all of the details. This approach provides a very fast and convenient way to experiment with Java code.

Next, let's look at how variables are supported. In JShell, you can declare a variable, assign the variable a value, and use it in any valid expressions. For example, enter the following line at the prompt:

```
int count;
```

After doing so you will see the following response:

```
count ==> 0
```

This indicates that **count** has been added to the synthetic class and initialized to zero. Furthermore, it has been added as a **static** variable of the synthetic class.

Next, give **count** the value 10 by entering this statement:

```
count = 10;
```

You will see this response:

```
count ==> 10
```

As you can see, **count**'s value is now 10. Because **count** is **static**, it can be used without reference to an object.

Now that **count** has been declared, it can be used in an expression. For example, enter this **println( )** statement:

```
System.out.println("Reciprocal of count: " + 1.0 / count);
```

JShell responds with

```
Reciprocal of count: 0.1
```

Here, the result of the expression **1.0 / count** is 0.1 because **count** was previously assigned the value 10.

In addition to demonstrating the use of a variable, the preceding example illustrates another important aspect of JShell: It maintains state information. In this case, **count** is assigned the value 10 in one statement, and then this value is used in the expression **1.0 / count** in the subsequent call to **println( )** in a second statement. Between these two statements, JShell stores **count**'s value. In general, JShell maintains the current state and effect of the code snippets that you enter. This lets you experiment with larger code fragments that span multiple lines.

Before moving on, let's try one more example. In this case, we will create a **for** loop that uses the **count** variable. Begin by entering this line at the prompt:

```
for(count = 0; count < 5; count++)
```

At this point, JShell responds with the following prompt:

```
...>
```

This indicates that additional code is required to finish the statement. In this case, the target of the **for** loop must be provided. Enter the following:

```
System.out.println(count);
```

After entering this line, the **for** statement is complete and both lines are executed. You will see the following output:

```
0
1
2
3
4
```

In addition to statements and variable declarations, JShell lets you declare classes and methods, and use import statements. Examples are shown in the following sections. One other point: Any code that is valid for JShell will also be valid for compilation by **javac**, assuming the necessary framework is provided to create a complete program. Thus, if a code fragment can be executed by JShell, then that fragment represents valid Java code. In other words, JShell code *is* Java code.

## List, Edit, and Rerun Code

JShell supports a large number of commands that let you control the operation of JShell. At this point, three are of particular interest because they let you list the code that you have entered, edit a line of code, and rerun a code snippet. As the subsequent examples become longer, you will find these commands to be very helpful.

In JShell, all commands start with a / followed by the command. Perhaps the most commonly used command is **/list**, which lists the code that you have entered. Assuming that you have followed along with the examples shown in the preceding section, you can list your code by entering **/list** at this time. Your JShell session will respond with a numbered list of the snippets you entered. Pay special attention to the entry that shows the **for** loop. Although it consists of two lines, it constitutes one statement. Thus, only one snippet number is used. In the language of JShell, the snippet numbers are referred to as *snippet IDs*. In addition to the basic form of **/list** just shown, other forms are supported, including those that let you list specific snippets by name or number. For example, you can list the **count** declaration by using **/list count**.

You can edit a snippet by using the **/edit** command. This command causes an edit window to open in which you can modify your code. Here are three forms of the **/edit** command that you will find helpful at this time. First, if you specify **/edit** by itself, the edit window contains all of the lines you have entered and lets you edit any part of it. Second, you can specify a specific snippet to edit by using **/edit** *n*, where *n* specifies the snippet's number. For example, to edit snippet 3, use **/edit 3**. Finally, you can specify a named element, such as a variable. For example, to change the value of **count**, use **/edit count**.

As you have seen, JShell executes code as you enter it. However, you can also rerun what you have entered. To rerun the last fragment that you entered, use **/!**. To rerun a specific snippet, specify its number using this form: /*n*, where *n* specifies the snippet to run. For example, to rerun the fourth snippet, enter **/4**. You can rerun a snippet by specifying its position relative to the current fragment by use of a negative offset. For example, to rerun a fragment that is three snippets before the current one, use **/-3**.

Before moving on, it is helpful to point out that several commands, including those just shown, allow you to specify a list of names or numbers. For example, to edit lines 2 and 4, you could use **/edit 2 4**. For recent versions of JShell, several commands allow you specify a range of snippets. These include the **/list**, **/edit**, and /*n* commands just described. For example, to list snippets 4 through 6, you would use **/list 4-6**.

There is one other important command that you need to know about now: **/exit**. This terminates JShell.

## Add a Method

As explained in Chapter 6, methods occur within classes. However, when using JShell it is possible to experiment with a method without having to *explicitly* declare it within a class. As mentioned earlier, this is because JShell automatically wraps code fragments within a synthetic class. As a result, you can easily and quickly write a method without having to provide a class framework. You can also call the method without having to create an object. This feature of JShell is especially beneficial when learning the basics of methods in Java or when prototyping new code. To understand the process, we will work through an example.

To begin, start a new JShell session and enter the following method at the prompt:

```
double reciprocal(double val) {
  return 1.0/val;
}
```

This creates a method that returns the reciprocal of its argument. After you enter this, JShell responds with the following:

```
|  created method reciprocal(double)
```

This indicates the method has been added to JShell's synthetic class and is ready for use.

To call **reciprocal( )**, simply specify its name, without any object or class reference. For example, try this:

```
System.out.println(reciprocal(4.0));
```

JShell responds by displaying 0.25.

You might be wondering why you can call **reciprocal( )** without using the dot operator and an object reference. Here is the answer: When you create a stand-alone method in JShell, such as **reciprocal( )**, JShell automatically makes that method a **static** member of the synthetic class. As you know from Chapter 7, **static** methods are called relative to their class, not on a specific object. So, no object is required. This is similar to the way that stand-alone variables become **static** variables of the synthetic class, as described earlier.

Another important aspect of JShell is its support for a *forward reference* inside a method. This feature lets one method call another method, even if the second method has not yet been defined. This enables you to enter a method that depends on another method without having to worry about which one you enter first. Here is a simple example. Enter this line in JShell:

```
void myMeth() { myMeth2(); }
```

JShell responds with the following:

```
|  created method myMeth(), however, it cannot be invoked until myMeth2()
   is declared
```

As you can see, JShell knows that **myMeth2( )** has not yet been declared, but it still lets you define **myMeth( )**. As you would expect, if you try to call **myMeth( )** at this time, you will see an error message since **myMeth2( )** is not yet defined, but you are still able to enter the code for **myMeth( )**.

Next, define **myMeth2( )** like this:

```
void myMeth2() { System.out.println("JShell is powerful."); }
```

Now that **myMeth2( )** has been defined, you can call **myMeth( )**.

In addition to its use in a method, you can use a forward reference in a field initializer in a class.

## Create a Class

Although JShell automatically supplies a synthetic class that wraps code snippets, you can also create your own class in JShell. Furthermore, you can instantiate objects of your class. This allows you to experiment with classes inside JShell's interactive environment. The following example illustrates the process.

Start a new JShell session and enter the following class, line by line:

```
class MyClass {
  double v;

  MyClass(double d) { v = d; }

  // Return the reciprocal of v.
  double reciprocal() { return 1.0 / v; }
}
```

When you finish entering the code, JShell will respond with

```
|  created class MyClass
```

Now that you have added **MyClass**, you can use it. For example, you can create a **MyClass** object with the following line:

```
MyClass ob = new MyClass(10.0);
```

JShell will respond by telling you that it added **ob** as a variable of type **MyClass**. Next, try the following line:

```
System.out.println(ob.reciprocal());
```

JShell responds by displaying the value 0.1.

As a point of interest, when you add a class to JShell, it becomes a **static** nested member of a synthetic class.

## Use an Interface

Interfaces are supported by JShell in the same way as classes. Therefore, you can declare an interface and implement it by a class within JShell. Let's work through a simple example. Before beginning, start a new JShell session.

The interface that we will use declares a method called **isLegalVal( )** that is used to determine if a value is valid for some purpose. It returns **true** if the value is legal and **false** otherwise. Of course, what constitutes a legal value will be determined by each class that implements the interface. Begin by entering the following interface into JShell:

```
interface MyIF {
  boolean isLegalVal(double v);
}
```

JShell responds with

```
| created interface MyIf
```

Next, enter the following class, which implements MyIF:

```
class MyClass implements MyIF {

  double start;
  double end;

  MyClass(double a, double b) { start = a; end = b; }

  // Determine if v is within the range start to end, inclusive.
  public boolean isLegalVal(double v) {
    if((v >= start) && (v <= end)) return true;
    return false;
  }

}
```

JShell responds with

```
| created class MyClass
```

Notice that **MyClass** implements **isLegalVal( )** by determining if the value **v** is within the range (inclusive) of the values in the **MyClass** instance variables **start** and **end**.

Now that both **MyIF** and **MyClass** have been added, you can create a **MyClass** object and call **isLegalVal( )** on it, as shown here:

```
MyClass ob = new MyClass(0.0, 10.0);

System.out.println(ob.isLegalVal(5.0));
```

In this case, the value **true** is displayed because 5 is within the range 0 through 10.

Because **MyIF** has been added to JShell, you can also create a reference to an object of type **MyIF**. For example, the following is also valid code:

```
MyIF ob2 = new MyClass(1.0, 3.0);
boolean result = ob2.isLegalVal(1.1);
```

In this case, the value of **result** will be **true** and will be reported as such by JShell.

One other point: enumerations and annotations are supported in JShell in the same way as classes and interfaces.

## Evaluate Expressions and Use Built-in Variables

JShell includes the ability to directly evaluate an expression without it needing to be part of a full Java statement. This is especially useful when you are experimenting with code and don't need to execute the expression in a larger context. Here is a simple example. Using a new JShell session, enter the following at the prompt:

```
3.0 / 16.0
```

JShell responds with

```
$1 ==> 0.1875
```

As you can see, the result of the expression is computed and displayed. However, note that this value is also assigned to a temporary variable called **$1**. In general, each time an expression is evaluated directly, its result is stored in a temporary variable of the proper type. Temporary variable names all begin with a **$** followed by a number, which is increased each time a new temporary variable is needed. You can use these temporary variables like any other variable. For example, the following displays the value of **$1**, which is 0.1875 in this case:

```
System.out.println($1);
```

Here is another example:

```
double v = $1 * 2;
```

Here, the value **$1** times 2 is assigned to **v**. Thus, **v** will contain 0.375.

You can change the value of a temporary variable. For example, this reverses the sign of **$1**:

```
$1 = -$1
```

JShell responds with

```
$1 ==> -0.1875
```

Expressions are not limited to numeric values. For example, here is one that concatenates a **String** with the value returned by **Math.abs($1)**:

```
"The absolute value of $1 is " + Math.abs($1)
```

This results in a temporary variable that contains the string

```
The absolute value of $1 is 0.1875
```

## Importing Packages

As described in Chapter 9, an **import** statement is used to bring members of a package into view. Furthermore, any time you use a package other than **java.lang**, you must import it. The situation is much the same in JShell, except that by default JShell imports several commonly used packages automatically. These include **java.io** and **java.util**, among several others. Since these packages are already imported, no explicit **import** statement is required to use them.

For example, because **java.io** is automatically imported, the following statement can be entered:

```
FileInputStream fin = new FileInputStream("myfile.txt");
```

Recall that **FileInputStream** is packaged in **java.io**. Since **java.io** is automatically imported, it can be used without having to include an explicit **import** statement. Assuming that you actually have a file called **myfile.txt** in the current directory, JShell will respond by adding the variable **fin** and opening the file. You can then read and display the file by entering these statements:

```
int i;
do {
  i = fin.read();
  if(i != -1) System.out.print((char) i);
} while(i != -1);
```

This is the same basic code that was discussed in Chapter 13, but no explicit **import java.io** statement is required.

Keep in mind that JShell automatically imports only a handful of packages. If you want to use a package not automatically imported by JShell, then you must explicitly import it as you do with a normal Java program. One other point: you can see a list of the current imports by using the **/imports** command.

# Exceptions

In the I/O example shown in the preceding section on imports, the code snippets also illustrate another very important aspect of JShell. Notice that there are no **try**/**catch** blocks that handle I/O exceptions. If you look back at the similar code in Chapter 13, the code that opens the file catches a **FileNotFoundException**, and the code that reads the file watches for an **IOException**. The reason that you don't need to catch these exceptions in the snippets shown earlier is because JShell automatically handles them for you. More generally, JShell will automatically handle checked exceptions in many cases.

# Some More JShell Commands

In addition to the commands discussed earlier, JShell supports several others. One command that you will want to try immediately is **/help**. It displays a list of the commands. You can also use **/?** to obtain help. Some of the more commonly used commands are examined here.

You can reset JShell by using the **/reset** command. This is especially useful when you want to change to a new project. By use of **/reset** you avoid the need to exit and then restart JShell. Be aware, however, that **/reset** resets the entire JShell environment, so all state information is lost.

You can save a session by using **/save**. Its simplest form is shown here:

/save *filename*

Here, *filename* specifies the name of the file to save into. By default, **/save** saves your current source code, but it supports several options, of which two are of particular interest. By specifying **-all**, you save all lines that you enter, including those that you entered incorrectly. You can use the **-history** option to save your session history (i.e., the list of the commands that you have entered).

You can load a saved session by using **/open**. Its form is shown next:

/open *filename*

Here, *filename* is the name of the file to load.

JShell provides several commands that let you list various elements of your work. They are shown here:

| Command | Effect |
|---|---|
| /types | Shows classes, interfaces, and enums |
| /imports | Shows import statements |
| /methods | Shows methods |
| /vars | Shows variables |

For example, if you entered the following lines:

```
int start = 0;
int end = 10;
int count = 5;
```

and then entered the **/vars** command, you would see

```
|   int start = 0;
|   int end = 10;
|   int count = 5;
```

Another often useful command is **/history**. It lets you view the history of the current session. The history contains a list of what you have typed at the command prompt.

# Exploring JShell Further

The best way to get proficient with JShell is to work with it. Try entering several different Java constructs and watching the way that JShell responds. As you experiment with JShell, you will find the usage patterns that work best for you. This will enable you to find effective ways to integrate JShell into your learning or development process. Also, keep in mind that JShell is not just for beginners. It also excels when prototyping code. Thus, even if you are an experienced pro, you will still find JShell helpful whenever you need to explore new areas.

Simply put: JShell is an important tool that further enhances the overall Java development experience.

# APPENDIX C

# Compile and Run Simple Single-File Programs in One Step

In Chapter 2, you were shown how to compile a Java program into bytecode using the **javac** compiler and then run the resulting **.class** file(s) using the Java launcher **java**. This is how Java programs have been compiled and run since Java's beginning, and it is the method that you will use when developing applications. However, beginning with JDK 11, it is possible to compile and run some types of simple Java programs directly from the source file without having to first invoke **javac**. To do this, pass the name of the source file, using the **.java** file extension, to **java**. This causes **java** to automatically invoke the compiler and execute the program.

For example, the following automatically compiles and runs the first example in this book:

```
java Example.java
```

In this case, the **Example** class is compiled and then run in a single step. There is no need to use **javac**. Be aware, however, that no **.class** file is created. Instead, the compilation is done behind the scenes. As a result, to rerun the program, you must execute the source file again. You can't execute its **.class** file because one won't be created.

One use of the source-file launch capability is to facilitate the use of Java programs in script files. It can also be useful for short one-time-use programs. In some cases, it makes it a little easier to run simple sample programs when you are experimenting with Java. It is not, however, a general-purpose substitute for Java's normal compilation/execution process.

Although this new ability to launch a Java program directly from its source file is appealing, it comes with some restrictions. First, the entire program must be contained in a single source file. However, most real-world programs use multiple source files. Second, it will always execute the first class it finds in the file, and that class must contain a **main( )** method. If the first class in the file does not contain a **main( )** method, the launch will fail. This means that you must follow a strict organization for your code, even if you would prefer to organize it otherwise. Third, because no **.class** files are created, using **java** to run a single-file program does not result in a class file that can be reused, possibly by other programs. As a result of these restrictions, using **java** to run a single-file source program can be useful, but it constitutes what is, essentially, a special-case technique.

As it relates to this book, it is possible to use the single source-file launch feature to try many of the examples; just be sure that the class with the **main( )** method is first in your file. That said, it is not, however, applicable or appropriate in all cases. Furthermore, the discussions (and many of the examples) in the book assume that you are using the normal compilation process of invoking **javac** to compile a source file into bytecode and then using **java** to run that bytecode. This is the mechanism used for real-world development, and understanding this process is an important part of learning Java. It is imperative that you are thoroughly familiar with it. For these reasons, when trying the examples in this book, it is strongly recommended that in all cases you use the normal approach to compiling and running a Java program. Doing so ensures that you have a solid foundation in the way Java works. Of course, you might find it fun to experiment with the single source-file launch option!

---

**NOTE** It is possible to execute a single-file program from a file that does not use the **.java** extension. To do so, you must specify the **--source** *APIVer* option, where *APIVer* specifies the JDK version number.

# Index

## A

## B

## C

## D

## E

## F

## G

## J

## K

## L



## M

## N

## Q



## R

## T

## U



## V